BERGIN AND GARFIELD'S

HANDBOOK *of* PSYCHOTHERAPY *and* BEHAVIOR CHANGE

SIXTH EDITION

EDITED BY

Michael J. Lambert

WILEY

John Wiley & Sons, Inc.

Cover image: © kgphoto/iStockphoto
Cover design: David Riedy

This book is printed on acid-free paper. ⊗

Library of Congress Cataloging-in-Publication Data:

Bergin and Garfield's handbook of psychotherapy and behavior change /
edited by Michael J. Lambert—6th ed.
    p. cm.
  Includes bibliographical references and index.
  ISBN 978-1-118-03820-8 (cloth); ISBN 978-1-118-43362-1 (ebk); ISBN 978-1-118-41868-0 (ebk);
ISBN 978-1-118-41592-4 (ebk)
  1. Psychotherapy.   2. Psychotherapy—Research.   I. Lambert, Michael J.   II. Title: Handbook
of psychotherapy and behavior change.   III. Title: Psychotherapy and behavior change.
  RC480.H286   2012
  616.89′14—dc23

                                                                        2012034369

Printed in the United States of America

10 9 8 7 6 5

This sixth edition of the handbook is dedicated to the patients and psychotherapists who have allowed their work together to be scrutinized for the benefit of those who are yet to participate. The research enterprise has often been undertaken by these individuals without personal compensation, but for the good of unknown others. It is a pleasure to see patients, professionals, and researchers work together for the common good of mankind.

CONTENTS

List of Contributors

Jay Amsterdam, MD
Depression Research Unit
University of Pennsylvania
Philadelphia, PA

Scott Baldwin, PhD
Department of Psychology
Brigham Young University
Provo, UT

Jacques P. Barber, PhD, ABPP
The Derner Institute of Advanced Psychological
    Studies
Adelphi University
Garden City, NY

Michael Barkham, PhD
Centre for Psychological Services Research
Department of Psychology
University of Sheffield
Sheffield, United Kingdom

Aaron Beck, MD
Department of Psychiatry
University of Pennsylvania
Philadelphia, PA

Arthur C. Bohart, PhD
Department of Psychology
California State University-Dominguez Hills
Carson, CA

Gary M. Burlingame, PhD
Department of Psychology
Brigham Young University
Provo, UT

Louis G. Castonguay, PhD
Department of Psychology
Pennsylvania State University
University Park, PA

Paul Crits-Christoph, PhD
Center for Psychotherapy Research
Department of Psychiatry
University of Pennsylvania
Philadelphia, PA

Jonathan S. Comer, PhD
Early Childhood Interventions Program
Center for Anxiety and Related Disorders
Department of Psychology
Boston University
Boston, MA

Mary Beth Connolly Gibbons, PhD
Center for Psychotherapy Research
Department of Psychiatry
University of Pennsylvania
Philadelphia, PA

Corinne Datchi, PhD
Department of Professional Psychology and
    Family Therapy
Seaton Hall University
South Orange, NJ

Robert J. DeRubeis
Department of Psychology
School of Arts and Sciences
University of Pennsylvania
Philadelphia, PA

Robert Elliott, PhD
School of Psychological Sciences and Health
University of Strathclyde
Glasgow, United Kingdom

Paul M. G. Emmelkamp, PhD
Royal Netherlands Academy of Arts and Sciences
Department of Clinical Psychology
University of Amsterdam
Amsterdam, The Netherlands

Lauren Evans
Center for Adolescent and Family Studies
Indiana University
Bloomington, IN

Nicholas R. Forand, PhD
Department of Psychology
University of Pennsylvania
Philadelphia, PA

Elizabeth S. Freier
The School of Education
King's College
Aberdeen, United Kingdom

Leslie S. Greenberg, PhD
York University
Toronto, Canada

Clara Hill, PhD
University of Maryland
College Park, MD

Steven D. Hollon, PhD
Vanderbilt University
Nashville, TN

Zac E. Imel, PhD
Department of Educational Psychology
University of Utah
Salt Lake City, UT

Anthony Joyce, PhD
Department of Psychiatry
University of Alberta
Edmonton, Canada

Jack Keefe
Perelman School of Medicine
University of Pennsylvania
Philadelphia, PA

Philip C. Kendall, PhD, ABPP
Department of Psychology
Temple University
Philadelphia, PA

Sarah Knox, PhD
Department of Counselor Education and
    Counseling Psychology
College of Education
Marquette University
Milwaukee, WI

Julie LaFollette
Center for Adolescent and Family Studies
Indiana University
Bloomington, IN

Michael J. Lambert, PhD
Department of Psychology
Brigham Young University
Provo, UT

Nancy Lau, AM
Department of Psychology
Harvard University
Cambridge, MA

Wolfgang Lutz, PhD
Department of Psychology
University of Trier
Trier, Germany

Sara Masland, AM
Department of Psychology
Harvard University
Cambridge, MA

Andrew McAleavey, MS
Department of Psychology
Pennsylvania State University
University Park, PA

Kevin Scott McCarthy
Chestnut Hill College
Philadelphia, PA

John McLeod, PhD
Tayside Institute for Health Studies (SHS)
University of Abertay Dundee
Dundee, United Kingdom

Dahlia Mukherjee, MA, MPhil
Center for Psychotherapy Research
Department of Psychiatry
University of Pennsylvania
Philadelphia, PA

J. Christopher Muran, PhD
Derner Institute for Advanced Psychological
    Studies
Adelphi University
Garden City, NY

Mei Yi Ng, AM
Department of Psychology
Harvard University
Cambridge, MA

Benjamin M. Ogles, PhD
College of Family, Home, & Social Sciences
Brigham Young University
Provo, Utah

Christopher Rutt, AM
Department of Psychology
Harvard University
Cambridge, MA

Thomas L. Sexton, PhD, ABPP
Center for Adolescent and Family Studies
Indiana University
Bloomington, IN

Timothy W. Smith, PhD
Department of Psychology
University of Utah
Salt Lake City, Utah

Bernhard Strauss, PhD
Institute of Psychosocial Medicine and
    Psychotherapy
University Hospital Jena
Jena, Germany

Ladislav Timulak, PhD
School of Psychology
Trinity College
Dublin, Ireland

Amy Wade, PhD
Private Practice
Chandler, AZ

Jeanne C. Watson, PhD
Ontario Institute for Studies in Education
Toronto, Canada

John R. Weisz, PhD, ABPP
Department of Psychology
Harvard University
Cambridge, MA
Judge Baker Children's Center
Boston, MA

Paula G. Williams, PhD
Department of Psychology
University of Utah
Salt Lake City, Utah 84112-0251

Lauren Wright
Center for Adolescent and Family Studies
Indiana University
Bloomington, IN

EDITORIAL BOARD

David Orlinsky, PhD
Department of Comparative Human
    Development
University of Chicago
Chicago, IL

Alan E. Kazdin, PhD, ABPP
Department of Psychology
Yale University
New Haven, CT

PREFACE

I am pleased to have played a part in the publication of this sixth edition of the *Handbook of Psychotherapy and Behavior Change*. Allen Bergin and Sol Garfield, the former editors of the first four editions of this standard reference book, published their first edition in 1971, the year I received my PhD. I met Allen that same year as we began faculty appointments at Brigham Young University. In 1973 I met Sol Garfield at the annual meetings of the Society of Psychotherapy Research. We shared a strong interest in psychotherapy and in its scientific foundations. The Society was a meeting point for many of the great minds in the field and a stimulus for integration of research and practice. Most of the authors who have contributed chapters to the handbook over the years discussed and debated the important issues of the day in the context of the Society and its international, multidisciplinary membership. Both Garfield and Bergin, after decades of creating the handbook, felt it was time to step aside. Given my past contributions to the handbook and long-standing association with them, I agreed to their suggestion that I edit the fifth, and now the sixth edition.

The influence of the handbook on the field of psychotherapy has been enormous. The early editions of the handbook have become citation classics. Reference to psychotherapy research is not complete without considering the comprehensive work of past handbook authors. Graduate education in psychology and the related professions would seem deficient without exposure to the empirical literature and past editions of the handbook have set the standard for balance and completeness. Without thoughtful review of the empirical literature on psychotherapy practitioners cannot expect to deliver services of the highest quality.

I began editing the fifth edition of the handbook with a full understanding of the book's importance to the field over the 30 years that Garfield and Bergin devoted to it. I also realized that it needed to measure up to expectations form readers of early editions. The sixth edition reflects the many changes that have influenced the field in the years since its inception. It is published now at a time when psychotherapy is expected to be supported by empirical evidence. I endeavored to invite outstanding authors to contribute to the sixth edition with the hope and intention that the handbook remains the most important overview of research findings in the field. This is no small task for the handbook authors since a great deal of research has been published in the past 10 years and since the field has become more specialized, making integration of findings more difficult than ever before. The authors work remains thorough and comprehensive, aiming to inform the reader while also appreciating the complexity of patients, of psychotherapy, and of scientific inquiry.

There continues to be overwhelming evidence for the effectiveness of psychotherapy and mechanisms of change, but also conflicting views about the value of certain treatment methods in relation to others, most effective processes, necessary and sufficient conditions for positive change, and the interpretation of some findings.

These conflicts provide an important source of discussion and wonder that will be stimulating to students and professionals. Certainly, these conflicts and their resolution will have great value for effectively treating patients.

The focus of the handbook remains on empirical studies based on traditional research designs, but a new chapter has been added that highlights qualitative research designs and methods for understanding emotional problems and processes of change. This chapter has replaced the chapter by Brent Slife on the philosophy of science included in the fifth edition. Another new chapter has been added that emphasizes research in naturalistic settings that capitalizes on the curiosity of providers of services. After the absence of a chapter on psychodynamic psychotherapy in the fifth edition, the current addition includes a thoughtful summary of research on this long-standing theoretical tradition and its effects. As in past handbooks, the current edition emphasizes practice-relevant findings, as well as methodological issues that will help direct future research. It is therefore meant to be both a summary of accumulated knowledge and a guide for the future practice of psychotherapy. I believe the reader will find the sixth edition of the handbook to be up to the same high standards maintained by Garfield and Bergin in the preceding four editions. The handbook authors have done their best to keep pace with the rapid changes that are taking place in the world and attempted to be forward looking in making recommendations for future research and practice.

I would like to thank the contributing authors for their careful reviews and long hours of thoughtful work. Because of their history of accomplishments and contributions to the field over many years, their wisdom is apparent and likely to be greatly appreciated by the reader. I hope that readers of the sixth edition of the *Handbook of Psychotherapy and Behavior Change* are able to use the information presented to augment their work with patients and that this research compendium stimulates and guides further examination of the scientific foundations and consequences of psychotherapeutic practice.

M.J.L.

HISTORICAL, METHODOLOGICAL, AND CONCEPTUAL FOUNDATIONS

•

CHAPTER 1

INTRODUCTION AND HISTORICAL OVERVIEW

MICHAEL J. LAMBERT

Psychotherapy has come a long way from its humble beginnings as a "new movement" at the beginning of the 20th century and continues to be a field characterized by changing emphases, new developments, and considerable controversy. It receives considerable attention from the news media, has a place in the popular media such as TV, novels, movies, the Internet (Barkham, Stiles, Connell, Twigg, Leach & Angus, 2008), and its methods feature prominently in the "self-help" industry. It is widely regarded as an indispensable form of treatment for a variety of mental health problems and personal crises, and remains a popular endeavor in which a growing number of professionals and paraprofessionals are actively involved. Its evolution has been nicely summarized in *The History of Psychotherapy: Continuity and Change* by Norcross, Vandenbos, and Freedheim (2011).

In contrast, research into the processes and effects of psychotherapy remains much less known and, to some degree, a minor aspect of the endeavors falling under the rubric of psychotherapy with its emphasis on theory and practical application. Nevertheless, a search of ISI Web of Knowledge (an Internet journal search engine) reveals that around 60,000 academic papers have been published on psychotherapy research in just the past 30 years. If each of these papers took 1 hour to read, a comprehensive reading of the literature would take about 13 years (working at one paper per hour nonstop for 12 hours a day) and that is not including all the book chapters, reports, and papers in nonacademic journals. The field of psychotherapy research is also a vital and evolving enterprise, which supplements the theory-based activities of therapists, and is quickly

becoming the foundation for treatment guidelines and "best practices" common in today's world.

The forms that research has taken over the years have evolved in many of the same ways as psychotherapy itself—moving in the direction of precisely understanding the factors that lead to patient improvement. This evolution has been nicely summarized in past editions of this handbook (Bergin & Garfield, 1971, 1994; Garfield & Bergin, 1978, 1986; Lambert, 2004).

Before discussing current trends and issues in psychotherapy research, an historical overview is presented for the purpose of putting current research in the context of past research practices and changes in society at large. This overview includes comments on trends in practice, basic training of providers, payment systems, and issues of general interest. Finally, an overview of the book's contents is provided.

HISTORICAL BACKGROUND

From the end of the 19th century to around 1960, the dominant influence in psychotherapy was Freud and his notable colleagues. Even after his death in 1939, Freud's followers persisted in defending psychoanalysis and in creating variations and significant modifications of his original scheme. Adler, Jung, Horney, and Sullivan, among others, while offering important modifications, retained traditional features of Freud's thinking, such as the importance of early life experiences, repressed conflict, unconscious motivation, defenses, and the like.

Research on these methods was published as early as 1924 (Bergin, 1971). Following the emergence of the Freudian influence, other approaches to psychotherapy began to appear. Client-centered therapy as developed by Carl Rogers (1942) was a significant departure from Freudian views where the therapist was considered the expert on the client. Rogers emphasized the client's potential for self-healing through the positive directional tendency found within, and the need for the therapist to provide an environment rich in respect, warmth, and empathic connection. Positive personality change was viewed as inevitable in such an environment. The use of interpretations common in Freudian treatment was seen not only as unhelpful, but potentially damaging.

Other more radical developments included the growth of learning-based approaches that appeared as early as the 1920s (Jones, 1924; O. Mowrer & Mowrer, 1938). Learning-based procedures emphasized patient behaviors, situational contingencies, and an active/directive role for the therapist. These approaches did not begin to have a dramatic impact on psychotherapy until the publication of Wolpe's *Psychotherapy by Reciprocal Inhibition* in 1958. Since then psychologists have been extremely influential in the development of learning-based approaches to behavior change.

Both the Rogerian position and that of the learning-based approaches placed greater emphasis on the importance of formally evaluating the effects of therapy than had been true of other orientations. Roger's research groups applied sound-recording techniques of actual sessions, allowing researchers to carefully examine the moment-by-moment encounter, thereby reducing the mystery of the therapeutic hour and identifying correlates of positive and negative change. Learning-based approaches put major emphasis on monitoring treatment response and its connection to therapist-guided interventions. Both methods were relatively brief (lasting weeks or months) as compared with psychoanalysis and related techniques (often taking years), a factor that increased the feasibility of research inquiries.

The emergence of cognitive therapy was a natural outgrowth of the limitations of the learning-based approaches with their emphasis on behavior at the expense of thought, but also represented dissatisfaction with the effects of psychodynamic treatments. Cognitive therapy was most notably advocated by Ellis (1962) and Beck (1970) and came to the forefront of theory-driven treatments by the mid-1970s with the publication of Beck's (1976) *Cognitive Therapy and the Emotional Disorders*. These and related developments, such as the emergence of social learning theory (Bandura, 1969), provided rich contrasts between cognitive theories and treatment methods and carried with them a strong research emphasis.

The decades of the 1950s and 1960s were an exciting and innovative period for the field of psychotherapy and mental health in general. The community mental health movement, along with additional forces from within psychology itself, resulted in further declines in the popularity of long-term treatments, with many psychodynamic assumptions about behavior change interventions being further challenged. These challenges were largely based on social forces that provided pressure to make affordable treatments widely available to all segments of the population. The necessity of reducing treatment length continue to this day and have even become more accelerated in the past two decades due to economic pressures and the costs involved in making therapy widely available. Within psychology, theoretical issues have been a strong driving force toward changes in treatment (DeLeon, Kenkel, Garcia-Shelton, & VandenBos, 2011), but research results have also been important and, as of this writing, have become a dominant force (e.g., *Evidence-Based Psychotherapy: Where Practice and Research Meet*, Goodheart, Kazdin, & Steinberg, 2006). Practical necessity aside, theoretical battles about the causes and cures of psychopathology have been prominent in the history of psychotherapy practice and research.

The brewing theoretical controversy between systems of treatment with their underlying assumptions and practices was crystallized in a controversial article published by British psychologist Hans Eysenck. He published an early review of 24 studies, concluding that there was no research evidence to support the effectiveness of psychotherapy compared to groups receiving no therapy, and that psychoanalysis was less effective than no treatment (Eysenck, 1952). This provocative conclusion was strongly criticized by numerous psychologists (e.g., Bergin, 1971; Lambert, 1976). Nonetheless, the Eysenck article was important in sparking considerable interest in scientific investigations of psychotherapy. Since that time there has been a dramatic increase in both the quantity and quality of research on psychotherapy, with the emerging conclusions that are the focus of this and the previous handbooks.

Since Eysenck's (1952) review, most reviews evaluating the efficacy of psychotherapy have been much more positive. By 1970 there were enough studies on the outcome of treatments that it took "the patience of Job and the mind of a bank auditor" to integrate the information (Meltzoff & Korneich, 1970). This job was undertaken by several reviewers (Bergin, 1971; Bergin & Lambert, 1978; Meltzoff & Korneich, 1970). With the emergence of meta-analytic statistical techniques, reviews of the growing literature were subjected to quantitative analysis, with large bodies of information summed across studies. Smith, Glass, and Miller's (1980) book was the most extensive reanalysis of the psychotherapy literature that dealt with treatment effects. Through an analysis of more than 475 studies it reaffirmed the findings of the earlier scholarly reviews: The effects of therapy are superior to no-treatment and placebo control conditions, and therapies appear to have equivalent effects when compared with each other across a variety of disorders (see Chapter 6, this volume, for an elaboration of this point). Since the Smith et al. (1980) review, the number of studies on psychotherapy has increased dramatically and, consequently, meta-analytic reviews are so numerous that just reviewing the reviews is a daunting task. Although not attempting to be comprehensive, the chapters in this book provide integrations of the effects of psychotherapy with an emphasis on recent research findings. They rely heavily on findings based on quantitative reviews. Meta-analytic reviews of the effects of psychotherapy have gone from rare in the 1980s to commonplace, providing more precise estimates of both the effects of psychological treatments and the contributing factors.

Several other developments have taken place in the field and are worthy of note here. The number and types of psychotherapy has expanded. The practitioners of psychotherapy have increased in number and diversity along with training programs. Reimbursement systems have changed dramatically and emerged as a powerful force in practice, and research, and great emphasis is being placed on providing the right treatment for the right disorder. All of these topics merit further discussion and are highlighted here as well as focused on by chapter authors.

ISSUES

A central issue for contemporary practice and research is the failure of clinicians to respond to and integrate research findings into daily activities and for researchers to make efforts to translate their findings into clinically useful recommendations for practice.

Integration of Research and Practice

Historically, the importance of research in guiding clinical practice has been limited. Theories that guide interventions have typically been developed and disseminated independent of research investigations. Despite considerable lip service to the importance of research for practice, many practitioners have not found treatment research, as reported in scientific journals, to be particularly useful to them. Research articles reporting clinical trials have not been rated highly among important sources of information on treatment (Cohen, Sargent, & Sechrest, 1986; Morrow-Bradley & Elliott, 1986). However, several dynamic forces have resulted in a renewed interest in outcome research and its integration into routine practice. These forces are both theoretical and economic. The emergence of cognitive-behavioral treatments and the increasing specificity of the *Diagnostic and Statistical Manual of Mental Disorders* (*DSM*) of the American Psychiatric Association (2000) have led to increased interest in developing specific treatments for specific disorders. In recent years we have seen more interest in what form of therapy is most effective within diagnostic classifications. Thus, research and practice have moved from an early emphasis on viewing symptoms as superficial, to considering the removal of symptoms as a central goal of treatment. This trend can be noted in both research designs that include only patients with a specific disorder as well as increased use of dependent measures that operationalize outcomes for specific disorders (as noted by Ogles, Chapter 5, this volume). The result has been unambiguous evidence for the efficacy of some treatments that are transportable from the laboratory to clinical settings (Burns & Hoagwood, 2005).

Changes in reimbursement systems in the form of managed care organizations have also had an impact on both practice and research. These organizations have emphasized the development of clinical guidelines that are intended to make treatment more uniform across practitioners and settings and, presumably, more effective. Despite a major emphasis placed on cost reductions (rather than treatment quality) by these organizations, they clearly have rekindled the need for evidence-based practice. Irrespective of an emphasis on financial considerations the resulting attention to acquiring more research-based evidence for effective and efficient practice promises to benefit patients in the long run if the evidence is translated into policy and practice.

From Empirically Validated Psychotherapies to the Emergence of Evidence-Based Practice

Based on the assumption that society is in need of treatments with known effects, and that behavioral health care specialists agree on the necessity of providing a firm base of empirical support for their activities, numerous efforts have been made to solidify evidence to guide practice. The most notorious of efforts in this area were those developed by Division 12 of the American Psychological Association (The Division of Clinical Psychology), which created criteria for what constitutes empirical support for treatments. The agenda of the original Task Force on Promotion and Dissemination of Psychological Procedures (1995) was to consider methods for educating clinical psychologists, third-party funders, and the public about effective psychotherapies. This Task Force (now called the Standing Committee on Science and Practice) generated and disseminated criteria for levels of empirical support, identified relevant treatment outcome studies, and weighed evidence according to defined criteria. This resulted in highly controversial lists of treatments that met criteria for different levels of empirical support, and lists of resources for training and treatment manuals (Woody & Sanderson, 1998), along with the phrase, empirically *validated*, to describe these treatments (Chambless, 1996; Chambless et al., 1996; Chambless & Hollon, 1998).

The controversies generated from the initial report came mainly from practitioners who saw the report as rigid, if not dogmatic, and as having an agenda that was biased in favor of a small number of therapies that were promoted by Task Force members (e.g., criteria were set up that would give an advantage to highly structured short-term behavioral and cognitive-behavioral treatments advocated by many Task Force members). But strong criticism came from psychotherapy researchers as well (Garfield, 1996; Nathan, 1998; Strupp, 1997). For example, Gavin Andrews (2000) who produced some of the first treatment guidelines stated his view of empirically supported treatments in a commentary:

> This is not to deny that identifying empirically supported treatments

carried out by a profession does not have important political advantages for the profession. Funders, providers, and consumers all like to pretend that efficacy is the same as effectiveness, and lists of empirically supported treatments feed this delusion. (p. 267)

Beutler (2000) among others provided an overview of the early efforts to set scientific standards both in the United States and abroad. He notes, however, that scientific standards for practice have been typically based on the subjective impressions of committee members rather than on the evidence itself (e.g., Nathan, Gorman, & Salkind's 2002 *Treating Mental Disorders: A Guide to What Works;* Roth & Fonagy's 2005 *What Works for Whom? A Critical Review of Psychotherapy Research*). The Task Force's initial response to these criticisms appeared defensive to many—they insisted on retaining terms such as empirically "validated" therapies (later changed to empirically *supported* therapies, Chambless, 1996) and seemed to lack the humility of recognizing the limitations of their own work, while being especially harsh on practitioners whose practices were often seen as not being based on empirical knowledge. This "methodolatry" did not seem like a hopeful way of bridging the gap between practice and research, creating greater distance rather than greater consensus.

Since the earlier efforts, the task of identifying effective treatments has become more sophisticated, but the job of privileging certain psychotherapies undertaken by committees is a difficult one that will never be completed because treatments are constantly being modified, and new treatments invented. Treatments evolve, as do research strategies, and the search for final conclusions that is being undertaken by committees must always recognize the tentative nature of the results that are forthcoming from research and practice. The ensuing efforts by American Psychological Association (APA) committees appear to be mindful of this reality and much more circumspect in its assertions than the original committee (Weisz, Hawley, Pilkonis, Woody, & Follette, 2000). Nevertheless, the committee continued toward the goal of developing "a single list of empirically supported treatments" and setting "standards of practice" (Weisz et al., 2000, p. 249). But this Committee on Science and Practice also pursued a three-part agenda (Weisz et al., 2000): (1) increasing the reliability of review procedures through standardization and rules of evidence; (2) improving research quality; and (3) increasing relevance and dissemination to the professions and public.

Given the number of disorders, treatment research paradigms, and means of measuring treatment effects, a valuable service would be to inform both practitioners and the public of developments in the field based on current research. Lists of "empirically supported treatments" are static and seem to offer only a false guarantee of effectiveness. Some would argue that even efforts at softening the term *validated* for the more modest term *supported* has not gone far enough.

More recently there have been additional attempts to further bridge the gap between practice and research. Perhaps the most important of these was undertaken by Alan Kazdin while president of the American Psychological Association (Kazdin, 2008). He helped to illuminate the various positions taken by researchers and practitioners with regard to empirical evidence noting that psychology as a discipline has increased its emphasis on what is commonly referred to as *evidence-based practice* in psychology (APA Presidential Task Force on Evidence-Based Practice, 2006). Key terms that are used to discuss treatments and the use of evidence reflect the differences and priorities of the various parties involved. For example, empirically supported or evidence-based *treatment* (EBT) refers to the specific interventions or techniques (e.g., exposure-based therapy for phobic disorders) that have produced therapeutic change in controlled trials. Evidence-based practice (EBP) is a broader term and refers to clinical practice that is informed by evidence about interventions, clinical expertise, and patient needs, values, and preferences and their integration, to make decisions about individual care (e.g., American Psychological Association [APA], 2005). In 2010 the American Psychological Association initiated a process for developing evidence-based practice and evaluation with treatment guidelines developed by a variety of organizations (Kurtzman & Bufka, 2011). In this effort a distinction is made between the narrow term *treatment guideline* and that of *practice guideline*.

Kazdin (2008) also notes that: "In the evolution of attempts to place psychotherapy practice on a stronger empirical footing the discussion of preferred treatment and delivery of services has moved into the public domain as part of the larger health-care landscape. There is an effort to provide resources that inform and make available current evidence-based interventions." For example, on web-based sites a single link can encompass more than 30 federal, state, professional, and university sites that enumerate these interventions (http://ucoll.fdu.edu/apa/lnksinter .html). The Substance Abuse and Mental Health Services Administration (http://www.nrepp .samhsa.gov) has provided an active and ever-expanding Web-based site that regularly evaluates and adds new treatment options.

One can applaud efforts to provide resources to agencies and practitioners for the purpose of improving services; but it is also clear that some are eager to be more forceful in insisting evidence-based treatments be exclusively used. There are efforts among third-party payers and states to prescribe what treatments are to be allowed and reimbursed. According to the Campaign for Mental Health Reform—a national group of mental health organizations including among others the American Psychiatric and Psychological Associations—the only remaining impediment to widespread use of evidence-based treatment is, "resistance to change by entrenched and threatened organizational structures, outdated reimbursement rules, lack of effective provider training, and, most importantly, lack of resources" (http://www.mhreform.org).

Serious questions can be raised about who (professionals, managed-care agencies, government agencies, or administrators) should be empowered to make treatment decisions *when the evidence applies to a specific client*. Researchers, practitioners, and health-care policy advocates continue to debate the merits of the evidence in behalf of various interventions, what counts as evidence, and how the evidence is to be used and integrated (e.g., Burns & Hoagwood, 2005; Goodheart et al., 2006; Hunsley, 2007; Tanenbaum, 2005; Wampold, 2001; Westen, Novotny, & Thompson-Brenne, 2004). Most would agree that the final decision must rest with practitioners.

From the point of view of many practitioners and researchers, another problem with evidence-based treatment guidelines is that reliance on the prevailing research paradigm (randomized clinical trials) has had the organizational effect of distancing some therapies and specific interventions from being considered as "evidence-based" because they have not relied on these procedures. This has a self-perpetuating effect, as research funding goes increasingly to research groups who have already completed large grant projects successfully. Some treatment procedures become set in stone, while others languish. Funding decisions and research evidence work together to shorten the list of treatments considered to be empirically supported. Although some might argue that ignoring treatments that do not have a strong evidence base is justified, they miss the real sociological and epistemological complexity of the scientific undertaking and such a view dooms regulatory and advisory bodies to marginalize some psychosocial interventions and remain restrictively focused on pharmacological interventions and on particular therapies and particular problems and client groups. This is a great loss of potential to maximize learning and uptake of learning for the benefit of the full population of people with mental health needs.

Although many practitioners and the public may be comforted by the notion that they are offering or receiving an empirically supported psychotherapy that works best, the fact is that success of treatment appears to be largely dependent on the client and the therapist, not on the use of "proven" empirically based treatments (see Chapters 6, 7, and 8, this volume). Proof of effective treatment needs to be based on the measurement of treatment response rather than merely provision of the "right" treatment (Lambert, 2010). We cannot be satisfied with providing the right treatment for the right disorder as a means of exercising our duty to patients who are suffering from the pain of psychological problems.

CONTINUING DOMINANCE OF INTEGRATIVE/ECLECTIC PRACTICE

A clear trend in psychotherapeutic interventions since the mid-1960s has been the proliferation not only of types of practitioners, but of the types and numbers of psychotherapies used alone and in combination in day-to-day practice. Garfield (1982) identified 60 forms of psychotherapy in use in the 1960s. In 1975 the Research Task Force of the National Institute of Mental Health, estimated that there were 125 different forms. Henrick (1980) listed more than 200 separate approaches, while Kazdin (1986) noted 400 variants of psychotherapy. Research on the effectiveness of each and every emerging form of therapy is nonexistent. As far back as the 1980s Parloff (1982), pointed out that "a systematic approach to dealing with a matrix of 250 psychosocial therapies and 150 classes of disorders would require approximately 47 million comparisons" (p. 723). Clearly the invention of separate psychotherapies took place independent of research evidence, and research results have not slowed the development and advocacy of various treatment methods. Note that Parloff made his comment more than 30 years ago and that what he said then holds even more so today: It is impossible for comparative testing of every existing or new therapy to be conducted even if the resources to make comparisons were available.

This dilemma becomes even more problematic because the proliferation of therapies has been accompanied by the continuing trend for therapists to disavow allegiance to a single system of treatment in the form of a purely theoretically based approach. *Eclecticism*, representing the use of procedures from different theoretical systems, and *integrationism*, representing the theoretical joining of two or more positions into a consistent approach, has replaced the dominance of major theories in therapeutic practice. Surveys of practitioners repeatedly indicate that one half to two thirds of providers prefer using a variety of techniques that have arisen from major theoretical schools (e.g., Jensen, Bergin, & Greaves, 1990: Norcross, Karg & Proshaska, 1997). Those therapists who identify with an eclectic orientation feel free to select techniques from any orientation that they deem to be in the best interest of a particular patient. Although taking great liberties in applying mixed interventions in routine practice is done to maximize therapist responsiveness to individual patient needs, such seemingly unsystematic practice bolsters the need for treatment guidelines.

Unfortunately, there appears to be little consensus among eclectic therapists about the specific techniques that are most helpful, and thus there is little likelihood that two eclectic therapists would use the same techniques with the same client. Garfield and Kurtz (1977) who studied 154 eclectic psychologists found 32 combinations of theoretical orientations were in use. Jensen et al. (1990) found comparable results but also a trend toward differences in preferred combinations across professional disciplines, with dynamic orientations more often used in psychiatry, systems theories in social work and marriage and family therapy, and cognitive and behavioral approaches in psychology. Preferences for certain types of theory-directed interventions appear to be largely based on traditions rather than empirical considerations.

Nevertheless, eclecticism reflects the fact that there are many diverse theoretical orientations with varying strengths. These strengths are widely recognized and occasionally supported by research evidence from the study of single theory approaches. The movement to combined use and integration of these approaches is likely to continue and appears inevitable given the diversity of concerns manifest in people who come for help. Consider for example the clear trend of cognitive-behavior therapy (CBT) to incorporate psychodynamic, client-centered/experiential approaches, along with mindfulness practices that come from Eastern religious traditions. It is readily observed that even "single school" approaches such as CBT are far more eclectic than the name implies, with substantial variations in CBT practices across the globe and over time. Even within the eclectic practice of CBT there are strong disagreements among theoreticians about the necessity and importance of specific procedures; it does not seem farfetched to suggest that two patients entering CBT treatment offered by different providers might receive nearly nonoverlapping treatments. Newer variations displace older ones for reasons that are sometimes just as much about human and social needs for identity, change and novelty, as the empirical evidence itself.

Eclectic and integrationist treatment approaches might also be explained in part by the diversity of individuals who are treated, even within specific diagnostic categories. Kazdin (2008), for example, notes that given the criteria for diagnosing conduct disorder, there are more than 32,000 combinations of symptoms that individuals can have and still meet the diagnosis. The same can be said for other disorders such as agoraphobia. Williams (1985) notes that: "The configuration of fears in agoraphobics is so highly idiosyncratic that it is substantially true that no two agoraphobics have exactly the same pattern of phobias and that two people with virtually no overlapping areas of phobia disability can both be called agoraphobic" (p. 112).

The integrative movement, which parallels eclectic practice, has the ambitious goal of being more systematic than eclecticism. Early attempts at theoretical integration of psychodynamic and behavioral procedures by Wachtel (1977) and the early work of Goldfried (1991) are fine examples of blending theoretical diversity. Integrationist activity and growth can also be noted by the formation and success of the Society for the Exploration of Psychotherapy Integration (SEPI). In addition to these movements, process research aimed at examining the in-session behavior of therapists across different theoretical orientations indicates that the distinctiveness of approaches in *practice* is less pronounced than it is at the abstract level of theory (Ablon & Jones, 1999; Norcross & Goldfried, 1992). Thus, theories of change are somewhat independent of the actual activities that therapists engage in and these activities show a large degree of overlap across theoretically diverse treatments. The overlap in behaviors are also a part of what has commonly been referred to as common factors in psychotherapy dealt with more extensively in Chapter 6 of this volume. These common factors can be shown to account for a significant amount of patient change. They include the facilitation of hope, the opportunity for emotional release, exploration and integration of one's problems, support, advice, and encouragement to try out new behaviors and ways of thinking.

Emphasis on common factors as central to the changes made in psychotherapy, a phenomenon that is distinct from eclecticism has the potential for reducing conflicts between particular theoretic views. Polarization based on claims of unique effectiveness for specific theoretical orientations has resulted in conflict within the field that has had positive consequences (e.g., stimulation of research studies), but has also caused considerable defensiveness and slowing of progress (e.g., through the overstatement of claims of success, and attempts to create exclusive lists of effective treatment). Eclectic and integrationist movements reflect similar attempts by many practitioners to be flexible in their approach to working with patients.

This handbook has been eclectic from its inception in 1967 and first publication by Bergin and Garfield in 1971. Empirical findings from all approaches are considered potentially important. Being open to research findings on any approach, both positive and negative, is the central mission of the handbook. This focus is consistent with the ideal goals of eclecticism—fostering what works for the patient. Openness to methods of investigating psychotherapy is also valued and represented by inclusion of chapters representing not only traditional research paradigms but diverse and competing methods that search for "practice-based evidence" from practice research networks, as well as a variety of qualitative methods that are now covered in the handbook (see Chapters 3 and 4, this volume).

THE PRACTITIONERS OF PSYCHOTHERAPY

The practitioners of psychotherapy are becoming more numerous and diverse. This phenomenon can be seen across other professions as well. In medicine, for example, many services, such as writing prescriptions or administering anesthesia, were once performed solely by MDs, but are now offered by nurses, medical assistants, and related personnel. Since Freud's time, the practitioners of psychotherapy were primarily physicians, and prior to World War II, clinical psychology was a relatively small and undeveloped profession with a major emphasis on the administration of psychological tests. After the war the shortage of psychiatrists, coupled with the unmet demand to care for veterans who had developed psychological disorders, led to government-supported graduate training in clinical and counseling psychology with psychotherapy becoming an important part of this training. Despite subsequent conflicts with organized medicine, the independent practice of psychotherapy by psychologists became a reality (Garfield, 1983).

Social work, school psychology, nursing, pastoral counseling, marriage and family therapy, licensed professional counseling, substance abuse counseling, as well as a host of paraprofessionals also participate in a variety of psychotherapeutic practices. The professionals responsible for training across disciplines as well as regulatory boards disagree about the type and extent of training needed to safely and effectively engage clients in psychological treatments. One might think that if we were able to agree on the most effective practices then there might be some agreement as to the training and qualification of providers—but this is not the case.

In the United States, as much as 60% of the psychotherapy that is conducted is now provided by social workers whose master's degree training in psychotherapy, at least from the point of view of psychology, is inadequate. A common practice in Europe and the United Kingdom is to license professionals within psychotherapy training programs that are single theory-based rather than profession-based and typically require a master's degree (in these training models the focus of training and credentialing is entirely on the practice of psychotherapy). Given such diverging views about ideal or even adequate training and necessary qualifications (in the United States and abroad) confusion reigns supreme, with regulatory bodies and a public unsure about differences and advantages that might come from selecting an available provider.

Selecting a provider based on knowledge of that provider's treatment effects is emerging as a possibility (Okiishi et al., 2006), but it is as rare in psychotherapy as it is in medicine to know the likely consequences of being treated by a particular provider. The kinds of professions involved in psychotherapeutic services has risen to meet the demands for service, especially as demands for service came from the needs of underserved populations such as the poor, substance abusing individuals, those in the criminal justice system, and the seriously and persistently mentally ill. The established professions both resisted and facilitated such developments. Because of fears about the negative consequences to the patient who would be treated by minimally trained persons and fear of competition from less trained providers, resistance was (and often is) the most common reaction from within the professions to new classes of providers.

However, the forces at work in society and within individuals appear to stretch the boundaries of who can be considered a trustworthy provider. Besides the needs of the underserved, and the fact that many treatments, once developed, can be routinely offered through the use of treatment manuals, economic forces play a large part in the movement toward using less trained persons (Bright, Baker, & Niemeyer, 1999; Weisz, Weisz, Ham, Granger, & Morton, 1995). Nowhere is this more evident than in recent developments in the United Kingdom where access to specialized mental health service has been characterized by long waitlists and immediate service provision in the hands of general practitioners who often simply prescribe medications (Carey, 2010; Carey & Spratt, 2009). Despite the fact that many mental health practitioners were available and could provide prescribed treatment an initiative titled Improving Access to Psychological Treatments (IAPT), which targets anxiety and depression through the use of circumscribed CBT, began in 2008. "CBT Workers" who do not need to be mental health professionals provide "low" and "high" intensity

CBT after a year of training. They carry a very heavy active load of 45 clients, seeing between 175 and 250 cases per year. Using 4-session CBT protocols, National Institute of Health and Clinical Excellence Guidelines (NICE), and a stepped-care approach to their patients that relies on the individual's self-management of their problems, a whole new profession was created (see http://www.iapt.nhs.uk, 2011).

Some of the more promising (and disturbing?) conclusions of psychotherapy research arose from its investigation of the effects of training on patient outcome. Within this context research has *not* shown a strong link between level or type of professional training and psychotherapy outcome. Durlak (1979), among others, reviewed early research in this area concluding that clients treated by paraprofessionals had outcomes that were essentially equivalent to those offered by professionals. This research was criticized on numerous grounds (Hattie, Sharpley, & Rogers, 1984; Nietzel & Fisher, 1981; Stein & Lambert, 1984, 1995) and detractors were quick to point out that most of this research was conducted by those who had an interest in showing the value of paraprofessionals. It was also noted that paraprofessionals were trained and supervised by professionals, rather than offering independent services. Nevertheless, few studies can be found that show the expected superiority for the highly trained professional.

The study by Strupp and Hadley (1979) comparing experienced psychotherapists with college professors who had campus reputations as counselors secured no significant differences between the two groups. A replication of this work using group psychotherapy had the same results (Burlingame & Barlow, 1996). An experimental program to provide therapy training for middle-aged homemakers who were college graduates also produced very positive results for the nonprofessionals (Rioch, 1971). Although research comparing more and less trained individuals has all but disappeared from the research literature (see Hill & Knox, Chapter 19, this volume) the topic is a vital one for both training programs and service delivery.

This research does raise questions about the value of clinical training and the uniqueness of psychotherapeutic interventions taught in graduate schools. Nevertheless, research in this area supports the value of psychotherapy regardless of the level or kind of training that typifies the separate professions and the paraprofessionals whom they train and employ as extensions of their influence. If taken seriously such findings support the widespread application of psychotherapeutic services and will ensure that they remain widely available. On the basis of research evidence no monopoly on superior service can be claimed by any one profession, and the thoughtful use of paraprofessionals should be encouraged not only for economic reasons, but because they have been found to be effective in a variety of circumscribed roles when properly supervised. A repeated finding of research studies aimed at satisfaction with service, suggests satisfaction is equal across mental health specialties, with 46% of more than 1,500 respondents indicating that psychotherapy made things "a lot better" and 45% said things were "somewhat better" (Consumer Reports, 2010). The current large-scale experiment being undertaken in the United Kingdom (IAPT) will become an important source of information over the next decade.

Perhaps one reason for the lack of difference between professions on psychotherapy outcome is that the training in psychotherapy that is received is highly diverse even within professions. Psychiatrists are trained first in medicine, and second in pharmacological solutions, with psychotherapy being a distant third in emphasis. Psychologists have typically been trained in academic departments of psychology, but now are often trained in freestanding professional schools as well. Both types of programs differ within and between themselves in the amount and intensity of didactic and supervised experience. One cannot distinguish the training (or its quality) a particular psychologist has received by virtue of knowing the type of degree that has been attained. Since the various programs may emphasize different theoretical orientations and different practicum experiences, the diversity in training can be extensive.

In addition, knowledge about professionals' credentials is not informative about their participation in widely available postdoctoral institutes, continuing education programs, workshops, professional meetings, and the like. The personal qualities of those who provide treatment can also be of great importance, but are seldom studied. Nevertheless, psychotherapy research has illuminated the widespread effectiveness of psychological interventions across a wide range of practitioners that offer services, and this effectiveness is highlighted in many of the chapters that follow, particularly Chapters 7 and 19.

Managed Care and Dose-Effect Research

For the first half of the 20th century effective psychotherapy was considered to be a long-term process, with briefer therapy considered superficial. Early providers of psychoanalytically oriented therapy prescribed years of treatment that was very costly. Voth and Orth (1973), for example, reported an average length of 835 sessions from their study of psychoanalysis. A clear trend in practice has been the movement toward relatively brief treatments, although a preference for longer treatment persists in some parts of the world, it certainly does not represent current practice patterns in the United States and many other countries. In a recent dinner conversation with a group of psychoanalysts from Germany, where the health system continues to support long-term therapy, the discussion turned to a recent controversy within psychoanalytically oriented providers, with some advocating three sessions per week instead of the traditional four sessions per week.

This less intense therapy was viewed by the more traditional providers as undermining the best interests of the patient. The author was a complete outsider in such a discussion, because in the United States brief therapy has become acceptable to most practitioners and certainly the common experience for most patients. In fact, most research is conducted on therapy offered once a week for no more than 14 to 20 weeks, and in most practice settings treatment actually averages closer to five sessions (Hansen, Lambert, & Forman, 2002). Earlier editions of this handbook included a chapter dedicated to brief therapy. Organized brief therapy programs tended to use interventions that lasted 6 to 10 sessions and generally reported positive results (Koss & Shiang, 1994). In the 2004 and current edition, no such chapter was included because it was seen as redundant with the study results reported in most other chapters, which seldom summarize long-term treatments. Almost all therapies that are studied (particularly in the United States) are "brief," lasting less than 20 sessions. For an understanding of longer-term treatments, one must consider older studies that were reviewed in earlier editions of the handbook, examine research from European countries where patients continue to receive treatments that last for years (that is often not available in English) or consult Chapter 12 of this volume.

One of the most profound developments in recent years that affects the length of treatment has been the advent of managed care organizations. Most health insurance plans place limits on the number of treatment sessions they will reimburse (hovering around eight sessions), and often instigate evaluative procedures to make certain that coverage does not extend beyond what they advocate as the basic necessary treatment length. This practice is undertaken with little regard for the fact that a majority of studies of empirically supported psychotherapy is based on at least weekly psychotherapy that extends over an average of 14 weeks. Because many people cannot afford self-paid treatment that goes beyond an insurance coverage limit, managed care organizations determine the length of treatment received by a large number of Americans and this same trend can be found in other countries.

Patients, for the most part, prefer to be helped as quickly as possible, and efficiency is also favored by funding services such as insurance companies and the government. Managed care itself arose, at least partially, as a response to spiraling health care cost in general. Limiting sessions is an obvious and relatively simple way of reducing costs. The amount of treatment available to those in need is often determined by the costs of providing services. Obviously, if as much can be gained from 10 sessions of treatment as 30, then curtailing the amount of therapy makes good economic sense. Brief therapy is an option that responds to the issue of efficiency, a topic that is on the minds of many. At this point in time psychotherapy researchers have not devoted much attention to cost-effectiveness studies that would simultaneously consider cost and outcome, although they have begun to investigate the relationship between "dose" of treatment and response with its obvious correlation with costs.

Early investigations within this latter topic were focused on demonstrating that brief therapy was as effective as longer therapies (e.g., Luborsky, Singer, & Luborsky, 1975). Contemporary studies have been more interested in understanding the dose–response relationship (how many sessions are needed for a meaningful treatment outcome?). This research has important implications for social policy and insurer decision making as well as client suffering. Howard, Kopta, Krause, Merton, and Orlinsky (1986) were the first to report data in a form that estimated the dose response relationship. In a mega-analysis of data from 2,431 patients drawn from previously reported studies using pre- and postchange, they used statistical modeling techniques to estimate the number of sessions needed to meet a defined standard of improvement. Their analysis suggested that positive gains made early in treatment were followed by less dramatic changes across later sessions. They also suggested that 75% of patients had improved after 26 treatment sessions (nearly 6 months of once-weekly psychotherapy).

Later research following this same paradigm, but using data from patients who rated their functioning on a weekly basis (obviating the need for statistical procedures that estimate weekly change), found the same general relationships— rapid change early in therapy is followed by smaller per session increments, but more therapy increases the likelihood of improvement and recovery in individual patients (e.g., Anderson & Lambert, 2001; Kadera, Lambert, & Andrews, 1996). It appears from this research and related studies summarized in Chapter 6 of this volume, that 50% of patients who enter treatment in clinical settings will show *clinically meaningful change* after 13 to 18 sessions of treatment. An additional 25% will meet the same standards after approximately 50 sessions of once weekly treatment (an estimate of sufficient dosage that exceeds that provided by Howard et al., 1986). More recently, researchers studying care in naturalistic settings have suggested that patients tend to withdraw from treatment when they have reliably improved or recovered. Barkham et al. (2006), for example, suggest that the impact of sessions does not diminish as dosage increases, a finding supported by Percevic, Lambert, and Kordy (2006).

These studies suggest that the movement toward briefer treatment is justified on empirical grounds for some patients; but that close to 50% of patients will not be well served by therapies that are intentionally limited to less than 18 sessions. They also suggest that the more disturbed a patient is when they begin treatment, the longer therapy will need to last for the patient to return to normal functioning. *Limiting treatment duration to eight sessions serves the interests of those patients who are least disturbed, but cannot be considered a fair and equitable practice for a majority of patients. Some recognition of this reality and its social consequences needs to find its way into the minds of the U.S. public, employers, and government, and be integrated into third-party payer guidelines and future social policy* decisions as well as theoretical suppositions about effective psychotherapy.

THE EMERGENCE OF EVIDENCE-BASED OUTCOME MONITORING

There are several trends in psychotherapy research and practice that appear to be highly promising for patients beyond the provision of evidence-based treatments and treatment practices. These promising new practice/research strategies are likely to make research more useful to providers and will probably have more impact on patients than offering "empirically supported treatments." Two distinct but potentially overlapping research paradigms hold this potential: patient-focused research and practice-based research.

Patient-focused research. Initial efforts to apply this alternative psychotherapy research paradigm were described in a special section of the *Journal of Consulting and Clinical Psychology* (Lambert, 2001). Variously termed, *patient-focused research*, *quality management*, and *outcome management*, this research strategy makes use of actuarial methods for modeling expected patient treatment response in relation to actual treatment response, feeding back this information to therapists, supervisors, and the patient. Thus the results of research become imbedded in routine care that includes session-by-session monitoring of mental health vital signs. Although most research has depended on statistical tests of differences between a treatment group and a control group, with differences reported through the use of group-based inferential statistics, patient-focused research uses clinically meaningful change criteria such as those elaborated upon by the late Neil Jacobson and his colleagues (Jacobson, Follette, & Ravenstorf, 1984; Jacobson & Truax, 1991) for the *individual* patient to inform the clinician when the patient has reliably improved or recovered. Outcome management research strategies are aimed at helping clinicians formally monitor patient treatment response, and make adjustments to treatments in real time. In contrast to other research strategies, outcome management makes empiricism a viable part of routine practice on a case-by-case basis, rather than a distant abstraction that practitioners find difficult to incorporate in practice. At this point in time enough research evidence has accumulated to show such methods significantly enhance patient outcomes (Lambert & Shimokawa, 2011; Shimokawa, Lambert, & Smart, 2010), but these methods are relatively new and they are in need of replication. In addition, there is considerable resistance among clinicians to making regular assessments of outcomes a routine practice (Jensen-Doss & Hawley, 2010).

Practice-based evidence. Barkham and Margison (2007) have provided a definition for this term: "Practice-based evidence is the conscientious, explicit, and judicious use of current evidence drawn from practice settings in making decisions about the care of individual patients." (Barkham & Margison, 2007, p. 446). These authors suggest that practice-based evidence results from integrating both individual clinical expertise and service-level parameters, with the best available evidence drawn from rigorous research activity carried out in routine clinical settings. Practice-based research examines how and which treatments or services are provided to individuals within service systems and evaluates how to improve treatment or service delivery at the clinic level. The aim is not so much to isolate or generalize the effect of an intervention across settings, but to examine variations in care and ways to implement research-based treatments. Much of the work in this area has been summarized by Barkham, Hardy, and Mellor-Clark (2010). The focus of their edited book is to show how practice-based evidence starts with a focus on the individual patient through monitoring treatment response, and then extends the use of this systematic data collection to providers, groups of providers, and systems of care. In the end, very large data sets become available and can be used in a wide variety of ways, from providing benchmarks that can be compared across services and within services over time, to identifying practices that are working and those that are not (Stiles, Barkham, Connell, & Mellor-Clark, 2008). Good examples of benchmarks can be found in a special issue of *Counselling & Psychotherapy Research* (2006), including completion rates for measures, frequency of unilateral termination, recovery and improvement rates, and waiting times (Trusler, Doherty, Grant, Mullin, & McBride, 2006). Benchmarking can also take the form of comparing effectiveness in a particular clinical setting against the outcomes obtained in efficacy studies (e.g., Barkham et al., 2008; Merrill, Tolbert, & Wade, 2003; Minami, Wampold, Serlin, Kircher, & Brown, 2007). Weisz and colleagues (2005) indicate that the most valid answers to questions about treatment outcome and change processes are more likely to come from research in "real-world" service settings than from controlled lab studies.

Based on the initial applications of these research methods it is clear that practice-based evidence research can be integrated into routine practice, thus narrowing the gap between practice and research, while improving treatment outcomes (see Chapter 4, this volume, for a more complete discussion).

ETHICS IN RESEARCH

Interest and concern over the ethics of research activities connected to psychotherapy have a long-standing history. For example, in the 1950s Rogers and Dymond (1954) raised concerns about the use of a no-treatment control group in their study of client-centered psychotherapy because it was clear that psychotherapy had been shown to be effective. The current climate for conducting studies of psychotherapy, and psychology in general, abounds with ethical and legal considerations aimed at protecting the participants in studies. The protection of "subjects'" rights and welfare has been a positive development, notwithstanding the sometimes-obvious inhibition on creativity and slowing of progress in the field. These protections have obvious impact on design and conduct of studies and have led to reductions in the use of no-treatment and placebo control groups as well as the rise in use of "standard treatment" or "usual treatment" control groups to overcome the problems associated with depriving individuals who need treatment with bona fide interventions (Spielmans, Gatlin, & McFall, 2010).

Other standards for conduct of research studies have remained more stable. Objectivity and honesty in recording, tabulating, analyzing, and reporting results are mainstays of all scientific endeavors. It is important to maintain such principles if the research enterprise is to exist and flourish. So far psychotherapy research has avoided notoriety for the kind of fraud that has been exposed in some fields (e.g., data tampering or even the creation of false data). One notable case in the field of psychotherapy recently involved accusations of filing false information involving discrepancies between the number of subject volunteers that were reported on progress reports that William Fals-Stewart submitted to the National Institute for Drug Abuse relating to grants for which he was the Principal Investigator, and his subsequent actions aimed at covering up this fraud. Such intentional deception as well as mishandling of data and its variations must be perceived as simply intolerable. However, within the field, instances of biased interpretation of data have been noted (e.g., Bergin & Garfield, 1994) and such activities can be harmful to patients, the status of scientific information, as well as the reputation and careers of those who are involved.

Some related problems are more subtle and complex, but nonetheless important to the field. For example, the presentation and interpretation of data by researchers leaves considerable wiggle room for partial truths to be presented as the entire picture. In fact, journal review procedures encourage routine summaries of procedures that make it all but certain that research reports will present the strongest possible case for rigor with little mention of significant limiting information. In the competitive world of publishing in the most respected journals, where editors and reviewers search for design and performance flaws and reject 85% of manuscripts, researchers are likely to emphasize the strengths of their research procedures and methods rather than providing a complete list of problems. Even the most rigorously executed research is imperfectly conducted but little is to be gained by elaborating on problems when submitting manuscripts for review.

For example, a common demand in clinical trials research is to test the effects of treatment on a single disorder. In the context of writing about selection and exclusion criteria for study patients, researchers are prone to emphasize the inclusion of homogeneously diagnostic patient samples. When being criticized for the lack of relevance of such research (with such carefully selected patients) for practice, however, these same researchers are likely to present a picture of these patients that is quite different when this criticism is raised. They argue that the patients are, after all, just like the patients seen in everyday practice. It is generally understood by avid readers of scientific reports that the politics of publishing influences the presentation of methods, and that these presentations are not an entirely accurate picture of all the findings that could be reported. Fortunately, the discussion of results by the authors (and the use of peer review) often point out many limitations of the research and soften the expression of implications for practice that might otherwise be made.

In addition, replication studies, as well as exposure of research to public scrutiny, eventually correct many of the important errors that find their way into the field. But this corrective action often takes years. The American Psychological Association has gone to great lengths to provide reporting standards (APA Publications and Communications Board, 2008). Aside from these remedies, it behooves readers of research to use caution in drawing more than tentative conclusions from any particular study. In the area of interpreting research findings, meta-analytic reviews present an opportunity to increase objectivity. Although such procedures are not entirely free of biasing choices (compare, for example, Anderson & Lambert, 1995; Crits-Christoph, 1992; Svartberg & Stiles, 1991; or results presented by Prioleau, Murdock, & Brody, 1983; Smith et al., 1980). Although meta-analytic procedures are not free from biasing choices, the decision rules are made explicit and made public, and thus a step in the direction of reducing biases in reviews of psychotherapy outcome literature can be achieved (see Chapter 2, this volume).

Psychotherapy researchers have considerable awareness that values are central in the therapeutic process as well as in the research that they conduct. An emphasis on values and their impact on research are often obscured by the focus on effective technologies and their evaluation in standard research paradigms. Yet researchers are well aware that their choices about what and how to study the changes that result from psychotherapy guide the phenomena that they seek to investigate. Psychotherapy and psychotherapy research are in fact guided by a host of value choices. Change in humans is so complex that it is difficult to study the full meaning of the changes that take place in treatment. Symptomatic changes often have a meaning component that is seldom studied in traditional research. The errors and oversimplification that inevitably arise in psychotherapy research often come from the complexity of a research task that is very daunting, rather than from carelessness, ignorance, or naiveté. Few studies even attempt to examine the full range of consequences of entering treatment at a propitious moment in the life of a client who is enmeshed in a family and social context. The research summaries in this book attempt to reduce the myriad methods and results of psychotherapy into a cohesive picture that has implications for practice, but in so doing, the values of reviewers effect the conclusions that are drawn.

Out of necessity, the chapters in this text, like the research studies that informed them, sometimes emphasize relatively narrow domains of personal functioning and include research studies that vary widely in sophistication and rigor. Though there are limitations in the research summaries that follow, they provide a foundation for broadening inquiries into the effects of psychotherapies that will enable future studies to move forward with questions of greater precision if not importance. Even with these limitations the research summaries included in this volume have important implications for the practice of psychotherapy and thereby the fabric of social life in the fullest sense of the word.

OVERVIEW OF THE BOOK

This handbook is divided into four sections. As in the previous five editions, each chapter can be read by itself and makes an independent contribution to the literature. The first five chapters focus on broad methodological issues. Following the present introductory chapter, Comer and Kendall summarize important principles and contemporary methods applied in traditional experimental research designs. The chapter helps the reader understand terminology, procedures, statistical methods, and what types of designs are suitable for answering particular research questions. The information in Chapter 2 is essential to understanding and evaluating the nuances of existing research findings. Chapter 3 (McLeod) provides an emphasis on *qualitative methods*, and their use in illuminating the subjective experience of research participants and in formulating research questions—and stands in stark contrast to the methods focused on in Chapter 2. The fourth chapter (Castonguay, Barkham, Lutz, and McAleavey) exposes the reader to relatively new research strategies aimed at improving service delivery and outcomes with an emphasis on research in routine care. The emphasis is on bridging the gap between psychotherapy research and psychotherapy practice. It has the important goal of greater cooperation between scientists and practitioners with positive consequences for patients. Chapter 5 (Ogles) focuses on an essential aspect of the scientific study of psychotherapy: methods of measuring the outcomes of psychotherapy. By reviewing contemporary measurement strategies and methods, this chapter brings clarity to how the variables of greatest interest are operationally

defined and handled within empirical evaluation. It is an especially important chapter for those who are planning research on behavior change and trying to understand its meanings.

The second section of this handbook moves away from methodological issues by examining findings in a broad context. Chapter 6 (Lambert) provides an overview of the general effects of therapy (efficacy and effectiveness) and deals with questions that are central to practice outside of specific treatments. Chapter 7 (Bohart and Wade) focuses on the patient's contribution to psychotherapy outcomes. Chapter 8 (Baldwin and Imel) summarizes the impact of the therapist on psychotherapy outcome. The final chapter (Crits-Christoph, Gibbons, and Mukherjee) in this section evaluates the role of processes and outcomes (activities and impacts) as studied simultaneously within single investigations. Together these five chapters, while overlapping to some degree, provide a broad picture of the most basic and general findings of psychotherapy research.

The third section of this handbook reviews research findings as they have arisen within four major schools of psychotherapy (and their variants). It includes chapters on behavior therapy (Emmelkamp), cognitive and cognitive-behavioral therapy (Hollon and Beck), psychodynamic psychotherapy (Barber, Murran, McCarthy, and Keefe) and experiential/humanistic interventions (Elliot, Greenberg, Watson, Timulak, and Freire).

The fourth and final section of the handbook—"Research on Applications in Special Groups and Settings"—is the longest section, with six chapters. Included are chapters on psychotherapies with child and adolescent patients (Weisz, Ng, Rutt, Lau, and Masland), couple and family therapies (Sexton, Datchi, Evans, LaFollette, and Wright) group psychotherapies (Burlingame, Strauss, and Joyce), behavioral medicine and health psychology (Smith and Williams). Chapter 18 (Forand, DeRubeis, and Amsterdam) reviews research on treating psychological problems with medications alone and in conjunction with psychotherapy. The psychotherapeutic practices in these chapters represent, to a certain extent, specialty areas that are distinct from each other, but also overlap, both in the patient problems that are addressed, and the interventions that are used. The final chapter (Hill and Knox) considers what we know from research about training, and supervision and their effects.

REFERENCES

Ablon, J. S., & Jones, E. E. (1999). Psychotherapy process in the National Institute of Mental Health Treatment of Depression Collaborative Research Program. *Journal of Consulting and Clinical Psychology*, *67*(1), 64–75.

American Psychiatric Association. (2000). *Diagnostic and statistical manual of mental disorders* (4th ed.). Washington, DC: Author.

American Psychological Association. (2005). *Determination and documentation of the need for practice guidelines.* www.apa.org/practice/guidelines/determination-documentation.pdf

Anderson, E. M., & Lambert, M. J. (1995). Short-term dynamically oriented psychotherapy: A meta-analysis. *Clinical Psychology Review*, *15*(5), 503–514.

Anderson, E. M., & Lambert, M. J. (2001). A survival analysis of clinically significant change in outpatient psychotherapy. *Journal of Clinical Psychology*, *57*, 875–888.

Andrews, G. (2000). A focus on empirically supported outcomes: A commentary on search for empirically supported treatments. *Clinical Psychology: Science and Practice*, *7*, 264–268.

APA Presidential Task Force on Evidence-Based Practice. (2006). Evidence-based practice in psychology. *American Psychologist*, *61*, 271–285.

APA Publications and Communications Board Working Group on Journal Article Reporting Standards. (2008). Reporting standards for research in psychology: Why do we need them? What might they be? *American Psychologist*, *63*, 839–851.

Bandura, A. (1969). *Principles of behavior modification.* New York, NY: Holt, Rinehart & Winston.

Barak, A., Hen, L., Boniel-Nissim, R., & Shapira, N. (2008). A comprehensive review and meta-analysis of the effectiveness of Internet-based psychotherapeutic interventions. *Journal of Technology in Human Services*, *26*, 109–160.

Barkham, M., Connell, J., Stiles, W. B., Miles, J. N. V., Margison, F., Evans, C., & Mellor-Clark, J. (2006). Dose-effect relations and responsive regulation of treatment duration: The good enough level. *Journal of Consulting and Clinical Psychology*, *74*, 160–167.

Barkham, M., Hardy, G., & Mellor-Clark, J. (2010). *Developing and delivering practice-based evidence: A guide for the psychological therapies* (pp. 21–62). New York, NY: Wiley-Blackwell.

Barkham, M., & Margison, F. (2007). Practice-based evidence as complement to evidence-based practice: From dichotomy to chiasmus. In C. Freeman & M. Power (Eds.), *Handbook of evidence-based psychotherapies: A guide for research & practice* (pp. 443–476). Chichester, United Kingdom: Wiley.

Barkham, M., Stiles, W. B., Connell, J., Twigg, E., Leach, C., ... Angus, L. (2008). Effects of psychological therapies in randomized clinical trials and practice-based studies. *British Journal of Clinical Psychology*, *47*, 397–415.

Beck, A. T. (1970). Cognitive therapy: Nature and relation to behavior therapy. *Behavior Therapy*, *1*, 184–200.

Beck, A. T. (1976). *Cognitive therapy and the emotional disorders.* New York, NY: International Universities Press.

Bergin, A. E. (1971). The evaluation of therapeutic outcomes. In A. E. Bergin & S. L. Garfield (Eds.), *Handbook of psychotherapy and behavior change: An empirical analysis* (pp. 217–270). New York, NY: Wiley.

Bergin, A. E., & Garfield, S. L. (Eds.). (1971). *Handbook of psychotherapy and behavior change.* New York, NY: Wiley.

Bergin, A. E., & Garfield, S. L. (Eds.). (1994). *Handbook of psychotherapy and behavior change* (4th ed.). New York, NY: Wiley.

Bergin, A. E., & Lambert, M. J. (1978). The evaluation of therapeutic outcomes. In S. L. Garfield & A. E. Bergin (Eds.), *Handbook of psychotherapy and behavior change* (2nd ed., pp. 139–189). New York, NY: Wiley.

Beutler, L. E. (2000). David and Goliath: When empirical and clinical standards of practice meet. *American Psychologist*, *55*, 997–1007.

Bright, J. I., Baker, K. D., & Niemeyer, R. A. (1999). Professional and paraprofessional group treatments for depression. A comparison of cognitive behavioral and mutual support interventions. *Journal of Consulting and Clinical Psychology*, *67*, 491–501.

Burlingame, G. M., & Barlow, S. H. (1996). Outcome and process differences between professional and nonprofessional therapists in time-limited group psychotherapy. *International Journal of Group Psychotherapy*, *46*, 455–478.

Burns, B., & Hoagwood, K. E. (Eds.). (2005). Evidence-based practice: Part I: Effecting change. *Child and adolescent psychiatric clinics of North America*, *14* (Whole No. 2).

Carey, T. A. (2010). Will you follow while they lead? Introducing a patient-led approach to low intensity CBT interventions. In J. Bennett-Levy, D. A. Richards, P. Farrand, H. Christensen, K. M. Griffiths, D. J. Kavanagh, ... C. Williams (Eds.), *Oxford guide to low intensity CBT interventions* (pp. 331–338). Oxford, United Kingdom: Oxford University Press.

Carey, T. A., & Spratt, M. B. (2009). When is enough enough? Structuring the organisation of treatment to maximise patient choice and control. *Cognitive Behaviour Therapist*, *2*, 211–226.

Chambless, D. L. (1996). In defense of dissemination of empirically supported psychological interventions. *Clinical Psychology: Science and Practice*, *3*(3), 230–235.

Chambless, D. L., & Hollon, S. D. (1998). Defining empirically supported psychological interventions. *Consulting and Clinical Psychology, 66*(1), 7–18.

Chambless, D. L., Sanderson, W. C., Shoham, V., Johnson, S. B., Pope, K. S., Crits-Christoph, P., ...McCurry, S. (1996). An update on empirically validated therapies. *Clinical Psychology, 49*(2), 5–14.

Cohen, L. H., Sargent, M. M., & Sechrest, L. B. (1986). Use of psychotherapy research by professional psychologists. *American Psychologist, 41*(2), 198–206.

Consumer Reports. (2010, July). *Depression and anxiety: Readers reveal the therapists and drugs that helped.* www.ConsumerReports.org

Crits-Christoph, P. (1992). The efficacy of brief dynamic psychotherapy: A meta-analysis. *American Journal of Psychiatry, 149*(2), 151–158.

DeLeon, P. H., Kenkel, M. B., Garcia-Shelton, L., & VandenBos, G. R. (2011). Psychotherapy, 1960 to the present. In J. C. Norcross, G. R. VandenBos, & D. K. Freedheim (Eds.), *History of psychotherapy: Continuity and change* (2nd ed., pp. 39–62). Washington, DC: American Psychological Association.

Durlak, J. A. (1979). Comparative effectiveness of paraprofessional and professional helpers. *Psychological Bulletin, 86*, 80–92.

Ellis, A. (1962). *Reason and emotion in psychotherapy.* New York, NY: Lyle Stuart.

Eysenck, H. F. (1952). The effects of psychotherapy: An evaluation. *Journal of Consulting Psychology, 16*, 319–324.

Garfield, S. L. (1982). Eclecticism and integration in psychotherapy. *Behavioral Therapy, 13*, 174–183.

Garfield, S. L. (1983). *Clinical Psychology: The study of personality and behavior* (2nd ed.). New York, NY: Aldine.

Garfield, S. L. (1996). Some problems associated with "validated" forms of psychotherapy. *Clinical Psychology: Science and Practice, 3*, 218–229.

Garfield, S. L., & Bergin, A. E. (Eds.). (1978). *Handbook of psychotherapy and behavior change* (2nd ed.). New York, NY: Wiley.

Garfield, S. L., & Bergin, A. E. (Eds.). (1986). *Handbook of psychotherapy and behavior change* (3rd ed.). New York, NY: Wiley.

Garfield, S. L., & Kurtz, R. (1977). A study of eclectic views. *Journal of Consulting and Clinical Psychology, 45*, 78–83.

Geddes, J. R., Burgess, S., Hawton, K., Jamison, K., & Goodwin, G. M. (2004). Long-term lithium therapy for bipolar disorder: Systematic review and meta-analysis of randomized controlled trials. *American Journal of Psychiatry, 161*, 217–222.

Goldfried, M. R. (1991). Research issues in psychotherapy integration. *Journal of Psychology Integration, 1*, 5–25.

Goodheart, C. D., Kazdin, A. E., & Steinberg, R. J. (2006). *Evidence-based psychotherapy: Where practice and research meet.* Washington, DC: American Psychological Association.

Hansen, N. B., Lambert, M. J., & Forman, E. M. (2002). The psychotherapy dose–response effect and its implications for treatment delivery services. *Clinical Psychology: Science and Practice, 9*, 329–343.

Hattie, J. A., Sharpley, C. F., & Rogers, H. J. (1984). Comparative effectiveness of professional and paraprofessional helpers. *Psychological Bulletin, 95*, 534–541.

Henrick, R. (Ed.). (1980). *The psychotherapy handbook: The A to Z guide to more than 250 different therapies in use today.* New York, NY: Meridian Books.

Howard, K. I., Kopta, S. M., Krause, M. S., Merton, S., & Orlinsky, D. E. (1986). The dose-effect relationship in psychotherapy. *American Psychologist, 41*(2), 159–164.

Hunsley, J. (2007). Addressing key challenges in evidence-based practice in psychology. *Professional Psychology: Research and Practice, 38*, 113–121.

Jacobson, N. S., Follette, W. C., & Revenstorf, D. (1984). Psychotherapy outcome research: Methods for reporting variability and evaluating clinical significance. *Behavior Therapy, 15*(4), 336–352.

Jacobson, N. S., & Truax, P. (1991). Clinical significance: A statistical approach to defining meaningful change in psychotherapy research. *Journal of Consulting and Clinical Psychology, 59*(1), 12–19.

Jensen, J. P., Bergin, A. E., & Greaves, D. W. (1990). The meaning of eclecticism: New survey and analysis of components. *Professional Psychology: Research and Practice, 21*, 124–130.

Jensen-Doss, A., & Hawley, K. M. (2010). Understanding barriers to evidence-based assessment: Clinician attitudes toward standardized assessment tools. *Journal of Clinical Child & Adolescent Psychology, 39*, 885–896.

Jones, M. C. (1924). The elimination of children's fears. *Journal of Experimental Psychology, 7*, 383–390.

Kadera, S. W., Lambert, M. J., & Andrews, A. A. (1996). How much therapy is really enough? A session-by-session analyses of the psychotherapy dose-effect relationship. *Journal of Psychotherapy Practice and Research, 5*, 132–151.

Kazdin, A. E. (1986). Comparative outcome studies of psychotherapy: Methodological issues and strategies. *Journal of Consulting and Clinical Psychology, 54*, 95–105.

Kazdin, A. E. (2008). Evidence-based treatment and practice—New opportunities to bridge clinical research and practice, enhance the knowledge base, and improve patient care. *American Psychologist, 63*(3), 146–159.

Koss, M. P., & Shiang, J. (1994). Research on brief psychotherapy. In A. E. Bergin & S. L. Garfield (Eds.), *Handbook of psychology and behavior change* (4th ed., pp. 664–700). New York, NY: Wiley.

Kurtzman, H., & Bufka, L. (2011). APA moves forward on developing clinical treatment guidelines. Washington, DC: APA.

Lambert, M. J. (1976). Spontaneous remission in adult neurotic disorders: A revision and summary. *Psychological Bulletin, 83*(1), 107–119.

Lambert, M. J. (2001). Psychotherapy outcome and quality improvement: Patient-focused research. *Journal of Consulting and Clinical Psychology, 69,* 147–149.

Lambert, M. J. (2004). *Bergin and Garfield's handbook of psychotherapy and behavior change* (5th ed.). Hoboken, NJ: Wiley.

Lambert, M. J. (2010). *Prevention of treatment failure: The use of measuring, monitoring, and feedback in clinical practice.* Washington, DC: American Psychological Association.

Lambert, M. J., & Shimokawa, K. (2011). Collecting client feedback. In J. C. Norcross (Ed.), *Psychotherapy relationships that work* (2nd ed., pp. 203–223). New York, NY: Oxford University Press.

Luborsky, L., Singer, B., & Luborsky, L. (1975). Comparative studies of psychotherapies: Is it true that "everyone has one and all must have prizes"? *Archive of General Psychiatry, 32,* 995–1008.

Meltzoff, J., & Korneich, M. (1970). *Research in psychotherapy.* New York, NY: Atherton Press.

Merrill, K. A., Tolbert, V. E., & Wade W. A. (2003). Effectiveness of cognitive therapy for depression in a community mental health center: A benchmarking study. *Journal of Consulting & Clinical Psychology, 71,* 404–409.

Minami, T., Wampold, B. E., Serlin, R. C., Kircher, J. C., & Brown, G. S. (2007). Benchmarks for psychotherapy efficacy in adult major depression. *Journal of Consulting & Clinical Psychology, 75,* 232–243.

Morrow-Bradley, C., & Elliott, R. (1986). Utilization of psychotherapy research by practicing psychotherapists. *American Psychologist, 41*(2), 188–197.

Mowrer, O. H., & Mowrer, W. (1938). Enuresis: A method of its study and treatment. *American Journal of Orthopsychiatry, 8,* 436–459.

Nathan, P. E. (1998). Practice guidelines: Not yet ideal. *American Psychologist, 53,* 290–299.

Nathan, P. E., Gorman, J. M., & Salkind, N. J. (2002). *Treating mental disorders: A guide to what works* (2nd ed.). New York, NY: Oxford University Press.

Nietzel, N. T., & Fisher, S. G. (1981). Effectiveness of professional and paraprofessional helpers: A comment on Durlak. *Psychological Bulletin, 89,* 555–565.

Norcross, J. C., & Goldfried, M. R. (Eds.). (1992). *Handbook of psychotherapy integration.* New York, NY: Basic Books.

Norcross, J. C., Karg, R. S., & Proshaska, J. O. (1997). Clinical psychologists in the 90's: Part 1. *The Clinical Psychologist, 50*(2), 4–9.

Norcross, J. C., Vanderbos, G. R., & Freedheim, D. K. (2011). *History of psychotherapy: Continuity & change* (2nd ed.). Washington, DC: American Psychological Association.

Okiishi, J. C., Lambert, M. J., Eggett, D., Nielsen, L., Dayton, D. D., & Vermeersch, D. A. (2006). An analysis of therapist treatment effects: Toward providing feedback to individual therapists on their clients' psychotherapy outcome. *Journal of Clinical Psychology, 62,* 1157–1172. doi: 10.1002/jclp

Parloff, M. B. (1982). Psychotherapy research evidence and reimbursement decisions: Bambi meets Godzilla. *American Journal of Psychiatry, 139,* 718–727.

Percevic, R., Lambert, M. J., & Kordy, H. (2006). What is the predictive value of responses to psychotherapy for its future course? Empirical explorations and consequences for outcome monitoring. *Psychotherapy Research, 16,* 364–373.

Prioleau, L., Murdock, M., & Brody, N. (1983). An analysis of psychotherapy versus placebo studies. *Behavioral and Brain Sciences, 6,* 275–285.

Report of the Research Task Force of the National Institute of Mental Health. (1975). *Research in the service of mental health* (DHEW Publication No. ADM 75–236). Rockville, MD.

Rioch, M. J. (1971). Two pilot projects in training mental health counselors. In R. R. Holt (Ed.), *New horizon for psychiatry* (pp. 294–311). New York, NY: International Universities Press.

Rogers, C. R. (1942). *Counseling and psychotherapy.* Boston, MA: Houghton Mifflin.

Rogers, C. R., & Dymond, R. F. (Eds.). (1954). *Psychotherapy and personality change.* Chicago, IL: University of Chicago Press.

Roth, A., & Fonagy, P. (2005). *What works for whom? A critical review of psychotherapy research* (2nd ed.). New York, NY: Guilford Press.

Shimokawa, K., Lambert, M. J., & Smart, D. W. (2010). Enhancing treatment outcome of patients at risk of treatment failure: Meta-Analytic and mega-analytic review of a psychotherapy quality assurance system. *Journal of Consulting & Clinical Psychology, 78,* 298–311.

Smith, M. L., Glass, G. W. V., & Miller, T. L. (1980). *The benefits of psychotherapy.* Baltimore, MD: Johns Hopkins University Press.

Spielmans, G. I., Gatlin, E. T., & McFall, J. P. (2010). The efficacy of evidence-based psychotherapies versus usual care for youths: Controlling confounds in a meta-reanalysis. *Psychotherapy Research, 20,* 234–246.

Stein, D. M., & Lambert, M. J. (1984). On the relationship between therapist experience and psychotherapy outcome. *Clinical Psychology Review, 4*(2), 127–142.

Stein, D. M., & Lambert, M. J. (1995). Graduate training in psychotherapy: Are therapy outcomes enhanced? *Journal of Consulting and Clinical Psychology, 63*(2), 179–183.

Stiles, W. B., Barkham, M. B., Connell, J., & Mellor-Clark, J. (2008). Responsive regulation of treatment duration in routine practice in United Kingdom primary care settings: Replication in a larger sample. *Journal of Consulting and Clinical Psychology, 76*, 298–305.

Strupp, H. H. (1997). On the limitation of therapy manuals. *Clinical Psychological Science and Practice, 4*(1), 76–82.

Strupp, H. H., & Hadley, S. W. (1979). Specific and nonspecific factors in psychotherapy. *Archives of General Psychiatry, 36*, 1125–1136.

Svartberg, M., & Stiles, T. C. (1991). Comparative effects of short-term psychodynamic psychotherapy: A meta-analysis. *Journal of Consulting and Clinical Psychology, 59*(5), 704–714.

Tanenbaum, S. J. (2005). Evidence-based practice as mental health policy: Three controversies and a caveat. *Health Affairs, 24*, 163–173.

Task Force on Promotion and Dissemination of Psychological Procedures. (1995). Training in and dissemination of empirically validated psychologist treatments: Report and recommendations. *Clinical Psychologist, 48*(1), 3–23.

Trusler, K., Doherty, C., Grant, S., Mullin, T., & McBride, J. (2006). Waiting times for primary counseling services. *Counselling & Psychotherapy Research, 6*, 23–32.

Voth, H. M., & Orth, M. H. (1973). *Psychotherapy and the role of the environment.* New York, NY: Behavioral Press.

Wachtel, P. L. (1977). *Psychoanalysis and behavior therapy.* New York, NY: Basic Books.

Wampold, B. E. (2001). *The great psychotherapy debate: Models, methods, and findings.* Mahwah, NJ: Erlbaum.

Weisz, J. R., Hawley, K. M., Pilkonis, P. A., Woody, S. R., & Follette, W. C. (2000). Stressing the (other) three Rs in the search for empirically supported treatments: Review procedures, research quality, relevance to practice and the public interest. *Clinical Psychology: Science and Practice, 7*(3), 243–258.

Weisz, J. R., Jensen, A. L., & McLeod, B. D. (2005). Development and dissemination of child and adolescent psychotherapies: Milestones, methods, and a new deployment-focused model. In E. D. Hibbs & P. S. Jensen (Eds.), *Psychosocial treatments for child and adolescent disorders: Empirically based strategies for clinical practice* (2nd ed., pp. 9–39). Washington, DC: American Psychological Association.

Weisz, J. R., Weisz, B., Ham, S. S., Granger, D. A., & Morton, T. (1995). Effects of psychotherapy with children and adolescents revisited: A meta-analysis of treatment outcome studies. *Psychological Bulletin, 117*, 450–468.

Wolpe, J. (1958). *Psychotherapy by reciprocal inhibition.* Stanford, CA: Stanford University Press.

Westen, D., Novotny, C. M., & Thompson-Brenne, H. (2004). The empirical status of empirically supported psychotherapies: Assumptions, findings, and reporting in controlled clinical trials. *Psychological Bulletin, 130*, 631–663.

Williams, S. L. (1985). On the nature and measurement of agoraphobia. *Progress in Behavior Modification, 19*, 109–144.

Woody, S. R., & Sanderson, W. C. (1998). Manuals for empirically supported treatments: 1998 update. *Clinical Psychology Review, 51*, 17–21.

CHAPTER 2

METHODOLOGY, DESIGN, AND EVALUATION IN PSYCHOTHERAPY RESEARCH

JONATHAN S. COMER AND PHILIP C. KENDALL

Even after 40 years it remains reasonable to note that in many ways Kiesler (1971) was right. In the first edition of this handbook (1971) in the chapter "Experimental Designs in Psychotherapy Research," he recommended that therapy researchers make consistent use of designs in which patient, therapist, and type of treatment are independent variables and dependent variables are examined over time (repeated measures). This approach provides the researcher with the opportunity to begin to answer the critical and often-restated question, "What therapist behaviors are effective with which types of clients in producing which kinds of patient change?" In the time since this valued directive, the field of therapy outcome evaluation has progressed—our knowledge about the outcomes of clinical interventions has been advanced by the accumulation of information gathered using this approach. Nevertheless, times have changed, new questions have been posed, and additional methodological niceties are now expected. In addition, the desire to bring empirically supported treatments based on experimental research designs to clinical practice has gained visibility.

In this chapter, in neo-Kiesler style, we present and discuss topics that pertain to the evaluation of the outcomes of psychological therapy. We begin with a brief description of principles that guide therapy researchers. We then describe and define the methodological issues that face therapy outcome researchers and discuss related questions concerning those treatments that have been evaluated. Specific methods for addressing the issues scientifically are described, and we consider both the problems that make definitive clinical outcome research difficult and the tactics developed by clinical researchers to handle these challenges. Last, we describe and comment on approaches to the cumulative examination of outcomes from multiple research studies. In general, sections of this chapter may stand alone, and the interested reader may go to any individual section for consideration of that specific content.

GUIDING PRINCIPLES

Two guiding principles merit preliminary consideration: (1) the role of the scientific practitioner in psychotherapy research and practice, and (2) the importance of empirically supported treatments.

The Scientist Practitioner

Treatment outcome research methods within psychology developed largely from the fundamental commitment of clinical psychologists to a scientist-practitioner model for training and professional practice (Shakow, 1976). This model has implications for research evaluations of therapy, and the empirical-clinical model of clinical practice and research developed as an operationalization of this guiding philosophy. Arguably, the scientist-practitioner model provides the framework (the adoption and refinement of the methods and guidelines of science) for continuously improving the clinical services offered to clients across the globe. Although the initial formulation of effective therapeutic strategies may result from activities other than rigorous research, such as careful observation or theoretical extrapolations, empirical evaluation of the efficacy and effectiveness of therapy is typically considered necessary before widespread utilization can be sanctioned. As a result, therapy researchers developed a sophisticated array of research methods for evaluating the outcome of therapeutic intervention.

The scientist-practitioner model is widespread. Indeed, both scientists who evaluate their work and their theories with rigor, and practitioners who utilize a research-based understanding of human behavior in social contexts to aid people in resolving psychological dysfunctions and enhancing their lives, follow the scientist-practitioner model. The ideal is not intended to create professional role confusion but rather to foster service providers who evaluate their interventions scientifically and researchers who study applied questions and interpret their findings with an understanding of the richness and complexity of human experience (Kendall & Norton-Ford, 1982). For treatment outcome studies to be meaningful, they must reflect both a fit within the guidelines of science and an understanding of the subtleties of human experience and behavior change. Exceptionally controlled investigations that are distant from the realities of therapy may offer only limited conclusions. Uncontrolled studies of therapy fail to pinpoint the effects that can be accurately attributed to therapy and provide at most, speculations. The scientist-practitioner develops a variety of methods for studying meaningful therapeutic interventions and outcomes in a scientific fashion. Indeed, one can find fairly widespread acceptance of the scientist-practitioner model and commitment to it when we consider the question, "What if we did not seek empirical evaluation of the effects of therapy?" (Beutler, 1998; Kendall, 1998). What process would replace it as we seek to advance our understanding of what treatments are effective for what types of client problems?

Empirically Supported Treatment(s)

The application of research methods to treatment outcome has amassed a sizable literature. Generalized conclusions about the efficacy of treatment (based on findings from studies using clinical practitioners) have begun to be reached, and the field has developed a set of criteria to be used when reviewing the cumulative literature on the outcomes of therapy. These criteria help determine whether or not a treatment can be considered "empirically supported."

Empirically supported treatments may be defined as treatments found to be efficacious when evaluated in randomized clinical trials (referred to as RCTs) with specified populations of patients (see American Psychological Association Task Force on Promotion and Dissemination of Psychological Procedures, 1995; Chambless & Hollon, 1998). Different perspectives exist on the utility of defining and delineating validated treatments, and the topic has been much debated in recent years (e.g., see articles in *Clinical Psychology: Science and Practice;* Weisz, Weersing, & Henggeler, 2004; Westen, Novotny, & Thompson-Brenner, 2004). Although the majority of researchers and clinicians would likely agree that the evaluation of treatment is necessary, not all agree on the best methods to identify effective treatments (Westen et al., 2004). The operational definition of empirically supported treatments focuses on the accumulated data on the *efficacy* of a psychological therapy. These demonstrations of treatment efficacy often involve an RCT in which an intervention is applied to cases that meet criteria for a specific disorder and analyzed against a comparison condition (e.g., wait list, alternative treatment, treatment-as-usual) to determine the degree or relative degree of beneficial change associated with treatments. The accumulated evidence comes from multiple studies whose aims were to examine the presence or absence of a treatment effect. Note that one study *does not* prove the benefits of therapy nor does a single study raise a treatment to the level of being considered empirically supported. Rather by accumulating evaluated outcomes, one can summarize the research and suggest that the beneficial effects of a given treatment have been supported empirically.

Even if a treatment has been supported empirically, however, the transport of the treatment from one setting (research clinic) to another (service clinic) represents a separate and important issue. A researcher who addresses this issue considers the *effectiveness* of treatment. Its effectiveness has to do with the generalizability, feasibility, and cost-effectiveness of the therapeutic procedures. The investigation of treatment effectiveness necessarily grows out of studies on treatment efficacy, and it seems reasonable to assert that RCTs are useful to address questions of both efficacy and effectiveness. For the research study to be valid, however, the study must include real patients (e.g., patients with comorbid disorders), must evaluate outcomes on more than narrow measures of improvement (i.e., focus on improvements in general functioning rather than improvements in specific symptoms), and cannot be limited to brief therapy without follow-up. Fortunately, many contemporary evaluations of treatment outcomes include both genuine cases with comorbid conditions, and measures of general functioning, examine therapies that are not always of short duration, and evaluate the maintenance of outcomes. Moreover, the methods of an RCT are pliable and can accommodate variations in the questions being asked. As a result, they can be used repeatedly for evaluation. When considering the efficacy and effectiveness of treatments, the evaluator of outcome needs to make informed decisions regarding both the internal and external validity of the study in question.

Managed care currently affects the mental health field. What role will treatment outcome research play in the future of mental health services vis-à-vis managed care? Although this chapter does not seek to address managed care, it does appear to us that the treatment outcome literature is now receiving a much more widespread readership. Parties involved in financing psychological treatments are paying increased attention to the data that inform us about the outcomes associated with different types of treatment. For better or worse, in the future, treatment outcome research is likely to prosper in part as a means of distilling the preferred interventions from the larger number of practiced treatments. Recognizing the utility of treatment outcome research in the healthcare system, Lambert, Huefner, and Reisinger (2000) proposed that this research should do more than simply provide evidence that some treatments are worthier of health care resources than others. Treatment outcome research can also offer valuable feedback to clinicians and health care providers. When integrated as part of a larger quality improvement system, outcome data can provide information about the progress of treatment gains and suggest viable alternate treatment plans. Treatment outcome research that integrates the finely honed results of efficacy RCTs with the nuanced complexities found by clinicians operating in the trenches is essential to the development of optimal mental health services.

CHAPTER OVERVIEW

In this chapter we focus on the design, methodology, and analysis of therapy evaluations in a manner that maximizes both scientific rigor and clinical relevance (for consideration of single case, multiple baseline, and small pilot trial designs, see Gallo, Comer, & Barlow, in press). Although all of the methodological and design ideals are rarely achieved within a single study, our discussions provide exemplars. We organize the present chapter around: (a) design considerations, (b) procedural considerations, (c) measurement considerations, (d) data analysis, and (e) reporting. For a comprehensive examination of specific research strategies, the reader is referred to Comer and Kendall (in press).

DESIGN CONSIDERATIONS

Clinical researchers use control procedures derived from experimental science to adequately assess the causal impact of a therapeutic intervention. The objective is to distinguish intervention effects from any changes that result from other factors, such as patient expectancies of change, the passage of time, therapist attention, repeated assessments, and simple regression to the mean. To have confidence that an intervention (i.e., the experimental manipulation) is responsible for observed changes, these extraneous factors must be "controlled." To elaborate, we turn our attention to the selection of random assignment, control conditions, evaluation of treatment response across time, and comparison of multiple treatments.

Random Assignment

Random assignment is essential to achieving baseline comparability between study conditions by ensuring that every participant has an equal chance of being assigned to the active treatment condition or the control condition(s). Importantly, however, random assignment does not guarantee comparability across conditions—simply due to chance one resultant group may be different on some variables (e.g., gender, impairment, income), especially if the groups are small. Appropriate statistical tests can be used to examine the comparability of participants across treatment conditions.

When random assignment is not applied, problems arise. Consider a situation in which participants do not have an equal chance of being assigned to the experimental and control conditions. Suppose a researcher were to allow anxious participants to decide for themselves whether to participate in the active treatment or in a no-treatment condition. If participants in the active treatment condition subsequently showed greater symptom reductions than no-treatment participants, the possibility that symptom differences could have resulted from prestudy differences between the participants (e.g., selection bias) cannot be ruled out. Participants who elected not to receive treatment may not be ready to work on their anxiety, and may be meaningfully different from those anxious participants who are ready to work on their distress.

Absolute assurance of participant comparability across conditions on all measures is not guaranteed by random assignment, but randomization procedures when sample sizes are large do maximize the likelihood of comparability, especially in the usual case where every variable that could be different cannot be measured. An alternative procedure, randomized blocks assignment, or assignment by stratified blocks, involves matching (arranging) prospective clients in subgroups that (a) contain clients that are highly comparable on key dimensions (e.g., baseline severity) and (b) contain the same number of clients as the number of conditions. For example, if the study requires two conditions—a standard treatment and an experimental treatment—participants can be paired off so that each pair is highly comparable. Members in each pair are then randomly assigned to either condition, in turn increasing the probability that each condition will contain relatively comparable participants while retaining a critical randomization procedure.

Selecting Control Condition(s)

Comparisons of participants randomly assigned to different treatment conditions are essential to control for factors other than treatment. In a "controlled" treatment evaluation, comparable persons are randomly placed into either the *treatment condition* composed of those who receive the intervention or a *control condition* composed of those who do not receive the intervention. By comparing the changes shown by participants across conditions, the efficacy of therapy over and above the outcome produced by extraneous factors (e.g., patient expectations) can be determined. Deciding which form of control condition (e.g., no-treatment, wait list, attention-placebo, standard treatment-as-usual) to select for a particular study requires careful deliberation (see Table 2.1 for recent examples).

In a *no-treatment* control condition, comparison participants are given the assessments on repeated occasions, separated by an interval of time equal in duration to the therapy provided to those in the experimental treatment condition. Any changes seen in the treated clients are compared to changes seen in the nontreated clients. When treated clients show significantly greater improvements relative to nontreated clients, the treatment may be credited with producing the changes. A number of important rival hypotheses are eliminated in a no-treatment design, including effects due to maturation, spontaneous remission, and regression to the mean. However, a no-treatment control condition does not rule out other potentially important confounding factors, such as seeing a warm and attentive therapist—independent of the specific treatment actually provided in the experimental condition. Accordingly, whereas a no-treatment control condition may be useful in earlier stages of treatment evaluation, other control procedures are preferred to establish broad empirical support for an intervention.

The *wait-list condition* is a more revealing variant of the no-treatment condition. Here, participants in the waitlist condition expect that after a certain period of time they will receive treatment, and accordingly may anticipate changes due to this treatment (which may affect their symptoms). Symptom changes are evaluated at uniform intervals across the experimental and wait-listed conditions, and if we assume the clients in the wait list and treatment conditions are comparable (e.g., gender, ethnicity, age, symptom severity at baseline, and client motivation), then we can infer that changes in the treated participants relative to wait-listed participants are likely due to the intervention rather than to expectations of impending change. As with no-treatment conditions, wait-list conditions offer limited value for treatments that have already been examined relative to "inactive" comparisons.

The use of no-treatment and wait-list conditions in study designs introduces important ethical considerations. For ethical purposes, the functioning of control participants needs to be carefully monitored to ensure that they are safely able to tolerate the treatment delay. Suppose a wait-list participant experiences a clinical emergency during the wait-list interval that requires immediate professional attention. The provision of emergency professional services will compromise the integrity of the wait-list condition. In addition, the duration of the control condition should be the same as the duration of the treatment condition to ensure that any differences across conditions in improvement

TABLE 2.1   Types of Control Conditions in Treatment Outcome Research

Control Condition	Definition	Recent Example in Literature	
		Description	Reference
No-treatment control	Control clients are administered assessments on repeated occasions, separated by an interval of time equal to the length of treatment.	Refugees in Uganda diagnosed with PTSD were randomly assigned to active trauma-focused treatments or a control condition. Individuals in the control condition received no treatment but were assessed on repeated occasions.	Neuner et al. (2008)
Wait-list control	Control clients are assessed before and after a designated duration of time, but receive the treatment following the waiting period. They may anticipate change due to therapy.	Socially phobic adults were randomly assigned to CBT, exposure therapy, or a wait-list control condition.	Hofmann (2004)
Attention-placebo/ common factors control	Control clients receive a treatment that involves common factors (e.g., attention, contact with a therapist)	Children with anxiety disorders were randomly assigned to cognitive-behavioral treatments or a control condition in which they received weekly attention and psycho-education.	Kendall, Hudson, Gosch, Flannery-Schroeder, and Suveg (2008)
Standard treatment/ routine care control	Control clients receive an intervention that is the current practice for treatment of the problem under study.	Depressed veterans were randomly assigned to either a telephone-administered CBT or standard care through community-based outpatient clinics.	Mohr, Carmody, Erickson, Jin, and Leader (2011)

cannot be attributed to differential passages of time. However, suppose a 20-session treatment takes 5 months to provide—is it ethical to withhold treatment for such a long wait period (see Bersoff & Bersoff, 1999)? The ethical response to this question varies across clinical conditions. It may be unethical to assign a depressed patient with multiple suicide attempts and active suicidal ideation to a long wait list, but there may be no ethical dilemma when assigning a shy child to a 2-week wait list prior to participation in an assertiveness training program. Moreover, with increasing waitlist durations, the problem of differential attrition arises, or waitlist participants may seek nonstudy care, each of which

compromise study interpretation. Wait lists can also induce feelings in participants that can compromise the integrity of the design. For example, participants assigned to a wait-list condition may become angry at being put off, an effect that is not simply due to the passage of time. If attrition rates are high in a wait-list condition, the sample in the control condition may be different from the sample in the treatment condition, and no longer representative of the larger group (e.g., the smaller wait-list group at the end of the study now only represents clients who could tolerate and withstand a prolonged wait-list period).

Attention-placebo (or common factors treatment) control conditions are an alternative to the wait list. Such conditions account for effects that might be due simply to meeting with and getting the attention of a warm and knowledgeable therapist. For example, in a recent randomized clinical trial (RCT), Kendall, Hudson, Gosch, Flannery-Schroeder, and Suveg (2008) randomly assigned children with anxiety disorders to receive cognitive-behavioral treatment (CBT; either individual or family CBT) or a manual-based family education, support, and attention (i.e., FESA) condition. Individual and family-based CBT showed superiority over FESA in reducing children's principal diagnosis. Given the attention/support nature of FESA, it was able to be inferred that gains associated with receiving CBT were not likely attributed to "common therapy factors" such as learning about anxiety and emotions, support from an understanding therapist, and opportunities to discuss the child's anxiety.

Attention-placebo control conditions offer advantages over no-treatment and wait-list conditions, but they are not without limitations (Parloff, 1986). Attention placebos must credibly instill positive expectations in participants and provide professional contact, while at the same time they must be devoid of therapeutic techniques hypothesized to be effective. For ethical purposes, clients must be fully informed of and willing to take a chance on receiving a psychosocial placebo condition. Even then, a credible attention-placebo condition may be difficult for the therapist to accomplish, particularly if they do not believe that the treatment will offer any benefit to the participant. Methodologically, it is difficult to ensure that therapists share comparable positive expectancies for their attention-placebo clients as they do for their clients in receiving more active intervention (Kendall, Holmbeck, & Verduin, 2002; O'Leary & Borkovec, 1978). "Demand characteristics" suggest that when therapists predict a favorable outcome, participants will tend to improve accordingly (Kazdin, 2003), which in turn can impact the interpretability of study findings. Similarly, clients in an attention-placebo condition may have high expectations at baseline, but may grow disenchanted when no specific changes are emerging. If study results show that an experimental therapy condition showed significantly better outcomes relative to an attention-placebo control condition, it is important that the researcher evaluate treatment credibility by assessing participant expectations for change across conditions.

The use of a *local standard treatment* (treatment-as-usual) as a comparison condition affords evaluation of an experimental treatment relative to the intervention that is currently available locally and being applied. Including local standard treatment as the control condition offers advantages over attention-placebo, wait-list, and no-treatment controls. Ethical concerns about no-treatment conditions are quelled, as care is provided to all participants, and attrition is likely to be minimized and common factors are likely to be equated (Kazdin, 2003). When the experimental treatment and the standard care intervention share comparable durations and participant and therapist expectancies, the researcher can evaluate the relative efficacy of the interventions. For example, Mufson and colleagues (2004) randomly assigned depressed adolescents to interpersonal psychotherapy (IPT-A) or to "treatment-as-usual" in school-based mental health clinics. Adolescents treated with IPT-A compared to treatment-as-usual showed greater symptom reduction and improved overall functioning. Given the nature of their comparison group the researchers were able to infer that gains associated with IPT-A outperformed the existing standard of care for depressed adolescents in the school settings. Importantly, in standard treatment comparisons, it is imperative that both the local standard (routine) treatment and the new treatment are implemented in a high-quality fashion (Kendall & Hollon, 1983). Researchers need to be cautious when utilizing a TAU comparison design, as recent meta-analytic work finds that such designs can overestimate experimental treatment effects by introducing a number of confounds, including discrepancies across treatment conditions in the extent to which treatments are bona fide, whether supervision is provided across conditions, whether the experimental treatment was provided by research staff, and whether specialized training was provided for providers of experimental therapies (see Spielmans et al., 2009).

Evaluating Treatment Response Across Time

For proper evaluation of treatment effects, it is essential to first evaluate participant functioning on the dependent variables (e.g., presenting symptoms) prior to the initiation of treatment. Such pretreatment (or "baseline") assessments provide key data to evaluate participant comparability across conditions at the beginning of treatment (i.e., between-groups comparisons), as well as the within-groups treatment response. Posttreatment assessments of clients are essential to examine the comparative efficacy of treatment versus control conditions. However, evidence of treatment efficacy immediately on therapy completion may not be indicative of long-term success (maintenance). Treatment effects may be appreciable at posttreatment but fail to exhibit maintenance at a follow-up assessment. Accordingly, it is highly recommended, and increasingly expected (Chambless & Hollon, 1998), that treatment outcome studies include a follow-up assessment. Follow-up assessments (e.g., 3 months, 6 months, 1 year) are essential to demonstrations of maintained treatment efficacy and are a signpost of methodological rigor. Evidence of maintenance is provided when the treatment produces results at the follow-up assessment that are at least comparable to those found at posttreatment (i.e., improvements from pretreatment and an absence of detrimental change from posttreatment to follow-up).

Repeated measures across treatment (e.g., weekly ratings) have been increasingly incorporated into clinical research designs and psychotherapy evaluations. Such data allow the researcher to go beyond traditional two-wave (pre- versus post-) designs and evaluate treatment responses that may be nonlinear (e.g., symptoms get worse before they get better, treatment response plateaus early but accelerates toward later sessions). The researcher with across-treatment repeated measurements is also able to evaluate the impact of various treatment components (e.g., introduction of exposure tasks in anxiety treatment; Kendall, Comer, Marker, et al., 2009) and to evaluate phases of sudden gains in treatment response.

Follow-up evaluations can help to identify differential treatment effects of considerable clinical utility. For example, two treatments may produce comparable effects at the end of treatment, but one may be more effective in the prevention of relapse (see Anderson & Lambert, 2001, for demonstration of survival analysis in clinical psychology). When two treatments show comparable gains at posttreatment, yet one is associated with a higher relapse rate over time, follow-up evaluations provide critical data to support the selection of one treatment over the other. For example, Brown, Evans, Miller, Burgess, and Mueller (1997) compared CBT and relaxation training for depression in alcoholism. When

considering the average (mean) days abstinent and drinks per day as dependent variables, measured at pretreatment and at 3 and 6 months posttreatment, the authors found that, although both treatments produced comparable initial gains, CBT was superior to relaxation training in maintaining the gains.

In addition, follow-up evaluations may detect continued improvement—the benefits of some interventions may accumulate over time, and possibly expand to other domains of functioning. Policy makers and researchers are increasingly interested in expanding intervention research to consider potential indirect effects on the prevention of secondary problems. In a long-term (7.4-year) follow-up of individuals treated with CBT for childhood anxiety disorders (Kendall, Safford, Flannery-Schroeder, & Webb, 2004), it was found that a meaningful percentage of those treated had maintained improvements in anxiety, and that positive responders relative to less-positive responders had reduced problems with substance use at the long-term follow-up (see also Kendall & Kessler, 2002). Importantly, gains identified at long-term follow-up are only fully attributable to the initial treatment after one determines that participants did not seek or receive additional treatments during the follow-up interval. When services have been rendered during the long-term follow-up interval, appropriate statistical tests are needed to account for any such differences across treatment conditions.

Multiple Treatment Comparisons

Researchers use between-groups designs with more than one active treatment condition to determine comparative (or relative) efficacy of therapeutic interventions. Such between-groups designs offer direct comparisons of one treatment with one or more alternative active treatments. Whereas larger effect sizes may be expected in evaluations comparing an active treatment to an inactive treatment, smaller differences are to be expected when distinguishing among multiple active treatments. Accordingly, sample size considerations are influenced by whether the comparison is between a treatment and a control condition or one treatment versus another known to be effective treatment (see Kazdin & Bass, 1989). Research aiming to identify reliable differences in response between two active treatments will need to evaluate a larger sample of participants than research comparing an active condition to an inactive treatment. Analyses can be performed by either comparing posttreatment scores across the two conditions, comparing posttreatment scores across the two conditions after controlling for pretreatment scores, or comparing change scores (i.e., post scores minus pre-, or pre- minus post) across the two conditions (see Rausch, Maxwell, & Kelley, 2003, for a comparison of analytic methods).

To prevent potential biases associated with researcher allegiances, care must be taken to ensure that proponents of all treatments evaluated be involved in the RCT design. For example, a multisite evaluation comparing the relative effects of CBT, antidepressant medication, and their combination for depression should optimally include researchers with expertise in CBT as well as researchers with primary expertise in pharmacologic interventions among the principal investigators responsible for designing and selecting outcome assessments. If a pharmacologic intervention typically takes 4 to 6 weeks to take effect, one could foresee such a trial designed solely by a researcher with pharmacology expertise might propose a 6-week mark for posttreatment evaluations. However, if the indicated CBT protocol for that condition typically takes 12 to 16 weeks to administer, having a CBT expert involved in the trial design might result in a more "fair" comparison between the two interventions—that is, a consensus design might evaluate the impact of intervention after both treatments have been fully administered. Selection of outcome measures will require the input of researchers with allegiances to each of the treatments evaluated. A measure that primarily evaluates patient self-talk may seem like an optimal outcome measure when considering the impact of CBT, but may not evaluate meaningful changes associated with antidepressant medication, for which the direct targeting patient self-talk is not a proposed mechanism of change.

Multiple treatment comparisons are optimal when each participant is randomly assigned to receive one and only one treatment condition, with assignment resulting in the initial comparability of participants receiving each intervention. As previously noted, a randomized block procedure, with participants blocked on an important variable (e.g., baseline severity), can be used. As in the above-mentioned designs, it is wise to check the comparability of the participants across conditions on other important variables (e.g., prior therapy experience, socioeconomic factors, treatment preferences/expectancies) before

continuing with statistical evaluation of the intervention effects.

We believe comparability across study therapists who are administering the different treatments is preferred, although in actual practice therapist comparability can never truly be achieved. Clinical researchers may aim for therapist equivalence across (a) training, (b) experience, (c) intervention expertise, (d) treatment allegiance, and (e) expectation that the intervention will be effective—although the extent to which each of these therapist variables are independently related to outcome remain unclear. To control for many of these therapist variables, one method has each study therapist conduct each type of intervention, with at least one client per intervention. This method is optimized when cases are randomly assigned to therapists who are equally expert and favorably disposed toward each intervention. For example, an intervention test would have reduced validity if a group of psychodynamic therapists were asked to conduct both a CBT (in which their expertise is low) and a psychodynamic therapy (in which their expertise is high). *Stratified blocking* offers a viable option to ensure that all intervention is conducted by several comparable therapists. It is wise to gather data on therapist variables (e.g., allegiance, expertise) and examine their relationships to outcomes.

For proper evaluation, intervention procedures across treatments must be equated for key variables such as (a) duration; (b) length, intensity, and frequency of contacts with clients; (c) credibility of the treatment rationale; (d) treatment setting; and (e) degree of involvement of persons significant to the client. These factors may be the basis for two alternative therapies (e.g., child- versus family-based treatment; conjoint versus individual marital therapy). In such cases, the nonequated treatment feature (e.g., number of out-of-session phone check-ins from therapists) constitutes an experimentally manipulated variable rather than a matter for control.

When two alternative treatments are being compared, what is the best method of measuring change? Importantly, measures should cover the range of functioning targeted for change, tap the costs and potential negative side effects, and be unbiased with respect to the alternate interventions. Measures should not be differentially sensitive to one treatment over another. Some have argued that therapy comparisons will be misleading if the assessments are not equally sensitive to the types of changes that are most likely caused by each intervention type, although there is at present little evidence that this is a problem.

Comparisons of psychological and psychopharmacological treatments (e.g., Beidel et al., 2007; Dobson et al., 2008; Marcus et al., 2007; MTA Cooperative Group, 1999; Pediatric OCD Treatment Study Team, 2004; Walkup et al., 2008) present special issues. For example, how and when placebo medications should be used in comparison to or with psychological therapy? How should expectancy effects be addressed? How should differential attrition be handled statistically and/or conceptually? How best to handle inherent differences in professional contact across psychological and pharmacologic interventions? Follow-ups become especially important after active treatments are discontinued. Psychological treatment effects may persist after treatment, whereas the effects of medications may not persist when medications are discontinued. (Readers interested in discussions of these issues are referred to Hollon, 1996; Hollon & DeRubeis, 1981; Jacobson & Hollon, 1996a, 1996b.)

PROCEDURAL CONSIDERATIONS

We now consider procedural matters related to (a) defining the independent variable (the use of manualized treatments), (b) checking the integrity of the independent variable (treatment fidelity checks), (c) sample selection, and (d) study setting.

Defining the Independent Variable: Manual-Based Treatments

When evaluating treatments, the treatment must be adequately described and detailed to replicate the evaluation, or to be able to show and teach others how to conduct the treatment. The use of treatment manuals is needed to achieve the required detail and description of the treatment. Treatment manuals enhance internal validity and treatment integrity, and afford comparison of treatments across contexts and formats, while at the same time reducing confounds (e.g., differences in the amount of contact, type, and amount of training). Therapist manuals facilitate training and contribute meaningfully to replication (Dobson & Hamilton, 2002; Dobson & Shaw, 1988).

Not all agree on the merits of manual-based treatments. Debate has ensued regarding the appropriate use of manual-based treatments versus a more variable approach typically found in practice (see Addis, Cardemil, Duncan, & Miller, 2006; Addis & Krasnow, 2000; Westen et al., 2004). It has been argued that manuals limit therapist creativity and place restrictions on the individualization that the clinicians use (see also Waltz, Addis, Koerner, & Jacobson, 1993; Wilson, 1995). Some therapy manuals may appear "cook-bookish," and some lack attention to the clinical sensitivities needed for implementation and individualization. Indeed, to the extent that manuals are overly directive, they can ignore the moment-to-moment clinical decisions that therapists make while providing therapy. Moreover, when manuals are inflexible they are less likely to be implemented and more likely to be rejected by practitioners. Fortunately, manuals are beginning to reflect a greater degree of flexibility. An empirical evaluation from our laboratory found that the use of a manual-based treatment for child anxiety disorders (Kendall & Hedtke, 2006) did not restrict therapist flexibility (Kendall & Chu, 1999). This is not always the case in the implementation of many manual-based treatments, and across every setting. Posthoc evaluations of treatment failures suggest that, among other variables, inflexible applications of manual-based protocols can interfere with optimal response (see special series of papers in Dimidjian & Hollon, 2011). Although it is not the goal of manual-based treatments to have clinicians perform treatment in a rigid manner, this perception has restricted some clinicians' openness to manual-based interventions (Addis & Krasnow, 2000).

Barlow (1989) noted that effective use of manual-based treatments must be preceded by adequate training. Interactive training, flexible application, and ongoing supervision are essential to ensure proper conduct of manual-based therapy: The goal can be referred to as *flexibility within fidelity* (Kendall & Beidas, 2007). Professionals are not likely to become proficient in the administration of therapy simply by reading a manual.

Several modern treatment manuals allow the therapist to attend to each client's specific circumstances, needs, concerns, and comorbid conditions without deviating from the core treatment strategies detailed in the manual. The goal is to include provisions for standardized implementation of therapy while using a personalized case formulation (Suveg, Comer, Furr, & Kendall, 2006). Importantly, potential for differential therapist effects are not eliminated through use of manual-based treatments. Within the context of manual-based treatments, researchers are examining therapist variables (e.g., warmth, therapeutic relationship-building behaviors) that frequently relate to treatment outcome (Creed & Kendall, 2005; Karver et al., 2008; Shirk, Gudmundsen, Kaplinski, & McMakin, 2008). A full consideration of designing, conducting, and evaluating therapy process research is provided in this handbook (see Chapters 3 and 9) and elsewhere (McLeod, Islam, & Wheat, in press).

Checking the Integrity of the Independent Variable: Treatment Fidelity Checks

Rigorous experimental research requires careful checking of the manipulated variable. In therapy outcome evaluations, the manipulated variable is typically treatment or a key characteristic of treatment. By experimental design, all clients are not treated the same. However, just because the study has been so designed does not guarantee that the independent variable (treatment) has been implemented as intended. In the course of a study—whether due to therapist variables, lack of manual specification, inadequate therapist training, insufficient therapist monitoring, client demand characteristics, or simple error variance—the treatment that was assigned may not in fact be the treatment that was provided (see also Perepletchikova & Kazdin, 2005).

To help ensure that the treatments are indeed implemented as intended, it is wise to require that a treatment plan be followed, that therapists are carefully trained, and that sufficient supervision is available throughout. An independent check on the manipulation should be conducted. For example, therapy sessions are recorded so that an independent rater can listen to and/or watch the recordings and conduct a manipulation check. Quantifiable judgments regarding key characteristics of the treatment provide the necessary check that the described treatment was indeed provided. Digital audio and video recordings are inexpensive, can be used for subsequent training, and can be analyzed to answer important research questions. Recordings of therapy sessions evaluated in outcome studies not only provide a check on the treatment within each separate study but also allow for a check on the comparability of treatments provided across studies. That is, the therapy provided as CBT in one clinician's study

could be checked to determine its comparability to other teams' CBT.

A recently completed clinical trial from our research program comparing two active treatment conditions for child anxiety disorders against an active attention control condition (Kendall et al., 2008) illustrates a procedural plan for integrity checks. We first developed a checklist of the content and strategies called for in each session by the respective treatment manuals. A panel of expert clinicians served as independent raters who used the checklists to rate randomly selected videotape segments from randomly selected cases. The panel of raters was trained on nonstudy cases until they reached an inter-rater reliability of Cohen's $\kappa \geq .85$. After ensuring reliability, the panel used the checklists to evaluate whether the appropriate content was covered for randomly selected segments that were representative of all sessions, conditions, and therapists. We computed an integrity ratio for each coded session: The number of checklist items covered by the therapist divided by the total number of items that should have been included. Integrity check results indicated that across the conditions, 85% to 92% of intended content was in fact covered. Therapists were able to adhere to the treatment manuals at rather high, albeit imperfect levels.

Evaluating the *quality* of treatment provided is also of interest. A therapist may strictly adhere to the manual and yet fail to administer the therapy in an otherwise competent manner. In both cases, the operational definition of the independent variable (i.e., the treatment manual) has been violated, treatment integrity impaired, and replication rendered impossible (Dobson & Shaw, 1988). When a treatment fails to demonstrate expected gains, one can examine the quality with which the treatment was implemented (see Hollon, Garber, & Shelton, 2005). It is also of interest to investigate potential variations in treatment outcome that may be associated with differences in the *quality* of the treatment provided (Garfield, 1998; Kendall & Hollon, 1983). Expert judges are needed to make determinations of differential quality prior to the examination of differential outcomes for high- versus low-quality therapy implementation (see Waltz et al., 1993). Whereas a compliance rating might capture whether a specific treatment task (e.g., exposure task for anxiety) was attempted at all in a given session, a quality rating might capture the extent to which the therapist implemented the task in a skillful manner. McLeod and colleagues (in press) provide a description of procedural issues in the conduct of quality assurance and treatment integrity checks.

Sample Selection

Careful deliberations are required when choosing a sample to best represent the clinical population of interest. Debate exists over the preferred samples for treatment outcome research. A *community subthreshold sample* refers to a nontreatment-seeking sample of participants who may benefit from treatment but who may otherwise only approximate clinically disordered individuals. Many of the most rigorous RCTs, by contrast, apply and evaluate treatments with actual treatment-seeking clients who meet diagnostic criteria for the disorder(s) of interest. Consider a study investigating the effects of Treatment A on depression. The researcher could use (a) a sample of treatment-seeking clients diagnosed with major depression via structured interviews (*genuine clinical sample*), (b) a sample consisting of a group of adults who self-report elevated dysphoric mood, but not necessarily clinical depression (an *analogue sample*), or (c) a sample of depressed persons after excluding cases with suicidal ideation, marital conflict, and/or a substance use (*highly select sample*). This last sample may meet diagnostic criteria for major depression but are nevertheless highly selected, and may accordingly be limited in their generalizability to the larger population of patients with major depression seeking care.

Analogue samples may afford a greater ability to control various conditions and minimize threats to internal validity, and from a feasibility standpoint researchers may find it easier to recruit these samples over genuine clinical samples (e.g., undergraduate students in the institution where a research study is being conducted). On the other hand, subthreshold and analogue samples compromise external validity—these individuals are not necessarily comparable to the spectrum of patients seen in typical clinical practice. With respect to depression, for instance, many question whether depression in genuine clinical populations compares meaningfully to self-reported dysphoria in adults (e.g., Coyne, 1994; Krupnick, Shea, & Elkin, 1986; Tennen, Hall, & Affleck, 1995; see also A. M. Ruscio & Ruscio, 2002, 2008). Researchers consider how the study results will be interpreted and generalized when deciding which type of sample to study.

Regrettably, nationally representative data show that standard exclusion criteria set for treatment studies for major depression (which may include strict comorbidity rule-outs) exclude up to 75% of individuals in the general population who suffer with major depression (Blanco et al., 2008).

Client diversity must be considered when deciding which samples to study. Historically, research supporting the efficacy of psychological treatments was conducted with predominantly European American samples—although this is rapidly changing (see Huey & Polo, 2008). Although ethnically diverse samples may be similar in many ways to single ethnicity samples, one can question the extent to which efficacy findings from European American samples can be generalized to ethnic minority samples (Bernal, Bonilla, & Bellido, 1995; Bernal & Scharron-Del-Rio, 2001; Hall, 2001; Olfson, Cherry, & Lewis-Fernandez, 2009; Sue, 1998). Investigations have also addressed the potential for bias in diagnoses and in the provision of mental health services to ethnic minority patients (e.g., Flaherty & Meaer, 1980; Homma-True, Green, Lopez, & Trimble, 1993; Lopez, 1989; Snowden, 2003).

A simple rule is that the research sample should reflect the population to which the study results will be generalized. To generalize to a diverse population, one must study a diverse sample. Barriers to care must be reduced and outreach efforts employed to inform minorities of available services (see Sweeney, Robins, Ruberu, & Jones, 2005; Yeh, McCabe, Hough, Dupuis, & Hazen, 2003) and include them in the research. Walders and Drotar (2000) provide guidelines for recruiting and working with ethnically diverse samples (e.g., hiring and training recruitment staff that represent the target population, develop plans to address potential barriers to diverse recruitment, pilot test recruitment strategies). Needless to say, this rule-of-thumb ideal is difficult to achieve in actual research practice.

After the fact, statistical analyses examine potential differential outcomes (see Arnold et al., 2003; Treadwell, Flannery-Schroeder, & Kendall, 1994). Grouping and analyzing research participants by racial or ethnic status is one approach. However, this approach is simplistic because it fails to address variations in individual client's degree of ethnic identity. It is often the degree to which an individual identifies with an ethno-cultural group or community, and not simply his or her ethnicity itself that may potentially moderate treatment outcome. For further consideration the reader is referred to Leong and Kalibatseva (in press).

Study Setting

It is not sufficient to demonstrate treatment efficacy within a highly selective setting. The question of whether the treatment can be transported to other settings requires independent evaluation (Southam-Gerow, Ringeisen, & Sherrill, 2006). Treatment outcome studies conducted in some settings (settings in which staff expertise, infrastructure, and resources—among other variables—may differ in important ways) may not generalize to other settings. Some have questioned whether the outcomes found at select research centers will transport to clinical practice settings. One should study, rather than assume, that a treatment found to be efficacious within a research clinical setting will be efficacious in a clinical service setting (see Hoagwood, 2002; Silverman, Kurtines, & Hoagwood, 2004; Southam-Gerow et al., 2006; Weisz, Donenberg, Han, & Weiss, 1995; Weisz, Weiss, & Donenberg, 1992).

Closing the gap between clinical research and practice requires transporting effective treatments (getting "what works" into practice) and identifying additional research into those factors (e.g., client, therapist, researcher, service delivery setting; see Kendall & Southam-Gerow, 1995; Silverman et al., 2004) that may be involved in successful transportation. Fishman (2000) suggested that an electronic journal of case studies be assembled so that patient, therapy, and environmental variables can be collected and compiled from within naturalistic therapy settings. Methodology issues relevant to the conduct of research evaluating the transportability of treatments to "real-world" settings can be found elsewhere (Beidas, Mehta, Atkins, Solomon, & Merz, in press).

MEASUREMENT CONSIDERATIONS

Among measurement considerations, the assessment of the dependent variable(s) merits particular attention.

Assessing the Dependent Variable(s)

There is no single measure that can serve as the sole indicator of clients' treatment-related gains. Rather, a variety of methods, measures, data sources, and sampling domains (e.g., symptomatic distress, functional impairment, quality of life) are used to assess outcomes. A contemporary and rigorous evaluation of therapy effects will consider using assessments of client self-report; client test/task performance; therapist judgments and ratings; archival or documentary records (e.g., health care visit and costs, work and school records); observations by trained, unbiased, blinded observers; rating by significant people in the client's life; and independent judgments by professionals. These issues have been discussed in earlier editions of this handbook (Hill & Lambert, 2004; Lambert, 1986), as well as in Chapter 5 of the current volume (Ogles, this volume). Outcomes have more compelling impact to outside observers when seen by independent (blind) evaluators than when based solely on the therapist's opinion or the client's self-reports (although this does not mean outside ratings are any more valid or important).

The *multi-informant strategy*, in which data on variables of interest are collected from multiple reporters (e.g., patient, family members, peers) can be particularly important when assessing children and adolescents. Features of cognitive development may compromise youth self-reports, and children may offer what they believe to be the desired responses. Thus, in RCTs with children and adolescents, collecting additional data from key adults in children's lives who observe them across different contexts (e.g., parents, teachers) is essential, particularly in research with children. However, because emotions and mood are partially internal phenomena, some symptoms may be less known to parents, teachers, and independent raters; and some observable symptoms may occur in situations outside the home or school. An inherent concern with multi-informant assessment is that discrepancies among informants are to be expected (Comer & Kendall, 2004). Research shows low-to-moderate concordance rates among informants in the assessment of children and adolescents (De Los Reyes & Kazdin, 2005), with agreement lowest among parental and child estimates of child internalizing symptoms (Comer & Kendall, 2004).

A *multimodal strategy* relies on multiple modes of assessment (e.g., observational data and self-reports) to evaluate an underlying construct of interest. For example, assessing family functioning may include family members completing self-report forms on their perceptions of family relationships, as well as conducting structured behavioral observations of family members interacting (to later be coded by independent raters). Statistical packages can integrate data obtained from multimodal assessment strategies. The increasing availability of handheld communication devices and personal digital assistants allows researchers to incorporate experience sampling methodology (ESM), in which people report on their emotions and behavior in the actual situation (*in situ*). These ESM data provide naturalistic information on patterns in day-to-day functioning (see Santangelo, Ebner-Priemer, & Trull, in press).

It is optimal and preferred that multiple targets be assessed in treatment evaluations. For example, one can measure the presence of a diagnosis, overall psychological adjustment, specific interpersonal skills, self-reported mood, cognitive functioning, life environment, vocational status, interpersonal relationships, and health-related quality of life. No one target captures all, and using multiple targets facilitates an examination of therapeutic changes when changes occur, and the absence of change when interventions are less beneficial. Inherent in a multiple-domain assessment strategy, however, is that it is rare that a treatment produces uniform effects across assessed domains. Suppose Treatment A, relative to a control condition, improves depressed clients' severity of depression, but not their overall psychological well-being. In an RCT designed to evaluate improved depression symptoms and psychological well-being, should Treatment A be deemed efficacious if only one of two measures showed gains? De Los Reyes and Kazdin (2006) propose the Range of Possible Changes model, which calls for a multidimensional conceptualization of intervention change. In this spirit, we recommend that researchers conducting RCTs be explicit about the domains of functioning expected to change and the relative magnitude of such expected changes. We also caution consumers of the treatment outcome literature against simplistic dichotomous appraisals of treatments as efficacious or not.

DATA ANALYSIS

Data do not "speak" for themselves. *Data analysis* is an active process through which we extract useful information from the data we have collected in ways that allow us to make statistical inferences about the larger population that a given sample was selected to represent. Although

a comprehensive statistical discussion for clinical trial evaluation is beyond the present scope (the interested reader is referred to Jaccard & Guilamo-Ramos, 2002a, 2002b; Kraemer & Kupfer, 2006; Kraemer, Wilson, Fairburn, & Agras, 2002; Rausch, in press; Wolf & Brown, in press) in this section, we discuss four areas that merit consideration in the context of research methods in clinical psychology: (1) addressing missing data and attrition, (2) assessing clinical significance, (3) mechanisms of change (i.e., mediators and moderators), (4) and cumulative outcome analysis. In addition, we mention cautions regarding the misuse of pilot data for the purposes of power calculations.

Addressing Missing Data and Attrition

Not all clients who are assigned to treatment actually complete their participation in the study. A loss of research participants (*attrition*) may occur just after randomization, during treatment, prior to posttreatment evaluation, or during the follow-up interval. Increasingly, clinical scientists are analyzing attrition and its predictors and correlates to elucidate the nature of treatment dropout, understand treatment tolerability, and to enhance the sustainability of mental health services in the community (Kendall & Sugarman, 1997; Reis & Brown, 2006; Vanable, Carey, Carey, & Maisto, 2002). However, from a research methods standpoint, attrition can be problematic for data analysis, such as when there are large numbers of noncompleters or when attrition varies across conditions (Leon et al., 2006; Molenberghs et al., 2004).

Regardless of how diligently researchers work to prevent attrition, data will likely be lost. Although attrition rates vary across studies and treated clinical populations, Mason (1999) estimated that most researchers can expect nearly 20% of their sample to withdraw or be removed from a study prior to completion. To address this matter, researchers can conduct and report two sets of analyses: (1) analyses of outcomes for treatment completers, and (2) analyses of outcomes for all participants who were included at the time of randomization (i.e., the *intent-to-treat sample*). An analysis of completers involves the evaluation of only those who actually completed treatment and examines what the effects of treatment are when someone completes a full treatment course. Treatment refusers, treatment dropouts, and participants who fail to adhere to treatment schedules would not be included in such analyses. Reports of such treatment outcomes may be somewhat high because they represent the results for only those who adhered to and completed the treatment. Intent-to-treat analyses, a more conservative approach to addressing missing data, require the evaluation of outcomes for all participants involved at the point of randomization. As proponents of intent-to-treatment analyses we say, "once randomized, always analyzed." Outcomes for these samples may produce low estimates of outcome since they include individuals who were not treated or only partially treated.

Selection of an appropriate analytic method to handle missing endpoint data requires careful consideration because different methods can produce different outcomes (see McKnight, in press). Delucchi and Bostrom (1999) summarized the effects of missing data on a range of statistical analyses. Researchers address missing endpoint data via one of several ways: (a) *last observation carried forward* (LOCF), (b) substituting pretreatment scores for post-treatment scores, (c) multiple imputation methods, and (d) mixed-effects models. A LOCF analysis assumes that participants who attrit remain constant on the outcome variable from their last assessed point through the post-treatment evaluation. For example, if a participant drops out at Week 9 of a 12-session protocol, the data from the Week 8 assessment would be substituted for their missing posttreatment assessment data.

A LOCF approach can be problematic, however, as the last data collected may not be representative of the dropout participant's ultimate progress or lack of progress at posttreatment, given that participants may change after dropping out of treatment. The use of pretreatment data as posttreatment data (a highly conservative and not recommended method because even some change typically occurs due to simple regression to the mean) simply inserts pretreatment scores for cases of attrition as posttreatment scores, assuming that participants who attrit make no change from their initial baseline state. Critics of the LOCF and pretreatment data substitution methods argue that these crude methods introduce systematic bias and fail to take into account the uncertainty of posttreatment functioning (see Leon et al., 2006).

Increasingly, journals are calling for missing data imputation methods to be grounded in statistical theory and to incorporate the uncertainty regarding the true value of the missing data.

Multiple imputation methods impute a range of values for the missing data (incorporating the uncertainty of the true values of missing data), generating a number of nonidentical datasets (typically five is considered sufficient; Little & Rubin, 2002). After the researcher conducts analyses on the nonidentical datasets, the results are pooled and the resulting variability addresses the uncertainty of the true value of the missing data. Moreover, *mixed-effects modeling*, which relies on linear and/or logistic regression to address missing data in the context of random (e.g., participant) and fixed effects (e.g., treatment, age, sex) (see Hedeker & Gibbons, 1994, 1997; Laird & Ware, 1982), can be used (see Neuner et al., 2008, for an example). Mixed-effects modeling may be particularly useful in addressing missing data if numerous assessments are collected throughout a treatment trial (e.g., weekly symptom ratings).

To minimize any potential error introduced by statistical imputation and modeling approaches to missing data, we recommend that researchers attempt to contact noncompleting participants and reevaluate them at the time when the treatment protocol would have ended. This method controls for the passage of time, because both dropouts and treatment completers are evaluated over time periods of the same duration. If this method is used, however, it is important to determine whether dropouts sought and/or received alternative treatments in the interim.

Clinical Significance

The data produced by research projects designed to evaluate the efficacy of therapy are submitted to statistical tests of significance. Mean scores for participants in each condition are compared, within-group and between-group variability is considered, and the analysis produces a numerical figure, which is then checked against critical values. *Statistical* significance is achieved if the magnitude of the mean difference is beyond what could have resulted by chance alone (conventionally defined as $p < .05$). Tests of statistical significance are essential as they inform us that the degree of change was likely not due to chance. However, statistical tests alone do not provide evidence of *clinical significance*. Sole reliance on statistical significance can lead to perceiving differences (i.e., treatment gains) as potent when in fact they may be *clinically* insignificant. For example, imagine that the results of a treatment outcome study demonstrate that mean Beck Depression Inventory (BDI) scores are significantly lower at posttreatment than pretreatment. An examination of the means, however, reveals only a small but reliable shift from a mean of 28 to a mean of 25. With large sample sizes, this difference may well achieve statistical significance at the $p < .05$ level (i.e., more than 95% chance that the finding is not due to chance alone), yet perhaps be of limited practical significance. At both pre- and posttreatment, the scores are within the range considered indicative of clinical levels of depressive distress (Kendall, Hollon, Beck, Hammen, & Ingram, 1987), and such a magnitude of change may have little effect on a person's perceived quality of life (Gladis, Gosch, Dishuk, & Crits-Christoph, 1999). Moreover, statistically meager results may disguise meaningful changes in client functioning. As Kazdin (1999) put it, sometimes a little can mean a lot, and vice versa.

Clinical significance refers to the meaningfulness or persuasiveness of the magnitude of change (Kendall, 1999). Whereas tests of statistical significance address the question "Were there treatment-related changes?" tests of clinical significance attempt to address the question "Were treatment-related changes convincing and meaningful?" Specifically, this can be made operational as changes on a measure of the presenting problem (e.g., depressive symptoms) that result in the client's being returned to within normal limits on that same measure. Clinical significance research has been conducted to evaluate dose–response relationships (e.g., how many sessions until clinically significant change has been achieved), and in outcome management systems that use it as a marker for clinical response or deterioration (see Anderson & Lambert, 2001). Moreover, clinical significance research has been applied to estimate the relative value of empirically supported therapy as examined in clinical trials relative to community practice (Hansen, Lambert, & Forman, 2002). Several approaches for measuring clinically significant change have been developed, two of which are *normative sample comparison* and *reliable change index*.

Normative Comparisons

Normative comparisons (Kendall & Grove, 1988; Kendall, Marrs-Garcia, Nath, & Sheldrick, 1999) can be conducted in several steps. First, the researcher selects a normative group for posttreatment comparison. Given that several well-established measures provide normative data (e.g., the Beck Depression Inventory, the Child Behavior Checklist), investigators may choose to rely on these preexisting normative samples. However, when normative data do not exist, or when the treatment sample is qualitatively different on key factors (e.g., age, socioeconomic status), it may be necessary to collect one's own normative data. In typical research, when using statistical tests to compare groups, the investigator assumes equivalency across groups (null hypothesis) and aims to find that they are not (alternate hypothesis). However, when the goal is to show that treated individuals are equivalent to "normal" individuals on some factor (i.e., are indistinguishable from normative comparisons), traditional hypothesis-testing methods are inadequate. To circumvent this problem, one uses an equivalency testing method (Kendall, Marrs-Garcia et al., 1999) that examines whether the difference between the treatment and normative groups is within some predetermined range. When used in conjunction with traditional hypothesis testing, this approach allows for conclusions about the equivalency of groups (see e.g., Jarrett, Vittengl, Doyle, & Clark, 2007; Kendall et al., 2008; Pelham et al., 2000; Westbrook & Kirk, 2007, for examples of normative comparisons), thus testing that a posttreatment case is within a normative range on the measure of interest, and by inference functioning as well as others.

The Reliable Change Index

A second popular method to examining clinically significant change is the Reliable Change Index (RCI; Jacobson, Follette, & Revenstorf, 1984; Jacobson & Truax, 1991). Jacobson's method first involves calculating the number of participants moving from a dysfunctional to a normative range based on a normative-dysfunctional cutoff score. Step two entails evaluating whether each individual's change was reliable (rather than simply measurement error). To assess this second step, the RCI was proposed, which is a calculation of a difference score (post- minus pretreatment) divided by the standard error of measurement (calculated based on the reliability of the measure). From these two steps, individual patients are classified as either recovered (i.e., passed both cutoff and RCI criteria), unchanged (i.e., passed neither criteria), improved (i.e., passed RCI but not cutoff criteria), or deteriorated (i.e., passed RCI criteria in the unintended direction; see McGlinchy, Atkins, & Jacobson, 2002). This approach assumes the existence of two populations (dysfunctional and normative) that each approximate normal distributions. The RCI is influenced by the magnitude of change and the reliability of the measure. The RCI has been used in clinical psychological research, although its originators point out that it has at times been misapplied (Jacobson, Roberts, Berns, & McGlinchey, 1999). When used in conjunction with reliable measures and appropriate cutoff scores, it can be a valuable tool for assessing clinical significance. But much research remains to be done to validate statistically based definitions of reliable change.

Since the original RCI proposal (Jacobson et al., 1984; Jacobson & Truax, 1991), a number of alternative calculations have been proposed, each with their own purported improvements over the Jacobson RCI approach. For example, following concerns that the RCI does not account for the expectation of regression to the mean (i.e., extreme scores will naturally become less extreme over repeated assessments regardless of treatment-related change), Hsu (1989) proposed methods that control for this potential confound. In another approach, Speer (1992) emphasizes confidence intervals to account for simple regression to the mean. In a recent empirical comparison among methods, Bauer, Lambert, and Nielson (2004) identified the original Jacobson and Truax (1991) calculation as the recommended method, given its favorable balance of both sensitivity and specificity properties, its continued popularity, and the relatively straightforward nature of its calculation. Although much progress has been made regarding clinical significance, some debate exists over how to improve the measurement of this construct. Whereas some researchers propose more advanced methods of normative comparison and analysis (e.g., using multiple normative samples), others suggest that clinical significance remain as a simple, client-focused, practical adjunct to statistical significance results (cf. Follette & Callaghan, 1996; Martinovich, Saunders, & Howard, 1996; Tingey, Lambert, Burlingame, & Hansen, 1996).

Both clinical and statistical significance are of great importance in the assessment of treatment outcome. Given the complex nature of change, it is essential to evaluate treatment with consideration of both approaches. Statistically significant improvements are not equivalent to "cures," and clinical significance is an additional, not a substitute, evaluative strategy. Statistical significance is required to document that changes were beyond those due to chance alone; yet it is also useful to consider if the changes returned dysfunctional clients to within normal limits on the measure of interest. For example, to be considered clinically significant, improvement beyond a minimum criterion could be set for dependent measures (e.g., within 1.5 standard deviations from the normative mean). Empirical reports show that the RCI and the normative comparison methods each provide unique information regarding clinical significance (Sheldrick, Kendall, & Heimberg, 2001), supporting the idea that from a research standpoint these two methods may optimally be used in conjunction with one another. Importantly, the researcher is also advised to include assessments of functional change and quality of life. The standards of evaluating clinical significance in symptom reports described above are not grounded in "real-world" referents (e.g., relationship satisfaction, role performance). Future work is needed to evaluate the extent to which clinically significant change generalizes to patient functioning (see also Kazdin, 2006).

Evaluating Mechanisms of Change: Mediators and Moderators of Treatment Response

It is often of interest to identify (a) the conditions that dictate when a treatment is more or less effective, and (b) the processes through which a treatment produces change. Addressing such issues necessitates the specification of *moderator* and *mediator* variables (Baron & Kenny, 1986; Holmbeck, 1997; Kraemer et al., 2002). A moderator is a variable that delineates the conditions under which a given treatment is related to an outcome. Conceptually, after Kiesler (1971), moderators identify *on whom* and *under what circumstances* which treatments have different effects (Kraemer et al., 2002). Functionally, a moderator is a variable that influences either the direction or the strength of a relationship between an independent variable (treatment) and a dependent variable (outcome). For example, if in a randomized clinical trial the experimental treatment was found to be more effective with women than with men, but this gender effect was not found in response to the control treatment, then gender would be considered a moderator of the association between treatment and outcome. Treatment moderators help clarify for clinicians (and other consumers of the treatment outcome literature) which clients might be most responsive to which treatments (and for which clients alternative treatment might be sought). When a variable is associated broadly with outcome across all treatment conditions, conceptually that variable is simply a *predictor*, and not a moderator (see Kraemer et al., 2002).

A mediator, on the other hand, is a variable that serves to explain the process by which a treatment impacts on an outcome. Conceptually, mediators identify *how* and *why* treatments have effects (Kraemer et al., 2002). The mediator effect elucidates the mechanism by which the independent variable (e.g., treatment) is related to outcome (e.g., treatment-related changes). Thus, mediational models are inherently causal models, and in the context of an experimental design (i.e., random assignment), significant meditational pathways tell us about causal relationships. If an effective treatment for child conduct problems was found to impact on the parenting behavior of mothers and fathers, which in turn was found to have a significant impact on child problem behavior, then parent behavior would be considered to mediate the treatment-to-outcome relationship (provided certain statistical criteria were met; see Holmbeck, 1997).

Specific statistical methods used to evaluate the presence of treatment moderation and mediation can be found elsewhere (MacKinnon, in press), but it is nonetheless worth providing a brief overview of these procedures here. A moderation effect is inherently an interaction effect. When using multiple regression, the predictor (e.g., treatment assignment, coded as treatment or no treatment) and proposed moderator (e.g., age of client) are main effects and entered into the regression first (along with any covariates or potential confounds, if applicable), followed by the interaction (product) of the predictor and the proposed moderator. Alternatively, if one is only interested in testing the significance of the interaction effect, all of these terms can be entered simultaneously (see Aiken & West, 1991; Holmbeck, 2002, for a discussion of the importance of "centering" main effects when testing moderator effects within a regression context). If one is using analysis of variance (ANOVA), the significance of the interaction between two main effects is tested in an analogous manner. A moderator, like an interaction effect, documents that the effects of one variable are different for different levels of another variable. Significant interactions are then probed by plotting and

testing the significance of simple regression line slopes for high and low values of the moderator variable (Holmbeck, 2002). Alternatively, one can test the significance of simple main effects when the predictor and moderator are both categorical variables and tested with ANOVA. Probing significant interactions allows the research to identify specifically under which conditions one condition is more or less effective than another condition in producing changes.

Importantly if the proposed moderator predicts treatment response across all conditions, without an interaction with treatment assignment (e.g., if age predicted worse outcome across an active treatment *and* a psychoeducational control condition), the proposed moderator is simply a "predictor." It is only when this predictive relationship differs across treatments (i.e., interacts with treatment) that the term *moderator* is appropriately applied.

To test for mediation, one examines whether the following are significant: (a) the association between the predictor (e.g., treatment assignment) and the outcome, (b) the association between the predictor and the mediator, and (c) the association between the mediator and the outcome, after controlling for the effect of the predictor. If all of these conditions are met, the researcher then examines whether the predictor-to-outcome effect is less after controlling for the mediator (Condition 4). A corollary of the first condition is that there initially should be a significant relationship between the treatment and the outcome for a mediator to serve its mediating role. In other words, if the treatment and outcome are not significantly associated, there is no significant effect to mediate. (Such a bivariate association between treatment and outcome is not required for moderated effects.)

The conditions necessary for mediated effects can be tested with three multiple regression analyses (Baron & Kenny, 1986). The strategy is similar to that employed when conducting a path analysis (Cohen & Cohen, 1983). The significance of the treatment-to-outcome path (Condition 1, above) is examined in the first regression after controlling for any covariates. The significance of the treatment-to-mediator path (Condition 2) is examined in the second regression. Finally, treatment and the proposed mediator are employed as predictors (entered simultaneously) in the third equation where the outcome is the dependent variable. Baron and Kenny (1986) recommend using simultaneous entry (rather than hierarchical entry) in the third equation so that the effect of the proposed mediator on the outcome is examined after controlling for treatment and the effect of the treatment on the outcome is examined after controlling for the proposed mediator (Cohen & Cohen, 1983). The significance of the mediator-to-outcome path in this third equation is a test of Condition 3. The relative effect of the treatment on the outcome in this equation (when the proposed mediator is controlled) in comparison to the effect of the treatment on the outcome in the first equation (when the proposed mediator is not controlled) is the test of the fourth condition. Specifically, the treatment should be less highly associated with the outcome in the third equation than was the case in the first equation.

One question that arises with meditational analysis is this: How much reduction in the total effect is necessary to claim the presence of mediation (see Holmbeck, 2002). Some researchers have reported whether the treatment-to-outcome effect drops from significance (e.g., $p < .05$) to nonsignificance ($p > .05$) after the proposed mediator is introduced into the model. This strategy is flawed, however, because a drop from significance to non-significance may occur, for example, when a regression coefficient drops from .28 to .27 but may not occur when it drops from .75 to .35. In other words, it is possible that significant mediation *has not* occurred when the test of the treatment-to-outcome effect drops from significance to nonsignificance after taking the mediator into account. On the other hand, it is also possible that significant mediation *has* occurred even when the statistical test of the treatment-to-outcome effect continues to be significant after taking the mediator into account. It appears that a test is needed to evaluate the significance of this drop.

One such approach is to evaluate the indirect effect, which is mathematically equivalent to a test of whether the drop in total effect is significant upon inclusion of the mediator in the model (see MacKinnon & Dwyer, 1993). Here, the significance test of the indirect effect is equivalent to a significance test of the difference between the total and direct effects, with the latter representing the drop in the total effect after the mediator is in the model. The indirect effect is the product of the predictor-to-mediator and mediator-to-outcome path coefficients. To conduct the statistical test for mediation, one needs unstandardized path coefficients from the model

as well as standard errors for these coefficients. One also needs the standard error of the indirect effect. Sobel (see Baron & Kenny, 1986) presents an equation for computing the standard error of the indirect effect. Full mediation occurs if 100% of the total effect is accounted for by the mediator (which is highly unlikely in most psychological therapy research). Thus, statistical analyses in the social sciences typically examine whether there is significant or nonsignificant *partial* mediation (Baron & Kenny, 1986).

These rather complicated statistical procedures are an essential part of scientific investigations aimed at understanding causality and identifying essential ingredients of psychotherapy. They help us evaluate the substance of theories of change and to modify theory, but they are also important in clinical practice and clinical training. For examples of what we know from such investigations the reader is referred to the handbook chapter analyzing the relationship between the processes of psychotherapy and the outcomes (see Chapter 9, this volume).

Cumulative Outcome Analyses

The literature examining the outcomes of diverse therapies is vast, and there is a vital need to synthesize that which we have learned in a systematic, coherent, and meaningful manner. Several major cumulative analyses have undertaken the challenging task of reviewing and reaching conclusions with regard to the effects of psychological therapy. Some of the reviews are strictly qualitative and are based on subjective conclusions, whereas others have used tabulations of the number of studies favoring one type of intervention versus that of competing interventions (e.g., Beutler, 1979; Luborsky, Singer, & Luborsky, 1975). This approach uses a "box score" summary of the findings, and reviewers would compare rates of treatment success to draw conclusions about outcomes. Still other reviewers have used multidimensional analyses of the impact of potential causal factors on therapy outcome: *meta-analysis* (Smith & Glass, 1977).

To understand the effects of psychological treatments, as well as the factors associated with variations in these effects, meta-analysis is a preferred tool with which to inform funding decisions, service delivery, and public policy. Meta-analytic procedures provide a quantitative, replicable, accepted, and respected approach to the synthesis of a body of empirical literature, and are themselves to be considered empirical reports. Impactful literature reviews are increasingly moving away from the qualitative summary of research to the quantitative analysis of the reported findings of the studies (Weisz, Doss, & Hawley, 2006; Weisz, McCarty, & Valeri, 2006). By summarizing the magnitude of overall relationships found across studies, determining factors associated with variations in the magnitude of such relationships, and establishing relationships by aggregate analysis, meta-analytic procedures provide more objective, exhaustive, systematic, and representative conclusions than do qualitative reviews (Field, in press; Rosenthal, 1984).

Meta-analytic techniques are highly informative because they quantitatively synthesize findings across multiple studies by converting the results of each data report into a common metric (e.g., the effect size). The outcomes of different types of treatments can then be compared with respect to the aggregate magnitude of change reflected in such statistics across studies. The effect size is typically derived by computing the difference between the reported means of the treatment group and control group at posttreatment, then dividing this difference by the pooled standard deviation of the two groups (Durlak, 1995). The more rigorous scientific journals now require authors to include effect sizes in their reports.

What are the steps involved in conducting a meta-analysis? After determining that a particular research area has developed to the point at which a meta-analysis is possible (i.e., numerous studies have evaluated the same question in a similar manner) and the results of such an analysis would be of interest to the field, one first conducts a literature search. Multiple methods of searching are often used, including computer database searches, reviews of reference sections from relevant articles, and sending a table of studies to be included to known experts in the area to review for potential missing citations. We strongly caution researchers interested in conducting a meta-analysis against relying solely on computer searches, because they routinely omit several important studies.

The meta-analyzer must now decide whether studies of varying quality should be included (Kendall, Flannery-Schroeder, & Ford, 1999; Kendall & Maruyama, 1985). On the one hand, it could be argued that poor-quality studies should not be included in the review, since such studies would not ordinarily be used to draw conclusions about the effectiveness of a given psychological therapy. On the other hand, decisions concerning whether a study is of poor versus good quality are often not straightforward. A study may have certain exemplary features and other less desirable features. By including studies that vary in quality, one can examine whether certain "quality" variables (e.g., subthreshold versus genuine clinical cases) are associated with differential outcomes. For example, in a recent meta-analysis (Furr, Comer, Edmunds, & Kendall, 2010), studies were rated in terms of their methodological rigor: one point for addressing missing data, one point for including appropriate comparison groups, one point for using psychometrically sound measures, and so on. One is then able to examine the extent to which methodological quality is related to results.

The next step entails coding the results of specific studies. Decisions need to be made regarding what types of variables will be coded and how interrater reliability among coders will be assessed. For example, in a study that examined the outcomes of a psychological therapy, one might code the nature of the intervention, whether the treatment was conducted in clinically representative conditions (Shadish, Matt, Navarro, & Phillips, 2000), the number of sessions, the types of participants, the diagnoses of the participants, the age range, the gender distribution, the therapy administration method (e.g., group versus individual), the qualifications of the therapists, the various features of the research design, and types of outcomes. Once variables such as these have been coded, the effect sizes are then computed. The methods employed to compute effect sizes should be specified.

Another consideration is whether effect sizes will be weighted (for example, based on the sample sizes of the studies reviewed, methodological rigor of studies, precision of measurement across studies). Using sample size to weight study findings has historically been employed in meta-analyses as a way to approximate the reliability of findings (i.e., larger samples would expectedly yield more reliable estimates than smaller samples). However, researchers are increasingly weighting studies by inverse variance weights (i.e., $1/[SE]^2$), where SE = standard error), rather than sample size, as this provides a more direct weighting of study findings by reliability. By weighting by inverse variance weights, the researcher is weighting by precision—the smaller the SE, the more precise the effect size, and consequently the greater you want that effect size represented when aggregating it with other effect sizes.

After computing the effect sizes and inverse variance weights across studies, and then computing an overall *weighted mean effect size* (and confidence interval) based on the inverse variance weights associated with each effect size, the researcher evaluates the adequacy of the mean effect size in representing the entire distribution of effects via homogeneity testing (i.e., homogeneity statistic, Q). This consists of comparing the observed variability in the effect size values with the estimate of variance that is expected from subject-level sampling error alone (Lipsey & Wilson, 2000). A stem-and-leaf plot can also be useful in determining the distribution of effect sizes. Often a researcher will specifically hypothesize that effect sizes will be significantly heterogenous, given that multiple factors (e.g., sample characteristics, study methodology) can systematically exert influences on documented treatment effects. If the distribution is not found to be homogeneous, the studies likely estimate different population mean effect sizes, and alternative procedures are required that are beyond the scope of this chapter (see Lipsey & Wilson, 2000).

Some cautions must be exercised in any meta-analysis. As noted earlier, one must check on the quality of the studies, eliminating those that cannot contribute meaningful findings due to basic inadequacies (Kraemer, Gardner, Brooks, & Yesavage, 1998). If the research evidence is methodologically unsound, it remains inadequate as a basis for either supporting or refuting treatment recommendations, and therefore it should not be included in cumulative analyses. If a study is methodologically sound, then regardless of the outcome, it must be included. Importantly, the researcher must define what constitutes a methodologically sound clinical trial to be included a priori, so as to avoid the potential for bias in the exclusion of specific studies in a literature.

Caution is paramount in meta-analyses in which various studies are said to provide evidence that treatment is superior to controls. The exact nature of the control condition in each specific study must be examined, especially in the case of attention-placebo control conditions. This caution arises from the potential vagaries inherent in the term attention-placebo control conditions. As noted earlier, one researcher's attention-placebo control condition may be serving as another researcher's therapy condition! Meta-analyzers cannot tabulate the number of studies in which treatment was found to be efficacious in relation to controls without examining the nature of the control condition.

Formal guidelines for conducting and reporting meta-analytic studies in psychology are now available (American Psychological Association, 2008)

Caution Concerning the Misuse of Pilot Data for the Purposes of Power Calculations

As addressed elsewhere (Cohen, 1988; Kraemer, in press; Kraemer & Thiemann, 1987), *power* refers to the probability of accurately rejecting a null hypotheses (e.g., the ability to reject that the compared treatments have comparable effects) when the null hypothesis is in fact untrue (one treatment condition performs better than the other condition). Designing an adequately powered RCT entails recruiting a sample large enough to adequately and reliably test different treatment responses across conditions.

To determine the minimum sample size required for an RCT, conventional calculations consider an *expected effect size* (in RCT data, typically the magnitude of difference in treatment response across groups) in the context of an acceptably low α level (i.e., the probability of rejecting the null hypothesis if it is indeed true; consensus typically stipulates a $\le .05$), and an acceptably high level of power (consensus typically stipulates power $\ge .80$).

Although conventions for sample size calculations stipulate acceptable α and power levels to incorporate, broad conventions do not stipulate an expected magnitude of effect size to include because this will vary widely across varied clinical populations and across diverse treatments. For example, whereas a behavioral treatment for an anxiety disorder may expectedly yield a relatively moderate effect size, a bibliotherapy treatment for polysubstance use disorder may expectedly yield a very small effect size. To estimate an expected effect size for the design of an adequately powered study, the researcher must rely on theory, as well as the magnitude of effects found in related research. In fact, expert guidelines instruct that rationale and justification for a study proposal should be drawn "from previous research" (Wilkinson & Task Force on Statistical Inference, 1999).

Often, a researcher will use data from a small pilot study to estimate an expected effect size for a proposed large-scale RCT. For example, if a small pilot RCT ($n = 18$) identified a large treatment effect at (e.g., $d = 0.9$), a researcher might use this effect size to guide power calculations for determining the sample size required for a proposed large-scale RCT. But as Kraemer, Mintz, Noda, Tinklenberg, and Yesavage (2006) mathematically demonstrate, this misguided practice can lead to the design of an underpowered study positioned to accept the null hypothesis when true treatment differences exist. Effect sizes drawn from underpowered studies (such as small pilot studies) result in effect size estimates that are unstable because a limited sample size can yield oversized variability in effects. In the earlier example, although a large treatment effect was found in the small pilot trial, the true treatment effect may actually be smaller but meaningful (e.g., $d = 0.45$). As larger sample sizes are required to reliably detect a moderate effect versus a large effect, a study designed to detect a large effect is at increased risk to accept the null hypothesis when there are true treatment differences. In this scenario, after a time- and resource-intensive RCT, the researcher could erroneously conclude that the treatment does not "work." However, an adequately powered study based on an accurate estimation of an expected moderate treatment effect size, would appropriately reject the null hypothesis. A researcher is better justified to rely on related work in the literature using adequately powered samples to evaluate the effect of similar treatment methods for neighboring clinical conditions than to rely on underpowered pilot work (see also Gallo et al., in press).

REPORTING

The final stage of conducting a treatment evaluation entails communicating study findings to the scientific community. A well-constructed and quality report will discuss outcomes in the context of previous related work (e.g., discussing how the findings build on and support previous work; discussing the ways in which findings are discrepant from previous work and why this may be the case), as well as consider limitations and shortcomings that can direct future theory and empirical efforts in the area. To prepare a quality report, the researcher must provide all of the relative information for the reader to critically appraise, interpret, and/or replicate study findings.

It has been suggested that there have been inadequacies in the reporting of RCTs (see Westen et al., 2004). Inadequacies in the reporting of RCTs can result in bias in estimating the effectiveness of interventions (Moher, Schulz, & Altman, 2001; Shulz, Chalmers, Hayes, & Altman, 1995). To maximize transparency in the reporting of RCTs, an international group of epidemiologists, statisticians, and journal editors developed a set of consolidated standards of reporting trials (i.e., CONSORT; see Begg et al., 1996), consisting of a 22-item checklist of study features that can bias estimates of treatment effects, or that are critical to judging the reliability or relevance of study findings, and consequently should be included in a comprehensive research report. A quality report will address each of these 22 items. For example, the title and abstract are to include how participants were allocated to interventions (e.g., randomly assigned), the methods must clearly detail eligibility criteria (i.e., inclusion/exclusion criteria) and how the sample size was determined, the procedures must indicate whether evaluators were blind to treatment assignment, and baseline demographic characteristics must be included for all participants. Importantly, participant flow must be characterized at each stage. The researcher reports the specific numbers of participants randomly assigned to each treatment condition, who received treatments as assigned, who participated in posttreatment evaluations, and who participated in follow-up evaluations. It has become standard practice for scientific journals to require a CONSORT flow diagram. See Figure 2.1 for an example of a flow diagram used in reporting to depict participant flow at each stage of an RCT.

The researcher's next decision is where to submit the report. We recommend that the researcher only consider submitting the report of their findings to a peer-reviewed journal. Publishing the outcomes of a study in a refereed journal (i.e., one that employs the peer-review process) signals that the work has been accepted and approved for publication by a panel of qualified and impartial reviewers (i.e., independent scientists knowledgeable in the area but not involved with the study). Consumers should be highly cautious of studies published in journals that do not place manuscript submissions through a rigorous peer-review process. Although the peer-review process slows down the speed with which one is able to communicate study results (much to the chagrin of the excited researcher who just

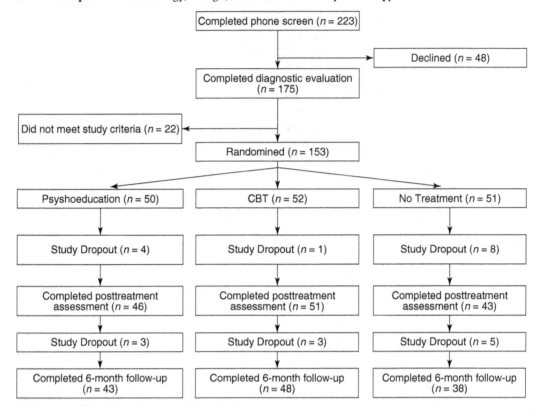

FIGURE 2.1 Example of flow diagram used in reporting to depict participant flow at each study stage.

completed an investigation), it is nonetheless one of the indispensable safeguards that we have to ensure that our collective knowledge base is drawn from studies meeting acceptable standards. Typically, the review process is "blind," meaning that the authors of the article do not know the identities of the peer-reviewers who are considering their manuscript. Many journals employ a double-blind peer-review process, in which the identities of study authors are also not known to the peer-reviewers.

CONCLUSION

One recognizes that no one single study, even with optimal design and procedures, can answer all of the relevant questions about the efficacy and effectiveness of therapy. Rather, a collection and series of studies, with varying approaches, is necessary for an incremental growth in our knowledge of optimal treatments for mental health problems. The criteria for determining empirically supported treatments and evidence-based practices have been proposed and accepted

(e.g., APA Task Force on Evidence Based Practice, 2006; Chambless & Hollon, 1998 in the United States; the National Institute for Health and Clinical Excellence [NICE] in the United Kingdom), and the quest for the continued identification and improvement of such treatments is underway. The goal is for the research to be rigorous, with the end goal being that the most promising procedures serve professional practice and those in need of services.

Treatment outcome research plays a vital role in facilitating a dialogue between scientist-practitioners and the public and private sector. Treatment outcome research is increasingly examined by both managed care organizations and professional associations with the intent of formulating practice guidelines for cost-effective care that provides optimal service to those in need. There is the risk that psychological science and practice will be co-opted and exploited in the service only of cost-containment and profitability. Psychotherapy outcome research must retain scientific rigor balanced with clinical relevance to enhance the ability of clinicians to deliver effective clinical procedures to individuals in need.

REFERENCES

Addis, M., Cardemil, E. V., Duncan, B., & Miller, S. (2006). Does manualization improve therapy outcomes? In J. C. Norcross, L. E. Beutler, & R. F. Levant (Eds.), *Evidence-based practices in mental health* (pp. 131–160). Washington, DC: American Psychological Association.

Addis, M., & Krasnow, A. (2000). A national survey of practicing psychologists' attitudes toward psychotherapy treatment manuals. *Journal of Consulting and Clinical Psychology, 68,* 331–339.

Aiken, L. S., & West, S. G. (1991). *Multiple regression: Testing and interpreting interactions.* Newbury Park, CA: Sage.

American Psychological Association. (2008). Reporting standards for research in psychology: Why do we need them? What might they be? *American Psychologist, 63,* 839–851.

American Psychological Association Task Force on Evidence-Based Practice. (2006). Report of the 2005 presidential task force on evidence-based practice. *American Psychologist, 61,* 271–285.

American Psychological Association Task Force on Promotion and Dissemination of Psychological Procedures. (1995). Training in and dissemination of empirically validated procedures: Report and recommendations. *Clinical Psychologist, 48,* 3–23.

Anderson, E. M., & Lambert, M. J. (2001). A survival analysis of clinical significant change in outpatient psychotherapy. *Journal of Clinical Psychology, 57,* 875–888.

Arnold, L. E., Elliott, M., Sachs, L., Bird, H., Kraemer, H. C., Wells, K. C., . . . Wigal, T. (2003). Effects of ethnicity on treatment attendance, stimulant response/dose, and 14-month outcome in ADHD. *Journal of Consulting and Clinical Psychology, 71,* 713–727.

Barlow, D. H. (1989). Treatment outcome evaluation methodology with anxiety disorders: Strengths and key issues. *Advances in Behavior Research and Therapy, 11,* 121–132.

Baron, R. M., & Kenny, D. A. (1986). The mediator-moderator variable distinction in social psychological research: Conceptual, strategic, and statistical consideration. *Journal of Personality and Social Psychology, 51,* 1173–1182.

Bauer, S., Lambert, M. J., & Nielsen, S. L. (2004). Clinical significance methods: A comparison of statistical techniques. *Journal of Personality Assessment, 82,* 60–70.

Begg, C. B., Cho, M. K., Eastwood, S., Horton, R., Moher, D., Olkin, I., . . . Stroup, D. F. (1996). Improving the quality of reporting of randomized controlled trials: The CONSORT statement. *Journal of the American Medical Association, 276,* 637–639.

Beidas, R. S., Mehta, T., Atkins, M., Solomon, B., & Merz, J. (in press). Dissemination and implementation science. Research models and methods. In J. S. Comer & P. C. Kendall (Eds.), *The Oxford handbook of research strategies for clinical psychology.* New York, NY: Oxford University Press.

Beidel, D. C., Turner, S. M., Sallee, F. R., Ammerman, R. T., Crosby, L. A., & Pathak, S. (2007). SET-C vs. fluoxetine in the treatment of childhood social phobia. *Journal of the American Academy of Child and Adolescent Psychiatry, 46,* 1622–1632.

Bernal, G., Bonilla, J., & Bellido, C. (1995). Ecological validity and cultural sensitivity for outcome research: Issues for the cultural adaptation and development of psychosocial treatments with Hispanics. *Journal of Abnormal Child Psychology, 23,* 67–82.

Bernal, G., & Scharron-Del-Rio, M. R. (2001). Are empirically supported treatments valid for ethnic minorities? Toward an alternative approach for treatment research. *Cultural Diversity and Ethnic Minority Psychology, 7,* 328–342.

Bersoff, D. M., & Bersoff, D. N. (1999). Ethical perspectives in clinical research. In P. C. Kendall, J. Butcher, & G. Holmbeck (Eds.), *Handbook of research methods in clinical psychology* (2nd ed., pp. 31–55). New York, NY: Wiley.

Beutler, L. E. (1998). Identifying empirically supported treatments: What if we didn't? *Journal of Consulting and Clinical Psychology, 66,* 37–52.

Beutler, L. (1979). Toward specific psychological therapies for specific conditions. *Journal of Consulting and Clinical Psychology, 47,* 882–897.

Blanco, C., Olfson, M., Goodwin, R. D., Ogburn, E., Liebowitz, M. R., Nunes, E. V., & Hasin, D. S. (2008). Generalizability of clinical trial results for major depression to community samples: Results from the national epidemiologic survey on alcohol and related conditions. *Journal of Clinical Psychiatry, 69,* 1276–1280.

Brown, R. A., Evans, M., Miller, I., Burgess, E., & Mueller, T. (1997). Cognitive-behavioral treatment for depression in alcoholism. *Journal of Consulting and Clinical Psychology, 65,* 715–726.

Chambless, D. L., & Hollon, S. D. (1998). Defining empirically supported therapies. *Journal of Consulting and Clinical Psychology, 66,* 7–18.

Cohen, J. (1988). *Statistical power analysis for the behavioral sciences* (2nd ed.). Hillsdale, NJ: Erlbaum.

Cohen, J., & Cohen, P. (1983). *Applied multiple regression/correlation analysis for the behavior sciences* (2nd ed.). Hillsdale, NJ: Erlbaum.

Comer, J. S., & Kendall, P. C. (2004). A symptom-level examination of parent–child agreement in the diagnosis of anxious youths. *Journal of the American Academy of Child and Adolescent Psychiatry, 43,* 878–886.

Comer, J. S., & Kendall, P. C. (Eds.). (in press). *The Oxford handbook of research strategies for clinical psychology.* New York, NY: Oxford University Press.

Coyne, J. C. (1994). Self-reported distress: Analog or ersatz depression? *Psychological Bulletin, 116,* 29–45.

Creed, T. A., & Kendall, P. C. (2005). Therapist alliance-building behavior within a cognitive-behavioral treatment for anxiety in youth. *Journal of Consulting and Clinical Psychology, 73*, 498–505.

De Los Reyes, A., & Kazdin, A. E. (2005). Informant discrepancies in the assessment of childhood psychopathology: A critical review, theoretical framework, and recommendations for further study. *Psychological Bulletin, 131*, 483–509.

De Los Reyes, A., & Kazdin, A. E. (2006). Conceptualizing changes in behavior in intervention research: The range of possible changes model. *Psychological Review, 113*, 554–583.

Delucchi, K., & Bostrom, A. (1999). Small sample longitudinal clinical trials with missing data: A comparison of analytic methods. *Psychological Methods, 4*, 158–172.

Dimidjian, S., & Hollon, S. (2011). What can be learned from when empirically supported treatments fail? *Cognitive and Behavioral Practice, 18*, 303–305.

Dobson, K. S., & Hamilton, K. E. (2002). The stage model for psychotherapy manual development: A valuable tool for promoting evidence-based practice. *Clinical Psychology: Science and Practice, 9*, 407–409.

Dobson, K. S., Hollon, S. D., Dimidjian, S., Schmaling, K. B., Kohlenberg, R. J., Gallop, R. J.,...Jacobson, N. S. (2008). Randomized trial of behavioral activation, cognitive therapy, and antidepressant medication in the prevention of relapse and recurrence in major depression. *Journal of Consulting and Clinical Psychology, 76*, 468–477.

Dobson, K. S., & Shaw, B. (1988). The use of treatment manuals in cognitive therapy. Experience and issues. *Journal of Consulting and Clinical Psychology, 56*, 673–682.

Durlak, J. A. (1995). Understanding meta-analysis. In L. G. Grimm & P. R. Yarnold (Eds.), *Reading and understanding multivariate statistics* (pp. 319–352). Washington, DC: American Psychological Association.

Field, A. P. (in press). Meta-analysis in clinical research. In J. S. Comer & P. C. Kendall (Eds.), *Oxford handbook of research strategies for clinical psychology*. New York, NY: Oxford University Press.

Fishman, D. B. (2000). Transcending the efficacy versus effectiveness research debate: Proposal for a new, electronic "Journal of Pragmatic Case Studies." *Prevention and Treatment, 3*, ArtID8.

Flaherty, J. A., & Meaer, R. (1980). Measuring racial bias in inpatient treatment. *American Journal of Psychiatry, 137*, 679–682.

Follette, W. C., & Callaghan, G. M. (1996). The importance of the principle of clinical significance— Defining significant to whom and for what purpose: A response to Tingey, Lambert, Burlingame, and Hansen. *Psychotherapy Research, 6*, 133–143.

Furr, J. M., Comer, J. S., Edmunds, J., & Kendall, P. C. (2010). Disasters and youth: A meta-analytic examination of posttraumatic stress. *Journal of Consulting and Clinical Psychology, 78*, 765–780.

Gallo, K., Comer, J. S., & Barlow, D. H. (in press). Single case, multiple-baseline, and small pilot trial designs. In J. S. Comer & P. C. Kendall (Eds.), *The Oxford Handbook of Research Strategies for Clinical Psychology*. New York, NY: Oxford University Press.

Garfield, S. (1998). Some comments on empirically supported psychological treatments. *Journal of Consulting and Clinical Psychology, 66*, 121–125.

Gladis, M. M., Gosch, E. A., Dishuk, N. M., & Crits-Christoph, P. (1999). Quality of life: Expanding the scope of clinical significance. *Journal of Consulting and Clinical Psychology, 67*(3), 320–331.

Hall, G. C. N. (2001). Psychotherapy research with ethnic minorities: Empirical, ethnical, and conceptual issues. *Journal of Consulting and Clinical Psychology, 69*, 502–510.

Hansen, N. B., Lambert, M. J., & Forman, E. M. (2002). The psychotherapy dose–response effect and its implications for treatment delivery services. *Clinical Psychology: Science and Practice, 9*, 329–343.

Hedeker, D., & Gibbons, R. D. (1994). A random-effects ordinal regression model for multilevel analysis. *Biometrics, 50*, 933–944.

Hedeker, D., & Gibbons, R. D. (1997). Application of random-effects pattern-mixture models for missing data in longitudinal studies. *Psychological Methods, 2*, 64–78.

Hill, C. E., & Lambert, M. J. (2004). Methodological issues in studying psychotherapy processes and outcomes. In M. J. Lambert (Ed.), *Bergin and Garfield's handbook of psychotherapy and behavior change* (5th ed., pp. 84–136). Hoboken, NJ: Wiley.

Hoagwood, K. (2002). Making the translation from research to its application: The je ne sais pas of evidence-based practices. *Clinical Psychology: Science and Practice, 9*, 210–213.

Hofmann, S. G. (2004). Cognitive mediation of treatment change in social phobia. *Journal of Consulting and Clinical Psychology, 72*(3), 392–399.

Hollon, S. D. (1996). The efficacy and effectiveness of psychotherapy relative to medications. *American Psychologist, 51*, 1025–1030.

Hollon, S. D., & DeRubeis, R. J. (1981). Placebo-psychotherapy combinations: Inappropriate representation of psychotherapy in drug-psychotherapy comparative trials. *Psychological Bulletin, 90*, 467–477.

Hollon, S. D., Garber, J., & Shelton, R. C. (2005). Treatment of depression in adolescents with cognitive behavior therapy and medications: A commentary on the TADS project. *Cognitive and Behavioral Practice, 12*, 149–155.

Holmbeck, G. N. (1997). Toward terminological, conceptual, and statistical clarity in the study of mediators and moderators: Examples from the child-clinical and pediatric psychology literatures.

Journal of Consulting and Clinical and Clinical Psychology, 65, 599–610.

Holmbeck, G. N. (2002). Post-hoc probing of significant moderational and mediational effects in studies of pediatric populations. *Journal of Pediatric Psychology, 27,* 87–96.

Homma-True, R., Greene, B., Lopez, S. R., & Trimble, J. E. (1993). Ethnocultural diversity in clinical psychology. *Clinical Psychologist, 46,* 50–63.

Hsu, L. M. (1989). Reliable changes in psychotherapy: Taking into account regression toward the mean. *Behavioral Assessment, 11,* 459–467.

Huey, S. J., & Polo, A. J. (2008). Evidence-based psychosocial treatments for ethnic minority youth. *Journal of Clinical Child and Adolescent Psychology, 37,* 262–301.

Jaccard, J., & Guilamo-Ramos, V. (2002a). Analysis of variance frameworks in clinical child and adolescent psychology: Issues and recommendations. *Journal of Clinical Child and Adolescent Psychology, 31,* 130–146.

Jaccard, J., & Guilamo-Ramos, V. (2002b). Analysis of variance frameworks in clinical child and adolescent psychology: Advanced issues and recommendations. *Journal of Clinical Child and Adolescent Psychology, 31,* 278–294.

Jacobson, N. S., Follette, W. C., & Revenstorf, D. (1984). Psychotherapy outcome research: Methods for reporting variability and evaluating clinical significance. *Behavior Therapy, 15,* 336–352.

Jacobson, N. S., & Hollon, S. D. (1996a). Cognitive-behavior therapy versus pharmacotherapy: Now that the jury's returned its verdict, it's time to present the rest of the evidence. *Journal of Consulting and Clinical Psychology, 74,* 74–80.

Jacobson, N. S., & Hollon, S. D. (1996b). Prospects for future comparisons between drugs and psychotherapy: Lessons from the CBT-versus-pharmacotherapy exchange. *Journal of Consulting and Clinical Psychology, 64,* 104–108.

Jacobson, N. S., Roberts, L. J., Berns, S. B., & McGlinchey, J. B. (1999). Methods for defining and determining the clinical significance of treatment effects. Description, application, and alternatives. *Journal of Consulting and Clinical Psychology, 67,* 300–307.

Jacobson, N. S., & Truax, P. (1991). Clinical significance: A statistic approach to defining meaningful change in psychotherapy research. *Journal of Consulting and Clinical Psychology, 59,* 12–19.

Jarrett, R. B., Vittengl, J. R., Doyle, K., & Clark, L. A. (2007). Changes in cognitive content during and following cognitive therapy for recurrent depression: Substantial and enduring, but not predictive of change in depressive symptoms. *Journal of Consulting and Clinical Psychology, 75,* 432–446.

Karver, M., Shirk, S., Handelsman, J. B., Fields, S., Crisp, H., Gudmundsen, G., & McMakin, D. (2008). Relationship processes in youth psychotherapy: Measuring alliance, alliance-building behaviors, and client involvement. *Journal of Emotional and Behavioral Disorders, 16,* 15–28.

Kazdin, A. E. (1999). The meanings and measurement of clinical significance. *Journal of Consulting and Clinical Psychology, 67,* 332–339.

Kazdin, A. E. (2003). *Research design in clinical psychology* (4th ed.). Boston, MA: Allyn & Bacon.

Kazdin, A. E. (2006). Arbitrary metrics: Implications for identifying evidence-based treatments. *American Psychologist, 61,* 42–49.

Kazdin, A. E., & Bass, D. (1989). Power to detect differences between alternative treatments in comparative psychotherapy outcome research. *Journal of Consulting and Clinical Psychology, 57,* 138–147.

Kendall, P. C. (1998). Empirically supported psychological therapies. *Journal of Consulting and Clinical Psychology, 66,* 19–36.

Kendall, P. C. (1999). Introduction to the special section: Clinical Significance. *Journal of Consulting and Clinical Psychology, 67,* 283–284.

Kendall, P. C., & Beidas, R. S. (2007). Smoothing the trail for dissemination of evidence-based practices for youth: Flexibility within fidelity. *Professional Psychology: Research and Practice, 38,* 13–20.

Kendall, P. C., & Chu, B. (1999). Retrospective self-reports of therapist flexibility in a manual-based treatment for youths with anxiety disorders. *Journal of Clinical Child Psychology, 29,* 209–220.

Kendall, P. C., Comer, J. S., Marker, C., Creed, T. A., Puliafico, A. C., … Hudson, J. L. (2009). In-session exposure tasks and therapeutic alliance across the treatment of childhood anxiety. *Journal of Consulting and Clinical Psychology, 77,* 517–525.

Kendall, P. C., Flannery-Schroeder, E., & Ford, J. (1999). Therapy outcome research methods. In P. C. Kendall, J. Butcher, & G. Holmbeck (Eds.), *Handbook of research methods in clinical psychology* (2nd ed., pp. 330–363). New York, NY: Wiley.

Kendall, P. C., & Grove, W. (1988). Normative comparisons in therapy outcome. *Behavioral Assessment, 10,* 147–158.

Kendall, P. C., & Hedtke, K. A. (2006). *Cognitive-behavioral therapy for anxious children* (3rd ed.). Ardmore, PA: Workbook.

Kendall, P. C., & Hollon, S. D. (1983). Calibrating therapy: Collaborative archiving of tape samples from therapy outcome trials. *Cognitive Therapy and Research, 7,* 199–204.

Kendall, P. C., Hollon, S., Beck, A. T., Hammen, C., & Ingram, R. (1987). Issues and recommendations regarding use of the Beck depression inventory. *Cognitive Therapy and Research, 11,* 289–299.

Kendall, P. C., Holmbeck, G., & Verduin, T. L. (2002). Methodology, design, and evaluation in psychotherapy research. In M. J. Lambert (Ed.), *Bergin and Garfield's handbook of psychotherapy and behavior change* (5th ed.). Hoboken, NJ: Wiley.

Kendall, P. C., Hudson, J. L., Gosch, E., Flannery-Schroeder, E., & Suveg, C. (2008). Cognitive-behavioral therapy for anxiety disordered youth: A randomized clinical trial evaluating child and family modalities. *Journal of Consulting and Clinical Psychology, 76*, 282–297.

Kendall, P. C., & Kessler, R. C. (2002). The impact of childhood psychopathology interventions on subsequent substance abuse: Policy implications, comments, and recommendations. *Journal of Consulting and Clinical Psychology, 70*, 1303–1306.

Kendall, P. C., & Maruyama, G. (1985). Meta-analysis: On the road to synthesis of knowledge? *Clinical Psychology Review, 5*, 79–89.

Kendall, P. C., Marrs-Garcia, A., Nath, S. R., & Sheldrick, R. C. (1999b). Normative comparisons for the evaluation of clinical significance. *Journal of Consulting and Clinical Psychology, 67*, 285–299.

Kendall, P. C., & Norton-Ford, J. D. (1982). *Clinical psychology: Scientific and professional dimensions.* New York, NY: Wiley.

Kendall, P. C., Safford, S., Flannery-Schroeder, E., & Webb, A. (2004). Child anxiety treatment: Outcomes in adolescence and impact on substance use and depression at 7.4-year follow-up. *Journal of the Consulting and Clinical Psychology, 72*, 276–287.

Kendall, P. C., & Southam-Gerow, M. A. (1995). Issues in the transportability of treatment: The case of anxiety disorders in youth. *Journal of Consulting and Clinical Psychology, 63*, 702–708.

Kendall, P. C., & Sugarman, A. (1997). Attrition in the treatment of childhood anxiety disorders. *Journal of Consulting and Clinical Psychology, 65*, 883–888.

Kiesler, D. J. (1971). Experimental designs in psychotherapy research. In A. E. Bergin & S. L. Garfield (Eds.), *Handbook of psychotherapy and behavior change.* New York, NY: Wiley.

Kraemer, H. C. (in press). Statistical power: Issues and proper applications. In J. S. Comer & P. C. Kendall (Eds.), *The Oxford handbook of research strategies for clinical psychology.* New York, NY: Oxford University Press.

Kraemer, H. C., Gardner, C., Brooks, J., & Yesavage, J. (1998). Advantages of excluding underpowered studies in meta-analysis: Inclusionist versus exclusionist viewpoints. *Psychological Methods, 3*, 23–31.

Kraemer, H. C., & Kupfer, D. J. (2006). Size of treatment effects and their importance to clinical research and practice. *Biological Psychiatry, 59*, 990–996.

Kraemer, H. C., Mintz, J., Noda, A., Tinklenberg, J., & Yesavage, J. A. (2006). Caution regarding the use of pilot studies to guide power calculations for study proposals. *Archives of General Psychiatry, 63*, 484–489.

Kraemer, H. C., & Thiemann, S. (1987). *How many subjects? Statistical power analysis in research.* Newbury Park, CA: Sage.

Kraemer, H. C., Wilson, G. T., Fairburn, C. G., & Agras, W. S. (2002). Mediators and moderators of treatment effects in randomized clinical trials. *Archives of General Psychiatry, 59*, 877–883.

Krupnick, J., Shea, T., & Elkin, I. (1986). Generalizability of treatment studies utilizing solicited patients.

Journal of Consulting and Clinical Psychology, 54, 68–78.

Laird, N. M., & Ware, J. H. (1982). Random-effects models for longitudinal data. *Biometrics, 38*, 963–974.

Lambert, M. J., Huefner, J. C., & Reisinger, C. W. (2000). Quality improvement: Current research in outcome management. In G. Stricker, W. G. Trow, & S. A. Shueman (Eds.), *Handbook of quality management in behavioral health* (pp. 95–110). New York, NY: Kluwer-Plenum.

Lambert, M. J., Shapiro, D. A., & Bergin, A. E. (1986). The effectiveness of psychotherapy. In S. L. Garfield & A. E. Bergin (Eds.), *Handbook of psychotherapy and behavior change* (3rd ed., pp. 157–211). New York, NY: Wiley.

Leon, A. C., Mallinckrodt, C. H., Chuang-Stein, C., Archibald, D. G., Archer, G. E., & Chartier, K. (2006). Attrition in randomized controlled clinical trials: Methodological issues in psychopharmacology. *Biological Psychiatry, 59*, 1001–1005.

Leong, F., & Kalibatseva, Z. (in press). Cross-cultural issues in clinical research. In J. S. Comer & P. C. Kendall (Eds.), *The Oxford handbook of research strategies for clinical psychology.* New York, NY: Oxford University Press.

Little, R. J. A., & Rubin, D. (2002). *Statistical analysis with missing data* (2nd ed.). Hoboken, NJ: Wiley.

Lipsey, M. W., & Wilson, D. B. (2000). Practical meta-analysis. *Applied social research methods series* (Vol. 49). Thousand Oaks, CA: Sage.

Lopez, S. R. (1989). Patient variable biases in clinical judgment: Conceptual overview and methodological considerations. *Psychological Bulletin, 106*, 184–204.

Luborsky, L., Singer, B., & Luborsky, L. (1975). Comparative studies of psychotherapy. *Archives of General Psychiatry, 32*, 995–1008.

Marcus, S. M., Gorman, J., Shea, M. K., Lewin, D., Martinez, J., Ray, S., . . . Woods, S. (2007). A comparison of medication side effect reports by panic disorder patients with and without concomitant cognitive behavior therapy. *American Journal of Psychiatry, 164*, 273–275.

MacKinnon, D. (in press). Evaluating treatment moderators and mediators. In J. S. Comer & P. C. Kendall (Eds.), *The Oxford handbook of clinical psychology.* New York, NY: Oxford University Press.

MacKinnon, D., & Dwyer, J. H. (1993). Estimating mediated effects in prevention studies. *Evaluation Review, 17*, 144–158.

Martinovich, Z., Saunders, S., & Howard, K. I. (1996). Some comments on assessing clinical significance. *Psychotherapy Research, 6*, 124–132.

Mason, M. J. (1999). A review of procedural and statistical methods for handling attrition and missing data. *Measurement and Evaluation in Counseling and Development, 32*, 111–118.

McGlinchey, J. B., Atkins, D. C., & Jacobson, N. S. (2002). Clinical significance methods: Which one to use and how useful are they? *Behavior Therapy, 33*, 529–550.

McKnight, P. E. (in press). Addressing missing data in clinical research. In J. S. Comer & P. C. Kendall (Eds.), *The Oxford handbook of research strategies for clinical psychology*. New York, NY: Oxford University Press.

McLeod, C., Islam, N., & Wheat, E. (in press). Designing, conducting, and evaluating therapy process research. In J. S. Comer & P. C. Kendall (Eds.), *The Oxford handbook of research strategies for clinical psychology*. New York, NY: Oxford University Press.

Moher, D., Schulz, K. F., & Altman, D. (2001). The CONSORT statement: Revised recommendations for improving the quality of reports of parallel-group randomized trials. *Journal of the American Medical Association, 285*, 1987–1991.

Mohr, D. C., Carmody, T., Erickson, L., Jin, L., & Leader, J. (2011). Telephone-administered cognitive behavioral therapy for veterans served by community-based outpatient clinics. *Journal of Consulting and Clinical Psychology, 79*(2), 261–265.

Molenberghs, G., Thijs, H., Jansen, I., Beunckens, C., Kenward, M. G., Mallinckrodt, C., & Carroll, R. (2004). Analyzing incomplete longitudinal clinical trial data. *Biostatistics, 5*, 445–464.

MTA Cooperative Group. (1999). A 14-month randomized clinical trial of treatment strategies for attention-deficit/hyperactivity disorder. *Archives of General Psychiatry, 56*, 1088–1096.

Mufson, L., Dorta, K. P., Wickramaratne, P., Nomura, Y., Olfson, M., & Weissman, M. M. (2004). A randomized effectiveness trial of interpersonal psychotherapy for depressed adolescents. *Archives of General Psychiatry, 61*, 577–584.

Neuner, F., Onyut, P. L., Ertl, V., Odenwald, M., Schauer, E., & Elbert, T. (2008). Treatment of posttraumatic stress disorder by trained lay counselors in an African refugee settlement: A randomized controlled trial. *Journal of Consulting and Clinical Psychology, 76*, 686–694.

O'Leary, K. D., & Borkovec, T. D. (1978). Conceptual, methodological, and ethical problems of placebo groups in psychotherapy research. *American Psychologist, 33*, 821–830.

Olfson, M., Cherry, D., & Lewis-Fernandez, R. (2009). Racial differences in visit duration of outpatient psychiatric visits. *Archives of General Psychiatry, 66*, 214–221.

Parloff, M. B. (1986). Placebo controls in psychotherapy research: A sine qua non or a placebo for research problems? *Journal of Consulting and Clinical Psychology, 54*, 79–87.

Pediatric OCD Treatment Study (POTS) Team. (2004). Cognitive-behavior therapy, sertraline, and their combination for children and adolescents with obsessive-compulsive disorder: The Pediatric OCD Treatment Study (POTS) randomized controlled trial. *Journal of the American Medical Association, 292*, 1969–1976.

Pelham, W. E. Jr., Gnagy, E. M., Greiner, A. R., Hoza, B., Hinshaw, S. P., Swanson, J. M., . . . McBurnett, K. (2000). Behavioral versus behavioral and psychopharmacological treatment in ADHD children attending a summer treatment program. *Journal of Abnormal Child Psychology, 28*, 507–525.

Perepletchikova, F., & Kazdin, A. E. (2005). Treatment integrity and therapeutic change: Issues and research recommendations. *Clinical Psychology: Science and Practice, 12*, 365–383.

Rausch, J. (in press). Data analysis in the randomized controlled trial. In J. S. Comer & P. C. Kendall (Eds.), *The Oxford handbook of research strategies for clinical psychology*. New York, NY: Oxford University Press.

Rausch, J. R., Maxwell, S. E., & Kelley, K. (2003). Analytic methods for questions pertaining to a pretest posttest follow-up design. *Journal of Clinical Child and Adolescent Psychology, 32*, 467–486.

Reis, B. F., & Brown, L. G. (2006). Preventing therapy dropout in the real world: The clinical utility of videotape preparation and client estimate of treatment duration. *Professional Psychology: Research and Practice, 37*, 311–316.

Rosenthal, R. (1984). *Meta-analytic procedures for social research*. Beverly Hills, CA: Sage.

Ruscio, A. M., & Ruscio, J. (2002). The latent structure of analogue depression: Should the Beck depression inventory be used to classify groups? *Psychological Assessment, 14*, 135–145.

Ruscio, J., & Ruscio, A. M. (2008). Categories and dimensions: Advancing psychological science through the study of latent structure. *Current Directions in Psychological Science, 17*, 203–207.

Santangelo, P. S., Ebner-Priemer, U. W., & Trull, T. J. (in press). Experience sampling methods in clinical psychology. In J. S. Comer & P. C. Kendall (Eds.), *The Oxford handbook of research strategies for clinical psychology*. New York, NY: Oxford University Press.

Shadish, W. R., Matt, G. E., Navarro, A. M., & Phillips, G. (2000). The effects of psychological therapies under clinically representative conditions: A meta-analysis. *Psychological Bulletin, 126*, 512–529.

Shakow, D. (1976). What is clinical psychology? *American Psychologist, 31*, 553–560.

Sheldrick, R. C., Kendall, P. C., & Heimberg, R. G. (2001). The clinical significance of treatments: A comparison of three treatments for conduct disordered children. *Clinical Psychology: Science and Practice, 8*, 418–430.

Shirk, S. R., Gudmundsen, G., Kaplinski, H., & McMakin, D. L. (2008). Alliance and outcome in cognitive-behavioral therapy for adolescent depression. *Journal of Clinical Child and Adolescent Psychology, 37*, 631–639.

Shulz, K. F., Chalmers, I., Hayes, R. J., & Altman, D. G. (1995). Empirical evidence of bias: Dimensions of methodological quality associated with estimates of treatment effects in clinical trials. *Journal of the American Medical Association, 273*, 408–412.

Silverman, W. K., Kurtines, W. M., & Hoagwood, K. (2004). Research progress on effectiveness, transportability, and dissemination of empirically supported treatments: Integrating theory and research. *Clinical Psychology: Science and Practice, 11,* 295–299.

Smith, M. L., & Glass, G. V. (1977). Meta-analysis of psychotherapy outcome studies. *American Psychologist, 32,* 752–760.

Snowden, L. R. (2003). Bias in mental health assessment and intervention: Theory and evidence. *American Journal of Public Health, 93,* 239–243.

Southam-Gerow, M. A., Ringeisen, H. L., & Sherrill, J. T. (2006). Integrating interventions and services research: Progress and prospects. *Clinical Psychology: Science and Practice, 13,* 1–8.

Speer, D. C. (1992). Clinically significant change: Jacobson and Truax (1991) revisited. *Journal of Consulting and Clinical Psychology, 60,* 402–408.

Spielmans, G. I., Gatlin, E. T., & McFall, J. P. (2009). The efficacy of evidence-based psychotherapies versus usual care for youths: Controlling confounds in a meta-analysis. *Psychotherapy Research, 20,* 234–246.

Sue, S. (1998). In search of cultural competence in psychotherapy and counseling. *American Psychologist, 53,* 440–448.

Suveg, C., Comer, J. S., Furr, J. M., & Kendall, P. C. (2006). Adapting manualized CBT for a cognitively delayed child with multiple anxiety disorders. *Clinical Case Studies, 5,* 488–510.

Sweeney, M., Robins, M., Ruberu, M., & Jones, J. (2005). African-American and Latino families in TADS: Recruitment and treatment considerations. *Cognitive and Behavioral Practice, 12,* 221–229.

Tennen, H., Hall, J. A., & Affleck, G. (1995). Depression research methodologies in the *Journal of Personality and Social Psychology*: A review and critique. *Journal of Personality and Social Psychology, 68,* 870–884.

Tingey, R. C., Lambert, M. J., Burlingame, G. M., & Hansen, N. B. (1996). Clinically significant change: Practical indicators for evaluating psychotherapy outcome. *Psychotherapy Research, 6,* 144–153.

Treadwell, K., Flannery-Schroeder, E. C., & Kendall, P. C. (1994). Ethnicity and gender in a sample of clinic-referred anxious children: Adaptive functioning, diagnostic status, and treatment outcome. *Journal of Anxiety Disorders, 9,* 373–384.

Vanable, P. A., Carey, M. P., Carey, K. B., & Maisto, S. A. (2002). Predictors of participation and attrition in a health promotion study involving psychiatric outpatients. *Journal of Consulting and Clinical Psychology, 70,* 362–368.

Walders, N., & Drotar, D. (2000). Understanding cultural and ethnic influences in research with child clinical and pediatric psychology populations. In D. Drotar (Ed.), *Handbook of research in pediatric and clinical child psychology* (pp. 165–188). New York, NY: Kluwer Academic/Plenum.

Walkup, J. T., Albano, A. M., Piacentini, J., Birmaher, B., Compton, S. N., . . . Kendall, P. C. (2008). Cognitive behavioral therapy, sertraline, or a combination in childhood anxiety. *New England Journal of Medicine, 359,* 1–14.

Waltz, J., Addis, M. E., Koerner, K., & Jacobson, N. S. (1993). Testing the integrity of a psychotherapy protocol: Assessment of adherence and competence. *Journal of Consulting and Clinical Psychology, 61,* 620–630.

Weisz, J., Donenberg, G. R., Han, S. S., & Weiss, B. (1995). Bridging the gap between laboratory and clinic in child and adolescent psychotherapy. *Journal of Consulting and Clinical Psychology, 63,* 688–701.

Weisz, J. R., Doss, A. J., & Hawley, K. M. (2006). Evidence-based youth psychotherapies versus usual clinical care: A meta-analysis of direct comparisons. *American Psychologist, 61,* 671–689.

Weisz, J. R., McCarty, C., & Valeri, S. M. (2006). Effects of psychotherapy for depression in children and adolescents: A meta-analysis. *Psychological Bulletin, 132,* 132–149.

Weisz, J. R., Weersing, V. R., & Henggeler, S. W. (2004). Jousting with straw men: Comment on Westen, Novotny, and Thompson-Brenner (2004). *Psychological Bulletin, 131,* 418–426.

Weisz, J. R., Weiss, B., & Donenberg, G. R. (1992). The lab versus the clinic: Effects of child and adolescent psychotherapy. *American Psychologist, 47,* 1578–1585.

Westbrook, D., & Kirk, J. (2007). The clinical effectiveness of cognitive behaviour therapy: Outcome for a large sample of adults treated in routine practice. *Behaviour Research and Therapy, 43,* 1243–1261.

Westen, D., Novotny, C., & Thompson-Brenner, H. (2004). The empirical status of empirically supported psychotherapies: Assumptions, findings, and reporting in controlled clinical trials. *Psychological Bulletin, 130,* 631–663.

Wilkinson, L., & Task Force on Statistical Inference. (1999). Statistical methods in psychology journals: Guidelines and explanations. *American Psychologist, 54,* 594–604.

Wilson, G. T. (1995). Empirically validated treatments as a basis for clinical practice: Problems and prospects. In S. C. Hayes, V. M. Follette, R. D. Dawes, & K. Grady (Eds.), *Scientific standards of psychological practice: Issues and recommendations* (pp. 163–196). Reno, NV: Context Press.

Wolf, E. J., & Brown, T. (in press). Structural equation modeling: Applications in the study of clinical psychology. In J. S. Comer & P. C. Kendall (Eds.), *The Oxford handbook of research strategies for clinical psychology.* New York, NY: Oxford University Press.

Yeh, M., McCabe, K., Hough, R. L., Dupuis, D., & Hazen, A. (2003). Racial and ethnic differences in parental endorsement of barriers to mental health services in youth. *Mental Health Services Research, 5,* 65–77.

CHAPTER 3

QUALITATIVE RESEARCH
Methods and Contributions

JOHN MCLEOD

INTRODUCTION

The counseling and psychotherapy research literature continues to be dominated by studies that are based on quantitative measurement. However, research carried out with the use of qualitative methods, such as the analysis of interviews or therapy recordings, has a strong appeal for many clinicians and students because, in contrast to quantitative research, it remains closer to the actual phenomena and lived experience of therapy. Qualitative research articles provide a sense of being able to hear the voice of the client or therapist, and offer an understanding of the meaning that various aspects of therapy hold for them. At the same time, there are concerns about the reliability and validity of qualitative studies, for instance around difficulties in generalizing from small samples and in the possibility of researcher bias. There are also important barriers to the conduct of qualitative research. For new researchers, the domain of qualitative inquiry can appear impossibly complex and fragmented, with a confusing array of competing methodologies clamoring for attention. In addition, qualitative research is time-consuming, and requires specialist training and supervision. Although previous editions of this handbook have endorsed the value of qualitative methods, they have not included a chapter dedicated to this approach to inquiry, and authors of chapters on substantive topics have made scant reference to the contribution of qualitative investigations. In some respects, therefore, the present chapter can be viewed as evidence for the "coming of age" of qualitative research within the field of psychotherapy research.

This chapter provides an overview of the current landscape of qualitative research in counseling and psychotherapy. Methodological principles that inform the design of qualitative psychotherapy research are examined. Underlying philosophical and methodological assumptions that inform the conduct of qualitative research are outlined. The main methods of data collection and analysis are described, and critical issues are discussed. The contribution of qualitative research to the evidence base for counseling and psychotherapy is reviewed in relation to three key areas: the outcomes of therapy, therapy process, and the characteristics of effective therapists. The chapter concludes by considering some possible future directions for qualitative research on therapy.

CONCEPTUAL AND METHODOLOGICAL FOUNDATIONS

To understand what qualitative research is trying to achieve, it is necessary to consider the contrasting philosophical assumptions that underpin mainstream quantitative research, on the one hand, and qualitative inquiry, on the other. The act of measurement is part of a long tradition in human society. People have always needed to count things, for practical purposes. From around the 17th century, a concept of *science* began to evolve, based on an assumption of an objective physical reality (e.g., atoms, molecules) that could be measured, and a realization that mathematical analysis of patterns within these numbers would yield theories or models that could be used to develop new technologies (e.g., machines, drugs) of immense value to human well-being. The act of making sense of the meaning of words or texts is also part of a long tradition in human society. The mythology or wisdom of a social group was initially conveyed through an oral tradition of stories and myths, then later through religious texts and other writings. But the meaning of these linguistic objects was not always clear—a different kind of "human science" needed to be developed, focusing on the interpretation of texts (Dilthey, 1977; Hiley, Bohman, & Shusterman 1991; Mueller-Vollmer, 1997; Packer & Addison, 1989; Taylor, 1971).

These alternative and competing knowledge-generating structures continue to exist in contemporary society. Although the "natural science" paradigm has enjoyed a dominant position within industrialized societies, in relation to public funding and influence over decision making, it is clear that interpretive forms of inquiry also play a significant role in cultural life. Bruner (1986) characterized these traditions as constituting discrete *ways of knowing*: a *paradigmatic* form of knowing that seeks to explain events in terms of abstract laws, and a *narrative* form of knowing that seeks to understand events in terms of contextualized, concrete stories. One of the barriers to the use of both of these forms of inquiry within the psychological research community has been the view that these forms of knowing are incommensurable—they provide competing perspectives that cannot be reconciled. However, it can be argued that the field of counseling and psychology represents a domain of practical knowledge that calls for clinicians and researchers to embrace both paradigmatic and narrative ways of knowing (Madill & Gough, 2008; McLeod, 2011). For example, a female client who seeks therapy to deal with her post-natal depression wishes to explore the effects of causal/paradigmatic factors such as hormonal changes and sleep deprivation, alongside interpretive/narrative themes such as the meaning of motherhood and the renegotiation of roles within her marriage.

The implication of this kind of everyday clinical scenario is that therapists (and therapy researchers) tend to find ways to integrate knowledge and understanding from apparently quite different ontological and epistemological paradigms or traditions. As a result, psychotherapy research has consistently moved in the direction of methodological pluralism (Howard, 1983) as it has matured as a field of inquiry in its own right and freed itself of the constraints of the assumptions of experimental psychology. The vision of psychotherapy research that has been most influential in recent years draws on a *pragmatic* image of knowledge as a basis for reasoned and responsible professional action (Fishman, 1999) that can be traced back to the ideas of William James, one of the founding figures of modern psychology. A pragmatic perspective is associated with the view that there is no single source of truth to which all knowledge claims can be reduced. All sources of knowledge are of potential value while at the same time being open to critical scrutiny.

Philosophical Sources

Although it is possible to argue that quantitative and qualitative traditions each have their place in the context of the bigger picture of the psychotherapy research literature as a whole, it is undoubtedly the case that, historically, the training and professional socialization of the majority of therapy researchers has resulted in the development of deep understanding and technical skills around quantitative methodologies, and at the cost of a relative lack of knowledge and experience in relation to qualitative research. In response to this bias, several writers have sought to explicate the nature of qualitative therapy research from philosophical "first principles" (Madill & Gough, 2008; McLeod, 2011; Morrow, 2007; Polkinghorne, 1988; Ponterotto, 2005; Rennie, 2000a). There have been two main aims of these writings. First, it is argued that the positivist and critical realist philosophical positions that underpin mainstream psychological and medical research are so ingrained in researchers that researchers need to be challenged to rethink their underlying (or taken-for-granted) assumptions about ontology and epistemology if they are to engage effectively with qualitative methodologies.

The second aim has been to increase appreciation of the potential contribution of qualitative research and the necessity of understanding the distinctive values and knowledge criteria that can be used to evaluate qualitative work. Widely used qualitative methods texts, such as Hill (2012) and Smith, Flowers, and Larkin (2009), reflect these principles in providing readers with detailed accounts of the epistemological grounding of the methods that they describe.

There is a broad agreement across writers on the methodology of qualitative psychotherapy research that qualitative inquiry is informed by a specific set of interlocking philosophical traditions. The earliest of these traditions, in respect of its position within the history of human thought, is represented by the field of *hermeneutics*, which refers to the principles that guide valid interpretation of the meaning of a text. The hermeneutic tradition encompasses such knowledge-generating activities such as arriving at an understanding of the meaning of such diverse texts as religious writings, legal cases, plays and movies, and architectural styles (Taylor, 1971). It is but a small step to move from these examples of interpretive inquiry to contemporary research applications such as interpreting the meaning of a research interview or a therapy transcript (Gergen, 1988).

Phenomenology represents another philosophical tradition that has been incorporated into the methodology of qualitative inquiry. Phenomenology seeks to attain true knowledge by systematically bracketing-off everyday assumptions (natural attitude) concerning the meaning of an experience (Finlay, 2008; Fischer, 2009). For example, a client being interviewed about his experience in therapy stated that:

> In the beginning, before therapy I blamed everything on me, everything that went wrong, I blamed it on me. But when I started speaking about it that kind of changed and my perspective changed.

Faced with this segment of interview transcript, a qualitative researcher might code it as "client perception of value of self-disclosure" and "gaining a perspective as an outcome of therapy." Given that the researcher might need to work through many hundreds of lines of transcript, it might seem reasonable to accept these codes as providing a satisfactory rendering of that segment of the text, and move on. However, the phenomenological discipline of "bracketing-off" requires the researcher to stay with the text and ask, "What else might be there?" Within that particular passage, the researcher might then find other threads of potential meaning: the repetition

and emphasis around "I blamed it on me," the subtle qualification of therapeutic benefit implied by "*kind of* changed," and the inclusion of time markers ("in the beginning," "started"). The aim of phenomenological inquiry is to describe the phenomenon in as much detail as possible, and arrive at an appreciation of its "essence." The process of bracketing-off slows down the researcher to a point at which a nuanced complexity can emerge and some sense of the "essential" quality of the experience being described can be at least partially grasped. The principles and practices of phenomenology have proved to be enormously useful for qualitative researchers aiming to move beyond surface or taken for granted understanding of the meaning of qualitative data and to achieve a deeper and more comprehensive appreciation of the possible layers of meaning in verbal accounts of experience.

There are two further areas of the philosophical literature that comprise essential sources of knowledge and understanding for those carrying out qualitative research: *rhetoric* and *critical theory*. The topic of rhetoric refers to the question of how an argument is constructed, to persuade an audience of its plausibility. Again, this is an area of philosophy that has substantial historical roots, and can be traced back to the origins of democracy in the open citizens debates that determined collective decision making in the ancient Greek city states (Eden, 1987; Perelman, 1982). An appreciation of rhetorical principles and structures is valuable for qualitative researchers because the basic data that are being handled (words) have been constructed by an informant in the light of his or her communicative goals in relation to their audience or interlocutor. Unlike numbers, qualitative data do not consist of bits of information that can be assembled and combined in different ways. Instead, the meaning of qualitative data, such as an interview transcript, always needs to be interpreted in relation to the context in which it was produced (Billig, 1996). A statement such as "before therapy, I blamed everything on me," might have a different meaning if the informant was responding to an open invitation to talk about his experience of therapy, as against a situation in which the interviewer had asked a specific question about self-blame. Beyond an appreciation of rhetorical aspects of the ways in which clients give accounts of their experience, ideas about rhetoric are also relevant for qualitative researchers in respect to the way in which their research findings are communicated.

Skilled qualitative researchers are sensitive to the task of explicating the personal stance of the researcher and conveying the distinctive *voice* or perspective of research participants. This concern with the rhetorical issues that are involved in reporting qualitative research has led to an interest within the qualitative research community in the ways in which scientific reports are written (Bazerman, 1988; Gergen, 1997; Nelson, Megill, & McCloskey, 1987; Rennie, 1995).

The notion of *critical theory* is of more recent origin, and is associated with the ideas of members of the Frankfurt School such as Jurgen Habermas (1972; Kincheloe & McLaren, 2005), and the writings of Michel Foucault (1972; Flyvbjerg, 2001) and Klaus Holzkamp (1992; Teo, 1998; Tolman, 2009). The primary focus of these social scientists, around methodological issues, has been to draw attention to the social role of science, and in particular to the ways in which science might appear to produce valid value-free knowledge but in reality was often conducted to support the interests of ruling elites. As result, it is essential for researchers to adopt a questioning and critical perspective in relation to the wider social meaning of their investigations. In the field of qualitative research, this position has translated into a concern for the power relationship between the researcher and the object of their research, and sensitivity to the ways in which dimensions of power and control are mediated and expressed in language and talk. This orientation toward a social justice agenda for research and practice is connected to similar developments within the field of psychotherapy as a whole (Goodman, Helms, Latta, Sparks, & Weintraub, 2004; Greenleaf & Williams, 2009).

It is possible to identify phenomenology, hermeneutics, rhetoric, and critical theory as essential methodological ingredients that constitute the practice of qualitative research. These ingredients can be combined in a range of different ways, depending on the aims and values of different researchers, and the topics that they are investigating. As a consequence, there does not exist, at the present time, a unified methodology for qualitative research. The absence of clearly defined principles and procedures for qualitative work can be confusing for those who are new to the field, and perplexing for those who have been trained in the quantitative-experimental tradition. It is therefore essential for training

in qualitative methods to address underlying philosophical issues, so that researchers can make informed methodological choices.

There are many methodological choice-points that arise during the design and conduct of any qualitative project. It is necessary, for example, for any qualitative researcher to take a position in relation to the issue of researcher reflexivity. From a positivist epistemological standpoint, the personal experience and motivation of the researcher is only of interest as a potential source of bias, to be eliminated. In qualitative research, by contrast, it is clear that the person of the researcher may play an important role in shaping the type of data that is collected, and how it is analyzed. For instance, in a qualitative study of the emotional impact of loss of sight, research participants acknowledged that they were able to be more open in their interviews because the researcher was visually impaired, and could identify with how they felt (Thurston, 2010). Guided by phenomenological and hermeneutic principles, Thurston (2010) therefore made sure to keep a personal diary of her responses to participants, invited interviewees to comment on the experience of taking part in the study, and wrote about these matters in the method section of the resulting research article.

From a critical theory perspective, however, this kind of "first-person" account is not encouraged. The perspective of qualitative methodologies that adopt a critical theory stance, is that any personal statement on the art of the researcher needs to be regarded as a piece of discourse, or speech act, is no different in status from the words of research participants, and must be open to critical analysis and deconstruction. Researchers whose work is predominantly located within a critical theory approach deal with the issue of researcher reflexivity by ensuring that substantial amounts of basic transcript data is included in the research report, so that what the researcher does with the data is transparent to the reader. The challenge of research reflexivity is discussed in more detail in a later section of this chapter. Other methodological choices that are faced by qualitative researchers include the extent to which a study adopts an action orientation (rather than merely seeking to generate academic knowledge), the kind of rationale and procedures that are used to support validity claims, and the way that the findings of a study is reported and disseminated.

The Constructivist Basis of Qualitative Research

Constructivism represents a core idea that forms a shared point of contact across hermeneutics, phenomenology, rhetoric, and critical theory. Constructivism is grounded in the idea that the real nature of things is not knowable, and that human life is organized around an active process of co-construction that involves attributing meaning to experience, and continually revising these meanings through collaboration and conflict between individuals and groups. From a constructivist perspective, the concepts and theories held by individuals do not comprise a mirror to nature, but instead can be regarded as comprising an ongoing conversation about the nature of things (Rorty, 1980). Constructivism refers to a broad set of ideas, which can be traced back to the earliest philosophical writings. A version of constructivism that has been particularly influential for some qualitative researchers is *social constructionism*, which places particular emphasis on the role of talk and language as the primary means through which processes of construction takes place (M. Gergen & Gergen, 2003; Lock & Strong, 2010). To a large extent, the existing counseling and psychotherapy literature is grounded in an assumption of naturalism, which holds that there is an objective external reality that can be measured and known (Slife, 2004). The methodology of the randomized clinical trial is an example of the way that the psychotherapy research community has sought to converge on a single right (or objective) answer to the question of which therapy is most effective. As a result, the epistemological pluralism (Ferrara, 2010; Rescher, 1993; Woody & Viney, 2009) that is inherent in constructivist and social constructionist ways of thinking (i.e., that there can be several valid answers to one question) is hard for many researchers to accept.

Qualitative research can be viewed as a process of inquiry that aims to elucidate the construction of social reality in specific contexts. In the domain of counseling and psychotherapy, the aim of qualitative research is to describe, analyze, and understand the means through which the phenomena of therapy (for example, the therapeutic relationship, or changes in client symptoms) are constructed by various stakeholders or participants. In general terms, quantitative research seeks to establish causal links between "factors" or "variables." So, for example, a typical quantitative study on the therapeutic relationship might aim to determine whether alliance scores at Session 3 predicted the ultimate outcome of therapy. By contrast, qualitative research into the client-therapist relationship aims to elucidate such topics as the meanings that clients attribute to different therapist activities (Bedi, Davis, & Williams, 2005), and the use of conversational strategies in arriving at a shared understanding of the goals of therapy (Davis, 1986). Quantitative and qualitative researchers are interested in the same fundamental question (what is a facilitative therapeutic relationship?). However, quantitative researchers approach the question from a perspective of trying to establish the validity of if-then statements or predictions. Qualitative researchers, by contrast, approach the question from a perspective of trying to describe the actions that people undertake in the light of the meaning structures that are available to them.

Qualitative research strives to maintain a balance between realism and relativism (Rennie, 2000b). The products of qualitative inquiry are based in a good-faith, accurate rendering of reality as it is experienced by all of those who have taken part in a study. At the same time, this product is of necessity a version, a construction of that reality, a particular reading. By including vivid examples, in the form of cases, quotes from informants or segments of therapy text, qualitative research attempts to show as well as tell, thus creating a space within which the reader has the possibility of arriving at his or her own interpretation of the material. The concept of the *hermeneutic circle* refers to the notion that any interpretation of reality, or story, can itself be reinterpreted or retold from a different viewpoint. There is therefore always a sense in which qualitative research recounts the history of a phenomenon or topic (Gergen, 1973). A powerful interpretive account of a phenomenon creates a temporary clearing, within which certain features of the terrain can be clearly seen (Heidegger, 1962). However, as these ideas become assimilated into the everyday, taken-for-granted understanding of participants in social life, that initial moment of clarity becomes overlaid with layers of further meaning. As a result, qualitative research is always, to some extent, a discovery-oriented activity. The qualitative researcher is like a reporter or archivist who documents and describes segments of everyday life, and at the same time an artist who is able to offer his or her audience a new way of seeing.

QUALITATIVE RESEARCH DESIGNS

At the present time, there is little agreement around the types of qualitative research design that are most appropriate to use in addressing different research questions in the field of counseling and psychotherapy. Most qualitative research textbooks (for example, Creswell, 2007; Flick, 2009; Harper & Thompson, 2011) locate questions of research design in a discussion of qualitative methodologies, such as phenomenology or narrative analysis, that are derived from underlying epistemological principles. One consequence of the widespread adoption of this strategy has been a situation in which researchers become adherents of particular methodologies, and as a result fail to acknowledge the relevance of competing methodologies. This state of affairs has contributed to a somewhat fragmented, conflictual, and inward-looking research community (Denzin & Lincoln, 2011; Lincoln, Lynham, & Guba, 2011; Preissle, 2006). Within the field of qualitative therapy research, Elliott and Timulak (2005) advocate the adoption of a generic qualitative method, applicable to all or most research questions. Also from a standpoint in psychotherapy research, Moertl, Gelo, and Pokorny (in press) have categorized qualitative methodologies along two dimensions: theory-confirming versus theory-building, and content-oriented versus structure-oriented. An alternative approach, adopted in the present chapter, is to differentiate between qualitative research designs that investigate therapy outcome and process in relation to three units of scale: macro, mid-range, and micro. Macro-level studies explore the social, cultural, and historical context within which therapy takes place. Mid-range studies examine the experience of therapy for participants. Finally, micro-level investigations consider moment-by-moment processes. Each of these units of analysis present distinctive opportunities and challenges for qualitative therapy researchers, and are associated with the use of specific methods of gathering and analyzing data.

Investigating the Context of Therapy

Any experienced clinicians will have their own ideas about the ways in which the historical and organizational context in which therapy takes

place has an impact on the work they are able to do with clients. Qualitative research has the potential to document and describe contextual factors, and interpret their meaning and implication in relation to therapy practice. A study by Cook, Biyanova, and Coyne (2009) provides an example of the use of qualitative methods to explore the role of contextual factors in therapy. In this research, interviews were conducted with therapists in two therapy clinics within the same health care system. One of the clinics had adopted eye-movement desensitization and reprocessing (EMDR) as a favored intervention for patients with posttraumatic stress disorder, while in the other clinic this technique was not used at all. Cook et al. (2009) were able to identify the events, values, and management decision making that resulted in the dissemination (or otherwise) of EMDR in these clinics. The findings of this study were also used to generate a model of diffusion of innovation that could be applied in other settings.

The Cook et al. (2009) study was able to rely on interviews with individual informants, because in each setting it was possible to identify a set of members who had been present throughout the period of time being investigated, and were able to report on what had happened. In some studies of contexts, however, the topic of investigation calls for the collection of further sources of data, such as observation and personal or institutional documents, in order to be able to capture the complexity of the slice of social reality that is being investigated, and overcome the limitations of each source. The method of ethnographic *participant observation* encompasses spending time with a group of people, watching what they do, conducting informal conversations and more formal interviews, and collecting examples of the artifacts produced by the group, such as writings, objects and images (McLeod, 2011; Suzuki, Ahluwalia, Mattis, & Quizon, 2005). An example of an ethnographic study of therapy can be found in the work of Waldram (2007), who investigated the delivery of cognitive-behavior therapy (CBT) in the context of a prison-based treatment program for sex offenders. This study was able to show that the therapists in this program possessed a detailed record of the offending behavior of each client in advance of meeting him, and employed this account as a "truth" against which the openness of the client's own account of their actions could be assessed. As a result, the use of CBT within this program was fundamentally different from the collaborative way of working espoused by therapists in outpatient or private-practice settings. Unlike the Cook et al. (2009) study, where it was possible to make use of informants who were able to articulate a reflective understanding of the operation of the social context within which they were located, Waldram (2007) needed to piece together his analysis of the social context being investigated by building up relationships over time with key informants that made it possible to engage in direct observation of therapy sessions, take part in informal personal conversations, and have access to case records.

A wider perspective on the context of therapy can be developed by examining the ways in which therapy practice is shaped by shifts in external cultural, social, and economic conditions. There have been two studies that have used a historical, hermeneutic-interpretive approach to analyze these factors. Lewis, Clark, and Morgan (1992) identified two main influences on the emergence of marriage guidance counseling in Britain in the years following World War II. During that period, marital breakdown represented a significant moral and social issue that needed to be addressed through voluntary and community-based initiatives. In addition, leading figures in professional therapy promoted the adoption and application of established models of counseling and psychotherapy within the field of marital work. In a study of the historical development of psychotherapy in the United States, Cushman (1995) demonstrated the links between the growth in popularity and accessibility of therapy that took place in the 1950s, and the establishment of consumerism and individualism within American culture as a whole. The historical scope of the Lewis, Clark, and Morgan (1992) and Cushman (1995) studies meant that interviews with key informants were of limited value, because each informant could only offer a limited and partial account of the events in question. These studies therefore largely relied on analysis of documentary evidence rather than on collecting primary evidence through interviews.

A further set of qualitative studies has examined the practice of therapy in relation to the everyday lives of clients, using ethnographic methods (Dreier, 2000, 2008) and solicited diaries (Mackrill, 2008a, 2008b, 2009). This line of research has provided evidence of the extent to which clients are exposed to, and make use of, "therapeutic" ideas and techniques that are available within everyday culture and discourse, and that clients frequently interpret the methods being used by their therapists in the light of these preexisting practices. This research also found that therapeutic change in the cases that were examined did not consist of shifts in the emotional or cognitive functioning of the client, but was expressed in clients' decisions to rearrange elements of the structure of their everyday lives (Dreier, 2008). These studies draw attention to the extent to which the everyday lives of clients are not visible to their therapists.

These examples of qualitative studies of the social context of therapy illustrate several key methodological principles. Qualitative contextual studies require the identification of a specific case to be examined. The case can be relatively limited in scope, for example one therapy program (Waldram, 2007), one family (Dreier, 2008), a case comparison of two programs (Cook et al., 2009), the relationship between the therapy profession and managed care organizations (Greer & Rennie, 2006), or the influence on clients of being participants in a randomized controlled trial (Anderson & Strupp, 1986). Alternatively, contextual studies can be much wider in scope, such as the "case" of therapy in the United States (Cushman, 1995) or psychotherapeutic responses to depression in Greek women (Peglidou, 2010). Sufficiently rich data need to be collected to enable cross-checking of interpretations and conclusions (triangulation) across different sources of evidence. Analysis of data usually consists of identifying a coherent narrative of the stages in the development of the ideas and practices that are being investigated. Within these general methodological principles, a range of specific data collection and analysis strategies may be employed, depending on the aims of each particular study. Although few qualitative contextual studies of psychotherapy have been carried out, it seems clear that this type of research has the potential to make a significant contribution to the counseling and psychotherapy literature as a whole. Essentially, these studies show that the type of therapy that is delivered, and the effectiveness of that therapy, may depend less on the level of empirical support for the approach being used, or the skillfulness of the therapists who are delivering it, than on the ways in which these ideas and skills are adapted and reconstructed in the light of local conditions.

Research Into the Experience of Therapy

The largest body of work within the field of qualitative research in counseling and psychotherapy consists of studies of the experiences of therapy participants. Although most of these studies have focused on client experiences, there have also been studies of therapist experiences of aspects of therapy (Arthern & Madill, 1999; Beck et al., 2005; Daniel & McLeod, 2006; Frontman & Kunkel, 1994; Goddard, Murray, & Simpson, 2008; O'Neill, 1998), and the experiences of third parties such as family members (Jensen et al., 2010; Roberts, 1996). The rationale for research into the experience of therapy is compelling: There is an endless curiosity about what it is "really" like to be a client or a therapist. This curiosity is reinforced by an appreciation that the process of training and professional socialization undertaken by therapists may make it difficult or impossible for clinicians to appreciate what it feels like to be a client who is in therapy for the first time, or who is on the receiving end of a routine intervention. The appeal of qualitative research into the experience of therapy is that it offers participants a voice, and helps to de-familiarize taken-for-granted practices in ways that allow clinicians to remain receptive and responsive to clients and trainees. The basic methodological strategy that is employed within this genre of qualitative research is to collect self-reports of experience from a group of informants who have been selected on the basis of their exposure to a particular type of therapy event (e.g., they have all completed therapy, or they have all undergone a particular type of intervention). These qualitative accounts are then systematically analyzed to identify constituent themes or categories. Ultimately, the researcher is trying to answer the question: How is this aspect of therapy constructed by participants, in terms of a set of meanings that they are able to articulate? The aim is to achieve a "thick description" of the phenomenon being investigated (Geertz, 1973). What the researcher is looking for is not to arrive at a simple rendering of an experience (for example, that it was helpful), but instead to generate a multifaceted, nuanced, or layered account that will enable the reader to arrive at a deeper understanding or insight of the topic. It is also important to make a distinction between qualitative research and content analysis.

The aim of content analysis is to count the number of times a word or topic occurs within a research text such as an interview transcript. For example, for some research purposes it may be of interest to count the frequency with which a client engages in storytelling or refers to particular emotional states. Qualitative research always seeks to go beyond an itemization of content categories, in order to make some kind of sense of the *meaning* that the category has for research participants. For example, it is valuable to know about the average number of times a client engages in storytelling in a typical therapy session (Luborsky & Crits-Christoph, 1990), because this information can sensitize a therapist to the potential clinical significance of an absence, or overabundance, of storytelling within the therapy discourse of a particular client. But what a qualitative study, such as Rennie (1994a), adds to this knowledge is an appreciation of what the client is *doing* when he or she uses time within a therapy session to recount a story of an everyday event. Using careful analysis of stimulated recall interviews with clients, Rennie (1994a) was able to demonstrate that storytelling could function as a means of delaying entry into difficult feelings, and that the act of telling the story involved a process of internal reflection and sense-making.

There are several alternative methodological procedures that have been developed to carry out qualitative research on the experience of therapy. It is possible to identify four specific qualitative methodologies that are widely used. The most straightforward and flexible approach is thematic analysis (Boyatzis, 1998; Braun & Clarke, 2006), which consists of conducting a careful line-by-line reading of interview transcripts to identify themes within informants accounts of the topic being explored. A second group of qualitative methodologies are similar in intention to thematic analysis, but have developed more elaborate protocols for data analysis. The most widely used of these approaches are grounded theory (Charmaz, 2006; Rennie, Phillips, & Quartaro, 1998), interpretive phenomenological analysis (IPA; Smith, Flowers, & Larkin, 2009) and consensual qualitative research (CQR; Hill, 2012; Hill, Thompson, & Nutt-Williams, 1997). Each of these qualitative methodologies provides researchers with substantial guidance around how to organize the analysis of data, and what the finished product should look like. There are relatively minor differences between these approaches, which may be helpful or hindering in relation to the goals of a particular project. For example, grounded theory analysis requires the researcher to be able to identify a single overarching category that encapsulates the core meaning of the phenomenon being studied. IPA encourages analysis on a case-by-case basis, and invites the researcher to attend to structural and linguistic aspects of informant accounts (for instance, the potential meaning of long silences during an interview). CQR allows for the use of a start list of categories derived from previous research, theory, or clinical experience, and requires the analysis to be conducted by a team of researchers. These differences in technique can be viewed as alternative routes to arrive at the same general destination. Essentially, grounded theory, IPA, and CQR represent epistemologically eclectic strategies for assembling a pragmatic account of the categories through which individuals construct the meaning of their experience of specific segments of social life.

A third tradition of qualitative research into individual experience has adopted a more epistemologically purist approach, informed by phenomenological philosophy. Qualitative methodologies such as grounded theory, IPA, and CQR seek to use the description of the meaning of experience as the basis for deriving some kind of interpretive structure or framework for understanding that experience. By contrast, the aim of phenomenological research is to elucidate the meaning of an experience through comprehensive description alone. This is a remarkably hard thing to accomplish, because it requires being able to encourage research informants to generate detailed accounts of their experiences, and a capacity on the part of the researcher to bracket-off his or her assumptions about what the informant is saying, to remain open to subtle or implicit meanings that are present. Several groups of phenomenological researchers have developed protocols for undertaking phenomenological analysis (Giorgi & Giorgi, 2003; Halling, Leifer, & Rowe, 2006; Wertz, 2005). Some versions of this style of qualitative inquiry use the phrase *phenomenological-hermeneutic* to describe their approach (Dahlberg, Drew, & Nystrom, 2001).

In recent years, a further group of qualitative researchers has sought to develop methodologies for using systematic analysis of the subjective, personal experience of the researcher as a basis for exploration of the meaning of aspects of social life. This genre of research has taken the form of *heuristic inquiry*, a phenomenologically inspired approach constructed by Moustakas (1990), and *autoethnography*, an integration of practices from autobiographical writing and ethnography (Chang, 2008). The rationale for these methodologies should be clear to anyone with firsthand experience of psychotherapy: The full meaning of an area of experience can never be adequately captured in a single interview with a stranger, but only emerges through weeks or months of disciplined self-attention. In practice, however, successful completion (to the point of publication) of heuristic or autoethnographic inquiry calls for a high level of emotional maturity and writing skill. As a result, at the present time few studies of this kind have been published within the field of counseling and psychotherapy.

The area of personal experience of therapy comprises a particularly fertile territory for qualitative researchers. There are a wide range of questions that can be asked and topics that can be explored, and virtually any competently managed study will produce findings that are interesting and surprising. Most of the studies in this area have used structured step-by-step inquiry protocols, such as IPA and CQR, because these frameworks force the researcher to engage closely with the material, and are associated with tried and trusted formats for the reporting of findings. These protocols are also valuable sources of guidance for students undertaking their first qualitative study, who remain the main source of published work in this area.

Qualitative Research Into Therapy Micro-Processes

Research into client or therapist experience of therapy can be regarded as similar to taking or making a picture of what the participant can see with their naked eye. Research into the context of therapy is like using a telescope or satellite camera to represent an image of a wider vista. Continuing this visual metaphor, studies of therapy micro-processes are concerned with the patterns that become visible through the use of devices such as microscopes. Micro-process research focuses on phenomena that are unseen and/or unseeable because they happen too quickly and are out of awareness.

There are two qualitative research designs that have been extensively used in the investigation of therapy micro-processes: interpersonal process recall (IPR) and conversation analysis (CA). IPR is derived from a training method developed by Kagan (1984) in which therapy trainees made audio or video recordings of their work with clients, then played back the recording, regularly pausing the tape at points of particular interest and talking about what they recalled of their experience at that moment in the original therapy session. Kagan (1984) hypothesized that if the recall interview took place soon after the therapy session (usually within 24 hours), the act of watching or hearing the recording would restimulate the person's memory of what they had been experiencing at that time. This technique was soon adopted by therapy researchers, who realized its potential to capture information about client and therapist experiences of hitherto transient aspects of the process of therapy. An example of therapy process research carried out with this approach can be found in studies by Angus and Rennie (1988, 1989) on the significance for the client of periods in therapy when metaphors arise during their conversations with their therapist. In these studies, audio recordings were made of therapy sessions. The researchers then identified episodes during the session when metaphoric language was being used. These segments of the recording were played back to the client, who was invited to report on what they had been experiencing during these parts of the therapy session.

The other qualitative methodology that has been used to explore therapy micro-processes is conversation analysis (CA; Madill, Widdicombe, & Barkham, 2001; Perakyla, Antaki, Vehvilainen, & Leudar, 2008). This approach originated in ethnomethodology, a branch of micro-sociology that examines the accomplishment of joint action (such as turn-taking, formulation of a problem, or arriving at an agreement) within conversation. Conversation analysis provides one of the earliest examples of rigorous qualitative research in psychotherapy, in the form of the analysis of a single session of therapy (Labov & Fanshel, 1977). Most CA studies are based on the analysis of a transcript of an example of "naturally occurring" talk (such as a therapy session), which has been prepared to a high level of precision using notation rules to indicate the length of pauses, intonation patterns, overlapping speech, and other aspects of conversational performance. The aim of the analysis is to identify the ways in which language is used in order to accomplish the institutional objectives of actors within a particular social context.

An example of how this methodology can be applied in the study of psychotherapy can be found in a study by Davis (1986), which examined the way in which a therapist used various conversational strategies to reformulate a problem presented by a client in her first session of therapy. Further examples can be found in an extensive body of work by Peräkylä and colleagues, involving analysis of conversational strategies used by therapists in facilitating decision making in

clients contemplating HIV testing (Peräkylä, 1995; Peräkylä & Silverman, 1991), making interpretations (Peräkylä, 2004), and encouraging client movement into immediacy (Kondratyuk & Peräkylä, 2011). Strong and Pyle (2009) have applied conversation analysis in the exploration of how therapists use particular forms of language to engage clients in solution-focused interventions. Some qualitative researchers have used CA analytic strategies with the somewhat broader interpretive framework afforded by discourse analysis (DA; Avdi & Georgaca, 2007; Madill, 2006). A key feature of discourse analytic research has been its use of the concept of "subject positioning" (Harre & Van Langenhove, 1999) to enable micro-analysis of subtle ways in which therapists offer their clients alternative ways of talking about their problems. This perspective has been applied within psychotherapy research to examine the discursive construction of moments of change in individual therapy (Madill & Barkham, 1997; Madill & Docherty, 1994), and attribution of responsibility in couples therapy (Kurri & Wahlström 2005, 2007), family therapy (Suoninen & Wahlström, 2009) and group therapy for perpetrators of domestic violence (Holma, Partanen, Wahlström, Laitila, & Seikkula, 2006; Partanen, Wahlström, & Holma, 2006).

A further variant of a broadly conversational analytic approach to psychotherapy research can be found in methodologies that have focused on the significance of client narratives within the overall flow of therapy talk. Boothe and von Wyl (2004), McLeod and Balamoutsou (2000, 2001) and Rober, Van Eesbeek, and Elliott (2006) have developed structured qualitative methods for exploring the role of specific storytelling events in the co-construction of meaning in therapy.

The genre of qualitative research represented by the conversation analysis, discourse analysis, and narrative analysis tradition is characterized by intensive analysis of single instances of therapy talk, selected as typical or theoretically significant. There has been some debate around the relevance of CA/DA research to counseling and psychotherapy practice, on the grounds that these approaches appear to deny the possibility of human agency and choice (Madill & Docherty, 1994) and are therefore grounded in a concept of the person that is hard to reconcile with most theories of therapy. Strong, Zeman, and Foskett (2006) have attempted to overcome this difficulty by combining techniques from IPR and CA, in inviting clients and therapists to comment on their experience of conversational patterns that have been identified through microanalysis of their discourse in a therapy session. Viklund, Holmqvist, and Nelson (2010) addressed this issue by asking clients to identify helpful events in therapy, and then conducting a conversation analysis of the interaction patterns that occurred within these episodes.

Sources of Qualitative Data

One of the potential strengths of qualitative research designs is that they make available a wide range of sources of data. The interview remains the most widely used method of data collection in qualitative research in counseling and psychotherapy (Knox & Burkard, 2009). However, many different forms of interview are possible. The structure of the interview schedule can vary, from highly structured to open-ended. Interviews can be carried out with individual informants, couples, families and groups. A range of strategies can be used to supplement the use of questions within an interview—for example, informants can be invited to listen to a recording of a therapy session in which they have participated, or to depict their experience as an image or drawing and then reflect on what they produced, or to comment on case vignettes.

The interpersonal style of the interviewer can be relatively formal, or more personal and self-disclosing. Interview questions may be provided to informants ahead of the interview, or used in a way that seeks to elicit an immediate spontaneous response. In many studies, only one interview is carried out with each participant, while in other studies a series of interviews are conducted. The interview method therefore represents a highly flexible tool for qualitative researchers. In addition to interviews, there are many other sources of qualitative data that have been used by therapy researchers: diaries, open-ended questionnaires, written reports, personal and official documents, transcripts of therapy sessions, observation, projective techniques, and photographs.

The diversity of data collection techniques that can be used within qualitative designs represents a valuable asset but also a significant challenge for researchers. The advantage lies in the capacity of qualitative research to gain access to vivid and intrinsically interesting examples of what can happen within a therapy session.

The existence of a range of data collection tools has allowed hidden or subtle aspects of therapy process to be uncovered, and silenced aspects of self to be heard. At the same time, a disadvantage of this diversity lies in the fact that there has been relatively little research into the attributes of qualitative research tools, and the types of information that are likely to be highlighted or occluded by the use of different methods. For example, in a study of client experiences of therapy, will different themes emerge if information is collected through weekly open-ended diaries, or by means of a single follow-up interview? At the present time, it is hard to answer this kind of question with any confidence, because of the absence of research into method factors in qualitative inquiry. This situation can be contrasted with the extensive literature that has accumulated around issues of reliability, validity and sensitivity to change in quantitative outcome and process measures.

A further methodological challenge for the qualitative research community arises in relation to the uncritical use of self-report methods, such as interviews and open-ended questionnaires. Although there is no doubt that valuable insights can flow from "just asking people," it is also the case that what a person reports in an interview, or writes in an open-ended questionnaire, needs to be understood as an act of communication within a particular context. Older traditions of qualitative research, such as ethnography (Fetterman, 2009) or introspection (Danziger, 1990), were characterized by high levels of sensitivity to these factors. Ethnographic researchers, for instance, are careful to balance interview material with observational data, and to interpret the former in the light of the quality of the relationship between informant and interlocutor. In the early years of laboratory-based psychology, research subjects were trained in systematic techniques of introspection, so that they could differentiate between their actual experience, and their assumptions around what the experimenter might expect them to experience.

Mixed Method Designs

In the main, qualitative and quantitative methodologies have tended to have been used in isolation from each other. The nature of research training has made an important contribution to this kind of methodological apartheid. For the most part, new researchers have concentrated on developing skills in one or the other of these paradigms, and as a result have lacked confidence in designing mixed method studies. However, in recent years, there has been a lot of interest in mixed methods designs within the broader social science research community, leading to the identification of methodological principles and guidelines (Hanson, Creswell, Plano-Clark, Petska, & Creswell, 2005). Until now, mixed methods research has been featured to only a limited extent within the counseling and psychotherapy literature.

A range of strategies has been developed for combining qualitative and quantitative methods in a single study, or within a broader program of research. One approach has been to treat both qualitative and quantitative data as material that is open to interpretation. The operation of this strategy, which is informed by hermeneutic principles (Maracek, 2011), can be seen in the work of Robert Elliott over many years, through the development of comprehensive process analysis (CPA; Elliott, 1984) and hermeneutic single case outcome studies (Elliott et al., 2009), and in the program of case-based research into the assimilation model of therapeutic change (Osatuke & Stiles, 2011).

An alternative mixed methods strategy involves building an understanding of a phenomenon through qualitative inquiry, then using quantitative methods to determine the prevalence of that phenomenon, or to investigate its co-occurrence with other factors. Examples of this approach include research into therapist presence (Geller & Greenberg, 2002; Geller, Greenberg, & Watson, 2010), self-esteem (Mruk, 2010), the process of coming to terms with loss (Lichtenthal, Currier, Neimeyer, & Keesee, 2010), and inter-action sequences in therapist-client discourse (Westerman, 2011). A further strategy consists of using quantitative research as a starting point, and then conducting a qualitative study to resolve ambiguities that have been identified in the quantitative analysis. An example of this kind of research is a study by Råbu, Halvorsen, Seeger, and Haavind (2011), which used qualitative methods to examine the process of a successful therapy in a case in which the therapist and client reported a poor alliance—a finding at odds with the results of quantitative studies of the working alliance. Another type of mixed methods design that seeks to use qualitative methods to "fill the gaps" in quantitative research can be found in Miller and Crabtree (2005), who have argued for the adoption of a "double helix" randomized trial

design, in which a qualitative strand of inquiry is wrapped around a standard randomized clinical trial, thereby enabling the meaning of quantitative results to be understood in the light of the experiences of clients and clinicians who were involved in the study. Although it is too early for this type of research to have been widely applied, its potential value is illustrated in the Allen, Bromley, Kuyken, and Sonnenberg (2009) study of client experiences of mindfulness-based cognitive therapy, which was embedded within a wider randomized trial of that form of therapy (Kuyken et al., 2008).

There have in fact been many qualitative studies of client experiences of cognitive, cognitive-behavioral and mindfulness-oriented therapies in recent years (Berg, Raminani, Greer, Harwood, & Safren, 2008; Borrill & Foreman, 1996; Clarke, Rees, & Hardy, 2004; Cunningham, Wolbert, & Lillie, 2004; Glasman, Finlay, & Bock, 2004; Mason & Hargreaves, 2001; McGowan, Lavender, & Garety, 2005; Messari & Hallam, 2003; Morone, Lynch, Greco, Tindle, & Weiner, 2008; Nilsson, Svensson, Sandell, & Clinton, 2007; Perseius, Öjehagen, Ekdahl, Åsberg, & Samuelsson, 2003; Smith, Graham, & Senthinathan, 2007; York, 2007). Although this body of research has not been explicitly interpreted within the cognitive-behavioral literature in the light of the double-helix model proposed by Miller and Crabtree (2005), there seems little doubt it shares similar goals and intentions. It can be argued that the methodologically pluralist research strategy adopted within the CBT professional community has made a major contribution to the construction of a comprehensive evidence base in support of that particular therapy orientation.

A final approach to combining qualitative and quantitative methods within a single study is to use a qualitative approach to collect rich descriptions of experience, then make use of a coding system that transforms that material into quantitative data. An example of how this approach has been used to good effect in psychotherapy research can be found in work on the process of narrative change in therapy (Adler, 2012; Adler & McAdams, 2007; Adler, Skalina, & McAdams, 2008; Angus, Levitt, & Hardtke, 1999).

The strength of mixed method designs are that they combine the capacity of quantitative measures to integrate data across large samples, and make comparisons across groups, with the ability of qualitative methodologies to capture the lived experience and complexity of the phenomena being investigated.

CRITICAL ISSUES IN QUALITATIVE RESEARCH

At the present time, there exists a number of critical methodological issues within the area of qualitative research design. Some of these issues reflect debates within the wider domain of qualitative inquiry in the social sciences as a whole, while other concerns are more specific to the application of qualitative methods within the field of psychotherapy research. It is possible to identify two broad categories of critical issues: challenges and dilemmas arising from the conduct of qualitative research, and barriers to the further development and practical utilization of qualitative methods.

Challenges and Dilemmas Arising From the Conduct of Qualitative Research

As discussed earlier, there are some well-established research designs that have been widely deployed within the field of qualitative research in psychotherapy, such as grounded theory, conversation analysis, interpretive phenomenological analysis, and consensual qualitative research. However, even within these tried and trusted methodologies, there are key critical choice points at which qualitative researchers need to make decisions that call on knowledge and understanding of underlying methodological, ethical, and epistemological issues. The most important of these decision-points centers on the adoption of validity procedures. Quantitative research designs are supported by criteria for reliability and validity of measures, statistical power estimates that inform sample size calculations, randomization strategies, and many other ways of determining the validity of a study. By contrast, the validity criteria that are appropriate to the conduct of qualitative research are less well-defined. Important contributions to the literature on the validity of qualitative research in psychotherapy have been made by Elliott, Fischer, and Rennie (1999), Morrow (2005), Stiles (1993), Williams and Hill (2012), and Williams and Morrow (2009), among others. There is now a general acceptance on the part of thesis supervisors and journal reviewers that some kind of external auditing or dialogue between co-researchers is

desirable within qualitative data analysis and that processes of data selection, condensation, and interpretation should be transparent to readers of qualitative reports. There is less agreement within the field around the value or feasibility of inviting research participants or informants about their views of the credibility and accuracy of findings.

In general the recent literature around the validity, plausibility, or trustworthiness of qualitative therapy research has tended to emphasize the principle that research findings are most credible when they emerge from a process of dialogue between participants in the research process. The field has tended to move away from the idea, expressed by Rennie (1994d) and other early adopters of grounded theory methodology, that adequacy of data analysis depends on immersion in the data by a single analyst. While acknowledging the necessity for immersion in the data, the current view is that sensitivity to implicit meaning within a qualitative text, is best facilitated by opening up the analysis to a plurality of perspectives. Influential examples of how teams of researchers can work together in the analysis of rich qualitative data can be found in Elliott et al. (2009), Halling, Leifer, and Rowe (2006), Hill (2012), Morrow (2007), and Schielke, Fishman, Osatuke, and Stiles (2009).

A particularly contentious area of debate within the qualitative research community centers on the role and significance of researcher reflexivity (Etherington, 2004; Finlay & Gough, 2003). It is clear that the personal involvement of the researcher has the potential to shape the type of data that are collected, as well as the subsequent analysis of these data. Typically, a participant in a qualitative research study will engage in a fairly intense exploration of personal experience, in the presence of an interviewer who has a powerful interest in the topic that is being discussed. This is a situation in which there may be subtle pressures on an informant to emphasize certain aspects of his or her story, in reaction to the responsiveness of the interviewer. Similarly, interview transcripts tend to incorporate ambiguous information that may be read by the researcher in ways that are consistent with his or her preexisting biases. It seems clear, in the light of these issues, that it is important for qualitative researchers to reflect on possible ways in which they might exert an influence on data collection and analysis.

What is less clear, at the present time, is how researcher reflexivity should be organized and reported. Researchers within the traditions of discourse analysis and conversation analysis argue that the data with which they work (segments of text) and the analysis that they carry out, are open to the scrutiny of readers, who are therefore in a position to make up their own minds around any possible researcher bias (see, for example, Parker, 1994, 2004). Within these traditions, it is also sometimes argued that reflexive statements on the part of the researcher are themselves example of text, requiring the same sort of deconstructive analysis that is applied to other sources of evidence. Researchers who use methods such as grounded theory, CQR, and IPA to explore the experience of therapy, usually include a brief paragraph within the method section of their papers, describing the professional identity and background of the members of the research team, their expectations for what they would find, and the mechanisms for addressing power imbalances within the team. By contrast, studies that make use of heuristic research and autoethnographic techniques typically report in detail on all aspects of the researcher's experience of conducting the study (see, for example, Meekums, 2008). Behind these differences in style of reporting lie further divergences in the attention that is paid during the research process to the systematic collection of information around the reflexive self-awareness of the researcher, such as the use of a research diary.

Some critics of qualitative research regard the issue of researcher reflexivity as a sign of an ineradicable degree of subjectivity within this form of inquiry, which makes its findings worthless in scientific terms. It is perhaps worth pointing out, in this context, that the problem of experimenter bias has been widely studied within experimental psychology (Rosnow & Rosenthal, 1997), and researcher allegiance effects have been demonstrated within randomized trials of the outcomes of psychotherapy (Berman & Reich, 2010; Luborsky, Diguer, & Seligman, 1999). It can be argued that well-conducted qualitative studies are well placed to address issues of researcher bias, because they force the researcher to engage with the experiences of research participants at a level of intensity that is likely to challenge his or her preexisting assumptions (Flyvbjerg, 2006).

A further critical issue that is associated with qualitative research concerns the challenge of how to convey the findings of such studies in an effective manner (McLeod, 2011; Ponterotto & Grieger, 2007). In quantitative research, large amounts of data can be summarized in a single numerical table. In qualitative research, by contrast, the researcher needs to find ways to condense the words of several informants into a limited set of quotations or exemplars, and to find appropriate phrases that will capture the meaning of themes or categories. There is an expectation in qualitative work that research reports will reflect the "lived experience" of participants. Not all researchers are equally skillful in writing.

In addition, the style formats adopted by APA (and other) journals have been largely developed to facilitate the reporting of quantitative studies, and are experienced by some qualitative researchers as restricting their capacity to do justice to their findings. It would seem useful for the qualitative therapy research community to consider the advantages and disadvantages of alternative communication formats. For example, O'Neill (1998) used a monograph-length report as a means of presenting detailed client accounts of their experiences of negotiating consent over the type of therapeutic intervention they were to receive. By contrast, some medical journals, such as the *British Journal of General Practice*, have created effective formats for 2,000-word qualitative articles that are intended to be highly accessible for practitioners. Elliott et al. (2009) have demonstrated how online supplementary documents can be used to allow readers to gain access to interview transcripts. Speedy (2008) has argued that some qualitative findings demand representation through various types of performance, as well as in written form.

There are distinctive ethical challenges that can arise in qualitative research (Brinkmann & Kvale, 2005; Guillemin & Gillam, 2004; Van den Hoonard, 2002). The experience of being interviewed may re-evoke personal issues for clients, and the inclusion of lengthy quotations in qualitative research reports may threaten the degree to which informant confidentiality can be maintained. The use of unstructured or semistructured interviews means that it can be hard for a researcher to predict what an informant will discuss, which raises difficulties for ethics committees and institutional review boards in terms of evaluating the type of risk management strategies that may be necessary. There are also ethical issues that center on the well-being of the researcher. For example, it can be emotionally demanding for qualitative researchers to listen to stories of abuse recounted by informants, and then to spend hours transcribing and analyzing these accounts.

The critical issues highlighted in this section reflect a need for ongoing conceptual and empirical investigations into the methodology of qualitative research. Some qualitative research communities have contributed to this task through critical review of methodologies such as IPA (Brocki & Wearden, 2006), CQR (Hill, 2012), IPR (Larsen, Flesaker, & Stege, 2008), heuristic inquiry (Sela-Smith, 2002), and solicited diaries (Mackrill, 2008b). In addition, Madill, Jordan, and Shirley (2000) have examined the validity implications of comparison of qualitative analysis carried out by different researchers on the same data. There have been projects that have explored the use of different qualitative methodologies in relation to analysis of a single set of data (Frost et al., 2011; Frost & Nolas, 2011). The latter initiative is part of a broader movement within qualitative research to question the application of predetermined research procedures and methodologies (such as grounded theory or CQR) and replace it with an image of the qualitative researcher as a "bricoleur" who "employ(s) methodological processes as they are needed in the unfolding context of the research situation" (Kincheloe, McLaren, & Steinberg, 2011, p. 168). These methodological initiatives, which intriguingly mirror some of the debates within the field of psychotherapy itself, around the relative merits of treatment manuals versus integrative or pluralistic ways of working with clients, have made valuable contributions to enhancing the rigor of qualitative studies. However, there remain a number of areas in which additional meta-methodological work on these issues would be useful.

Barriers to the Further Development and Practical Utilization of Qualitative Methods

The relevance of qualitative research for counseling and psychotherapy practice is contingent on two factors. First, there needs to be a sufficient number of high-quality published studies on key topics to allow an accumulation of qualitative evidence. Second, there need to be rational and transparent procedures for reviewing the cumulative findings of these studies, in a manner that will enable credible implications for policy and practice to be derived.

TRAINING IN QUALITATIVE METHODS

Although the proportion of qualitative studies being published in counseling and psychotherapy journals has increased over the past decade, it is still the case that fewer than 20% of therapy research studies make use of these approaches (McLeod, 2011; Munley et al., 2002; Rennie, Watson, & Monteiro, 2002). The impact of the qualitative papers that are published is further constrained by the fragmented nature of this literature—there have been no coordinated, large-scale programs of research that have used qualitative methods. Informal scrutiny of bibliographic databases, as well as personal experience, suggests that many more qualitative studies are completed as dissertation work, than are ever published. This phenomenon possibly reflects the challenges involved in reducing dissertation-length qualitative studies to comply with the word count requirements of research journals. It may also reflect differential career trajectories, in which students who undertake qualitative research for their dissertation tend to become clinicians, while those who conduct quantitative studies are relatively more likely to end up in academic positions. Behind these publication patterns are a series of critical issues around the nature of research training.

Relatively few counseling and psychotherapy training programs include sufficient training in qualitative methodologies to enable students to develop the competence and confidence required to produce publishable qualitative work. Effective training in qualitative research is time-consuming, incorporating experiential learning within an expert-apprentice relationship, the development of practical skills around interviewing and data analysis, and the acquisition of an understanding of critical conceptual and methodological issues (Eisenhart & Jarrow, 2011; Hansen & Rapley, 2008; Josselson, Lieblich, & McAdams, 2003). If the field of counseling and psychotherapy research is to embrace methodological pluralism in a manner that creates a more equitable balance among quantitative, qualitative, and mixed methods approaches, it may be necessary to initiate a process of review of the extent to which current models of research training produce graduates who are comfortable reading and conducting studies across the quantitative-qualitative continuum. Of course such a recommendation has implications for the expertise of faculty mentors and the need to include individuals with such expertise among the faculty.

Qualitative Metasynthesis

The question of how best to bring together the findings of qualitative studies continues to stimulate debate within the social sciences (Dixon-Woods, Booth, & Sutton, 2007; Paterson et al., 2009). Within the field of quantitative research, highly sophisticated methods of meta-analysis have been evolved that enable findings from multiple studies to be combined (Borenstein, Hedges, Higgins, & Rothstein, 2009; Higgins & Green, 2008). Essentially, the logic of quantitative meta-analysis relies on an ability to differentiate between good- and poor-quality studies, and to aggregate treatment outcomes in terms of effect sizes. In addition, the establishment of agreed criteria for inclusion in systematic reviews has meant that quantitative researchers conduct and write up their studies in ways that are conducive to subsequent meta-analyses. At the present time, none of these factors can be readily mapped onto the task of carrying out a systematic review of qualitative studies of psychotherapy process or outcome. It may therefore be misleading to use the term *meta-analysis* in relation to reviews of the findings of qualitative studies. As a result, some qualitative research groups use the term *metasynthesis* to describe the process of conducting a systematic review of the cumulative findings of a set of qualitative studies. Narrative reviews of qualitative research have been carried out in relation to negative experiences in therapy (Hill, 2010), and grounded theory research into the client's experience of therapy (Rennie, 2000a). These reviews offered summaries of key studies, discussion of areas of agreement and disagreement between studies, and implications for practice. Timulak (2009) developed a systematic approach to metasynthesis of qualitative psychotherapy research that compared themes or categories reported in the results sections of published studies, leading to identification of shared categories and deviant categories. The fruits of this method can be found in two metasyntheses of qualitative research into client and therapist experiences of significant events in psychotherapy (Timulak, 2007, 2010), and one review of qualitative outcomes in person-centered and experiential psychotherapy (Timulak & Creaner, 2010). A further example of this type of qualitative metasynthesis has been carried out by Khan,

Bower, and Rogers (2007) in a review of qualitative studies of patient experiences of guided self-help in primary care mental health, and by Hill, Knox, and Hess (2012), in the context of an appraisal of participants reasons for taking part in CQR studies. The Khan et al. (2007) review is notable in the level of detailed implications for practice that were generated.

Timulak (2009) and Hill et al. (2012) have called for the psychotherapy community to carry out further qualitative metasynthesis projects, to enable further refinement and extension of qualitative meta-analytic methodology. There is an inevitable tension within qualitative metasynthesis, between seeking to identify recurring categories, and the wish to retain the rich narrative data that give meaning to these categories. A strategy that might enable metasynthesis to incorporate more descriptive data might be to map the multiple meanings of a single theme or category, across a number of studies. For example, Timulak (2010) reported that clients in several studies described insight events as being highly meaningful. It would be useful to go back to the accounts of such events, in the original publications, to develop a more nuanced appreciation of the process and impact on insight, than would be possible in a review that aimed to consider all categories of significant events. Another approach to qualitative meta-analysis that may be valuable would be to strengthen the link between research and practice by analyzing qualitative findings not in terms of categories but in terms of therapeutic principles (Levitt, Neimeyer, & Williams, 2005; Williams & Levitt, 2007a, 2007b).

A further challenge in this area consists of finding ways to carry out systematic reviews that incorporate findings from both qualitative and quantitative studies (Dixon-Woods et al. 2006). A review of research into the impact on clinicians of participating in their own personal therapy, by Orlinsky, Norcross, Rønnestad, and Wiseman (2005) provides an example of how qualitative findings are merely used to support the conclusions of a review of quantitative evidence, rather than as findings that may have something more to offer. At least these reviewers acknowledged the existence of qualitative studies; most systematic reviews of psychotherapy research tend to disregard this source of evidence. An important task, for reviewers seeking to integrate evidence from quantitative, qualitative, and mixed methods studies, will be to find ways to give equal weighting to findings derived from different types of study.

Contributions to Theory and Practice

Qualitative research has made a made a contribution to many aspects of contemporary theory and practice in counseling and psychotherapy. This section explores the nature of that contribution in relation to four areas: therapy outcome, the process of therapy, the client-therapist relationship, and therapist development.

Qualitative Research Into the Outcomes of Therapy

Historically, research into the outcomes of therapy represents the domain of therapy research that has had the most impact on practice. The adoption by governments and health care provider organizations of service-delivery policies based on principles of evidence-based or empirically validated treatment, has created a direct link between the findings of outcome research, and the types of therapy that are offered to clients. Almost all of the evidence base for the effectiveness of psychotherapy is derived from research in which symptoms are measured before therapy and on completion of treatment. Few qualitative outcome studies have been carried out. However, the findings of qualitative studies offer a significant challenge to assumptions about outcome that derive from mainstream quantitative research on this topic, in relation to two key questions: how outcome is conceptualized, and the overall effectiveness of therapy.

In principle, there are a number of qualitative methods that might be employed to explore client experiences of outcome, such as diaries, analysis of therapy transcripts, and ethnographic observation. In practice, almost all qualitative outcome studies have relied on interviews in which clients have been invited to describe, in their own terms, the effect that therapy has had on their lives. Some studies have used only posttherapy interviews, while other studies have interviewed clients at the start of therapy and at follow-up. McKenna and Todd (1997) interviewed clients who had received several episodes of therapy over the course of their lives, and found that the outcome of each episode was evaluated in relation to its position within a wider therapy trajectory. Participants reported that they mainly evaluated the success of their first encounter with therapy not in terms of symptom reduction or the amelioration of distress, but

in terms of the extent to which they gained a sense of whether that kind of treatment might in principle be useful in resolving their problems at some point in the future. By contrast, subsequent involvement in therapy was evaluated in relation to the degree to which problems were resolved. Finally, further therapy episodes were evaluated on the basis of whether the client was able to use treatment to maintain earlier gains. This study suggests that, from the point of view of the client, the effectiveness of therapy may be evaluated in quite different ways at different stages in a treatment career. If replicated by other studies, the results obtained by McKenna and Todd (1997) could have important implications for the way in which therapy effectiveness is understood. Up to now, the therapy outcome literature is organized around research of the impact of a single therapy episode, whose effectiveness is defined in terms of symptom and behavioral change. From the client's perspective, by contrast, it seems likely that "good" therapy may sometimes involve measurable symptom or behavioral change, but in other instances may involve learning about the possible value of therapy, or engaging in relapse prevention that maintains previous gains. In addition, the usefulness of therapy may depend to some extent on the promise or availability of on-going care across the life course (Cummings, 2007).

More detailed elaboration of the categories that clients use to assess the effectiveness of therapy can be found in the findings of qualitative outcome studies by Kuhnlein (1999) and Valkonen, Hanninen, and Lindfors (2011). What these studies have shown is that clients enter therapy with preexisting ideas about the reasons for their distress, and the type of treatment experience that is necessary to help them. These studies have yielded complex results, which at the present time are not easily assimilated into a single model. However, a common theme across this set of studies is the finding that there are at least three broad types of client understanding. One group of clients views current difficulties as arising from early childhood difficulties, and evaluates therapy in terms of the extent to which it enables them to come to terms with these early events. A second group of clients view themselves as generally enjoying positive psychological and emotional functioning, other than a temporary inability to cope with certain stressful events. These clients evaluate therapy in terms of the degree to which they have acquired coping skills.

A third group of clients understand their distress as arising from a lack of meaning in their lives, and evaluate outcome in relation to what they have learned around cultivating sources of meaning. In these studies, several examples are offered of clients who received what they regarded as the "wrong" type of treatment. These clients described their therapists as caring and competent, but not able to provide them with what they needed. Broadly similar findings have been reported by further qualitative studies of client "ideas of cure," carried out by Lilliengren and Werbart (2005), Philips, Wennberg, and Werbart (2007) and Philips, Werbart, Wennberg, and Schubert (2007). An important implication of this line of research is that estimates of treatment effectiveness should take clients' criteria for success into account.

When clients in qualitative studies have been invited to describe the changes that they have experienced as a result of therapy, they frequently report various forms of enhanced personal agency, such as a capacity to apply insights or skills that they learned from their therapist (Burnett, 1999; Carey et al., 2007; Clarke et al., 2004; Glasman, Finlay, & Brock, 2004; Perren, Godfrey, & Rowland, 2009). Other qualitative studies have found that clients' account for the success of their therapy in terms of their acquisition of a benign or wise internal representation of their therapist (Knox, Goldberg, Woodhouse, & Hill, 1999; Mosher & Stiles, 2009; Myers & White, 2010). These clients report that, in moments of stress, they are able to recall the words of their therapists, or even to engage in internal dialogue with an imagined therapist. Phillips and Daniluk (2004) found that survivors of child sexual abuse reported that changes in their fundamental sense of identity were more salient, as therapy outcomes, than amelioration of symptoms.

One study, by Nilsson et al. (2007), compared accounts of outcome offered by clients in two different forms of therapy—psychodynamic and cognitive-behavioral. The satisfied recipients of psychodynamic therapy described what they had learned in terms of an enhanced capacity to manage relationships. The satisfied cognitive-behavioral clients described what they had learned in terms of an enhanced capacity to manage anxiety. Within the context of the field of psychotherapy outcome research as a whole, the Nilsson et al. (2007) study is of particular significance because it suggests a possible resolution to the "equivalence" paradox—the consistent finding that very different forms of therapy report similar levels of outcome. The groups of psychodynamic of CBT clients studied by Nilsson et al. (2007) were equally satisfied with their therapy, but gained in different ways.

There have been few qualitative studies that have examined client perceptions of the extent to which they have gained from therapy. In many of these studies, information about how the client evaluates the outcome of their therapy is embedded within a wider exploration of their experience of therapy as a whole. As a result, the experience of outcome is discussed in a limited way, with a lack of detail. There is a need for further qualitative research that focuses directly on outcome. Nevertheless, despite these limitations, it is possible to identify some emerging themes. All the studies carried out in this area have found that clients are able to provide a considered, nuanced appraisal of the helpfulness of the therapy they have received. In general, when clients are given time and space to talk at length about the outcomes of their therapy, they tend to offer a somewhat more critical account, when contrasted with the findings of quantitative outcome studies (Dale, Allen, & Measor, 1998; Howe, 1996; Morris, 2005) that merely report changes in level of functioning.

In most of these studies, a phenomenon that emerges is that of clients who are mainly positive about the benefits of therapy, yet express a theme of disappointment: They are aware of what they wished to gain from therapy, and did not receive. Other clients may be generally satisfied and comment that that the problem that motivated them to enter therapy remains a factor in their lives: They have learned to live with the problem, and manage it, rather than having been able to arrive at a complete resolution of their difficulties (Osborn & Smith, 2008). These qualitative outcome studies are based on relatively small samples of clients, which raises questions about the extent to which the findings that are reported are typical of all clients. Morris (2005) observed that participants in her qualitative study of the outcomes of psychodynamic psychotherapy who were less positive about their therapy experience required a considerable amount of encouragement and support to get to a point of being able to engage in the study. The implication here is that there may be a tendency for qualitative outcome studies to be more likely to recruit those clients who were satisfied with treatment, unless vigorous efforts are made (as in Morris, 2005) to reach out to the less-satisfied group. In the light of these issues, it is all the more striking that, compared to the high effect sizes reported in most quantitative outcome studies, the picture that emerges from qualitative outcome research is characterized by a significant degree of client disappointment and ambivalence with respect to the benefits that they have gained from therapy.

Mixed methods outcome studies, in which both qualitative and quantitative outcome data have been collected, make it possible to directly compare the outcome information from each source. Svanborg, Bäärnhielm, and Wistedt (2008) reported a high degree of overlap between qualitative and quantitative estimates of outcome. By contrast, Elliott et al. (2009) and Klein and Elliott (2006) reported a lack of correspondence between estimates of success from qualitative and quantitative data sources. At the present time, too few studies of this type have been carried out to allow firm conclusions to be reached regarding the factors that might contribute to convergence or divergence between qualitative and quantitative analyses of therapeutic success. Given the powerful investment in quantitative methods within the psychotherapy research community, it may be tempting to argue that the qualitative findings must be wrong. However, there does exist a coherent, if somewhat neglected, body of work that has identified important conceptual limitations in current strategies for quantitative assessment of therapy outcomes (Kazdin, 2006; McLeod, 2001; Meier, 2008; Michell, 1999, 2011). Mixed methods outcome research represents an important area for further research, because it has the potential of generating ways of evaluating outcome that is sensitive to the interests and perspectives of different stakeholders, particularly clients.

Taken together, the findings of qualitative studies into the outcomes of counseling and psychotherapy raise a number of important questions for further investigation. It is clear that more qualitative outcome studies need to be carried out, both to establish the generalizability of current findings, and to develop better solutions to methodological issues around recruitment participation, data collection strategies, and data reporting. However, what seems clear even at this stage is that mainstream symptom-oriented outcome measures may be missing dimensions of outcome that are also important to clients (Binder, Holgersen, & Nielsen, 2010). In addition, qualitative outcome research appears to yield an understanding of outcome that is somewhat less optimistic than the version that is conveyed through quantitative studies. When clients are provided with opportunities to evaluate outcome in their own terms, many of them describe their therapy as having been a valuable experience, but one that was only partially successful is resolving the problems in living for which they originally sought help.

The Process of Therapy

Qualitative methodologies have proved to be particularly suitable for the task of exploring the process of therapy. The range of qualitative process studies that has been carried out is too extensive to provide comprehensive coverage within this section. Instead, three specific areas of process research are discussed: the client's experience of the moment-by-moment process of therapy; assimilation of problematic experiences over the course of therapy; and the characteristics of significant events within therapy. These topics represent areas in which qualitative research has made a distinctive contribution to theory and practice.

There have been a number of studies that have interviewed clients about their experience of being involved in the moment-by-moment work of therapy. In some of these studies, clients have been invited to reflect on their experience in a recent session, while other studies have employed a stimulated recall technique in which a recording of a session is played back to the participant, who is asked to pause the tape at any point where they were able to recall what they had been experiencing at that moment in the session. The findings reported in a stimulated recall by Fessler (1983) illustrate the way that this approach yields insight into the co-constructed nature of the therapy process:

> Therapist and...patient do not take turns speaking and listening. Rather they participate in a speech that is taking place between and through them—a speech that is both spoken and listened to simultaneously. (Fessler, 1983, p. 44)

A series of studies by Rennie and his colleagues (Rennie, 1994a, 1994b, 1994c, 2000a; Watson & Rennie, 1994) exemplifies the theoretical and practical implications of qualitative research into clients' experiences of therapy process. Using a grounded theory method of analysis, these studies generated a conceptual model of client involvement in therapy that highlighted the interplay between client agency and reflexivity in a relational context. In other words, during therapy the client is actively pursuing his or her track or implicit sense of where the conversation needs to go. At the same time, the client is engaged in reflexively monitoring his or her experience, and deciding on what to say, and how to say it, in the light of his or her perception of the responsiveness of the therapist. The implications for practice of this model have been explored by Bohart and Tallmann (1999) and Rennie (1998).

The assimilation model, developed by Stiles (2002; Stiles & Angus, 2000) represents an important example of the use of qualitative research to develop a theory of therapy process. The assimilation model proposes that a central goal of therapy is to enable clients to come to terms with problematic experiences in their lives that remain outside of their primary sense of self, and are experienced in the form of disruptive or puzzling thoughts, behaviors, and feelings. The evolution of the assimilation model has been based on a series of qualitative case studies, in which assimilation stages, and the client and therapist actions that facilitate movement between stages, are analyzed through systematic interpretation of therapy session transcript material by a research team. Some of these studies have used ideas and techniques from dialogical sequence analysis, a form of discourse analysis, to enable micro-processes of therapist-client interaction to be scrutinized (Stiles et al., 2006). The assimilation process literature is distinctive in its use of case-level data to investigate processes that can take several sessions to unfold, and also in its adoption of an explicit theory-building orientation.

The largest single body of research into the process of therapy consists of studies that have elicited clients' views of significant events, or helpful/hindering events, within the therapy that they have received. Some of these studies have involved postsession interviews with clients, while other studies have been based on client written accounts. In a few studies, similar data are collected from therapists, enabling comparison between client and therapist views of what was helpful. A systematic metasynthesis of this research has been carried out by Timulak (2007), which concluded that there are several different types of experience that clients report as valuable within their therapy: awareness/insight/self-understanding; behavioral change/problem solution; exploring feelings/emotional experiencing; empowerment; relief; feeling understood; client involvement; reassurance/support/safety; personal contact. The lessons for practice that can be derived from these studies offer support to integrative and pluralistic approaches to therapy, which seek to facilitate client engagement in a range of change processes, in contrast to approaches that focus on a more limited set of change mechanisms.

Other qualitative research into the helpfulness of therapy events has examined client experiences of specific interventions that are considered by clinicians to have particular relevance to the effectiveness of the kind of therapy that they offer. O'Connor, Meakes, Pickering, and Schuman (1997) and Young and Cooper (2008) have explored client experiences of narrative therapy techniques such as externalizing their problem. Client experiences of specific interventions have also been explored in relation to a structured, task-oriented methods of working on problematic reactions (Watson & Rennie, 1994), receiving letters from their therapist (Hamill, Reid, & Reynolds, 2008), motivational interviewing procedures (Angus & Kagan, 2009), receiving intensive psychotherapy in a day center (Mörtl & Von Wietersheim, 2008), person-centered therapy for alcohol misuse (Moerman & McLeod, 2006), psychodynamic therapy (Poulsen, 2004; Poulsen, Lunn, & Sandros, 2010), minimal intervention therapy (Macdonald, Mead, Bower, Richards, & Lovell, 2007), couples therapy (Rautiainen & Seikkula, 2009), cognitive analytic therapy (Rayner, Thompson, & Walsh, 2011), and participation in mindfulness training (Allen, Bromley, Kuyken, & Sonnenberg, 2009; Chadwick, Kaur, Swelam, Ross, & Ellett, 2011; Fitzpatrick, Simpson, & Smith, 2010; Moss, Waugh, & Barnes, 2008; Proulx, 2008; Stelter, 2009). Qualitative studies have also been used to explore client experiences of generic processes that occur in all forms of therapy. Dalenberg (2004) analyzed the views of clients on the issue of how their therapists responded to their anger. Hanson (2005), Burkard, Knox, Groen, Perez, & Hess (2006), and Knox, Hess, Petersen, and Hill (1997) investigated client experiences of therapist self-disclosure. Roe, Dekel, Harel, Fennig, and Fennig (2006), Knox, Adrians, Everson, Hess, Hill, and Crook-Lyon (2011), and others, have interviewed clients on their experience of termination of therapy.

In relation to qualitative research into client experiences of specific interventions, a series of studies on the role of metaphor in collaborative meaning-making in psychotherapy is of particular interest. Angus and Rennie (1988, 1989) used recall interviews to invite clients and therapists to describe their experiences during segments of therapy that were identified as involving the use of metaphor. Two patterns of therapist-client interaction were observed. In some cases, the therapist and client used the shared metaphor to access networks of associative meaning, which were highly productive in relation to overall progress of therapy. In other cases, there were misunderstandings around the meaning that the metaphor held for each participant, with the consequence that attention to the metaphor was not therapeutically productive.

Rasmussen and Angus (1996) and Rasmussen (2000) extended this work into a study in which metaphor-oriented experience of clients with borderline personality disorder characteristics and those without such characteristics were compared. For those without such characteristics, the emergence of a shared metaphor contributed to the development of a stable theme for the session. However, shared exploration of the meanings of metaphors that arose in-session did not appear to occur in the cases with borderline characteristics. Angus (1996), Levitt, Korman, and Angus (2000) and Long and Lepper (2008) tracked the occurrence of metaphor themes across multiple sessions of therapy, using qualitative analysis of therapy transcripts. In both studies, it was found that consistent metaphor themes (clusters of metaphors that drew on the same underlying meaning, such as "My marriage is like a battleground" and "I have to defend myself against him") represented central topic threads within the therapy, and that client change was marked by metaphor shift.

Long and Lepper (2008) identified specific types of client reflective processing that were linked to shifts in metaphor use. Other studies have identified ways in which cultural metaphors enter therapy discourse, for example in clients with issues around depression (Levitt, Korman, & Angus, 2000; McMullen, 1999) and addiction (Shinebourne & Smith, 2010). These qualitative studies of metaphor use as a therapeutic process indicate the potential of qualitative process research, in being able to extend an initial inquiry (Angus & Rennie, 1988, 1989) into new areas, and gradually construct a comprehensive model.

At the same time, this set of studies also illustrates the limitations of contemporary qualitative process research in terms of the small number of studies that are published. Making the step beyond exploring metaphor process, to using these ideas to inform practice, requires further replication studies to be carried out.

This brief account of some representative areas of qualitative research into client experience of the process of counseling and psychotherapy cannot do justice to the richness and clinical relevance of the studies that have been outlined. The distinctive contribution of qualitative methodologies, in this area of research in counseling and psychotherapy, is that it facilitates understanding of the complexity of the process of therapy as it unfolds over time, in a manner that represents both client and therapist as co-creators of meaning.

The Client-Therapist Relationship

The conceptualization by Bordin (1979) of the therapeutic relationship as a "working alliance" characterized by a secure emotional bond between therapist and client, and agreement around the goals and tasks of therapy, has functioned for more than 20 years as a cornerstone of counseling and psychotherapy research. A generation of researchers has used this framework to develop measures that have been used to examine the links between alliance and outcome, the nature of failed alliances, and the effectiveness of methods for training therapists to form better alliances with their clients (Muran & Barber, 2010). In recent years, however, it has become apparent that although the alliance perspective can be seen as a metaphor that has served the field well in respect of highlighting important dimensions of the therapeutic relationship, it has also had the effect of diverting attention from other aspects of the relationship that are of clinical significance (Safran & Muran, 2006; Stiles & Goldsmith, 2010). In this context, the role of qualitative research into relationship factors has been to go "beyond the alliance," to identify relationship phenomena that challenge and extend the prevailing alliance perspective.

One area in which qualitative research has uncovered aspects of the therapeutic relationship that are not explicitly addressed within alliance theory and research concerns the extent to which the client-therapist relationship involves negotiating issues of power, control, and status.

Interview research by Rennie (1994a, 1994c) has identified the extent to which clients defer to their therapists—when they believe that the therapist has misunderstood them, or made an unhelpful interpretation or suggestion, they are likely to say nothing. Conversation analysis studies of therapist use of language demonstrates that clinicians take control of the course of therapy by redefining client problem statements so that they correspond with the theoretical model of the therapist (Antaki, Barnes, & Leudar, 2007; Davis, 1986) or steer client discourse in the direction of certain solutions (Peräkylä, 1995; Peräkylä & Silverman, 1991). Clients who view themselves as lower in social status than their therapists report that they typically held back on engagement in the therapeutic process, and did not expect that therapy would be helpful (Balmforth, 2006). Similar results have been found in qualitative research into the experiences of black and ethnic minority clients (Chang & Berk, 2009; Chang & Yoon, 2011; Thompson, Bazile, & Akbar, 2004; Ward, 2005).

A further set of findings from qualitative research into the therapeutic relationship suggests that on some occasions the client-therapist relationship is more than an alliance between two people working together to tackle a problem, and represents a potent curative experience in its own right. Some studies into client and therapist experience of the therapeutic relationship have collected accounts of moments in therapy when each participant is open to the other and experiences a sense of profound interpersonal contact (Grafanaki & McLeod, 1999; McMillan & McLeod, 2006). This sense of mutual connectedness or "relational depth" (Cooper, 2005; Knox, 2008; Knox & Cooper, 2010, 2011; McMillan & McLeod, 2006) can in some cases come to form a continuing strand within the ongoing relationship. Clients who have experienced this phenomenon describe it as representing as highly memorable, and as a turning point in their capacity to enter into meaningful relationships with other people in their life as a whole (Knox, 2008). Along similar lines, Schnellbacher and Leijssen (2009) found some clients who believed that the level of authenticity of their therapist as having been a central curative factor. When it occurs, this new type of relationship schema may be retained by the client as an internal dialogue with a supportive "other" that can be drawn upon at times of stress (Knox et al., 1999; Mosher & Stiles, 2009; Myers & White, 2010).

Other qualitative research into the process of therapy has highlighted the value for clients of working with a therapist who cares about them (Bachelor, 1995). Clients interviewed by Bedi, Davis, and Williams (2005), Levitt, Butler, and Hill (2006), and MacCormack et al. (2001) described how much they appreciated the fact that their therapists actively cared about them, and were "willing to go the extra mile" (e.g., by allowing session to go over time, or visiting them at home) to help them. Similarly, Binder, Moltu, Hummelsund, Sagen, and Holgersen (2011) reported that adolescent clients formed stronger relationships with clinicians who they perceived as being comfortable and confident in the role of therapist. These findings can be interpreted as being consistent with an image of the therapist-client relationship as similar to a relationship with a caregiver or good parent.

A theme that has emerged within some qualitative studies of client experience of therapy has been the finding that clients do not readily differentiate between "interventions" and "relationships" (for example, in studies by Bedi et al., 2005, and Borrill & Foreman, 1996). Clients may view the use of specific therapy techniques as indicative of their therapist's commitment to them, or may be willing to persevere with emotionally challenging activities because of their trust in their therapist. These findings imply that the search for causal links between alliance and outcome may be in danger of oversimplifying what, in the eyes of clients, is a process of reciprocal causality in which interventions and the quality of the relationship mutually interact in complex ways. Qualitative research into the therapeutic relationship provides an example of how the discovery-oriented nature of qualitative inquiry can be used within a professional community to sustain creative dialogue around important issues of theory and practice. The concept of the working alliance has made a massive contribution to the field of psychotherapy over more than three decades. However, the generativity of the alliance paradigm, as a source of ideas for research and practice, has perhaps run its course (Safran & Muran, 2006). It may be that an overreliance on quantitative methods has limited the capacity of the psychotherapy research community to do justice to the complexity of the client-therapist relationship. Stiles and Goldsmith (2010) have argued that there is a tendency for forms of psychological measurement to reduce to a single dimension of "evaluation" (i.e., a general sense of how good something is). What seems to have been happening within the domain of qualitative research into the client-therapist relationship is a gradual opening up of other dimensions of the relationship. This process of discovery can be regarded as beginning to provide confirmation, within the field of psychotherapy, of the relevance of multidimensional models of interpersonal relationships (Josselson, 1996, 2003; Stiles & Goldsmith, 2010). There have been relatively few qualitative studies into relationship factors in therapy, and the theoretical and clinical implications of the findings of these studies have yet to be incorporated into practice. Nevertheless, what has emerged from these investigations points toward a concept of the client-therapist relationship as involving multiple points of negotiation (Safran & Muran, 2006) between client and therapist around a fairly broad set of possible ways of constructive engagement.

Therapist Development

Qualitative methods have been used to examine the meaning of being a therapist, the experience of training, and the shifts in perspective that occur over the course of a career. A key starting point for this area of work has been the classic Rønnestad and Skovholt (2003, 2012; Skovholt & Rønnestad, 1995) study of counselor professional development. This study is of special significance in identifying a set of stages of counselor development that have served as a basis for further focused inquiry, and establishing high standards of methodological rigor that have remained influential within this domain of research. The Skovholt and Rønnestad (1995, 2003) model of counselor development suggests that therapists pass through six phases during their professional lifetime: lay helper; beginning student; advanced student; novice professional; experienced professional; and senior professional. Each of these phases is associated with its own set of developmental challenges. Subsequent qualitative research has explored the experiences of therapists at each of these stages, adding further detail to the understanding of therapist development that is available. One of the most striking features of recent research on therapist development has been an increasing use of autoethnographic methods, in which clinicians systematically reflect on their own experience of training and practice (Grant, 2006, 2010a, 2010b; Moxnes, 2006). Possibly the most methodologically satisfying

example of this type of work can be found in a study by McIlveen (2007), in which the author analyses the factors that influenced his own development as a theorist and researcher. McIlveen (2007) uses biographical material to question the validity of a conventional scientist-practitioner account of the links between research and practice, and to offer an alternative model that places the meaning of research within a life history perspective.

Qualitative studies have examined the experiences of therapists in relation to formative learning experiences, such as different types of training (Armstrong, 2003; Carlsson, Norberg, Sandell, & Schubert, 2011; Nerdrum & Rønnestad, 2002; Smith, 2011), and engagement in personal therapy (Grimmer & Tribe, 2001; Mackey & Mackey, 1993; Macran, Stiles, & Smith, 1999; Moller, Timms, & Alilovic 2009; Murphy, 2005; Rake & Paley, 2009; Rizq & Target, 2008a, 2008b; Wiseman & Shefler, 2001). The bibliography of CQR studies assembled by Chui, Jackson, Liu, and Hill (2012) lists a total of 23 qualitative studies on topics related to different aspects of counselor development. Taken together, these studies contribute a nuanced account of what it means to become and be a therapist. Unfortunately little is known about the relationships between these developmental and training factors and client outcomes.

One of the most influential domains of current research in counseling and psychotherapy comprises the accumulating body of work that confirms striking differences in effectiveness across therapists (Kraus, Castonguay, Boswell, Nordberg, & Hayes, 2011). Qualitative research has made a significant contribution to this area in exploring the personal characteristics of senior and "master" therapists, clinicians nominated by their peers as the "best of the best"—the therapists that they would recommend a family member to consult. The value of these studies lies in their capacity to use the broader perspective available to highly successful practitioners, who have survived the hazards of practice and thrived, as a means of highlighting the attitudes and strategies that are associated with excellence in the field of counseling and psychotherapy (Jennings & Skovholt, 1999; Levitt & Williams, 2010; Miller, 2007; Skovholt & Jennings, 2004; Skovholt, Rønnestad, & Jennings, 1997). In the first of this series of studies, Jennings and Skovholt (1999) interviewed 10 master therapists, representing a wide range of theoretical orientations. All of these therapists worked full time in private practice. The conclusions that emerged from this study were that master therapists are:

- Voracious learners;
- Sensitive to and value cognitive complexity and the ambiguity of the human condition;
- Emotionally receptive, self-aware, reflective, nondefensive, and open to feedback;
- Mentally healthy and mature individuals who attend to their own emotional well-being;
- Aware of how their emotional health affects the quality of their work;
- In possession of strong relationship skills;
- Convinced that the foundation for therapeutic change is a strong working alliance;
- Experts at using their exceptional relationship skills in therapy;
- Able to use their accumulated life and professional experiences as a major resource in their work.

These conclusions have been largely supported by the findings of subsequent studies. The findings, along with the results of other qualitative research on therapist training, suggest that the therapist role incorporates a high level of integration of personal experience and professional knowledge. Implications for practice based on qualitative research on master therapists are discussed in Skovholt and Jennings (2004) and O'Donohue, Cummings, and Cummings (2006). Unfortunately two major problems have emerged from this research. The first is that the identification of "master therapists" did not include the actual effects of their treatments on clients. That is, no evidence was presented that they were unusually effective, other than peer nominations. The second problem was that the research design did not call for qualitative study of typical or poorly regarded therapists, who may turn out to share many of the values, attitudes, and behaviors that are demonstrated by their more highly regarded colleagues. Further research into these issues is required to determine the validity and general applicability of the "master therapist" literature.

CONCLUSIONS

Qualitative methods have been used to investigate a wide range of questions that have been of interest to counseling and psychotherapy practitioners

and researchers. Qualitative research can be seen to complement mainstream measurement-oriented research in a variety of ways—by opening up new topics of inquiry, representing complex phenomena, and introducing a perspective that is grounded in the phenomenological world of the participant. The practice-focused nature of psychotherapy research requires the pursuit of methodologically pluralist research strategies that build on clinical experience. The practitioner status of qualitative therapy researchers, and their willingness to acknowledge the value of measurement-based approaches, has resulted in qualitative psychotherapy research inhabiting a methodological space somewhat apart from current debates within the wider field of qualitative inquiry. For example, the most recent edition of the authoritative *Handbook of Qualitative Research* (Denzin & Lincoln, 2011) makes no mention of qualitative research in psychotherapy. The relative isolation of the qualitative therapy research community is both a strength and a weakness. It is a weakness because it inhibits exploitation of new ideas and methods around the process of qualitative inquiry that have been developed within cognate disciplines such as education, health studies and management studies. It is a strength because qualitative researchers in the field of counseling and psychotherapy have, for the most part, avoided being drawn into "paradigm wars" and have therefore been able to retain their focus on the task of producing knowledge for practice.

The contribution of qualitative research to the counseling and psychotherapy evidence base is limited by a number of factors. Qualitative research relies on the "power of example" (Flyvbjerg, 2001), in the form of descriptions or accounts of key moments of action and interaction. Being able to communicate such segments of lived experience effectively remains a challenge both for researchers and journal editors—all too often the meaning and significance of a qualitative investigation is hidden behind dead writing. The descriptive basis of qualitative research also presents difficulties at the level of meta-analysis, or metasynthesis of findings. In a good qualitative study, the meaning of a theme or category is carried not merely in the title of the category, but in "thick descriptions" that are provided within the text: Qualitative papers are intended to be read all the way through.

For qualitative work to have its full impact on policy and practice, methods are needed for synthesizing results across studies. Since quantitative research syntheses like meta-analysis are having a powerful impact on public policy and practice decisions it is tempting to try to mimic these procedures for qualitative research integration. The work of Timulak (2007) and Hill et al. (2012) have moved in this direction. Hill et al. (2012) suggest that around 12 studies on a specific topic are necessary in order to generate a plausible qualitative meta-analysis. At the present time, there are few areas of qualitative therapy research that have accumulated anything approaching this number of studies. Alongside an uplift in the number of published qualitative studies, it is also important for researchers to provide sufficient information around sampling, validity procedures, exemplification of categories, and other basic reporting requirements, to enable those carrying out meta-analyses to arrive at well-founded conclusions.

It would also be valuable for the field of counseling and psychotherapy research to take greater advantage of the possibilities afforded by mixed methods research designs. One way of moving forward on this goal would be for qualitative and quantitative researchers to work together to plan and participate in multisite programs around key research priority areas.

It is possible to identify three tentative priority areas for qualitative therapy research over the next decade. The first priority is devote effort and resources, using the whole range of qualitative methodologies, to the issue of understanding how therapy outcomes are co-constructed, by clients, clinicians and other stakeholders, on the basis of cultural discourses around the meaning of suffering, well-being, and cure. This area of inquiry is of particular importance because an appreciation of "what works for whom" is of immense practical and economic significance, and because early returns from the small number of qualitative outcome studies that have been carried out suggest that there is a risk that outcome estimates based on standardized measures may not be telling the whole story. Within the broader field of mental health research, there has been increasing willingness to involve service users in the design and conduct of studies, as a means of maximizing the relevance of research findings in relation to the needs and wishes of recipients of care (Faulkner, 2000; Wallcraft, Schrank & Amering, 2009). Although qualitative research in psychotherapy has done a great deal to explore and document the experiences of therapy clients, few researchers have taken the next step of engaging in a collaborative process of inquiry with clients. This kind of development could do a great deal to enhance the impact of qualitative outcome research in psychotherapy.

A second priority area for qualitative therapy research is to examine the ways in which therapists actually make decisions about how to respond to clients. Gabbay and Le May (2011) used ethnographic methods to analyze the role of theory and research in shaping the clinical decisions of doctors. What they found was that the physicians in their study were certainly scientifically informed, but that they had little time for clinical guidelines, and in practice took a complex range of contextual factors into account in arriving at a view on how to treat each patient. This kind of investigation has major implications for the delivery of evidence-based treatment, for the type of treatment research that is carried out, and for the training, supervision, support and working conditions of clinicians.

A third priority area for qualitative research is to follow through on the potential and promise of certain areas of qualitative therapy research, to the point where learning from that research can directly influence practice in ways that can be evaluated. Being able to point to some examples of practical questions where qualitative research findings have yielded tangible improvements in efficacy, will transform the way that qualitative methodologies are perceived within the clinical, academic, and policy communities.

In conclusion, it can be suggested that it is essential for the knowledge base of counseling and psychotherapy to maintain a balanced commitment to the pursuit of practical knowledge through both quantitative and qualitative methodologies. Qualitative research yields nuanced, contextualized knowledge (Seikkula & Arnkil, 2006) that seeks to describe and make sense of the complexity of what is happening at ground level, and which provides a counterpoint to the more simplified, broad-brush general statements that are typically derived from quantitative studies.

REFERENCES

Adler, J. M. (2012). Living into the story: Agency and coherence in a longitudinal study of narrative identity development and mental health over the course of psychotherapy. *Journal of Personality & Social Psychology, 102*, 367–389.

Adler, J. M., & McAdams, D. P. (2007). The narrative reconstruction of psychotherapy. *Narrative Inquiry, 17*, 179–202.

Adler, J. M., Skalina, L. M., & McAdams, D. P. (2008). The narrative reconstruction of psychotherapy and psychological health. *Psychotherapy Research, 18*, 719–734.

Allen, M., Bromley, A., Kuyken, W., & Sonnenberg, S. J. (2009). Participants' experiences of mindfulness-based cognitive therapy: "It changed me in just about every way possible." *Behavioural & Cognitive Psychotherapy, 37*, 413–430.

Anderson, T., & Strupp, H. H. (1986). The ecology of psychotherapy research. *Journal of Consulting and Clinical Psychology, 64*, 716–782.

Angus, L. (1996). An intensive analysis of metaphor themes in psychotherapy. In J. S. Mio, & A. Katz (Eds.), *Metaphor: pragmatics and Applications* (pp. 73–84). New York, NY: Erlbaum.

Angus, L., Levitt, H., & Hardtke, K. (1999). The narrative process coding system: Research applications and implications for psychotherapy practice. *Journal of Clinical Psychology, 55*, 1255–1270.

Angus, L. E., & Kagan, F. (2009). Therapist empathy and client anxiety reduction in motivational interviewing: "she carries with me, the experience." *Journal of Clinical Psychology, 65*, 1156–1167.

Angus, L. E., & Rennie, D. L. (1988). Therapist participation in metaphor generation: Collaborative and noncollaborative styles. *Psychotherapy, 25*, 552–560.

Angus, L. E., & Rennie, D. L. (1989). Envisioning the representational world: The client's experience of metaphoric expressiveness in psychotherapy. *Psychotherapy: Theory, research, practice and training, 26*, 373–379.

Antaki, C., Barnes, R., & Leudar, I. (2007). Members' and analysts' interests: "Formulations" in psychotherapy. In A. Hepburn & S. Wiggins (Eds.), *Discursive research in practice: New approaches to psychology and interaction* (pp. 166–181). Cambridge, United Kingdom: Cambridge University Press.

Armstrong, J. (2003). Training for paraprofessional counsellors: Evaluating the meaning and impact of a common factors approach. *Counselling & Psychotherapy Research, 3*, 270–277.

Arthern, J., & Madill, A. (1999). How do transition objects work? The therapist's view. *British Journal of Medical Psychology, 72*, 1–21.

Avdi, A., & Georgaca, E. (2007). Discourse analysis and psychotherapy: A critical review. *European Journal of Psychotherapy & Counselling, 9*, 157–176.

Bachelor, A. (1995). Clients perception of the therapeutic alliance, a qualitative analysis. *Journal of Counseling Psychology, 42*, 323–337.

Balmforth, J. (2006). Clients' experiences of how perceived differences in social class between a counsellor and client affect the therapeutic relationship. In G. Proctor, M. Cooper, P. Sanders, & B. Malcolm (Eds.), *Politicizing the person-centred approach: An agenda for social change* (pp. 215–224). Ross-on-Wye, United Kingdom: PCCS Books.

Bazerman, C. (1988). *Shaping written knowledge: The genre and activity of the experimental article in science.* Madison: University of Wisconsin Press.

Beck, B., Halling, S., McNabb, M., Miller, D., Rowe, J. O., & Schulz, J. (2005). On navigating despair: Stories from psychotherapists. *Journal of Religion and Health, 44*, 187–205.

Bedi, R. P., Davis, M. D., & Williams, M. (2005). Critical incidents in the formation of the therapeutic alliance from the client's perspective. *Psychotherapy: Theory, Research, Practice, Training, 41*, 311–323.

Berg, C., Raminani, S., Greer, J., Harwood, M., & Safren, S. (2008). Participants' perspectives on cognitive-behavioral therapy for adherence and depression in HIV. *Psychotherapy Research, 18*, 271–280.

Berman, J. S., & Reich, C. M. (2010). Investigator allegiance and the evaluation of psychotherapy outcome research. *European Journal of Psychotherapy & Counselling, 12*, 11–21.

Billig, M. (1996). *Arguing and thinking: A rhetorical approach to social psychology* (2nd ed.). Cambridge, United Kingdom: Cambridge University Press.

Binder, P., Moltu, C., Hummelsund, D., Sagen, S. H., & Holgersen, H. (2011). Meeting an adult ally on the way out into the world: Adolescent patients' experiences of useful psychotherapeutic ways of working at an age when independence really matters. *Psychotherapy Research, 21*, 554–566.

Binder, P. E., Holgersen, H., & Nielsen, G. H. (2010). What is a "good outcome" in psychotherapy? A qualitative exploration of former patients' point of view. *Psychotherapy Research, 20*, 285–294.

Bohart, A. C., & Tallman, K. (1999). *How clients make therapy work: The process of active self-healing.* Washington, DC: American Psychological Association.

Boothe, B., & von Wyl, A. (2004). Story dramatology and personal conflict: JAKOB—A tool for narrative understanding and psychotherapy practice. In L. E. Angus & J. McLeod (Eds.), *The handbook of narrative and psychotherapy: Practice, theory, and research* (pp. 283–296). Thousand Oaks, CA: Sage.

Bordin, E. S. (1979). The generalizability of the psychoanalytic concept of working alliance. *Psychotherapy: Theory, Research, Practice, 16*, 252–260.

Borenstein, M., Hedges, L. V., Higgins, J. P. T., & Rothstein, H. R. (2009). *Introduction to meta-analysis.* Oxford, United Kingdom: Wiley-Blackwell.

Borrill, J., & Foreman, E. I. (1996). Understanding cognitive change: a qualitative study of the impact of cognitive-behavioural therapy on fear of flying. *Clinical Psychology and Psychotherapy, 3,* 62–74.

Boyatzis, R. E. (1998). *Transforming qualitative information: Thematic analysis and code development.* Thousand Oaks, CA: Sage.

Braun, V., & Clarke, V. (2006). Using thematic analysis in psychology. *Qualitative Research in Psychology, 3,* 77–101.

Brinkmann, S., & Kvale, S. (2005). Confronting the ethics of qualitative research. *Journal of Constructivist Psychology, 18,* 157–181.

Brocki, J. M., & Wearden, A. J. (2006). A critical evaluation of the use of interpretative phenomenological analysis (IPA) in health psychology. *Psychology & Health, 21,* 87–108.

Bruner, J. (1986). *Actual minds, possible worlds.* Cambridge, MA: Harvard University Press.

Burkard, A. W., Knox, S., Groen, M., Perez, M., & Hess, S. (2006). European American therapist self-disclosure in cross-cultural counseling. *Journal of Counseling Psychology, 53,* 15–25.

Burnett, P. C. (1999). Assessing the structure of learning outcomes from counselling using the SOLO autonomy: An exploratory study. *British Journal of Guidance & Counselling, 27,* 567–580.

Carey, T. A., Carey, M., Stalker, K., Mullan, R. J., Murray, L. K., & Spratt, M. B. (2007). Psychological change from the inside looking out: A qualitative investigation. *Counselling and Psychotherapy Research, 7,* 178–187.

Carlsson, J., Norberg, J., Sandell, R., & Schubert, J. (2011). Searching for recognition: The professional development of psychodynamic psychotherapists during training and the first few years after it. *Psychotherapy Research, 21,* 141–153.

Chadwick, P., Kaur, H., Swelam, M., Ross, S., & Ellett, L. (2011). Experience of mindfulness in people with bipolar disorder: A qualitative study. *Psychotherapy Research, 21,* 277–285.

Chang, D. F., & Berk, A. (2009). Making cross-racial therapy work: A phenomenological study of clients' experiences of cross-racial therapy. *Journal of Counseling Psychology, 56,* 521–536.

Chang, D. F., & Yoon, P. (2011). Ethnic minority clients' perceptions of the significance of race in cross-racial therapy relationships. *Psychotherapy Research, 21,* 567–582.

Chang, H. (2008). *Autoethnography as method.* Walnut Creek, CA: Left Coast Press.

Charmaz, K. (2006). *Constructing grounded theory.* Thousand Oaks, CA: Sage.

Chui, H. T., Jackson, J. L., Liu, J., & Hill, C. E. (2012). Annotated bibliography of studies using consensual qualitative research. In C. E. Hill (Ed.), *Consensual qualitative research. A practical resource for investigating social science phenomena* (pp. 213–266). Washington, DC: American Psychological Association.

Clarke, H., Rees, A., & Hardy, G. E. (2004). The big idea: Clients' perspectives of change processes in cognitive therapy. *Psychology and Psychotherapy: Theory, Research and Practice, 77,* 67–89.

Cook, J. M., Biyanova, T., & Coyne, J. C. (2009). Comparative case study of diffusion of eye movement desensitization and reprocessing in two clinical settings: Empirically supported treatment status is not enough. *Professional Psychology: Research and Practice, 40,* 518–524.

Cooper, M. (2005). Therapists' experiences of relational depth: A qualitative interview study. *Counselling and Psychotherapy Research, 5,* 87–95.

Creswell, J. W. (2007). *Qualitative inquiry and research design: Choosing among five approaches* (2nd ed.). Thousand Oaks, CA: Sage.

Cummings, N. A. (2007). Interruption replaces termination in focused, intermittent psychotherapy throughout the life cycle. In W. T. O'Donohue & M. Cucciare (Eds.), *Terminating psychotherapy: A clinician's guide* (pp. 99–120). New York, NY: Routledge.

Cunningham, K., Wolbert, R., & Lillie, B. (2004). It's about me solving my problems: Clients' assessments of dialectical behavior therapy. *Cognitive & Behavioral Practice, 11,* 248–256.

Cushman, P. (1995). *Constructing the self, constructing America: A cultural history of psychotherapy.* Reading, MA: Addison-Wesley.

Dahlberg, K., Drew, N., & Nystrom, M. (2001). *Reflective lifeworld research.* Lund, Sweden: Studentlitteratur.

Dale, P., Allen, J., & Measor, L. (1998). Counselling adults who were abused as children: Clients' perceptions of efficacy, client-counsellor communication, and dissatisfaction. *British Journal of Guidance & Counselling, 26,* 141–158.

Dalenberg, C. J. (2004). Maintaining the safe and effective therapeutic relationship in the context of distrust and anger: Countertransference and complex trauma. *Psychotherapy: Theory, Research, Practice, Training, 41,* 438–447.

Daniel, T., & McLeod, J. (2006). Weighing up the evidence: A qualitative analysis of how person-centred counsellors evaluate the effectiveness of their practice. *Counselling and Psychotherapy Research, 6,* 244–249.

Danziger, K. (1990). *Constructing the subject. Historical origins of psychological research.* Cambridge, United Kingdom: Cambridge University Press.

Davis, K. (1986). The process of problem (re)formulation in psychotherapy. *Sociology of Health and Illness, 8,* 44–74.

Denzin, N. K., & Lincoln, Y. S. (Eds.). (2011). *The Sage handbook of qualitative research* (4th ed.). Thousand Oaks, CA: Sage.

Dilthey, W. (1977). *Descriptive psychology and historical understandings*. The Hague, The Netherlands: Martinus Nijhoff. (Original work published 1894)

Dixon-Woods, M., Bonas, S., Booth, A., Jones, D. R., Miller, T. Sutton. A. J.,...Young, B. (2006). How can systematic reviews incorporate qualitative research? A critical perspective. *Qualitative Research, 6*, 27–44.

Dixon-Woods, M., Booth, A., & Sutton, A. J. (2007). Synthesizing qualitative research: A review of published reports. *Qualitative Research, 7*, 375–422.

Dreier, O. (2000). Psychotherapy in clients' trajectories across contexts. In C. Mattingly & L. Garro (Eds.), *Narratives and the cultural construction of illness and healing* (pp. 237–258). Berkeley: University of California Press.

Dreier, O. (2008). *Psychotherapy in everyday life*. New York, NY: Cambridge University Press.

Eden, K. (1987). Hermeneutics and the ancient rhetorical tradition. *Rhetorica, 5*, 59–86.

Eisenhart, M., & Jarrow, A. S. (2011). Teaching qualitative research. In N. K. Denzin & Y. S. Lincoln (Eds.), *The Sage handbook of qualitative research* (4th ed., pp. 691–744). Thousand Oaks, CA: Sage.

Elliott, R. (1984). A discovery-oriented approach to significant change events in psychotherapy, interpersonal process recall and comprehensive process analysis. In L. N. Rice & L. S. Greenberg (Eds.), *Patterns of change; Intensive analysis of psychotherapy process* (pp. 249–286). New York, NY: Guilford Press.

Elliott, R., Fischer, C. T., & Rennie, D. L. (1999). Evolving guidelines for the publication of qualitative research studies in psychology and related fields. *British Journal of Clinical Psychology, 38*, 215–229.

Elliott, R., Partyka, R., Wagner, J., Alperin, R., Dobrenski, R., Messer, S. B.,...Castonguay, L. G. (2009). An adjudicated hermeneutic single case efficacy design study of experiential therapy for panic/phobia. *Psychotherapy Research, 19*, 543–557.

Elliott, R., & Timulak, L. (2005). Descriptive and interpretive approaches to qualitative research. In J. Miles & P. Gilbert (Eds.), *A handbook of research methods in clinical and health psychology* (pp. 147–159). Oxford, United Kingdom: Oxford University Press.

Etherington, K. (2004). *Becoming a reflexive researcher: Using our selves in research*. London, United Kingdom: Kingsley.

Faulkner, A. (2000). *Strategies for living: A report of user-led research into people's strategies for living with mental distress*. London, United Kingdom: Mental Health Foundation.

Ferrara, A. (2010). Reflexive pluralism. *Philosophy & Social Criticism, 36*, 353–364.

Fessler, R. (1983). Phenomenology and the "talking cure", "research on psychotherapy." In A. Giorgi,

A. Barton, & C. Macs (Eds.), *Duquesne studies in phenomenological psychology* (Vol. 4, pp. 33–46). Pittsburgh, PA: Duquesne University Press.

Fetterman, D. M. (2009). *Ethnography: Step-by-step*. Thousand Oaks, CA: Sage.

Finlay, L. (2008). A dance between the reduction and reflexivity: Explicating the "phenomenological psychological attitude." *Journal of Phenomenological Psychology, 39*, 1–32.

Finlay, L., & Gough, B. (Eds.). (2003). *Reflexivity: A practical guide for researchers in health and social sciences*. Oxford, United Kingdom: Blackwell.

Fischer, C. T. (2009). Bracketing in qualitative research: Conceptual and practical matters. *Psychotherapy Research, 19*, 583–590.

Fishman, D. B. (1999). *The case for pragmatic psychology*. New York: New York University Press.

Fitzpatrick, L., Simpson, J., & Smith, A. (2010). A qualitative analysis of mindfulness-based cognitive therapy (MBCT) in Parkinson's disease. *Psychology & Psychotherapy: Theory, Research and Practice, 83*, 179–92.

Flick, U. (2009). *An introduction to qualitative research* (4th ed.). London, United Kingdom: Sage.

Flyvbjerg, B. (2001). *Making social science matter. Why social inquiry fails and how it can succeed again*. New York, NY: Cambridge University Press.

Flyvbjerg, B. (2006). Five misunderstandings about case-study research. *Qualitative Inquiry, 12*, 219–245.

Foucault, M. (1972). *The archaeology of knowledge* (A. S. Smith, Trans.). New York, NY: Harper & Row.

Frontman, K. C., & Kunkel, K. A. (1994). A grounded theory of counselors' construal of success in the initial session. *Journal of Counseling Psychology, 41*, 492–499.

Frost, N. A., Holt, A., Shinebourne, P., Esin, C., Nolas, S., Mehdizadeh, L., & Brooks-Gordon, B. (2011). Collective findings, individual interpretations: An illustration of a pluralistic approach to qualitative data analysis. *Qualitative Research in Psychology, 8*, 93–113.

Frost, N. A., & Nolas, S. (2011). Exploring and expanding on pluralism in qualitative research in psychology. *Qualitative Research in Psychology, 8*, 115–119.

Gabbay, J., & Le May, A. (2011). *Practice-based evidence for healthcare. Clinical mindlines*. London, United Kingdom: Routledge.

Geertz, C. (1973). *The interpretation of cultures. Selected essays*. New York, NY: Basic Books.

Geller, S. M., & Greenberg, L. S. (2002). Therapeutic presence: Therapists' experience of presence in the psychotherapeutic encounter. *Person-Centered & Experiential Psychotherapies, 1*, 71–86.

Geller, S. M., Greenberg, L. S., & Watson, J. C. (2010). Therapist and client perceptions of therapeutic presence: The development of a measure. *Psychotherapy Research, 20*, 599–610.

Gergen, K. J. (1988). If persons are texts. In S. B. Messer, L. A. Sass, & R. L. Woolfolk (Eds.), *Hermeneutics and psychological theory, interpretive perspectives on personality, psychotherapy and psychopathology* (pp. 28–51). New Brunswick, NJ: Rutgers University Press.

Gergen, K. J. (1973). Social psychology as history. *Journal of Personality & Social Psychology, 26,* 309–320.

Gergen, K. J. (1997). Who speaks and who replies in human science scholarship? *History of the Human Sciences, 10,* 151–173.

Gergen, M., & Gergen, K. J. (Eds.). (2003). *Social construction: A reader.* Thousand Oaks, CA: Sage.

Giorgi, A. P., & Giorgi, B. M. (2003). The descriptive phenomenological psychological method. In P. M. Camic, J. E. Rhodes, & L. Yardley (Eds.), *Qualitative research in psychology: Expanding perspectives in methodology and design* (pp. 43–73). Washington, DC: American Psychological Association.

Glasman, D., Finlay, W. M. L., & Brock, D. (2004). Becoming a self-therapist: Using cognitive-behavioural therapy for recurrent depression and/or dysthymia after completing therapy. *Psychology and Psychotherapy: Theory, Research and Practice, 77,* 335–51.

Goddard, A., Murray, C. D., & Simpson, J. (2008). Informed consent and psychotherapy: An interpretative phenomenological analysis of therapists' views. *Psychology and Psychotherapy: Theory, Research and Practice, 81,* 177–191.

Goodman, B. L., Helms, J. E., Latta, R. E., Sparks, E., & Weintraub, S. R. (2004). Training counseling psychologists as social justice agents: Feminist and multicultural principles in action. *Counseling Psychologist, 32,* 793–837.

Grafanaki, S., & McLeod, J. (1999). Narrative processes in the construction of helpful and hindering events in experiential psychotherapy. *Psychotherapy Research, 9,* 289–303.

Grant, A. (2006). Testimony: God and aeroplanes: My experience of breakdown and recovery. *Journal of Psychiatric & Mental Health Nursing, 13,* 456–457.

Grant, A. (2010a). Autoethnographic ethics and rewriting the fragmented self. *Journal of Psychiatric & Mental Health Nursing, 17,* 111–116.

Grant, A. (2010b). Writing the reflexive self: An autoethnography of alcoholism and the impact of psychotherapy culture. *Journal of Psychiatric & Mental Health Nursing, 17,* 577–582.

Greenleaf, A. T., & Williams, J. M. (2009). Supporting social justice advocacy: A paradigm shift towards an ecological perspective. *Journal for Social Action in Counseling & Psychotherapy, 2,* 1–14.

Greer, L. A., & Rennie, D. L. (2006). Providers' and payers' endorsements of empirically-supported therapy: A power-knowledge relationship? *Psychotherapy Research, 16,* 67–79.

Grimmer, A., & Tribe, R. (2001). Counselling psychologists' perceptions of the impact of mandatory personal therapy on professional development—An exploratory study. *Counselling Psychology Quarterly, 14,* 287–301.

Guillemin, M., & Gillam, L. (2004). Ethics, reflexivity and "ethically important moments" in research. *Qualitative Inquiry, 10,* 261–280.

Habermas, J. (1972). *Knowledge and human interests.* London, United Kingdom: Heinemann.

Halling, S., Leifer, M., & Rowe, J. O. (2006). Emergence of the dialogal approach: Forgiving another. In C. T. Fischer (Ed.), *Qualitative research methods for psychologists: Introduction through empirical examples* (pp. 173–212). New York, NY: Academic Press.

Hamill, M., Reid, M., & Reynolds, S. (2008). Letters in cognitive analytic therapy: The patient's experience. *Psychotherapy Research, 18,* 573–583.

Hansen, S., & Rapley, M. (2008). Editorial: Special issue of *Qualitative Research in Psychology* on "Teaching Qualitative Methods." *Qualitative Research in Psychology, 5,* 171–172.

Hanson, J. (2005). Should your lips be zipped? How therapist self-disclosure and non-disclosure affects clients. *Counselling and Psychotherapy Research, 5,* 96–104.

Hanson, W. E, Creswell, J. W., Plano-Clark, V. L., Petska, K. S., & Creswell, J. D. (2005). Mixed methods research designs in counseling psychology. *Journal of Counseling Psychology, 52,* 4–35.

Harper, D., & Thompson, A. R. (Eds.). (2011). *Qualitative research methods in mental health and psychotherapy: A guide for students and practitioners.* Oxford, United Kingdom: Wiley-Blackwell.

Harre, R., & Van Langenhove, L. (Eds.). (1999). *Positioning theory.* Oxford, United Kingdom: Blackwell.

Heidegger, M. (1962). *Being and time.* Oxford, United Kingdom: Blackwell.

Higgins, J. P. T., & Green, S. (Eds.). (2008). *Cochrane handbook for systematic reviews of interventions.* Oxford, United Kingdom: Wiley-Blackwell.

Hiley, D. R., Bohman, J. F, & Shusterman, R. (Eds.). (1991). *The interpretive turn: Philosophy, science, culture.* Ithaca, NY: Cornell University Press.

Hill, C. E. (2010). Qualitative studies of negative experiences in psychotherapy. In J. C. Muran, & J. P. Barber (Eds.), *The therapeutic alliance. An evidence-based guide to practice* (pp. 63–73). New York, NY: Guilford Press.

Hill, C. E. (Ed.). (2012). *Consensual qualitative research. A practical resource for investigating social science phenomena.* Washington, DC: American Psychological Association.

Hill, C. E., Knox, S., & Hess, S. A. (2012). Qualitative meta-analysis of consensual qualitative research studies. In C. E. Hill (Ed.), *Consensual qualitative research. A practical resource for investigating social science phenomena* (pp. 159–171). Washington, DC: American Psychological Association.

Hill, C. E., Thompson, B. J., & Nutt-Williams, E. (1997). A guide to conducting consensual qualitative research. *Counseling Psychologist, 25,* 517–572.

Holma, J., Partanen, T., Wahltsrom, J., Laitila, A., & Seikkula, J. (2006). Narratives and discourses in groups for male batterers. In M. Libschitz (Ed.), *Domestic violence and its reverberations* (pp. 84–10). New York, NY: Nova Science.

Holzkamp, K. (1992). On doing psychology critically. *Theory & Psychology, 2,* 193–204.

Howard, G. S. (1983). Toward methodological pluralism. *Journal of Counseling Psychology, 30,* 19–21.

Howe, D. (1996). Client experiences of counselling and treatment interventions, a qualitative study of family views of family therapy. *British Journal of Guidance and Counselling, 24,* 367–376.

Jennings, L., & Skovholt, T. M. (1999). The cognitive, emotional and relational characteristics of master therapists. *Journal of Counseling Psychology, 48,* 3–11.

Jensen, T. K., Haavind, H., Gulbrandsen, W., Mossige, S., Reichelt, S., & Tjersland, O. A. (2010). What constitutes a good working alliance in therapy with children who may have been sexually abused? *Qualitative Social Work, 9,* 461–478.

Josselson, R. (1996). *The space between us: Exploring the dimensions of human relationships.* Thousand Oaks, CA: Sage.

Josselson, R. (2003). The space between in group psychotherapy: Application of a multidimensional model of relationship. *Group, 27,* 203–219.

Josselson, R., Lieblich, A., & McAdams, D. P. (Eds.). (2003). *Up close and personal: The teaching and learning of narrative research.* Washington, DC: American Psychological Association.

Kagan, N. (1984). Interpersonal process recall, basic methods and recent research. In D. Larsen (Ed.), *Teaching psychological skills* (pp. 229–244). Monterey, CA: Brooks/Cole.

Kazdin, A. E. (2006). Arbitrary metrics in psychology: implications for identifying evidence-based treatments. *American Psychologist, 61,* 42–49.

Khan, N., Bower, P., & Rogers, A. (2007), Guided self-help in primary care mental health. Meta-synthesis of qualitative studies of patient experience. British Journal of Psychiatry, *191,* 206–211.

Kincheloe, J. L., & McLaren, P. (2005). Rethinking critical theory and qualitative research. In N. K. Denzin & Y. S. Lincoln (Eds.), *The Sage handbook of qualitative research* (3rd ed., pp. 303–342). Thousand Oaks, CA: Sage.

Kincheloe, J. L., McLaren, P., & Steinberg, S. R. (2011). Critical pedagogy, and qualitative research: Moving to the bricolage. In N. K. Denzin & Y. S. Lincoln (Eds.), *The Sage handbook of qualitative research* (4th ed., pp. 163–178). Thousand Oaks, CA: Sage.

Klein, M. J., & Elliott, R. (2006). Client accounts of personal change in process-experiential psychotherapy: A methodologically pluralistic approach. *Psychotherapy Research, 16,* 91–105.

Knox, R. (2008). Clients' experiences of relational depth in person-centred counselling. *Counselling and Psychotherapy Research, 8,* 118–124.

Knox, R., & Cooper, M. (2010). Relationship qualities that are associated with moments of relational depth: The client's perspective. *Person-Centered and Experiential Psychotherapies, 9,* 236–256.

Knox, R., & Cooper, M. (2011). A state of readiness: An exploration of the client's role in meeting at relational depth. *Journal of Humanistic Psychology, 51,* 61–81.

Knox, S., & Burkard, A. W. (2009). Qualitative research interviews. *Psychotherapy Research, 19,* 566–575.

Knox, S., Adrians, N., Everson, E., Hess, S., Hill, C., & Crook-Lyon, R. (2011). Clients' perspectives on therapy termination. *Psychotherapy Research, 21,* 154–167.

Knox, S., Goldberg, J. L., Woodhouse, S. S., & Hill, C. E. (1999). Clients' internal representations of their therapists. *Journal of Counseling Psychology, 46,* 244–56.

Knox, S., Hess, S. A., Petersen, D. A., & Hill, C. E. (1997). A qualitative analysis of client perceptions of the effects of helpful therapist self-disclosure in long-term therapy. *Journal of Counseling Psychology, 44,* 274–283.

Kondratyuk, N., & Peräkylä, A. (2011). Therapeutic work with the present moment: A comparative conversation analysis of existential and cognitive therapies. *Psychotherapy Research, 21,* 316–330.

Kraus, D. R., Castonguay, L., Boswell, J. F., Nordberg, S. S., & Hayes, J. A. (2011). Therapist effectiveness: Implication for accountability and patient care. *Psychotherapy Research, 21,* 267–276.

Kuhnlein, I. (1999). Psychotherapy as a process of transformation: the analysis of posttherapeutic autobiographical narrations. *Psychotherapy Research, 9,* 274–288.

Kurri, K., & Wahlström, J. (2005). Placement of responsibility and moral reasoning in couple therapy. *Journal of Family Therapy, 27,* 357–369.

Kurri, K., & Wahlström, J. (2007). Reformulations of agentless talk in psychotherapy. *Text & Talk, 27,* 315–338.

Kuyken, W., Byford, S., Taylor, R. S., Watkins, E., Holden, E., White, K., . . . Teasdale, J. D. (2008). Mindfulness-based cognitive therapy to prevent relapse in recurrent depression. *Journal of Consulting & Clinical Psychology, 76,* 966–978.

Labov, W., & Fanshel, D. (1977). *Therapeutic discourse.* New York, NY: Academic Press.

Larsen, D., Flesaker, K., & Stege, R. (2008). Qualitative interviewing using interpersonal process recall: Investigating internal experiences during professional-client conversation. *International Journal of Qualitative Methods, 7,* 18–37.

Levitt, H., Korman, Y., & Angus, L. (2000). A metaphor analysis in treatments of depression: Metaphor as a marker of change. *Counselling Psychology Quarterly, 13,* 23–35.

Levitt, H. M., Butler, M., & Hill, T. (2006). What clients find helpful in psychotherapy: Developing principles for facilitating moment-to-moment change. *Journal of Counseling Psychology, 53,* 314–324.

Levitt, H. M., Neimeyer, R. A., & Williams, D. (2005). Rules versus principles in psychotherapy: Implications of the quest for universal guidelines in the movement for empirically supported treatments. *Journal of Contemporary Psychotherapy, 35,* 117–129.

Levitt, H. M., & Williams, D. C. (2010). Facilitating client change: Principles based upon the experience of eminent psychotherapists. *Psychotherapy Research, 20,* 337–352.

Lewis, J., Clark, D., & Morgan, D. (1992). *Whom God hath joined together: The work of marriage guidance.* London, United Kingdom: Routledge.

Lichtenthal, W., Currier, J. M., Neimeyer, R. A., & Keesee, N. J. (2010). Sense and significance: A mixed methods examination of meaning making after the loss of one's child. *Journal of Clinical Psychology, 66,* 791–812.

Lilliengren, P., & Werbart, A. (2005). A model of therapeutic action grounded in the patients' view of curative and hindering factors in psychoanalytic psychotherapy. *Psychotherapy: Theory, Research, Practice, Training, 3,* 324–399.

Lincoln, Y. S., Lynham, S. A., & Guba, E. G. (2011). Paradigmatic controversies, contradictions, and emerging confluences, revisited. In N. K. Denzin & Y. S. Lincoln (Eds.), *The Sage handbook of qualitative research* (4th ed., pp. 97–128). Thousand Oaks, CA: Sage.

Lock, A., & Strong, T. (2010). *Social constructionism: Sources and stirrings in theory and practice.* Cambridge, United Kingdom: Cambridge University Press.

Long, P. S., & Lepper, G. (2008). Metaphor in psychoanalytic psychotherapy: A comparative study of four cases by a practitioner-researcher. *British Journal of Psychotherapy, 24,* 343–364.

Luborsky, L., Diguer, L., & Seligman, D. A. (1999). The researcher's own therapy allegiances: A "wild card" in comparisons of treatment efficacy. *Clinical Psychology: Science and Practice, 6,* 95–106.

Luborsky, L., & Crits-Christoph, P. (Eds). (1990). *Understanding transference: The CCRT method.* New York, NY: Basic Books.

MacCormack, T., Simonian, J., Lim, J., Remond, L, Roets, D., Dunn, S., & Butow, P. (2001). "Someone who cares": A qualitative investigation of cancer patients' experiences of psychotherapy. *Psycho-Oncology, 10,* 52–65.

Macdonald, W., Mead, N., Bower, P., Richards, D., & Lovell, K. (2007). A qualitative study of patients' perceptions of a "minimal" psychological therapy. *International Journal of Social Psychiatry, 53,* 23–33.

Mackey, R. A., & Mackey, E. F. (1993). The value of personal psychotherapy to clinical practice. *Clinical Social Work Journal, 21,* 97–110.

Mackrill, T. (2008a). Exploring psychotherapy clients' independent strategies for change while in therapy. *British Journal of Guidance and Counselling, 36,* 441–453.

Mackrill, T. (2008b). Solicited diary studies of psychotherapeutic practice—Pros and cons. *European Journal of Psychotherapy and Counselling, 10,* 5–18.

Mackrill, T. (2009). A cross-contextual construction of clients' therapeutic practice. *Journal of Constructivist Psychology, 22,* 283–305.

Macran, S., Stiles, W. B., & Smith, J. A. (1999). How does personal therapy affect therapists' practice? *Journal of Counseling Psychology, 46,* 419–431.

Madill, A. (2006). Exploring psychotherapy with discourse analysis: Chipping away at the mortar. In C. T. Fischer (Ed.), *Qualitative research methods for psychologists: Introduction through empirical case studies* (pp. 23–58). San Diego, CA: Academic Press.

Madill, A., & Barkham, M. (1997). Discourse analysis of a theme in one successful case of brief psychodynamic-interpersonal psychotherapy. *Journal of Counseling Psychology, 44,* 232–244.

Madill, A., & Docherty, K. (1994). "So you did what you wanted then," discourse analysis, personal agency, and psychotherapy. *Journal of Community & Applied Social Psychology, 4,* 261–273.

Madill, A., & Gough, B. (2008). Qualitative research and its place in psychological science. *Psychological Methods, 13,* 254–271.

Madill, A., Jordan, A., & Shirley, C. (2000). Objectivity and reliability in qualitative analysis, realist, contextualist and radical constructionist epistemologies. *British Journal of Psychology, 91,* 1–20.

Madill, A., Widdicombe, S., & Barkham, M. (2001). The potential of conversation analysis for psychotherapy research. *Counseling Psychologist, 29,* 413–434.

Marecek, J. (2011). Numbers and interpretations: What is at stake in our ways of knowing? *Theory & Psychology, 21,* 220–240.

Mason, O., & Hargreaves, I. (2001). A qualitative study of mindfulness-based cognitive therapy for depression. *British Journal of Medical Psychology, 74,* 197–212.

McGowan, J. F., Lavender, T., & Garety, P. A. (2005). Factors in outcome of cognitive behavioural therapy for psychosis: Users' and clinicians' views. *Psychology and Psychotherapy: Theory, Research and Practice, 78,* 513–529.

McIlveen, P. (2007). The genuine scientist-practitioner in vocational psychology: an autoethnography. *Qualitative Research in Psychology, 4*, 295–311.

McKenna, P. A., & Todd, D. M. (1997). Longitudinal utilization of mental health services, a time-line method, nine retrospective accounts, and a preliminary conceptualization, *Psychotherapy Research, 7*, 383–396.

McLeod, J. (2001). An administrative reality: Some problems with the use of self-report questionnaire measures of adjustment in counselling/psychotherapy outcome research. *Counselling and Psychotherapy Research, 1*, 215–226.

McLeod, J. (2011). *Qualitative research in counselling and psychotherapy* (2nd ed.). London, United Kingdom: Sage.

McLeod, J., & Balamoutsou, S. (2000). Narrative process in the assimilation of a problematic experience: Qualitative analysis of a single case. *Zeitshcrift fur qualitative Bildungs - Beratungs - und Sozialforschung, 2*, 283–302.

McLeod, J., & Balamoutsou, S. (2001). A method for qualitative narrative analysis of psychotherapy transcripts. In J. Frommer & D. Rennie (Eds.), *Qualitative psychotherapy research: Methods and methodology* (pp. 18–35). Lengerich, Germany: Pabst.

McMillan, M., & McLeod, J. (2006). Letting go: The client's experience of relational depth. *Person-Centered & Experiential Psychotherapies, 5*, 277–293.

McMullen, L. M. (1999). Metaphors in the talk of "depressed" women in psychotherapy. *Canadian Psychology, 40*, 104–111.

Meekums, B. (2008). Embodied narratives in becoming a counselling trainer: An autoethnographic study. *British Journal of Guidance & Counselling, 36*, 287–301.

Meier, S. T. (2008). *Measuring change in counseling and psychotherapy*. New York, NY: Guilford Press.

Messari, S., & Hallam, R. (2003). CBT for psychosis: A qualitative analysis of clients' experiences. *British Journal of Clinical Psychology, 42*, 171–188.

Michell, J. (1999). *Measurement in psychology: Critical history of a methodological concept*. New York, NY: Cambridge University Press.

Michell, J. (2011). Qualitative research meets the ghost of Pythagoras. *Theory & Psychology, 21*, 241–259.

Miller, B. (2007). What creates and sustains commitment to the practice of psychotherapy? *Psychiatric Services, 58*, 174–176.

Miller, W. I., & Crabtree, B. F. (2005). Clinical research. In N. K. Denzin & Y. S. Lincoln (Eds.), *The Sage handbook of qualitative research* (3rd ed., pp. 605–640). Thousand Oaks, CA: Sage.

Moerman, M., & McLeod, J. (2006). Person-centred counselling for alcohol-related problems: The client's experience of self in the therapeutic relationship. *Person-Centered & Experiential Psychotherapies, 5*, 21–35.

Moertl, K., Gelo, O., & Pokorny, D. (in press). Qualitative methods in psychotherapy process research. In O. Gelo, A. Pritz, & B. Rieken (Eds.), *Psychotherapy research. General issues, outcome and process*. New York: Springer-Verlag.

Moller, N. P., Timms, J., & Alilovic, K. (2009). Risky business or safety net? Trainee perceptions of personal therapy: A qualitative thematic analysis. *European Journal of Psychotherapy, Counselling & Health, 11*, 369–384.

Morone, N. E., Lynch, C. S., Greco, C. M., Tindle, H. A., & Weiner, D. K. (2008). "I felt like a new person." The effects of mindfulness meditation on older adults with chronic pain: Qualitative narrative analysis of diary entries. *Journal of Pain, 9*, 841–848.

Morris, B. (2005). *Discovering bits and pieces of me: research exploring women's experiences of psychoanalytical psychotherapy*. London, United Kingdom: Women's Therapy Centre.

Morrow, S. L. (2005). Quality and trustworthiness in qualitative research in counselling psychology. *Journal of Counseling Psychology, 52*, 250–260.

Morrow, S. L. (2007). Qualitative research in counseling psychology: Conceptual foundations. *Counseling Psychologist, 35*, 209–235.

Mörtl, K., & Von Wietersheim, J. (2008). Client experiences of helpful factors in a day treatment program: A qualitative approach. *Psychotherapy Research, 18*, 281–293.

Mosher, J. K., & Stiles, W. B. (2009). Clients' assimilation of experiences of their therapists. *Psychotherapy, 46*, 432–447.

Moss, D., Waugh, M., & Barnes, R. (2008). A tool for life? Mindfulness as self-help or safe uncertainty. *International Journal of Qualitative Studies on Health and Well-Being, 3*, 132–142.

Moustakas, C. (1990). *Heuristic research: Design, methodology and applications*. Thousand Oaks, CA: Sage.

Moxnes, P. (2006). Group therapy as self-management training: A personal experience. *Group Analysis, 39*, 215–234.

Mruk, C. J. (2010). Integrated description: A qualitative method for an evidence-based world. *Humanistic Psychologist, 38*, 305–316.

Mueller-Vollmer, K. (Ed.). (1997). *The hermeneutics reader: Texts of the German tradition from the enlightenment to the present*. New York, NY: Continuum.

Munley, P. H., Anderson, M. Z., Briggs, D., Devries, M. R., Forshee, W. J., & Whisner, E. A. (2002). Methodological diversity of research published in selected psychology journals in 1999. *Psychological Reports, 91*, 411–420.

Muran, J. C., & Barber, J. P. (Eds.). (2010). *The therapeutic alliance. An evidence-based guide to practice*. New York, NY: Guilford Press.

Murphy, D. (2005). A qualitative study into the experience of mandatory personal therapy during training. *Counselling & Psychotherapy Research, 5,* 27–32.[1]

Myers, S. A., & White, C. M. (2010). The abiding nature of empathic connections: A 10-year follow-up study. *Journal of Humanistic Psychology, 50,* 77–95.

Nelson, J. S., Megill, A., & McCloskey, D. (Eds.). (1987). *The rhetoric of the human sciences: Language and argument in scholarship and public affairs.* Madison: University of Wisconsin Press.

Nerdrum, P., & Rønnestad, M. H. (2002). The trainees' perspective: A qualitative study of learning empathic communication in Norway. *Counseling Psychologist, 30,* 609–629.

Nilsson, T., Svensson, M., Sandell, R., & Clinton, D. (2007). Patients' experiences of change on cognitive-behavioral therapy and psychodynamic therapy: A qualitative comparative study. *Psychotherapy Research, 17,* 553–566.

O'Connor, T. S., Meakes, E., Pickering, R., & Schuman, M. (1997). On the right track: Client experience of narrative therapy. *Contemporary Family Therapy, 19,* 479–496.

O'Donohue, W., Cummings, N., & Cummings, J. (Eds). (2006). *Clinical strategies for becoming a master therapist.* New York, NY: Academic Press.

O'Neill, P. (1998). *Negotiating consent in psychotherapy.* New York, NY: New York University Press.

Orlinsky, D. E., Norcross, J. C., Rønnestad, M. H., & Wiseman, H. (2005). Outcomes and impacts of the psychotherapists' own psychotherapy: A research review. In J. D. Geller, J. C. Norcross, & D. E. Orlinsky (Eds.), *The psychotherapist's own psychotherapy* (pp. 214–230). New York, NY: Oxford University Press.

Osatuke, K., & Stiles, W. B. (2011). Numbers in assimilation research. *Theory & Psychology, 21,* 200–219.

Osborn, M., & Smith, J. A. (2008). The fearfulness of chronic pain and the centrality of the therapeutic relationship in containing it: An interpretative phenomenological analysis. *Qualitative Research in Psychology, 5,* 276–288.

Packer, M., & Addison, R. B. (Eds.). (1989). *Entering the circle, hermeneutic investigation in psychology.* Albany, NY: State University of New York Press.

Parker, I. (1994). Reflexive research and the grounding of analysis, social psychology and the psy-complex. *Journal of Community and Applied Social Psychology, 4,* 239–252.

Parker, I. (2004). Criteria for qualitative research in psychology. *Qualitative Research in Psychology, 1,* 95–106.

Partanen, T., Wahlström, J., & Holma, J. (2006). Loss of self-control as an excuse in group-therapy conversations for intimately violent men. *Communication & Medicine, 3,* 171–183.

Paterson, B. L., Dubouloz, C. Chevrier, J., Hull, G., Ashe, B. King, J., & Moldoveanu, M. (2009). Conducting qualitative metasynthesis research: Insights from a metasynthesis project. *International Journal of Qualitative Methods, 8,* 22–33.

Peglidou, A. (2010). Therapeutic itineraries of "depressed" women in Greece: Power relationships and agency in therapeutic pluralism. *Anthropology & Medicine, 17,* 41–57.

Peräkylä, A. (1995). *AIDS counselling, institutional interaction and clinical practice.* Cambridge, United Kingdom: Cambridge University Press.

Peräkylä, A. (2004). Making links in psychoanalytic interpretations: A conversation analysis perspective. *Psychotherapy Research, 14,* 289–307.

Peräkylä, A., & Silverman, D. (1991). Reinterpreting speech-exchange systems, communication formats in AIDS counselling. *Sociology, 25,* 627–651.

Peräkylä, A., Antaki, C., Vehvilainen, S., & Leudar, I. (Eds.). (2008). *Conversation analysis and psychotherapy.* Cambridge, United Kingdom: Cambridge University Press.

Perelman, C. H. (1982). *The realm of rhetoric.* Notre Dame, IN: University of Notre Dame Press.

Perren, S., Godfrey, M., & Rowland, N. (2009). The long-term effects of counselling: The process and mechanisms that contribute to ongoing change from a user perspective. *Counselling & Psychotherapy Research, 9,* 241–249.

Perseius, K.-I., Öjehagen, A., Ekdahl, S., Åsberg, M., & Samuelsson, M. (2003). Treatment of suicidal and deliberate self-harming patients with borderline personality disorder using dialectical behavioral therapy: The patients' and the therapists' perceptions. *Archives of Psychiatric Nursing, 17,* 218–227.

Philips, B., Wennberg, P., & Werbart, A. (2007). Ideas of cure as a predictor of premature termination, early alliance and outcome in psychoanalytic psychotherapy. *Psychology and Psychotherapy: Theory, Research and Practice, 80,* 229–245.

Philips, B., Werbart, A., Wennberg, P., & Schubert, J. (2007). Young adults' ideas of cure prior to psychoanalytic psychotherapy. *Journal of Clinical Psychology, 63,* 213–232.

Phillips, A., & Daniluk, J. C. (2004). Beyond "survivor": How childhood sexual abuse informs the identity of adult women at the end of the therapeutic process. *Journal of Counseling & Development, 82,* 177–184.

Polkinghorne, D. E. (1988). *Narrative knowing and the human sciences.* Albany: State University of New York Press.

Ponterotto, J. G. (2005). Qualitative research in counseling psychology: A primer on research paradigms and philosophy of science. *Journal of Counseling Psychology, 52,* 126–136.

Ponterotto, J. G., & Grieger, I. (2007). Effectively communicating qualitative research. *Counseling Psychologist, 35,* 404–430.

Poulsen, S. (2004). De-privatization: Client experience of short-term dynamic group psychotherapy. *Group, 28,* 31–50.

Poulsen, S., Lunn, S., & Sandros, C. (2010). Client experience of psychodynamic psychotherapy for bulimia nervosa. *Psychotherapy Theory, Research, Practice, Training, 47,* 469–483.

Preissle, J. (2006). Envisioning qualitative inquiry: A view across four decades. *International Journal of Qualitative Studies in Education, 19,* 685–695.

Proulx, K. (2008). Experiences of women with bulimia nervosa in a mindfulness-based eating disorder treatment group. *Eating Disorders, 16,* 52–72.

Råbu, M., Halvorsen, M. S., & Haavind, H. (2011). Early relationship struggles: A case study of alliance formation and reparation. *Counselling & Psychotherapy Research, 11,* 23–33.

Rake, C., & Paley, G. (2009). Personal therapy for psychotherapists: The impact on therapeutic practice. *A qualitative study using interpretative phenomenological analysis. Psychodynamic Practice, 15,* 275–294.

Rasmussen, B. (2000). Poetic truths and clinical reality: Client experiences of the use of metaphor by therapists. *Smith College Studies in Social Work, 27,* 355–373.

Rasmussen, B., & Angus, L. (1996). Metaphor in psychodynamic psychotherapy with borderline and non-borderline clients: A qualitative analysis. *Psychotherapy, 33,* 521–530.

Rautiainen, E., & Seikkula, J. (2009). Clients as co-researchers: How do couples evaluate couple therapy for depression? *Journal of Systemic Therapies, 28,* 41–60.

Rayner, K., Thompson, A. R., & Walsh, S. (2011). Clients' experience of the process of change in cognitive analytic therapy. *Psychology and Psychotherapy: Theory, Research and Practice, 84,* 299–313

Rennie, D. (1998). *Person-centred counselling: An experiential approach.* London, United Kingdom: Sage.

Rennie, D. L. (1994a). Clients' deference in psychotherapy. *Journal of Counseling Psychology, 41,* 427–437.

Rennie, D. L. (1994b). Storytelling in psychotherapy, the client's subjective experience. *Psychotherapy, 31,* 234–243.

Rennie, D. L. (1994c). Clients' accounts of resistance in counselling, a qualitative analysis. *Canadian Journal of Counselling, 28,* 43–57.

Rennie, D. L. (1994d). Strategic choices in a qualitative approach to psychotherapy process research, a personal account. In L. Hoshmand & J. Martin (Eds.), *Method choice and inquiry process, Lessons from programmatic research in therapeutic psychology* (pp. 198–220). New York, NY: Teachers Press.

Rennie, D. L. (1995). On the rhetorics of social science, lets not conflate natural science and human science. *Humanistic Psychologist, 23,* 321–332.

Rennie, D. L. (2000a). Experiencing psychotherapy, grounded theory studies. In D. Cain & J. Seeman (Eds.), *Handbook of research in humanistic psychotherapies* (pp. 117–144). Washington, DC: American Psychological Association.

Rennie, D. L. (2000b). Grounded theory methodology as methodological hermeneutics, reconciling realism and relativism. *Theory and Psychology, 10,* 481–502.

Rennie, D. L., Phillips, J. R., & Quartaro, J. K. (1988). Grounded theory, a promising approach for conceptualization in psychology? *Canadian Psychology, 29,* 139–150.

Rennie, D. L., Watson, K. D., & Monteiro, A. (2002). The rise of qualitative research in psychology. *Canadian Psychology, 43,* 179–189.

Rescher, N. (1993). *Pluralism: Against the demand for consensus.* Oxford, United Kingdom: Oxford University Press.

Rizq, R., & Target, M. (2008a). "Not a little Mickey Mouse thing": How experienced counselling psychologists describe the significance of personal therapy in clinical practice and training. Some results from an interpretative phenomenological analysis. *Counselling Psychology Quarterly, 21,* 29–48.

Rizq, R., & Target, M. (2008b). "The power of being seen": An interpretative phenomenological analysis of how experienced counselling psychologists describe the meaning and significance of personal therapy in clinical practice. *British Journal of Guidance & Counselling, 36,* 131–153.

Rober, P., Van Eesbeek, D., & Elliott, R. (2006). Talking about violence: A micro-analysis of narrative processes in a family therapy session. *Journal of Marital & Family Therapy, 32,* 313–338.

Roberts, J. (1996). Perceptions of the significant other of the effects of psychodynamic psychotherapy, implications for thinking about psycho-dynamic and systems approaches. *British Journal of Psychiatry, 168,* 87–93.

Roe, D., Dekel, R., Harel, G., Fennig, S., & Fennig, S. (2006). Clients' feelings during termination of psychodynamically oriented psychotherapy. *Bulletin of the Menninger Clinic, 70,* 68–81.

Rønnestad, M. H., & Skovholt, T. M. (2003). The journey of the counselor and therapist: Research findings and perspectives on professional development. *Journal of Career Development, 30,* 5–44.

Rønnestad, M. H., & Skovholt, T. M. (2012). *The developing practitioner: Growth and stagnation of therapists and counselors.* New York, NY: Routledge.

Rorty, R. (1980). *Philosophy and the mirror of nature.* Oxford, United Kingdom: Blackwell.

Rosnow, R. L., & Rosenthal, R. (1997). *People studying people: Artifacts and ethics in behavioural research.* New York, NY: Freeman.

Safran, J. D., & Muran, J. C. (2006). Has the concept of the therapeutic alliance outlived its usefulness? *Psychotherapy: Theory, Research, Practice, Training, 43,* 286–291.

Schielke, H. J., Fishman, J. L., Osatuke, K., & Stiles, W. B. (2009). Creative consensus on interpretations of qualitative data: The Ward method. *Psychotherapy Research, 19,* 558–565.

Schnellbacher, J., & Leijssen, M. (2009). The significance of therapist genuineness from the client's perspective. *Journal of Humanistic Psychology, 49,* 207–228.

Seikkula, J., & Arnkil, T. E. (2006). *Dialogical meetings in social networks.* London, United Kingdom: Karnac.

Sela-Smith, S. (2002). Heuristic research: A review and critique of Moustakas's method. *Journal of Humanistic Psychology, 42,* 53–88.

Shinebourne, P., & Smith, J. A. (2010). The communicative power of metaphors: An analysis and interpretation of metaphors in accounts of the experience of addiction. *Psychology and Psychotherapy: Theory, Research and Practice, 83,* 59–73.

Skovholt, T. M., & Jennings, L. (2004). *Master therapists: Exploring expertise in therapy and counseling.* New York, NY: Allyn & Bacon

Skovholt, T. M., & Rønnestad, M. H. (1995). *The evolving professional self: Stages and themes in therapist and counselor development.* Chichester, United Kingdom: Wiley.

Skovholt, T. M., & Rønnestad, M. H. (2003). Struggles of the novice counselor and therapist. *Journal of Career Development, 13,* 45–58.

Skovholt, T. M., Rønnestad, M. H., & Jennings, L. (1997). Searching for expertise in counseling, psychotherapy and professional psychology. *Educational Psychology Review, 9,* 361–369.

Slife, B. D. (2004). Theoretical challenges to therapy practice and research: the constraint of naturalism. In M. J. Lambert (Ed.), *Bergin and Lambert's handbook of psychotherapy and behavior change* (pp. 44–83). Hoboken, NJ: Wiley.

Smith, A., Graham, L., & Senthinathan, S. (2007). Mindfulness-based cognitive therapy for recurring depression in older people: A qualitative study. *Aging & Mental Health, 11,* 346–357.

Smith, I. C. (2011). A qualitative investigation into the effects of brief training in solution-focused therapy in a social work team. *Psychology and Psychotherapy: Theory, Research and Practice, 84,* 335–348.

Smith, J. A., Flowers, P., & Larkin, M. (2009). *Interpretative phenomenological analysis: Theory, method and research.* London, United Kingdom: Sage.

Speedy, J. (2008). *Narrative inquiry and psychotherapy.* Basingstoke, United Kingdom: Palgrave Macmillan.

Stelter, R. (2009). Experiencing mindfulness meditation: A client narrative perspective. *International Journal of Qualitative Studies on Health & Well-Being, 4,* 145–158.

Stiles, W. B. (1993). Quality control in qualitative research. *Clinical Psychology Review, 13,* 593–618.

Stiles, W. B. (2002). Assimilation of problematic experiences. In J. C. Norcross (Ed.), *Psychotherapy relationships that work* (pp. 357–365), New York, NY: Oxford University Press.

Stiles, W. B., & Angus, L. (2000). Qualitative research on clients' assimilation of problematic experiences in psychotherapy. In J. Frommer & D. L. Rennie (Eds.), *Qualitative Psychotherapy Research, Methods and Methodology* (pp. 111–126). Berlin, Germany: Pabst.

Stiles, W. B., & Goldsmith, J. Z. (2010). The alliance over time. In J. C. Muran & J. P. Barber (Eds.), *The therapeutic alliance: An evidence-based approach to practice* (pp. 44–62). New York, NY: Guilford Press.

Stiles, W. B., Leiman, M., Shapiro, D. A., Hardy, G. E., Barkham, M., Detert, N. B., & Llewelyn, S. P. (2006). What does the first exchange tell? Dialogical sequence analysis and assimilation in very brief therapy. *Psychotherapy Research, 16,* 408–421.

Strong, T., & Pyle, N. R. (2009). Constructing a conversational "miracle": Examining the "miracle question" as it is used in therapeutic dialogue. *Journal of Constructivist Psychology, 22,* 328–353.

Strong, T., Zeman, D., & Foskett, A. (2006). Introducing new discourses into counselling interactions: A microanalytic and retrospective examination. *Journal of Constructivist Psychology, 19,* 67–89.

Suoninen, E., & Wahlström, J. (2009). Interactional positions and the production of identities: Negotiating fatherhood in family therapy talk. *Communication and Medicine, 6,* 199–209.

Suzuki, L. A., Ahluwalia, M. K., Mattis, J. S., & Quizon, C. A. (2005). Ethnography in counseling psychology research: Possibilities for application. *Journal of Counseling Psychology, 52,* 206–214.

Svanborg, C., Bäärnhielm, S., Wistedt, A. A., & Lützen, K. (2008). Helpful and hindering factors for remission in dysthymia and panic disorder at 9-year follow-up: A mixed methods study. *BMC Psychiatry, 8,* 52. http://www.biomedcentral.com/1471-244X/8/52

Taylor, C. (1971). Interpretation and the sciences of man, *Review of Metaphysics, 25,* 3–51.

Teo, T. (1998). Klaus Holzkamp and the rise and decline of German critical psychology. *History of Psychology, 1,* 235–253.

Thompson, V. L. S., Bazile, A., & Akbar, M. (2004). African Americans' perceptions of psychotherapy and psychotherapists. *Professional Psychology: Research and Practice, 35,* 19–26.

Thurston, M. (2010). An enquiry into the emotional impact of sight loss and the counselling experiences and needs of blind and partially sighted adults. *Counselling & Psychotherapy Research, 10,* 3–12.

Timulak, L. (2007). Identifying core categories of client identified impact of helpful events in psychotherapy—A qualitative meta-analysis. *Psychotherapy Research, 17,* 305–314.

Timulak, L. (2009). Meta-analysis of qualitative studies: A tool for reviewing research findings in psychotherapy. *Psychotherapy Research, 19,* 591–600.

Timulak, L. (2010). Significant events in psychotherapy: An update of research findings. *Psychology and Psychotherapy: Theory, Research and Practice, 83,* 421–447.

Timulak, L., & Creaner, M. (2010). Qualitative meta-analysis of outcomes of person-centered and experiential psychotherapies. In M. Cooper, J. C. Watson, & D. Holldampf (Eds.), *Person-centered and experiential therapies work. A review of the research on counseling, psychotherapy and related practices* (pp. 65–90). Ross-on-Wye, United Kingdom: PCCS Books.

Tolman, C. W. (2009). Holzkamp's critical psychology as a science from the standpoint of the human subject. *Theory & Psychology, 19*, 149–160.

Valkonen, J., Hanninen, V., & Lindfors, O. (2011). Outcomes of psychotherapy from the perspective of the users. *Psychotherapy Research, 21*, 227–240.

Van den Hoonard, W. C. (2002). *Walking the tightrope: Ethical issues for qualitative researchers.* Toronto, Canada: University of Toronto Press.

Viklund, E., Holmqvist, R., & Nelson, K. Z. (2010). Client-identified important events in psychotherapy: Interactional structures and practices. *Psychotherapy Research, 20*, 151–164.

Waldram, J. B. (2007). Narrative and the construction of "truth" in a prison-based treatment program for sexual offenders. *Ethnography, 8*, 145–160.

Wallcraft, J., Schrank, B., & Amering, M. (Eds.). (2009). *Handbook of service user involvement in mental health research.* Oxford, United Kingdom: Wiley-Blackwell.

Ward, E. C. (2005). Keeping it real: A grounded theory study of African American clients engaged in counseling at a community mental health agency. *Journal of Counseling Psychology, 52*, 471–481.

Watson, J. C., & Rennie, D. L. (1994). Qualitative analysis of clients subjective experience of significant moments during the exploration of problematic reactions. *Journal of Counseling Psychology, 41*, 500–509.

Wertz, F. J. (2005). Phenomenological research methods for counseling psychology. *Journal of Counseling Psychology, 52*, 167–177.

Westerman, M. A. (2011). Conversation analysis and interpretive quantitative research on psychotherapy process and problematic interpersonal behavior. *Theory & Psychology, 21*, 155–178.

Williams, D. C., & Levitt, H. M. (2007a). Principles for facilitating agency in psychotherapy. *Psychotherapy Research, 17*, 66–82.

Williams, D. C., & Levitt, H. M. (2007b). A qualitative investigation of eminent therapists' values within psychotherapy: Developing integrative principles for moment-to-moment psychotherapy practice. *Journal of Psychotherapy Integration, 17*, 159–184.

Williams, E. N., & Hill, C. E. (2012). Establishing trustworthiness in consensual qualitative research studies. In C. E. Hill (Ed.), *Consensual qualitative research. A practical resource for investigating social science phenomena* (pp. 175–186). Washington, DC: American Psychological Association.

Williams, E. N., & Morrow, S. L. (2009). Achieving trustworthiness in qualitative research: A pan-paradigmatic perspective. *Psychotherapy Research, 19*, 576–582.

Wiseman, H., & Shefler, G. (2001). Experienced psychoanalytically oriented therapists' narrative accounts of their personal therapy: Impacts on professional and personal development. *Psychotherapy: Theory, Research, Practice, Training, 38*, 129–141.

Woody, W. D., & Viney, W. (2009). A pluralistic universe: An overview and implications for psychology. *Journal of Mind & Behavior, 30*, 107–110.

York, M. (2007). A qualitative study into the experience of individuals involved in a mindfulness group within an acute inpatient mental health unit. *Journal of Psychiatric and Mental Health Nursing, 14*, 603–608.

Young, K., & Cooper, S. (2008). Toward co-composing an evidence base: The narrative therapy re-visiting project. *Journal of Systemic Therapies, 27*, 67–83.

CHAPTER 4

PRACTICE-ORIENTED RESEARCH
Approaches and Applications

LOUIS CASTONGUAY, MICHAEL BARKHAM, WOLFGANG LUTZ,
AND ANDREW MCALEAVEY

There are many controversies in the field of psychotherapy. Numerous debates remain ongoing, for example, about what treatments are (or are not) effective for certain disorders and what variables are responsible for change. Although these debates are of great conceptual and clinical significance, they fade in comparison to the gravity of the schism that is at the core of clinical and counseling psychology. While these disciplines, as well as many training programs in other mental health professions, are based on the scientist-practitioner model, it is well documented that psychotherapists are not frequently and substantially influenced by empirical findings when they conduct their case formulations, treatment plan, and implementations (e.g., Cohen, Sargent, & Sechrest, 1986; Morrow-Bradley & Elliott, 1986).

There are a number of ways to explain the apparent indifference of clinicians toward psychotherapy research. To begin with, many scientific investigations are perceived as being limited in terms of their clinical relevance. The emphasis on internal validity, especially in traditional randomized controlled trials (RCTs), has sometimes come at a cost in terms of external validity. For instance, the focus on setting, a priori, the number of sessions and inclusion/exclusion criteria, among other constraints required for controlled research, may well reduce

error variance. However, the generalization of the findings to everyday practice is not always clear-cut (for further elaboration see Chapters 1, 3, and 14, this volume). It has also been argued that researchers pay limited attention to the concerns that therapists have when working with their clients (Beutler, Williams, Wakefield, & Entwistle, 1995). As described elsewhere (Castonguay, Boswell, et al., 2010), this could be viewed as a consequence or a reflection of "empirical imperialism" that has prevailed in many programs of research in which individuals who see very few clients per week decide what should be studied and how it should be investigated, to understand and facilitate the process of change.

The argument has also been made that clinicians would pay more attention to research findings if they were involved in research (e.g., Elliott & Morrow-Bradley, 1994). However, a number of obstacles can interfere with such involvement. Many therapists conducted research projects during graduate training that were unrelated to their clinical work. Similarly, not every clinician had the opportunity to work with an advisor who was conducting research while also treating psychotherapy clients of their own. Consequently, many clinicians lacked an early-career model based on conducting scientifically rigorous and clinically relevant studies that would then help them identify questions that could make a difference in their clinical work, or to help identify the most appropriate methods to investigate these questions. Full-time clinicians, even those

The authors are most grateful for the tremendous help provided by Soo Jeong Youn in preparing this chapter.

who were mentored by ideal scholars, are also confronted with pragmatic obstacles that can seriously interfere with an involvement in research, such as limited time, lack of resources, and difficulties in keeping up-to-date with methodological and statistical advances.

Needless to say, many have lamented over the gap between science and practice, and, over the six decades since the inception of the scientific-practitioner model (Raimy, 1950), several efforts have been made to foster and/or repair this concept (e.g., Soldz & McCullogh, 2000; Talley, Strupp, & Butler, 1994). The various avenues that are currently being promoted (and debated) to define evidence-based practice reflect a resurgence of the need to build stronger links between research and practice (e.g., Goodheart, Kazdin, & Sternberg, 2006; Norcross, Beutler, & Levant, 2006). Interestingly, it could also be argued that the current attention given to evidence-based practice has been triggered by the delineation and advocacy of empirically supported treatments (ESTs; Chambless & Ollendick, 2001). Although several scholars have warned that the promulgation of ESTs could deepen the schism between research and clinicians (e.g., Elliott, 1998), there seems to be no doubt that the EST movement has galvanized diverse efforts to foster the use of empirical information in the conduct of clinical tasks.

Directly related to the EST movement are the empirical investigations that have been conducted to test whether treatments shown to be effective under the stringent criteria of controlled trials also work when delivered in naturalistic settings. These effectiveness, as opposed to efficacy, studies are guided by the rationale that scientific advances will improve mental health care if it can be demonstrated that effective treatments (i.e., yielding large effect sizes) for specific and debilitating problems can be implemented and adopted in routine clinical care (Tai et al., 2010). A related effort has been the publication of important books and articles aimed at disseminating the research findings on ESTs, with the goal of offering a list of "treatments that work" (e.g., Nathan & Gorman, 2002). Complementing such publications are a large number of books describing how clinicians can apply specific ESTs. In fact, a number of these well known books are published versions of treatment manuals that have been used in clinical trials (e.g., Beck, Rush, Shaw, & Emery, 1979; Klerman, Weissman, Rounsaville, & Chevron, 1984). As argued elsewhere (Castonguay, Schut,

Constantino, & Halperin, 1999), such treatment manuals provide specific guidelines for interventions that can be extremely helpful to clinicians, as long as they are not imposed as the only form of therapy to be reimbursed. Nor that they are prescribed or used rigidly without being individualized to the needs of particular clients, and without consideration of other empirical data that can help foster process and outcome.

In response to the effort to bring science into practice via the validation and dissemination of specific treatments for particular disorders, came other initiatives emphasizing different variables and methodologies. These included the task forces on empirically supported therapeutic relationships (Norcross, 2011) and empirically based principles of change (Castonguay & Beutler, 2005a). The books that emerged from these task forces not only review the literature about variables related to the client and relationship, but also offer clinical guidelines derived from the empirical literature. In addition, noteworthy contributions (e.g., texts by Cooper [2008] and Lebow [2006]), have successfully taken on the challenge of presenting, without jargon, how research findings can be used in clinical practice.

Even though the efforts reported above focus on different variables and rely on different avenues of dissemination, they all share a top-down approach: that is, science is transmitted, and potentially adopted, via researchers informing therapists about the issues that have been studied and the lessons that can be derived from the findings. For example, in the United Kingdom some of these findings, derived from traditional RCTs and related meta-analytic studies, largely determine the national treatment guidelines to which practitioners and services are required to adhere. In this chapter, we refer to these efforts as manifestations of the paradigm of evidence-based practice. Although such efforts have and will continue to provide useful information to therapists, they nevertheless all reflect a more or less benign form of empirical imperialism.

One possible way to avoid or reduce empirical imperialism is for clinicians to be actively engaged in the design and/or implementation of research protocols. Such *practice-orientated research*, conducted not only for but also, at least in some way, by clinicians, reflects a bottom-up approach to building and using scientific knowledge. This approach is likely to create new pathways of connections between science and practice, both in terms of process and outcome. By fostering a sense of shared ownership and mutual collaboration between researchers and clinicians (e.g., in deciding what data to collect and/or how to collect it), this actionable approach can build on complementary expertise, compensate for limitations of knowledge and experience, and thus foster new ways of conducting and investigating psychotherapy. By emerging directly from the context in which therapists are working, practice-oriented research is likely to be intrinsically relevant to their concerns and can optimally "confound" research and practice: that is, when the design of studies leads clinicians to perform activities that are simultaneously and intrinsically serving both clinical and scientific purposes.

The primary goal of this chapter is to describe three main approaches within the overarching paradigm of practice-oriented research: *patient-focused research*, *practice-based evidence*, and *practice research networks*. All three approaches share commonalities, the most notable being the collection of data within naturalistic settings. However, they also represent, in the order that they are presented in this chapter, a gradual variation on two crucial dimensions: first, in terms of the focus of research knowledge (from very specific to very broad), and second, in terms of active involvement of practitioners in the design, implementation, and dissemination of research. Although this chapter does not stand as a comprehensive review, it provides examples of psychotherapy studies that have been conducted within each of the three approaches highlighted and their application to practice. The chapter also briefly addresses some additional lines of inquiry that are aimed at fostering the link between research and practice.

We hasten to say that we do not view the strategies of accumulation and dissemination of empirical knowledge described in this chapter (i.e., practice-oriented research) as being superior to those typically associated with the evidence-based practice movement. Rather, we would argue for adopting a position of equipoise between these two complementary paradigms. Although traditional RCTs are often viewed as the gold standard within a hierarchy of evidence, this position has been challenged: "The notion that evidence can be reliably placed in hierarchies is illusory. Hierarchies place RCTs on an undeserved pedestal, for . . . although the technique has advantages it also has significant disadvantages"

(Rawlins, 2008).[1] And in relation to the potential of practice-based evidence, Kazdin (2008) has written that "[W]e are letting the knowledge from practice drip through the holes of a colander." The *colander effect* is a salutary reminder of the richness of data that is potentially collectable but invariably lost every day from routine practice. A position of equipoise would advocate that neither paradigm alone—evidence-based practice or practice-oriented research—is able to yield a robust knowledge base for the psychological therapies. Furthermore, it is important to recognize that the methods typically associated with these approaches are not mutually exclusive. As we describe later, for example, RCTs have been designed and implemented within the context of practice research networks. Hence, rather than viewing these two approaches as dichotomous, a robust knowledge-base needs to be considered as a chiasmus that delivers *evidence-based practice and practice-oriented evidence* (Barkham & Margison, 2007).

PATIENT-FOCUSED RESEARCH

This section on patient-focused research has the goal of presenting one way of thinking about the scientist-practitioner gap from a scientist's as well as a practitioner's perspective. The main tool to achieve this goal is the careful study of patterns of patient change as well as tracking individual patients' progress over the course of treatment and feeding back the actual treatment progress into clinical practice. Patient-focused research provides tools in order to support, but *not* replace, clinical decision-making with actual ongoing research data and specially developed decision support tools. The goal is, for example, to identify negative and positive developments early on in treatment and then to feed these back to therapists so they can combine science and practice immediately during the ongoing treatment. This is akin to physicians using lab test data and vital sign measures to manage physical ailments such as diabetes (see Lambert, 2010).

Importantly, the models discussed in this section are based on a generic approach to psychotherapy. Psychotherapies are viewed as a class of treatments defined by overlapping techniques, mechanisms, and proposed outcomes. Outcomes

---

[1] Sir Michael Rawlins has been Chairman of the United Kingdom's National Institute for Health and Clinical Excellence (NICE) since its inception in 1999.

are measured by summing items related to many disorders. Instead of identifying particular treatments for particular diagnoses as is the case in clinical trials, patient-focused research focuses more on the (real time) improvement of the actual treatment as implemented and the development of tools in order to achieve that task (Lutz, 2002). Overall, it supports a research perspective more focused on outcomes and the improvement of actual clinical practice based on empirical knowledge and less based on a debate about therapeutic schools (e.g., Goldfried, 1984; Grawe, 1997). Accordingly, the core of this approach requires research to be conducted on the course of patient change for individual clients/patients to learn about differences in patient change as well as subgroups of patients with specific patterns of change.

To date, the field of psychotherapy research has studied different types of psychopathology and accumulated a large amount of knowledge in terms of specific treatments for particular diagnostic subgroups (e.g., Barlow, 2007; Nathan & Gorman, 2002; Schulte, 1998). However, considerably less is known about different types of patient change. This situation is puzzling given that research has provided support for patient variability as a substantial source in explaining outcome variance, which Norcross and Lambert (2012) have estimated to be in the region of 30%. In contrast, treatment techniques have been reported as explaining only a small portion of the outcome variance (e.g., Lambert & Ogles, 2004; Wampold, 2001). Accordingly, careful examinations of how and when patients progress during treatment, or fail to do so, may both increase our understanding of psychotherapy and provide us with tools that could improve its effectiveness.

The following section is organized in three parts. First, a short introduction sets out the history of patient-focused research (dosage and phase models of therapeutic progress). Second, the main focus and themes of patient-focused research are described and discussed (rationally and empirically derived methods, nearest neighbors techniques, and new ways of detecting patterns of patient change and variability). And finally, the evidence-base for applying these methods to yield feedback to therapists is considered.

Dosage and Phase Models of Therapeutic Progress

The theoretical origins of patient-focused psychotherapy research, often described in the

literature as the "expected treatment response model," are the dosage and phase models of psychotherapy. The dosage model of psychotherapeutic effectiveness established a positive, but negatively accelerating, relationship between the number of sessions (dose) and the probability of patient improvement (effect) such that increased number of sessions is associated with diminishing returns (Howard, Kopta, Krause, & Orlinsky, 1986). In subsequent work, Howard, Lueger, Maling, and Martinovich (1993) as well as Kadera, Lambert, and Andrews (1996) interpreted findings as representing rapid improvement early in treatment while in later phases increasing numbers of sessions were needed to reach a higher percentage of changed patients (see also Chapter 6, this volume). For instance, Howard et al. (1986), analyzing data on 2,431 patients from 15 studies, found that after 2 sessions 30% of patients had shown positive results. The percentages increased to 41% after 4 sessions, 53% after 8 sessions, and 75% after 26 sessions. In an extended analysis, Lambert, Hansen, and Finch (2001), using survival statistics and a more refined clinically significant change criteria, showed that these rates of improvement were overestimates of the speed of improvement and were dependent on patients' pretreatment functioning. Their results showed that 50% of the patients who were in the dysfunctional range before treatment needed 21 sessions of treatment to reach the criteria for clinically significant change. However, for 70% of patients in the dysfunctional range to reach clinically significant change, more than 35 sessions were necessary. Further research has shown differential patient change rates by diagnosis and symptoms (Barkham et al., 1996; Kopta, Howard, Lowry, & Beutler, 1994; Maling, Gurtman, & Howard, 1995). In addition, Hansen, Lambert, and Forman (2002) reported that in clinical practice success rates are lower when treatment plans do not allow for enough sessions. Hence, a variety of factors will impact on the rate of change for each individual patient. An extension of this line of research can be seen in the good-enough level of change concept (e.g., Barkham et al., 2006; Stiles, Barkham, Connell, & Mellor-Clark, 2008; see later in this chapter).

The phase model further amplifies the dose-effect model by focusing on which specific dimensions of outcome are changing and in what temporal sequence (Howard et al., 1993). It proposes three sequential and progressive phases of the therapeutic recovery process and assumes sequential improvement in the following areas of patient change: (1) *remoralization*, the enhancement of well-being; (2) *remediation*, the achievement of symptomatic relief; and (3) *rehabilitation*, the reduction of maladaptive behaviors, cognitions, and interpersonal problems that interfere with current life functioning (e.g., self-management, work, family, and partner relationships). In applying the dose-effect and phase models to therapeutic change, the decelerating curve of improvement can be related to the increasing difficulty of achieving treatment goals over the course of psychotherapy. Moreover, a causal relationship between changes in these dimensions was proposed with the phase model. That is, improvement in well-being is assumed to be necessary, but not sufficient, for a reduction of symptoms, which is assumed to be necessary for the subsequent enhancement in life functioning (cf. Stulz & Lutz, 2007).

In a replication study, Stulz and Lutz (2007) identified three patient subgroups on the basis of their development over the course of treatment in the dimensions of the phase model. In all of these subgroups, well-being increased most rapidly, followed by symptom reduction, while improvement in life-functioning was slowest. This finding supports the notion of differential change sensitivity for the three dimensions. Further, approximately two thirds of cases were consistent with the predicted temporal sequencing of phases (i.e., well-being to symptoms to functioning). However, a smaller but significant proportion of patients, approximately 30%, violated at least one of the two predicted sequences (e.g., moving directly from well-being to functioning). In addition, results suggested that the phase model seemed to be less powerful in describing treatment progress among more severely disturbed patients. A similar finding was also reported by Joyce, Ogrodniczuk, Piper, and McCallum (2002). In light of the earlier findings, further refinement focusing on differential change sequences between individuals is important.

Patient-Focused Research and Expected Treatment Response

The dosage and phase models define the process of recovery in psychotherapy for an average patient. However, patterns of improvement for individuals can vary significantly from the general trend (Krause, Howard, & Lutz, 1998). Thus, to accommodate this individuality, a model could be helpful that estimates an expected course of recovery for individual patients based on their progress-relevant pretreatment characteristics. Indeed, this was the starting point for patient-focused psychotherapy research (Howard, Moras, Brill, Martinovich, & Lutz, 1996). Patient-focused research is concerned with the monitoring, prediction, and evaluation of individual treatment progress during the course of therapy by means of the repeated assessment of outcome variables, the evaluation of these outcome variables through decision rules, and the feedback of this information to therapists and patients (e.g., Lambert, Hansen, et al., 2001; Lutz, 2002). Such quality management efforts have been recognized not only as a promising method but as evidence-based practice that identifies patients at risk for treatment failure, supports adaptive treatment planning during the course of treatment, and, as a result, enhances the likelihood of positive treatment outcomes (Lambert, 2010; Shimokawa, Lambert, & Smart, 2010).

Patient-focused research asks how well a particular treatment works for the actual treated patient (i.e., whether the patient's condition is responding to the treatment he or she is currently engaged in). The evaluation of progress depends on the idiosyncratic presentation of the patient with respect to his or her expected treatment response. For example, minimal progress by Session 8 might be insufficient for many patients to consider their treatment as a success. However, for a highly symptomatic patient with comorbid levels of impairment (e.g., multiple symptoms as well as interpersonal problems) such moderate progress might be considered a success (Lutz, Stulz, & Köck, 2009). As a result, feedback systems to support clinical decision making in psychotherapy should include decision rules that are able to evaluate treatment progress based on the individual patient's status (Barkham, Hardy, & Mellor-Clark, 2010; Lambert, 2010; Lutz, 2002; see also Chapter 6, this volume).

Two distinct approaches to decision rules have been used to determine expected progress and to provide feedback (cf. Lambert, Whipple, et al., 2002; Lutz, Lambert, et al., 2006). One approach comprises rationally derived methods that are based on predefined judgments about progress using clinicians' ratings based on changes in mental health functioning over sessions of psychotherapy. The other approach comprises empirically derived methods that, in contrast, are based on statistically derived expected treatment response (ETR) curves based on large available data sets that are respecified for each individual client.

Rationally Derived Methods

Rationally derived methods of patient-focused research use psychometric information based on standardized measures (e.g., the Brief Symptom Inventory [BSI]; Derogatis, 1993) to make an a priori definition about a patient's status and change. This then serves as a benchmark for his or her expected change and the evaluation of progress. A classic example of the rationally derived method can be seen in the concept of reliable and clinically significant change (Jacobson & Truax, 1991). The first component in this concept focuses on the actual amount of change achieved by the patient, which has to be greater than expected by measurement error of the instrument alone. The measurement error of an instrument depends on its reliability, hence the term *reliable change* (which comprises both *reliable improvement* and *reliable deterioration*). The second component, *clinically significant change* (or, more precisely, *clinically significant improvement*), occurs if a client who before treatment was more likely to belong to a patient sample is, at the final assessment, more likely to belong to a nonpatient sample (e.g., a community sample). Consequently, a patient has achieved *reliable and clinically significant improvement* if his or her score on the primary outcome measure meets both these criteria, indicating that the extent of improvement exceeds measurement error and the endpoint score is more likely to be drawn from a nonclinical population.

The following example of a rationally derived method used within a large feedback study is somewhat more complex. In a large-scale study funded by a German health insurance company comprising 1,708 patients within three regions of Germany, a rationally derived decision rule based on an extension of clinically significant change criteria was used (e.g., Lutz, Böhnke, & Köck, 2011). Feedback to the therapists was based on a patient's presentation at intake and on his or her amount of change by a certain session. This information was implemented into a graphical report, which was then fed back to clinicians who had the option to discuss these results via progress charts with patients.

To give feedback on initial patient status and patient progress to therapists at every assessment, all patients completed three instruments: the BSI, the Inventory for Interpersonal Problems (IIP; Horowitz, Rosenberg, Baer, Ureño, & Villaseñor, 1988), and a disorder-specific instrument (e.g., a patient diagnosed with a depressive disorder would complete the Beck Depression Inventory; Beck, Ward, Mendelson, Mock, & Erbaugh, 1961). Patients were first classified into three categories by each instrument according to their initial impairment. For example, patients were categorized as initially "highly impaired" if their pretreatment score on that specific instrument was above the mean of an outpatient sample. Initially "moderately impaired" patients scored below the mean of that reference sample, but above the cutoff score of a nonpatient population for that instrument (e.g., Jacobson & Truax, 1991). Patients who scored below that cutoff score were categorized as "minimally impaired."

The feedback and evaluation of progress were based on the following decision rules. For the "minimally impaired" patients, each positive change resulted in a positive evaluation. For "moderately impaired" patients, change was considered positive only if improvement reached at least the predefined amount of the reliable change index (RCI) for that instrument. Finally, treatment change of "highly impaired" patients was viewed as positive only if patients fulfilled the criteria of reliable and clinically significant change. A negative reliable change was rated as deterioration independent of initial scores. The ratings for each of the three instruments were then integrated into a global score by summing them. Furthermore, the therapist could also be informed of the stability of treatment progress by reporting on progress over several administrations of the measures (for further details, see Lutz, Böhnke, & Köck, 2011; Lutz, Stulz, et al., 2009). The outcome findings of this study are briefly summarized in the subsequent section on feedback.

Empirically Derived Methods

Empirically derived methods define the expected treatment course based on previously treated patients with similar intake characteristics. These patient-specific databases are then used to determine the expected change for future patients. Furthermore, confidence or prediction intervals can be assigned around the predicted courses of improvement. Hence it is possible to provide an estimate of how much a patient's actual progress diverges from the expected course of change together with the probabilities of a successful outcome.

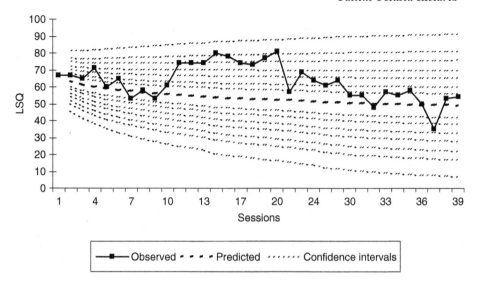

FIGURE 4.1 Predicted individual treatment response and confidence intervals (patient example) for the Outcome Questionnaire-30 (LSQ) and nearest neighbor predictive methods.

Source: Reprinted from "The Probability of Treatment Success, Failure, and Duration—What Can Be Learned From Empirical Data to Support Decision Making in Clinical Practice?" by W. Lutz, M. J. Lambert, S. C. Harmon, A. Tschitsaz, E. Schürch, and N. Stulz, 2006, in *Clinical Psychology and Psychotherapy*, *13*, p. 227. Copyright 2006 by John Wiley & Sons, Inc.

In an application of empirically derived ETRs, Lutz, Martinovich, and Howard (1999) analyzed data from 890 psychotherapy outpatients and identified a set of seven intake variables that allowed prediction of individual change (e.g., initial impairment, chronicity, previous treatment, patient's expectation of improvement). Figure 4.1 shows the ETR profile (predicted change based on intake variables) and the actual treatment progress of one selected patient with the Outcome Questionnaire-30 (OQ-30) as a dependent variable from an extended study with 4,365 patients (Lutz, Lambert, et al., 2006). To further explore the empirical decision system, different prediction intervals from 67% to 99.5% were considered around the predicted course of each patient. Using this schema, it was shown that the greater the number of actual scores a patient receives outside a confidence interval and the higher the interval, then the higher is the predictive validity of the actual score for the end of treatment.

In this way, actual treatment progress can be compared to the expected course of treatment and warning signals can be developed if a patient's progress falls below a predefined failure boundary. As the number of observed values falling below this failure boundary increases, for example between Sessions 2 and 8, then the probability of treatment failure increases. Also vice versa, as the number of observed values occurring above this failure boundary increases, then the probability of treatment success increases. Thus, the more and the further any extreme positive deviations are detected, then the higher is the probability for treatment success. Similarly, the more and the further any extreme negative deviations occur (e.g., early in treatment), then the higher the probability is for treatment failure (Lutz, Lambert, et al., 2006). These resulting percentages over the course of treatment can be employed as supporting tools by practitioners to adapt and potentially reevaluate their treatment strategy to enhance the patient's actual outcome. For example, a deviation from the ETR profile in a specific session might result in a "warning" feedback signal to the therapists and supervisors or other clinicians involved in the case (e.g., Finch, Lambert, & Schaalje, 2001; Lambert, Whipple, et al., 2002; Lueger et al., 2001; Lutz, 2002). Different approaches to ETR models have been developed that provide information to understand individual patient progress and to assist in improving treatment strategies. For example, the application of ETR models has been extended to different diagnostic groups or symptom patterns as well as being applied to the study of therapist effects. The models have also been improved by adding patient change information during the early course of treatment as predictors in order to have an adapted ETR model that is better able to predict patient change later in treatment (e.g., Lutz, Martinovich, Howard, & Leon, 2002; Lutz, Stulz, Smart, & Lambert, 2007). Two further extensions are presented here: One concerns how to identify subgroups of patients for developing ETRs, and the second concerns adjusting ETRs to different shapes or patterns of patient change.

Nearest Neighbors Techniques to Generate ETR Curves

To refine the prediction of ETR curves, Lutz et al. (2005) introduced an extended growth curve methodology that employs nearest neighbors (NN) techniques. This approach is based on research in areas other than psychotherapy in which large databases with many kinds of potentially relevant parameters (e.g., temperature and barometric pressure) recorded on a daily basis are used to make predictions of alpine avalanches (e.g., Brabec & Meister, 2001). This methodology was adapted by Lutz et al. (2005) in a sample of 203 psychotherapy outpatients seen in the United Kingdom to predict the individual course of psychotherapy based on the most similar previously treated patients (nearest neighbors). Similarity among patients was defined in terms of Euclidean distances between these variables. In a subsequent study, Lutz, Saunders, et al. (2006) tested the predictive validity and clinical utility of the approach in generating predictions for different treatment protocols (cognitive-behavioral therapy [CBT] versus an integrative CBT and interpersonal treatment [IPT] protocol). The NN method created clinically meaningful patient-specific predictions between the treatment protocols for 27% of the patients, even though no average significant difference between the two protocols was found. Using a sample of 4,365 outpatients in the United States, Lutz, Lambert, et al. (2006) further demonstrated the NN technique to be superior to a rationally derived decision rule with respect to the prediction of the probability of treatment success, failure, and treatment duration using the Outcome Questionnaire (OQ-45; e.g., Lambert, 2007).

In summary, these findings suggest that models of identifying similar patients could be an alternative approach to predicting individual treatment progress and to identifying patients at risk for treatment failure. It might be used in clinical settings either to evaluate the progress of an individual patient in a given treatment protocol, or to determine what treatment protocol (e.g., CBT or IPT) or treatment setting (e.g., individual, family, or group) is most likely to result in a positive outcome based on similar already treated patients. Furthermore, if used in the context of a clinical team, the model could be used to identify therapists who are most effective in working with a particular group of already treated patients (nearest neighbors) who could then provide consultation on treatment plans or supervision for a trainee or novice therapist working with the new case.

New Ways of Detecting Patterns of Patient Change and Variability

The models discussed previously take into account differences in patient change but they are built on the assumption that there is one specific shape of change (e.g., log-linear) for all patients in the data set. Although this assumption makes sense in order to estimate a general trend over time, actual patient change may follow highly variable temporal courses and this variation might not just be due to measurement error, but rather be clinically meaningful (e.g., Barkham et al., 2006; Barkham, Stiles, & Shapiro, 1993; Krause et al., 1998). Growth mixture models (GMM) relax this single population assumption and allow for parameter differences across unobserved subgroups by implementing a categorical latent variable into a latent growth-modeling framework (e.g., Muthén, 2001, 2004). This technique assumes that individuals tend to cluster into distinct subgroups or patterns of patient change over time and allows the estimation of different growth curves for a set of subgroups. Such GMMs have been used to analyze psychotherapy data in naturalistic settings (Lutz et al., 2007; Stulz & Lutz, 2007; Stulz, Lutz, Leach, Lucock, & Barkham, 2007) and from randomized controlled trials (Lutz, Stulz, & Köck, 2009).

Figure 4.2 shows an application of a GMM in a sample of 192 patients drawn from the U.K. database mentioned earlier (Stulz et al., 2007). These patients completed the short-form versions of the Clinical Outcome in Routine Evaluation-Outcome Measure (CORE-SF; Cahill et al., 2006). In this example, shapes or patient clusters of early change (up to Session 6) have been identified to predict later outcome and treatment duration. Figure 4.2a displays the five different shapes of early change identified with the GMM. As can be seen, one cluster can be characterized

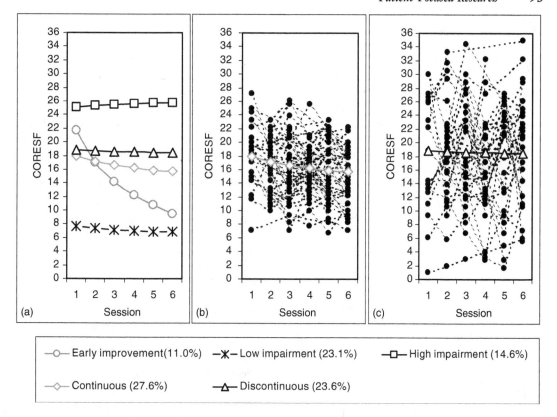

FIGURE 4.2 The five different shapes of early change (up to Session 6) identified in a sample of $N = 192$ psychotherapy outpatients using GMM (Figure 4.2a), and the observed individual growth curves for the continuous group (Figure 4.2b) and the discontinuous group (Figure 4.2c).

Source: Reprinted from "Methodological Background of Decision Rules and Feedback Tools for Outcomes Management in Psychotherapy," by W. Lutz, N. Stulz, Z. Martinovich, S. Leon, and S. M. Saunders, 2009, *Psychotherapy Research*, *19*(4), p. 507. Copyright 2009 Routledge.

by "early improvement" (11%). Patients in this cluster start with high scores on the CORE-SF but improve rapidly and substantially—more than 90% of those patients still show a substantial improvement at the end of treatment. A second cluster can be characterized by "high impairment" (23.1%) with little or no early patient change. The third cluster includes patients with "low impairment" (14.6%) who seem to have little or no early change until Session 6. The two remaining clusters in Figure 4.2a show two moderately impaired groups with similar average growth curves but, interestingly, very different individual treatment courses. Figures 4.2b and 4.2c display the plots of the actual individual treatment courses around the average growth curves in these two groups. Figure 4.2b presents the growth curves of the 27.6% of patients categorized into the "continuous" group who

showed modest session-to-session variation in the early phase of treatment. These can be contrasted to the individual growth curves displayed in Figure 4.2c. These patients (23.6%) were categorized into the "discontinuous" group as they demonstrated fairly substantial session-to-session variation. When using the reliable change criterion (Jacobson & Truax, 1991) to evaluate pretreatment to posttreatment change in these two groups, results revealed a higher rate of reliably improved patients in the "discontinuous" group than in the "continuous" group (44% versus 19%). Importantly, however, treatment duration was not different between the two groups ($M = 24.63$ versus $M = 25.55$ sessions, n.s.). Conversely, the rate of reliably deteriorated patients was also higher in the "discontinuous" patient group relative to the "continuous" group (13% versus 0%). The results from this study suggest that instability during early treatment phases seems to result in higher chances for positive treatment outcomes but also higher risk for negative treatment outcomes.

To date, research on the advantages and disadvantages of rationally derived and empirical approaches has yielded mixed results. For example, Lambert, Whipple, et al. (2002) compared a rationally derived method to predict patient treatment failure with a statistical growth curve technique. The results showed broad equivalence between both methods but the empirical approach was somewhat more accurate. Other research also indicates that the empirically derived methods might be slightly superior (e.g., Lutz, Lambert, et al., 2006; Lutz, Saunders, et al., 2006). Irrespective of the selected approach (rationally derived or empirical), further research on differential patterns of change is necessary to clarify typical patterns for subgroups of patients as well as relating these empirical findings to clinical theories. Clinical theories that have a simple concept of treatment progress (i.e., a patient has a problem, a treatment approach is applied, the patient becomes healthy) appear oversimplistic and need to be adapted to take into account empirically defined change patterns. They could be further enhanced by considering related mediators and moderators causing different patterns of change that can then be used to guide or support clinical decisions (Kazdin, 2009).

Research on patterns of change is still in a preliminary phase. More studies are needed to further validate and replicate the findings obtained so far, and consideration needs to be given to the development of simpler methods. However, this research has the potential to provide therapists with decision guidelines that are individualized to each of their patients, especially early in treatment, as well as to identify and better understand the meaning of discontinuous treatment courses.

Provision of Feedback to Therapists and Patients

The above methods provide actuarial and predictive information on the course of treatment that has the potential to be used to enhance patient outcomes. At the practice level, the most apparent self-corrective function of routinely collected data derived from measurement systems is when it is used in the form of feedback to the practitioner, an area of research that has been espoused by the APA Presidential Task Force on Evidence-Based Practice (2006). Indeed, despite the small differences in predictive accuracy, research on feedback appears to be a powerful tool for enhancing outcomes, especially for patients who are at risk of treatment failure (e.g., Carlier et al., 2012; Lambert, 2010; Lutz, Böhnke, & Köck, 2011; Newnham & Page, 2010; Shimokawa et al., 2010). In this subsection, we consider the evidence base for using feedback routinely in clinical practice.

Recognizing Failing Patient Outcomes

The need for corrective feedback has been shown in comparisons between practitioners' and actuarial predictions of patient deterioration. Hannan et al. (2005) reported data from 48 therapists (26 trainees, 22 licensed) who were informed that the average rate of deterioration, defined as reliable deterioration on the OQ-45, was likely to be in the region of 8%. Given this base rate, the therapists were tasked with identifying, from a data set of 550 patients, how many would deteriorate by the end of treatment. Actual outcome data indicated that 40 clients (7.3%)—very close to the base rate—deteriorated by the end of therapy. Use of the actuarial predictive methods led to the identification of 36 of these 40 deteriorated cases. By contrast, the therapists predicted that a total of only 3 of the 550 clients would deteriorate, and only 1 of these had, in actuality, deteriorated at the end of therapy. Such data provides a powerful argument for investing in methods and procedures that enhance practitioners' treatment responses and planning in relation to patients who may be on course to fail in therapy.

Meta-Analyses and Reviews of Feedback

Carlier et al. (2012) carried out a review of 52 trials of feedback, 45 of which were based in mental health settings. The two largest subgroups of studies comprised those using global outcome measures ($N = 24$), of which 13 studies supported feedback, and depression measures ($N = 11$), of which 7 studies supported feedback. Overall, 29 of the 45 studies supported the superiority of providing feedback. Although providing a broad evidence base for feedback, this review lacked the precision afforded by a meta-analytic approach. A number of meta-analyses of outcomes feedback studies have been carried out (e.g., Knaup, Koesters, Schoefer, Becker, & Puschner, 2009; Lambert et al., 2003; Shimokawa et al., 2010). Lambert et al. (2003) completed a meta-analytic review of three large-scale studies[2] in which the findings suggested that formally monitoring patient progress has a significant impact on clients who show a poor initial response to treatment. Implementation of a feedback system reduced client deterioration by between 4% and 8% and increased positive outcomes. Knaup et al. (2009) reviewed 12 studies[3] and reported a small but significant positive short-term effect ($d = .10$; 95% CI .01 to .19). However, health gains were not sustained.

Lambert and Shimokawa (2011) carried out a meta-analysis of patient feedback systems relating to the Partners for Change Outcome Management System (PCOMS) and the OQ System. Three studies covering the PCOMS, drawn from two published reports (Anker, Duncan, & Sparks, 2009; Reese, Norsworthy, & Rowlands, 2009), indicated that the average client in the feedback group was better off than 68% of those in the treatment-as-usual group. Results indicated that patients in the feedback group had 3.5 times higher odds of experiencing reliable improvement while having half the odds of experiencing reliable deterioration. In terms of the OQ system, Lambert and Shimokawa (2011; see also Shimokawa et al., 2010) reanalyzed the combined data set ($N = 6,151$) from all six OQ feedback studies published to date.[4] The three main comparisons were: no feedback, OQ-45 feedback, and OQ-45 plus clinical support tools (CST). Based on intent-to-treat analyses, the combined effects, using Hedges's g, of mean posttreatment OQ-45 scores for feedback only, patient/therapist feedback, and CST feedback were −0.28, −0.36, and −0.44 respectively. Shimokawa et al. (2010) concluded that all forms of feedback were effective in improving outcomes while reducing treatment failures (i.e., deterioration), with the exception of

patient/therapist feedback for reducing treatment failures.

Even though this area of research is still relatively recent, research on feedback in clinical practice is already an internationally studied area of investigation. A program of research in Australia on feedback, subsequent to the above review and meta-analyses, has considered the impact of providing feedback given at a specific time-point during the course of treatment and at follow-up (Byrne, Hooke, Newnham, & Page, 2012; Newnham, Hooke, & Page, 2010). Newnham et al. (2010) employed a historical cohort design to evaluate feedback for a total of 1,308 consecutive psychiatric and inpatients completing a 10-day CBT group. All patients (inpatients and day patients), whose diagnoses were primarily depressive and anxiety disorders, completed the World Health Organization's Wellbeing Index (WHO-5; Bech, Gudex, & Johansen, 1996) routinely during a 10-day cognitive-behavioral therapy group. The first cohort ($n = 461$) received treatment-as-usual. The second cohort ($n = 439$) completed monitoring measures without feedback, and for patients in the third cohort ($n = 408$), feedback on progress was provided to clinicians and patients midway through the treatment period. Feedback was effective in reducing depressive symptoms in patients at risk of poor outcome. In a 6-month follow-up study, Byrne et al. (2012) compared the no-feedback cohort with the feedback cohort. Feedback was associated with fewer readmissions over the 6-month period following completion of the therapy program for patients who, at the point of feedback, were on track to make clinically meaningful improvement by treatment termination. Importantly, the authors argued that the findings suggested feedback could result in cost saving in addition to being associated with improved outcomes following treatment completion for patients deemed on track during therapy.

Besides recently published meta-analyses or reviews (e.g., Carlier et al., 2012; Shimokawa et al., 2010), several advances have also been made to adapt feedback systems to different patient populations and settings. For example, Reese, Toland, Slone, and Norsworthy (2010) carried out a randomized trial comparing feedback with treatment-as-usual for couple psychotherapy ($N = 46$ couples) within a routine service setting. The setting was a training clinic and the therapists were practicum trainees. At the level of the individual client, rates of clinically significant change

---

[2]The three studies comprised Lambert et al. (2001); Lambert, Whipple, Bishop, et al. (2002); Whipple et al. (2003).

[3]The 12 studies comprised the following: Ashaye, Livingston, & Orrell (2003); Bauer (2004); Berking, Orth, & Lutz (2006); Brodey et al. (2005); Hawkins, Lambert, Vermeersch, Slade, & Tuttle (2004); Lambert et al. (2001); Lambert, Whipple, Vemeersch, et al. (2002); Marshall et al. (2004); Schmidt et al. (2006); Slade et al. (2006); Trudeau (2001); Whipple et al. (2003).

[4]The six studies comprised: Harmon et al. (2007); Hawkins et al. (2004); Lambert et al. (2001); Lambert, Whipple, Bishop, et al. (2002); Slade, Lambert, Harmon, Smart, & Bailey (2008); Whipple et al. (2003).

TABLE 4.1 Patients' Evaluations of the Quality Monitoring Project: Absolute Number and Percentage of Patients in the Respective Response Categories

Question	N*	Completely Right N (%)	Partially Right N (%)	Neither N (%)	Partially Wrong N (%)	Completely Wrong N (%)
I like the idea of having a project monitoring the quality of outpatient psychotherapy.	597	374 (62.6)	177 (29.6)	41 (6.9)	3 (0.5)	2 (0.3)
I find it important to monitor the results of psychotherapeutic treatments.	597	399 (66.8)	156 (26.1)	30 (5.0)	8 (1.3)	4 (0.7)
The time I needed to answer the questions was appropriate.	597	389 (66.8)	181 (30.3)	14 (2.3)	12 (2.0)	1 (0.2)
I had a hard time answering the questions because they affected me too much.	594	21 (3.5)	32 (5.4)	50 (8.4)	159 (26.8)	332 (55.9)
My therapist showed me the feedback and discussed it with me.	275	182 (66.2)	46 (16.7)	10 (3.6)	10 (3.6)	27 (9.8)
The information was very important to me.	258	85 (32.9)	105 (40.7)	35 (13.6)	13 (5.0)	20 (7.8)
The feedback was very helpful to me.	258	73 (28.3)	98 (38.0)	52 (20.2)	16 (6.2)	19 (7.4)
The feedback reflected my own assessment.	257	62 (24.1)	119 (46.3)	44 (17.1)	18 (7.0)	14 (5.4)
I felt like I could deal more responsibly with my psychological problems because of the feedback.	256	46 (18.0)	75 (29.3)	72 (28.1)	26 (10.2)	37 (14.5)

Note. *The questions in the lower part of the table were only given to patients in the feedback condition.

for the feedback versus nonfeedback groups were 48.1% and 26.3% respectively while for reliable change the rates were 16.7% and 5.3% respectively. This advantage to the feedback condition also held when the couple was used as the unit of analysis, with 29.6% of couples in the feedback condition meeting clinically significant change versus 10.5% (no feedback). Respective rates for reliable change only were 14.8% versus 5.3%.

Bickman, Kelley, Breda, de Andrade, and Riemer (2011) carried out a randomized trial of feedback for youths within naturalistic settings comprising 28 services across 10 states.[5] Services were randomly assigned to a control condition comprising access to feedback every 90 days, or an experimental condition comprising weekly access to feedback. Because many of the youths in the 90-day condition ended treatment prior to their practitioners accessing the feedback, the authors considered this condition as a no-feedback control. Effect size (Cohen's d) advantages to the

[5]The study originally comprised 49 services randomized, of which 10 control and 11 experimental services subsequently withdrew.

feedback condition held regardless of the source of the outcome: .18 (youths), .24 (clinicians), and .27 (caregivers). The authors argued that although the effect sizes were small, they showed how outcomes could be improved without invoking new evidence-based treatment models. Feedback has also been evaluated in a nonrandomized study for substance-abuse patients (Crits-Cristoph et al., 2012). The design employed a two-phase implementation (Phase 1, weekly outcomes; Phase 2, feedback) with results showing advantages to the feedback phase. Crucially, however, these methods cannot be the sole basis for making clinical decisions—it can only be a support tool in aid of making clinical decisions, which always stays in the hands of the clinician.

In the feedback study carried out in Germany that was reported earlier, therapists received feedback for their patients several times during the course of treatment. Table 4.1 and Figure 4.3 show how they responded to the feedback provided. On approximately 70% of occasions, therapists made some use of the feedback either by taking some action or by drawing some consequence concerning their treatment formulation.

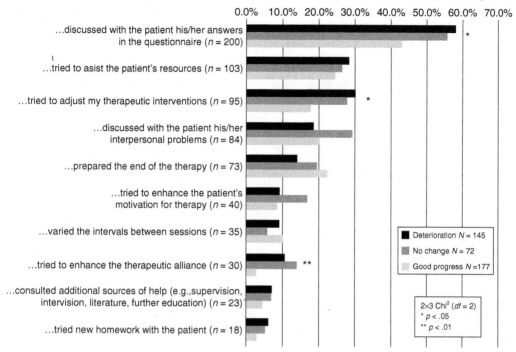

Due to the feedback, I...(multiple choices possible; 701 responses on *N* = 394 patients)

FIGURE 4.3 Consequences and modifications therapists did due to feedback related to patients' progress.

This is a high rate of action by therapists in response to the feedback information, especially given that most of the feedback was indeed positive feedback about the progress of patients. As can be seen in Figure 4.3, however, if patients showed negative progress early in treatment, then therapists, after receiving feedback, responded with a significant increase in the frequency of discussing the results with patients, adapting their treatment strategy, or trying to improve the therapeutic alliance (Lutz, Böhnke, Köck, & Bittermann, 2011). The positive evaluation from the patients participating in this study was also high, even when taking into account that not all of the patients responded. On almost all questions (see Table 4.1), the positive response rate exceeded 80%.

The above reviews, meta-analyses, and empirical reports provide an evidence-base that feedback to practitioners on patients shown not to be on-track enhances their outcomes across an increasing diversity of therapeutic modalities and patient populations. An early focus on university settings has broadened into wider samples of patient presentations. Research and development

foci have moved to considering the most effective clinical support tools to aid the practitioner's decision making in how best to respond to a patient who is not on track.

In addition, there have been calls for the development of a theory for feedback (see Bickman et al., 2011; Carlier et al., 2012), a call similar to those seeking a theoretical model for the impact of routine outcome measurement (see Greenhalgh, Long, & Flynn, 2005). From a viewpoint of differing paradigms, this area of work shows how both practice-oriented research and trials methodology can yield a robust evidence base for one area of clinical activity. Moreover, it shows how the former can provide a platform for more intensive trial work that might enable a more fine-grained investigation into the mechanisms and theory-building of how feedback achieves better patient outcomes for those patients deemed not to be on-track.

Summary

Patient-focused research has provided the field with new insights about how patients change, with regard to the relationship between the amount of treatment received and outcome, as well as with respect to various patterns of progress, or lack thereof, experienced by different groups of clients. In addition, feedback on outcome progress has been found to be an effective tool to support treatment, especially for patients at risk of treatment failure (e.g., Carlier et al., 2012; Lambert, 2010; Lutz, Böhnke, & Köck, 2011; Newnham & Page, 2010; Shimokawa, et al., 2010). Furthermore, combining clinical support tools with such feedback has enhanced its effect (cf. Shimokawa et al., 2010). In this way research on outcomes feedback has two clinical implications: First, it allows therapists to track clinical progress on an individual level in order to determine, as early as possible, if a patient is moving in the right direction; and second, it has led to the delineation of decision support tools based on the variability and patterns in patient change. However it is important to emphasize, that clinically, outcome feedback can only serve as information to guide or support the decision-making process; the actual decisions of what goals or tasks to pursue, as well as when to continue, intensify, or terminate treatment remain to be made by the clinician and the patient.

Practice-Based Evidence

This section focuses on a further form of practice oriented research, namely *practice-based evidence*, which is a reversal of the term *evidence-based practice*. Together, these two terms generate a chiasmus[6]—*evidence-based practice and practice-based evidence*—that has the potential for yielding a rigorous and robust knowledge base for the psychological therapies (Barkham & Margison, 2007). As the term suggests, practice-based evidence is rooted in routine practice and aims to reprivilege the role of the practitioner as a central focus and participant in research activity (for a detailed description, see Barkham, Stiles, Lambert, & Mellor-Clark, 2010). Although the approach shares much in common with patient-focused research, the hallmarks of repeated measurement and a primary focus on patients that underpin patient-focused research are not

sine qua non for practice-based evidence. Accordingly, practice-based evidence encompasses a broader, looser—less focused—collection of activities but takes its starting point as what practitioners do in everyday routine practice. At its heart, practice-based evidence is premised on the adoption and ownership of a *bona fide measurement system* and its implementation as standard procedure within routine practice. Implementation may be in the form of a pre- and posttherapy administration, repeated measurement intervals, or on a session-by-session basis. In terms of the yield of practice-based evidence, results can be considered at two broad levels: first, at the level of the individual practitioner whether working alone in private practice or within a community of practitioners in which the aim is to use data to *improve their practice*, and second, at a collective level in which the aim is to pool data such that it can contribute to and *enhance the evidence base* for the psychological therapies. With these two central aims, practice-based evidence delivers anew to the scientist-practitioner agenda.

This section provides illustrative examples of the yield of practice-based research by summarizing four key areas. First, a brief summary is provided of the development of selected measurement and monitoring systems, as representative of the field. Then illustrative findings are reported focusing on three successive levels of routine practice: the level of practitioners, then at the level of single services or providers, and finally, multiple services.

Measurement and Monitoring Systems

Although there are numerous features of practice-based evidence, the central component is the adoption and implementation of a measurement and monitoring system as part of routine practice. In contrast to stand-alone outcome measures, measurement and monitoring systems collect information on context and outcomes that are then used to improve practice and enhance the evidence base of the psychological therapies. The drive toward the adoption of measurement *systems* grew out of a developing trend for health insurance companies to seek evidence of outcomes and also from a growing frustration with the fragmented state regarding outcome measurement generally. The latter was illustrated in a review of 334 outcome studies from 21 major journals over a 5-year period (January 1983 to October

---

[6]Technically this is an *antimetabole* in which the same words are repeated in inverse order. All antimetaboles are, by definition, *chiastic*, which is the generic term used to refer to this grammatical structure in which there is a criss-cross (Greek: Chi χ) of words.

1988) that showed 1,430 outcome measures were cited, of which 851 were used only once (Froyd, Lambert, & Froyd, 1996). In routine practice, decisions on the selection of outcome measures were determined by factors such as those used in trials, which were invariably proprietary measures carrying a financial cost, or determined by idiosyncratic, historical, or local influences.[7] These factors combined to militate against building a cumulative body of evidence derived from routine practice settings that could complement the evidence derived from trials methodology.

Measurement Systems

Measurement systems began to be developed in the 1990s with the first outcomes management system being named COMPASS (Howard et al., 1996; Sperry, Brill, Howard, & Grissom, 1996). The COMPASS system—comprising evaluations of current state of well-being, symptoms, and life functioning—together with subsequent research reported by Lueger et al. (2001) provided the basis for other outcomes management systems that drew upon the phase model as a conceptual foundation. These included the Treatment Evaluation and Management (TEaM) instrument (Grissom, Lyons, & Lutz, 2002) and the Behavioral Health Questionnaire (Kopta & Lowry, 2002).

Subsequently other measurement systems have been developed. Examples of systems developed include:

- The Outcome Questionnaire-45 and associated measures (OQ-45; Lambert, Hansen, & Harmon, 2010; Lambert, Lunnen, Umphress, Hansen, & Burlingame, 1994): The OQ Psychotherapy Quality Management System has, at its heart, the OQ-45, which assesses three main components: symptoms, especially depression and anxiety; interpersonal problems; and social role functioning. For more information, see Lambert, Hansen, and Harmon (2010); also www.oqmeasures.com
- The Treatment Outcome Package (TOP; Kraus & Castonguay, 2010; Kraus, Seligman, & Jordan, 2005; Youn, Kraus, & Castonguay, 2012): The TOP comprises 58 items that assess 12 symptom and functioning domains: work functioning, sexual functioning, social conflict, depression, panic, psychosis, suicidal

ideation, violence, mania, sleep, substance abuse, and quality of life. In addition, the TOP measures demographics, health, stressful life events, treatment goals, and satisfaction with treatment. For further information, see www.OutcomeReferrals.com

- CelestHealth System for Mental Health and College Counseling Settings (CHS-MH; Kopta & Lowry, 2002): The Behavioral Health Measure (BHM) comprises four instruments that (a) assess complete behavioral health, (b) alert at the first session whether the client is at risk to do poorly in psychotherapy, and (c) evaluate the relationship between the therapist and the client. For more information, see www.celesthealth.com
- Partners for Change Outcome Management System (PCOMS; Miller, Duncan, Brown, Sparks, & Claud, 2003; Miller, Duncan, Sorrell, & Brown, 2005): The PCOMS comprises two 4-item scales: the Outcome Rating Scale (ORS; Miller et al., 2003) and the Session Rating Scale (SRS; Duncan & Miller, 2008). The ORS targets key components of mental health functioning while the SRS focuses on aspects of the therapeutic alliance. For more information, see www.heartandsoulofchange.com
- The Clinical Outcomes in Routine Evaluation system (CORE; Barkham, Mellor-Clark, et al., 2010; Mellor-Clark & Barkham, 2006; Evans et al., 2002): The CORE-OM (Barkham et al., 2001; Evans et al., 2002) is a pan-theoretical outcome measure comprising 34 items tapping the domains of subjective well-being, problems, functioning, and risk. It lies at the heart of the broader CORE System, which provides contextual information on the provision of the service received by the patient (Mellor-Clark & Barkham, 2006). A family of measures is available for differing uses and for specific populations and translations are available in 20 languages. For more information, see www.coreims.co.uk

Outcomes systems have also been developed for specific populations and treatment modalities. For example, the Contextualized Feedback Intervention Training (CFIT) has been developed for youths (Bickman, Riemer, Breda, & Kelley, 2006) and the Integrative Problem Centered Metaframeworks for family therapy (IPCM; Pinsoff, Breunlin, Russell, & Lebow, 2011).

Although each outcome system differs on any number of particular features, they reflect a

---

[7]For a summary of the status of outcome measures, see Whipple and Lambert (2011).

common aim, namely to measure and monitor patient outcomes *routinely* from which data is then used—fed back—to improve service delivery and patient outcomes. A resulting feature of practice-based evidence is, therefore, its ability to provide self-correcting information or evidence at the levels of practice and science within a short time frame. The following three subsections provide illustrative examples of the research yield at the levels listed earlier: practitioners, single services, and multiple services.

Practitioner Level: Effective Therapists and Therapist Effects

Reprivileging the therapist as a central focus of practice-based research redresses the balance in which the focus on treatments has long been dominant. Given that practitioners are the greatest resource—and cost—of any psychological delivery service, an equal investment in and prioritizing of practitioners is required to that already committed to the development and implementation of evidence-based treatments. The development of models of treatment based on the identification and observation of the practices of practitioners in the community who empirically obtain the most positive outcomes was a key recommendation of the APA Presidential Task Force on Evidence-Based Practice (2006). Research activity, especially trials, has predominantly used the patient rather than the practitioner as the primary unit upon which design features and analyses have been powered and premised. However, patients allocated to conditions within trials and observational studies are nested within therapists. This means that the outcomes of patients for any given therapist will be related to each other and likely different from those for patients seen by another (or other) therapist(s). Where a hierarchical structure is present but ignored in the analyses, assumptions about the independence of patient outcomes are violated, standard errors are inflated, p-values exaggerated, and the power of the trial reduced (e.g., Walwyn & Roberts, 2010).

A focus on what has come to be termed *therapist effects* developed following an article by Martindale (1978) and a subsequent meta-analysis in this area by Crits-Cristoph et al. (1991) as well as a critique of design issues (Crits-Christoph & Mintz, 1991). Wampold's (2001) text *The Great Psychotherapy Debate* followed, in which he concluded the impact of therapist effects as

being in the region of 8%. Subsequent reanalyses of therapist effects in the NIMH Treatment of Depression Collaborative Research Program (TDCRP; Elkin et al., 1989) by Elkin, Falconner, Martinovitch, and Mahoney (2006), and Kim, Wampold, and Bolt (2006) highlighted the problems of low power and of attempting to determine therapist effects from trials that were originally designed to assess treatment effects. Elkin et al.'s (2006) advice was clear, namely that therapist effects would be best investigated using (very) large samples drawn from managed care or practice networks—that is, routine settings. Subsequent reports on therapist effects and effective practitioners have been consistent with this advice (e.g., Brown, Lambert, Jones, & Minami, 2005; Kraus, Castonguay, Boswell, Nordberg, & Hayes, 2011; Lutz, Leon, Martinovich, Lyons, & Stiles, 2007; Okiishi, Lambert, Nielsen, & Ogles, 2003; Okiishi et al., 2006; Saxon & Barkham, 2012; Wampold & Brown, 2005).

A series of studies utilizing data from Pacifi-Care Behavioral Health, a managed behavioral health care organization, focused on various aspects of therapist effects and effectiveness (Brown & Jones, 2005; Brown et al., 2005; Wampold & Brown, 2005). Brown et al. (2005) evaluated the outcomes of 10,812 patients treated by 281 therapists between January 1999 and June 2004. Mean residual change scores, obtained by multiple regression, were used to adjust for differences in case mix among therapists. Raw change scores as well as mean residualized change scores were compared between the 71 psychotherapists (25%) identified as highly effective and the remaining 75% of the sample. During a cross-validation period—used as a more conservative estimate accounting for regression to the mean—the highly effective therapists achieved an average of 53.3% more change in raw change scores than the other therapists. Results could not be explained by case mix differences in diagnosis, age, sex, intake scores, prior outpatient treatment history, length of treatment, or therapist training/experience.

Wampold and Brown (2005) analyzed data comprising a sample of 581 therapists and 6,146 patients, the latter completing a 30-item version of the OQ-45. Multilevel modeling yielded a therapist effect of 5%, somewhat lower than the 8% the authors reported as an estimate from clinical trials. To explain this counterintuitive finding, they reasoned that the restricted severity range employed in trials, thereby leading to a more homogeneous sample, yielded a smaller denominator when calculating the therapist effect.

The above studies focused on overall therapist effects. However, it might be that therapists are differentially effective depending on the specific focus of the clinical presentation. This question was addressed in an archive data set comprising services contracted with Behavioral Health Laboratories (BHL). Kraus et al. (2011) analyzed the outcomes of 6,960 patients seen by 696 therapists (i.e., 10 clients per therapist) in the context of naturalistic treatment in which the TOP was used. The specific aim was to investigate the effectiveness across the 12 domains in the TOP. With the exception of Mania, which had a low base rate, the reliability of the remaining 11 domains ranged from .87 to .94. Therapists were defined as effective, harmful, or neither based on categories of change using the criterion of the reliable change index (RCI) as follows: *effective* therapist if their average client reliably improved, *harmful* if their average client reliably deteriorated, and *ineffective/unclassifiable* if their average client neither improved nor worsened. Hence therapists were deemed effective or otherwise according to average change scores on each domain of the TOP, where a specific therapist could be classified as effective in treating depression (for example) and ineffective or harmful in treating substance abuse. In all, 96% of therapists were classified as effective in treating at least one TOP domain while classifications varied widely across 11 of the 12 domains (Mania was excluded due to low base rate.) Effective therapists displayed large positive treatment effects across domains (Cohen's $d = 1.00$ to 1.52). For example, in the domain of depression 67% of therapists were rated as effective (i.e., their average patient achieved reliable change in the domain of depression) with an average treatment effect size of 1.41. Harmful therapists demonstrated large, negative treatment effect sizes ($d = -0.91$ to -1.49). An important finding was that therapist domain-specific effectiveness correlated poorly across domains, suggesting that therapist competencies may be specific to domains or disorders rather than reflecting a core attribute or underlying therapeutic skill construct. This study highlights the distinction between seeking and analyzing competencies in specific domains of patient experience versus averaging the therapist effects by analyzing total scores across their patients. For a discussion of the advantages and limitations of these two approaches in outcome monitoring, see McAleavey, Nordberg, Kraus, and Castonguay (2012).

The notion that some therapists are more effective than others caught attention with the use of the term *supershrink* (Ricks, 1974) in relation to a report on a very effective practitioner, with Bergin and Suinn (1975) labeling its opposite as *pseudoshrink*. Okiishi and colleagues addressed the concept of the exceptional therapist in consecutive studies (Okiishi et al., 2003, 2006). They utilized data from a large data pool in a university counseling center in which clients completed the OQ-45 on a regular basis. Both studies selected cases in which there were at least 3 data points. In addition, the initial study sampled practitioners who had seen a minimum of 15 clients each yielding a target sample of 56 therapists and 1,779 clients. This sample was extended in the second study and the criterion for the number of clients seen per therapist was increased to 30, yielding a target sample of 71 therapists and 6,499 clients (Okiishi et al., 2006). In this latter study, analyses focused on the average ranking of these 71 therapists based on their combined rankings according to their effectiveness (i.e., patient outcomes) and efficiency (i.e., number of sessions delivered). The authors examined and contrasted the top and bottom 10% of therapists (i.e., the ends of the distribution). The seven most effective therapists saw their clients for an average of 7.91 sessions, with clients making gains of 1.59 OQ points per session and resulting in a pre-posttherapy average change score on the OQ-45 of 13.46 ($SD = .76$). By contrast, the seven least effective therapists saw their clients for an average of 10.59 sessions, making gains of .48 OQ points per session and a pre-postaverage OQ-45 change score of 5.33 ($SD = 1.66$). Hence, these analyses suggested the most effective therapists achieved threefold gains for their patients compared with the least effective. Classifying clients seen by these most- and least-effective therapists according to the clinical significance of their change on pre-posttherapy scores (Jacobson & Truax, 1991; recovered, improved, no change, or deteriorated) showed therapists at the top end of the distribution had an average recovery rate of 22.4% with a further 21.5% improved while therapists at the bottom end of the distribution had a recovery rate of 10.61% with a further 17.37% improved. In addition, bottom-ranked therapists had a 10.56% deterioration rate while the equivalent percentage was 5.20% for top-ranked therapists.

The finding that some therapists achieve appreciably better outcomes than average highlights the naturally occurring variability in outcomes for therapists. For example, Saxon and Barkham (2012) investigated this phenomenon using a large U.K. data set in which clients completed the CORE-OM. Like Okiishi et al. (2006), the authors employed the recommendation of Soldz (2006) with each practitioner seeing a minimum of 30 patients. They investigated the size of therapist effects and considered how this therapist variability interacted with key case-mix variables, in particular, patient severity and risk. The study sample comprised 119 therapists and 10,786 patients. Multilevel modeling, including Markov chain Monte Carlo procedures, was used to derive estimates of therapist effects and to analyze therapist variability.

The model yielded a therapist effect of 7.8% that reduced to 6.6% by the inclusion of therapist caseload variables. Effects for the latter rate varied between 1% and 10% as patients' scores reflecting their levels of subjective well-being, symptoms, and overall functioning became more severe. The authors concluded that a significant therapist effect existed, even when controlling for case mix, and that the effect increased as patient severity increased. Patient recovery rates, using Jacobson's criteria for reliable and clinically significant improvement, for individual therapists ranged from 23.5% to 95.6%. Overall, two-thirds of therapists ($n = 79$, 66.4%) could be termed as average in that the 95% confidence intervals surrounding their residual score crossed zero and could not, therefore, be considered different from the average therapist. The mean patient recovery rate for this group of therapists was 58.0%. For 21 (17.7%) therapists their outcomes were better than average with a mean patient recovery rate of 75.6%, while for 19 (16.0%) therapists their outcomes for patients were poorer than average with a mean recovery rate of 43.3%.

The studies by Okiishi et al. (2003, 2006) as well as by Saxon and Barkham (2012) highlight the considerable differences that exist in therapist effectiveness when comparing the two ends of the distribution of therapists. Although the majority of therapists cannot be differentiated from each other (i.e., are not significantly different from the average), differences between the extremes are real and meaningful for patients and, when considered in relation to the population of therapists as a whole, have significant implications for professional policy and practice. Variability is a phenomenon that is inherent in all helping professions and it would seem important to understand the extent of this phenomenon in routine practice. Developing supportive ways of providing feedback at both the individual therapist and organizational level is an area that needs attention.

Single Service Level and Benchmarking in Routine Settings

A service or professional center providing psychological therapy will have, as a priority, a focus on its effectiveness, efficiency, quality, and cost, while patients, as consumers, will increasingly want to be assured they are seeking help from a professional agency (i.e., mental health center or service) that is effective. Current work has built on ideas dating back to the seminal work of, for example, Florence Nightingale (1820–1910)—who suggested a simple 3-point health-related outcome measure for her patients of relieved, unrelieved, and dead—and Ernest Codman (1869–1940), who implemented an "end results cards" system for collating the outcomes and errors on all patients in his hospital in Boston. However, while using a measurement system provides data on the actual service, practice data requires a comparator or standard against which to locate its own outcomes or other data. This requirement has led to the practice of benchmarking service data (for a summary, see Lueger & Barkham, 2010). Benchmarking can either involve comparisons with similar types of service (i.e., outcomes of other practice-based studies) or against the results of trials (i.e., assumed to be the gold standard). Persons, Burns, and Perloff (1988) provided an early example in which they compared cognitive therapy as delivered in a private practice setting with outcomes from two trials (Murphy, Simons, Wetzel, & Lustman, 1984; Rush, Beck, Kovacs, & Hollon, 1977). The authors concluded that their results were broadly consistent with those from the trials. Subsequently, although better described as effectiveness studies rather than practice-based, Wade, Treat, and Stuart (1998) as well as Merrill, Tolbert, and Wade (2003) provided examples of research that transported treatments into more routine settings and evaluated them using a benchmarking approach. Subsequent methods for determining benchmarks have been devised that enable comparisons with trials (see Minami, Serlin, Wampold, Kircher, & Brown, 2006; Minami, Wampold, Serlin, Kircher, & Brown, 2007).

Benchmarking as an approach has burgeoned across a range of service settings and patient populations whereby routine services and/clinics have been able to establish their relative effectiveness. Examples include the following: service comparisons year-on-year (e.g., Barkham et al., 2001; Gibbard & Hanley, 2008) and with national referential data (Evans, Connell, Barkham, Marshall, & Mellor-Clark, 2003), OCD in childhood (Farrell, Schlup, & Boschen, 2010) and in adults (Houghton, Saxon, Bradburn, Ricketts, & Hardy, 2010), group CBT (e.g., Oei & Boschen, 2009), psychodynamic-interpersonal therapy (e.g., Paley et al., 2008), CBT with adults (e.g., Gibbons et al., 2010; Westbrook & Kirk, 2005) and with adolescents (e.g., Weersing, Iyengar, Kolko, Birmaher, & Brent, 2006). These benchmarking studies, which are only a sample, all share a common aim of providing an evidence base regarding the effectiveness of interventions as delivered in routine services. But it is also possible to see specific themes by which studies can be grouped. These include, underrepresented approaches (e.g., non-CBT interventions), new or innovative interventions, and extensions to broader populations and/or settings.

In terms of *underrepresented* approaches, Gibbard and Hanley (2008), for example, reported a study employing data from a single service over a 5-year period using the CORE-OM, in which counselors delivered person centered therapy (PCT). In this study, a total of 1,152 clients were accepted into therapy and the data sample comprised 697 clients who completed CORE-OM forms at both pre- and posttherapy (i.e., 63% completion rate). Rates for reliable improvement[8] calculated for each year separately ranged between 63.1% (second year) and 73.5% (third year) with an overall rate for the 5-year period of 67.7%. The authors concluded that PCT was an effective intervention in primary care. Moreover, based on a smaller subset of data ($n = 196$), they concluded that PCT was also effective for moderate to severe problems of longer duration.

Similarly, Paley et al. (2008) reported the outcomes of a single service delivering psychodynamic-interpersonal (PI) therapy. Full data was available for 62 of the 67 patients who were referred by either their general practitioner or psychiatrist to receive psychotherapy. Outcomes were obtained for the CORE-OM and

the BDI and were then benchmarked against data reported from other practice-based studies. The pre-posttherapy BDI effect size for the PI service was .76 compared with a benchmark of .73 derived from CBT delivered at the Oxford-based CBT clinic (Westbrook & Kirk, 2005). When only those clients who initially scored above clinical threshold were considered, the pre-posttherapy effect size for PI therapy was .87 compared with an effect size of 1.08 for the CBT routine clinic. Rates of reliably and significant improvement (Jacobson & Truax, 1991) were identical for both services at 34%, indicating broad equivalence in outcomes of the contrasting therapeutic approaches in routine settings. Both these studies illustrate the effectiveness of interventions in routine practice settings that are underrepresented when national bodies determine treatment interventions of first choice. Addressing this issue requires either the necessary funding to secure an evidence-base sufficient to satisfy national bodies (e.g., NICE) or, more radically, a reevaluation of how we define the nature of evidence.

Studies of *new interventions or applications* of evidence-based interventions within a novel package are exemplified by, for example, Richards and Suckling (2009) who reported on data from a single service following a U.K. government initiative to improve access to evidence-based psychological therapies (see Layard, 2006). This government initiative provided initial investment in new posts and training focused on low-intensity (i.e., self-help) and high-intensity (i.e., traditional) cognitive-behavioral therapy. One feature of its implementation was the requirement for patients at each session to complete the PHQ-9 (Kroenke, Spitzer, & Williams, 2001) and GAD-7 (Spitzer, Kroenke, Williams, & Löwe, 2006). This enabled outcome data to be reported on all patients (i.e., including those leaving treatment unilaterally). Of 2,795 patients assessed, 2,017 received more than one session, and change indices were reported for the 689 patients who completed treatment (i.e., 43% of those receiving more than 1 session; 24% of those assessed). Pre-posttreatment effect sizes, using the posttreatment SD as the denominator, were 1.38 for depression and 1.38 for anxiety (here recalculated as 1.46 and 1.52 respectively using the pre-treatment SD as the denominator).

The authors benchmarked these outcomes against a number of published data drawn from trials, practice-based studies, and reviews. Although they concluded that the outcomes fell within the range of comparator studies, the ranges

---

[8]The authors used reliable improvement rather than reliable and clinically significant improvement.

for the comparator benchmark effect sizes were sufficiently large as to lack precision: 0.80 to 1.46 for depression, and 0.73 to 2.1 for anxiety. However, the specific pre- to posttherapy effect sizes for depression and anxiety based on the PHQ-9 and GAD-7 respectively were very similar to data reported by Stiles, Barkham, Mellor-Clark, and Connell (2008a) in which a subset of counselors self-reporting to use CBT ($N = 1,045$ patients) for mixed diagnosis yielded an effect size of 1.34 (here adjusted to 1.30 when based on pretherapy SD). It would be important to note, however, that although the Richards and Suckling study contains many of the features of practice-based evidence as outlined earlier, it was reporting a government-funded initiative and was therefore well resourced, targeted CBT, and used mandated condition-specific outcome measures. Hence it better reflects a hybrid of both evidence-based practice and practice-based evidence.

In relation to extending interventions originally tested in trials into *new clinical populations or settings* in routine settings, there are numerous studies using a benchmarking approach. For example, Oei and Boschen (2009) adopted this approach in evaluating group-based CBT as delivered in a community setting. The authors compared the pre-posttreatment effect size of 0.64 obtained from the community setting with the pre-post effect sizes reported from other studies, including that of Westbrook and Kirk (2005), and considered the outcomes to be broadly similar. Other researchers have employed a similar strategy across a wide range of situations: for example, an outpatient setting for adolescents presenting with OCD (Farrell et al., 2010), CBT in a pain clinic (Morley, Williams, & Hussain, 2008), and cognitive-analytic therapy in routine practice (Marriott & Kellett, 2009). Common to them all has been the intention of extending the findings of efficacy trials into routine practice settings with the aim of building a broader evidence base.

Overall, results have shown interventions in routine practice to be effective but, in most cases, to fall short of the gains achieved in efficacy trials. One comparison between practice-based data and a selection of trials in depression showed the outcomes of trials to be approximately 12% superior to those of practice-based studies based on mean pre-posttreatment change (Barkham et al., 2008). A similar difference was found when methods of reliable and clinically significant improvement were applied. However, the differences were larger when comparing pre-posttherapy effect

sizes. This result was likely due to the tendency for trials to have restrictions on patient inclusions leading to reduced variance (and consequently higher effect sizes). Regardless of which metric is used, superior outcomes, on average, in trials compared with practice-based studies is what would be expected given the highly selective and more protective environment in which trials are implemented. However, while average outcomes from routine settings may, in general, fall short of efficacy studies, the likely greater variation in individual therapist outcomes in practice-based studies might mean that there are therapists in routine setting who achieve consistently better outcomes than the top ranked therapists in trials. The above results suggest the need for policy makers to consider a broader evidence base than provided by trials alone.

Although benchmarking appears an attractive and relatively low-cost strategy for securing a comparator for practice-based studies, it is not without problems. First, comparisons often do not take into account the differential dose received by patients in routine services compared with trials. For example, a review of the clinical trials literature showed between 57.6% and 67.2% of patients improved within an average of 12.7 sessions. By contrast, naturalistic data showed that the average number of sessions received in a national database of more than 6,000 patients was less than five sessions with the rate of improvement in this sample being approximately 20% (Hansen et al., 2002).

Second, an intrinsic difficulty with adopting a benchmarking strategy concerns the selection of the benchmark used, which invariably differs across studies, thereby making comparisons study-specific. For example, two studies cited earlier using benchmarking approaches for CBT for depression with adults used different benchmarks: one with a specific focus on depression (Gibbons et al., 2010) and the other employing a more generic sample (Westbrook & Kirk, 2005). Although both studies employed the BDI as one of their primary outcome measures, in their selection of a benchmarking study Westbrook and Kirk used data from Persons, Bostrom, and Bertagnolli (1999) and the NIMH TDCRP (Elkin et al., 1989) while Gibbons et al. (2010) used unpublished data derived from DeRubeis et al. (2005). In both studies there were specific reasons for the selection of the benchmarks used that made the direct comparisons credible, but at the expense of adopting a common comparator.

Other studies have used benchmarks from, for example, three or more comparator studies. A logical strategy is to use the most recent study or studies as benchmarks, thereby generating successively new (and different) comparators over time. To reduce the arbitrary decision of which benchmark to select, one strategy would be to benchmark any new study against the cumulative body of previous studies. Houghton and colleagues (2010) adopted this strategy and determined a benchmark from nine published studies on OCD. Adopting such an approach would mean that as new studies are published and added to the body of evidence, the benchmark should become increasing robust (i.e., less vulnerable to the influence of any single study) and have ever-increasing tighter confidence intervals. Another approach would be extending the procedures applied to depression by Minami et al. (2007) to other clinical presentations. Either way, the aim would be to use a benchmark that better represents the collective body of trials evidence rather than any single trial alone.

Multiple Services: Effectiveness of Psychological Therapies in Routine Settings

In this subsection, we review evidence derived from the investigation of data from multiple services in which the aim is to move beyond statements that are specific to any single service toward considering data as contributing to the knowledge base about psychological therapies in general. Specifically, we focus on analyses of routine data sets that address issues of the overall effectiveness of therapies as well as how much therapy is considered enough.

Meta-Analyses of Practice-Based and Effectiveness Studies

In a meta-analysis of practice-based studies addressing common mental health problems, Cahill, Barkham, and Stiles (2010) reported the average pre-posttreatment effect size from 10 studies for the treatment of depressive symptomatology, using a fixed effect model, to be 1.29 (95% CI 1.26 to 1.33). However, using a fixed effect model restricts the extent to which the findings can be generalized in that the results pertain only to the sample of therapists used in the studies. Using a random effects model allows the results to be generalized to the population of patients as a whole and this analysis

yielded an overall pre-post effect size of 1.14 (95% CI 0.96 to 1.32). Applying Jacobson and Truax's (1991) criteria of clinical change to seven studies using the CORE-OM yielded a mean rate of 56% of patients meeting the threshold for reliable and clinically significant improvement, with an additional 18% achieving reliable improvement only, and 25% showing no reliable change.

Stewart and Chambless (2009) carried out a meta-analysis of 56 effectiveness studies—as opposed to practice-based studies—of CBT across five adult anxiety disorders: panic disorder, social anxiety disorder, PTSD, generalized anxiety disorder, and obsessive-compulsive disorder. The authors rated studies on nine dimensions reflecting clinical representativeness in relation to: settings, referrals, therapists, structure, monitoring, no pretherapy training of therapists, no randomization, clinically representative patients, and allowance of medication. Studies were included if they scored 3 or more on a 9-point scale. Further, inspection of the supplementary data shows only 2 of the 56 studies received a maximum rating (i.e., 9) as indicating being clinically representative on all dimensions (http://dx.doi.org/10.1037/a0016032.supp). Indeed, the authors stated: "The real-world mental health practitioner may not agree that studies included in this meta-analysis are clinically representative" (p. 601). Pre-post effect sizes for each condition were compared to three benchmark studies (i.e., trials) targeting each specific presenting condition. Results indicated the pre-posttreatment effect sizes for the effectiveness studies in three of the conditions (social anxiety $ES = 1.04$; generalized anxiety disorder $ES = 0.92$; and obsessive-compulsive disorder $ES = 1.45$) to be within the range of the efficacy benchmarks, while findings for PTSD ($ES = 2.59$) exceeded those of trials. Only the results for panic disorder ($ES = 1.02$) were below the lower range of the benchmark studies.

Overall, results from both these meta-analyses indicate that interventions delivered in routine practice are effective, yielding mainly large pre-posttherapy effect sizes. Hence, with the exception of the finding that PTSD as delivered in effectiveness studies exceeded those of trials, the pre-posttreatment effect sizes all fell within the range 0.90 to 1.45; that is, the average patient at posttreatment was better than between 83% and 93% of people prior to treatment.

Practice-Based Studies of Comparative Treatment Outcomes

While the above meta-analytic studies have focused on the effects for clinically defined presentations, empirical studies have addressed the comparative effectiveness of differing schools of interventions (e.g., Stiles, Barkham, Twigg, Mellor-Clark, & Cooper, 2006; Stiles, Barkham, Mellor-Clark, et al., 2008a). Stiles et al. (2006) utilized data drawn from 58 services in the United Kingdom from which a subset of 1,309 patients were selected who, according to the therapists self-reported accounts, received either cognitive-behavioral therapy (CBT), person-centered therapy (PCT), or psychodynamic therapy (PDT). Patients completed the CORE-OM at the beginning and end of their treatment and therapists indicated which treatment approaches were used. Hence, results focused only on patients who completed treatment. Comparisons were made between six subgroups: three comprising CBT, PCT, or PDT only (i.e., pure), and three treated with one of these plus one additional approach used by the therapist (e.g., integrative, supportive, art). These latter three groups were designated as CBT + 1, PCT + 1 or PDT + 1 respectively. All six groups averaged marked improvement with an overall pre-posttherapy effect size of 1.36. Treatment approach and degree of purity (i.e., "pure" versus "+1") each accounted for statistically significant but comparatively very small proportions of the variance in CORE-OM scores.

Stiles et al. (2008a) replicated this study drawing on an original data pool comprising 33,587 patients, which, after excluding incomplete data from either patients and/or therapists, yielded complete data on 12,162 patients. The study focused on the same six subgroups as in the previous study yielding a sample of 5,613 patients. All six groups began treatment with equivalent CORE-OM scores, and all averaged marked improvement with an overall pre-posttherapy effect size of 1.39. Figure 4.4 presents notched boxplots of the extent of change across the six groups. Distributions of change scores were all similar. Although the authors signaled caution because of limited treatment specification, non-random assignment, incomplete data, and other issues, the study was criticized on these same grounds (see Clark, Fairburn, & Wessley, 2008), criticisms that in turn were rebutted (see Stiles, Barkham, Mellor-Clark, & Connell, 2008b). The debate exemplifies the tensions surrounding the use and interpretation of data from routine practices. However, Stiles and colleagues concluded that these routine treatments were effective for patients who complete them but that those who fail to complete, or indeed even begin, treatment deserve attention by researchers and policymakers.

The impact of using a sample of completer patients versus an intention-to-treat sample has a direct impact on the reporting of outcomes in routine practice. Using the CORE database comprising 33,587 patients, Barkham, Stiles, Connell, and Mellor-Clark (2012) calculated rates of reliable and clinically significant improvement, as defined by Jacobson and Truax (1991), based on completer and intention-to-treat samples drawn from this data set. The particular focus was on the different ways in which the total sample can be defined as follows: all patients referred to the service (referred), only those patients assessed (assessed), only those patients accepted into treatment and attending at least one session (attenders), or only patients completing treatment (completers). The rates, as would be expected, were highly dependent on which definition of the sample was used and, to a lesser extent, on the statistic used for determining improvement or recovery (i.e., reliable and clinically significant improvement, or case versus not case).

The recovery rate for the completer sample using the criteria of reliable and clinically significant improvement was 58.3%. However, this rate fell to 36.7% when calculated on an intent-to-treat sample based on those patients who were assessed and attended at least one session. Moreover, the attender sample comprised only 50% of the original full sample. Although criticisms might be leveled at studies using only completer samples, they do provide a test of the treatment as received by the patient and having an agreed ending between patient and therapist. By contrast, intent-to-treat analyses in routine settings are likely to reflect a combination of treatment and service effects. However, more than anything else, these findings attest to the need to invest in efforts to retain patients in therapy. The delivery of efficacious treatments is a necessary but not sufficient condition for maximizing the personal and social benefits of the psychological therapies.

Dose-Effect Relations

A continuing question within psychotherapy research has been the issue of how much therapy

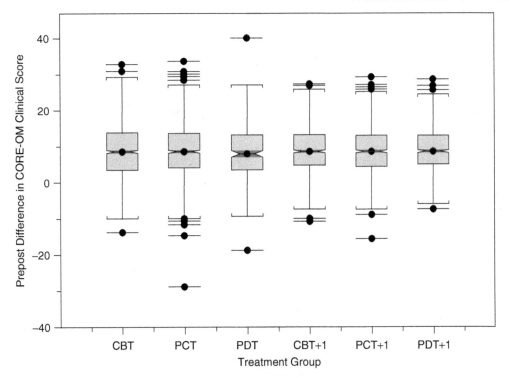

FIGURE 4.4 Notched boxplots showing pre-/postdifferences in CORE-OM clinical scores.

Note. The notch shows the 95% confidence interval around the median. The boxes show the middle 50% of the distribution. The whiskers show the range, except that observations falling 1.5 times the interquartile range or more away from the top or bottom of the box are considered outliers and are shown separately. CBT, Cognitive, behavioral, or cognitive/behavioral therapy ($n = 1,045$); PCT, person-centered therapy ($n = 1,709$); PDT, psychodynamic/psychoanalytic therapy ($n = 261$); CBT+1, CBT combined with one other therapy ($n = 1,035$); PCT+1, PCT combined with one other therapy ($n = 1,033$); PDT+1, PDT combined with one other therapy ($n = 530$).

Reprinted from "Effectiveness of Cognitive-Behavioural, Person-Centred, and Psychodynamic Therapies in UK Primary Care Routine Practice: Replication with a Larger Sample," by W.B. Stiles, M. Barkham, J. Mellor-Clark, & J. Connell, 2008, *Psychological Medicine, 38*, pp. 677–688. Cambridge, United Kingdom: Cambridge University Press.

is enough. As previously mentioned, Howard et al. (1986) characterized the path of client improvement as a negatively accelerating function of treatment length, which has usually been interpreted as reflecting the diminishing strength of each successive session. Successive studies using data from naturalistic studies have been carried out using measurement of client dysfunction on a session-by-session basis and a binomial classification of dysfunction—recovered or not recovered—at each session (e.g., Anderson & Lambert, 2001; Hansen & Lambert, 2003; Hansen, Lambert, & Forman, 2002; Harnett, O'Donovan, & Lambert, 2010; Kadera, Lambert, & Andrews, 1996). The results from these studies suggest a range of 11 to 18 sessions as the number of sessions needed to achieve clinically significant change for half of the sample starting therapy.

The usual interpretation in psychotherapy research has considered the aggregate curves as representing an average of individual dose–effect curves that are also negatively accelerated, modeled as log-linear functions of session number. There are, however, other possibilities. Barkham et al. (1996) observed that session-by-session plots of improvement in particular symptoms for up to 16 sessions tended to look more or less linear and noted that, in the dose–effect studies by Howard et al. (1986), clients had varying lengths of treatment, so that different aggregations of clients were represented at each successive point. To encompass these results, Barkham and colleagues suggested that problems might be assumed to improve at a steady (i.e., linear) rate across sessions until it reaches a *good enough level* (GEL), at which point the client and therapist either redeploy therapeutic efforts to other problems or discontinue therapy.

Subsequent work has provided support for the GEL model. Barkham et al. (2006) studied clients ($N = 1,868$) seen for a variety of problems in routine primary care mental health practices, who attended 1 to 12 sessions, had planned endings, and completed the CORE-OM at the beginning and end of their treatment. The percentage of clients achieving reliable and clinically significant improvement (RCSI) on the CORE-OM did not increase with the number of sessions attended. For clients who began treatment above the CORE-OM clinical cutoff ($n = 1,472$), the RCSI rate ranged from 88% for clients who attended 1 session down to 62% for clients who attended 12 sessions ($r = -.91$).

A replication study was carried out by Stiles et al. (2008) who examine rates of improvement in psychotherapy in United Kingdom primary care settings as a function of the number of sessions attended. Included in the study were adult clients who returned valid assessments at the beginning and the end of their treatment, had planned endings, began treatment above the clinical cutoff score, and were seen for 20 or fewer sessions ($N = 9,703$). Clients' average assessment scores improved substantially across treatment, with a pre-post treatment effect size of 1.96 with 62.0% achieving reliable and clinically significant improvement (RCSI). Clients' mean pre-post treatment change were broadly constant regardless of treatment duration (in the range of 0 to 20 sessions) and the RCSI rate decreased slightly with treatment duration, as fewer clients fell below the cutoff at longer durations. The results were consistent with therapists and clients tending to make appropriately responsive decisions about treatment duration (see also Chapter 8, this volume).

In a comparison between the competing predictions of the dose-effect and good enough level models, Baldwin, Berkeljon, Atkins, Olsen, and Nielsen (2009) examined the relationship between rate of change and total dose in 4,676 psychotherapy patients who received individual psychotherapy. Patients attended 6.46 sessions on average ($SD = 4.14$, range $= 3$–29, $Mdn = 5$). Results were most consistent with the GEL model with rate of change being related to total dose of treatment. That is, small doses were related to relatively fast rates of change, whereas large doses were related to slow rates of change.

In a further study, Reese, Toland, and Hopkins (2011) sought to replicate the GEL model and explore if session frequency moderates the influence that the number of sessions has on the rate of change in psychotherapy. They used an archival naturalistic data set with a U.S. university counseling center sample ($n = 1,207$), with treatment progress measured using the OQ-45. Results were consistent with the GEL model (i.e., clients who attended fewer sessions evidenced faster rates of change). Findings also indicated that the rate of change was influenced by session frequency (i.e., clients who attended more sessions on average per week demonstrated more rapid improvement).

In light of the above findings, session frequency needs to be considered at the level both of practice but also in terms of definitions of dose within research. Practice-based evidence can be used to establish clinical decisions and, consequently, policy about the needed length of therapy—something that clinical trials have failed to address because of the restriction of defining a set dosage when, in fact, some individuals will need more and some less than the fixed dose.

Summary

The studies reported in this section have set out both the yield and potential of an approach that goes part way to redressing the balance with trials methodology as well as promoting a strategy for ensuring better capture and use of data from routine practice. Crucially, however, it reprivileges the practitioner as both a focus and an active agent in the research endeavor by investigating their effects and effectiveness, both as individual therapists and also as the key resource defining any psychological service. Collectively, findings from this approach indicate therapist effects to account for between approximately 5% and 8% of outcome variance, with some therapists yielding considerably better patient outcomes than other therapists. Where evaluations of individual services have been carried out and benchmarked against other studies, findings suggest they are effective but invariably not to the same extent as in trials. And comparisons between differing treatment approaches have yielded broadly equivalent outcomes while investigations into how much therapy is enough suggests that fixed durations of treatment may not be the best way of allocating valuable resources.

PRACTICE RESEARCH NETWORKS

There is no doubt that practitioners are at the center of, and substantially contribute to, the investigations that are conducted within both the patient-focused and practice-based research approaches. Clinicians are directly involved in data collection, and this data collection is aimed at understanding or improving the practice of psychotherapy, including their own, in naturalistic environments. The level of engagement of clinicians in research tends to be even greater in the third approach of practice-oriented research: practice research networks (PRNs). As stated by Parry, Castonguay, Borkovec, and Wolfe (2010), PRNs:

> "[H]ave been alternately defined as a group of practicing clinicians that co-operates to collect data and conduct research study" (Zarin, Pincus, West, & McIntyre, 1997), and "large numbers of practicing clinicians and clinical scientists brought together in collaborative research on clinically meaningful questions in the naturalistic setting for the sake of external validity and employing rigorous scientific methodology for the sake of internal validity" (Borkovec, 2002, p. 313).

When based on a partnership of practitioners and researchers, PRNs involve, optimally, collaboration on all aspects of investigation: from the generation of ideas to the design, implementation, and publication of studies. This collaboration aims to foster a sense of equality, shared ownership, and mutual respect between researchers and clinicians, and promoting diversity of scholarship (i.e., different ways of understanding and investigating complex phenomena). It also capitalizes on the complementary expertise, knowledge, and experiences of each stakeholder to provide unique opportunities for two-way learning in order to conduct studies that are both clinically relevant and scientifically rigorous. Also characteristic of PRNs is the consideration of respective needs and resources of both clinicians and researchers in designing protocols that balance issues of internal validity and feasibility, which can sometimes compete and at other times be synergistic. By having practitioners involved in deciding what studies should be conducted

and how they should be implemented, PRNs also provide practitioners with an active voice in "setting the research agenda" (Zarin et al., 1997) and a vehicle for shaping the empirical evidence upon which practice could be based. For more discussion on the defining features of PRNs, as well as strengths, weaknesses, and challenges associated with research conducted within them, see Garland, Hurlburt, and Hawley (2006), McMillen, Lenze, Hawley, and Osborne (2009), Parry et al. (2010), and Zarin et al. (1997).

The first PRNs were created in the 1950s to meet the needs of specific healthcare fields, such as primary care in rural areas, and nursing (see Bradley, Sexton, & Smith, 2005; McMillen et al., 2009; Zarin et al., 1997). However, it was not until four decades later that behavioral or psychological health PRNs began to emerge. Currently, there are several PRN infrastructures that are devoting at least part of their focus to research related to psychotherapy. Although these infrastructures vary considerably, they can be clustered into three categories identifying the main groups of clinicians involved: PRNs based primarily on *professional organizations*, *specific disorders*, and *common clinical settings*. This section presents brief descriptions of some of the PRNs within each of these clusters as well as some examples (it is not a comprehensive survey) of psychotherapy studies conducted in each.

As the three approaches of practice-oriented research presented in this chapter focus on the utilization and delivery of care in naturalistic settings, it will be no surprise that some of the studies conducted in PRNs address topics also investigated in patient-focused and/or practice-based research. However, in part because the ideas for studies in PRNs tend to rely more on a diversity of voices, reflecting both clinicians' and researchers' perspectives, investigations carried out within PRNs cover a wider range of topics than those conducted in the two approaches described earlier.

Professional Organization PRNs

A number of PRNs have been created or sponsored by professional organizations representing several fields of mental health, including psychiatry, psychology, social work, marriage and family therapy, and art therapy. Although the studies conducted within these PRNs cover a wide range of interests, they do reflect an apparent desire for research on actual practice that is shared by therapists of different training backgrounds.

The American Psychiatric Institute for Research and Education

The American Psychiatric Institute for Research and Education's PRN (APIRE-PRN) was originally conceived as a nationwide network of psychiatrists, collaborating on data collection and conducting research on a variety of issues related to clinical services delivery, health services, and health policy (West & Zarin, 1995). It was established in 1993 in response to the understanding that more research relevant to practice was needed in psychiatry. The psychotherapy studies conducted within this PRN have been mostly observational, short in duration, as well as simple to implement and adaptable to different office practices in order to avoid interfering with clinical routines. While we cover some of the most psychotherapy-relevant studies here, it should be noted that recent studies associated with this PRN have involved large-scale investigations that are based on randomly selected psychiatrists from the American Psychiatric Association Physician Masterfile, rather than on the more limited (and thus less representative) samples of psychiatrists that participated in earlier investigations.

Drawing from a broad range of patients, treatments, and treatment settings, the infrastructure of the PRN allows for multiple areas of research. One such area is how patients' characteristics affect clinical care. For example, Herbeck et al. (2004) explored variations in the use of second-generation antipsychotic medications by race and found that, even after controlling for potential confounds, African Americans were less likely to be prescribed second-generation antipsychotic medications, considered to be the treatment of choice by psychiatrists, compared to Whites.

Another study, by Duffy et al. (2008), assessed the feasibility and helpfulness in adding a depression severity monitoring measure to 19 psychiatric practices. The results suggested that the inclusion of the measure was both feasible and helpful for treatment: 93% of psychiatrists reported utilizing the instrument, and in 40% of patient visits it led to treatment changes such as dosage, medication change, or recommendation for psychotherapy and medication.

Data collected through the APIRE-PRN has also allowed researchers to conduct studies on issues related to therapeutic processes. For example, Herbeck et al. (2005) examined various factors related to treatment noncompliance in patients with substance use disorders. The results suggested that several variables, such as presence of a personality disorder, low Global Assessment of Functioning (GAF; American Psychiatric Association, 2000) scores, side effects from medications, and seeing psychiatrists at a discounted service fee, were associated with an increased probability of treatment noncompliance.

Trends in psychiatric practice are another major area investigated in this PRN. West, Wilk, Rae, Narrow, and Regier (2003) compared the fees that psychiatrists receive for providing a psychotherapy session (with a medical evaluation) with three medication management sessions and found that psychotherapy sessions were reimbursed $74.52 less than medication management sessions. Wilk, West, Rae, and Reiger (2006) studied the patterns and predictors of psychotherapy use in psychiatric patients and found that two-thirds of patients received psychotherapy as part of their treatment and more than half of these were with their treating psychiatrist.

A study conducted by Zarin, Johnson, and West (2005) addressed an issue related to clinical relevance of traditional research: the comparability of clients in RCTs and general practice. They compared patients diagnosed with bipolar and schizophrenia across several demographic, clinical (such as principal diagnoses, comorbidity, medical history), and treatment (medications and dosages) variables. Overall, the results supported the conclusion that the patients and treatments in RCTs are not representative of clinical practice: PRN patients were predominantly white, female, and older, with more comorbid diagnoses compared to RCT patients. Approximately 40% of the patients with schizophrenia and 50% of the bipolar patients in the PRN would not have met inclusion criteria for an RCT.

The Pennsylvania Psychological Association

Originally created by a full-time academician (Thomas Borkovec) and a full-time clinician (Stephen Ragusea), the Pennsylvania Psychological Association PRN (PPA-PRN) has been devoted to the conduct of psychotherapy research in outpatient clinics in Pennsylvania. In all investigations of this PRN, clinicians and researchers have fully collaborated in the specification of the goals, design, implementation, and dissemination of the findings. Based on the coordinated work of three committees (core assessment, study protocol, and ethics), the first study was conducted for the sole purpose of evaluating the feasibility of a research infrastructure in naturalistic outpatient psychotherapy (Borkovec, Echmendia, Ragusea,

& Ruiz, 2001). This led to the adoption of a standardized outcome measure by more than 50 private practitioners, who used it as an assessment tool in routine care. Although clearly stating that their intention "was not to draw specific conclusions from the results of the PRN study for either theoretical or applied purposes" (p. 159), members of the PRN reported a number of findings that could (with additional studies aimed at determining mechanisms of change, as well as cause and effect relationships) lead to clarification of how therapy works and how it can be improved. Specifically, in addition to indicating that significant improvement took place during treatment across a number of outcome dimensions (e.g., symptoms, interpersonal problems, and life functioning), the results suggest that some client and therapist characteristics were associated with improvement. For example, while clients' initial expectancy for a positive outcome was predictive of greater change, interpersonal distress was negatively related to improvement. Interestingly, female clients showed more therapeutic change than male clients regarding family relationships, and clients of male therapists showed greater changes in intimacy than clients of female therapists. Moreover, while a higher number of clients in a therapist's caseload was predictive of worse outcome, better outcome was associated with the number of sessions received (Borkovec et al., 2001; Ruiz et al., 2004). A number of lessons for future PRN efforts were also derived from this study, such as the need to provide incentives to participants, as well as securing grants from funding agencies and psychological associations.

A second investigation was developed and carried out by 13 clinicians of varying theoretical orientations who, for a period of 18 months, invited all of their new clients (adults, adolescents, and children) to participate, except when psychotherapists judged such participation to be clinically contra-indicated. The study, involving a total of 146 clients, was a randomized clinical trial aimed at examining two general questions. First, clinicians wanted to know what clients and therapists find the most helpful and hindering during therapy. The second goal was to determine whether the provision of such feedback at the end of every session improves the effectiveness of therapy. The study led to the collection and coding of close to 1,500 events that were reported as being helpful or detrimental during sessions. Among the results obtained, the therapists' efforts to foster clients' awareness of their emotions, thoughts, and behaviors were perceived as

particularly helpful by both clients and therapists. Events leading to the strengthening of the alliance were also reported by therapists as particularly helpful. Furthermore, therapists identified as particularly hindering some omissions that they themselves committed (e.g., failure to provide needed structure) during sessions (Castonguay, Boswell, et al., 2010). The difficulty of collecting outcome measures at the end of treatment, however, prevented the researchers/clinicians from answering the second question of the study. After the completion of this study, participating therapists were interviewed regarding their experience of designing and implementing the research protocol within their private practice (Castonguay, Nelson, et al., 2010). A qualitative analysis of these interviews revealed a number of benefits. The therapists reported, for example, that receiving feedback from clients about helpful and hindering events allowed them to adjust their interventions toward clients' needs, and that writing down their thoughts after each session provided clients with the opportunity to consolidate therapeutic material. They also reported that their involvement in the study fostered new learning, as well as a sense of community with other professionals with shared goals. Therapists also reported that clients perceived their research participation as intrinsically meaningful in that it provided them with an opportunity to contribute to scientific knowledge. However, there were a number of difficulties reported, such as having to depart from their clinical routine, remembering detailed procedures of the research protocol, and finding time to complete and review questionnaires. At times, research tasks were perceived as interfering with clients' needs (e.g., when an explanation of the study took away time to establish rapport early in therapy).

A number of recommendations for future PRN studies were also generated by the analyses of the interviews, including the design of research procedures that are as simple and clear as possible, direct and easily available consultation to address problems of data collection, and strategies aimed at increasing clients' and therapists' motivation (such as financial incentives for clients to help reduce the problem of post-treatment data collection mentioned above). Perhaps the most important recommendation for future PRN endeavors was the need to develop and conduct studies in which the empirical and clinical goals are confounded. That is, "studies for which it is impossible to fully distinguish whether the nature of the questions investigated, tasks implemented, or the data collected are empirical or clinical" (Castonguay, Nelson, et al., 2010, p. 352).

Additional Professional Organization PRNs

At least six other professional organizations have sponsored PRNs: American Association for Marriage and Family Therapy (AAMFT), American Counseling Association (ACA), Association for Cognitive Analytic Therapy, American Psychological Association (APA), Art Therapy Practice, and the National Association of Social Workers (NASW). At this point in time, the studies that have been conducted in these PRNs have been mostly surveys (often nationally representative), which primarily examine practitioner and client characteristics, practice settings, as well as treatment and services patterns (e.g., Bradley et al., 2005; Huet, Springham, & Evans, 2008; Northey, 2002; Simmons & Doherty, 1995; Smith, Whitaker, & Weismiller, 2006). Some of the findings of these surveys have revealed important information. For instance, Smith, Whitaker, and Weismiller (2006), from the NASW PRN, reported that more than 25% of the clients treated by social workers were diagnosed with a substance use disorder, but fewer than half of the sample's social workers had received specific training in treatment of substance abuse during the previous 12-month period. The authors interpreted these findings as suggesting that social workers may not be receiving adequate training in the types of problems they need to treat. It should also be mentioned that the ACA-PRN has begun to examine outcomes of treatments provided by counselors. Smith, Sexton, and Bradley (2005) reported preliminary outcomes from a study of 143 clients seen by 26 counselors in routine practice. In this study, clients completed the OQ-45 before and after treatment, and scores were examined for differences. Though the authors described this study as preliminary, and a complete description of findings was not presented, they did find significant overall improvement in symptom distress after counseling for those clients who were significantly distressed at the start of treatment. This study is noteworthy since a substantial amount of work that organization-based PRNs have conducted to date has been focused on documenting practices in routine care, rather than addressing outcomes. Studies like this one suggest that these PRNs, given their wide reach, may be able to provide meaningful information as to rates of treatment success as well as potential obstacles to therapeutic improvement.

Disorder-Specific PRNs

Several PRN initiatives have focused on specific clinical problems, such as substance abuse, disruptive behavioral problems in children, child maltreatment, eating disorders, and autism. Like the PRN infrastructures described in the previous sections, they have led to a variety of studies in terms of topics and complexity. This variety no doubt reflects variation in the longevity and resources across these different PRNs. It also represents the wide range of interests that drives clinicians and researchers in their inquiries about psychotherapy-related issues.

The National Drug Abuse Treatment Clinical Trials Network

The National Drug Abuse Treatment Clinical Trials Network (CTN) is a particularly well-developed PRN infrastructure. Created by the National Institute on Drug Abuse as a way "to bring drug abuse researchers into the real world of the treatment clinic while creating opportunities that allow practitioners to participate in treatment research" (Hanson, Leshner, & Tai, 2002, p. 69), the CTN has not only conducted numerous studies on psychotherapy and behavioral health interventions for drug abuse, but has also developed a model infrastructure for promoting high-quality experimental research in a large, clinic-based network (Tai et al., 2010). This PRN has produced 271 published journal articles at the time of this writing (National Drug Abuse Treatment Clinical Trials Network, 2011).

Explicit collaboration between researchers and providers, including clinicians and directors of treatment programs, is built into the infrastructure of this PRN. This is accomplished at both regional and national levels. In the CTN, regional "nodes" include university-based researchers and clinic-based practitioners who meet, discuss, plan, and conduct research projects within a particular part of the country. Nodes often collaborate in CTN-funded studies that require at least three nodes to participate, increasing external validity. As described in Tai et al. (2010), research projects that are conducted through this infrastructure are approved and supported nationally by NIDA, which provides input on research design and oversees the study progress. A centralized management corporation provides an overall structure to this PRN by coordinating clinical research training, given by providers and researchers, as well as managing data and providing statistical expertise. The governance of the CTN is assumed by a steering committee that comprises an equal representation of providers and researchers with representation from each node. Exchanges between researchers and providers have also been promoted through more than 20 special interest groups, in which many research ideas are developed and issues in need of research are advocated. It is noteworthy that while much of the research conducted in the CTN is largely indistinguishable from traditional clinical research, what makes it a PRN is the active participation of practice sites, their directors, and their clinicians in the design and implementation of each project. This demonstrates the potential for PRNs to conduct highly rigorous studies that emphasize both internal and external validity, as well as the potential for clinicians to value, utilize, and conduct such research.

As of 2011, 52 primary research studies have been conducted or funded, including over 20 RCTs along with several surveys and process studies (National Drug Abuse Treatment Clinical Trials Network, 2011). Although many of the studies conducted by this PRN have tested the efficacy of pharmacologic interventions, several have provided large-scale, field trial clinical investigations of psychotherapeutic and behavioral treatments. For instance, Robbins et al. (2011) conducted a multisite RCT to evaluate treatment-as-usual (TAU) and brief strategic family therapy (BSFT) for adolescent substance users. In the main outcome of this study (i.e., urinalysis, which only assesses the previous week at posttreatment), the researchers found no significant differences between treatment types. However, they did find evidence of better retention, treatment engagement, and parent-reported family functioning for the BSFT condition, as well as a significant difference between groups in self-reported drug use.

In another study, Carroll et al. (2006) trained drug counselors in motivational interviewing (MI) techniques, and integrated these techniques into a single session of intake and initial assessment for drug abuse patients. This study showed that the MI procedures increased retention rates for the first month of treatment, an important factor in drug counseling. Ball et al. (2007) also tested a brief motivation enhancement therapy (MET) against usual counseling and found significant effects on retention. Both studies also suggested that there was meaningful variability between sites in the CTN as well as differences in the types of substances being treated in terms of the effectiveness of the motivational interventions.

Additionally, the CTN has produced a large amount of research on the effectiveness of empirically supported treatments when delivered to particularly underserved populations, which are not always well represented in large-scale RCTs (Burlew et al., 2011). Studies have included a specific focus on, among others, African Americans (e.g., Montgomery, Burlew, Kosinski, & Forcehimes, 2011), Spanish speakers (e.g., Carroll et al., 2009), and American Indians (e.g., Forcehimes et al., 2011).

The variety of methods and research topics of studies conducted within the CTN is expansive and clearly illustrates the potential for high-quality research in naturalistic settings. Studies in the CTN have focused on therapist characteristics (e.g., Suarez-Moreles et al., 2010), client pretreatment characteristics (e.g., Hartzler, Donovan, & Huang, 2010), dissemination of efficacious treatments into the community (e.g., Walker et al., 2010), brain imaging (e.g., Upadhyay et al., 2010), surveys (e.g., Pinto, Yu, Spector, Gorroochurn, & McCarty, 2010), and statistical and research methodology (e.g., Morgan-Lopez, Saavedra, Hien, & Fals-Stewart, 2010). Such breadth of research topics suggests that there are many areas of research in which clinicians are potentially interested.

It is important to note that in addition to this research, work from the CTN has also touched on practitioners' views of participating in research. Knudsen, Ducharme, and Roman (2007) surveyed practitioners in the CTN and found that counselors' perceptions of increased stress due to research (e.g., larger workload, emotional stress) were associated with intentions to discontinue working at their clinic. In contrast, the perception that research was helpful to patients and the clinic (e.g., increasing retention rates, increasing sense of teamwork) was positively associated with counselors' intentions to stay. This has clear implications for any research studies developed in PRNs in the future.

Practice and Research: Advancing Collaboration

A researcher-practitioner partnership (the Practice and Research: Advancing Collaboration [PRAC]), focusing on the treatment of disruptive behavioral problems (DBP) in children, has been developed by Garland and her colleagues at the University of California at San Diego (Garland, Hurlburt, & Hawley, 2006). The primary goal of this partnership is to understand the therapeutic processes and the associated clinical outcomes in the treatment of DBP, in a naturalistic setting. As described in Garland et al., clinicians representing six clinical sites collaborated with researchers in the planning (e.g., selection and adaption of measures, refinement of the methodological design, increase of feasibility and clinical relevance), implementation (e.g., recruitment of participants, problem solving), and interpretation of a large study. This study, involving more than 80 therapists of various professional backgrounds and more than 200 children, examined how principles of change underlying evidence-based practice (EBP) for DBP were consistent with common practices for this problem in usual care. Based on observational coding of psychotherapy sessions with children and their family conducted in community outpatient clinics, the specific aims were to describe the therapeutic process in terms of treatment strategy and relationship variables, and examine the relationship between practice elements (evidence-based and practitioner-based) and outcome. The study also aimed to investigate pre-treatment characteristics of clients and therapists. Recently published results (Brookman-Frazee, Haine, Baker-Ericzen, Zoffness, & Garland, 2010) indicate that, even though EBP elements were used in almost all the 1,215 sessions that were coded, the overall intensity (i.e., how extensively the treatment element was delivered) of these elements was low for both caregivers and children. The implication was that the use of EBP elements was brief. Brookman-Frazee et al. (2010) also reported that the child's age (older) and therapists identifying themselves as cognitive behavioral or behavioral in orientation were significantly associated with higher EBP use.

Similar to the procedures carried out in the PPA-PRN, a qualitative analysis was conducted to learn how the clinicians and researchers viewed their collaboration at the beginning and during the PRAC project, as well as their recommendations for future collaborative projects (Garland, Plemmons, & Koontz, 2006). Both challenges (such as tensions related to group dynamics, conceptual issues, and communication) and positive experiences (perceived trust in others, increase in knowledge, and changes in their views of research

and practice) were reported. In particular, an emphasis on clinical concerns and observations in the formulation and development of research questions was highlighted as a characteristic of an ideal collaboration.

The Healthy Families America Research Practice Network

The Healthy Families America Research Practice Network (HFA RPN) is aimed at the prevention of child maltreatment. To this end, it has grouped academic researchers with community-based evaluators. As of 2007, HFA RPN comprised, as part of its researchers and practitioners council, 25 researchers and 15 clinicians (Galano & Schellenbach, 2007). Although this infrastructure is focused on prevention, it shares many of the same goals as the PRNs focused on treatment and psychotherapy based interventions (e.g., facilitate communication between researchers and clinicians, integration of research based practices in naturalistic settings, identification of most clinically relevant questions, and strategies to investigate them). It has emerged, in part, because of similar perceived limitations of traditional research in social sciences. As in a few of the PRN infrastructures described above, it has led to a common standardized database, as well as the conduct of a large study involving 100 sites across nine states and aimed, in part, at implementing evidence-based intervention strategies. Interestingly, the building of infrastructure and conduct of research within community interventions involves issues that are not typically addressed in psychotherapy, but that might be worth considering in our attempt to improve mental health care, such as the involvement of policy makers and human services agencies.

Additional Disorder-Specific PRNs

Some researchers have also employed a practice research network approach as a way to recruit practicing clinicians to conduct studies on specific disorders. For example, Westen, Shedler, Durrett, Glass, and Martens (2003) used this approach in order to randomly select and contact clinicians who were members of either the American Psychological Association or American Psychiatric Association, and asked them to provide data on their patients for a national study looking at psychopathology in adolescents. Thompson-Brenner, Boisseau, and Satir (2010) used a similar approach and sample of clinicians when conducting a study looking at eating disorders in adolescents. Other researchers have established collaborations with community providers to promote cooperative and symbiotic efforts in the dissemination of evidence-based practices and decrease the research-practice gap. Stahmer and colleagues (Brookman-Frazee, Stahmer, Searcy, Feder, & Reed, 2012; Stahmer, Brookman-Frazee, Lee, Searcy, & Reed, 2011), for example, developed the BRIDGE (Bond-Regulate-Interact-Develop-Guide-Engage) Collaborative, a group comprised of researchers, providers, parents, and funding agencies, aimed at implementing interventions in community early intervention settings for infants and toddlers who are at risk of autism spectrum disorders (ASD). Similarly, researchers and community stakeholders collaborated to develop a mental health intervention protocol and corresponding therapist training model for school-age children with ASD treated in community mental health settings. Results of a pilot study indicated that community mental health therapists can be trained in a short period of time to implement (with fidelity and promising effectiveness) interventions drawn from evidence-based practice for this clinical population (Brookman-Frazee, Drahota, & Stadnick, 2011).

PRNs Based on Common Settings

Another type of PRN is aimed at conducting studies that may address various clinical problems and may involve therapists of different training backgrounds. In contrast with those described earlier, these PRNs have been developed to better understand and improve practice in specific clinical settings. Two examples of such PRNs are presented next. One examines services provided in college counseling centers, and the other operates in a psychotherapy training clinic.

The Center for Collegiate Mental Health

The Center for Collegiate Mental Health (CCMH) is an infrastructure that has been created to foster mutually beneficial bridges between a large number of collaborators (mental health treatment providers, psychological and information science researchers, industry leaders, and university administrators), all of whom are invested in the collection of data to enhance the mental health services provided to college students (Castonguay, Locke, & Hayes, 2011; Hayes, Locke, & Castonguay, 2011; Locke, Bieschke, Castonguay, & Hayes, 2012). This infrastructure now includes

more than 150 college counseling centers across the United States. These centers are using the same instruments in routine practice, allowing for a collection and "real-time" processing of a massive flow of standardized (and Institutional Review Board-approved) data. The first instrument, the Standardized Data Set (SDS) covers a range of basic issues such as client/counselor demographics, mental health history, and living situation. The second measure (the Counseling Center Assessment of Psychological Symptoms [CCAPS]; Locke et al., 2011; McAleavey et al., 2012) is a multidimensional assessment of clients' difficulties and treatment outcome. A short version of the CCAPS has now been validated to allow for the purposes of repeated assessments (Locke, McAleavey, et al., 2012). While routine data collection is primarily administrated at the center level (each counseling center has autonomy to set their own schedule of administrations), research studies and access to data of the national sample is centralized at CCMH.

A pilot study of more than 19,000 clients seen at counseling centers in the fall semester of 2008 led to the examination of the clinical difficulties and use of counseling services by college students of ethnic and/or sexual minorities. One of the questions investigated, for example, was whether students who represent a double minority status, racial/ethnic and sexual, experience more intense and/or specific types of clinical problems as compared to students who are members of only one minority group (Hayes, Chun-Kennedy, Edens, & Locke, 2011). Another question examined was whether eating disorder and body image problems, both predominant foci of psychological services provided in counseling centers, should be viewed as a problem predominantly experienced by white women or if college students from a variety of backgrounds express similar concerns (Nelson, Castonguay, & Locke, 2011). Two other investigations found that different groups of sexual orientation minorities (e.g., gay, lesbian, and bisexual clients) and gender minorities (e.g., transgender clients) experience different types of psychological difficulties, some of them being extremely severe (Effrig, Bieschke, & Locke, 2011; McAleavey, Castonguay, & Locke, 2011).

A second wave of studies has begun to address issues related to therapeutic change. For example, Boswell, McAleavey, Castonguay, Hayes, and Locke (2012) have investigated how the particular client pre-treatment characteristic of prior treatment history affects outcomes in routine treatment. Despite their expectations, the authors found that clients who had previously been in counseling, but not previously taken psychiatric medications or been hospitalized for mental illness, were slower to respond to a course of counseling and evidenced less overall improvement than other clients. Lockard, Hayes, McAleavey, and Locke (2012) have also reported on a counseling outcome study stemming from the CCMH PRN infrastructure. In this study the authors used data from clients at two clinics on one university campus and compared them to a group of nonclinical peers from the same university. These authors report that the mean level of academic distress among those students in counseling decreased significantly over 6 weeks of counseling, while it remained stable in the nonclinical group. This finding provides support for the effect of counseling and also demonstrates the value of collaboration between counselors at different clinics.

Also within the context of the CCMH infrastructure, a qualitative study was recently conducted on the experience of both doctoral students and their clients in using the CCAPS on a repeated basis (Martin, Hess, Ain, Nelson, & Locke, 2012). As in the PPA-PRN and the PRAC studies mentioned above, obstacles, such as limited time available to devote to collecting data, were reported, but so were benefits. For example, 62% of clients reported that completing the CCAPS helped them think differently about their problems. Similarly, 64% of the therapists reported using the outcome scores to modify the case formulation of their clients' difficulties. In addition, the therapists, all of whom were trainees, reported discussing their clients' CCAPS scores during supervision. This study provides an example of how the collection and use of data in naturalistic settings can simultaneously serve research, clinical, and training purposes (Castonguay, 2011).

The Pennsylvania State University Training Clinic PRN

With the goal of fostering a seamless integration of research, practice, and psychotherapy training, the Department of Psychology at Penn State University has transformed its training clinic into a PRN. This has been achieved by incorporating four major components into its training program (see Castonguay et al., 2004; Parry et al., 2010): a core outcome battery, the Treatment Outcome Package (TOP; Kraus et al., 2005); standardized

diagnostic assessment procedures; a selection committee for the evaluation of research proposals (including representatives from the faculty, clinical staff, students, and practitioners from the community); and an innovative agreement with the office of research protection to efficiently streamline the Institutional Review Board (IRB) review process. This infrastructure has enabled several students to find themselves in a situation in which they are seeing clients, meeting their clinical hour requirements, and collecting their masters and/or dissertation data. Studies by students, postdoctoral fellows, and faculty members are conducted in this infrastructure only if they are judged to be clinically relevant, to reflect the clinic's mission of promulgating and integrating rigorous (and pluralistic) research within clinical services and training, and judged to be minimally invasive to the functioning of the clinic. At this point in time, more than 10 studies have been launched; a few of them are briefly described next.

Boswell, Castonguay, and Wasserman (2010) reported on a study of training, psychotherapeutic intervention use, and perceived session quality in this PRN. The authors had PRN therapists complete measures of training variables and then had clients and therapists complete measures of psychotherapy techniques use and session outcome after each session of psychotherapy. This process study tracked 19 therapists with 42 clients across an average of 10 sessions per client using quantitative self-report methods.

Interestingly, the authors found that several training-relevant variables (e.g., self-identified psychotherapeutic orientation, years in training, degree status, practicum orientation) were not related to the kinds of psychotherapy techniques reported in sessions. This was surprising, and suggests that the types of techniques used in therapy may not be a simple function of training. In addition, these authors found a complex relationship between technique use and session quality as rated by clients, suggesting that, overall, clients reported the most benefit from sessions involving greater frequency of techniques associated with interpersonal therapy and behaviors considered to be "common factors" across therapy orientations. In addition, an interesting result was found for clients who received especially frequent common factors (compared to other clients of the same therapist) from therapists who reported a particularly high frequency of common factors behaviors (compared to other therapists). These clients indeed reported diminished session quality when their therapists used more CBT techniques than usual. This suggests an important lesson for trainees and experienced therapists: The implementation of CBT interventions should proceed with careful consideration of the current context of treatment, especially when therapy with a client has relied heavily on common factors (the basic helping skills and therapeutic environment), because the client is likely to experience these as less helpful when compared with other clients.

In another study, Nordberg, Castonguay, Fisher, Boswell, & Kraus (2008) examined outcomes of treatment in this PRN. Using the TOP, these authors sought to replicate and extend earlier work carried out in naturalistic settings of psychotherapy (see Stulz et al., 2007). Specifically, using growth mixture modeling of outcome data in treatment, this study found support for the identification of three latent classes of clients with depressive symptoms: low-distress slow responders, high-distress slow responders, and high-distress fast responders. This study used archival information derived through the PRN's unique data generation process to identify depression chronicity as a potential discriminator between the two high-distress groups.

Summary

Reflecting clinicians' wide arrays of interests, a very broad range of topics has been investigated in psychotherapy PRN studies, such as the clinical problems and utilization of services by ethnic and/or sexual minorities, and the impact of clients' characteristics on prescribed care, treatment compliance and outcome. Different procedures related to clinical care have also been examined, including the feasibility and impact of assessment measures on routine practice, types of treatments and interventions used by therapists, the link between therapists' interventions and the impact of the session on clients, as well as helpful and hindering events in sessions. Several studies have also investigated the outcome of therapy from a variety of angles, such as the examination of patterns of change in a training clinic, effectiveness of treatment-as-usual in clinical practice, as well as the effectiveness (via randomized trials conducted in naturalistic settings) of specific interventions and empirically supported treatments for underserved populations. These issues represent a large array of questions that are pertinent to the practice and effectiveness of psychotherapy. While some of these issues

are consistent with the interests of academic researchers and/or the priorities of funding agencies, others more directly reflect the concerns and questions of those practitioners working within the demands and pressures of everyday routine practice. Such convergence and diversity are no doubt indicative of the complexity of psychotherapy, as well as showing the likely benefit of recognizing the merits of different research strategies, and the relevance of their findings, to further understand and improve therapeutic practice.

OTHER INITIATIVES TO CLOSE THE SCIENCE-PRACTICE GAP

There have been numerous and diverse attempts to bridge the science-practice gap in addition to the three approaches discussed earlier (practice-based evidence, patient-focused research, and practice research networks). Here we briefly present a few major trends in this work.

A number of authors have identified ways to facilitate practicing psychotherapists conducting research in the context of their own practice, (e.g., Goldfried, 1984; Kazdin, Kratochwill, & VandenBos, 1986). The clinical case study is perhaps the original model for clinicians interested in contributing to empirical knowledge. In recent years, there has been an increasing call for such in-depth analyses of single cases as an essential form of knowledge (e.g., Barlow & Nock, 2009; Borckardt et al., 2008; Dattilio, Edwards, & Fishman, 2010; Iwakabe & Gazzola, 2009; Kazdin, 2008, 2010). This call has also come as the available methods of case study analysis have expanded to include numerous diverse approaches to maximize empirical and theoretical knowledge derived from single cases. Stiles (2007, 2010) has proposed that a unique benefit of case study research is that it can identify ways in which existing theories are inadequate and need to be developed. Stiles proposed methods by which psychotherapists can implement a case study with the explicit goal of building new and modified theories that could later be tested with other methods (2007), as well as ways in which these case studies can constitute practice-based evidence (2010). Elliott and colleagues (Elliott, 2002; Elliott et al., 2009) described a hermeneutic single-case efficacy design, which was developed explicitly to test whether psychotherapy has been an active and meaningful contributor to client improvement. This method relies on quantitative as well as qualitative assessment strategies to make this interpretive decision. Numerous models like these have been developed specifically to enable case-based research in applied settings of psychotherapy (e.g., Beeson & Robey, 2006; Borckardt et al., 2008; Galassi & Gersh, 1993; Hayes, 1981; Mayott-Blum et al., 2011). However, it is likely the case that countless clinical theories have not been adequately documented using such case study research methods, and many of the clinical lessons that could be learned from such case studies are not rapidly or systematically integrated into researchers' studies. This is perhaps a particular instance of the colander effect mentioned earlier: numerous pieces of knowledge slipping through the grates.

Aside from case studies, there has also been considerable encouragement offered to practicing clinicians in conducting research within their everyday clinical work (e.g., Goldfried, 1984). Clinicians/researchers such as Jacqueline Persons (e.g., Persons et al., 1988; Persons, Roberts, Zalecki, & Brechwald, 2006) and David Burns (e.g., Burns & Nolen-Hoeksema, 1991, 1992) have provided the field with exemplary models of how process and outcome data can be collected in private practice in order to shed light on therapeutic change. Research in applied settings has also included large-scale quantitative evaluations of treatment programs (e.g., Hardy, Weatherford, Locke, DePalma, & D'Iuso, 2011; Steinfeld, Coffman, & Keyes, 2009). In addition, there have been calls for the application of controlled qualitative research methods, primarily through detailed analysis of cases and aggregating this information within a practice, to improve conceptualization of clients' presenting problems and strengthen effectiveness of future services (e.g., Silverstein, Auerbach, & Levant, 2006). Moreover, researchers have described tools to aid clinicians conducting research, including quantitative methods for analyzing and better understanding naturalistic psychotherapy data (e.g., Crosbie, 1993; Jones, 2003; Speer & Greenbaum, 1995).

There has been a developing trend toward increasing the clinical relevance of research, based on the belief that much research, especially internally valid RCTs, may not suffice to inform the clinical situation (e.g., Persons & Silberschatz, 1998). For instance, journals have been launched that are dedicated to promoting clinicians' participation in and/or consumption

of research. These have included the *Journal of Clinical Psychology: In Session* and *Pragmatic Case Studies in Psychotherapy*, to name just two. Other journals, such as *Psychotherapy*, have recently put out specific calls for papers meeting the criteria for a "practice review," a literature review with clinical implications and discussion (e.g., Davis & Hayes, 2011) and "empirically based case studies," which incorporate clinical material with predefined quantitative process and outcome data.

Additional methods for increasing the clinical relevance of research have included other initiatives to seek out clinicians' feedback on existing research and to direct future research. For instance, Goldfried (2011) described a feedback mechanism for clinicians to provide input on the problems and difficulties encountered when attempting to implement ESTs in their practice. Experienced clinicians have also been invited to provide their perspective about the current state of research in psychotherapy. That is, how findings confirm what they already knew, are inconsistent with what they believed or have observed, and provide them with new information or perspectives about therapy. In addition, their views have been sought about dimensions, issues, or questions that have not been covered in the empirical literature but would be important to investigate (e.g., Castonguay, Adam-Term, et al., 2010). Similarly, as described earlier, Martin et al. (in press) and Garland et al. (2006), as well as Castonguay et al. (2011), have provided qualitative analyses of psychotherapists' experiences participating in research projects.

There has been an additional trend in the literature towards exploring ways to optimally train graduate students for careers that balance research and practice. For instance, Stricker and Trierweiler (1995) suggested that if clinicians adopted the role of a "local clinical scientist," they could incorporate empirical findings from research while developing local expertise relating to their own clients through repeated and systematic clinical work. Goldfried (1984) suggested that training programs should in fact explicitly aim to encourage their students to engage in research once out of training, in order to close the divide between research and practice.

Recently, the Association for Psychological Science has sponsored an effort to further encourage graduate programs to emphasize research in training. As described by Baker, McFall, and Shoham (2009), the Psychological

Clinical Science Accreditation System is designed to accredit only those programs that train graduates who "can generate and apply psychological clinical science effectively" (p. 88). This system may have significant effects on the way that many clinical psychologists approach research and practice. There have been other endeavors at closing the science-practice gap through training, including a current initiative of the American Psychological Association's Division 12 (Society for Clinical Psychology) to make recommendations to training programs about how to implement evidence-based practice (Beck et al., 2012). Among the sources of knowledge that have been considered for such recommendations are the efforts in health fields, such as medicine, in order to foster the translation and implementation of research evidence into clinical practice (see Gray, 2004; Guyatt & Rennie, 2002; Straus, Glasziou, Richardson, & Haynes, 2011). Regardless of how the gap between research and practice is addressed, it is highly likely that training will be a key component.

CONCLUSION: CONVERGENCE AND FUTURE DIRECTIONS

There are a number of convergences between the three main research approaches, as well as with the other avenues noted above, that have attempted to integrate science and practice. Crucially, these studies are conducted in naturalistic settings rather than highly controlled research environments. As such, a priority is placed on external validity. In addition, with the exception of some descriptive and survey studies, the research conducted within each approach of the paradigm of practice-oriented research is based on the adoption and implementation of a standardized measurement system as part of routine practice (e.g., CCAPS, CORE, OQ, TOP). Furthermore, while the degree to which clinicians are involved in the design of the studies varies within and across the various approaches, four unifying goals of the paradigm of practice-oriented research can be identified. First, to provide practitioners with the opportunity to be *active participants* in scientific endeavors and have ownership of the data collected. This goal represents a fundamental shift away from traditional efficacy research. Second, to use data as it is being collected to inform their interventions during therapy, thereby seamlessly integrating or *confounding science and practice*. Third, to rely on this data, collected

individually or aggregated from groups of clinicians, to examine questions that *they perceive as relevant to their practice*. Hence, a key driver is the desire for local knowledge such that the results have a direct bearing and relevance on everyday practice. And fourth, to allow practitioners to *contribute to the accumulation of rigorous knowledge* aimed at better describing, understanding, and ultimately improving psychotherapy. This goal is consistent with the aims of more traditional psychotherapy research guided and conducted by full-time researchers and demonstrates the complementarity of evidence-based practice and practice-oriented research.

Interestingly, although a wide range of research topics has been investigated, a number of themes have emerged as the foci of studies in two, or all three, approaches of practice-oriented research described in this chapter. Among these themes are the following: therapist effects, dose-effect relationship, differential trajectories of change, description of routine practice and its effectiveness, as well as the investigation and comparison of therapeutic approaches. Moreover, a variety of research methodologies have been used, more or less extensively, in different types of practice-oriented research, including descriptive, correlational, and experimental designs. In addition, the application of multilevel modeling to large data sets has become an increasing hallmark of practice-oriented research.

It should be mentioned that with the conduct of practice-oriented research there frequently comes a number of methodological and pragmatic challenges. For example, there are considerable hurdles to implementing the routine monitoring of individual treatment progress that is at the core of many patient-focused and practice-based studies. These include administrative costs, the need to bring clinicians and administrative staff on board, the need for sufficient expertise to produce timely decision algorithms and reports, and training in how to interpret and evaluate the information provided. Ongoing consultation with researchers and among clinicians, help from research assistants in collecting and managing data, as well as a considerable amount of time devoted to the design and learning of research protocols are among the strategies that have been emphasized to prevent or resolve obstacles encountered in PRN studies. Like most meaningful professional tasks, the conduct of research for and by clinicians requires additional work and is facilitated by resources and funding that are not always available in routine treatment settings.

As with any type of research, including RCTs, a number of limitations have been identified with studies conducted within the paradigm of practice-oriented research (see McMillen et al., 2009; Parry et al., 2010; Stiles et al., 2008a; Zarin et al., 1997). Some of these, especially with regard to internal validity, are not likely to be addressed in future investigations. For example, it is neither possible nor advisable for clinicians to have every prospective new client assigned to repeated and blind assessments before and after treatment, so that reliable judgment of the diagnoses of research participants can be ascertained. However, improvements could be made to address current limitations. For example, practice-based research can be criticized for the lack of assessment of therapists' treatment adherence and competence, thereby precluding confident statements about what interventions therapists used and how well they implemented them in studies investigating or comparing different forms of therapy. Although no doubt costly in terms of time and expertise, checklists or observer assessment of therapists' delivery of therapy should be considered in future studies, perhaps building on the therapist and client reports of techniques conducted session-by-session that have been collected in some PRN studies (e.g., Boswell et al., 2010). Crucially, however, such procedures need to be integrated into routine practice, thereby delivering on the confounding of research and practice activities.

Practice-oriented research has offered contributions to the field that are beneficial to therapists and their clients and should be recognized both by psychotherapy scholars, irrespective of their methodological preferences, and by policy makers. At a clinical level, for instance, repeated assessment and immediate feedback of a patient's mental health functioning during the course of therapy can alert therapists to patient nonresponse or negative response, support decisions on treatment planning and strategies (e.g., when and how to repair alliance ruptures), and help determine when treatment has been sufficient. These tools can be used by practitioners of all theoretical orientations and levels of experience when making complex and individualized decisions in their day-to-day practice.

At a scientific and policy-making level, the studies reported in this chapter set out both the yield and potential of an overarching paradigm that goes part way to redressing the balance with trials methodology as well as promoting a strategy for ensuring better capture and use of data from routine practice; that is, addressing the colander effect (Kazdin, 2008). As demonstrated in studies described in the patient-focused section, for example, the quality of patient care has been improved for those patients who have been deemed to be off-track as a result of a program of trials carried out in routine settings and extended to routine settings as one component of good practice (see Lambert, 2010). As also illustrated in the practice-based section, the combination of multilevel modeling to reflect the hierarchical structure of the data (i.e., patients nested within practitioners, who are nested within services, see Adelson & Owen, 2012), together with very large data sets and intelligent data capture methods has reprivileged practitioners and services in generating robust evidence of their effectiveness. In addition, these data can be used to address service delivery issues not amenable to trials methodology. For example, therapist effects may be related to practitioners' abilities to retain a patient in treatment rather than dropping out, which may in turn be more crucial than differences between treatment orientations for those patients remaining in treatment. Similarly, dosage in trials is fixed whereas the weight of evidence from studies based in routine practice settings suggests that some patients require fewer sessions while others require more and that patients themselves may be the best arbiter of the question "how much therapy is enough." Also based on multilevel modeling methods, studies reported in the practice-research network section suggest that while some types of events can be perceived as particularly helpful (even when accounting for variability across sessions, patients, and therapists), some specific types of interventions (e.g., CBT techniques) can be associated with negative impact when used by particular therapists with particular clients.

Taken as a whole, these examples indicate that studies conducted using the three research approaches described in this chapter are increasingly able to capture and analyze data that reflect the complex structure and processes involved in delivering psychological therapies in the real world. This evidence base from routine practice needs to be considered in conjunction with RCT evidence by bodies informing national policies to realize the full potential from the chiasmus of evidence-based practice and practice-oriented evidence.

More issues remain to be investigated and further scientific, as well as clinical, advances are likely to be achieved with increased utilization of a diversity of research methods. Among the numerous recommendations that can be made for future research, a few appear particularly worthy of attention. First, practice-oriented collaborators might be encouraged to pursue studies exploring the interaction of participant (i.e., client and therapist) characteristics, relationship variables (e.g., alliance), and technical factors (common to several forms of psychotherapy or unique to particular approaches). Examining the moderating and mediating roles that some of these elements may have on treatment outcome could well capture intricate details of the change process in applied settings. Second, and complementing these complex quantitative analyses, we would also suggest that particular emphasis be given to extensive qualitative analyses of significant episodes during therapy. Third, large practice-oriented infrastructures have been described as optimal contexts to implement sophisticated experimental methods (e.g., additive, dismantling, and parametric designs) to simultaneously test the effectiveness of new approaches of psychotherapy and examine cause-effect relationships between interventions and outcome (see Borkovec & Castonguay, 1998), thereby offering another avenue for the seamless integration of clinical and scientific pursuits.

The same recommendations for future investigations can, and have been, made toward research conducted outside of the approaches described in this chapter (see Castonguay & Beutler, 2005b). Such convergence should be viewed as a warning sign of a possible false dichotomy between traditional (i.e., evidence-based) and practice-oriented research paradigms. Not only do these lines of research share important goals including, as mentioned above, the quest to better understand and improve psychotherapy, but they can also focus on similar issues and use identical research methods, including randomized clinical trials. This is exemplified in the trials designs used in the research on feedback (e.g., Harmon et al., 2007). There are, obviously, important distinctions between these two strategies in how studies are designed and conducted. For example, the starting point of traditional effectiveness studies—a relatively practice-oriented type of traditional trials-based research—is a manualized and well-controlled treatment that is then imported into the naturalistic environment.

By contrast, in most studies conducted within practice-oriented research, the starting point is ongoing psychotherapy that is then studied and sometimes manipulated, via randomized trials, to gradually improve its potency. However, perhaps the most important distinction is the guiding force of the investigations conducted. Whereas most traditional investigations are guided, and often funded, by the research programs of academicians, studies in practice-oriented infrastructure are based on the active participation of clinicians in collaborative research endeavors. This means that the recommendations for future research mentioned above should be viewed as tentative suggestions. Presenting them as priorities or imperatives would amount to empirical imperialism: researchers telling clinicians what to study and how to study it.

In terms of future directions, the most important issue in relation to practice-oriented research is not what studies need to be conducted, but what can be done to facilitate the collaboration of researchers and clinicians in designing and conducting studies in which they wish to invest their time and energy. On this, we can only provide a glimpse of ideals that could be pursued. On a pragmatic level, it would be beneficial to foster the following initiatives. First, embed practice-oriented research during training. This could be facilitated by implementing repeated measurements and the use of feedback within clinical training and supervision, as well as by providing opportunities for students to do research that is not only clinically relevant but that interfaces with their clinical experiences. As noted elsewhere, it could be argued "that simultaneous, seamless, and repeated integration of science and practice activities as early as possible in a psychotherapist's career might create an intellectual and emotional (hopefully secure) attachment to principles and merits of the Boulder model" (Castonguay, 2011, p. 135). Second, "ask and tell" by surveying clinicians about what they want to know and what kind of study they would like to build and implement with others, and then publish the results of these studies to inform and stimulate the field into action. Third, work locally but collaborate globally. This could be done, for example, by creating large networks that connect smaller groups of clinicians and researchers collecting data on the same variables at different sites (see Borkovec, 2002; Castonguay, 2011). Fourth, use data that is already available—that is, archived or secondary data sets. Many studies can be carried out by taking advantage of archival data open to researchers (e.g., NIDA, CCMH).

Finally, we would argue that the engagement of practice-oriented collaborators could be most fruitfully carried forward by the adoption of three guiding principles. First, cover the colander that leaks clinically based knowledge. To maximize the ability of practice-oriented research to generate new and actionable findings, let alone to foster its collaborative spirit, it would be most beneficial to conduct studies that address clinicians' questions and that are designed, in part, on their knowledge and observations. Second, as far as possible, avoid constructing studies requiring tasks that are not immediately relevant to the conduct of therapy. In other words, we need to think beyond the "bridge" between science and practice. Indeed, rather than trying to connect science and practice, as if they stand on different river banks, we should strive to confound the two activities to create a new, unified landscape of knowledge and action. And third, make the research for and by clinicians count. There is a robust argument to be made to funders and policy makers to ensure that the evidence derived from practice-oriented research contributes in equal measure to the development of national, local, and professional guidelines. Methodologists within the wider discipline of public health have argued that "if the health professions and their sponsors want more widespread and consistent evidence-based practice, they will need to find ways to generate more practice-based evidence that explicitly addresses external validity and local realities" (Green & Glasgow, 2006, p. 128). We would also argue that this is a two-way street. Although it is clear that our understanding and conduct of psychotherapy can be improved by the scientific contributions of practice-oriented research, clinicians are more likely to engage in designing, implementing, and disseminating studies if there is clear evidence that the merit and impact of these studies will be fairly considered and duly recognized by scholars, researchers, and policy makers.

REFERENCES

Adelson, J. L., & Owen, J. (2012). Bringing the psychotherapist back: Basic concepts for reading articles examining therapist effects using multilevel modeling. *Psychotherapy*, *49*, 152–162.

American Psychiatric Association. (2000). *Diagnostic and Statistical Manual of Mental Disorders* (4th ed., text rev.). Washington, DC: American Psychiatric Association.

American Psychological Association. (2006). Evidence-based practice in psychology: APA Presidential task force on evidence-based practice. *American Psychologist*, *61*, 271–285.

Anderson, E. M., & Lambert, M. J. (2001). A survival analysis of clinically significant change in outpatient psychotherapy. *Journal of Clinical Psychology*, *57*, 875–888.

Anker, M. G., Duncan, B. L., & Sparks, J. A. (2009). Using client feedback to improve couple therapy outcomes: A randomized clinical trial in a naturalistic treatment setting. *Journal of Consulting and Clinical Psychology*, *77*, 693–704.

Ashaye, O. A., Livingston, G., & Orrell, M. W. (2003). Does standardized needs assessment improve the outcome of psychiatric day hospital care for older people? A randomized controlled trial. *Aging and Mental Health*, *7*, 195–199.

Baker, T. B., McFall, R. M., & Shoham, V. (2009). Current status and future prospects of clinical psychology: Toward a scientifically principled approach to mental and behavioral health care. *Psychological Science in the Public Interest*, *9*, 67–103.

Baldwin, S. A., Berkeljon, A., Atkins, D. C., Olsen, J. A., & Nielsen, S. L. (2009). Rates of change in naturalistic psychotherapy: Contrasting dose-effect and good-enough level models of change. *Journal of Consulting and Clinical Psychology*, *77*, 203–211.

Ball, S. A., Martino, S., Nich, C., Frankforter, T. L., Van Horn, D., Crits-Christoph, P., . . . Carroll, K. M. (2007). Site matters: Multisite randomized trial of motivational enhancement therapy in community drug abuse clinics. *Journal of Consulting and Clinical Psychology*, *75*, 556–567.

Barkham, M., Connell, J., Stiles, W. B., Miles, J. N. V., Margison, J., Evans, C., & Mellor-Clark, J. (2006). Dose-effect relations and responsive regulation of treatment duration: The good enough level. *Journal of Consulting and Clinical Psychology*, *74*, 160–167.

Barkham, M., Hardy, G. E., & Mellor-Clark, J. (Eds.). (2010). *Developing and delivering practice-based evidence: A guide for the psychological therapies*. Chichester, United Kingdom: Wiley.

Barkham, M., & Margison, F. (2007). Practice-based evidence as a complement to evidence-based practice: From dichotomy to chiasmus. In C. Freeman & M. Power (Eds.), *Handbook of evidence-based psychotherapies: A guide for research and practice* (pp. 443–476). Chichester, United Kingdom: Wiley.

Barkham, M., Margison, F., Leach, C., Lucock, M., Mellor-Clark, J., Evans, C., . . . McGrath, G. (2001). Service profiling and outcomes benchmarking using the CORE-OM: Towards practice-based evidence in the psychological therapies.

Journal of Consulting and Clinical Psychology, 69, 184–196.

Barkham, M., Mellor-Clark, J., Connell, J., Evans, R., Evans, C., & Margison, F. (2010). The CORE measures & CORE system: Measuring, monitoring, and managing quality evaluation in the psychological therapies. In M. Barkham, G. E. Hardy, & J. Mellor-Clark (Eds.), *Developing and delivering practice-based evidence: A guide for the psychological therapies* (pp. 175–219). Chichester, United Kingdom: Wiley.

Barkham, M., Rees, A., Stiles, W. B., Shapiro, D. A., Hardy, G. E., & Reynolds, S. (1996). Dose-effect relations in time-limited psychotherapy for depression. *Journal of Consulting and Clinical Psychology, 64,* 927–935.

Barkham, M., Stiles, W. B., Connell, J., & Mellor-Clark, J. (2012). The meaning of treatment effectiveness in routine NHS primary care psychological therapy services. *Psychology and Psychotherapy: Theory, Research and Practice, 85,* 1–16.

Barkham, M., Stiles, W. B., Connell, J., Twigg, E., Leach, C., Lucock, M.,...Angus, L. (2008). Effects of psychological therapies in randomized trials and practice-based studies. *British Journal of Clinical Psychology, 47,* 397–415.

Barkham, M., Stiles, W. B., Lambert, M. J., & Mellor-Clark, J. (2010). Building a rigorous and relevant knowledge-base for the psychological therapies. In M. Barkham, G. E. Hardy, & J. Mellor-Clark (Eds.), *Developing and delivering practice-based evidence: A guide for the psychological therapies* (pp. 21–61). Chichester, United Kingdom: Wiley.

Barkham, M., Stiles, W. B., & Shapiro, D. A. (1993). The shape of change in psychotherapy: Longitudinal assessment of personal problems. *Journal of Consulting and Clinical Psychology, 61,* 667–677.

Barlow, D. (Ed.). (2007). *Clinical handbook of psychological disorders.* New York, NY: Guilford Press.

Barlow, D. H., & Nock, M. K. (2009). Why can't we be more idiographic in our research? *Perspectives on Psychological Science, 4,* 19–21.

Bauer, S. (2004). Outcome monitoring and feedback: Strategies for optimisation of inpatient psychotherapy. Doctoral Thesis (PhD), Faculty of Social and Behavioral Sciences, University of Tubingen, Germany, 2004.

Bech, P., Gudex, C., & Johansen, K. S. (1996). The WHO (Ten) well-being index: Validation in diabetes. *Psychotherapy and Psychosomatics, 65,* 183–190.

Beck, A. T., Rush, A. J., Shaw, B. F., & Emery, G. (1979). *Cognitive therapy of depression.* New York, NY: Guilford Press.

Beck, A. T., Ward, C. H., Mendelson, M., Mock, J., & Erbaugh, J. (1961). An inventory for measuring depression. *Archives of General Psychiatry, 4,* 561–571.

Beck, J. G., Castonguay, L. G., Chronis-Tuscano, A., Klonsky, E. D., McGinn, L., & Youngstrom, E. (2012, November). *Giving students a fish versus teaching students to fish: Evidence-based training principles and practical guidelines.* Symposium presented at the 46th Annual Convention of the Association for Behavioral and Cognitive Therapies. National Harbor, MD.

Beeson, P. M., & Robey, R. R. (2006). Evaluating single-subject treatment research: Lessons learned from the aphasia literature. *Neuropsychological Review, 16,* 161–169.

Bergin, A. E., & Suinn, R. M. (1975). Individual psychotherapy and behavior therapy. *Annual Review of Psychology, 26,* 509–556.

Berking, M., Orth, U., & Lutz, W. (2006). Effects of systematic feedback to the therapist on patient progress. An empirical study in a cognitive-behavioral inpatient setting (in German). *Zeitschrift für Klinische Psychologie und Psychotherapie, 35,* 21–29.

Beutler, L. E., Williams, R. E., Wakefield, P. J., & Entwistle, S. R. (1995). Bridging scientist and practitioner perspectives in clinical psychology. *American Psychologist, 50,* 984–994.

Bickman, L., Kelley, S. D., Breda, C., de Andrade, A. R., & Riemer, M. (2011). Effects of routine feedback to clinicians on mental health outcomes of youths: Results of a randomized trial. *Psychiatric Services, 62,* 1423–1429.

Bickman, L., Riemer, M., Breda, C., & Kelley, S. D. (2006). CFIT: A system to provide a continuous quality improvement infrastructure through organizational responsiveness, measurement, training, and feedback. *Report on Emotional & Behavioral Disorders in Youth, 6,* 86–87, 93–94.

Borckardt, J. J., Nash, M. R., Murphy, M. D., Moore, M., Shaw, D., & O'Neil, P. (2008). Clinical practice as natural laboratory for psychotherapy research: A guide to case-based time-series analysis. *American Psychologist, 63,* 77–95.

Borkovec, T. D. (2002). Training clinic research and the possibility of a national training clinics practice research network. *Behavior Therapist, 25,* 98–103.

Borkovec, T. D., & Castonguay, L. G. (1998). What is the scientific meaning of "Empirically Supported Therapy"? *Journal of Consulting and Clinical Psychology, 66,* 136–142.

Borkovec, T. D., Echemendia, R. J., Ragusea, S. A., & Ruiz, M. (2001). The Pennsylvania practice research network and future possibilities for clinically meaningful and scientifically rigorous psychotherapy research. *Clinical Psychology: Science and Practice, 8,* 155–168.

Boswell, J. F., Castonguay, L. G., & Wasserman, R. H. (2010). Effects of psychotherapy training and intervention use on session outcome. *Journal of Consulting and Clinical Psychology, 78,* 717–723.

Boswell, J. F., McAleavey, A. A., Castonguay, L. G., Hayes, J. A., & Locke, B. D. (2012). The effect of previous mental health service utilization on change in counseling clients' depressive symptoms. *Journal of Counseling Psychology*, *59*, 368–378.

Brabec, B., & Meister, R. (2001). A nearest-neighbor model for regional avalanche forecasting. *Annals of Glaciology*, *32*, 130–134.

Bradley, L. J., Sexton, T. L., & Smith, H. B. (2005). The American counseling association practice research network (ACA-PRN): A new research tool. *Journal of Counseling & Development*, *83*, 488–491.

Brodey, B. B., Cuffel, B., McCulloch, J., Tani, S., Maruish, M., Brodey, I., & Unutzer, J. (2005). The acceptability and effectiveness of patient reported assessments and feedback in a managed behavioral healthcare setting. *American Journal of Managed Care*, *11*, 774–780.

Brookman-Frazee, L. I., Drahota, A., & Stadnick, N. (2011). Training community mental health therapists to deliver a package of evidence-based practice strategies for school-age children with autism spectrum disorders: A pilot study. *Journal of Autism and Developmental Disorders*. doi: 10.1007/s10803–011–1406–7

Brookman-Frazee, L., Haine, R. A., Baker-Ericzen, M., Zoffness, R., & Garland, A. F. (2010). Factors associated with the use of EBP strategies in usual care youth psychotherapy. *Administration and Policy in Mental Health*, *37*, 254–269.

Brookman-Frazee, L., Stahmer, A., Searcy, L. K., Feder, J., Reed, S. (2012). Building a research-community collaborative to improve preventative care for children at-risk for autism spectrum disorders. *Journal of Community Psychology*, *40*, 715–734.

Brown, G. S., & Jones, E. R. (2005). Implementation of a feedback system in a managed care environment: What are patients teaching us? *Journal of Clinical Psychology/In Session*, *61*, 187–198.

Brown, G. S., Lambert, M. J., Jones, E. R., & Minami, T. (2005). Identifying highly effective therapists in a managed care environment. *American Journal of Managed Care*, *8*, 513–520.

Burlew, A. K., Larios, S., Suarez-Morales, L., Holmes, B. W., Venner, K. L., & Chavez, R. (2011). Increasing ethnic minority participation in substance abuse clinical trials: Lessons learned in the national institute on drug abuse's clinical trials network. *Cultural Diversity and Ethnic Minority Psychology*, *17*, 345–356.

Burns, D. D., & Nolen-Hoeksema, S. (1991). Coping styles, homework compliance, and the effectiveness of cognitive-behavioral therapy. *Journal of Consulting and Clinical Psychology*, *59*, 305–311.

Burns, D. D., & Nolen-Hoeksema, S. (1992). Therapeutic empathy and recovery from depression in cognitive-behavioral therapy: A structure equation model. *Journal of Consulting and Clinical Psychology*, *60*, 441–449.

Byrne, S. L., Hooke, G. R., Newnham, E. A., & Page, A. C. (2012). The effects of progress monitoring on subsequent readmission to psychiatric care: A six-month follow-up. *Journal of Affective Disorders*, *137*, 113–116.

Cahill, J., Barkham, M., & Stiles, W. B. (2010). Systematic review of practice-based research on psychological therapies in routine clinic settings. *British Journal of Clinical Psychology*, *49*, 421–454.

Cahill, J., Barkham, M., Stiles, W. B., Twigg, E., Rees, A., Hardy, G. E., & Evans, C. (2006). Convergent validity of the CORE measures with measures of depression for clients in brief cognitive therapy for depression. *Journal of Counseling Psychology*, *53*, 253–259.

Carlier, I. V. E., Meuldijk, D., Van Vliet, I. M., Van Fenema, E., Van der Wee, N. J. A., & Zitman, F. G. (2012). Routine outcome monitoring and feedback on physical or mental health status: evidence and theory. *Journal of Evaluation in Clinical Practice*, *18*, 104–110.

Carroll, K. M., Ball, S. A., Nich, C., Martino, S., Frankforter, T. L., Farentinos, C., . . . Woody, G. E. for the National Institute on Drug Abuse Clinical Trials Network. (2006). Motivational interviewing to improve treatment engagement and outcome in individuals seeking treatment for substance abuse: A multisite effectiveness study. *Drug and Alcohol Dependence*, *81*, 301–312.

Carroll, K. M., Martino, S., Ball, S. A., Nich, C., Frankforter, T. L., Anez, L., . . . Farentinos, C. (2009). A multisite randomized effectiveness trial of motivational enhancement therapy for Spanish-speaking substance users. *Journal of Consulting and Clinical Psychology*, *77*, 993–999.

Castonguay, L. G. (2011). Psychotherapy, psychopathology, research and practice: Pathways of connections and integration. *Psychotherapy Research*, *21*, 125–140.

Castonguay, L. G., Adam-Term, R., Cavanagh, T., Hill, B., Johnson, B., Magnavita, J., . . . Spayd, C. (2010). *What do clinicians think about research?* Structured discussion presented at the meeting of the Society for Psychotherapy Research, Asilomar, California.

Castonguay, L. G., & Beutler, L. E. (Eds.). (2005a). *Principles of therapeutic change that work.* New York, NY: Oxford University Press.

Castonguay, L. G., & Beutler, L. E. (2005b). Common and unique principles of therapeutic change: What do we know and what do we need to know? In L. G. Castonguay & L. E. Beutler (Eds.), *Principles of therapeutic change that work.* New York, NY: Oxford University Press.

Castonguay, L. G., Boswell, J. F., Zack, S., Baker, S., Boutselis, M., Chiswick, N., . . . Grosse Holtforth, M. (2010). Helpful and hindering events in psychotherapy: A practice research network study. *Psychotherapy: Theory, Research, Practice, and Training*, *47*, 327–344.

Castonguay, L. G., Locke, B. D., & Hayes, J. A. (2011). The center for collegiate mental health: An example of a practice-research network in university counseling centers. *Journal of College Student Psychotherapy, 25,* 105–119.

Castonguay, L., Nelson, D., Boutselis, M., Chiswick, N., Damer, D., Hemmelstein, N., . . . Borkovec, T. (2010). Clinicians and/or researchers? A qualitative analysis of therapists' experiences in a practice research network. *Psychotherapy: Theory, Research, Practice, and Training, 47,* 345–354.

Castonguay, L. G., Pincus, A. L., Arnett, P. A., Roper, G., Rabian, R., & Borkovec, T. B. (2004, November). *Psychology training clinic as a research practice network: Integrating research and clinical practice in graduate school.* Paper presented at the annual meeting of the North American Society for Psychotherapy Research, Springdale, Arizona.

Castonguay, L. G., Schut, A. J., Constantino, M. J., & Halperin, G. S. (1999). Assessing the role of treatment manuals: Have they become necessary but non-sufficient ingredients of change? *Clinical Psychology: Science and Practice, 6,* 449–455.

Chambless, D. L., & Ollendick, T. H. (2001). Empirically supported psychological interventions: Controversies and evidence. *Annual Review of Psychology, 52,* 685–716.

Clark, D. M, Fairburn, C. G., & Wessely, S. (2008). Psychological treatment outcomes in routine NHS services: a commentary on Stiles et al. (2007). *Psychological Medicine, 38,* 629–634.

Cohen, L. H., Sargent, M. M., & Sechrest, L. B. (1986). Use of psychotherapy research by professional psychologists. *American Psychologist, Special Issue: Psychotherapy Research, 41,* 198–206.

Cooper, M. (2008). *Essential research findings in counseling and psychotherapy: The facts are friendly.* London, United Kingdom: Sage.

Crits-Christoph, P., Baranckie, K., Kurcias, J., Beck, A., Carroll, K., Perry, K., . . . Zitrin, C. (1991). Meta-analysis of therapist effects in psychotherapy outcome studies. *Psychotherapy Research, 1,* 81–91.

Crits-Christoph, P., & Mintz, J. (1991). Implications of therapist effects for the design and analysis of comparative studies of psychotherapy. *Journal of Consulting and Clinical Psychology, 54,* 20–26.

Crits-Christoph, P., Ring-Kurtz, S., Hamilton, J. L., Lambert, M. J., Gallop, R., McClure, B., . . . Rotrosen, J. (2012). A preliminary study of the effects of individual patient-level feedback in outpatient substance abuse treatment programs. *Journal of Substance Abuse Treatment, 42,* 301–309.

Crosbie, J. (1993). Interrupted time-series analysis with brief single-subject data. *Journal of Consulting and Clinical Psychology, 61,* 966–974.

Dattilio F. M., Edwards, D. J. A., & Fishman, D. B. (2010). Case studies within a mixed methods paradigm: Toward a resolution of the alienation between researcher and practitioner in psychotherapy research. *Psychotherapy: Theory, Research Practice, Training, 47,* 427–441.

Davis, D. M., & Hayes, J. A. (2011). What are the benefits of mindfulness? A practice review of psychotherapy-related research. *Psychotherapy, 48,* 198–208.

Derogatis, L. R. (1993). *BSI. Brief symptom inventory. Administration, scoring, and procedures manual* (4th ed.). Minneapolis, MN: National Computer Systems.

DeRubeis, R. J., Hollon, S. D., Amsterdam, J. D., Shelton, R. C., Young, P. R., Salomon, R. M., . . . Gallop, R. (2005). Cognitive therapy vs. medications in the treatment of moderate to severe depression. *Archives of General Psychiatry, 62,* 409–416.

Duffy, F. F., Chung, H., Trivedi, M., Rae, D. S., Regier, D. A., & Katzelnick, D. J. (2008). Systematic use of patient-rated depression severity monitoring: Is it helpful and feasible in clinical psychiatry? *Psychiatric Services, 59,* 1148–1154.

Duncan, B. L., & Miller, S. D. (2008). *The Outcome and Session Rating Scales: The revised administration and scoring manual, including the Child Outcome Rating Scale.* Chicago: Institute for the Study of Therapeutic Change.

Effrig, J., Bieschke, K. J., & Locke, B. D. (2011). Examining victimization and psychological distress in transgender college students. *Journal of College Counseling, 14,* 143–157.

Elkin, I., Falconner, L., Martinovich, Z., & Mahoney, C. (2006). Therapist effects in the national institute of mental health treatment of depression collaborative research program. *Psychotherapy Research, 16,* 144–160.

Elkin, I., Shea, M. T., Watkins, J. T., Imber, S. D., Sotsky, S. M., Collins, J. F., . . . Parloff, M. B. (1989). National Institute of Mental Health Treatment of Depression Collaborative Research Program. *Archives of General Psychiatry, 46,* 971–892.

Elliott, R. (1998). Editor's introduction: A guide to the empirically supported treatments controversy. *Psychotherapy Research, 8,* 115–125.

Elliott, R. (2002). Hermeneutic single-case efficacy design. *Psychotherapy Research, 12,* 1–21.

Elliott, R., & Morrow-Bradley, C. (1994). Developing a working marriage between psychotherapists and psychotherapy researchers: Identifying shared purposes. In P. F. Talley, H. H. Strupp, & S. F. Butler (Eds.), *Psychotherapy research and practice: Bridging the gap* (pp. 124–142). New York, NY: Basic Books.

Elliott, R., Partyka, R., Wagner, J., Alperin, R., Dobrenski, R., Messer, S. B., . . . Castonguay, L. G. (2009). An adjudicated hermeneutic single case efficacy design study of experiential therapy for panic/phobia. *Psychotherapy Research, 19,* 543–557.

Evans, C., Connell, J., Barkham, M., Margison, F., Mellor-Clark, J., McGrath, G., & Audin, K. (2002). Towards a standardised brief outcome measure: Psychometric properties and utility of the CORE-OM. *British Journal of Psychiatry, 180,* 51–60.

Evans, C., Connell, J., Barkham, M., Marshall, C., & Mellor-Clark, J. (2003). Practice-based evidence: Benchmarking NHS primary care counselling services at national and local levels. *Clinical Psychology & Psychotherapy, 10,* 374–388.

Farrell, L. J., Schlup, B., & Boschen, M. J. (2010). Cognitive–behavioral treatment of childhood obsessive–compulsive disorder in community-based clinical practice: Clinical significance and benchmarking against efficacy. *Behaviour Research and Therapy, 48,* 409–417.

Finch, A. E., Lambert, M. J., & Schaalje, B. G. (2001). Psychotherapy quality control: The statistical generation of expected recovery curves for integration into an early warning system. *Clinical Psychology and Psychotherapy, 8,* 231–242.

Forcehimes, A. A., Venner, K. L., Bogenschutz, M. P., Foley, K., Davis, M. P., Houck, J. M., . . . Begaye, P. (2011). American Indian methamphetamine and other drug use in the southwestern United States. *Cultural Diversity and Ethnic Minority Psychology, 17,* 366–76.

Froyd, J. E., Lambert, M. J., & Froyd, J. D. (1996). A review of practices of psychotherapy outcome measurement. *Journal of Mental Health, 5,* 11–16.

Galano, J., & Schellenbach, C. J., (2007). Healthy families America research practice network: A unique partnership to integrate prevention sciences and practice. *Journal of Prevention and Integration in the Community, 34,* 39–66.

Galassi, J. P., & Gersh, T. L. (1993). Myths, misconceptions, and missed opportunity: Single-case designs and counseling psychology. *Journal of Counseling Psychology, 40,* 525–531.

Garland, A. F., Hurlburt, M. S., & Hawley, K. M. (2006). Examining psychotherapy processes in a services research context. *Clinical Psychology: Science and Practice, 13,* 30–46.

Garland, A. F., Plemmons, D., & Koontz, L. (2006). Research-practice partnership in mental health: lessons from participants. *Administration and Policy in Mental Health and Mental Health Services, 33,* 517–528.

Gibbard, I., & Hanley, T. (2008). A five-year evaluation of the effectiveness of person-centred counselling in routine clinical practice in primary care. *Counselling and Psychotherapy Research, 8,* 215–222.

Gibbons, C. J., Fourner, J. C., Stirman, S. W., DeRubeis, R. J., Crits-Christoph, P., & Beck, A. T. (2010). The clinical effectiveness of cognitive therapy for depression in an outpatient clinic. *Journal of Affective Disorders, 125,* 169–176.

Goldfried, M. R. (1984). Training the clinician as scientist-professional. *Professional Psychology: Research and Practice, 15,* 477–481.

Goldfried, M. R. (2011). Generating research questions from clinical experience: Therapists' experiences in using CBT for panic disorder. *Behavior Therapist, 34,* 57–62.

Goodheart, C. D., Kazdin, A. E., & Sternberg, R. J. (2006). *Evidence-based practice: Where practice and research meet.* Washington, DC: American Psychological Association.

Grawe, K. (1997). Research-informed psychotherapy. *Psychotherapy Research, 7,* 1–19.

Gray, G. E. (2004). *Evidence-based psychiatry.* Washington, DC: American Psychiatric Association.

Green, L. W., & Glasgow, R. E. (2006). Evaluating the relevance, generalizability, and applicability of research: Issues in external validation and translational methodology. *Evaluation & the Health Professions, 29,* 126–153.

Greenhalgh, J., Long, A. F., & Flynn, R. (2005). The use of patient reported outcome measures in routine clinical practice: Lack of impact or lack of theory? *Social Science & Medicine, 60,* 833–843.

Grissom, G. R., Lyons, J. S., & Lutz, W. (2002). Standing on the shoulders of a giant: Development of an outcome management system based on the dose model and phase model of psychotherapy. *Psychotherapy Research, 12,* 397–412.

Guyatt, G. H., & Rennie, D. (Eds.). (2002). *Users' guides to the medical literature.* Chicago, IL: AMA Press.

Hannan, C., Lambert, M. J., Harmon, C., Nielsen, S. L., Smart, D. W., Shimokawa, K., & Sutton, S. W. (2005). A lab test and algorithms for identifying clients at risk for treatment failure. *Journal of Clinical Psychology: In Session, 61,* 155–163.

Hansen, N., & Lambert, M. (2003). An evaluation of the dose–response relationship in naturalistic treatment settings using survival analysis. *Mental Health Services Research, 5,* 1–12.

Hansen, N. B., Lambert, M. J., & Forman, E. M. (2002). The psychotherapy dose–response effect and implications for treatment delivery services. *Clinical Psychology: Science and Practice, 9,* 329–343.

Hanson, G. R., Leshner, A. I., & Tai, B. (2002). Putting drug abuse research to use in real-life settings. *Journal of Substance Abuse Treatment, 23,* 69–70.

Hardy, J. A., Weatherford, R. D., Locke, B. D., DePalma, N. H., & D'luso, N. T. (2011). Meeting the demand for college student concerns in college counseling centers: Evaluating a clinical triage system. *Journal of College Student Psychotherapy, 25,* 220–240.

Harmon, S. C., Lambert, M. J., Smart, D. W., Hawkins, E. J., Nielsen, S. L., Slade, K., & Lutz, W. (2007). Enhancing outcome for potential treatment failures: Therapist/client feedback and clinical support tools. *Psychotherapy Research, 17,* 379–392.

Harnett, P., O'Donovan, A., & Lambert, M. J. (2010). The dose response relationship in psychotherapy: Implications for social policy. *Clinical Psychologist, 14,* 39–44.

Hartzler, B., Donovan, D. M., & Huang, Z. (2010). Comparison of opiate-primary treatment seekers with and without alcohol use disorder. *Journal of Substance Abuse Treatment, 39,* 114–123.

Hawkins, E. J., Lambert, M. J., Vermeersch, D. A., Slade, K., & Tuttle, K. (2004). The effects of providing patient progress information to therapists and patients. *Psychotherapy Research, 14*, 308–327.

Hayes, J. A., Chun-Kennedy, C., Edens, A., & Locke, B. D. (2011). Do double minority students face double jeopardy? Testing minority stress theory. *Journal of College Counseling, 14*, 117–126.

Hayes, J. A., Locke, B. E., & Castonguay, L. G. (2011). The center for collegiate mental health: Practice and research working together. *Journal of College Counseling, 14*, 101–104.

Hayes, S. C., (1981). Single case experimental design and empirical clinical practice. *Journal of Consulting and Clinical Psychology, 49*, 193–211.

Herbeck, D. M., Gitek, D. J., Svikis, D. S., Montoya, I. D., Marcus, S. C., & West, J. C. (2005). Treatment compliance in patients with comorbid psychiatric and substance use disorders. *American Journal on Addictions, 14*, 195–207.

Herbeck, D. M., West, J. C., Ruditis, I., Duffy, F. F., Fitek, D. J., Bell, C. C., & Snowden, L. R. (2004). Variations in use of second-generation antipsychotic medication by race among adult psychiatric patients. *Psychiatric Services, 55*, 677–684.

Horowitz, L. M., Rosenberg, S. E., Baer, B. A., Ureño, G., & Villaseñor, V. S. (1988). Inventory of interpersonal problems: Psychometric properties and clinical applications. *Journal of Consulting and Clinical Psychology, 56*, 885–892.

Houghton, S., Saxon, D., Bradburn, M., Ricketts, T., & Hardy, G. E. (2010). The effectiveness of routinely delivered cognitive behavioural therapy for obsessive-compulsive disorder: A benchmarking study. *British Journal of Clinical Psychology, 49*, 473–489.

Howard, K. I., Kopta, M., Krause, M. S., & Orlinsky, D. E. (1986). The dose-effect relationship in psychotherapy. *American Psychologist, 41*, 159–164.

Howard, K. I., Lueger, R. J., Maling, M. S., & Martinovich, Z. (1993). A phase model of psychotherapy: Causal mediation of outcome. *Journal of Consulting and Clinical Psychology, 61*, 678–685.

Howard, K. I., Moras, K., Brill, P., Martinovich, Z., & Lutz, W. (1996). The evaluation of psychotherapy. *American Psychologist, 52*, 1059–1064.

Huet, V., Springham, N., & Evans, C. (2008). Art therapy practice research network. http://www.baat.org/atprn.html

Iwakabe, S., & Gazzola, N. (2009). From single-case studies to practice-based knowledge: Aggregating and synthesizing case studies. *Psychotherapy Research, 19*, 601–611.

Jacobson, N. S., & Truax, P. (1991). Clinical significance: A statistical approach to defining meaningful change in psychotherapy research. *Journal of Consulting and Clinical Psychology, 59*, 12–19.

Jones, W. P. (2003). Single-case time series with Bayesian analysis: A practitioner's guide. *Measurement and Evaluation in Counseling and Development, 36*, 28–39.

Joyce, A. S., Ogrodniczuk, J., Piper, W. E., & McCallum, M. (2002). A test of the phase model of psychotherapy change. *Canadian Journal of Psychiatry, 47*, 759–766.

Kadera, S. W., Lambert, M. J., & Andrews, A. A. (1996). How much therapy is really enough: A session-by-session analysis of the psychotherapy dose-effect relationship. *Journal of Psychotherapy Practice and Research, 5*, 132–151.

Kazdin, A. E. (2008). Evidence-based treatment and practice: New opportunities to bridge clinical research and practice, enhance the knowledge base, and improve patient care. *American Psychologist, 63*, 146–159.

Kazdin, A. E. (2009). Understanding how and why psychotherapy leads to change. *Psychotherapy Research, 19*, 418–428.

Kazdin, A. E. (2010). *Single-case research designs: Methods for clinical and applied settings* (2nd ed.). New York, NY: Oxford University Press.

Kazdin, A. E., Kratochwill, T. R., & VandenBos, G. R. (1986). Beyond clinical trials: Generalizing from research to practice. *Professional Psychology: Research and Practice, 17*, 391–398.

Kim, D-M, Wampold, B. E., & Bolt, D. M. (2006). Therapist effects in psychotherapy: A random-effects modeling of the National Institute of Mental Health Treatment of Depression Collaborative Research Program data. *Psychotherapy Research, 16*, 161–172.

Klerman, G. L., Weissman, M. M., Rounsaville, B. J., & Chevron, E. S. (1984). *Interpersonal therapy of depression.* New York, NY: Basic Books.

Knaup, C., Koesters, M., Schoefer, D., Becker, T., & Puschner, B. (2009). Effect of feedback of treatment outcome in specialist mental healthcare: Meta-analysis. *British Journal of Psychiatry, 195*, 15–22.

Knudsen, H. K., Ducharme, L., J., & Roman, P. M. (2007). Research participation and turnover intention: An exploratory analysis of substance abuse counselors. *Journal of Substance Abuse Treatment, 33*, 211–217.

Kopta, S. M., Howard, K. I., Lowry, J. L., & Beutler, L. E. (1994). Patterns of symptomatic recovery in time-unlimited psychotherapy. *Journal of Consulting and Clinical Psychology, 62*, 1009–1016.

Kopta, S. M., & Lowry, J. L. (2002). Psychometric evaluation of the behavioral health questionnaire-20: A brief instrument for assessing global mental health and the three phases of psychotherapy outcome. *Psychotherapy Research, 12*, 413–426.

Kraus, D., & Castonguay, L. G. (2010). Treatment outcome package (TOP)—Development and use in naturalistic settings. In M. Barkham, G. E. Hardy, & J. Mellor-Clark (Eds.), *Developing and delivering practice-based evidence: A guide for the psychological therapies* (pp. 155–174). Chichester, United Kingdom: Wiley.

Kraus, D. R., Castonguay, L., Boswell, J. F., Nordberg, S. S., & Hayes, J. A. (2011). Therapist effectiveness: Implications for accountability and patient care. *Psychotherapy Research, 21,* 267–276.

Kraus, D. R., Seligman, D. A., & Jordan, J. R. (2005). Validation of a behavioral health treatment outcome and assessment tool designed for naturalistic settings: The treatment outcome package. *Journal of Clinical Psychology, 61,* 285–314.

Krause, M. S., Howard, K. I., & Lutz, W. (1998). Exploring individual change. *Journal of Consulting and Clinical Psychology, 66,* 838–845.

Kroenke, K., Spitzer, R. L., & Williams, J. B. (2001). The PHQ-9: Validity of a brief depression severity measure. *Journal of General Internal Medicine, 16,* 606–613.

Lambert, M. J. (2007). Presidential address: What we have learned from a decade of research aimed at improving psychotherapy outcome in routine care. *Psychotherapy Research, 17,* 1–14.

Lambert, M. J. (2010). *Prevention of treatment failure: The use of measuring, monitoring, and feedback in clinical practice.* Washington, DC: American Psychological Association.

Lambert, M. J., Hansen, N. B., & Finch, A. E. (2001). Patient-focused research: Using patient outcome data to enhance treatment effects. *Journal of Consulting and Clinical Psychology, 69,* 159–172.

Lambert, M. J., Hansen, N. B., & Harmon, S. C. (2010). Outcome questionnaire system (the OQ system): Development and practical applications in healthcare settings. In M. Barkham, G. E. Hardy, & J. Mellor-Clark (Eds.), *Developing and delivering practice-based evidence: A guide for the psychological therapies* (pp.141–154). Chichester, United Kingdom: Wiley.

Lambert, M. J., Lunnen, K., Umphress, V., Hansen, N., & Burlingame, G. M. (1994). Administration and scoring manual for the outcome questionnaire (*OQ-45.1*). Salt Lake City, UT: IHC Center for Behavioral Healthcare Efficacy.

Lambert, M. J., & Ogles, B. M. (2004). The efficacy and effectiveness of psychotherapy. In M. J. Lambert (Ed.), *Bergin and Garfield's handbook of psychotherapy and behavior change* (5th ed., pp. 139–193). Hoboken, NJ: Wiley.

Lambert, M. J., & Shimokawa, K. (2011). Collecting client feedback. *Psychotherapy, 48,* 72–79.

Lambert, M. J., Whipple, J. L., Bishop, M. J., Vermeersch, D. A., Gray, G. V., & Finch, A. E. (2002). Comparison of empirically derived and rationally-derived methods for identifying patients at risk for treatment failure. *Clinical Psychology and Psychotherapy, 9,* 149–164.

Lambert, M. J., Whipple, J. L., Hawkins, E. J., Vermeersch, D. A., Nielsen, S. L., & Smart, D. W. (2003). Is it time for clinicians to routinely track patient outcome?: A meta-analysis. *Clinical Psychology: Science & Practice, 10,* 288–301.

Lambert, M. J., Whipple, J. L., Smart, D. W., Vermeersch, D. A., Nielsen, S. L., & Hawkins, E. J. (2001). The effects of providing therapists with feedback on client progress during psychotherapy: Are outcomes enhanced? *Psychotherapy Research, 11,* 49–68.

Lambert, M. J., Whipple, J. L., Vermeersch, D. A., Smart, D. W., Hawkins, E. J., Nielsen, S. L., & Goates, M. K. (2002). Enhancing psychotherapy outcomes via providing feedback on client progress: A replication. *Clinical Psychology and Psychotherapy, 9,* 91–103.

Layard, R. (2006). The case for psychological treatment centres. *British Medical Journal, 332,* 1030–1032.

Lebow, J. (2006). *Research for the psychotherapist: From science to practice.* New York, NY: Routledge.

Lockard, A. J., Hayes, J. A., McAleavey, A. A., & Locke, B. D. (2012). Change in academic distress: Examining differences between a clinical and nonclinical sample of college students. *Journal of College Counseling, 15,* 233–246. doi: 10.1002/j.2161-1882.2012.00018.x

Locke, B. D., Bieschke, K. J., Castonguay, L. G., & Hayes, J. A. (2012). The center for collegiate mental health (CCMH): Studying college student mental health through an innovative research infrastructure that brings science and practice together. *Harvard Review of Psychiatry, 20,* 233–245.

Locke, B. D., Buzolitz, J. S., Dowis, J. D., Lei, P., Boswell, J. F., McAleavey, A. A.,…Hayes, J. A. (2011). Development of the counseling center assessment of psychological symptoms. *Journal of Counseling Psychology, 58,* 97–109.

Locke, B. D., McAleavey, A. A., Zhao, Y., Lei, P. W., Hayes, J. A., Castonguay, L. G.,…Lin, Y. C. (2012). Development and initial validation of the counseling center assessment of psychological symptoms-34 (CCAPS-34). *Measurement and Evaluation in Counseling and Development, 45,* 151–169.

Lueger, R. J., & Barkham, M. (2010). Using benchmarks and benchmarking to improve quality of practice and services. In M. Barkham, G. E. Hardy, & J. Mellor-Clark (Eds.), *Developing and delivering practice-based evidence: A guide for the psychological therapies* (pp. 223–256). Chichester, United Kingdom: Wiley.

Lueger, R. J., Howard, K. I., Martinovich, Z., Lutz, W., Anderson, E. E., & Grissom, G. (2001). Assessing treatment progress of individual patients using expected treatment response models. *Journal of Consulting and Clinical Psychology, 69,* 150–158.

Lutz, W. (2002). Patient-focused psychotherapy research and individual treatment progress as scientific groundwork for an empirical based clinical practice. *Psychotherapy Research, 12,* 251–273.

Lutz, W., Böhnke, J., & Köck, K. (2011). Lending an ear to feedback systems: Evaluation of recovery and non-response in psychotherapy in a German outpatient setting. *Community Mental Health Journal, 47,* 311–317.

Lutz, W., Böhnke, J. R., Köck, K., & Bittermann, A. (2011). Diagnostik und psychometrischer Verlaufsrückmeldungen im Rahmen eines Modellprojektes zur Qualitätssicherung in der ambulanten Psychotherapie [Diagnostic and psychometric feedback within a pilot project on quality assurance in outpatient psychotherapy]. *Zeitschrift für Klinische Psychologie und Psychotherapie, 40,* 283–297.

Lutz, W., Lambert, M. J., Harmon, S. C., Tschitsaz, A., Schürch, E., & Stulz, N. (2006). The probability of treatment success, failure and duration—What can be learned from empirical data to support decision making in clinical practice? *Clinical Psychology and Psychotherapy, 13,* 223–232.

Lutz, W., Leach, C., Barkham, M., Lucock, M., Stiles, W. B., Evans, C., . . . Iverson, S. (2005). Predicting change for individual psychotherapy clients based on their nearest neighbors. *Journal of Consulting and Clinical Psychology, 73,* 904–913.

Lutz, W., Leon, S. C., Martinovich, Z., Lyons, J. S., & Stiles, W. B. (2007). Therapist effects in outpatient psychotherapy: A three-level growth curve approach. *Journal of Counseling Psychology, 54,* 32–39.

Lutz, W., Martinovich, Z., & Howard, K. I. (1999). Patient profiling: An application of random coefficient regression models to depicting the response of a patient to outpatient psychotherapy. *Journal of Consulting and Clinical Psychology, 67,* 571–577.

Lutz, W., Martinovich, Z., Howard, K. I., & Leon, S. C. (2002). Outcomes management, expected treatment response and severity adjusted provider profiling in outpatient psychotherapy. *Journal of Clinical Psychology, 58,* 1291–1304.

Lutz, W., Saunders, S. M., Leon, S. C., Martinovich, Z., Kosfelder, J., Schulte, D., . . . Tholen, S. (2006). Empirically and clinically useful decision making in psychotherapy: Differential predictions with treatment response models. *Psychological Assessment, 18,* 133–141.

Lutz, W., Stulz, N., & Köck, K. (2009). Patterns of early change and their relationship to outcome and follow-up among patients with major depressive disorders. *Journal of Affective Disorders, 118,* 60–68.

Lutz, W., Stulz, N., Martinovich, Z., Leon, S., & Saunders, S. M. (2009). Methodological background of decision rules and feedback tools for outcomes management in psychotherapy. *Psychotherapy Research, 19,* 502–510.

Lutz, W., Stulz, N., Smart, D. W., & Lambert, M. J. (2007). Die Identifikation früher Veränderungsmuster in der ambulanten Psychotherapie [Patterns of early change in outpatient therapy]. *Zeitschrift für Klinische Psychologie und Psychotherapie, 36,* 93–104.

Maling, M. S., Gurtman, M. B., & Howard, K. I. (1995). The response of interpersonal problems to varying doses of psychotherapy. *Psychotherapy Research, 5,* 63–75.

Marriott, M., & Kellett, S. (2009). Evaluating a cognitive analytic therapy service; practice-based outcomes and comparisons with person-centred and cognitive-behavioural therapies. *Psychology and Psychotherapy: Theory, Research and Practice, 82,* 57–82.

Marshall, M., Lockwood, A., Green, G., Zajac-Roles, G., Roberts, C. & Harrison, G. (2004). Systematic assessments of need and care planning in severe mental illness. *Cluster randomised controlled trial. British Journal of Psychiatry, 185,* 163–168.

Martin, J. L., Hess, T. R., Ain, S. C., Nelson, D. L., & Locke, B. D. (2012). Collecting multi-dimensional client data using repeated measures: Experiences of clients and counselors using the CCAPS-34. *Journal of College Counseling, 15,* 247–261. doi: 10.1002/j.2161-1882.2012.00019.x

Martindale, C. (1978). The therapist-as-fixed-effect fallacy in psychotherapy research. *Journal of Consulting and Clinical Psychology, 46,* 1526–1530.

Mayotte-Blum, J., Slavin-Mulford, J., Lehmann, M., Pesale, F., Becker-Matero, N., & Hilsenroth, M. (2011). Therapeutic immediacy across long-term psychodynamic psychotherapy: An evidence-based case study. *Journal of Counseling Psychology, 59,* 27–40.

McAleavey, A. A., Castonguay, L. G., & Locke, B. D. (2011). Sexual orientation minorities in college counseling: Prevalence, distress, and symptom profiles. *Journal of College Counseling, 14,* 127–142.

McAleavey, A. A., Nordberg, S. S., Hayes, J. A., Castonguay, L. G., Locke, B. D., & Lockard, A. J. (2012, September 3). Clinical validity of the Counseling Center Assessment of Psychological Symptoms-62 (CCAPS-62): Further evaluation and clinical applications. *Journal of Counseling Psychology.* Advance online publication. doi: 10.1037/a0029855

McAleavey, A. A., Nordberg, S. S., Kraus, D. R., & Castonguay, L. G. (2012). Errors in treatment outcome monitoring: Implications for real-world psychotherapy. *Canadian Psychology, 53,* 105–114.

McMillen, J. C., Lenze, S. L., Hawley, K. M., & Osbourne, V. A. (2009). Revisiting practice based research networks as a platform for mental health services research. *Administration and Policy in Mental Health, 36,* 308–321.

Mellor-Clark, J., & Barkham, M. (2006). The CORE system: Developing and delivering practice-based evidence through quality evaluation. In C. Feltham & I. Horton (Eds.), *Handbook of counselling and psychotherapy* (2nd ed., pp. 207–224). London, United Kingdom: Sage.

Merrill, K. A., Tolbert, V. E., & Wade, W. A. (2003). Effectiveness of cognitive therapy for depression in a community mental health center: A benchmarking study. *Journal of Consulting and Clinical Psychology, 71,* 404–409.

Miller, S. D., Duncan, B. L., Brown, J., Sparks, J. A., & Claud, D. A. (2003). The outcome rating scale: A preliminary study of the reliability, validity, and feasibility of a brief visual analog measure. *Journal of Brief Therapy, 2,* 91–100.

Miller, S. D., Duncan, B. L., Sorrell, R., & Brown, G. S. (2005). The partners for change outcome system. *Journal of Clinical Psychology: In Session, 61,* 199–208.

Minami, T., Serlin, R. C., Wampold, B. E., Kircher, J. C., & Brown, G. S. (2006). Using clinical trials to benchmark effects produced in clinical practice. *Quality & Quantity, 42,* 513–525.

Minami, T., Wampold, B. E., Serlin, R. C., Kircher, J. C., & Brown, G. S. (2007). Benchmarks for psychotherapy efficacy in adult major depression. *Journal of Consulting and Clinical Psychology, 75,* 232–243.

Montgomery, L., Burlew, A. K., Kosinski, A. S., & Forcehimes, A. A. (2011). Motivational enhancement therapy for African American substance users: A randomized clinical trial. *Cultural Diversity and Ethnic Minority Psychology, 17,* 357–365.

Morgan-Lopez, A. A., Saavedra, L. M., Hien, D. A., & Fals-Stewart, W. (2010). Estimating statistical power for open-enrollment group treatment trials. *Journal of Substance abuse Treatment, 40,* 3–17.

Morley, S., Williams, A., & Hussain, S. (2008). Estimating the clinical effectiveness of cognitive behavioural therapy in the clinic: Evaluation of a CBT informed pain management programme. *Pain, 137,* 670–680.

Morrow-Bradley, C., & Elliott, R. (1986). Utilization of psychotherapy research by practicing psychotherapists. *American Psychologist, Special Issue: Psychotherapy Research, 41,* 188–197.

Murphy, G. E., Simons, A. D., Wetzel, R. D., & Lustman, P. J. (1984). Cognitive therapy and pharmacotherapy, singly and together, in the treatment of depression. *Archives of General Psychiatry, 41,* 33–41.

Muthén, B. O. (2001). Second-generation structural equation modeling with a combination of categorical and continuous latent variables. In L. M. Collins & A. G. Sayer (Eds.), *New methods for the analysis of change* (pp. 291–332). Washington, DC: American Psychological Association.

Muthén, B. O. (2004). Latent variable analysis: Growth mixture modeling and related techniques for longitudinal data. In D. Kaplan (Ed.), *Handbook of quantitative methodology for social sciences* (pp. 345–368). Newbury Park, CA: Sage.

Nathan, P. E., & Gorman, J. M. (2002). (Eds.). *A guide to treatments that work* (2nd ed.). New York, NY: Oxford University Press.

National Drug Abuse Treatment Clinical Trials Network. (2011, December 21). *Dissemination library.* Retrieved from http://ctndissemination library.org/

Nelson, D. L., Castonguay, L. G., & Locke, B. D. (2011). Challenging stereotypes of eating and body image concerns among college students: Implications for diagnosis and treatment of diverse populations. *Journal of College Counseling, 14,* 158–172.

Newnham, E. A., Hooke, G. R., & Page, A. C. (2010). Progress monitoring and feedback in psychiatric care reduces depressive symptoms. *Journal of Affective Disorders, 127,* 139–146.

Newnham, E. A., & Page, A. C. (2010). Bridging the gap between best evidence and best practice in mental health. *Clinical Psychology Review, 30,* 127–142.

Norcross, J. C. (2011). *Psychotherapeutic relationships that work* (2nd ed.). New York, NY: Oxford University Press.

Norcross, J. C., Beutler, L. E., & Levant, R. F. (2006). *Evidence-based practice in mental health: Debate and dialogue on the fundamental questions.* Washington, DC: American Psychological Association.

Nordberg, S. S., Castonguay, L. G., Fisher, A. J., Boswell, J. F., & Kraus, D. (2008, June). *Measuring the shape of change: Results from three years of repeated assessment in a university clinic.* Paper presented as part of a symposium at the annual meeting of the Society for Psychotherapy Research. Barcelona, Spain.

Northey, W. F., Jr. (2002). Characteristics and clinical practices of marriage and family therapists: A national survey. *Journal of Marital and Family Therapy, 28,* 487–494.

Oei, T. P. S., & Boschen, M. J. (2009). Clinical effectiveness of a cognitive behavioral group treatment program for anxiety disorders: A benchmarking study. *Journal of Anxiety Disorders, 23,* 950–957.

Okiishi, J. C., Lambert, M. J., Eggett, D., Nielson, S. L., Dayton, D. D., & Vermeersch, D. A. (2006). An analysis of therapist treatment effects: Toward providing feedback to individual therapists on their patients' psychotherapy outcome. *Journal of Clinical Psychology, 62,* 1157–1172.

Okiishi, J., Lambert, M. J., Nielsen, S. L., & Ogles, B. M. (2003). Waiting for supershrink: An empirical analysis of therapist effects. *Clinical Psychology & Psychotherapy, 10,* 361–373.

Paley, G., Cahill, J., Barkham, M., Shapiro, D. A., Jones, J., Patrick, S., & Reid, E., (2008). The effectiveness of psychodynamic-interpersonal psychotherapy in routine clinical practice: A benchmarking comparison. *Psychology and Psychotherapy: Theory, Research and Practice, 85,* 157–175.

Parry, G., Castonguay, L. G., Borkovec, T. D., & Wolfe, A. W. (2010). Practice research networks and psychological services research in the UK and USA. In M. Barkham, G. E. Hardy, & J. Mellor-Clark (Eds.), *Developing and delivering practice-based evidence: A guide for the psychological therapies.* Hoboken, NJ: Wiley.

Persons, J. B., Bostrom, A., & Bertagnolli, A. (1999). Results of randomized controlled trials of cognitive therapy for depression generalize to private practice. *Cognitive Therapy and Research, 23,* 535–548.

Persons, J. B., Burns, D. D., & Perloff, J. M. (1988). Predictors of dropout and outcome in cognitive therapy for depression in a private practice setting. *Cognitive Therapy and Research, 12,* 557–575.

Persons, J. B., Roberts, N. A., Zalecki, C. A., & Brechwald, W. A. G. (2006). Naturalistic outcome of case-formulation-driven cognitive-behavioral therapy for anxiety depressed outpatients. *Behaviour Research and Therapy, 44,* 1041–1051.

Persons, J. B., & Silberschatz, G. (1998). Are results of randomized controlled trials useful to psychotherapists? *Journal of Consulting and Clinical Psychology, 66,* 126–135.

Pinsoff, W., Breunlin, D. C., Russell, W. P., & Lebow, J. (2011). Integrative problem-centered metaframeworks therapy II: Planning, conversing, and reading feedback. *Family Process, 50,* 314–336.

Pinto, R. M., Yu, G., Spector, A. Y., Gorroochurn, P., & McCarty, D. (2010). Substance abuse treatment providers' involvement in research is associated with willingness to use findings in practice. *Journal of Substance Abuse Treatment, 39,* 188–194.

Raimy, V. (Ed.). (1950). *Training in clinical psychology.* New York, NY: Prentice-Hall.

Rawlins, M. D. (2008). De testimonio: On the evidence for decisions about the use of therapeutic interventions. The Harveian Oration of 2008. Royal College of Physicians. Reprinted in *The Lancet* (2008), *372,* 2152–2161.

Reese, R. J., Norsworthy, L., & Rowlands, S. (2009). Does a continuous feedback system improve psychotherapy outcome? *Psychotherapy: Theory, Research, Practice, & Training, 46,* 418–431.

Reese, R. J., Toland, M. D., & Hopkins, N. B. (2011). Replicating and extending the good enough level model of change: Considering session frequency. *Psychotherapy Research, 21,* 608–619.

Reese, R. J., Toland, M. D., Slone, N. C., & Norsworthy, L. (2010). Effect of client feedback on couple psychotherapy outcomes. *Psychotherapy Theory, Research, Practice, Training, 47,* 616–630.

Richards, D. A., & Suckling, R. (2009). Improving access to psychological therapies: Phase IV prospective cohort study. *British Journal of Clinical Psychology, 48,* 377–396.

Ricks, D. F. (1974). Supershrink: Methods of a therapist judged successful on the basis of adult outcomes of adolescent patients. In D. F. Ricks, M. Roff, & A. Thomas (Eds.), *Life history in research in psychopathology.* Minneapolis: University of Minnesota Press.

Robbins, M. S., Feaster, D. J., Horigian, V. E., Rohrbaugh, M., Shoham, V., Bachrach, K., ... Szapocznik, J. (2011). Brief strategic family therapy versus treatment as usual: Results of a multi-site randomized trial for substance using adolescents. *Journal of Consulting and Clinical Psychology, 79,* 713–727.

Ruiz, M. A., Pincus, A. L., Borkovec, T. B., Echemendia, R., Castonguay, L. G., & Ragusea, S., (2004). Validity of the inventory of interpersonal problems (IIP-C) for predicting treatment outcome: An investigation with the Pennsylvania practice research network. *Journal of Personality Assessment, 83,* 213–222.

Rush, A. J., Beck, A. T., Kovacs, M., & Hollon, S. (1977). Comparative efficacy of cognitive therapy and pharmacotherapy in the treatment of depressed outpatients. *Cognitive Therapy and Research, 1,* 17–38.

Saxon, D., & Barkham, M. (2012). Patterns of therapist variability: Therapist effects and the contribution of patient severity and risk. *Journal of Consulting and Clinical Psychology, 80,* 535–546.

Schmidt, U., Landau, S., Pombo-Carril, M. G., Bara-Carril, N., Reid, Y., Murray, K., ... Katzman, K. (2006). Does personalized feedback improve the outcome of cognitive-behavioural guided self-care in bulimia nervosa? A preliminary randomized controlled trial. *British Journal of Clinical Psychology, 45,* 111–121.

Schulte, D. (1998). *Therapieplanung [Treatment planning]* (2nd ed.). Göttingen: Hogrefe.

Simmons, D. S., & Doherty, W. J. (1995). Defining who we are and what we do: Clinical practice patterns of marriage and family therapists in Minnesota. *Journal of Marital and Family Therapy, 21,* 403–407.

Shimokawa, K., Lambert, M. J., & Smart, D. W. (2010). Enhancing treatment outcome of patients at risk of treatment failure: Meta-analytic and mega-analytic review of a psychotherapy quality assurance system. *Journal of Consulting and Clinical Psychology, 78,* 298–311.

Silverstein, L. B., Auerbach, C. F., & Levant, R. F. (2006). Using qualitative research to strengthen clinical practice. *Professional Psychology: Research and Practice, 37,* 351–358.

Slade, K., Lambert, M. J., Harmon, S. C., Smart, D. W., & Bailey, R. (2008). Improving psychotherapy outcome: The use of immediate electronic feedback and revised clinical support tools. *Clinical Psychology & Psychotherapy, 15,* 287–303.

Slade, M., McCrone, P., Kuipers, E., Leese, M., Cahill, S., Parabiaghi, A., ... Thornicroft, G. (2006). Use of standardised outcome measures in adult mental health services. *British Journal of Psychiatry, 189,* 330–334.

Smith, H. B., Sexton, T. L., & Bradley, L. J. (2005). The practice research network: Research into practice, practice into research. *Counselling and Psychotherapy Research, 5,* 285–290.

Smith, M. J. W., Whitaker, T., & Weismiller, T. (2006). Social workers in the substance abuse treatment field: A snapshot of service activities. *Health & Social Work, 31*, 109–115.

Soldz, S. (2006). Models and meanings: Therapist effects and the stories we tell. *Psychotherapy Research, 16*, 173–177.

Soldz, S., & McCullough, L. (Ed.). (2000). *Reconciling empirical knowledge and clinical experience: The art and science of psychotherapy.* Washington, DC: American Psychological Association.

Speer, D. C., & Greenbaum, P. E. (1995). Five methods for computing significant individual client change and improvement rates: Support for an individual growth curve approach. *Journal of Consulting and Clinical Psychology, 63*, 1044–1048.

Sperry, L., Brill, P. L., Howard, K. I., & Grissom, G. R. (1996). *Treatment outcomes in psychotherapy and psychiatric interventions.* New York, NY: Brunner/Mazel.

Spitzer, R. L., Kroenke, K., Williams, J. B. W., & Löwe, B. (2006). A brief measure for assessing generalized anxiety disorder: The GAD-7. *Archives of Internal Medicine, 166*, 1092–1097.

Stahmer, A. C., Brookman-Frazee, L., Lee, E., Searcy, K., & Reed, S. (2011). Parent and multidisciplinary provider perspectives on earliest intervention for children at risk for autism spectrum disorders. *Infants & Young Children, 24*, 344–363.

Steinfeld, B. I., Coffman, S. J., & Keyes, J. A. (2009). Implementation of an evidence-based practice in a clinical setting: What happens when you get there? *Professional Psychology: Research and Practice, 40*, 410–416.

Stewart, R. E., & Chambless, D. L. (2009). Cognitive–behavioral therapy for adult anxiety disorders in clinical practice: A meta-analysis of effectiveness studies. *Journal of Consulting and Clinical Psychology, 77*, 595–606.

Stiles, W. B. (2007). Theory-building cases studies of counselling and psychotherapy. *Counselling and Psychotherapy Research, 7*, 122–127.

Stiles, W. B. (2010). Theory-building case studies as practice-based evidence. In M. Barkham, G. E. Hardy, & J. Mellor-Clark (Eds.), *Developing and delivering practice-based evidence: A guide for the psychological therapies* (pp. 91–108). Chichester, United Kingdom: Wiley-Blackwell.

Stiles, W. B., Barkham, M., Connell, J., & Mellor-Clark, J. (2008). Responsive regulation of treatment duration in routine practice in United Kingdom primary care settings. *Journal of Consulting and Clinical Psychology, 76*, 298–305.

Stiles, W. B., Barkham, M., Mellor-Clark, J., & Connell, J. (2008a). Effectiveness of cognitive-behavioural, person-centred, and psychodynamic therapies in UK primary care routine practice: Replication with a larger sample. *Psychological Medicine, 38*, 677–688.

Stiles, W. B., Barkham, M., Mellor-Clark, J., & Connell, J. (2008b). Routine psychological treatment and the Dodo Verdict: A rejoinder to Clark et al. (2007). *Psychological Medicine, 38*, 905–910.

Stiles, W. B., Barkham, M., Twigg, E., Mellor-Clark, J., & Cooper, M. (2006). Effectiveness of cognitive-behavioural, person-centred, and psychodynamic therapies as practiced in UK national health service settings. *Psychological Medicine, 36*, 555–566.

Straus, S. E., Glasziou, P., Richardson, W. S., & Haynes, R. B. (2011). *Evidence-based medicine: How to practice and teach EBM* (4th ed.). New York, NY: Churchill Livingstone.

Stricker, G., & Trierweiler, S. J. (1995). The local clinical scientist: A bridge between science and practice. *American Psychologist, 50*, 995–1002.

Stulz, N., & Lutz, W. (2007). Multidimensional patterns of change in outpatient psychotherapy: The phase model revisited. *Journal of Clinical Psychology, 63*, 817–833.

Stulz, N., Lutz, W., Leach, C., Lucock, M., & Barkham, M. (2007). Shapes of early change in psychotherapy under routine outpatient conditions. *Journal of Consulting and Clinical Psychology, 75*, 864–874.

Suarez-Morales, L., Martino, S., Bedregal, L., McCabe, B. E., Cuzmar, I. Y., Paris, M., Jr., . . . Szapocznik, J. (2010). Do therapist cultural characteristics influence the outcome of substance abuse treatment for Spanish-speaking adults? *Cultural Diversity and Ethnic Minority Psychology, 16*, 199–205.

Tai, B., Straus, M. M., Liu, D., Sparenborg, S., Jackson, R., & McCarty, D. (2010). The first decade of the national drug abuse treatment clinical trials network: Bridging the gap between research and practice to improve drug abuse treatment. *Journal of Substance Abuse Treatment, 38*(Suppl. 1), S4–S13.

Talley, P. F., Strupp, H. H., & Butler, S. F. (1994). (Eds). *Psychotherapy research and practice: Bridging the gap.* New York, NY: Basic Books.

Thompson-Brenner, H., Boisseau, C. L., & Satir, D. A. (2010). Adolescent eating disorders: Treatment and response in a naturalistic study. *Journal of Clinical Psychology, 66*, 277–301.

Trudeau, L. S. (2001). *Effects of a clinical feedback system on client and therapist outcomes in a rural community mental health center.* Doctoral Thesis (PhD), Institute for Social and Behavioral Research, Iowa State University, Iowa.

Upadhyay, J., Maleki, N., Potter, J. S., Elman, I., Rudrauf, D., Knudsen, J., . . . Borsook, D. (2010). Alterations in brain structure and functional connectivity in prescription opioid-dependent patients. *Brain, 13*, 2098–2114.

Wade, W. A., Treat, T. A., & Stuart, G. L. (1998). Transporting an empirically supported treatment for panic disorder to a service clinic setting: A benchmarking strategy. *Journal of Consulting and Clinical Psychology, 66*, 231–239.

Walker, N. R., Rosvall, T., Field, C. A., Allen, S., McDonald, D., Salim, Z., ... Adinoff, B. H. (2010). Disseminating contingency management to increase attendance in two community substance abuse treatment centers: Lessons learned. *Journal of Substance Abuse Treatment, 39*, 202–209.

Walwyn, R., & Roberts, C. (2010). Therapist variation within randomised trials of psychotherapy: Implications for precision, internal and external validity. *Statistical Methods in Medical Research, 19*, 291–315.

Wampold, B. E. (2001). *The great psychotherapy debate: Models, methods, and findings*. Mahwah, NJ: Erlbaum.

Wampold, B. E., & Brown, G. (2005). Estimating therapist variability in outcomes attributable to therapists: A naturalistic study of outcomes in managed care. *Journal of Consulting and Clinical Psychology, 73*, 914–923.

Weersing, V. R., Ivengar, S., Kolko, D. J., Birmaher, B., & Brent, D. A. (2006). Effectiveness of cognitive-behavioral therapy for adolescent depression: A benchmarking investigation. *Behavior Therapy, 37*, 36–48.

West, J. C., Wilk, J. E., Rae, D. S., Narrow, W. E., & Regier, D. A. (2003). Economic grand rounds: Financial disincentives for the provision of psychotherapy. *Psychiatric Services, 54*, 1582–1583, 1588.

West, J. C., & Zarin, D. A. (1995). Practice-relevant research findings: APA's psychiatric research network. *Behavioral Healthcare Tomorrow, 4*(3), 38–39.

Westbrook, D., & Kirk, J. (2005). The clinical effectiveness of cognitive behaviour therapy: Outcome for a large sample of adults treated in routine practice. *Behaviour Research and Therapy, 45*, 1243–1261.

Westen, D., Shedler, J., Durrett, C., Glass, S., & Martens, A. (2003). Personality diagnoses in adolescence: DSM-IV axis II diagnoses and an empirically derived alternative. *The American Journal of Psychiatry, 160*, 952–966.

Whipple, J. L., & Lambert, M. J. (2011). Outcome measures for practice. *Annual Review of Clinical Psychology, 7*, 87–111.

Whipple, J. L., Lambert, M. J., Vermeersch, D. A., Smart, D. W., Nielsen, S. L., & Hawkins, E. J. (2003). Improving the effects of psychotherapy: The use of early identification of treatment failure and problem solving strategies in routine practice. *Journal of Counseling Psychology, 58*, 59–68.

Wilk, J. E., West, J. C., Rae, D. S., & Regier, D. A. (2006). Patterns of adult psychotherapy in psychiatric practice. *Psychiatric Services, 57*, 472–476.

Youn, S. J., Kraus, D. R., & Castonguay, L. G. (2012). The treatment outcome package: Facilitating practice and clinically relevant research. *Psychotherapy, 49*, 115–122.

Zarin, D. A., Johnson, J. L., & West, J. C. (2005). Challenges to evidence-based medicine: A comparison of patients and treatment in randomized controlled trials with patients and treatments in the APA practice research network. *Social Psychiatry and Psychiatric Epidemiology, 40*, 27–35.

Zarin, D. A., Pincus, H. A., West, J. C., & McIntyre, J. S. (1997). Practice-based research in psychiatry. *American Journal of Psychiatry, 154*, 1199–1208.

CHAPTER 5

MEASURING CHANGE IN PSYCHOTHERAPY RESEARCH

BENJAMIN M. OGLES

It is possible that uncritical scientists in a particular area could, for socio-historical reasons, come to misunderstand a concept such as measurement and use it in ways inconsistent with its wider theoretical commitments.

—Joel Michell

Treatment studies include four basic methodological elements: time, a program or treatment, observations or measures, and groups or individuals (Trochim & Land, 1982). These elements can be combined to create a design that is appropriate for the treatment research question and setting of the study. While other chapters in this handbook take a more in depth look at various aspects of treatment studies (e.g., Chapter 2, quantitative research designs; Chapter 3, qualitative research designs; Chapter 4, practice-based evidence; along with the results of studies in the bulk of the chapters), this chapter takes a more narrow look at an essential and important aspect of all psychotherapy research—the observations or instruments that are necessary for assessing or measuring change.

Any attempt to substantiate the efficacy or effectiveness of a psychological intervention relies heavily on measurement instruments that can assess change. The purpose of psychotherapy and other similar treatment methods is to facilitate client change. Clients enter treatment seeking and hoping for personal change. Therapists hope to be effective in their work to assist with client-desired change. Insurance companies and other payers fund treatment with the idea that interventions will improve (change) the functioning of the client and alter their well-being or quality of life. Others in the client's life hope that treatment will help the client to achieve changes

they (the client) desires or that the other desires for the client in order to maintain or improve the quality of the relationship. Indeed, the very title of this volume—*Bergin and Garfield's Handbook of Psychotherapy and Behavior Change*—illustrates the necessity of identifying a method for assessing change. Although this book appropriately focuses primarily on the effect of treatments, there would be no effect without a dependent variable—a measure of change.

Unfortunately, the study of and development of change measures often takes a secondary or tertiary place when compared to treatment development and other treatment-related research questions (Doucette & Wolf, 2009). Psychotherapy researchers exhibit far more interest in developing the newest, improved treatment for a given disorder than in the development of a measure of change. Similarly, more researchers focus on identifying the treatment, therapist, and client processes and characteristics that influence successful intervention than on measuring change. Investigators certainly acknowledge the need for high-quality outcome assessment devices and devote significant time to selecting or creating measures to be used in treatment studies, but the bulk of the time is concentrated on the development, delivery, and understanding of treatments and exploring the avenues of their effectiveness. Similarly, researchers reviewing treatment outcome studies or providing instructions for conducting clinical trials typically devote more space to the topic of treatments and experimental design than to outcome measures. Even Campbell and Stanley (1963) in their classic chapter on quasi-experimental design devoted less time and space to measurement issues.

An examination of studies published in the leading psychotherapy research journals will quickly reveal that articles devoted to the advancement of outcome assessment are infrequent when compared to treatment development and testing or investigations examining mediators, moderators, or processes of change. Given the need to treat clients with significant mental health disorders, it is not surprising that researchers focus first on developing methods for relieving pain, alleviating suffering, and helping the ill. This is an appropriate and needed focus. To validate these methods, however, requires a way to capture the status of the clients prior to treatment and track their improvement during and following the intervention. As a result, a focus on outcome measurement is also warranted and a chapter devoted to the philosophical, scientific, and practical issues involved in the measurement of change is rightly situated along with other methodological issues in the early part of this handbook.

PHILOSOPHICAL ISSUES

From the most abstract point of view, the measurement of psychotherapy outcome fits within the context of all psychological measurement and faces the challenges of those who criticize the assignment of numbers to people. These philosophers, psychometricians, and methodologists are dissatisfied with the assumptions and methods inherent in quantifying people or their characteristics. Some suggest that most forms of contemporary psychological measurement are inaccurate or inappropriate representations of the people, their attributes, or the relationship among attributes. For example, Michell (1999) stated that "there is a particularly pernicious form of Pythagoreanism, according to which the ostensively qualitative features of human life are squeezed, insensitively and without second thought, into a quantitative mould" (p. xiv, see Michell, 1999, for an excellent overview and history of the issues). On the other hand, most psychologists, including psychotherapy researchers have accepted the basic assumptions of representational measurement theory and are

willing to live with the weaknesses of assigning numerical scores to persons or characteristics of persons. Not that these researchers are naive to the implications of accepting these quantitative measurement assumptions and methods—they recognize that scores on a survey are imperfect representations of people and their attributes. Yet these representations make it possible to apply mathematical and statistical procedures (with their own set of philosophical assumptions) to the analysis and understanding of change. In the end, though replete with assumptions that can and ought to be questioned, it is a pragmatic choice to use the best indicators and methods available to us today to examine the effectiveness of psychological interventions.

Because of the strength and breadth of the acceptance of the extant measurement tradition or paradigm, there are only a few philosophical or methodological writers who are currently exploring alternatives to our typical forms of measurement. Some qualitative research attempts to present a more broad and complex picture of change without quantification, but even within qualitative methodologies it is not unusual for researchers to quantify human attributes and to use statistical analysis of these numerical representations all within the current paradigm. A more complete essay justifying the current paradigm or considering contemporary extensions or objections will not be presented here, but it is important to note that future advances in the assessment of change may necessitate a significant paradigm shift and could involve advances in qualitative or quantitative methods of measurement. For the remaining portions of this chapter, I will accept the underlying philosophical assumptions of our measurement methods and review the current literature from the perspective of one deeply embedded within the current psychotherapy research worldview that making scientific advancements requires representational quantitative measurement.

DEFINITION OF OUTCOME

What is the desired outcome of psychotherapy and other behavioral change interventions? At first thought, the answer may seem obvious, but with further contemplation, the definition of outcome becomes more complex than one might expect. Some examples may help illustrate the broad range of perspectives concerning outcome. Luborsky (1984) in his treatment manual for supportive-expressive psychoanalytic therapy describes "what it is that changes" during treatment within the context of numerically outlining the basic principles and premises of the psychoanalytic theory of change (I begin with Premise 3):

> 3. The theory covers both change and stability in behavior as multiply determined by the interaction of psychological and physical, biological, and cultural factors. This interaction has experiential representation within the individual personality—the entity which is changing and is at the same time the intervening variable between external impacts and behavioral change. General and specific improvement in the main symptoms are the most obvious changes to take place in the personality; the symptoms most likely to improve are those that are related to the treatment goals.
>
> 4. Within the personality it is the psychological conflicts that most require change.
>
> 5. During the sessions it is the relationship problems that are the most accessible and therapeutically usable expression of these conflicts; they tend to be directly involved in the patients suffering and therefore to require change. The conflicts expressed in the core conflictual relationship patterns are transference potentials; they are ready to be actualized in relationship after relationship, like a theme and variations on a theme. Freud has referred to the transference potentials as relationship "stereotype plates" since certain of their components get reproduced repeatedly in nearly identical versions, in spite of their self-hurtful nature. The patient's treatment goals reflect the desire to change some of these relationship components. (pp. 17–18)

As can be seen, change in psychoanalytic therapy is thought to involve changes in symptoms, psychological conflict, and relationship problems. Later, Luborsky summarizes more succinctly this thinking in table form and indicates that the change includes "Patient's increased

understanding of the symptoms and the related core conflictual relationship theme (CCRT) problems, some of which the patient had been unaware of. The understanding leads to changes in symptoms and greater mastery over the deleterious expressions of the CCRT problems as well as some changes in the components of the CCRT" (p. 16). So we see that change from this perspective includes increased understanding of the symptoms, increased understanding of core patterns of conflict, change in symptoms, greater mastery over relationship problems, and personality change as evidenced in structural alterations in the core conflictual relationship themes.

Alternatively, Kanfer and Goldstein (1991) define the goals or outcomes of treatment in this way:

> A good treatment program is built with a clear conception of treatment goals, developed jointly by the helper and the client. It is possible to differentiate among five long-term treatment objectives: (a) change of a particular problem behavior, such as poor interpersonal skills; (b) insight or a clear rational and emotional understanding of one's problems; (c) change in one's subjective emotional comfort, including changes in anxiety or tension; (d) change in one's self-perceptions, including goals, self-confidence, and sense of adequacy; and (e) change in one's lifestyle, or "personality restructuring," an objective aimed at a sweeping change in the client's way of living. The selection of any one of these goals does not eliminate the secondary achievement of other objectives. (pp. 9–10)

As illustrated by these two lengthy quotes, the definition(s) of desired therapy outcomes can vary widely from symptoms or problems to psychological conflicts that surface in relationships problems or even personality restructuring. As we see later, the indicators that are selected to measure different domains vary even more than the definitions.

Strupp and Hadley (1977) further argue that the definition of positive outcome (and its corresponding opposite negative effects) depends on ones vantage point. They suggest that there are three primary stakeholders or "interested parties" (p. 188) that have differing perspectives on outcome: society, the individual patient, and the mental health professional. They argue society tends to define mental health in terms of "behavioral stability, predictability, and conformity to the social code" while the individual patient defines mental health in terms of "highly subjective feelings of well-being" such as feeling happy or having a sense of contentment. The mental health professional defines mental health in reference to a "theoretical model of a 'healthy' personality structure," which may transcend the social adaptation and subjective well-being perspectives of society and the individual. Strupp and Hadley's (1977) model suggests that to obtain a "comprehensive picture of the individual" one must obtain evaluations from all three vantage points.

Difficulties with narrowly defining outcomes are not limited to mental health interventions. Researchers and service providers in medical, educational, and other services face equally challenging circumstances when attempting to define successful outcomes. For example, even in a circumstance where the desired outcome would seem simple such as in assisted reproduction technology (ART) where the birth of a child would seem like the obvious and easily defined outcome, researchers differ on their definitions for the standards of success. Some argue that a single standard of success—"the singleton term gestation live birth rate per ART cycle initiated"—should be the standard index of success (Min, Breheny, MacLachlan, & Healy, 2004). Others argue that multiple parameters—(a) number of oocytes per aspiration, (b) number of ongoing implantations per embryo transferred, and (c) number of deliveries per embryo transferred—should be used to better represent all phases of the ART process (Pinborg, Loft, Ziebe, & Nyboe Andersen, 2004). Issues such as whether the pregnancy must be full term to be considered successful and whether nonsingleton births should be considered successful are debated within the literature. Importantly, both sides of the argument agree that the goal of homogeneous reporting of success rates in the research literature is desirable so that appropriate comparisons and aggregating of studies can be accomplished. Similarly, the definition of outcome for individuals with brain injury can vary from "simple measures useful for epidemiology" to "detailed symptom descriptions," "single indices of community re-entry such as return to work," or "detailed operational statements of the minutiae of individual and family outcome"

(Brooks, 1989, p. 325). These examples illustrate that psychotherapy research is not unique in its struggle with the definition of outcome. Medical, educational, and other service industries all wrestle with the myriad potential definitions and operationalizations of outcome used to examine their effectiveness.

Some might be troubled by the lack of clarity about the desired outcome of therapy. Keisler (1971) argues, however, that, "there is no one answer to the criterion problem. There are as many answers as our theoretical and research ingenuity can establish. There are no best measures that one can recommend for evaluating the outcome of psychotherapy. There are as many measures as are relevant and required by the theoretically specific constructs of patient change involved" (p. 45). In short, the definitions and measurements of positive outcome in studies of the efficacy and effectiveness of treatment vary widely depending on the theoretical framework of the researcher, the vantage point of the outcome evaluator, and other characteristics of the study. No one clear definition of outcome is superior though we see later that there are de facto perspectives and definitions that are more frequently used and preferred in the research literature.

It is clear that there are many different perspectives and issues to be considered when defining outcome measurement. The patient, family, therapist, and society all have an established interest and potentially valuable perspectives from which to view therapy outcome. Additionally, matters pertaining to values and theory will influence the choice of therapeutic goals and consequently what is considered to be a desirable outcome (Bergin, 1980; Keisler, 1971). Within each treatment study, researchers must carefully define their expected outcomes and the methods that are used to assess those outcomes. In the end, there is no one definition of outcome for psychotherapy and investigators often address this issue through using multiple definitions and multiple measures. And, in fact, some argue that "multiple reliable and valid outcome measures should be administered in every controlled trial with each measure given equal weight" since no single "gold standard" measure exists "to test the efficacy of any treatment, for any diagnostic condition, for any treatment population" (p. 833; De Los Reyes, Kundy, & Wang, 2011). Importantly, whatever methods of assessment are used, they all need to be rigorous, psychometrically sound, and reproducible.

PSYCHOMETRIC CHARACTERISTICS

An important part of the development of any instrument used for psychological assessment involves gathering data regarding the psychometric properties of the instruments. Researchers selecting among instruments for the assessment of change must consider both the usual psychometric properties of assessment devices such as reliability and validity, along with characteristics relevant to the measurement of change (i.e., sensitivity to change and clinical utility).

Guidelines for psychological assessment are included both in the *American Psychological Association Ethical Principles of Psychologists and Code of Conduct* (2010; see especially Standard 9: Assessment) and, in much greater detail, in the American Educational Research Association's *Standards for Educational and Psychological Testing* (1999). These sources provide extensive guidance and instruction regarding the development and use of tests and measures. Although a complete cataloging of these guidelines is not necessary for this review, it is worth noting that outcome measures must meet the general standards for appropriate use in psychological assessment. Importantly, following the guidelines not only results in ethical research and practice, but also improves the quality of research since using instruments with poor psychometric properties would lead to unreliable or spurious findings in treatment outcome studies. As a result, researchers are interested in the statistical characteristics of measures available for assessing change both for ethical and scientific reasons. For the purposes of this review, a look at reliability, validity, sensitivity to change and clinical utility with specific focus on application to measures of change is provided.

Reliability

Internal and inter-rater consistency or reliability are important components of outcome assessment devices and are examined through the usual methods of test development—typically through use of Cronbach's alpha for internal consistency and through measures of agreement (such as kappa) for interrater reliability. Test-retest reliability in the specific case of outcome measures, however, is more troubling both conceptually and practically.

Test-retest reliability indices give the researcher an estimate of the true variation of a given personal characteristic over time while considering the influence of random sources of error.

Conceptually, the notion that an instrument must demonstrate consistency over time stands in direct tension with the need for the instrument to be used specifically as a measure of change (by definition inconsistency over time). Indeed, outcome measures differ from some classes of psychological assessment by their need to be sensitive to change. (Further discussion of methods for assessing sensitivity to change is described later.) As a result, the assessment of test-retest reliability for outcome measures is a more delicate and thorny issue. A stable measure with excellent test-retest reliability over extended times may be less sensitive to change. On the other hand, a measure that is prone to fluctuate may be sufficiently unreliable that changes occurring during treatment could be attributed to factors other than treatment. Or, real changes occurring during treatment in a measure of a characteristic that fluctuates may be of marginal meaning since the change due to treatment may be easily reversed or altered as a result of other events.

In the typical treatment study, the client is assessed prior to treatment and then repeatedly at predetermined intervals both during and following treatment. The passage of time may result in differences in test scores through any of a host of random or systematic sources of variation including true change in the construct being measured, variation associated with response to treatment, or change associated with sources of error such as test taking environment, characteristics of the test, or item sampling (Campbell & Stanley, 1963). Importantly, the potential error variance associated with a change score is larger than the error variance associated with any single administration of the measure.

Researchers typically approach this conundrum by attempting to find constructs that are important indicators of change and that are likely to respond to treatment, but that also have sufficient stability and reliability to be measured and monitored in a dependable way. Short to moderate time frames for assessing test-retest reliability for these instruments (e.g., a few days to several weeks) are more typical. As a result, these instruments can be both dependable representations of the construct at a single point in time and reasonable representations of change occurring in treatment while also being sensitive to change.

Another way of looking at the reliability of outcome measures is through a conception of stability. The more stable a characteristic or trait, the less likely it is to respond to treatment.

Thus, measures with high test-retest reliability especially over long periods of time are more stable and more difficult to change. Effect sizes for stable, trait-like, and personality characteristics are smaller in treatment studies (Ogles, Lambert, Weight, & Payne, 1990; Smith, Glass, & Miller, 1980). However, changes in these variables are also potentially an indication of a more powerful and durable effect of treatment. Less stable variables such as mood and affect may have lower reliability estimates especially for longer periods of time and are more likely to have larger effect sizes in response to treatment. However, these changes may not be as durable and can occur in response to less powerful interventions. For these reasons, researchers often include a range of measures to assess the multifaceted nature of change. For example, Howard, Lueger, Maling, and Martinovich (1993) proposed a phase model of change in psychotherapy in which participants in treatment experience change in a succession of stages—remoralization, remediation, and rehabilitation. In short, the model proposes that clients first gain hope (remoralization) in the early stages of treatment. This renewed hope is followed by an improvement in symptoms (remediation) with continued treatment. Finally, as treatment continues and symptoms continue to abate, the individual experiences improvement in life functioning (rehabilitation). Howard's research group (Grissom & Howard, 2000) developed the COMPASS outcome system based on this model with measures of hopefulness, symptom severity, and life functioning. The underlying assumption is that the more stable and durable changes would be last to surface and the most difficult to detect. It is clear that the tension between reliability/stability and sensitivity to change will continue and additional research and innovation in this area could bear fruitful results.

Validity

Validity is the key characteristic of any assessment device. Evidence that an instrument provides a genuine index of a given construct in a specific circumstance is essential in order to trust the data. The validity of an instrument can be assessed in a variety of ways including through examination of the content (content validity), correlations with other criteria to establish expected relationships (criterion validity), correlation with future events or criteria (predictive validity), or through combined examination of relationships between

the variable of interest and other variables in the "nomological network" (construct validity; Cronbach & Meehl, 1955). In the outcome assessment arena, outcome measures are subjected to the traditional evaluation of validity through efforts to establish that the measure genuinely represents the construct being examined at a given point in time. However, evidence that changes in an instrument represent actual change in the characteristics of the person is an even more central question in treatment research. Although sensitivity to change (discussed later) provides evidence that the measure can detect change as it occurs, validity suggests both point in time representative accuracy of the construct (measure x is a valid representation of construct y at a given point in time) and accurate time concurrent representation of a change occurring in the person (change in measure x is a valid representation of change in the person). Evidence of the second type of validity is much scarcer in the literature. At the same time, one might argue that the vibrant area of research on clinical significance discussed later in this chapter is in reality a fundamental evaluation of the validity of change measurement—Do changes identified through the administration of an instrument before and after treatment represent real, meaningful, or clinically significant changes? This issue is discussed more fully later.

Sensitivity to Change

Instruments used in the evaluation of change should meet an additional standard beyond reliability and validity. A measure of change must be capable of identifying or detecting differences as they occur over time—they must be sensitive to change. Some may argue that this is a special case of validity, but regardless of its categorization, sensitivity to change is an important characteristic of psychotherapy change measures.

A few methods have been used to assess a measure's sensitivity to change. The most elementary and least persuasive method is to administer a measure before or early in treatment and then to administer it again later or following treatment. If statistically significant differences are found that are in a direction consistent with theoretically expected changes, then the measure is considered to be sensitive to change. For example, Valen, Ryum, Svartberg, Stiles, and McCullough (2011) examined the sensitivity to change of the Achievement of Therapeutic Objectives Scale (ATOS) in this way. In a study comparing the effects of Short Term Dynamic Psychotherapy with Cognitive Therapy, judges rated the entire 6th and 36th sessions for the 50 patients who were receiving treatment because they met criteria for one or more Cluster C personality disorders. Statistically significant changes were observed in all seven of the ATOS subscales between early and late session ratings. As a result, the investigators indicated that the ATOS was sensitive to change. The potential problem with this method for evaluating sensitivity to change is the lack of evidence that real change occurred. In fact, Valen et al. (2011) did have other outcome data for the clients, but ATOS scores were not compared or correlated with the other data in any way to determine if outcomes were concordant.

A more persuasive method for examining sensitivity to change is conducted by using another measure (usually an established measure) as the anchor comparison. The new measure is then administered simultaneously with the "gold" standard measure. If individuals who change on the measure of interest are also found to change on the anchor measure and individuals who do not change on the first measure show no change on the anchor measure (or stated using the language of covariance—the difference scores for the two measures are correlated) then the measure of interest is said to be sensitive to change. For example, Shiner, Watts, Pomerantz, Young-Xu, and Schnurr (2011) examined the sensitivity of the SF-36 to PTSD symptom change by comparing it with changes on the PTSD Checklist-Military Version (PCL-M). Veterans receiving treatment ($n = 167$) completed both the SF-36 and the PCL-M at 2 times. Using the reliable change index and the PCL-M, clients were categorized into three groups: better, unchanged, worse. Changes on each of the eight subscales and the two summary scales of the SF-36 were then analyzed for concordance with the three PCL-M categories using analysis of variance. The mental component summary scale and three of the subscales showed significant mean differences between all three categories. Other subscales also showed changes that were consistent with the groups though not all differences were significant. The investigators concluded that sufficient evidence existed to suggest that the SF-36 was sensitive to changes in PTSD symptoms. As PTSD symptoms improved on the PCL-M, general functioning as measured by the SF-36 also improved. As PTSD symptoms worsened or increased, functioning on the SF-36 also declined.

A final method for examining sensitivity to change involves the use of hierarchical linear modeling. McClendon, Warren, Green, Burlingame, Eggett, and McClendon (2011) compared three measures of youth outcome in terms of their sensitivity to change. In this study, youth and parents rated youth changes in response to treatment at a community mental health center on at least two occasions on three measures (CBCL, YOQ, BASC-2) administered on a monthly basis. A subgroup of the youth, those having made reliable change as determined by the reliable change index, was analyzed to determine if the aggregated slopes (sensitivity to change) differed among the three measures. In fact, all three measures captured change occurring during treatment, but the Y-OQ was more sensitive (steeper slope) to change in parent-reported symptoms. This additional sensitivity was present both for cases in which the youth improved and in cases where the youth's symptoms increased. There were no sensitivity differences in youth-reported symptoms.

Vermeersch, Lambert, and Burlingame (2000) used a similar method to examine the sensitivity to change of individual items on the Outcome Questionnaire (OQ-45). Two criteria were used to determine if an item was sensitive to change: (1) clients changed in the expected direction (lower scores), and (2) average changes for treated clients showed significantly more improvement than changes for untreated individuals. Treated clients included in the analysis had participated in one of several studies conducted in different settings (university training clinic, private practice clinicians through a managed care organization, EAP clients through managed care, and a university counseling center). Untreated individuals were participants in a test-retest reliability study of the OQ-45 or a sample that was administered the OQ-45 on a biweekly basis for 12 weeks to assess for the presence of test-retest artifacts. Hierarchical linear modeling was used to estimate the slope of change for each item. For treated clients, 43 of the 45 items exhibited change in the expected direction (negative slope). Forty of the 43 slopes were significantly different from zero. For the nonclinical sample, 29 items demonstrated a negative slope with 16 items having slopes that were significantly different from zero. When comparing the item slopes for treated individuals with the nonclinical sample, 37 of the items met the second criterion. Subscale scores and the total score also met both criteria. A follow-up study using a clinical sample from

40 university counseling centers found that 34 of 45 OQ items, all 3 subscales, and the total score of the OQ-45 were sensitive to change using the same criteria (Vermeersch et al., 2004).

These studies illustrate a growing trend in the literature toward examining the sensitivity to change of outcome measures. Although several recent studies are presented, many instruments have not been subjected to serious examination for sensitivity to change. Much future work can be conducted to examine existing measures and where needed to modify and improve measures with regard to their sensitivity to change. Hierarchical linear modeling can be used to examine the slopes of change aggregated across individuals and sessions to help with this line of research.

Clinical Utility

Typically, clinical utility would not be an essential topic for a review chapter on outcome assessment in research. However, a major recent addition to the outcome literature involves the gathering of evaluation data in practice leading to published research (practice-based research). Although practice-based research typically does not have the control and internal validity of randomized clinical trials (RCTs) and other more rigorous experimental and quasi-experimental designs, it does play a role in broadening the generalizability of research findings into clinical settings. Various labels are used to describe this research including dissemination, effectiveness, practice-based, or patient-oriented clinical research (Howard, Moras, Brill, Martinovich, & Lutz, 1996). As a result of this emerging research area and the need to have useful measures to conduct these types of studies, some brief discussion of clinical utility in outcome measurement is included here.

As part of the recent movement toward refining treatment and assessment through empirical evidence, Hunsley and Mash (2007) suggest that in "evidence based assessment" there must be "consensus on the psychometric qualities necessary for an instrument to merit its use in clinical services" (p. 42). They go on to suggest that it would be "ideal" if the measures met the following criteria: brief, inexpensive, robust evidence of reliability and validity, and practical (that is, straight forward to administer, score, and interpret). Reliability, validity, and sensitivity to change were previously discussed. The practical criteria (brief, inexpensive, straight forward administration, scoring, and interpretation) might fall under the broad heading of clinical utility.

Although researchers are also interested in efficiency and practical issues when conducting controlled research, studies conducted in clinical settings have even more emphasis on practical issues for gathering data. When evaluation is incorporated into the clinical setting, the measures must be reasonably priced, require little time of the clinician and client, and be quickly and easily administered (Ishak, Burt, & Sederer, 2002; Ogles, Lambert, & Fields, 2002). If the outcome measures are being used by a researcher who gathers the individual data, combines it with other cases, analyzes and ultimately publishes aggregated findings (as in evaluation studies), then the practical nature of scoring and interpretation may not be as critically important. However, in studies where quick clinically oriented feedback from the measures is important (as used in monitoring and feedback studies) then the ability to easily score and interpret the measure is also an essential part of the clinical utility package.

One can imagine a process for collecting blood sugar or blood pressure data that was onerous, expensive, and time consuming. In such an instance, the data gathering would likely be relegated to the most sophisticated and expensive research protocols. When technological advances provide quick, inexpensive, and less painful methods for gathering this data, the findings can be expanded from the essential experimental studies to those based in data gathered during routine clinical care. Similarly, in effectiveness research, the use of measures having clinical utility may result in findings from therapy outcome data gathered in routine clinical practice. Technological advances in measurement have and will continue to assist with the gathering of data (e.g., handheld devices, phone surveys, web-based services). Measures that are brief, easy to understand, easy to complete, and easy to score are the most likely to be used in practice-based research. Several research groups have developed measures to be used in this practice oriented research (e.g., CORE: Barkham, Hardy, & Mellor-Clark, 2010; COMPASS: Grissom & Howard, 2000; OQ-45: Lambert et al., 1996; Ohio Scales for Youth: Ogles, Melendez, Davis, & Lunnen, 2001; SF–36: Ware & Sherbourne, 1992; YOQ: Burlingame, Lambert, Wells, & Cox, 2004) resulting in a variety of interesting findings that are discussed later in this chapter and in other chapters (e.g., Castonguay et al., Chapter 4, this volume). The development and use of practical measures combined with innovative technologies will increase the likelihood of more publications of data gathered in routine practice. These studies have the potential to expand the research base through less-controlled but more broadly generalizable findings, and therefore, the ongoing development of measures with clinical utility will be an important future direction for the assessment of change.

HISTORY OF OUTCOME ASSESSMENT

The earliest studies of psychotherapy effectiveness relied primarily on therapist ratings of outcome. For example, Bergin (1971), and later Bergin and Lambert (1978) in the first two editions of this handbook, reviewed the data collected at the Berlin Psychoanalytic Institute in the 1920s. In this study, psychoanalysts reviewed written case notes and files then classified clients as uncured, improved, much improved, or cured. No other method of assessing outcome was incorporated into the study. Over time, psychotherapy researchers began to focus on developing a broader variety and more rigorous methods of assessing change in outcome studies. Standardized measures from the clinician's perspective were first to be developed, but standardized measures from other perspectives (client, independent judge, significant other) soon followed. Measures also evolved in their specificity with global measures of change used primarily in earlier studies. Later studies tended to have greater measurement specificity, with instruments selected to assess the diagnostic criteria for a given disorder. Measures have also gradually become less attached to therapy orientation with greater focus on diagnoses. For the most part, gone are the days of using the Rorschach, TAT, Q-sort, self-actualization scales and other orientation generated scales (Lambert, Christensen, & DeJulio, 1983; Lambert, Shapiro, & Bergin, 1986). Instead, researchers are more focused on symptoms and quality of life in a more pragmatic approach to the assessment of outcome.

Self-report measures are certainly the staple of the typical study today. Self-report measures provide a unique and important source of information regarding change occurring during psychotherapy. Self-report measures are particularly appealing in clinical practice where customer's view of success is more important than research aims. In addition, when external entities fund treatment, they are prone to anticipate a therapist bias toward proving their treatment works. As a result, external funders typically expect evidence of effectiveness from a source other than the treatment provider. In addition, self-report measures require less clinician time. Some concern remains, however, regarding the exclusive use of patient self-report as a means of evaluating treatment outcome. Smith, Glass, and Miller (1980) felt that self-report measures may be too reactive and overestimate treatment changes. In addition, since clients are an integral part of the therapy process, they may have a limited perspective about changes occurring during treatment. In short, self-report measures provide an important perspective yet it is still only one view of the therapy outcome.

As research methodologies advanced and researchers considered the problems associated with therapist and client rated measures, some investigators turned to the use of persons not involved in therapy who were blind to treatment status as raters or judges of outcome. These independent raters utilized scales of both global and specific natures. In addition, many of the rating scales targeted overt behaviors, which was particularly important for evaluating the effectiveness of behavioral therapies. Structured and semi-structured clinical interviews also became a more common method of assessing clients entering therapy studies. In some cases, the interviews are used only at intake to qualify clients for the study or to identify characteristics of the client at the beginning of treatment that may predict treatment success. In other studies, however, the interview is administered at the end of the treatment to assess the degree to which treatment has altered the current symptom presentation and diagnosis. For example, Lester, Artz, Resick, and Young-Xu (2010) examined racial differences in drop out and outcome for clients receiving treatment for PTSD. One of the instruments used to assess outcome in the study was the Clinician Administered PTSD Scale (CAPS; Blake et al., 1990, 1995). The CAPS can be used to provide both a PTSD diagnosis and a measure of symptom severity. The clinician conducts the interview and then rates the client on each of the diagnostic symptoms (frequency and intensity). In the Lester et al. (2010) study, the CAPS was used to assess PTSD prior to treatment, at the end of treatment, and at follow-up. Findings regarding diagnosis were not reported, but clients did improve on average using the symptom severity measure of the CAPS and diagnosis could be determined both before and after treatment. Similarly, Barrett, Dadds, and Rapee (1996) conducted a study to intervene with childhood anxiety. They reported that 70% of the children who were treated in either treatment condition no longer met the criteria for an anxiety disorder while 26% of children in the wait-list condition no longer met the criteria for an anxiety disorder. Importantly, clinicians who conducted the diagnostic interviews were not the therapists and were blind to treatment condition. Although it may have been easy to determine who was in the wait-list condition, there was an attempt to have the diagnosis independent of treatment.

As the therapy research literature matured, other sources of outcome were also added to the research mix as investigators sought to expand the evidence for validity of treatment effects. So-called objective measures such as physiological indices and environmentally generated data or unobtrusive measures (e.g., student grades, hospital readmissions, physiological data, recidivism, and marital status) were used to evaluate outcome in treatment studies. Although appealing for their lack of any obvious human bias, these measures also have their shortcomings. For example, change in subjective experience often does not correspond with change in physiological measures. Environmental data are also subject to a host of confounding influences including policy decisions and other factors that are extraneous to therapy and generally considered to be irrelevant to measuring treatment outcome (e.g., having insurance coverage). For example, new policies or practices regarding the oversight of foster care placement could substantially alter findings for family therapy oriented treatment where reunification with the biological family was specified as an outcome of interest. Similarly, changing societal norms regarding marriage and divorce could significantly influence the interpretation of divorce/nondivorce as a potential outcome for couples treatment. Each type of measurement has potential benefits and weaknesses, which must be carefully considered when selecting among instruments for use in a study. Because no one measure satisfies all criteria, researchers often use several indicators of outcome based on the desired perspectives and practical limitations of the methods.

As can be seen, the measurement of psychotherapy outcome has substantially evolved from the earliest studies of therapy efficacy. The first studies tended to use unstandardized, global, one-dimensional, unidirectional assessment while more recent studies have turned to assessment of multiple perspectives and methods using standardized rating scales for specific treatment related issues (Hill & Lambert, 2004). Current research is much improved and generates useful information from a variety of sources regarding multiple potential outcomes of psychological treatments.

PERENNIAL ISSUES

Within the history of outcome measurement several persistent and sometimes controversial issues continue to perturb the psychotherapy researcher. A few of the most salient issues are presented here. Researchers are faced with problems associated with multidimensional outcome assessment, the search for a core battery of outcome measures to be used across studies, conceptually organizing outcome measurement, the pros and cons of individualized versus standardized measurement, and the problem of concordance among multiple measures (particularly in research about child interventions).

Multidimensional Chaos

While the evolution of outcome measurement has resulted in steady improvements in the breadth and quality of assessment strategies available for outcome studies, the multidimensional assessment of therapy outcome also brings with it several problems. For example, multidimensional assessment in some studies is limited to multiple self-report instruments while leaving other sources of information (e.g., trained observers, significant others, clinicians) untapped. Even when measuring multiple *sources* of outcome data, there is no guarantee that the rich content and complexity of change will be adequately captured. The use of multiple measures can also be an obstacle to aggregating findings across studies. In fact, reviewers and researchers conducting meta-analyses often lament the limits of cross study comparisons created through the use of different dependent variables (Ogles et al., 1990). Much of what occurs in outcome research appears to be lacking in any conceptual or organizational consistency and there is still a wide range of opinion among practicing clinicians concerning desirable patient change measures.

A number of researchers (e.g., Froyd, Lambert, & Froyd, 1996; Lambert et al., 1983;

Ogles et al., 1990) have surveyed treatment studies over the years in order to capture and describe the breadth of the outcome landscape. In their book on outcome assessment, Lambert, Christensen, and DeJulio (1983) summarized the measures used in 216 outcome studies published in 5 years of the *Journal of Consulting and Clinical Psychology*. They noted that self-report outcome measures were the most frequently used and in one third of the studies were the only measures used. Seventy-five percent of the studies used from two to six measures, but even when multiple measures were used nearly half of the studies included multiple measures from a single source. A total of 254 different self-report measures were used in the 216 studies with the State-Trait Anxiety Inventory being the most frequently used measure in 22 (8.7%) of the studies. Other self-report measures included the MMPI, Rotter Internal External Locus of Control Scale, Marital Adjustment Test, Rathus Assertiveness Scale, Social Avoidance and Distress Scale, Beck Depression Inventory and others. Froyd, Lambert, and Froyd (1996) later examined 348 studies published in 20 journals between 1983 and 1989 and found 1,430 different outcome measures. Amazingly, of this total, 840 measures were used in a single study!

A subsequent review was conducted that examined only studies of agoraphobia outcome published during the 1980s (Ogles et al., 1990; Ogles & Lambert, 1989). In this survey, 98 different outcome measures were used in 106 studies and ranged from unstandardized researcher-created measures applied in a single study to well-validated measures that were used in as many as 55% of the studies (Phobic Anxiety and Avoidance Scales; Watson & Marks, 1971). Still, the diversity among measures was significant even when considering a narrow set of studies for one disorder that is typically treated with an equally narrow range of interventions, mainly behavioral and cognitive/behavioral therapies.

While preparing to write this chapter, 3 years of the *Journal of Consulting and Clinical Psychology* were examined to quickly assess the degree to which the outcome measurement scene had shifted since these previous overviews were conducted. In a 3-year period, 163 of the 302 studies published in JCCP included some assessment of intervention outcome as a related component of the study. Some studies were the typical examination of treatment efficacy while others were more targeted toward the examination of mediators or moderators of outcome. The outcome measures used in these studies varied widely mostly as a direct result of the clinical population being treated. A total of 435 unique outcome measures were used in the 163 studies—371 outcome measures were used in a single study. For example, carbon monoxide breath analysis and self-report of smoking (often using a timeline follow back protocol) were the two most common outcome measures for studies of smoking interventions, but other measures were added to these in one or another of the studies. Other disorder/problem specific measures were used in studies of interventions for those disorders/problems. In studies of depression, the Beck Depression Inventory (both I and II) and the Hamilton Depression Rating Scale (17 and 24 items versions) were the most frequently used measures of outcome but a variety of other measures were used either as the primary outcome measure (e.g., Center for Epidemiological Studies for Depression Scale, COMPASS–Depression subscale) or as supplementary outcomes (e.g., anxiety measures, attribution measures). The typical study uses multiple measures—3.89 measures of outcome were used on average and ranged from 1 measure to 14. Physiological measures such as CO breath testing, urine screening, and cortisol levels were used in 12% of the studies. Unlike earlier descriptive studies, significant other reports were used more frequently—24% of the outcome studies included an outcome from a spouse, parent, and so on. About 30% of the studies relied exclusively on self-report measures of outcome. Importantly, only 5% of the studies included an unstandardized measure (one with no prior reliability or validity data).

When considering this collection of studies describing outcome measurement practices as a whole, the results might be summarized in the following themes:

1. There is great variety in outcome measurement—typically as many measures as studies. Even within a more circumscribed area such as agoraphobia (e.g., Ogles et al., 1990) nearly 100 different measures were used in 106 studies of treatment outcome.

2. Researchers often develop their own outcome measure or measures (some standardized and some not), which may be used by other researchers, but researchers tend to have their favorite battery of measures for their treatments and studies.

3. Most modern studies include more than one outcome measure in order to obtain a multifactored view of outcome. Unfortunately, even studies with multiple measures sometimes limit their view of outcome to a single source (e.g., self-report).

4. The use of unstandardized measures with no psychometric data has become a less pressing problem over the years. Many studies 30 to 50 years ago included a single unstandardized measure, but more recent studies tend to use measures with psychometric data available in published format.

5. Increasingly, certain measures (e.g., BDI, State-Trait Anxiety Inventory) are used more frequently across studies and provide some opportunity to aggregate and compare across studies that did not exist earlier.

6. As studies become more and more specific, new outcome measures are developed for assessing the outcome of a treatment for a more narrow, disorder specific population.

When considering the range of measures used across studies, the lack of organization and direction for current practices and procedures is striking and outcome measurement has become increasingly chaotic. There are probably many reasons for this including the fact that clients often participate in multifaceted treatments and that change is a multidimensional phenomenon. It is much too simple to routinely expect clients to show invariable and integrated improvement as a result of therapy. Consequently methodological divergence is to be expected and, within limits, encouraged. Yet the lack of consistency, replication, and organization that characterizes outcome measurement likely slows progress in the field.

The Search for a Core Battery

With such diversity in measurement, it should come as no surprise that some reviewers continue to call for a core battery of outcome measures that can be used across studies. For example, as early as 1975, the National Institute of Mental Health sponsored an outcome measures project culminating in publication of *Psychotherapy Change Measures* edited by Waskow and Parloff (1975). This text suggested a core battery of assessment procedures to be used in addressing patient change. Unfortunately, this important and well-meaning effort to bring consistency to outcome assessment has not resulted in widespread use of the core battery. In hindsight, it appears that

few researchers or practitioners adopted the recommendations of the NIMH consultants in the ensuing years.

According to the advocates of the core battery, there is a need to have common measures in studies across laboratories, diagnoses, treatment types, and so on, to compare findings and have indices or metrics for change across the diverse circumstances for research. Even prior to the NIMH conference mentioned above, Bergin (1971) called for a core battery in the first edition of this book. Lambert et al. (1983) and Ciarlo, Brown, Edwards, Kiresuk, and Newman (1986) also wrote about the need for common measures. A later conference organized by Hans Strupp and colleagues (Horowitz, Lambert, & Strupp, 1997) in Nashville once again attempted to move in the direction of a core battery. The general idea for all of these efforts is that if researchers include the same measures in their treatment studies, greater comparability across studies will be possible and conclusions that could be attributable to differences in measurement methodology will be eliminated. This desire is especially frequent among meta-analytic researchers who wonder about the consequences of aggregating effect sizes across multiple measures of outcome. Their concern has empirical support—an outcome measure can influence the size of effect produced in a treatment study.

For example, Lambert, Hatch, Kingston, and Edwards (1986) in a study of three commonly used measures of outcome for treatment of depression discovered that effect sizes can vary as a direct result of the measure selected to assess change in treatment. They found that the Hamilton Rating Scale for Depression (HRSD) produced significantly larger effect sizes than both the Beck Depression Inventory (BDI) and the Zung Self-Rating Depression Scale. A more recent meta-analysis found similar results (Cuijpers, Li, Hofmann, & Andersson, 2010). In 48 randomized controlled studies of treatments for depression, 2,462 participants completed a self-report measure of outcome and were also rated on a clinician rated outcome measure. Clinician-rated outcome measures produced a significantly larger effect size (delta $g = .20$) than self-report measures of outcome. When comparisons were limited to just one self-report measure (BDI) and one clinician rated measure (HRSD), the difference between clinicians and self-report was smaller, but still statistically different, with the HRSD having a consistently larger effect size.

A similar meta-analysis was conducted examining the effect sizes of different outcome instruments used in primary studies assessing the efficacy of treatments for agoraphobia (Ogles et al., 1990). As in the previous studies, different measures of outcome produced statistically different effect sizes. In this case, more specific measures of agoraphobia outcome (like the Phobic Anxiety and Avoidance Scale) produced larger effect sizes than more global measures (such as the Fear Survey Schedule). Not surprisingly, the behavioral approach test and heart rate produced smaller effect sizes. The investigators concluded that "the size of treatment effects and judgments of improvement are highly dependent on which outcome measures are used in a given study" (p. 323). A more recent meta-analysis of treatment studies for panic disorder (Sánchez-Meca, Rosa-Alcázar, Marín-Martínez, & Gómez-Conesa, 2010), found similar differences among measures (see Table 5.1). The largest effect sizes were found with measures of panic $d = 1.015$ (95% CI: 0.855, 1.175), followed by a cluster of measures associated with other anxiety symptoms (global adjustment, bodily sensations, agoraphobia, and, general anxiety). Measures of change on depression and other measures produced slightly lower effect sizes. As

TABLE 5.1 Summary Results for the Effect Size as a Function of the Outcome Measure and Type of Measurement Instrument

Outcome/Report Type	k	d+	(95% C.I.)	Q	I2
Panic:					
Self-reports	50	1.037	(0.848; 1.227)	180.78	72.9
Clinician	25	1.182	(0.924; 1.441)	86.44	72.2
Combined	61	1.015	(0.855; 1.175)	202.77	70.4
Agoraphobia:					
Self-reports	40	0.784	(0.621; 0.948)	93.81	58.4
Clinician	7	1.961	(1.608; 2.315)	8.48	29.2
Combined	42	0.856	(0.679; 1.033)	118.03	65.3
General anxiety:					
Self-reports	41	0.773	(0.609; 0.936)	98.90	59.6
Clinician	18	1.128	(0.949; 1.307)	20.44	16.8
Combined	44	0.840	(0.686; 0.994)	99.59	56.8
Depression:					
Self-reports	35	0.689	(0.539; 0.840)	50.19	32.3
Clinician	12	0.545	(0.270; 0.820)	24.23	54.6
Combined	42	0.645	(0.500; 0.791)	72.08	43.1
Bodily sensations (self-reports only)	18	0.874	(0.656; 1.092)	33.04	48.5
Global adjustment:					
Self-reports	20	0.919	(0.648; 1.189)	75.33	74.8
Clinician	10	0.840	(0.481; 1.200)	31.05	71.0
Combined	25	0.895	(0.665; 1.126)	87.03	72.4
Other outcomes:					
Self-reports	21	0.644	(0.450; 0.838)	38.99	48.7
Clinician	3	0.586	(−0.051; 1.223)	5.25	61.9
Combined	24	0.627	(0.446; 0.808)	44.09	47.8
Global results:					
Self-reports	59	0.811	(0.686; 0.936)	117.27	50.5
Clinician	34	1.080	(0.864; 1.296)	115.50	71.4
Total (self-reports + clinician)	65	0.784	(0.663; 0.905)	136.91	53.3

k: number of studies. d+: weighted mean effect size. 95% C.I.: 95% confidence interval around the mean effect size. Q: heterogeneity Q statistic. I2: I2 heterogeneity index (%).

$p < .05$.

$p < .01$.

Source: From "Psychological Treatment of Panic Disorder with or without Agoraphobia: A Meta-Analysis," by J. Sánchez-Meca, A. I. Rosa-Alcázar, F. Marín-Martínez, and A. Gómez-Conesa, 2010, Clinical Psychology Review, 30(1), 37–50. Reprinted with permission.

in the previous studies, self-reports gave slightly lower effect sizes than clinician assessments in the anxiety related measures, but were reversed for the depression, global adjustment and other measures. In all four studies cited in the previous two paragraphs, the outcomes following treatment as measured by different instruments were not as concordant as might be expected. As a result, an investigator could influence the size of treatment effects solely through the decision of which instrument to use for measuring change.

Not only do different measures produce different effect sizes, but a single measure may in reality be more diverse than one might assume given what is reported. Grundy, Lunnen, Lambert, Ashton, and Tovey (1994) examined studies that reported using the Hamilton Rating Scale for Depression (Hamilton, 1967) and discovered that in fact a variety of HRSD versions were used across different studies. For example, 17 item and 21 item versions of the HSRD were most frequently used, but other investigator and study specific changes to the instrument in more than 10% of the studies produced variations in the final HRSD version used to assess outcome. It seems clear from this study that the Hamilton Rating Scale for Depression is actually not a simple scale, but a scale with many variants (Grundy, Lunnen, Lambert, Ashton, & Tovey, 1994).

With the variety of measures used, variation in uses of a single measure, and clear evidence that different measures produce different results (i.e., effect sizes), it is not surprising that those conducting reviews and meta-analyses of the literature call for greater consistency in the selection of measures especially within a group of studies for a specific disorder. In the end, however, most reviews either (a) select a class of measures that are thought to be most representative of the specified treatment(s) or (b) average across measures of outcome in order to produce estimates of treatment effectiveness across multiple studies. The search for a core battery has largely failed to date.

One consolation for the lack of a core battery is that over time investigators have naturally included certain measures in an increasingly higher frequency of studies. For example, Nietzel, Russell, Hemmings, and Gretter (1987) reported that 70% of the studies in their meta-analysis of treatments for depression used the Beck Depression Inventory as a measure of outcome. Similarly, Nietzel and Trull (1988) and Ogles et al. (1990) both found that the Fear Questionnaire was used as a measure of outcome

in 30% and 39% of agoraphobia outcome studies respectively. A more recent meta-analysis also indicated that the Fear Questionnaire was the most frequently used measure of agoraphobic symptoms in 65 studies (Sánchez-Meca et al., 2010). If researchers continue to move in this direction, a time may come when one index of outcome is common to most studies with other measures used in the various studies having much greater diversity.

One potential reason for the increasing use of at least one common measure is the medical model methodology of identifying a primary outcome measure. The identification of a primary outcome measure can benefit the field through greater parsimony in reporting and greater ability to compare and aggregate across studies, yet De Los Reyes, Kundy, and Wang (2011) argue that in mental health treatments, the use of a primary outcome measure is problematic. They propose an alternative to the primary outcome measure approach that emphasizes the deliberate use of multiple measures from multiple perspectives and then examining the extent to which there is evidence of replicability across findings for the multiple measures.

Developing a Conceptual Organization

Although some investigators call for a core battery or common index of treatment outcome within a given area of treatment, other investigators attempt to bring order to the outcome measurement through the development of taxonomies, grids, or conceptual schemes to help organize thinking about measures. Curious readers are referred to works by Strupp and Hadley (1977), Gelso (1979), Ciarlo et al. (1986), Lambert et al. (1983), Lambert, Ogles, and Masters (1992), McGlynn (1996), and Elliot (1992). These efforts to organize the assessment of outcome have been largely motivated by the need to create a body of treatment studies that all use similar instruments or categories of instruments.

Keisler (1971) developed a "grid model" (p. 42) for theory and research in psychotherapy with three dimensions: kind of change, patients, and interventions. The change dimension or "surface" of the grid "represents specification of the kind of changes that should occur" within the respective subgroups of the other two dimensions in the model. In other words, different outcomes can be specified for different kinds of patients and interventions (the other two dimensions of the grid). His grid is based on the notion that variety in measures is not only inevitable, but necessary, and that a model for organizing thinking can lead to a more systematic approach to selecting measures both within and across studies depending on the patients and interventions.

Keisler is not the only researcher to try and bring a greater degree of organization and conceptual understanding to outcome assessment. For example, Rosenblatt and Attkisson (1993) developed a conceptual framework for classifying outcomes for individuals with severe or persistent mental disorders. Three dimensions of outcomes were proposed, including (1) the respondent type; (2) the social context; and (3) the domain of treatment outcomes. Each dimension is further subdivided with respondent types into five subcategories: the client, the family, the extended social network, the clinician, and the scientist. Social contexts include four subcategories: the individual, the family, work/school, and the broader community. Domains of treatment outcome include clinical status (the symptom domain), functioning, life satisfaction and fulfillment, and safety and welfare. The three-dimensional framework can be used to identify and evaluate measures and to assess the degree to which treatments and studies are addressing or capturing information regarding the various domains of outcome.

A similar conceptual and organizational scheme was developed by Lambert and colleagues and originated in reviews of the outpatient psychotherapy outcome literature (Bergin & Lambert, 1978; Lambert et al., 1983; Lambert et al., 1986). The taxonomy has evolved over time (Lambert et al., 1983; Lambert & Hill, 1994; Lambert, Masters, & Ogles, 1991; Lambert, Ogles, & Masters, 1992; Ogles, Lambert, & Masters, 1996) to include five dimensions: content, social level, source, technology, and time orientation. Although they are not completely independent, the dimensions provide a consistent and useful way to organize outcome measures.

The content dimension answers the question of what psychological area is being measured. This includes consideration of behavioral, cognitive, and affective content areas. (Physiological measures are incorporated within the behavioral category.) The social level dimension represents a continuum depicting the degree to which an instrument measures intrapsychic (internal) attributes of the client versus more broadly defined characteristics of the client's interpersonal

(external) world using three arbitrary anchors: intrapsychic, interpersonal, and social. The dimension considering source of outcome information answers the question: Who is making the assessment? It is divided into five categories: client self-report, therapist rating, relevant others (e.g., spouse, friend, work mate), trained observers or judges, or institutional referents (e.g., work and hospitalization records, public records of arrest). This dimension approximates a hierarchy of participation in treatment beginning with the most involved sources (i.e., client and therapist) and moving to the more remote ones (i.e., others and institutions). The fourth dimension is currently called the technology dimension because instruments vary in terms of their methodology or technology of data collection using the following subcategories: descriptive, evaluative, observer, and status. The final dimension included in this conceptual scheme is time orientation. The time orientation dimension reflects the degree to which the instrument attempts to measure a stable, trait-like characteristic versus an unstable, state-like characteristic.

Reviewers have used variations of the Lambert conceptual scheme as a way of evaluating outcome assessment over a large number of studies in a particular area (e.g., Froyd et al., 1996; Lambert et al., 1992; Ogles et al., 1990). For example, one review (Froyd et al., 1996) found over a 5-year period that the typical study in a major journal included 3.5 measures that most often assessed the affective (content), intrapsychic (social level), using self-report ratings (source), symptom specific (descriptive technology) measures. This suggests that certain content areas, sources, and technologies of measures are preferred and repeated in the treatment outcome literature. Similarly, Ogles et al. (1990) categorized measures used in the agoraphobia outcome literature and discovered that measures representing the self-report source and descriptive technology were used in 90% of the studies. The intrapersonal or intrapsychic social level with some assessment of the behavioral content area was ubiquitous with 99% of the studies including a measure of this sort. Areas of relative neglect included measures assessing social role performance and institutional sources of data such as work attendance.

Reviews using taxonomies point to the fact that studies naturally gravitate to measures that are relevant and practical such as client self-report of the symptoms being treated and that more distal outcomes or outcomes that are more difficult and costly to gather are less likely to be collected (e.g., physiological measures, significant others, social role functioning). It is clear that not every perspective or technology need be evaluated yet the clustering of methods across studies may indicate some fruitful avenues of additional study that may provide informative data regarding the benefits of treatments. Of particular interest is the correlated nature of the various methods and perspectives. Correlated measures need not be administered simultaneously in studies, but the taxonomy does provide a way to categorize the breadth of outcome measurement occurring in the field across the various dimensions of the model. This may lead us to further study of the multidimensional nature of change.

Individualized or Standardized

Another repeating theme in the outcome assessment literature involves the question of whether to identify and measure individualized outcomes that may be unique for each client or to develop standardized measures that can be used for every client. Each has advantages and disadvantages. Individualized measures can be tailored to the circumstance and tend to be more sensitive to change (e.g., Ogles et al., 1990). Standardized measures can be used to compare the individual client with a normative sample and are more easily aggregated to look at programs, therapists, agencies, and so on. A common approach in research studies is to use both individualized and standardized measures. For example, in the NIMH Treatment for Depression Collaborative Research Program (TDCRP; Elkin et al., 1989), multiple standardized measures of outcome were used such as the SCL-90 and BDI, but an individualized measure of outcome was also used—the Target Complaints as completed by both therapist and client. Several measures for assessing individualized change are available in addition to the Target Complaints such as Goal Attainment Scaling (Kiresuk, Smith, & Cardillo, 1994) and Progress Evaluation Scales (Ihilevich & Gleser, 1982). Primary outcome measures in published studies tend to be standardized measures. The individualized measures then provide supplemental data regarding individual variation in targets for treatment and changes in those targets. At this point, however, the individualized measures receive far less attention in the literature and could be a useful source of future research regarding the rich and complex nature of individual client responses to intervention.

Measurement Concordance

A final ongoing issue in the measurement of change involves the agreement or disagreement among various sources of outcome. Especially in the child treatment literature where parents and youth often provide their perspective on outcome, the degree of concordance among sources becomes relevant and troublesome. While the typical outcome study with adults relies primarily on patient self-report of change, youth studies often discount self-report measures since the youth may not be sufficiently mature enough to provide accurate information regarding their mental health or they may deny or minimize their symptoms (Cantwell, Lewinsohn, Rhode, & Seeley, 1997). As a result, both researchers and clinicians typically obtain information from multiple parties when assessing youth. Though self-report is not as suspect in the adult research, discrepancy among sources is also relevant to the adult literature. In the youth literature, however, the agreement among sources is more crucial to understanding and has led to a body of research regarding discrepancy among sources (cf. Achenbach, McConaughy, & Howell, 1987; De Los Reyes & Kazdin, 2005).

For example, Achenbach, McConaughy, and Howell (1987) conducted a widely cited meta-analysis that examined agreement among various pairs of raters/informants in the child literature (e.g., parent–parent, parent–teacher, parent–mental health worker). Individuals in similar roles had the highest agreement levels (as estimated by Pearson rs). For example, one parent compared with the other parent had an average correlation of .59 while one teacher with another teacher had an average correlation of .64. Parent and teacher agreement in contrast was not as highly correlated, $r = .27$. These data clearly indicate that different sources of assessment data provide discrepant points of view.

In a more recent review, De Los Reyes and Kazdin (2005) confirm "what has become one of the most robust findings in clinical child research: Different informants' (e.g., parents, children, teachers) ratings of social, emotional, or behavior problems in children are discrepant (e.g., rs often in the .20s)" (p. 483). They go on to summarize the literature regarding the factors thought to contribute to these discrepancies and formulate a theoretical model—the Attribution Bias Context Model—to help guide future studies. Importantly, the data in the original meta-analysis, most studies since that time, and the more recent review are all heavily based on assessment of childhood problems prior to treatment and do not reflect any potential implications of measurement discrepancy for the *assessment of change*. Examining agreement in various informants point of view on change could be even more discordant given the well-known issues with the reliability of change measurement. Indeed, the absence of studies about different informants' views of change leaves a significant hole in the literature regarding informant discrepancy. De Los Reyes and Kazdin (2005) raise the issue of post treatment assessment in their discussion of the Attribution Bias Context Model (see p. 501), but none of the existing reviews provide good estimates of concordance among various informants when assessing change.

Ogles, Lambert, and Sawyer (1995) did compare the concordance between self-report (Beck Depression Inventory and Hopkins Symptom Checklist) and clinician rated (Hamilton Depression Rating Scale) change in the NIMH Treatment for Depression Collaborative Research Program data and found that more than 70% of clients were classified as either clinically improved, no change, or deterioration by all measures. More studies that extend the findings of discrepancy at one point in time to the possibilities for measurement of change are needed to fill in our understanding of outcome from different perspectives.

INNOVATIONS IN OUTCOME MEASUREMENT

Since the last edition of this handbook, several outcome measurement trends have taken more visible roles within the treatment evaluation literature including the increasing use of physiological/neurological measures of change, the patient-oriented research movement, and additional attention to definitions and methods used to examine the clinical significance of change.

Physiological/Neurological Outcomes

A variety of studies are beginning to use new methods for examining a broader range of physiological or neurological outcomes in response to psychological interventions. Studies investigating the effectiveness of treatments for anxiety disorders have used physiological variables such as heart rate or galvanic skin response as outcome

measures for many years (Ogles et al., 1990). Similarly, physiological outcomes for addiction interventions such as Breathalyzer and CO_2 testing are being used in addition to self-report measures of substance use. Beyond these more typical uses of physiological measures, some interesting newer measures are surfacing or being used with greater frequency. A few examples of this budding research area may illustrate some of the possibilities.

Stress Hormones

Some researchers are examining the potential health outcomes of therapy interventions through examination of physiological markers of the stress response. One frequently used method involves the assessment of hormones of the hypothalamus-pituitary-adrenal (HPA) axis, which are known to effect cardiovascular, immune, metabolic, and emotional processes and can, with extended release, result in detrimental physical and emotional consequences. Studies have demonstrated that psychologically oriented interventions can result in HPA axis hormone changes. For example, Storch, Gaab, Küttel, Stüssi, and Fend (2007) studied a resource-activating stress management training intervention in healthy adults and found decreased cortisol responses to a standardized stress test 3 months following intervention. This replicated the findings of earlier studies (Gaab, Blättler, Menzi, Pabst, Stoyer, & Ehlert, 2003; Hammerfald et al., 2006) using a more problem-focused stress management intervention, which also found changes in the psychobiological stress response following treatment. Holt-Lunstad, Birmingham, and Light (2011) examined the effects of a supportive intervention in healthy married couples on both plasma and salivary collected oxytocin levels. They found that "the warm touch enhancement intervention had a measurable beneficial effect in lowering stress-enhanced oxytocin among the men and women with subclinical depression" (p. 1253).

HPA axis hormones have also been used as outcome measures in studies using clinical samples. Evans, Douglas, Bruce, and Drummond (2008) conducted an exploratory study of changes in salivary cortisol in response to treatment for chronic pain. Patients ($n = 18$) participated in a 4-week pain-management program including physiotherapy, psychoeducational seminars, and relaxation training and demonstrated improvements on a variety of self-report measures in addition to providing saliva samples that were used to examine cortisol secretion. Changes in pain level were correlated with changes in waking cortisol levels and changes in depression were correlated with changes in late morning and evening cortisol levels. Siegmund et al., (2011) examined cortisol responses during discrete sessions of exposure treatment and correlated them with other measures of outcome. In this case, as in many other studies in the recent literature, the stress response was not examined as an outcome measure, but rather as a predictor of outcome or as a marker for various subtypes of a disorder.

McKay and Zakzanis (2010) conducted a meta-analysis of studies assessing pre- to post-treatment changes in HPA axis hormones (cortisol and ACTH) in response to treatment for unipolar major depression. Interestingly, studies that used psychotherapy were not included in the final meta-analysis because they "either did not fulfill inclusion criteria or did not report sufficient statistics" (p. 187). Still, 34 primary studies (including 1,049 patients) receiving medications, ECT, or transcranial magnetic stimulation as treatment for depression were included in the final analysis. Approximately 56% of the patients had similar levels of cortisol before and after treatment and responders did not statistically differ from nonresponders in terms of change in cortisol measures. Cortisol changes were similarly unrelated to type of treatment, but were related to response to treatment within subtypes of depression (in a small sample of studies including information about subtypes). Although the findings were decidedly mixed and the majority of patients with unipolar depression showed no change in cortisol levels in response to treatment, the authors concluded that the utility of cortisol as a measure of outcome cannot be ruled out at this point in time since its usefulness as a measure may be limited to certain subtypes of depression.

Neurocognitive and Imaging

An even more recent development in measurement technology involves the use of neurocognitive approaches and imaging to assess the outcome of therapy (Linden, 2008). For example, Lavoie, Imbriglio, Stip, and O'Connor (2011) examined neurocognitive changes following CBT treatment of 24 individuals with Tourette syndrome or chronic tic conditions. Outcomes were assessed with both traditional clinical measures along with neurocognitive and electrophysiological measures including the Purdue pegboard and EEG event related

potentials (ERPs) gathered through a standardized procedure (Traffic Light Task). Changes in movement associated potentials (MAP) were found in response to CBT treatment. Similarly, Nedeljkovic, Kyrios, Moulding, and Doron (2011) assessed changes in neuropsychological functioning in 26 patients undergoing treatment for obsessive compulsive disorder (OCD) using selected tasks from the Cambridge Neuropsychological Test Automated Battery (CANTAB; Morris, Evendon, Sahakian, & Robbins, 1987).

Several studies examine pre-post treatment changes using functional magnetic resonance imagining (fMRI) or positron emission tomography (PET) scanning and their variations. For example, Brody et al. (2001) used PET scanning and found regional brain metabolic changes (in the direction of normalization) in patients receiving medications (paroxetine) or therapy (interpersonal psychotherapy) for depression. The same research team (Saxena et al., 2002) found regional brain metabolic changes in patients with OCD and depression. Interestingly, changes differed significantly by diagnostic group and treatment response.

Other researchers have used fMRI to assess brain changes following treatment. For example, Paquette et al. (2003) observed fMRI changes in patients following treatment for spider phobia. They studied 12 phobic subjects and 13 controls who viewed film excerpts of spiders and butterflies at the time of the imaging. Phobic subjects then participated in treatment followed by a second fMRI session. Changes in brain functioning following treatment for a variety of other disorders using several imaging methods are now available in the literature including spider phobia/fMRI (Schienle, Schäfer, Hermann, Rohrmann, & Vaitl, 2007; Schienle, Schafer, Stark, & Vaitl, 2009), major depression/PET/fMRI (Goldapple et al., 2004; Kennedy et al. 2007; Konarski, McIntyre, Soczynska, & Kennedy, 2007), obsessive compulsive disorder/PET/SPECT (Baxter et al., 1992; Hendler et al., 2003), obsessive compulsive disorder/fMRI (Nabeyama et al., 2008), specific phobia/fMRI (Straube, Glauer, Dilger, Mentzel, & Miltner, 2006), and social phobia/PET (Furmark et al., 2002). Clearly a modern frontier in therapy outcome will include continuing use of imaging technology along with improvements in methodology and findings.

It should be noted that the findings of imaging studies to date are entirely reliant on traditional outcome measurement strategies. Response to treatment is first determined using the typical behavioral indicators of outcome applied in the literature. Investigators then note brain functioning differences for patients who respond to treatment. Brain-functioning differences that are identified are only assumed to be relevant by the nature of their correspondence with the traditional measures of outcome. Much additional work needs to be done before greater specificity and causality can be attributed to the imaging work of today (Keller, 2003). In addition, as Kaplan (1990) has correctly and insightfully demonstrated, it is easy to become fascinated with physiological measures and their apparent "objectivity" at the expense of behavioral assessment. He argues convincingly that physiological measures are only important insofar as they predict or relate to some behavioral outcome. Nevertheless, imaging studies provide a fruitful avenue of continuing research within the therapy outcome literature.

IRT in Outcome

Another more recent avenue of exploration in the measurement of outcome involves the increasing use of Item Response Theory (IRT) for the development and evaluation of outcome measures. IRT-based measures and models have been available in the achievement testing literature for some time, but because of the computational complexity and limited availability of appropriate software, the use of IRT in psychotherapy research has been slower to catch on (Doucette & Wolf, 2009). In the past decade more researchers have begun the process of applying IRT to measures used in psychotherapy research. For example, Doucette and Wolf (2009) use clinical samples from a commercial health plan in the United States to both define the basics of IRT theory and practice and to illustrate the possible benefits of IRT on an outcome measure developed using classical true score theory.

Similarly, Elliott et al. (2006) use Rasch analysis (the basic form of IRT theory) to examine the psychometric characteristics of the SCL-90R. They found that the SCL-90R item rating categories did in fact advance monotonically, but clients did not effectively discriminate among the 5 categories of the rating scale. Collapsing the 5 categories into 3 categories (by combining categories 1 and 2, and 3 and 4) improved the scale. In addition, three misfitting items were dropped. Using the person-item separation statistics also allowed the researchers to identify groups of items

that denoted increasingly severe symptomatology from mild medical concerns and aches and pains (least severe) to serious psychosis (most severe). Interestingly, these groups of symptoms roughly matched the order of change in symptoms as found in an earlier conventional study of the SCL-90R (Kopta, Howard, Lowry, & Beutler, 1994). The researchers go on to make other empirically guided suggestions for improving the SCL-90R (e.g., dropping redundant items) and for developing algorithms using the improved scale and Rasch models to create clinically useful indices. This study presents an excellent example of the potential use of IRT theory for the evaluation and improvement of psychotherapy outcome measures, but it is focused on the SCL-90R scores at one point in time. Pastor and Beretvas (2006) used Rasch modeling to examine outcome scores with longitudinal data from students receiving treatment at one of ten counseling centers. Rasch analysis allowed them to examine changes in individual items over time. Four items were identified with questionable validity and the advantages of using multilevel item response theory models with longitudinal outcomes data were described. Studies such as the three briefly mentioned here and others that build on this early foundation are likely to be an important and useful line of scholarship in outcome assessment in the coming years.

Practice-Based Research

One of the more obvious advances in outcomes measurement is the move toward using outcome in practice to monitor treatment and its companion practice-based or patient oriented research studies. In fact, Andrews and Page (2005) suggest that

[O]ne of the most exciting developments among clinicians is the expansion of thinking from the measurement of an outcome, to include the monitoring of clinical practice. Monitoring refers to the periodic assessment of an intervention to permit inferences about the nature and extent of observed patient changes. Progress monitoring is aimed at determining deviations from the expected course of improvement; whereas outcomes monitoring focuses upon the aspects of the intervention process that bring about change. Thus, if measurement is like a speedometer, monitoring is akin to a pilot landing an airplane, using multiple readouts to determine if the vehicle is in the right glide path. Clinicians can monitor progress against typical and atypical treatment pathways and this assists matching patients to treatment options thereby maximizing outcomes. For instance, the routine feedback to clinicians of monitoring data doubled the rate of patients demonstrating clinically significant outcomes. (p. 650)

Andrews and Page (2005) are lauding the opportunity for clinicians to apply outcome measurement in practice and are not referring to the consequences of routine assessment for the research literature. A variety of others join the chorus of those encouraging routine assessment in practice (Hatfield & Ogles, 2007; Lambert, Okiishi, Finch, & Johnson, 1998; Lambert & Vermeersch, 2008; Maruish, 1999; Ogles, Lambert, & Fields, 2002; Sederer & Dickey, 1996; Whipple & Lambert, 2011). These publications and others note a significant side benefit of having more practical measures combined with technology and greater information about treatment expectancies. Practitioners are using outcome measures, thus bridging the gap between science and practice.

Importantly, and more directly related to the purposes of this chapter, as practitioners, agencies, and payers join the ranks of those conducting outcome assessment, the opportunities to publish patient-oriented or practice-based research is also increased (Barkham, Hardy et al., 2010; Cahill, Barkham, & Stiles, 2010). As a result, the last decade has seen an increase in the number of published studies conducted in treatment settings. These studies are typically conducted with fewer experimental controls (e.g., no standardized training or supervision of therapists, no control group, no strict subject inclusion strategy) yet they make a contribution through their immediate relevance and generalizability. For example, Connell, Barkham, and Mellor-Clark (2008) examined the data from 11 U.K. student counseling services (1,189 clients) using the CORE system measures, which include both client self-report and clinician ratings (Barkham, Mellor-Clark, et al., 2010). Clients presented with a variety of problems and completed measures before and after treatment. Therapists also completed ratings of the client at the intake session and when the client ended treatment or stopped attending. No controls were used to govern treatment, client selection, or other aspects of the measurement. Indeed, pre- and post data were available for only 323 (38%) of the complete sample. Approximately one half of the clients (56%) with complete data achieved clinically significant change and 70% made reliable improvements. Those who completed a course of therapy had better outcomes than those who dropped out of treatment.

In a similar study using data gathered from primary care mental health practice in the United Kingdom, Stiles, Barkham, Mellor-Clark, and Connell (2008) compared outcomes for patients ($n = 4,954$) receiving cognitive-behavioral therapy, person-centered therapy or psychodynamic therapy. Again outcomes were measured by the CORE-OM system before and after treatment and clients presented with a wide variety of problems and disordered behavior. On average clients improved significantly pre- to posttreatment and outcomes were similar across therapeutic orientations. Additional detail regarding the study is not necessary since I am limiting my focus here to the research possibilities afforded by routine outcome assessment in practice. Both of these illustrative studies involved the gathering of data in routine practice with no experimental controls and were possible as a result of the implementation of outcome assessment in two very different clinical settings.

Some may argue that this naturalistic gathering of data has extremely limited usefulness given the lack of experimental controls. Barkham et al. (2008) address these concerns and discuss the benefits of using heterogeneous samples treated under routine clinical practice conditions. Most importantly the generalizability of the results (external validity) precipitates outcome findings that have relevance to practitioners. Barkham et al. (2008) take an additional step by comparing the findings of practice-based studies with those found in randomized trials. The randomized trials were represented by six studies including 477 clients while the practice-based studies included four published studies and 4,196 clients. The clients participating in treatment through usual practice averaged 12.3% less improvement (using transformed outcome measures) than clients completing treatment through a randomized protocol that included manualized treatment, training of therapists, selective intake procedures, and so on. Other methods of comparing the treatments (effect sizes, change scores) each with unique pros and cons, found bigger or smaller differences between the randomized studies and practice-based studies and a number of limitations make these findings seem preliminary. Still, the consistent pre-post treatment change identified in studies without significant controls suggests that the practice-based research methodology can and does contribute to the ongoing dialogue. Future research will hopefully better iron out the specifics of the relationship between practice-based and controlled studies of therapy effectiveness.

Some studies conducted in naturalistic settings attempt to modify treatment or introduce some degree of experimental control. For example, the series of studies conducted by the Lambert research team on the benefit of providing feedback using the OQ-45 (Lambert & Shimokawa, 2011) to clinicians regarding client progress provide an example of this type of study (e.g., Lambert et al., 2001; Slade, Lambert, Harmon, Smart, & Bailey, 2008; Whipple & Lambert, 2011). Each of these studies builds on the basic foundation of session-by-session outcome assessment administered in the treatment center with the added introduction of feedback and other procedures delivered to some portion of the clients. Clients complete the OQ-45 prior to each session. Several different interventions (mostly involving some form of feedback to therapists with a variety of supplements) have been tested and are described in greater detail in Chapter 5 of this volume. The key point for this chapter, however, is that the session-by-session outcome assessment provides an opportunity to ask some interesting clinical questions and to explore them using modest experimental interventions with random assignment and minimal controls. This type of practice-based research is likely to continue and may be amplified by the development of additional practical measures and improved technology that will make ongoing outcome assessment even more possible. Perhaps the day will come when psychological outcome measurement is as common as the routine temperature, pulse, and blood pressure assessment delivered with each visit to a physician or the daily monitoring of blood glucose as in diabetes (Lambert, 2010).

Clinical Significance

One of the more clear trends in outcome measurement over the past two decades is the effort to provide additional data regarding the clinical meaning of changes observed in treatment outcome studies. In fact, just one year after the previous edition of this handbook was published, the *Journal of Consulting and Clinical Psychology* became the first journal to require that outcome studies include some analysis of clinical significance in the results section of submitted manuscripts. No one method of assessing clinical significance was specified though several common methods were cited (La Greca, 2005). Studies published in other journals are also including analysis of clinical significance in addition to the traditional tests of statistical effects and the effect size statistic. It would not be surprising if in the future such analyses were routine for all outcome studies.

As illustrated earlier in this chapter, the validity of outcome measurement has been a perennial issue and in many ways connects directly to the philosophical concerns (reductionism, quantification) of assigning numbers to people in the first place. How can a 15-point change in a survey instrument score be an accurate representation of a person's change occurring inside of therapy? Although the problems associated with reducing people and their attributes to numbers cannot be resolved within the current psychotherapy research paradigm, there have been attempts to bring greater meaning to changes in scores within the paradigm under the rubric of clinical significance. Importantly, methods for assessing clinical significance have also improved over time. Discussion of clinical significance within the literature occurs under several names including social validity, clinical significance, applied importance, ecological validity, and so on (Foster & Mash, 1999). A brief history of some key features along with several examples and more recent findings follows.

Social Validity

Beginning in the 1970s, behavioral researchers developed a line of research focused on further exploring the "social validity" of changes occurring in response to treatment. Two general ways for evaluating the question of social validity have been proposed: (1) the subjective evaluation method, and (2) the social comparison method (Foster & Mash, 1999; Kazdin, 1977; Wolf, 1978).

In the subjective evaluation method the client's behavior is evaluated by individuals who are "likely to have contact with the client or in a position of expertise" (Kazdin, 1998, p. 387). This allows the researcher to tap whether the client has made qualitative changes that are in turn observable by relevant others outside the therapy situation. For example, Feldman, Condillac, Tough, Hunt, and Griffiths (2002) evaluated the effectiveness of positive behavioral intervention for individuals with developmental disabilities who displayed self-injurious, aggressive, and disruptive behaviors. To assess the ecological and social validity of the outcomes, the clients were videotaped in a variety of settings. Primary care workers then observed pre- and postintervention videotape segments and provided their perspective on severity of the participant's target behaviors using a researcher-developed questionnaire that tapped four dimensions: frequency, intensity, duration, and pervasiveness of the behavior. The addition of this external and subjective perspective helps to provide evidence of the meaningfulness of change. Similar studies over the years have included a range of outside observers who rate the "social validity" of the improvement in both naturalistic and analog settings (see, for example, Carr, Austin, Britton, Kellum, & Bailey, 1999, for a review of social validity studies published in the *Journal of Applied Behavior Analysis*).

Subjective evaluations, however, are also limited by a number of important considerations. Kazdin (1977) initially worried that the subjective evaluations would be stretched beyond their applicability and used as a type of prescriptive guideline. In the intervening years, however, this has not proven to be the case. Subjective evaluation also weights the societal view more heavily than the client or therapist point of view. As we have already seen earlier in this chapter (e.g., Strupp & Hadley, 1977), the client, therapist, society and others (e.g., payers) may have a legitimate stake in therapy so a multidimensional view of outcome is the ideal. The subjective evaluations of those external to therapy need not be considered the most important source of outcome.

The second method for evaluating the social validity of outcome is the social comparison method. In this method treatment effectiveness is evaluated based on pre- and postevaluations of the client's behavior with a reference group of "nondeviant" peers. A variety of methods can be used to make this comparison and the statistical methods for comparing treated with normative groups have evolved into the most commonly used methods for assessing clinical significance. In the social validity context, a social comparison is performed through direct observational ratings.

Nondeviant or nondysfunctional peers are compared to treated individuals both before and after treatment using an observational method for examining change in behavioral targets.

Although the social validity methodologies presented here do not completely satisfy the question of how to determine clinically significant improvement, they do provide promising methods for evaluating meaningfulness of change (some of which continue to be used) and pave the way for newer approaches.

From the foundation of social validity, a number of specific methodologies have been developed to examine the clinical meaningfulness of change. These methods are more narrowly focused on researcher defined or "clinical" definitions of significant change. The three most prominent definitions of clinically significant change include: (1) treated clients make statistically reliable improvements as a result of treatment (improvement), (2) treated clients are empirically indistinguishable from "normal" or nondeviant peers following treatment (recovery), or (3) a combination of return to normal functioning plus reliable improvement (clinical significance). Note that Definition 1 is a statistical variation of the subjective evaluation method and Definition 2 is largely a statistical variation of the social comparison method within social validity. Many researchers use the terms clinically significant change and recovery interchangeably.

Reliable Change Index

Jacobson and Truax (1991) developed the most commonly used measure of assessing statistically reliable change—the reliable change index (RCI). The RCI is based in the social validity idea that clients make meaningful change when that change is sufficiently large that it is easily noticed by others (Wolf, 1978). The RCI is calculated for each individual based on the pretreatment score (X_{pre}), the posttreatment score (X_{post}) and the standard error of the difference between two test scores (S_{diff}):

$$\text{RCI} = \frac{X_{post} - X_{pre}}{S_{diff}}$$

The change is considered reliable, or unlikely to be the product of measurement error, if the change index (RCI) is greater than 1.96. The change is categorized as improvement when the individual has a change score greater than 1.96 and as deterioration when the individual has a change score less than −1.96. This reliable change index (RCI) is the most frequently used method for examining improvement in the literature (Ogles, Lunnen, & Bonesteel, 2001). Alternative methods and their calculation along with differences in their classification rates were summarized by Lambert, Hansen, and Bauer (2008). The primary criticism of the RCI is that it does not take into account regression to the mean (Hsu, 1989, 1999; Speer, 1992; Speer & Greenbaum, 1995). Regression to the mean implies that in repeated assessments with the same (not perfectly reliable) outcome measure, more extreme scores naturally become less extreme over time. In spite of the criticisms, the Jacobson-Truax RCI approach is the most frequently used and two recent studies comparing methods for calculating reliable change suggest slight improvements in the formulae for calculating the RCI result in little difference among the methods in terms of individuals classified as improved (Atkins, Bedics, McGlinchey, & Beauchine, 2005; Bauer, Lambert, & Nielsen, 2004).

Other methods outside of the RCI and its variations are available for examining improvement. For example, investigators studying treatments for headaches use client headache diaries to calculate the percent improvement based on the frequency and severity of headaches per week (Blanchard & Schwarz, 1988).

Percent Improvement

$$= 100 \times \frac{\text{Pretreatment} - \text{Posttreatment}}{\text{Pretreatment}}$$

A 50% reduction in headache activity, in the absence of increased medication, is defined as clinically significant improvement (Blanchard & Schwarz, 1988). The use of percent improvement in headache research is likely connected to the common use of this index in the pharmacological literature (Hiller, Schindler, & Lambert, 2011). Importantly, the percent improvement index of improvement resolves one of the weaknesses of the RCI—that it does not adapt to the client's level of pretreatment disturbance.

For example, depending on the normative sample used, the amount of change necessary to be considered improved using the RCI on the BDI would be 8.46 points (see Seggar, Lambert, & Hansen, 2002). Using the Percent Improvement (PI) approach, the amount of change needed on the BDI to obtain a 50% reduction in symptoms would vary depending on the pretreatment level of disturbance. Hiller, Schindler, and Lambert (2011) illustrate this principle using Figure 5.1.

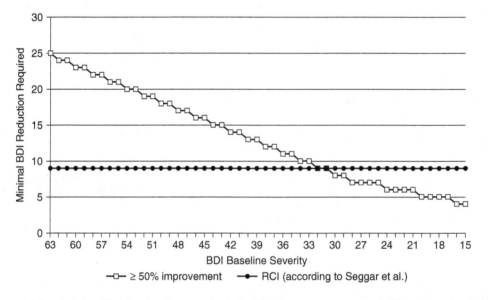

FIGURE 5.1 Minimal BDI reduction required for 50% improvement or reliable change by baseline severity.

Source: Reprinted with permission from "Defining Response and Remission in Psychotherapy Research: A Comparison of the RCI and the Method of Percent Improvement," by W. Hiller, A. C. Schindler, and M. J. Lambert, 2011, *Psychotherapy Research.* doi: 10.1080/10503307.2011.616237 Reprinted with permission.

As can be seen, the amount of client self-report change on the BDI that is needed from pre-treatment to post-treatment to be considered improved fluctuates significantly depending on their initial score.

Hiller et al. (2011) further examine the differences between the RCI and PI methods through an analysis of response to treatment in a sample of 395 consecutive admissions to an outpatient clinic at the University of Mainz, Germany. They found that the PI approach produced slightly and statistically higher rates of response (66.3% in the intent to treat sample and 76.2% in the completer sample) than the RCI (59.2% in the intent to treat sample and 68.5% in the completer sample). Because the PI method takes into account the pre-treatment severity and is independent of "arbitrarily chosen reliabilities and reference populations" (p. 1), they recommend the PI method as a potentially useful extension to the RCI. Other improvement methods have been developed within subsets of the treatment literature (Ogles et al., 2001).

Although changes from pre- to posttreatment may be large enough to be statistically reliable for a given individual, this does not guarantee that the changes will be noticeable. Ankuta and Abeles (1993) were the first to address this issue. They compared clients who demonstrated clinically significant improvement using the RCI and the SCL-90R with the client's self-reported change as measured on the Patient Questionnaire (Strupp, Fox, & Lessler, 1969). Clients who improved using the RCI cutoff reported higher levels of self-reported change than those who did not improve. Similarly, Lunnen and Ogles (1998) performed a multiperspective, multivariable analysis of the RCI. Clients in outpatient therapy were divided into three groups based on their change scores on the Outcome Questionnaire (OQ-45; Lambert et al., 1996): improvers, no-changers, and deteriorators. When clients demonstrated reliable change—either improvement or deterioration—they were matched with clients who were unchanged. Clients then rated perceived change, satisfaction with treatment, and the therapeutic alliance. Similarly therapists and significant others rated perceived change and the therapists rated the therapeutic alliance. Perceived change and therapeutic alliance were significantly higher for individuals who reliably improved than for nonchangers and deteriorators from both client and therapist perspectives. Clients demonstrating reliable deterioration were not significantly different from nonchangers on

any of the outcome variables reported by any of the three perspectives. They concluded that the RCI is an effective way of evaluating improvement, but that it is less effective for identifying deterioration. These two studies began the process of demonstrating that improvement based on the RCI statistical method is also noticeable to the client, the therapist, and others. Several other studies have continued exploring this area of work (e.g., Åsenlöf, Denison, & Lindberg, 2006; Newnham, Harwood, & Page, 2007; Openshaw, Waller, & Sperlinger, 2004). For example, Newnham et al. (2007) found that clients classified as recovered, improved, no change, or deteriorated using the SF-36 had corresponding levels of self-rated quality of life and clinician rated overall distress. This suggests that the Jacobson categories are valid indicators of real differences in behavior on other important areas of functioning from multiple perspectives. This series of studies appears to be a fruitful avenue for continuing exploration.

Recovery

Kendall and Grove (1988) suggest taking the perspective of the "skeptical potential consumer" of psychological treatments to better understand the concept of clinical meaningfulness. To convince the skeptic, an intervention should lead to "changes that materially improve the client's functioning" (p. 148) and suggest that the most convincing demonstrations of successful treatment provide evidence that once troubled clients are now "not distinguishable from a . . . representative non-disturbed reference group" (p. 148). Kendall and Grove's statistical approach (1988) is based on normative distributions of outcome measures. Clients' post treatment scores are compared with the normative distribution to determine if they have recovered or not following treatment.

A variety of methods can be used to determine cutoff scores or percentile levels at which recovery is defined (Kendall & Grove, 1988; Kendall, Marrs-Garcia, Nath, & Sheldrick, 1999; Jacobson & Truax, 1991; Nasiakos, Cribbie, & Arpin-Cribbie, 2010). Kendall's method (Kendall, Marrs-Garcia, Nath, & Sheldrick, 1999) involves using traditional statistical tests to explore the hypothesis that treated and non-clinical groups are equivalent within a given range. For example, Moleiro and Beutler (2009) examined the clinical significance of change for patients receiving treatment for depression. Using four archival samples, post treatment scores were compared with normative data for the BDI. Six of the eight treatment groups from the four samples had scores that were statistically significant and clinically equivalent to the normative sample following intervention.

Another method for assessing recovery involves setting a priori expectations for end-of-treatment client scores on the outcome measures. For example, Elkin et al. (1989) considered the clinical significance of the NIMH TDCRP by identifying the number of clients who "met a predefined level of clinical recovery" (p. 974). Recovery was defined as a score of 6 or less on the Hamilton Rating Scale for Depression (HRSD; Hamilton, 1967) or 9 or less on the Beck Depression Inventory (BDI; Beck, Ward, Mendelson, Mock, & Erbaugh, 1961). Cutoffs were loosely determined by previous research indicating that few remaining symptoms of depression occurred at scores in this range. Similarly, agoraphobia researchers developed criteria for identifying "end-state functioning" (Michelson, Mavissakalian, & Marchione, 1985). High end-state functioning was defined as a score of 3 or 4, medium end-state functioning was defined as a score of 1 or 2, and low end-state functioning was defined as a score of zero. Scores represented the aggregate end of treatment outcome for each client on a combination of four measures used in the study. The presence and then absence of meeting criteria for a diagnosis through pre- and post diagnostic interviewing would be another similar method for assessing recovery. Individuals would be expected to meet diagnostic criteria for a disorder prior to treatment, but not following treatment.

Jacobson and colleagues method (Jacobson, 1988; Jacobson, Follette, & Revenstorf, 1984; Jacobson, Roberts, Berns, & McGlinchey, 1999; Jacobson & Truax, 1991) for assessing recovery requires that clients' scores on the outcome measures move from the dysfunctional to functional range. When the functional and dysfunctional distributions are overlapping, different cutoff points (or clinical cutoff indices) may be used to determine criterion when the client has returned to the normal range.

Combining Improvement and Recovery

The most conservative criterion for clinical significance proposed by Jacobson and Truax (1991) requires that the client make reliable improvement (using the RCI) and end of treatment recovery. They define this as clinically significant change. For example, Ogles et al. (1995) examined the clinical significance of the TDCRP data. When combining estimates across three empirically supported treatments (interpersonal psychotherapy—IPT, cognitive-behavior therapy—CBT, and imipramine plus clinical management) and three measures, they found that 69 (55%) of the 125 clients who participated in a minimum of 12 sessions and 15 weeks of treatment met the criteria for clinically meaningful change on all three measures. Hansen, Lambert, and Forman (2002) summarized 28 clinical trials that studied a variety of disorders and treatment methods and found that 58% of patients met the criteria for clinically significant change at the end of treatment (average 13 sessions). Other reviews have examined both the statistical and clinical significance of findings over a broad range of studies (e.g., Nietzel, Russell, Hemmings, & Gretter, 1987; Ogles et al., 1995; Ogles et al., 2001). Clearly, the methods for examining clinical significance are making a contribution to the assessment of change in psychotherapy research.

Criticisms

Although the methods presented here provide novel approaches to demonstrating the meaningfulness of change occurring during treatment, a variety of issues have been noted in the literature.

1. Regression to the mean and its potential impact on the RCI is the most frequent criticism mentioned (e.g., Speer, 1992).
2. The lack of normative data for some instruments makes calculation of recovery difficult in those instances (Lambert & Ogles, 2009; Ogles et al., 2001).
3. The potential discordance of measures when used to assess clinical significance within the same study is a problem that this method shares with the general outcome literature (Lunnen & Ogles, 1998; Ogles et al., 1995).
4. Patients sometimes enter treatment with scores in the normal range. This presents a problem for determining if they recovered or not (Lambert & Ogles, 2008).
5. A similar issue involves the problem of assessing recovery for individuals with chronic conditions. Should some form of modified recovery cutoffs be used in these circumstances? (Grundy et al., 1994; Grundy, Lambert, & Grundy, 1996; Tingey, Lambert, Burlingame, & Hansen, 1996).

6. Hsu (1996) argues that methods for classifying clients who move from the dysfunctional to functional distributions do not consider the base rate of movement between the two distributions. As a result, he proposes modifications to the formulas that strengthen conclusions made when categorizing clients into groups based on their post treatment scores.

7. The variability in methods used, even within the Jacobson-Truax approach, make it difficult to compare across studies regarding the ultimate clinical meaning of results since the parameters, formulas, and calculation decisions in each study may result in divergent findings (Kazdin, 2003; Lambert & Ogles, 2008; Odgaard & Fowler, 2010).

8. Some may suspect that the changing of continuous outcome data into discrete categories (e.g., improved, not improved) may limit variability and influence statistical findings. However, Cuijpers, Smit, Hollon, and Andersson (2010) found little difference in effect sizes between continuous and dichotomous outcome measures in a meta-analysis of studies testing treatments for depression. They specifically note that many of the dichotomous measures involved the RCI or other tests of clinical significance.

These and other issues will likely become the subjects of future research and the continuing investigation of methods for validating the meaningfulness of change will remain an important area of discovery.

CONCLUSIONS

In the first edition of this handbook, Allen Bergin (1971) devoted seven pages to the "issues and techniques" of "criterion measurement" used to evaluate therapeutic outcomes. He summarized the status of criterion measurement in five conclusions: (1) patient change is multifactorial, (2) the decision to use external/behavioral versus internal/experiential measures was the most central issue of the day, (3) a growing trend favored more specific and even individualized measurement of change criteria in favor of global improvement indices, (4) adequate measurement in psychotherapy evaluation is dependent on advances in personality measurement in general, and (5) he added brief commentary on several outcome criteria, including assessment interviews, the MMPI, behavioral assessment,

self-concept measures, thematic stories, checklists and self-ratings, factor analytic batteries, mood ratings, the Personal Orientation Inventory, self-regulation measures, and peer ratings. In the 40 intervening years, outcome measurement has evolved and improved even though some perennial issues noted by Bergin continue to be relevant. After considering the wide range of issues included in this chapter, a brief summary of the central contemporary issues may be useful:

1. The long-standing philosophical issues regarding representational measurement theory are largely ignored by contemporary psychotherapy researchers. However, the next major paradigm shift in psychotherapy research may well be connected to a breakthrough or innovation in measurement methods. Psychotherapy researchers would do well to consider working with psychometricians who are working on the forefront of new philosophies and methods of measuring humans and human attributes. In this regard, the recent exploration of Item Response Theory and Rasch model applications to outcome measurement may help lead the way.

2. Outcome measures require the usual analysis of reliability and validity, but also have unique requirements for sensitivity to change and clinical utility. Additional work on the tension between the stability of traits and durable effects of treatment and continued efforts to develop measures that can be clinically useful for practice-based research (potentially through innovative technologies) may be fruitful avenues for future research.

3. The history of outcome measurement clearly demonstrates a productive and evolving pattern of improvement in outcome assessment including a broader range of contents and sources using newer methods. Outcome measurement has moved from the orientation/ theory specific to the practical and diagnostic.

4. No core battery is widely accepted and all previous attempts to unite researchers within an area of study around a core group of measures have failed. Nevertheless, a small group of measures are widely used (e.g., BDI, Fear Questionnaire) within certain content areas and may eventually become the de facto norm.

5. Attempts to bring greater theoretical coherence and order to the selection and examination of outcome measures using taxonomies or categorical schemes are well-intentioned but

infrequently used. Researchers may expand the breadth of the findings for effective treatments by including measures from corners of these taxonomies that are rarely included in the contemporary literature. Typically, however, this will result in more expensive and time-consuming methods for collecting some outcome data.

6. Standardized measures have largely become the norm though some studies do continue to use an individualized measure of outcome as part of a package of outcome measures. New strategies for addressing the tension between individual and standardized measures may not only benefit science, but also help to bridge the research-clinical gap.

7. Several innovations in outcome assessment appear to be gaining momentum and all show promise for continuing exciting work.

   a. Neuroimaging appears to be an especially exciting avenue of exploration for the coming years, but to the degree that is remains reliant on standard outcome measures for initial classification it will be stunted in its contribution.

   b. Practice based research is helping to move the field beyond the use of outcome measures to quantify overall treatment effects when a study is complete to the ongoing use of measures *during the course of therapy* to enhance treatment effects, prompt decisions to alter ongoing treatments, and study patterns of change. This use of outcome measures is an important leap toward greater value and usefulness of these measures—modifying treatments in real time, rather than years after the results of single outcome studies are published.

   c. Clinical significance and its variants are moving from useful add-on to standard operating procedure for outcome studies and several interesting lines of exploration are evolving (e.g., concordance among various measures/sources; variants of the methods such as percent improvement; and increased focus on client deterioration during treatment).

This chapter leads to an increased interest in this important methodological aspect of every treatment outcome study. The measurement of change continues to be essential and some of the most intriguing findings regarding treatments undoubtedly are connected with improved methods for tracking change. Therapy research to date has gradually improved and broadened the horizons for measuring change yet much work remains to develop the theories, methods, and analytic strategies for conducting this work. A number of possibilities have been presented here and certainly many others both easily conceptualized and previously unimagined will be at the disposal of the creative researcher. I look forward to seeing the continuing evolution of this exciting field.

REFERENCES

Achenbach, T. M., McConaughy, S. H., & Howell, C. T. (1987). Child/adolescent behavioral and emotional problems: Implications of cross-informant correlations for situational specificity. *Psychological Bulletin, 101*(2), 213–232. doi: 10.1037/0033–2909.101.2.213.

American Educational Research Association. (1999). *Standards for educational and psychological testing.* Washington, DC: American Psychological Association.

American Psychological Association. (2010). *American Psychological Association ethical principles of psychologists and code of conduct.* Retrieved from http://www.apa.org/ethics/code/index.aspx

Ankuta, G. Y., & Abeles, N. (1993). Client satisfaction, clinical significance, and meaningful change in psychotherapy. *Professional Psychology: Research and Practice, 24*(1), 70–74. doi: 10.1037/0735–7028.24.1.70

Andrews, G., & Page, A. C. (2005). Outcome measurement, outcome management and monitoring. *Australian and New Zealand Journal of Psychiatry, 39*(8), 649–651. doi: 10.1111/j.1440–1614.2005.01648.x

Åsenlöf, P., Denison, E., & Lindberg, P. (2006). Idiographic outcome analyses of the clinical significance of two interventions for patients with musculoskeletal pain. *Behaviour Research and Therapy, 44*(7), 947–965. doi: 10.1016/j.brat.2005.07.005

Atkins, D. C., Bedics, J. D., McGlinchey, J. B., & Beauchaine, T. P. (2005). Assessing clinical significance: Does it matter which method we use? *Journal of Consulting and Clinical Psychology, 73*(5), 982–989. doi: 10.1037/0022–006X.73.5.982

Barkham, M., Hardy, G., & Mellor-Clark, J. (Eds.). (2010). *Developing and delivering practice-based evidence: A guide for the psychological therapies.* Hoboken, NJ: Wiley-Blackwell. doi: 10.1002/9780470687994

Barkham, M., Mellor-Clark, J., Connell, J., Evans, C., Evans, R., & Margison, F. (2010). Clinical outcomes in routine evaluation (CORE)—The CORE measures and system: Measuring, monitoring and managing quality evaluation in the psychological therapies. In M. Barkham, G. E. Hardy, & J. Mellor-Clark (Eds.), *Developing and delivering practice-based evidence: A guide for the psychological therapies* (pp. 175–219). Hoboken, NJ: Wiley-Blackwell. doi: 10.1002/9780470687994.ch8

Barkham, M., Stiles, W. B., Connell, J., Twigg, E., Leach, C., Lucock, M., . . . Angus, L. (2008). Effects of psychological therapies in randomized trials and practice-based studies. *British Journal of Clinical Psychology, 47*(4), 397–415. doi: 10.1348/014466508X311713

Barrett, P. M., Dadds, M. R., & Rapee, R. M. (1996). Family treatment of childhood anxiety: A controlled trial. *Journal of Consulting and Clinical Psychology, 64*(2), 333–342. doi: 10.1037/0022–006X.64.2.333

Bauer, S., Lambert, M. J., & Nielsen, S. (2004). Clinical significance methods: A comparison of statistical techniques. *Journal of Personality Assessment, 82*(1), 60–70. doi: 10.1207/s15327752jpa8201_11

Baxter, L., Schwartz, J., Bergman, K., Szuba, M., Guze, B., Mazziotta, J., & Munford, P. (1992). Caudate glucose metabolic rate changes with both drug and behavior therapy for obsessive-compulsive disorder. *Archives of General Psychiatry, 49*(9), 681–689.

Beck, A. T., Ward, C. H., Mendelson, M. M., Mock, J. J., & Erbaugh, J. J. (1961). An inventory for measuring depression. *Archives of General Psychiatry, 4,* 561–571.

Bergin, A. E. (1971). The evaluation of therapeutic outcomes. In S. L. Garfield & A. E. Bergin (Eds.), *The handbook of psychotherapy and behavior change.* New York, NY: Wiley.

Bergin, A. E. (1980). Psychotherapy and religious values. *Journal of Consulting and Clinical Psychology, 48*(1), 95–105. doi: 10.1037/0022–006X.48.1.95

Bergin, A. E., & Lambert, M. J. (1978). The evaluation of therapeutic outcomes. In S. L. Garfield & A. E. Bergin (Eds.), *Handbook of psychotherapy and behavior change* (2nd ed., pp. 139–189). New York, NY: Wiley.

Blake, D., Weathers, F. W., Nagy, L. M., & Kaloupek, D. G. (1995). The development of a Clinician-Administered PTSD Scale. *Journal of Traumatic Stress, 8*(1), 75–90. doi: 10.1002/jts.2490080106

Blake, D. D., Weathers, F. W., Nagy, L. M., Kaloupek, D. G., Klauminzer, G., Charney, D. S., & Keane, T. M. (1990). A clinician rating scale for assessing current and lifetime PTSD: The CAPS-1. *Behavior Therapist, 18,* 187–188.

Blanchard, E. B., & Schwarz, S. P. (1988). Clinically significant changes in behavioral medicine. *Behavioral Assessment, 10*(2), 171–188. doi: 10.1007/BF00962642

Brody, A., Saxena, S., Stoessel, P., Gillies, L., Fairbanks, L., Alborzian, S., & Baxter, L. (2001). Regional brain metabolic changes in patients with

major depression treated with either paroxetine or interpersonal therapy: Preliminary findings. *Archives of General Psychiatry, 58*(7), 631–640.

Brooks, N. (1989). Defining outcome. *Brain Injury: [BI], 3*(4), 325–329.

Burlingame, G. M., Wells, M., Lambert, M. J., & Cox, J. C. (2004). Youth Outcome Questionnaire (Y-OQ). In M. E. Maruish (Ed.), *The use of psychological testing for treatment planning and outcomes assessment: Volume 2: Instruments for children and adolescents* (3rd ed., pp. 235–273). Mahwah, NJ: Erlbaum.

Cahill, J., Barkham, M., & Stiles, W. B. (2010). Systematic review of practice-based research on psychological therapies in routine clinic settings. *British Journal of Clinical Psychology, 49*(4), 421–453. doi: 10.1348/014466509X470789

Campbell, D. T., & Stanley, J. C. (1963). *Experimental and quasi-experimental designs for research.* Chicago, IL: Rand McNally.

Cantwell, D. P., Lewinsohn, P. M., Rohde, P., & Seeley, J. R. (1997). Correspondence between adolescent report and parent report of psychiatric diagnostic data. *Journal of the American Academy of Child & Adolescent Psychiatry, 36*(5), 610–619. doi: 10.1097/00004583–199705000–00011

Carr, J. E., Austin, J. L., Britton, L. N., Kellum, K., & Bailey, J. S. (1999). An assessment of social validity trends in applied behavior analysis. *Behavioral Interventions, 14*(4), 223–231. doi: 10.1002/(SICI)1099–078X(199910/12)14:4<223::AID-BIN37>3.0.CO;2-Y

Ciarlo, J. A., Brown, T. R., Edwards, D. W., Kiresuk, T. J., & Newman, F. L. (1986). *Assessing mental health treatment outcome measurement techniques* (DHHS Publication No. ADM 86–1301). Washington, DC: Superintendent of Documents, U.S. Government Printing Office.

Connell, J., Barkham, M., & Mellor-Clark, J. (2008). The effectiveness of UK student counselling services: An analysis using the CORE system. *British Journal of Guidance & Counselling, 36*(1), 1–18. doi: 10.1080/03069880701715655

Cronbach, L. J., & Meehl, P. E. (1955). Construct validity in psychological tests. *Psychological Bulletin, 52*(4), 281–302. doi: 10.1037/h0040957

Cuijpers, P., Li, J., Hofmann, S. G., & Andersson, G. (2010). Self-reported versus clinician-rated symptoms of depression as outcome measures in psychotherapy research on depression: A meta-analysis. *Clinical Psychology Review, 30*(6), 768–778. doi: 10.1016/j.cpr.2010.06.001

Cuijpers, P., Smit, F., Hollon, S. D., & Andersson, G. (2010). Continuous and dichotomous outcomes in studies of psychotherapy for adult depression: A meta-analytic comparison. *Journal of Affective Disorders, 126*(3), 349–357. doi: 10.1016/j.jad.2010.01.001

De Los Reyes, A., & Kazdin, A. E. (2005). Informant discrepancies in the assessment of childhood psychopathology: A critical review, theoretical framework, and recommendations for further study. *Psychological Bulletin, 131*(4), 483–509. doi:10.1037/0033-2909.131.4.483

De Los Reyes, A., Kundey, S. A., & Wang, M. (2011). The end of the primary outcome measure: A research agenda for constructing its replacement. *Clinical Psychology Review, 31*(5), 829–838. doi: 10.1016/j.cpr.2011.03.011

Doucette, A., & Wolf, A. W. (2009). Questioning the measurement precision of psychotherapy research. *Psychotherapy Research, 19*(4–5), 374–389. doi: 10.1080/10503300902894422

Elkin, I., Shea, T, Watkins, J. T., Imber, S. D., Sotsky, S. M., Collins, J. F., ... Parloff, M. B. (1989). National Institute of Mental Health Treatment of Depression Collaborative Research Program. *Archives of General Psychiatry, 46*, 971–982.

Elliot, R. (1992). A conceptual analysis of Lambert, Ogles, and Masters's conceptual scheme for outcome assessment. *Journal of Counseling & Development, 70*(4), 535–537.

Elliott, R., Fox, C. M., Beltyukova, S. A., Stone, G. E., Gunderson, J., & Zhang, X. (2006). Deconstructing therapy outcome measurement with Rasch analysis of a measure of general clinical distress: The symptom checklist-90-revised. *Psychological Assessment, 18*(4), 359–372. doi: 10.1037/1040-3590.18.4.359

Evans, K., Douglas, B., Bruce, N., & Drummond, P. D. (2008). An exploratory study of changes in salivary cortisol, depression, and pain intensity after treatment for chronic pain. *Pain Medicine, 9*(6), 752–758. doi: 10.1111/j.1526-4637.2006.00285.x

Feldman, M. A., Condillac, R. A., Tough, S., Hunt, S., & Griffiths, D. (2002). Effectiveness of community positive behavioral intervention for persons with developmental disabilities and severe behavior disorders. *Behavior Therapy, 33*(3), 377–398. doi: 10.1016/S0005-7894(02)80034-X

Foster, S. L., & Mash, E. J. (1999). Assessing social validity in clinical treatment research: Issues and procedures. *Journal of Consulting and Clinical Psychology, 67*(3), 308–319. doi: 10.1037/0022-006X.67.3.308

Froyd, J. E., Lambert, M. J., & Froyd, J. D. (1996). A review of practices of psychotherapy outcome measurement. *Journal of Mental Health, 5*(1), 11–15. doi: 10.1080/09638239650037144

Furmark, T., Tillfors, M., Marteinsdottir, I., Fischer, H., Pissiota, A., Långström, B., & Fredrikson, M. (2002). Common changes in cerebral blood flow in patients with social phobia treated with citalopram or cognitive-behavioral therapy. *Archives of General Psychiatry, 59*(5), 425–433.

Gaab, J. J., Blättler, N. N., Menzi, T. T., Pabst, B. B., Stoyer, S. S., & Ehlert, U. U. (2003). Randomized controlled evaluation of the effects of cognitive-behavioral stress management on cortisol responses to acute stress in healthy subjects. *Psychoneuroendocrinology, 28*(6), 767–779. doi: 10.1016/S0306-4530(02)00069-0

Gelso, C. J. (1979). Research in counseling: Methodological and professional issues. *Counseling Psychologist, 8*(3), 7–35. doi: 10.1177/001100007900800303

Goldapple, K., Segal, Z., Garson, C., Lau, M., Bieling, P., Kennedy, S., & Mayberg, H. (2004). Modulation of cortical-limbic pathways in major depression: Treatment-specific effects of cognitive behavior therapy. *Archives of General Psychiatry, 61*(1), 34–41.

Grissom, G. R., & Howard, K. I. (2000). Directions and COMPASS-PC. In M. E. Maruish (Ed.), *Handbook of psychological assessment in primary care settings* (pp. 255–275). Mahwah, NJ: Erlbaum.

Grundy, C. T., Lambert, M. J., & Grundy, E. M. (1996). Assessing clinical significance: Application to the Hamilton rating scale for depression. *Journal of Mental Health, 5*(1), 25–33. doi: 10.1080/09638239650037162

Grundy, C. T., Lunnen, K. M., Lambert, M. J., Ashton, J. E., & Tovey, D. (1994). Hamilton rating scale for depression: One scale or many? *Clinical Psychology—Science & Practice, 1*, 197–205.

Hamilton, M. (1967). Development of a rating scale for primary depressive illness. *British Journal of Social and Clinical Psychology, 6*, 278–296.

Hammerfald, K. K., Eberle, C. C., Grau, M. M., Kinsperger, A. A., Zimmermann, A. A., Ehlert, U. U., & Gaab, J. J. (2006). Persistent effects of cognitive-behavioral stress management on cortisol responses to acute stress in healthy subjects—A randomized controlled trial. *Psychoneuroendocrinology, 31*(3), 333–339. doi: 10.1016/j.psyneuen.2005.08.007

Hansen, N. B., Lambert, M. J., & Forman, E. M. (2003). The psychotherapy dose-effect in naturalistic settings revisited: Response to Gray. *Clinical Psychology: Science and Practice, 10*, 507–508.

Hatfield, D. R., & Ogles, B. M. (2007). Why some clinicians use outcome measures and others do not. *Administration and Policy in Mental Health and Mental Health Services Research, 34*(3), 283–291. doi: 10.1007/s10488-006-0110-y

Hendler, T., Goshen, E., Zwas, S., Sasson, Y., Gal, G., & Zohar, J. (2003). Brain reactivity to specific symptom provocation indicates prospective therapeutic outcome in OCD. *Psychiatry Research: Neuroimaging, 124*(2), 87–103. doi: 10.1016/S0925-4927(03)00091-X

Hill, C. E., & Lambert, M. J. (2004). Methodological issues in studying psychotherapy processes and outcomes. In Lambert, M. J. (Ed.), *Bergin & Garfield's handbook of psychotherapy and behavior change* (pp. 84–136). Hoboken, NJ: Wiley.

Hiller, W., Schindler, A. C., & Lambert, M. J. (2011). Defining response and remission in psychotherapy research: A comparison of the RCI and the method of percent improvement. *Psychotherapy Research*. doi: 10.1080/10503307.2011.616237

Holt-Lunstad, J., Birmingham, W., & Light, K. C. (2011). The influence of depressive symptomatology and perceived stress on plasma and salivary oxytocin before, during and after a support enhancement intervention. *Psychoneuroendocrinology*, *36*(8), 1249–1256. doi: 10.1016/j.psyneuen.2011.03.007

Horowitz, L. J., Lambert, M. J., & Strupp, H. H. (Eds.). (1997). *Measuring patient change in mood, anxiety, and personality disorders: Toward a core battery*. Washington, D C: American Psychological Association Press.

Howard, K. I., Lueger, R. J., Maling, M. S., & Martinovich, Z. (1993). A phase model of psychotherapy outcome: Causal mediation of change. *Journal of Consulting and Clinical Psychology*, *61*(4), 678–685. doi: 10.1037/0022–006X.61.4.678

Howard, K. I., Moras, K., Brill, P. L., Martinovich, Z., & Lutz, W. (1996). Evaluation of psychotherapy: Efficacy, effectiveness, and patient progress. *American Psychologist*, *51*(10), 1059–1064. doi: 10.1037/0003–066X.51.10.1059

Hsu, L. M. (1989). Reliable changes in psychotherapy: Taking into account regression toward the mean. *Behavioral Assessment*, *11*, 459–467.

Hsu, L. M. (1996). On the identification of clinically significant client changes: Reinterpretation of Jacobson's cut scores. *Journal of Psychotherapy and Behavioral Assessment*, *18*(4), 371–385. doi: 10.1007/BF02229141

Hsu, L. M. (1999). Caveats concerning comparisons of change rates obtained with five methods of identifying significant client changes: Comment on Speer and Greenbaum (1995). *Journal of Consulting and Clinical Psychology*, *67*, 594–598.

Hunsley, J., & Mash, E. J. (2007). Evidence-based assessment. *Annual Review of Clinical Psychology*, 329–351. doi: 10.1146/annurev.clinpsy.3.022806.091419

Ihilevich, D., & Gleser, G. C. (1982). *Evaluating mental health programs: The progress evaluation scales*. Lexington, MA: Lexington Books.

Ishak, W., Burt, T., & Sederer, L. (Eds.). (2002). *Outcome measurement in psychiatry: A critical review*. Washington, DC: American Psychiatric Association.

Jacobson, N. S. (1988). Defining clinically significant change: An introduction. *Behavioral Assessment*, *10*, 131–132.

Jacobson, N. S., Follette, W. C., & Revenstorf, D. (1984). Psychotherapy outcome research: Methods for reporting variability and evaluating clinical significance. *Behavior Therapy*, *15*, 336–352.

Jacobson, N. S., Roberts, L. J., Berns, S. B., & McGlinchey, J. B. (1999). Methods for defining and determining the clinical significance of treatment effects: Description, application, and alternatives. *Journal of Consulting and Clinical Psychology*, *67*, 300–307.

Jacobson, N. S., & Truax, P. (1991). Clinical significance: A statistical approach to defining meaningful change in psychotherapy research. *Journal of Consulting and Clinical Psychology*, *59*, 12–19.

Kanfer, F. H., & Goldstein, A. P. (1991). *Helping people change*. New York, NY: Pergamon Press.

Kaplan, R. M. (1990). Behavior as the central outcome in health care. *American Psychologist*, *45*(11), 1211–1220. doi: 10.1037/0003–066X.45.11.1211

Kazdin, A. E. (1977). Assessing the clinical or applied importance of behavior change through social validation. *Behavior Modification*, *1*, 427–452.

Kazdin, A. E. (1998). *Research design in clinical psychology* (3rd ed.). Boston, MA: Allyn & Bacon.

Kazdin, A. E. (2003). Clinical significance: Measuring whether interventions make a difference. In: A. E. Kazdin (Ed.), *Methodological issues & strategies in clinical research* (3rd ed., pp. 691–710). Washington, DC: American Psychological Association.

Keisler, D. J. (1971). Experimental designs in psychotherapy research. In A. E. Bergin & S. L. Garfield (Eds.), *Handbook of psychotherapy and behavior change* (pp. 36–74). New York, NY: Wiley.

Keller, M. B. (2003). Past, present, and future directions for defining optimal treatment outcome in depression: Remission and beyond. *JAMA*, *289*(23), 3152–3160. doi: 10.1001/jama.289.23.3152

Kendall, P. C., & Grove, W. M. (1988). Normative comparisons in therapy outcome. *Behavioral Assessment*, *10*(2), 147–158.

Kendall, P. C., Marrs-Garcia, A., Nath, S. R., & Sheldrick, R. C. (1999). Normative comparisons for the evaluation of clinical significance. *Journal of Consulting and Clinical Psychology*, *67*, 285–299.

Kennedy, S., Konarski, J., Segal, Z., Lau, M., Bieling, P., McIntyre, R., & Mayberg, H. (2007). Differences in brain glucose metabolism between responders to CBT and venlafaxine in a 16-week randomized controlled trial. *American Journal of Psychiatry*, *164*(5), 778–788.

Kiresuk, T. J., Smith, A., & Cardillo, J. E. (Eds.). (1994). *Goal attainment scaling: Applications, theory, and measurement*. Hillsdale, NJ: Erlbaum.

Konarski, J., McIntyre, R., Soczynska, J., & Kennedy, S. (2007). Neuroimaging approaches in mood disorders: technique and clinical implications. *Annals of Clinical Psychiatry: Official Journal of the American Academy of Clinical Psychiatrists*, *19*(4), 265–277.

Kopta, S., Howard, K. I., Lowry, J. L., & Beutler, L. E. (1994). Patterns of symptomatic recovery in psychotherapy. *Journal of Consulting and Clinical Psychology*, *62*(5), 1009–1016. doi: 10.1037/0022–006X.62.5.1009

La Greca, A. M. (2005). Editorial. *Journal of Consulting and Clinical Psychology*, *73*(1), 3–5. doi: 10.1037/0022–006X.73.1.3

Lambert, M. J. (2010). *Prevention of treatment failure: The use of measuring, monitoring, and feedback in clinical practice*. Washington, DC: American Psychological Association. doi:10.1037/12141-000

Lambert, M. J., Burlingame, G. M., Umphress, V., Hansen, N. B., Vermeersch, D. A., Clouse, G. C., & Yanchar, S. C. (1996). The reliability and validity of the Outcome Questionnaire. *Clinical Psychology and Psychotherapy*, *3*, 249–258.

Lambert, M. J., Christensen, E. R., & DeJulio, S. S. (1983). *The assessment of psychotherapy outcome*. New York, NY: Wiley.

Lambert, M. J., Hansen, N. B., & Bauer, S. (2008). Assessing the clinical significance of outcome results. In A. M. Nezu & C. Nezu (Eds.), *Evidence-based outcome research: A practical guide to conducting randomized controlled trials for psychosocial interventions* (pp. 359–378). New York, NY: Oxford University Press.

Lambert, M. J., Hatch, D. R., Kingston, M. D., & Edwards, B. C. (1986). Zung, Beck, and Hamilton rating scales as measures of treatment outcome: A meta-analytic comparison. *Journal of Consulting and Clinical Psychology*, *54*(1), 54–59. doi: 10.1037/0022–006X.54.1.54

Lambert, M. J., & Hill, C. (1994). Assessing psychotherapy outcomes and processes. In A. E. Bergin & S. L. Garfield, *Handbook of psychotherapy and behavior change* (4th ed., pp. 72–113). New York, NY: Wiley.

Lambert, M. J., Masters, K. S., & Ogles, B. M. (1991). Outcome research in counseling. In C. E. Watkins & L. J. Schneider (Eds.), *Research in counseling* (pp. 51–83). Hillsdale, NJ: Erlbaum.

Lambert, M. J., & Ogles, B. M. (2009). Using clinical significance in psychotherapy-outcome research: The need for a common procedure and validity data. *Psychotherapy Research*, *19*, 493–501. doi: 10.1080/10503300902849483

Lambert, M. J., Ogles, B. M., & Masters, K. S. (1992). Choosing outcome assessment devices: An organizational and conceptual scheme. *Journal of Counseling and Development*, *70*, 538–539.

Lambert, M. J., Okiishi, J. C., Finch, A. E. & Johnson, L. D. (1998). Outcome assessment: From conceptualization to implementation. *Professional Psychology: Research & Practice*, *29*, 63–70.

Lambert, M. J., Shapiro, D. A., & Bergin, A. E. (1986). The effectiveness of psychotherapy. In S. L. Garfield & A. E. Bergin (Eds.), *Handbook of psychotherapy and behavior change* (3rd ed.). New York, NY: Wiley.

Lambert, M. J., & Shimokawa, K. (2011). Collecting client feedback. *Psychotherapy*, *48*(1), 72–79. doi: 10.1037/a0022238

Lambert, M. J., & Vermeersch, D. A. (2008). Measuring and improving psychotherapy outcome in routine practice. In S. D. Brown, R. W. Lent, S. D. Brown, & R. W. Lent (Eds.), *Handbook of counseling psychology* (4th ed., pp. 233–248). Hoboken, NJ: Wiley.

Lambert, M. J., Whipple, J. L., Smart, D. W., Vermeersch, D. A., Nielsen, S. L., & Hawkins, E. J. (2001). The effects of providing therapists with feedback on patient progress during psychotherapy: Are outcomes enhanced? *Psychotherapy Research*, *11*, 49–68.

Lavoie, M. E., Imbriglio, T. V., Stip, E., & O'Connor, K. P. (2011). Neurocognitive changes following cognitive-behavioral treatment in Tourette syndrome and chronic tic disorder. *International Journal of Cognitive Therapy*, *4*(1), 34–50. doi: 10.1521/ijct.2011.4.1.34

Lester, K., Artz, C., Resick, P. A., & Young-Xu, Y. (2010). Impact of race on early treatment termination and outcomes in posttraumatic stress disorder treatment. *Journal of Consulting and Clinical Psychology*, *78*(4), 480–489. doi: 10.1037/a0019551

Linden, D. E. J. (2008). Brain imaging and psychotherapy: Methodological considerations and practical implications. *European Archives of Psychiatry Clinical Neuroscience*, *258*(Suppl. 5), 71–75. doi: 10.1007/s00406–008–5023–1.

Luborsky, L. (1984). *Principles of psychoanalytic psychotherapy: A manual for supportive-expressive treatment*. New York, NY: Basic Books.

Lunnen, K. M., & Ogles, B. M. (1998). A multiperspective, multivariable evaluation of reliable change. *Journal of Consulting and Clinical Psychology*, *66*, 400–410. doi: 10.1037/0022–006X.66.2.400

Maruish, M. E. (Ed.). (1999). *The use of psychological testing for treatment planning and outcomes assessment* (2nd ed.). Mahwah, NJ: Erlbaum.

McClendon, D. T., Warren, J. S., Green, K. M., Burlingame, G. M., Eggett, D. L., & McClendon, R. J. (2011). Sensitivity to change of youth treatment outcome measures: A comparison of the CBCL, BASC-2, and Y-OQ. *Journal of Clinical Psychology*, *67*(1), 111–125. doi: 10.1002/jclp.20746

McGlynn, E. A. (1996). Domains of study and methodological challenges. In L. I. Sederer & B. Dickey (Eds.), *Outcomes assessment in clinical practice*. Baltimore, MD: Williams & Wilkins.

McKay, M. S., & Zakzanis, K. K. (2010). The impact of treatment on HPA axis activity in unipolar major depression. *Journal of Psychiatric Research*, *44*(3), 183–192. doi: 10.1016/j.jpsychires.2009.07.012

Michell, J. (1999). *Measurement in psychology critical history of a methodological concept*. New York, NY: Cambridge University Press.

Michelson, L., Mavissakalian, M., & Marchione, K. (1985). Cognitive and behavioral treatments of agoraphobia: Clinical, behavioral, and psychophysiological outcomes. *Journal of Consulting and Clinical Psychology*, *53*, 913–925. doi: 10.1037/0022–006X.53.6.913

Min, J., Breheny, S., MacLachlan, V., & Healy, D. (2004). What is the most relevant standard of success in assisted reproduction? The singleton, term gestation, live birth rate per cycle initiated: The BESST endpoint for assisted reproduction. *Human Reproduction* (Oxford, England), *19*(1), 3–7.

Moleiro, C., & Beutler, L. E. (2009). Clinically significant change in psychotherapy for depressive disorders. *Journal of Affective Disorders, 115*(1–2), 220–224. doi: 10.1016/j.jad.2008.09.009

Morris, R. G., Evenden, J. L., Sahakian, B. J., & Robbins, T. W. (1987). Computer-aided assessment of dementia: Comparative studies of neuropsychological deficits in Alzheimer-type dementia and Parkinson's disease. In S. M. Stahl, S. D. Iversen, & E. C. Goodman (Eds.), *Cognitive neurochemistry* (pp. 21–36). New York, NY: Oxford University Press.

Nabeyama, M., Nakagawa, A., Yoshiura, T., Nakao, T., Nakatani, E., Togao, O., . . . Kanba, S. (2008). Functional MRI study of brain activation alterations in patients with obsessive-compulsive disorder after symptom improvement. *Psychiatry Research: Neuroimaging, 163*(3), 236–247. doi: 10.1016/j.pscychresns.2007.11.001

Nasiakos, G., Cribbie, R. A., & Arpin-Cribbie, C. A. (2010). Equivalence-based measures of clinical significance: Assessing treatments for depression. *Psychotherapy Research, 20*(6), 647–656. doi: 10.1080/10503307.2010.501039

Nedeljkovic, M., Kyrios, M., Moulding, R., & Doron, G. (2011). Neuropsychological changes following cognitive-behavioral treatment of obsessive-compulsive disorder (OCD). *International Journal of Cognitive Therapy, 4*(1), 8–20. doi: 10.1521/ijct.2011.4.1.8

Nietzel, M. T., & Trull, T. J. (1988). Meta-analytic approaches to social comparisons: A method for measuring clinical significance. *Behavioral Assessment, 10,* 159–169.

Nietzel, M. T., Russell, R. L., Hemmings, K. A., & Gretter, M. L. (1987). The clinical significance of psychotherapy for unipolar depression: A meta-analytic approach to social comparison. *Journal of Consulting and Clinical Psychology, 55,* 156–161. doi: 10.1037/0022–006X.55.2.156

Newnham, E. A., Harwood, K. E., & Page, A. C. (2007). Evaluating the clinical significance of responses by psychiatric inpatients to the mental health subscales of the SF-36. *Journal of Affective Disorders, 98,* 91–97. doi: 10.1016/j.jad.2006.07.001.

Odgaard, E. C., & Fowler, R. L. (2010). Confidence intervals for effect sizes: Compliance and clinical significance in the journal of consulting and clinical psychology. *Journal of Consulting and Clinical Psychology, 78*(3), 287–297. doi: 10.1037/a0019294

Ogles, B. M., & Lambert, M. J. (1989). A meta-analytic comparison of twelve agoraphobia outcome measures. *Phobia Practice and Research Journal, 2,* 117–127.

Ogles, B. M., Lambert, M. J., & Fields, S. (2002). *Essentials of outcome assessment.* Hoboken, NJ: Wiley.

Ogles, B. M., Lambert, M. J., & Masters, K. S. (1996). *Assessing outcome in clinical practice.* Boston: Allyn & Bacon.

Ogles, B. M., Lambert, M. J., & Sawyer, J. D. (1995). Clinical significance of the National Institute of Mental Health Treatment of Depression Collaborative Research Program data. *Journal of Consulting and Clinical Psychology, 63,* 321–326. doi: 10.1037/0022–006X.63.2.321

Ogles, B. M., Lambert, M. J., Weight, D. G., & Payne, I. R. (1990). Agoraphobia outcome measurement in the 1980's: A review and meta-analysis. *Psychological Assessment, 2,* 317–325. doi: 10.1037/1040–3590.2.3.317

Ogles, B. M., Lunnen, K. M., & Bonesteel, K. (2001). Clinical significance: History, application, and current practice. *Clinical Psychology Review, 21,* 421–446. doi: 10.1016/S0272–7358(99)00058–6

Ogles, B. M., Melendez, G., Davis, D. C., & Lunnen, K. M. (2001). The Ohio scales: Practical outcome assessment. *Journal of Child and Family Studies, 10,* 199–212.

Openshaw, C., Waller, G., & Sperlinger, D. (2004). Group cognitive-behavior therapy for bulimia nervosa: Statistical versus clinical significance of changes in symptoms across treatment. *International Journal of Eating Disorders, 36,* 363–375.

Pastor, D. A., & Beretvas, S. (2006). Longitudinal Rasch modeling in the context of psychotherapy outcomes assessment. *Applied Psychological Measurement, 30*(2), 100–120. doi: 10.1177/0146621605279761

Paquette, V., Lévesque, J., Mensour, B., Leroux, J., Beaudoin, G., Bourgouin, P., & Beauregard, M. (2003). "Change the mind and you change the brain": Effects of cognitive-behavioral therapy on the neural correlates of spider phobia. *Neuroimage, 18*(2), 401–409.

Pinborg, A., Loft, A., Ziebe, S., & Nyboe Andersen, A. (2004). What is the most relevant standard of success in assisted reproduction? Is there a single "parameter of excellence"? *Human Reproduction, 19*(5), 1052–1054.

Rosenblatt, A., & Attkisson, C. C. (1993). Assessing outcomes for sufferers of severe mental disorder: A conceptual framework and review. *Evaluation and Program Planning, 16,* 347–363.

Sánchez-Meca, J., Rosa-Alcázar, A. I., Marín-Martínez, F., & Gómez-Conesa, A. (2010). Psychological treatment of panic disorder with or without agoraphobia: A meta-analysis. *Clinical Psychology Review, 30*(1), 37–50.

Saxena, S., Brody, A., Ho, M., Alborzian, S., Maidment, K., Zohrabi, N., & Baxter, L. (2002). Differential cerebral metabolic changes with paroxetine treatment of obsessive-compulsive disorder vs major depression. *Archives of General Psychiatry, 59*(3), 250–261.

Schienle, A., Schäfer, A., Hermann, A., Rohrmann, S., & Vaitl, D. (2007). Symptom provocation and reduction in patients suffering from spider phobia: An fMRI study on exposure therapy. *European Archives of Psychiatry and Clinical Neuroscience, 257*(8), 486–493.

Schienle, A., Schäfer, A., Stark, R., & Vaitl, D. (2009). Long-term effects of cognitive behavior therapy on brain activation in spider phobia. *Psychiatry Research, 172*(2), 99–102.

Sederer, L. I., & Dickey, B. (Eds.). (1996). *Outcomes assessment in clinical practice*. Baltimore, MD: Williams & Wilkins.

Seggar, L. B., Lambert, M. J., & Hansen, N. B. (2002). Assessing clinical significance: Application to the Beck depression inventory. *Behavior Therapy, 33,* 253–269.

Shiner, B., Watts, B. V., Pomerantz, A., Young-Xu, Y., & Schnurr, P. P. (2011). Sensitivity of the SF-36 to PTSD symptom change in veterans. *Journal of Traumatic Stress, 24,* 111–115. doi: 10.1002/jts.20613

Siegmund, A., Köster, L., Meves, A. M., Plag, J., Stoy, M., & Ströhle, A. (2011). Stress hormones during flooding therapy and their relationship to therapy outcome in patients with panic disorder and agoraphobia. *Journal of Psychiatric Research, 45*(3), 339–346. doi: 10.1016/j.jpsychires.2010.07.002

Slade, K., Lambert, M. J., Harmon, S., Smart, D. W., & Bailey, R. (2008). Improving psychotherapy outcome: The use of immediate electronic feedback and revised clinical support tools. *Clinical Psychology & Psychotherapy, 15*(5), 287–303. doi: 10.1002/cpp.594

Smith, M. L., Glass, G. V., & Miller, T. I. (1980). *The benefits of psychotherapy*. Baltimore, MD: Johns Hopkins University Press.

Speer, D. C. (1992). Clinically significant change: Jacobson and Truax (1991) revisited. *Journal of Consulting and Clinical Psychology, 60,* 402–408.

Speer, D. C., & Greenbaum, P. E. (1995). Five methods for computing significant individual client change and improvement rates: Support for an individual growth curve approach. *Journal of Consulting and Clinical Psychology, 63,* 1044–1048.

Stiles, W. B., Barkham, M., Mellor-Clark, J., & Connell, J. (2008). Effectiveness of cognitive-behavioural, person-centred, and psychodynamic therapies in UK primary-care routine practice: Replication in a larger sample. *Psychological Medicine: A Journal of Research in Psychiatry and the Allied Sciences, 38*(5), 677–688. doi: 10.1017/S0033291707001511

Storch, M., Gaab, J., Küttel, Y., Stüssi, A., & Fend, H. (2007). Psychoneuroendocrine effects of resource-activating stress management training. *Health Psychology, 26*(4), 456–463. doi: 10.1037/0278-6133.26.4.456

Straube, T., Glauer, M., Dilger, S., Mentzel, H., & Miltner, W. (2006). Effects of cognitive-behavioral therapy on brain activation in specific phobia. *Neuroimage, 29*(1), 125–135.

Strupp, H. H., Fox, R. E., & Lessler, K. (1969). *Patients view their psychotherapy*. Oxford, United Kingdom: Johns Hopkins Press.

Strupp, H. H., & Hadley, S. W. (1977). A tripartite model of mental health and therapeutic outcome: With special reference to negative effects in psychotherapy. *American Psychologist, 32,* 187–196.

Tingey, R. C., Lambert, M. J., Burlingame, G. M., & Hansen, N. B. (1996). Assessing clinical significance: Proposed extensions to method. *Psychotherapy Research, 6*(2), 109–123. doi:10.1080/10503309612331331638

Trochim, W., & Land, D. (1982). Designing designs for research. *Researcher, 1,* 1–6. http://www.socialresearchmethods.net/kb/desdes.php

Valen, J., Ryum, T., Svartberg, M., Stiles, T. C., & McCullough, L. (2011, April 25). The achievement of therapeutic objectives scale: Interrater reliability and sensitivity to change in short-term dynamic psychotherapy and cognitive therapy. *Psychological Assessment*. Advance online publication. doi: 10.1037/a0023649

Vermeersch, D. A., Lambert, M. J., & Burlingame, G. M. (2000). Outcome questionnaire: Item sensitivity to change. *Journal of Personality Assessment, 74*(2), 242–261. doi: 10.1207/S15327752JPA7402_6

Vermeersch, D. A., Whipple, J. L., Lambert, M. J., Hawkins, E. J., Burchfield, C. M., & Okiishi, J. C. (2004). Outcome questionnaire: Is it sensitive to changes in counseling center clients? *Journal of Counseling Psychology, 51*(1), 38–49. doi: 10.1037/0022-0167.51.1.38

Ware, J. E., & Sherbourne, C. D. (1992). The MOS 36-item short-form health survey (SF-36). I. Conceptual framework and item selection. *Medical Care, 30,* 473–483. doi: 10.1097/00005650-199206000-00002

Waskow, I. E., & Parloff, M. B. (1975). *Psychotherapy change measures*. Rockville, MD: National Institute of Mental Health.

Watson, J. P., & Marks, I. M. (1971). Relevant and irrelevant fear in flooding—A crossover study of phobic patients. *Behavior Therapy, 2,* 275–293.

Whipple, J. L., & Lambert, M. J. (2011). Outcome measures for practice. *Annual Review of Clinical Psychology, 7,* 87–111. doi: 10.1146/annurev-clinpsy-040510-143938

Wolf, M. M. (1978). Social validity: The case for subjective measurement or how applied behavior analysis is finding its heart. *Journal of Applied Behavior Analysis, 11,* 203–214.

EVALUATING THE INGREDIENTS OF THERAPEUTIC EFFICACY

•

CHAPTER 6

THE EFFICACY AND EFFECTIVENESS OF PSYCHOTHERAPY

MICHAEL J. LAMBERT

In this chapter, the status of empirical evidence on the efficacy and effectiveness of psychotherapy—mainly with adult outpatients—is reviewed. A variety of related issues, including the nature, permanence, relevance, and generalizability of therapy, curative factors, common and specific therapy factors as agents of change, and potential methods for improving the potency of therapies is considered. With the ever-growing number of interventions that are applied in a variety of contexts (e.g., medical, Internet, educational) with patients who have diverse problems, coupled with the growing number of researchers and journals showing interest in studying treatment efficacy, a complete cataloging of all studies and reviews in the area of behavior change is not possible. As a result and in keeping with previous editions of the handbook, here the practice of individual therapy with adults is considered. Full accounts of the major approaches to therapy are reserved for other chapters, but in this chapter the focus is on an integration and comparison of results along with issues of central importance to the effectiveness of all therapies. Occasionally, other literature is reported (e.g., group therapy) to help emphasize the breadth and consistency of the behavior change literature.

Research on therapy outcome from the 1930s through the early 2000s was summarized in the five previous editions of this chapter (Bergin, 1971; Bergin & Lambert, 1978; Lambert & Bergin, 1994; Lambert & Ogles, 2004; Lambert, Shapiro, & Bergin, 1986). Review of this literature and the related controversies is well documented. The interested reader is invited to examine earlier editions of this chapter to gain an appreciation of the historical context of the current chapter, the nature and quality of prior research, and the controversies that have attended analyses of therapeutic outcomes such as spontaneous remission. For the most part, studies conducted in the past decade are emphasized in the present chapter.

THE EFFECTIVENESS OF PSYCHOTHERAPY

A huge body of literature has been generated to examine the benefits of psychotherapy. It is a formidable task to broadly review the main findings produced by numerous scholars using both qualitative and quantitative techniques. To provide some organization to the general findings regarding the efficacy of psychotherapy, a number of specific questions are addressed: (a) Is psychotherapy efficacious? (b) Do patients make changes that are clinically meaningful? (c) Do the benefits of therapy exceed placebo? (d) Do patients maintain their gains? (e) How much therapy is necessary? (f) Do some patients get worse? (g) Does efficacy research generalize to applied settings? and, (h) What is the contribution of the individual therapist?

Is Psychotherapy Efficacious?

The historical controversy regarding the effects of psychotherapy compared to no treatment and to placebo controls (e.g., Bergin, 1971; Bergin & Lambert, 1978; Eysenck, 1952; Rachman &

Wilson, 1980) has been settled largely through the use of meta-analyses. Meta-analyses provide an efficient and replicable integrative summary of primary studies and apply the methods and principles of empirical research to the process of reviewing literature. Following a systematic search of the literature to locate studies meeting predefined inclusion criteria, the findings of individual studies are quantified using a common metric such as an effect size statistic. The most common effect size statistic in outcome research is Cohen's d (Cohen, 1969), which is the standardized difference between the mean of groups; say a treatment group and a no-treatment control group. The aim of d and related statistics is to describe the magnitude of treatment response. An effect size of zero indicates the complete lack of differences (i.e., the means of the two groups were identical), while an effect size of 1.0 indicates that one group, on average, is one standard deviation superior to the other group, on average. Since effect size can be understood in terms of the percent of patients responding to treatment, it provides an easy way to estimate the magnitude of effects a treatment has had.

Table 6.1 displays the meanings of various effect sizes that might be reported in studies and summed in meta-analytic reviews. If the effect size being examined refers to the difference between a group receiving a treatment and a no-treatment control group, then an effect size of zero would indicate that 50% of treated patients would be below the average of those who do not receive treatment (with 50% above as well). If an effect size were 1, then 84% of those receiving treatment would have a better outcome than the average patient who did not receive treatment (i.e., who is at the 50th percentile, keeping in mind that 50% of the no treatment group is better off than the other 50%). For an effect of this size, it would be expected that 72% of patients receiving treatment would experience a "success" versus 28% of untreated patients (using Table 6.1).

Meta-analysis essentially is a statistical means to test hypotheses by synthesizing the results of a set of studies addressing the same research question. The typical meta-analytic hypothesis is that the aggregate effect size is different from zero. In meta-analysis an effect is calculated for each study and then aggregated; the aggregate is then tested against zero. If an aggregate effect for treatment versus no-treatment is significantly greater than zero, then it can be concluded that the treatment is more effective than no treatment. However, meta-analysis can also be used to determine whether there are moderators of the effects obtained from the various studies. For example,

TABLE 6.1 Effect Sizes With Various Interpretations

Cohen's Designation and d	Proportion of Untreated Controls Below Mean of Treated Persons	Proportion of Variability in Outcomes Due to Treatment	Success Rate of Untreated Persons	Success Rate of Treated Persons
Small				
0.0	.500	.000	.500	.500
0.1	.540	.002	.475	.525
0.2	.579	.010	.450	.550
Medium				
0.3	.618	.022	.426	.574
0.4	.655	.038	.402	.598
0.5	.691	.059	.379	.621
0.6	.726	.083	.356	.644
0.7	.758	.109	.335	.665
Large				
0.8	.788	.138	.314	.686
0.9	.816	.168	.295	.705
1.0	.841	.200	.276	.724

Source: From *The Great Psychotherapy Debate: Models, Methods, and Findings* (p. 53, Table 2.4), by B. E. Wampold, 2001, Mahwah, NJ: Erlbaum. Copyright 2001 by Lawrence Erlbaum Associates. Adapted with permission.

it may well be that the effects are larger in studies for which the researcher has an allegiance to a type of psychotherapy than for studies in which the researcher has no allegiance. Meta-analysis can be used to identify and test moderating variables. Another important statistical concept that is used to characterize the effects of treatment is clinical significance, a topic that will be addressed later in this chapter.

Broad Meta-Analyses of Therapy Efficacy

Early applications of meta-analysis to psychotherapy outcomes (Smith & Glass, 1977; Smith, Glass, & Miller, 1980) addressed the overall question of the extent of benefit associated with psychotherapy as evidenced in the literature as a whole, compared the outcomes of different treatments, and examined the impact of methodological features of studies on the reported effectiveness of treatments. Smith et al. (1980) found an aggregate effect size of .85 standard deviation units over 475 studies comparing treated and untreated groups. Using the second column in Table 6.1 this indicates that, at the end of treatment, the average treated person is better off than about 80% of the untreated sample. The third column suggests that the proportion of variability in outcome that is due to treatment is about 15% (with the remaining variance due to client variables such as degree of disturbance, error of measurement, and the like), with the percent of successful untreated patients being about 30% compared to 70% for those who are treated (columns 4 and 5).

A second wave of meta-analytic reviews included both critical replications using the same database as Smith et al. (1980) (Andrews & Harvey, 1981; Landman & Dawes, 1982) and independent analyses of other large samples of studies (Shapiro & Shapiro, 1982). These studies substantiated the consistent effect of treatment as opposed to no treatment controls. A large number of meta-analyses have been conducted in the intervening 30 years since Glass and his colleagues' early work. These have often focused on more narrow bodies of literature with more specific questions than the earliest meta-analyses. For example, multiple meta-analyses focused on the effects of treatments on depression (e.g., Robinson, Berman, & Neimeyer, 1990). In the previous handbook chapter Lambert and Ogles (2004) provided a series of tables summarizing outcome by disorders, listing more than 25 meta-analytic reviews on anxiety disorders alone.

One unusually broad review (Lipsey & Wilson, 1993) summarized the results of 302 meta-analyses (not studies!) of psychological, educational, and behavioral treatments. By examining a subset of these meta-analytic studies using the most stringent inclusion criteria they concluded that the average treatment effect for this limited sample (156 *meta-analyses*) was .47. One obvious difference between the Smith et al. (1980) conclusions and the Lipsey and Wilson (1993) findings is the relatively large difference in overall effect size (e.g., .85 versus .47). Nevertheless, Lipsey and Wilson (1993) suggested that "the evidence from meta-analysis indicates that the psychological, educational, and behavioral treatments studied by meta-analysts generally have positive effects" (p. 1198).

It is clear that the use of meta-analysis to summarize efficacy literature is critical for the field. That being said, meta-analyses are just as prone to poor methods and misinterpretation as other methods of research and there are three main threats to their validity that are frequently overlooked by researchers and clinicians. These include the *file drawer* problem (the tendency for studies with small or no effects to never be published); the *garbage in, garbage out* problem (mixing poor-quality and high-quality studies), and the *apples and oranges* problem (combining studies of very different phenomena). Statistical methods can be employed to make adjustments to effect size estimates, such as calculating Q or I^2 to understand how heterogeneous effect sizes are (Sharpe, 1997). Heterogeneity is partially determined by the quality of the studies included in a meta-analysis.

Several researchers have reexamined the question of the size of the effect of psychotherapy by taking into account such methodological issues, all of which tend to lower effect size estimates. For example, Cuijpers, Smit, Bohlmeijer, Hollon, and Anderson (2010) estimated that the average effect size of treatments for depression should be adjusted from .67 to .42 (across 51 studies) by examining the quality of the studies. The unadjusted effect size across 115 randomized control trials of depression in a review by Cuijpers, van Straten, Bohlmeijer, Hollon, and Andersson (2010) was .74; however, after controlling for methodological quality, the effect across more rigorous studies was .22.

Reanalyses of older reviews as well as newer meta-analytic reviews have tended to produce smaller effect sizes than the original estimates.

Nevertheless, the broad finding of therapy benefit across a range of treatments for a variety of disorders remains since even the smaller effects show treatments are working. Indeed, psychotherapy is more effective than many "evidence-based" medical practices, some of which are costly and produce significant side effects, including almost all interventions in cardiology (e.g., beta-blockers, angioplasty, statins), geriatric medicine (e.g., calcium and alendronate sodium for osteoporosis), and asthma (e.g., budesonide); influenza vaccine; and cataract surgery, among other treatments (Wampold, 2007). Considering the high burden of illness manifest in psychological disorders, and the fact that the psychotherapies studied last only weeks, the consequences of entering treatment versus having no formal treatment are dramatic. Even if the effect size between treated and untreated individuals is as small as $d = .40$, this would still lead to an estimate of the success rate in treated persons of 60% compared to that of 40% for untreated persons.

Meta-Analyses Focused on Particular Disorders

Estimates of treatment effects, based on studies of specific disorders with well-defined psychotherapies, provide a more refined baseline for average treatment effects. Common in contemporary research, the focus of investigation is on specific disorders and (as it turns out) findings for the efficacy of psychotherapy do change when we consider which kinds of patients are being treated. In the following, treatment effects are described in relation to various mood and anxiety disorders.

Mood Disorders

Numerous meta-analytic reviews suggest that patients undergoing many diverse kinds of psychotherapy for depression surpass no-treatment and wait-list control patients. For example, Dobson, in an early analysis (1989), reported that 98% of clients treated with Beck's cognitive therapy (CT) had a better outcome than the average patient not receiving any treatment. Positive but less dramatic results were reported by Robinson, Berman, and Neimeyer (1990) who found that behavioral, cognitive behavioral and, to a lesser extent, general verbal therapies, all had positive effects on outcome compared to controls, with an average effect across studies of .84. Gloaguen, Cottraux, Cucherat, and Blackburn (1998) found

the general size of the treatment effect for depression to be .82. These older reviews support the finding that a range of therapeutic interventions result in improvement in mood and other symptoms for patients with depression compared to waitlist controls.

In the past three decades, more than 40 *meta-analyses* have been conducted in this area (Cuijpers & Dekker, 2005). Results in treating depression have shown that most psychological treatments that have been studied produce substantial effects, in terms of symptom reduction in depression and increased well-being (Cuijpers, van Straten, Warmerdam, & Andersson, 2008). These meta-analyses also have shown that psychological treatments are effective in specific populations, including adults, older adults (Cuijpers, van Straten, & Smit, 2006), women with postpartum depression (Lumley, Austin, & Mitchell, 2004) and patients with both depression and general medical disorders, including multiple sclerosis (Mohr & Goodkin, 1999), stroke (Hackett, Anderson, & House, 2004), and cancer (Sheard & Maguire, 1999). In contrast to meta-analyses on major depression, there are a limited number of meta-analyses that examine the effects of psychotherapy on chronic depression and dysthymia. It is estimated that 20% of all depressed individuals (over their lifetime) and up to 47% of the patients treated in mental health care suffer from chronic depression (Cuijpers, van Straten, Schuurmans et al., 2010). Meta-analyses have shown that psychotherapy has a small but significant effect ($d = 0.23$) on chronic depression when compared to control groups (Cuijpers, van Straten, Schuurmans, et al, 2010). Another example of psychotherapy benefit within specific mood disorders is its value in treating bipolar disorder. There are few meta-analyses that examine psychological treatments. For several decades, lithium was overwhelmingly the most widespread treatment and has been shown to be more effective than placebo in preventing manic relapse (Geddes, Burgess, Hawton, Jamison, & Goodwin, 2004; Perlis, Welge, Vornik, Hirschfeld, & Keck, 2006). Adding psychotherapies to a mood stabilizer regimen has been shown to reduce rates of relapse over 1 to 2 years (Miklowitz & Scott, 2009). It appears that therapies that specifically target increases in medication adherence, teach self-monitoring and early intervention with emergent episodes, and enhance interpersonal functioning and family communication help to prevent relapse (Miklowitz & Scott, 2009). There is certainly a place for psychological treatments in managing what many consider a biologically based disorder.

There has been considerable interest in comparing the efficacy of psychotherapy to pharmacological treatments for depression (a topic also dealt with in Chapters 11 and 18, this volume). Overall, the effects of both types of treatment are comparable (e.g., Imel, McKay, Malterer, & Wampold, 2008; Robinson et al., 1990) at termination, although there is some evidence that medications may be superior to psychotherapy for dysthymia (Imel et al., 2008). More generally, medication can prevent depression symptom relapse as long as medication is not discontinued (Hollon et al., 2005; Nelson, Delucchi, & Schneider, 2008). The combination of psychotherapy and medication appears to be somewhat more effective than treatment with pharmacotherapy alone, according to some reviews (Friedman et al., 2004; Pampanolla, Bollini, Tibaldi, Kupelnick, & Munizza, 2004). Pharmacotherapy, especially selective serotonin reuptake inhibitors (SSRIs), for those with chronic depression, appears to be more effective than psychotherapy alone ($d = 0.45$; Cuijpers, van Straten, Schuumans et al., 2010; Cuijpers, van Straten, van Open, Andersson, 2008). But, importantly, combined treatment appears to be more effective than pharmacotherapy alone ($d = 0.23$), suggesting there is a place for psychological treatments with these difficult to treat individuals.

Similar to meta-analyses that focus on adults, studies that have focused on psychological treatments for depression in older adults have found moderate to large effects for psychological treatments with no differences between individual, group, or bibliotherapy formats, or between cognitive-behavior therapy and other types of psychological treatment (Cuijpers et al., 2006). The finding that psychotherapies produce comparable or superior effects to medication with moderate and mild cases of depression is significant and persistent over time (Dobson et al., 2008; Hollon, 2011; Hollon & Ponniah, 2010; Robinson et al., 1990). For example, an early meta-analysis examined the comparative benefits of cognitive-behavioral therapy (CBT) and medication in 17 direct comparisons (Gloaguen et al., 1998). This study found that cognitive-behavioral therapy (CBT) was more effective than antidepressant medication (comparative effect size .38). When examining eight of the studies that included a minimum of 1-year follow up data, CBT treatments exhibited an average relapse rate of 29.5%, while the antidepressant medication groups average relapse rate was 60%. This suggests that, especially in the long run, CBT is superior to antidepressant medications.

Similar results were reported in a newer meta-analytic review by de Maat, Dekker, Schoevers, and de Jonghe (2006) who found that pharmacotherapy and psychotherapy did not differentially affect remission of depression at termination (35% versus 38%, respectively), but that the relapse rate during follow-up was nearly double in pharmacotherapy (57%) compared to psychotherapy (27%). Obviously with disorders like depression that are subject to relapse, long-term consequences are highly important (see Chapter 18, this volume, for further discussion of this topic).

It is clear that psychotherapy has proven to be effective in the treatment of depression and that the number of effective psychotherapies is rising over time. APA's Division 12 Task force on empirically supported psychotherapies now lists 12 separate treatments for depression, six with strong evidence and six with lesser evidence. Patients suffering from mood disorders who enter a variety of treatments can expect considerable relief, with the number who will experience a full remission varying with the type of mood disorder, and its chronicity. The range of remission probably hovers somewhere between 35% and 70%.

Anxiety Disorders

Considerable research has been aimed at evaluating outcomes in patients with anxiety-based disorders ranging from disorders that might be expected to show high improvement rates (e.g., panic) to those where improvement is more difficult to attain (e.g., chronic posttraumatic stress disorder). The most dramatic and consistent findings over time have been reported with the behavioral and cognitive-behavioral treatment of panic disorder. In this domain well developed research programs aimed at examining Barlow's, Clark's, and related protocols have shown positive results with an average effect size of .64 compared to waitlist comparisons (Norton & Price, 2007). Early estimates suggested that 70% to 80% of individuals treated in clinical trials with CBT were panic-free at termination. When normal end-state functioning was used as the criterion, 50% to 70% of patients succeeded (Barlow,

Craske, Cerny, & Klosko, 1989). Lower rates are reported when agoraphobia symptoms are also present and when follow-up data are examined (Dow et al., 2007; Haby, Donnelly, Corry, & Vos, 2006; Norton & Price, 2007). In an unusually long follow-up study, Butler, Chapman, Forman, and Beck (2006) found only 18.5% of panic-free individuals at termination relapsed over a 5- to 7-year period. Importantly, Habey et al. (2006) found the relapse rate to be 50% higher with psychoactive medications when compared to psychotherapy. While CBT studies have dominated research investigations, other treatments have also been found to be effective. For example, Milrod et al. (2007) found that a 12-week, panic-focused psychodynamic psychotherapy delivered twice weekly over 12 weeks far superior to applied relaxation training, with 73% of individuals responding to the psychodynamic treatment.

Generalized Anxiety Disorder (GAD)

Patients treated with CBT have been shown to benefit from treatment. Meta-analyses suggest that, on average, about 50% of clients with GAD achieve high end-state functioning (Borkovec & Ruscio, 2001). Mitte (2005) compared CBT with pharmacotherapy, finding them equally effective. At the same time she suggested that across the 65 studies that were examined, the various CBT interventions were highly effective and superior to both wait-list and placebo conditions ($ES = .82$; success rate about 70%). Indeed the CBT treatments for GAD affected specific GAD symptoms, depression, and quality of life, but to different degrees, with the strongest effects on GAD specific symptoms.

One important area of dysfunction common to GAD is interpersonal dysfunction, which is not specifically addressed in most CBT protocols. Similar to its failure to address interpersonal problems, CBT for GAD has failed to include interventions that target emotional avoidance and discomfort (Newman, Castonguay, Borkovec, & Molnar, 2004). In a study by Borkovec and Costello (1993), the level of emotional processing was found to be significantly lower in CBT than in a reflective listening condition. This finding is consistent with some process research literature suggesting that CBT attempts to control or reduce patient's feelings (Blagys & Hilsenroth, 2000, p. 172). Interestingly, studies have also found that higher levels of emotional experiencing were associated with a positive

outcome in CBT (e.g., Castonguay, Goldfried, Wiser, & Raue, 1996). Taken together, these basic and applied findings suggest that adding techniques specifically designed to help GAD clients deeply experience and process uncomfortable emotions may help them to reduce their chronic worrying.

Posttraumatic Stress Disorder (PTSD)

PTSD is a common disorder that as many as 20+% of people may develop after being exposed to a life-threatening event, has been found to yield to psychological interventions. Psychological treatments from various theoretical perspectives have been found to be effective for PTSD in previous reviews (Bisson et al., 2007). Some of the earlier reviews had to rely on uncontrolled trials as well as controlled ones, and on uncontrolled effect sizes. There are now sufficient numbers of randomized controlled trials of psychological treatments of PTSD to allow meta-analysis of effect sizes in such trials. In recent years, findings suggest that specific therapies, such as CBT, exposure-based therapy and cognitive therapy are equally effective, and more effective than supportive techniques, including psychodynamic and supportive therapy (Mendes, Mello, Ventura, Passarela, & Mari, 2008). Hofmann and Smits (2008) found trauma-focused CBT treatments compared to placebo controls had an effect size of .62 (a 64% rate compared to 36% for *placebo* treatments).

Certainly one of the most important considerations in interpreting studies of individuals with PTSD is that there is a spectrum of disturbance ranging from individuals with more mild symptoms and more recent onset to individuals who are more highly disturbed, have had multiple and constant threats, as well as decades of symptomatic problems. Although patient factors such as severity may affect the rate of change for individuals who respond to treatment, there is little doubt that receiving treatment is superior to being on a wait list. The majority of patients treated with psychotherapy for PTSD in randomized trials improve. These exposure-based approaches are some of the most effective psychosocial treatments devised, and yet, in the community, polysymptomatic presentations in many cases lessen the portion of positive response, which can be very low. The majority of patients with complex PTSD continue to have substantial residual symptoms if the conditions are chronic at the onset of treatment. Cloitre et al. (2009) notes that clinicians can be confident that

PTSD symptoms will improve through trauma-focused-CBT (TF-CBT) and eye-movement desensitization and reprocessing (EMDR) as well as other trauma-based therapies, but that much more effort needs to be expended on helping the most disturbed individuals. Seidler and Wagner (2006) argue that the case has been made for both TF-CBT and EMDR and that research should now focus on identifying which clients respond best to these treatments and on finding ways to reduce drop-out rates from an average of 30%.

Although many researchers and practitioners accept the notion that *trauma-focused treatments* are superior to nontrauma-focused treatments for posttraumatic stress disorder (PTSD), Benish, Imel, and Wampold (2008a) recently published a meta-analysis of clinical trials directly comparing "bona fide" nonexposure-based PTSD treatments with exposure-based treatments that found that exposure-based treatments are not uniquely effective. They concluded that the results of previous meta-analysis favoring exposure-based treatments compared to alternative treatments may have been influenced by several confounds, including the use of alternative treatments that were not actually bona fide interventions, thus overstating the relative efficacy of specific PTSD treatments. Ehlers et al. (2010) claim that the selection procedures of the Benish et al.'s meta-analysis were biased and cite results from individual studies and previous meta-analyses that suggest trauma-focused psychological treatments are superior to nontrauma-focused treatments. Benish, Imel, and Wampold (2008b) in response to these criticisms offer a review and justification of the coding criteria and procedure used in their original meta-analysis (Benish et al., 2008a). In addition, they discuss the appropriateness of utilizing treatments designed to control for nonspecifics or common factors such as "supportive therapy" for determining the relative efficacy of specific PTSD treatments. Finally, they note several additional confounds, such as therapist effects, allegiance, and alteration of alternate treatment protocols to lessen their effects in PTSD research. They describe conceptual problems involved in the classification scheme used to determine "trauma focus" of interventions, which lead to inappropriate conclusions about what works best in the treatment of PTSD. This interesting debate does not question the efficacy of "exposure-based" treatments, but the necessity and superiority of incorporating some specific exposure methods. The jury may still be out on the superiority of exposure-based treatments when compared to other bona fide psychotherapies.

Obsessive Compulsive Disorder (OCD)

It is becoming clearer that patients respond to exposure and response prevention for treating OCD. Not surprisingly it appears that an active ingredient includes exposure to situations that provoke obsessions and compulsive acts, while inhibiting the expression of the compulsive act. Early reviews (Abramowitz, 1997; Abramowitz, Franklin, & Foa, 2002; Eddy Dutra, Bradley, & Westen, 2004) are consistent with more recent findings (Rosa-Alcázar, Sánchez-Meca, Gómez-Conesa, & Marín-Martínez, 2008; see also Chapter 10, this volume). The effect sizes in the Rosa-Alczar review suggest a rather strong impact of treatment across 19 controlled trials with 24 comparison groups. The treated versus controlled effect size for exposure treatments was a large *d* equal to 1.13. Similarly, the *d* for cognitive restructuring was 1.09, while combined treatments attained a *d* of 99.80. These figures suggest that about 73% of treated cases achieve a positive outcome in contrast to 27% of untreated cases.

A caveat in considering this analysis is that the cognitive restructuring intervention was only examined in three studies. There was considerable heterogenaiety of effect sizes in this review but few variables could be found to account for this variability. The interventions, although quite specific, not only effected OCD symptoms, but also general anxiety, social adjustment, and depression, albeit less than OCD specific problems. Despite the generally positive effects of treatment across patient problem areas, a sizable minority of patients do not respond, and dropout rates can be among the highest in psychotherapy. Of even greater interest and importance is that there is evidence that the majority of individuals who enter treatment with a *psychiatrist* never undergo exposure and response prevention for OCD (about 7%), with the majority of patients receiving only an SSRI (Blanco et al., 2006). Less is known about the practices of other mental health professionals, and one can only hope that the frequency of using exposure and response prevention is greater, especially among psychologists.

Social Anxiety Disorder

A variety of treatments are used to help patients diagnosed with social anxiety disorder. This is a disorder where group psychotherapy comes into prominence (as discussed in Chapter 16, this volume). In Hofmann and Smits (2008) meta-analysis of CBT treatments compared to placebo they found a range of effects sizes (.51 to .94) across studies. Similarly, Acarturk, Cuijpers, van Straten, and de Graff (2009) examined outcomes across 29 RCTs with various control conditions. They found treatments for social anxiety to be moderately to highly effective with an average effect size of .70 (67% of treated individuals compared to 33% of control group patients would have a positive outcome). This general outcome was found on both specific outcome measures and more general measures including depressive symptoms. Effect sizes were smaller when the active treatments (almost all variations of exposure, CBT, social skills training, relaxation, and varied combinations) were contrasted with placebo controls or TAU ($d = .36$; 58% versus 42% positive outcomes). Effect sizes were much smaller when the patients in the study met strict criteria for the disorder than when they were subclinical and when ITT comparisons were contrasted instead of completer samples ($d = .45$ versus .80).

Summary of the General Effects of Psychotherapy

The pervasive theme derived from meta-analyses of the large body of psychotherapy research, whether it concerns broad summaries of the field or outcomes of specific disorders and specific treatments must remain the same as in past reviews—psychotherapy has proven to be highly beneficial. Psychotherapies clearly show effectiveness compared to wait-list and no-treatment control comparison groups (e.g., Gava et al., 2007; Hofmann & Smits, 2008). Mood-disordered patients respond well to the wide variety of psychotherapies that have been studied. Psychological therapies, in general, have been found to be highly effective for anxiety-based problems. The family of cognitive and behavior therapies have been studied most often and extensively (see Chapters 10, 11, and 16, this volume) and found to be highly effective in reducing anxiety and related symptoms (e.g., OCD, PTSD; see, Hunot, Churchill, Silva de Lima, & Teixeira, 2007) but there is evidence for other treatments as well (also see Chapters 12 and 13, this volume). There is growing evidence that medications used to treat depression (antidepressants) can be helpful for people who suffer from anxiety disorders as well, but seldom

more effective than psychotherapy, especially in the long run (e.g., see Chapter 18, this volume). The consistent finding of positive psychotherapy effects—across decades, thousands of studies and hundreds of meta-analyses, examining diverse disorders and therapies—is seemingly undebatable at this point in time. The size of treatment effects hovers around an effect size of .60 (.40 to .80), meaning that about 65% of treated patients will have a positive outcome compared to 35% of patients who are on a wait list for the same time period. As a result, researchers have turned to other important questions that take us beyond the issue of whether an average positive change occurs in treated cases compared to the untreated.

Do Patients Make Changes That Are Clinically Meaningful?

The scientific study of psychotherapy efficacy has focused primarily on testing whether a group of patients who received treatment had a better outcome than a group of persons who did not receive treatment. The effect size statistics that are derived from the typical efficacy study *estimate* change in standardized units, as we have discussed. Discussing change in this way obscures whether the change actually made by each patient is clinically important. During the past 3 decades, many researchers have supplemented statistical comparisons between groups and the use of the effect size statistics with additional analyses that investigate the clinical significance of changes that occur as a result of psychotherapy. The most popular statistical method for estimating meaningful change possess two criteria that each patient must meet before their change is considered meaningful: (1) treated clients make statistically *reliable* improvements as a result of treatment (Jacobson & Truax, 1991), and (2) treated clients are statistically indistinguishable from "normal" or nondeviant peers following treatment (Kendall, Marrs-Garcia, Nath, & Sheldrick, 1999).

As one might expect applying these criteria to individual patient changes provides a lower estimate of the portion of patients helped by psychotherapy while increasing the standard for making such judgments (Ogles, Lunnen, & Bonesteel, 2001). A general review of methods has been reported by Lambert and Bailey (2012). Bauer, Lambert, and Nielsen (2004) compared five statistical methods with a sample of 386 outpatients treated with a variety of psychotherapies and found that improvement estimates ranged between 30% and 46% with Jacobson and Truax's Reliable Change Index (RCI) method providing a moderate estimate of 35% improving. A recent review (Eisen, Ranganathan, Seal, & Spiro, 2007) of community-based inpatient and outpatient mental health treatment centers compared the reliable change index (RCI), proposed by Jacobson and Truax (1991) the effect size statistic (ES), and standard error of measurement (SEM). The RCI, ES, and SEM analyses all showed patterns of improvement across indices but they each classified a different proportion of individuals as reliably improved, with the RCI being the most conservative estimate followed by ES and SEM, respectively. For example, only 38% of inpatient admission-discharge periods of care showed reliable improvement based on the RCI, whereas 67% and 73% did when ES or SEM were used, respectively.

Further evidence that the effect size statistic *d* overestimates (relative to other methods) the proportion of patients with positive outcomes can be found in a meta-analysis by Shimokawa, Lambert, and Smart (2010) comparing feedback and clinician decision tools with treatment-as-usual, the treatment effect was a *d* of .70 in the completer sample (*n* = 217 and 318, respectively). The binomial effect size display (in Table 6.1) estimates the percent of positive outcome in the treatment group to be 66% while in the treatment-as-usual it is 34%. The Jacobson and Truax method estimates that 52% of the feedback participants and 22% of the treatment-as-usual participants had a positive outcome (improved or recovered), with the remaining patients either deteriorating or failing to respond.

The proportion of individuals considered improved also is a function of specific outcome measures. Ogles, Lambert, and Sawyer (1995) examined the clinical significance of the Treatment of Depression Collaborative Research Program (TDCRP) data (Elkin, 1994). This multisite study compared two types of psychotherapy, medication, and a medication placebo with unipolar depressed patients. When combining estimates across three treatments (interpersonal psychotherapy—IPT, cognitive-behavior therapy—CBT, and imipramine plus clinical management) and three measures, they found that 69 (55%) of the 125 clients who participated in a minimum of 12 sessions and 15 weeks of treatment met the Jacobson and Truax (1991) criteria for clinically meaningful change based on all three depression measures. The percent of patients who

were regarded as recovered depended on the measure that was used as well as the kind of treatment that was offered. The lowest recovery estimate came from outcome in the placebo treatment measured with the Beck Depression Inventory (46% clinically significant change). The highest estimate came from the Hopkins Symptom Checklist with patients treated with IPT (85%). When speaking of the impacts of treatment on the functioning of patients treated with arguably our best documented treatments it appears that more than half (50% to 85%) recovered while the placebo group that included an inert substance, and regular contact and support from a psychiatrist had a recovery rate of 46% to 62% depending on which measure was used.

Cost Offset

A related body of research that suggests treatment effects produce clinically significant change and broad effects across a person's life is that on medical cost offset. Medical cost offset studies suggest that many patients who enter psychotherapy have concurrent medical and psychological needs. Mumford, Schlesinger, Glass, Patrick, and Cuerdon (1984) were the first to conduct a meta-analysis regarding the cost offset effect. They concluded that those who participated in psychological interventions were less likely to use inpatient medical services. In a selective review of methodologically rigorous studies (Gabbard, Lazar, Hornberger, & Spiegel, 1997), a second meta-analysis found that significant cost savings, as a result of reductions in inpatient treatment, were associated with services for individuals with chronic mental illness.

Chiles, Lambert, and Hatch (1999) conducted meta-analysis to examine the cost offset literature. They examined 91 studies conducted in a variety of treatment settings in which different therapeutic interventions with diverse patient groups were implemented in an effort to reduce medical utilization. The primary finding suggests that on average treated clients had a 15.7% reduction in utilization of medical services as opposed to a 12.27% increase in use of medical services by individuals assigned to control conditions, for a combined 25.08% difference in medical utilization between treatment and control groups. For studies that used hospital days as the dependent variable, an average reduction of 2.52 hospital days per person was associated with participation in psychological treatment. The savings were greatest among those patients who over utilized services and for behavior medicine interventions, but can also be found across treatment types and particular medical and psychological conditions.

For example, family therapy has been shown to be a cost-effective treatment and one that appears to reduce the number of health care visits and physical health care costs among those who participate in it (Crane, 2008; Crane & Christenson, 2008). Results of this study found a 21% reduction in health care use for individuals who participated in marital/couple or family therapy. Their examination of high utilizers of medical services (four or more doctor visits in a 6-month period) found that high utilizers of health care significantly decreased their use of health care after receiving psychosocial treatment. Reductions were found to go as high as 50% for individuals receiving marital/couples or family therapy with reductions highest in acute care utilizations (78%).

Evidence of a medical cost offset has been found for specific diseases and illnesses where one might expect an effect such as panic disorder, cancer, and depression. For example, Davidson, Gidron, Mostofsky, and Trudeau (2007) conducted a randomized controlled trial examining the hospitalization cost offset of a hostility intervention for coronary heart disease patients. At 6-month follow-up, therapy patients in this study were found to have significantly shorter hospital stays and average hospitalization costs in the treatment group were also found to be significantly lower than those in the control group. More specifically, for every $1 spent in therapy, an approximate savings of $2 in hospitalization costs was found. Examining somatoform disorders, Hiller, Fichter, and Rief (2003) examined the effects of providing cognitive-behavioral therapy and then examined medical cost calculations obtained from insurance companies for 2-year periods before treatment and after treatment and compared them to the medical cost calculations of a regular clinical group without somatoform disorders. Results of the study found significant treatment-related cost offsets of –24.5% for outpatients and –36.7% for inpatients in the treatment group compared to the regular clinical nonsomatoform disorder group. Furthermore, indirect costs from lost workdays were found to decrease by –35.3% in the treatment group, showing the same consequences that research aimed at altering work productivity have documented (e.g., Trotter et al., 2009).

These findings document the life-functioning outcomes that can result from psychological interventions and it is important for practitioners and the public at large (not to mention insurers and employers) to realize the far-reaching effects of psychological interventions. The authors of these reviews plead for more research to be done on this topic and for insurance companies and other third-party payers to pay heed to the results in the hopes that a change in the health care system can occur. In an edited book Lazar (2010) took an extensive look at both medical cost offset, reaffirming the large savings that can be made particularly in patients with physical disorders. For a more complete discussion of this topic the interested reader is referred to Smith and Williams, Chapter 17 (this volume).

Summary

Not only are psychological interventions statistically superior to control conditions, but the size of this effect is larger than the effects of many medical treatments across a variety of conditions. Although the effect size statistic overestimates the proportion of individuals who experience clinically meaningful changes, there is substantial evidence that the psychotherapies also produce outcomes that are clinically meaningful. Both primary studies and meta-analytic reviews find that many clients improve to levels that might be considered a full recovery.

In addition, the medical cost offset literature provides evidence that individuals who have emotional difficulties also benefit medically (physical health) when they participate in psychological interventions, especially if they are high utilizers of medical services. In this age of accountability, the ability of behavioral health professionals to demonstrate that their interventions are not just reliable but have practical consequences that are economical is an important discovery. The fact that psychological interventions have real-life impacts and economic consequences as well helps to verify that psychosocial interventions are meaningful to clients, therapists, and society. The study of clinical significance and meaningful change will remain a promising field for investigation in the years to come.

Does Therapy Exceed Placebo?

In medical research, the effects of an active pharmacological agent are contrasted with the effects of a pharmacologically inert or nontherapeutic substance—a "placebo." This contrast makes good sense with respect to drug therapies and many other medical interventions, for their success to be attributed to the pharmacological agent rather than to the psychological effects of being "treated" or taking "medicines." Placebo controls appear to make less sense, however, when extended to psychotherapy research where the benefits of treatments and placebos both depend on psychological mechanisms. Many authors entirely reject the placebo concept in psychotherapy research because it is not conceptually consistent with testing the efficacy of *psychological* mechanisms of change (e.g., Wilkins, 1984).

Placebos have also been labeled as *nonspecific* factors (e.g., Oei & Shuttlewood, 1996). This conceptualization, however, raises serious questions about the definition of *nonspecific*. For example, once a nonspecific factor is labeled and operationally defined, does it then become a specific factor and fall outside the domain of a placebo effect? Similarly, if an influence like *therapist accurate empathy* is considered to be a placebo because it is not a theory-specific technique, how can it also be a substantial factor in client change as theorized by person-centered therapists?

Although psychotherapy is statistically and clinically beneficial when compared to various no-treatment control conditions and therefore surpasses improvement based on "spontaneous remission," one might conclude that the benefits of therapy are not caused by the specific treatments, but rather by a generalized placebo effect (i.e., that psychotherapists are merely "placebologists"; see Prioleau, Murdock, & Brody, 1983). Psychotherapy researchers have pursued the relative benefit of therapy when compared to placebo controls that focus on leading people to believe they are getting a bona fide intervention when they are not. More currently such comparisons have come from studies comparing psychoactive medications with an inert substance and with psychotherapy. But contemporary psychotherapy outcome studies seldom use the placebo term, preferring instead to control for all factors that are common to all treatments not just expectancy effects. Others have suggested the term *common factors* in recognition that many therapies have ingredients that are not unique to a specific treatment but healing nonetheless. Thus, research on placebo effects would be better conceptualized as research on common factors versus the specific effects of a particular technique. Common factors are those dimensions of the treatment setting

(e.g., therapist belief in treatment, a confidential, legally protected activity; client expectations of a positive outcome) that are not specific to any particular theoretically based approach. Research on the broader concept of common factors will be discussed later in this chapter, but here it is important to note that those factors common to most therapies (such as expectation for improvement, installation of hope, persuasion, warmth and attention, understanding, encouragement, and the like) should not be viewed as theoretically inert or as trivial. Indeed, these factors are central to psychological interventions in both theory and practice. They play an active role in patient improvement, and can be specified and taught (see Chapter 19, this volume).

A number of historical articles address the issue of treatments' superiority to "placebo" (e.g., Barker, Funk, & Houston, 1988; Dush, 1986; Prioleau et al., 1983; Sheperd, 1984; Smith et al., 1980), with the Smith meta-analysis of 32 trials indicating an effect size of only .15 between placebo and psychotherapy. Lipsey and Wilson (1993) addressed the placebo issue as part of their extensive review of meta-analyses. A subset ($n = 30$) of the meta-analyses reviewed by Lipsey and Wilson (1993) included comparisons of treatment with no-treatment control groups and placebo control groups. They report an effect size of .67 between psychotherapy and wait list, and .44 between psychotherapy and placebo. They concluded that "there are quite likely some generalized placebo effects that contribute to the overall effects of psychological treatment, but their magnitude does not seem sufficient to fully account for those overall effects" (pp. 1196–1197). These findings are also supported by many of the meta-analytic reviews conducted since their review of meta-analyses.

Grissom (1996) examined the relationship of therapy to no treatment control, therapy to placebo, placebo to no treatment control, and therapy to therapy across 46 meta-analytic reviews. Using the "probability of superior estimate" (PS) to "estimate the probability that a randomly sampled client from a population given treatment 1 will have an outcome ... that is superior to that ... of a randomly sampled client from a population given treatment 2" (Grissom, 1996, p. 973) he found the effect size to be .75 for psychotherapy versus no treatment, .44 for placebo versus no treatment, .58 for therapy versus placebo, and .23 for differences between therapies.

In a more narrow review, Hofmann and Smits (2008) conducted a meta-analysis contrasting outcomes for anxiety disordered patients who received either CBT or a placebo. Twenty-seven studies were identified with a portion including intention to treat (ITT) analysis as well as completer samples. Their analysis of completer samples provided a pooled effect size of .73 on anxiety measures and this effect was obtained whether the placebo control was a medication or a psychological placebo. The ITT analysis found smaller but still significant differences. There is no comparable recent analysis of other types of psychotherapy, so the rather large size of this effect may be limited to CBT treatments of anxiety-based problems.

Among the controversies about placebo controls is the question of what composes the control group. Baskin, Tierney, Minami, and Wampold (2003) note that the placebo term connotes deception and charade and that in psychotherapy research it is more common to label these controls as supportive therapy, nondirective therapy, common factor control, and the like. Thus they prefer the term *common factor control* for placebo and suggest that these placebo controls rarely include all the components (common factors) they could and thereby overestimate the difference between active treatments and these controls. In their study they coded "structural" components of these controls (number and duration of sessions, training of therapists, format, and restriction of topics pursued in therapy). They found that when the placebo (common factor) controls were structurally equivalent the outcomes for them and the comparison group were very similar ($d = .15$) while structurally nonequivalent control versus the active treatment favored the active treatment ($d = .46$).

In a meta-analysis of placebo effects in medicine, Hróbjartsson and Gøtzsche (2004) estimated that the effects in medical conditions were small. A reanalysis of a subset of these studies was published by Wampold, Minami, Tierney, Baskin, and Bhati (2005) who suggested that the effects are large. These contrasting positions were followed by a number of commentaries including those of the original authors (Hróbjartsson & Gøtzsche, 2007a, 2007b) and Wampold, Imel, and Minami (2007) as well as Hunsley and Westmacott (2007). Hunsley and Westmacott (2007) point out in their commentary that both meta-analytic reviews reported nearly identical effect sizes for the placebo active treatment

comparisons, but provided different interpretations of these findings. The large discrepancies in their conclusions were due to ambiguity of interpreting numbers and words. They suggest alternative methods for representing and interpreting the magnitude of effect size estimates. They also suggest that the effect size, .29, for placebos in medicine and psychotherapy based on continuous measures is small but cannot be dismissed as unimportant.

Although estimates of the effects of psychotherapy compared to placebo controls are variable, it is also clear that psychotherapy surpasses placebo effects sometimes by large margins. Psychotherapy effects go beyond the installation of hope.

Do Patients Maintain Their Gains?

Although early outcome research focused primarily on the immediate posttreatment status of patients who participated in therapy, hundreds of studies have now considered the maintenance of treatment gains. Similarly, many meta-analytic reviews consider outcome immediately following treatment and at follow-up. There is no reason to believe that a single course of psychotherapy (especially as practiced in the United States where average doses hover around 4 to 5 sessions in routine care; or 4 to 20 sessions in an RCT; Hansen, Lambert, & Forman, 2002), should inoculate a person forever from relapse and the development of new symptoms. Yet, many patients who undergo therapy achieve healthy adjustment for long periods of time. This is true even though some have had a long history of recurrent problems. At the same time, there is clear evidence that a portion of patients who are improved at termination do relapse and continue to seek help from a variety of mental health providers, including their former therapists. Several problems such as alcohol and drug dependence, smoking, obesity, and possibly depression are so likely to recur that they are not considered properly studied without data collection at least one year after treatment. Yet even among alcoholic patients 30% stay dry during follow-ups of this length, and an additional 30% or more show a reduced level of drinking at follow-up (Carroll et al., 1994).

In an older review, Bakker, van Balkom, Spinhoven, Blaauw, and van Dyck (1998) examined the follow-up status of patients engaged in treatments for panic with and without agoraphobia. Follow-up periods ranged from 4 weeks to

8 years (average 62 weeks). The pretreatment to follow-up effect size was 1.28 for panic and 1.41 for agoraphobia, indicating a remarkable endurance for treatment benefits, including a continuing gain between the end of treatment and follow-up for agoraphobic symptoms. In a more recent meta-analysis of similar literature, Emmelkamp and Powers (2010) examined follow-up reports from 4 to 9 years after relatively brief treatments concluding that the results of exposure therapy with agoraphobia (with its life-impairing consequences) are long-lasting for many individuals. Generally, improvements brought about by the treatment were, on average, maintained. Other meta-analyses also find that treatment benefits are maintained for a range of disorders over a variety of mostly short (within 1 year) follow-up periods (Carlson & Hoyle, 1993; Fettes & Peters, 1992; Gould, Otto, & Pollack, 1995; Marrs, 1995; Murtagh & Greenwood, 1995; Sherman, 1998; Taylor, 1996).

On the other hand estimates suggest that approximately 83% of individuals who experience a depressive episode *and who drop out of treatment early* will experience a relapse within 2 years (Jarrett et al., 2001) a rate much higher than that found in patients who complete treatment. Prevalence of relapse for individuals who completed treatment for major depression can be equally concerning with some of the higher-end estimates averaging around 42% (Koppers, Peen, Niekerken, Van, & Dekker, 2011) to 49% (Jarrett et al., 2001) after 5 years. Risk of relapse increases with each successive relapse (Solomon et al., 2000; ten Doesschate, Bockting, Koeter, & Schene, 2010). Using data from a 10-year prospective multicenter study, Solomon and colleagues (2000) estimated risk of relapse increases 16% with each subsequent depressive episode. On the other hand, risk of relapse progressively decreases as recovery length increases, such that the probability of relapse diminishes from 20% within the first 6 months following a depressive episode to 9% after 3 years of maintaining gains (Solomon et al., 2000).

Maintenance of gains seems unrelated to specific type of treatment, or even treatment length. Marchand, Roberge, Primiano, and Germain (2009) followed patients treated for panic with agoraphobia who received one of three separate versions of CBT at 1 and 2 years following treatment. Regardless of treatment condition (14-session individual psychotherapy, 14-session group treatment, or 7-session individual

treatment) patients recovered at the same rate and maintained their gains equally well. With anxiety disorders a high proportion of patients maintain gains 6 months to 2 years following treatment. For example, Foa et al. (1999) examined the long-term benefit for 64 patients who completed treatment for PTSD. All three active treatments were superior to the wait list at the end of the treatment period, and improvements in all three treated groups were maintained at 12-month follow-up. Feske and Chambless (1995) conducted an analysis of 21 studies of cognitive-behavioral and exposure-only treatment for social phobia. They found that both treatments produced significant pre- to post-treatment gains that were maintained at follow-up 1 to 12 months later.

The CBT package of Dugas and colleagues for treatment of generalized anxiety disorder was found to be more effective than a waiting list control condition (Dugas et al., 2003; Dugas et al., 2010; Ladouceur et al., 2000) and "nondirective therapy" (Gosselin, Ladouceur, Morin, Dugas, & Baillargeon, 2006). Interestingly, in the studies by Dugas and colleagues (2003, 2010) level of worry further decreased from post treatment to 2-year follow-up, showing that gains were not only maintained but further gains accrued.

A number of follow-up studies reveal that the effects of exposure in vivo and response prevention are maintained after 2 years (Whittal, Robichaud, Thordarson, & McLean, 2008), 4 years (van Oppen, van Balkom, De Haan, & van Dyck, 2005), and 7 years (Rufer et al., 2005). Resick, Williams, Suvak, Monson, and Gradus (2012) have now reported 5- to 10-year follow-up results of their cognitive-processing therapy and prolonged exposure treatments of PTSD in female rape victims. They were able to follow three fourths of the original sample. Gains were maintained in both treatment conditions, neither proved superior to the other. About 18% to 22% of these individuals still met criteria for PTSD.

In contrast to the proceeding findings, Durham et al., (2005) examined the long-term (2 to 14 years following treatment) outcome of participants in clinical trials of cognitive-behavior therapy for anxiety disorders (GAD, panic, and PTSD). They attempted to contact and interview participants in eight studies conducted in Scotland. They found that 50% of individuals met criteria for at least one diagnosis at follow-up, with comorbidity and health status scores similar to the lowest 10% of the general population. Only 36% of patients had not sought additional treatment in the interim for anxiety with 19% receiving almost constant treatment. Although CBT patients had, on average, surpassed control conditions at termination, the positive effects had eroded over time with the most positive outcomes associated with less complex and less severe cases at intake, completion of initial treatment (regardless of the kind), and amount of treatment during the follow-up period.

In some cases gains are maintained where we might least expect them. For example, Bateman and Fonagy (2008) reported a 5-year follow-up of patients treated for borderline personality disorder following 18 months of partial hospitalization who received either mentalization-based treatment or treatment-as-usual (mainly medication and support). Following another 18 months, where less intensive treatment was provided, the active treatment period ended and the follow-up period began. After the subsequent 5-year follow-up only 13% of mentalization patients still met criteria for BPD, while 87% of TAU patients did so. Suicidality continued to be a problem for 74% of TAU patients, but only 23% of mentalization patients had high suicide ratings. The use of polypharmacy had been reduced in the mentalization group but not TAU (.02 versus 1.9 years of taking three or more medications).

Overall this study demonstrated rather remarkable treatment effects that became even more apparent and dramatic 5 years following termination. Similar results for psychodynamic psychotherapy were reported by Najavits and Gunderson (1995) who examined the 3-year outcome of clients treated for borderline personality disorder. Although the study was uncontrolled, the evidence suggested that even clients with serious and chronic disorders maintained improvement over the course of three years following treatment.

Certainly many patients and clinicians have reason to be optimistic about the likelihood that their work together will have a lasting impact, and even more so if specific attempts are made to make psychotherapy effects more durable and to target those at risk for relapse.

Strategies to Maximize Maintenance

A growing number of studies have looked at individual difference variables that may influence which patients are more likely to maintain treatment gains or relapse. This is especially the case with affective disorders because of their high prevalence rates compared to other disorders and high comorbidity with other disorders (Burcusa & Iacono, 2007; Kessler et al., 1994). Using survival analytic techniques, Ilardi, Craighead, and Evans (1997) examined the influence of Axis II psychopathology on the relapse rates of patients who were hospitalized with affective disorders. They report that "patients without a personality disorder have an expected survival (i.e., remission) period approximately 7.4 times longer than that of patients who met *DSM-III-R* criteria for at least one Axis II disorder" (Ilardi et al., 1997, p. 388). The greatest risk occurred in the first 6 months following discharge from the hospital. Patients with personality disorders had much higher rates of relapse (77%) when compared to patients with no comorbid diagnosis (14%). Obviously such findings call for more extensive efforts by treatment providers and patients to address personality issues more completely after patients leave the hospital.

Other clinical factors, spanning across patient, therapist, and therapeutic variables, have been a predominant focus of much of the relapse risk research and it should be noted that many of these factors that influence relapse rates in MDD, also seem to contribute to relapse rates in other mood, anxiety, and substance use disorders (Bodkin et al., 2011; Bradizza, Stasiewicz, & Paas, 2006; Degenhardt, Gatz, Jacob, & Tohen, 2012; Nakajima & al'Absi, 2012; Thuile, Christian, & Rouillon, 2009). Among these clinical factors that seem to influence risk of relapse are number of depressive episodes (Solomon et al., 2000; Burcusa & Iacono 2007; Richards, 2011), severity of initial depressive episode (Barkow et al., 2003; Burcusa & Iacono 2007; Rucci et al., 2011; Solomon et al., 2004; Solomon et al., 2008), response to acute treatment (Dew et al., 2001), residual symptoms following treatment (Jarrett, Vittengl, & Clark, 2008; Richards, 2011; Taylor, Walters, Vittengl, Krebaum, & Jarrett, 2010; Yang et al., 2010), psychopathological and medical comorbidities (Barkow et al., 2003; Bercusa & Iacono, 2007; Conradi, de Jonge, & Ormel, 2008; Dombrovski et al., 2008; Taylor et al., 2010), family history of depression and other psychopathology (Bercusa & Iacono, 2007; Conradi et al., 2008; Taylor et al., 2010), treatment type and duration (Hollon et al., 2005; de Maat et al., 2006; Nelson et al., 2008), treatment adherence (Gopinath, Katon, Russo, & Ludman, 2007), and the therapeutic alliance (Weck et al., 2012). Clinicians can keep such information in mind as they consider the need to engage particular patients in some kind of continuation therapy or related techniques for enhancing maintenance of treatment gains, such as preparing patients for relapse. There are many alternatives within specific theoretical systems. One of the more recent to emerge is mindfulness-based cognitive therapy (MBCT).

MBCT was developed specifically to "reduce relapse and recurrence in depression" (Beshai, Dobson, Bockting, & Quigley, 2011; Godfrin & van Heeringen, 2010). Utilizing mindfulness training to empower patients with the ability to be internally calm regardless of one's emotional state, MBCT has demonstrated the ability to perform as well or better than psychoactive medications in preventing depression recurrence. When patients in remission discontinued (Segal et al., 2010) or tapered from (Kuyken, 2008) their antidepressants and attended group sessions of MBCT, they experienced the same low recurrence rates as did those who stayed on their maintenance medication. Segal et al. (2010) concluded "for depressed patients achieving stable or unstable clinical remission, MBCT offers protection against relapse/recurrence on a par with that of maintenance antidepressant pharmacotherapy." In a similar vein, Bondolfi et al. (2010) observed depressed patients who incorporated MBCT into their treatment plans as compared to those with "treatment as usual" (TAU); over a period of 14 months, the two groups experienced similar relapse rates but the time preceding the relapse varied substantially. Individuals not engaged in MBCT relapsed in a median 69 days, while those with MBCT added to TAU averaged 204 days before relapse. This is consistent with research by Godfrin and van Heeringen (2010), who found not only increased times before a first relapse, but also reduced rates of relapse. MBCT plus TAU groups also indicated reductions in "short and longer-term depressive mood and better mood states and quality of life" (p. 475).

As previously discussed, relapse rates for psychotherapy (27%) are almost half when compared to pharmacotherapy (57%) in depression (de Maat et al., 2006), unless pharmacotherapy is continued (see Hollon & Beck, this volume; Hollon et al., 2005; Nelson et al., 2008). Despite continued debate surrounding which psychotherapy provides superior maintenance of therapeutic gains, a cursory examination of risk ratios from 24 studies provided by Beshai, Dobson, Bockting, and Quigley (2011) representing probability of relapse between cognitive therapy (CT; range of risk ratios = .25–1.32), mindfulness-based cognitive therapy (MBCT; range of risk ratios = .29–1.80), and interpersonal therapy (IPT; range of risk ratios = 0.51–1.23) suggest menial differences between therapy type with a possible small advantages for MBCT.

The use of Internet chat groups and related procedures as an alternative for in-person maintenance therapy shows some promise. For example, Bauer, Wolf, Haug, and Kordy (2011) using Kaplan Meier survival analysis, showed 1 year following discharge from inpatient treatment, patients who participated in an online chat group exhibited significantly smaller relapse rates (22.2%) in comparison to patients who did not participate (46.5%).

Despite these overall impressively positive findings, several methodological problems hinder conclusions about how well patients do maintaining treatment gains over the long term. First, attrition between the end of treatment and collection of follow up data is a significant problem. For example, in the Bakker et al., (1998) meta-analysis, only 15% of patients (202 of 1,346) in the medication conditions were present at the follow-up point. Other studies also show significant amounts of attrition following treatment. Indeed, attrition during treatment presents a challenging problem in many studies, amplifying the effects of dropout that occurs following treatment. Second, most studies do not continue to follow control groups after treatment ends. Thus, findings regarding follow-up must remain "naturalistic" in most cases. Results from studies and reviews of follow-up are encouraging, and therefore greater selection in the application of follow-up designs is recommended. For example, continuing use of follow-up studies on depression outcome is recommended, but only if the length of the follow-up time is extended to at least 1 year. For the most part, short-term follow-up studies are no longer needed for establishing the durability of effects.

Summary

Therapy researchers continue to make progress in the study of long-term maintenance of treatment gains. Many high-quality studies have been conducted in the past decade that follow clients for several years after treatment. These studies generally find that treatment effects are maintained *for those who continue to participate in the data collection*. New studies are documenting the effects of interventions aimed at increasing treatment effects beyond termination. This area of research will continue to be extremely important for the practice of psychotherapy in the years to come.

Demonstrating that treatments are beneficial for longer periods of time, identifying clients who are at risk of relapse, and developing methods of improving treatments that have acute as well as long-term benefits will be important future projects. For now, it appears that a variety of treatments provided to a broad range of client problems do offer long-term benefit for many clients. This is especially true when comparisons are made with psychoactive medications, where psychotherapy usually has substantial advantages. The many methodological difficulties of longitudinal research with therapy participants (e.g., dropout, uncontrolled designs, and clients seeking extra-study treatment) make definitive conclusions difficult. Thus, the maintenance of treatment gains remains a rich, yet difficult, area of study.

How Much Therapy Is Necessary?

An important issue for patients, policy makers, and psychotherapists is the optimal "dosage" of therapy needed to reduce impairment and increase positive life functioning. Howard, Kopta, Krause, and Orlinsky (1986) reported a meta-analysis on 2,431 patients from published research covering a 30-year period. Their analysis showed a stable pattern across studies reflecting the relationship of amount of therapy to patient improvement. They concluded that the relationship between the number of sessions and client improvement took a form similar to that evidenced by many medications—"a positive relationship characterized by a negatively accelerated curve; that is, the more psychotherapy, the greater the probability of improvement, with diminishing returns at higher doses" (Kopta, Howard, Lowry, & Beutler, 1994, p. 1009). Their analysis of the data indicated that 14% of clients improved before attending the initial session, 53% were improved following 8 weekly sessions, 75% by 26 sessions, and 83% after 52 sessions.

The Howard et al. (1986) study supports the meta-analytic findings that treatment produces a benefit that surpasses spontaneous remission rates by demonstrating that clients receiving treatments make substantial gains early in treatment. McNeilly and Howard (1991) used the same analytic methods to reconsider Eysenck's

(1952) original data set from which Eysenck drew the conclusion that psychotherapy was no more effective than spontaneous remission. Using probit analysis of the untreated sample, they demonstrated that psychotherapy produced in 15 sessions the same recovery rate as spontaneous remission after 2 years! Ironically, Eysenck's own data confirm that therapy is beneficial. The more rapid effect of psychotherapy versus no treatment is particularly important because suffering is relieved faster.

A limitation of both the Howard et al. (1986) meta-analysis and the McNeilly and Howard (1991) study was their reliance on pre-postestimates of patient improvement to model change over time, rather than session-by-session ratings of improvement. Reliance on pre-postratings makes it difficult to identify the exact time to recovery for individual patients. Later studies relying on session-by-session mental health ratings and follow-up data (Anderson & Lambert, 2001; Kadera, Lambert, & Andrews, 1996) suggest that the review by Howard et al. (1986) overestimated the speed of recovery and indicated that 50% of patients needed 13 sessions of therapy before they reached criteria for clinically significant change and 75% of patients met criteria after more than 50 sessions. This finding was partially replicated in an Australian population, where 50% of clients at two university training clinics were estimated to recover after 14 sessions and 70% required 23 sessions (Harnett, O'Donovan, & Lambert, 2010). Anderson and Lambert (2001) also found that patients tended to maintain or show additional improvement at follow-up. They noted a relationship between initial levels of distress and time to recovery, with more disturbed patients reaching criteria for recovery at a slower rate.

In an extension, Lambert, Hansen, and Finch (2001) reported recovery rates from a more diverse national sample of patients ($n = 6,072$) undergoing treatment in various routine care settings (employee assistance programs, private practice, university counseling centers, and community mental health centers). Results of the analysis are illustrated in Figure 6.1. The findings suggest that 50% of patients who begin treatment in the dysfunctional range can be expected to achieve clinically significant change (recovery) following 21 sessions of psychotherapy. More than double this number of treatment sessions is necessary, however, before 75% of patients reach this same criterion. Using a lesser

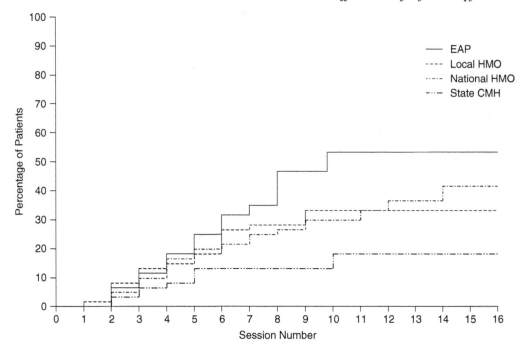

FIGURE 6.1   Time to recovery using clinically significantly improvement criteria.

standard of improvement (reliable change) and including patients who began treatment in the functional range, we find that 50% are estimated to improve following 7 sessions and 75% following 14 sessions.

In this naturalistic database (as opposed to clinical trials) the dosage of therapy needed to meet the criterion of success depended on the criterion of success selected and initial level of disturbance, not the type of psychotherapy or patient diagnosis. In the 1990s many attempts were made to refine variables that moderated time to recovery and thereby make estimates more precise. These methods usually tried to refine the type of outcome of interest, such as the restoration of morale versus characterological change or change in acute versus chronic distress (Barkham et al., 1996; Kopta et al., 1994; Maling, Gurtman, & Howard, 1995; Thompson, Thompson, & Gallagher-Thompson, 1995), but few replications support these initial efforts to specify what changes when.

Research now suggests some modification to the idea that more therapy will lead to better outcomes (also see Chapter 4, this volume). The earlier research in this area combined data across patients who varied in their total dose of therapy

and assumed that the rate of change during therapy is constant across different doses. In contrast, Barkham et al. (2006) and Stiles, Barkham, Connell, and Mellor-Clark (2008) suggested that there is a "good enough" dose of therapy and that the rate of change will be related to the total dose of therapy. In other words, rather than a negatively accelerating curve, where a session of psychotherapy incrementally contributes to change, individual rate of change determines the dose, rather than the number of sessions predicting recovery. Barkham et al. (2006) theorized that the speed of recovery would predict the number of sessions. This model was termed the "good-enough level" (GEL) model of psychotherapy change.

Baldwin, Berkeljon, Atkins, Olsen, and Nielsen (2009) evaluated these competing predictions by examining the relationship between rate of change and total dose in 4,676 psychotherapy patients who received individual psychotherapy. The initial aggregate model replicated the negative accelerating curve described in the dose-effect literature. When the sample was stratified by number of sessions, however, the model indicated that although patients improved during treatment, patients' rate of change varied as a

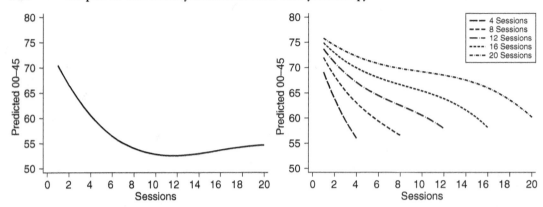

FIGURE 6.2 Predicted rate of change in Outcome Questionnaire-45 (OQ-45) scores across sessions in treatment. The top panel represents the aggregate model, which averaged the rate of change across all patients, ignoring the number of sessions they attended. The bottom panel represents the stratified model, which stratified rate of change across the total number of sessions patients attended.

Source: Baldwin et al. (2009). Reprinted with permission of the American Psychological Association.

function of total dose of treatment. Small doses of treatment were related to relatively fast rates of change, whereas large doses of treatment were related to slower rates of change, as illustrated in Figure 6.2. Interestingly, this suggests that equal amounts of change occur over the course of therapy but at different rates for different patients. Some clients require only 4 sessions to achieve recovery, and others more than 20. A statistically significant dose-response relationship was found, as the early research suggested, but this relationship was slight and detected only in the first eight sessions; as the dosage increased beyond that limit, the dose response relationship became insignificant. This phenomenon is depicted in Figure 6.2 as well, where it can be seen that the expected percentage of patients recovering remains depends on response more than dose. Overall, these findings indicate that the GEL model of psychotherapy change, where patients remain in therapy until they recover, is a better description of the relationship between dose and individual patient recovery than earlier dose-response models.

The results indicated that although patients improved during treatment, patients' rate of change varied as a function of total dose of treatment. Small doses of treatment were related to relatively fast rates of change, whereas large doses of treatment were related to slower rates of change. Total dose had a nonlinear relationship with the likelihood of clinically significant change. It appears that there is a dose-response

relationship as the early research suggested, but possibly that this relationship is most clear in just the first eight sessions, as the dosage increases beyond that limit the dose response relationship becomes less detectable (see also Chapter 4, this volume). Reese, Toland, and Hopkins (2011) have drawn similar conclusions but also found a significant influence of session frequency on the rate of recovery, a finding that has important implications for patients and providers since spaced sessions produced slower recovery.

For policy makers and therapists alike the dose response literature has important implications for routine care. Given the variability in rates of change, it appears that time limits for treatment uniform to all patients would not adequately serve patients' needs. Standard, fixed, low doses of treatment are not justified for the majority of individuals who enter treatment and are akin to establishing a set minimal time to keep a broken leg in a cast, rather than removing the cast when sufficient healing has taken place. A major unanswered question is how long to continue treatment that the patient has not yet responded to.

Sudden Gains and Related Patterns of Change

Other important questions related to the dose-effect relationship have come into their own as the practice of monitoring patient treatment response has become more widespread. One particularly important phenomenon is that dealing with dramatic treatment response, in contrast to session-by-session change. The progress of clients in psychotherapy has often been assumed to be linear in nature and fairly similar among clients. For example, evidence-based treatments are usually tested in protocols with fixed session limits hovering around 12 to 16 sessions based on the assumption that a standard treatment protocol of this length is necessary and sufficient. In the past 20 years much more attention has been placed on researching the timing and sequence of psychotherapy based on the finding that an individual client's recovery path is likely to differ from the group mean in some way (Ilardi & Craighead, 1994; Tang & DeRubeis, 1999a). In reality, many different courses of progress are present even within similar disorders, seemingly similar clients, and similar psychotherapies. A recently studied, and often observed, phenomenon of psychotherapy course has been that of dramatic between session and within (Bornas, Gelabert, Llabres, Balle, & Tortella-Feliu, 2011) session response and its ties to psychotherapy outcomes.

Early work using rudimentary measures of the phenomena such as a > 50% change in BDI scores from initiation of treatment (Renaud et al., 1998) and response within the first 2 weeks of treatment (Fennell & Teasdale, 1987) were related to better outcomes at the end of treatment and even at up to 24-month follow-up (Renaud et al., 1998). However, the mechanisms, definition, and even what to label these phenomena has varied from study to study. Labels used have included "Sudden Gains" (Tang & DeRubeis, 1999b), "Rapid Response" (Fennell & Teasdale, 1987), "Early Response" (Ilardi & Craighead, 1994), "Large Sudden Improvements" (Gaynor et al., 2003), "Rapid Early Response" (Haas, Hill, Lambert, & Morrell, 2002), and "Early Sudden Gains" (Stiles et al., 2003). Consequently, clarification is needed among terms and descriptions of terms. Spurred on by the work of Ilardi and Craighead (1994), Tang & DeRubeis (1999a) reconsidered the idea of drastic between session changes in depression symptomology. In their initial study they offered a precise definition of the phenomena, and defined many aspects of sudden gains which are investigated to this day. They proposed three requirements: An intersession change that was "large (a) in absolute terms, (b) relative to depressive symptom severity before the gain, and (c) relative to symptom fluctuations preceding and following the gain" (Tang & DeRubeis, 1999b). This was later translated

into operational terms for depression stating that a sudden gain occurred when (a) the gain was ≥ 7 BDI points (absolute magnitude), (b) the gain represented at least 25% of the pre-gain session's BDI score (relative magnitude), and (c) the difference between the mean BDI score of the three sessions before the gain and the three sessions after the gain was at least 2.78 times greater than the pooled standard deviations of these sessions' BDI scores (i.e., relative to symptom fluctuation) (Tang, DeRubeis, Hollon, Amsterdam, & Shelton, 2007).

This definition, while specific, is not without controversy. The criteria are somewhat arbitrary in nature, but have been used in many of the succeeding studies to some degree, despite these validity concerns. Using this definition evidence of sudden gains was found in 39% of Tang and DeRubeis (1999b) clients. Those with sudden gains showed an average of 11.2 points of change on the Beck Depression Inventory. This change accounted for 51% of the total change of these clients by the end of treatment. Of those who experienced sudden gains, 79% reached the status of "recovered" by the end of treatment compared to 41% in the contrast group. At follow-up, 6 months and 18 months after the end of treatment, those who experienced sudden gains exhibited significantly reduced amounts of depressive symptoms on the BDI compared to those who had not experienced sudden gains (Tang & DeRubeis, 1999b). Instances of dramatic improvement during the course of psychotherapy proves to be highly important to having a positive outcome and the permanence of the improvement.

Subsequent studies using much of the same criteria as Tang and DeRubeis (1999b; Gaynor et al., 2003; Hardy et al., 2005; Hofmann, Schulz, Meuret, Moscovitch, & Suvak, 2006; Stiles et al., 2003; Tang & DeRubeis, 1999b; Tang, DeRubeis, Beberman, & Pham, 2005; Tang et al., 2007; Tang, Luborsky, & Andrusyna, 2002; Vittengl, Clark, & Jarrett, 2005) exhibited many similar results. Sudden gains were found in 17% (Stiles et al., 2003) to 50% (Gaynor et al., 2003) of the treated clients. In studies using the BDI, the mean magnitude of the sudden gains found was remarkably similar, ranging from 10.21 to 13.25 (Hardy et al., 2005; Tang et al., 2002; Tang et al., 2005; Tang et al., 2007; Vittengl, et al., 2005). Typically, sudden gains accounted for at least 50% of the total change in the course of therapy (Gaynor et al., 2003; Hardy et al., 2005; Hofmann et al., 2006; Stiles et al., 2003; Tang et al., 2002; Tang et al., 2005; Tang, et al., 2007; Tang & DeRubeis, 1999b; Vittengl, et al., 2005). All but one study (Stiles et al., 2003) hovered within a range between 50% and 65% of total change. Multiple, but not all studies, showed significant maintenance of treatment gains at some period of follow-up (Gaynor et al., 2003; Hardy et al., 2005; Stiles et al., 2003; Tang et al., 2007; Tang & DeRubeis, 1999b).

Across studies, the median session at which sudden gains occurred was commonly five (Hardy et al., 2005; Stiles et al., 2003; Tang et al., 2002; Tang et al., 2005; Tang & DeRubeis, 1999b). In two studies, however, the median occurrence was Session 8 (Tang et al., 2005; Vittengl et al., 2005). Overall, remarkable consistency is shown. Even in RCT trials of 12 to 20 sessions, sudden gains often occur very early in treatment, ironically, before the bulk of therapeutic work typically occurs.

An alternative definition of sudden gains was operationalized and applied in a study of routine clinical care from a naturalistic (as opposed to RCT) database by Haas, Hill, Lambert, and Morrell (2002). These researchers examined the psychotherapy outcome of 147 clients diagnosed with a variety of mood, anxiety, and adjustment disorders treated with a variety of monotherapy and eclectic interventions, mainly CBT. They were followed for 6 months to 2 years after they completed therapy. Rather than stipulating that an absolute score was necessary for identifying sudden gains, these researchers used the degree to which each patient changed in relation to patients with an identical intake score. Thus a sudden gain was based on the difference between average patient change (expected change) and actual change adjusted for functioning at intake and amount of psychotherapy. This procedure results in taking into account regression to the mean by requiring high scoring individual to change more than low scoring individuals rather than imposing an absolute standard. In addition, rather than identifying sudden gains with a single score, scores representing the first three sessions were averaged. Thus, the study contrasted the treatment outcomes of dramatic early (first three sessions) treatment responders with those who failed to show such a pattern.

Results using these procedures indicated that 31% (46/147) of the clients met criteria for early dramatic response. These individuals made up 84% of those who either improved or recovered by the end of treatment, while those who responded more slowly and less dramatically made up the remaining 16%. At follow-up, an average of 1-year posttreatment, the early dramatic responders tended to maintain their treatment gains, with 80% of patients classified as improved or recovered at follow-up being early dramatic responders.

In contrast to the findings of studies of antidepressant medication (e.g., Quitkin, McGrath, Stewart, Taylor, & Klein, 1996) that show dramatic early response is related to *relapse* at follow up, the Haas et al. (2002) study found that early (within the first three sessions) extreme positive response to psychotherapy predicted final treatment status as well as follow up status, being stable for at least 1 to 2-years. Certainly such findings provide a strong challenge to our assumptions about the amount of therapy required for a positive treatment outcome, and even more importantly, about what happens during psychotherapy that makes it so powerful that such lasting changes (for about a third of patients) can be facilitated with so little treatment. Many patients who respond to therapy make gains early on and these gains precede rather than follow the specific techniques deemed to be essential by most theories of psychotherapeutic intervention. Such findings beg for additional research into these change processes, but also encourage weekly routine monitoring of patient treatment response (Lambert, 2010). This would allow therapists (and systems of care) to end therapy with such patients sooner, freeing up space for patients that have been wait-listed.

Summary

The question, how much therapy is enough, is important for both practical and theoretical reasons. Research on this topic can help therapists and patients make reasonable decisions in treatment planning. Such research can inform policy decisions about the amount of services that are necessary for sufficient medical coverage. It also allows for theory-driven exploration of variables that modify dosage models. Significant progress has been made in this area over the past decade and a half. Research suggests that a sizable portion of patients reliably improve after 7 sessions and that 75% of patients will meet more rigorous criteria for success after about 50 sessions of treatment. Limiting treatment sessions to less than 20 will mean that about 50% of patients will not achieve a substantial benefit from therapy (as measured by standard self-report scales).

Aspects of patient functioning show differential response to treatment, with more characterological (e.g., perfectionism) and interpersonal aspects of functioning responding more slowly than psychological symptoms. Future research may illuminate which, if any, specific interventions are more efficient in producing patient change. At this point in time, the results of research into the dose-effect relationship should serve as a guide to employers, government agencies, and insurance companies. Most patients are being underserved by current session limits. Policy makers, if they are interested in quality care, should do more to encourage greater, not less, utilization of psychotherapy service.

Do Some Patients Get Worse?

Although negative effects are difficult, if not impossible, to study in an experimentally controlled way, research clearly indicates that some patients are worse at the time therapy is terminated than when they started. It appears that negative outcomes can be observed across a variety of treatment modalities, including group and family therapies as well as across theoretical orientations. This does not mean that all instances of worsening are the product of therapy. Some cases may be on a progressive decline that no therapist effort can stop. Other cases may experience highly negative life events that therapy is unable to protect them from (such as a new medical condition or loss of a loved one). The extent or rate of such negative change or of "spontaneous" deterioration in untreated groups has never been determined, so there is no baseline from which to judge deterioration rates observed in treated groups. The alternative is to observe negative change in experiments using treated versus control conditions (such as waitlisted patients) and in studies of specific connections between therapy processes and patient responses.

Prior work (Bergin & Lambert, 1978; Lambert, Bergin, & Collins, 1977) described evidence (based on more than 50 studies) about the incidence, prevalence, and magnitude of negative change. That process involved piecing together obscure bits of evidence since there were few, if any, definitive studies. There has been considerable hesitation to address this issue directly, and most early outcome studies did not even include a category of "worse" as a descriptor for categorizing patient treatment response. However, the evidence is slowly changing as studies

improve. There is a paradoxical fact, however, that as precision of inquiry into this question is improving, the quality of therapy may also be improving (especially as represented by RCTs). The research itself stimulates better quality control and inclusion of especially competent therapists in outcome studies, so the study of negative effects may decrease its extent and its visibility.

Many early studies documented rates of deterioration in patients, even in those who participated in carefully controlled research protocols (cf. Beutler, Frank, Schieber, Calvert, & Gaines, 1984; Doherty, Lester, & Leigh, 1986; Emmelkamp, De Haan, & Hoogduin, 1990; Henry, Schacht, & Strupp, 1986; Jacobson et al., 1984; Mohr et al., 1990; Orlinsky & Howard, 1980). Those studies that use controls usually show that deterioration is lower in controls than in treated samples. For example, Ogles et al. (1995) in a reanalysis of the NIMH TDCRP data found that 8% of the clients in the completer sample (the 162 clients who completed at least 12 sessions and 15 weeks of treatment) deteriorated as measured with the Hamilton Rating Scale for Depression (HRSD). None of the clients who deteriorated participated in the placebo plus clinical management control group. Scogin et al. (1996) using a liberal definition of negative outcome: any client making even a 1-point increase (worsening) in scores on the self-report or clinician measures, found that 1% of clients were identified as having a negative outcome using the clinician rated outcome, and 9% were identified as having a negative outcome using the self-report measure of outcome.

In a review of outcomes reported in a cross sampling of clinical trials investigating the effects of treating a variety of specific adult disorders (2,109 patients) with a variety of specific treatments (89 different treatment conditions, mostly CBT) the rate of recovery was 58% with an additional 9% of patients reliably improved (Hansen, Lambert, & Forman, 2002). In general we can say that about two-thirds of adults who enter treatment in RCTs have a positive outcome in about 14 sessions, but about a third either show no benefit or worsen. These same authors examined outcome in *routine practice settings* ranging from employee assistance programs to community mental health centers. Outcomes for these unselected naturalistic samples totaling more than 6,000 patients are presented in Table 6.2. As can be seen the adult clients did not fare nearly as

TABLE 6.2 Number of Patients, by Site, Who Demonstrated Reliable Negative Change (Deteriorated), Did Not Demonstrate Reliable Change (No Change), Demonstrated Reliable Positive Change (Improved), and Demonstrated Reliable Change Into the Functional Range (Recovered) and Treatment Dosage

Site	Average Treatment Length (SD)	Deteriorated	No Change	Improved	Recovered
EAP	3.6 (2.0)	216 (6.6%)	1911 (58.5%)	645 (19.7%)	497 (15.2%)
UCC	5.8 (5.4)	115 (9.7%)	684 (57.6%)	239 (20.1%)	150 (12.6%)
Local HMO	3.3 (2.4)	84 (14.1%)	321 (53.9%)	122 (20.5%)	68 (11.4%)
National HMO	5.1 (4.0)	40 (7.5%)	258 (48.1%)	153 (28.5%)	85 (15.9%)
Training CMH	9.5 (6.8)	4 (3.2%)	57 (45.6%)	39 (31.2%)	25 (20.0%)
State CMH	4.1 (2.8)	37 (10.2%)	219 (60.7%)	74 (20.5%)	31 (8.6%)
Total N = 6,072	4.3 (3.5)	496 (8.2%)	3448 (56.8%)	1272 (20.9%)	856 (14.1%)

Note. EAP = Employee Assistance Program; UCC = University Counseling Center; Local HMO = Health Maintenance Organization in Utah; National HMO = outpatient psychotherapy clinics and practitioners from across the United States; Training CMH = Clinical Psychology training clinic; State CMH = Community mental health center funded by state and local government. From "The Psychotherapy Dose-Response Effect and Its Implications for Treatment Delivery Services" by N. B. Hansen, M. J. Lambert, & E. V. Forman, 2002, in *Clinical Psychology: Science and Practice, 9,* 337. Copyright 2002 American Psychological Association. Reprinted with permission.

well as those in clinical trials, with only about one third showing improvement or recovery, while an average of 8% deteriorated (Range, 3% to 14%) and more than 50% did not respond.

The situation for child outcome in routine care is even more sobering. The small body of outcome studies in community-based usual care settings has yielded an overall mean effect size near zero (Weiss, Catron, Harris, & Phung, 1999; Weisz, 2004; Weisz, Donenberg, Han, & Weiss, 1995), yet millions of youth are served each year in these systems of care (National Advisory Mental Health Council, 2001; Ringel & Sturm, 2001). Furthermore, although the broader research base that considers controlled studies with children and adolescents is more impressive, significant concerns exist regarding the applicability and generalizability of these studies to usual clinical care (Garland, Hurlburt, & Hawley, 2006; Weisz, 2004; Weisz, Doss, & Hawley, 2005). Warren, Nelson, Mondragon, Baldwin, and Burlingame (2010) examined outcomes of children being treated in community mental health (N = 936)

or through managed care (N = 3,075) and found deterioration rates in these settings to be a staggering 24% and 14%, respectively.

In a relevant special section of *Cognitive and Behavioral Practice*, Dimidjian and Hollon (2011) asked researchers and clinicians to discuss treatment failures within the context of clinical trials of very specific therapies for specific disorders. It is noted that the term *treatment failure* can have multiple definitions, with client worsening being a unique type of failure that is distinct from "failing to respond." Unfortunately there is no generally agreed upon definition of treatment failure and this is reflected in the diversity of definitions used by the authors in this special issue. Most often authors interpreted treatment failure to mean that the patient did not seem to respond to treatment by the time it was terminated. In the case examples that were provided in this issue, treatment failure cases ranged from patients who actually had a good outcome by termination but whose course of therapy was marked by very rough progress and a need to modify usual procedures (Eisendrath, Chartier, & McLane, 2011; Newman, 2011); or who had a positive outcome at termination only to relapse soon after (Arch & Craske, 2011), to clients who have more or less been untouched by treatment delivered in a highly structured and time-limited format.

When the various articles are seen as a whole, and when treatment failure (nonresponse) is highlighted, it becomes obvious that as effective as these treatments are, there is still plenty of room for improvement. This is true even where therapists had success in returning patients to a state of normal functioning (e.g., 50% to 70% in panic; Arch & Craske, 2011), but especially true for the more difficult disorders (e.g., at best less than 50% of eating disordered patients gain a full recovery; Cooper, 2011). The editors guided authors to consider the full range of reasons for nonresponse—including client factors, treatment model factors (the wrong treatment, applying treatments that do not cover a full range of client problems, inadequate conceptualization), as well as poor delivery of treatment. This helped focus the special section and give it some uniformity with regards to analyzing how and why treatment failed. Authors of each article were free to emphasize what seemed most important to them, what they learned from retrospectively examining the failure of some clients to change, and what to do about it.

In general, those who did not respond to treatment provided special challenges to practitioners and these tended to take three general forms: poor motivation, complicated problems, and resistance to therapist prescriptions and suggestions. These variables are largely client contributions. While DBT training explicitly forbids therapists from attributing failure to clients undergoing DBT, one cannot read the case example presented by Rizvi (2011) of the treatment of BPD without sensing that a major goal of the patient was to defeat the therapist at every turn. In the case of family focused therapy (FFT) for bipolar disorder, the therapist appeared to side too much with the adolescent (and father) while seeing the mother as overinvolved and needing to give up control, but here there was also the problem of substance abuse that the adolescent kept hidden from the parents and the therapist. The shear multitude of problems in the family dynamics, in addition to bipolar disorder and unreported substance abuse appeared to doom the treatment.

Clearly client contributions to treatment failure are central in explaining its occurrence but often we are not blessed with the knowledge to know beforehand if client problems will prove too difficult to overcome in specific cases, even when patients are selected to be a good match for an empirically supported treatment and similar to individuals who have profited in the past. Even though there are ideal candidates for specific treatments we cannot refuse treatment to less than ideal clients, and one of the functions of this series was to push the field to consider the treatment of patients presenting with substantial complexity and comorbidity.

Each article in this series found instances where *therapist mistakes in delivery* may have interfered with patient outcome, but also they place considerable emphasis on the technical aspects of treatment and the modification of treatment protocols to increase and broaden their impact for reducing nonresponse. This practice stands in contrast to the bulk of recommendations that have been emphasized in the deterioration literature—where therapist relational failures have been emphasized.

Perhaps the clearest example of attending to nonresponders and then modifying a treatment protocol is Cooper and Fairburn (2011) who provide an enhanced cognitive-behavior therapy for eating disorders based on examination of nonresponders. They propose one to four elements be added to their eating disorder treatment *in particular cases*: increased focus on clinical perfectionism, mood intolerance, low self-esteem, and interpersonal difficulties. Addition of these treatment foci increases the basic protocol to 20 sessions delivered over 20 weeks in order to broaden the focus of treatment for patients at risk for nonresponse.

Another example can be found in adapting adult behavioral activation interventions to depressed adolescents (McCauley, Schloredt, Gudmundsen, Martell, & Dimidjian, 2011). Pilot testing the adaptation with a small number of cases including the one presented, suggested that with youth the therapist needed to be more flexible, including putting aside worksheets and other prepreparated material if responded to negatively by the adolescent. This flexibility also included adapting the order of presenting core skills. Although a fixed order was suitable for the majority of patients, it needed to be modified for some in relation to feedback from them. There appeared to be a need to make greater attempts to strike a balance between insistence on following a preset structure and individualization based on patient reactions.

They also added weekly assessment of suicide to the assessment that was already in place and tapering of sessions to make the end of treatment more responsive to individual cases. Ongoing flexible contact with families was another innovation that was proposed as a method to enhance treatment for particular clients. In general, it appears that in order to enhance treatment outcomes, treatment protocols needed to cover more aspects of dysfunction and more treatment targets tailored to specific clients. In routine practice clinicians may already make such accommodations because they do not feel compelled to follow manuals, while in research protocols the treatments are being tested for efficacy and need to be more restricted—including being offered in a standard dosage.

This special series of studies on negative outcomes provides overlapping explanations with earlier reviews of deterioration. For example, Mohr (1995) found evidence for increased rates of negative outcome among patients treated for borderline personality disorder and obsessive compulsive disorder. Two client variables were related to negative outcome: high levels of interpersonal difficulties and more severe problems at intake. Therapist variables that were identified as potential contributors to negative outcome included lack of empathy, underestimation of patient's problem severity, and negative countertransference. Finally, there was evidence that experiential therapies may have a higher propensity to produce negative outcome and that minimal intervention for severely distressed patients may result in deterioration. These findings were strikingly similar to earlier conclusions about causal factors (e.g., Lambert et al., 1977).

The literature on negative effects suggests that although the studies contain many methodological shortcomings and ambiguities, the evidence that psychotherapy can and does harm a portion of those it is intended to help is substantial. The relatively consistent portion of adults (5% to 10%) and a shockingly high proportion of children (14% to 24%) who deteriorate while participating in treatment—especially in routine care—beg for solutions. The study of negative change has important implications for the selection of students for graduate study, the selection of clients for treatment, the suitability

of specific procedures for some clients, and the selection, training, and monitoring of therapists. Several of these issues are discussed later in the chapter.

Does Efficacy Research Generalize to Practice?

Use of the term *efficacy* in addition to *effectiveness* was deliberate in the title of this chapter, based on an increasing interest in the empirical substantiation of treatments in applied versus laboratory settings (see Chapter 4, this volume, for a more complete discussion). In the past decades, therapy researchers have applied more distinct definitions for these terms (Seligman, 1995). The efficacy of treatment is determined by a clinical trial or trials in which many variables are carefully controlled in order to demonstrate that the causal relationship between the treatment and outcome are relatively unambiguous (see Chapter 2, this volume). Efficacy studies emphasize the internal validity of experimental design through a variety of means, including (a) controlling the types of patients included in the study (e.g., limiting the number of clients with comorbid disorders), (b) using manuals to standardize treatment delivery, (c) training therapists prior to the study, monitoring therapist adherence to the treatment during the study, and supervising therapists to ensure they do not deviate from the treatment protocol, (d) managing the "dose" of treatment through analyses that include only patients who have received a specified amount of treatment, and (e) random assignment of clients to treatments, and (f) the use of blinding procedures for raters. These and other strategies are used to enhance the investigator's ability to make causal inferences based on the findings.

In contrast, the *effectiveness* of a treatment is considered in clinical situations when the intervention is implemented without the same level of internal validity. Effectiveness studies emphasize the external validity of the experimental design and attempt to demonstrate that the treatment can be equally beneficial in a clinical setting. Typically, clients are not as carefully preselected, treatment dose is less controlled, and therapist adherence is neither monitored nor modified to be a pure-form, manually determined treatment. Therapists tend to be those working in the settings and may or may not receive the same level of prestudy training as that of the efficacy study. At the same time, many clinically representative studies have high internal validity because they have random assignment and minimize attrition (Shadish, Navarro, Matt, & Phillips, 2000). Nevertheless, effectiveness studies differ from efficacy studies based on "the joint effects of a constellation of variables that might pertain to clinical relevance" (Shadish et al., 1997, p. 356).

Much of the research concerning the benefits of treatment is not easily categorized into these two categories. For example, the numerous studies included in the Smith, Glass, and Miller (1980) meta-analysis have extremely varied experimental designs, some of which may be viewed as efficacy studies and others of which may be viewed as effectiveness studies. With the increasing use of meta-analysis, however, many reviewers narrowed the focus of their meta-analyses to include only methodologically superior studies with specified experimental controls or ratings of study quality. As a result, the strongest findings for the benefits of psychotherapy involve the efficacy of treatments in controlled conditions. Fewer studies have examined the effectiveness of treatments. Several of the original meta-analyses examined the relationship of therapy setting, therapist experience, or other variables that are related to this issue, but few studies directly examined the differences related to efficacy versus effectiveness studies.

Weisz, Weiss, and Donenberg (1992) examined four meta-analyses of the child and adolescent treatment literature. A consistent positive benefit for treatment was noted across more than 200 studies. When comparing the effect sizes for treatments conducted in research settings with treatments conducted in clinic settings, however, they found significant differences. They suggested that "most clinic studies have not shown significant effects" (Weisz et al., 1992, p. 1578). Spurred by the findings of Weisz et al. (1992), several important studies considered whether treatment works in clinically representative conditions. Shadish et al. (1997, 2000) conducted two secondary analyses to consider the benefits of therapy conducted in clinically representative conditions. The first meta-analysis identified 54 studies from 15 previous meta-analyses that varied in the degree to which they were conducted in clinically representative conditions. For example, studies conducted in community settings with patients entering treatment using typical routes were considered to be more representative of clinical settings than studies conducted in university settings with patients recruited through ads and carefully screened to select a homogeneous sample. When comparing outcome studies along the continuum of representativeness, Shadish et al. (1997) found that the effects of clinically representative studies were the same as effects reported in the original meta-analyses. But bear in mind many of these effectiveness studies mimicked RCTs and exercised considerable control, that is, they were not studying therapy the way it might unfold outside of the research protocol.

The second meta-analysis (Shadish et al., 2000) improved on the first study with several methodological changes and the inclusion of a larger sample of studies. Three samples were analyzed to investigate the influence of clinical representativeness of studies on their effects. Criteria for determining clinical representativeness included the following study characteristics: (a) client problems, (b) setting, (c) referral source, (d) therapists, (e) treatment structure, (f) treatment monitoring, (g) problem heterogeneity, (h) pretherapy training, (i) therapy freedom, and (j) flexible number of sessions. Both random and fixed-effect analyses found that studies that were representative of clinical conditions produced similar effects to those that were not representative of clinical conditions.

During the past decade, the issue of treatment effectiveness in applied settings has become an important area of study (see Chapter 4, this volume). The dissemination or transportability of efficacious treatments may be one of the most fertile areas of study for the next decade. With diminishing resources and increasing accountability, those who fund the delivery of mental health services are clamoring for "best practices" and empirically supported interventions. The ability of researchers and evaluators to demonstrate that "laboratory treatments" also work in the real world will eventually lead to a better understanding of the effects of therapy as it is typically offered. At this time it appears that RCTs can and do generalize to clinical settings, but not always. In addition, the likelihood of this occurring depends to a great deal on the degree to which the studies are similar in design to the RCT. The more they depart from what is done in the RCT the smaller the impact of treatment is compared to the RCT. This is well illustrated by the meta-analysis of multisystemic therapy where the RCTs attained an effect size of .81 while the effectiveness studies effect size was .26 (for a more complete discussion of this topic see Chapter 15, this volume).

COMPARISON AND CAUSATIVE FACTORS

In this section, research is reviewed that further clarifies the factors associated with improvement during psychotherapy. This research, to a large extent, employs research designs that are aimed at discovering the effects of specific therapies by contrasting an established treatment with a new treatment (comparison studies), an effective treatment with one or more of its component factors, or an effective treatment with a different effective treatment on a group of patients with special characteristics. First, evidence that deals with the differential effectiveness of different schools of therapy is explored. Next, other causal factors will be discussed, including factors that are common across therapies.

Is One Treatment More Effective Than Another?

Historically, there has been a clear difference of approach between "schools" of therapy associated with psychodynamic and humanistic theories on the one hand ("verbal" or "insight" therapies), and behavioral and cognitive theories ("action" therapies), on the other. It cannot be assumed that such global and philosophical divisions between treatment approaches are faithfully or functionally represented in the actual procedures implemented in the delivery of their respective therapies. The use of "manuals" to specify treatment activities characteristic of the different schools results in objectively discriminable therapist behaviors (e.g., Luborsky & DeRubeis, 1984; Rounsaville, O'Malley, Foley, & Weissman, 1988) that are true to conceptions of what is wrong and how it can be changed. The use of therapy manuals and more experienced therapists also have been found to reduce the *variability* in outcome due to the therapist-as-a-person, allowing for more accurate comparisons of treatment techniques in comparative outcome studies (Crits-Christoph et al., 1991). Whether these differences hold up in everyday routine clinical practice, however, is an open question and even more so because practicing therapists often combine techniques developed within schools.

Many older reviews have analyzed studies comparing the psychotherapies (e.g., Bergin & Lambert, 1978; Beutler, 1979; Goldstein & Stein, 1976; Kellner, 1975; Lambert & Bergin, 1973; Meltzoff & Kornreich, 1970; Rachman & Wilson, 1980). The conclusion of most, but not all, of these reviews is similar to that drawn by Luborsky, Singer, and Luborsky (1975), who suggested a verdict similar to that of the Dodo bird in Alice in Wonderland: "Everyone has won and all must have prizes." These reviews used traditional scholarly methods of reaching conclusions without reference to meta-analytic procedures. However, meta-analytic methods have now been extensively applied to large groups of comparative studies, and these reviews generally offer similar conclusions, that is, little or no substantial difference between therapies with regard to client outcome.

Early meta-analytic reviews often showed a small, but consistent, advantage for cognitive and behavioral methods over traditional verbal and relationship-oriented therapies (e.g., Dobson, 1989; Dush, Hirt, & Schroeder, 1989; Nicholson & Berman, 1983; Robinson et al., 1990; D. A. Shapiro & Shapiro, 1982; Smith et al., 1980; Svartberg & Stiles, 1991). This was not always the case (e.g., Shoham-Salomon & Rosenthal, 1987), but certainly when differences were found they often favored, even if marginally, cognitive or behavioral approaches across a variety of patient diagnostic categories.

Some meta-analytic reviews present evidence for the superiority of one treatment over another without considering potential reasons for the differences (e.g., analogue studies, measurement biases). For example, (Svartberg & Stiles, 1991) examined the effects of short-term dynamic psychotherapy (STDP) in 19 studies published in the period between 1978 and 1988. Their analysis showed that while STDP was superior to no-treatment, it was less effective than alternative therapies even at a 1-year follow-up. However, two subsequent meta-analyses updated this review (Anderson & Lambert, 1995; Crits-Christoph, 1992) and found short-term dynamic therapy to be equivalent to other treatments using a larger database of studies.

Robinson et al. (1990) conducted a comprehensive review of comparative outcome studies of treatments with depressive disorders. In their analysis of direct comparisons (i.e., within-study comparisons) of cognitive, behavioral, and cognitive behavioral, or general verbal therapies, they found equivalence between cognitive and cognitive-behavioral approaches, with the latter treatment showing some superiority to a strictly behavioral approach. Verbal therapies were less effective than all three alternative therapies with which they were compared. However, when two independent raters judged investigator allegiance toward a treatment on a 5-point scale, the differences between treatments vanished. Ratings were based on reading and rating the introduction of the study. Some investigators had strong theoretical preferences for a particular treatment. In some cases, preferences had to be inferred. Preferred therapies produced more improvement than their less favored counterparts, but when this bias was eliminated through statistical adjustments, therapies were equivalent. Similar results were reported for analysis of drug versus psychotherapy comparisons. The evidence that favored psychotherapies over medication disappeared when comparisons took into account experimenter allegiance.

In addition to reanalyzing Dobson's meta-analysis, Gaffan, Tsaousis, and Kemp-Wheeler (1995) conducted a second analysis using 35 new published studies of cognitive therapy for depression that used the Beck Depression Inventory as the measure of outcome. Within this second set of studies, cognitive therapy was again superior to other psychotherapies and pharmacotherapy. However, behavior therapy produced larger effect sizes than cognitive therapy (with just four comparisons). Importantly, ratings of investigator allegiance were not correlated with effect sizes in this more recent sample of studies.

Wampold et al. (1997) also conducted a meta-analysis comparing treatments, drawing in part on the summary of comparative studies in an earlier version of the handbook (Lambert, Shapiro, & Bergin, 1986). This meta-analysis differed from earlier comparisons between treatments in several ways. First, only studies that directly compared two or more treatments were included in the meta-analysis. This eliminates the potential confounds associated with comparing treatments administered in different studies (Shadish & Sweeney, 1991). Second, the treatments were not divided into general types or categories. Third, only "bona fide" treatments were included in the meta-analysis. That is, studies in which the treatment was delivered "by trained therapists and were based on psychological principles, were offered to the psychotherapy community as viable treatments . . . or contained specified components" were included in the meta-analysis. Thus, studies in which a viable treatment was compared to an alternative therapy that was "credible" to participants in the study but not intended to be "therapeutic" were excluded (Wampold et al., 1997, p. 205).

To test whether one treatment was superior to another, effect sizes calculated comparing two treatments were randomly given a positive or negative sign. The distribution of effects was then tested to see if variability in effects was homogeneously centered around zero. Using several databases with different numbers of effect sizes—"none of the databases yielded effects that vaguely approached the heterogeneity expected if there were true differences among bona fide psychotherapies" (Wampold et al., 1997, p. 205). Further analyses also indicated that more sophisticated methods associated with more recent studies were not related to increased differences between treatments and theoretically dissimilar treatments did not produce larger effect sizes. Both of these findings provide additional evidence for the substantial equivalence of bona fide treatments.

In addition to studies comparing various orientations or methods of treatment, some studies examine the comparative benefit of differing modes of therapy (e.g., family versus individual treatment). Some of the earliest meta-analyses compared the various modalities of therapy using between-group comparisons (Robinson et al., 1990; Smith et al., 1980). Although the number of studies is typically small and the detailed results vary somewhat, these studies generally find no difference between group and individual therapy (McRoberts, Burlingame, & Hoag, 1998; Tillitski, 1990; see Chapter 16, this volume), marital/family therapies and individual therapy (see Chapter 15, this volume). The foregoing meta-analyses that examine the comparative effectiveness of differing theories of psychotherapy or modes of psychotherapy reveal a mixed picture.

There is a strong trend toward no differences between techniques or modes in amount of change produced, which is counterbalanced by indications that, under some circumstances, certain methods (generally cognitive-behavioral) or modes (family therapy) are superior. The potential confounds of cross-study comparisons (e.g., where CBT is examined in one study and compared to psychodynamic treatment from another study) include differences in measurement, samples studied, and investigator allegiance, complicate the process of making general conclusions. An examination of selected exemplary studies allows us to explore this matter further. When examining these well-designed studies that compare different therapeutic orientations, the findings are consistently small or negligible. Indeed, studies comparing two bona fide therapeutic approaches that find significantly different outcomes may be more unusual than not. The finding of relative equivalence of differing approaches has significant implications for theories regarding the processes of change and the relative importance of theory-specific techniques versus common factors as agents of change.

Among the most rigorous designs for evaluating causative mechanisms are studies that take an effective treatment and break it down into its various components (i.e., they subtract treatment elements and thereby dismantle it) or studies that add elements to an existing treatment and then contrast the outcomes. In general, the results from comparative, dismantling, and components analysis studies suggest the general equivalence of treatments based on different theories and techniques. Ahn and Wampold (2001) examined component analyses conducted over an 18-year period and found that adding or removing components of treatment did not change the effects of the core treatment. Wampold (2001) believes that the lack of findings within these dismantling and constructive designs suggests that "there is little evidence that specific ingredients are necessary to produce psychotherapeutic change" (p. 126). It appears that subtracting elements that are considered essential to the success of a treatment does not lessen its effectiveness.

Is One Therapist More Effective Than Another Therapist?

In addition to the comparison of treatment orientations, modalities, and components, differences among therapists within treatments (so-called therapist effects) is another avenue of investigation into causal factors in therapy research. The specific therapist contributions to client outcome have long been a concern of the therapy researcher and are widely accepted as important in clinical practice. Few clinicians refer patients to just any practitioner. It is assumed that some therapists obtain large positive effects, many obtain modest effects, and a few may be by-and-large ineffective. Several important historical studies have examined this issue. Just a few examples of findings in this area will suffice to make the point.

Orlinsky and Howard (1980) conducted a retrospective study based on case files to examine differences among therapists. The outcome ratings of 143 female cases seen by 23 traditional verbal psychotherapists were listed therapist by therapist. Six of the 23 therapists were rated ✓+, which means that at least 70% of their cases were improved and none was rated worse. Overall, 84% of patients treated by these six therapists were improved at termination. Five of the 23 therapists, on the other hand, were X-rated, which means that 50% or fewer of their cases improved while more than 10% were worse. Overall, 44% of their 25 cases improved. The study provided some of the first evidence showing significant differences in effectiveness among therapists.

Luborsky, McClellan, Woody, O'Brien, and Auerbach (1985) reported the results of their analysis of the differential outcome of clients seen by nine different therapists who were treating opiate-dependent addicts. The therapists were trained to offer the prescribed treatment using detailed treatment manuals. Despite careful selection, training, monitoring, and supervision, patients of therapists offering the same treatments had highly divergent results. In their analysis of the therapy process, Luborsky et al. (1985) found that the differences in outcome between therapists could be attributed to a number of therapist variables. Three therapist qualities were identified as distinguishing the more helpful from the less helpful therapists: (1) the therapist's adjustment, skill, and interest in helping patients; (2) the purity of the treatment they offered; and (3) the quality of the therapist/patient relationship.

Crits-Christoph and Mintz (1991) presented further evidence that the contribution of individual therapists should not be ignored in research designs and statistical analysis of data. Their meta-analysis of 15 studies and 27 treatment groups revealed an average therapist effect accounting for 9% of outcome variance. One study showed therapist effects accounting for 49% of the outcome variance, while other studies showed no independent therapist effect.

Blatt, Sanislow, Zuroff, and Pilkonis (1996) found relatively large differences among the therapists in the NIMH Collaborative Depression study even after the rigorous selection and training process. Based on an examination of the average composite outcome score for their clients there were significant differences among therapists, but these differences were independent of the type of treatment, the research site, and the general experience level of the clinician. More effective therapists had a more psychological approach (rather than biological) to the treatment of depression, and more psychologists (and fewer psychiatrists) were included in the more effective group.

Analysis of data from routine care settings where the selection, training, and supervision of therapists are much less controlled, the number of clients per therapist is much larger, and length of treatment is variable, also opens a window into therapist effects. Okiishi, Lambert, Nielsen, and Ogles (2003) examined routine care outcomes by therapist and replicated the study as more clients became available for each clinician (Okiishi et al., 2006). The client samples for these studies consisted of college students seen at a university counseling center for individual psychotherapy. Although 11,736 students were seen at the center over the 6-year period of data collection, the analysis being used for this study required at least 3 data points (a pretest and two additional measurements), so individuals with less than three treatment sessions including the intake were not included in the sample. This selection criterion yielded a data set of 7,628 patients who had been seen for a total of 64,103 sessions.

Patients at the center presented with a wide range of problems from simple homesickness to personality disorders and more serious problems. The most common diagnoses in the final data set were mood disorders (36%), anxiety disorders (22%) and adjustment disorders (17%). One hundred forty nine therapists contributed data to the entire data pool of 7,628 patients. A minimum of 30 clients per therapist was set, and using this criterion, as well as the 3 data-point minimum described above, 71 therapists who had seen a total of 5,427 patients were left in the sample. The therapists in this final data set had seen an average of 76 patients each, for an average of 9.71 sessions. Data were also collected on a variety of therapist variables: level of training (preinternship, internship, and postinternship), type of training (clinical psychology, counseling psychology, social work, marriage and family therapy), sex (M, F), and primary theoretical orientation (cognitive-behavioral, behavioral, humanistic, psychodynamic). The modal therapist was a male, licensed, counseling psychology PhD, who identified their primary theoretical orientation as cognitive-behavioral.

Therapist variables (level of training, primary theoretical orientation, type of training, and gender) were coded in order to answer the question: "Do available therapist variables account for differences in patients' outcome?" Furthermore, an ANOVA was performed on patient's initial OQ-45 scores by therapist to answer the question: "Do some therapists see patients whose average initial disturbance is greater than other therapists?" Following this initial check of therapist variables two ways of ranking therapists were examined. The first method was based on HLM slopes to examine the modeled *rate* at which patients' OQ-45 scores decreased over sessions of psychotherapy. This gave an indication of which therapists' patients improved significantly more *rapidly* than expected and which therapists' patients improved at a rate much slower than expected. This is an important index both from a cost/benefit perspective, where improvement is accomplished with fewer sessions, but also with regard to length of suffering, with faster response more quickly relieving the burden of illness carried by the patient.

Another method of examining therapist effectiveness was based on the traditional pre- to postchange score. These were computed for each patient by subtracting the patient's last OQ-45 score from their initial OQ-45 score. These change scores were averaged for all patients within therapists. This provided the actual amount of change experienced by patients seen by a therapist rather than a change index based on a statistical model of change and slope (line of best fit as computed by the HLM analysis). Pre- to post-treatment ignores speed of change (number of sessions delivered to patients). Once these average change scores had been computed, therapists were again ranked from most to least effective.

Outcome by therapist showed considerable variability, with the most effective therapist's patients showing both rapid and substantial treatment response, while the least effective therapist's patients showed an *average worsening* in functioning. There was no evidence that the same degree of variability and superiority could be found for outcomes analyzed on the basis of therapist self-identified treatment orientation. Client outcomes were unrelated to the type of therapy a therapist claimed to practice even when they held strong allegiance to a particular theory-based approach. No systematic difference between experienced and inexperienced therapists could be found, except that licensed psychologists attained positive outcomes with fewer sessions of care. One of the more dramatic findings was that a typical client seeing the most *efficient* therapist would need between six and seven sessions of treatment to recover, while the average client seeing the least efficient therapist would need 94 sessions, nearly 2 years of weekly treatment.

The outcome of the top 10% ($n = 7$) of therapists and the bottom 10% ($n = 7$) was examined in order to illustrate the size of the differences in patient outcome. The most effective therapists had an average HLM slope $3\frac{1}{2}$ that of the less effective therapists and overall change that was twice as much. Top therapists had an average recovery rate of 22% while bottom ranked therapists had a recovery rate of 15%. Conversely, bottom-ranked therapists had an 11% rate of deterioration, while the top ranked therapists' only had 5% of their patients deteriorate.

Anderson et al. (2009) attempted to identify the extent to which therapist interpersonal skills could account for differences in outcome. Available therapists in the two Okiishi studies were invited to complete the Facilitative Interpersonal Skills (FIS) Performance Task (Anderson, Patterson, & Weis, 2007). FIS is defined as a set of qualities that correspond to a person's ability to perceive, understand, and communicate a wide range of interpersonal messages, as well as a person's ability to persuade others with personal problems to apply suggested solutions to their problems and abandon maladaptive patterns. The performance task was designed as a means of measuring therapists' abilities to respond to *challenging* therapy situations based on viewing video recordings. Four problematic therapy process segments were selected from the videotaped archives of a study that focused on problematic interpersonal interactions between patients and therapists (Strupp, 1993). In addition, four unique interpersonal patient styles were selected to represent a range of challenging interpersonal patterns, including (1) a confrontational and angry patient ("You can't help me"), (2) a passive, silent, and withdrawn patient ("I don't know what to talk about"), (3) a confused and yielding patient (only the therapist's opinion matters), and (4) a controlling and blaming patient (implies that others, including the therapist, are not worthy of him).

Thus, two cases were designed to include patients who were highly self-focused, negative, and self-effacing, and the remaining two cases were designed to be highly other-focused, friendly, but highly dependent clients. Therapist responses were rated across 10 interpersonal "skills": verbal fluency, emotional expression, persuasiveness, hopefulness, warmth, empathy, alliance-bond capacity, and problem focus. An important aspect of this methodology was that this material was collected independent of the services provided by therapists and was remote in time from the collection of client outcome data. Using this methodology assumes that the skills measured are trait-like and would also be present in the psychotherapy offered. Results indicated a high relationship between FIS ratings from the analogue material and client outcomes in routine care ($r = .47$, $d = 1.07$).

These results, were they replicated and causal, suggest that the way particular therapists characteristically react to challenging client presentations partially explains why some therapists are more effective than others. Whether making a referral, hiring a new therapist at a group practice, selecting a therapist for inclusion in a panel of providers, or deciding who to go to for one's own therapy, judgments about the best providers are being made on a daily basis. Despite the need for making these important decisions (about who is and who is not an effective therapist, or who will be an effective therapist with a particular client), little effort has been expended on using empirical data based on specific therapists to help make decisions. Using actual treatment outcomes based on the effects of the individual therapist to directly improve patient outcome is almost never attempted. Hesitancy to use such information is hardly limited to behavioral health care. Millenson (1997) has documented a plethora of examples in the field of medicine where resistance to analyzing outcomes within hospitals and physicians has had disastrous consequences for patients.

Additional information on therapist outcomes in routine care is summarized in this handbook in Chapter 4 as well as Chapter 8. Of course, the studies cited in those chapters and here constitute a mere beginning to examining the contribution of the individual therapist. What we do know at this time is that there are intriguing possibilities for new discoveries here, and that the issue of the individual therapist's contribution has been ignored to a surprising degree. Researchers, influenced by mechanistic models, have placed their bets more on technique factors as the powerful ones in therapeutic change. In this view the differences in effectiveness between therapists are likely to reflect variations in technical skill rather than personal qualities. More and less effective psychotherapy looked at on a therapist-by-therapist basis may well be to differences in applying school-based techniques. To the extent that this is true, studies of techniques have been contaminated by heterogeneity in the purity or quality of techniques being applied. However, findings like those just cited suggest that, selection of therapists, training and even treatment manuals have not consistently remedied this problem. Consequently, monitoring of individual therapist variation in skill (and personal qualities like empathic attunement or flexibility) is essential in outcome studies in which specific causal mechanisms are explored.

It is possible that too much energy is being devoted to technique studies at the expense of examining therapists as persons and in interaction with techniques, as well as patient characteristics. Therapist-by-technique-by-patient interaction effects will need to be more carefully conducted. Such studies may well show not only potent therapist outcome but also that technique differences are inseparably bound with therapist and patient differences. A logical extension of research on therapist outcome is to encourage research focused on the "empirically supported psychotherapist" rather than on empirically supported treatments. This type of research might have an immediate impact on practice and might also lead to a greater probability of ensuring positive patient outcomes.

COMMON FACTORS AND OUTCOME

The general finding of no difference or very little difference in the outcome of therapy for clients who have participated in highly diverse therapies has a number of alternative explanations: (a) different therapies can achieve similar goals through different processes; (b) different outcomes do occur but are not detected by past research strategies; and (c) different therapies embody common factors that are curative, though not emphasized by the theory of change central to a particular school. At this time, any of the above interpretations can be advocated and defended because of the ambiguity of the data or because there is not enough evidence available to rule out alternative explanations. Clearly, different therapies require the client to undergo different experiences and to engage in different behaviors all of which could be helpful. Diverse therapies could be effective for different reasons, but we do not yet know enough about the boundaries of effectiveness for each therapy to discuss alternative (a) and its merits. Alternative (b), the inadequacy of past research, will not be fully discussed here. Suffice it to say

that there are many methodological reasons for failing to reject the null hypothesis. Kazdin and Bass (1989), for example, have questioned the value of the majority of comparative studies on the basis of a "lack of statistical power." There are also serious problems in accurately measuring behavioral change (see Chapter 5, this volume). In fact, any of a host of methodological problems could result in a failure to detect differences between diverse therapies. The third alternative (c), emphasizing common factors in different therapies, is the possibility that has received the most research attention and that has the clearest implications for practice. It was first hypothesized by Rosenzweig (1936) in reference to similarities in outcome manifest in treatments available at that time. Alternative (c) is not only an interpretation of the results of comparative outcome literature, but is based on other research aimed at discovering the active ingredients of psychotherapy. Alternative (c) is also consistent with the results of the placebo literature discussed earlier.

Table 6.3 is provided to help the reader understand the kinds of variables that might be subsumed under the rubric of common factors. Here the common factors have been grouped into Support, Learning, and Action categories. These categories were chosen to represent a sequence that might be presumed to operate in psychotherapies. Together they suggest the possibility that all therapies provide for a cooperative working endeavor in which the patient's increased sense of trust, security, and safety, along with decreases in tension, threat, and anxiety, lead to changes in conceptualizing his or her problems and ultimately in acting differently by reframing fears, taking risks, and working through problems. The variables and constructs organized in Table 6.3 were derived from readings of empirical research and theory. Most have been operationally defined and then correlated with outcome in research studies of therapy. The developmental sequence is at least partially mediated through factors common across therapies. The developmental nature of this sequence presumes that the supportive functions precede changes in beliefs and attitudes, which precede the therapist's attempts to encourage patient action. This table lists a variety of common factors attributable to the therapist, therapy procedures, and the client.

Lambert (1992) attempted to illustrate the place of common factors in psychotherapy outcome by representing variables that cause change into a pie chart that illustrated various

TABLE 6.3   Sequential Listing of Common Factors Present Across Psychotherapies

Support Factors	Learning Factors	Action Factors
Catharsis/release of tension	Advice	Facing fears
Mitigation of isolation	Affective re-experiencing	Cognitive mastery
Structure/organization	Assimilating problematic experiences	Encouragement of experimenting with new behaviors
Positive relationship	Cognitive learning	Taking risks
Reassurance	Corrective emotional experience	Mastery efforts
Safe environment	Feedback	Modeling
Identification with therapist	Insight	Practice
Therapeutic alliance	Rationale	Reality testing
Therapist/client active participation	Exploration of internal frame of reference	Success experiences
Recognition of therapist expertness	Changing expectations of personal effectiveness	Working through
Therapist warmth, respect, empathy, acceptance, genuineness	Reframing of self-perceptions	Behavioral/emotional regulation
Trust/open exploration		

contributions (see Figure 6.3). The proportion of outcome due to various factors was rationally derived based on extensive readings of the psychotherapy outcome literature. It is really difficult to partition and compare sources of variability in psychotherapy because no single study encapsulates all the variables of interest. Nevertheless the pie chart suggests a crude picture of outcome from an empirical point of view. As can be seen the client (and the world external to treatment) can be regarded as making the largest

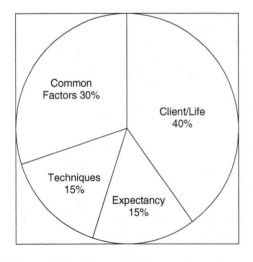

FIGURE 6.3   Percent of improvement in psychotherapy patients as a function of therapeutic factors.

contribution, followed by factors common across therapies, with specific techniques accounting for a rather small portion of the changes clients experienced while in treatment.

Only recently have attempts been made to test the empirical basis for the original conception. Cuijpers et al., (2012) meta-analyzed studies ($n = 31$) that examined outcomes of depression in clinical trials in which common factors control groups were used and compared to active treatments and no treatment controls. These common factor controls are sometimes also labeled nondirective supportive therapy (NDST). Some researchers intentionally create such interventions as "intention to fail" controls (Baskin, Tierney, Minami, & Wampold, 2003), while a minority of other researchers regard such treatment groups as likely to provide patient benefits. The results of this review suggested that the patient (and his or her environment) as captured by change in wait-list controls (pre- to post) was responsible for 33.3% of the improvement that was found. In contrast, common factors (NDST compared to waitlist) accounted for 49% of patient improvement, while specific therapy factors contributed 17.1% of changes in depressive symptoms. When researcher allegiance to the active treatments was taken into account the portion of variance associated with active treatments was cut nearly in half.

Given that these results were based on 2,508 patients, they seem to be reliable estimates, at least for the treatment of depression. As the authors point out, the results of their study must be considered tentative as they are based on a variety of assumptions. But they also note the similarity with the Lambert (1992) estimates. They write: "These results are remarkably similar to the estimates made almost two decades ago with respect to psychotherapy in general for all disorders by Lambert (1992). Lambert further estimated that the therapeutic relationship and patient expectations (both non-specific placebo effects) taken together were responsible for 45% of the improvement (we found that nonspecific factors were responsible for 49.6%)" (p. 18).

Among the limitations to keep in mind regarding this meta-analysis is the fact that follow-up data were infrequent enough to disallow examination of long-term effects, and that those with severe depression were underrepresented. Since placebo effects appear to have less effect on the severely depressed (Driessen, Cuijpers, Hollon, & Dekker, 2010; Fournier et al., 2010) and therefore are most influential with the samples that were studied in this review, the NDST estimate may be inflated relative to all patients who undergo treatment. The relative strength of the various contributors to outcome represented in the pie chart across different forms of psychotherapy and psychological disorders needs further scrutiny.

Many specific variables can be subsumed under the common factor rubric. Reviewers are virtually unanimous in their opinion that the therapist-patient *relationship* is a common factor critical to positive outcome. An important contribution to the literature in this area is *Psychotherapy Relationships That Work*: *Evidence-Based Responsiveness* (Norcross, 2011), which summarizes a variety of relationship variables and their contribution to patient change, providing new meta-analytic findings. This project was sponsored by the American Psychological Association's Divisions of Clinical Psychology and Psychotherapy. Each relationship element is rated with regard to the strength of the evidence supporting its contribution as: "demonstrably effective," "probably effective," or "promising but insufficient evidence." After examining evidence from more than two dozen reviews an independent panel rated the evidence and made recommendations for practice, training, and research. Among the more important conclusions was that: "The therapy relationship makes substantial and consistent contributions to psychotherapy outcome independent of

the specific type of treatment." And that "Practice and treatment guidelines should explicitly address therapist behaviors and qualities that promote facilitative therapy relationship." "Efforts to promulgate best practices" or "evidence-based practices (EBPs) without including the relationship are seriously incomplete and potentially misleading" (Norcross & Wampold, 2011, pp. 423–424).

Early research on the relationship was extensively studied by client-centered therapists who operationally defined accurate empathy, unconditional positive regard, nonpossessive warmth, and the like. The importance of the therapeutic relationship has been bolstered in recent years by investigations of the therapeutic alliance, an aspect of the relationship. Although most of the early work was generated by psychodynamically oriented researchers, more recent studies include most orientations. The therapeutic alliance has been conceptualized and defined differently by a host of interested investigators. Like the "necessary and sufficient" client-centered dimensions, it can be measured by client ratings, therapist ratings, and judges' ratings.

There is more disagreement about the therapeutic alliance construct than there was with the client-centered conditions. This lack of consensus may prove to be a hindrance in drawing conclusions in this area because there are now several popular methods for measuring this construct, rather than the limited number of scales evidenced in the client-centered literature (cf. Martin, Garske, & Davis, 2000). In addition, the alliance is seen as a necessary, but not sufficient, condition for personality change, and so it assumes a less important theoretical position in what causes change. Ratings of the therapeutic alliance also contain a heavy emphasis on patient variables and focus mainly on the client's ability to participate productively in therapy. Since alliance ratings go well beyond measuring therapist behaviors, they can be expected to correlate more highly with outcome than the client-centered measures, but have fewer implications for training since alliance ratings may not lead directly into modification of specific therapist attitudes and behavior.

In an important conceptual article, Gaston (1990) integrated the various constructs that have been offered to describe the therapeutic alliance and suggested that four core components of the alliance are measured by some but not all current rating scales: (1) the patient's affective relationship to the therapist; (2) the patient's capacity to purposefully work in therapy; (3) the therapist's empathic understanding and involvement; and (4) the patient-therapist agreement on the goals and tasks of therapy. These core components are considered in many of the conceptual and research articles published since that time.

Research literature on the alliance has been reviewed elsewhere in this volume (in particular, Chapters 7, 8, 9, 12, and 13, this volume). Most recently Horvath, Del Re, Fluckinger, and Symonds (2011) examined 201 studies with 190 comparisons and found the correlation between the alliance and outcome to be $r = .275$ ($d = .57$). They also noted that there were more than 30 different therapeutic alliance measures in this literature. Correlations were higher when the same source provided both alliance and outcome ratings and there was only 50% agreement between therapist and client ratings of the alliance, a finding that suggests the need for therapists to gather self-report alliance ratings from their clients in routine care if they want to have a chance to correct their view of this important variable. Formal assessment of the alliance or the client-centered variables would allow therapists to improve the alliance.

Alliance ratings correlate with psychotherapy outcome across a variety of types of treatment and patient populations. In children these alliance and outcome correlations average $r = .19$ (Shirk, Karver, & Brown, 2011). In family and couple therapy the average correlation is $r = .26$ (Friedlander, Escudero, Heatherington, & Diamond, 2011). In group psychotherapy correlations between the cohesion felt by group members and patient outcome correlates around .25 (Burlingame, McClendon, & Alonso, 2011).

Similar findings can be found for constructs coming from the client-centered tradition. Elliott, Bohart, Watson, and Greenberg (2011) report that therapist empathy correlates with outcome at an average r of .30 (based on 224 comparisons). While Farber and Doolin (2011) found positive regard to correlate with outcome at an $r = .27$. For the most part this correlational evidence cannot be assumed to be causal and these various constructs overlap and cannot be assumed to be independent (e.g., alliance ratings include ratings of therapist empathy as well as collaboration). Nevertheless the size of the ratings of relationship variables produce results that are reasonably consistent in suggesting the quality of the relationship correlates more highly with positive outcomes than specific treatments. Such ratings indicate that relationship variables not only predict positive change but may produce it as well (see Chapters 8 and 9, this volume), although the alliance and related variables sometimes fail to predict outcome or produce associations that are quite small.

The alliance has also been found to be important in pharmacotherapy (Krupnick et al., 1996). In the NIMH depression study, both the clinical management and placebo drug control group and imipramine plus clinical management groups had equivalent levels of the therapeutic alliance to the two psychotherapies (CBT and IPT). Surprisingly, the relationship between the alliance and outcome was consistent across both pharmacological and psychological treatments (accounting for 21% of the variance in combined self-report and expert-rated outcome).

Summary

Common factors loom large as mediators of treatment outcome. The research base for this conclusion is substantial and multidimensional (Wampold, 2001). When considered as a whole, common factors are probably much more powerful than the contribution of specific techniques. Although there is considerable resistance to acknowledging the importance of common factors, possibly as Frank (1976) states because "little glory derives from showing that the particular method one has mastered with so much effort may be indistinguishable from other methods in its effects" (p. 74). It seems imperative that we continue moving toward an understanding of how change occurs in psychotherapy through common and unique mechanisms. The evidence on the alliance strengthens arguments for common factors as major mediators of change and this fact needs to be acknowledged by bodies that develop treatment guidelines, training programs, and the like. Learning how to engage the client in a collaborative process is more central to positive outcomes than which process (theory of change) is provided.

The Search for Larger Effects

While the field struggles to find ways of integrating evidence-based practices into routine care as the central contemporary method of improving patient outcomes, it is also obvious that treatments (even empirically supported ones) are constantly being modified and broadened with the hope that more patients will be affected. The history of psychotherapy reveals its constant modification over time in an attempt to find larger effects. Even the practice of blending techniques and procedures that result in a majority of practitioners practicing eclectic and integrative approaches can be seen in this same light (see Chapter 1, this volume). In addition to these traditional efforts, and administrative pressures to use evidence-based treatments and practices, research directed at decreasing the variability of responses to treatment (particularly eliminating deterioration) may push the average treatment gain in the direction of improvement. Much of this research has been described in Chapter 4 (this volume) where efforts to use practice-based evidence (in addition to evidence-based practice) have been summarized.

Using Feedback and Problem-Solving Tools to Enhance Treatment Outcomes

As has been documented in this chapter and others in this handbook, a significant portion of patients (perhaps 40% to 60%) fail to respond to treatment, even when they are evidence-based (Hansen et al., 2002). Unfortunately therapists regularly fail to identify who these nonresponding and negatively responding individuals are before they leave treatment. Evidence for this assertion comes from a variety of sources. For example, Regan and Hill (1992) asked patients and therapists to report on thoughts or feelings that they were unable to express in treatment. They then asked the therapists to guess what patients had left unsaid. Results indicated that for both patients and therapists, most things left unsaid were negative. In addition, therapists were only aware of 17% of the things patients left unsaid. Rhodes, Hill, Thompson, and Elliott (1994), in another qualitative study, asked therapists and therapists-in-training to recall events from their own treatment and performed a qualitative analysis of the events. Although some of the patients were able to talk openly about their negative feelings toward the therapist, patients who felt uncomfortable addressing misunderstanding of events were able to conceal them from their therapists and the misunderstandings remained unaddressed, often leading to termination.

Hill, Thompson, Cogar, and Denman (1993) extended the investigation into patient covert processes (reactions to in-session events) to include things left unsaid and secrets. As in their previous studies, they found that therapists were often unaware of patients' unexpressed reactions. They also found that patients were particularly likely to hide negative feelings and that even experienced, long-term therapists were only able to guess when patients had hidden negative feelings 45% of the time. Furthermore, 65% of the patients in the study left something unsaid (most often negative), and only 27% of the therapists were accurate in their guesses about what their patients were withholding.

In a later study, Hill, Nutt-Williams, Heaton, Thompson, and Rhodes (1996) conducted a qualitative analysis of therapists' recollections of impasse events that had ended in termination. In retrospect, therapists identified multiple variables they associated with the impasses including lack of agreement about the tasks and goals of therapy, transference, possible therapist mistakes, and therapists' personal issues, among others. Perhaps most significant, however was the finding that, as in the Rhodes et al. (1994) study, patients did not reveal their dissatisfaction until they quit therapy. Moreover, therapists reported that they became aware of patients' dissatisfaction only with the announcement of termination and were often taken by surprise.

Hatfield, McCullough, Franz, and Krieger (2009) noted the failure of therapists to record in weekly case notes any indication of client worsening in 70% of the cases in which it occurred, even when the negative change was extreme. In a more direct study of predictive accuracy, Hannan et al. (2005) examined therapist accuracy by asking 40 therapists (20 trainees and 20 experienced professionals), at the end of each session with each of their clients, if they believed the client would leave treatment in a deteriorated state, and, in addition, if the client was worse off at this particular session than when they entered treatment. Hannan et al. (2005) expected that experienced clinicians, given their extensive contact with clients over the years, would be more accurate in their judgments and predictions than trainees (who ranged from first-year graduate students to intern-level providers).

During a 3-week period predictions were made for 550 clients who participated in therapy sessions. In some cases therapists made three predictions, two predictions, or a single prediction based on the number of sessions a client attended over the 3 weeks. In every other way treatment continued as usual and clients' progress was followed until they terminated treatment, at which time their intake functioning could be compared with their end of treatment functioning. Although 40 clients were deteriorated at the termination of treatment only 3 of 550 clients (.01%) were predicted by their therapist to leave treatment worse off than when they began, one of whom actually deteriorated based on self-reported functioning. In general, clients' eventual deterioration was not forecast by clinicians who were attempting to do so. Rather than *experienced clinicians* being more able to predict the phenomenon, they *did not identify a single client who deteriorated* —the only accurate prediction out of the three predictions that were made was made by a trainee (see also, Breslan, Sobell, Sobell, Buchan, & Cunningham, 1997; Lunnen & Ogles, 1998).

In contrast to therapist clinical judgment, statistical algorithms can identify the vast majority of cases who go on to deteriorate before they leave treatment (see Chapter 4, this volume). A program of research aimed at improving treatment response through prediction of treatment failure and feedback has been summarized by Lambert (2010). Contextualized Feedback Theory (Riemer & Bickman, 2011) suggests that for feedback to improve performance it needs to be provided in a timely manner and provide novel information about performance, especially errors, along with ameliorative actions that can be taken. In this case the novel information provided to therapists is that the patient is not making expected progress and is so far off that they are likely to have a negative outcome. In addition the therapist is provided with problem-solving strategies for changing the course of therapy.

The effects of quality assurance interventions that incorporate feedback consistent with this theoretical foundation appear to be substantial in reducing deterioration rates and enhancing positive outcomes in patients predicted to be treatment failures. Among other findings, a meta-mega-analysis of six randomized clinical trials (Shimokawa, Lambert, & Smart, 2010) found that deterioration rates could be reduced from the baseline of 20% in predicted treatment failures to 13% when therapists were alerted to patient progress status. The problem-solving intervention further reduced deterioration rates to about 5.5% while doubling positive outcomes. More recent studies within this program of research (Crits-Christoph et al., 2012; Simon, Lambert, Busath, et al., in press; Simon, Lambert, Harris, Busath, & Vazquez, 2012) have partially replicated these findings with substance abusing individuals, eating disordered in-patients, and a hospital-based outpatient population, suffering mainly with depression.

Several advantages to such quality assurance systems for enhancing outcome in routine care include: They provide clinicians with information they do not generally have (lab test data that alerts of impending treatment failure); they can be applied with most patient populations; and across a wide variety of treatment orientations and modalities, including medication management; training in their use is minimal (about 2 hours); they are minimally intrusive on patient time (take about 5 minutes of patient time and 30 seconds of clinician time each week; and they are relatively inexpensive. They also provide therapists with information about problematic alliance items with cut-off scores that can lead to resolution of alliance ruptures.

The greatest barrier to widespread use appears to be therapist reluctance to add such tools (client feedback based on assessment) to their treatment routine. Walfish et al. (2012) in a survey of practitioners found that therapists probably inflate rates of recovery in their patients (seeing 85% as improved; overvalue their own effectiveness relative to their peers—with all therapists seeing themselves as above average and 90% seeing themselves as above the 75th percentile). With self-assessments that are this far inflated, and confidence in their ability to predict treatment outcome and the therapeutic alliance, therapists are not rushing to use this innovation, just as there is reluctance to adopt other evidence-based practices.

CONCLUSIONS

Research on psychotherapy outcomes has resulted in 12 important conclusions that have implications for theory, research, social policy, and clinical practice.

1. Many formal, theory-driven, psychotherapies that have been subjected to empirical study over the past 50 years have demonstrable effects on a variety of clients. From 40% to 60% of clients show a substantial benefit in carefully controlled research protocols, although far fewer attain this degree of benefit in routine practice.

2. Those clients that undergo formal treatment have better outcomes than individuals who are on a wait list or who receive no treatment.

3. Patients who undergo control treatments meant to simulate aspects of being treated show considerable improvement depending on the procedures used. Bona fide interventions are superior at promoting change than control conditions that encompass only some of the ingredients of effective treatments. The degree of inferiority depends on the nature of the control condition.

4. The effects of treatment are not only statistically significant but also clinically meaningful. Psychotherapy facilitates the remission of symptoms and improves everyday functioning. Psychological treatments not only speed up the natural healing process but also often provide additional coping strategies and methods for dealing with future problems. Providers as well as patients can be assured that a broad range of therapies, when offered by skillful, wise, and stable therapists, are likely to result in appreciable gains for the client, including a return to normal functioning.

5. We now have better general estimates of the amount of therapy needed in order to bring about clinically meaningful change. For patients who begin therapy in the dysfunctional range, 50% can be expected to achieve clinically significant change (recovery) after about 20 sessions of psychotherapy. More than 50 sessions are needed for 75% of patients to meet this criterion. Using the lesser standard of reliable improvement, it appears that 50% of patients respond by the 8th session and 75% are predicted to need at least 14 sessions to experience this degree of relief. Therapists and policy makers can use this general estimate to develop treatment plans and make policy decisions. Patients can be encouraged to anticipate a course of therapy of these durations if they want to experience meaningful change. Data support the use of brief therapies for many patients and cast doubt on their value for others. The issue of efficiency promises to be an important area of future study because of its practical, economic, and ethical consequences. Therapy is highly efficient for a large minority of clients, perhaps 30% of whom attain a lasting benefit after only three sessions.

6. The effects of therapy tend to be lasting. Although some problems, such as addictive disorders, tend to recur, the gains many patients make in therapy endure (with perhaps the striking finding that only 25% of depressed psychotherapy patients relapse, while 50% of those who received antidepressant medication do so). This is probably because most therapists are interested in enduring changes rather than temporary improvements. Research suggests that therapists consider expending greater systematic efforts on helping patients solidify the gains made in therapy and focus attention near the end of treatment on the meaning of improvement to the patient and methods of coping with future problems. As difficult as it is to study the long-term effects of therapy, the field would be well-served if continued effort was devoted to conducting long-term follow up studies and on strategies that are intended to increase the permanence of change in patients who have recurrent disorders.

7. Although research continues to support the efficacy of those therapies that have been rigorously tested, differences in outcome between various forms of therapy are not as pronounced as might have been expected or hoped for. Behavioral therapy, cognitive therapy, and eclectic mixtures of these methods have shown marginally superior outcomes to traditional verbal therapies in several studies on specific disorders, but this is by no means the general case. When this superiority is evidenced, the results are often diminished by the extent to which researchers do not enthusiastically and carefully implement alternative treatments.

The current interest in generating lists of "empirically supported" therapies for specific disorders is controversial and probably places too much emphasis on small differences in outcome associated with some treatments. Thankfully evidence-based treatments are effective and can be promoted, but the size of the differences and their reliability does not really justify the hope that is placed in them as uniquely effective. To advocate empirically supported therapies as preferable or superior to other treatments is probably premature. Not only is this endeavor impractical (after all how many different therapies can one person learn execute effectively) and expensive, but sufficient research evidence is lacking in many cases. Listed therapies are constantly evolving and new treatments are emerging. Nonetheless, behavioral and cognitive methods appear to add an incremental advantage with respect to a number of problems (e.g., panic, phobias, and compulsions) and to provide useful methods with a number of nonneurotic problems with which traditional therapies have shown little effectiveness (e.g., childhood aggression. psychotic behavior).

8. Given the growing evidence that there are probably some specific technique effects as well as large common effects across treatments, the vast majority of therapists have become eclectic in orientation. This appears to reflect a healthy response to empirical evidence and a rejection of previous trends toward rigid allegiances to schools of treatment. It also opens up the possibility of matching techniques to client dispositions, personality traits, and other diagnostic differences, but this is more a hope than a reality.

9. Positive affective relationships and positive interpersonal encounters, that characterize most psychotherapy and are common across therapies, still loom large as stimulators of patient improvement. It should come as no surprise that helping others deal with depression, anxiety, confusion, inadequacy, and inner conflicts, as well as helping them form viable relationships and meaningful directions for their lives, can be greatly facilitated in a therapeutic relationship that is characterized by trust, understanding, acceptance, kindness, warmth, and human consideration.

These relationship factors are probably crucial even in the more technical therapies that generally minimize relationship factors and emphasize the importance of technique in their theory of behavior change. This is not to say that techniques are irrelevant but that their power for change is limited when compared with personal influence. Common factors that help explain improvement in therapy also include exposure to anxiety-provoking situations, and encouragement to participate in other risk-taking behavior rather than avoiding the difficult and painful. Facing reality and problem-solving rather than avoiding are at the heart of most treatments.

10. Although the individual therapist can play a surprisingly large role in treatment outcome even when treatment is being offered within the stipulations of manual-guided therapy, recognition of the important place held by a therapist should in no way be construed as suggesting that technical proficiency has no unique contribution to make. The current trend to provide therapy in a systematic way, as characterized by the use of treatment manuals, and further studies of the process of therapy may yet allow for more definitive conclusions regarding the contribution of technique factors. Research suggests that clients would be wise to pick a therapist as-a-person at least in parity with the selection of a kind of psychotherapy.

11. The development and use of meta-analytic procedures for integrating outcome research is a methodological advancement that has enabled scholars and clinicians to better understand research findings. However, as more meta-analytic reviews are published, it is becoming obvious that this group of techniques has not reduced the controversies surrounding the interpretation of research findings. Meta-analysis is not a panacea and cannot be used to create worthwhile information if it is based on poorly designed studies or is biased. An important task of future meta-analytic reviews will be to translate the abstract review into clinically meaningful terms.

12. Although the broad, positive statements about psychotherapy can be made with more confidence than ever before, it is still important to point out that average positive effects mask considerable variability in outcomes. Wide variations exist among therapists. The therapist factor, as a contributor to outcome, looms large in the assessment of outcomes. Some therapists appear to be unusually effective, while others may not even help the majority of patients who seek their services. It is apparent that a portion of those whom therapy is intended to help are actually harmed through inept application of treatments, negative attitudes, or poor combinations of treatment technique and patient problem. Current research, based on monitoring patient treatment response and alarm signals following each treatment session, can provide a powerful method for reducing negative change and enhancing outcome through timely feedback to providers. Such quality management efforts appear to be well worth the cost of employing them in routine practice.

The public deserves treatments that are based not only on our best clinical judgment but also on systematic research conducted under controlled and naturalistic conditions. It is our duty to be sensitive to both the positive and negative effects of therapy and to base our treatment efforts on a broad empirical foundation as we routinely monitor the effects of our ongoing efforts with each person we see.

REFERENCES

Abramowitz, J. S. (1997). Effectiveness of psychological and pharmacological treatments for obsessive-compulsive disorder: A quantitative review. *Journal of Consulting and Clinical Psychology, 65*, 44–52.

Abramowitz, J. S., Franklin, M. E., & Foa, E. B. (2002). Empirical status of cognitive-behavioral therapy for obsessive-compulsive disorder: A meta-analytic review. *Romanian Journal of Cognitive & Behavioral Psychotherapies, 2*(2), 89–104.

Acarturk, C. C., Cuijpers, P. P., van Straten, A. A., & de Graaf, R. R. (2009). Psychological treatment of social anxiety disorder: A meta-analysis. *Psychological Medicine: A Journal of Research in Psychiatry and the Allied Sciences, 39*(2), 241–254. doi: 10.1017/S0033291708003590

Ahn, H., & Wampold, B. E. (2001). Where oh where are the specific ingredients? A meta-analysis of component studies in counseling and psychotherapy. *Journal of Counseling Psychology, 48*, 251–257.

Anderson, E. M., & Lambert, M. J. (1995). Short-term dynamically oriented psychotherapy: A review and meta-analysis. *Clinical Psychology Review, 15*, 503–514.

Anderson, E. M., & Lambert, M. J. (2001). A survival analysis of clinically significant change in outpatient psychotherapy. *Journal of Clinical Psychology, 57*, 875–888.

Anderson, T., Ogles, B. M., Patterson, C. L., Lambert, M. J., & Vermeersch, D. A. (2009). Therapist effects: Facilitative interpersonal skills as a predictor of therapist success. *Journal of Clinical Psychology, 65*(7), 755–768. doi: 10.1002/jclp.20583

Anderson, T., Patterson, C. L., & Weis, A. C. (2007). *Facilitative interpersonal skills performance analysis rating method*. Unpublished coding manual, Department of Psychology, Ohio University, Athens, Ohio.

Andrews, G., & Harvey, R. (1981). Does psychotherapy benefit neurotic patients: A re-analysis of the Smith, Glass, & Miller Data. *Archives of General Psychiatry, 38*, 1203–1208.

Arch, J. J., & Craske, M. G. (2011). Addressing relapse in cognitive behavioral therapy for panic disorder: Methods for optimizing long-term treatment

outcomes. *Cognitive and Behavioral Practice, 18*(3), 306–315. doi: 10.1016/j.cbpra.2010.05.006

Bakker, A., van Balkom, A. J. L. M., Spinhoven, P., Blaauw, B. M. J. W., & van Dyck, R. (1998). Follow up on the treatment of panic disorder with or without agoraphobia. *Journal of Nervous and Mental Disease, 186*, 414–419.

Baldwin, S. A., Berkeljon, A., Atkins, D. C., Olsen, J. A., & Nielsen, S. L. (2009). Rates of change in naturalistic psychotherapy: Contrasting dose-effect and good-enough models of change. *Journal of Consulting and Clinical Psychology, 77*, 203–211.

Barker, S. L., Funk, S. C., & Houston, B. K. (1988). Psychological treatment versus nonspecific factors: A meta-analysis of conditions that engender comparable expectations for improvement. *Clinical Psychology Review, 8*, 579–594.

Barkham, M., Connell, J., Stiles, W. B., Miles, J. N. V., Margison, J., Evans, C., & Mellor-Clark, J. (2006). Dose-effect relations and responsive regulation of treatment duration: The good enough level. *Journal of Consulting and Clinical Psychology, 74*, 160–167.

Barkham, M., Rees, A., Shapiro, D. A., Stiles, W. B., Agnew, R. M., Halstead, J., . . . Harrington, V. M. G. (1996). Outcomes of time-limited psychotherapy in applied settings: Replicating the second Sheffield psychotherapy project. *Journal of Consulting and Clinical Psychology, 64*, 1079–1085.

Barkow, K., Maier, W., Üstün, T. B., Gänsicke, M., Wittchen, H., & Heun, R. (2003). Risk factors for depression at the 12-month follow-up in adult primary health care patients with major depression: An international prospective study. *Journal of Affective Disorders, 76*, 157–169.

Barlow, D. H., Craske, M. G., Cerny, J. A., & Klosko, J. S. (1989). Behavioral treatment of panic disorder. *Behavior Therapy, 20*, 261–282.

Baskin, T. W., Tierney, S., Minami, T., & Wampold, B. E. (2003). Establishing specificity in psychotherapy: A meta-analysis of structural equivalence of placebo controls. *Journal of Consulting and Clinical Psychology, 71*(6), 973–979. doi: 10.1037/0022–006X.71.6.973

Bateman, A. & Fonagy, P. (2008). 8-year follow-up of patients treated for borderline personality disorder—mentalization based treatment versus treatment as usual. *American Journal of Psychiatry, 165*, 631–638.

Bauer, S., Lambert, M. J., & Nielsen, S. (2004). Clinical significance methods: A comparison of statistical techniques. *Journal of Personality Assessment, 82*(1), 60–70. doi: 10.120.1207/s15327752jpa8201_11

Bauer, S., Wolf, M., Haug, S., & Kordy, H. (2011). The effectiveness of internet chat groups in relapse prevention after inpatient psychotherapy. *Psychotherapy Research, 21*, 219–226.

Benish, S. G., Imel, Z. E., & Wampold, B. E. (2008a). The relative efficacy of bona fide psychotherapies for treating post-traumatic stress disorder: A meta-analysis of direct comparisons. *Clinical Psychology Review, 28*(5), 746–758. doi: 10.1016/j.cpr.2007.10.005

Benish, S. G., Imel, Z. E., & Wampold, B. E. (2008b). Corrigendum to "The relative efficacy of bona fide psychotherapies for treating post-traumatic stress disorder: A meta-analysis of direct comparisons." *Clinical Psychology Review, 28*(5), 766–775. doi:10.1016/j.cpr.2008.06.001

Bercusa, S. L., & Iacono, W. G. (2007). Risk for recurrence in depression. *Clinical Psychology Review, 27,* 959–985.

Bergin, A. E. (1971). The evaluation of therapeutic outcomes. In A. E. Bergin & S. L. Garfield (Eds.), *Handbook of psychotherapy and behavior change* (pp. 217–270). New York, NY: Wiley.

Bergin, A. E., & Lambert, M. J. (1978). The effectiveness of psychotherapy. In S. L. Garfield & A. E. Bergin (Eds.), *Handbook of psychotherapy and behavior change* (2nd ed.). New York, NY: Wiley.

Beshai, S., Dobson, K. S., Bockting, C. L. H., & Quigley, C. (2011). Relapse and recurrence prevention in depression: Current research and future prospects. *Clinical Psychology Review, 31,* 1349–1360.

Beutler, L. E. (1979). Toward specific psychological therapies for specific conditions. *Journal of Consulting and Clinical Psychology, 47,* 882–897.

Beutler, L. E., Frank, M., Schieber, S. C., Calvert, S., & Gaines, J. (1984). Comparative effects of group psychotherapies in a short-term inpatient setting: An experience with deterioration effects. *Psychiatry, 47,* 66–76.

Bisson, J., Ehlers, A., Matthews, R., Pilling, S., Richards, D., & Turner, S. (2007). Psychological treatments for chronic post-traumatic stress disorder: Systematic review and meta-analysis. *British Journal of Psychiatry, 190,* 97–104. doi: 10.1192/bjp.bp.106.021402

Blagys, M. D., & Hilsenroth, M. J. (2000). Distinctive feature of short-term psychodynamic-interpersonal psychotherapy: A review of the comparative psychotherapy process literature. *Clinical Psychology: Science & Practice, 7*(2). doi: 10.1093/clipsy/7.2.167

Blanco, C., Olfson, M., Stein, D. J., Simpson, H., Gameroff, M. J., & Narrow, W. H. (2006). Treatment of obsessive-compulsive disorder by U.S. psychiatrists. *Journal of Clinical Psychiatry, 67*(6), 946–951. doi: 10.4088/JCP.v67n0611

Blatt, S. J., Sanislow, C. A., Zuroff, D. C., & Pilkonis, P. A. (1996). Characteristics of effective therapists: Further analyses of data from the National Institute of Mental Health Treatment of Depression Collaborative Research Program. *Journal of Consulting Clinical Psychology, 64*(6), 1276–1284.

Bodkin, J. A., Allgulander, C., Llorca, P. M., Spann, M. E., Walker, D. J., Russell, J. M., & Ball, S. G. (2011). Predictors of relapse in a study of duloxetine treatment for patients with generalized anxiety disorder. *Human Psychopharmacology: Clinical and Experimental, 26,* 258–266.

Bondolfi, G., Jermann, F., Van der Linden, M., Gex-Fabry, M., Bizzini, L., Rouget, B. W., . . . Bertschy, G. (2010). Depression relapse prophylaxis with mindfulness-based cognitive therapy: Replication and extension in the Swiss health care system. *Journal of Affective Disorders, 122,* 224–231.

Borkovec, T. D., & Costello, E. (1993). Efficacy of applied relaxation and cognitive-behavioral therapy in the treatment of generalized anxiety disorder. *Journal of Consulting and Clinical Psychology, 61*(4), 611–619. doi: 10.1037/0022–006X.61.4.611

Borkovec, T. D., & Ruscio, A. M. (2001). Psychotherapy for generalized anxiety disorder. *Journal of Clinical Psychiatry, 62,* 37–45.

Bornas, X., Gelabert, J. M., Llabres, J., Balle, M., & Tortella-Feliu, M. (2011). Slope of change throughout exposure treatment for flight phobia: The role of autonomic flexibility. *Journal of Clinical Psychology, 67,* 550–560. doi: 10.1002/jclp.20780

Bradizza, C. M., Stasiewicz, P. R., & Paas, N. D. (2006). Relapse to alcohol and drug use among individuals diagnosed with co-occurring mental health and substance use disorders: A review. *Clinical Psychology Review, 26,* 162–178.

Breslan, F., Sobell, M. B., Sobell, L. C., Buchan, G., & Cunningham, J. (1997). Toward a stepped-up care approach to treating problem drinkers: The predictive validity of written treatment variables and therapist prognostic ratings. *Addiction, 92,* 1479–1489.

Burcusa, S. L., & Iacono, W. G. (2007). Risk for recurrence in depression. *Clinical Psychology Review, 27,* 959–985.

Burlingame, G. M., McClendon, D., & Alonso, J. (2011). Cohesion in group therapy. *Psychotherapy, 48*(1), 34–42.

Butler, A. C., Chapman, J. E., Forman, E. M., & Beck, A. T. (2006). The empirical status of cognitive-behavioral therapy: A review of meta-analyses. *Clinical Psychology Review, 26,* 17–31.

Carlson, C. R., & Hoyle, R. H. (1993). Efficacy of abbreviated progressive muscle relaxation training: A quantitative review of behavioral medicine research. *Journal of Consulting and Clinical Psychology, 61,* 1059–1067.

Carroll, K. M., Rounsaville, B. J., Nich, C., Gordon, L. T., Wirtz, P. W., & Gawin, F. (1994). One-year follow-up of psychotherapy and pharmacotherapy for cocaine dependence. *Archives of General Psychiatry, 51,* 989–997.

Castonguay, L. G., Goldfried, M. R., Wiser, S., & Raue, P. J. (1996). Predicting the effect of cognitive therapy for depression: A study of unique and common factors. *Journal of Consulting and Clinical Psychology, 64,* 497–504.

Chiles, J. A., Lambert, M. J., & Hatch, A. L. (1999). The impact of psychological interventions on medical cost offset: A meta-analytic review. *Clinical Psychology: Science & Practice, 6*, 204–220.

Cloitre, M., Stolbach, B. C., Herman, J. L., van der Kolk, B., Pynoos, R., Wang, J., & Petkova, E. (2009). A developmental approach to complex PTSD: Childhood and adult cumulative trauma as predictors of symptom complexity. *Journal of Traumatic Stress, 22*, 399–408.

Cohen, J. (1969). *Statistical power analysis for the behavioral sciences.* New York, NY: Academic Press.

Conradi, H. J., de Jonge, P., & Ormel, J. (2008). Prediction of the three-year course of recurrent depression in primary care patients: Different risk factors for different outcomes. *Journal of Affective Disorders, 105*, 267–271.

Cooper, M. J. (2011). Working with imagery to modify core beliefs in people with eating disorders: A clinical protocol. *Cognitive & Behavioral Practice, 18*(4), 454–465.

Cooper, Z., & Fairburn, C. G. (2011). The evolution of "enhanced" cognitive behavior therapy for eating disorders: Learning from treatment nonresponse. *Cognitive and Behavioral Practice, 18*, 394–402.

Crane, D. (2008). The cost-effectiveness of family therapy: A summary and progress report. *Journal of Family Therapy, 30*(4), 399–410.

Crane, D., & Christenson, J. D. (2008). The medical offset effect: Patterns in outpatient services reduction for high utilizers of health care. *Contemporary Family Therapy: An International Journal, 30*(2), 127–138.

Crits-Christoph, P. (1992). The efficacy of brief dynamic psychotherapy: A meta-analysis. *American Journal of Psychiatry, 149*, 151–158.

Crits-Christoph, P., Baranackie, K., Kurcias, J. S., Beck, A. T., . . . Zitrin, C. (1991). Meta-analysis of therapist effects in psychotherapy outcome studies. *Psychotherapy Research, 1*, 81–91.

Crits-Christoph, P., & Mintz, J. (1991). Implications of therapist effects for the design and analysis of comparative studies of psychotherapies. *Journal of Consulting and Clinical Psychology, 59*, 20–26.

Crits-Christoph, P., Ring-Kurtz, S., Hamilton, J., Lambert, M. J., Gallop, R., McClure, B., . . , Rotrosen, J. A (2012). A preliminary study of the effects of individual patient-level feedback in outpatient substance abuse treatment programs. *Journal of Substance Abuse Treatment*.

Cuijpers, P., & Dekker, J. (2005). Psychological treatment of depression: A systematic review. *Nederlands Tijdschrift Voor Geneeskunde, 149*, 1892–1897.

Cuijpers, P., Driessen, E., Hollon, S. D., van Oppen, P., Barth, J. & Andersson, G. (2012). The efficacy of non-directive supportive psychotherapy for adult depression: A meta-analysis. *Clinical Psychology Review, 32*(4), 280–291.

Cuijpers, P., Smit, F., Bohlmeijer, E., Hollon, S. D., & Andersson, G. (2010). Efficacy of cognitive-behavioral therapy and other psychological treatments for adult depression: Meta-analytic

study of publication bias. *British Journal of Psychiatry, 196*(3), 173–178.

Cuijpers, P. P., van Straten, A. A., Bohlmeijer, E. E., Hollon, S. D., & Andersson, G. G. (2010). The effects of psychotherapy for adult depression are overestimated: A meta-analysis of study quality and effect size. *Psychological Medicine: A Journal of Research in Psychiatry & the Allied Sciences, 40*(2), 211–223. doi: 10.1017/S0033291709006114

Cuijpers, P., van Straten, A., Schuurmans, J., van Oppen, P., Hollon, S., & Andersson, G. (2010). Psychotherapy for chronic major depression and dysthymia: A meta-analysis. *Clinical Psychology Review, 30*, 51–62.

Cuijpers, P., van Straten A., & Smit, F. (2006). Psychological treatment of late-life depression: A meta-analysis of randomized controlled trials. *International Journal of Geriatric Psychology, 21*, 1139–1149.

Cuijpers, P., van Straten, A., van Oppen, P., & Andersson, G. (2008). Psychotherapy for depression in adults: A meta-analysis of comparative outcome studies. *Journal of Consulting and Clinical Psychology, 76*(6), 909–922.

Cuijpers, P., van Straten, A., Warmerdam, L., & Andersson, G. (2008). Psychological treatment of depression: A meta-analytic database of randomized studies. *BMC Psychiatry, 8.* doi: 10.1186/1471–244X-8-36

Davidson, K. W., Gidron, Y., Mostofsky, E., & Trudeau, K. J. (2007). Hospitalization cost offset of a hostility intervention for coronary heart disease patients. *Journal of Consulting and Clinical Psychology, 75*(4), 657–662. doi: 10.1037/0022–006X.75.4.657

Degenhardt, E. K., Gatz, J. L., Jacob, J., & Tohen, M. (2012). Predictors of relapse or recurrence in bipolar I disorder. *Journal of Affective Disorders, 136*, 733–739.

De Maat, S., Dekker, J., Schoevers, R., & De Jonghe, F. (2006). Relative efficacy of psychotherapy and pharmacotherapy in the treatment of depression: A meta-analysis. *Psychotherapy Research, 16*(5), 562–572. doi: 10.1080/10503300600756402

Dew, M. A., Reynolds, C. F. III, Mulsant, B., Frank, E., Houck, P. R., Mazumdar, S. . . . Kupfer, D. J. (2001). Initial recovery patterns may predict which maintenance therapies for depression will keep older adults well. *Journal of Affective Disorders, 65*, 155–166.

Dimidjian, S., & Hollon, S.D. (2011). What can be learned when empirically supported treatments fail? *Cognitive & Behavioral Practice, 18*(3), 303–305.

Dobson, K. S. (1989). A meta-analysis of the efficacy of cognitive therapy for depression. *Journal of Consulting and Clinical Psychology, 57*, 414–419.

Dobson, K. S., Hollon, S. D., Dimidjian, S., Schmaling, K. B., Kohlenberg, R. J., Gallop, R. J., . . . Jacobson, N. S. (2008). Randomized trial of behavioral activation, cognitive therapy, and antidepressant medication in the prevention of relapse and recurrence in major depression. *Journal of Consulting and Clinical Psychology, 76,* 468–477.

Doherty, W. J., Lester, M. E., & Leigh, G. K. (1986). Marriage encounter weekends: Couples who win and couples who lose. *Journal of Marital and Family Therapy, 12,* 49–61.

Dombrovski, A. Y., Cyranowski, J. M., Mulsant, B. H., Houck, P. R., Buysse, D. J., Andreescu, C., . . . Frank, E. (2008). Which symptoms predict recurrence of depression in women treated with maintenance interpersonal psychotherapy? *Depression and Anxiety, 25,* 1060–1066.

Dow, M. G., Kenardy, J. A., Johnston, D. W., Newman, M. G., Taylor, C. B., & Thomson, A. (2007). Prognostic indices with brief and standard CBT for panic disorder: II. Moderators of outcome. *Psychological Medicine, 37*(10), 1503–1509.

Driessen, E., Cuijpers, P., Hollon, S. D., & Dekker, J. M. (2010). Does severity moderate the efficacy of psychological treatment of adult outpatient depression? A meta-analysis. *Journal of Consulting & Clinical Psychology, 78*(5), 668–680. doi: 10.1037/a0020570

Dugas, M. J., Brillon, P., Savard, P., Turcotte, J., Gaudet, A., Ladouceur, R., . . . Gervais, N. J. (2010). A randomized clinical trial of cognitive-behavioral therapy and applied relaxation for adults with generalized anxiety disorder. *Behavior Therapy, 41,* 46–58.

Dugas, M. J., Ladouceur, R., Leger, E., Freeston, M. H., Langlois, F., . . . Provencher, M. (2003). Group cognitive-behavioral therapy for generalized anxiety disorder: Treatment outcome and long-term follow-up. *Journal of Consulting and Clinical Psychology, 71,* 821–825.

Durham, R. C., Chambers, J. A., Power, K. G., Sharp, D. M., Macdonald, R. R., Major, K. A., . . . & Gumley, A. (2005). Long term outcome of cognitive behavioural therapy clinical trials in central Scotland. *Health Technology Assessment, 9,* 22–30.

Dush, D. M. (1986). The placebo in psychosocial outcome evaluations. *Evaluation & the Health Professions, 9,* 421–438.

Dush, D. M., Hirt, M. L., & Schroeder, J. E. (1989). Self-statement modification in the treatment of child behavior disorders: A meta-analysis. *Psychological Bulletin, 106,* 97–106.

Eddy, K. T., Dutra, L., Bradley, R., & Westen, D. (2004). A multidimensional meta-analysis of psychotherapy and pharmacotherapy for obsessive-compulsive disorder. *Clinical Psychology Review, 24,* 1011–1030.

Ehlers, A., Bisson, J., Clark, D. M., Creamer, M., Pilling, S., Richards, D., . . . Yule, W. (2010). Do all psychological treatments really work the same in posttraumatic stress disorder? *Clinical Psychology Review, 30*(2), 269–276. doi: 10.1016/j/cpr.2009.12.001

Eisen, S. V., Ranganathan, G., Seal, P., & Spiro, A. (2007). Measuring clinically meaningful change following mental health treatment. *Journal of Behavioral Health Services & Research, 34*(3), 272–289. doi: 10.1007/s11414–007–9066–2

Eisendrath, S., Chartier, M., & McLane, M. (2011). Adapting mindfulness-based cognitive therapy for treatment-resistant depression. *Cognitive & Behavioral Practice, 18,* 362–370.

Elkin, I. (1994). The NIMH treatment of depression collaborative research program: Where we began and where we are. In A. E. Bergin & S. L. Garfield (Eds.), *Handbook of psychotherapy and behavior change* (4th ed., pp. 114–142). New York, NY: Wiley.

Elliott, R., Bohart, A. C., Watson, J. C., & Greenberg, L. S. (2011). Empathy. *Psychotherapy, 48*(1), 43–49.

Emmelkamp, P. M., de Haan, E., & Hoogduin, C. A. (1990). Marital adjustment and obsessive-compulsive disorder. *British Journal of Psychiatry, 156,* 55–60.

Emmelkamp, P. M. G., & Powers, M. B. (2010). Agoraphobia. In J. Thomas & M. Hersen (Eds.), *Handbook of clinical psychology competencies* (pp. 723–758). New York, NY: Springer.

Eysenck, H. J. (1952). The effects of psychotherapy: An evaluation. *Journal of Consulting Psychology, 16,* 319–324.

Farber, B. A., & Doolin, E. M. (2011). Positive regard and affirmation. In J. C. Norcross (Eds.), *Psychotherapy relationships that work: Evidence-based responsiveness* (2nd ed., pp. 168–186). New York, NY: Oxford University Press.

Fennell, M. J., & Teasdale, J. D. (1987). Cognitive therapy for depression: Individual differences and the process of change. *Cognitive Therapy & Research, 11*(2), 253–271. doi: 10.1007/BF01183269

Feske, U., & Chambless, D. L. (1995). Cognitive behavioral versus exposure only treatment for social phobia: A meta-analysis. *Behavior Therapy, 26,* 695–720.

Fettes, P. A., & Peters, J. M. (1992). A meta-analysis of group treatments for bulimia nervosa. *International Journal of Eating Disorders, 11,* 97–110.

Foa, E. B., Dancu, C. V., Hembree, E. A., Jaycox, L. H., Meadows, E. A., & Street, G. P. (1999). A comparison of exposure therapy, stress inoculation training, and their combination for reducing posttraumatic stress disorder in female assault victims. *Journal of Consulting and Clinical Psychology, 67,* 194–200.

Fournier, J. C., DeRubeis, R. J., Hollon, S. D., Dimidjian, S., Amsterdam, J. D., Shelton, R. C., & Fawcett, J. (2010). Antidepressant drug effects and depression severity: A patient-level meta-analysis. *Journal of the American Medical Association, 303*(1), 47–53. doi: 10.1001/jama.2009.1943

Frank, J. D. (1976). Psychotherapy and the sense of mastery. In R. L. Spitzer & D. F. Klein (Eds.), *Evaluation of psychotherapies: Behavioral therapies, drug therapies, and their interactions* (pp. 47–56). Baltimore, MD: Johns Hopkins University Press.

Friedlander, M. L., Escudero, V., Heatherington, L., & Diamond, G. M. (2011). Alliance in couple and family therapy. *Psychotherapy, 48*(1), 25–33. doi: 10.1037/a0022060

Friedman, M. A., Detweiler-Bidell, J. B., Leventhal, H. E., Horne, R., Keitner, G. I., & Miller, I. W. (2004). Combined psychotherapy and pharmacotherapy for the treatment of major depressive disorder. *Clinical Psychology: Science & Practice, 11*, 47–68.

Gabbard, G. O., Lazar, S. G., Hornberger, J., & Spiegel, D. (1997). The economic impact of psychotherapy: A review. *American Journal of Psychiatry, 154*, 147–155.

Gaffan, E. A., Tsaousis, I., & Kemp-Wheeler, S. M. (1995). Researcher allegiance and meta- analysis: The case of cognitive therapy for depression. *Journal of Consulting and Clinical Psychology, 63*, 966–980.

Garland, A. F., Hurlburt, M. S., & Hawley, K. M. (2006). Examining psychotherapy processes in a services research context. *Clinical Psychology: Science & Practice, 13*(1), 30–46. doi: 10.1111/j/1468-2850.2006.00004.x

Gaston, L. (1990). The concept of the alliance and its role in psychotherapy: Theoretical and empirical considerations. *Psychotherapy, 27*, 143–153.

Gava, I., Barbui, C., Aguglia, E., Carlino, D., Churchill, R., De Vanna, M., & McGuire, H. F. (2007). Psychological treatments versus treatment as usual for obsessive compulsive disorder (OCD). *Cochrane Database of Systematic Reviews* (2), CD005333.

Gaynor, S. T., Weersing, V., Kolko, D. J., Birmaher, B., Heo, J., & Brent, D. A. (2003). The prevalence and impact of large sudden improvements during adolescent therapy for depression: A comparison across cognitive-behavioral, family, and supportive therapy. *Journal of Consulting and Clinical Psychology, 71*(2), 386–393. doi: 10.1037/0022-006.71.2.386

Geddes, J. R., Burgess, S., Hawton, K., Jamison, K., & Goodwin, G. M. (2004). Long-term lithium therapy for bipolar disorder: Systematic review and meta-analysis of randomized controlled trials. *American Journal of Psychiatry, 161*, 217–222.

Gloaguen, V., Cottraux, J., Cucherat, M., & Blackburn, I. M. (1998). A meta-analysis of the effects of cognitive therapy in depressed patients. *Journal of Affective Disorders, 49*, 59–72.

Godfrin, K. A., & van Heeringen, C. (2010). The effects of a mindfulness-based cognitive therapy on recurrence of depressive episodes, mental health and quality of life: A randomized controlled study. *Behavior Research and Therapy, 48*, 738–746.

Goldstein, A. P., & Stein, N. (1976). *Prescriptive psychotherapies.* New York, NY: Pergamon.

Gopinath, S., Katon, W. J., Russo, J. E., & Ludman, E. J. (2007). Clinical factors associated with relapse in primary care patients with chronic or recurrent depression. *Journal of Affective Disorders, 101*, 57–63.

Gosselin, P, Ladouceur, R., Morin, C.M., Dugas, M. J., & Baillargeon, L. (2006). Benzodiazepine discontinuation among adults with GAD: A randomized trial of cognitive-behavioral therapy. *Journal of Consulting and Clinical Psychology, 74*(5), 908–19.

Gould, R. A., Otto, M. W., & Pollack, M. H. (1995). A meta-analysis of treatment outcome for panic disorder. *Clinical Psychology Review, 15*(8), 819–844.

Grissom, R. J. (1996). The magical number .7 +- .2: Meta-meta-analysis of the probability of superior outcome in comparisons involving therapy, placebo, and control. *Journal of Consulting and Clinical Psychology, 64*, 973–982.

Haas, E., Hill, R., Lambert, M. J., & Morrell, B. (2002). Do early responders to psychotherapy maintain treatment gains? *Journal of Clinical Psychology, 58*, 1157–1172.

Haby, M. M., Donnelly, M., Corry, J., & Vos, T. (2006). Cognitive behavioral therapy for depression, panic disorder and generalized anxiety disorder: A meta-regression of factors that may predict outcome. *Australian and New Zealand Journal of Psychiatry, 40*(1), 9–19.

Hackett, M., Anderson, C., & House, A. (2004). Letters to the editor: Pharmacologic treatment of post stroke depression: A systematic review of the literature. *Topics in Stroke Rehabilitation, 11*(1), viii.

Hannan, C., Lambert, M. J., Harmon, C., Nielsen, S., Smart, D. W., Shimokawa, K., & Sutton, S. W. (2005). A lab test and algorithms for identifying clients at risk for treatment failure. *Journal of Clinical Psychology, 61*(2), 155–163. doi: 10.1002/jclp.20108

Hansen, N., Lambert, M. J., & Forman, E. M. (2002). The psychotherapy dose-response effect and its implication for treatment delivery services. *Clinical Psychology: Science and Practice, 9*, 329–343.

Hardy, G. E., Cahill, J., Stiles, W. B., Ispan, C., Macaskill, N., & Barkham, M. (2005). Sudden gains in cognitive therapy for depression: A replication and extension. *Journal of Consulting and Clinical Psychology, 73*(1), 59–67. doi: 10.1037/0022–006X.73.1.59

Harnett, P., O'Donovan, A., & Lambert, M. J. (2010). The dose response relationship in psychotherapy: Implications for social policy. *Clinical Psychologist, 14*, 39–44.

Hatfield, D., McCullough, L., Frantz, S., & Krieger, K. (2009). Do we know when our clients get worse? An investigation of therapists' ability to detect negative client change. *Clinical Psychology & Psychotherapy, 17*, 25–32. doi: org/10.1002/cpp.656

Henry, W. P., Schacht, T. E., & Strupp, H. H. (1986). Structural analysis of social behavior: Application to a study of interpersonal process in differential psychotherapeutic outcome. *Journal of Consulting and Clinical Psychology, 54*, 27–31.

Hill, C. E., Nutt-Williams, E., Heaton, K. J., Thompson, B. J., & Rhodes, R. H. (1996). Therapist retrospective recall impasses in long-term psychotherapy: A qualitative analysis. *Journal of Counseling Psychology, 43*(2), 207–217.

Hill, C. E., Thompson, B. J., Cogar, M. C., & Denman, D. W. (1993). Beneath the surface of long-term therapy: Therapist and client report of their own and each other's covert processes. *Journal of Counseling Psychology, 40*(3), 278–287. doi: 10.1037/0022-0167.40.3.278

Hiller, W., Fichter, M. M., & Rief, W. (2003). A controlled treatment study of somatoform disorders including analysis of healthcare utilization and cost-effectiveness. *Journal of Psychosomatic Research, 54*(4), 369–380. doi: 10.1016/S0022-3999(02)00397-5

Hofmann, S. G., Schulz, S. M., Meuret, A. E., Moscovitch, D. A., & Suvak, M. (2006). Sudden gains during therapy of social phobia. *Journal of Consulting and Clinical Psychology, 74*(4), 687–697. doi: 10.1037/0022-006X.74.4.687

Hofmann, S., & Smits, J. (2008). Cognitive-behavioral therapy for adult anxiety disorders: A meta-analysis of randomized placebo-controlled trials. *Journal Clinical Psychiatry, 69*, 621–632.

Hollon, S. D. (2011). Cognitive and behavior therapy in the treatment and prevention of depression. *Depression and Anxiety, 28*, 263–266.

Hollon, S. D., DeRubeis, R. J., Shelton, R. C., Amsterdam, R. M., Solomon, J. P., O'Reardon, M. L., ... Gallop, R. (2005). Prevention of relapse following cognitive therapy vs. medications in moderate to severe depression. *Archives of General Psychiatry, 62*, 417–422. doi:10.1001/archpsyc.62.4.417

Hollon, S. D., & Ponniah, K. (2010). A review of empirically supported psychological therapies for mood disorders in adults. *Depression and Anxiety, 27*, 891–932.

Horvath, A. O., Del Re, A. C., Flückiger, C., & Symonds, D. (2011). Alliance in individual psychotherapy. *Psychotherapy, 48*(1), 9–16. doi: 10.1037/a0022186

Howard, K. I., Kopta, S. M., Krause, M. S., & Orlinsky, D. E. (1986). The dose-effect relationship in psychotherapy. *American Psychologist, 41*, 159–164.

Hróbjartsson, A., & Gøtzsche, P. C. (2004) Placebo interventions for all clinical conditions. *Cochrane Database of Systematic Reviews, (3)*, CD003974.

Hróbjartsson, A., & Gøtzsche, P. C. (2007a). Powerful spin in the conclusion of Wampold et al.'s reanalysis of placebo versus no-treatment trials despite similar results as in original review. *Journal of Clinical Psychology, 63*(4), 373–377. doi: 10.1002/jclp.20357

Hróbjartsson, A., & Gøtzsche, P. C. (2007b). Wampold et al.'s reiterate spin in the conclusion of a re-analysis of placebo versus no-treatment trials despite similar results as in original review. *Journal of Clinical Psychology, 63*(4), 405–408. doi: 10.1002/jclp.20356

Hunot, V., Churchill, R., Silva de Lima, M., & Teixeira, V. (2007). Psychological therapies for generalised anxiety disorder. *Cochrane Database of Systematic Reviews* (24), CD001848.

Hunsley, J., & Westmacott, R. (2007). Interpreting the magnitude of the placebo effect: Mountain or molehill. *Journal of Clinical Psychology, 63*(4), 391–399. doi: 10.1002/jclp.20356

Ilardi, S. S., & Craighead, W. E. (1994). The role of non-specific factors in cognitive-behavior therapy for depression. *Clinical Psychology: Science & Practice, 1*, 138–156.

Ilardi, S. S., Craighead, W. E., & Evans, D. D. (1997). Modeling relapse in unipolar depression: Effects of dysfunctional cognitions and personality disorders. *Journal of Consulting and Clinical Psychology, 65*, 381–391.

Imel, Z. E., Malterer, M. B., McKay, K. M., & Wampold, B. E. (2008). A meta-analysis of psychotherapy and medication in unipolar depression and dysthymia. *Journal of Affective Disorders, 110*(3), 197–206. doi: 10.1016/j.jad.2008.03.018

Jacobson, N. S., Follette, W. C., Revenstorf, D., Baucom, D. H., Hahlweg, K., & Margolin, G. (1984). Variability in outcome and clinical significance of behavioral marital therapy: A re-analysis of outcome data. *Journal of Consulting and Clinical Psychology, 52*, 497–504.

Jacobson, N. S., & Truax, P. (1991). Clinical significance: A statistical approach to defining meaningful change in psychotherapy research. *Journal of Consulting and Clinical Psychology, 59*, 12–19.

Jarrett, R. B., Kraft, D., Doyle, J., Foster, B. M., Eaves, G. G., & Silver, P. C. (2001). Preventing recurrent depression using cognitive therapy with and without a continuation phase-A randomized clinical trial. *Archives of General Psychiatry, 58*, 381–388.

Jarrett, R. B., Vittengl, J. R., & Clark, L. A. (2008). How much cognitive therapy, for which patients, will prevent depressive relapse? *Journal of Affective Disorders, 111*, 185–192.

Kadera, S. W., Lambert, M. J., & Andrews, A. A. (1996). How much therapy is really enough? A session-by-session analysis of the psychotherapy dose-effect relationship. *Psychotherapy: Research and Practice, 5*, 1–21.

Kazdin, A. E., & Bass, D. (1989). Power to detect differences between alternative treatments in comparative psychotherapy outcome research. *Journal of Consulting and Clinical Psychology, 57*, 138–147.

Kellner, R. (1975). Psychotherapy in psychosomatic disorders. A survey of controlled studies. *Archives of General Psychiatry, 32*, 1021–1028.

Kendall, P. C., Marrs-Garcia, A., Nath, S. R., & Sheldrick, R. C. (1999). Normative comparisons for the evaluation of clinical significance.

Journal of Consulting and Clinical Psychology, 67, 285–299.

Kessler, R. C., McGonagle, K. A., Zhao, S., Nelson, C. B., Hughes, M., Eshleman, S., . . . Kendler, K. S. (1994). Lifetime and 12-month prevalence of DSM-III-R psychiatric disorders in the United States. *Archives of General Psychiatry, 51,* 8–19.

Koppers, D. D., Peen, J. J., Niekerken, S. S., Van, R. R., & Dekker, J. J. (2011). Prevalence and risk factors for recurrence of depression five years after short term psychodynamic therapy. *Journal of Affective Disorders, 134,* 468–472. doi: 10.1016/j.jad.2011.05.027

Kopta, S. M., Howard, K. I., Lowry, J. L., & Beutler, L. E. (1994). Patterns of symptomatic recovery in psychotherapy. *Journal of Consulting and Clinical Psychology, 62,* 1009–1016.

Krupnick, J. L., Sotsky, S. M., Elkin, I., Simmens, S., Moyer, J., Watkins, J., & Pilkonis, P. A. (1996). The role of the therapeutic alliance in psychotherapy and pharmacotherapy outcome: Findings in the national institute of mental health treatment of depression collaborative research program. *Journal of Consulting and Clinical Psychology, 64,* 532–539.

Kuyken, W., Byford, S., Taylor, R. S., Watkins, E., Holden, E., White, K., . . . Teasdale, J. D. (2008). Mindfulness-based cognitive therapy to prevent relapse in recurrent depression. *Journal of Consulting and Clinical Psychology, 76,* 966–978.

Ladouceur, R., Dugas, M. J., Freeston, M. H., Léger, E., Gagnon, F., Thibodeau, N. (2000). Efficacy of a new cognitive-behavioral treatment for generalized anxiety disorder: Evaluation in a controlled clinical trial. *Journal of Consulting and Clinical Psychology, 68,* 957–964.

Lambert, M. J. (1992). Psychotherapy outcome research: Implications for integrative and eclectic therapists. In J. C. Norcross & M. R. Goldfried (Eds.), *Handbook of psychotherapy integration* (pp. 94–129). New York, NY: Basic Books.

Lambert, M. J. (2010). *Prevention of treatment failure: The use of measuring, monitoring, & feedback in clinical practice.* Washington, DC: American Psychological Association Press.

Lambert, M. J., & Bailey, R. J. (2012). Measures of clinically significant change. In H. Cooper, P. M. Camic, D. L. Long, A. T. Panter, D. Rindskopf, & K. J. Sher (Eds.), *APA handbook of research methods in psychology, Vol 3: Data analysis and research publication* (pp. 147–160). Washington, DC: American Psychological Association. doi: 10.103/13621–007

Lambert, M. J., & Bergin, A.E. (1973). Psychotherapeutic outcomes and issues related to behavioral and humanistic approaches. *Cornell Journal of Social Relations, 8,* 47–61.

Lambert, M. J., & Bergin, A. E. (1994). The effectiveness of psychotherapy. In A. E. Bergin & S. L. Garfield (Eds.), *Handbook of psychotherapy and behavior change* (4th ed., pp. 143–189). New York, NY: Wiley.

Lambert, M. J., Bergin, A. E., & Collins, J. L. (1977). Therapist-induced deterioration in psychotherapy. In A. S. Gurman & A. M. Razin (Eds.), *Effective psychotherapy: A handbook of research* (pp. 452–481). New York, NY: Pergamon.

Lambert, M. J., Hansen, N. B., & Finch, A. E. (2001). Patient-focused research: Using patient outcome data to enhance treatment effects. *Journal of Consulting and Clinical Psychology, 69,* 159–172.

Lambert, M.J., & Ogles, B. M. (2004). The efficacy and effectiveness of psychotherapy. In M. J. Lambert (Ed.), *Bergin and Garfield's handbook of psychotherapy and behavior change* (5th ed., pp. 139–193). Hoboken, NJ: Wiley.

Lambert, M. J., Shapiro, D. A., & Bergin, A. E. (1986). The effectiveness of psychotherapy. In S. L. Garfield & A. E. Bergin (Eds.), *Handbook of psychotherapy and behavior change* (3rd ed., pp. 157–211). New York, NY: Wiley.

Landman, J. T., & Dawes, R. M. (1982). Smith and Glass' conclusions stand up under scrutiny. *American Psychologist, 37,* 504–516.

Lazar, S. G. (2010). *Psychotherapy is worth it.* Arlington, VA: American Psychiatric Press.

Lipsey, M. W., & Wilson, D. B. (1993). The efficacy of psychological, educational, and behavioral treatment: Confirmation from meta-analysis. *American Psychologist, 48,* 1181–1209.

Luborsky, L., & DeRubeis, R. J. (1984). The use of psychotherapy treatment manuals—A small revolution in psychotherapy research style. *Clinical Psychology Review, 4,* 5–14.

Luborsky, L., McClellan, A. T., Woody, G. E., O'Brien, C. P., & Auerbach, A. (1985). Therapist success and its determinants. *Archives of General Psychiatry, 42,* 602–611.

Luborsky, L., Singer, J., & Luborsky, L. (1975). Comparative studies of psychotherapy. *Archives of General Psychiatry, 32,* 995–1008.

Lumley, J., Austin, M. P., & Mitchell, C. (2004) Intervening to reduce depression after birth: A systematic review of the randomized trials. *International Journal of Technology Assessment in Health Care, 20*(2), 128–144.

Lunnen, K. M., & Ogles, B. M. (1998). A multiperspective, multivariable evaluation of reliable change. *Journal of Consulting and Clinical Psychology, 66,* 400–410.

Maling, M. S., Gurtman, M. B., & Howard, K. I. (1995). The response of interpersonal problems to varying doses of psychotherapy. *Psychotherapy Research, 5,* 63–75.

Marrs, R. W. (1995). A meta-analysis of bibliotherapy studies. *American Journal of Community Psychology, 23,* 843–870.

Marchand, A., Roberge, P., Primiano, S., & Germain, V. (2009). A randomized, controlled clinical trial of standard, group and brief cognitive-behavioral therapy for panic disorder with agoraphobia: A two-year follow-up. *Journal of Anxiety Disorders, 23*(8), 1139–1147. doi: 10.1016/j.janxdis.2009.07.019

Martin, D. J., Garske, J. P., & Davis, M. K. (2000). Relation of the therapeutic alliance with outcome and other variables: A meta-analytic review. *Journal of Consulting and Clinical Psychology, 68*, 438–450.

McCauley, E., Schloredt, K., Gudmundsen, G., Martell, C, & Dimidjian, S. (2011). Expanding behavioral activation to depressed adolescents: Lessons learned in treatment development. *Cognitive and Behavioral Practice, 18*, 371–383.

McNeilly, C. L., & Howard, K. I. (1991). The effects of psychotherapy: A reevaluation based on dosage. *Psychotherapy Research, 1*, 74–78.

McRoberts, C. H., Burlingame, G. M., & Hoag, M. J. (1998). Comparative efficacy of individual and group psychotherapy: A meta-analytic perspective. *Group Dynamics: Theory, Research, & Practice, 59*, 101–111.

Meltzoff, J., & Kornreich, M. (1970). *Research in psychotherapy*. New York, NY: Atherton.

Mendes, D. D., Mello, M. F., Ventura, P., Passarela, C. M., & Mari, J. J. (2008). A systematic review on the effectiveness of cognitive behavioral therapy for posttraumatic stress disorder. *International Journal of Psychiatry & Medicine, 38*(3), 241–259.

Miklowitz, D. J., & Scott, J. (2009). Psychosocial treatments for bipolar disorder: Cost-effectiveness, mediating mechanisms, and future directions. *Bipolar Disorders, 11*, 110–122.

Millenson, M. L. (1997). *Demanding medical excellence: Doctors and accountability in the information age*. Chicago, IL: University of Chicago Press.

Milrod, B., Leon, A. C., Busch, F., Rudden, M., Schwalberg, M., Clarkin, J., . . . Shear, M. K. (2007). A randomized controlled clinical trial of psychoanalytic psychotherapy for panic disorder. *The American Journal of Psychiatry, 164*(2), 265–272. doi: 10.1176/appi.ajp.164.2.265

Mitte, K. (2005). Meta-analysis of cognitive-behavioral treatments for generalized anxiety disorder: A comparison with pharmacotherapy. *Psychological Bulletin, 131*, 785–795.

Mohr, D. C. (1995). Negative outcome in psychotherapy: A critical review. *Clinical Psychology: Science and Practice, 2*, 1–27.

Mohr, D. C., Beutler, L. E., Engle, D., Shoham-Salomon, V., Bergan, J., Kaszniak, A. W., & Yost, E. B. (1990). Identification of patients at risk for nonresponse and negative outcome in psychotherapy. *Journal of Consulting and Clinical Psychology, 58*, 622–628.

Mohr, D. C., & Goodkin, D. E. (1999). Treatment of depression in multiple sclerosis: Review and meta-analysis. *Clinical Psychology: Science & Practice, 6*(1). doi: 10.1093/clipsy/6.1.1

Mumford, E., Schlesinger, H. J., Glass, G. V., Patrick, C., & Cuerdon, T. (1984). A new look at evidence about reduced cost of medical utilization following mental health treatment. *Journal of Psychotherapy Practice and Research, 7*, 68–86.

Murtagh, D. R. R., & Greenwood, K. M. (1995). Identifying effective psychological treatments for insomnia: A meta-analysis. *Journal of Consulting and Clinical Psychology, 63*, 79–89.

Najavits, L. M., & Gunderson, J. G. (1995). Better than expected: Improvements in borderline personality disorder in a 3-year prospective outcome study. *Comprehensive Psychiatry, 36*, 296–302.

Nakajima, M. & al'Absi, M. (2012). Predictors of risk for smoking relapse in men and women: A prospective examination. *Psychology of Addictive Behaviors*. doi: 10.1037/a0027280

National Advisory Mental Health Council. (2001). *Blueprint for change: Research on child and adolescent mental health. A report by the National Advisory Mental Health Council's Workgroup on Child and Adolescent Mental Health Intervention Development and Deployment*. Bethesda. MD: National Institutes of Health/National Institute of Mental Health.

Nelson, J. C., Delucchi, K., & Schneider, L. S. (2008). Efficacy of second generation antidepressants in late-life depression: A meta-analysis of the evidence. *American Journal of Geriatric Psychiatry, 16*, 558–567.

Newman, C. F. (2011). When clients' morbid avoidance and chronic anger impede their response to cognitive-behavioral therapy for depression. *Cognitive & Behavioral Practice, 18*(3), 350–361. doi: 10.1016/j.cbpra.2010.07.004

Newman, M. G., Castonguay, L. G., Borkovec, T. D., & Molnar, C. (2004). Integrative psychotherapy. In R. G. Heimberg, C. L. Turk, D. S. Mennin, R. G. Heimberg, C. L. Turk, & D. S. Mennin (Eds.), *Generalized anxiety disorder: Advances in research and practice* (pp. 320–350). New York, NY: Guilford Press.

Nicholson, R. A., & Berman, J. S. (1983). Is follow up necessary in evaluating psychotherapy? *Psychological Bulletin, 93*, 261–278.

Norcross, J. (Ed.). (2011). *Psychotherapy relationships that work: Evidence-based responsiveness* (2nd ed.). New York, NY: Oxford University Press.

Norcross, J. C., & Wampold, B. E. (2011). Evidence-based therapy relationships: Research conclusions and clinical practices. In J. C. Norcross (Eds.), *Psychotherapy relationships that work: Evidence-based responsiveness* (2nd ed., pp. 423–430). New York, NY: Oxford University Press.

Norton, P. J., & Price, E. C. (2007). A meta-analytic review of adult cognitive-behavioral treatment outcome across the anxiety disorders. *Journal of Nervous &Mental Disease, 195*(6), 521–531. doi: 10.1097/01.nd.0000253843.70149.9a

Oei, T. P. S., & Shuttlewood, G. J. (1996). Specific and nonspecific factors in psychotherapy: A case of cognitive therapy for depression. *Clinical Psychology Review, 16*, 83–103.

Ogles, B. M., Lambert, M. J., & Sawyer, J. D. (1995). Clinical significance of the national institute of mental health treatment of depression collaborative research program data. *Journal of Consulting and Clinical Psychology, 63*, 321–326.

Ogles, B. M., Lunnen, K. M., & Bonesteel, K. (2001). Clinical significance: History, definitions, and applications. *Clinical Psychology Review, 21*, 421–446.

Okiishi, J. C., Lambert, M. J., Eggett, D., Nielsen, L., Dayton, D. D., & Vermeersch, D. A. (2006). An analysis of therapist treatment effects: Toward providing feedback to individual therapists on their clients' psychotherapy outcome. *Journal of Clinical Psychology, 62*(9), 1157–1172. doi: 10.1002/jclp.20272

Okiishi, J., Lambert, M. J., Nielsen, S. L., & Ogles, B. M. (2003). Waiting for super shrink: An empirical analysis of therapist effects. *Clinical Psychology & Psychotherapy, 10*(6), 361–373. doi: 10.1002/cpp.383

Orlinsky, D. E., & Howard, K. I. (1980). Gender and psychotherapeutic outcome. In A. M. Brodsky & R. T. Hare-Mustin (Eds.), *Women and psychotherapy* (pp. 3–34). New York, NY: Guilford Press.

Pampanolla, S., Bollini, P., Tibaldi, G., Kupelnick, B., & Munizza, C. (2004). Combined pharmacotherapy and psychological treatment for depression: A systematic review. *Archives of General Psychiatry, 61*, 714–719.

Perlis, R. H., Welge, J. A., Vornik, L. A., Hirschfeld, R. M., & Keck, P. E., Jr. (2006). Atypical antipsychotics in the treatment of mania: A meta-analysis of randomized, placebo-controlled trials. *Journal of Clinical Psychiatry, 67*, 509–516.

Prioleau, L., Murdock, M., & Brody, N. (1983). An analysis of psychotherapy versus placebo studies. *Behavioral & Brain Sciences, 6*, 275–310.

Quitkin, F. M., McGrath, P. J., Stewart, J. W., Taylor, B. P., & Klein, D. F. (1996). Can the effects of antidepressants be observed in the first two weeks of treatment? *Neuropsychopharmacology, 15*, 390–394.

Rachman, S. J., & Wilson, G. T. (1980). *The effects of psychological therapy* (2nd ed.). New York, NY: Pergamon.

Reese, R. J., Toland, M. D., & Hopkins, N. B. (2011). Replicating and extending the good-enough level model of change: Considering session frequency. *Psychotherapy Research, 21*, 608–619.

Regan, A. M., & Hill, C. E. (1992). Investigation of what clients and counselors do not say in brief therapy. *Journal of Counseling Psychology, 39*(2), 168–174.

Renaud, J., Brent, D. A., Baugher, M., Birmaher, B., Kolko, D. J., & Bridge, J. (1998). Rapid response to psychosocial treatment for adolescent depression: A two-year follow-up. *Journal of the American Academy of Child & Adolescent Psychiatry, 37*(11), 1184–1190. doi: 10.1097/00004583–199811000–00019

Resick, P. A., Williams, L. F., Suvak, M. K., Monson, C. M., & Gradus, J. L. (2012). Long-term outcomes of cognitive-behavioral treatments for posttraumatic stress disorder among female rape survivors. *Journal of Consulting and Clinical Psychology, 80*, 201–210.

Rhodes, R. H., Hill, C. E., Thompson, B. J., & Elliott, R. (1994). Client retrospective recall of resolved and unresolved misunderstanding events. *Journal of Counseling Psychology, 41*(4), 473–483. doi: 10.1037/0022–0167.41.4.473

Richards, D. (2011). Prevalence and clinical course for depression: A review. *Clinical Psychology Review, 31*, 1117–1125.

Riemer, M., & Bickman, L. (2011). Using program theory to link social psychology and program evaluation. In M. M. Mark, S. I. Donaldson, & B. Campbell (Eds.), *Social psychology and evaluation* (pp. 104–139). New York, NY: Guilford Press.

Ringel, J. S., & Sturm, R. (2001). Financial burden and out-of-pocket expenditures for mental health across difference socioeconomic groups: Results from healthcare for communities. *Journal of Mental Health Policy & Economics, 4*(3), 141–150.

Rizvi, S. L. (2011). Treatment failure in dialectical behavior therapy. *Cognitive and Behavioral Practice, 18*(3), 403–412. doi: 10.1016/j.cbpra.2010.05.003

Robinson, L. A., Berman, J. S., & Neimeyer, R. A. (1990). Psychotherapy for the treatment of depression: A comprehensive review of controlled outcome research. *Psychological Bulletin, 108*, 30–49.

Rosa-Alcázar, A. I., Sánchez-Meca, J., Gómez-Conesa, A., & Marín-Martínez, F. (2008). Psychological treatment of obsessive-compulsive disorder: A meta-analysis. *Clinical Psychology Review, 28*(8), 1310–1325. doi: 10.1016/j.cpr.2008.07.001

Rosenzweig, S. (1936). Some implicit common factors in diverse methods of psychotherapy. *American Journal of Orthopsychiatry, 6*, 412–415.

Rounsaville, B. J., O'Malley, S., Foley, S., & Weissman, M. M. (1988). Role of manual-guided training in the conduct and efficacy of interpersonal psychotherapy for depression. *Journal of Consulting and Clinical Psychology, 56*, 681–688.

Rucci, P., Frank, E., Scocco, P., Calugi, S., Miniati, M., Fagiolini, A., & Cassano, G. B. (2011). Treatment-emergent suicidal ideation during 4 months of acute management of unipolar major depression of SSRI pharmacotherapy or interpersonal psychotherapy in a randomized clinical trial. *Depression & Anxiety, 28*, 303–309.

Rufer, M., Hand, I., Alsleben, H., Braatz, A., Ortmann, J., Katenkamp, B., . . . Peter, H. (2005). Long-term course and outcome of obsessive-compulsive patients after cognitive-behavioral therapy in combination with either fluvoxamine or placebo: A 7-year follow-up of a randomized double-blind trial. *European Archives of Psychiatry and Clinical Neuroscience, 255*, 121–1288.

Scogin, F., Floyd, M., Jamison, C., Ackerson, J., Landreville, P., & Bissonnette, L. (1996). Negative outcomes: What is the evidence on self-administered treatments? *Journal of Consulting and Clinical Psychology, 64*, 1086–1089.

Segal, Z. V., Bieling, P., Young, T., MacQueen, G., Cooke, R., Martin, L,..., Levitan, R. D. (2010). Antidepressant monotherapy vs. sequential pharmacotherapy and mindfulness-based cognitive therapy, or placebo, for relapse prophylaxis in recurrent depression. *Archives of General Psychiatry, 67*, 1256–1264.

Seidler, G. H., & Wagner, F. E. (2006). Comparing the efficacy of EMDR and trauma-focused cognitive-behavioral therapy in the treatment of PTSD: A meta-analytic study. *Psychological Medicine: A Journal of Research in Psychiatry & The Allied Sciences, 36*(11), 1515–1522. doi: 10.1017/S0033291706007963

Seligman, M. E. P. (1995). The effectiveness of psychotherapy: The Consumer Reports study. *American Psychologist, 50*, 965–974.

Shadish, W. R., Matt, G. E., Navarro, A. M., Siegle, G., Crits-Christoph, P., Hazelrigg, M. D.,...Weiss, B. (1997). Evidence that therapy works in clinically representative conditions. *Journal of Consulting and Clinical Psychology, 65*, 355–365.

Shadish, W. R., Navarro, A. M., Matt, G. E., & Phillips, G. (2000). The effects of psychological therapies under clinically representative conditions: A meta-analysis. *Psychological Bulletin, 126*, 512–529.

Shadish, W. R., & Sweeney, R. B. (1991). Mediators and moderators in meta-analysis: There's a reason we don't let dodo birds tell us which psychotherapies should have prizes. *Journal of Consulting and Clinical Psychology, 59*, 883–893.

Shapiro, D. A., & Shapiro, D. (1982). Meta-analysis of comparative therapy outcome studies: A replication and refinement. *Psychological Bulletin, 92*, 581–604.

Shirk, S. R., Karver, M. S., & Brown, R. (2011). The alliance in child and adolescent psychotherapy. *Psychotherapy, 48*(1), 17–24. doi: 10.1037/a0022181

Sharpe, D. (1997). Of apples and oranges, file drawers and garbage: Why validity issues in meta-analysis will not go away. *Clinical Psychology Review, 17*, 881–901.

Sheard, T., & Maguire, P. (1999). The effect of psychological interventions on anxiety and depression in cancer patients: Results of two meta-analyses. *British Journal of Cancer, 80*(11), 1770–1780.

Sheperd, M. (1984). What price psychotherapy? *British Medical Journal, 288*, 809–810.

Sherman, J. J. (1998). Effects of psychotherapeutic treatments for PTSD: A meta-analysis of controlled clinical trials. *Journal of Traumatic Stress, 11*, 413–435.

Shimokawa, K., Lambert, M. J., & Smart, D. W. (2010). Enhancing treatment outcome of patients at risk of treatment failure: Meta-analytic and mega-analytic review of a psychotherapy quality assurance system. *Journal of Consulting and Clinical Psychology, 78*(3), 298–311. doi: 10.1037/a0019247

Shirk, S. R., Karver, M. S., & Brown, R. (2011). The alliance in child and adolescent psychotherapy. *Psychotherapy, 48*(1), 17–24. doi: 10.1037/a0022181

Shoham-Salomon, V., & Rosenthal, R. (1987). Paradoxical interventions: A meta-analysis. *Journal of Consulting and Clinical Psychology, 55*, 22–28.

Simon, W., Lambert, M. J., Busath, G., Vazquez, A., Berkeljon, A., Hyer, K.,..., Berrett, M. (in press). Effects of providing patient progress feedback and clinical support tools to psychotherapists in an inpatient eating disorders treatment program: A randomized controlled study.

Simon, W., Lambert, M. J., Harris, M. W., Busath, G., & Vazquez, A. (2012, July 4). Providing patient progress information and clinical support tools to therapists: Effects on patients at risk for treatment failure. *Psychotherapy Research*. Advance online publication.

Smith, M. L., & Glass, G. V. (1977). Meta-analysis of psychotherapy outcome studies. *American Psychologist, 32*, 752–760.

Smith, M. L., Glass, G. V., & Miller, T. I. (1980). *The benefits of psychotherapy*. Baltimore, MD: Johns Hopkins University Press.

Solomon, D. A., Keller, M., Leon, A. C., Mueller, T. I., Lavori, P. W., Shea, M. T.,...Endicott, J. (2000). Multiple recurrences of major depressive disorder. *American Journal of Psychiatry, 157*, 229–233.

Solomon, D. A., Leon, A. C., Endicott, J., Mueller, T. I., Coryell, W., Shea, M. T., & Keller, M. B. (2004). Psychosocial impairment and recurrence of major depression. *Comprehensive Psychiatry, 45*, 423–430.

Solomon, D. A., Leon, A. C., Mueller, T. I., Posternak, M., Endicott, J., & Keller, M. B. (2008). Predicting recovery from episodes of major depression. *Journal of Affective Disorders, 107*, 285–291.

Stiles, W. B., Barkham, M., Connell, J., & Mellor-Clark, J. (2008). Responsive regulation of treatment duration in routine practice in United Kingdom primary care settings: Replication in a larger sample. *Journal of Consulting and Clinical Psychology, 76*, 298–305.

Stiles, W. B., Leach, C., Barkham, M., Lucock, M., Iveson, S., Shapiro, D. A., & Hardy, G. E. (2003). Early sudden gains in psychotherapy under routine clinic conditions: Practice-based evidence. *Journal of Consulting and Clinical Psychology, 71*(1), 14–21. doi: 10.1037/0022-006X.71.1.14

Strupp, H. H. (1993). The Vanderbilt psychotherapy studies: Synopsis. *Journal of Consulting and Clinical Psychology, 61*(3), 431–433. doi: 10.1037/0022–006X.61.3.431

Svartberg, M., & Stiles, T. C. (1991). Comparative effects of short-term psychodynamic psychotherapy: A meta-analysis. *Journal of Consulting and Clinical Psychology, 59,* 704–714.

Tang, T. Z., & DeRubeis, R. J. (1999a). Reconsidering rapid early response in cognitive behavioral therapy for depression. *Clinical Psychology: Science & Practice, 6*(3), 283–288. doi: 10.1093/clipsy/6.3.283

Tang, T. Z., & DeRubeis, R. J. (1999b). Sudden gains and critical sessions in cognitive-behavioral therapy for depression. *Journal of Consulting and Clinical Psychology, 67*(6), 894–904. doi: 10.1037/0022–0066x.67.6.894

Tang, T. Z., DeRubeis, R. J., Beberman, R., & Pham, T. (2005). Cognitive changes, critical sessions, and sudden gains in cognitive-behavioral therapy for depression. *Journal of Consulting and Clinical Psychology, 73*(1), 168–172. doi: 10.103/0022–006X.73.1.168

Tang, T. Z., DeRubeis, R. J., Hollon, S. D., Amsterdam, J., & Shelton, R. (2007). Sudden gains in cognitive therapy of depression and depression relapse/recurrence. *Journal of Consulting and Clinical Psychology, 75*(3), 404–408. doi: 10.1037/0022–006X.75.3.404

Tang, T. Z., Luborsky, L., & Andrusyna, T. (2002). Sudden gains in recovering from depression: Are they also found in psychotherapies other than cognitive-behavioral therapy. *Journal of Consulting and Clinical Psychology, 70*(2), 444–447. doi: 10.1037/0022–006X.70.2.444

Taylor, S. (1996). Meta-analysis of cognitive-behavioral treatment for social phobia. *Journal of Behavior Therapy and Experimental Psychiatry, 27,* 1–9.

Taylor, D. J., Walters, H. M., Vittengl, J. R., Krebaum, S., & Jarrett, R. B. (2010). Which depressive symptoms remain after response to cognitive therapy of depression and predict relapse and recurrence? *Journal of Affective Disorders, 123,* 181–187.

ten Doesschate, M. C., Bockting, C. H., Koeter, M. J., & Schene, A. H. (2010). Prediction of recurrence in recurrent depression: A 5.5-year prospective study. *Journal of Clinical Psychiatry, 71*(8), 984–991. doi: 10.4088/JCP.08m04858blu

Thompson, M. G., Thompson, L., & Gallagher-Thompson, D. (1995). Linear and nonlinear changes in mood between psychotherapy sessions: Implications for treatment outcome and relapse risk. *Psychotherapy Research, 5,* 327–336.

Thuile, J., Christian, E., & Rouillon, F. (2009). Long-term outcome of anxiety disorders: A review of double-blind studies. *Current Opinion in Psychiatry, 22,* 84–89. doi: 10.1097/YCO.0b013e32831a726d

Tillitski, C. J. (1990). A meta-analysis of estimated effect sizes for group versus individual versus control treatments. *International Journal of Group Psychotherapy, 40,* 215–224.

Trotter, V. K., Lambert, M. J., Burlingame, G. M., Rees, F., Carpenter, B. N., Steffen, P. R., & Eggett, D. (2009). Measuring work productivity with a mental health self-report measure. *Journal of Occupational and Environmental Medicine, 51*(6), 739–746. doi: 10.1097/JOM.0b013e3181a83567

van Oppen, P., van Balkom, A. J., de Haan, E., & van Dyck, R. (2005). Cognitive therapy and exposure in vivo alone and in combination with fluvoxamine in obsessive-compulsive disorder: A 5-year follow-up. *Journal of Clinical Psychiatry, 66*(11), 1415–22.

Vittengl, J. R., Clark, L., & Jarrett, R. B. (2005). Validity of sudden gains in acute phase treatment of depression. *Journal of Consulting and Clinical Psychology, 73*(1), 173–182.

Walfish, S., McAlister, B., O'Donnell, P., & Lambert, M. J. (2012). An investigation of self-assessment bias in mental health providers. *Psychological Reports, 110*(2), 1–6. doi: 10.2466/02.07.17

Wampold, B. E. (2001). *The great psychotherapy debate: Models, methods, and findings.* Mahwah, NJ: Erlbaum.

Wampold, B. E. (2007). Psychotherapy: The humanistic (and effective) treatment. *American Psychologist, 62*(8), 857–873. doi: 10.1037/0003–006X.62.8.857

Wampold, B. E., Imel, Z. E., & Minami, T. (2007). The placebo effect: "Relatively large" and "robust" enough to survive another assault. *Journal of Clinical Psychology, 63*(4), 401–403. doi: 10.1002/jclp.20350

Wampold, B. E., Minami, T., Tierney, S., Baskin, T. W., & Bhati, K. S. (2005). The placebo is powerful: Estimating placebo effects in medicine and psychotherapy from randomized clinical trials. *Journal of Clinical Psychology, 61*(7), 835–854. doi: 10.1002/jclp.20129

Wampold, B. E., Mondin, G. W., Moody, M., Stich, F., Benson, K., & Ahn, H. (1997). A meta-analysis of outcome studies comparing bona fide psychotherapies: Empirically, "all must have prizes." *Psychological Bulletin, 122,* 203–215.

Warren, J. S., Nelson, P. L., Mondragon, S. A., Baldwin, S. A., & Burlingame, G. M. (2010). Youth psychotherapy change trajectories and outcomes in usual care: Community mental health versus managed care settings. *Journal of Consulting and Clinical Psychology, 78*(2), 144–155. doi: 10.1037/a0018544

Weck, F., Weigel, M., Hautzinger, M., Barocka, A., Schlösser, R. G., & Stangier, U. (2012). Relapses in recurrent depression 1 year after psychoeducational treatment: The role of therapist adherence and competence, and the therapeutic alliance. *Psychiatry Research, 30,* 51–55.

Weiss, B., Catron, T., Harris, V., & Phung, T. M. (1999). The effectiveness of traditional child psychotherapy. *Journal of Consulting and Clinical Psychology, 67*(1), 82–94. doi: 10.1037/0022–006X.67.1.82

Weisz, J. R. (2004). *Psychotherapy for children and adolescents: Evidence-based treatments and case examples.* New York, NY: Cambridge University Press.

Weisz, J. R., Donenberg, G. R., Han, S. S., & Weiss, B. (1995). Bridging the gap between laboratory and clinic in child and adolescent psychotherapy. *Journal of Consulting and Clinical Psychology, 63*(5), 688–701. doi: 10.1037/0022–006X63.5.688

Weisz, J. R., Doss, A., & Hawley, K. M. (2005). Youth psychotherapy outcome research: A review and critique of the evidence base. *Annual Review of Psychology, 56*, 337–363. doi: 10.1146/annurev.psych.55.090902.141449

Weisz, J. R., Weiss, B., & Donenberg, G. R. (1992). The lab versus the clinic: Effects of child and adolescent psychotherapy. *American Psychologist, 47*, 1578–1585.

Wilkins, W. (1984). Psychotherapy: The powerful placebo. *Journal of Consulting and Clinical Psychology, 52*, 570–573.

Whittal, M. L., Robichaud, M., Thordarson, D. S., & McLean, P. D. (2008). Group and individual treatment of obsessive-compulsive disorder using cognitive therapy and exposure plus response prevention: A 2-year follow-up of two randomized trials. *Journal of Consulting and Clinical Psychology, 76*, 1003–1014.

Yang, H., Chuzi, S., Sinicropi-Yao, L., Johnson, D., Chen, Y., Clain, A...Fava, M. (2010). Type of residual symptom and risk relapse during the continuance/maintenance phase treatment of major depressive disorder with the selective serotonin reuptake inhibitor fluoxetine. *European Archives of Psychiatry & Clinical Neuroscience, 260*, 145–150.

CHAPTER 7

THE CLIENT IN PSYCHOTHERAPY

ARTHUR C. BOHART AND AMY GREAVES WADE

In recent years there has been a shift toward greater recognition of the client's role as an active participant in psychotherapy. In 1994 Bergin and Garfield said, "Another important observation regarding the client variable is that it is the client more than the therapist who implements the change process. If the client does not absorb, utilize, and follow through on the facilitative efforts of the therapist, then nothing happens. Rather than argue over whether or not 'therapy works,' we could address ourselves to the question of whether "the client works"! In this regard, there needs to be a reform in our thinking about the efficacy of psychotherapy. Clients are not inert objects on whom techniques are administered. They are not dependent variables upon whom independent variables operate" (pp. 825–826).

There is evidence that clients make the single strongest contribution to outcome. Lambert (1992) places "extratherapeutic factors," consisting of the client and factors in the client's life, at 40% of the variance in final outcome. This compares to 30% for common factors (such as the therapeutic relationship), 15% for techniques, and 15% for placebos. Wampold (2001) estimates that all therapy factors combined account for about 13% of outcome variance. Wampold (2010) states that most of the remaining 87% is likely due to the client. Norcross and Lambert (2011) suggest that 40% of the variance in outcome is unexplained. Of the remaining 60%, they attribute 30% to the client and 30% to all other factors combined. Orlinsky, Grawe, and Parks

(1994) and Orlinsky, Rønnestadt, and Willutski (2004) have documented that various client factors are the best predictors of improvement. Orlinsky et al. (1994) concluded, "the quality of the patient's participation in therapy stands out as the most important determinant of outcome" (p. 361). In keeping with these scholarly conclusions, there is evidence that clients benefit from a wide range of therapy approaches (i.e., the "Dodo bird" verdict, Luborsky, Singer, & Luborsky, 1975; Wampold, 2010). Furthermore, they benefit from self-help (Norcross, 2006) and Internet-provided procedures (Caspar & Berger, 2011) as much or nearly as much as from face-to-face therapy. Bohart and Tallman (1999, 2010) have explained this phenomenon by arguing that clients are at the center of the healing process. They are able to utilize widely differing methods of promoting change in order to grow. Bohart and Tallman have suggested this is the most parsimonious explanation for the Dodo bird verdict, that is, that psychotherapies have equal effects.

In this chapter we highlight the role of the client as an active learner and problem solver who contributes to therapy process and outcome. This continues an evolution in how the client's contribution has been conceptualized. Garfield's earlier reviews in this handbook (1971, 1978, 1986, 1994) emphasized research on specific client variables and their relationship to premature termination and outcome. Results of these studies were generally mixed. This led Clarkin and Levy (2004) to emphasize a more dynamic view of the client-therapy relationship. They suggested that these earlier results were due to the fact that, from the start of therapy, client variables begin to dynamically interact with therapist and treatment

The authors wish to thank Michelle Yep-Martin and Makenna Berry for their assistance in the literature search.

variables. Therefore it is unlikely that simple relationships will be found. This was seconded by Beutler and colleagues (2004). They argued that the reason no clear relationship between interventions and outcome has been found is that clients react differently to different interventions.

From a research perspective, we consider a change toward looking at therapy from the client's side of the interaction to be something of a paradigm shift. Most research and theory focuses on therapists' interventions and on how clients receive and respond to them. However, clients are not passive recipients of treatment like patients in surgery. Rather, they actively intersect with what therapists have to offer (even if that "activity" sometimes consists of adopting a passive or resistant stance). How they learn involves their degree of involvement, their resonance with therapists and methods, how much effort they put in, their own creativity, and how they interpret and implement the input they receive.

There is one sense in which it has always been held that clients' perspectives and actions matter. This has usually been interpreted negatively: Clients' distortions, transference relationships, and dysfunctional beliefs get in the way of therapy. Although this happens, research findings support a more proactive view. One finding, for instance, is that clients' perspectives and beliefs correlate positively with outcome, suggesting the possibility that how they construe therapy either contributes to or reflects a positive therapy process.

Viewing the client as an active contributor is compatible with American Psychological Association (2006) policy on evidence-based practice. Clients' preferences, values, and perceptions should be included in therapeutic decision making. The client is also featured in recent efforts to reform the behavioral health care system (Bohanske & Franzcik, 2010). The President's New Freedom Commission on Mental Health (2003) argued that consumers should be placed "at the *center* of the system of care" (p. 27).

The recovery movement has also emphasized empowering consumers of mental health services. Recovery focuses less on treating pathology and more on supporting client strength (Bohanske & Franzcik, 2010). Compatible with this, Bergin and Garfield (1994) concluded: "As therapists have depended more upon the client's resources, more change seems to occur" (p. 826). Research has begun to substantiate this view. Gassman and Grawe (2006) found, for instance, that successful

therapists paid attention to clients' strengths starting in the first session, while unsuccessful therapists focused on problems but neglected strengths.

As in previous editions of this handbook, we focus on research that is linked to outcome. However, we also consider studies of client participation and experience in therapy that have not yet been linked to outcome. Participation and experience are important because of their direct link to psychotherapy and the action of therapists. For instance, we review studies on clients' views of what is helpful. A skeptic could argue that what a client thinks may have nothing to do with what is actually helpful. However, what clients think and want is sometimes discrepant with what professional models of therapy focus on. This may be particularly clear in terms of what clients want out of therapy in contrast to what professionals are measuring (primarily symptom reduction; see our sections on clients' views of good outcome and on goal consensus). It is important to investigate clients' views of what is helpful because they may be picking up things that are being overlooked by researchers and by theories. This may be particularly true because the change processes postulated by theories have so far not been shown to explain very well how therapy works (see Crits-Christoph et al. this volume).

In addition, there is evidence that many clients' perceptions, expectations, and preferences do relate to outcome. It may behoove therapists to be aware of the research on clients' views about therapy so they can anticipate the kinds of things clients are thinking, perceiving, wanting, and needing, in order to (a) strengthen the therapeutic alliance, and (b) to capitalize on ways to mobilize client participation.

There are methodological issues that we do not have space to consider. Several are mentioned in Crits-Christoph et al. (this volume). Of most importance is the issue of correlation not implying causation. Many of the findings we consider are correlational. Therefore conclusions we draw must have this as a caveat. In addition, we have included a number of qualitative research findings. Recent editions of this handbook have included favorable comments on qualitative research (e.g., Hill & Lambert, 2004; Slife, 2004). However, for the most part, qualitative research has not previously been included. We break with this precedent because (a) much of the recent research on the client's role in therapy has been qualitative, and (b) because these qualitative studies offer rich findings that invite future quantitative investigation. We note the limitations of qualitative research: (a) samples are often small and nonrandom so that findings may not be generalizable, (b) functionally the studies are correlational in nature, and (c) there have rarely been attempts to link findings to outcome in a formal way. However, there have been attempts to develop qualitative and/or mixed qualitative/quantitative methods for assessing outcome and its links to process (Bohart, Tallman, Byock, & Mackrill, 2011; Elliott, 2002; R. B. Miller, 2011). We cannot consider them here (but see Elliott et al., Chapter 13, this volume; and McLeod, Chapter 3, this volume).

We have chosen to do a narrative review that incorporates recent research evidence, meta-analytic reviews when available, and past narrative summaries. There are now many available reviews of specific aspects of client functioning but none give a comprehensive picture of the client in therapy. Our goal is to give an overview of what is known about clients' participation in psychotherapy and what it means for effective practice. Too many client variables have been studied for us to consider all of them. We have focused on certain variables that have traditionally been studied, as well as newer ones that seem of importance. One final note: Although we prefer the term "clients," we use both "clients" and "patients" in this chapter to reflect the terms used in the various studies we review.

CLIENT ATTENDANCE IN THERAPY

Entering Psychotherapy

Many potential clients never enter into treatment, and many more who do enter, do not stay. Corrigan (2004) suggested that estimates ranged anywhere from 40% to 90% of individuals in need of professional care either received no treatment or had less treatment than needed. In addition to the lack of benefits that clients may receive, this may cause researchers to mis-estimate the effects of treatment because we only know the outcome for those who enter and stay in our care.

Research reviewers have concluded that several variables predict nonattendance and these variables appear to be consistent over time: lower socioeconomic status, ethnic minority status, being older, being male, fear of being stigmatized, and being a person who causes stress to others but has less psychological distress him- or herself (Clarkin & Levy, 2004; Garfield, 1994). However, Zane, Hall, Sue, Young, and Nunez (2004) concluded that studies on utilization of services by ethnic minorities have found conflicting results, with Asian Americans having the only consistent pattern of underutilization.

A variety of variables have been proposed as to why many individuals do not choose to enter psychotherapy. Life circumstances may play a role, particularly with individuals with lower socioeconomic status (e.g., it may be difficult for them to get to the office, find child care). Another factor is the possible discrepancy between clients' ideas about problem etiology and treatment and the ideas of the mental health establishment (Garfield, 1994). Fears of stigmatization may play a role. It was found that those who hold negative stereotypes about mental disorders (Corrigan, 2004) or experience shame over their problems (Leaf, Bruce, & Tischler, 1986) are less likely to seek treatment themselves. Obviously there is a strong need to improve the degree to which those who are not entering treatment do so—based on the assumption that they will benefit despite their negative attitudes.

Early Termination (ET)

Premature, or early, termination (ET) can be costly both to clients and service providers. Many clients who drop out early not only fail to improve but may get worse (Reis & Brown, 1999). In addition to its impact on clients, dropping out before a benefit has been realized is a drain on mental health resources (Barrett, Chua, Crits-Christoph, Connolly Gibbons, & Thompson, 2008; Garfield, 1994; Reis & Brown, 1999) and consequently on the quality of care of even those who do attend treatment (through long wait lists and spaced treatment).

Estimates of the dropout rate have varied widely. Wierzbicki and Pekarik (1993) did a meta-analysis of 125 studies and estimated that the mean early terminator rate was about 47%. A more recent comprehensive meta-analysis of a staggering 669 studies found an average dropout rate of 19.7%; however, there was considerable heterogeneity, with rates ranging from 0% to 74% (Swift & Greenberg, 2012). One reason for such heterogeneity may have to do with the definition of an early terminator (Garfield, 1994; Hatchett & Park, 2003). Definitions in individual studies have included those who have an appointment scheduled but fail to return, those who stop therapy yet are rated as premature terminators by therapists, or those who terminate before attending a certain number of sessions. However, failing to return and/or terminating before a certain number of sessions may not necessarily indicate that therapy was a failure. Therapists' ratings depend on personal judgments that vary from therapist to therapist. Recently, Swift, Callahan, and Levine (2009) have suggested using as a definition of ET, those who terminate before reaching a level of clinically significant change. However, as of this writing, there is still no consensus in the literature on how ET is defined. Unless otherwise noted, studies reviewed below typically relied upon multiple criteria, or did not specify the criteria for dropout utilized.

Decades of research has been done to identify client variables and factors associated with dropout. There are now a number of reviews and meta-analyses available. (e.g., Barrett et al., 2008; McMurran, Huband, & Overton, 2010; Reis & Brown, 1999; Swift & Greenberg, 2012). For the most part, results for demographic variables have been inconsistent or weak. This is true for gender (Garfield, 1994; Reis & Brown, 1999; Swift & Greenberg, 2012). On clients' age Garfield (1994) and Reis and Brown (1999) did not find a clear relationship. However, the meta-analysis by Swift and Greenberg (2012) found that younger clients showed a greater tendency to drop out, although the effect size was small ($d = .16$). Other variables that reviewers have sometimes concluded are important are socioeconomic status (Barrett et al., 2008; Garfield, 1994; Reis & Brown, 1999), education (Barrett et al., 2008; Garfield, 1994), and ethnicity/minority status (Barrett et al., 2008; Garfield, 1994; Reis & Brown, 1999). However, the most recent and comprehensive meta-analysis by Swift and Greenberg (2012) did not find any consistent relationship of these variables and early termination. Zane and colleagues (2004) concluded that the results were inconsistent on whether persons of color drop out of therapy more often.

Overall, as we also see with outcome, the results of correlating demographic variables with ET has not been particularly productive. Clarkin and Levy (2004) have suggested that looking at what these variables mean may be more fruitful. Consider gender. Men appear to be less likely to enter therapy, although it is not clear that they drop out more or have worse outcomes (Bedi & Richards, 2011). Bedi and Richards (2011) have

suggested that this may be due to the norms and values some men hold. In particular, men who hold traditional North American values are more likely to question the value of therapy.

Some research suggests that masculine norms may influence how clients construe the therapy experience. Bedi and Richards had men sort statements about what strengthened the therapeutic alliance. They found that the categories men created were different from those women created. For instance, the most important category for men was that the therapist helped them talk about important issues, while for women it was that the therapist provided education and validation. Owen, Wong, and Rodolpha (2010) found that clients who held masculine norms, whether men or women, were more likely to see helpful therapist actions in terms of insight or relationship value provided, while those who did not hold masculine norms focused more on information. These findings were not related to early termination or outcome. Nonetheless, taking a more differentiated look like this may ultimately prove more fruitful than simply focusing on gender per se.

Research reviews have also looked at personal characteristics that impact on early termination. Reviewers have concluded that individuals diagnosed with a personality disorder have increased likelihood of ET (Barrett et al., 2008; McMurran et al., 2010; Swift & Greenberg, 2012), as do those with some other disorders such as eating disorders (Flückiger et al., 2011; Swift & Greenberg, 2012), sexual offending, and psychopathy (Olver & Wong, 2011). A variety of characteristics have been found to relate to dropout. These include low motivation, resistance, and relationship issues in psychopathy (Olver & Wong, 2011); and impulsivity, hostility, and low self-esteem in eating disorders (Flückiger et al., 2011). For clients with personality disorders, having a greater number of and more severe problems, having characteristics that interfered with commitment to treatment (e.g., avoidance), and deficient ego strength all related to premature termination (McMurran et al., 2010).

With regard to expectations, there is evidence that many clients expect that therapy will work more quickly than it actually does (Swift & Callahan, 2008). Garfield (1994) and Barrett et al. (2008) have concluded that such an expectation increases the odds of premature dropout. However, the Constantino, Glass, Arnkoff, Ametrano, and Smith review (2011) found the evidence was unclear. Nonetheless, Swift and Callahan (2011) have shown that educating clients about how long it takes on average for therapy to have its effect led to reduced dropout ($d = 0.55$). As for expectations regarding treatment rationale, clients who did not believe in the treatment rationale were more likely to drop out (Davis & Addis, 2002; Westmacott, Hunsley, Best, Rumstein-McKean, & Shindlera, 2010). There is not much consistent evidence, but these results on expectations suggest that it may be useful for therapists to initiate regular discussions about expectations for the duration of treatment both at the start and during the course of psychotherapy and also to continuously make sure that the client still buys into the therapist's rationale for treatment as a way of preventing dropout.

When asked about their reasons for dropping out, clients' reasons have included being disappointed in treatment and making less progress (Garfield, 1994; Knox et al., 2011; Westmacott et al., 2010). This fits with evidence from Lambert, Harmon, Slade, Whipple, and Hawkins (2005). These researchers used an outcomes management system in which clients' progress was tracked on a session-by-session basis. They found that clients whose progress was below what was expected (compared to other clients with the same level of disturbance) were more likely to drop out. Similarly, clients who dropped out also often reported dissatisfaction with their therapists and with the alliance (Knox et al., 2011; Westmacott et al., 2010). A meta-analysis by Sharf, Primavera, and Diener (2010) of 11 studies looked at the relationship of the weakness of the alliance to dropout. They found a moderately strong relationship ($d = .55$). The results on both dissatisfaction with progress, and with the therapist and alliance, suggest that therapists need to monitor client satisfaction. One way to do this is by regularly collecting client feedback (see section on client feedback).

Clients also drop out because of therapy-interfering life circumstances. Kazdin, Holland, Crowley, and Breton (1997) found that life barriers, such as those related to transportation or scheduling issues (which are highly related to socioeconomic level), were associated with dropout. Barrett et al. (2008) concluded that factors such as distance the client has to travel, having to wait to get treatment, difficulty in finding child care, and the like, are associated with higher likelihood of drop out. Limited health care coverage also played a role.

Finally, it may be "therapist-centric" to exclusively look at client dropout as a problem/failure of treatment. Despite what therapists believe about how much treatment clients need, clients may not agree. Westmacott et al. (2010) compared clients who terminated unilaterally with those whose decision to terminate was made mutually with their therapists. These authors found that unilateral terminators were more likely to see their distress as lower when they terminated while their therapists were more likely to see them as unchanged. It is possible that these clients got just what they wanted from the therapy or that an extra-therapeutic factor remitted their distress. Likewise, Barrett et al. (2008) summarized studies that showed that some clients end treatment because in their eyes they have attained sufficient relief, even if professionals' criteria for clinically significant improvement or recovery have not been met. A study by Cahill and colleagues (2003) found that the majority of clients who unilaterally left treatment had achieved at least reliable improvement (70%). However, only 13% of them reached the level of clinically significant change, compared to a rate of 71% of those who remained in treatment for the full length of time. In a study reexamining the dose-effect relationship in psychotherapy, Barkham and colleagues (2006) found that more than 50% of clients who attended only one or two sessions achieved a reliable and clinically significant change in symptoms.

Conclusion

Clients appear to drop out for a variety of reasons. First, personal characteristics, such as demographics, type of disorder, level of motivation, impulsivity, or hostility interfere with connecting with the therapist and treatment. Second, and overlapping with the first, from their perspective clients are not receiving the kind of treatment they believe they need, in terms of progress made, relationship with the therapist, or beliefs and expectations about the nature of treatment. Third, life space issues, such as lack of funds or transportation problems, can get in the way. Fourth, some drop out because they perceive they have gotten the help they need even though therapists may not agree. It is likely that most of these issues can be affected by therapist behaviors and attitudes and are matters for training programs and mental health professionals to address.

CLIENT CONTRIBUTIONS TO THERAPY PROCESS AND OUTCOME

In this section we look at the role of clients and their contribution to how therapy works. We first consider individual differences in clients' change trajectories. Then we look at client characteristics. Next we consider clients' perceptions, beliefs, and actions and how they relate to the therapeutic process. Finally we look at client constructive activity in therapy.

Early Responders and Trajectories of Change

It has been found that clients follow different change trajectories. Of particular interest has been the identification of *early responders*. Early responders show significant positive change within a small number of sessions, and this occurs across diagnoses and therapy approaches (Haas, Hill, Lambert, & Morrell, 2002). Furthermore, they may enter therapy with high levels of impairment (Stulz, Lutz, Leach, Lucock, & Barkham, 2007). There has been no one definition used to identify an early responder. It might be based on clinician ratings, reduction of symptoms, deviations from expected rates of improvement, or other methods (Haas et al., 2002). Early responders have been found to have more positive outcomes, and the outcomes last.

Hansen and Lambert (2003) have speculated about causes. These include the possibility that early responders are more ready to change, that they are clients who achieve a better fit with their therapists, or that they are clients who are more organized and better able to maintain a focus in therapy.

Studies have identified other trajectories (e.g., Brown, Burlingame, Lambert, Jones, & Vaccaro, 2001; Stulz et al., 2007; Vermote et al., 2009). For instance, Stulz et al. (2007) found five different slopes of change. These slopes included those who showed high initial impairment followed by improvement, those who showed low initial impairment and improvement, early responders (early improvement), a group that started out with a medium level of impairment and then showed continuous improvement, and a group that started out with a medium level of impairment and showed discontinuous improvement. This latter pattern consisted of periods of both improvement and regression, although the trajectory overall was upwards. Of the two medium-impaired groups at intake, the discontinuous change group showed more reliable change than the continuous improvement group (44% to 19%). Stulz et al. also found that a discontinuous pattern of change did not necessarily predict poor outcome. However, some members of this group showed greater deterioration than those in the continuous change group.

Findings that different clients have different trajectories of change have implications both for understanding how therapy works and for treatment. Brown et al. (2001) found that different trajectories did not depend on the theoretical orientation of the therapist. They concluded, "the most tenable hypothesis is that the patients themselves are the primary determinant of duration of treatment and that the decision to terminate treatment is based on the rate of improvement...the faster the improvement, the sooner treatment is terminated" (p. 8). Client characteristics, in combination with type of therapy, may make a difference. Vermote et al. (2009) studied hospitalization-based psychoanalytic treatment. They found that two groups of clients, both with moderate symptomatology, one successful and one unsuccessful, differed in pretreatment personality characteristics. The more successful group presented with characteristics similar to that of an introjective style focused on matters of self-definition (Blatt, Quinlan, Pilkonis, & Shea, 1995). Vermote et al. suggest that such a style may match up with an insight-oriented approach better. On the other hand, Lambert (2010), speaking specifically to client deterioration, noted that we can predict deterioration before it occurs by utilizing information about the client's level of distress and disturbance at the start of therapy and the client's response to treatment in early sessions. He also noted that other variables, such as diagnosis, age, sex, ethnicity, type of treatment, and experience of the therapist, added relatively little once level of distress and disturbance were taken into account. Further research is needed to understand how different trajectories of change are generated and what it means for treatment.

Client Demographic Variables and Outcome

Decades of research on the relationship of demographic variables to outcome have replicated the pattern found between demographic variables and premature termination; that is, results are generally inconsistent, although there is evidence of weak trends. Clarkin and Levy (2004) found no relationship between age and outcome other than possibly for substance abuse, where there was evidence that younger adults did less well. Reviews of dysphoric, anxiety, substance abuse, and personality disorders identified an effect only for dysphoric/mood disorders (Castonguay & Beutler, 2006a). Older clients did less well than younger ones. This was supported by a randomized trial of both cognitive therapy and medication for depression (Fournier et al., 2009). However, two meta-analyses of treatment for depression by Cuijpers, van Straten, Smit, and Andersson (2009) and Oxman and Sengupta (2002) did not find evidence that older adults were less responsive.

Prior reviews have not found that gender consistently makes a difference in outcome either (see reviews of client characteristics in Castonguay & Beutler, 2006b; Clarkin & Levy, 2004). Furthermore, reviews of studies on matching therapist to client on gender have led to mixed results (Bowman, Scogin, Floyd, & McKendree-Smith, 2001; Clarkin & Levy, 2004). There are occasional studies where gender has been found to make some difference. For instance, Pertab, Nielsen, and Lambert (in press) studied more than 17,000 students at a university counseling center and found that female clients were more likely to end treatment in the "improved" category. However, by-and-large this study found little difference in outcome regardless of gender matches and mismatches with therapists. Ogrodniczuk (2006) found that men benefited more from interpretative short-term psychodynamic therapy than from supportive short-term psychodynamic therapy, while the reverse was true of women. Thus, there may be something about gender that can play a role in outcome, but consistent findings are yet to emerge than can be used prescriptively.

Garfield (1994) concluded that there was a small positive relationship between client educational level and staying in treatment. He also concluded that there was little evidence of a relationship between socio-economic status (SES) and therapy outcome. If there is a pattern, it is that lower SES predicts less improvement; but once again results are inconsistent. For instance, in a review on treatment of anxiety disorders Newman, Crits-Christoph, Connolly Gibbons, and Erickson (2006) found that in five of eight studies low SES clients were more likely to drop out and to have decreased treatment response. However, the authors concluded that the heterogeneity of

definitions and the confounding effects of race and ethnicity prohibited drawing firm conclusions.

Research on clients' social support suggests that it too shows a weak relationship to outcome. There are individual studies that have found a relationship (e.g., Fournier et al., 2009, for cognitive therapy of depression, and Kazdin & Whitley, 2006, for parent management training). Roehrle and Strouse (2008) did a meta-analysis of 27 studies of clients with various problems in various types of therapy. They found a small effect size of $r = 0.13$. Narrative reviews for dysphoric, anxiety, personality, and substance abuse disorders only found clear evidence of an effect for dysphoric disorders (Castonguay & Beutler, 2006a). Thus, social support makes some difference in some cases. Although the relationships are weak, it may make sense for therapists to systematically measure amount of social support present at the inception of therapy and then use methods to bolster social support with individuals' whose support is especially low.

Cultural diversity has been of major concern in the provision of psychological services. Castonguay and Beutler (2006a) concluded that, for the treatment of depression, "patients representing underserved ethnic or racial groups achieve fewer benefits from conventional psychotherapy than Anglo-American groups" (p. 355). However there were no differential effects for treatment of anxiety disorders, personality disorders, or substance abuse disorders. Other studies have not found differential effects. For instance, Lambert et al. (2006) studied archival data on clients who had come to a university counseling center. Each ethnic minority group member was matched with a Caucasian client based on important variables including initial level of disturbance. There were no differences in outcome between any ethnic group and their Caucasian counterparts.

Although there is no consistent evidence that ethnic-minority clients on average do worse in therapy, there has been interest in the idea of matching clients with therapists of their own ethnicity. Zane et al. (2004) concluded that such matching improved both outcome and staying in therapy, although results were mixed. Beutler and colleagues (2004) reported statistical significance in outcome in favor of matching, but the effect size was near zero ($r = .02$). Meta-analyses of matching studies found similar small effects sizes of $r = .01$ (Maramba & Hall, 2002) and $d = .09$ (Cabral & Smith, 2011). Thus the evidence that ethnic matching has any substantial impact on outcome is minimal. However, Cabral and Smith (2011) did find an effect size of .63 for who clients preferred to work with in terms of their ethnicity (not that this produced better outcomes). Farsimaden, Draghi-Lorenze, and Ellis (2007) studied clients who expressed a preference for matching. Those who got their preference had better outcomes, although the size of this effect was not provided. Possibly matching might work better where clients care about it, but studies of outcomes with this subgroup is limited. Further research is needed in this area, though matching with minority clients and therapists has serious practical limitations with only limited evidence that it would improve outcomes if it could be done.

The provision of culturally adapted treatments has been investigated. Smith, Rodriguez, and Bernal (2011) did a meta-analysis of 65 quasi-experimental and experimental studies where treatments for mental illness, distress, family problems, and problem behaviors were provided in culturally adapted ways. They based their conception of culturally adapted treatments on a schemata of eight criteria provided by Bernal and Sáez-Santiago (2006). Examples include providing treatment in the appropriate language, and using culturally appropriate metaphors. They found a moderate effect size of $d = .46$. The effects varied by ethnicity. The effect size for Asian Americans was $d = 1.18$, while it was $d = .22$ for Native Americans. Interventions designed for specific cultural groups were more effective ($d = .51$) than interventions delivered to mixed groups ($d = .18$).

There is a problem of interpretation with these results. Not all of the studies compared culturally adapted treatment with a nonculturally adapted version of the same treatment. In some cases the comparison was to an untreated control group. Thus, while the data can be read as supporting the usefulness of culturally adapted treatment, it is less clear that it supports an interpretation that such treatment is superior to non-culturally adapted treatment. On the other hand, it was found that culturally adapted treatment correlated with outcome $r = .28$ when studies were rated on their *degree* of cultural adaptation. Furthermore, using symbols and metaphors that matched clients' cultural worldview also correlated with outcome ($b = .37$, $p = .02$). These findings suggest there can be utility in adapting treatment in a culturally sensitive way.

The issue of working with culturally diverse clients merits much more research. Furthermore,

we did not review evidence on other kinds of diversity/minority statuses such as that of sexual orientation because we were unable to locate sufficient research.

Conclusion

With the possible exception of culturally adapted treatments there is little evidence that demographic variables significantly moderate psychotherapy outcome. In one sense this is good news. It means that psychotherapy is broadly applicable. In another sense, it suggests that looking for simple relationships between individual demographics and outcome no longer seems fruitful. As Clarkin and Levy (2004) have noted, and as we have previously commented, it is time for research to move on from studying simple correlations between age, gender, and so on, and outcome, and develop more sophisticated hypotheses about the psychological variables that may moderate and mediate treatment effects.

Client Pathology

In this section we review evidence on the relationship of the severity of client problems and comorbidity to outcome.

Severity of Problems

Clarkin and Levy (2004) concluded that severity of symptoms and functional impairment led to poorer prognosis, and that individuals with more severe symptoms needed more sessions to show improvement. In addition, higher functioning before impairment predicted a better prognosis. Recent reviews on anxiety disorders (Newman et al., 2006) and on dysphoric/depressive disorders (Beutler, Blatt, Alimohamed, Levy, & Angtuaco, 2006) have drawn similar conclusions. However greater severity does not always lead to poorer outcome. Two studies of parent management training for children with conduct problems found that greater severity led to better outcomes (Hautmann et al., 2010; Kazdin & Whitley, 2006). It is unclear what about parent management training led to results that contradict the general trend in other studies.

In apparent contradiction to the general findings on severity, there is a evidence that a higher level of distress at the start of therapy is the best predictor of outcome, more so than the client's diagnosis, problem chronicity, or treatment population. Brown et al. (2001) studied clients who had received treatment through a major health care organization. The most severe patients, as rated on the OQ-45, showed the most change. Two other studies (Hansen & Lambert, 2003; Hansen, Lambert, & Forman, 2002) also found that higher pretreatment distress predicted greater change.

A resolution of this inconsistency can be found by considering that, although clients with higher levels of distress may show the most *change*, they do not necessarily achieve the most positive outcomes in an absolute sense (Michael Lambert, personal communication, October, 2011). For instance, Brown et al. (2001) found that although such clients showed the most change, the most severe patients did not improve to the 50% level of a nontreatment control group. In the context of these findings (based on extremely large patient samples), when discussing the relationship between initial levels of disturbance and outcome it is important to know if outcome means amount of change or final status (return to normal levels of functioning).

Comorbidity

Earlier reviews have found that clients with comorbid problems are less likely to do well. Clarkin and Levy (2004) concluded that personality disorder comorbidity has been almost uniformly found to predict poorer outcome, with one exception: Cluster A and C personality disorders did not predict poorer outcome with eating disordered patients. Newman et al. (2006), based on their review of research on treatments for anxiety disorders, concluded that comorbidity for depression, personality disorders, and substance abuse all negatively impacted outcome. Beutler et al. (2006) summarized factors influencing treatment of dyshporic/depressive disorders and found that in 15 of 20 studies personality disorder comorbidity negatively affected outcome. Haaga, Hall, and Haas (2006) concluded that substance abusers with comorbid psychiatric diagnoses had less favorable treatment outcomes.

The results on severity and comorbidity imply that policy makers need to be willing to adjust treatment limits to take into account clients' initial levels on these variables. Since these are variables that the client comes with and treatments are aimed at changing these variables, treatment may need to be prolonged or adjusted to deal with them. This may include providing sessions more than on a once-weekly basis, or utilizing adjunctive treatments.

Personal Characteristics

Personal characteristics have to do with clients' styles and competencies for relating to self and others. In previous reviews, such characteristics as internal locus of control, social competence, learned resourcefulness, ego strength, coping style, and defense style were found to predict outcome in therapy (Clarkin & Levy, 2004; Piper, 1994). Below, we look at motivation, styles of attachment in forming relationships, manner of coping with stressors, degree of psychological mindedness, relating to emotion and inner experiencing in an open manner, and tendencies towards self-criticism.

Client Motivation

Research shows that client involvement and engagement are strongly associated with outcome (Orlinsky et al., 1994; Orlinsky et al., 2004). Therefore, it might be expected that client motivation would also be associated with outcome. However, Garfield (1994) concluded that the effects of motivation had not received strong support. On the other hand Orlinsky et al. (2004) concluded that more highly motivated clients, defined as clients who saw themselves as engaged and motivated help seekers, or who were seen that way by their therapists, had better outcomes. Results were stronger when motivation was rated by clients. In their summary of research on anxiety disorders, Newman et al. (2006) concluded that four of five studies that assessed motivation found a positive relationship with treatment outcomes.

In part, the issue may have to do with what kind of motivation we are considering. Donovan and Rosengren (1999) observed that the motivation to enter psychotherapy may be different than the motivation to change. Another possible dimension has to do with whether the motivation is internal or external. Research on personality (e.g., Sheldon, 2004) has found that internal motives, such as those that arise from an individual's intrinsic interests, or those that represent their personally chosen or "identified" values, sustain effort and behavior better than external motives, such as external rewards or punishments, or introjected "shoulds."

Motivation also overlaps with constructs like expectation and hopefulness. Clients who do not believe they can change, and who feel hopeless, may accordingly feel low motivation to participate. Finally motivation overlaps with why clients are in therapy (e.g., personal choice versus external pressure), their views on the nature of problems, their concerns with stigmatization, and their views on what kind of treatment will benefit them.

In general, it appears that clients who are "ready to change" (i.e., more internally motivated) are more likely to benefit. The stages of change model (Norcross, Krebs, & Prochaska, 2011) takes a systematic look at how clients progress, from being unready to change to ready to actively invest in change. The model's first stage, that of precontemplation, is the stage where clients are not internally motivated because they do not recognize that a problem exists. Clients in the next stage, contemplation, have moved to where they recognize there is a problem, but are not ready to take action. By the next stage, preparation for action, clients are showing readiness to change, that is, more self-generated motivation. This continues through the remaining two stages. In a recent meta-analysis of 39 studies, Norcross et al. (2011) looked at the client's readiness to change prior to therapy and its relationship to therapy outcome. The overall effect size was $d = .46$, a medium effect size. Effect sizes did vary somewhat by client diagnostic category, but still were in the medium to large range for all.

Zuroff and colleagues (2007) looked at readiness to change in a different way. They studied autonomy motivation, defined as the degree to which clients experienced participation in therapy as freely chosen. Autonomy motivation was a better predictor of outcome than was the therapeutic alliance. However, the degree of perceived autonomy, measured at the third session, was not entirely determined by the client. Therapists who were perceived as supporting autonomy motivation had clients who were higher in it. McBride and colleagues (2010) also found evidence that autonomy motivation related positively to outcome and that "controlled" (external) motivation related negatively.

In contrast to these findings, clients who are mandated to be in treatment, that is, those whose motivation is more likely to be external, often do not fare as well. A meta-analysis of 129 studies of offenders referred for correctional treatment in the criminal justice system found that mandated treatment was ineffective, while voluntary treatment was effective (Parhar, Wormith, Derkzen, & Beauregard, 2008).

Finally, clients will not be ready to change if they are resistant. Resistance is related to poorer outcome in therapy (e.g., Beutler, Moliero, & Talebi, 2002). Beutler, Harwood, Michelson, Song, and Holman (2011) have used the concept of *reactance* to explain resistance. Highly reactant individuals are those who are particularly sensitive to interpreting external direction as threats to their freedom (Brehm, 1966). Beutler, Harwood, Michelson, and Holman (2011) have argued that clients high in reactance are more likely to show resistance when working with therapists who are directive. In a meta-analysis they located 12 studies that looked at the relationship of the directiveness of the treatment to the level of client reactance. The effect size for matching was $d = .82$. That is, clients who were high in reactance and got treatments lower in directiveness did better than clients high in reactance who got treatments high in directiveness. The reverse was true for clients low in reactance.

In conclusion, results suggest that when clients' motivation to work comes from within, either in terms of their readiness to change, their autonomy motivation, or therapy not activating their resistance, they are more likely to do well. This suggests that therapists need to find ways of mobilizing clients' internal reasons for change. Approaches such as Motivational Interviewing (e.g., W. R. Miller & Rollnick, 2002) explicitly attempt to do this.

Attachment Style

Attachment style has to do with clients' ways of relating to other people, although it also impacts how they relate to themselves. Two attachment constructs—that of the client's relationships with people outside of therapy, and within therapy relationships—are addressed in the research. The impact of attachment style on both outcome and process variables has been investigated. Change to attachment style is also an outcome variable in and of itself.

Bowlby (1969, 1988) saw the importance of an attachment relationship as different from other relationships in the sense that the attachment figure was used as a safe haven from distressing events. The attachment figure also functioned as a secure base from which to explore the environment and express oneself. Attachment patterns are formed in infancy through interactions with the primary caregiver. Four main attachment styles have been identified: secure/autonomous, anxious/preoccupied, avoidant (dismissive or fearful), and disorganized; the first three have received the most research attention. Attachment in adulthood can be understood in terms of one's perception of self and others with securely attached individuals having a positive view of self and others; preoccupied/anxious attached individuals having a negative view of self and a positive view of others; and avoidant (fearful/dismissive) attached individuals have a positive view of self and a negative view of others (Levy, Ellison, Scott, & Bernecker, 2011).

Therapists are more likely to see clients with global attachment styles that are secure or anxious/preoccupied whereas those with avoidant attachment styles are more distrustful and less interested in seeking psychotherapy (Obegi & Berant, 2008). The therapy relationship and therapist offer many components of an attachment figure (someone who is strong, a consistent figure that the client can form an emotional connection with, a secure base for exploration or retreat, and who may trigger separation anxiety). Clients may utilize the relationship as a corrective emotional experience (Mallinckrodt, 2010).

In a recent meta-analysis of 19 data sets, Levy et al. (2011) found a significant positive correlation between global assessments of clients' secure attachment and outcome ($r = .182$). Additionally, they found a significant negative correlation between global assessments of attachment anxiety and outcome ($r = -.224$) and a negligible relationship between attachment avoidance and outcome. Likewise, in a group therapy context, secure clients had better outcomes than preoccupied clients (Strauss et al., 2006). Levels of attachment anxiety were significantly correlated with clients' levels of distress at the outset of treatment (Sauer, Anderson, Gormley, Richmond, & Preacco, 2010). Different attachment patterns were correlated with specific symptom patterns, although they were unrelated to personality variables (Bachelor & Meunier, 2010). Sauer et al.'s (2010) findings suggested that secure attachment *to the therapist* had more predictive value for treatment progress than did global measures of secure attachment.

A recent meta-analysis of 17 studies linking attachment and alliance showed a significant effect size for securely attached clients having better alliances and insecurely attached clients having weaker alliances (Diener & Monroe, 2011). Clients' self-reported global attachment style had a higher correlation with client-rated alliance than therapist-rated alliance. Diener and Monroe postulated that clients may be viewing their attachment and their working relationship with the therapist from a more similar framework than therapists who may distinguish more fully between the two.

Bachelor and Meunier (2010) also found clients' attachment to their therapists was more predictive of alliance than either personality variables or symptomatology. Avoidant-fearful attachment scores were negatively correlated with alliance scores; however, there was no significant relationship between clients' preoccupied attachment scores and alliance. Bachelor and Meunier did find that a significant moderator of the relationship between preoccupied attachment and alliance was the degree of clients' distress.

Attachment also affects clients' in-therapy behavior. Increased self-disclosure and positive feelings about disclosure were associated with clients' secure attachment styles and negatively correlated with fearful attachment styles (Saypol & Farber, 2010). The amount of exploration and session depth was also predicted by clients' secure attachment to their therapist, and therapists' own global attachment style served as a moderator in this association (Romano, Fitzpatrick, & Janzen, 2008).

In conclusion, clients' attachment styles impact how they enter into therapy. Both their global attachment styles and their specific attachments to their therapists impact outcome, as well as the alliances they form and specific therapy behaviors such as self-disclosing and amount of exploration. This suggests that it may help for therapists to understand how clients are construing their relationship to therapy in terms of attachment, and to accordingly find ways to work with that (see Wallin, 2007).

Coping Style

Coping style has to do with how individuals deal with change and/or stress (Beutler, Harwood, Kimpara, Verdirame, & Blau, 2011). Two styles have been identified. According to Beutler, Harwood, Alimohamed, and Malik (2002), *externalizers* have been defined as, "those who are impulsive, action or task-oriented, gregarious, aggressive, hedonistic, stimulation-seeking, and lacking in insight," while *internalizers* are, "shy, retiring, self-critical, withdrawn, constrained, over-controlled, self-reflective, worried, and inhibited" (p. 148). In a "box score" analysis, Beutler et al. (2002) found that internalizers were more likely to benefit from insight-oriented therapy, while externalizers benefitted from symptom-focused, or behavioral-skills approaches. In a recent meta-analysis Beutler, Harwood, Kimpara, Verdirame, and Blau (2011) replicated this finding. Overall, based on 12 studies that had been selected for meeting a variety of research criteria, they found a medium effect size ($d = 0.55$), when matching coping style with treatment approach. Based on these findings Beutler, Harwood, Kimpara et al. (2011) recommend that therapists assess clients' coping style and then match treatment based on that assessment.

Psychological Mindedness

Psychological mindedness (PM) is the tendency of a person to turn inward and to seek psychological explanations of behavior or to try to understand people and problems in psychological terms. Studies have found that PM is positively related to staying in therapy (Barrett et al., 2008). However, results with outcome are mixed. In the previous review, Clarkin and Levy (2004) identified 5 studies. Two found a relationship of PM to outcome, two did not, and one found that it related to outcome in one form of therapy but not in three other forms. McCallum, Piper, Ogrodniczuk, and Joyce (2003) examined both psychological mindedness and alexithymia and their relationship to outcome. The data came from two separate trials comparing interpretive to supportive psychotherapy. Both psychological mindedness and alexithymia were found to predict outcome. Nyklíček, Majoor, and Schalken (2010) found that increases in the insight scale of psychological mindedness over the course of therapy predicted increased symptom reduction. On the other hand, Kronström and colleagues (2009) studied the effects of psychological mindedness on outcome in short-term psychodynamic therapy with major depressive disorder. They did not find any relationship between baseline psychological mindedness and outcome.

In conclusion, the mixed findings on psychological mindedness reported in Clarkin and Levy's (2004) review were replicated here. Although there are not enough studies, the roughly 50–50 split in results suggest there may be some relationship to outcome in some cases and further research is needed. There is not as yet enough clarity or consistency in findings in order to use the research to modify the kind of treatment delivered to clients.

Access to Emotion and Experiencing

Access and awareness of emotions have been postulated to be qualities that foster therapeutic change. Therefore, clients who have difficulties with these ought to have more problems benefiting from therapy. We first look at research on alexithymia.

Alexithymia has to do with difficulty in identifying feelings, difficulty in communicating feelings to others, constricted imagination, and an externally oriented cognitive style in regard to how people understand their experience. Defined as such, alexithymia bears some conceptual similarities to low levels of experiencing (Klein, Mathieu-Coughlan, & Kiesler, 1986), particularly in the focus on difficulties in identifying internal experiencing and in adopting a more distal, intellectual perspective.

Several studies have found that high levels of alexithymia predict poorer outcome, but primarily in psychodynamic and not cognitive-behavior therapy. McCallum and colleagues (2003) found that alexithymia was associated with poorer outcome in both interpretive and supportive brief psychotherapy. Leweke, Bausch, Leichsenring, Walter, and Stingl (2009) studied patients in psychodynamically oriented therapy. They found high initial alexithymia total scores significantly predicted worse treatment outcome, although the predictive values were small. Patients with alexithymia still were able to benefit from therapy. On the other hand Spek, Nyklíček, Cuijpers, and Pop (2008) found that alexithymia at the start of cognitive-behavior therapy for depression did not predict outcome. Instead they found that alexithymia varied as a function of depression, suggesting the possibility that depression may in part impact or cause alexithymia. Rufer and colleagues (2010) studied alexithymia in clients in group cognitive-behavior therapy for panic disorder. They found that initial levels of alexithymia did not predict outcome.

Access to emotion has also been studied by experiential psychotherapists. They typically have utilized ratings of early in-therapy emotional openness. Boritz, Angus, Monette, Hollis-Walker, and Warwar (2011) found that higher proportions of autobiographical memories that contained specific concrete emotions which were shared early in therapy predicted outcome. Pos, Greenberg, and Warwar (2009) found that clients lower in emotional processing at the beginning of experiential therapy had poorer outcomes on a measure of interpersonal skills. Watson, McMullen, Prosser, and Bedard (2011) studied 66 clients who received either cognitive-behavioral therapy or experiential therapy for depression. Their findings suggested that, early in therapy, clients' level of affect regulation, which included level of emotional awareness, had a significant impact on the quality of their in-session processing and on outcome.

Clients who are receptively open to their internal experiencing also have been shown to have better outcomes (Elliott, Greenberg, & Lietaer, 2004; Hendricks, 2002; Orlinsky et al., 2004). Inner experiencing is a broader construct than emotion. It includes thoughts, images, and what Gendlin (1996) has called "bodily felt meanings." It has been found that this kind of receptive openness is something clients enter therapy with (Gendlin, Beebe, Cassens, Klein, & Oberlander, 1968), although therapy can promote it as well (Goldman, Greenberg, & Pos, 2005). Findings on whether openness to experiencing correlates with outcome in cognitive therapy have been mixed (e.g., Castonguay, Goldfried, Wiser, Raue, & Hayes, 1996; Rudkin, Llewelyn, Hardy, Stiles, & Barkham, 2007; Watson & Bedard, 2006).

In conclusion clients' openness to emotion and inner experiencing appears to be beneficial, particularly for psychodynamic and experiential approaches, but less consistently so in cognitive-behavior therapy. The findings suggest the possibility of favoring cognitive-behavior therapy for those high in alexithymia.

Perfectionism and Self-Criticism

In contrast to being acceptantly open to emotions and experiencing, clients may have a perfectionistic, critical stance toward the self. If inner openness is important, a critical stance could be expected to be associated with poorer outcome. Hawley, Ho, Zuroff, and Blatt (2006) cite studies that are in accord with this hypothesis. For instance, Blatt et al. (1995) found that high levels of pretreatment perfectionism had a negative impact on psychotherapy outcome. Hawley et al. (2006) tracked the impact of perfectionism across sessions. They found that reduction in perfectionism significantly predicted therapeutic change across sessions.

Along with the findings on openness to inner experiencing and emotion, the research on perfectionism suggests that the *manner* in which clients relate to themselves can either facilitate or inhibit therapeutic processing. Facilitating more effective processing, therefore, may become a prime focus of intervention, although the methods needed to accomplish this and degree to which it can change await further investigation.

Conclusion on Personal Characteristics

Overall certain client characteristics appear to predispose clients to better outcomes. Some of these are styles and competencies that would be expected to make for more adaptive functioning in general (e.g., secure attachment, high ego strength, lower self-criticism). Others appear to particularly influence the quality of the client's participation in therapy. These include motivation, openness to experiencing and emotion, possibly psychological mindedness, and how certain characteristics such as reactance and coping style match up with the particular therapy approach offered.

How Clients Perceive, Construe, and Experience Psychotherapy

As might be expected, there is evidence that clients' perceptions of and beliefs about psychotherapy process and outcome often correlate positively with outcome. Furthermore, their perceptions, such as of the therapeutic alliance, correlate more highly with outcome than do those of therapists. Yet clients' perceptions and beliefs often do not coincide with those of therapists (e.g., Levitt & Rennie, 2004).

This suggests that clients' constructions of therapy may selectively influence how they interact with and process what is going on. An alternative possibility is that their constructions are a consequence of how much they are benefiting from therapy. However, some research has shown that clients' perceptions of the alliance early in therapy are independent of how much benefit they are experiencing (Horvath, Del Re, Flückiger, & Symonds, 2011). In any case, it is important to pay attention to clients' constructions and perhaps to formally measure them during psychotherapy.

Client Perceptions and Experience of the Therapeutic Relationship

The importance of the therapy relationship is not just statistically established; there are more than 100 studies where clients themselves point to the relationship as one of the most helpful aspects of therapy (Norcross, 2010). As previously noted, there can be important differences in how clients and therapists perceive their interactions (Eugster & Wampold, 1996; Levitt & Rennie, 2004). Here we highlight the client's perspective.

Clients' Perceptions of the Working Alliance

Horvath et al.'s (2011) most recent meta-analysis of 190 independent data sets shows a highly reliable ($p < .001$) relationship between alliance and outcome, independent of how either is measured, by whom, or when. Confirming results of a prior meta-analysis (Horvath & Bedi, 2002), clients' alliance scores were significantly related to outcome ($r = .282$) and had higher correlations with outcome than therapists' ($r = .196$), challenging the notion that clients distort the therapy relationship and its impact.

Nonetheless, meta-analytic reviews show there is a moderate amount of reciprocity within client-therapist dyads regarding perceptions of the strength of the working alliance (Marcus, Kashy, & Baldwin, 2009). Clients' degree of disturbance can increase the discrepancy between therapist and client perspectives, although generally speaking clients' ratings of the alliance are higher than those of therapists (Tryon, Blackwell, & Hammel, 2007). Explanations of clients' more generous views of the relationship are not known, although it may serve a purpose in the healing process. In two studies that used multilevel modeling techniques, aggregate client ratings of the alliance were able to predict which therapists would have better than average outcomes for their overall caseload, whereas therapist ratings did not have predictive value even in their own case load (Baldwin, Wampold, & Imel, 2007; Marcus et al., 2009). This lends further support to the idea that clients can be finely tuned into critical aspects of a good working alliance.

Marcus et al. (2009) found that clients of the same therapist differed greatly in rating the strength of the therapeutic alliance. However, if a particular client's alliance ratings were especially stronger than the therapist's other clients, this was predictive of a better outcome for that particular client. This suggests that therapists do not construct the same type of alliance with each client; rather, each unique pairing of therapist and client results in a somewhat unique quality of therapeutic alliance. It also suggests that if a client felt that he or she was able to form an especially strong alliance with his or her therapist, this had a positive impact on treatment progress. As a collective whole, client ratings of the alliance were predictive of which therapists were more proficient than others, which lends further support to the unique vantage point of clients in detecting relevant and helpful therapist stances (Marcus et al., 2009).

Clients' Perceptions of the Real Relationship

As defined by Gelso (2009) the real relationship is "the personal relationship existing between two or more people reflected in the degree to which each is genuine with the other and perceives and experiences the other in ways that befit the other" (pp. 254–255). From a psychodynamic point of view the real relationship is distinguished from transferential and countertransferential aspects of the therapy relationship. Lo Coco, Cullo, Prestano, and Gelso (2011) found that clients' perceptions of the real relationship predicted outcome although therapists' perceptions did not. This was particularly true for the genuineness component. Fuertes and colleagues (2007) found that both clients' and therapists' assessment of the real relationship was associated with clients' view of treatment progress. On the other hand, Marmarosh and colleagues (2009) found that clients' ratings of the real relationship did not have a significant correlation with treatment progress, whereas therapists' perceptions did. But Marmarosh et al. also found that clients' perceptions of the genuine qualities of the real relationship did accurately predict therapists' views of the working alliance, although the reverse was not found. Thus two of three studies found that clients' perceptions of the real relationship correlated with outcome. In addition, their perceptions of the genuineness component appeared to be particularly important.

Client Relationship Preferences

There is evidence that clients have preferences for the kinds of relationship qualities they receive in psychotherapy. In addition to prizing genuineness and realness from the therapist, clients also prize "therapeutic presence" (Geller, Greenberg, & Watson, 2011). This is defined by Geller and Greenberg (2002) as the therapist being completely in the moment in terms of physical, spiritual, cognitive, and emotional engagement of the whole self. Geller et al. (2011) have found that clients' perceptions of presence correlate with outcome higher than do therapists' perceptions. Clients also reveal preferences about the kind of atmosphere they would like their therapist to create. Martin (2008) found that clients mainly wanted an environment that reduced stigma to talk about difficult things, and that enhanced clients' sense of self-efficacy. This environment was facilitated when therapists' were open, respectful, and worked at earning trust (Beretta et al., 2005; Martin, 2008). Clients noted that they sometimes tested their therapist before opening up about vulnerable things. Therapists' "invitations" in the form of slowing down the pace of therapy, giving the clients their full attention, and making themselves vulnerable in some way all seemed to help therapists "pass the test." Nilsson, Svensson, Sandell, and Clinton (2007) reported similar findings with clients preferring therapists that were adaptive to clients' needs, accepting, and patient such that clients felt free to take their time. These clients also reported that while they appreciated emotional support, neutrality and some interpersonal distance were also important.

Clients of ethnically diverse backgrounds reported better experiences when therapists were open to seeing the strengths in clients' cultural heritage, discerned clients' unique positioning within their culture, and acted with awareness about the impact of ethnic differences within the therapeutic relationship (Cardemil & Battle, 2003). Clients' perceptions of therapists' multicultural awareness and sensitivity were positively correlated with perceptions of alliance and the real relationship (Owen, Tao, Leach, & Rodolfa, 2011). The alliance was a mediator between perceptions of therapists' multicultural orientation and measures of psychological well-being, indicating that multicultural competence fostered a relationship in which good therapeutic work could occur. Likewise, similarity between therapist and client in religious or spiritual orientation was less important to clients than having a therapist who was trained to address spiritual matters and who was open and nonjudgmental (Knox, Catlin, Casper, & Schlosser, 2005; Pieper & van Uden, 1996).

There are several studies that identify clients' contraindications for their therapists' relational stances. One study found that confrontation proved unhelpful (W. R. Miller, Wilbourne, & Hettema, 2003). Another study found that clients generally were mistrustful of confrontational therapists, unless the client was being manipulative or avoidant in which case it was appreciated (Levitt, Butler, & Hill, 2006). Clients were sensitive to therapists becoming critical or rejecting of them (Constantino et al., 2007). Von Der Lippe, Monsen, Rønnestad, and Eilertsen (2008) found that with clients who showed little change or were worse after treatment, therapists had *initiated* more disparaging comments and dismissive interactions than with clients who had positive outcomes. Nilsson and colleagues' (2007) reported that clients who were dissatisfied in therapy frequently identified their therapist as treating them more like a "thing" than a person, acted as if being a therapist was "just a job," and were emotionally absent or hiding something.

Client Preferences for Therapist and Therapy

Clients have preferences for their experiences in psychotherapy. For example, King and colleagues (2000) gave clients descriptions of cognitive-behavior therapy and person-centered therapy and the option of choosing what they received. Not all patients decided to choose one or the other. Of those who did, 60% chose CBT and 40% chose person-centered counseling. In another study, Swift and Callahan (2010) had clients rate their preferences for treatment by comparing variables such as empirical support for treatment to common factors. It was found that clients were more likely to choose variables such as a satisfactory therapeutic relationship, that their therapist would have a greater level of experience, and that they, the clients, would be able to do more of the talking, over whether interventions had empirical support.

Swift, Callahan, and Vollmer (2011) did a meta-analysis that broke client preferences down into three areas: role preferences, therapist preferences, and treatment preferences. Role preferences had to do with the activities and behaviors that clients preferred for themselves and therapists to engage in. Examples given by Swift et al. (2011) included having the therapist play an active advice-giving role versus adopting more of a listening role, or preferring group therapy over individual therapy. Therapist preferences included things like: therapist years of experience, preferring a therapist of a particular ethnic background or of a particular gender, or preferring therapists who were empathic. Treatment preferences included clients preferring one "brand" of therapy over the other, or preferring to have either psychotherapy or pharmacotherapy.

Swift et al. (2011) found 35 studies that looked at whether clients got their preferences for role, therapist, or treatment; 18 studies looked at premature termination. Using an odds ratio calculation, a significant effect was found at the $p <$ .001 level that clients who received their preferred conditions were less likely to prematurely drop out of therapy. Of the 35 studies, 33 also looked at outcome. The overall effect size for outcome was $d = .31$, a small but significant effect size. The average effect of psychotherapy versus pharmacotherapy was $d = .36$; for one therapy against another, $d = .21$. The only client characteristic that mattered was client diagnosis/problem. Matching client preferences positively influenced treatment outcomes for anxiety, depression, and substance abuse disorders.

There was no difference among the type of preference and its bearing on dropout rates, or on outcome, suggesting that matching clients to their preferred role, therapist, or treatment all had similar effects. Swift et al. (2011) reported that patient preferences themselves have been found to be influenced by a number of other variables, such as demographic characteristics, beliefs about the nature of problems, level of symptom severity, previous experience with therapy, expectations for therapy, and other life experiences.

These findings suggest that therapists should monitor client preferences, particularly if the client is having difficulty engaging in the therapy. It does not mean that a client who does not get his or her therapy preference will not be able to benefit. However, if clients' preferences present obstacles therapists may wish to take appropriate action, such as either referring the client or finding a way of more comfortably coordinating what they are doing with the client's pre-existing beliefs.

Therapy Expectations

The topic of client expectations overlaps with that of client preference, but is conceptually different. Frank (1961) referred to it as a preeminent factor in client outcomes. Further spawning the interest in this variable was Lambert's (1992) estimation that 15% of outcome variance could be tied to client expectations about treatment. There are many different angles from which the topic of client expectations has been investigated—expectations in terms motivation for change, preferences for the type of therapy or therapist, theories explaining human transformation, expectations about how the process of therapy should work, and finally, about the efficacy of therapy and whether it will really work for *them*. The first three topics related to expectations are addressed in other sections of this chapter; here we focus on the latter two.

Role Expectations for Therapist and Client

There are mixed findings concerning the relationship between role expectations and outcome. Role expectations have to do with how clients expect therapy to operate. Arnkoff, Glass, and Shapiro's (2002) review listed 19 studies finding a positive correlation, 9 studies that showed no correlation, and 12 studies with mixed findings.

However, clients' expectations for how both they and their therapists will behave influences how the process of therapy unfolds. For instance, clients in one study who reported expectations that they would work hard and come regularly also reported stronger alliances by the end of the third session (Patterson, Uhlin, & Anderson, 2008). These clients' emphasis on their own role had predictive value whereas there was no correlation between their ratings of alliance and their prior anticipation of a warm, accepting therapist or a therapist with great expertise.

It is useful to catalog the variety as well as predominant trends regarding the specifics of what clients anticipate in the therapy environment. In a qualitative study examining expectations, clients reported surprise that they worked so hard in therapy, both in the case of good and poor outcome (Westra, Aviram, Barnes, & Angus, 2010). Despite their surprise that they worked hard, they had expected "to be 'grilled,' 'rushed,' 'pushed,' 'restrained,' and 'made to do things' and were pleasantly surprised when the therapist relied on them for direction" (Westra et al., 2010, pp. 439–440). In general, clients with good outcomes did not expect therapy to be so collaborative, to feel so free to direct the process, or feel so comfortable with the therapist. Clients were also surprised that their therapists were nonjudgmental. This was the case in both good and poor outcome cases. Westra et al. (2010) also found support for the idea that if *negative* expectations about the clients' role were *disconfirmed*, this could draw clients' attention to positive target behaviors. This made these behaviors more likely and led to better outcomes.

Client Characteristics Impacting Expectations

High scores on adaptive perfectionism measures were associated with clients' positive expectations towards the therapeutic process and positive outcomes (Oliver, Hart, Ross, & Katz, 2001). In a similar vein, clients who were high in psychological mindedness did not tend to expect more from their therapist but did expect more from themselves (Beitel et al., 2009). Specifically, they expected themselves to be active in the counseling process by sharing openly, sticking with the process when it became difficult, and taking responsibility for the course of therapy. Beitel and colleagues (2009) found that a *general trait* of optimism was not significantly related to overall client expectations (Beitel et al.,

2009). However, a general measure of client hopelessness did correlate with lower outcome expectations (Goldfarb, 2002).

Diagnostic differences can contribute to differences in expectancy/outcome correlations. Depressed clients reported higher pessimism with regard to improvement and suitability of treatment than those with anxiety or comorbid diagnoses, although this difference disappeared mid-treatment (Schulte, 2008). Clients with more severe symptomatology were more likely to have lower outcome expectations (Safren, Heimberg, & Juster, 1997). Also, clients who had received prior therapy were more likely to have higher expectations about therapy success (MacNair-Semands, 2002).

Expectations Regarding Outcome

In a recent statistical meta-analysis using 46 samples, Constantino and colleagues (2011) reported a small ($r = .12$) but significant effect size for the relationship between clients' expectancy of treatment success and outcome. It also appeared that moderate expectations had the best predictive power. Noble, Douglas, and Newman's (2001) review of studies published prior to 1980 also evidenced a curvilinear relationship between expectations for success and outcome; those with moderate expectations had the best outcome compared with those with very high and very low expectations. Extreme expectations in both directions were also correlated with attrition. In one study, clients were seven times more likely to drop out of therapy if their scores were outside the normative range for expectancy (Aubuchon-Endsley, & Callahan, 2009).

Expectations and Role Induction

Role-induction protocols have been shown to modify expectations and increase successful outcomes (Constantino et al., 2011; Noble et al., 2001). Less has been done on modifying outcome expectations (Constantino et al., 2011). Constantino et al. (2011) offer a number of suggestions for how therapists can both assess and help clients productively modify expectations. Intuitively, it makes sense to try to help clients to have realistic expectations. However, diminishing expectations that are unrealistically high runs the risk of discouraging some patients. Further understanding of the effects of specific methods of changing outcome expectations on specific kinds of clients is needed.

Clients' Views of Problem Etiology and Theories of Change

Clients' views about who/what is responsible for the cause of the problem are important to consider. Studies have shown that when the therapist is aligned with client's attributional theories, it is predictive of client satisfaction and outcome (Hayes & Wall, 1998; Tracey, 1988). Furthermore, therapists who align with clients' attribution of responsibility are deemed more credible and understanding (Worthington & Atkinson, 1996).

This does not mean that clients do not change their theories about causes of problems. Clients in Mackrill's (2008) qualitative study had definite ideas going into therapy about what was the cause of problems and the strategy to resolve them. The cases represented a mixture of clients sticking with their theories and/or modifying their understanding when confronted with an alternate explanation that made sense to them.

Clients' understanding regarding the root of current problems can have an impact on their motivation for the type of treatment offered. When Meyer and Garcia-Roberts (2007) administered the Reasons for Depression and the Motivation for Intervention measures to clients, it was found that clients who saw their depression as rooted in interpersonal issues were more motivated for interventions that were interpersonal in nature. Similar results were found for the categories of characterological issues, childhood issues, biological roots, achievement, and relationship issues. Clients with these reasons were motivated for therapy that was personality changing, past-focused, pharmacological, goal setting, or relationship-focused, respectively. Conversely, clients who endorsed more complex reasons for their depression (as measured by their citing multiple reasons) were less motivated for behavioral approaches, possibly because they did not see their problems as being fixed by simply changing behaviors.

There is also congruence between how clients see themselves and how they see the path of change. Kühnlein (1999) interviewed clients 2 years posttherapy and pulled for a narrative history, what the perceived usefulness of therapy was, and the meaning of recovery. She identified four types of clients' models of change and labeled them: *Overburdened, Deviation, Deficit,* and *Developmental-Disturbance*. Clients' narratives about their problem category were congruent with their perceived path of change. For instance, those who fit under the Deficit type described their history primarily in terms of their shortcomings. Therapy was seen as a means for learning self-improvement techniques, a learning process that would be ongoing after therapy ended. Although the therapy approach was cognitive-behavioral, clients' narratives involved themes that went beyond formal CBT learning processes, and explanations went beyond the change narratives offered by their therapists. However, evidence that clients construct or retain their own change narrative independent of the therapy model offered is mixed. Like Kühnlein, some studies have found that clients maintained an independent theory (e.g., Clarke, Rees, & Hardy, 2004; Orford et al., 2009). However, Valkonen, Hänninen, and Lindfors (2011) found that clients' problem etiology and resulting change narrative either happened to match the therapy offered or clients accommodated to the therapist's theory.

In conclusion, clients can have their own theories of what is wrong. These can influence their experience in therapy and may impact outcome. Clients may or may not modify their theories to match the theory of the therapist. However, change may happen even if their theories do not match their therapists' theories.

Clients' Report of Impactful Processes

Numerous studies, especially in the past 25 years, have investigated clients' views of therapeutic processes that lead to change. These studies can be categorized in three ways. One category, "significant events," refers to investigations into a specific point in time. Clients (and therapists) provide a narrative of processes that had a significant impact on the proceedings of therapy (either positive or negative). These events are usually richly described and sometimes are associated with recordings of the session (e.g., interpersonal process recall methods). Inquiries into significant events often highlight therapeutic micro-processes that can be woven together to construct a view of how change comes about (see Elliott, 1985).

Alternatively, inquiries categorized as "helpful and hindering processes" tend to invite clients to reflect more globally on what occurs during either the course of therapy or during a particular therapy hour, again either positive or negative. Although there can be significant specificity in this type of inquiry, there is not usually a causal weaving together of a sequence of events as is the case with the "significant events" inquiry

method. A third inquiry, addressed in the previous section, invites clients to reflect on their "theory of change," allowing clients to not just reflect on what *did* help the change process but also to prospectively talk about what processes *could* facilitate change, thereby adding an element of their philosophy along with specific change processes.

In a qualitative meta-analysis involving seven studies looking at significant events, Timulak (2007) identified nine core categories: personal contact; behavioral change/problem solution; exploring feelings/emotional experiencing; empowerment; relief; feeling understood; client involvement; reassurance/support/safety; and awareness/insight/self-understanding. The last two categories were reported in all seven studies. Timulak (2010) also performed a qualitative meta-analysis of 41 additional studies of significant events. He noted that significant events findings can be complex and that while clients may label a sequence of therapy as being *helpful*, it may also include elements that are hindering. The "significant event" can really only be understood in the context of the larger picture of the therapy endeavor and clients have vastly different understandings of these events than do their therapists. One difference Timulak (2010) found between therapists and clients' understandings was that clients tended to focus on the emotional and relational factors of a significant event whereas therapists placed value on the cognitive components of an event.

Castonguay and colleagues (2010) similarly found there was little overlap in the types of activities reported as helpful by clients and therapists. In another study, Altimir and colleagues (2010) found that clients who were deemed successful tended to report more numerous change processes than their therapists or observers. However, Altimir and colleagues reported that clients and therapists did agree on the basic content of the change process even if they did not agree on the specific change moments. The fact that clients picked up on more change processes may mean that therapists' preexisting schemas for what counts as helpful are less comprehensive and therapists could stand to benefit from paying closer attention to clients' more nuanced perceptions. These are important findings that suggest what clinicians think, teach, and write about with regard to change processes can be generally and importantly different than what clients believe, leaving therapists in a position of not fully understanding client experience.

Studies of helpful processes have yielded a number of findings. Clients identified internal processes that facilitated change, including self-acceptance (Castonguay et al., 2010; Davidson et al., 2005; Nilsson et al., 2007), reflection and insight about self and others (Castonguay et al., 2010; Orford et al., 2009; Paulson, Truscott, & Stuart, 1999), and learning to reason with self (Svanborg, Åberg, & Svanborg, 2008). Negotiation of the client's role was mentioned in several studies as an important element of the therapy: working through a commitment to therapy (Levitt et al., 2006), feeling free to choose the focus of the therapy (Bowman & Fine, 2000), and feeling comfortable with self-disclosure (Orford et al., 2009). Clients also pointed to helpful processes that occurred outside of therapy: trying something new or transferring skills (Mörtl & Von Wietersheim, 2008), testing things out (Clarke et al., 2004), continued processing between sessions (Bowman & Fine, 2000; Levitt et al., 2006), exerting self-control, utilizing environmental supports, and taking medication (Davidson et al., 2005; Orford et al., 2009). The relationship with the therapist and the therapists' facilitative stance was identified as an important element (Binder, Holgersen, & Neilsen, 2009; Bowman & Fine, 2000; Levitt et al., 2006), including an attachment to the therapist (Svanborg et al., 2008) and particular therapist interventions (Paulson et al., 1999). Variety in the client responses to questions about helpful processes may be due to idiosyncratic elements of the treatment, the nature of the questions asked, the time lapse between therapy and the client's report (ranging from a few minutes to 17 years), or the depth of the information that can be obtained from different assessment methods such as using a one-item questionnaire or doing a 3-hour interview.

Clients' Views of Good Outcome

To understand more fully what a good therapeutic outcome is, Valkonen and her colleagues (2011) suggested getting the different viewpoints of researchers, therapists, and clients. Arguably, researchers have paid significantly more attention to good outcome as is defined by reduction in symptoms at the expense of other elements of change that are deemed valuable by clients (Connolly & Strupp, 1996). Klein and Elliott (2006) employed both quantitative and qualitative free-response measures in their study of outcome. They found overlap between the quantitative measures with clients' perspectives on the qualitative measure. However, clients also spoke of discreet changes that were not accounted for in the various quantitative measures but were nonetheless significant to them. Klein and Elliott (2006) suggest that pluralistic methods for gathering therapeutic results be utilized to include both client and researcher/therapist constructed outcome data.

In addition to symptom reduction, clients in Binder, Holgersen, and Nielsen's (2010) study focused on healthier relationship patterns, an increase in self-understanding that led to freedom and avoidance of destructive behavior, and a stronger valuing of the self. Others have also noted clients' emphasis on changes in self-concept and other-relatedness (Connolly & Strupp, 1996; Svanborg et al., 2008; Castonguay et al., 2010). Knowing when to take responsibility and when to let go was identified with the concept of a good outcome (Clarke et al., 2004). Klein and Elliott (2006) categorized two types of clients' self-reported outcomes. First were changes within the self, which included affective changes, self-improvement, and experiential awareness of self and others. Second were significant changes in terms of their life functioning, such as changes in interpersonal relationships and life status/role changes (e.g., getting a job or reconciling with a spouse).

This broadening of the view of what constitutes a "good outcome" is reflected in both the academic literature and in mental health consumer advocate groups. A panel of 110 experts published a statement that reflects the transformation of "recovery" defined traditionally as stabilization of symptoms to a definition that includes a focus on clients' abilities to participate fully in relationships, work, learning, and in society (National Consensus Conference on Mental Health Recovery and Mental Health Systems Transformation, 2004). Davidson et al.'s (2005) interviews confirmed the importance of this broadened definition of "good outcome"; patients spoke of recovery in terms of reengaging in meaningful work and social roles and a restoration of their sense of self-respect as individuals that are not wholly defined by psychosis.

Conclusion

Research on clients' perspectives supports the idea of the client as someone who plays an active, agentic role in therapy. Where such relationships have been studied, clients' perspectives tend to correlate with outcome, often more highly than those of their therapists. Their views of the nature of their problems, of what they want in therapy, and how those views match up with therapists' interventions can influence both their motivation and outcome. Their views may also influence how they construe change. Furthermore they see themselves as actively contributing through such activities as working hard, learning to reason with themselves, reflecting, and trying something new. Finally, as agents, they value being understood by the therapist and being involved in a genuine, mutual relationship.

Client Constructive Activity

In this section we review evidence demonstrating that clients often contribute proactively to the change process. We first look at client agency, then at how clients contribute to the therapeutic alliance. We then consider how clients carry therapy experiences into everyday life. Finally, we consider two models of client processing.

Client Agency

The concept of client agency assumes that clients are not merely "absorbers" of what therapists offer, but generators of change as well. Through a series of interviews using interpersonal process recall (IPR) methods, Rennie documented clients' agency in the form of awareness of themselves and the activities they engaged in to negotiate change (Rennie, 2002). Rennie (2010) has called this self-awareness *reflexivity* and asserted that clients are also aware of their self-awareness, which he referred to as *radical reflexivity*. Rennie (1992, 2002, 2010) found that clients actively thought to themselves about what was going on while listening to therapists, gained insights they did not share, sometimes resisted therapists' influence, acted upon therapists' directives, were aware of deferring to therapists' expertise, and provided their own interpretation of the meaning of a specific technique or of relationship factors. Mackrill (2009) recommended psychotherapeutic research take a more contextual approach that accounts for agency both in and outside of the therapy room. He pointed to the qualitative work of Dreier's (2008) cross-contextual approach as evidence of clients' agentic ways of transforming everyday life based on what they learned in therapy. Mackrill's (2007, 2008) diary studies provide additional examples of cross-contextual agency: clients learned from and acted upon their environment both in and out of therapy, made connections between the different contexts,

and these connections then influenced how they participated in each context.

Levitt's (2004) interviews with 26 clients revealed that clients idiosyncratically reacted to interventions and managed their therapists' style in order to gain what they personally needed from the session. She noted that manualized interventions that are a one-size-fits-all approach would not be sensitive to the way these clients were agentically interacting with the therapy provided. Greaves and Carl (2009) interviewed group therapy participants using interpersonal process recall methods and found that clients were aware of and able to reflect on their intentions behind their actions in the group. Clients indicated that they facilitated an environment where they could receive specific support, could use others as a foil to understand themselves, and set up situations in group that allowed them to practice new behaviors.

The 11 participants in a qualitative study of individual psychotherapy by Hoener, Stiles, Luka, and Gordon (2012) attributed the change they experienced to their own agentic efforts. They worked within the various therapy approaches they were offered and highlighted ways that a particular approach facilitated their agency. For example, more directive approaches were valued for the responsibility placed on them to do homework whereas less-directive approaches lent them freedom to explore.

Studies that allow for the construct of agency to be measured are a rarity. Research shows that measures of well-being are related to clients' agency-laden thoughts and narratives. For instance, one study coded and then rated clients' narratives for content that reflected a sense of empowerment to overcome rather than be at the mercy of circumstances (Adler, Skalina, & McAdams, 2008). The quantified measure of agency correlated significantly with a composite score of subjective well-being measures ($r = .55$). In another study, following a five-session pretherapy group addressing the topics of hope and agency, clients were given measures of agency and subjective well-being (Irving et al., 2004). In a hierarchical regression analysis, agency scores were predictive of higher subjective well-being scores.

Clients' Contribution to the Therapeutic Relationship

Often when the therapeutic relationship is discussed in the literature, it is referred to as something that is *built* by therapists for the "benefit" of clients. Recent publications, though, give rise to the notion of clients that positively contribute to the therapy relationship in unique ways. To be more in tune with clients, it is wise for therapists to understand ways in which the client, too, is building the relationship (Soares, Botella, & Corbella, 2010).

Assessing clients' contribution is tricky. Use of self-report measures to determine clients' views of their impact on the formation of a solid therapy relationship may underestimate the client's role, especially if clients see the relationship similar to a parent–child relationship (e.g., Fitzpatrick, Janzen, Chamodraka, & Park, 2006) or a doctor-patient relationship. For instance, Bachelor's (1995) study with open-ended questions inviting clients to talk about what made up a good therapy relationship resulted in clients predominantly talking about therapists' contributions to the alliance. However, in an in-depth transcript-analysis of nearly 100 sessions where the focus was solely on *client* initiated sequences of alliance building, it was found that clients played a role in fostering healing qualities in the therapist (Greaves, 2006). This study found that by being "present" themselves and engaging with the therapist in a "real" way, above and beyond their role as a client, they appeared to influence similar responses in the therapist. It was also found that clients' vulnerable expressions of pain fostered empathy in their therapists and alternatively, clients' expressions of hope and optimism about treatment progress seemed to inspire a reciprocal hope in the therapists' responses.

Clients have reported being aware of a "state of readiness" and making conscious decisions to become vulnerable and to open up about difficult material (Knox & Cooper, 2011). Clients also noted seemingly reciprocal openness from their therapists as they were able to become vulnerable. It may be assumed that clients' perceived impact on their therapists' vulnerability may be tied with increases in the "bond" of the relationship (e.g., liking, trust, safety, comfort). Fitzpatrick and colleagues (2006) found that as the bond increased, so did clients' "expressive openness." And clients' gradual reduction of self-concealment was found to be a unique predictor of distress reduction (Wild, 2005). Clients also paid tribute to their own openness to the interventions of the therapist. Fitzpatrick et al. (2006) called this "receptive openness." As clients attributed positive meaning to their therapists' responses, this also contributed to more positive emotions or more exploration. This kind of receptive openness was found in a qualitative study with patients treated for psychosis (McGowan, Lavender, & Garety, 2005). As these patients were able to move into the frame of reference of their therapists, they were able to progress in the treatment. Both receptive and expressive openness seem to be important activities that move the client along in the therapeutic process and are in part facilitated by clients' capacity to experience positive feelings of liking or being liked by their therapist.

Greaves (2006) found that clients were active in building this rapport with their therapists through prosocial behaviors like being appreciative of their therapist or being accommodative of therapists' schedule changes. Clients cultivated mutuality with their therapist by responding to the humor or "realness" of the therapist, building upon a common language base, or creating shared stories about the therapy experience which were referred to time and again. Further impacting the therapeutic bond, clients also took the initiative to make process comments about relationship dynamics. It is clear from Krupnick et al.'s (1996) study examining the relative impact of clients' versus therapists' contributions to the alliance that clients' contributions had more impact on outcome. In this study, external ratings of Patient Exploration, Patient Participation, and Patient Hostility on the Vanderbilt Therapeutic Alliance Scale were significantly correlated with outcome whereas none of the therapists' contributions related to outcome and for each unit of increase in client alliance contributions, there was a threefold increase in odds of remission.

Ablon and Jones (1999) found an inverse relationship between negative patient interpersonal behaviors and improvement in therapy. Items that were significantly correlated in the reverse were: Patient rejects therapist's comments, is suspicious, verbalizes negative feelings, is shy and provocative. There was only one item on the Psychotherapy Process Q-Set that measured a positive interpersonal process initiated by the patient: Patient seeks greater intimacy with the therapist. This item was positively correlated with outcome. Thus it may be inferred that in the absence of these negative behaviors, patients were accepting, trusting, affirming, assertive, and tactful. Once again, the clear importance of client relationship-building behaviors highlights the need to have process and alliance measures that explicitly query for positive and active client contributions.

Clients' Repair of Alliance Ruptures

Research has supported the usefulness of therapists attending to and helping repair ruptures in the alliance (Safran, Muran, & Eubanks-Carter, 2011). However clients, too, contribute to rupture repairs. Often clients do not attempt to repair ruptures and instead choose to resolve the matter by terminating therapy, perhaps because they see no need to waste time in repairing a mismatched relationship. It makes sense that clients themselves would take on the burden of repairing a salvageable relationship since they have invested both time *and* money in it and face a setback if they were to switch to another therapist or give up.

Rhodes, Hill, Thompson, and Elliott (1994) found that a differentiating quality between good and poor therapy outcomes was the way that misunderstandings were handled. Good outcome cases involved having a previously established good relationship combined with clients' assertiveness about negative feelings and therapists' flexible and accepting attitude. Williams and Levitt (2008) found that some clients were equipped to manage these differences. One client-therapist dyad had a cue that acknowledged when they were at odds. Another client made special allowances for the therapist based on the fact that the therapist was in training. Resolving disagreements enhanced another client's sense of efficacy when the client was able to get the therapist to see an alternate viewpoint.

There is no shortage of errors that therapists make including inaccurate interpretations, mixing up clients' stories, showing lack of interest, cutting clients off, and misunderstanding cultural differences (Williams & Levitt, 2008). Greaves (2006) found that some clients not only confronted therapists' errors but queried therapists' intentions in order to understand the root of the mistake. One client overlooked the mistake, then addressed it later by asking for something opposite of the therapist's original response. The work of forgiveness was evident on both the part of clients and therapists. These clients both worked to offer forgiveness and renewed faith in the relationship after ruptures as well as offer their own apologies and promises to change when they were the offending party. It should be noted, though, that clients may not reveal negative feelings and this may be due to an assumption that their feelings are irrational or that they would lose the approval of the therapist (Rennie, 1992). It has been shown that when clients do not assert themselves and bring up negative reactions or if they do and therapists do not discuss or acknowledge them, it may lead to poor outcomes or early termination (Rhodes et al., 1994). Westra et al. (2011) found that clients dropped their expectations for improvement by 25% following alliance rupture situations and that expectations were a key moderator on the impact of ruptures on outcome.

Conclusion

Clients, not just therapists, can play a role in actively coping with and managing the therapeutic relationship. When they do not, this fact needs to become a serious topic of discussion.

Goal Consensus

The construct of the therapeutic alliance is deeply rooted in concepts related to goal consensus: agreeing on the direction of healthy change for the clients, agreeing on the path and goals that lead there, and actively structuring the treatment to be in line with those goals with client buy-in regarding expectations of therapy (Bordin, 1979; Tryon & Winograd, 2011). Goal consensus has been identified as an important ingredient in effective psychotherapy (Steering Committee, 2002). The most recent meta-analysis of the relationship between goal consensus and therapy outcome found an effect size of .34 (Tryon & Winograd, 2011).

Mackrill (2011) identified four different sets of goals: those for life (e.g., repairing a significant relationship) and those for the psychotherapy endeavor (e.g., emotional expression), with therapists and clients each having their own perspectives on each. When addressing the goals for life, diagnosis is not all that therapists need in order to make a treatment plan. Collaboration with clients around treatment goals is an important step in tailoring the treatment plan to meet clients' wishes, not just to remit certain symptoms. For instance, Rajkarnikar (as cited in Cooper & McLeod, 2010) found that for the diagnosis of social anxiety, only a little more than half of the clients were wanting to work on issues of social avoidance or performance anxiety and many instead wanted to focus on other issues like sexuality, work problems, or, the largest category—self-esteem/confidence.

Consensus also needs to be reached for goals regarding the process of psychotherapy (e.g., the quality of therapeutic relationship to be built, degree of emotional expressiveness, insight to be gained). Wampold and colleagues (2006) cited mounting empirical data that better outcomes were associated with therapists explaining the rationale behind the proposed treatment plan and how it fit with clients' presenting concerns, while making room for discussion and negotiation. If clients and therapists agree about the in-session goals and how they relate to the clients' life goals as well as to the in-session tasks, the process of therapy will most likely make more sense to clients and this will mobilize their active participation.

Cooperation and Collaboration

Client cooperation and particularly collaborative participation, has often been cited as one of the primary factors contributing to change (Orlinsky et al., 2004; Lambert, 1992). In a recent meta-analysis, Tryon and Winograd (2011) confirmed a correlation ($r = .33$) between clients' cooperative behaviors and successful outcomes. But collaboration implies more than just cooperation and much more than compliance. However, of the 19 studies included in the meta-analysis, 13 measured "collaboration" via some form of homework compliance (11) and/or treatment adherence (2). Even the value of homework *compliance* has changed in light of recent research showing that homework links to better outcome if clients can "buy in" to the rationale behind it (Scheel, Hanson, & Razzhavaikina, 2004) or if clients are explicitly involved in the creation of the homework assignments (Kazantzis, Deane, & Ronan, 2000). Furthermore, evidence suggests that clients may not follow the homework as prescribed and instead mold their therapists' requests into what fits for them (Greaves, 2006; Mackrill, 2008; Rennie, 1992).

Most of the remaining six studies in Tryon and Winograd's (2011) meta-analysis used an alliance measure as a means of determining collaboration. For instance, the California Psychotherapy Alliance Scale (Gaston, 1991) defines the client's involvement with two separate scales: Patient Commitment (e.g., trust, willingness to make sacrifices and experience painful moments) and Patient Working Capacity (e.g., disclosure, introspection, and experience emotion). Although this scale is classified as an Alliance scale, it has significant overlap with much of what is considered collaboration. On the other hand, scales that have been explicitly designed to measure collaboration do not properly elucidate the clients' involvement in comparison to the therapist's. This deficit is important since collaboration and its relative impact on outcome can only be studied as thoroughly as it is operationally defined. Bachelor, Laverdière, Gamache, and Bordeleau (2007) point out that some measures of collaboration are simply one item or are only vaguely related

to the construct. For instance, the Psychotherapy Process Q-Set is a 100-item measure that contains both positive and negative statements about client and therapist activities (Jones, 2000). Of the 100 statements, there are only nine that are positively worded statements about clients' active rather than passive involvement. In an NIMH depression study, of the 11 Q-Set items that were linked to outcome, nine of them were these same active client processes (Ablon & Jones, 1999). It would seem then that there are disproportionately fewer positive client activities being measured despite these having the most elucidating power to predict what works in therapy.

Other scales tend to have more favorable constructs for the therapist than for the client. One example of this imbalance is the Collaborative Interaction Scale (Colli & Lingiardi, 2009). In this scale, therapists are rated on 12 Positive Interventions and 8 Negative Interventions with regard to collaboration; however for the client, there are only 3 "positive" items ascribed to the Client Collaborative Processes and the remaining 18 items are either Direct or Indirect Rupture Markers. Conceivably, many of the positive behaviors that therapists are rated on could also apply to the client but are left out.

In an effort to enrich the construct of collaboration, Bachelor et al. (2007) invited clients to share details of a "good experience of collaboration in your therapy" (p. 178). Through a qualitative analysis of their answers, three categories of client collaboration were constructed: Active Collaboration Mode (26.7% of clients), where clients see themselves as primarily responsible for the change process; Mutual Collaboration Mode (36.7%), where there is a shared sense of responsibility and activity, and Dependent Collaboration Mode (33.3%), where clients highlighted the importance of the therapists' collaborative efforts. An interesting finding was the restricted range of collaborative actions clients reported about *themselves* in this qualitative study in comparison to those that clients were able to articulate about their therapist (Bachelor et al., 2007). One possibility for this disproportion is that therapists are collaborating more; another possibility is that clients take for granted what they are contributing to the therapy process and instead focus on the strengths of their therapy partner.

As an alternative to self-report, session transcript analysis revealed that clients did intervene in the therapy in a myriad of ways, although these were not explicit strategies that they announced one day in session or that were formalized in treatment planning (Greaves, 2006). Greaves pointed to a similar finding in sociological studies of groups where those who were the underdog often appeared to defer on the surface, leaving the *strategic* moves to those in power, and instead exerted their influence in the grit of the interactions through *tactical* means (see Certeau, 1984).

Although it is clear that collaboration as it is currently defined has a significant impact on measures of process and outcome, more elaboration is needed both in terms of client actual processes as well as the intricate combining of client and therapist activities for the formation of a true collaborative effort.

Client Feedback

An influential development has been that of utilizing ongoing client feedback to enhance the effectiveness of therapy (e.g., Lambert & Shimokawa, 2011). Client feedback can also be seen as a form of collaboration since it adds the client's voice to the practice of therapy management.

Lambert and Shimokawa (2011) pointed out that an estimated 5% to 10% of adult clients participating in clinical trials left therapy worse off than they began. To improve outcome, it has been shown to be useful to regularly monitor and track client responses to therapy and to provide therapists with this information. This is particularly important because therapists often overestimate client performance. Tracking is done by having clients regularly fill out measures of progress, typically on a session-by-session basis.

There are two major approaches to the use of client feedback. The first is that of Lambert and his colleagues (e.g., Lambert & Shimokawa, 2011). Here, collecting client feedback is primarily used to help therapists improve performance. The focus is on cases where clients are not making sufficient progress. This is measured by comparing the client's progress to normed data on clients with similar symptom patterns. Therapists receive feedback on how clients are doing and may use this to make adjustments. In addition, they may also be given tools to help them improve performance if clients are lagging behind. Research has shown that this significantly improves outcomes ($g = .70$; Shimokawa, Lambert, & Smart, 2010).

In one variant of the Lambert approach, clients who were at-risk were also given information as to their progress. The effect size for studies in which clients were given progress information was $g = .55$ (Shimokawa et al., 2010). This was similar to the effect size for the therapist-only feedback group ($g = .53$). Thus there was no clear evidence that giving clients information enhanced outcomes. However, a closer look revealed that giving clients progress information appeared to have a polarizing effect; 15% of clients deteriorated when both themselves and their therapists were given feedback. This compared to 9% deteriorating when only therapists where given feedback. On the other hand, more clients achieved clinically significant change (45% to 38%) when both therapists and clients were given feedback. This suggests that feedback can be beneficial for some clients, and harmful to others. Further research is needed to unpack these results, although it makes intuitive sense that learning you are not progressing as rapidly as most clients could have a motivating effect on some and a discouraging effect on others.

The Partners for Change Outcome Management Systems (PCOMS; S. D. Miller, Duncan, Sorrell, & Brown, 2005) focuses on utilizing client feedback for the purposes of therapists collaborating with clients in the therapy session. Clients fill out a short (four-item) outcome rating scale (the ORS) at the start of each session, which purports to measure subjective well-being, interpersonal relations, social functioning, and overall sense of well-being. At the end of the session clients fill out a four-item session rating scale (the SRS), which basically is a measure of the alliance. The scales are then utilized by the therapist to engage the client in dialogue.

With regard to the PCOMS approach, three studies have supported its effectiveness (Anker, Duncan, & Sparks, 2009; Reese, Norsworthy, & Rowlands, 2009). For example, Reese and colleagues (2009) conducted two studies comparing treatment outcome of clients receiving PCOMS feedback and those receiving no feedback. Patients were randomly assigned to either a feedback or treatment-as-usual (TAU) condition. In the first study they reported that 80% of clients in the feedback group experienced reliable change, while 54% of clients in TAU experienced reliable change. Deterioration was lower in the feedback group (4% to 13%). Lambert and Shimokawa (2011) aggregated these three studies and did a meta-analysis. The combined effect size was $g = 0.48$, which is a moderate effect size favoring the client feedback condition.

It is difficult to know how much the effects of collecting client feedback are due to an increase in including clients as active agents in therapy or due to increased therapist effectiveness. In the Lambert system the focus is on the therapist who is given a choice about sharing the feedback with the client. However, when clients are given feedback it is clear that it has an impact, with some improving and others deteriorating. In the PCOMS system, clients routinely discuss their ratings of progress with their therapists. In either case, including client feedback makes therapy more of an interactive, responsive process (Stiles, Honos-Webb, & Zurko, 1998). Further research is needed to see just how these methods work.

Clients' Learning and Processing Activities Outside of Therapy

Studies have shown that how clients relate to therapy experiences between sessions, specifically in terms of internalizing therapist and therapy experience, can have either a positive or negative effect on outcome. Hartmann, Orlinsky, Weber, Sandholz, and Zeeck (2010) concluded, "it appears that differences in the way patients 'absorb' and 'metabolize' their therapy may emerge more clearly *between* sessions, when patients are not actually in contact with their therapists, than in the therapeutic process observed *during* therapy sessions" (p. 357). Research with eating-disordered clients has found that therapy-related intersession experiences were related to client outcome (Hartmann, 1997; Zeeck, 2004; Zeeck & Hartmann, 2005). In one study of bulimic clients, 86% of successful clients and 68% of unsuccessful clients could be identified from their intersession experience. Zeeck (2004) found that positive therapy-related intersession experiences predicted good outcome while negative intersession experiences predicted poor outcome. Different aspects were important in different phases of therapy. In the beginning of therapy clients who had positive experiences thinking about their therapist and therapy between sessions had better outcomes. Hartmann et al. (2010) found that clients who thought more about the therapist and therapy had a lower risk of failure. On the other hand, clients who specifically recreated therapeutic dialogues involving negative emotions such as feeling hurt, rejected, or misunderstood between sessions were more likely to have a heightened risk of failure at 3-month follow-up. However, Nichols (2009) found that while greater negative internalizations were associated with greater negative change, greater positive internalizations were not associated with greater positive change.

There is evidence that different clients internalize in different ways. Knox (2000) reported that some internalized more than others. They were the ones who were more likely to use their representations of the therapist to soothe or support themselves. Farber and Geller (1994) found that women were more likely to use representations of their therapists when working on problems outside of therapy. Bender (1996) found that avoidant, dependent, passive-aggressive, self-defeating, and schizotypal character styles were less likely to benignly internalize the therapist. As noted, a failure to benignly internalize the therapist was associated with less successful outcomes. Zeeck, Hartmann, and Orlinsky (2006) found that clients who received borderline personality diagnoses were more likely to experience their therapists between sessions as offensive or as making them insecure.

Three studies have recently addressed other aspects of client intersession experience. Mörtl and Von Wietersheim (2008) did a qualitative study of clients in a day treatment program. Day treatment experiences became a resource in the home environment. Clients used day treatment experiences as homework at home. They reflected on experiences at the day treatment center with relatives at home, involved people at home in the development of what they had been learning, and used what they had been learning to confront problems at home. Conversely, they compared and contrasted relationships at home with relationships in the day treatment program and learned from that. Overall, they saw the day treatment program as a kind of "practice field" for everyday life.

Mackrill (2008) studied four clients in a program for adult children of alcoholics. Both therapists and clients kept diaries of their experiences. In addition, sessions were taped and qualitatively analyzed. Clients participated on the average for ten sessions. He found that clients were therapeutically active outside the session. For instance, they created their own experiments and other healing experiences without necessarily having them suggested or even implied by the therapist. In addition, clients used their own ideas of what was helpful to structure their experience of therapy, which allowed for a kind of "seamless" translation between therapy and the natural environment. Clients also compared what they were learning from their therapists with what others were telling them in their everyday lives, such as romantic partners or talk show hosts. They were more likely to use what the therapist said if it fit with what someone else had told them.

Finally, Khurgin-Bott and Farber (2011) studied 135 clients in individual psychotherapy and how much they disclosed about their therapy to confidants in everyday life. On average, most clients moderately self-disclosed. They reported having positive feelings about doing so, and the amount of their self-disclosure correlated with the benefit from psychotherapy.

In conclusion, clients work with their therapy experiences outside of therapy. This can either enhance or detract from outcome, depending on how it is done.

Models of Client Processing Activity

Next we consider two models of how clients process information to help get them "out of the box" of the problems in which they have previously been trapped.

ASSIMILATION OF PROBLEMATIC EXPERIENCES Stiles' (2002) Assimilation of Problematic Experiences approach models how clients gradually acquire insight and move beyond it to process problematic experiences. It has been studied with psychodynamic-interpersonal, cognitive-behavioral, and experiential therapy approaches. The model construes the self as a community of voices. The goal of therapy is to build communicative bridges among the voices. It describes a series of steps. In the first stage, the problematic experience is warded off or dissociated. In the second stage, it emerges as an unwanted thought and is avoided. In the third stage the client acknowledges there is a problem but cannot formulate it clearly. In the next stage there is now clarity about the nature of the problem. However, the experience is still one of being stuck. In the fifth stage, the client gains understanding and insight. Understanding is construed as a "meaning bridge" between conflicting internal "voices" or perspectives. In the sixth stage clients use the understanding to work on the problem. In the seventh stage, there is problem resolution. In the eighth stage, there is mastery and integration. The client uses the problem resolution as a new resource for solving future problems.

The method of Stiles and colleagues for validating the model has been to utilize a series of case histories. As one example, Detert, Llewelyn, Hardy, Barkham, and Stiles (2006) contrasted four good outcome cases with four poor outcome cases. These were drawn from a research project where depressed clients received two sessions of either cognitive-behavioral or interpersonal-psychodynamic therapy one week apart, followed by a third session 3 months later. There were no differences in mean assimilation ratings between the two approaches. However, good outcome cases had significantly higher mean ratings on the assimilation scale than did poor outcome cases. Insight was associated with symptom reduction.

INNOVATIVE MOMENTS The concept of innovative moments (IMs; Gonçalves, Ribiero, et al., 2010) is derived from narrative therapy theory although it has been used to study other approaches. The theory holds that psychopathology is the result of a rigid dominant self-narrative. It is assumed that this self-narrative wards off minority "voices" that might change it in more productive directions. IMs are thoughts, feelings, intentions, projects, or other things that periodically emerge to challenge the dominant self-narrative. However, the question is: Does the client ward them off or does the client integrate them in, thereby changing the dominant self-narrative?

There are five different types of innovative moments: the emergence of a new action, a moment of new thinking or feeling, a moment of actively challenging the problem, a moment of reconceptualizing the problem, and a moment of performing change, which consists of anticipating or planning new experiences or projects. Studies of brief psychotherapy have shown that poor- and good-outcome cases have different profiles of IMs. "Reconceptualization" IMs are more frequent in good outcome cases while rarely being found in poor outcome cases. Performing change IMs, in which new aims, experiences, activities, or projects emerge, also are found more in good outcome cases (Gonçalves, Mendes, Ribiero, Angus, & Greenberg, 2010; Matos, Santos, Gonçalves, & Martins, 2009; Mendes, Ribierto, Angus, & Gonçalves, 2010).

What processes block the path of change in poor-outcome cases? According to a study by Gonçalves, Ribiero, et al. (2010), one process involves what they call *mutual in-feeding*, in which clients resolve the threat to the dominant self narrative by quickly returning to it, thereby not giving the person the chance to integrate the IM in. This minimizes the threat to the dominant self-narrative and preserves its stability.

Research on the assimilation of problematic experiences, and on the integration of innovative moments, is still in formative stages. Nonetheless, it illustrates the possibility that achieving a better understanding of clients' active processing can help therapists intervene more effectively. For instance, familiarity with the assimilation research has helped therapists sensitively identify where a client was in the process of change in order to choose how to more effectively proceed (Carol Humphreys, personal communication, February 10, 2012).

Conclusion on Client Processing Activity

Overall the research demonstrates that clients can take an active role in mining and managing their therapy experiences. Clients are "co-authors" of therapy. They may silently work to themselves while simultaneously participating in activities with their therapists; they may help manage the therapeutic relationship; most of them are interested in collaboration, and collaboration correlates with outcome; and many of them work between sessions and such work relates to outcome. Furthermore, actively involving them by seeking their feedback impacts on outcome. Finally, clients progress by assimilating problematic material and by attending to innovative moments.

CONCLUSION

In our introductory section, we cited Orlinsky et al.'s (1994) conclusion that the quality of clients' participation played the most important role in making psychotherapy work. The findings of this review are compatible with this. A number of client characteristics as well as the degree of psychological dysfunction correlate with both early termination and with outcome. However, more so than these, the best predictors of outcome appear to be how distressed clients are when they enter therapy, and their actual in-therapy behavior. This is suggested by research on early responders, trajectories of change, and on predicting deterioration.

Research also shows that clients are as much independent variables operating on therapy as they are "dependent variables" influenced by therapist operations. Findings on early responders demonstrate that many clients do well regardless of the type of therapy they are in. Clients' preferences, beliefs, motivations, and expectations have been found to influence outcome. Their perceptions correlate with outcome. Yet their perceptions may differ from those of their therapists, while correlating with outcome more highly than those of their therapists. This suggests the possibility that how they construe therapy influences what they get out of it.

Findings also show that clients view themselves, and operate, as active agents. They see themselves as working hard and as playing an integral role in producing outcome. They process information and achieve their own insights. They work to develop, maintain, and repair the therapeutic alliance. They may build bridges between their in-session experiences and their between-session everyday lives. They interpret what they are learning in terms of their individual beliefs, schemas, and goals. Some of this research is of a qualitative nature on small client samples. Furthermore, not all of the research has been related to outcome. Nonetheless the research illustrates the existence of client agentic activity.

Implications for Practice

The most important implication of our review for psychotherapy practice has to do with the potential usefulness of the information for individualizing treatment. There are two general ways to do this. One is to use aptitude-by-treatment interaction information to match clients to a therapy practice based on preexisting client characteristics. We have reviewed evidence that suggests that client reactance, coping style, ethnicity, and preference for different therapy practices might differentially match up better with different ways of providing therapy such as, in the case of ethnicity, the utilization of culturally adapted treatments.

Studies on matching continue to be done. For instance, Conrod and colleagues (2000) have studied the match between client personality traits and variations in substance abuse treatment. Shoham and Insel (2011) have advocated exploring theory-derived mechanisms of problem-formation or problem maintenance and matching intervention to clients on the basis of that exploration. However, there has been controversy over the value of matching (Shoham & Insel, 2011), and not all of the results we have cited are strong.

The other way to use the information is to enhance therapists' capacities for effective *responsiveness* (Stiles et al., 1998). Responsiveness has to do with therapists' ability to be aware of and adjust to the evolving context. Therapists can utilize the evidence presented here to heighten their empathic awareness. They may be reminded that clients, in some sense, are in many ways the mirror images of themselves in the relationship. As are therapists, clients are thinking to themselves, trying to understand what is going on, trying to decide what to do next, try to figure out how best to connect with or deal with the other person, how best to deal with frustration when things are not going well, and how best to make the situation work. Using this awareness, therapists may be in a better position to sensitively tailor the emerging context to help the client. For instance, knowing that clients often interpret what is going on differently than therapists do might help therapists become aware of such moments when they are occurring. They then can make appropriate adjustments, or, through listening to the client, learn how the client's interpretation may even be helping the client progress at that point.

In terms of responsiveness, we support the recent focus on gathering session-by-session client feedback. Not only does the evidence support its usefulness, but it is another way of heightening therapists' sensitivity to the emerging treatment context.

Research Directions

If clients really do play a central role in therapy outcome, then more research needs to focus on how clients do this. We have previously mentioned that simply correlating client characteristics with early termination and with outcome frequently has not proved to be fruitful. It seems more useful to investigate what these characteristics mean, and then study how they might facilitate or detract from the degree and quality of clients' participation. For instance, given a negative relationship of client impulsiveness to outcome, what does that mean from the client's side of the coin? Does impulsiveness detract because clients are unable to stay involved in the process? Or does it in some way negatively impact on their information processing? Or is it possible that our current therapies do not offer the kinds of affordances that would help such clients successfully involve themselves? These are the kinds of questions that would be fruitful to ask.

In terms of understanding how clients process information, a research direction that has not been extensively pursued so far, but is likely to be in the future is to look at neuropsychological underpinnings of psychotherapy and behavior change (e.g., Wampold, Hollon, & Hill, 2011). There is now considerable research devoted to the neuropsychological correlates of both psychopathology and social behavior (e.g., De Haan & Gunnar, 2009). Such research has demonstrated, for instance, that there are many ways in which social interaction directly affects the physiology and brain functioning of individuals. This kind of research may help clarify perennial issues of debate in psychotherapy such as how much change is based on insight and how much it may be based on direct "reprogramming" of the brain as a result of relational interaction.

Much of the recent research on clients has been qualitative in nature. However, as we noted in the introduction, qualitative studies often have small n. Furthermore they are often based on nonrandom samples. This makes it difficult to generalize results. Nevertheless, qualitative studies are of value in demonstrating the existence of phenomena. They can show that something is *possible*. This has been true for studies we have considered. Furthermore, qualitative studies can add a richness of understanding often lacking in quantitative studies. The next step will be to see how widespread some of the phenomena we have considered are and to assess their relative impact on outcome.

From our perspective, we encourage more research from a stance of looking at therapy from the client's vantage point. Current attempts to maximize outcomes place enormous amounts of time and energy in treatment protocols, while comparatively neglecting clients' contributions. Typically therapy research has focused on what therapists do and how it impacts on clients. However, when one looks at therapy from the client's side, either through interpersonal process recall methods (e.g., Rennie, 2002), or by analyzing transcripts by focusing on the client as an active agent (e.g., Greaves, 2006), one gets a different picture. Imagine as a thought experiment that therapy is a co-constructive activity of two creative learners. Furthermore, assume that it is clients who ultimately are the ones to take what happens and to use it to change. Then ask: How do they do it? We still know relatively little about this.

In this regard, many previous studies on clients experiences have focused on their retrospective accounts. Although these have been useful, we believe that looking at therapy from the client's side of the coin means more than asking about his or her experience. Some qualitative studies, for instance those of Rennie (1992), Greaves (2006), and Mackrill (2008), have utilized other methods such as tape-assisted recall, ongoing diaries, or intensive analyses of therapy transcripts to get closer to how clients are actually processing and utilizing therapy. Models of how clients process information can also be utilized to explore how they contribute to change. Examples include Stiles and colleagues' assimilation of problematic experiences approach (e.g., Stiles, 2002), the "innovative moments" approach (e.g., Gonçalves, Ribeiro, et al., 2010), and the task analytic approach of Greenberg, Elliott, and colleagues (e.g., Greenberg, Rice, & Elliott, 1993).

Traditionally psychotherapy theory has focused on the idea of the client as someone whose dysfunctionality gets in the way of therapy. Certainly there is evidence for this. However, the assumption that clients are active co-constructors of a positive process may lead to new insights. For instance, one of us (Amy Wade) has observed that many clients seem to have an order and purpose in the material they present. Just at the time where the therapist feels stuck about what to do next, clients may volunteer information that is relevant and that helps the therapy move along in the proper direction. Some clients seem to have this intuitiveness, whereas others do not. Insight processes can be dependent on clients volunteering just the right information that allows clinicians to make connections so that they can offer up a brilliant insight. Observations such as these, if validated by research, may help therapists find new ways of helping.

A key way that therapists therefore can be responsive to clients' therapy-enhancing activities is to first become aware of what these processes look like. The more the research literature identifies specific client contributions in facilitating the change process, in response to and in interaction with what therapists are doing, and the more these contributions find their way into process measures, the more they can then be distinctly connected to successful (or unsuccessful) outcome. This can then find its way into the training of novice therapists.

The creation of precise and thorough conceptualizations of the change process will not evolve as long as researchers are focused on unidirectional theories of influence (i.e., therapist to client; Dorn, 1984) or easily observable but unimportant therapeutic phenomena (Hill & Corbett, 1993). However, slowly building a database that captures the variety of client processes, intentions, and experiences of therapy would serve as a reference point for the possibilities of productive therapeutic endeavors. Clinicians, clients, and researchers alike could refer to this database of "lived knowledge" as a way to recognize or even anticipate the potential influence the client is having on the therapy endeavor and respond accordingly (Polkinghorne, 1999). As the client's

contribution is understood, then paired with the therapist's contribution, the truly dialogic aspects of therapy can be better accounted for.

There is an abundance of data that points to the crucial nature of client contributions to therapy outcome and yet it may be easier to return to researching what we know and what we can most readily control, that of technique, interventions, and therapist relational stances. We believe this would be a mistake. We urge researchers and clinicians alike to expand the comprehensiveness and complexity of research and theories linking process and outcome so as to include the dialogic interplay of client, therapist, theory, and technique.

REFERENCES

Ablon, J. S., & Jones, E. E. (1999). Psychotherapy process in the national institute of mental health treatment depression collaborative research program. *Journal of Consulting and Clinical Psychology, 67*, 64–75.

Adler, J., Skalina, L., & McAdams, D. (2008). The narrative reconstruction of psychotherapy and psychological health. *Psychotherapy Research, 18*, 719–734.

Altimir, C., Krause, M., Dagnino, P., Tomicic, A., Valdés, N., Perez, J. C., . . . Vilches, O. (2010). Clients', therapists', and observers' agreement on the amount, temporal location, and content of psychotherapeutic change and its relation to outcome. *Psychotherapy Research, 20*, 472–487.

American Psychological Association Presidential Task Force on Evidence-Based Practice. (2006). Evidence-based practice in psychology. *American Psychologist, 61*, 271–285.

Anker, M. G., Duncan, B. L., & Sparks, J. A. (2009). Using client feedback to improve couple therapy outcomes: A randomized clinical trial in a naturalistic treatment setting. *Journal of Consulting & Clinical Psychology, 77*, 693–704.

Arnkoff, D. B., Glass, C. R., & Shapiro, D. A. (2002). Expectations and preferences. In J. C. Norcross (Ed.), *Psychotherapy relationships that work* (pp. 335–356). New York, NY: Oxford University Press.

Aubuchon-Endsley, N., & Callahan, J. L. (2009). The hour of departure: Predicting attrition in the training clinic from role expectancies. *Training & Education in Professional Psychology, 3*, 120–126.

Bachelor, A. (1995). "Clients" perception of the therapeutic alliance: A qualitative analysis, *Journal of Counseling Psychology, 42*, 323–337.

Bachelor, A., Laverdière, O., Gamache, D., & Bordeleau, V. (2007). Collaboration in the therapeutic relationship: The client's perspective. *Psychotherapy: Theory, Research, Training, and Practice, 44,* 175–192.

Bachelor, A., & Meunier, G. (2010). Client attachment to therapist: Relation to client personality and symptomatology, and their contributions to the therapeutic alliance. *Psychotherapy Theory, Research, Practice, Training, 47,* 454–468.

Baldwin, S., Wampold, B., & Imel, Z. (2007). Untangling the alliance–outcome correlation: Exploring the relative importance of therapist and patient variability in the alliance. *Journal of Consulting and Clinical Psychology, 75,* 842–852.

Barkham, M., Connell, J., Stiles, W. B., Miles, J. N. V., Margison, F., Evans, C., & Mellor-Clark, J. (2006). Dose-effect relations and responsive regulation of treatment duration: The good enough level. *Journal of Consulting and Clinical Psychology, 74,* 160–167.

Barrett, M. S., Chua, W. J., Crits-Christoph, P., Connolly Gibbons, M. B., & Thompson, D. (2008). Early withdrawal from mental health treatment: Implications for psychotherapy practice. *Psychotherapy: Theory, Research, Practice, Training, 45,* 247–267.

Bedi, R. P., & Richards, M. (2011). What a man wants: The male perspective on therapeutic alliance formation. *Psychotherapy, 48*(4), 381–390.

Beitel, M., Hutz, A., Sheffield, K., Gunn, C., Cecero, J., & Barry, D. (2009). Do psychologically minded clients expect more from counselling? *Psychology and Psychotherapy: Theory, Research and Practice, 82,* 369–383.

Bender, D. (1996). *The relationship of psychopathology and attachment to patients' representations of self, parents, and therapist in the early phase of psychodynamic psychotherapy.* Unpublished doctoral dissertation, Teachers College, Columbia University, New York.

Beretta, V., De Roten, Y. Stigler, M., Drapeau, M., Fischer, M., & Despland, J. (2005). The influence of patient's interpersonal schemas on early alliance building. *Swiss Journal of Psychology, 64,* 13–20.

Bernal, G., & Sáez-Santiago, E. (2006). Culturally centered psychosocial interventions. *Journal of Community Psychology, 34,* 121–132.

Bergin, A. E., & Garfield, S. L. (1994). Overview, trends, and future issues. In A. E. Bergin & S. L. Garfield (Eds.), *Handbook of psychotherapy and behavior change* (4th ed., pp. 821–830). New York, NY: Wiley.

Beutler, L. E., Blatt, S. J., Alimohamed, S., Levy, K. N., & Angtuaco, L. A. (2006). Participant factors in treating dysphoric disorders. In L. G. Castonguay & L. E. Beutler (Eds.), *Principles of therapeutic change that work* (pp. 13–64). New York, NY: Oxford University Press.

Beutler, L. E., Harwood, T. M., Alimohamed, S., & Malik, M. (2002). Functional impairment and coping style. In J. C. Norcross (Ed.), *Psychotherapy relationships that work: Therapist contributions and responsiveness to patients* (pp. 145–170). New York, NY: Oxford University Press.

Beutler, L. E., Harwood, T. M., Michelson, A., Song, X., & Holman, J. (2011). Reactance/resistance level. In J. C. Norcross (Ed.), *Psychotherapy relationships that work: Evidence-based responsiveness* (2nd ed., pp. 261–278). New York, NY: Oxford University Press.

Beutler, L. E., Harwood, M. T., Kimpara, S., Verdirame, D., & Blau, K. (2011). Coping style. In J. C. Norcross (Ed.), *Psychotherapy relationships that work: Evidence-based responsiveness* (2nd ed., pp. 336–353). New York, NY: Oxford University Press.

Beutler, L. E., Malik, M., Alimohamed, S., Harwood, T. M., Talebi, H., Noble, S., & Wong, E. (2004). Therapist variables. In M. J. Lambert (Ed.), *Bergin and Garfield's handbook of psychotherapy and behavior change* (5th ed., pp. 227–306). Hoboken, NJ: Wiley.

Beutler, L. E., Moleiro, C. M., & Talebi, H. (2002). Resistance. In J. C. Norcross (Ed.), *Psychotherapy relationships that work* (1st ed., pp. 129–144.). New York, NY: Oxford University Press.

Binder, P. E., Holgersen, H., & Nielsen, G. H. (2009). Why did I change when I went to therapy? A qualitative analysis of former patients' conceptions of successful psychotherapy. *Counselling and Psychotherapy Research, 9,* 250–256.

Binder, P. E., Holgersen, H., & Nielsen, G. H. (2010). What is a "good outcome" in psychotherapy? A qualitative exploration of the former patient's point of view. *Psychotherapy Research, 20,* 285–294.

Blatt, S. J., Quinlan, D. M., Pilkonis, P. A., & Shea, T. M. (1995). Impact of perfectionism and need for approval on the brief treatment of depression: The national institute of mental health treatment of depression collaborative research program revisited. *Journal of Consulting and Clinical Psychology, 63,* 125–132.

Bohanske, R. T., & Franzcik, M. (2010). Transforming public behavioral health care: A case example of consumer-directed services, recovery, and the common factors. In B. L. Duncan, S. D. Miller, B. E. Wampold, & M. A. Hubble (Eds.), *The heart & soul of change: Delivering what works* (2nd ed., pp. 299–322). Washington, DC: American Psychological Association.

Bohart, A. C., & Tallman, K. (1999). *How clients make therapy work: The process of active self-healing.* Washington, DC: American Psychological Association.

Bohart, A. C., & Tallman, K. (2010). Clients as active self-healers: Implications for the person-centered approach. In M. Cooper, J. C. Watson, & D. Hölldampf (Eds.), *Person-centered and experiential therapies work* (pp. 91–131). Ross-on-Wye, United Kingdom: PCCS Books.

Bohart, A. C., Tallman, K. L., Byock G., & Mackrill, T. (2011). The "Research Jury Method": The application of the jury trial model to evaluating the validity of descriptive and causal statements about psychotherapy process and outcome. *Pragmatic Case Studies in Psychotherapy*, 7(Module 1, Article 8), 101–144. Online journal: http://pcsp.libraries.rutgers.edu

Bordin, E. S. (1979). The generalizability of the psychoanalytic concept of the working alliance. *Psychotherapy: Theory, Research & Practice*, 16, 252–260.

Boritz, T. Z., Angus, L., Monette, G., Hollis-Walker, L., & Warwar, S. (2011). Narrative and emotion integration in psychotherapy: Investigating the relationship between autobiographical memory specificity and expressed emotional arousal in brief emotion-focused and client-centered treatment of depression. *Psychotherapy Research*, 21, 16–26.

Bowlby, J. (1969). *Attachment and Loss: Vol. 1. Attachment*. New York, NY: Basic Books.

Bowlby, J. (1988). *A secure base: Parent–child attachment and healthy human development*. New York, NY: Basic Books.

Bowman, L., & Fine, M. (2000). Client perceptions of couples therapy: Helpful and unhelpful aspects. *American Journal of Family Therapy*, 28, 295–310.

Bowman, D., Scogin, F., Floyd, M., & McKendree-Smith, N. (2001). Psychotherapy length of stay and outcome: A meta-analysis of the effect of therapist sex. *Psychotherapy: Theory, Research, Practice, Training*, 38, 142–148.

Brehm, J. W. (1966). *A theory of psychological reactance*. New York, NY: Academic Press.

Brown, G. S., Burlingame, G. M., Lambert, M. J., Jones, E., & Vaccaro, J. (2001). Pushing the quality envelope: A new outcomes management system. *Psychiatric Services*, 52, 925–934.

Cabral, R. C., & Smith, T. B. (2011). Racial/ethnic matching of clients and therapists in mental health services: A meta-analytic review of preferences, perceptions, and outcomes. *Journal of Counseling Psychology*, 58, 537–554.

Cahill, J., Barkham, M., Hardy, G., Rees, A., Shapiro, D. A., Stiles, W. B., & Macaskill, N. (2003). Outcomes of patients completing and not completing cognitive therapy for depression. *British Journal of Clinical Psychology*, 42, 133–143.

Cardemil, E. V., & Battle, C. (2003). Guess who's coming to therapy? Getting comfortable with conversations about race and ethnicity in psychotherapy. *Professional Psychology: Research & Practice*, 34, 278–286.

Caspar, F., & Berger, T. (2011). Internet-delivered psychological treatments and psychotherapy integration. *Psychotherapy Bulletin*, 46, 7–11.

Castonguay, L. G., & Beutler, L. E. (2006a). Common and unique principles of therapeutic change: What do we know and what do we need to know? In L. G. Castonguay & L. E. Beutler (Eds.), *Principles of therapeutic change that work* (pp. 353–370). New York, NY: Oxford University Press.

Castonguay, L. G., & Beutler, L. E. (Eds.). (2006b). *Principles of therapeutic change that work*. New York, NY: Oxford University Press.

Castonguay, L. G., Boswell, J. F., Zack, S., Baker, S., Boutselis, M., Chiswick, N., . . . Grosse Holtforth, M. (2010). Helpful and hindering events in psychotherapy: A practice research network study. *Psychotherapy: Theory, Research, Practice, and Training*, 47, 327–344.

Castonguay, L. G., Goldfried, M. R., Wiser, S., Raue, P. J., & Hayes, A. M. (1996). Predicting the effect of cognitive therapy for depression: A study of unique and common factors. *Journal of Consulting and Clinical Psychology*, 64, 497–504.

Certeau, M. (1984). *The practice of everyday life* (S. Rendall, Trans.). Berkeley: University of California Press.

Clarke, H., Rees, A., & Hardy, G. E. (2004). The big idea: Clients' perspectives of change processes in cognitive therapy. *Psychology and Psychotherapy: Theory, Research and Practice*, 77, 67–89.

Clarkin, J. F., & Levy, K. N. (2004). The influence of client variables on psychotherapy. In M. J. Lambert (Ed.), *Bergin and Garfield's handbook of psychotherapy and behavior change* (5th ed., pp. 194–226). Hoboken, NJ: Wiley.

Colli, A., & Lingiardi, V. (2009). The collaborative interactions scale: A new transcript-based method for the assessment of therapeutic alliance ruptures and resolutions in psychotherapy. *Psychotherapy Research*, 19, 718–734.

Connolly, M. B., & Strupp, H. H. (1996). Cluster analysis of patient reported psychotherapy outcomes. *Psychotherapy Research*, 6, 30–42.

Conrod, P. J., Stewart, S. H., Pihl, R. O., Côté, S., Fontaine, V., & Dongier, M. (2000). Efficacy of brief coping skills interventions that match different personality profiles of female substance abusers. *Psychology of Addictive Behaviors*, 14(1), 231–242.

Constantino, M. J., Manber, R., Ong, J., Kuo, T. F., Huang, J. S., & Arnow, B. A. (2007). Patient expectations and therapeutic alliance as predictors of outcome in group cognitive-behavioral therapy for insomnia. *Behavioral Sleep Medicine*, 5, 210–228.

Constantino, M., Glass, C. R., Arnkoff, D. B., Ametrano, R. M., & Smith, J. Z. (2011). Expectations. In J. C. Norcross (Ed.), *Psychotherapy relationships that work: Evidence-based responsiveness* (2nd ed., pp. 354–376). New York, NY: Oxford University Press.

Cooper, M., & McLeod, J. (2010). *Pluralistic counselling and psychotherapy*. Thousand Oaks, CA: Sage.

Corrigan, P. (2004). How stigma interferes with mental health care. *American Psychologist*, 59, 614–625.

Cuijpers, P., van Straten, A., Smit, F., & Andersson, G. (2009). Is psychotherapy for depression equally effective in younger and older adults? A meta-regression analysis. *International Psychogeriatrics, 21,* 16–24.

Davidson, L., Borg, M., Marin, I., Topor, A., Mezzina, R., & Sells, D. (2005). Processes of recovery in serious mental Illness: Findings from a multinational Study. *American Journal of Psychiatric Rehabilitation, 8,* 177–201.

Davis, M. J., & Addis, M. E. (2002). Treatment expectations, experiences, and mental health functioning predict attrition status in behavioural medicine groups. *Irish Journal of Psychology, 23,* 37–51.

De Haan, M., & Gunnar, M. R. (Eds.). (2009). *Handbook of developmental social neuroscience.* New York: Guilford Press.

Detert, N. B., Llewelyn, S., Hardy, G. E., Barkham, M. & Stiles, W. B. (2006). Assimilation in good- and poor-outcome cases of very brief therapy for mild depression: an initial comparison. *Psychotherapy Research, 16,* 393–407.

Diener, M. J., & Monroe, J. M. (2011). The relationship between adult attachment style and therapeutic alliance in individual psychotherapy: A meta-analytic review. *Psychotherapy, 48,* 237–48.

Donovan, D. B., & Rosengren. D. B. (1999). Motivation for behavior change and treatment among substance abusers. In J. A. Tucker, D. M. Donovan, & A. G. Marlett (Eds.), *Changing addictive behavior: Bridging clinical and public health strategies,* (pp. 127–159). New York, NY: Guilford Press.

Dorn, F. J. (1984). The social influence model: A cautionary note on counseling psychology's warm embrace. *Journal of Counseling Psychology, 31,* 111–115.

Dreier, O. (2008). *Psychotherapy in everyday life.* Cambridge, UK: Cambridge University Press.

Elliott, R. (1985). Helpful and nonhelpful events in brief counseling interviews: An empirical taxonomy. *Journal of Counseling Psychology, 32,* 307–322.

Elliott, R. (2002). Hermeneutic single case efficacy design. *Psychotherapy Research, 12,* 1–21.

Elliott, R., Greenberg, L. S., & Lietaer, G. (2004). Research on experiential psychotherapies. In M. Lambert (Ed.), *Bergin and Garfield's handbook of psychotherapy and behavior change* (5th ed., pp. 493–540). Hoboken, NJ: Wiley.

Eugster, S. L., & Wampold, B. (1996). Systematic effects of participant role on the evaluation of the psychotherapy session. *Journal of Consulting and Clinical Psychology, 64,* 1020–1028.

Farber, B. A., & Geller, J. S. (1994). Gender and representation in psychotherapy. *Psychotherapy, 31,* 318–326.

Farsimaden, F., Draghi-Lorenze, R., & Ellis, J. (2007). Process and outcome of therapy in ethnically similar and dissimilar therapeutic dyads. *Psychotherapy Research, 17,* 567–575.

Fitzpatrick, M. R., Janzen, J., Chamodraka, M., & Park, J. (2006). Client critical incidents in the process of early alliance development: A positive emotion-exploration spiral. *Psychotherapy Research, 16,* 486–498.

Flückiger, C., Meyer, A., Wampold, B. E., Gassman, D., Messerli-Bürgy, & Munsch, S. (2011). Premature termination within a randomized controlled trial for binge-eating patients. *Behavior Therapy, 42,* 716–725.

Fournier, J. C., DeRubeis, R. J., Shelton, R. C., Hollon, S. D., Amsterdam, J. D., & Gallop, R. (2009). Prediction of response to medication and cognitive therapy in the treatment of moderate severe depression. *Journal of Consulting and Clinical Psychology, 77,* 775–787.

Frank, J. D. (1961). *Persuasion and healing.* Baltimore, MD: Johns Hopkins University Press.

Fuertes, J. N., Mislowack, A., Brown, S., Gur-Arie, S., Wilkinson, S., & Gelso, C. J. (2007). Correlates of the real relationship in psychotherapy: A study of dyads. *Psychotherapy Research, 17,* 423–430.

Garfield, S. L. (1971). Research on client variables in psychotherapy. In A. E. Bergin & S. L. Garfield (Eds.), *Handbook of psychotherapy and behavior change: An empirical analysis.* New York, NY: Wiley.

Garfield, S. L. (1978). Research on client variables in psychotherapy. In S. L. Garfield & A. E. Bergin (Eds.), *Handbook of psychotherapy and behavior change* (2nd ed., pp. 191–232). New York, NY: Wiley.

Garfield, S. L. (1986). Research on client variables in psychotherapy. In S. L. Garfield & A. E. Bergin (Eds.), *Handbook of psychotherapy and behavior change* (3rd ed., pp. 213–256). New York, NY: Wiley.

Garfield, S. L. (1994). Research on client variables in psychotherapy. In A. E. Bergin & S. L. Garfield (Eds.), *Handbook of psychotherapy and behavior change* (4th ed., pp. 190–228). New York, NY: Wiley.

Gassman, D., & Grawe, K. (2006). General change mechanisms: The relation between problem activation and resource activation in successful and unsuccessful therapeutic interactions. *Clinical Psychology and Psychotherapy, 13,* 1–11.

Gaston, L. (1991). Reliability and criterion-related validity of the California psychotherapy alliance scales—Patient version. *Psychological Assessment: A Journal of Consulting and Clinical Psychology, 3,* 68–74.

Geller, S. M., & Greenberg, L. S. (2002). Therapeutic presence: Therapists' experience of presence in the psychotherapy encounter. *Person-Centered & Experiential Psychotherapies, 1,* 71–86.

Geller, S. M., Greenberg, L. S., & Watson, J. C. (2011). Therapist and client perceptions of therapeutic presence: The development of a measure. *Psychotherapy Research, 20,* 599–610.

Gelso, C. L. (2009). The real relationship in a postmodern world: Theoretical and empirical explorations. *Psychotherapy Research, 19,* 253–264.

Gendlin, E. T. (1996). *Focusing-oriented psychotherapy: A manual of the experiential method*. New York, NY: Guilford Press.

Gendlin, E. T., Beebe, J. III, Cassens, J., Klein, M., & Oberlander, M. (1968). Focusing ability in psychotherapy, personality, and creativity. In J. M. Shlien (Ed.), *Research in psychotherapy* (Vol. *III*, pp. 217–241). Washington, DC: American Psychological Association.

Goldfarb, D. E. (2002). College counseling center clients' expectations about counseling: How they relate to depression, hopelessness, and actual-ideal self-discrepancies. *Journal of College Counseling, 5*, 142–152.

Goldman, R. N., Greenberg, L. S., & Pos, A. E. (2005). Depth of emotional experience and outcome. *Psychotherapy Research, 15*, 248–260.

Gonçalves, M. M., Mendes, I., Ribeiro, A. P., Angus, L., & Greenberg, L. (2010). Innovative moments and change in emotion-focused therapy: The case of Lisa. *Journal of Constructivist Psychology, 23*, 267–294.

Gonçalves, M. M., Ribeiro, A. P. Stiles, W. B., Conde, T., Matos, M., Martins, C., & Santos, A. (2010). The role of mutual in-feeding in maintaining problematic self-narratives: Exploring one path to therapeutic failure. *Psychotherapy Research, 21*, 27–40.

Greaves, A. L. (2006). *The active client: A qualitative analysis of thirteen clients' contribution to the psychotherapeutic process*. Unpublished doctoral dissertation, University of Southern California.

Greaves, A. L., & Carl, B. (2009). *How clients as active self-healers make use of group therapy*. Paper presented at the Conference of the Society for Psychotherapy Research, Santiago, Chile.

Greenberg, L. S., Rice, L. N., & Elliott, R. (1993). *Facilitating emotional change: The moment-by-moment process*. New York, NY: Guilford Press.

Haaga, D. A. F., Hall, S. M., & Haas, A. (2006). Participant factors in treating substance abuse disorders. In L. G. Castonguay & L. E. Beutler (Eds.), *Principles of therapeutic change that work* (pp. 275–292). New York, NY: Oxford University Press.

Haas, E., Hill, R. D., Lambert, M. J., & Morrell, B. (2002). Do early responders to psychotherapy maintain treatment gains? *Journal of Clinical Psychology, 58*(9), 1157–1172.

Hansen, N. B., & Lambert, M. (2003). An evaluation of the dose–response relationship in naturalistic treatment settings using survival analysis. *Mental Health Services Research, 5*, 1–11.

Hansen, N. B., Lambert, M. J., & Forman, E. M. (2002). The psychotherapy dose–response effect and its implications for treatment delivery services. *Clinical Psychology: Science and Practice, 9*, 329–343.

Hartmann, A., Orlinsky, D., Weber, S., Sandholz, A., & Zeeck, A. (2010). Session and intersession experience related to treatment outcome in bulimia nervosa. *Psychotherapy: Theory, Research, Practice, Training, 47*, 355–370.

Hartmann, A. (1997). Therapie zwischen den Stunden. Explorationen von Intersession-Prozessen. [Therapy between the hours. Exporations of intersession processes] Frankfurt/M: Peter Lang Europäischer Verlag der Wissenschaften. [As referenced in Hartman, A., Orlinsky, D., Weber, S., Sandholz, A., & Zeeck, A. (2010)].

Hatchett, G. T., & Park, H. L. (2003). Comparison of four operational definitions of premature termination. *Psychotherapy: Theory, Research, Practice, Training, 40*, 226–231.

Hautmann, C., Eichelberger, I., Hanisch, C., Plück, J., Walter, D., & Döpfner, M. (2010). The severely impaired do profit most: Short-term and long-term predictors of therapeutic change for a parent management training under routine care conditions for children with externalizing problem behavior. *European Child & Adolescent Psychiatry, 19*, 419–430.

Hawley, L. L., Ho, M. R., Zuroff, D. C., & Blatt, S. J. (2006). The relationship of perfectionism, depression, and therapeutic alliance during treatment for depression: Latent difference score analysis. *Journal of Consulting and Clinical Psychology, 74*, 930–942.

Hayes, J. A., & Wall, T. N. (1998). What influences clinicians' responsibility attributions? The role of problem type, theoretical orientation, and client attribution. *Journal of Social and Clinical Psychology, 17*, 69–74.

Hendricks, M. N. (2002). Focusing-oriented/experiential psychotherapy. In D. J. Cain & J. Seeman (Eds.), *Humanistic psychotherapies: Handbook of research and practice* (pp. 221–252). Washington, DC: American Psychological Association.

Hill, C. E., & Corbett, M. M. (1993). A perspective on the history of process and outcome research in counseling psychology. *Journal of Counseling Psychology, 40*, 3–24.

Hill, C. E., & Lambert, M. J. (2004). Methodological issues in studying psychotherapy processes and outcomes. In M. J. Lambert (Ed.), *Bergin and Garfield's handbook of psychotherapy and behavior change* (5th ed., pp. 84–136). Hoboken, NJ: Wiley.

Hoener, C., Stiles, W. B., Luka, B. J., & Gordon, R. A. (2012). Client experiences of agency in therapy. *Person-Centered & Experiential Psychotherapies, 11*(1), 64–82.

Horvath, A. O., Del Re, A. C., Flückiger, C., & Symonds, D. (2011). Alliance in individual psychotherapy. In J. C. Norcross (Ed.), *Psychotherapy relationships that work: Evidence-based responsiveness* (2nd ed., pp. 25–69). New York, NY: Oxford University Press.

Horvath, A. O., & Bedi, R. P. (2002). The alliance. In J. C. Norcross (Ed.), *Psychotherapy relationships that work: Therapist contributions responsiveness to patients* (pp. 37–70). New York, NY: Oxford University Press.

Irving, L. M., Snyder, C. R., Cheavens, J., Gravel, L., Hanke, J., Hilberg, P., & Nelson, N. (2004). The relationships between hope and outcomes at the pretreatment, beginning, and later phases of psychotherapy. *Journal of Psychotherapy Integration, 14*, 419–443.

Jones, E. E. (2000). *Therapeutic action: A guide to psychoanalytic therapy*. Northvale, NJ: Aronson.

Kazantzis, N., Deane, F. P., & Ronan, K. R. (2000). Homework assignments in cognitive and behavioral therapy: A meta-analysis. *Clinical Psychology: Science and Practice, 7*, 189–202.

Kazdin, A. E., & Whitley, M. K. (2006). Comorbidity, case complexity, and effects of evidence-based treatment for children referred for disruptive behavior. *Journal of Consulting and Clinical Psychology, 74*, 455–467.

Kazdin, A. E., Holland, L., Crowley, M., & Breton, S. (1997). Barriers to treatment participation scale: Evaluation and validation in the context of child outpatient treatment. *Journal of Child Psychology and Psychiatry, 38*, 1051–1062.

Khurgin-Bott, R., & Farber, B. (2011). Patients' disclosures about therapy: Discussing therapy with spouses, significant others, and best friends. *Psychotherapy, 48*, 330–335.

King, M., Sibbald, B., Ward, E., Bowers, P., Lloyd, M., Gabbay, M., & Byford, S. (2000). Randomised controlled trial of non-directive counselling, cognitive-behaviour therapy and usual general practitioner care in the management of depression as well as mixed anxiety and depression in primary care. *Health Technology Assessment, 4*, 1–83.

Klein, M. H., Mathieu-Coughlan, P., & Kiesler, D. J. (1986). The experiencing Scales. In L. S. Greenberg & W. M. Pinsof (Eds.), *The psychotherapeutic process: A research handbook* (pp. 21–72). New York, NY: Guilford Press.

Klein, M. J., & Elliott, R. (2006). Client accounts of personal change in process–experiential psychotherapy: A methodologically pluralistic approach. *Psychotherapy Research, 16*, 91–105.

Knox, S. (2000). Clients' internal representations of their therapists: A qualitative study. *Dissertation Abstracts International: Section B: The Sciences and Engineering*, 4230.

Knox, S., Adrians, N., Everson, E., Hess, S., Hill, C., & Crook-Lyon, R. (2011). Clients' perspectives on therapy termination. *Psychotherapy Research, 21*(2), 154–167.

Knox, R., & Cooper, M. (2011). A state of readiness: An exploration of the client's role in meeting at relational depth. *Journal of Humanistic Psychology, 51*, 61–81.

Knox, S., Catlin, L., Casper, M., & Schlosser, L. Z. (2005). Addressing religion and spirituality in psychotherapy: clients' perspectives. *Psychotherapy Research, 15*, 287–303.

Kronström, K., Salminen, J. K., Hietala, J., Kajande, J., Vahlberg, T., Markkula, J., . . . Karlss, H. (2009). Does defense style or psychological mindedness predict treatment response in major depression? *Depression and Anxiety, 26*, 689–695.

Krupnick, J. L., Sotsky, S. M., Simmens, A. Moyer, J., Elkin, I., Watkins, J., & Pilkonis, P. A. (1996). The role of the therapeutic alliance in psychotherapy and pharmacotherapy outcome: Findings in the national institute of mental health treatment of depression collaborative research program. *Journal of Consulting and Clinical Psychology, 64*, 532–539.

Kühnlein, I. (1999). Psychotherapy as a process of transformation: Analysis of post-therapeutic autobiographical narrations. *Psychotherapy Research, 9*, 274–288.

Lambert, M. J. (1992). Psychotherapy outcome research: Implications for integrative and eclectic therapists. In J. C. Norcross & M. R. Goldfried (Eds.), *Handbook of psychotherapy integration* (pp. 94–129). New York, NY: Basic Books.

Lambert, M. J. (2010). "Yes, it is time for clinicians to routinely monitor treatment outcome." In B. L. Duncan, S. D. Miller, B. E. Wampold, & M. A. Hubble (Eds.), *The heart and soul of change: Delivering what works* (2nd ed., pp. 239–266). Washington, DC: American Psychological Association.

Lambert, M. J., & Shimokawa, K. (2011). Collecting client feedback. In J. C. Norcross (Ed.), *Psychotherapy relationships that work: Evidence-based responsiveness* (2nd ed., pp. 203–223). New York, NY: Oxford University Press.

Lambert, M. J., Smart, D. W., Campbell, M. P., Hawkins, E. J., Harmon, C., & Slade, K. L. (2006). Psychotherapy outcome as measured by the OQ-45 in African American, Asian/Pacific Islander, Latino/a, and Native American clients compared with matched Caucasian clients. *Journal of College Student Psychotherapy, 20*, 17–29.

Lambert, M. J., Harmon, C., Slade, K., Whipple, J. L., & Hawkins, E. J. (2005). Providing feedback to psychotherapists on their patients' progress: Clinical results and practice suggestions. *Journal of Clinical Psychology, 61*, 165–174.

Leaf, P. J., Bruce, M. L., & Tischler, G. L. (1986). The differential effect of attitudes on the use of mental health services. *Social Psychiatry, 21*, 187–192.

Levitt, H. M. (2004, November). What client interviews reveal about psychotherapy process: Principles for the facilitation of change in psychotherapy. Paper presented at the meeting of the North American Society for Psychotherapy Research, Springdale, Utah.

Levitt, H. M., & Rennie, D. L. (2004). Narrative activity: Clients' and therapists' intentions in the process of narration. In L. E. Angus & J. McLeod (Eds.), *The handbook of narrative and psychotherapy* (pp. 299–314). Thousand Oaks, CA: Sage.

Levitt, H., Butler, M., & Hill, T. (2006). What clients find helpful in psychotherapy: Developing principles for facilitating moment-to-moment change. *Journal of Counseling Psychology*, *53*, 314–324.

Levy, K. N., Ellison, W. D., Scott, L. N., Bernecker, S. L. (2011). Attachment style. In J. C. Norcross (Ed.), *Psychotherapy relationships that work* (2nd ed., pp. 377–401). New York, NY: Oxford University Press.

Leweke, F., Bausch, S., Leichsenring, F., Walter, B., & Stingl, M. (2009). Alexithymia as a predictor of outcome of psychodynamically oriented inpatient treatment. *Psychotherapy Research*, *19*, 323–331.

Lo Coco, G., Cullo, S., Prestano, C., & Gelso, C. L. (2011). Relation of the real relationship and the working alliance to outcome of brief psychotherapy. *Psychotherapy*, *48*(4), 368–373.

Luborsky, L., Singer, B., & Luborsky, L. (1975). Comparative studies of psychotherapies: Is it true that "everyone has won and all must have prizes"? *Archives of General Psychiatry*, *32*, 995–1008.

Mackrill, T. (2007). Using a cross-contextual qualitative diary design to explore client experiences of psychotherapy. *Counselling & Psychotherapy Research*, *7*, 233–239.

Mackrill, T. (2008) *The therapy journal project: A cross-contextual qualitative diary study of psychotherapy with adult children of alcoholics*. PhD Dissertation. Copenhagen, Denmark: Institute for Psychology, Copenhagen University.

Mackrill, T. (2009). Constructing client agency in psychotherapy research. *Journal of Humanistic Psychology*, *49*, 193–206.

Mackrill, T. (2011). Differentiating life goals and therapeutic goals: Expanding our understanding of the working alliance. *British Journal of Guidance & Counselling*, *39*, 25–39.

MacNair-Semands, R. R. (2002). Predicting attendance and expectations for group therapy. *Group Dynamics: Theory, Research, and Practice*, *6*, 219–228.

Mallinckrodt, B. (2010). The psychotherapy relationship as attachment: Evidence and implications. *Journal of Social and Personal Relationships*, *27*, 262–270.

Maramba, G. G., & Hall, G. C. N. (2002) Meta-analysis of ethnic match as a predictor of dropout, utilization, and level of functioning. *Cultural Diversity and Ethnic Minority Psychology*, *8*, 290–297.

Marcus, D. K., Kashy, D. A., & Baldwin, S. A. (2009). Studying psychotherapy using the one-with-many design: The therapeutic alliance as an exemplar. *Journal of Counseling Psychology*, *56*, 537–548.

Marmarosh, C. L., Gelso, C. J., Markin, R. D., Majors, R., Mallery, C., & Choi, J. (2009). The real relationship in psychotherapy: Relationships to adult attachments, working alliance, transference, and therapy outcome. *Journal of Counseling Psychology*, *56*, 337–350.

Martin, J. (2008). Male client's perceptions of positive therapeutic alliance. *Dissertation Abstracts International*: *Section B*: *The Sciences and Engineering*, p. 6972.

Matos, M., Santos, A., Gonçalves, M. M., & Martins, C. (2009). Innovative moments and change in narrative therapy. *Psychotherapy Research*, *19*, 68–80.

McBride, C., Zuroff, D. C., Ravitz, P., Koestner, R., Moskowitz, D. S., Quilty, L., & Bagby, R. M. (2010). Autonomous and controlled motivation and interpersonal therapy for depression: Moderating role of recurrent depression. *British Journal of Clinical Psychology*, *49*, 529–545.

McCallum, M., Piper, W. E., Ogrodniczuk, J. S., & Joyce, A. S. (2003). Relationships among psychological mindedness, alexithymia and outcome in four forms of short-term psychotherapy. *Psychology and Psychotherapy: Theory, Research and Practice*, *76*, 133–144.

McGowan, J. R., Lavender, T., & Garety, P. A. (2005). Factors in outcome of cognitive-behavioural therapy for psychosis: Users' and clinicians' views. *Psychology and Psychotherapy: Theory, Research and Practice*, *78*, 513–529.

McMurran, M., Huband, N., & Overton, E. (2010). Non-completion of personality disorder treatments: A systematic review of correlates, consequences, and interventions. *Clinical Psychology Review*, *30*, 277–287.

Mendes, I., Ribeiro, A., Angus, L., Greenberg, L., & Gonçalves, M. M. (2010). Narrative change in emotion-focused therapy: How is change constructed through the lens of the innovative moments coding system? *Psychotherapy Research*, *20*, 692–701.

Meyer, B. & Garcia-Roberts, L. (2007). Congruence between reasons for depression and motivations for specific interventions. *Psychology and Psychotherapy: Theory, Research and Practice*, *80*, 525–542.

Miller, S. D., Duncan, B. L., Sorrell, R., & Brown, G. S. (2005). The partners for change outcome system. *Journal of Clinical Psychology: In Session*, *61*, 199–208.

Miller, R. B. (2011). Real clinical trials (RCT)—Panels of psychological inquiry for transforming anecdotal data into clinical facts and validated judgments: Introduction to a pilot test with the case of "Anna." *Pragmatic Case Studies in Psychotherapy*, *7*(Module 1, Article 2), 6–36. Online journal: http://pcsp.libraries.rutgers.edu

Miller, W. R., & Rollnick, S. (2002). *Motivational interviewing: Preparing people for change* (2nd ed.). New York, NY: Guilford Press.

Miller, W. R., Wilbourne, P. L., & Hettema, J. E. (2003). What works? A summary of alcohol treatment outcome research. In R. K. Hester & W. R. (Eds.), *Handbook of alcoholism treatment approaches: Effective Miller* (3rd ed., pp. 13–63). Boston, MA: Allyn & Bacon.

Mörtl, K., & Von Wietersheim, J. (2008). Client experiences of helpful factors in a day treatment program: A qualitative approach. *Psychotherapy Research*, *18*, 281–293.

National Consensus Conference on Mental Health Recovery and Mental Health Systems Transformation. (2004). www.samhsa.gov

Newman, M. G., Crits-Christoph, P., Connolly Gibbons, M. B., & Erickson, T. M. (2006). Participant factors in treating anxiety disorders. In L. G. Castonguay & L. E. Beutler (Eds.), *Principles of therapeutic change that work* (pp. 121–154). New York, NY: Oxford University Press.

Nichols, S. (2009). The process of internalization in psychotherapy and its relationship to the working alliance and therapeutic change. *Dissertation Abstracts International: Section B: The Sciences and Engineering*, 2581.

Nilsson, T., Svensson, M., Sandell, R., & Clinton, D. (2007). Patients' experiences of change in cognitive-behavioral therapy and psychodynamic therapy: A qualitative comparative study. *Psychotherapy Research, 17*, 553–566.

Noble, L. M., Douglas, B. C., & Newman, S. P. (2001). What do patients expect of psychiatric services? A systematic and critical review of empirical studies. *Social Science & Medicine, 52*, 985–998.

Norcross, J. C. (2006). Integrating self-help into psychotherapy: 16 practical suggestions. *Professional Psychology: Research and Practice, 37*, 683–693.

Norcross, J. C. (2010). The therapeutic relationship. In B. L. Duncan, S. D. Miller, B. E. Wampold, & M. A. Hubble (Eds.), *The heart & soul of change: Delivering what works* (2nd ed., pp. 113–142). Washington, DC: American Psychological Association.

Norcross, J. C., & Lambert, M. J. (2011). Evidence-based therapy relationships. In J. C Norcross, (Ed.), *Psychotherapy relationships that work: Evidence-based responsiveness* (pp. 3–24). New York, NY: Oxford University Press.

Norcross, J. C., Krebs, P. M., & Prochaska, J. O. (2011). Stages of change. In J. C. Norcross (Ed.), *Psychotherapy relationships that work: Evidence-based responsiveness* (2nd ed., pp. 279–300). New York, NY: Oxford University Press.

Nyklíček, I., Majoor, D., & Schalken, P. A. A. M. (2010). Psychological mindedness and symptom reduction after psychotherapy in a hetereogeneous psychiatric sample. *Comprehensive Psychiatry, 51*, 492–496.

Obegi, J., & Berant, E. (2008). Introduction. In J. H. Obegi & E. Berant (Eds.), *Attachment theory and research in clinical work with adults* (pp. 1–16). New York, NY: Guilford Press.

Ogrodniczuk, J. S. (2006). Men, women, and their outcome in psychotherapy. *Psychotherapy Research, 16*, 453–462.

Oliver, J. M., Hart, B. A., Ross, M. J., & Katz, B. M. (2001). Healthy perfectionism and positive expectations about counseling. *North American Journal of Psychology, 3*, 229–242.

Olver, M. E., & Wong, S. (2011). Predictors of sex offender treatment dropout: Psychopathy, sex offender risk, and responsivity implications. *Psychology, Crime & Law, 17*, 457–471.

Orford, J., Hodgson, R., Copello, A., Wilton, S., Slegg, G., & UKATT Research Team. (2009). To what factors do clients attribute change? Content analysis of follow-up interviews with clients of the UK Alcohol Treatment Trial. *Journal of Substance Abuse Treatment, 36*, 49–58.

Orlinsky, D. E., Grawe, K., Parks, B. K. (1994). Process and outcome in psychotherapy—Noch einmal. In A. E. Bergin & S. L. Garfield (Eds.), *Handbook of psychotherapy and behavior change* (4th ed., pp. 270–378). New York, NY: Wiley.

Orlinsky, D. E., Rønnestad, M. H., &Willutzki, U. (2004). Fifty years of psychotherapy process-outcome research: Continuity and change. In M. J. Lambert (Ed.), *Bergin and Garfield's handbook of psychotherapy and behavior change* (5th ed., pp. 307–390). Hoboken, NJ: Wiley.

Oxman, T. E., & Sengupta, A. (2002). Treatment of minor depression. *American Journal of Geriatric Psychiatry, 10*, 256–264.

Owen, J. J., Wong, Y. J., & Rodolfa, E., (2010). The relationship between clients' conformity to masculine norms and their perceptions of helpful therapist actions. *Journal of Counseling Psychology, 57*, 68–78.

Owen, J. J., Tao, K., Leach, M. M., & Rodolfa, E. (2011). Clients' perceptions of their psychotherapists' multicultural orientation. *Psychotherapy, 48*, 274–282.

Parhar, K. K., Wormith, J. S., Derkzen, D. M., & Beauregard, A. M. (2008). Offender coercion in treatment: A meta-analysis of effectiveness. *Criminal Justice and Behavior, 35*, 1109–1135.

Patterson, C. L., Uhlin, B., & Anderson, T. (2008). Clients' pretreatment counseling expectations as predictors of the working alliance. *Journal of Counseling Psychology, 55*, 528–534.

Paulson, B. L., Truscott, D., & Stuart J. (1999). Client's perceptions of helpful experiences in counseling. *Journal of Counseling Psychology, 46*(3), 317–324.

Pertab, J., Nielsen, S. L., & Lambert, M. J. (in press). *Does client-therapist gender matching influence therapy course or outcome in psychotherapy?* Department of Psychology, Brigham Young University, Provo, UT.

Pieper, J., & van Uden, R. (1996). Religion in mental health care: Patients' views. In P. J. Verhagen & G. Glas (Eds.), *Psyche and faith: Beyond professionalism* (pp. 69–83). Uitgeverij Boekencentrum, The Netherlands: Zoetermeer.

Piper, W. E. (1994). Client variables. In A. Fuhriman & G. M. Burlingame (Eds.), *Handbook of group psychotherapy: An empirical and clinical synthesis* (pp. 83–113). New York, NY: Wiley.

Polkinghorne, D. E. (1999). Traditional research and psychotherapeutic practice. *Journal of Clinical Psychology, 55*, 1429–1440.

Pos, A. E., Greenberg, L. S., & Warwar, S. H. (2009). Testing a model of change in the experiential treatment for depression. *Journal of Consulting and Clinical Psychology, 77*, 1055–1066.

President's New Freedom Commission on Mental Health. (2003). *Achieving the promise: Transforming mental health care in America. Final report* (DHHS Pub. No. SMA-03-3832).

Reese, R. J., Norsworthy, L., & Rowlands, S. (2009). Does a continuous feedback system improve psychotherapy outcomes? *Psychotherapy: Theory, Research, Practice, & Training, 46*, 418–431.

Reis, B. F., & Brown, L. G. (1999). Reducing psychotherapy dropouts: Maximizing perspective convergence in the psychotherapy dyad. *Psychotherapy, 36*, 123–136.

Rennie, D. L. (1992). Qualitative analysis of the client's experience of psychotherapy: The unfolding of reflexivity. In S. G. Toukmanian & D. L. Rennie (Eds.), *Psychotherapy process research: Paradigmatic and narrative approaches* (pp. 211–233). Newbury Park, CA: Sage.

Rennie, D. L. (2002). Experiencing psychotherapy: Grounded theory studies. In D. J. Cain (Ed.), *Humanistic psychotherapies: Handbook of research and practice* (pp. 117–144). Washington, DC: American Psychological Association.

Rennie, D. L. (2010). Humanistic psychology at York university: Retrospective: Focus on clients' experiencing in psychotherapy: Emphasis of radical reflexivity. *Humanistic Psychologist, 38*, 40–56.

Rhodes, R., Hill, C. E., Thompson, B. J., & Elliott, R. (1994). Client retrospective recall of resolved and unresolved misunderstanding events. *Journal of Counseling Psychology, 41*, 473–483.

Roehrle, B., & Strouse, J. (2008). Influence of social support on success of therapeutic interventions: A meta-analytic review. *Psychotherapy: Theory, Research, Practice, Training, 45*(4), 464–476.

Romano, V., Fitzpatrick, M., & Janzen, J. (2008). The secure-base hypothesis: Global attachment, attachment to counselor, and session exploration in psychotherapy. *Journal of Counseling Psychology, 55*, 495–504.

Rudkin, A., Llewelyn, S., Hardy, G., Stiles, W. B., & Barkham, M. (2007). Therapist and client processes affecting assimilation and outcome in brief psychotherapy. *Psychotherapy Research, 17*, 613–621.

Rufer, M., Albrecht, P., Zaum, J., Schnyder, U., Mueller-Pfeiffer, C., Hand, I., & Schmidt, O. (2010). Impact of alexithymia on treatment outcome: A naturalistic study of short-term cognitive-behavioral group therapy for panic disorder. *Psychopathology, 43*, 170–179.

Safran, J. D., Muran, J. C., & Eubanks-Carter, C. (2011). Repairing alliance ruptures. In J. C. Norcross (Ed.), *Psychotherapy relationships that work: Evidence-based responsiveness* (pp. 224–238). New York, NY: Oxford University Press.

Safren, S. A., Heimberg, R. G., & Juster, H. R. (1997). Clients' expectancies and their relationship to pretreatment symptomatology and outcome of cognitive-behavioral group treatment for social phobia. *Journal of Consulting and Clinical Psychology, 65*, 694–698.

Sauer, E. M., Anderson, M. Z., Gormley, B., Richmond, C. J., & Preacco, L. (2010). Client attachment orientations, working alliances, and responses to therapy: A psychology training clinic study, *Psychotherapy Research, 6*, 702–711.

Saypol, E., & Farber, B. A. (2010). Attachment style and patient disclosure in psychotherapy. *Psychotherapy Research, 20*, 462–471.

Schulte, D. (2008). Patients' outcome expectancies and their impressions of suitability as predictors of good treatment. *Psychotherapy Research, 18*, 481–494.

Scheel, M. J., Hanson, W. E., & Razzhavaikina, T. I. (2004). The process of recommending homework in psychotherapy: A review of therapist delivery methods, client acceptability, and factors that affect compliance. *Psychotherapy: Theory, Research, Practice, Training, 41*, 38–55.

Sharf, J., Primavera, L. H., & Diener, M. J. (2010). Dropout and therapeutic alliance: A meta-analysis of adult individual psychotherapy. *Psychotherapy: Theory, Research Practice, Training, 47*, 637–645.

Sheldon, K. M. (2004). *Optimal human being: An integrated multi-level perspective*. Mahwah, NJ: Erlbaum.

Shimokawa, K., Lambert, M. J., & Smart, D. W. (2010). Enhancing treatment outcome of patients at risk of treatment failure: Meta-analytic and mega-analytic review of a psychotherapy quality assurance system. *Journal of Consulting & Clinical Psychology, 78*, 298–311.

Shoham, V., & Insel, V. R. (2011). Rebooting for whom? Portfolios, technology, and personalized intervention. *Perspectives on Psychological Science, 6*, 478–482.

Slife, B. D. (2004). Theoretical challenges to therapy practice and research: The constraint of naturalism. In M. J. Lambert (Ed.), *Bergin and Garfield's handbook of psychotherapy and behavior change* (5th ed., pp. 44–83). Hoboken, NJ: Wiley.

Smith, T. R., Rodriguez, M. D., & Bernal, G. (2011). Culture. In J. C. Norcross (Ed.), *Psychotherapy relationships that work: Evidence-based responsiveness* (2nd ed., pp. 316–335). New York, NY: Oxford University Press.

Soares, L., Botella, L., & Corbella, S. (2010). The co-constructed therapy alliance and the technical and tactical quality of the therapist interventions in psychotherapy. *European Journal of Psychotherapy and Counselling, 12*, 173–187.

Spek, V., Nyklíček, I., Cuijpers, P, & Pop, V. (2008). Alexithymia and cognitive behaviour therapy outcome for subthreshold depression. *Acta Psychiatrica Scandinavica, 118*, 164–167.

Steering Committee. (2002). Empirically supported therapy relationships: Conclusions and recommendations on the Division 29 Task Force. In J. C. Norcross (Ed.), *Empirically supported therapy relationships: Psychotherapy relationships that work. Therapist contributions and responsiveness to patients* (pp. 441–443). New York, NY: Oxford University Press.

Stiles, W. B. (2002). Assimilation of problematic experience. In J. C. Norcross (Ed.), *Psychotherapy relationships that work* (1st ed., pp. 357–366). New York, NY: Oxford University Press.

Stiles, W. B., Honos-Webb, L., & Zurko, M. (1998). Responsiveness in psychotherapy. *Clinical Psychology: Science and Practice, 5,* 439–458.

Strauss, B., Kirchmann, H., Eckert, J., Lobo-Drost, A., Marquet, A., Papenhausen, R.... Höger, D. (2006). Attachment characteristics and treatment outcome following inpatient psychotherapy: Results of a multisite study. *Psychotherapy Research, 16,* 573–586.

Stulz, N., Lutz, W., Leach, C., Lucock, M., & Barkham, M. (2007). Shapes of change in psychotherapy under routine outpatient conditions. *Journal of Consulting and Clinical Psychology, 75,* 864–874.

Svanborg, C., Åberg, W. A., Svanborg, P. (2008). Long-term outcome of patients with dysthymia and panic disorder: A naturalistic 9-year follow-up study. *Nordic Journal of Psychiatry, 62,* 17–24.

Swift, J. K., & Callahan, J. L. (2008). A delay discounting measure of great expectations and the effectiveness of psychotherapy. *Professional Psychology: Research and Practice, 39,* 581–588.

Swift, J. K., & Callahan, J. L. (2010). A comparison of client preferences for intervention: Empirical support versus common therapy variables. *Journal of Clinical Psychology, 66,* 1217–1231.

Swift, J. K., & Callahan, J. L. (2011). Decreasing treatment dropout by addressing expectations for treatment length. *Psychotherapy Research, 21*(2), 193–200.

Swift, J. K., Callahan, J., & Levine, J. C. (2009). Using clinically significant change to identify premature termination. *Psychotherapy: Theory, Research, Practice, Training, 46,* 328–335.

Swift, J. K., & Greenberg, R. P. (2012). Premature discontinuation in adult psychotherapy: A meta-analysis. *Journal of Consulting and Clinical Psychology, 80*(4), 547–559.

Swift, J. K., Callahan, J. L., & Vollmer, B. M. (2011). Preferences. In J. C. Norcross (Ed.), *Psychotherapy relationships that work: Evidence-based responsiveness* (2nd ed., pp. 301–315). New York, NY: Oxford University Press.

Timulak, L. (2007). Identifying core categories of client-identified impact of helpful events in psychotherapy: A qualitative meta-analysis. *Psychotherapy Research, 17,* 305–314.

Timulak, L. (2010). Significant events in psychotherapy: An update of research findings. *Psychology and Psychotherapy: Theory, Research and Practice, 83,* 421–447.

Tracey, T. J. (1988). Relationship of responsibility attribution congruence to psychotherapy outcome. *Journal of Social and Clinical Psychology, 7,* 131–146.

Tryon, G. S., Blackwell, S. C., & Hammel, E. F. (2007). A meta-analytic examination of client-therapist perspectives of the working alliance. *Psychotherapy Research, 17,* 629–642.

Tryon, G. S., & Winograd, G. (2011). Goal consensus and collaboration. *Psychotherapy, 48,* 50–57.

Valkonen, J., Hänninen, V., & Lindfors, O. (2011). Outcomes of psychotherapy from the perspective of the users. *Psychotherapy Research, 21,* 227–240.

Vermote, R., Fonagy, P., Vertommen, H., Verhaest, Y., Stroobants, R., Vandeneede, B.,...Peuskens, J. (2009). Outcome and outcome trajectories of personality disordered patients during and after a psychoanalytic hospitalization-based treatment. *Journal of Personality Disorders, 23,* 294–307.

Von Der Lippe, A. L., Monsen, J. T., Rønnestad, M. H., & Eilertsen, D. E. (2008). Treatment failure in psychotherapy: The pull of hostility. *Psychotherapy Research, 18,* 420–432.

Wallin, D. J. (2007). *Attachment in psychotherapy*. New York, NY: Guilford Press.

Wampold, B. E. (2001). *The great psychotherapy debate: Models, methods, and findings*. Mahwah, NJ: Erlbaum.

Wampold, B. E. (2010). The research evidence for common factors models: A historically situated perspective. In B. L. Dunca, S. D. Miller, B. E. Wampold, & M A. Hubble (Eds.), *The heart & soul of change: Delivering what works* (2nd ed., pp. 49–82). Washington, DC: American Psychological Association.

Wampold, B. E., Hollon, S. D., & Hill, C. E. (2011). Unresolved questions and future directions in psychotherapy research. In J. C. Norcross, G. R. VandenBos, & D. K. Freedheim (Eds.), *History of psychotherapy: Continuity and change* (2nd ed., pp. 333–356). Washington, DC: American Psychological Association.

Wampold, B. E., Imel, Z. E., Bhati, K. S., & Johnson, M. D. (2006). Insight as a common factor. In L. G. Castonguay & C. E. Hill (Eds.), *Insight in psychotherapy* (pp. 119–140). Washington, DC: American Psychological Association.

Watson, J. C., & Bedard, D. (2006). Clients' emotional processing in psychotherapy: A comparison between cognitive-behavioral and process-experiential psychotherapy. *Journal of Consulting and Clinical Psychology, 74,* 152–159.

Watson, J. C., McMullen, E. J., Prosser, M. C., & Bedard, D. L. (2011). An examination of the relationships among clients' affect regulation, in-session emotional processing, the working alliance, and outcome. *Psychotherapy Research, 21,* 86–96.

Westmacott, R., Hunsley, J., Best, M., Rumstein-McKean, O., & Schindlera, D. (2010). Client and therapist views of contextual factors related to termination from psychotherapy: A comparison between unilateral and mutual terminators. *Psychotherapy Research, 20,* 423–435.

Westra, H. A., Aviram, A., Barnes, M., & Angus, L. (2010). Therapy was not what I expected: A preliminary qualitative analysis of concordance between client expectations and experience of cognitive-behavioral therapy. *Psychotherapy Research, 20,* 436–446.

Westra, H. A., Constantino, M. J., & Aviram, A. (2011). The impact of alliance ruptures on client outcome expectations in cognitive behavioral therapy. *Psychotherapy Research, 21,* 472–481.

Wierzbicki, M., & Pekarik, G. (1993). A meta-analysis of psychotherapy dropout. *Professional Psychology: Research and Practice, 24,* 190–195.

Wild, N. D. (2005). Self-concealment as a predictor of psychotherapy outcome. *Dissertation Abstracts International: Section B: The Sciences and Engineering,* 3734.

Williams, D., & Levitt, H. M. (2008). Clients' experiences of difference with therapists: Sustaining faith in psychotherapy. *Psychotherapy Research, 18,* 256–270.

Worthington, R. L. & Atkinson, D. R. (1996). Effects of perceived etiology attribution similarity on client ratings of counselor credibility. *Journal of Counseling Psychology, 43,* 423–429.

Zane, N., Hall, G. C., Sue, S., Young, K., & Nunez, J. (2004). Research on psychotherapy with culturally diverse populations. In M. J. Lambert (Ed.), *Bergin and Garfield's handbook of psychotherapy and behavior change* (5th ed., pp. 767–804). Hoboken, NJ: Wiley.

Zeeck, A. (2004). Tagesklinische Psychotherapie: Stellenwert des Settings mit Einem Schwerpunkt in der Behandlung von Essstörungen. [Psychotherapy in a day treatment hospital: Evaluations of the setting with a focus on eating disorders]. Habilitationsschrift Universitität Freiburg im Breisgau. [As referenced in Hartman, A., Orlinsky, D., Weber, S., Sandholz, A., & Zeeck, A. (2010)].

Zeeck, A., & Hartmann, A. (2005). Relating therapeutic process to outcome: Are there predictors for the short-term course in anorexic patients? *European Eating Disorders Review, 13,* 245–254.

Zeeck, A., Hartmann, A., & Orlinsky, D. E. (2006). Internalization of the therapeutic process: Differences between borderline and neurotic patients. *International Journal of Personality Disorders, 20,* 22–41.

Zuroff, D. C., Koestner, R., Moskowitz, D. S., McBride, C., Marshall, M., & Bagby, M. (2007). Autonomous motivation for therapy: A new common factor in brief treatment for depression. *Psychotherapy Research, 17,* 137–147.

CHAPTER 8

Therapist Effects

Findings and Methods

Scott A. Baldwin and Zac E. Imel

Evaluation can be threatening. It exposes whether our performance is superior, comparable, or inferior to our peers. However, without evaluation it is difficult to know where we stand and how we can improve. In 2010, the *Los Angeles (LA) Times* ran a controversial series on teacher effectiveness (http://projects.latimes.com/value-added/). The paper posted standardized test scores online for third- through fifth-grade teachers who taught in the Los Angeles area between 2004 and 2010. On the *LA Times* site, one can search for particular teachers and schools or retrieve a listing of the top 100 teachers with respect to standardized test scores. Not surprisingly, many have questioned the use of test scores to identify good teachers and the precision of the statistical methods used to estimate differences in teacher effectiveness (Dillon, 2010). The *LA Times* acknowledged the limitations of their methodology but also noted that it does provide some information that the parents and the public in general should be able to access (http://projects.latimes.com/value-added/).

The *LA Times* series is highly controversial among the teachers and teachers' unions in the Los Angeles area. The president of the United Teachers Los Angeles union called for a boycott of the *LA Times* stating: "You're [i.e., the *LA Times*] leading people in a dangerous direction, making it seem like you can judge the quality of a teacher by...a test" (Song & Felch, 2010, para. 4). The union also raised concerns about privacy for teachers and whether the *LA Times* report was an unwarranted intrusion into teacher privacy (Song & Felch, 2010).

Despite the controversy, few will disagree that some teachers are better than others. Likewise, few will disagree that some therapists are better than others. But evaluation of therapists, like teachers, is difficult and threatening. There will be winners and losers and by definition some therapists will be identified as poor. Euphemisms such as "underperforming" do not lessen the blow. Mental health professionals, like teachers, have largely been able to operate without oversight regarding their effectiveness and have not been able to compare their effectiveness to the effectiveness of their peers. Provided they do not violate ethical mandates and follow the law, mental health professionals are left alone to practice as they see fit. This is a comfortable, but tenuous position. With continued calls for professional accountability, this position is unlikely to be sustainable and probably is not in the best interest of mental health service recipients. Like teachers, mental health professionals need to demonstrate that they provide effective treatment to their patients.

Identifying effective therapists presents significant practical and methodological hurdles. The *LA Times* story highlights some important questions. How much do therapists actually differ from each other? What methods can or should be used to identify effective therapists? How should the results of these analyses be interpreted? Can we account for why some therapists outperform others? In this chapter we attempt to provide an initial answer to these questions by reviewing the literature on the differential effects of therapists on outcome and the literature on some prominent variables that could account for differential effects.

In previous editions of the *Handbook of Psychotherapy and Behavior Change*, the therapist chapters have reviewed literature focused on the relationship between therapist characteristics and outcome. The fourth and fifth editions divided therapist variables into four quadrants: (1) observable traits (e.g., age, sex, ethnicity), (2) observable states (e.g., training), (3) inferred traits (e.g., personality style), and (4) inferred states (e.g., therapeutic relationship; Beutler et al., 2004; Beutler, Machado, & Neufeldt, 1994). These reviews contain a wealth of information about the relationship between therapist variables in each of these domains and outcomes. We believe the literature published since the publication of the fifth edition has little to add to previous versions. No major findings about the relationship between variables in the four quadrants and outcome have been published in the past 8 years. Thus, an update of the previous chapter produces little fruit. In the current chapter, we have chosen to narrow our focus to issues related to the differential effectiveness of therapists. We then focus on new methodological approaches to explaining the differential effectiveness of therapists in the hopes that these approaches may eventually be extended into other areas of inquiry.

The outline of the chapter is as follows. First, we define therapist effects and critically review the methods typically used to study them. Second, we review published estimates of therapist effects and discuss some of the challenges in interpreting these effects. Third, we review the literature on two variables that could account for differential effectiveness of therapists: the therapeutic alliance and adherence to a treatment protocol. Fourth, we conclude with a brief discussion of what we believe are important directions for this literature. We hope this discussion spurs the mental health professionals to talk with one another regarding how to increase accountability and improve outcomes for patients.

HOW MUCH DO THERAPISTS DIFFER IN THEIR OUTCOMES?

Very closely related to such implicit factors is the indefinable effect of the therapist's personality. Though long recognized, this effect still presents an unsolved problem. Even the personal qualities of the good therapist elude description for, while the words *stimulating, inspiring*, etc., suggest themselves, they are far from adequate. For all this, observers seem intuitively to sense the characteristics of the good therapist time and again in particular instances, sometimes being so impressed as almost to believe that the personality of the therapist could be sufficient in itself, apart from everything else, to account for the cure of many a patient by a sort of catalytic effect.

—(Rosenzweig, 1936, p. 413)

Historically, researchers tried to identify effective therapists by relying on the "intuitive sense," to use Rosenzweig's notion, of supervisors and experts to correctly distinguish between effective and ineffective therapists (Luborsky, McLellan, Diguer, Woody, & Seligman, 1997). Further, developers of treatment approaches are often viewed as master-clinicians because they developed the treatment and write about it. Little attention was paid to measuring the client outcomes of the therapists who created the treatment or determining who produced the best outcomes (Holt & Luborsky, 1958; Luborsky, 1952). Relying on ratings of supervisors and experts as well as the therapist's reputation probably sounds familiar to anyone who has worked in a mental health setting. When evaluating and assessing trainees—for example, to determine whether the trainees are ready for a clinical internship or licensure—we typically assess whether trainees behave ethically, develop a working relationship with patients, and use a coherent and empirically supported treatment model. We may have formal assessment procedures for these characteristics. If a particular trainee falls short in a domain, we may recommend that he or she receives additional supervision or takes an additional course. During this process, we rarely, if ever, document how much the trainees' patients improved. To be sure, a growing number of training programs require trainees to track treatment outcomes with standardized measures as part of the therapy process, but those treatment outcomes are not used to assess whether a particular therapist is ready to apply to be a licensed, independent practitioner.

For the purposes of this chapter we define *therapist effects* as the effect of a given therapist *on patient outcomes* as compared to another therapist. Therapist effects may be related to particular characteristics or behaviors of a given therapist but our definition does not depend on knowing what variables account for differences among therapists. Within this definition, high-quality therapists are not identified by supervisor- or peer-nominations nor are they identified by adhering to a particular treatment protocol. Instead, high-quality therapists are identified by actually measuring their patients' outcomes and determining who consistently does the best. Therapists can be tracked in many ways. Possible metrics include posttreatment outcome averaged across their patients, long-term outcome of their patients, variability in outcome within their caseload, average change per session or week, or value-added over and above a previous therapist. Regardless of the metric or even the specific outcome chosen, identifying effective therapists involves systematically tracking outcomes and making comparisons.

Although researchers have been interested in therapist effects since the beginning of psychotherapy research, the literature on therapist effects is small and is in many ways in its infancy, especially compared to the literature on specific treatment packages. The literature on designing, executing, and analyzing clinical trials comparing treatments is huge, as is the literature reporting the results of clinical trials. In contrast, there is no agreement on the best way to study therapist effects and, with a few key exceptions (Crits-Christoph & Gallop, 2006; Elkin, Falconnier, Martinovich, & Mahoney, 2006; Wampold & Bolt, 2006, 2007), there is not even debate about methodology. Few studies are designed to examine therapists—they are more often designed to minimize therapist differences via standardization and extensive supervision (Crits-Christoph & Gallop, 2006; Wampold & Brown, 2005). Further, most data sets used to study therapists include small numbers of therapists treating small numbers of patients (e.g., Kim, Wampold, & Bolt, 2006). Even studies that use large data sets often have so much heterogeneity among the patients that therapist differences may be masked (e.g., Wampold & Brown, 2005). In what follows, we review the therapist effects literature against the backdrop of these limitations. Additionally, we provide commentary on the primary methodological challenges and how the field can address those challenges.

Ways to Study Therapist Effects

Approaches for studying therapist effects fall into two categories. The first category is fixed effects studies. Fixed effects studies quantify how much two or more therapists differ from one another and the parameters estimated focus on differences among the particular therapists in the sample. For example, these studies estimate how much Harry's outcomes differ from Ron's and how much they differ from Hermione's and so on. Thus, the most salient result in fixed effects studies are estimates of differences among the particular therapists used in the study. The second category is random effects studies. Random effects studies also quantify how much two or more therapists differ from one another but the parameters estimated focus on the variability among therapists' outcomes in the population of therapists. That is, these studies treat Harry, Ron, and Hermione as a sample from a broader population of therapists and use their data to estimate how much therapists' outcomes differ from one another in the population. Thus, the most salient result in random effects analyses is an estimate of the amount of variance in outcome that is associated with therapists. The literature on therapist effects includes both fixed and random effects studies as well as studies that mix the approaches. We tend to favor random effects or their combination with fixed effects analyses[1] because therapists in the study are not typically the only therapists of interest. Instead, we see the particular therapists in a study as realizations from a broader population of therapists, much the same way that we typically see patients in a study as representative of a broader population of patients (see Martindale, 1978, for a readable introduction to fixed and random effects as they pertain to therapists). Consequently, we want to see how much variability exists in the population of therapists.

---

[1] Actually, we favor random effects analyses over combination studies. Random effects studies can also produce estimates of the differences among the particular therapists in a study. These estimates are sometimes called *empirical Bayes* or *shrunken estimates*. The statistical details of empirical-bayes estimates are beyond the scope of this chapter. Raudenbush and Bryk (2002) provide a thorough discussion of empirical Bayes estimates in the social sciences. Suffice it to say, empirical Bayes estimates provide similar information as fixed effects studies while still treating therapists as being sampled from a population of therapists.

Researchers and clinicians typically talk about therapists with reference to a distribution and thus are implicitly thinking about therapists from a random effects perspective. For example, we typically talk about clinicians as being average or in the top or bottom quartiles. That is, we compare clinicians to a normative distribution and place them within that distribution (the normative distribution is often an informal, intuitive distribution rather than a formal, explicitly defined distribution). In contrast, researchers and clinicians do not talk about treatments with reference to distributions. That is, we do not say that cognitive therapy for depression is in the top quartile of treatments for depression whereas interpersonal therapy is below average. Instead, we usually just talk about the direct differences between cognitive therapy and interpersonal therapy. Thus, we think about treatment types in a fixed effects way because we are typically interested in the particular therapies in our study—we are not trying to generalize to other therapy types not included in the study.

The distinction between fixed and random effects studies, particularly the distinction between the parameters estimated in each, provides a framework for understanding the therapist effects literature. Although fixed effects analyses provide information about the differential effectiveness of therapists, they can be challenging to interpret when making inferences to similar therapists not included in the study. In contrast, random effects analyses provide a description of the variability of similar therapists and thus better facilitate inferences to that population.[2]

As an illustration of the inferential issues related to fixed effects, consider one of the original therapist effects studies, Ricks' (1974) supershrink study. Ricks compared the long-term outcomes of 28 emotionally disturbed, delinquent adolescent boys seen by one of two therapists, Therapist A or B. The primary outcome was whether the boys were diagnosed with schizophrenia as adults. Ricks identified the 28 boys by reviewing the long-term outcomes of 121 adults, 61 of whom had developed schizophrenia. Ricks then identified the therapists that had worked with the 121 boys and found two therapists who had seen a sufficient number of the boys, allowing comparisons to be made between the therapists. Together these therapists saw the 28 boys that make up the sample of interest. Of the 15 boys seen by Therapist A, 4 (27%) developed schizophrenia as adults. Of the 13 boys seen by Therapist B, 11 (85%) developed schizophrenia as adults. Therapist A was nicknamed "supershrink" by the boys in the treatment center where the therapists worked. Ignore for a moment this study's monumental design problems and note the inferential difficulties when all we know is the difference in outcome between Therapist A and B. Namely, what can this difference tell us about what to expect of other therapists working with this population of adolescents and how Therapist A and B fit within the population? Consider the following thought experiment. Suppose the distribution of therapists' outcomes working with severely distressed boys is normally distributed (one could select other distributional forms but that does not change our point). Inferences about the population of therapists, as well as about Therapist A and B, changes depending on where Therapists A and B are within the distribution of therapists.

Figure 8.1 illustrates this point. Panels 1 to 3 represent three possible populations from which Therapist A and B could have been drawn. In Panel 1 the average therapist has 30% of his or her patients develop schizophrenia as an adult. In Panel 2 the average therapist has 50% of his or her patients develop schizophrenia as an adult. In Panel 3 the average therapist has 70% of his or her patients develop schizophrenia as an adult. In all panels, Therapist A and B have the same percentage of patients develop schizophrenia as reported by Ricks. In Panel 1 Therapist A is not a supershrink at all, at least relative to the rest of the distribution; Therapist A is similar to the majority of therapists. Therapist B, in contrast, is an extreme outlier in the negative outcome direction. In Panel 2 both Therapist A and B are far away from the mean and represent opposite ends of the distribution. Finally, in Panel 3, Therapist B is fairly close to the mean whereas Therapist A is an extreme outlier in the positive outcome direction. In Panels 2 and 3, Therapist A might well be classified as a supershrink but in Panel 1 Therapist A is average. Therefore, when interpreting the results described below one must remember that differences among particular therapists are one part of the story; how those differences fit in within the broader population of therapists is the other.

---

[2] Like any statistical model, random effects models come with assumptions that need to be considered (cf. Serlin, Wampold, & Levin, 2003; Siemer & Joorman, 2003a, 2003b).

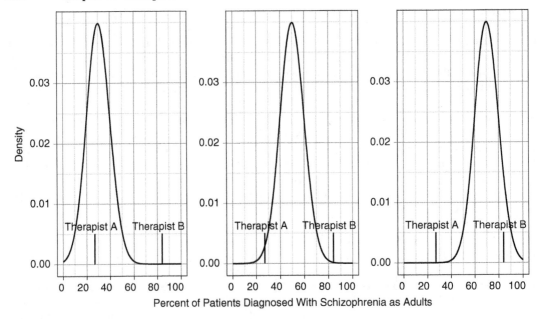

FIGURE 8.1 Three hypothetical distributions from which Therapist A and Therapist B from Ricks (1974) may have been drawn.

Studies Comparing Outcomes of Therapists

We searched the literature to locate fixed and random effects studies. In what follows, we report the results of these studies and highlight key findings.

Identification of Studies

We identified therapist effects studies in three ways. First, we conducted a search using PsycINFO, PubMed, and PsycAbstracts, with the search terms *therapist effects*, *therapist outcome*, *differential effects of therapists*, *therapist and intraclass correlation*, *therapist and multilevel* or *hierarchical linear modeling* or *mixed models*, *effective therapist*, *ineffective therapist*, and *therapist variance*. Second, we reviewed the reference lists of studies of therapist effects. Third, we reviewed studies reported in reviews of therapist effects (Baldwin et al., 2011; Crits-Christoph et al., 1991; Crits-Christoph & Mintz, 1991). All studies from Baldwin et al. (2011) were included and 10 of 18 studies from Crits-Christoph's and colleagues (1991) work were included. Data from seven studies included in Crits-Christoph et al. (1991) were no longer available. For the remaining study from Crits-Christoph et al. (1991) we had estimates of therapist effects from more current reports (Elkin

et al., 2006; Kim et al., 2006). For the reasons discussed below, we did not include studies that only reported that they tested for therapist effects but none were significant.

Fixed Effects Studies

Twenty-five studies reported a fixed effects analysis of therapist differences. We extracted the number of therapists (k), number of patients per therapist (m), treatment, outcome, and type of comparison among therapists made for the fixed effects studies. We made no attempt to extract all reported comparisons in a given study because of the quantity and variability in the comparisons used. As is apparent from the results of our review, there is little consistency in how therapist differences are defined in the fixed effects literature. Each study defines what constitutes an effective versus ineffective therapist. Consequently, we report what we determined to be the clearest comparison among therapists in a given fixed effects analysis. We refer readers who want more details regarding the results of a given study to the primary study reports.

Random Effects Studies

Forty-six studies reported a random effects analysis of therapist differences or provided sufficient information that we could compute a random effects analysis. All studies reported in Baldwin et al. (2011), Crits-Christoph et al. (1991), and Crits-Christoph and Mintz (1991) were random effects analyses. A measure of effect size in random effects studies is the intraclass correlation (ICC), which is computed as:

$$ICC = \frac{\sigma_t^2}{\sigma_t^2 + \sigma_e^2},$$

where σ_t^2 is the variance in the outcome variable associated with therapists and σ_e^2 is the residual variance in the outcome. A common interpretation of the ICC is the proportion of variance in the data associated with therapists.[3] The ICC can be computed using a multilevel model that estimates therapist variance or using an ANOVA where therapist is included as a factor. For each study we report the number of therapists (k), number of patients per therapist (m), treatment, outcomes, and ICCs. The values for k and m are the number of each that contributed to any given ICC. Where possible we report the ICCs by outcome measure, although in some cases only study-level ICCs were available (Crits-Christoph & Mintz, 1991).

We used meta-analysis to synthesize the ICCs. We used random effects meta-analysis techniques specifically designed for combining ICC estimates. See Blitstein, Hannan, Murray, and Shadish (2005) for details regarding the methodology. We first computed an average, aggregate effect for the 45 studies that reported sufficient information to be included in the

---

[3] An alternative conceptualization of the ICC is the correlation among observations within therapists. Unlike the ICC defined as the ratio of variances, this ICC can be both negative and positive. Considering ICCs as representing correlations among observations is especially important when estimating treatment effects (Baldwin et al., 2011). However, when focused on estimating the proportion of variance in outcome due to therapist, which is the primary question of this chapter, the conceptualization of the ICC discussed above is more natural. It turns out that the correlation and proportion of variance conceptualizations will provide identical results when the ICC is positive. When the ICC is negative, the correlation conceptualization will produce a negative value whereas the proportion of variance conceptualization will be fixed at zero (because proportions cannot be less than 0). Consequently, the negative ICCs from Baldwin et al. (2011) were fixed at zero in this chapter.

meta-analysis. Then, we estimated unique aggregate estimates for naturalistic/effectiveness studies and efficacy studies because it has been suggested that ICCs will be larger in naturalistic studies than in efficacy studies (cf. Crits-Christoph & Gallop, 2006; Elkin et al., 2006). For studies with multiple estimates, we averaged the estimates within the study so that each study only contributed a single ICC value to the overall analysis. In order to be included in the analysis, the study had to provide information about the number of therapists and patients per therapist. Only one study did not provide sufficient information in this regard (Zitrin, Klein, & Woerner, 1978). Two studies reported ICC estimates, computed from slightly different analyses, from the same data (Elkin et al., 2006; Kim et al., 2006). We included the Kim et al. (2006) estimate in the meta-analysis because the estimates in Elkin et al. (2006) use a method known to underestimate the ICC (Wampold & Bolt, 2007).

Results From Fixed Effects Studies

Table 8.1 presents the results of the 25 fixed effects studies. The studies in Table 8.1 are heterogeneous with respect to the number of therapists (k), number of patients per therapist (m), intervention, patient population, and outcome measures. Furthermore, the studies varied widely with respect to how differences among therapists were defined and tested. Generally, across the studies in Table 8.1, therapists differed in their outcomes. Some of the differences observed are quite large. For example, Okiishi, Lambert, Nielsen, and Ogles (2003) estimated therapist effects by computing the rate of change by session for each therapist using the OQ-45 (Lambert et al., 2004) as the outcome measure. Negative values indicated a reduction in symptoms from one session to the next. The top three therapists had changes rates of -7.97, -5.51, and -5.19. The bottom three therapists had change rates of -0.13, 0.05, and 0.68. This is a remarkable difference—four sessions with the best three therapists would lead to a 20 to 30 OQ-45 point reduction, which would be considered reliable and significant change (Lambert et al., 2004), whereas four sessions with the worst three therapist would lead to either no change or an increase in symptoms. Likewise, Brown, Lambert, Jones, and Minami (2005) found that patients of effective therapists showed 3 times as much change as the rest of the patients in their study.

TABLE 8.1 Selected Outcomes From Studies Reporting a Fixed-Effects Comparison Among Therapists

Study	k	m	Treatment	Outcome	Comparisons	Results
Blatt, Sanislow, Zuroff, and Pilkonis, 1996	24	4.5	CBT, IPT, and imipramine for depression	1. Composite measure of BDI, GAS, HRSD, HSCL, SAS	ANOVA to determine significance of therapist factor	1. No statistically significant therapist effects until the sample of therapists is divided into two groups consisting of the eight most-effective therapists and the seven least-effective therapists
Brown et al., 2005	281	26.5	TAU	1. LSQ or YLSQ	Separated therapists into an "effective" category ($k = 71$) or "other" category ($k = 210$). Effective therapists were those who averaged a residualized change score of 2.8 or greater on the Y/LSQ	1. Patients of effective therapists showed three times as much change as patients of therapists in the "other" category
Huppert et al., 2001	14	13.1	CBT for panic	1. PDSS	Percentage of a therapist's caseload that achieved clinically significant change among the above average outcome and below average outcome therapists	1. 66% of patients of above-average therapists achieved clinically significant change; 45% of patients of below-average therapists achieved clinically significant change
Kraus, Castonguay, Boswell, Nordberg, and Hayes, 2011	696	10	TAU	1. 12 domains from TOP	Effective therapists defined as achieving reliable change for their average patient	1. 301 (43%) therapists were effective in 4 or fewer domains; 393 (57%) therapists were in 5 to 11 domains
Luborsky et al., 1986	9	6.9	Cognitive or affective insight therapy	1. BDI 2. HSCL 3. PSAS (patient rated) 4. PSAS (therapist rated) 5. TC 1 (patient) 6. TC 2 (patient) 7. TC 1 (therapist) 8. TC 2 (therapist) 9. Therapist rating of patient TC 1 10. Therapist rating of patient TC 2	Examined statistical significance of therapist main effect	1–10: Significant therapist main effect on two (20%) measures

264

Study			Treatment	Measures	Analysis	Results
Luborsky et al., 1986	4	10	Psychodynamic	1. Discomfort 2. IBI 3. Improvement (patient rating) 4. Improvement (therapist rating) 5. Severity 6. TC (patient)	Examined statistical significance of therapist main effect	1–6: Significant therapist main effect on four (66%) measures
Luborsky et al., 1986	3	26.3	Short- or long-term therapy (individual and group)	1. CHS 2. CITS 3. DA-PSS 4. Disturbance (externally rated) 5. Disturbance (patient rated) 6. Disturbance (therapist rated) 7. IBS 8. SSLAM 9. Symptom Change 10. Usefulness	Examined statistical significance of therapist main effect	1–10: Significant therapist main effect on two (20%) measures
Luborsky et al., 1997	3	10	CBT for opiate addiction	1. BDI 2. ASI	Pre-post effect size for each therapist (d)	1. BDI d's: .94, .57, .29 2. ASI d's: .49, .21, .14
Luborsky et al., 1997	3	7.33	DC for opiate addiction	1. BDI 2. ASI	Pre-post effect size for each therapist (d)	1. BDI d's: .20, .08, −.07 2. ASI d's: .10, .04, .13
Luborsky et al., 1997	3	7.33	DC for opiate addiction	1. BDI 2. ASI	Pre-post effect size for each therapist (d)	1. BDI d's: .22, .07, −.06 2. ASI d's: .07, .05, .10
Luborsky et al., 1997	5	3.2	SE for chronic depression	1. BDI 2. GAS 3. HDRS	Therapist average percentage change in symptoms from pretreatment to posttreatment	1. BDI: 81, 71, 68, 64, −4 2. GAS: 29, 10, 26, 20, 12 3. HDRS: 65, 69, 73, 70, 14
Luborsky et al., 1997	4	9.25	SE for depression	1. BDI 2. GAS 3. HDRS	Therapist average percentage change in symptoms from pretreatment to posttreatment	1. BDI: 55, 50, 46, 28 2. GAS: 38, 36, 28, 24 3. HDRS: 56, 55, 47, 42
Luborsky et al., 1997	3	8.67	SE for opiate addiction	1. BDI 2. ASI	Pre-post effect size for each therapist (d)	1. BDI d's: 1.14, .58, .11 2. ASI d's: 1.01, .42, −.01

(continued)

TABLE 8.1 *(Continued)*

Study	k	m	Treatment	Outcome	Comparisons	Results
Luborsky et al., 1997	5	10.8	SE for opiate addiction	1. BDI 2. ASI	Pre-post effect size for each therapist (d)	1. BDI d's: 1.35, .94, .76, .39, .25 2. ASI d's: .65, .69, .49, –.02, .01
McLellan, Woody, Luborsky, and Goehl, 1988	4	15.3	Methadone Maintenance Program	1. Urinalysis 2. Methadone dose 3. Medication use 4. Employment 5. Arrests	Statistical tests before and after transfer of cases	1–5. No significant differences among counselors prior to transfer of cases. After reassignment, significant differences among therapists on all outcomes except arrests.
Miller and Taylor, 1980	9	4.6	BSCT, BSCT + relaxation, communication, & assertion training, or BSCT + individually tailored broad-spectrum approaches for teaching moderation in drinking	1. Improvement in drinking (at least a 30% or more reduction in drinking as compared to baseline)	Percentage of clients who showed improvement by therapist	1. Improvement ratings by therapists (from worst to best): 25%, 33%, 40%, 60%, 75% 75%, 75%, 100%, 100%
Najavits and Strupp, 1994	16	5	TLDP	1. GAS 2. GOR 3. PSS 4. PTE 5. SASB 6. SCL-90	Grouping of therapists into effective and less-effective categories. Effective therapists "ranked at the top in outcome, had no negative outcome cases, and had no patients leave before session 16" (p. 118). Ineffective therapists "were in the lower half on outcome, had at least one negative outcome case, and had two or more patients leave treatment before session 16" (p. 118).	1–6. Three therapists identified as effective; three therapists identified as ineffective
Okiishi et al., 2006	71	92	TAU	1. OQ-45	Percentage of patients seen by the top 10% of therapists who recovered or deteriorated as compared to the bottom 10% of therapists	1. Top 10% of therapists had 22.4% of patients recover whereas bottom 10% had 10.6%; top 10% of therapists had 5.2% of patients deteriorate and bottom 10% had 10.6% of patients deteriorate.

Study	k	m	Treatment	Outcome measures	Analysis	Findings
Okiishi et al., 2003	56	21.1	TAU	1. OQ-45	Descriptive comparison of change rates (OQ-45 change per session) for top three therapists versus bottom three therapists	1. The top three therapists' change rates were −7.97, −5.51, and −5.19; the bottom 3 therapists' change rates were −0.13, 0.05, 0.68
Orlinsky and Howard, 1980	23	6.21	TAU	1. Rater's retrospective ratings of symptom improvement	√-rated therapists had at least 70% of patients improve and less than 10% get worse; X-rated therapists had 50% or less of patients improve and more than 10% get worse	1. 11 (48%) were √-rated; 5 (22%) were X-rated
Project MATCH Research Group, 1998	54	32	CBT, MET, or TSF for alcohol problems	1. Client satisfaction 2. Percent days abstinent 3. Standard drinks per drinking day 4. Treatment retention	Computed proportion of variance attributable to therapists using η^2	1–4: η^2 ranged from .04 to .12
Shapiro, Firth-Cozens, and Stiles, 1989	4	10	CBT or interpersonal treatment	1. BDI 2. PSE 3. SAS 4. SCL-90 5. SES	Examined statistical significance of therapist main effect	1–5: Statistical tests of therapist effects were not significant except for the PSE
Wampold and Brown, 2005	73	9+	TAU	1. LSQ	Pre-post effect size for each therapist in the top and bottom quartiles (d)	1. Top quartile: $d = 0.47$; Bottom quartile: $d = 0.20$
Westra, Constantino, Arkowitz, and Dozois, 2011	4	8	CBT for GAD	1. PSWQ	Direct comparison of outcomes among the four therapists	1. The therapist by time interaction account for 29% of the outcome variance; some significant differences among the specific therapists
Whitehorn and Betz, 1954	14	7.1	Inpatient treatment for schizophrenia	1. Improvement at discharge	Improvement at discharge was evaluated by the physician who treated the patient and by second psychiatrist	1. 75% of patients seeing effective therapists had improved at discharge; 26.9% of patients seeing ineffective therapists had improved at discharge

Note: k = number of therapists; m = average number of patients per therapist. We do not report the results of the Penn-VA project as reported in Luborsky et al. (1986) because it is dealt with in Luborsky et al. (1997). ASI = Addiction Severity Index; BDI = Beck Depression Inventory; BSCT = Behavioral Self-Control Training; CBT = Cognitive Behavioral Therapy; CHS = Cattell H Scale; DA-PSS = Depression-Anxiety subscale of Psychiatric Status Scale; DC = Drug Counseling; GAD = Generalized Anxiety Disorder; GAS = Global Assessment Scale; GOR = Global Outcome Rating; HRSD = Hamilton Depression Rating Scale; HSCL = Hopkins-Symptom Checklist; IBI = Interpersonal Behavior Inventory; IBS = Interpersonal Behavior Scale; LSQ = Life-Status Questionnaire; MET = Motivational Enhancement Therapy; OQ-45 = Outcome Questionnaire-45; PDSS = Panic Disorder Severity Scale; PSAS = Personal and Social Adjustment Scale; PSE = Present State Examination; PSS = Problem Severity Scale; PSWQ = Penn-State Worry Questionnaire; PTE = Post-Therapy Evaluation; SAS = Social Adjustment Scale; SASB = Structural Analysis of Social Behavior; SCL_90 = Symptom-Checklist-90; SE = Supportive Expressive Psychotherapy; SES = Self-Esteem Scale; SSIAM = Structured and Scaled Interview to Assess Maladjustment; TC = Target Complaint; TOP = Treatment Outcome Package; YLSQ = Youth Life-Status Questionnaire; TSF = Twelve-step Facilitation

These studies also provide some information on the stability of therapist effects. Brown et al. (2005) and Wampold and Brown (2005) both provide some cross-validation data with respect to time. Wampold and Brown (2005) divided therapists' caseloads into half with respect to time. The first half constituted the predictor sample and the second half constituted the criterion sample. Thus, if a therapist saw 18 patients, the first 9 patients constituted the predictor sample and the last 9 the criterion sample. They divided therapists into quartiles based on the outcomes of the predictor sample. They then evaluated the therapists a second time based on the outcomes of the criterion sample. The results showed stability of therapist effects. For example, therapists in the best quartile had pre-post effect sizes in the criterion sample that were twice as large as therapists in the worst quartile.

Brown et al. (2005) provided evidence over a longer period of time. They divided their sample of therapists into two groups: highly effective therapists and other therapists. The highly effective therapists were identified by examining patient outcomes over a 3-year baseline period. After the baseline period was over, Brown et al. examined patient outcomes for the two groups of therapists over the next 18 months. The difference between the highly effective therapists and other therapists reduced some during the cross-validation period. This was likely due to regression to the mean, but a noticeable difference remained. More studies of the consistency of therapist effects across time are needed. However, the initial evidence suggests that therapist effects are reasonably consistent across time.

Results From Random Effects Studies

Table 8.2 presents the results of the 46 random effects studies. The studies in Table 8.2 are heterogeneous with respect to the number of therapists contributing the ICC (k), number of patients per therapist (m), intervention, population, and outcome measures. Summing across the 46 studies, there were a total of 1,281 therapists and 14,519 patients. The median number of therapists in a study was 9 and the range was 2 to 581. The median number of patients per therapist was 7.6 and the range was 1.3 to 51.1. These median values are quite small and we later discuss some of the problems that small numbers of therapists and patients per therapist create. The studies were both naturalistic/effectiveness studies (37%) and efficacy studies (63%).

Study-level ICCs ranged from 0 to 0.55 (25th percentile = 0.02, 50th percentile = 0.04, 75th percentile = 0.08). There was moderate between-study variability ($I^2 = 61.9$). Averaging across studies, the random effects mean ICC was 0.05 (95% CI = 0.03–0.07). This indicates that, on average, approximately 5% of the variance in outcomes is associated with therapists. This value is a bit smaller than the 8.6% estimate provided in a previous meta-analysis (Crits-Christoph et al., 1991).

Estimating an aggregate estimate separately from naturalistic/effectiveness studies and efficacy studies revealed differences between the two designs. Study-level ICCs for naturalistic/effectiveness studies ranged from 0 to 0.55 (25th percentile = 0.03, 50th percentile = 0.05, 75th percentile = 0.1). Study level ICCs for efficacy studies ranged from 0 to 0.22 (25th percentile = 0.01, 50th percentile = 0.04, 75th percentile = 0.07). Among naturalistic/effectiveness studies, the random effects mean ICC was 0.07 (95% CI = 0.05–0.1), indicating that approximately 7% of the variance in outcomes is associated with therapists in naturalistic/effectiveness studies. Among the efficacy studies, the random effects mean ICC was 0.03 (95% CI = 0.01–0.05), indicating that approximately 3% of the variance in outcomes is associated with therapists in efficacy studies. The difference between naturalistic/effectiveness studies and efficacy studies was statistically significant ($p < .05$). The lower ICC in efficacy studies may be due to the high amounts of training, supervision, and structure common in efficacy studies. This would be consistent with Crits-Christoph et al.'s (1991) finding that studies that used treatment manuals had smaller ICCs than nonmanualized studies.

Several problems with the estimation of the therapist effects should be considered. Biased estimation of therapist effects can occur for three reasons. The first two reasons would lead to overestimation of the aggregate effects and the third reason would lead to an underestimate. The first reason for overestimation is that ICCs are defined as the proportion of variance associated with therapists have a lower bound of zero, which in the long run will lead to an upwardly biased estimate of the ICC (see Baldwin et al., 2011, for details). We can overcome this problem by defining the ICC as the correlation among observations within a therapist, but that is not the statistic we most care about when discussing

TABLE 8.2   Outcome Intraclass Correlations (ICC) Associated With Therapists

Study	k	m	Treatment	Outcome	ICC	Other
Abramowitz, Foa, and Franklin, 2003[d]	5	2.9	ERP for OCD	1. BDI 2. YBOCS	1. 0.18 2. 0.13	Estimated using ANOVA; Posttreatment controlling for baseline
Almlov, Carlbring, Berger, Cuijpers, and Andersson, 2009	10	10.3	Internet delivered CBT for MDD	1. BAI 2. BDI 3. MADRS 4. QOLI	1. 0 2. 0.11 3. 0.07 4. 0.11	Estimated using ANOVA
Anker, Duncan, and Sparks, 2009	10	20.5	TAU for couple distress	1. ORS	1. 0.02	Estimate using a multilevel model; posttreatment controlling for baseline
Baldwin, Wampold, and Imel, 2007	80	4.1	TAU	1. OQ-45	1. 0.03	Estimated as a multilevel model; posttreatment controlling for baseline
Barber, Crits-Christoph, and Luborsky, 1996[b]	4	7.3	SE for depression	Specific outcomes not specified[b]	1–2: Mean = 0[c]	Estimated using ANOVA
Beck, Hollon, Young, Bedrosian, and Budner, 1985; Rush, Beck, Kovacs, and Hollon, 1977[b]	36[e]	1.3[e]	CBT for depression	Specific outcome not specified[b]	1. 0.00	Estimated using ANOVA
Borkovec and Mathews, 1988[b]	4	7.5	CBT, CSD, or ND for nonphobic anxiety	Specific outcomes not specified[b]	1–10: Mean = 0.03[c]	Estimated using ANOVA
Boswell, Castonguay, and Wasserman, 2010	19	2.2	TAU	1. SPS	1. 0.55	Estimated as a multilevel model; 3-level model
Brooker and Wiggins, 1983	8	24.3	BT for anxiety	1. FQ 2. General anxiety	1. 0.04 2. 0.05	Estimated using ANOVA
Carlbring et al., 2006[d]	3	7.4	CBT for panic disorder (Internet-based)	1. ACQ 2. BAI 3. BDI 4. BSQ 5. MADRS 6. MIA-AC 7. MIA-AL 8. QLI	1. 0.0 2. 0.03 3. 0.0 4. 0.0 5. 0.0 6. 0.03 7. 0.0 8. 0.0	Estimated using ANOVA; posttreatment controlling for baseline

(continued)

TABLE 8.2 (Continued)

Study	k	m	Treatment	Outcome	ICC	Other
Carroll et al., 2004[d]	5.3	3.9	CBT + Disulfram, IPT + Disulfram, CBT + Placebo, or IPT + Placebo	1. 84 day cocaine use 2. Days of cocaine use during treatment 3. Urinalysis	1. 0.1 2. 0.1 3. 0.08	Estimated using ANOVA; posttreatment controlling for baseline
Cella, Stahl, Reme, and Chalder, 2011	12	31.2	CBT for chronic fatigue	1. Fatigue 2. Disability	1. 0.0 2. 0.02	Estimated as a multilevel model; posttreatment controlling for baseline
Christensen et al., 2004[d]	7	8.4	IBCT or TBCT for marital distress	1. AC 2. CS 3. DAS 4. GDS 5. MHID 6. MSI 7. PSC	1. 0.02 2. 0.07 3. 0.01 4. 0.01 5. 0.07 6. 0.05 7. 0.03	Estimated using ANOVA; posttreatment controlling for baseline
Dinger, Strack, Leichsenring, Wilmers, and Schauenburg, 2008	50	51.1	Inpatient treatment	1. GSI 2. Impairment score	1. 0.03 2. 0.17	Estimated as a multilevel model; posttreatment controlling for baseline
Ehlers et al., 2003[d]	3	8.3	CBT for PTSD	1. BAI 2. BDI 3. CAPS-D 4. CAPS-DIS 5. CAPS-F 6. PDS-D 7. PDS-F 8. SDS	1. 0.08 2. 0.0 3. 0.0 4. 0.0 5. 0.0 6. 0.0 7. 0.0 8. 0.0	Estimated using ANOVA; posttreatment controlling for baseline
Elkin et al., 2006[a]	17	5.1	CBT or IPT for depression	1. BDI 2. GAS 3. HRSD 4. Social 5. Work	1. 0.02 2. 0.03 3. 0.0 4. 0.0 5. 0.04	Estimated as a multilevel model; 3-level model

Study			Treatment	Outcome measure		Notes
Hollon et al., 1992[b]	4	26.8	CBT or CBT + imipramine for depression	Specific outcome not specified[b]	1. 0.05	Estimated using ANOVA
Huppert et al., 2001*	14	13.07	CBT for panic	1. AntAnx 2. ADIS-R 3. ASI 4. CGI 5. FPA 6. HRSA 7. HRSD 8. PDSS 9. SSS	1. 0.02 2. 0.12 3. 0.14 4. 0.03 5. 0.01 6. 0.06 7. 0.04 8. 0.06 9. 0.03	Estimated using ANOVA; posttreatment outcome controlling for baseline
Kim et al., 2006	17	5.1	CBT or IPT for depression	1. BDI 2. GAS 3. HRSD 4. HSCL-90	1. 0.09 2. 0.08 3. 0.03 4. 0.01	Estimated using a multilevel model; posttreatment outcome controlling for baseline; intent-to-treat sample
Koch, Spates, and Himle, 2004[d]	4	3.62	BE or CBE for animal phobia	1. BAT-D 2. BAT-SP 3. BAT-SUDS 4. BAT-TP 5. BCSAQ-C 6. BCSAQ-S 7. CSAQ-C 8. CSAQ-S 9. EST 10. FSS-III A 11. FSS-III F 12. SPQ-A 13. SPQ-CB 14. SPQ-P 15. SPQ-Total 16. SPQ-V 17. TC-NI 18. TC-PI	1. 0.0 2. 0.0 3. 0.1 4. 0.0 5. 0.0 6. 0.1 7. 0.0 8. 0.02 9. 0.0 10. 0.0 11. 0.09 12. 0.04 13. 0.0 14. 0.0 15. 0.0 16. 0.05 17. 0.0 18. 0.16	Estimated using ANOVA; posttreatment controlling for baseline

(continued)

TABLE 8.2 (Continued)

Study	k	m	Treatment	Outcome	ICC	Other
Kuyken, 2004[d]	20	3.3	CBT for depression	1. BDI-II	1. 0.11	Estimated using ANOVA; posttreatment controlling for baseline
Lange et al., 2003[d]	18	2.9	Internet-based therapy for traumatic stress	1. IES-A 2. IES-I 3. SCL-90 Anxiety 4. SCL-90 depression 5. SCL-90 somatization 6. SCL-90 Sleep	1. 0.0 2. 0.0 3. 0.0 4. 0.0 5. 0.0 6. 0.0	Estimated using ANOVA; posttreatment controlling for baseline
Lincoln, Rief, Hahlweg, Frank, and von Witzelben, 2003[d]	9.5	2.9	CBT for social phobia	1. BDI 2. SCL-90 interpersonal sensitivity	1. 0.05 2. 0.04	Estimated using ANOVA; posttreatment controlling for baseline
Luborsky et al., 1997*	4	9.3	SE for depression	1. BDI 2. GAS 3. HRSD	1. 0 2. 0 3. 0.01	Estimated using a multilevel model; posttreatment outcome controlling for baseline
Lutz, Leon, Martinovich, Lyons, and Stiles, 2007[a]	60	20	TAU	1. MHI	1. 0.08; 0.17	Estimated as a multilevel model; 3-level model; first ICC is the ratio of therapist variance to all variance; second ICC is the ratio of therapist variance to just patient variance
Marcus et al., 2011	14	25	CBT, MET, family-support network, community reinforcement, or MDFT for cannabis use	1. Cannabis use 2. SPI	1. 0.05 2. 0	Estimated as a multilevel model
McKay, Imel, and Wampold, 2006	9	12.4	Imipramine or placebo for depression	1. BDI 2. HRSD	1. 0.09 2. 0.07	Estimated as a multilevel model; posttreatment controlling for baseline

Study			Treatment	Outcomes		Notes
Merrill, Tolbert, and Wade, 2003[d]	8	17.2	CBT	1. BDI 2. GAF	1. 0.0 2. 0.07	Estimated using ANOVA; posttreatment controlling for baseline
Nash et al., 1965[b]	4	10	Dynamic	Specific outcomes not specified[b]	Mean = 0.14[c]	Estimated using ANOVA
Okiishi et al., 2003	56	21.1	TAU	1. OQ-45	1. 0.04	Estimated as a multilevel model; 3-level model; ICC is the ratio of therapist variance to patient variance
Owen, Leach, Wampold, and Rodolfa, 2011	31	4.6	TAU	1. SOS-10	1. 0.09	Estimated as a multilevel model; posttreatment controlling for baseline
Owen, Rhoades, Stanley, and Markman, 2011	31	3.8	Premarital education	1. Confidence 2. NComm 3. PComm 4. RA	1. 0.10 2. 0.05 3. 0.05 4. 0.01	Estimated as a multilevel model; posttreatment controlling for baseline level
Owen, Tao, Leach, and Rodolfa, 2011	33	5.3	TAU	1. SOS-10	1. 0.03	Estimated as a multilevel model
Owen, Tao, and Rodolfa, 2010	37	3.3	TAU	1. SOS-10	1. 0	Estimated as a multilevel model
Pilkonis, Imber, Lewis, and Rubinsky, 1984[b]	9	7.1	Individual, conjoint, and group	Specific outcomes not specified[b]	Mean = 0.08[c]	Estimated using ANOVA
Piper, Debbane, Bienvenu, and Garant, 1984[b]	3	26.3	Short- or long-term therapy (individual and group)	Specific outcomes not specified[b]	1–10: Mean = 0.05[c]	Estimated Using ANOVA
Szapocznik et al., 2004[d]	3	18.4	PC or SET for HIV-positive African American women	1. BSI 2. Hassles scale 3. SSQ	1. 0.0 2. 0.0 3. 0.0	Estimated using ANOVA; posttreatment controlling for baseline
Taylor et al., 2003[d]	2	7.8	EMDR, exposure, or relaxation	1. BDI 2. CAPS-A 3. CAPS-H 4. CAPS-N 5. CAPS-R	1. 0.06 2. 0.12 3. 0.14 4. 0.06 5. 0.18	Estimated using ANOVA; posttreatment controlling for baseline

(continued)

TABLE 8.2 *(Continued)*

Study	k	m	Treatment	Outcome	ICC	Other
The Marijuana Treatment Project Research Group, 2004[d]	12	7.0	2-session MET or 9-session MET + CBT + CM	1. BDI 2. Joints per day 3. Marijuana dependence 4. Marijuana problems 5. Periods smoked per day 6. Days smoked in last 90 days 7. STAI	1. 0.002 2. 0.01 3. 0.004 4. 0.08 5. 0.02 6. 0.0 7. 0.0	Estimated using ANOVA; posttreatment controlling for baseline
Thompson, Gallagher, and Breckenridge, 1987[b]	10	7.6	BT, CBT, or dynamic	Specific outcomes not specified[b]	1–3. Mean = 0[c]	Estimated using ANOVA
Trepka, Rees, Shapiro, Hardy, and Barkham, 2004[d]	6	4.2	CBT for depression	1. BDI	1. 0.14	Estimated using ANOVA; posttreatment controlling for baseline
van Minnen, Hoogduin, Keijsers, Hellenbrand, and Hendriks, 2003[d]	5	2.5	BT for trichotillomania	1. BDI 2. Hair-loss ratings 3. MGHHS – pulling 4. MGHHS – total 5. SCL-90	1. 0.0 2. 0.29 3. 0.15 4. 0.35 5. 0.31	Estimated using ANOVA; posttreatment controlling for baseline
Wampold and Brown, 2005	581	9.68	TAU	1. LSQ	1. 0.05	Estimated as a multilevel model: posttreatment controlling for baseline
Watson, Gordon, Sterman, Kalogerakos, and Steckely, 2003[d]	7.5	4.3	CBT or PET for depression	1. BDI 2. DYAS 3. IIP 4. PFC-RA 5. PFC-RF 6. PFC-S 7. RSI 8. SCL-90	1. 0.04 2. 0.13 3. 0.0 4. 0.08 5. 0.08 6. 0.0 7. 0.08 8. 0.05	Estimated using ANOVA; posttreatment controlling for baseline

Study	Treatment	k	m	Outcomes	ICC	Method
Woody, McLellan, Luborsky, and O'Brien, 1995[b]	SE for opiate addiction	5	11.4	Specific outcomes not specified[b]	1–9: Mean = 0.04[c]	Estimated using ANOVA
Zitrin et al., 1978[b]	BT + imipramine, ST + imipramine, or BT + placebo	NR	NR	Specific outcomes not specified[b]	Mean = 0.04[c]	Estimated using ANOVA

Note: k = number of therapists contributing to the intraclass correlation;* ICCs computed based on information reported in the study; a = these studies anchored patients' rate of change over time to the baseline value of the outcome, which has been shown to lead to biased estimates of therapist effects (Wampold & Bolt, 2007); b = as reported in Crits-Christoph and Mintz (1991); c = only the average ICC across measures is available; d = estimates were drawn from Baldwin et al. (2011). Estimates were calculated per measure at the condition-level. We then aggregated the condition-level estimates to the study-level; e = we assumed that all therapists described in these studies provided the therapy; AC = Affective Communication; ACQ = Agoraphobic Cognitions Questionnaire; AntAnx = Anticipatory anxiety; ADIS-R = Anxiety Disorders Interview Schedule-Revised; ASI = Anxiety Sensitive Index; BAI = Beck Anxiety Inventory; BAT-D = Behavioral Approach Test - Distance Score; BAT-SP = Behavioral Approach Test - Patient Rating of Severity; BAT-TP = Behavioral Approach Test - Therapist Rating of Severity; BCSAQ-C = BAT Cognitive Somatic Anxiety Questionnaire - Cognitive Subscale; BCSAQ-S = BAT Cognitive Somatic Anxiety Questionnaire - Somatic Subscale; BDI = Beck Depression Inventory; BSI = Brief Symptoms Inventory; BSQ = Body Sensations Questionnaire; CAPS-A = Clinician Administered PTSD Scale - Avoidance; CAPS-D = Clinician Administered PTSD Scale - Distress; CAPS-DIS = Clinician Administered PTSD Scale - Disability; CAPS-F = Clinician Administered PTSD Scale - Frequency; CAPS-H = Clinician Administered PTSD Scale - Hyperarousal; CAPS-N = Clinician Administered PTSD Scale - Numbing; CAPS-R = Clinician Administered PTSD Scale - Re-experiencing; CBT = Cognitive Behavioral Therapy; CGI = Clinical Global Impressions scale; CM = Case Management; CS = Current Symptoms; CSAQ-C = Cognitive Somatic Anxiety Questionnaire - Cognitive Subscale; CSAQ-S = Cognitive Somatic Anxiety Questionnaire - Somatic Subscale; CSD = coping desensitization; DAS = Dyadic Adjustment Scale; DYAS = Dysfunctional Attitudes Scale; ERP = Exposure and Response Prevention; EST = Expected Success of Treatment; FQ = Fear Questionnaire; FPA = frequency of panic attacks; FSS-III A = Fear Survey Schedule-III Animal Item; FSS-III F = Fear Survey Schedule-III Factor Score; GAF = Global Assessment of Functioning; GDS = Global Distress Scale; GSI = Global Severity Index from the Symptom Checklist-90; HRSA = Hamilton Rating Scale for Anxiety; HRSD = Hamilton Rating Scale for Depression; IBCT = Integrative Behavioral Couples Therapy; IES-A = Impact of Events Scale - Avoidance; IES-I = Impact of Events Scale - Intrusion; IIP = Inventory of Interpersonal Problems; IPT = Interpersonal Therapy; LSQ = Life-Status Questionnaire; MADRS = Montgomery Asberg Depression Rating Scale; MDD = Major Depressive Disorder; MDFT = Multidimensional Family Therapy; MET = Motivational Enhancement Therapy; MIA-AC = Mobility Inventory for Agoraphobia - Accompanied; MIA-AL = Mobility Inventory for Agoraphobia - Alone; MGHHS = Massachusetts General Hospital Hairpulling Scale; MHI = Mental Health Index; MHID = Mental Health Index; MSI = Marital Status Inventory; NComm = Negative Communication; ND = nondirective therapy; NR = Not reported; OQ-45 = Outcome Questionnaire-45; ORS = Outcome Rating Scale; PC = Person Centered; PComm = Positive Communication; PDS-D = Posttraumatic Diagnostic Scale-Distress; PDS-F = Posttraumatic Diagnostic Scale-Frequency; PDSS = panic disorder severity scale; PET = Process Experiential Therapy; PFC-RA = Problem-Focused Coping - Reactive; PFC-RF = Problem-Focused Coping - Reflective; PFC-S = Problem-Focused Coping - Suppressive; PSC = Problem Solving Communication; QLI = Quality of Life Inventory; RA = Relationship Adjustment; RSI = Rosenberg Self-Esteem Inventory; SCL-90 = Symptom Checklist-90; SDS = Sheehan Disability Scale; SET = Structural Ecosystems Therapy; SOS-10 = Schwartz Outcome Scale-10; SPI = Substance Problem Index; SPQ-A = Specific Phobia Questionnaire - Avoidance; SPQ-CB = Specific Phobia Questionnaire - Cognitive-Behavioral; SPQ-P = Specific Phobia Questionnaire - Preoccupation; SPQ-Total = Specific Phobia Questionnaire - Total; SPQ-V = Specific Phobia Questionnaire - Vigilance; SPS = Session Progress Scale; SSQ = Social Support Questionnaire; SSS = Subjective symptom scale; STAI = State-Trait Anxiety Inventory; TAU = Treatment as Usual; TBCT = Traditional Behavioral Couples Therapy; TC-NI = Thought Checklist - Negative Items; TC-PI = Thought Checklist - Positive Items; YBOCS = Yale-Brown Obsessive-Compulsive Scale therapist effects. If we define ICCs as the proportion of variance associated with therapists, there is not much that can be done about this problem, except to design sufficiently large enough studies so that boundary estimates due to sampling error are rare. The second reason the aggregate effect may be overestimated is publication bias. Specifically, researchers may only publish information about therapist effects when there is indeed an effect or therapist effects may only be briefly mentioned if the significance test for the effect is not significant (Crits-Christoph & Gallop, 2006). Thus, the published ICC estimates may not include these null effects and the aggregate estimate will be too large.

To investigate publication bias we used four statistical methods: (1) funnel plots (Light & Pillemer, 1984), (2) Begg's rank correlation test (Begg & Mazumdar, 1994), (3) Egger's regression test (Egger, Davey Smith, Schneider, & Minder, 1997), and (4) a trim-and-fill analysis (Duval & Tweedie, 2000). Each of these methods provides evidence regarding whether our sample of ICC estimates is truncated such that null or tiny effects are missing. None of the methods suggested the presence of publication bias. In fact, the trim-and-fill analysis suggested that, if anything, the sample of ICC estimates is skewed toward small estimates not large estimates. Thus, there is little evidence that our aggregate estimate is biased by missing small effect studies.

Studies that only briefly mention therapists because the test of therapist effects was nonsignificant are difficult to treat appropriately. On the one hand, these studies are directly relevant to a meta-analysis of therapist effects. On the other hand, these studies typically only report that the therapist effect was not statistically significant but do not provide an ICC estimate. However, failing to reject the null hypothesis does not mean that the population therapist effect is actually zero. Further, tests of therapist effects will typically be so underpowered that we actually expect a nonsignificant test most of the time, even when the null is false. For example, Crits-Christoph and Gallop (2006) identified Taylor et al. (2003) as an example of a study that did not find statistically significant therapist effects and only briefly mentioned this in a preliminary analysis. One option for the meta-analysis is to include Taylor et al. (2003) but set the ICC = 0. This would be conservative. Table 8.2 presents the ICCs for Taylor et al. (2003), all of which are above zero and some substantially so. To be sure, these ICCs

are not statistically significant but power is low. If the population ICC = .05 and we design a study with two therapists each seeing eight patients, the power to detect a significant therapist effect is 10%. Thus, using statistical significance as a criterion for determining whether an effect is 0 is problematic in studies of this size. Further, a benefit of meta-analysis is that it pools the ICCs from Taylor et al. (2003) with 44 other studies, which will dramatically increase the precision of the estimate (Baldwin & Shadish, 2011). The aggregate ICC and its standard error from the meta-analysis will be based on hundreds or thousands of therapists rather than just the two from Taylor et al.

Together, the data from Taylor et al. (2003) and the publication bias analysis suggest that it is not likely that the aggregate estimate from our analysis is overestimated due to publication bias. In the end, the only certain way to rule the publication bias out is for researchers to routinely report ICC estimates for therapists (statistically significant or not) or make their data available so that meta-analysts can compute the ICC.

The meta-analytic aggregate estimate may also underestimate the true therapist effect. The underestimation may occur because studies are rarely, if ever, designed for the purpose of studying therapist effects. For example, two thirds of the studies contributing to the meta-analysis were efficacy studies. In efficacy studies, therapist behavior is often constrained via selection, manualization, and supervision, which increases the homogeneity of the therapist behaviors and decreases the degree of between-therapist variability (and ICCs). In naturalistic/effectiveness studies, by contrast, the degree of heterogeneity among patients is huge because nearly all patients are included. Thus, the within-therapist variability will dominate between-therapist variability and ICCs will be small. In any case, neither study is ideal for isolating therapist effects. Alternative designs where therapists provide a consistent treatment but are not supervised in a way that produces uniformity of behavior and where patient variability is reduced via careful selection or the use of "standardized patients" may be better for understanding therapist effects (Baer et al., 2009).

Interpreting Between-Therapist Variability

It is clear from the studies in Tables 8.1 and 8.2 that some therapists outperform others. The

ICCs indicate that therapist assignment accounts for about 5% of the variance in outcomes. This may not seem like much variance, but it is reasonably large for psychotherapy. For example, most meta-analyses comparing an active treatment to a wait-list control have posttest effect sizes at or below $d = 1.0$ (cf. Lambert & Bergin, 1994; Wampold, 2001), which corresponds to about 20% of the variance in outcome. Thus, psychotherapy as a whole and all the constructs it entails—specific factors, common factors, therapist factors, alliance, adherence, and so on—accounts for only 20% of the variance in outcomes. As we discuss below, the therapeutic alliance appears to account for about 5% of the variance in outcomes and therapist adherence to the treatment protocol 0% of the variance in outcomes. Relatively speaking, 5% of the variance is not so bad.

What does 5% of the outcome look like? To help visualize this relationship we simulated a sample of 50 therapists each seeing 100 patients. We simulated one dataset assuming the ICC was .05 and, as a reference, a second dataset assuming the ICC was .15. We standardized the outcome variable to have a normal distribution with a mean of 0 and standard deviation of 1. Thus in both data sets, the average outcome for all therapists averaging over all patients was 0. Negative values indicate outcomes below average and positive values indicate outcome above average. Figure 8.2 provides a boxplot for each therapist's outcomes stratified by ICC. The line in the center of each box represents the therapist's median outcomes. The width of the box represents the difference between outcomes at the 75th and 25th percentile (i.e., the interquartile range) for each therapist and the lines extending from the box represent

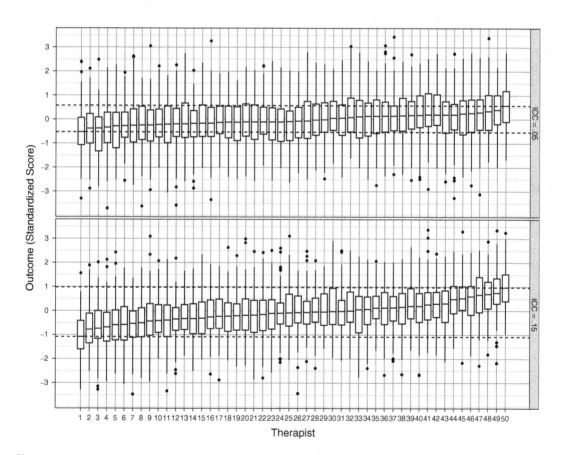

FIGURE 8.2   Boxplots representing outcomes of a simulated sample of 50 therapists seeing 100 patients each for two values of the intraclass correlation (ICC).

The outcome variable was simulated to have a mean of 0 and standard deviation of 1 (positive values indicate better outcomes). The dashed lines represent the median outcome of the best therapist (top line in each panel) and worst therapist (bottom line in each panel).

outcomes within 1.5 times the interquartile range. Lastly, the points extending beyond the lines for each therapist represent extreme observations for that therapist. We ordered the therapists from worst outcomes (1) to best outcomes (50). Within each panel of the graph, the top dashed line represents the median outcome for the best therapist and the bottom dashed line represents the median outcome for the worst therapist. These dashed lines help to visualize how any given therapist compares to the best and worst therapists.

Figure 8.2 illustrates five characteristics about between-therapist variability. First, 5% of the variance associated with therapists looks like it sounds—small but distinct differences among therapists. Second, the increased between-therapist variability when the ICC is .15 as compared to .05 results in a bigger discrepancy between one therapist to the next. Third, differences between any two therapists from the middle two thirds of the distribution are small, even when the ICC = .15. Differences are most prominent when comparing therapists from the opposite tails of the distribution. Fourth, the difference between the median outcome of the best and the worst therapist is about one standard deviation when the ICC = .05 and two standard deviations when ICC = .15. Fifth, when the ICC = .05, the interquartile range for the middle two thirds of therapists includes the median outcome value for the best and worst therapists. This was not the case when the ICC = .15 given the additional between-therapist variability. However, this indicates that with any given client, the predicted outcome of a client seen by the best therapist could also be generated by the worst therapist (and vice versa).

The impact of small effects will be played out in the long run. In baseball, the difference between a player who has a career batting average of .275 and one with .300 is only one hit every 2 weeks. If we consider that a baseball season is about 6 months long, then the difference is about 12 hits per year. Over a 15-year career the difference is 180 hits—that's many more times on base and could be the difference between a solid career and hall-of-fame career. However, if you were to watch both players in 15 games (out of 162), there is a 40% chance that the .275 hitter will have more hits in those games (Lewis, 2003).

The impact of 5% of the variance in outcome being between therapists will also be seen in the long run. For example, if we eliminated the bottom 20% of therapists from the top panel of

Figure 8.2, the mean outcome for patients would go up by a 10th of a standard deviation. This will not be a huge difference if we just consider 1 month of these therapists' careers. However, in the long run, perhaps 30 years, that 10th of a standard deviation begins to add up and has a real impact on patients' functioning. Okiishi et al. (2003) provide information that can be used to illustrate this point. They divided their sample of therapists into the best 10% and the worst 10%. Patients of the worst therapists had a deterioration rate of 11% and patients of the best therapists had a deterioration rate of 5%. Suppose that in a given year the best therapists, as a group, see 100 patients and the worst therapists, as a group, see 100 patients. We would expect the worst therapists to have 6 more patients deteriorate than the worst therapists. After 10 years the worst therapists would have 60 more patients deteriorate. After 30 years, the worst therapists would have 180 more patients deteriorate. If we could eliminate the bottom 10% either by training or by encouraging them to find other careers, we could reduce a lot of poor outcomes.

Interpreting Within-Therapist Variability

We have to be careful not to make too much of the between-therapist variability—5% of the variability in outcome is still just 5%. This also means that 95% of the variance lies within therapist caseloads. The issue of within-therapist variability has been present since early on in this literature. In their initial study of therapist effects, Luborsky et al. (1986) noted that one of the key findings of their analyses was that there was substantial variability in outcomes *within* therapists' caseloads. This raises the question of how much of a difference does the *particular* therapist a patient sees make? That is, if a patient sees the best therapist at a clinic, what probability does that patient have of achieving an above average outcome as compared to an average therapist at the clinic or as compared to the worst therapist?

These questions are not long-run questions like those we considered earlier. Instead of asking what is going to happen for many patients seeing the same group of therapists over a long period of time, we are now asking what is going to happen for a particular patient during his or her course of treatment. With respect to therapists, we are asking what is going to happen if the patients see Therapist A versus Therapist B. When 5% of the variance is between therapists, we expect the differences between Therapist A and B to not make much of a difference unless Therapist A and B are in the extremes of the distribution. Even at the extremes there is still a fair amount of overlap and, as a consequence, even if a patient sees the worst therapist, there is still a decent chance that he or she will have an above average outcome (see the top panel of Figure 8.2).

When we are dealing with a therapist in the middle part of the distribution rather than those at the extremes, the differences are quite small. Figure 8.3 provides the distribution of patient outcomes for a therapist at the 50th percentile and a therapist at the 75th percentile. We standardized outcomes so that an outcome of zero is an average outcome, negative values a below average outcome, and positive values an above average outcome. The left panel of Figure 8.3 provides outcomes assuming an ICC = .05 and the right panel assumes an ICC = .15. When the ICC = .05, patients seeing a therapist at the 50th percentile have a 50% chance of having an above average outcome because 50% of the distribution for a therapist at the 50th percentile is above 0. This 50% probability is represented by the light shading in Figure 8.3. When the ICC = .05, patients seeing a therapist at the 75th percentile have a 56% chance of having an above average outcome because 56% of the distribution for a therapist at the 75th percentile is above 0. Thus the difference in probability of an above average outcome for a patient seeing a therapist at the 50th percentile as compared to a therapist

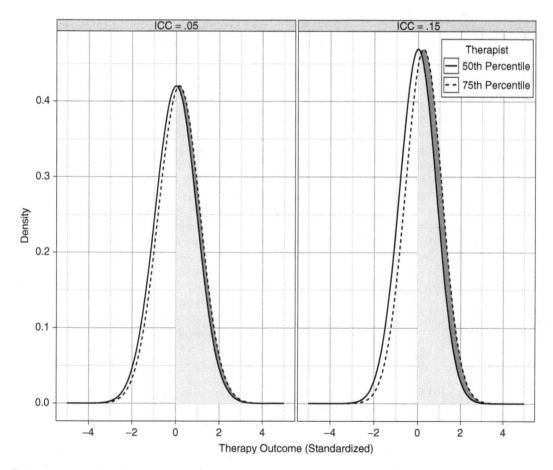

FIGURE 8.3   The distribution of patient outcomes for a therapist at the 50th percentile and a therapist at the 75th percentile assuming an intraclass correlation (ICC) of .05 or .15.

Outcomes are standardized so that an outcome of zero is an average outcome, negative values a below average outcome, and positive values an above average outcome. The light shading represents the probability (.5) of an above average outcome for a patient of a therapist at the 50th percentile. The dark shading represents the difference in probability of an above average outcome for patients seeing a therapist at the 75th percentile as compared to a therapist at the 50th percentile.

at the 75th percentile is 6 percentage points. This difference is represented by the dark shading in Figure 8.3. The size of the dark shading increases when the ICC increases (see the right panel of Figure 8.3), but the increase in probability of an above average outcome from seeing the better therapist still remains small. Indeed, the vast majority of the area in the distributions for a therapist at the 50th percentile and at the 75th percentile overlaps, which suggests that there is a high probability that a patient would have a similar outcome regardless of which therapist he or she saw.

To make this more concrete, consider again the data from Okiishi et al. (2003). Table 8.3 presents the clinical significance data from Okiishi et al. (2003), specifically the percentage of patients who fell into one of the four clinical significance categories (recovered, improved, no change, or deteriorated) for the best 10% and worst 10% of therapists. To be sure, a patient who sees one of the bottom 10% of therapists has half the probability of being in the recovered or improved category and more than twice the probability of being in the no change or deteriorated category as compared to the top 10%. Patients would surely want to know about this difference. However, within-therapist differences remain most important. Even if a patient sees one of the top 10% of therapists, he or she has a 50% probability of being in the no change category. In fact, the most likely outcome for patients seeing therapists in this setting who are in the top 10% is to be in the no change category. This is also true for the patients seeing therapists in the bottom 10%.

The Problem With Small Sample Sizes

Like any research area, small sample sizes in therapist effect studies cause problems. Specifically,

small sample sizes lead to imprecise estimates of therapist effects. There are two sample sizes to consider in therapist studies: the number of therapists and the number of patients per therapist. Both numbers are critically important. When the number of therapists is small, estimates of the therapist variance will vary widely simply due to sampling error. This variability is evident in our sample of studies where the median number of therapists contributing to ICC estimates was 9 and the range of study-level ICC estimates ranged from 0 to 0.55. To be sure, a lot of that variability is due to between-study differences but a large portion is also due to sampling error. This sampling error and the consequent imprecision in estimates lead to confusion regarding how important therapist effects are. Two sources of confusion are worth noting. First, power will be low with small numbers of therapists so statistical tests of between-therapist variability or the ICC have a high probability of being nonsignificant even when the null is false. Second, estimates of between-therapist variances will run into boundary problems (i.e., be estimated as zero) more frequently when therapist sample sizes are small.

When the number of patients per therapist is small, estimates of therapist mean outcomes will be less reliable (cf. Crits-Christoph, Gibbons, Hamilton, Ring-Kurtz, & Gallop, 2011), which will make comparisons among therapists suspect. The studies in our meta-analysis had a median of 7.6 patients per therapist. Although reliability of therapist means is not solely a function of the number of patients per therapist, seven to eight patients per therapist is not sufficient to obtain reliable estimates of therapist means (Crits-Christoph et al., 2011).

Advancement in our understanding of therapist effects will likely only come from larger studies of therapist effects. Granted, it is difficult and expensive to conduct large studies and we are quite sympathetic to that concern. However, saying that it is difficult does not solve the problem of imprecision and confusion. Meta-analysis can help with some of these sample size problems by aggregating data from multiple studies. However, this is not ideal as it does not reduce the imprecision reported in the original studies. Researchers will likely need to collaborate and pool resources to obtain sufficient amounts of data. It is a challenge but a challenge we must face if we are to move this literature forward.

TABLE 8.3 Clinical Significance Data from Okiishi et al. (2003)

	Best Therapists	Worst Therapists
Recovered	22.4	10.61
Improved	21.54	17.37
No Change	50.86	61.46
Deteriorated	5.2	10.56
	$N = 407$ patients	$N = 452$ patients

Summary of Therapist Effects

The literature to date has demonstrated that some therapists are more effective than others. In general, the effect of therapists is small in an absolute sense (5% of outcome variance) but similar in size to some process variables (e.g., alliance) and larger than other process variables (e.g., adherence). Although therapist effects are relatively small, in the long run, the differences among therapists may have a substantial impact on public health. Thus, it is important that we learn why some therapists are better than others and seek to improve the outcomes of poor performing therapists. Additionally, it is clear that within-therapist variability is huge. Consequently, an important research area for the future is to understand why therapists work well with some patients but not with others. We now turn our attention to data that could explain both between- and within-therapist variability in outcomes. We see, however, that most studies have not been designed or analyzed in a way that speaks to between- and within-therapist variability. Thus, we focus on how studies could be improved to help us better understand between- and within-therapist variability.

ACCOUNTING FOR DIFFERENCES AMONG THERAPISTS

It would be convenient if the best therapists could be identified by the type of treatment they provide; that is, the best therapists use the ideal treatment for the patient. However, even in medicine this does not always distinguish the best providers from other providers. Consider an illustration from the treatment of Cystic fibrosis (CF)—a fatal genetic disorder that results in a disruption in the flow of digestive enzymes and a dramatic reduction in lung capacity. For 40 years, the Cystic Fibrosis Foundation has maintained a data registry that archives outcome data for all 117 accredited CF treatment centers. In 2003, the average life expectancy for someone with CF was 33 years. However, at the best CF center it was approximately 47 years, an improvement of about 30%. The best predictor of survival for patients with CF is lung function. At the median center, the mean level of lung functioning was 75% of normal. At top centers, lung functioning was indistinguishable from children who did not have CF (Gawande, 2004).

So far, so good. It must be that the top centers are adhering to the best treatment guidelines and other centers would improve if they implemented those same guidelines. It turns out that this is not likely the case. All 117 CF centers complete a rigorous certification process that requires adherence to the same detailed treatment guidelines. Patients at the top center purportedly receive the same treatments as other treatment centers. Something besides well-established treatment protocols separates the best CF centers from the average ones (Gawande, 2004).

The source of provider differences in psychotherapy is even less clear. Although psychotherapy itself is as low technology as it gets (it involves people talking), the mechanisms are likely complex and embedded in sometimes upward of 20 hours of conversation. There is no national database that tracks treatment outcomes to provide exemplars of the most successful providers. Finally, there is no agreed on mediator of treatment success as there is in CF (i.e., lung function). In contrast, the processes that are responsible for successful outcomes in psychotherapy continue to be debated.

Differences among therapists are presumably tied to some component of therapists' behavior. However, the role of therapists in the relationship between process and outcome measures is a continued source of controversy. As noted at the beginning of the chapter, Beutler et al. (2004) reviewed the influence of a wide range of therapist characteristics including age, race or ethnic match, sex, professional training and discipline, therapist interpersonal style, directiveness, homework assignments, therapeutic interpretations, emotive versus supportive interventions, personality and coping patterns, dominance, and the therapeutic relationship, among many others. To ease interpretation, Beutler et al. (2004) divided these characteristics into four quadrants. The first (observable traits such as such as age, sex, gender), second (observed states such as training and experience), and third quadrants (inferred traits such as values, attitudes, well-being) revealed no consistent effects on outcome. The authors noted that characteristics in the fourth quadrant—inferred states—had received the most attention and empirical support. These traits include therapist adherence to specific and technical behaviors like those in relaxation training or exposure and nonspecific treatment components that cut across treatment approaches such as therapists' attempt to establish a strong therapeutic relationship.

Unfortunately, the methods used in most existing research are not sufficient for isolating the therapist contribution to these treatment processes and outcome. Specific questions include whether the therapist is responsible for the quality of the therapeutic alliance (e.g., DeRubeis, Brotman, & Gibbons, 2005), and how, or even if, therapist adherence to treatment protocols impacts treatment outcome (Webb, DeRubeis, & Barber, 2010). In this section, we discuss the role of the therapist in measures of the alliance and adherence as well as their relationship to treatment outcome. We focus on these two constructs because both are often conceptualized as dependent on therapists and are regarded as critical aspects of psychotherapy process. We first review the literature on alliance-outcome and adherence-outcome correlations. We then discuss how the majority of studies in this literature are not able to isolate the contribution of the therapist to either process or outcome. We show how "social relations modeling" and multilevel modeling provide the conceptual and statistical means for understanding the contribution of therapists to process-outcome literatures. Throughout this discussion, we highlight studies that have used these multilevel modeling techniques to test hypotheses regarding the impact of both therapists on treatment process and outcome.

Alliance, Adherence, and Outcome

Most explanations of process-outcome correlations assume that the therapist is responsible for a portion of variability in the process measure. For example, consider a measure of the relational component of psychotherapy such as the working alliance. Measures of the working alliance involve patients, therapists, or external raters indicating the degree to which patients and therapist agree on the tasks and goals of therapy as well as the quality of the therapeutic bond (Horvath & Greenberg, 1989). Although the working alliance as a concept has its roots in psychodynamic theory, it has been widely incorporated into most approaches to psychotherapy as a basic skill of any therapist. Meta-analyses of the alliance-outcome correlation suggest a consistent relationship between strong alliances and good therapy outcomes (Horvath & Bedi, 2002; Horvath, Del Re, Flückiger, & Symonds, 2011; Horvath & Symonds, 1991; Martin, Garske, & Davis, 2000). The most recent meta-analysis

included 190 independent studies. The aggregate alliance-outcome correlation was $r = .28$, which indicates that the alliance is associated with 7.8% of the variability in outcomes (Horvath et al., 2011).[4] Thus, therapist skill in forming an alliance may indeed be important.

Another therapist behavior that is thought to be central to achieving positive clinical outcomes is therapist adherence to specific treatment protocols. To assess adherence, raters who are trained by experts in a given therapy approach either derive frequency counts of a therapist utilizing specific techniques or provide more global indices that assess "treatment purity" or the "extensiveness" of a therapeutic style (see Luborsky, McLellen, Woody, O'Brien, & Auerbach, 1985). For example, in the motivational interviewing (MI) literature there are a variety of scales that are supposed to capture the extent a therapist behaved in a manner consistent with MI. The Motivational Interviewing Treatment Integrity Scale (MITI) provides behavioral counts (i.e., the number of open or closed questions asked by a therapist or the number MI inconsistent behaviors). In addition, the MITI provides global scales such as MI-spirit, which includes therapist evocation, collaboration, and support throughout the session (Moyers, Martin, Manuel, Miller, & Ernst, 2010).

Opinion regarding the influence of treatment adherence on outcome is varied. Specifically, if therapist behaviors that are prescribed by a treatment manual or even by a general treatment approach are responsible for treatment outcomes, then measures of adherence to a treatment protocol should relate to clinical outcomes. On the

---

[4]Crits-Christoph et al. (2011) used generalizability theory (Shavelson & Webb, 1991) to test how the "dependability" of alliance scores—where dependability is similar to reliability—attenuates the observed relationship between the alliance and outcome. At the patient level, Crits-Christoph et al. found that four assessments of the alliance were necessary to obtain a generalizability coefficient of .90. The vast majority of alliance studies are based on only one assessment of the alliance. Consequently, the percent of variance in outcome associated with the alliance in meta-analyses is likely to be an underestimate of the true effect. When observations of the alliance averaged across multiple sessions, Crits-Christoph et al. report that the alliance may account for 10.1% to 16.7% of the variance in depression symptoms. If their results generalize, this suggests that the meta-analytic estimate reported above may underestimate the true alliance-outcome correlation.

other hand, adherence to the structure provided by a manual may unintentionally impede the intended spirit of some treatments by detracting from the client and therapist interacting collaboratively in a genuine and spontaneous manner (Ball et al., 2007; Hettema, Steele, & Miller, 2005). Essentially, adherence to the *letter* but not the *spirit* of a treatment may attenuate change. As concluded by psychodynamic researchers who found a negative relationship between adherence and outcome, "although 'the *treatment* was delivered'...the *therapy* did not always occur" (Henry, Strupp, Butler, Schacht, & Binder, 1993, p. 438, italics added).

Adherence-outcome studies have provided mixed results. A meta-analysis of 32 studies of the adherence-outcome correlation indicated that the aggregate correlation was $r = .02$ and not statistically significant (Webb et al., 2010). There was a moderate amount of between-study heterogeneity, suggesting the variability observed exceeds what we would expect based on sampling error alone. It is possible that there is a distinct subset of studies where the adherence-outcome correlation is positive (or negative). Several studies have provided evidence of quadractic effects of adherence on clinical outcomes, wherein very high and very low adherence was associated with negative outcomes (Barber et al., 2006). Thus, the evidence does not consistently support a strong relationship between adherence and outcome, which may indicate that therapists' adherence to a treatment approach—as currently operationalized—does not impact outcomes. However, the current state of the evidence is not sufficient to fully draw these conclusions.

Although the interpretation of alliance-outcome and adherence-outcome correlations is often based on the assumption that therapists are responsible for variability in the alliance and adherence scores, the correlations do not tell us about the therapist contribution. Process measures such as the alliance and adherence are dyadic in nature. They are obtained in the context of an ongoing interaction between therapists and patients and thus any observed variability in process measures may be the result of a combination of therapist influence, patient influence, and/or the mutual influence of therapists and patients on each other. Accordingly, we cannot yet say, based on zero-order process-outcome correlations, how much therapists contribute to variability in these process variables and whether this variability explains differences in the effectiveness of therapists. To address these questions, we need to use methods that are suited for partitioning variance in process and outcome measures into patient, therapist, and patient × therapist interactions. Two methods that can partition the variance in this way and thus can isolate the role of therapists in process and outcome of psychotherapy are (1) the social relations model and (2) multilevel modeling.

Patient, Therapist, and Dyadic Variability in Alliance and Adherence

The social relations model (SRM; Kenny, Kashy, & Cook, 2006) provides a framework for partitioning sources of variability in psychotherapy data. According to the SRM, interpersonal behavior can differ as a result of three main components: (1) the actor, (2) the partner, and (3) the relationship, which map onto the patient, therapist, and dyadic components in psychotherapy.

To isolate the therapist contribution in alliance and adherence, sources of variability in measures of these processes need to be separated into each of the three components noted earlier. The between-therapist component of variance is a measure of consensus—the similarity of ratings for a given therapist compared to other therapists. High between-therapist components in adherence or alliance ratings indicate that some therapists receive consistently higher (or lower) ratings as compared to other therapists. The patient and relationship/dyad components are measures of uniqueness. The patient component indexes the degree to which adherence or alliance ratings are unique to a particular client, for example, the degree to which clients are prone to give high ratings. The relationship or dyad component indexes the degree to which adherence or alliance ratings are unique to a given patient-therapist dyad (Marcus, Kashy, & Baldwin, 2009).

The structure of most psychotherapy data sets provides an opportunity for obtaining an estimate of consensus. Psychotherapy data is usually nested in structure—one therapist treats multiple patients and each patient is treated by one and only one therapist. Consequently, we can estimate the percentage of variability in alliance or adherence ratings that is between therapists (e.g., between caseloads) relative to the variability within therapist (e.g., within caseloads). Note that this maps directly onto the methods used to isolate therapist variability in treatment outcomes. A large percentage of variability between therapists would indicate high levels of consensus and consistency among therapists in alliance and adherence. For example, a between-therapist component of .80 for therapist adherence would indicate that therapists are highly consistent in their adherence behavior across patients in their caseload and that there are relatively large differences between therapists. Put another way, a therapist who adheres, always adheres, no matter the client (e.g., two clients treated by the same therapist are likely to receive the same level of adherence). On the other hand, therapists with low adherence scores will fail to adhere regardless of clients. A much smaller therapist component of .05 would indicate considerable variability in adherence within therapist caseloads—therapists' adherence score was almost entirely dependent on the patient they happened to be treating at the time (e.g., two clients treated by the same therapist are not likely to receive the same level of adherence).

Unfortunately, most psychotherapy data only allows us to separate therapist variability from patient and dyadic variability. Patient and dyadic variability remain confounded. Because patients are treated by only one therapist, variability within a caseload may be the result of client characteristics (e.g., patients with difficult interpersonal presentations may elicit lower skills) or the unique relationship between a particular patient and a therapist (e.g., a therapist may be more adherent to a protocol with a given patient, but other therapists may be less adherent with this patient). Round robin designs in which patients are treated by multiple therapists are necessary to separate relationship or dyad effects from patient effects. Unfortunately, this design is typically infeasible in applied clinical studies.

We conducted a random effects meta-analysis of studies that have utilized social relations modeling procedures to isolate therapist contributions to the alliance. Table 8.4 presents alliance ICCs associated with therapists from 15 samples (Imel, Hubbard, Rutter, & Simon, 2011, contained analyses from two independent samples). Similar to the studies contributing effect sizes for therapist difference in outcomes, studies in Table 8.4 are heterogeneous with respect to the number of therapists contributing the ICC (k), number of patients per therapist (m), intervention, population, and alliance measures. Studies included patients from outpatient managed care settings (Imel, Hubbard, et al., 2011; Nissen-Lie, Monsen, & Ronnestad, 2010), psychodynamically

oriented intensive inpatient programs (Dinger, Strack, Leichsenring, Wilmers, & Schauenburg, 2008), college counseling centers (Hatcher, Barends, Hansell, & Gutfreund, 1995; Marcus et al., 2009; Owen, Quirk, Hilsenroth, & Rodolfa, 2011; Owen, Tao, Leach, & Rodolfa, 2011; Owen, Tao, & Rodolfa, 2010), clinical trials for substance abuse (Crits-Christoph et al., 2009; Marcus, Kashy, Wintersteen, & Diamond, 2011) and major depression (Zuroff, Kelly, Leybman, Blatt, & Wampold, 2010), and a family educational program (Owen, Rhoades, Stanley, & Markman, 2011). Across the 15 effects, there were a total of 838 therapists and 10,287 patients. The median number of therapists in a study was 35 and the range was 14 to 318. The median number of patients per therapist was 5.35 and the range was 2.96 to 51.08. Study-level ICCs ranged from 0.001 to 0.33. Between-study variability was quite large ($I^2 = 94.65$). Averaging across studies, the random effects mean ICC was 0.09 [95% CI = 0.02, 0.18]. This indicates that, on average, approximately 9% of the variance in alliance is associated with therapists. However, effects were extremely variable across studies.

The largest ICC observed was 0.33. If the therapist accounts for 33% of the variability in alliance scores *at most*, the majority of variability in alliance measures is at patient/dyad level of analysis, which is a combination of patient, dyad, and error variance. As noted earlier, typical clinical data sets in which one therapist treats many patients but patients do not see multiple therapists do not allow further separation of these components. Accordingly, it is not possible to determine if large patient/dyad components are due to the relational nature of the alliance or other components. However, in two separate papers (Marcus et al., 2009; Marcus et al., 2011) that included both patient and therapist ratings of the alliance, there was strong evidence of dyadic reciprocity, which is evidence of a relational component to the alliance. Dyadic reciprocity, which is measured by the correlation of the client relationship effect with the therapist relationship effect (see Marcus et al., 2011, p. 450), indicates that if the client reported a particularly strong alliance (better than those of other patients treated by the same therapist), the therapist was also likely to report a particularly strong alliance.

Perhaps it is not surprising that the primary source of variability in alliance is the patient/dyad; the alliance is intended to measure the qualities about the work between a patient and therapist.

TABLE 8.4 Therapeutic Alliance Intraclass Correlations (ICC) Associated With Therapists

Study	k	m	Treatment/Setting	Alliance Measure	ICC
Crits-Christoph et al., 2009	30	10.63	Motivational enhancement therapy; treatment as usual	1. HAQ	0.13
Dinger et al., 2008	50	51.08	Intensive inpatient psychodynamic psychotherapy	1. HAQ	0.34
Hatcher et al., 1995	38	3.79	Training clinic	1. WAI	0.06
				2. HAQ	0.06
				3. CALPAS	0.00
Imel, Hubbard et al., 2011	82	46.11	Outpatient HMO group model	1. WAI (3-item)	0.02
	315	5.37	Outpatient HMO Network model	1. WAI (3 item)	0.08
Marcus et al., 2009	65	3.49	Counseling center	1. WAI	0.06
Marcus et al., 2011	14	28.43	Counseling center	1. WAI	0.05
Nissen-Lie et al., 2010	68	4.93	General outpatient	1. HAQ	0.18
Owen & Hilsenroth 2011	23	2.96	Pyschodynamic	1. CASF-P	0.24
Owen, Quirk et al., 2011	25	3.00	Counseling center	1. WAI	0.003
Owen, Rhoades et al., 2011	31	7.61	Family education	1. WAI	0.29
Owen et al., 2010	37	3.43	Counseling center	1. WAI	0.001
				2. RRI-C	0.030
Zuroff et al., 2010	27	5.81	Interpersonal therapy; cognitive therapy	1. BLRI	0.10

Note: k = number of therapists contributing to the intraclass correlation; *m* = average number of patients per therapist; WAI = Working Alliance Inventory; HAQ = Helping Alliance Questionnaire; CALPAS = California Psychotherapy Alliance Scale; CASF-P = Combined Alliance Short Form – Patient; BLRI = Barrett Leonard Relationship Inventory.

However, the patient and dyad contributions also could impact measures of adherence. Measures of therapist adherence assess therapist behavior that occurs during the work between a patient and therapist. Consequently, the meaning of a score on an adherence scale is also potentially multidetermined. For example, therapists may adhere more closely to a manual with "easy" patients or may provide more of a given intervention (be more adherent) when a patient does not respond to treatment (Imel, Baer, Martino, Ball, & Carroll, 2011).

For example, an analysis of a multisite trial of Motivational Enhancement Therapy (MET; Ball et al., 2007) suggested that as much of the variability in therapist adherence was due to the patient/dyad component as the therapist (Imel, Baer, et al., 2011). For example, 14% of the variability in therapist adherence to fundamental MET skills (i.e., basic motivational interviewing skills such as skill in using open-ended questions, reflections) was due to the patient/dyad, whereas 12% was between therapists (i.e., differences between therapists' average ratings). Alternatively, utilization of MI inconsistent strategies (e.g., confrontation) was highly variable across therapists (32% of variability in ratings was between therapists) with relatively less variability within therapist caseloads (9%). These findings can be interpreted in several ways. First, it may be that some ratings of therapist adherence are not stable indicators of a therapist's ability, but a momentary state that is influenced by patients. Alternatively, there may be relatively little between-therapist variability in some adherence measures because initial trainings and ongoing supervision have successfully limited variability in therapist behavior—an indicator of a successful efficacy trial.

Total Correlations Versus Between- and Within-Therapist Correlations

Thus far we have focused on separating patient and therapist variability in alliance and adherence measures. As we have described, variability within alliance and adherence scores comes from multiple sources, including the patient, therapist, and the interaction between patient and therapist (i.e., the dyad; cf. Baldwin, Wampold, & Imel, 2007; DeRubeis et al., 2005; Marcus et al., 2009), although the ratings are provided by a single rater. Likewise, those three sources of variance also contribute to outcome variance. However, almost all studies of the alliance-outcome correlation and the adherence-outcome correlation do not distinguish between these sources of variability when computing alliance-outcome or adherence-outcome correlations. Consequently, the correlations reported in most studies are called *total* correlations because they represent the correlations between process-outcome that combine multiple sources of variance.

Reliance on the total correlation can lead to an error in inference known as the *contextual fallacy* (Snijders & Bosker, 1999). Consider the alliance-outcome correlation—there are three "levels" of relationship involved in that total correlation. First, there is a relationship at the therapist level or the *between*-therapist correlation. The therapist level gets at the following question: Does therapists' average alliance score across clients in their caseload relate to their clients' average outcome? Second, there is a relationship at the patient level or the *within*-therapist correlation. The patient level correlation answers the following question: Do patients of a given therapist who have a high alliance relative to other patients of the same therapist have better outcomes? Third, the final level is the interaction between the patient and therapist level and answers the following question: Does the relationship between alliance and outcome depend on the combination of a therapists' average alliance score and clients' alliance score within therapists?

The contextual fallacy occurs when we assume that the correlation between process and outcome measures is the same at both the therapist and patient levels (and we assume no interaction), when in fact they are not. Relationships between variables can, and often do, differ

across levels both in magnitude and direction (Snijders & Bosker, 1999). The most common example of this phenomenon is from education wherein the correlation between student socioeconomic status (SES) and math scores is larger between schools (i.e., schools with students from higher SES backgrounds have high math scores) than within schools (i.e., variability in students' SES with a school is not as strongly related to their math scores; Raudenbush & Bryk, 2002). We can index the size of the difference between the within- and between-school effects using what is called a *contextual effect*. In the school example, the contextual effect indicates how educational outcomes would differ between students with the same SES but who attended schools that differed in average SES.

Figure 8.4 from Baldwin et al. (2007) uses simulated data to provide a general illustration of separating the total alliance-outcome correlation into within- and between-therapist components. Although we focus here on the alliance-outcome correlation, we extend these concepts to the adherence-outcome correlation below. The X's note the alliance scores for Therapist 1, asterisks Therapist 2, and open circles Therapist 3. The three dotted lines for each therapist indicate a small or near-zero relationship between the alliance and outcome within a therapist's caseload—the within-therapist correlation. The open squares refer to each therapist's mean alliance score. The solid line connecting the open squares reflects a relatively strong relationship between alliance and outcome between therapists—the between-therapist correlation. The stronger the therapist's mean alliance score across patients in his or her caseload, the fewer symptoms reported by a typical patient in his or her caseload. As the total correlation is a composite of the between- and within-therapist correlations (Kreft, De Leeuw, & Aiken, 1995), the total correlation would overestimate the within-therapist correlation and would underestimate the between-therapist correlation, which illustrates how the contextual fallacy noted above can obscure the interpretation of the true alliance-outcome correlation.

Between- and Within-Therapist Alliance-Outcome Correlations

Three studies have separated the between- and within-therapist correlations in the alliance. All three studies used multilevel modeling, which can partition the total correlation into between and

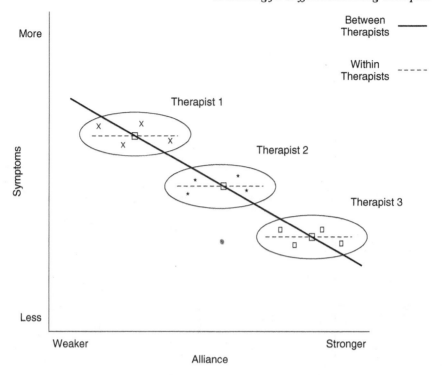

FIGURE 8.4   Illustration of between- and within-therapist relationships between the therapeutic alliance and outcome.

Source: Reprinted from Baldwin et al. (2007).

within therapist components. The first study was Baldwin et al. (2007). They used data obtained from the Research Consortium of Counseling and Psychological Services in Higher Education (Brownson, 2004) and included 331 patients seen by 80 therapists. Results were generally consistent with the pattern depicted in Figure 8.4. The within-therapist alliance-outcome correlation was small and not significant, whereas the between-therapist alliance-outcome correlation was negative and statistically significant. This indicates that patients who were treated by therapists with higher average alliance ratings had better outcomes, whereas variability in alliance scores within a caseload had little impact on treatment outcome.

Two subsequent studies have replicated the significant between-therapist alliance-outcome correlation. However, subsequent studies have differed from Baldwin et al. (2007) with respect to the size of the within-therapist correlation. In a reanalysis of the Treatment of Depression Collaborative Research Protocol, Zuroff et al. (2010) replicated the finding of a significant between-therapist correlation, but also found

a significant within-therapist correlation, indicating that variability in alliance scores both within- and between-therapist caseloads was correlated with outcome. Similarly, Crits-Christoph et al. (2009) reported a significant between- and within-therapist relationship between the alliance and outcome.

Between- and Within-Therapist Adherence-Outcome Correlations

We are not aware of any attempts to examine between- and within-therapist adherence-outcome correlations. However, it is possible to speculate regarding the potential outcomes of such an analysis. Figure 8.5 illustrates several different ways in which measures of treatment adherence may be related to outcome. Each row corresponds to a different between-therapist effect and each column represents a different within-therapist effect. We briefly provide an explanation and potential interpretation of each panel, although there are likely to be many other interpretations that we do not cover in this chapter. Admittedly, the plausibility and interpretation of each pattern of effects may vary

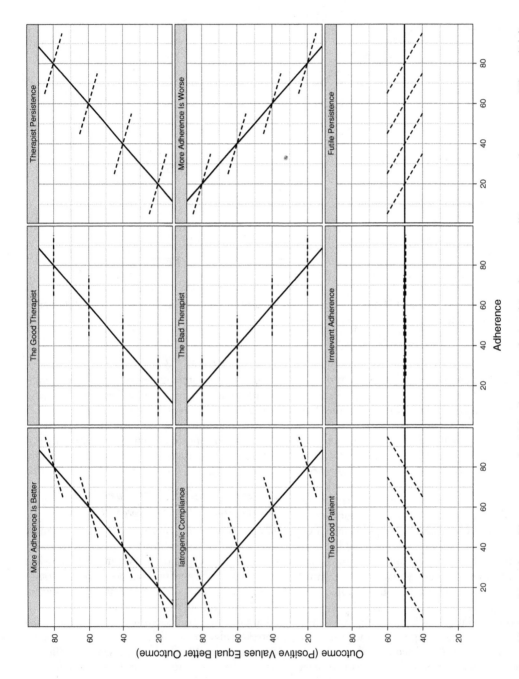

FIGURE 8.5 Possible combinations of between- and within-therapist relationships between adherence and outcome. The solid line represents the between-therapist relationship and dashed line represents the within-therapist relationship.

depending on the specific treatment, disorder, and patient population. However, our goal is to provide an initial illustration of how between- and within-therapist adherence-outcome correlations may address more specific questions regarding treatment process than the total correlation alone.

In the top row (Panels 1 to 3) the between-therapist effect is positive, indicating that some portion of the adherence outcome correlation is due to the therapist—some therapists consistently adhere to a treatment across patients in their caseload and those therapist's patients have better outcomes. However, the effect of within-therapist variance is different across panels in Row 1. In Panel 1—*"More Adherence Is Better"*—both between- and within-therapist effects are in the same positive direction. This result would provide different information than a total correlation if the size of the between- and within-therapist correlations are different. In Panel 2—*"The Good Therapist"*—the within-therapist effect is zero. This pattern suggests that good therapists consistently adhere to treatment protocols but that variability within their caseload is unrelated to outcomes. This would suggest that the effect of adherence is dependent, at least in part, on some therapist characteristic that is indexed by the therapist's average level of adherence (e.g., experience), but not just adherence itself. Specifically, positive outcomes were not strictly dose-dependent. Two patients with identical adherence scores seen by therapists who differed in their average adherence score would have different predicted outcomes. In other words, it matters which specific therapist a patient saw, but not the absolute level of adherence (it is not the gift, but the giver). However, in Panel 3—*"Therapist Persistence"*—there is a positive between-therapist effect and a negative within-therapist effect. This suggests that patients who experienced the highest levels of adherence within therapist caseloads did the worst. One plausible explanation might be that patient presentation is driving adherence wherein the therapist is doing more with those patients who do not respond to initial attempts (Carroll et al., 1998; Gibbons et al., 2010). Those patients who had lower adherence ratings may not have required a larger dose of treatment to respond. The positive between-therapist effect indicates that the best therapists stick with the treatment despite failed attempts and their persistence may buffer potentially worse outcomes for patients who struggle in treatment.

In the second row (Panels 4 to 6), there is a negative between-therapist effect of adherence on outcome, suggesting that therapists with consistently higher adherence ratings had clients who did poorly compared to those of other therapists. In Panel 4—*"Iatrogenic Compliance"*—there is a negative between-therapist effect, but a positive within-therapist effect. Here it may be that compliant patients, who make some progress, allow therapists to perform more of a given intervention, but a therapist's tendency to use the technique itself resulted in worse outcomes. Advocates of trauma-focused therapies for posttraumatic stress disorder might predict such a pattern in control treatments (e.g., present-centered therapy) designed to encourage avoidance of traumatic memories (see McDonagh et al., 2005). In Panel 5—*"The Bad Therapist"*—there is a negative between-therapist effect, but no within-therapist effect. This pattern is the mirror image of Panel 2, and suggests that some therapist characteristic associated with a tendency to adhere was associated with negative outcomes, but that there was no dose–response relationship. Specifically, therapists who adhered more consistently had worse outcomes, but the level of adherence within their caseload was not related to outcome. In Panel 6—*"More Adherence Is Worse"*—both between- and within-therapist effects are in the same negative direction, suggesting more adherence was associated with worse outcomes.

In the final row (Panels 7 to 9), the between-therapist effect of adherence on outcome is zero, suggesting that there were no predictable differences in outcomes between therapists who differed in their average adherence scores. In Panel 7—*"The Good Patient"*—there is a positive within-therapist effect, and no between-therapist effect. As there is no effect of therapist adherence on outcome, the positive adherence outcome correlation is entirely due to patients. The positive within-therapist correlation may be the result of good patients (i.e., nonresistant, motivated patients with sufficient psychological resources) facilitating therapist adherence to a benign therapeutic ingredient that has no actual beneficial effect. In Panel 8—*"Irrelevant Adherence"*—there is no effect of adherence between- or within-therapists, suggesting that adherence had no predictable relationship with outcome. Finally, in Panel 9—*"Futile Persistence"*—there is no between-therapist effect of adherence on outcome, but a negative within-therapist effect.

This might indicate that therapists attempted to utilize more of a given therapeutic technique with patients who were not responding to treatment, but that these efforts were not successful. This would be the equivalent of increasing the dose of an over-the-counter pain medication to treat patients with severe pain. This treatment would likely result in a negative relationship between dose and pain, when the medication actually had no effect in either direction.[5]

Summary

Social relations modeling and the separation of total correlations into between- and within-therapist components provide tests of the therapist contribution to psychotherapy process and outcome. We have provided evidence that there are therapist differences in measures of the alliance and adherence, and with respect to the alliance there is growing evidence that these differences account for a portion of variability in therapist success. Although we are not aware of any evidence for between/within therapist correlations in the adherence literature, the statistical approach offers an opportunity to test a variety of novel hypotheses about how therapist behavior impacts treatment outcome.

One finding that emerged from partitioning variability in the alliance is that the therapist contribution appears to be extremely variable across studies (the therapist contribution was variable across adherence and competence measures in the one study available). This suggests that in many contexts adherence and alliance are not likely to be strong therapist indicators and thus may not account for therapist effects (though there are some between-therapist correlations even when therapist variability in the alliance is small). Accordingly, the large contribution of the patient/dyad to both variability in alliance and some measures of adherence should temper the expectation that process measures can be reliably used to discriminate between effective and ineffective therapists. When it comes to alliance and adherence in typical clinical datasets we may want to focus on what they teach us about

therapeutic dyads, rather than specific therapists. However, it may also be important to consider alternative designs that offer the opportunity to isolate various aspects of psychotherapy process. As noted earlier, a potential design is one in which standardized patients are used. In such designs a sample of therapists each conduct sessions with a set of actors trained to portray patient scenarios (see Baer et al., 2009, for an example from motivational interviewing). This would likely reduce patient variability, provide the opportunity for more detailed observation of treatment process, and allow the use of the round robin design wherein the same patient is treated by multiple therapists, which provides the opportunity to separate therapist, patient, and dyad components.

CONCLUSIONS AND FUTURE DIRECTIONS

> What does the therapist contribute to the effectiveness of psychotherapy? That question is not researchable. We cannot design a basic research study to answer it. The question is too broad and abstract. It identifies a topic of interest rather than a research problem.
> —(Fiske, 1977, p. 38)

Fiske was skeptical that much of anything can be learned about therapists' contributions to outcome. Suffice it to say, we do not fully share that skepticism. Therapists differ in their effectiveness; the differences are small but reliable. We reviewed research that has attempted to understand therapist contributions to outcome via the therapeutic alliance and treatment adherence. Finally, we discussed several design, statistical, and conceptual issues to help guide future research on therapist effects.

Even if Fiske is more correct than we would like to think, calls for increased accountability will require that we grapple with the question of therapist effects. Generally speaking, therapists have been able to operate professionally with little oversight regarding the effectiveness of their services. As noted earlier, operating without oversight is comfortable and is a position that is not likely to be given up lightly. Nevertheless, we live in an era of accountability and mental health care will not likely avoid the scrutiny other professions, such as education and medicine, have begun to face. Accountability is not a bad

---

[5]The adherence-outcome correlation could be accounted for by the interaction between therapists and patients or it is possible that adherence could be the result of positive client change (e.g., good outcomes early in treatment may reinforce therapist adherence). As with any correlation, directionality (cause) cannot be determined.

thing; it is a chance for mental health professionals to show others what we can do. If we have a "good product," which presumably most therapists believe they do, then we ought to be able to demonstrate it—to patients, to those who provide payment, and to the community at large. Furthermore, ignoring accountability may be detrimental to our patients and to the mental health field. If stakeholders do not see the value of the services we provide, they will pull funding and patients will have reduced access to services, a situation that will not only affect suffering but also their contributions to society through work performance and family life.

An appropriate place to start with accountability is therapist effectiveness. The evidence presented above suggests that therapists differ in their effectiveness. Specifically, therapists are associated with a small but consistent effect on outcomes—5% of the outcome variance aggregating across 45 studies. This effect is similar in size to some of the best predictors of therapy outcome, such as the therapeutic alliance. Although this effect is small at any given point in time, this effect will add up over time and have important consequences for patients. However, there are many questions left to consider. In what follows, we raise 10 issues we believe are important future directions for research and clinical practice.

1. *We need to more consistently track therapists' outcomes and identify the best and worst therapists.* To do this, therapists, administrators, insurance providers, patients, and other stakeholders will need to demand that patient-treatment response be tracked and that information about therapist effectiveness be used to improve patient care. To be sure, implementing an outcome monitoring system would require an investment of time and money. However, if our primary goal is to improve therapist performance and thereby patient outcomes, then we need to know what those outcomes are.

2. *We need to better understand what separates the most effective therapists from the least effective therapists.* Once we consistently track patient outcomes, we can identify the most and least effective therapists. Such identification will allow us to study their behaviors and see whether there are clear differences between the most and least effective therapists.

3. *We need more discussion and research regarding what to do with less effective therapists.* One option for less effective therapists is to provide more training. However, that option assumes that we know what to train them in. Potential training options include methods of assessment and case conceptualization, empirically supported treatment packages, and therapy micro-skills and relationship building. If we had good answers from Number 2 above, we may be able to provide training consistent with those answers. A second option is to provide real-time feedback to therapists regarding their patients' outcomes. Therapists are typically poor at accurately predicting the outcomes of their patients and thus poor performing therapists may benefit from an outcome feedback system such as the one developed by Lambert (2010).

4. *We need more studies that address potential confounds in therapist effect studies.* Nearly all of the studies in Tables 1 and 2 did not randomly assign clients to therapist. Consequently, the possibility remains that "third" variables may account for the therapist effects observed. For example, some therapists may consistently see more difficult patients or some therapists might refer challenging patients. More methodological research focusing on how to equate therapists' caseloads is needed.

5. *We need to better attend to the relative contributions of therapists, patients, and therapist-patient dyads in process-outcome research.* As we have shown earlier, variability in process measures such as alliance and treatment adherence have multiple sources, including therapists, patients, and therapist-patient dyads. Attending to these different sources of variance will help elucidate how patients and therapists contribute to the relationship between process and outcome. For example, the evidence suggests that therapist variability in the alliance had a distinct relationship with outcome as compared to patient variability. Similar results may occur with adherence-outcome correlations and we have outlined the ways between- and within-therapist variability may be related to outcome.

6. *We do not need any more zero-order alliance-outcome correlations.* There is not much to be gained by continuing to evaluate whether ratings of the alliance are related to outcome, without partitioning the variance of the alliance and outcome. Indeed, the

meta-analytic evidence is clear regarding the size and direction of the alliance-outcome correlations and there is no reason to believe that conclusion will change. Likewise, we do not believe that much is to be gained from zero-order adherence-outcome correlations.

7. *We need to attend to and learn more about within-therapist differences.* As we have shown earlier, within-therapist differences dominate outcomes. Thus, it is critical that we begin to understand why a given therapist has an above average outcome with some clients but below average with other clients. Variables that could explain within-therapist differences are at the patient and patient-therapy dyad level.

8. *Studies of therapist effects should use a random effects analysis or at least provide an intraclass correlation for therapist.* Table 8.1 is challenging to make sense of because of the wide variety of ways therapist effects were defined and reported. The intraclass correlation can be used as a standard effect size for therapist effects and is easily computed. Furthermore, methods for meta-analytically combining intraclass correlations are available.

9. *Studies of therapist effects are generally going to need to be larger.* As we noted earlier, advancements in our understanding of therapist effects will likely only come from larger studies. Consequently, researchers and practitioners will likely need to pool resources to address this problem.

10. *We need more studies of therapist effects that were designed from the outset to be therapist effect studies.* We have designs for isolating the effects of a treatment and we even have some designs for isolating the effects of patients or patients by treatment interactions. Little research has been done on isolating the effects of therapists. The social relations model provides a natural framework for designing therapist effects studies. Additionally, studies that explicitly select therapists based on skill or that use standardized patients to control for patient variability are nicely suited to study therapists (Baer et al., 2009).

REFERENCES

Abramowitz, J. S., Foa, E. B., & Franklin, M. E. (2003). Exposure and ritual prevention for obsessive-compulsive disorder: Effects of intensive versus twice-weekly sessions. *Journal of Consulting and Clinical Psychology*, 71, 394–398.

Almlov, J., Carlbring, P., Berger, T., Cuijpers, P., & Andersson, G. (2009). Therapist factors in internet-delievered cognitive behavioural therapy for major depressive disorder. *Cognitive Behaviour Therapy*, 38, 247–254. doi: 10.1080/16506070903116935

Anker, M. G., Duncan, B. L., & Sparks, J. A. (2009). Using client feedback to improve couple therapy outcomes: A randomized clinical trial in a naturalistic setting. *Journal of Consulting and Clinical Psychology*, 77, 693–704. doi: 10.1037/a0016062

Baer, J. S., Wells, E. A., Rosengren, D. B., Hartzler, B., Beadnell, B., & Dunn, C. (2009). Agency context and tailored training in technology transfer: A pilot sevaluation of motivational interviewing training for community counselors. *Journal of Substance Abuse Treatment*, 37, 191–202. doi: 10.1016/j.jsat.2009.01.003

Baldwin, S. A., Murray, D. M., Shadish, W. R., Pals, S. L., Holland, J. M., Abramowtiz, J. S., . . . Watson, J. (2011). Intraclass correlation associated with therapists: Estimates and applications in planning psychotherapy research. *Cognitive Behaviour Therapy*, 40, 15–33.

Baldwin, S. A., & Shadish, W. R. (2011). A primer on meta-analysis in clinical psychology. *Journal of Experimental Psychopathology*, 2, 294–317. doi: 10.5127/jep.009610

Baldwin, S. A., Wampold, B. E., & Imel, Z. E. (2007). Untangling the alliance-outcome correlation: Exploring the relative importance of therapist and patient variability in the alliance. *Journal of Consulting and Clinical Psychology*, 75, 842–852. doi: 10.1037/0022-006X.75.6.842

Ball, S. A., Martino, S., Nich, C., Frankforter, T. L., Van Horn, D., Crits-Christoph, P., . . . Carroll, K. M. (2007). Site matters: Multisite randomized trial of motivational enhancement therapy in community drug abuse clinics. *Journal of Consulting and Clinical Psychology*, 75, 556–567. doi: 10.1037/0022-006X.75.4.556

Barber, J. P., Crits-Christoph, P., & Luborsky, L. (1996). Effects of therapist adherence and competence on patient outcome in brief dynamic therapy. *Journal of Consulting and Clinical Psychology*, 64.

Barber, J. P., Gallop, R., Crits-Christoph, P., Frank, A., Thase, M. E., Weiss, R. D., & Connolly Gibbons, M. B. (2006). The role of therapist adherence, therapist competence, and alliance in predicting outcome of individual drug counseling: Results from the national institute drug abuse collaborative cocaine treatment study. *Psychotherapy Research*, 16, 229–240. doi: 10.1080/10503300500288951

Beck, A. T., Hollon, S. D., Young, J. E., Bedrosian, R. C., & Budenz, D. (1985). Treatment of depression with cognitive therapy and amitriptyline. *Archives of General Psychiatry, 42,* 142–148.

Begg, C. B., & Mazumdar, M. (1994). Operating characteristics of a rank correlation test for publication bias. *Biometrics, 50,* 1088–1101.

Beutler, L. E., Machado, P. P. P., & Neufeldt, S. (1994). Therapist variables. In S. L. Garfield & A. E. Bergin (Eds.), *Handbook of psychotherapy and behavior change* (4th ed., pp. 259–269). New York, NY: Wiley.

Beutler, L. E., Malik, M., Alimohamed, S., Harwood, T. M., Talebi, H., Noble, S., & Wong, E. (2004). Therapist variables. In M. J. Lambert (Ed.), *Bergin and Garfield's handbook of psychotherapy and behavior change* (5th ed., pp. 227–306). Hoboken, NJ: Wiley.

Blatt, S. J., Sanislow, C. A., Zuroff, D. C., & Pilkonis, P. A. (1996). Characteristics of effective therapists: Further analyses of data from the national institute of mental health treatment of depression collaborative research program. *Journal of Consulting and Clinical Psychology, 64,* 1276–1284.

Blitstein, J. L., Hannan, P. J., Murray, D. M., & Shadish, W. R. (2005). Increasing the degrees of freedom in existing group randomized trials: The df* approach. *Evaluation Review, 29,* 241–267. doi: 10.1177/0193841X04273257

Borkovec, T., & Mathews, A. (1988). Treatment of nonphobic anxiety disorders: A comparison of nondirective, cognitive, and coping desensitization therapy. *Journal of Consulting and Clinical Psychology, 56,* 877–884.

Boswell, J. F., Castonguay, L. G., & Wasserman, R. (2010). Effects of psychotherapy training and intervention use on session outcome. *Journal of Consulting and Clinical Psychology, 5,* 717–723. doi: 10.1037/a0020088

Brooker, C., & Wiggins, R. D. (1983). Nurse therapist trainee variability: The implications for selection and training. *Journal of Advanced Nursing, 8,* 321–328.

Brown, G. S. J., Lambert, M. J., Jones, E. R., & Minami, T. (2005). Identifying highly effective psychotherapists in a managed care environment. *American Journal of Managed Care, 11,* 513–520.

Brownson, C. (2004). *The research consortium of counseling and psychological services in higher education: Report of activities.* Retrieved from http://www.utexas.edu/student/cmhc/research/rescon.html

Carlbring, P., Bohman, S., Brunt, S., Buhrman, M., Westling, B. E., Ekselius, L., & Andersson, G. (2006). Remote treatment of panic disorder: A randomized trial of internet-based cognitive behavior therapy supplemented with telephone calls. *American Journal of Psychiatry, 163,* 2119–2225.

Carroll, K. M., Connors, G. J., Cooney, N. L., DiClemente, C. C., Donovan, D. M., Kadden, R. R., ...Zweben, A. (1998). Internal validity of Project MATCH treatments: Discriminability and integrity. *Journal of Consulting and Clinical Psychology, 66,* 290–303.

Carroll, K. M., Fenton, L. R., Ball, S. A., Nich, C., Frankforter, T. L., Shi, J., & Rounsaville, B. J. (2004). Efficacy of disulfiram and cognitive behavioral therapy in cocaine-dependent outpatients: A randomized placebo-controlled trial. *Archives of General Psychiatry, 61,* 264–272.

Cella, M., Stahl, D., Reme, S. E., & Chalder, T. (2011). Therapist effects in routine psychotherapy practice: An account from chronic fatigue syndrome. *Psychotherapy Research, 21,* 168–178. doi: 10.1080/10503307.2010.535571

Christensen, A., Atkins, D. C., Berns, S., Wheeler, J., Baucom, D. H., & Simpson, L. E. (2004). Traditional versus integrative behavioral couples therapy for significantly and chronically distressed married couples. *Journal of Consulting and Clinical Psychology, 72,* 176–191.

Crits-Christoph, P., Baranackie, K., Kurcias, J. S., Beck, A. T., Carroll, K., Perry, K., ...Zitrin, C. (1991). Meta-analysis of therapist effects in psychotherapy outcome studies. *Psychotherapy Research, 1,* 81–91. doi: 10.1080/10503309112331335511

Crits-Christoph, P., & Gallop, R. (2006). Therapist effects in the national institute of mental health treatment of depression collaborative research program and other psychotherapy studies. *Psychotherapy Research, 16,* 178–181. doi: 10.1080/10503300500265025

Crits-Christoph, P., Gallop, R., Temes, C. M., Woody, G., Ball, S. A., Martino, S., & Carroll, K. M. (2009). The alliance in motivational enhancement therapy and counseling as usual for substance use problems. *Journal of Consulting and Clinical Psychology, 77,* 1125–1135. doi: 10.1037/a0017045

Crits-Christoph, P., Gibbons, M. B. C., Hamilton, J., Ring-Kurtz, S., & Gallop, R. (2011). The dependability of alliance assessments: The alliance–outcome correlation is larger than you might think. *Journal of Consulting and Clinical Psychology, 79,* 267–278. doi: 10.1037/a0023668

Crits-Christoph, P., & Mintz, J. (1991). Implications of therapist effects for the design and analysis of comparative studies of psychotherapies. *Journal of Consulting and Clinical Psychology, 59,* 20–26.

DeRubeis, R. J., Brotman, M. A., & Gibbons, C. J. (2005). A conceptual and methodological analysis of the nonspecifics argument. *Clinical Psychology: Science and Practice, 12,* 174–183.

Dillon, S. (2010, August 31). Formula to grade teachers' skill gains acceptance, and critics. *New York Times.* Retrieved from http://www.nytimes.com/2010/09/01/education/01teacher.html

Dinger, U., Strack, M., Leichsenring, F., Wilmers, F., & Schauenburg, H. (2008). Therapist effects on outcome and alliance in inpatient psychotherapy.

Journal of Clinical Psychology, 64, 344–354. doi: 10.1002/jclp.20443

Duval, S., & Tweedie, R. (2000). A nonparametric "trim and fill" method of accounting for publication bias in meta-analysis. *Journal of the American Statistical Association, 95,* 89–98.

Egger, M., Davey Smith, G., Schneider, M., & Minder, C. (1997). Bias in meta-analysis detected by a simple, graphical test. *British Medical Journal, 315,* 629–634.

Ehlers, A., Clark, D. M., Hackmann, A., McManus, F., Fennell, M., Herbert, C., & Mayou, R. (2003). A randomized controlled trial of cognitive therapy, a self-help booklet, and repeated assessments as early interventions for posttraumatic stress disorder. *Archives of General Psychiatry, 60,* 1024–1032.

Elkin, I., Falconnier, L., Martinovich, Z., & Mahoney, C. (2006). Therapist effects in the national institute of mental health treatment of depression collaborative research program. *Psychotherapy Research, 16,* 144–160. doi: 10.1080/10503 300500268540

Fiske, D. N. (1977). Methodological issues in research on the psychotherapist. In A. S. Gurman & A. M. Razin (Eds.), *Effective psychotherapy: A handbook of research* (pp. 23–43). New York, NY: Pergamon Press.

Gawande, A. (2004, December). The bell curve. *New Yorker, 88.* Retrieved from http://www .newyorker.com/archive/2004/2012/2006/041206 fa_fact

Gibbons, C. J., Steinberg, K., Nich, C., Roffman, R. A., Kadden, R. M., Corvino, J., . . . Carroll, K. M. (2010). Treatment process, alliance and outcome in brief versus extended treatments for maijuana dependence. *Addiction, 105,* 1799–1808.

Hatcher, R. L., Barends, A., Hansell, J., & Gutfreund, M. J. (1995). Patients' and therapists' shared and unique views of the therapeutic alliance: An investigation using confirmatory factor analysis in a nested design. *Journal of Consulting and Clinical Psychology, 63,* 636–643.

Henry, W. P., Strupp, H. H., Butler, S. F., Schacht, T. E., & Binder, J. L. (1993). Effects of training in time-limited psychotherapy: Changes in therapist behavior. *Journal of Consulting and Clinical Psychology, 61,* 434–440.

Hettema, J., Steele, J., & Miller, W. R. (2005). Motitvational interviewing. *Annual Review of Psychology, 1,* 91–111. doi: 10.1146/annurev.clinpsy .1.102803.143833

Hollon, S. D., DeRubeis, R. J., Evans, M. D., Wiemer, M. J., Garvey, M. J., Grove, W. M., & Tuason, V. B. (1992). Cognitive therapy, pharmacotherapy and combined cognitive-pharmacotherapy in the treatment of depression. *Archives of General Psychiatry, 49,* 774–781.

Holt, R. R., & Luborsky, L. (1958). *Personality patterns of psychatrists: A study of selection techniques* (Vol. 2). Topeka, KS: Menninger Foundation.

Horvath, A. O., & Bedi, R. P. (2002). The allilance. In J. C. Norcross (Ed.), *Psychotherapy relationships that work: Therapist contributions and responsiveness to patients* (pp. 37–70). New York, NY: Oxford University Press.

Horvath, A. O., Del Re, A. C., Flückiger, C., & Symonds, D. (2011). Alliance in individual psychotherapy. *Psychotherapy, 48,* 9–16. doi: 10.1037/a0022186

Horvath, A. O., & Greenberg, L. S. (1989). Development and validation of the working alliance inventory. *Journal of Counseling Psychology, 36,* 223–233.

Horvath, A. O., & Symonds, B. D. (1991). Relation between working allianc eand outcome in psychotherapy: A meta-analysis. *Journal of Counseling Psychology, 38,* 139–149.

Huppert, J. D., Bufka, L. F., Barlow, D. H., Gorman, J. M., Shear, M. K., & Woods, S. W. (2001). Therapists, therapist variables, and cognitive-behavioral therapy outcome in a multicenter trial for panic disorder. *Journal of Consulting and Clinical Psychology, 69,* 747–755. doi: 10.1037//0022–006X.69.5.747

Imel, Z. E., Baer, J. S., Martino, S., Ball, S. A., & Carroll, K. M. (2011). Mutual influence in therapist competence and adherence to motivational enhancement therapy. *Drug and Alcohol Dependence.* doi: 10.1016/j.drugalcdep.2010.11.010

Imel, Z. E., Hubbard, R., Rutter, C., & Simon, G. E. (2011). *Consistency of provider effects in mental health care: A multivariate approach.* Unpublished manuscript, Group Health Research Institute, Seattle, Washington.

Kenny, D. A., Kashy, D. A., & Cook, W. L. (2006). *Dyadic data analysis.* New York, NY: Guilford Press.

Kim, D.-M., Wampold, B., & Bolt, D. (2006). Therapist effects in psychotherapy: A random-effects modeling of the national institute of mental health treatment of depression collaborative research program data. *Psychotherapy Research, 16,* 161–172. doi: 10.1080/10503300500264911

Koch, E. I., Spates, C. R., & Himle, J. A. (2004). Comparison of behavioral and cognitive-behavioral one-session exposure treatments for small animal phobia. *Behaviour Research and Therapy, 42,* 1483–1504.

Kraus, D., Castonguay, L., Boswell, J., Nordberg, S., & Hayes, J. (2011). Therapist effectiveness: Implications for accountability and patient care. *Psychotherapy Research, 21,* 267–276. doi: 10.1080/10503307.2011.563249

Kreft, I., De Leeuw, J., & Aiken, L. (1995). The effect of different forms of centering in hierarchical linear models. *Multivariate Behavioral Research, 30,* 1–21.

Kuyken, W. (2004). Cognitive therapy outcome: The effects of hopelessness in a naturalistic outcome study. *Behaviour Research and Therapy, 42,* 631–646.

Lambert, M. J. (2010). *Prevention of treatment failure: The use of measuring, monitoring, and feedback in clinical practice.* Washington, DC: American Psychological Association.

Lambert, M. J., & Bergin, A. E. (1994). The effectiveness of psychotherapy. In A. E. Bergin & S. L. Garfield (Eds.), *Handbook of psychotherapy and behavior change* (4th ed., pp. 143–189). New York, NY: Wiley.

Lambert, M. J., Morton, J. J., Hatfield, D., Harmon, C., Hamilton, S., Reid, R. C., . . . , Burlingame, G. M. (2004). *Adimistration and scoring manual for the OQ-45.2.* Orem, UT: American Professional Credentialing Services.

Lange, A., Rietdeijk, D., Hudcovicova, M., van de Ven, J.-P., Schrieken, B., & Emmelkamp, P. M. G. (2003). Interapy: A controlled randomized trial of the standardized treatment of posttraumatic stress through the internet. *Journal of Consulting and Clinical Psychology, 71,* 901–909.

Lewis, M. (2003). *Moneyball: The art of winning an unfair game.* New York, NY: Norton.

Light, R. J., & Pillemer, D. B. (1984). *Summing up: The science of reviewing research.* Cambridge, MA: Harvard University Press.

Lincoln, T. M., Rief, W., Hahlweg, K., Frank, M., & von Witzelben, I. (2003). Effectiveness of an empirically supported treatment for social phobia in the field. *Behaviour Research and Therapy, 41,* 1251–1269.

Luborsky, L. (1952). The personality of the psychotherapist. *Menninger Quarterly, 6,* 1–6.

Luborsky, L., Crits-Christoph, P., McLellan, A. T., Woody, G., Piper, W., Liberman, B., . . . Pilkonis, P. (1986). Do therapists vary much in their success? Findings from four outcome studies. *Psychotherapy, 56,* 501–512.

Luborsky, L., McLellan, A. T., Diguer, L., Woody, G., & Seligman, D. A. (1997). The psychotherapist matters: Comparison of outcomes across twenty-two therapists and seven patient samples. *Clinical Psychology: Science and Practice, 4,* 53–65.

Luborsky, L., McLellen, A. T., Woody, G. E., O'Brien, C. P., & Auerbach, A. (1985). Therapist success and its determinants. *Archives of General Psychiatry, 42,* 602–611.

Lutz, W., Leon, S. C., Martinovich, Z., Lyons, J. S., & Stiles, W. B. (2007). Therapist effects in outpatient psychotherapy: A three-level growth curve approach. *Journal of Counseling Psychology, 54,* 32–39. doi: 10.1037/0022–0167.54.1.32

Marcus, D. K., Kashy, D. A., & Baldwin, S. A. (2009). Studying psychotherapy using the one-with-many design: The therapeutic alliance as an exemplar. *Journal of Counseling Psychology, 56,* 537–548. doi: 10.1037/a0017291

Marcus, D. K., Kashy, D. A., Wintersteen, M. B., & Diamond, G. S. (2011). The therapeutic alliance in adolescent substance abuse treatment: A one-with-many analysis. *Journal of Counseling Psychology, 58,* 449–455. doi: 10.1037/a0023196

The Marijuana Treatment Project Research Group. (2004). Brief treatments for cannabis dependence: Findings from a randomized multisite trial. *Journal of Consulting and Clinical Psychology, 72,* 455–466.

Martin, D. J., Garske, J. P., & Davis, M. K. (2000). Relation of the therapeutic alliance with outcome and other variables: A meta-analytic review. *Journal of Consulting and Clinical Psychology, 68,* 438–450.

Martindale, C. (1978). The therapist-as-fixed-effect fallacy in psychotherapy research. *Journal of Consulting and Clinical Psychology, 46,* 1526–1530.

McDonagh, A., Friedman, M., McHugo, G., Ford, J., Sengupta, A., Mueser, K., . . . Descamps, M. (2005). Randomized trial of cognitive-behavioral therapy for chronic posttraumatic stress disorder in adult femal survivors of childhood sexual abuse. *Journal of Consulting and Clinical Psychology, 73,* 515–524.

McKay, K. M., Imel, Z. E., & Wampold, B. E. (2006). Psychiatrist effects in the psychopharmacological treatment of depression. *Journal of Affective Disorders, 92,* 287–290. doi: 10.1016/j.jad.2006.01.020

McLellan, A. T., Woody, G. E., Luborsky, L., & Goehl, L. (1988). Is the counselor an "active ingredient" in substance abuse rehabilitation? An examination of treatment success among four counselors. *Journal of Nervous and Mental Disease, 176,* 423–430.

Merrill, K. A., Tolbert, V. E., & Wade, W. (2003). Effectiveness of cognitive therapy for depression in a community mental health center: A benchmarking study. *Journal of Consulting and Clinical Psychology, 71,* 404–409.

Miller, W., & Taylor, C. (1980). Focused versus broad-spectrum behavior therapy for problem drinkers. *Journal of Consulting and Clinical Psychology, 48,* 590–601.

Moyers, T. B., Martin, T., Manuel, J. K., Miller, W. R., & Ernst, D. (2010). *Motivational interviewing treatment integrity (MITI) coding system. 3.1.1.* Unpublished manuscript, University of New Mexico, Albuquerque, New Mexico.

Najavits, L. M., & Strupp, H. H. (1994). Differences in the effectiveness of psychodynamic therapists: A process-outcome study. *Psychotherapy: Theory, Research, Practice, Training, 31,* 114–123. doi: 10.1037/0033–3204.31.1.114

Nash, E., Hoehn-Sacric, R., Battle, C., Stone, A., Imber, S. D., & Frank, J. (1965). Systematic preparation of patients for short-term psychotherapy: 2. Relation to characteristics of patient, therapist, and the psychotherapeutic process. *Journal of Nervous and Mental Disorders, 140,* 374–383.

Nissen-Lie, H. A., Monsen, J. T., & Ronnestad, M. H. (2010). Therapist predictors of early patient-rated working alliance: A multilevel approach. *Psychotherapy Research, 20*, 627–646.

Okiishi, J. C., Lambert, M. J., Eggett, D., Nielsen, L., Dayton, D. D., & Vermeersch, D. A. (2006). An analysis of therapist treatment effects: Toward providing feedback to individual therapists on their clients' psychotherapy outcome. *Journal of Clinical Psychology, 62*, 1157–1172. doi: 10.1002/jclp

Okiishi, J. C., Lambert, M. J., Nielsen, S. L., & Ogles, B. M. (2003). Waiting for supershrink: An empirical analysis of therapist effects. *Clinical Psychology and Psychotherapy, 10*, 361–373. doi: 10.1002/cpp.383

Orlinsky, D. E., & Howard, K. I. (1980). Gender and psychotherapeutic outcome. In A. M. Brodsky & R. T. Hare-Mustin (Eds.), *Women and psychotherapy* (pp. 3–34). New York, NY: Guilford Press.

Owen, J. J., & Hilsenroth, M. J. (2011). The interaction between alliance and technique in the prediction of therapy outcomes during short-term psychodynamic therapy. *Journal of Nervous and Mental Disorders, 199*, 384–389.

Owen, J. J., Leach, M. M., Wampold, B., & Rodolfa, E. (2011). Client and therapist variability in clients' perceptions of their therapists' multicultural competencies. *Journal of Counseling Psychology, 58*, 1–9. doi: 10.1037/a0021496

Owen, J. J., Quirk, K., Hilsenroth, M. J., & Rodolfa, E. (2011). Working through: In-session processes that promote between-session thoughts and activities. *Journal of Counseling Psychology*. Advance online publication. doi: 10.1037/a0022065

Owen, J. J., Rhoades, G. K., Stanley, S. M., & Markman, H. J. (2011). The role of leaders' working alliance in premarital education. *Journal of Family Psychology, 25*, 49–57. doi: 10.1037/a0022084

Owen, J. J., Tao, K., Leach, M. M., & Rodolfa, E. (2011). Clients' perceptions of their psychotherapists' multicultural orientation. *Psychotherapy*. doi: 10.1037/a0022065

Owen, J. J., Tao, K., & Rodolfa, E. (2010). Microaggressions and women in short-term psychotherapy: Initial evidence. *Counseling Psychologist, 38*, 923–946. doi: 10.1177/0011000010376093

Pilkonis, P. A., Imber, S. D., Lewis, P., & Rubinsky, P. (1984). A comparative outcome study of individual, group, and conjoint psychotherapy. *Archives of General Psychiatry, 41*, 431–437.

Piper, W. E., Debbane, E. G., Bienvenu, J. P., & Garant, J. (1984). A comparative study of four forms of psychotherapy. *Journal of Consulting and Clinical Psychology, 52*, 268–279.

Project MATCH Research Group. (1998). Therapist effects in three treatments for alcohol problems. *Psychotherapy Research, 8*, 455–474. doi: 10.1080/10503309812331332527

Raudenbush, S. W., & Bryk, A. S. (2002). *Hierarchical linear models: Applications and data analysis methods*. Thousand Oaks, CA: Springer.

Ricks, D. F. (1974). Supershrink: Methods of a therapist judged successful on the basis of adult outcomes of adolescent patients. In D. F. Ricks, M. Roff, & A. Thomas (Eds.), *Life history research in psychopathology* (Vol. 3, pp. 275–297). Minneapolis: University of Minnesota Press.

Rosenzweig, S. (1936). Some implicit common factors in diverse methods of psychotherapy. *American Journal of Orthopsychiatry, 6*, 412–415.

Rush, A. J., Beck, A. T., Kovacs, M., & Hollon, S. D. (1977). Comparative efficacy of cognitive therapy and pharmacotherpay in the treatment of depressed outpatients. *Cognitive Therapy and Research, 1*, 17–37.

Serlin, R. C., Wampold, B. E., & Levin, J. R. (2003). Should providers of treatment be regarded as a random factor? If it ain't broke, don't "fix" it: A comment on Siemer and Joorman (2003). *Psychological Methods, 8*, 524–534. doi: 10.1037/1082-989X.8.4.524w

Shapiro, D. A., Firth-Cozens, J., & Stiles, W. B. (1989). The question of therapists' differential effectiveness. A Sheffield psychotherapy project addendum. *British Journal of Psychiatry, 154*, 383–385.

Shavelson, R. J., & Webb, N. M. (1991). *Generalizability theory: A primer*. Thousand Oaks, CA: Sage.

Siemer, M., & Joorman, J. (2003a). Assumptions and consequences of treating providers in therapy studies as fixed versus random effects: Reply to Crits-Christoph, Tu, and Gallop (2003) and Serline, Wampold, and Levin (2003). *Psychological Methods, 8*, 535–544. doi: 10.1037/1082-989X.8.4.535

Siemer, M., & Joorman, J. (2003b). Power and measures of effect size in analysis of variance with fixed versus random nested factors. *Psychological Methods, 5*, 425–433. doi: 10.1037/1082-989X.8.4.524s

Snijders, T. A. B., & Bosker, R. (1999). *Multilevel analysis: An introduction to basic and advanced multilevel modeling*. London, United Kingdom: Sage.

Song, J., & Felch, J. (2010, August 15). Union leader calls on L.A. teachers to boycott Times. *Los Angeles Times*. Retrieved from http://articles.latimes.com/2010/aug/15/local/la-me-teachers-react-20100816

Szapocznik, J., Feaster, D. J., Mitrani, V. B., Prado, G., Smith, L., Robinson-Batista, C., . . . Robbins, M. S. (2004). Structural ecosystems therapy for HIV-serpositive African American women: Effects of psychological distress, family hassles, and family support. *Journal of Consulting and Clinical Psychology, 72*, 288–303.

Taylor, S., Thordarson, D. S., Maxfield, L., Fedoroff, I. C., Lovell, K., & Ogrodniczuk, J. (2003). Comparative efficacy, speed, and adverse effects of three PTSD treatments: Exposure therapy, EMDR, and relaxation training. *Journal of Consulting and Clinical Psychology, 71,* 303–338.

Thompson, L. W., Gallagher, D., & Breckenridge, J. S. (1987). Comparative effectiveness of psychotherapies for depressed elders. *Journal of Consulting and Clinical Psychology, 55,* 385–390.

Trepka, C., Rees, A., Shapiro, D. A., Hardy, G. E., & Barkham, M. (2004). Therapist competence and outcome of cognitive therapy for depression. *Cognitive Therapy and Research, 28,* 143–157.

van Minnen, A., Hoogduin, K. A. L., Keijsers, G. P. J., Hellenbrand, I., & Hendriks, G.-J. (2003). Treatment of trichotillomania with behavioral therapy or fluoxetine. *Archives of General Psychiatry, 60,* 517–522.

Wampold, B. E. (2001). *The great psychotherapy debate: Models, methods, and findings.* Mahwah, NJ: Erlbaum.

Wampold, B. E., & Bolt, D. M. (2006). Therapist effects: Clever ways to make them (and everything else) disappear. *Psychotherapy Research, 16,* 184–187. doi: 10.1080/10503300500265181

Wampold, B. E., & Bolt, D. M. (2007). The consequences of "anchoring" in longitudinal multilevel models: Bias in the estimation of patient variability and therapist effects. *Psychotherapy Research, 17,* 509–514. doi: 10.1080/10503300701250339

Wampold, B. E., & Brown, G. S. (2005). Estimating variability in outcomes attributable to therapists: A naturalistic study of outcomes in managed care. *Journal of Consulting and Clinical Psychology, 73,* 914–923. doi: 10.1037/0022–006X.73.5.914

Watson, J. C., Gordon, L. B., Sterman, L., Kalogerakos, F., & Steckely, P. (2003). Comparing the effectiveness of process-experiential with cognitive-behavioral psychotherapy in the treatment of depression. *Journal of Consulting and Clinical Psychology, 71,* 773–781.

Webb, C. A., DeRubeis, R. J., & Barber, J. P. (2010). Therapist adherence/competence and treatment outcome: A meta-analytic review. *Journal of Consulting and Clinical Psychology, 78,* 200–211. doi: 10.1037/a0018912

Westra, H. A., Constantino, M. J., Arkowitz, H., & Dozois, D. J. A. (2011, June 20). Therapist differences in cognitive-behavioral psychotherapy for generalized anxiety disorder: A pilot study. *Psychotherapy: Theory, Research, Practice, Training. Advance online publication.* doi: 10.1037/a0022011

Whitehorn, J. C., & Betz, B. J. (1954). A study of psychotherapeutic relationships between physicians and schizophrenic patients. *American Journal of Psychiatry, 111,* 321–331.

Woody, G. E., McLellan, A. T., Luborsky, L., & O'Brien, C. P. (1995). Psychotherapy in community methadone programs: A validation study. *American Journal of Psychiatry, 152,* 1302–1308.

Zitrin, C. M., Klein, D. F., & Woerner, M. G. (1978). Behavior therapy, supportive psychotherapy, imipramine, and phobias. *Archives of General Psychiatry, 35,* 307–316.

Zuroff, D. C., Kelly, A. C., Leybman, M. J., Blatt, S. J., & Wampold, B. E. (2010). Between-therapist and within-therapist differences in the quality of the therapeutic relationship: Effects on maladjustment and self-critical perfectionism. *Journal of Clinical Psychology, 66,* 681–697.

CHAPTER 9

PSYCHOTHERAPY PROCESS-OUTCOME RESEARCH

PAUL CRITS-CHRISTOPH, MARY BETH CONNOLLY GIBBONS, AND DAHLIA MUKHERJEE

What happens during psychotherapy sessions that helps patients improve their functioning, reduce symptoms, and enjoy life more? Over many decades, researchers have attempted to answer this question by conducting psychotherapy process-outcome studies. The goal of this chapter is to provide an understanding of the relationship between psychotherapy process and outcome through examination of the available research literature. There are estimated to be more than 2,000 published process-outcome studies of psychotherapy (Orlinsky, Rønnestad, & Willutzki, 2004). Exhaustive reviews of this large body of scientific studies are available in previous editions of this handbook (Orlinsky et al., 2004). These reviews, however, have mostly focused on a generic model of psychotherapy that emphasizes common factors (e.g., patient–therapist relationship) across various psychotherapies. Although common factors are an important part of the process of various psychotherapies, clinical advances in the applications of psychotherapies, and scientific advances in our understanding of specific psychotherapies, are also likely to be influenced by process-outcome research that examines the key theoretical dimensions of treatment process that guide the application of specific psychotherapies. Therefore, in this chapter, in addition to summarizing and updating the research literature on such common process factors in relation to treatment outcome, we organize the literature on process-outcome studies from the perspective of the major theories of psychotherapy.

This shift in emphasis from common factors to factors specific to theoretical models also parallels historical changes in the field of psychotherapy research. Many studies of psychotherapy process conducted during the 1970s, 1980s, and 1990s used samples of naturalistic psychotherapy rather than a single standardized psychotherapy. With the advent of psychotherapy treatment manuals in the 1980s, the majority of studies of psychotherapy during the 1990s and 2000s were randomized clinical trials examining the efficacy of specific standardized psychotherapies. Many studies that have been published more recently utilized tape-recorded treatment sessions from the trials and considered this to be the basis for studying the process of these specific psychotherapies.

Because we review here studies of the theoretical mechanisms of action of specific psychotherapies, there is likely some overlap between studies reviewed in the current chapter and studies reviewed in other chapters in this volume that focus on a particular psychotherapeutic procedure and modality such as group or family therapy. In addition, much of the psychotherapy process-outcome literature has been reviewed previously (e.g., Orlinsky et al., 2004). Therefore, we conduct the current review differently in two major ways from previous reviews. First, rather than reviewing the large number of studies of generic, unspecified psychotherapy, we focus our review primarily on studies of the process (in relation to outcome) of specific models of psychotherapy. Thus, although we devote some attention to the state of knowledge regarding central cross-theoretical constructs (i.e., therapeutic alliance), this chapter is structured around what we know, and what we do not know, from existing process-outcome studies about the hypothesized theoretical mechanisms of action of behavioral, cognitive-behavioral, psychodynamic, experiential, and other specific forms of psychotherapy. The second distinguishing feature of the current review is that we evaluate the existing process-outcome literature in terms of certain methodological issues that constrain knowledge gained from such studies. Our goal in pointing out weaknesses in the evidence base for certain hypothesized curative factors in psychotherapy is to provide a road map for further process-outcome research.

Before launching into our review of the literature, we need to define what we mean by "psychotherapy process" and "process-outcome." We generally follow Orlinsky et al.'s (2004) description of psychotherapy process as "(primarily) the actions, experiences, and relatedness of patient and therapist in therapy sessions when they are physically together, and (secondarily) the actions and experiences of participants specifically referring to one another that occur outside of therapy sessions when they are not physically together" (p. 311). In our definition of process research, however, we also include changes occurring within the patient over the course of psychotherapy that are hypothesized to have a causal relation with treatment outcome. Doss (2004) describes these as "change mechanisms" that are distinct from "change processes." Because these changes that occur within the patient are thought to be triggered by the events that take place in therapy sessions, and the fact that such changes are occurring as therapy progresses over time, we view such changes as part of the overall process of psychotherapy that subsequently leads to positive treatment outcomes. Others might view such patient changes occurring during the course of therapy as short-term "outcomes" rather than "process," and at times it is admittedly difficult to distinguish the two. We make the distinction by attending to the nature of the construct being measured. For purposes of this chapter, we define outcome as improvements in patient-presenting problems, symptoms, and functioning. Process includes the events in psychotherapy sessions, or constructs thought to change during, or in

between, therapy sessions as a consequence of therapeutic interactions and *that subsequently lead to change in problems, symptoms, and functioning*. For example, insight is gained during therapy sessions (or in between sessions as one reflects on therapy conversations) and is hypothesized to then lead to improvements in patient symptoms and functioning. Thus, the relation of insight to treatment outcome is viewed here as a process-outcome relationship. However, to distinguish changes within the patient from events occurring in therapy sessions, we follow the terminology of Doss (2004) and refer to the former as "change mechanisms" and the latter as "change processes."

Having defined what this chapter is about, we also describe what is not included in the chapter. First, we constrain the focus of this chapter to the process of individual psychotherapy. Chapters in this volume on group and family psychotherapy provide some information on process-outcome research relevant to those formats of treatment. Second, our primary emphasis is on studies that link psychotherapy process to treatment outcome. There is a wealth of studies that examine what happens during psychotherapy sessions, but do not link those events and processes to treatment outcome. Single case studies, qualitative studies, microanalysis of sequential processes in session, and investigation of critical events in psychotherapy are examples of other forms of process research (Elliott, 2010). Such studies are essential building blocks to understanding the nature of psychotherapy; however, the impact of those forms of research on clinical practice and the training of psychotherapists is more speculative when outcome is not part of the empirical investigation. Although our primary focus is on process-outcome studies, we do mention some studies that shed light on the antecedents of important process variables so that the reader has a clear understanding of the construct that has been associated with treatment outcome. Third, although we cover a wide range of studies, our review is not an exhaustive review of all available process-outcome studies. Our focus is on major trends in the literature, especially as related to important models of psychotherapy. Readers can refer to earlier versions (e.g., Orlinsky et al., 2004) of this handbook to obtain, in particular, a historical account of process-outcome research and a more detailed review of the many individual facets of the therapeutic relationship component of the psychotherapy process in relation to outcome. Here, we cover the therapeutic alliance and other relationship factors, but only from a broader perspective.

METHODOLOGICAL CONCERNS WITHIN PROCESS-OUTCOME RESEARCH

Throughout our review of studies, we consistently describe how results may be affected by certain methodological issues. There are a wide range of methodological and design issues that might influence the nature and interpretation of findings from psychotherapy process-outcome studies. These issues include, among others, topics such as training and reliability of judges who make ratings of therapy sessions, the unit (e.g., therapist or patient statement; brief segment of a session; whole sessions) of therapy sampled, and the perspective of evaluation (client report, therapist report, independent observer ratings). These issues have been explicated elsewhere (Elliott, 2010; Hill & Lambert, 2004).

Our focus in this chapter is on five specific methodological issues that can greatly impact the findings from a process-outcome study and also affect the interpretation of results in terms of clinical recommendations that can be made from the studies. The first is the dependability of the process measure. In generalizability theory, dependability refers to the adequacy of generalizing over sampling units (e.g., sessions, patients, therapists) to the universe of such units from which the samples were selected (Cronbach, Rajaratnam, & Gleser, 1963; Shavelson & Webb, 1991). Most relevant to psychotherapy process-outcome research is the question of whether assessment of a single treatment session (or particular week in therapy) is adequate to generalize to the process that occurred in other treatment sessions. If, for example, a single session is sampled in a study of patient emotion expressed in therapy, but there is variability from session to session in patient emotion expressed, the single session sampled may not be representative of the typical level of emotion expressed in other sessions. This lack of dependability of the scores from a single session as a measure of typical level of emotion expressed will affect the size of any potential correlation between this process variable and outcome (because of the "error" added to the scores from the randomly higher or lower scores that are a consequence of sampling only a single session). Clinical recommendations need to be based on whether

a detected effect is "clinically meaningful" (i.e., large enough to make a difference in actual clinical practice), and, therefore, studies that underestimate actual effects because of inadequate sampling of sessions might provide misleading results. To provide a sense of the size of effects, we consistently have converted, when needed, the effects found in individual studies to a correlation coefficient (r). To reduce confusion, we also use a convention throughout that a positive correlation is indicative of an effect in the hypothesized direction and a negative correlation is indicative of an effect in the opposite direction from that hypothesized (note: this convention may deviate from what is provided in the original study because for some outcome measures, a lower score reflects improvement, and for other outcome measures, a higher score reflects improvement).

A second methodological problem is that the vast majority of process-outcome studies are correlational (i.e., not randomized experiments) and therefore are constrained by the standard limitations of correlational designs in regard to making causal inferences. These limitations relate to time precedence (i.e., does the process variable occur before the outcome variable?) and the potential influence of third variables. There are methods that attempt to address these concerns, and we indicate in our review when such methods have been employed. If no attempt has been made to address issues of causal direction and/or the role of third variables, any clinical recommendations would need to be made cautiously, if at all.

A third concern is the issue of therapist and patient responsiveness (Stiles, 1988; Stiles, Honos-Webb, & Surko, 1998). Responsiveness in psychotherapy refers to patient and therapist behavior that is affected by the emerging context. Such responsiveness can affect process-outcome correlations in various ways, particularly when the process variable is a count of the occurrence of therapist interventions in treatment sessions. For example, the use of Socratic questioning by the therapist is thought to be an important technique within cognitive therapy. One might, therefore, hypothesize that greater use of Socratic questioning in therapy sessions would be associated with better treatment outcomes. However, a cognitive therapist might well increase the use of Socratic questioning when the therapist observes that a patient is not progressing in treatment and decrease the use of Socratic questioning for a different patient who has already achieved great progress. If a researcher samples the treatment sessions that occurred after the therapist altered the frequency of certain interventions based on the patients' clinical state, the relation between frequency of use of Socratic questioning and treatment outcome might be attenuated, zero, or even a negative correlation (i.e., higher levels of Socratic questioning associated with relatively poorer outcomes). Process variables that are evaluative (i.e., the session was "good" or "skillful") rather than based on frequency counts are likely to be less affected by responsiveness. As we review process-outcome studies, we comment on the possibility that responsiveness may be affecting the reported results.

A fourth methodological concern is that individual psychotherapy is not based just on an individual: It is a dyadic relationship consisting of a patient and a therapist. In most studies, each therapist in the study has treated more than one patient. From a statistical point of view, such a study is therefore a *multilevel* study with patients nested within therapists. Either the patient or the therapist, or both, might be contributing to the level of a process variable measured in treatment sessions and therefore be responsible for the connection between that process variable and treatment outcome. Baldwin, Wampold, and Imel (2007) illustrate how process-outcome relationships could be occurring in opposite directions at the patient and therapist levels. Ignoring the multilevel nature of the data may therefore produce misleading findings. Modern statistical techniques of multilevel modeling (Bryk & Raudenbush, 1992) can sort out the therapist contribution and patient contribution to any process-outcome correlation. These techniques, however, have not been commonly applied until recently. Knowing that the patient, the therapist, or both are contributing to a process-outcome relationship has clear implications for any clinical recommendations in terms of how best to maximize the process variable to achieve positive outcomes. Thus, it is difficult to make clinical recommendations from research that fails to take into account the multilevel nature of psychotherapy data.

A fifth methodological issue relevant to process-outcome and mechanism of change studies is whether the research has examined if the effects are specific to a particular form of psychotherapy. For example, cognitive therapy for depression is hypothesized to work by changing dysfunctional depressogenic cognitions. If such change in dysfunctional cognitions (and symptoms) occurs to the same degree in a different form of psychotherapy as in cognitive therapy, there would be no need to specifically recommend cognitive therapy for depression. As an alternative to obtaining data from a comparison psychotherapy, investigators can address this issue by examining variability in the use of cognitive therapy techniques within cognitive therapy sessions in relation to change in dysfunctional cognitions. This linking of change processes (e.g., therapist techniques) to change mechanisms (e.g., change in cognitions), and in turn to treatment outcome, can provide a stronger test of a theoretical model of psychotherapy and therefore allow for greater confidence in making clinical recommendations. Ultimately, however, our view is that to have the strongest base for causal inferences, findings from correlational process-outcome studies should be followed by studies that experimentally manipulate key elements of the process of specific psychotherapies (such experimental studies are not reviewed in the current chapter).

It is important to emphasize that the vast majority of studies do not address any of the five major methodological issues that can potentially affect the interpretation of process-outcome correlational studies. However, where available, we consistently bring attention to the available studies that do address one or more of these issues so we have a better understanding of what we know, and what we don't know, about the relation of a certain process variable to treatment outcome and so that we have a clearer sense of the limitations on any clinical recommendations that can be made from such studies.

COMMON FACTORS: THE THERAPEUTIC RELATIONSHIP

In the past three decades, research findings have repeatedly demonstrated the therapeutic relationship as perhaps the most important common factor component to the therapeutic process. Most of the research is centered on the concept of the therapeutic alliance. The concept of therapeutic alliance originated with psychodynamic therapy but its role in the therapeutic process has been generalized to orientations other than just psychodynamic therapy (Horvath & Symonds, 1991). The therapeutic alliance may be broadly defined as the collaborative and affective relationship between the therapist and the client (Bordin, 1979). The collaborative aspects of the alliance include the extent of agreement between therapist and client about (a) the goals of therapy, and (b) techniques that will be implemented to achieve these goals. The affective component of the alliance is the "bond" between the participants, and includes mutual trust, liking, respect, and caring between the patient and therapist.

Alliance-Outcome Studies

Despite extant research, there are mixed views on the importance of the therapeutic alliance in treatment outcome. Some researchers have minimized the importance of the therapeutic relationship, pointing to research indicating that technical treatment intervention factors predict outcome more strongly than the alliance or that the alliance does not predict outcome once other variables have been controlled (DeRubeis, Brotman, & Gibbons, 2005; DeRubeis & Feeley, 1990; Feeley, DeRubeis, & Gelfand, 1999; Gaston, 1990; Kokotovic & Tracey, 1990; Strunk, Brotman, DeRubeis, & Hollon, 2010). In general, however, meta-analytic reviews have concluded that there is substantial evidence for a link between the alliance and treatment outcome (Horvath, 2001; Horvath, Del Re, Flückiger, & Symonds, 2011; Horvath & Symonds, 1991; Martin, Garske, & Davis, 2000). The most recent review (Horvath et al., 2011) included 190 independent data sources covering more than 14,000 patients. This meta-analysis found a small to moderate relation between the alliance and therapeutic outcome ($r = .27$).

Despite the large literature documenting an association between the therapeutic alliance and psychotherapy outcome (Horvath, 2001), important questions remain as to whether the alliance has a causal impact on the outcome of psychotherapy or whether the association is spurious or even runs in the opposite direction, with change in symptoms influencing the alliance (Feeley et al., 1999; Strunk et al., 2010). Temporal precedence is difficult to establish within the context of a process-outcome correlational study. Typically, a process-outcome study measures outcome as change from baseline to termination of treatment. The alliance is then typically measured at some point during treatment, such as Session 5. The alliance at Session 5 is then correlated with change in patient symptoms or functioning from baseline to termination, and the resultant correlation is described as evidence that the alliance is an important determinant of treatment outcome. But another possible interpretation is that the alliance-outcome relationship goes in the other direction: Patient improvement from baseline

to Session 5 "causes" a good alliance and such early-in-treatment improvement is often highly associated with outcome at treatment termination (Barber et al., 1999). This then produces an artificial relationship between the alliance at Session 5 and change in symptoms from baseline to termination.

To address this potential artifact, Barber et al. (1999) assert that, ideally, an investigator should examine the relation between the alliance and subsequent symptom change (e.g., change in symptoms from Session 5 to termination, if the alliance is measured at Session 5), controlling for prior change (change in symptoms from baseline to Session 5). Barber (2009) reviewed studies that took one or both criteria into consideration. An updated review of these studies (four additional studies were located and have been published subsequent to the Barber, 2009, review) is given in Table 9.1. Overall, the median correlation between the alliance and subsequent symptom change, and/or controlling for prior symptom change, across the studies listed in Table 9.1 is .24 (mean = .19). This value is slightly lower than the average effect (.27) found in the most recent meta-analysis of all alliance-outcome studies (Horvath et al., 2011). It is important to note, however, that studies that control for prior symptom change when examining the alliance-outcome correlation are likely to underestimate the impact of the alliance on outcome because the alliance may also be responsible, in part, for some of the prior symptom change. Thus, in general, there appears to be little evidence that controlling for prior symptom change substantially reduces or eliminates the alliance-outcome correlation. This conclusion, however, is tempered by the wide variability in the results of the studies shown in Table 9.1. These studies varied in their (a) types of treatment (cognitive, dynamic), (b) types of patient population (depression, substance use), (c) use/nonuse of multilevel modeling to separate out the patient and therapist components to the alliance-outcome relation, and (d) attention to reliability/dependability of alliance assessment. Any or all of these factors may explain the variability in the results of the studies, with some showing no relation of alliance to outcome, controlling for prior change, and others showing strong relations of alliance to outcome. Because of this variability across studies, comments about several specific studies are addressed next.

Two studies of cognitive therapy for depression showed relatively little association of the

TABLE 9.1 Studies Examining the Relation Between Alliance and Outcome That Addressed Reverse Causality

Study	Sample	Therapy	Sessions Sampled	Process Measure	Effect Size (*r*) With Outcome
Barber et al. (1999)	Cocaine Addicts (*n* = 252)	Cognitive therapy, drug counseling, or supportive expressive therapy	Session 5	Use of cocaine from pre-treatment to 1 month posttherapy (controlling for change up to Session 5)	.24 (completer sample)
Barber, Connolly, Crits-Christoph, Gladis, and Siqueland (2000)	Chronic depression (n = 11) GAD (*n* = 44) Avoidant PD (*n* = 19) OCPD (*n* = 14)	Dynamic Therapy	Session 2	Change in depressive symptoms at the end of treatment (controlling for change up to the session of alliance assessment)	.30**
Crits-Christoph et al. (2009)	Substance users (*n* = 257)	Motivational enhancement therapy counseling as usual	Session 2	Self-reported days of primary substance use during weeks 4 to 16 (controlling for prior change in drug use)	.21**
Crits-Christoph, Gibbons, M., Hamilton, Ring-Kurtz, and Gallop. (2011)	Depression (*n* = 45)	Alliance Fostering Psychotherapy	Average of Sessions 3 to 9	Change in depressive symptoms from pre- to posttherapy (controlling for change up to the session of alliance assessment)	.38*
DeRubeis & Feeley (1990)	Depression (*n* = 25)	Cognitive therapy	4 in total Early: 2 or 3 Other: 3 randomly selected	Change in depressive symptoms from pre- to posttherapy (controlling for change up to the session of alliance assessment)	.10
Feeley et al. (1999)	Depression (*n* = 32)	Cognitive therapy with or without medication	3 in total Session 2. Rest randomly selected	Change in depressive symptoms from pre- to posttherapy (controlling for change up to the session of alliance assessment)	–.27

(continued)

TABLE 9.1 *(Continued)*

Study	Sample	Therapy	Sessions Sampled	Process Measure	Effect Size (r) With Outcome
Gaston, Marmar, Gallagher, and Thompson (1991)	Depression ($n = 54$)	Behavior therapy, cognitive therapy, brief dynamic therapy	Session 5	Change in depressive symptom from pretreatment to termination (controlling for a change up to the session of alliance assessment)	.42
Klein et al. (2003)	Chronic depression ($n = 341$)	CBASP with or without medication	Session 2	Change in depressive symptoms between Weeks 3 and 12 (controlling for the effects of treatment condition and baseline Week 2)	.14**
Ryum, Stiles, and Vogel (2009)	Anxiety and depressive disorders ($n = 55$)	Naturalistic psychotherapy (mostly cognitive–behavioral)	Session 3	Change in symptoms and interpersonal problems (controlling for prior improvement on these measures)	.25
Webb et al.(2011)	Depression ($n = 105$)	Cognitive therapy	Session 3	Change in depressive symptoms subsequent to alliance assessment	.28**
Zuroff and Blatt (2006)	Depression ($n = 99$)	Cognitive therapy or interpersonal therapy	Session 2	Change in depressive symptoms subsequent to measurement of alliance (controlling for effects of early improvement on the alliance)	.07 (average of two treatments)

Note. A negative r indicates the finding was in the opposite direction from that hypothesized.
* $p < .05$; ** $p < .01$.

alliance with outcome once prior symptom change was controlled (DeRubeis & Feeley, 1990; Feeley et al., 1999). Similarly, another study (Strunk et al., 2010) by this research group also showed no relation of the alliance to change in depressive symptoms from session to session (this study is not shown in Table 9.1 because it did not relate the alliance to eventual treatment outcome). However, in a more recent publication, this same research group found that two components of the alliance (agreement on goals; agreement on tasks) predicted outcome controlling for prior improvement, but the third component (bond) appeared to be more of a consequence of prior improvement (Webb et al., 2011). Thus, the authors acknowledge that some aspects of the alliance may be part of the process of change in cognitive therapy for depression. Although the three components of the alliance are often highly correlated, other studies should investigate if the findings of the Webb et al. (2011) study showing no causal role for the bond component of the alliance replicate. This would be an important distinction because the therapeutic bond is often thought to be at the heart of the alliance concept. It should also be noted that the Webb et al. (2011) study used data from a controlled clinical trial. Alliance ratings from such trials often are highly constricted at the upper levels of alliance scales because of the use of highly experienced and trained therapists. Examination of a potential causal role of the therapeutic bond should ideally be done within a naturalistic sample that contained sufficient variability on alliance scales.

Klein et al. (2003) examined the alliance-outcome relation in a study of 367 chronically depressed patients treated with cognitive-behavioral analysis system of psychotherapy (CBASP) administered either alone or with medication. This study investigated the relationship between the alliance and subsequent change on depressive symptoms after controlling for two potential sources of confounding: (1) prior change in symptomatology, and (2) patient characteristics that may contribute to both a poor alliance and a poor outcome. The results showed that early alliance significantly predicted subsequent improvement in depressive symptoms, even after controlling for prior and concurrent levels of depressive symptoms, gender, chronicity, comorbid anxiety, substance use, personality disorders, highest level of social functioning in the past

five years, and a history of abuse and neglect in childhood. Another important methodological issue avoided in this study was shared method variance. The alliance and depressive symptoms were measured independently using different methods. Hence, the association between the alliance and outcome was not inflated by shared method variance.

In another study (Crits-Christoph et al., 2009), multilevel modeling was used to reveal that the therapist component to the alliance-outcome relation was significant (controlling for prior improvement), but not the patient component, in a community sample of substance users. In addition, alliance scores demonstrated a curvilinear relationship to drug use with the impact of the alliance having a negative impact at very high levels. The findings of an alliance-outcome relation at the therapist level, but not the patient level, replicate the results of an earlier study (Baldwin et al., 2007) that did not control for prior improvement. It would be informative if future examinations of the causal role of the alliance also use a multilevel approach to separate out the patient and therapist levels of analysis. In addition, it would be useful for studies to routinely test for curvilinear effects. The examination of curvilinear effects would have important clinical implications: extremely positive alliance is not necessarily a good thing for positive treatment outcomes.

Taking prior changes into consideration before assessing the relationship between the alliance and outcome is not the only important factor that has been missing in the methodology of alliance studies. Another important methodological concern for studies of the relation between alliance and outcome is attention to the dependability of alliance assessments. In a recent study, Crits-Christoph et al. (2011) showed that adequately assessing the alliance using multiple patients per therapist and at least four treatment sessions per patient is crucial to fully understanding the size of the alliance-outcome relationship. At the therapist level, a large number of patients (about 60) per therapist is needed to provide a dependable therapist-level alliance score. At the patient level, generalizability coefficients revealed that a single assessment of the alliance is only marginally acceptable. Very good (> .90) dependability at the patient level is only achieved through aggregating four or more assessments of the alliance. The study also suggests that early treatment alliance scores should be used to predict outcome because late sessions are influenced by prior symptomatic change. A single early session alliance score explained 4.7% of outcome variance but the average of six early sessions explained 14.7% of outcome variance, controlling for prior change in symptoms of depression. It may be that the average effect for the alliance on outcome (.27) reported by the most recent meta-analysis (Horvath et al., 2011) is attenuated by the inadequate dependability of alliance measurement utilized in most investigations.

Most of the studies in Table 9.1 involved the treatment of patients with depressive disorders. One study that included both anxiety and depressive disorders (Ryum et al., 2009) found that the alliance predicted change in symptoms more highly for those with depressive disorders compared to anxiety disorders. No studies have examined the alliance as a predictor of outcome, controlling for prior improvement, within the context of a specific anxiety disorder. It may be that the alliance plays more of a causal role in relation to outcome for patients with a disorder like depression that is characterized by isolation from others, loneliness, and low self-esteem, compared to other disorders.

Treatment Characteristics and the Alliance-Outcome Relation

The importance of the alliance with respect to treatment outcome has led to the investigation of its impact in different theoretical orientations. Alliance has been investigated in different types of psychotherapy treatment. This includes, among other treatments, cognitive therapy (e.g., DeRubeis & Feely, 1990), gestalt therapy (e.g., Horvath & Greenberg, 1989), and psychodynamic therapy (e.g., Eaton, Abeles, & Gutfreund, 1988; Horowitz & Marmar, 1985; Luborsky, 1976; Luborsky & Auerbach, 1985; Marmar, Horowitz, Weiss, & Marziali, 1986; Marziali, Marmar, & Krupnick, 1981).

Relationship Factors Overlapping With the Alliance Construct

Although the alliance is often thought of as the essence of the therapeutic relationship, researchers have investigated a large number of specific components of the therapeutic relationship that, though likely correlated highly with the alliance, may also be partly independent of the alliance. The previous edition of this handbook provides a detailed review of these factors

(Orlinsky et al., 2004). In this previous review, these other aspects of the therapeutic relationship are organized into the following domains: personal role investment, interactive coordination, expressive attunement, affective attitude, and experiential congruence. Here we provide a brief summary of studies of these aspects of the therapy relationship.

Personal Role Investment

Personal role investment is a construct defined by the level of involvement demonstrated by the participants in the therapeutic process. Factors associated with personal role investment include therapist role engagement and credibility. Orlinsky et al. (2004) reviewed 37 studies and found that the majority of studies ($n = 21$) supported that therapists who were viewed as positively engaged and credible helpers had better patient outcomes. Since 2004, therapist credibility has received less attention and the focus has shifted more toward treatment credibility and preference (e.g., Hilsenroth, Ackerman, Blagys, Baity, & Mooney, 2003). Of the three more recent studies that looked into therapist credibility, two determined a positive relationship with treatment outcome (Goates-Jones, 2006; Westra, Constantino, Arkowitz, & Dozois, 2011), and the third found therapist bond was a stronger predictor of outcome than therapist credibility (Farsimadan, Draghi-Lorenz, & Ellis, 2007).

Orlinsky et al. (2004) reviewed 54 studies focusing on patient role engagement, 35 of which showed a positive relationship with treatment outcome. In regard to patient motivation, half of the 28 studies reviewed by Orlinsky et al. (2004) reported a positive association with treatment outcome. Three more recent studies investigating patient motivation also found a positive relationship with treatment outcome (Huppert, Barlow, Gorman, Shear, & Woods, 2006; Simon & Siwiak-Kobayashi, 2008; Steketee et al., 2011). However, one investigation did not find any association between motivation and treatment outcome (Vogel, Hansen, Stiles, & Gibson, 2006). Although the findings on personal role investment predominantly demonstrate a positive relationship with therapeutic outcome, the findings are dependent on who rates the sessions. Specifically, studies using observer ratings generally did not show a positive association between the above factors and outcome (Orlinsky et al., 2004).

Interactive Coordination

This construct includes the quality of the inter-action process between the therapist and client. The interaction may be defined by a collaborative process between the therapist and client or may be represented by a process directed by the therapist. The type of treatment may influence the level of directiveness involved in the treatment process. For example, in cognitive-behavior therapy the therapist directs most sessions with specific ses-sion goals in mind. Psychodynamic therapy, in contrast, calls for the patient to provide relevant content for the therapist to address in sessions. Orlinsky et al. (2004) reported that 36 studies investigated interactive coordination, and the findings of these studies were mixed. However, when assessing a therapists' collaborative versus controlling behavior during therapy, Orlinsky et al. (2004) report that 24 studies consistently suggest a better treatment outcome for patients when a more collaborative relational style is implemented. A more recent study (Cao, 2011) disputes such findings and reports better treat-ment outcome for patients when using more direct methods.

One reason for such mixed findings may be the interaction of this process variable with patient characteristics. For instance, Karno and Longabaugh (2005) found only high-level reac-tance patients with substance abuse responded poorly to direct behavior by therapists, not the middle or low-level reactant patients. A recent meta-analysis by Beutler, Harwood, Michelson, Song, and Holman (2011) supports these findings. Based on 12 studies, the meta-analysis supported the hypothesis that patients exhibiting low levels of trait-like resistance respond better to direc-tive types of treatment, while patients with high levels of resistance respond best to less directive treatments. Since the psychotherapy interac-tion involves both the patient and the therapist, research exploring interactive coordination needs to account for the characteristics and behaviors of both participants.

Expressive Attunement

Expressive attunement includes the quality of communication between the client and the ther-apist, including therapist expressiveness, patient expressiveness, the patient's empathic under-standing in therapy, and communicative rapport. The Orlinsky et al. (2004) review found that 7 of 16 studies showed a positive relationship between therapist expressiveness and outcome while 32 of 51 studies showed a significant relationship between positive patient expressiveness and treat-ment outcome. There is also support for a positive association between communicative rapport and therapeutic outcome (26 of 42 studies; Orlinsky et al., 2004).

Affective Attitude

This construct focuses on the feelings that the client and therapist have towards one another. In Orlinsky et al.'s (2004) review, therapist affir-mative behavior was found to demonstrate a predominantly positive impact (87 of 154 stud-ies) on treatment outcome and is considered an effective component of successful therapeutic relationships. Patient affirmative behavior toward the therapist also showed a positive relationship (41 of 57 studies; Orlinsky et al., 2004) with out-come. Studies focusing on the joint affirmative behavior of both therapist and client also revealed a positive impact (25 of 32 studies; Orlinsky et al., 2004) on outcome. A more recent study, Hof-fart, Hedley, Thornes, Larsen, and Friis (2006) examined emotional reactions to patients as a mediator in cognitive-behavior therapy of panic disorder with agoraphobia and found therapist reactions did not affect symptomatic treatment outcome of patients. Another recent empiri-cal investigation of therapists' feelings toward patients using psychodynamic therapy revealed that symptom change was positively correlated with positive therapists' feelings toward patients and negatively correlated with negative feelings (Rossberg, Karterud, Pedersen, & Friis, 2010).

Experiential Congruence

Kivlighan and Arthur (2000) reported that the degree to which client and therapist agree on how they experience their session from a relational perspective is positively related to outcome. How-ever, two recent studies investigating experiential congruence concluded that level of congruence between therapist and patient did not impact either alliance (Fitzpatrick, Iwakabe, & Stalikas, 2005) or outcome (Swift & Callahan, 2009). Thus, it is difficult to draw any conclusions about the role of experiential congruence at this time.

Therapeutic Relationship: Summary and Future Directions

From the 1970s through the 1990s, a large body of research consistently documented that the quality of the therapeutic relationship was associated with psychotherapy outcome in a wide variety of patient populations and types of treatment. Following these initial findings, research on the therapeutic relationship over the past decade has delved more deeply into the nature of this relationship. Within the limitations of correlational (i.e., nonexperimental) research design, recent research supports the potential causal role that a positive therapeutic alliance plays in leading to relatively better treatment outcomes. The degree to which the alliance influences therapy outcomes is more difficult to specify with any certainty, as the size of the relationship is influenced by factors such as how many treatment sessions are sampled, which sessions are sampled (early versus later in treatment), type of patient population, and the type of psychotherapy. Studies have generally found evidence that a variety of aspects of the therapeutic relationship (e.g., personal role investment, interactive coordination, expressive attunement, affective attitude) measured in treatment sessions correlate positively with therapy outcomes. These studies, however, have not been conducted with attention to issues of reverse causality, dependability of assessments, multilevel modeling, or specificity of effects. It is, therefore, difficult to draw firmer conclusions about causal influence from the studies of other facets of the therapeutic relationship. Hopefully, in the years to come, studies of these variables will incorporate greater attention to methodological issues that will allow for stronger conclusions. Future research will need to unpack the contribution of the alliance to the outcome of specific treatments for specific patients, using designs that control for prior symptom course and third variables and using measurements that are reliable and dependable if we are to fully grasp the role of the therapeutic alliance in the process of psychotherapy.

Having reviewed current knowledge about common factors such as the therapeutic relationship, we now move on to focus on specific process features of major theoretical approaches.

THE PROCESS OF EXPOSURE-BASED THERAPY FOR ANXIETY DISORDERS

Behavior therapy for anxiety disorders typically consists of imaginal and/or in vivo exposure techniques. A clear theory about how the process

of such treatments should relate to treatment outcome was described by Foa and Kozak (1986). Their emotional processing theory hypothesizes that successful outcome requires activation of the fear structure during exposure (as assessed by physiological responses and self-report), a gradual reduction (i.e., habituation) of the degree of fear reactions after repeated presentation of fear stimuli during sessions (i.e., habituation within sessions), and a reduction in the degree of fear reactions across exposure sessions (i.e., habituation across sessions). Table 9.2 describes studies that have examined these process variables in relation to the outcome of behavior therapy for anxiety disorders. When multiple outcome measures were presented within a study, a measure of symptoms of the primary disorder was selected. Studies of a single session of exposure with volunteers were not included; nor were studies that did not examine individual differences in process in relation to outcome.

Overall, a strong relationship between the degree of activation of physiological indicators of fear during exposure sessions and treatment outcome was evident (mean r of heart rate with outcome = .66, $N = 3$ studies; facial coding of fear, $r = .61$, $N = 1$ study). Using patient reports of anxiety, three studies (Kozak et al., 1988; Rauch et al., 2004; van Minnen & Hagenaars, 2002) reported no significant relation between fear activation during sessions and outcome. In addition, one study (Foa et al., 1983) found a significant relationship in the opposite direction (i.e., higher fear activation was associated with relatively poor outcome). Three of four studies used patient ratings from the first exposure session, and the fourth (Kozak et al., 1988) sampled only two sessions. The reliability and dependability of simple fear ratings based on one or two imaginal exposures is likely to be limited; this issue may have hindered uncovering a relation between self-report of fear and outcome in the studies. Along these lines, a study that used a more dependable average fear rating for imagined fearful scenes across all of treatment found a significant relationship ($r = .57$) in the predicted direction between fear activation and treatment outcome (Crits-Christoph & Singer, 1984). The idea, however, that activation of the specific phobic fear is needed for successful outcome is challenged by a study by Watson and Marks (1971) who found that activation of irrelevant ("normal") fears correlated with treatment outcome but activation of relevant (phobic) fears did not.

TABLE 9.2 Process-Outcome Studies of Exposure-Based Behavior Therapy

Study	Sample	Sessions Sampled and Overall Treatment Length	Outcome Measure	Process Measures	Effect Size (*r*) With Outcome
Kozak, Foa, and Steketee (1988)	Obsessive compulsive disorder	Sessions 6 and 14 of 15-session treatment	Raw change from pre- to posttreatment in composite measure of OCD symptoms, averaging ratings by patient, therapist, and independent assessor	**Fear activation during sessions**	
				Self-report	.00
				Heart rate	.54*
				Habituation within sessions	Not significant
				Habituation across sessions	
				Self-report	.36
				Heart rate	.44*
Lang, Melamed, and Hart (1970)	9 female snake phobics	Average of 6 images that elicited fear drawn from 11 automated desensitization sessions	Average rank across snake phobia measures	**Fear activation during sessions**	
				Heart rate	.75*
				Habituation within sessions	
				Heart rate	.91**
Watson and Marks (1971)	6 specific phobics and 10 agoraphobics	8 exposure sessions targeting main phobia; 8 exposure sessions targeting "normal fears"	Sum of main phobia anxiety and avoidance ratings by therapist and patient	**Fear activation during sessions**	
				Therapist rated anxiety for "normal fears" at 10-minute intervals during all sessions	.60*
Pitman Orr, Altman, and Longpre (1996)	20 veterans with PTSD	2 of 12 flooding sessions	Intrusive memories per day measured using a daily log over 3 days	**Fear activation during sessions**	
				Heart rate	.70*
				Habituation within sessions	
				Heart rate	.51*
				Habituation across sessions	
				Heart rate	.46*

(*continued*)

TABLE 9.2 *(Continued)*

Study	Sample	Sessions Sampled and Overall Treatment Length	Outcome Measure	Process Measures	Effect Size (r) With Outcome
Foa et al. (1983)	50 patients with OCD	Average of 11 to 12 sessions	Percent change in obsessive compulsive symptoms	**Fear activation during sessions** Patient ratings of anxiety at first exposure	−.41*
				Habituation within sessions Decrease in self-reported anxiety within the session involving the most feared stimuli	.47**
				Habituation across sessions Decrease in self-reported anxiety from the session involving the most feared stimuli to anxiety in session 10	.50**
Rauch, Foa, Furr, and Filip (2004)	69 women with PTSD	Between 9 and 12 sessions of prolonged exposure (PE) or PE plus cognitive restructuring	Posttreatment PTSD symptoms	**Fear activation during sessions** Patient reported anxiety in first session	.09
				Habituation across sessions Decrease in self-reported anxiety, from the first to last session, in response to imaginal exposure	.36**
Crits-Christoph and Singer (1984)	19 patients with specific phobias	12 sessions of imaginal exposure	Change from pre- to posttreatment in ratings fear relevant to target phobia	**Fear activation during sessions** Patient-rated fear during presentation of phobic images throughout treatment (averaged)	.57*

Study	Sample	Treatment	Definition	Measure	r
Foa, Riggs, Massie, and Yarczower (1995)	12 patients with PTSD	9 sessions of prolonged exposure	Average percent improvement summing 3 measures of PTSD symptoms	**Fear activation during sessions** Facial movements indicative of fear during the 15 seconds prior to the highest level of distress reported in the first exposure session	.61*
van Minnen and Hagenaars (2002)	34 patients with PTSD	9 sessions of prolonged exposure	Improvers defines as having both a 50% or greater decrease in PTSD symptoms from baseline to end of treatment and below the posttreatment sample mean on depression and anxiety symptoms	**Fear activation during sessions** Peak patient ratings of fear during first session minus beginning level	.24
				Habituation within sessions Peak session 1 minus end session 1 anxiety rating	.20
				Habituation across sessions Peak session 1 minus peak session 2 anxiety rating	.36**

Note. A negative r indicates the finding was in the opposite direction from that hypothesized.
* $p < .05$; ** $p < .01$.

Support also exists for the theoretical proposition that habituation within sessions is needed for successful treatment outcome. Three studies (Table 9.2) reported moderately high correlations between reductions in fear (either self-report or physiological indicators) and outcome (Foa et al., 1983; Lang et al., 1970; Pitman et al., 1996); two studies reported no significant relationships (Kozak et al., 1988; van Minnen & Hagenaars, 2002). In this latter study the authors report that most patients showed within session habituation resulting in limited variability on within session habituation measures, and, therefore, this study may not have been an adequate test of the hypothesis. Taking all five studies into account (setting the nonsignificant result to zero), the mean r was equal to .42, a noteworthy effect.

Similarly, there is empirical support for the theoretical notion that habituation across treatment sessions is linked to therapeutic outcomes (Table 9.2). Two studies (Kozak et al., 1988; Pitman et al., 1996) measured heart rate habituation across sessions and each found a significant relation to outcome (mean $r = .45$). Three studies examined habituation on self-report measures of fear, with two of these studies (Foa et al., 1983; Rauch et al., 2004) reporting statistically significant relationships and one study reporting a nonsignificant relationship (Kozak et al., 1988) (mean $r = .41$ across three studies).

One concern about studies on habituation in relation to outcome is that habituation assessments (i.e., measures of change in fear levels across sessions) are essentially markers for ongoing symptomatic improvement. In studies of anxiety disorders and phobias, outcome is typically measured in terms of fear reduction. Thus, the process variables (fear reduction) and the outcome variable (fear reduction) are overlapping if not the same construct, perhaps different only in the timeframe addressed within the assessment instruments. None of the process-outcome studies of exposure therapy examined whether the process variable predicted *subsequent* change in the outcome measure controlling for prior change in the outcome measure. Thus, habituation across sessions may not "cause" good outcome. Rather, other factors (e.g., nonspecific elements of therapy) might be causing both the ongoing fear reduction across sessions and the final fear reduction seen at treatment termination.

Another consideration not addressed in these studies of the process of exposure therapy is the possibility that similar findings would be evident in other psychotherapies; that is, the specificity of these effects has not been examined. Exposure therapy is likely somewhat unique in the extent of increasing fear during treatment sessions, but other psychotherapies (i.e., emotion-focused experiential therapies) also focus on the elicitation of emotions during therapy. It may be a certain amount of elicitation of emotion is needed in therapy, but excessive elicitation of emotion is not needed. Other psychotherapies, such as emotion-focused experiential therapy, may elicit an adequate amount to activate fear structures and produce habituation, but going beyond that level to the more extreme levels of activation found in exposure therapy does not produce incremental benefits. This would suggest a curvilinear relationship between fear activation during sessions and treatment outcome in which outcome increases as fear activation increases, but then outcome reaches an asymptote once fear achieves a certain level. None of the studies we reviewed tested for such curvilinear relationships or identified an optimum threshold of fear activation.

In reviewing much of this same literature on process-outcome studies of exposure therapy, Craske et al. (2008) concluded that, contrary to our view, the evidence in support of the Foa and Kozak (1986) model is weak. These authors suggest that alternative explanations of the process of exposure therapy are needed. In particular, Craske et al. (2008) hypothesize that exposure treatment works through facilitating inhibitory learning (i.e., learning new nonthreatening associations that compete with the fearful association). However, research using actual psychotherapeutic treatments has not yet addressed the inhibitory learning models of the process of exposure therapy.

In addition to the studies reviewed above that examine "change processes" in exposure therapy for anxiety disorders, there have been several other studies that have examined "change mechanisms" in the behavioral or cognitive-behavioral treatment of anxiety disorders. In particular, two studies have addressed the extent to which improvement in exposure-based therapies for agoraphobia is mediated by change in cognitive variables. Smits, Powers, Cho, and Telch (2004) found that improvements in "fear of fear" partially mediate the outcome of exposure-based therapy for panic disorder. The cognitive variables and the outcome variables were measured only at baseline and termination of treatment, and, therefore, causal direction of the effects is unclear. Vögele et al. (2010) found that change in cognitions about physical catastrophes mediated symptom change for patients with agoraphobia, and changes in cognitions about loss of control mediated symptom change for both patients with agoraphobia and those with social phobia. Once again, however, both the mediator and outcomes were measured at the same point in time (6 weeks after the termination of therapy) and therefore the causal directions of these effects could not be isolated.

An additional study (Hofmann et al., 2007) investigated whether change in panic-related cognitions mediates the outcomes of cognitive-behavior therapy for panic disorder. These authors examined the role of physical catastrophes cognitions (thoughts of having a heart attack), mental catastrophes cognitions (thoughts of going crazy), and social catastrophes cognition (thoughts of making a fool of oneself) as mediators, measured at baseline, posttreatment, and 6-month follow-up. Results indicated that all three cognition scales were partial mediators of the change in panic symptoms over time, with change in cognitions accounting for 20% to 30% of the change in panic symptoms in cognitive-behavior therapy but not in medication treatment. However, temporal precedence of the mediators in relation to change in panic symptoms was not examined in this study.

A final study (Smits, Rosenfield, McDonald, & Telch, 2006) examined whether change in cognitions mediated change in social anxiety symptoms over the course of exposure therapy for social phobia. The cognitive variables in this study were reduction in the tendency to associate fearful stimuli with an unrealistic high probability of harm ("probability bias") and reduction in the tendency to exaggerate the negative consequences of an anticipated harmful event ("cost bias"). It was found that reduction in probability bias was associated with subsequent improvement in fear, but reductions in cost bias were a consequence of improvement in fear.

In summary, what we know from existing studies of the process of exposure therapy for anxiety disorders and phobias is that relatively high correlations between fear activation, habituation within sessions, and habituation across sessions have been reported. What we do not know is whether such correlations of process with outcome in exposure therapy are causal (i.e., predict subsequent change in symptoms), whether activation of the specific fear is crucial (as opposed to "normal" fears), or whether the effects are specific

to exposure therapy. Nevertheless, the consistently large effect sizes linking process to outcome found in this literature are noteworthy. Moreover, the findings for activation of fear in sessions cannot be explained away as a confound between the process variable and the outcome variable, as is the case for habituation assessments, because the finding is in the opposite direction of such a confound (i.e., higher fear in sessions is associated with lowered fear at the end of treatment). Thus, regardless of whether fear activation is specific to exposure therapy, we conclude that the empirical evidence is consistent with fear activation being a likely important aspect of the process of change for anxiety disorders and phobias. We can, therefore, recommend that clinicians attend to fear activation when conducting exposure therapy with such clients. Clinical measurement of fear activation, using simple patient-report fear ratings, should be an essential aspect of any exposure treatment so that the clinician can monitor the degree of fear activation that occurs. Although we have some confidence in these recommendations, it would also be important that further studies of the role of fear activation and habituation in exposure therapies be conducted to rule out third-variables and reverse causation (particularly in the case of habituation assessments).

Studies of change mechanisms for exposure-based studies of anxiety disorders have been scarce. Although some evidence exists for the role of cognitive variables, existing studies have generally not addressed reverse causation or third variables that might have influenced obtained correlations between changes in cognitions and treatment outcomes. Evidence for the mediating role of reductions in "probability bias" in the exposure treatment of social anxiety is promising, but thus far only one study has examined this variable and its specificity to exposure therapy has not been investigated.

THE PROCESS OF COGNITIVE THERAPY FOR DEPRESSION

In the next section, we first review research on change processes in cognitive therapy for depression. The major focus of this research has been on the relation of cognitive therapy techniques to treatment outcome. This is followed by a section on change mechanisms in cognitive therapy for depression (i.e., studies of change in depressogenic cognitions in relation to change in depressive symptoms).

Change Processes in Cognitive Therapy for Depression

Several studies have examined the use of cognitive therapy (CT) techniques in therapy sessions in relation to the outcome of CT for major depressive disorder (MDD). Table 9.3 provides a summary of these studies, drawn from the review by Webb, DeRubeis, and Barber (2010) (supplemented with additional studies not included in that review). From these studies we extracted (or calculated) the correlations of the technique variables with treatment outcome. If a study presented results for multiple sessions, we selected the findings from the earliest sessions because results from later sessions can often be influenced by the problem of therapist responsiveness discussed earlier in this chapter. If more than one outcome measure was presented, we selected (if available) an interview-based measure of depressive symptoms (e.g., Hamilton Rating Scale for Depression; Hamilton, 1960). If results were presented with and without controlling for other important variables (e.g., alliance), we selected the results that controlled for these potential confounding variables (so that the unique role of treatment techniques could be isolated).

Webb et al. (2010) conclude that across studies of different therapies correlations of adherence and competence with outcome are not significantly different from zero, and that this effect does not vary by treatment modality. Despite this overall lack of relation between adherence/competence scales and treatment outcome, several specific studies are notable among those that examined treatment techniques within CT. Webb et al. (2010) averaged effect sizes from the Castonguay et al., (1996) and Feeley et al. (1999) studies (both of whom used data from the Hollon et al., 1992, clinical trial of CT and CT plus imipramine for MDD), with this average showing no effect. However, the measures of treatment techniques used in the Castonguay et al. (1996) and Feeley et al. (1999) studies were quite different. In fact, the Feeley et al. (1999) study found a large effect ($r = .60$) between the use of concrete CT techniques in Session 2 (e.g., "set and followed an agenda"; "reviewed homework"; "asked for specific examples of beliefs"; "practiced rational responses with patient"; "asked patient to record thoughts") and treatment outcome measured *subsequent* to the assessment of the process variables (controlling for alliance, use of abstract techniques, and therapist facilitative conditions). Symptom change prior to Session 2 was unrelated to the use of CT concrete techniques in Session 2, thereby ruling out a temporal confound of symptom change. The use of abstract CT techniques was unrelated to subsequent improvement. The finding for CT concrete techniques replicated an earlier study (DeRubeis & Feeley, 1990) that also found that use of CT concrete techniques predicted subsequent change in depressive symptoms ($r = .53$), and that prior symptomatic change was unrelated to use of CT concrete techniques.

In another study, Ablon and Jones (2002) found that, using ratings of Sessions 4 and 12 for 29 patients who received CT in the NIMH Treatment of Depression Collaborative Research Program (TDCRP; Elkin et al., 1989), the extent to which therapy adhered to an ideal prototype of cognitive-behavioral therapy was positively associated with treatment outcome ($r = .49$). This investigation, however, examined outcome from pre- to posttherapy and did not control for the temporal confound of prior symptom improvement.

CT competence, rated from treatment sessions, has also been found to predict treatment outcome. The most compelling study is a recent investigation in which CT competence was found to predict subsequent change in depressive symptoms ($r = .33$) (Strunk et al., 2010). In an earlier study, Shaw et al. (1999), using sessions from the TDCRP study, found that supervisor's ratings of CT competence, controlling for CT adherence and ratings of "facilitative conditions," predicted change in depressive symptoms from pre- to posttreatment of CT for MDD ($r = .39$). One concern about this study is that the competence ratings were averaged over the full course of treatment (ratings obtained on Sessions 1, 2, 4, 6, 7, 10, 15, 18, and 19). Supervisors were likely aware of the clinical progress of patients and therefore competence ratings, particularly of the latter in treatment sessions, may have been confounded by this knowledge of clinical progress (i.e., the therapists for the patients who had substantially reduced their depression may have received higher competence ratings based on these good outcomes). A second related concern is that outcome from pre- to posttherapy, rather than outcome subsequent to the process measurements, was predicted. Another issue is that the meaning of CT competence controlling for CT adherence is not clear, especially because similar items appear on the CT competence and CT adherence scales.

TABLE 9.3   Therapist Techniques Predicting Outcome of Cognitive Therapy for MDD

Study	Sample	Outcome Measure	Process Measure	Effect Size (r) With Outcome
Use of CT Techniques				
Feeley et al. (1999)	25 patients with MDD who received CT alone or CT plus imipramine from Hollon et al. (1992) study	Change in depressive symptoms subsequent to session rated for process variable	Frequency of CT concrete techniques in Session 2 (controlling for alliance and facilitative conditions)	.60**
			Frequency of CT abstract techniques in Session 2	.00
DeRubeis and Feeley (1990)	25 patients with MDD treated with CT	Change in depressive symptoms subsequent to session rated for process variable	Frequency of CT concrete techniques in one early session	.53*
			Frequency of CT abstract techniques in early session	.13
Ablon and Jones (2002)	29 patients with MDD who received CT from the TDCRP (Elkin et al., 1989)	Change in depressive symptoms from pre- to posttherapy	Extent to which therapy adhered to an ideal prototype of cognitive–behavioral therapy in Sessions 4 and 12	.49*
Hayes, Castonguay, and Goldfried (1996)	30 depressed patients treated with CT or CT plus medication from Hollon et al. (1992) study	Change in depressive symptoms from pre- to posttherapy	Therapist focuses on intrapersonal cognitive change in one session drawn from first 4 weeks	−.28
Castonguay, Goldfried, Wiser, Raue, and Hayes (1996)	30 patient with MDD who received CT alone or CT plus medication from Hollon et al. (1992) study	Change in depressive symptoms from pre- to posttherapy	Intrapersonal links: Therapist highlights the cause and effect connection between two components of patient's functioning, rated in one early session (controlling for alliance)	−.32
Competence Using CT Techniques				
Shaw et al. (1999)	36 patients with MDD who received CT in the TDCRP (Elkin et al. 1989)	Change in depressive symptoms from pre- to posttherapy	CT competence, averaged across nine sessions rated (controlling for adherence and facilitative conditions)	.39*
Trepka, Rees, Shapiro, Hardy, and Barkham (2004)	30 patients with MDD who received CT in clinical practice	Change in depressive symptoms from pre- to posttherapy	CT global competence rated on one session chosen at random between Sessions 3 and 19 of 20 sessions (controlling for alliance)	.21
Strunk et al. (2010)	60 patients with MDD who received CT	Change in depressive symptoms subsequent to measuring competence	CT competence averaged over Sessions 1 to 4	.33

Note. A negative r indicates the finding was in the opposite direction from that hypothesized.

* $p < .05$; ** $p < .01$.

In a third study, CT global competence was rated on one session chosen at random between Session 3 and 19 (of 20 sessions) for 30 patients with MDD who received CT in normal clinical practice settings (Trepka et al., 2004). Controlling for levels of alliance, CT competence was not found to significantly predict change in depressive symptoms from pre- to posttherapy ($r = .21$). The use of only one session in this study may have attenuated the correlation with outcome. In addition, no attempt to control for prior symptom improvement was implemented in this investigation.

Overall, the literature on CT techniques used in the treatment of MDD is mixed. Some studies have suggested that the use of CT techniques, particularly "concrete" techniques, such as setting an agenda for the sessions, reviewing homework, and practicing rational responses, is associated with improved outcomes, and these effects are not due to the influence of prior symptomatic change. Other studies found that a focus on intrapersonal cognitive change was unrelated to outcome. These latter studies, however, failed to control for prior symptom change. In addition, all studies of CT techniques with the exception of Shaw et al. (1999) and Strunk et al. (2010) examined only a single treatment session for each patient. Nevertheless, we conclude that the use of more specific ("concrete") techniques in CT for MDD is clinically indicated. This conclusion is based on two studies (DeRubeis & Feeley, 1990; Feeley et al., 1999) that predicted subsequent symptom improvement, controlled for the alliance, and found relatively large effects. More tentatively, we also conclude that CT competence is related to treatment outcome (though one study was negative). The extent to which scales for CT competence measure something unique to CT or capture general psychotherapy skill is not clear.

Three studies have examined the role of interpersonal/psychodynamic techniques within the context of CT for MDD. Jones and Pulos (1993), using transcripts from the same Hollon et al. (1992) study used in the Feeley et al. (1999) article, reported that use of psychodynamic techniques (e.g., therapist emphasizes feelings to help the patient experience feelings more deeply; therapist is neutral; therapist interprets warded off or unconscious wishes, feelings, or ideas) in CT was positively related ($r = .33$) to outcome for 25 depressed patients treated with CT or CT plus medication. However, results were based on averaging process ratings across Sessions 1, 5,

and 14, and outcome was assessed from pre- to posttherapy. Thus, improvement subsequent to the assessment of the process variables was not examined. It is also likely that the techniques used in Session 14 (out of an average treatment length of 14.4 sessions; maximum of 20 sessions) are somewhat different than the techniques used in early treatment sessions.

Hayes et al. (1996) also examined transcripts from the Hollon et al. (1992) study. In this study, one session for each patient, drawn randomly from the first 4 weeks of treatment, was coded for the extent to which the therapist focused on cognitive, interpersonal, and developmental issues. It was found that interventions that addressed the interpersonal and developmental domains (exploration of early experiences with parents) were significantly associated with greater improvement in CT ($r = .40$), while interventions that addressed intrapersonal cognitive change were not ($r = -.28$). A greater focus on exploration of early experiences with parents was also associated with a longer time until relapse over the course of 2 years following termination of treatment.

Crits-Christoph, Gibbons, Temes, Elkin, and Gallop (2010) examined the interpersonal accuracy of therapist interventions using transcripts of treatment sessions (typically Sessions 2, 3, 4, and 5) for 72 patients who were being treated with cognitive or interpersonal therapy for MDD through the NIMH Treatment of Depression Collaborative Research Program (TDCRP). Interpersonal accuracy of therapist interventions was measured by first having judges determine from session transcripts the central relationship themes for each patient and then having separate judges rate the extent to which each patient's relationship themes were addressed by the therapist in their primary intervention statements to patients. Outcome was assessed subsequent to the measurement of the process variables, and change prior to the measurement of the process variables was statistically controlled. Results indicated that the role of interpersonal accuracy of interventions in relation to outcome differed for the two types of treatments. Higher levels of interpersonal accuracy on the patient's central wish during early treatment sessions was associated with relatively poorer outcomes for patients receiving CT ($r = -.32$) but relatively better outcomes for patients in interpersonal therapy.

Based on three available studies, the role of psychodynamic/interpersonal techniques within CT for MDD is not clear. Although two studies

(Hayes et al., 1996; Jones & Pulos, 1993) reported that using psychodynamic techniques is beneficial, these studies failed to control for prior symptom change. The one study that did control for prior symptom change reported that greater interpersonal accuracy of intervention was associated with relatively poorer outcome in CT for MDD. Whether the differences between the results of these studies are a function of the different process assessments, different sampling of sessions, or controlling/failing to control for prior improvement, is not known. Thus, it is difficult to draw broad conclusions or make clinical recommendations regarding the use of psychodynamic/interpersonal techniques in CT for MDD at this time.

One final comment relates to the rather meager evidence base regarding change processes for CT in the treatment of MDD. It is somewhat surprising that, despite the widespread influence of CT for MDD and the relatively large number of outcome studies that have been conducted to date on this treatment, that more and better studies of techniques used in CT for MDD in relation to outcome have not been conducted. The available process-outcome studies have largely concentrated on tapes/transcripts from two randomized clinical trials, with three studies (Ablon & Jones, 2002; Crits-Christoph et al., 2010; Shaw et al., 1999) conducted using sessions from the TDCRP, and four studies (Castonguay et al., 1996; Feeley et al., 1999; Hayes et al., 1996; Jones & Pulos, 1993) conducted using sessions from the Hollon et al. (1992) trial. Much more research is needed to determine whether the specific techniques of CT are responsible for symptom change in the treatment of MDD.

Change Mechanisms in Cognitive Therapy for MDD

CT of MDD specifies that depressogenic cognitions contribute to the emergence of depressive symptoms. At the deepest level (i.e., not readily accessible) of cognition are depressogenic "schemas," which are long-held underlying negative beliefs about the self. At a more "surface" level of conscious experience, depressed individuals engage in negative automatic thoughts that arise from such depressogenic schemas. At an intermediate level, it is possible to group automatic thoughts into patterns of dysfunctional attitudes. Various theoretical ideas about how cognitions change over the course of CT have been proposed, with one model hypothesizing

that the core cognitions (dysfunctional attitudes or schemas) are actually modified (Hollon, Evans, & DeRubeis, 1990), another model hypothesizing that core schemas are deactivated but remain intact (Ingram & Hollon, 1986), and a third model proposing that individuals learn compensatory skills that help suppress depressogenic cognitions in the context of stressful situations that would normally activate such cognitions (Barber & DeRubeis, 1992; Hollon et al. 1990). Compensatory skills emphasized in cognitive therapy include the generation of initial explanations followed by alternative explanations for negative events and thoughts as well as the creation of concrete problem-solving plans to resolve difficult situations.

A review of research examining cognitive change in relation to symptom change for CT of MDD in 31 studies has been provided by Garratt, Ingram, Rand, and Sawalani (2007). Several of these studies, however, did not compare CT to another treatment or control group. Of the 16 studies that did, the average within group sample size was 24 consumers, thus statistical power for correlations and for between group comparisons (interactions) was highly limited. Among the studies investigating change in cognitions in relation to treatment outcome and consisting of a sample size of approximately 50 or more per group, the following six results were evident: (1) Bieling, Beck, and Brown (2004) found responders to CT had greater change on a measure of fear of criticism and rejection than nonresponders to CT; (2) Oei and Sullivan (1999) found responders to CT decreased more on negative automatic thoughts than nonresponders; (3) Teasdale et al. (2001) predicted relapse following either 20 weeks of combined CT and pharmacotherapy and pharmacotherapy alone for consumers with residual depression who had failed to respond to a previous trial of an antidepressant medication. Week 8 cognitive measures (attributional style, dysfunctional attitudes, perceived uncontrollability of depression, self-blame for depression, meta-cognitive awareness) failed to predict relapse. A measure of extreme scores (in either direction) across the cognitive measures at Week 8 did predict relapse, though the authors do not clarify whether extremely healthy scores actually contribute to the prediction of relapse. Furthermore, change in cognitions was not examined in this study (only Week 8 level of negative cognitions was used as a predictor). (4) Kuyken (2004) found that early change in hopelessness predicted change in depressive symptoms for CT; (5) Seligman et al.

(1988) found that change in attributional style was associated with change in depressive symptoms; (6) Jacobson et al. (1996) found that when comparing three types of therapies that varied in their emphasis on cognitive interventions (behavioral activation, behavioral activation plus cognitive interventions targeting automatic thoughts, and a full CT package of interventions), all treatments equally reduced automatic thoughts and attributional style, and that early changes in attributional style predicted change in depression only for the behavioral activation group.

An additional study (Quilty, McBride, & Bagby, 2008), published after the review by Garratt et al. (2007), also addressed whether cognitive changes from pre to post treatment mediated symptom change in CT. This study found evidence that changes in dysfunctional attitudes mediated symptom reduction in CT, but not interpersonal therapy. In pharmacotherapy, change in depressive symptoms mediated changes in dysfunctional attitudes.

None of the studies reviewed above meet criteria for cognitive changes mediating change in depression using the Baron and Kenny (1986) approach to establishing mediation. Four of the seven studies did not have a control/comparison group; the Jacobson et al. (1996) study failed to find an effect specific to CT on cognitive measures; the Teasdale et al. (2001) study did not measure change in cognitions (and the effects for level of extreme responsiveness at Week 8 may be due to a preexisting personality tendency to relapse rather than a meditational effect tied to change in cognitions). Thus, focusing on studies of reasonably large sample sizes, the body of literature on cognitive changes in CT has largely shown that both cognitive therapy and medication are capable of deactivating self-reported negative thinking. However, all but Quilty et al. (2008) failed to find a unique mechanism for CT, and few studies document that changes in cognitions precede changes in depressive symptoms.

A study that did demonstrate change in cognitions preceded change in depressive symptoms is the investigation by DeRubeis and Feeley (1990). In this study, change in dysfunctional attitudes and hopelessness from intake to mid-phase predicted change in depressive symptoms from mid-phase to termination for CT, but not pharmacotherapy, for MDD. In contrast to measures of dysfunctional attitudes and hopelessness, measures of automatic thoughts and attributional style did not show significant differences between

CT and pharmacotherapy in the prediction of subsequent change in depressive symptoms. However, sample sizes were limited ($n = 32$ per group) and the role of the cognitive variables in an alternative psychotherapy was not examined in this study.

The above studies all relied on self-report measures of surface cognitions. To test the mechanism of CT for MDD, one recent study (Dozois et al., 2009) used a computerized cognitive task that is thought to measure the degree of underlying schema consolidation or interconnectedness of self-relevant information. This study randomly assigned patients either to CT plus pharmacotherapy ($n = 21$) or to pharmacotherapy alone ($n = 21$). Both groups evidenced significant and similar reductions in level of depression as well as self-report measures of automatic thoughts and dysfunctional attitudes. However, patients in the CT plus pharmacotherapy group had significantly larger changes in cognitive organization, as measured by the computerized cognitive task, compared to those who received pharmacotherapy alone. Although promising, this study did not demonstrate that the changes in cognitive structure were correlated with changes in depressive symptoms, nor did the study show that cognitive change precedes symptom change. Nevertheless, the Dozois et al. (2009) study suggests that CT may work by changing underlying cognitive structures. Earlier work by Segal and Gemar (1997) using a modified Stroop task following CT also suggests that patients successfully treated with CT may experience a shift in the organization of their underlying negative self-structures (however, the interconnectedness of the self-schema was inferred from reaction times in this study).

Three studies have examined the hypothesis that CT works by changing compensatory skills. Barber and DeRubeis (2001) found that after 12 weeks of CT for MDD, patients employed compensatory skills more adeptly. In the second study, the level of compensatory skills at posttreatment (controlling for pretreatment scores) was found to predict the likelihood of relapse among patients with MDD treated with CT (Strunk, DeRubeis, Chiu, & Alvarez, 2007). The third study was an investigation of the mechanisms of both CT and supportive-expressive (SE) psychodynamic therapy that used a pooled database that combined studies of the treatment of MDD, generalized anxiety disorder, borderline personality disorder, panic disorder, and adolescent anxiety disorders (Connolly Gibbons et al., 2009). The assessment of compensatory skills was conducted at intake and 4 months (the termination point for all but one of the studies), while symptoms were assessed at intake, Month 4, and follow-up (6 months following termination). The results of the study were that change on the measure of compensatory skills was significantly correlated with change in depression and anxiety symptom measures (from intake to Month 4); but, CT did not produce more change on this measure than SE therapy, and the correlations between change in compensatory skills and change in symptoms did not differ by treatment (no significant treatment by mediator interaction). The effects in this study were largely driven by a decrease in depressotypic reactions as measured by the negative compensatory skills subscale. There was little change evident on the positive compensatory skills subscale that directly assessed the acquisition of positive skills hypothesized to predict symptom reduction. In addition, change in compensatory skills from intake to termination was associated with *subsequent* change in symptoms (at least for anxiety symptoms) from termination to follow-up. Thus, this study provides some support that improvement in compensatory skills may be part of the mechanism of symptom change in CT, but this mechanism is not specific to CT. Limitations of this study were that the patient sample was heterogeneous and the mechanism measures were only assessed at intake and termination (thus, time precedence for mediation of symptom change from intake to termination could not be definitively demonstrated).

In summary, theories of the mechanism of change in CT have proposed that CT works by changing the following in the patient: (a) dysfunctional attitudes; (b) underlying schemas; and/or (c) compensatory skills. No fully adequate test of these potential mediators has been done to date. Existing studies either (a) fail to have a control/comparison group to look for specificity of effects, (b) have inadequate sample sizes, or (c) fail to assess the mediator before symptom change, thereby failing to rule out reverse causation. However, some data supportive of the role of change in cognitions in CT for MDD do exist, suggesting that further research is needed to understand which variables mediate the effects of CT, and to what degree such variables are specific to CT. There are promising data related to the role of learning of compensatory skills in CT as a predictor of relapse. This effect, however, does not appear to be specific to CT.

THE PROCESS OF COGNITIVE-BEHAVIOR THERAPY FOR OTHER DISORDERS

There exists a limited amount of research that examines process-outcome relationships within cognitive-behavior therapy for disorders besides anxiety disorders or MDD. Studies of change mechanism in CBT treatments for borderline personality disorder, panic disorder, eating disorders, and cocaine dependence are reviewed below.

Borderline Personality Disorder

One study has examined acquisition of skills in the treatment of borderline personality disorder as a mediator of outcome over the course of 1 year of treatment (Neacsiu, Rizvi, & Linehan, 2010). The study used pooled data from three studies of dialectical-behavior therapy (DBT) for borderline personality disorder. The self-report DBT skills measure included questions about how the patient coped with stress in the past month, such as "Counted my blessings," "Concentrated on something good that could come out of the whole thing," and "Talked to someone about how I've been feeling." Patients treated with DBT reported using 3 times more skills at the end of treatment than patients who received a control treatment. DBT skills use was measured at baseline and 4, 8, 12, and 16 months after baseline and was found to fully mediate the relation of time in treatment to decrease over time in number of suicide attempts and depression, and the increase in control of anger over time, across both DBT and control conditions. Unlike most studies, change in the mediator was assessed prior to change in the outcome measures. Thus, this study demonstrated that staying in treatment longer was associated with increased skill use and with better outcomes, that increased skill use was associated with better outcomes, and that the relation between time in treatment and outcome was reduced (i.e., mediated by) by an increase in the use of DBT skills.

Although this study is one of the better studies in terms of addressing the temporal relation of change mechanism variables (the mediator) and outcome, the focus of the investigation was on the relation of time in treatment to outcome rather than the treatment effect of DBT (i.e., comparison of DBT to control groups) and therefore the study does not directly address the mechanism of change of DBT. Rather, skill acquisition was examined as a nonspecific variable common to multiple treatments and, indeed, the coping strategies assessed by the scale appear to be strategies that might be learned in a variety of psychotherapies. Nevertheless, the study does provide evidence that acquiring such skills is associated with treatment outcome. Whether DBT is uniquely a treatment that enhances the acquisition of such skills is a question that should be addressed in future research.

Eating Disorders

Wilson, Fairburn, Agras, Walsh, and Krae-mer (2002) examined mediators of cognitive-behavioral and interpersonal therapies for bulimia nervosa. The authors found that eating frequency at posttreatment was associated with change in dietary restraint from baseline to Week 4, and also baseline to Week 6, and change in eating behavior self-efficacy from baseline to Week 10 mediated change in binge eating frequency from base-line to posttreatment (Week 20). Improvement in purge frequency from baseline to posttreat-ment was mediated by three factors: (1) change in dietary restraint from baseline to Weeks 4 and 6, (2) change in affective self-efficacy from baseline to Week 10, and (3) change in eating behavior self-efficacy from baseline to Week 10. These meditational effects, however, did not differ for cognitive behavior therapy compared to interpersonal therapy. The authors also did not demonstrate that change in the mediator predicted subsequent outcome because outcome was only measured at baseline and termination. Using data from the same trial, Loeb et al. (2005) examined the relation of adherence to outcome in cognitive-behavior therapy, and also to interper-sonal therapy, in the treatment of bulimia nervosa. Adherence was rated on Sessions 6, 12, and 18 of a 19-session treatment. No significant relations were found for either treatment ($r = -.19$ for cog-nitive behavior therapy; $r = .05$ for interpersonal therapy; taken from Webb et al., 2010).

Alcohol and Substance Dependence

Skill acquisition has been examined as a key mech-anism variable in a number of studies of alcohol dependence, with several studies suggesting that cognitive-behavioral treatments, relative to con-trol/comparison groups, increase skills to avoid relapse and cope with cravings (e.g., Chaney, O'Leary, & Marlatt, 1978; Hawkins, Catalano, & Wells, 1986). Other studies, however, failed to detect such effects (Kadden, Litt, Cooney, & Busher, 1992; Wells, Peterson, Gainey, Hawkins, & Catalano, 1994).

Further support for the role of coping skills comes from a study by Carroll, Nich, Frankforter, and Bisighini (1999), using data from several pre-vious studies of the treatment of cocaine depen-dence. The authors reported that: (a) patients in cognitive-behavioral therapy evidenced more coping plans than did patients in either 12-step facilitation treatment or clinical management, and (b) patients in cognitive-behavioral therapy, 12-step facilitation, and clinical management groups demonstrated greater change, respec-tively, on the types of coping response specific to each treatment modality. However, type of response at posttreatment was not associated with outcome (number of days abstinent during treatment). More importantly for understanding the mechanism of treatment, the degree of acqui-sition of skills over the course of treatment was not examined in relation to outcome.

Crits-Christoph et al. (2003) examined medi-ators of the outcome of several treatments for cocaine dependence. A measure of dysfunctional beliefs about addiction was found to correlate moderately with drug use outcomes in cogni-tive therapy. However, beliefs about addiction improved significantly more in individual drug counseling, compared to cognitive therapy, and the correlation between improvement in beliefs about addiction and change in drug use was the same in both cognitive therapy and individual drug counseling ($r = .43$).

In summary, findings from process-outcome studies of cognitive-behavioral treatments for alcohol/substance dependence are mixed, and no studies in this area have provided support for the causal direction of change in cognitive/skill vari-ables leading to reductions in alcohol/substance use. Thus, at this point in time, the evidence is not compelling that the theoretical notions of skill acquisition, or changes in dysfunctional beliefs, are central elements to the process of change for cognitive behavioral treatments for alcohol or substance dependence.

THE PROCESS OF PSYCHODYNAMIC THERAPY

To put process-outcome research of psychody-namic therapy in perspective, we begin with a brief overview of the nature of psychodynamic therapy. There are actually a variety of psychodynamic psychotherapy models that have been researched and disseminated clinically. These psychodynamic models share a focus on psychotherapy as an educational experience in which therapist interpretations help patients gain understanding of their relationship experiences. This gain in understanding has been traditionally referred to as insight but the term *insight* has been used differentially across models. In classical analytic theory, insight has been used to refer to patients' gains in uncovering repressed traumatic experiences, whereas later psychodynamically oriented psychotherapies have used the term *insight* to refer more generally to patients' gains in understanding their maladaptive relationship patterns. To differentiate these terms, some models such as supportive-expressive psychodynamic psychotherapy (Luborsky, 1984) have used the term *self-understanding* to more precisely refer to the primary change mechanism of modern dynamic psychotherapies. Whether one uses the term insight or self-understanding, psychodynamic psychotherapies share the premise that what patients learn about themselves and their relationships, through interventions such as interpretations, leads to symptom reduction by helping patients utilize more adaptive beliefs and responses in their important relationships.

In classic psychoanalysis as well as modern theories of brief or focal psychodynamic therapy, interpretation is the central therapist intervention designed to increase insight. For example, the interpretation of problematic relationships within a patient's life is often seen as a key technique in promoting patient insight within modern dynamic psychotherapies such as Luborsky's (1984) supportive-expressive therapy (SE) and Strupp and Binder's (1984) time-limited dynamic psychotherapy. These therapeutic models promote techniques that enable patients to recognize maladaptive relationship patterns, to understand the history of the development of the pattern, and to see ways in which the pattern is related to their present symptoms. Within these therapies, the therapist uses interpretations to help patients understand their relationship patterns outside of therapy and specifically transference interpretations to help patients understand their relationship patterns within the therapeutic relationship.

Related change mechanisms that are important for understanding the complex process of change across dynamic psychotherapy include changes in defensive functioning and reflective functioning. Within dynamic models of psychotherapy, defenses are viewed as expressions of unconscious conflicts, needs, and motivations. Defenses range from less mature defenses such as passive aggression and devaluation to more mature, adaptive defenses such as self-observation. Freud (1964) understood defenses as a means of avoiding psychic pain that could be both adaptive under stressful situations and pathological. In dynamic psychotherapy, therapists must recognize and work with patients to decrease the use of less mature defenses and find more adaptive ways to handle internal and external stressors.

In dynamic psychotherapies especially for personality disorders, improvements in reflective functioning are considered central to helping patients understand their own behaviors as well as predict and explain the behaviors of others. Bateman and Fonagy (2003) understand reflective functioning as one's capacity to recognize and understand mental processes in both one's self and others. The patient's ability to understand and change his or her maladaptive interpersonal patterns, including both perceptions of others' responses to them as well as his or her own interpersonal response patterns is dependent on the patient's ability to improve reflective functioning across treatment.

This section of this chapter specifically reviews the research literature on dynamic psychotherapy linking the use of dynamic psychotherapy change process, including the use of specific dynamic interventions, the quality of specific dynamic interventions, and the overall quality of dynamic interventions to symptomatic and functional outcomes. In addition, the relation of change mechanisms, including changes in self-understanding, defensive functioning, and reflective functioning to the outcome of dynamic psychotherapy are reviewed. Because there is very little research linking dynamic change processes and change mechanisms to the outcome of treatment for specific diagnostic groups, we review the literature across diagnostic groups indicating where relevant when recommendations can be made for specific patient groups.

Change Processes in Dynamic Therapy

There have been a number of studies that have specifically evaluated the relation between specific dynamic psychotherapy change processes and treatment outcome. These include studies that examined the frequency and quality of specific psychodynamic interventions as well as studies that examine overall adherence and competence to psychodynamic interventions.

Therapist Use of Dynamic Techniques

Most investigations that have examined the utilization of dynamic techniques within the process of dynamic psychotherapy have specifically examined the proportion of therapist dynamic interpretations. Table 9.4 summarizes studies that directly assessed the use of dynamic interpretations within sessions in relation to treatment outcome. Two investigations examined the relation between the proportion of interpretations delivered in a psychotherapy and treatment outcome. Hill et al. (1988) evaluated eight patients who received between 12 and 20 sessions of psychotherapy, although no specific treatment manual was mentioned. Three judges rated therapist speaking turns from transcripts of each session. Due to the small sample size, the proportion of interpretations used per case was not significantly related to treatment outcome, although there was a small effect for predicting change in depressive symptoms ($r = .38$). Piper, Debbane, deCarufel, and Bienvenu (1987) examined 21 patients who received 6 months of psychoanalytically oriented individual psychotherapy. Eight audiotaped sessions per patient were rated by two judges using a therapist intervention rating scale. The proportion of dynamic interpretations was significantly associated with the therapist ratings of overall usefulness of treatment ($r = .61$).

Regarding transference interpretations, two early investigations (Malan, 1976; Marziali, 1984) suggested that higher proportions of transference interpretations predicted good psychotherapy outcome. Malan (1976) estimated therapist use of transference interpretations from therapists' progress notes rather than from direct ratings of therapy. Using audiotapes of sessions, Marziali (1984) rated the frequency of interpretations that connected feelings toward persons in the past with feelings towards the therapist. The average frequency of transference interpretations across sessions was not significantly correlated with patient or therapist symptom measures (correlations of nonsignificant effects not reported) but was correlated with independent judge ratings on the Dynamic Outcome Scales ($r = .57$). The reliability of ratings of transference interpretation was questionable as the kappa scores for interjudge agreement were marginal, and the number

of judges rating each session across the sample was not specified.

Three more recent investigations used reliable rating systems to evaluate the relation between the proportion of transference interpretations and the outcome of dynamic psychotherapy and specifically took into account important patient moderator variables. Piper, Azim, Joyce, and McCallum (1991) found that high levels of transference interpretations were associated with poor treatment outcomes only for patients with high quality of object relations at treatment baseline. Piper et al. (1991) rated eight sessions for each of 64 patients treated with twenty sessions of dynamically oriented psychotherapy and found a moderately strong effect ($r = -.58$) for the prediction of outcome among the patients with high quality of object relations. In contrast, Connolly, Crits-Christoph, Shappell, et al. (1999) and Ogrodniczuk et al. (1999) found that high levels of transference interpretations were associated with poor treatment outcome for patients with poor quality of relationships at treatment baseline. In the Connolly, Crits-Christoph, Shappell, et al. (1999) investigation, a pool of three judges classified therapist interventions from three early sessions of treatment for each of 29 patients treated with supportive-expressive dynamic psychotherapy for MDD and found a significant interaction between the percentage of transference interpretations and quality of interpersonal relationships in the prediction of subsequent symptom course, controlling for symptom change that occurred prior to the measurement of the process variable. For patients rated with poor quality of relationships at treatment baseline, there was a moderate effect for the percentage of transference interpretations predicting poor treatment outcome ($r = -.40$). Ogrodniczuk et al. (1999) rated the presence of transference interpretations across sessions 3, 7, 9, 11, 15, and 19 for 40 patients with mixed diagnoses treated with 20 weeks of interpretive dynamic psychotherapy. For patients with low quality of object relations, the average frequency of transference interpretations across therapy was significantly associated with poor treatment outcome ($r = -.48$). Although these investigations appear contradictory, Connolly, Crits-Christoph, Shappell, et al. (1999) explain how the results may actually be complimentary given the different patient samples included in the two investigations as well as the differences in ranges of transference interpretations found in these dynamic treatments.

TABLE 9.4 Process-Outcome Effects for Utilization of Dynamic Interpretations in Dynamic Psychotherapy

Study	Sample	Overall Treatment Length	Process Measures	Effect Size (*r*) With Outcome
Interpretations				
Hill et al. (1988)	8 patients with mixed diagnoses	12–20 sessions	Proportion of interpretations	.38
Piper et al. (1987)	21 patients with mixed diagnoses	6 months	Proportion of dynamic interpretations	.61*
Transference Interpretations				
Marziali (1984)	25 patients	20 sessions	Frequency of transference interpretation	.57**
Piper et al. (1991)	64 patients with mixed diagnoses	20 sessions	Proportion of transference interpretation	–.58*(within subgroup with high quality of object relations)
Connolly, Crits-Christoph, Shappell, et al. (1999)	29 patients	16 sessions	Proportion of transference interpretation	–.40*(within subgroup with low quality of interpersonal relationships)
Ogrodniczuk, Piper, Joyce, and McCallum (1999)	40 patients with mixed diagnosis	20 weeks	Frequency of transference interpretation	–.48*(within subgroup with low quality of object relations)

Note. A negative *r* indicates the finding was in the opposite direction from that hypothesized.
* $p < .05$; ** $p < .01$.

Two dismantling studies specifically evaluated the role of transference interpretations to the outcome of dynamic psychotherapy, although neither specifically looked at session process measures in relation to outcome. Høglend et al. (1993) randomized 43 patients with mixed diagnoses to dynamic psychotherapy that was either relatively high in the use of transference interpretations or where transference interpretation was avoided. There was a negative main effect for the use of high transference interpretation in the prediction of dynamic change at 4 years ($r = -.39$). Likewise, Høglend et al. (2008) randomized 100 patients with mixed diagnoses to 1 year of dynamic psychotherapy with or without the inclusion of transference interpretation. In this investigation, patients with poor quality of object relations had better outcomes, as assessed by psychodynamic functioning, in the condition that used high levels of transference interpretation.

There were also a small number of investigations that examined the role of other therapist activities beyond therapist interpretations. Multiple investigations used the Inventory for Therapeutic Strategies (Gaston & Ring, 1992) to rate the degree to which therapist interventions were exploratory versus supportive. Although this measure does not rate the utilization of dynamic interventions per se and could be easily applied to alternative therapeutic modalities, Gaston and Ring (1992) demonstrated that therapist interventions in dynamic psychotherapy were rated significantly higher on the exploratory scale than therapist interventions in cognitive-behavioral therapy. In contrast, therapist statements in cognitive-behavioral therapy were rated higher on the supportive subscale. Gaston, Piper, Debbane, Bienvenu, and Garant (1994) rated an early, middle, and late session of treatment for 32 patients with mixed diagnoses randomly assigned to either a 22-week short-term or a 24-month long-term dynamic psychotherapy. Although there were no significant effects for the ratings of exploratory interventions for the short-term group, patients with a better therapeutic alliance had improved therapeutic outcomes when the therapist interventions were rated higher (patient working capacity alliance subscale, $r = .50$; patient commitment subscale, $r = .40$) on the exploratory scale in the long-term dynamic psychotherapy condition. Gaston, Thompson, Gallagher, Cournoyer, and Gagnon (1998) further examined the degree to which therapist interventions were exploratory for 30 patients treated with brief dynamic psychotherapy as part of a randomized trial of brief dynamic therapy, cognitive therapy, and behavior therapy for elderly depressed patients. The average ratings on the exploratory scale were not significantly predictive of treatment outcome, but the ratings from Session 10 interacted significantly with patient working capacity to predict positive treatment outcome ($r = .30$).

Horowitz, Marmar, Weiss, DeWin, and Rosenbaum (1984) rated a variety of therapist activities in a sample of 52 bereavement patients treated with 12 sessions of dynamic psychotherapy for stress response syndromes. The therapist action checklist was rated by three independent judges on Sessions 2, 5, 8, and 11. None of the therapist activities significantly correlated with outcome, although multiple effects were moderated by patient characteristics. Greater levels of therapist interventions focusing on real versus fantasized meanings of the stressful event were significantly predictive of positive therapeutic outcome for patients rated lower on motivation ($r = .46$) and developmental level of self-concept ($r = .33$). In addition, greater levels of therapist actions that focused on relating reactions to parental figures to the therapist were significantly predictive of better treatment outcome for patients rated high on motivation ($r = .42$). Finally, Diener, Hilsenroth, and Weinberger (2007) conducted a meta-analysis of 10 investigations, which examined the role of therapist interventions that focused on affect in the process of short-term dynamic psychotherapy. They report a moderate average effect size ($r = .30$) for the prediction of outcome from therapist affective focus.

In summary, multiple investigations have specifically related the use of dynamic interventions, which were assessed directly from therapy process ratings, to the outcome of psychotherapy. For the proportion of dynamic interpretations, in general, there was a moderate average effect (mean $r = .50$) across two investigations demonstrating that more dynamic interpretations were associated with better treatment outcome. For transference interpretations specifically, there was a moderate negative effect (mean $r = -.49$) for higher levels of transference interpretations to predict poor treatment outcome for subsets of patients. For therapist affective focus, the meta-analysis by Diener et al. (2007) further suggests a moderate effect (mean $r = .30$) indicating that greater emphasis on affect within dynamic interventions may be predictive of better therapeutic outcome.

Overall, these results imply that the use of dynamic interpretations in general is related to positive therapeutic effects in dynamic psychotherapy, but that use of transference interpretations at particularly high levels might not be therapeutic for certain patients. These clinical implications are limited by the small number of investigations exploring this process outcome relationship and by methodological constraints. Most of these investigations explored the relation of proportion of dynamic interventions and outcome using mixed diagnostic outpatient samples, thus limiting the generalizability of results to specific diagnostic groups. In addition, only the Connolly, Crits-Christoph, Shappell, et al. (1999) investigation was able to examine the relation of transference interpretations to subsequent symptom course controlling for prior symptom change. The other investigations did not parse out the temporal relation between the variables, leaving open the possibility that therapists were able to use more dynamic interventions with cases that were progressing well (i.e., reverse causation). Many studies averaged the therapeutic process across sessions sampled across the full course of treatment, with no attention to the role of early symptom change on subsequent therapeutic process. Measures of counts of interventions are also likely to be influenced by therapist responsiveness. Therapists may be increasing the rate of interpretations, or transference interpretations, for patients who have not responded previously to such interpretations. This can attenuate the correlations between counts of interventions and outcome, or even produce negative correlations (i.e., more interpretations associated with poor outcome). This phenomenon may explain the inconsistency of effects across studies for transference interpretations. Finally, none of the studies reported the dependability of the process measures. Although three investigations sampled eight or more sessions, the Connolly, Crits-Christoph, Shappell, et al. (1999) study sampled only three sessions from the early sessions of treatment.

Therapist Quality of Interpretations

Beyond simple frequency of interventions, it may be more important to examine the average quality of dynamic interventions in the prediction of treatment outcome. It could be that the quality or accuracy of a therapist interpretation has more impact on the course of treatment than the raw number of interpretations implemented. Several studies have evaluated the relation between the quality of interpretations and the outcome of dynamic psychotherapy.

Silberschatz, Fretter, and Curtis (1986) conducted a small study of the extent to which therapist interpretations addressed each patient's strategy, or plan, for disconfirming pathogenic beliefs across three cases of chronic depression. The effects were small to moderate (range $r = .25$ to $.54$) across the three cases for the relation between the "plan" compatibility of therapist interventions and session outcomes. Norville, Sampson, and Weiss (1996) expanded this study to seven cases and found a significant correlation between the average plan compatibility of interpretations and the patient's self-reported plan attainment ratings ($r = .48$).

Two larger scale investigations also demonstrated significant associations between the quality of dynamic interpretations and therapeutic outcome. Crits-Christoph, Cooper, and Luborsky (1988) evaluated 43 patients with a variety of diagnoses engaged in dynamically oriented therapy ranging from 21 to 149 weeks. The therapists' average accuracy of interpreting the patients' wishes and response across three early sessions was significantly associated with treatment outcome ($r = .44$). Piper, Joyce, McCallum, and Azim (1993) found a small but significant association ($r = .22$) between the average correspondence of therapist interpretations and treatment outcome for 64 patients who received outpatient dynamic psychotherapy. However, when patients with a poor quality of object relations were examined separately, a moderate inverse relation was found ($r = -.49$) indicating that high correspondence of interpretations for patients with a history of poor relationships led to poor treatment outcome.

The small number of studies of quality of dynamic interpretations precludes drawing any definitive clinical inferences. The four studies that evaluated the quality of therapist interpretations all suggest that higher levels of therapist accuracy in interpreting interpersonal conflicts are predictive of better therapeutic outcome (mean $r = .42$). However, none of these investigations were able to demonstrate the causal pathway indicating that accurate interpretations cause positive outcome rather than the alternative explanation that cases that are improving allow therapists to provide more accurate interpretations. In addition, none of the investigations comment on the dependability of the process ratings, usually including ratings from three to eight sessions.

Furthermore, it is possible that the measures of "accuracy," "correspondence," and "plan compatibility" in the above studies are simply capturing therapist empathy, a more generic psychotherapy process variable, rather than anything specifically psychodynamic in nature.

Therapist Adherence and Competence

Nine investigations to date have evaluated the relation of therapist adherence scores to the outcome of dynamic psychotherapy, although some methodological issues and application of measures to a variety of distinct patient samples preclude firm conclusions at this point. Four investigations evaluated the relation between adherence to dynamic techniques and the outcome of dynamic psychotherapy for mixed diagnostic samples. Ogrodniczuk and Piper (1999; see also Ogrodniczuk, 1997) evaluated adherence to interpretive versus supportive techniques in a sample of 144 patients with mixed diagnoses treated by eight therapists in either of two dynamically oriented psychotherapies, interpretive psychotherapy, or supportive therapy. Adherence was assessed by one rater (from a pool of 10 raters) on odd number sessions and represented a relative emphasis on interpretive techniques versus supportive techniques. Adherence to interpretive techniques did not correlate significantly with treatment outcome ($r = .09$), but results are limited by the fact that only one judge was used per session and adherence was averaged across the entire treatment not accounting for the role of prior symptom change. DeFife, Hilsenroth, and Gold (2008) used patient ratings on the Comparative Psychotherapy Process Scale for 55 patients with mixed diagnoses treated with dynamic psychotherapy in a university-based community center. Patient adherence ratings from Session 3 correlated significantly with improvements in psychological well-being ($r = .30$) but not symptoms ($r = .10$). However, patient ratings of adherence may be particularly prone to responsiveness bias and may not capture the subtle aspects of treatment adherence recognized by experts.

Owen and Hilsenroth (2011) also evaluated adherence to dynamic techniques in a mixed diagnostic sample. The Comparative Psychotherapy Rating Scale was rated on one early session (number of judges not specified) for 68 cases treated with open-ended psychodynamic psychotherapy. The psychodynamic-interpersonal subscale did not significantly predict outcome as measured by the patient estimate of improvement ($r = .02$);

however, the psychodynamic-interpersonal scale significantly interacted with ratings of the therapeutic alliance ($r = .35$) in predicting therapeutic outcome, indicating that greater adherence to psychodynamic techniques in the context of a strong therapeutic alliance was associated with better treatment outcome. Also validating the importance of examining therapist adherence in the context of the therapeutic alliance, Spektor (2008) evaluated the role of adherence to brief relational therapy interventions specifically during alliance ruptures for 14 patients with mixed diagnoses. Adherence assessed by the Beth Israel Adherence Scale on 15-minute segments from an early rupture session and one late rupture session significantly predicted residual change on the SCL-90 ($r = .41$).

Two investigations specifically examined therapist adherence to dynamic psychotherapy for depressive disorders. Hilsenroth et al. (2003) had two independent judges rate adherence to psychodynamic-interpersonal techniques for seven sessions across 57 weeks using the Comparative Psychotherapy Process Scale for a sample of 29 patients with depressive disorders treated in open-ended psychodynamic therapy. Adherence to psychodynamic-interpersonal techniques significantly predicted reliable change on the SCL-90R ($r = .49$). Connolly Gibbons et al. (2012) evaluated the relation of treatment adherence to outcome for a sample of 32 patients treated in either supportive-expressive dynamic psychotherapy, or treatment as usual, in the treatment of MDD in a community mental health setting. There was a moderate significant effect ($r = .47$) for adherence to expressive techniques to predict change in depression across treatment for the full sample. These two investigations suggest that adherence to dynamic techniques may be predictive of symptom course for depressive disorders, although neither investigation adequately assessed the temporal course of the relation.

A variety of other specific diagnostic groups have a single study supporting an association between adherence to dynamic techniques and therapeutic outcome. Goldman and Gregory (2009) evaluated 10 patients with borderline personality disorder plus alcohol use disorders treated with 12 months of Dynamic Deconstructive Psychotherapy. Independent observer ratings of adherence for two raters averaged across ratings from Months 3, 6, 9, and 12 correlated significantly with outcome ($r = .64$), although results are limited by the inclusion of the author as a rater. Slavin-Mulford, Hilsenroth, Weinberger, and Gold (2011) rated the Comparative Psychotherapy Process Scale on one early session of open-ended psychodynamic psychotherapy for anxiety disorders. Ratings on the psychodynamic-interpersonal scale significantly predicted residual change on the brief symptom inventory ($r = .51$). Finally, Luborsky, McLellan, Woody, O'Brien, and Auerbach (1985) assessed adherence to dynamic psychotherapy for 41 drug dependent male veterans randomized to either supportive-expressive dynamic psychotherapy, cognitive-behavioral therapy, or drug counseling alone. Average adherence to dynamic techniques across three early sessions significantly predicted change on the SCL-90 ($r = .40$) across all treatments (correlations within treatment groups not specified).

These nine investigations of adherence to dynamic techniques suggest a moderate association between treatment adherence and therapeutic outcome (average $r = .37$). However, conclusions are limited by a number of methodological problems. The variety of diagnostic groups examined preclude conclusions about the role of therapist adherence in specific diagnostic groups, although two studies did demonstrate moderate effects (average $r = .31$) for the association between treatment adherence and outcome for depressive disorders. None of the investigations examined were able to adequately unpack the temporal course of change between symptoms and therapist adherence, limiting conclusions regarding the causal role of therapist adherence. It could be that therapists are able to use more adherent interventions with patients who are improving across the early sessions of treatment.

Ratings of therapist competence in utilizing dynamic interventions may be a more accurate assessment of the role of therapist interventions in the therapeutic process. Three investigations to date have specifically examined therapist competence in dynamic interventions. Svartberg and Stiles (1992) evaluated 15 highly educated patients with anxiety disorders treated with short-term anxiety provoking psychotherapy. A single rater assessed the fourth session of treatment. Therapist competence weighted by patient difficulty, was not significantly related to improvement ($r = .36$) but the small sample size limited the power to detect the effect. Barber, Crits-Christoph, and Luborsky (1996) evaluated a sample of 29 patients treated with 16 sessions of supportive expressive dynamic psychotherapy for MDD. Competence to dynamic interventions

was rated on audiotapes of Session 3 by trained independent judges and demonstrated a moderate effect ($r = .53$) in the prediction of subsequent depressive symptoms, controlling for symptom change that occurred prior to Session 3. Finally, Barber et al. (2008) evaluated therapist competence for 108 cocaine dependent patients treated with 24 weeks of supportive-expressive dynamic psychotherapy. For this patient sample, therapist adherence predicted worse drug use outcome ($r = -.21$) as did therapist competence ($r = -.20$).

There is some evidence that competence to dynamic interventions is predictive of the outcome of dynamic psychotherapy, at least for anxiety and depressive disorders. The variety of patient samples examined precludes drawing strong conclusions about specific diagnostic groups. Evidence is accumulating to support the role of adherence and competence to dynamic techniques specifically for patients with depressive disorders. In fact, the Barber et al. (1996) investigation is the only study of adherence or competence to dynamic techniques to specifically address the temporal relation between symptoms and therapist technique by showing that competence in dynamic interventions predicted subsequent symptom course after controlling for prior symptom reduction. Further research will be needed to definitively unpack the temporal relation between adherence and competence to dynamic techniques and treatment course. Finally, many studies assessed treatment adherence and competence at a single session. It is not likely that one early session is a large enough sample to provide a dependable estimate of the effect, suggesting that the relation between adherence and competence of dynamic techniques to the outcome of dynamic psychotherapy may actually be larger than suggested by these investigations.

Change Mechanisms in Dynamic Therapy

Studies of change mechanisms in dynamic therapy have focused on self-understanding, reflective functioning, or defenses. We summarize the literature on these change mechanisms in the next sections.

Change in Patient Self-Understanding

There is now a substantial body of research accumulating validating self-understanding of interpersonal patterns as a central change mechanism in dynamic psychotherapy. We summarize below research that evaluates whether self-understanding changes across dynamic psychotherapy, whether changes in self-understanding are predictive of therapeutic symptom course, and finally whether these changes are specific to psychotherapies that use dynamic interventions to specifically address interpersonal patterns.

Eight studies specifically evaluated the relation of change in self-understanding/insight to outcome across the course of dynamic psychotherapy. Seven of the eight investigations demonstrated significant change in self-understanding across the course of dynamic psychotherapy for a variety of patient samples including mixed diagnostic outpatients (Connolly Gibbons et al., 2009; Høglend, Engelstad, Sørbye, Heyerdahl, & Amlo, 1994; Johansson et al., 2010), patients with generalized anxiety disorder (Connolly, Crits-Christoph, Shelton, et al., 1999), patients with Cluster C personality disorders (Kallestad et al., 2010), patients seeking psychotherapy for relationship problems (Kivlighan, Multon, & Patton, 2000), and a mixed diagnostic sample of inpatients (Grande, Rudolf, Oberbracht, & Pauli-Magnus, 2003). Only one study (Crits-Christoph, 1984; Luborsky, Crits-Christoph, Mintz, & Auerbach, 1988) reported no significant change in self-understanding across dynamic psychotherapy, although this investigation evaluated change across a very short period of time from Session 3 to 5.

Three of these investigations also suggest that changes in self-understanding of interpersonal patterns are specific to dynamic psychotherapy. Connolly, Crits-Christoph, Shelton, et al. (1999) evaluated changes in self-understanding across 16 sessions of dynamic psychotherapy for generalized anxiety disorder compared to 16 weeks of medication. Self-understanding changed significantly more in the psychotherapy group compared to the medication group despite comparable changes in anxiety across the treatments. Connolly Gibbons et al. (2009) evaluated changes in self-understanding across a pooled database of 138 outpatients who participated in a pilot trial of dynamic psychotherapy, cognitive therapy, or a supportive control psychotherapy. There was significantly greater change in self-understanding in the dynamic psychotherapy group compared to the other treatment groups. Kallestad et al., (2010) evaluated changes in insight for 49 patients randomized to 40 weekly sessions of either short-term dynamic psychotherapy or cognitive therapy for cluster C personality disorders (Svartberg,

Stiles, & Seltzer, 2004). Insight rated by paired judges from videotapes of Sessions 6 and 36 demonstrated significant change within the dynamic psychotherapy group but no significant change within the cognitive therapy group. Across a variety of patient samples, research evidence is accumulating to support that changes in self-understanding of interpersonal patterns can be demonstrated through self-report and observer rated measures across dynamic psychotherapy. There are now three investigations that indicate that changes in self-understanding may be specific to the process of dynamic psychotherapy.

Table 9.5 summarizes the findings relating changes in self-understanding across the course of dynamic psychotherapy to therapeutic outcome for the investigations that demonstrated change in self-understanding across treatment. Five investigations demonstrated a small to moderate effect for change in self-understanding in relation to symptomatic course across treatment (mean $r = .52$). Høglend et al. (1994) reported a significant association between change in insight levels over a 2-year period of dynamic psychotherapy and a rating of overall dynamic change ($r = .60$) for a mixed diagnostic outpatient sample. Kivlighan et al. (2000) found that gains in insight, rated by independent judges based on patient responses to five questions following each session, were related to improvements in target complaints for 12 patients who had received 20 sessions of psychotherapy for relationship problems ($r = .53$). In this study, a time series analysis was used indicating that changes in insight at one session were followed by lower target complaints at the next therapy sessions, indicating a causal relationship between improvements in insight and symptom course. Grande et al. (2003) evaluated 49 clients who received 12 weeks of inpatient psychodynamic psychotherapy using the Heidelberg Structural Change Scale. Improvements in insight across a hierarchy from the problem being unconscious to dealing with the problem in a naturalistic fashion were significantly associated with positive changes in the patient's external life ($r = .42$).

For the dynamic psychotherapy subgroup of the Connolly Gibbons et al. (2009) investigation, there were small but significant effects for changes in self-understanding across treatment to predict improvements in depressive symptoms ($r = .46$) and quality of life ($r = .35$) using the revised Self-Understanding of Interpersonal Patterns scale. In addition, there was a small effect for changes

TABLE 9.5   Process-Outcome Effects for Change in Self-Understanding in Dynamic Psychotherapy

Study	Sample	Overall Treatment Length	Process Measures	Effect Size (r) With Outcome
Høglend et al. (1994)	43 patients with mixed diagnoses	2 years	Change in insight	.60*
Connolly et al. (1999)	33 patients with GAD	16 sessions	Change in self-understanding of interpersonal patterns	.01
Kivlighan et al. (2000)	12 patients with relationship problems	20 sessions	Change in insight	.53*
Grande et al. (2003)	49 inpatients with mixed diagnoses	12 weeks	Change in insight	.42*
Connolly Gibbons et al. (2009)	52 patients mixed diagnoses	4 months to 1 year	Change in self-understanding of interpersonal patterns	.46*
Johansson et al., 2010	100 patients with mixed diagnosis	1 year	Change in insight	.59*

Note. *$p < .05$.

in self-understanding across treatment to predict symptoms across the treatment follow-up period, controlling for symptomatic improvement across the treatment phase ($r = .51$). An investigation by Kallestad et al. (2010), not provided in Table 9.5 because the relevant statistics were not reported, found that change in insight from Session 6 to Session 36 significantly predicted symptom slope across the 2-year follow-up controlling for early symptom improvement across the first half of treatment for the short-term dynamic psychotherapy group.

Høglend et al. (2006) implemented an experimental design to evaluate the role of transference interpretations in the process of dynamic psychotherapy for patients with mixed diagnoses. One hundred patients were randomized to either dynamic therapy with transference interpretation or dynamic therapy without transference interpretations. The authors report that patients with low quality of object relations had greater improvements in the treatment that included transference interpretation, with later reports indicating that the effect was moderated by patient symptom severity and interpersonal problems (Høglend, Johansson, Marble, Bøgwald, & Amlo, 2007), gender (Ulberg, Johansson, Marble, & Høglend, 2009), and alliance (Høglend et al., 2011). Johansson et al. (2010) specifically examined observer ratings of insight in the Høglend et al. (2006) sample and found that change in

insight across treatment significantly predicted long-term improvement in interpersonal functioning. Johansson et al. (2010) further provide some evidence that changes in insight preceded changes in interpersonal functioning.

Only Connolly, Crits-Christoph, Shelton et al. (1999) found no relation between change in self-understanding and symptom course across dynamic psychotherapy for a sample treated with 16 sessions of dynamic psychotherapy for generalized anxiety disorder ($r = .01$). It should be noted that the lack of findings in this investigation might be a result of problems with the original self-understanding of interpersonal patterns scale used in this investigation. Connolly Gibbons et al. (2009) describe several limitations to this original measure including a ceiling effect for the measure that may have hindered the possibility of finding a process outcome correlation and that led to the development of the revised measure implemented by Connolly Gibbons et al. (2009).

In summary, a review of the literature suggests that changes in self-understanding are an important part of the therapeutic process of dynamic psychotherapy. Results suggest that across a variety of patient samples, self-understanding changes across dynamic psychotherapy, changes in self-understanding may be specific to dynamic therapy, and these changes in self-understanding are predictive of change in symptoms over the course of treatment.

Although these results are promising in validating this important therapeutic process, there is a substantial amount that we still do not know about the role of self-understanding in the process of psychotherapy. The studies reviewed here involve a variety of patient samples and mixed diagnostic groups. Although change in self-understanding is postulated to be an important part of the process of dynamic psychotherapies for a variety of disorders, patient diagnosis is likely to influence the degree of change achievable across treatment. More research is needed to understand the process of change in self-understanding for specific patient samples across specific time frames. Further, measurement of mechanism variables such as self-understanding is costly and time-consuming. None of the investigations reviewed specifically addressed the dependability of self-understanding assessments, with most studies including only a few assessment points, decreasing the possibility of a stable effect size estimate.

Further, much research is needed to understand the temporal course of changes in self-understanding in relation to symptom course and to understand the specificity of effects to dynamic interventions. Two investigations provide the first evidence that changes in self-understanding might proceed and predict subsequent symptom course. Investigations with repeated assessments of self-understanding and symptoms are needed to fully unpack this temporal relationship. The specificity of effects has been mostly overlooked in the literature relating process change to psychotherapy outcome. With a multitude of studies indicating that different therapeutic models are equally effective at producing symptom change, identifying whether changes in self-understanding are specific to dynamic psychotherapies will help validate that it is the active ingredient of dynamic psychotherapies that is responsible for the process outcome effects demonstrated. Finally, the studies that evaluate changes in self-understanding often rely on patient self-report measures outside of psychotherapy with the assumption that gains in skills can be attributed to the interventions that occur within the therapeutic hour. Studies that link the use of specific therapeutic techniques with gains in self-understanding and subsequent improvement in symptoms would be needed to definitively validate this central construct within models of dynamic psychotherapy.

Change in Reflective Functioning

Only recently have studies begun to explore changes in reflective functioning in the process of dynamic psychotherapy for personality disorders. Although Levy et al. (2006) demonstrated significant change in reflective functioning across transference focused psychotherapy, and showed specificity of such changes to the dynamic psychotherapy compared to dialectical behavior therapy, this investigation did not take the next step to explore the relation of changes in reflective functioning to symptom course. Only one investigation (Vermote et al., 2010) evaluated the relation of change in reflective functioning to the outcome of dynamic psychotherapy. This investigation evaluated 44 patients who received psychodynamic inpatient services for personality disorders. There was no evidence that reflective functioning changed across this inpatient treatment and change in reflective functioning was not associated with change in symptoms ($r = .03$).

It is too early to summarize any results for the role of changes in reflective functioning in the process of dynamic psychotherapy. Given the potential importance of this variable in helping patients with personality disorders to explore and unpack their impairing relationship conflicts, and the fact that Levy et al. (2006) demonstrated specificity of reflective functioning change to dynamic psychotherapy, this construct warrants further investigations as a mechanism of dynamic psychotherapy.

Change in Defenses

Only recently have investigations begun to explore changes in defensive functioning and its relation to the outcome of dynamic psychotherapy. Although a number of studies have evaluated the role of baseline defensive functioning in the course of dynamic psychotherapy, only four of these evaluated whether the changes in defenses hypothesized in dynamic models of psychotherapy predict symptom course. Winston, Samstag, Winston, and Muran (1994) evaluated changes in defenses across 40 sessions of dynamic psychotherapy for 28 patients with personality disorders. The frequency of intermediate defenses was assessed from the videotapes of four sessions sampled across the four quartiles of treatment. There was a small but significant effect for a decrease in intermediate defenses across dynamic psychotherapy to predict a composite outcome measure ($r = .28$). Bond and Perry (2004) also found a large effect for the relation between change in overall defensive function and decrease in depression for a sample of 53 patients with a variety of Axis I and Axis II disorders who engaged in 3 to 5 years of psychoanalytic psychotherapy ($r = .64$). Kramer, Despland, Michel, Drapeau, and deRoten (2010) found a moderately small but significant effect ($r = .37$) for improvements in overall defensive functioning in the predictions of change in symptoms for 32 university students treated with up to a year of therapy for adjustment disorders. Johansen, Krebs, Svartberg, Stiles, and Holen (2011) evaluated overall defensive functioning in the sample of 50 Cluster C personality disorder patients randomized to 40 sessions of either short-term dynamic psychotherapy or cognitive therapy (Svartberg et al., 2004). Change in overall defensive functioning significantly predicted change in symptoms from pretreatment to 2-year follow-up ($r = .34$).

The variability in effects demonstrated across these three investigations may be a result of the different patient populations sampled. Large effects were demonstrated for the studies that included patients with severe Axis I disorders and/or personality disorders where use of less mature defenses is hypothesized to be an important part of the psychopathology. In comparison, the study that demonstrated a very small effect for change in defensive functioning included patients with adjustment disorders for whom problems with immature defenses might not be central to the presenting problem. Although two studies demonstrate that changes in defensive functioning may be a very important part of the process of dynamic psychotherapy, at least for patients with personality disorders, more research is needed to understand the role of this therapeutic mechanism.

An important part of exploring changes in defensive functioning in the process of dynamic psychotherapy will be to unpack the temporal relation between changes in defensive functioning and symptom course. For the Bond and Perry (2004) investigation, change in defensive functioning was related to residual change in symptoms from Session 20 to treatment termination because symptom course was flat across the first 20 sessions with this seriously mentally ill sample. With such samples that demonstrate change across longer periods of time, it will be important to determine whether changes in defensive functioning proceed and predict symptom course or whether they are a result of decreased symptoms. The specific techniques, if any, that lead to reductions in defensive functioning also need further investigation.

THE PROCESS OF EXPERIENTIAL THERAPY

Experiential therapy (see Chapter 13, this volume) is another psychotherapeutic modality that has clear views on the curative processes that occur in psychotherapy sessions. Like exposure-based behavior therapy, in experiential therapy it is important that the patient activates, attends to, and tolerates emotions during therapy sessions. However, unlike exposure-based behavior therapy, experiential therapy also focuses on optimum emotional processing that involves the integration of cognition and affect. Therapists in experiential psychotherapy also encourage patients to explore, reflect on, and make sense of their emotions. This process includes exploring beliefs relating to emotions, giving voice to emotional experience, and identifying needs that can motivate change in personal meanings and beliefs (Elliott, Watson, Goldman, & Greenberg, 2004).

Process-outcome research on experiential therapy has been extensively reviewed previously (Elliott, Greenberg, & Lietaer, 2004). Central aspects of experiential therapy that have been examined in relation to outcome include emotional arousal and processing and therapist empathy. Other elements of the techniques and process of experiential therapy, such as two-chair dialogue, empty-chair dialogue, evocative unfolding, and creation of meaning in emotional crises, have largely been examined in terms of their immediate session outcome rather than eventual treatment outcome.

A number of early studies found that emotional processing, as measured by the Experiencing Scale (Klein, Mathieu, Gendlin, & Kiesler, 1969), was predictive of the outcome of client centered psychotherapy, a therapy that bears some similarity to experiential therapy (Elliott, Greenberg, et al., 2004). Studies of emotional processing in experiential therapy for depression have also found evidence linking higher levels in early sessions with treatment outcome ($r = .41$, Pos, Greenberg, Goldman, & Korman, 2003; $r = .44$, Watson & Bedard, 2006). A subsequent study by Pos, Greenberg, and Warwar (2009) that combined data from the Pos et al. (2003)

study with data from another study of experiential therapy for depression found that emotional processing in the "working" phase of treatment (between Session 4 and the fourth to last session) was particularly correlated ($r = .44$) with change in depressive symptoms. However, complicating studies of emotional processing is a recent finding that emotional arousal, a prerequisite for emotional processing, shows a nonlinear relation with outcome in experiential therapy, with a moderate level of emotional arousal being optimal (Carryer & Greenberg, 2010). In regard to therapist empathy, there has been consistent evidence linking empathy with treatment outcome in both experiential therapy and other therapies, with a mean r of .31 across studies (Elliott, Bohart, Watson, & Greenberg, 2011).

Despite evidence linking two key clinical aspects (emotional processing; therapist empathy) of the process of experiential therapy to outcome, studies of this treatment have failed to address the types of methodological issues that we have raised in this chapter. In particular, no studies of the process of experiential therapy have predicted outcome subsequent to the measurement of the process variables (controlling for prior improvement), nor have they examined the dependability of the process variables. Pos et al. (2003) report a correlation of .40 between emotional processing in Session 2 and the second to last session (of a 14 to 20 session treatment), suggesting that a single session measurement is likely to be inadequate to characterize the typical level of experiencing in a therapy dyad. No process-outcome studies of experiential therapy have yet used multilevel modeling to separate out therapist and patient contributions to correlations with outcome. Nevertheless, a number of other types of studies not reviewed here, primarily focusing on a microanalysis of significant events in experiential therapy, have provided some support for the important clinical constructs of experiential therapy (Elliott, 2010).

OVERALL SUMMARY

As we have mentioned, it is difficult to make firm clinical recommendations from correlational studies. In fact, there have been cases of serious errors in medicine occurring because of reliance on correlational studies. For example, many correlational studies appeared to show that women receiving hormone replacement therapy had relatively lower rates of coronary heart disease compared to women not receiving hormone replacement therapy. Based on these correlational data, doctors suggested to patients that hormone replacement therapy was protective against coronary heart disease. Randomized clinical trials subsequently showed the opposite: hormone replacement therapy resulted in a small increase in rates of coronary heart disease (Lawlor, Davey Smith, & Ebrahim, 2004). A confounding third variable (socioeconomic status, which was correlated with the tendency to exercise and have a healthier diet) produced the artifactual correlations between use of hormone replacement therapy and lower rates of coronary heart disease. Like this example, it may be that correlational studies that find that relatively higher levels of certain psychotherapy process variables are associated with better or worse treatment outcome are misleading due to unmeasured confounding variables.

Because of this inherent problem in correlational studies, we have reviewed process-outcome correlational studies of psychotherapy in this chapter with an eye toward studies that attempt to address at least one common confounding third variable: prior symptom improvement. We have also highlighted other methodological issues (therapist responsiveness, dependability of measurement over sessions, multilevel nature of psychotherapy) that can substantially alter the size and nature of correlations in process-outcome studies. Our conclusions from process-outcome correlational studies of psychotherapy are offered, therefore, not with confidence that such conclusions are definitively accurate, but as a snapshot of what the best available evidence suggests at this moment in time. We base our final conclusions on (a) consistent findings that are at least moderate in size and have been replicated across studies, and (b) where available, studies that have attempted to address the methodological issues we have raised.

The strongest conclusion that can be made from the large body of process-outcome studies is that the alliance is an important aspect of outcome across a range of psychotherapies. Studies of the alliance in relation to outcome have controlled for the influence of prior symptomatic improvement, have addressed dependability of measurement, and have begun to examine the alliance-outcome relation at both the patient and therapist level. No other areas of process-outcome research have addressed all three of these methodological issues.

A second conclusion is that arousal of emotion in exposure-based behavior therapy for anxiety disorders is likely to be an essential ingredient in achieving positive outcomes. Although studies on this topic have not controlled for prior improvement or examined dependability of measurement, the effect sizes are large and the finding is in the opposite direction (i.e., increasing fear in sessions leads to decreases in phobic fear by treatment termination) of what might be expected if it was due to a confound of prior improvement on the process variable.

A third tentative conclusion (because it is based on only two studies, but prior improvement was controlled in both) is that the use of "concrete" techniques in cognitive therapy for depression leads to better outcome. There is also some evidence that CT competence is related to outcome in the treatment of MDD. A fourth tentative conclusion is that gains in self-understanding lead to improvements in symptoms in psychodynamic therapy. This result has been replicated across studies, and change in self-understanding has been found to predict subsequent change in symptoms.

These empirical findings for the alliance, emotional arousal during behavior therapy for anxiety disorders, use of "concrete" techniques in CT for MDD, and gains in self-understanding in psychodynamic therapy, lead to our recommendation that clinicians attend to these processes as important determinants of treatment outcome. The findings for CT competence have clear relevance for the training and dissemination of CT: Training/dissemination programs should train to an acceptable level of competence and mechanisms for maintaining competence over time should be considered.

Of equal importance is what has not been adequately established about the mechanisms of various psychotherapies through process-outcome research. Despite the large outcome literature supporting the efficacy of CT for MDD and other disorders, the theory-relevant mediators of change in this treatment have not been demonstrated with reasonable certainty. In particular, evidence supporting the temporal sequence of cognitive changes preceding symptom change has remained elusive. It may be that this is simply a difficult question to address empirically because the time interval between cognitive change and symptom change is very short, or because the time interval varies from patient to patient. Most promising has been research showing that gains in compensatory skills over the course of CT for MDD predict subsequent symptom course

(relapse). This result, however, has only been found in one study to date, and other research suggests that the finding may not be specific to CT. Research on the role of therapist techniques in psychodynamic psychotherapy has also not reached our threshold for making clinical recommendations with confidence. There has been little attention to potential confounding factors in the studies of psychodynamic techniques in relation to outcome, particularly the role of prior improvement, with the exception of the study by Barber et al. (1996). Most studies are likely sampling too few treatment sessions (typically only one), and no investigations have examined the dependability over sessions of measures of psychodynamic techniques.

Based on our methodological critique of process-outcome studies, it would be easy to conclude that the large number of such studies has yielded little definitive evidence for the mechanisms of specific psychotherapies. However, the evidence base for theoretical mechanisms is building, with pieces of the puzzle beginning to fall into place for several psychotherapies. Our hope is that future studies will be able to complete the picture by addressing some of the methodological limitations of existing studies. These future process-outcome studies, taken together with empirical evidence from a wide range of other types of studies, will be crucial for refining existing treatment models and providing a better understanding of the nature of change in psychotherapy.

REFERENCES

Ablon, J. S., & Jones, E. E. (2002). Validity of controlled clinical trials of psychotherapy: Findings for the NIMH treatment of depression collaborative research program. *American Journal of Psychiatry, 159*, 775–783.

Baldwin, S. A., Wampold, B. E., & Imel, Z. E. (2007). Untangling the alliance-outcome correlation: Exploring the relative importance of therapist and patient variability in the alliance. *Journal of Consulting and Clinical Psychology, 75*, 842–852.

Barber, J. P. (2009). Toward a working through of some core conflicts in psychotherapy research. *Psychotherapy Research, 19*(1), 1–12.

Barber, J. P., Connolly, M. B., Crits-Christoph, P., Gladis, L., & Siqueland, L. (2000). Alliance predicts patients' outcome beyond in-treatment change in symptoms. *Journal of Consulting and Clinical Psychology, 68*(6), 1027–1032.

Barber, J. P., Crits-Christoph, P., & Luborsky, L. (1996). Effects of therapist adherence and competence on patient outcome in brief dynamic therapy. *Journal of Consulting and Clinical Psychology*, *64*(3), 619–622.

Barber, J. P., & DeRubeis, R. J. (1992). The ways of responding: A scale to assess compensatory skills taught in cognitive therapy. *Behavioral Assessment*, *14*(1), 93–115.

Barber, J. P., & DeRubeis, R. J. (2001). Change in compensatory skills in cognitive therapy for depression. *Journal of Psychotherapy Practice Research*, *10*(1), 8–13.

Barber, J. P., Gallop, R., Crits-Christoph, P., Barrett, M. S., Klostermann, S., McCarthy, K. S., & Sharpless, B. A. (2008). The role of the alliance and techniques in predicting outcome of supportive-expressive dynamic therapy for cocaine dependence. *Psychoanalytic Psychology*, *25*, 461–482.

Barber, J. P., Luborsky, L., Crits-Christoph, P., Thase, M. E., Weiss, R., Frank, A., . . . Gallop, R. (1999). Therapeutic alliance as a predictor of outcome in treatment of cocaine dependence. *Psychotherapy Research*, *9*(1), 54–73.

Baron, R. M., & Kenny, D. A. (1986). The moderator–mediator variable distinction in social psychological research: Conceptual, strategic, and statistical considerations. *Journal of Personality and Social Psychology*, *51*(6), 1173–1182.

Bateman, A. W., & Fonagy, P. (2003). The development of an attachment-based treatment program for borderline personality disorder. *Bulletin of the Menninger Clinic*, *67*(3), 187–211.

Beutler, L. E., Harwood, T. M., Michelson, A., Song, X., & Holman, J. (2011). Resistance/reactance level. *Journal of Clinical Psychology*, *67*, 133–142.

Bieling, P. J., Beck, A. T., & Brown, G. K. (2004). Stability and change of sociotropy and autonomy subscales in cognitive therapy of depression. *Journal of Cognitive Psychotherapy: An International Quarterly*, *18*(2), 135–148.

Bond, M., & Perry, J. C. (2004). Long-term changes in defense styles with psychodynamic psychotherapy for depressive, anxiety, and personality disorders. *American Journal of Psychiatry*, *161*(9), 1665–1671.

Bordin, E. S. (1979). The generalizability of the psychoanalytic concept of the working alliance. *Psychotherapy: Theory, Research & Practice*, *16*(3), 252–260.

Bryk, A., & Raudenbush, S. W. (1992). *Hierarchical linear modeling: Applications and data analysis methods*. Thousand Oaks, CA: Sage.

Cao, J. (2011). The credibility of psychotherapy: Psychological reactance and Chinese students' impressions of directive and nondirective approaches. *Dissertation Abstracts International: Section B: The Sciences and Engineering*. Retrieved from http://search.proquest.com/docview/62205 6886?accountid=14707

Carroll, K. M., Nich, C., Frankforter, T. L., & Bisighini, R. M. (1999). Do patients change in the ways we intend? Assessing acquisition of coping skills among cocaine-dependent patients. *Psychological Assessment*, *11*, 77–85.

Carryer, J. R., & Greenberg, L. S. (2010). Optimal levels of emotional arousal in experiential therapy of depression. *Journal of Consulting and Clinical Psychology*, *78*(2), 190–199.

Castonguay, L. G., Goldfried, M. R., Wiser, S., Raue, P. J., & Hayes, A. M. (1996). Predicting the effect of cognitive therapy for depression: A study of unique and common factors. *Journal of Consulting and Clinical Psychology*, *64*, 497–504.

Chaney, E. F., O'Leary, M. R., & Marlatt, G. A. (1978). Skill training with problem drinkers. *Journal of Consulting and Clinical Psychology*, *46*, 1092–1104.

Connolly, M. B., Crits-Christoph, P., Shappell, S., Barber, J. P., Luborsky, L., & Shaffer, C. (1999). The relation of transference interpretations to outcome in the early sessions of brief supportive-expressive psychotherapy. *Psychotherapy Research*, *9*(4), 485–495.

Connolly, M. B., Crits-Christoph, P., Shelton, R. C., Hollon, S., Kurtz, J. E., Barber, J. P., . . . Thase, M. E. (1999). The reliability and validity of a measure of self-understanding of interpersonal patterns. *Journal of Counseling Psychology*, *46*(4), 472–482.

Connolly Gibbons, M. B., Crits-Christoph, P., Barber, J. P., Wiltsey Stirman, S., Gallop, R., Goldstein, L. A., . . . Ring-Kurtz, S. (2009). Unique and common mechanisms of change across cognitive and dynamic psychotherapies. *Journal of Consulting and Clinical Psychology*, *77*(5), 801–813.

Connolly Gibbons, M. B., Thompson, S. M., Scott, K., Schauble, L. A., Mooney, T., Thompson, D., . . . Crits-Christoph, P. (2012). Supportive-expressive dynamic psychotherapy in the community mental health system: A pilot effectiveness trial for the treatment of depression. *Psychotherapy: Theory, Research, Practice, Training*, *49*(3), 303–316.

Craske, M. G., Kircanski, K., Zelikowsky, M., Mystkowski, J., Chowdhury, N., & Baker, A. (2008). Optimizing inhibitory learning during exposure therapy. *Behaviour Research and Therapy*, *46*(1), 5–27.

Crits-Christoph, P. (1984). *The development of a measure of self-understanding of core relationship themes*. Paper presented at NIMH workshop on methodological challenges in psychodynamic research, Washington, DC.

Crits-Christoph, P., Cooper, A., & Luborsky, L. (1988). The accuracy of therapists' interpretations and the outcome of dynamic psychotherapy. *Journal of Consulting and Clinical Psychology*, *56*(4), 490–495.

Crits-Christoph, P., Gallop, R., Temes, C. M., Woody, G., Ball, S. A., Martino, S., & Carroll, K. M. (2009). The alliance in motivational enhancement therapy and counseling as usual for substance use problems. *Journal of Consulting and Clinical Psychology*, 77(6), 1125–1135.

Crits-Christoph, P., Gibbons, M. B., Barber, J. P., Gallop, R., Beck, A. T., Mercer, D., . . . Frank, A. (2003). Mediators of outcome of psychosocial treatments for cocaine dependence. *Journal of Consulting and Clinical Psychology*, 71, 918–925.

Crits-Christoph, P., Gibbons, M. B. C., Hamilton, J., Ring-Kurtz, S., & Gallop, R. (2011). The dependability of alliance assessments: The alliance–outcome correlation is larger than you might think. *Journal of Consulting and Clinical Psychology*, 79(3), 267–278.

Crits-Christoph, P., Gibbons, M. B. C., Temes, C. M., Elkin, I., & Gallop, R. (2010). Interpersonal accuracy of interventions and the outcome of cognitive and interpersonal therapies for depression. *Journal of Consulting and Clinical Psychology*, 78(3), 420–428.

Crits-Christoph, P., & Singer, J. L. (1984). An experimental investigation of the use of positive imagery in the treatment of phobias. *Imagination, Cognition and Personality*, 3(4), 305–323.

Cronbach, L. J., Rajaratnam, N., & Gleser, G. C. (1963). Theory of generalizability: A liberalization of reliability theory. *British Journal of Statistical Psychology*, 16(2), 137–163.

DeFife, J. A., Hilsenroth, M. J., & Gold, J. R. (2008). Patient ratings of psychodynamic psychotherapy session activities and their relation to outcome. *Journal of Nervous and Mental Disease*, 196, 538–547.

DeRubeis, R. J., Brotman, M. A., & Gibbons, C. J. (2005). A conceptual and methodological analysis of the nonspecifics argument. *Clinical Psychology: Science and Practice*, 12(2), 174–183.

DeRubeis, R. J., & Feeley, M. (1990). Determinants of change in cognitive therapy for depression. *Cognitive Therapy and Research*, 14(5), 469–482.

Diener, M. J., Hilsenroth, M. J., & Weinberger, J. (2007). Therapist affect focus and patient outcomes in psychodynamic psychotherapy: A meta-analysis. *American Journal of Psychiatry*, 164, 936–941.

Doss, B. D. (2004). Changing the way we study change in psychotherapy. *Clinical Psychology: Science and Practice*, 11(4), 368–386.

Dozois, D. J. A., Bieling, P. J., Patelis-Siotis, I., Hoar, L., Chudzik, S., McCabe, K., & Westra, H. A. (2009). Changes in self-schema structure in cognitive therapy for MDD: A randomized clinical trial. *Journal of Consulting and Clinical Psychology*, 77(6), 1078–1088.

Eaton, T. T., Abeles, N., & Gutfreund, M. J. (1988). Therapeutic alliance and outcome: Impact of treatment length and pretreatment symptomatology.

Psychotherapy: Theory, Research, Practice, Training, 25(4), 536–542.

Elkin, I., Shea, M. T., Watkins, J. T., Imber, S. D., Sotsky, S. M., Collins, J. F., . . . Parloff, M. B. (1989). National institute of mental health treatment of depression collaborative research program: General effectiveness of treatments. *Archives of General Psychiatry*, 46(11), 971–982.

Elliott, R. (2010). Psychotherapy change process research: Realizing the promise. *Psychotherapy Research*, 20(2), 123–135.

Elliott, R., Bohart, A., Watson, J., & Greenberg, L. S. (2011). Empathy. *Psychotherapy*, 48(1), 43–49.

Elliott, R., Greenberg, L. S., & Lietaer, G. (2004). Research on experiential psychotherapies. In M. Lambert (Ed.), *Bergin and Garfield's handbook of psychotherapy and behavior change* (5th ed., pp. 493–539). Hoboken, NJ: Wiley.

Elliott, R., Watson, J. C., Goldman, R. N., & Greenberg, L. S. (2004). *Learning emotion-focused therapy: The process-experiential approach to change*. Washington, DC: American Psychological Association.

Farsimadan, F., Draghi-Lorenz, R., & Ellis, J. (2007). Process and outcome of therapy in ethnically similar and dissimilar therapeutic dyads. *Psychotherapy Research*, 17(5), 567–575.

Feeley, M., DeRubeis, R. J., & Gelfand, L. A. (1999). The temporal relation of adherence and alliance to symptom change in cognitive therapy for depression. *Journal of Consulting and Clinical Psychology*, 67(4), 578.

Fitzpatrick, M. R., Iwakabe, S., & Stalikas, A. (2005). Perspective divergence in the working alliance. *Psychotherapy Research*, 15(1–2), 69–79.

Foa, E. B., Grayson, J. B., Steketee, G. S., Doppelt, H. G., Turner, R. M., & Latimer, P. R. (1983). Success and failure in the behavioral treatment of obsessive-compulsives. *Journal of Consulting and Clinical Psychology*, 51(2), 287–297.

Foa, E. B., & Kozak, M. J. (1986). Emotional processing of fear: Exposure to corrective information. *Psychological Bulletin*, 99(1), 20–35.

Foa, E. B., Riggs, D. S., Massie, E. D., & Yarzower, M. (1995). The impact of fear activation and anger on the efficacy of exposure treatment for post-traumatic stress disorder. *Behavior Therapy*, 26(3), 487–499.

Freud, S. (1964). Studies on hysteria. In J. Strachey (Ed. and Trans.), *The standard edition of the complete psychological works of Sigmund Freud* (Vol. 2, pp. 3–181). London, United Kingdom: Hogarth.

Garratt, G., Ingram, R. E., Rand, K. L., & Sawalani, G. (2007). Cognitive processes in cognitive therapy: Evaluation of the mechanisms of change in the treatment of depression. *Clinical Psychology: Science and Practice*, 14(3), 224–239.

Gaston, L. (1990). The concept of the alliance and its role in psychotherapy: Theoretical and empirical considerations. *Psychotherapy*, 27, 143–153.

Gaston, L., Marmar, C. R., Gallagher, D., & Thompson, L. W. (1991). Alliance prediction of outcome beyond in-treatment symptomatic change as psychotherapy processes. *Psychotherapy Research, 1*(2), 104–112.

Gaston, L., Piper, W. E., Debbane, E. G., Bienvenu, J. P., & Garant, J. (1994). Alliance and technique for predicting outcome in short and long term analytic psychotherapy. *Psychotherapy Research, 4,* 121–135.

Gaston, L., & Ring, J. M. (1992). Preliminary results on the inventory of therapeutic strategies. *Journal of Psychotherapy Practice & Research, 1*(2), 135–146.

Gaston, L., Thompson, L., Gallagher, D., Cournoyer, L., & Gagnon, R. (1998). Alliance, technique, and their interactions in predicting outcome of behavioral, cognitive, and brief dynamic therapy. *Psychotherapy Research, 8,* 190–209.

Goates-Jones, M. (2006). Client preferences for insight-oriented and action-oriented psychotherapy. *Dissertation Abstracts International: Section B: The Sciences and Engineering.* Retrieved from http://search.proquest.com/docview/621576428?accountid=14707

Goldman, G. A., & Gregory, R. J. (2009). Preliminary relationships between adherence and outcome in dynamic deconstructive psychotherapy. *Psychotherapy: Theory, Research, Practice, Training, 46,* 480–485.

Grande, T., Rudolf, G., Oberbracht, C., & Pauli-Magnus, C. (2003). Progressive changes in patients' lives after psychotherapy: Which treatment effects support them? *Psychotherapy Research, 13,* 43–58.

Hamilton, M. (1960). A rating scale for depression. *Journal of Neurology, Neurosurgery & Psychiatry, 23,* 56–61.

Hawkins, J. D., Catalano, R. F., & Wells, E. A. (1986). Measuring effects of a skills training intervention for drug abusers. *Journal of Consulting and Clinical Psychology, 54,* 661–664.

Hayes, A. M., Castonguay, L. G., & Goldfried, M. R. (1996). Effectiveness of targeting the vulnerability factors of depression in cognitive therapy. *Journal of Consulting and Clinical Psychology, 64*(3), 623–627.

Hill, C. E., Helms, J. E., Tichenor, V., Spiegel, S. B., O'Grady, K. E., & Perry, E. S. (1988). Effects of therapist response modes in brief psychotherapy. *Journal of Counseling Psychology, 35*(3), 222–233.

Hill, C. E., & Lambert, M. J. (2004). Methodological issues in studying psychotherapy processes and outcomes. In M. Lambert (Ed.), *Bergin and Garfield's handbook of psychotherapy and behavior change* (5th ed., pp. 84–135). Hoboken, NJ: Wiley.

Hilsenroth, M. J., Ackerman, S. J., Blagys, M. D., Baity, M. R., & Mooney, M. A. (2003). Short-term psychodynamic psychotherapy for depression: An examination of statistical, clinically significant, and technique-specific change. *Journal of Nervous and Mental Disease, 191*(6), 349–357.

Hoffart, A., Hedley, L. M., Thornes, K., Larsen, S. M., & Friis, S. (2006). Therapists' emotional reactions to patients as a mediator in cognitive behavioural treatment of panic disorder with agoraphobia. *Cognitive Behaviour Therapy, 35*(3), 174–182.

Hofmann, S. G., Meuret, A. E., Rosenfield, D., Suvak, M. K., Barlow, D. H., Gorman, J. M., . . . Woods, S. W. (2007). Preliminary evidence for cognitive mediation during cognitive-behavioral therapy of panic disorder. *Journal of Consulting and Clinical Psychology, 75*(3), 374–379.

Høglend, P., Amlo, S., Marble, A., Bøgwald, K. P., Sørbye, Ø., Sjaastad, M. C., & Heyerdahl, O. (2006). Analysis of the patient-therapist relationship in dynamic psychotherapy: An experimental study of transference interpretations. *American Journal of Psychiatry, 163,* 1739–1746.

Høglend, P., Bøgwald, K. P., Amlo, S., Marble, A., Ulberg, R., Sjaastad, M. C., & Johansson, P. (2008). Transference interpretations in dynamic psychotherapy: Do they really yield sustained effects? *American Journal of Psychiatry, 165,* 763–771.

Høglend, P., Engelstad, V., Sørbye, Ø., Heyerdahl, O., & Amlo, S. (1994). The role of insight in exploratory psychodynamic psychotherapy. *British Journal of Medical Psychology, 67*(4), 305–317.

Høglend, P., Hersoug, A. G., Bøgwald, K. P., Amlo, S., Marble, A., Sørbye, Ø., . . . Crits-Christoph, P. (2011). Effects of transference work in the context of therapeutic alliance and quality of object relations. *Journal of Consulting and Clinical Psychology, 79,* 697 – 706.

Høglend, P., Heyerdahl, O., Amlo, S., Engelstad, V., Fossum, A., Sørbye, Ø., & Sørlie, T. (1993). Interpretations of the patient-therapist relationship in brief dynamic psychotherapy. *Effects on long-term mode specific changes. Journal of Psychotherapy Practice and Research, 2,* 296–306.

Høglend, P., Johansson, P., Marble, A., Bøgwald, K. P., & Amlo, S. (2007). Moderators of the effects of transference interpretations in brief dynamic psychotherapy. *Psychotherapy Research, 17,* 160–171.

Hollon, S. D., DeRubeis, R. J., Evans, M. D., Wiemer, M. J., Garvey, M. J., Grove, W. M., & Tuason, V. B. (1992). Cognitive therapy and pharmacotherapy for depression: Singly and in combination. *Archives of General Psychiatry, 49*(10), 774–781.

Hollon, S. D., Evans, M. D., & DeRubeis, R. J. (1990). Cognitive mediation of relapse prevention following treatment for depression: Implications of differential risk. In R. E. Ingram (Ed.), *Contemporary psychological approaches to depression: Theory, research, and treatment* (pp. 117–136). New York, NY: Plenum Press.

Horowitz, M., & Marmar, C. (1985). The therapeutic alliance with difficult patients. In R. Hales &

A. Frances (Eds.), *Psychiatry update annual review* (pp. 573–584). Washington, DC: American Psychiatric Press.

Horowitz, M. J., Marmar, C. R., Weiss, D. S., DeWin, K. N., & Rosenbaum, R. (1984). Brief psychotherapy of bereavement reactions: The relationship of process to outcome. *Archives of General Psychiatry*, *41*, 43–48.

Horvath, A. O. (2001). The alliance. *Psychotherapy: Theory, Research, Practice, Training*, *38*(4), 365–372.

Horvath, A. O., Del Re, A. C., Flückiger, C., & Symonds, D. (2011). Alliance in individual psychotherapy. *Psychotherapy*, *48*(1), 9–16.

Horvath, A. O., & Greenberg, L. S. (1989). Development and validation of the working alliance inventory. *Journal of Counseling Psychology*, *36*(2), 223–233.

Horvath, A. O., & Symonds, B. D. (1991). Relation between working alliance and outcome in psychotherapy: A meta-analysis. *Journal of Counseling Psychology*, *38*(2), 139–149.

Huppert, J. D., Barlow, D. H., Gorman, J. M., Shear, M. K., & Woods, S. W. (2006). The interaction of motivation and therapist adherence predicts outcome in cognitive behavioral therapy for panic disorder: Preliminary findings. *Cognitive and Behavioral Practice*, *13*(3), 198–204.

Ingram, R. E., & Hollon, S. D. (1986). Cognitive therapy for depression from an information processing perspective. In R. E. Ingram (Ed.), *Information processing approaches to clinical psychology* (pp. 259–281). San Diego, CA: Academic Press.

Jacobson, N. S., Dobson, K. S., Truax, P. A., Addis, M. E., Koerner, K., Gollan, J. K., ... Prince, S. E. (1996). A component analysis of cognitive-behavioral treatment for depression. *Journal of Consulting and Clinical Psychology*, *64*(2), 295–304.

Johansen, P. Ø., Krebs, T. S., Svartberg, M., Stiles, T. C., & Holen, A. (2011). Change in defense mechanisms during short-term dynamic and cognitive therapy in patients with cluster C personality disorders. *Journal of Nervous and Mental Disease*, *199*, 712–715.

Johansson, P. Høglend, P., Ulberg, R., Amlo, S., Marble, A., Bøgwald, K. P., ... Heyerdahl, O. (2010). The mediating role of insight for long-term improvements in psychodynamic therapy. *Journal of Consulting and Clinical Psychology*, *78*, 438–448.

Jones, E. E., & Pulos, S. M. (1993). Comparing the process in psychodynamic and cognitive-behavioral therapies. *Journal of Consulting and Clinical Psychology*, *61*(2), 306–316.

Kadden, R. M., Litt, M. D., Cooney, N. L., & Busher, D. A. (1992). Relationship between role-play measures of coping skills and alcoholism treatment outcome. *Addictive Behaviors*, *17*, 425–437.

Kallestad, H., Valen, J., McCullough, L., Svartberg, M., Høglend, P., & Stiles, T. C. (2010). The relationship between insight gained during therapy and long-term outcome in short-term dynamic psychotherapy and cognitive therapy for cluster C personality disorders. *Psychotherapy Research*, *20*, 526–534.

Karno, M. P., & Longabaugh, R. (2005). An examination of how therapist directiveness interacts with patient anger and reactance to predict alcohol use. *Journal of Studies on Alcohol*, *66*(6), 825–832.

Kivlighan, D. M. Jr., & Arthur, E. G. (2000). Convergence in client and counselor recall of important session events. *Journal of Counseling Psychology*, *47*(1), 79–84.

Kivlighan, D. M. Jr., Multon, K. D., & Patton, M. J. (2000). Insight and symptom reduction in time-limited psychoanalytic counseling. *Journal of Counseling Psychology*, *47*(1), 50–58.

Klein, D. N., Schwartz, J. E., Santiago, N. J., Vivian, D., Vocisano, C., Castonguay, L. G., ... Keller, M. B. (2003). Therapeutic alliance in depression treatment: Controlling for prior change and patient characteristics. *Journal of Consulting and Clinical Psychology*, *71*(6), 997–1006.

Klein, M. H., Mathieu, P. L., Gendlin, E. T., & Kiesler, D. J. (1969). *The Experiencing Scale: A research and training manual*. Madison, WI: Wisconsin Psychiatric Institute.

Kokotovic, A. M., & Tracey, T. J. (1990). Working alliance in the early phase of counseling. *Journal of Counseling Psychology*, *37*(1), 16–21.

Kozak, M. J., Foa, E. B., & Steketee, G. (1988). Process and outcome of exposure treatment with obsessive-compulsives: Psychophysiological indicators of emotional processing. *Behavior Therapy*, *19*(2), 157–169.

Kramer, U., Despland, J.-N., Michel, L., Drapeau, M., & de Roten, Y. (2010). Change in defense mechanisms and coping over the course of short-term dynamic psychotherapy for adjustment disorder. *Journal of Clinical Psychology*, *66*(12), 1232–1241.

Kuyken, W. (2004). Cognitive therapy outcome: The effects of hopelessness in a naturalistic outcome study. *Behaviour Research and Therapy*, *42*(6), 631–646.

Lang, P. J., Melamed, B. G., & Hart, J. (1970). A psychophysiological analysis of fear modification using an automated desensitization procedure. *Journal of Abnormal Psychology*, *76*(2), 220–234.

Lawlor, D. A., Davey Smith, G., & Ebrahim, S. (2004). Commentary: The hormone replacement-coronary heart disease conundrum: Is this the death of observational epidemiology? *International Journal of Epidemiology*, *33*(3), 464–467.

Levy, K. N., Meehan, K. B., Kelly, K. M., Reynoso, J. S., Weber, M., Clarkin, J. F., & Kernberg, O. F. (2006). Change in attachment patterns and reflective function in a randomized control trial of transference-focused psychotherapy for borderline personality disorder. *Journal of Consulting and Clinical Psychology*, *74*(6), 1027–1040.

Loeb, K. L., Wilson, G. T., Labouvie, E., Pratt, E. M., Hayaki, J., Walsh, B. T., . . . Fairburn, C. G. (2005). Therapeutic alliance and treatment adherence in two interventions for bulimia nervosa: A study of process and outcome. *Journal of Consulting and Clinical Psychology*, *73*, 1097–1107.

Luborsky, L. (1984). *Principles of psychoanalytic psychotherapy: A manual for supportive-expressive treatment*. New York, NY: Basic Books.

Luborsky, L., & Auerbach, A. (1985). The therapeutic relationship in psychodynamic psychotherapy: The research evidence and its meaning for practice. *Psychiatry Update: American Psychiatric Association Annual Review*, *4*, 550–561.

Luborsky, L., Crits-Christoph, P., Mintz, J., & Auerbach, A. (1988). *Who will benefit from Psychotherapy?* New York, NY: Basic Books.

Luborsky, L., McLellan, A. T., Woody, G. E., O'Brien, C. P., & Auerbach, A. (1985). Therapist success and its determinants. *Archives of General Psychiatry*, *42*, 602–661.

Malan, D. H. (1976). *Towards the validation of dynamic psychotherapy: Replication*. New York, NY: Plenum Medical Books.

Marmar, C. R., Horowitz, M. J., Weiss, D. S., & Marziali, E. (1986). The development of the therapeutic alliance rating system. In L. S. Greenberg & W. M. Pinsof (Eds.), *The psychotherapeutic process: A research handbook* (pp. 367–390). New York, NY: Guilford Press.

Martin, D. J., Garske, J. P., & Davis, M. K. (2000). Relation of the therapeutic alliance with outcome and other variables: A meta-analytic review. *Journal of Consulting and Clinical Psychology*, *68*(3), 438–450.

Marziali, E. A. (1984). Prediction of outcome of brief psychotherapy from therapist interpretive interventions. *Archives of General Psychiatry*, *41*, 301–304.

Marziali, E., Marmar, C., & Krupnick, J. (1981). Therapeutic alliance scales: Development and relationship to psychotherapy outcome. *American Journal of Psychiatry*, *138*(3), 361–364.

Neacsiu, A. D., Rizvi, S. L., & Linehan, M. M. (2010). Dialectical behavior therapy skills use as a mediator and outcome of treatment for borderline personality disorder. *Behaviour Research and Therapy*, *48*(9), 832–839.

Norville, R., Sampson, H., & Weiss, J. (1996). Accurate interpretations and brief psychotherapy outcome. *Psychotherapy Research*, *6*(1), 16–29.

Oei, T. P. S., & Sullivan, L. M. (1999). Cognitive changes following recovery from depression in a group cognitive–behaviour therapy program. *Australian and New Zealand Journal of Psychiatry*, *33*(3), 407–415.

Ogrodniczuk, J. S. (1997). Therapist adherence to treatment manuals and its relation to the therapeutic alliance and therapy outcome: Scale development and validation (Doctoral dissertation). Available from Pro-Quest Dissertations and Theses database. (UMI No. NQ23049)

Ogrodniczuk, J. S., & Piper, W. E. (1999). Measuring therapist technique in psychodynamic psychotherapies, development, and use of a new scale. *Journal of Psychotherapy Practice and Research*, *8*, 142–154.

Ogrodniczuk, J. S., Piper, W. E., Joyce, A. S., & McCallum, M. (1999). Transference interpretations in short-term dynamic psychotherapy. *Journal of Nervous and Mental Disease*, *187*, 571–578.

Orlinsky, D. E., Rønnestad, M. H., & Willutzki, U. (2004). Fifty years of psychotherapy process-outcome research: Continuity and change. In M. Lambert (Ed.), *Bergin and Garfield's handbook of psychotherapy and behavior change* (5th ed., pp. 307–389). Hoboken, NJ: Wiley.

Owen, J., & Hilsenroth, M. J. (2011). Interaction between alliance and technique in predicting patient outcome during psychodynamic psychotherapy. *Journal of Nervous and Mental Disease*, *199*, 384–389.

Piper, W. E., Azim, H. F., Joyce, A. S., & McCallum, M. (1991). Transference interpretations, therapeutic alliance, and outcome in short-term individual psychotherapy. *Archives of General Psychiatry*, *48*(10), 946–953.

Piper, W. E., Debbane, E. G., de Carufel, F. L., & Bienvenu, J. P. (1987). A system for differentiating therapist interpretations from other interventions. *Bulletin of the Menninger Clinic*, *51*(6), 532–550.

Piper, W. E., Joyce, A. S., McCallum, M., & Azim, H. F. (1993). Concentration and correspondence of transference interpretations in short-term psychotherapy. *Journal of Consulting and Clinical Psychology*, *61*(4), 586–595.

Pitman, R. K., Orr, S. P., Altman, B., & Longpre, R. E. (1996). Emotional processing and outcome of imaginal flooding therapy in Vietnam veterans with chronic posttraumatic stress disorder. *Comprehensive Psychiatry*, *37*(6), 409–418.

Pos, A., Greenberg, L. S., Goldman, R. N., & Korman, L. M. (2003). Emotional processing during experiential treatment of depression. *Journal of Consulting and Clinical Psychology*, *71*(6), 1007–1016.

Pos, A., Greenberg, L. S., & Warwar, S. H. (2009). Testing a model of change in the experiential treatment of depression. *Journal of Consulting and Clinical Psychology*, *77*(6), 1055–1066.

Quilty, L. C., McBride, C., & Bagby, R. M. (2008). Evidence for the cognitive meditational model of cognitive behavioural therapy for depression. *Psychological Medicine*, *38*(11), 1331–1341.

Rauch, S. A. M., Foa, E. B., Furr, J. M., & Filip, J. C. (2004). Imagery vividness and perceived anxious arousal in prolonged exposure treatment for PTSD. *Journal of Traumatic Stress*, *17*(6), 461–465.

Rossberg, J. I., Karterud, S., Pedersen, G., & Friis, S. (2010). Psychiatric symptoms and countertransference feelings: An empirical investigation. *Psychiatry Research*, *178*(1), 191–195.

Ryum, T., Stiles, T. C., & Vogel, P. A. (2009). Therapeutic alliance as a predictor of outcome in the treatment of depression and anxiety disorders. *Journal of the Norwegian Psychological Association*, *46*, 651–657.

Segal, Z. V., & Gemar, M. (1997). Changes in cognitive organisation for negative self-referent material following cognitive therapy for depression: A primed Stroop study. *Cognition and Emotion*, *11*(5–6), 501–516.

Seligman, M. E. P., Castellon, C., Cacciola, J., Schulman, P., Luborsky, L., Ollove, M., & Downing, R. (1988). Explanatory style change during cognitive therapy for unipolar depression. *Journal of Abnormal Psychology*, *97*(1), 13–18.

Shavelson, R. J., & Webb, N. M. (1991). Generalizability theory: A primer. *Measurement methods for the social sciences series* (Vol. *1*). Thousand Oaks, CA: Sage.

Shaw, B. F., Elkin, I., Yamaguchi, J., Olmsted, M., Vallis, T. M., Dobson, K. S., . . . Imber, S. D. (1999). Therapist competence ratings in relation to clinical outcome in cognitive therapy of depression. *Journal of Consulting and Clinical Psychology*, *67*(6), 837–846.

Silberschatz, G., Fretter, P. B., & Curtis, J. T. (1986). How do interpretations influence the process of psychotherapy? *Journal of Consulting and Clinical Psychology*, *54*(5), 646–652.

Simon, W., & Siwiak-Kobayashi, M. (2008). The motivational factors of activity versus helplessness and the psychotherapeutic change. *Archives of Psychiatry and Psychotherapy*, *10*(3), 51–60.

Slavin-Mulford, J., Hilsenroth, M., Weinberger, J., & Gold, J. (2011). Therapeutic interventions related to outcome in psychodynamic psychotherapy for anxiety disorder patients. *Journal of Nervous & Mental Disease*, *199*, 214–221.

Smits, J. A. J., Powers, M. B., Cho, Y., & Telch, M. J. (2004). Mechanism of change in cognitive-behavioral treatment of panic disorder: Evidence for the fear of fear mediational hypothesis. *Journal of Consulting and Clinical Psychology*, *72*(4), 646–652.

Smits, J. A., Rosenfield, D., McDonald, R., & Telch, M. J. (2006). Cognitive mechanisms of social anxiety reduction: An examination of specificity and temporality. *Journal of Consulting & Clinical Psychology*, *74*(6), 1203–1212.

Spektor, D. (2008). Therapists' adherence to manualized treatments in the context of ruptures (Doctoral dissertation). Dissertations and Theses database. (UMI No. 3333897).

Steketee, G., Siev, J., Fama, J. M., Keshaviah, A., Chosak, A., & Wilhelm, S. (2011). Predictors of treatment outcome in modular cognitive therapy for obsessive-compulsive disorder. *Depression and Anxiety*, *28*(4), 333–341.

Stiles, W. B. (1988). Psychotherapy process-outcome correlations may be misleading. *Psychotherapy: Theory, Research, Practice, Training*, *25*(1), 27–35.

Stiles, W. B., Honos-Webb, L., & Surko, M. (1998). Responsiveness in psychotherapy. *Clinical Psychology: Science and Practice*, *5*(4), 439–458.

Strunk, D. R., Brotman, M. A., DeRubeis, R. J., & Hollon, S. D. (2010). Therapist competence in cognitive therapy for depression: Predicting subsequent symptom change. *Journal of Consulting and Clinical Psychology*, *78*(3), 429–437.

Strunk, D. R., DeRubeis, R. J., Chiu, A. W., & Alvarez, J. (2007). Patients' competence in and performance of cognitive therapy skills: Relation to the reduction of relapse risk following treatment for depression. *Journal of Consulting and Clinical Psychology*, *75*(4), 523–530.

Strupp, H. H., & Binder, J. L. (1984). *Psychotherapy in a new key: A guide to time-limited psychotherapy*. New York, NY: Basic Books.

Svartberg, M., & Stiles, T. C. (1992). Predicting patient change from therapist competence and patient-therapist complementarity in short-term anxiety-provoking psychotherapy: A pilot study. *Journal of Consulting and Clinical Psychology*, *60*(2), 304–307.

Svartberg, M., Stiles, T. C., & Seltzer, M. H. (2004). Randomized, controlled trial of the effectiveness of short-term dynamic psychotherapy and cognitive therapy for cluster C personality disorders. *American Journal of Psychiatry*, *161*(5), 810–817.

Swift, J., & Callahan, J. (2009). Early psychotherapy processes: An examination of client and trainee clinician perspective convergence. *Clinical Psychology & Psychotherapy*, *16*, 228–236.

Teasdale, J. D., Scott, J., Moore, R. G., Hayhurst, H., Pope, M., & Paykel, E. S. (2001). How does cognitive therapy prevent relapse in residual depression? Evidence from a controlled trial. *Journal of Consulting and Clinical Psychology*, *69*(3), 347–357.

Trepka, C., Rees, A., Shapiro, D. A., Hardy, G. E., & Barkham, M. (2004). Therapist competence and outcome of cognitive therapy for depression. *Cognitive Therapy and Research*, *28*(2), 143–157.

Ulberg, R., Johansson, P., Marble, A., & Høglend, P. (2009). Patient sex as moderator of effects of transference interpretation in a randomized controlled study of dynamic psychotherapy. *Canadian Journal of Psychiatry*, *54*, 78–86.

Van Minnen, A., & Hagenaars, M. (2002). Fear activation and habituation patterns as early process predictors of response to prolonged exposure treatment in PTSD. *Journal of Traumatic Stress*, *15*(5), 359–367.

Vermote, R., Lowyck, B., Luyten, P., Vertommen, H., Corveleyn, J., Verhaest, Y., . . . Peuskens, J.

(2010). Process and outcome in psychodynamic hospitalization-based treatment for patients with a personality disorder. *Journal of Nervous and Mental Disease*, *198*(2), 110–115.

Vogel, P. A., Hansen, B., Stiles, T. C., & Götestam, K. G. (2006). Treatment motivation, treatment expectancy, and helping alliance as predictors of outcome in cognitive behavioral treatment of OCD. *Journal of Behavior Therapy and Experimental Psychiatry*, *37*(3), 247–255.

Vögele, C., Ehlers, A., Meyer, A. H., Frank, M., Hahlweg, K., & Margraf, J. (2010). Cognitive mediation of clinical improvement after intensive exposure therapy of agoraphobia and social phobia. *Depression and Anxiety*, *27*, 294–301.

Watson, J. C., & Bedard, D. L. (2006). Clients' emotional processing in psychotherapy: A comparison between cognitive-behavioral and process-experiential therapies. *Journal of Consulting and Clinical Psychology*, *74*(1), 152–159.

Watson, J. P., & Marks, I. M. (1971). Relevant and irrelevant fear in flooding: A crossover study of phobic patients. *Behavior Therapy*, *2*(3), 275–293.

Webb, C. A., DeRubeis, R. J., Amsterdam, J. D., Shelton, R. C., Hollon, S. D., Dimidjian, S. (2011). Two aspects of the therapeutic alliance: Differential relations with depressive symptom change. *Journal of Consulting and Clinical Psychology*, *79*(3), 279–283.

Webb, C. A., DeRubeis, R. J., & Barber, J. P. (2010). Therapist adherence/competence and treatment outcome: A meta-analytic review. *Journal of Consulting and Clinical Psychology*, *78*(2), 200–211.

Wells, E. A., Peterson, P. L., Gainey, R. R., Hawkins, J. D., & Catalano, R. F. (1994). Outpatient treatment for cocaine abuse: A controlled comparison of relapse prevention and Twelve Step approaches. *American Journal of Drug and Alcohol Abuse*, *20*, 1–17.

Westra, H. A., Constantino, M. J., Arkowitz, H., & Dozois, D. J. A. (2011). Therapist differences in cognitive–behavioral psychotherapy for generalized anxiety disorder: A pilot study. *Psychotherapy*, *48*(3), 283–292.

Wilson, G. T., Fairburn, C. G., Agras, W. S., Walsh, B. T., & Kraemer, H. C. (2002). Cognitive behavior therapy for bulimia nervosa: Time course and mechanisms of change. *Journal of Consulting and Clinical Psychology*, *70*, 267–274.

Winston, B., Samstag, L. W., Winston, A., & Muran, J. C. (1994). Patient defense/therapist interventions. *Psychotherapy: Theory, Research, Practice, Training*, *31*(3), 478–491.

Zuroff, D. C., & Blatt, S. (2006). The therapeutic relationship in the brief treatment of depression: Contributions to clinical improvement and enhanced adaptive capacities. *Journal of Consulting and Clinical Psychology*, *74*(1), 130–140.

PART III

MAJOR APPROACHES

CHAPTER 10

BEHAVIOR THERAPY WITH ADULTS

PAUL M. G. EMMELKAMP

This chapter provides an overview of the current status of behavior therapy with adult disorders. Emphasis throughout is on the application of behavioral procedures on clinical patients. Separate chapters in this volume are devoted to health psychology, behavior therapy with children, and (behavioral) marital therapy for marital distress, so these topics are not dealt with in this chapter. Cognitive interventions are covered only insofar as they are contrasted with behavioral procedures or form an integral part of cognitive-behavioral procedures. For a more detailed discussion of cognitive therapy, the reader is referred to Chapter 11 (this volume). As an aside, to separate procedures that are purely behavioral from procedures that are purely cognitive is rather artificial. Most cognitive procedures have clear behavioral techniques in them, and although less obvious, most behavioral procedures also contain cognitive elements.

In the early days of behavior therapy the emphasis was on the idiosyncratic approach: the individualized case formulation, firmly based in theory (Sturmey, 2007). Evidently, the once close relationship between theory and practice in behavior therapy has changed considerably over the past decades. Today the dominant paradigm is the evidence-based treatment paradigm. This is a normative approach with an emphasis on group means rather than on individual cases. Throughout the years both the normative and the idiosyncratic approaches have had their proponents, but the relative emphasis has changed considerably over time (Emmelkamp, Ehring, & Power, 2010).

The scope of this chapter is limited to those disorders for which the behavioral approach has been most influential. As in previous editions of this handbook, this chapter reviews the state-of-the-art of current behavioral procedures for anxiety disorders, depression, substance abuse, and personality disorders. Given that research into behavioral interventions for sexual dysfunction and schizophrenia has not substantially advanced since the last edition (Emmelkamp, 2004), these subjects are not reviewed.

ANXIETY DISORDERS

In this section the principles of behavioral treatment strategies for simple phobia, panic disorder with agoraphobia, social phobia, obsessive compulsive disorder, generalized anxiety disorder and posttraumatic stress disorder are presented, followed by a review of empirical findings on their effectiveness.

Exposure therapy for anxiety disorders consists of exposing patients to situations they fear (Emmelkamp, 1982). Others use a more broad definition of exposure, for example, Brady and Raines (2009), who describe exposure therapy as a process of "deliberately confronting some ordinarily avoided stimulus that provokes an undesired response, in order to reduce the strength of that response" (p. 51). Cognitive therapists acknowledge the value of exposure as an important element in cognitive therapy (e.g., Clark, 1999). Similarly, also in acceptance-based approaches exposure is seen as an important component of therapy (Orsillo, Roemer, Block Lerner, & Tull, 2004).

Exposure as treatment for anxiety disorders can be carried out in three ways: (1) in imagination, in which patients must imagine themselves to be in a fearful situation, (2) in vivo, in which patients are actually exposed to this situation, or (3) in virtual reality, in which patients are exposed to virtual environments. The treatment is based on the notion that anxiety subsides through a process of habituation after a person has been exposed to a fearful situation for a prolonged period of time, without trying to escape. According to the emotional processing theory (Foa, Huppert, & Cahill, 2006; Foa & Kozak, 1986) two basic conditions have to be fulfilled for successful therapy. The fear structure of the patient has to be activated and information, which is incompatible with the existing anxiety structure has to be presented and emotionally processed. Habituation of fear plays a key role as shown in (a) within-session habituation, as reflected in decreases in the magnitude of fear indices; and (b) between-session habituation, as reflected in gradual reductions in the peak anxiety across sessions.

Considerable evidence exists, on subjective as well as on physiological measures, that anxiety decreases by staying in the situation, a process that is called *extinction of fear* or *habituation*. Exposure in vivo is usually more effective than exposure in imagination (for review see Emmelkamp, 1994). Other important variables in exposure treatments are the degree of anxiety and the duration of exposure trials. Exposure tasks can be ordered hierarchically from low anxiety to high anxiety (gradual exposure) or patients can be confronted with the most difficult situation from the start (flooding). Exposure can be either self-controlled (i.e., patients decide for themselves when to enter a more difficult situation), or controlled by the therapist. The most succesful programs are those carried out in vivo, during a long uninterrupted period of time (prolonged), and in which escape and avoidance of the situation are prevented (van Hout & Emmelkamp, 2002).

If anxious patients escape the situation that they fear, anxiety usually will subside. This escape behavior, however, will reinforce the anxiety and hence lead to further avoidance and escape behavior in the future. Therefore, in exposure programs it is often necessary to deal with this escape behavior by response prevention, which means that the patients are no longer allowed to perform escape behavior. Response prevention is an essential part of treatment with obsessive-compulsive disorder, but also plays a part in the treatment of social phobia and agoraphobia.

The Process of Exposure

Exposure is usually explained in terms of habituation. Habituation refers to a decline in fear responses, particularly the physiological responses, overrepeated exposures to fear-provoking stimuli. The classical habituation theory predicts that habituation would not occur if (baseline) arousal was high. Then, arousal would further increase and lead to *sensitization* (i.e., increase in fear responses after repeated exposures to fear-provoking stimuli). However, the literature revealed that a reduction instead of a further increase in psychophysiological and subjective anxiety could be expected, for instance, during exposure to high fear-provoking stimuli (e.g., flooding therapy). Recent habituation theories have been extended to accommodate these findings. These dual-process theories decribe complex interactions between habituation and sensitization, in which habituation can eventually occur after exposure to high fear-provoking stimuli (van Hout & Emmelkamp, 2002).

Several studies have provided supportive evidence for the role of habituation in exposure therapy, with self-reported fear and physiological arousal showing a declining trend across exposures, consistent with habituation (e.g., Meyerbröker, Powers, van Steegeren, & Emmelkamp, 2012; van Hout, Emmelkamp, & Scholing, 1994). Results of studies investigating whether within session habituation and between session habituation are associated with outcome are inconclusive (Craske et al., 2008; Norton, Hayes-Skelton, & Klenck, 2011). There is some evidence that indicators of emotional processing may be more related to outcome during the later exposure sessions than during the initial exposure session (e.g., Hayes, Hope, & Heimberg, 2008).

The success of exposure in vivo has also been explained by the acquisition of fresh, disconfirmatory evidence, which weakens the catastrophic cognitions. From this perspective, exposure is viewed as a critical intervention through which catastrophic cognitions may be tested. This is in line with the cognitive therapy based on the perceived danger theory according to Beck and colleagues (Beck, Emery, & Greenberg, 1985). Within this model, exposure (i.e., behavioral experiments) is generally regarded as a necessity for testing the validity of dysfunctional thoughts next to other strategies such as Socratic questioning of probabilities.

Clinicians hold that cognitive avoidance during exposure is detrimental to its effects.

Distraction is one of the safety measures used by phobic patients. As predicted by the emotional processing theory of Foa and Kozak (1986), a number of studies have shown that distraction during exposure inhibits habituation, but results are inconclusive (see Emmelkamp, 2004). For example, Johnstone and Page (2004) found that distraction of the patient during exposure enhanced successful fear reduction. As suggested by Foa et al. (2006), whether distraction helps or hinders emotional processing may depend on the type of anxiety disorder. Although distraction might facilitate progress in exposure for specific phobia, it might hinder progress in exposure for agoraphobia, social phobia, and obsessive-compulsive disorder.

SPECIFIC PHOBIA

Specific phobias are especially responsive to behavioral treatment; exposure therapy has proven successful in alleviating symptoms of specific phobia (Emmelkamp, 2004). Since the first controlled studies had demonstrated the effectiveness of one session of exposure in vivo in specific phobias (Emmelkamp & Felten, 1985; Öst, Salkovskis, & Hellström, 1991), results have been replicated in a large number of studies for a variety of specific phobias (see Zlomke & Davis, 2008). Öst's one-session exposure procedure involves cognitive and behavioral interventions to facilitate change, but it is unclear what the additional benefit of cognitive interventions is. Neither in the study of Emmelkamp and Felten (1985) nor in a study of Koch, Spates, and Himleb (2004) led the addition of cognitive methods to the one-session exposure treatment to enhancement of outcomes in terms of behavioral, cognitive, and somatic phobic symptoms. Also in a recent study (Raes, Koster, Loeys, & De Raedt, 2011), in which pure exposure in vivo was compared with exposure in vivo framed within a cognitive context, were both treatments equally effective. Interestingly, in the Koch et al. (2004) study and the Raes et al. (2011) study both treatments were equally effective in promoting cognitive change, which does not support the idea that cognitions have to be explicitly challenged to elicit cognitive change in exposure treatment.

Blood Injury Phobia

Although prolonged exposure in vivo seems to be the treatment of choice for most specific phobias, it has been suggested that in blood-injury phobia additional measures may be required, given the unusual pattern of physiological responses. Instead of an increase in heart rate and respiration as typically seen in phobics, blood phobics show bradycardia and a decrease in blood presure, which may result in fainting (but see Ritz, Meuret, & Ayala, 2010). In such cases adding applied tension to exposure in vivo has been recommended. With applied tension, patients are taught to tense their muscles when exposed to a series of slides of wound injuries and blood. In later sessions, patients have to donate blood and observe open-heart or lung surgery. Patients learn to recognize the earliest sign of a drop in blood pressure and to apply the tension technique to reverse it. Although Öst, Fellenius, and Sterner (1991) reported that exposure plus applied tension was more effective than exposure to blood stimuli alone, more recent studies, however, are inconclusive. In contrast to the generally accepted view that in blood-injury phobias applied tension is superior to exposure alone, this is not corroborated by a number of recent controlled studies (Ayala, Meuret, & Ritz, 2009). Actually, exposure in vivo outperformed other treatments, including applied tension, on measures of the degree of phobia.

Virtual Reality Exposure

There is now robust evidence that exposure can be conducted using virtual reality technology. Virtual reality (VR) integrates real-time computer graphics, body tracking devices, visual displays, and other sensory inputs to immerse individuals in a computer-generated virtual environment. VR exposure has several advantages over exposure in vivo. The treatment can be conducted in the therapist's office rather than the therapist and patient having to go outside to do the exposure exercises in real phobic situations. Hence, treatment may be more cost-effective than therapist-assisted exposure in vivo. Further, VR treatment can also be applied on patients who are too anxious to undergo real-life exposure in vivo.

Especially in specific phobias virtual reality exposure therapy has been found to be at least as effective as the state-of-the-art treatment exposure in vivo (see Meyerbröker & Emmelkamp, 2010; Powers & Emmelkamp, 2008). It should be noted that most of the randomized controlled trials (RCTs) within this research field have been limited to subjects with acrophobia and fear of flying. Research concerning the effectiveness of virtual reality exposure therapy (VRET) in other specific phobias has hardly been conducted.

In sum, VRET is an effective treatment for acrophobia and fear of flying. In fear of flying clear advantages in costs are obvious, because treatment can be done in virtual airplanes, rather than having to take a real flight.

Cognitive Enhancers

A new class of drugs (cognitive enhancers) holds particular promise for the future. Examples of novel pharmacological enhancers include d-cycloserine, yohimbine hydrochloride, methylene blue, and oxytocin. D-cycloserine (DCS) is a partial n-methyl-d-aspartate (NMDA) glutamate agonist. Administration of DCS prior to exposure therapy enhances treatment outcome among patients with height phobia (Ressler et al., 2004).

Yohimbine hydrochloride is a selective alpha2-adrenergic receptor antagonist that enhances extinction learning in animals (Morris & Bouton, 2007). In the first study of yohimbine in humans Powers and colleagues (2009) showed that yohimbine administration prior to exposure-based treatment of claustrophobic participants enhanced treatment outcome at medication free follow-up (Powers et al., 2009), but results were not replicated in patients with fear of flying (Meyerbröker et al., 2012). Studies are currently underway in other anxiety disorders.

PANIC DISORDER AND AGORAPHOBIA

Panic disorder is characterized by recurrent panic attacks, which are discrete periods of intense fear and discomfort, often occurring unexpectedly. Panic attacks are accompanied by a number of symptoms, such as shortness of breath, dizziness, palpitations, trembling, sweating, choking, abdominal distress, depersonalization or derealization, fear of dying, or fear of going crazy. Panic disorder often leads to extensive avoidance behavior, because these patients fear being in places or situations from which it is difficult to escape, or in which there is no help at hand in case of a panic attack.

Exposure in Vivo

There exists a number of evidence-based interventions focusing either on panic or the agoraphobic avoidance behavior. One core element in most treatments is exposure to anxiety arousing cues. *Exposure* therapy in the case of agoraphobia consists of exposing patients to situations they fear. Exposure in vivo is well documented in numerous randomized controlled clinical trials (see reviews and meta-analyses by Craske & Barlow, 2007; Emmelkamp & Powers, 2010; Mitte, 2005a; Sánchez-Meca, Rosa-Alcázar, Marin-Martínez, & Gómez-Conesa, 2010). Results of these reviews and meta-analyses are usually consistent, indicating that exposure in vivo has a substantial effect size for agoraphobic symptoms. A total of 60% to 80% of all treated agoraphobics benefit significantly from exposure. Thus, exposure has become the gold standard treatment of agoraphobic patients.

Although prolonged exposure has been found to be superior to short exposure, this does not mean that having the opportunity to escape during exposure in vivo has detrimental effects as once thought (Craske, 1999). Although exposure therapies can be conducted as self-help programs with instructions by a live therapist, by a computer, or by phone (Emmelkamp, 2005; Schneider, Mataix-Cols, Marks, & Bachofen, 2005), there is some evidence that therapist guidance may lead to superior results. In a large RCT (Gloster et al., 2011), therapist-guided exposure was more effective than exposure without therapist guidance both in reducing the number of panic attacks and avoidance behavior, and improvement of global functioning. Such therapist-guided exposure in vivo resulted in quicker and stronger improvement than when exposure exercises were planned but patients had to do the exercises on their own without the therapist being present during the exposure in vivo.

Exposure in vivo not only leads to a reduction of anxiety and avoidance, but also to a reduction of panic attacks (Emmelkamp, 2004) and a reduction of negative self-statements (e.g., Meyerbröker et al., 2012). The results of exposure therapy with agoraphobics are long-lasting. Follow-up reports ranging from 4 to 9 years after treatment have been published. Generally, improvements brought about by the treatment were maintained (Emmelkamp & Powers, 2010). In a study by Peter, Brückner, Hand, Rohr, and Rufer (2008) a total of 40% of patients reached a level within a normal range 3 to 9 years after treatment. In two-thirds of the patients, treatment outcome was stable during follow-up.

Exposure in Vivo Versus Cognitive Therapy

A number of cognitively oriented researchers have stressed psychological factors in accounting for panic attacks (Clark, 1986; Ehlers & Margraf, 1989). In these models it is assumed that patients misinterpret bodily sensations as a sign of a serious physical danger (e.g., a heart attack). The common element is that patients are likely to mislabel such bodily sensations and attribute them to a threatening disease and as a result may panic. Central to the cognitive conceptualization of panic is that bodily sensations are interpreted as dangerous. A positive feedback loop between physiological arousal and anxiety is postulated that leads to an ascending "spiral" ending in the full-blown panic attack.

Those formulations of panic have led to development of cognitive therapy focusing on the bodily sensations. The cognitive therapy of Clark (1986) consists of explanation and discussion of the way hyperventilation induces panic, breathing exercises, interoceptive exposure, and relabeling of bodily symptoms. This treatment has been found effective in patients with panic disorder (Emmelkamp, 2004). There is convincing evidence that cognitive therapy dealing with misinterpretations of bodily sensations is highly effective in reducing panic attacks. However, this does not necessarily lead to a reduction of the avoidance behavior in severe agoraphobic patients.

The cognitive-behavioral treatment of panic disorder includes interoceptive exposure, which involves inducing the feared bodily sensations associated with panic attacks through various exercises in order to reduce the fear associated with these physical sensations through habituation. These exposure exercises are designed to mimic the physiological sensations that patients experience during panic attacks (i.e., sweating, heart palpitations, and dizziness) through assignments such as brief vigorous physical exercise, hyperventilation, and spinning.

Craske and Barlow (2006) developed a comprehensive package consisting of exposure to interoceptive stimuli, imaginal exposure, breathing retraining, cognitive restructuring, and exposure in vivo. In a large multicenter trial (Barlow, Gorman, Shear, & Woods, 2000) this package was found to be as effective as imipramine and both active treatments were more effective than placebo. A combined treatment of cognitive-behavior therapy (CBT) and imipramine was not significantly superior to CBT plus placebo. Barlow et al. (2000) included only patients with no or mild agoraphobia. In another study (van Apeldoorn et al., 2008) a combined treatment consisting of SSRI plus CBT was more effective than CBT alone. Although most patients had agoraphobia, in the CBT condition the first 10 sessions consisted solely of cognitive therapy rather than exposure in vivo. From Session 10 onward, both cognitive therapy and exposure in vivo were offered in the form of homework assignments. The emphasis on one of the two was left to "the clinical judgment of the therapist" (p. 263). The postponing of exposure in vivo to the 10th session and the reliance on the clinical wisdom of the therapist make the results difficult to interpret.

A few studies investigated the effects of various components of a cognitive behavioral treatment package. Craske, Rowe, Lewin, and Noriega-Dimitri (1997) and Schmidt et al. (2000) demonstrated that interoceptive exposure is a more powerful component of CBT for panic disorder than breathing retraining. Results of both studies revealed that breathing retraining added little to other components of the CBT intervention. Antony, Ledley, Liss, and Swinson (2006) instructed participants to complete 13 interoceptive exposure exercises and found that breathing through a very thin straw for 2 minutes, was the most potent exposure exercise, followed by spinning around while standing for 1 minute, hyperventilation for 1 minute, and pressing a tongue depressor down at the back of the tongue for half a minute.

In agoraphobia, exposure-based interventions are usually superior to cognitive interventions (e.g., Emmelkamp, 2004; Moscovitch, Antony, & Swinson, 2009; Sánchez-Meca et al., 2010). There is no evidence that additional components (e.g., cognitive restructuring, breathing retraining) do increase outcomes above exposure alone (e.g., Craske et al., 1997; Öst, Thulin, & Ramnero, 2004).

Given this state of affairs cognitive therapy (without exposure in vivo) cannot be recommended for panic patients with severe agoraphobia.

Virtual Reality Exposure Therapy

Few studies have investigated the effects of VRET in patients with agoraphobia and results are inconclusive. In one study cognitive therapy plus VRET was compared with cognitive therapy plus exposure in vivo in patients with panic disorder with or without agoraphobia (Botella et al., 2007). In this study with 37 patients VRET was found to be as efficacious as exposure in vivo, but a number of patients did not have agoraphobia.

In a more recent study (Meyerbröker, Morina, Kerkhof, & Emmelkamp, in press) patients with panic disorder with severe agoraphobia ($N = 55$) were randomly assigned to receive four sessions of cognitive therapy followed by either six sessions of virtual reality exposure therapy (VRET) or six sessions of exposure in vivo or to a waiting list control condition. Both active treatment packages were more effective than no treatment and there was a slight superiority for exposure in vivo. The results show clear synchrony of temporal processes involved in VRET and exposure in vivo, not only on weekly panic and avoidance measures but on weekly cognitive measures as well. Thus, whether VRET may offer an alternative for exposure in vivo for patients with severe agoraphobia is still open to debate.

CBT and Comorbid Substance Abuse and Dependence

In case of comorbid substance abuse or dependence, the task of the clinician is to determine the temporal relationship between the syndromes identified. For example, panic attacks are often associated with withdrawal syndromes. Although it has been claimed that comorbid anxiety disorders predict poor outcome of alcoholism treatment (e.g., Kushner et al., 2005), results are inconclusive given the many methodological problems in most studies (Emmelkamp & Vedel, 2006; Marquenie et al., 2006). Further, concurrent SUDs did not moderate treatment outcomes in CBT treatment focusing on anxiety disorders (McEvoy & Shand, 2008).

In cases where panic disorder/agoraphobia precede development of substance abuse, it has been suggested that many patients may ingest alcohol or drugs as self-medication to cope with the psychiatric symptoms. Would a combination of cognitive behavior strategies focusing on both the panic disorder/agoraphobia and substance abuse enhance treatment effects? Unfortunately, the results of the few studies that investigated whether dual treatments focusing both on the alcohol dependence as well as on panic disorder/agoraphobia are more effective

than treatment focusing on either disorder on its own are negative (e.g., Kushner et al., 2009). The combined treatment focusing on both disorders rather than on SUD alone was not more effective than treatment focusing only on SUD in terms of substance use. In the Bowen, D'Arcy, Keegan, and Van Senthilsel (2000) study the addition of 12 hours of cognitive-behavioral therapy directed at panic and agoraphobia led neither to enhanced outcome on drinking measures nor on mood and anxiety symptoms. In a study by Schadé et al. (2005) the addition of the treatment directed at the anxiety neither enhanced treatment outcome in terms of abstinence or a reduction in days of heavy drinking, nor reduced relapse. The additional therapy reduced the anxiety symptoms, but it had no significant effect on the outcome of alcohol treatment programs.

Because there is considerable evidence that substance abuse may perpetuate or exacerbate anxiety symptoms, it is therapeutically wise to wait and see what happens with the anxiety symptoms when the substance use is stopped or substantially reduced. Generally, cognitive-behavior therapy targeting the substance abuse is not only likely to result in a reduction of substance use but in a reduction of anxiety symptoms as well, so within the perspective of a stepped-care approach, in most cases treatment should be directed at the substance abuse first (Emmelkamp & Vedel, 2006). If the anxiety symptoms remain prevalent after a period of at least 4 weeks of abstinence, there is reason to consider more detailed assessment and treatment directed toward the panic disorder/agoraphobia. If anxiety does not improve after reduction of substance abuse, adding treatment components directly addressing the anxiety disorder might be indicated.

Effect of Personality Disorders

Comorbid personality disorders are common in patients with anxiety disorders, the avoidant and dependent personality disorders (PDs) being most frequent (Emmelkamp & Kamphuis, 2007). Although there is some evidence that some personality traits are associated with poorer outcome in CBT, there is no evidence that the presence of personality disorders per se results in poorer outcome when personality disorder diagnosis is formally established with a structured interview (see Emmelkamp & Kamphuis, 2007).

CBT: The Role of the Therapist

There is some evidence that cognitive behavior therapy can be applied with reduced therapist contact (Cote, Gauthier, Laberge, & Cormier, 1994), or can be conducted by competent nurse-therapists (Kingdon, Tyrer, Seivewright, Ferguson, & Murphy, 1996). Results with respect to the efficacy of bibliotherapy are inconclusive (e.g., Fanner & Urquhartt, 2008). One study found that telephone-based collaborative care for panic disorder and generalized anxiety disorder is more effective than usual care in terms of anxiety reduction (Rollman et al., 2005).

More recently, a number of studies have shown that CBT can also be delivered through the Internet, which studies were reviewed by Gallego and Emmelkamp (2012). There are 12 controlled studies in this area, but Internet-based treatments for PD have been compared with face-to-face treatments in only two controlled studies (Carlbring et al., 2005; Kiropoulos et al., 2008). The attrition rate for the Internet-based PD studies has been variable. The mean dropout for all Internet conditions was 19.27% in contrast to 8.6% for the face-to-face treatments. The Internet-based treatments for PD were found to be more effective than a variety of control conditions (waiting list, self-monitoring, and information-only), and to be equally effective as face-to-face treatments and a therapist-assisted self-help manual (see also Ruwaard et al., 2012). Generally, treatment adherence is higher for face-to-face treatments than for Internet-based interventions.

CBT and Pharmacotherapy

Many studies have been reported that investigated the relative contribution of cognitive-behavioral procedures and psychopharmaca, which would be difficult to discuss in any detail. Different classes of drugs have been investigated, including antidepressants (TCAs and SSRIs), (high-potency) benzodiazepines, and cognitive enhancers.

Antidepressants have been demonstrated to be effective in preventing panic attacks, and in improving anticipatory anxiety and avoidance behavior. In a meta-analysis Furukawa, Watanabe, and Churchill (2007) investigated the relative effectiveness of CBT, antidepressants, and the combination of both treatment approaches. In the acute phase treatment, the combined therapy was superior to antidepressant pharmacotherapy or CBT. The combined therapy led to more dropouts due to side effects than CBT. After termination of the active treatment, the combined therapy was as effective as CBT and more effective than antidepressants alone. Thus, results of this meta-analysis suggest that either combined therapy or CBT alone may be chosen as first line treatment for panic disorder with or without agoraphobia, depending on patient preference. A more recent study of Marchand et al. (2008) suggest, however, that a combination of CBT and antidepressant medication is not more effective that CBT plus placebo.

High-potency benzodiazepines have been shown to display a rapid onset of anti-anxiety effect and have beneficial effects during the first few days of treatment and are therefore often prescribed; however, the use of benzodiazepines is associated with a number of negative side effects, including sedation, cognitive impairments, and development of dependence and tolerance. Often a rebound of panic attacks occurs during tapering off. Results of studies investigating the effects of combining CBT with benzodiazepines are mixed. Combined treatment of alprazolam and exposure or CBT results in poorer maintenance of remission of panic disorder than CBT alone (Marks et al., 1993; Otto, Pollack, & Sabatino, 1996; Spiegel & Bruce, 1997), but can facilitate discontinuation of alprazolam therapy in patients who have been treated with alprazolam only (Bruce, Spiegel, Gregg, & Nuzzarello, 1995). A recent review concluded that there is a paucity of high quality studies in this area: "Based on limited available published and unpublished data, however, the combined therapy is probably to be recommended over benzodiazepine alone for panic disorder with agoraphobia. The combination might be superior to behavior therapy alone during the acute phase, but afterwards this trend may be reversed" (Watanabe, Churchill, & Furukawa, 2007). Few studies have evaluated the effects of cognitive enhancers in panic disorder and agoraphobia. Research sofar has been limited to d-cycloserine (DCS). DCS enhanced the effect of CBT involving interoceptive exposures in patients with a panic disorder (Otto et al., 2010). Siegmund et al. (2011) investigated the potential of DCS to improve the effect of CBT including in vivo exposure in patients with agoraphobia with panic disorder. DCS did not significantly improve outcome, but only 3 out of 11 sessions involved exposure in vivo.

Benchmarking of CBT for Panic Disorder With or Without Agoraphobia

There is an ongoing debate over the extent to which results from randomized controlled trials (RCTs) of psychological treatments can be generalized to routine clinical practice. Questions that have to be addressed are whether (a) patients and therapists in RCTs are truly representative of those seen in clinical practice; and (b) manualized treatment is used in routine practice (Powers & Emmelkamp, 2009). In RCTs, so-called efficacy studies, often relatively homogeneous samples of patients are recruited specifically for the study, patients are randomly assigned to treatment or control groups, and therapists are trained in a specific intervention and supervised so that they will implement the intervention in a manner consistent across therapists. In contrast, in routine clinical practice therapists are used who are already working in a clinical setting with patients who are routinely referred for services.

A number of studies have compared the typical RCTs with so called effectiveness studies in clinical practice in order to benchmark the treatments. In a recent review of research in this area Hunsley and Lee (2007) found across the adult effectiveness studies, most results were comparable with the efficacy-based outcome benchmarks. With respect to the treatment of panic disorder/agoraphobia, four of seven effectiveness trials had results comparable with the benchmark, with one study having a lower improvement rate and two having a higher improvement rate. Taken together, the results of the benchmark studies suggest that the results are generalizable to routine clinical practice.

SOCIAL PHOBIA

A social phobia is characterized by a marked and persistent fear of possible scrutiny by other people. Patients with this disorder are often inclined to avoid situations in which they could be criticized, which usually leads to significant interference in social relationships and occupational functioning (American Psychiatric Association, 1994). Studies on treatment outcome with social phobics concentrated on exposure in vivo, social skills training, cognitive strategies, and treatments in which cognitive and behavioral strategies were integrated.

Exposure in Vivo

As discussed earlier, exposure in vivo is the gold standard for treatment of phobias. With exposure in vivo, patients are exposed to gradually more anxiety arousing situations for prolonged periods of time per session until anxiety dissipates and habituation occurs. One of the problems with exposure in vivo with social phobics is that it is difficult to build a hierarchy of gradually more difficult social situations to be practiced during treatment, given the unpredictability of reactions of other people. Moreover, many social interactions are time-limited, often not long enough for habituation of anxiety to occur. These aspects are a serious drawback for the normal use of exposure in vivo for social phobics and may explain why treatment with exposure in vivo with social phobics is generally less effective than with individuals with specific phobia such as fear of heights or claustrophobia (Emmelkamp, 2004).

Virtual Reality Exposure Therapy

Exposure using virtual reality may solve many of the problems currently associated with conducting exposure therapy with social phobics. In virtual reality exposure to virtual social situations can be repeated over and over again until habituation occurs. Moreover, the therapist can control a hierarchy of increasing difficulty within and between the virtual social scenes. Further, in clinical practice treatment often consists of group therapy, which might be too aversive for socially anxious patients. Taken these considerations into account, VRET could be an ideal treatment for patients with social anxiety since exposure can be better controlled and VRET is given individually rather than in a group. Unfortunately, until to date few studies have investigated this possibility. In one study (Klinger et al., 2005) individually conducted VRET was compared to group treatment consisting of cognitive-behavior therapy and found to be equally effective. Results are difficult to interpret for a variety of reasons, including non random allocation to treatment conditions, no behavioral measure to investigate generalization to real rather than virtual social situations, and no control group. The only RCT on the treatment of social phobia with VRET was reported by Wallach, Safir, and Bar-Zvi (2009) and involved subjects with a specific social phobia: fear of public speaking. Results indicated that cognitive behavior therapy plus VRET was not more effective than standard cognitive behavior therapy for fear of public speaking. Both treatments were superior to the control condition on anxiety measures and on a behavioral avoidance measure (BAT). Twice as many subjects dropped out of the cognitive behavioral condition than out of the cognitive behavioral plus VRET condition, which suggests that VRET made the treatment less aversive and more palatable for patients. Thus, although the first results of VRET in public speaking are promising, further controlled studies are needed in other forms of social phobia before this treatment can be recommended for social phobic patients.

Social Skills Training

The rationale for social skills training for social phobia is that a number of individuals with social phobia, especially generalized social anxiety disorder, are characterized by deficits in social performance, which may reflect actual skills deficits. Social skills training has been shown to be an effective treatment (e.g., Bögels & Voncken, 2008; Herbert et al., 2006). In view of the fact that inadequate social skills seem less important in the etiology and maintenance of social fears as was once thought, questions about the effective ingredients of the treatment have been raised. It is possible that skills training is mainly useful in enhancing patients' self-confidence. In addition it must be noted that the effects of social skills training, when conducted in groups (as is usually the case), can be explained in terms of in vivo exposure, both in the group sessions and in homework assignments.

Empirical Results of Behavioral and Cognitive Treatment Strategies

A growing number of studies have accumulated over the past 30 years that support the CBT treatment of social anxiety disorder as shown in reviews and meta-analyses (Bandelow, Seidler–Brandler, Becker, Wedekind, & Ruther, 2007; Emmelkamp, 2004; Fedoroff & Taylor, 2001; Feske & Chambless, 1995; Gould, Buckminster, Pollack, Otto, & Yap, 1997; Meca, Alcazar, & Rodriguez, 2004; Moreno, Carrillo, & Meca, 2001; Ponniah & Hollon, 2007; Taylor, 1996). Powers, Sigmarsson, and Emmelkamp (2008) conducted a meta-analysis for social anxiety disorder by combining multiple randomized controlled trials. The meta-analysis of 32 ($n = 1,479$) randomized controlled trials found that CBT outperformed wait list ($d = 0.86$) and placebo conditions ($d = 0.38$) across outcome domains and at follow-up. No significant differences were found between combined treatment (exposure with cognitive therapy) and exposure or cognitive methods alone. It is interesting to note that while not significantly different, exposure methods produced the largest controlled effect size ($d = 0.89$) relative to cognitive ($d = 0.80$) or combined ($d = 0.61$). In addition, exposure methods showed significant improvement on both behavioral ($d = 0.75$) and cognitive ($d = 0.55$) measures. Likewise, cognitive methods showed significant improvement on both behavioral ($d = 0.48$) and cognitive ($d = 0.51$) measures.

Thus, there is considerable evidence that exposure is an effective treatment for social anxiety disorder. Adding cognitive therapy does not enhance the outcome. Exposure not only leads to improvement in anxiety, but also leads to cognitive changes. Despite these results, CBT does not produce improvement in all patients, and even among those who do respond, most remain at least somewhat symptomatic following treatment, especially among patients with the generalized subtype of SAD, whose fear and avoidance involves most social situations. It has been suggested that this may be due to the heterogeneity of social phobics. In the past, several attempts have been made to divide patients into more homogenous subgroups and to match treatment strategies to specific patient characteristics. The research strategy usually includes the following design. Patients are divided into two groups, showing different response patterns (e.g., behavioral reactors low in social skills, cognitive reactors, or physiological reactors). Within each group, half of the patients receive a consonant treatment, matching the reactor type (e.g., relaxation in the case of physiological reactors, social skills training in the case of behavioral reactors; cognitive therapy in the case of cognitive reactors), whereas the other half receive a treatment that does not fit the response pattern. In all, it appears that matched and standardized treatments both led to improvement, and that they were equally effective (see Emmelkamp, 2004).

As far as long-term follow-up data are available, generally, results of CBT are maintained up to 1 year after treatment. A few studies evaluated longer follow-up periods (Mersch, Emmelkamp, & Lips, 1991; Scholing & Emmelkamp, 1996a, 1996b; Turner, Beidel, & Cooley-Quille, 1995). Generally, treatment gains were maintained up to 2 years after treatment

(Turner et al., 1995). For individual patients the results are divergent. Scholing and Emmelkamp (1996a) found that between the posttest and the 18-month follow-up, 58% of the patients still functioned at their posttest level, 20% had relapsed, and 22% had further improved.

Group Treatment Versus Individual Treatment

It can be expected that, especially for social phobia, group treatments have clear advantages above individual treatments. Group treatment provides a continuous exposure to a group—for many social phobics one of the most anxiety provoking situations. However, only few studies have directly compared group and individual treatments for social phobics. With repect to CBT programs involving exposure in vivo, few differences were found between both modalities either on process measures (Hayes et al., 2008) or on outcome (Scholing & Emmelkamp, 1993, 1996a). In contrast, in cognitive therapy individual treatment was superior to group treatment (Mortberg, Clark, Sundin, & Wistedt, 2007; Stangier, Heidenreich, Peitz, Lauterbach, & Clark, 2003).

Internet-Based CBT

Internet-based treatments for social phobia have been intensively studied in the past few years (see Gallego & Emmelkamp, 2012). Results reveal that Internet-based treatment for social phobia was more effective than waiting list. There was one exception: A self-guided Internet intervention without any contact with the therapist did not do better than waiting-list control (Titov, Andrews, Choi, Schwencke, & Mahoney, 2008). Face-to-face treatment for fear of public speaking was as effective and acceptable as the same treatment applied over the Internet without any contact with a therapist (Botella et al., 2010). Nevertheless, contact with the therapist during treatment increases treatment compliance and enhances treatment outcome (Titov, Andrews, Choi et al., 2008; Titov, Andrews, Choi, Schwencke, & Johnston, 2009). In a recent study (Gallego, Emmelkamp, Kooij, & Mees, 2011) an exposure-based Internet treatment "Talk to me" was compared with a waiting-list control group. Internet-based cognitive-behavioral treatment resulted in significant improvement from pretest to posttest on all social phobia measures and in social and work impairment. Talk to me

was significantly more effective than the control group on a number of measures: fear and avoidance to the target behaviors, fear of public speaking, and work impairment. Regarding the effect size (Cohen-d) for the measures related to social phobia, the Internet treatment had a high within-group ($d = 1.13$) and between-groups effect size ($d = .86$). The effect sizes achieved with the "Talk to me" program are comparable to results of face-to-face treatment of social phobia (Powers et al., 2008).

Concluding Remarks

Considering the clinical relevance of the data, it must be concluded that the improvements in social phobia following CBT are encouraging but many patients still report substantial fear at the end of treatment. On the basis of the empirical findings, treatments for social phobia should at least include a considerable amount of in vivo exposure. Although there is a trend toward the development of integrated treatments consisting of different strategies, results to date do not support the view that a combination of cognitive therapy and exposure in vivo is more effective than exposure in vivo as stand-alone treatment.

GENERALIZED ANXIETY DISORDER

In recent years a number of studies have been conducted that investigated the effectiveness of behavioral and cognitive procedures on patients with generalized anxiety disorder (GAD). Although exposure procedures are effective when anxiety is triggered by external stimuli, avoidance is less obvious in GAD. Therefore, the emphasis is on reducing the excessive psychophysiological activation characteristic of GAD by means of relaxation procedures, and on changing the worrying by cognitive and behavioral techniques.

Worry is the key cognitive aspect of GAD. A number of primarily CBT interventions have been developed to target worry in GAD clients. Research into the effect of these treatments are discussed below. Most evidence-based treatments for GAD include a complex package of treatment strategies aimed to target the cognitive, behavioral, and emotional processes thought to underlie pathological worry. These treatments are based on theoretical models of GAD, such as Borkovec's cognitive avoidance model (Borkovec, Alcaine, & Behar, 2004; Borkovec, Ray, & Stöber,

1998) or the intolerance of uncertainty model by Dugas, Gagnon, Ladouceur, and Freeston (1998). Both models share an underlying commonality in their specific focus on worrying.

Borkovec and colleagues (2004) suggest that worry serves as a cognitive-avoidance strategy by suppressing anxious arousal. In this model, worry is primarily seen as a cognitive-verbal activity that inhibits emotional processing. In the multi-component CBT approach based on this model, clients are imaginally exposed to situations they are worrying about and to the associated physiological arousal which is then paired with a relaxation response (Borkovec, Newman, Pincus, & Lytle, 2002). This is combined with additional techniques, such as cognitive restructuring, applied relaxation, and stimulus control. In the model developed by Dugas and colleagues (1998), intolerance of uncertainty is held to result from a set of negative beliefs about uncertainty and its implications. In the CBT intervention developed on the basis of this model, clients are instructed to separate their worries into two categories, namely worries that are amenable to problem solving and worries that are not. In the former case, clients are taught problem-solving strategies and in case that the problems cannot be changed, worry exposure is used (Dugas & Robichaud, 2006). In addition, cognitive restructuring is used to directly target intolerance of uncertainty. The goal of this approach is to help clients with GAD to develop beliefs about uncertainty that are less negative, rigid, and pervasive.

Empirical Evidence for CBT

The CBT package of Borkovec et al. (2004) has been found effective in a number of controlled studies, in that it reduced symptoms of anxiety as well as levels of worry (Covin, Ouimet, Seeds, & Dozois, 2008; Fisher, 2006; Gould, Safren, Washington, & Otto, 2004; Mitte, 2005b). The goal of a recent study by Newman and colleagues (2011) was to test whether the addition of techniques aimed at fostering emotional deepening and improving interpersonal functioning would increase the effect of the CBT package of Borkovec et al. (2004). Results revealed that interpersonal emotion focused therapy did not enhance the effects of the standard CBT approach. Further, the CBT package of Borkovec et al. (2004) was significantly superior to psychodynamic therapy on worrying, trait-anxiety, and depressed mood (Leichsenring et al., 2009).

The CBT package of Dugas and colleagues has been found to be more effective than a waiting list control condition (Dugas et al., 2003; Dugas et al., 2010; Ladouceur et al., 2000) and nondirective therapy (Gosselin, Ladouceur, Morin, Dugas, & Baillargeon, 2006). Interestingly, in the studies by Dugas and colleagues (2003, 2010), level of worry further decreased from posttreatment to 2-year follow-up.

In sum, both treatments described so far have been found to be effective. However, as these multicomponent packages both include a number of different strategies, it remains unclear which of these is responsible for the observed effects. In the following list, studies focusing on one of the techniques only are presented.

Worry exposure. To date, only one study investigated worry exposure as a stand-alone treatment for GAD (Hoyer et al., 2009). In this study, worry exposure led to clinically significant changes on anxiety, depression, and worry. Worry exposure was more effective than a waiting list condition and as effective as applied relaxation.

Applied relaxation and anxiety management. Relaxation forms an essential ingredient in anxiety management training and in applied relaxation. In both procedures, patients are trained to recognize the physiological cues of tension and to apply relaxation whenever tension is perceived. Anxiety management includes additional procedures for reducing anxiety symptoms, such as distraction, controlling upsetting thoughts, and panic management. Both anxiety management and applied relaxation have been found to be effective in GAD (see Emmelkamp, 2004). Results of studies reveal that applied relaxation results in reduced anxiety, worrying, and depressed mood. In a study of Borkovec and Costello (1993), applied relaxation was as effective as the multicomponent package based on the avoidance model of GAD. More recently, effects of applied relaxation were compared with the CBT package of Dugas and Robichaud (2006) described above. Results revealed that both treatments were more effective than no treatment, and that the multicomponent CBT approach was slightly superior to applied relaxation (Dugas et al., 2010). Importantly, CBT did not lead to a statistically greater change in worry than applied relaxation. As described earlier, Hoyer and colleagues (2009) found applied relaxation to be as effective as worry exposure, not only on anxiety, but on severity of worry as well. Interestingly, although neither applied relaxation nor worry exposure involved cognitive restructuring, both treatments led to cognitive and metacognitive change.

Cognitive therapy. According to the cognitive model, anxiety is maintained by an individual's catastrophic misinterpretations of generally benign stimuli thus creating a self-perpetuating cycle of increasingly intensified anxiety (Beck, Emery, & Greenberg, 1985). As described earlier, cognitive restructuring techniques are part of most multicomponent CBT packages for treating CBT. Siev and Chambless (2007) conducted a meta-analysis of studies that compared cognitive therapy and relaxation. Cognitive therapy proved equally efficacious in treating GAD in terms of anxiety, anxiety-related cognitions, and depression.

In contrast to the cognitive-behavioral theories where worrying has been proposed as a form of emotional avoidance (Borkovec et al., 2004) or as resulting from beliefs leading to an intolerance of uncertainty (Dugas et al., 1998), the meta-cognitive model of Wells (2010) holds that pathological worry is the result of negative beliefs about worrying and counterproductive strategies of mental control. Central to the development of GAD is worry about worry or meta-worry. In Wells's view when negative beliefs about worrying are activated this will lead to negative appraisal of the worry process as uncontrollable and dangerous. Meta-cognitive therapy therefore focuses on challenging these meta-cognitive beliefs. A small RCT comparing meta-cognitive therapy to applied relaxation (Wells et al., 2010), showed that meta-cognitive therapy was superior to applied relaxation on most measures across 12-month follow-up. In a large study conducted in the Netherlands (van de Heiden, Muris, & van der Molen, 2012), meta-cognitive therapy was compared with a treatment based on the intolerance of uncertainty model described earlier. Both treatments led to significant improvements on worry, anxiety, and depressed mood, meta-cognitive therapy was significantly superior to intolerance of uncertainty treatment immediately after treatment at the posttest, but not at follow-up.

Concluding Remarks

Results of studies into behavior therapy and cognitive therapy with GAD patients are promising, but results are generally less than in specific phobia, social phobia, or panic disorder (Emmelkamp, 2004).

OBSESSIVE-COMPULSIVE DISORDER

Obsessions are experienced as senseless or repugnant thoughts, which the patient attempts to ignore or suppress. Compulsions are repetitive, apparently purposeful behaviors that are intentionally produced and performed according to certain rules or in a stereotyped fashion. Compulsions serve to neutralize or to prevent discomfort and/or anxiety. Rituals or compulsions usually accompany obsessions. The majority of obsessive-compulsive patients have obsessions as well as compulsions. Generally, obsessions are anxiety inducing and the performance of compulsions leads to anxiety reduction. Obsessive-compulsive patients not only try to neutralize discomfort or anxiety with compulsions, but also try to avoid stimuli that might provoke discomfort or anxiety. In a number of patients, neutralizing thoughts (cognitive rituals) serve the same function as rituals, that is, undoing the expected harmful effects of the obsession.

Exposure in Vivo and Response Prevention

Obsessive-compulsive problems are among the most difficult problems to treat, yet it is in this area that behavioral research has made significant advances. Exposure in vivo and response prevention are effective with a substantial number of obsessive-compulsive patients, resulting in large effect sizes (see meta-analyses of Abramowitz, 1996; Eddy, Dutra, Bradley, & Westen, 2004; Fisher & Wells, 2005; Hofmann & Smits, 2008; Rosa-Alcazar, Sanchez-Meca, Gomez-Conesta, & Marin-Martinez, 2008). Further, exposure and response prevention results in a considerable improvement of quality of life (Diefenbach, Abramowitz, Norberg, & Tolin, 2007). Positive results of exposure in vivo and response prevention are not restricted to patients treated in experimental studies, but generalize to OCD patients treated in clinical settings (Franklin, Abramowitz, Kozak, Levitt, & Foa, 2000; Nakatani et al., 2009, Rothbaum & Shahar, 2000).

With exposure and response prevention, patients are exposed to stimuli that trigger obsessions and urges to ritualize but are prevented from performing the rituals. Since the first controlled studies into exposure and response prevention, which were conducted in the United Kingdom

(Marks, Hodgson, & Rachman, 1975) and the Netherlands (Boersma, Dekker, & Emmelkamp, 1976) nearly 40 years ago and were published, numerous controlled studies have determined what the essential ingredients of successful treatment are (see Emmelkamp, 1994, 2004). There is no need to elicit high anxiety during treatment because gradual exposure in vivo is equally effective as flooding in vivo. As gradual exposure evokes less tension and is easier for the patient to carry out by her- or himself, it is to be preferred to flooding. Both exposure to distressing stimuli and response prevention of the ritual are essential components (Abramowitz, 1996; Emmelkamp, 1994). Exposure led to more anxiety reduction but less improvement of rituals, while the reverse was found for response prevention. Further, although results of a meta-analysis suggest that exposure in vivo carried out by the patient him- or herself and response prevention in his or her natural environment is slightly less effective than therapist-controlled exposure (Abramowitz, 1996), results of controlled studies found therapist-controlled and self-controlled exposure equally effective (Emmelkamp, 1994; van Oppen et al., 2010). Further, given that massed exposure is as effective as spaced exposure (Abramowitz, Foa, & Franklin, 2003; Emmelkamp, Linden van den Heuvell, Rüphan, & Sanderman, 1989; Storch et al., 2007, 2008), a frequency of two sessions a week can be recommended.

Although treatment by exposure and response prevention was originally applied when the patient was hospitalized, treatment is now usually administered by the patient in his natural environment. Admission to a hospital is not necessary for most OCD patients, as the same results can be achieved if the treatment is provided in their own environment (van den Hout, Emmelkamp, Kraaykamp, & Griez, 1988). Exposure in vivo and response prevention have succesfully been applied in a group format (e.g. van Noppen, Pato, Marsland, & Rasmussen, 1998), but there is some evidence that individual treatment is more effective (Anderson & Rees, 2007; Jaurrieta et al., 2008; O'Connor, Freeston, et al., 2005).

Emmelkamp, Bouman, and Blaauw (1994) studied whether treatment based on a functional analysis would be better than a standardized exposure/response prevention program. Obsessive-compulsive patients were randomly assigned to two conditions. In one condition the patients were treated with the standardized behavioral program of exposure in vivo and response prevention. The other treatment program was individually tailored to the needs of the patient. Therefore, four to five interviews were held with *all* patients by an experienced behavior therapist to enable him to make a functional analysis and a treatment plan based on this analysis. Neither on obsessive-compulsive complaints nor on depression and general psychopathology were the treatments (individually tailored versus exposure and response prevention) found to be differentially effective.

Bibliotherapy is less effective than therapist-directed exposure (Tolin et al., 2007). There is some evidence, however, that exposure and response prevention can be administered by computer programs. Bachofen et al. (1999) evaluated the effects of a computer program that was designed to assist OCD patients in carrying out self-exposure and response prevention. Patients used a touchtone telephone to access computer-driven interviews via an Interactive Voice Response system. This program resulted in statistically and clinically significant improvement in OCD symptomatology. However, nearly half of the patients dropped out of the study. More recent studies show that computer-delivered treatment is less effective than therapist-assisted exposure and response prevention (Tumur, Kaltenthaler, Ferriter, Beverley, & Parry, 2007). To date the evidence base for technology-enhanced OCD treatments is limited and there is a clear need of better studies (Lovell & Bee, 2011).

Family members are often involved in the rituals of OCD patients and this often results in a heavy burden (Amir, Freshman, & Foa, 2000). Although a substantial number of patients have relationship problems, there is no evidence that involving the patient's partner in the treatment is more effective than treating the patient on his or her own (Emmelkamp, de Haan, & Hoogduin, 1990).

Exposure Versus Cognitive Therapy

A number of studies have compared the effectiveness of exposure in vivo plus response prevention and cognitive therapy. Various cognitive procedures have been evaluated: self-instruction training, rational emotive therapy (RET), and cognitive therapy. Self-instruction training did not prove to increase the effectiveness of exposure in vivo and response prevention (Emmelkamp, Helm, van der Zanten, & Plochg, 1980). RET was as effective as exposure in vivo

(Emmelkamp, Visser, & Hoekstra, 1988), but adding RET to exposure and response prevention did not enhance the effects of exposure in vivo (Emmelkamp & Beens, 1991). In the studies on RET, cognitive therapy was provided "pure," that is, patients were not instructed to change their behavior.

More recently, the emphasis has been on evaluating therapy based on the "cognitive appraisal model" (Obsessive Compulsive Cognitions Working Group, 1997). A number of studies have compared cognitive therapy based on the cognitive appraisal model with exposure and response prevention and results suggest that both treatments are about equally effective (Belloch, Cabedo, & Carrio, 2008; Cottraux et al., 2001; McLean, Whittal, & Thordarson, 2001; O'Connor, Aardema, et al., 2005; Whittal, Thordarson, & McLean, 2005). Interestingly, exposure in vivo and response prevention leads to comparable cognitive changes as cognitive therapy (Belloch et al., 2008; Emmelkamp, van Oppen, & van Balkom, 2002; O'Connor, Aardema, et al., 2005; Whittal et al., 2005). Unfortunately, studies into the long-term effects of cognitive therapy are lacking.

Exposure Versus Pharmacotherapy

Over the past decades, a number of controlled studies have been carried out on the effect of drugs, which concentrate on the disrupted serotenergic neurotransmission: clomipramine, fluvoxamine and fluoxetine. Two studies focused on the question of whether a combination of clomipramine and behavior therapy (exposure in vivo and response prevention) was more effective than behavior therapy on its own or clomipramine on its own. Behavior therapy proved to be more effective than clomipramine, but the combination of clomipramine and behavior therapy was not more effective than behavior therapy on its own (Marks et al., 1988). In a more recent study (Foa, Liebowitz et al., 2005), clomipramine, exposure, and response prevention and the combination of both treatments were found to be superior to placebo. Exposure and response prevention outperformed clomipramine, and adding clomipramine to exposure and response prevention did not enhance outcome.

Van Balkom et al. (1998) compared cognitive, behavior therapy, a combination of cognitive therapy and fluvoxamine, and a combination of behavior therapy and fluvoxamine. Results revealed that cognitive and behavior therapy were

no less effective than the combined treatment approaches. More recently, Hohagen et al. (1998) found behavior therapy plus fluvoxamine not to be more effective than behavior therapy plus placebo on compulsions. In severely depressed patients the fluvoxamine-behavior therapy combination was superior to the placebo-behavior therapy combination.

In a meta-analysis of Kobak, Greist, Jefferson, Katzelnick, and Henry (1998), exposure in vivo and response prevention was found to be superior to treatment with serotonin reuptake inhibitors. It is important to note that stopping the antidepressant medication usually results in a relapse, in contrast to stopping exposure and response prevention (Marks, 1997; Simpson et al., 2004). Thus exposure and response prevention appears to be cost-effective and is the first choice of treatment for OCD (Expert Consensus Panel for Obsessive-Compulsive Disorder, 1997). However, antidepressant medication may be a useful adjunct to exposure and response prevention when OCD is accompanied by severe comorbid depression.

Long-Term Results and Relapse Prevention

A number of follow-up studies reveal that the effects of exposure in vivo and response prevention are maintained after 2 years (Kasvikis & Marks, 1988; Whittal et al., 2008), 4 years (van Oppen, van Balkom, De Haan, & van Dyck, 2005; Visser, Hoekstra, & Emmelkamp, 1992) and 7 years (Rufer et al., 2005).

PROGNOSTIC FACTORS

Few robust prognostic factors have been found: Most predictor variables (e.g., demographic variables, severity and type of OCD problem, anxiety, depression, and patient adherence) were not consistenly associated with outcome across studies (see Emmelkamp, 2004; Simpson et al., 2011). Thus, the literature is inconclusive about whether pretreatment depression, anxiety, or severity predict outcome. Other variables, however, may affect treatment outcome. These include a type of OCD with hoarding having a worse prognosis (Abramowitz et al., 2003; Mataix-Cols, Marks, Greist, Kobak, & Baer, 2002; Rufer, Fricke, Moritz, Kloss, & Hand, 2006), overvalued ideation (Basoglu, Lax, Kasvikis, & Marks, 1988; Foa, Steketee, Grayson, & Doppel, 1983;

Himle, Van Etten, Janeck, & Fischer, 2006), dissociation (Rufer, Held, et al., 2006), expressed emotionality/hostility (Chambless & Steketee, 1999; Emmelkamp, Kloek, & Blaauw, 1994), and negative parental rearing (Visser et al., 1992).

POSTTRAUMATIC STRESS

Posttraumatic stress disorder (PTSD) is a prevalent and disabling psychological disorder with onset after traumatic experiences. In the past 20 years, a number of different psychological treatments for this disorder have been developed and have been evaluated in more than 40 randomized controlled trials. In recent meta-analyses, two different types of psychological treatments have been found to be clearly effective in the treatment of PTSD, namely trauma-focused cognitive-behavioral treatment (TF-CBT) on the one hand and eye-movement desensitization and reprocessing (EMDR) on the other hand (Bisson et al., 2007; Bradley, Greene, Russ, Dutra, & Westen, 2005; van Etten & Taylor, 1998; Powers, Halpern, Ferenschak, Gillihan, & Foa, 2010; Seidler & Wagner, 2006). Trauma-focussed CBT varies, but include (prolonged) exposure in imagination to the trauma and often assignment of in vivo exposure homework to avoided trauma cues. Eye-movement desensitization and reprocessing (EMDR) entails brief imaginal exposure to traumatic images while saccadic eye movements are induced by tracking a therapist's finger as it is moved rapidly from side to side. The mechanism underlying EMDR remains poorly understood. EMDR is believed to restore the disrupted physiological balance between excitatory and inhibitory systems in the brain produced by exposure to trauma (Shapiro, 1995), but recently alternative explanations have been suggested, including taxing of the working memory (Gunter & Bodner, 2008) and reciprocal activation by eye movements of brain areas involved in REM-sleep (Elofsson, von Scheele, Theorell, & Söndergaard, 2008).

Empirically Supported Treatments

According to the current evidence, the two types of treatment can be regarded as equally effective in treating PTSD following *single-event traumas*. A number of studies have investigated whether cognitive therapy would enhance the outcome of trauma-focused CBT. Marks, Lovell, Noshirvani, Livanou, and Trasher (1998) compared exposure,

cognitive therapy and a combined cognitive-exposure treatment with relaxation control. All three active treatments were more effective than relaxation control up to 6-month follow-up. Combining cognitive therapy with exposure did not result in added value above exposure alone or cognitive therapy alone. Exposure yielded the greatest number of participants achieving good end-state functioning (53% for exposure, 32% for cognitive therapy, 32% for the combined approach, and 15% for relaxation). Two other studies found that combining cognitive therapy and exposure actually was *less* effective than imaginal exposure alone (Foa et al., 2005; Paunovic & Ost, 2001). In contrast, Bryant et al. (2008) found that combining trauma-focused CBT and cognitive therapy led to greater reductions in PTSD than did trauma-focused exposure alone. Interestingly, exposure leads to cognitive change without formal cognitive therapy (Foa & Rauch, 2004; Paunovic & Ost, 2001).

Cognitive-processing therapy is an alternative treatment for PTSD and consists of cognitive restructuring with a small dose of exposure (two sessions) in the form of written trauma accounts. Resick, Nishith, Weaver, Astin, & Feuer (2002) found that cognitive-processing therapy and imaginal exposure alone resulted in comparable gains. In a dismantling study, the combination of cognitive therapy and exposure through writing accounts did not outperform the results of writing accounts alone (Resick et al., 2008). A writing assignment as stand-alone treatment has been proven to be effective before (e.g., Lange et al., 2003) and is as effective as trauma-focused CBT (van Emmerik, Kamphuis, & Emmelkamp, 2008). Similarly, there is also considerable evidence that narrative exposure therapy, which involves emotional exposure to the memories of traumatic events and the reorganization of these memories into a coherent chronological narrative is an effective trauma-focused treatment (see Robjant & Fazel, 2010).

Treatment for Type II Trauma

For patients suffering from PTSD symptoms following repeated or chronic interpersonal trauma, such as sexual or physical abuse in childhood, little research on the efficacy of treatment outcome has been done yet (Taylor & Harvey, 2010). Problems in the treatment of PTSD following this type of trauma, also called *type II trauma*, are worsening of symptoms, high dropout and compliance problems (Levitt & Cloitre, 2005). Nevertheless some studies have shown that patients with chronic interpersonal trauma may benefit from trauma-focused CBT. In a study by McDonagh et al. (2005) trauma-focused CBT was compared with a present-centered problem-solving therapy in adult female survivors of childhood sexual abuse. Trauma-focused CBT was more effective than problem-solving therapy.

Some type II trauma survivors may have only the core PTSD symptoms, while others have multiple ancillary problems (van der Kolk, Roth, Pelcovitz, Sunday, & Spinazzola, 2005), including pervasive personality disturbance, particularly impaired affect modulation, self-destructive and impulsive behavior, identity disturbance, and impaired relationships.

PTSD following type II trauma is considered to be more difficult to treat than PTSD following single-event trauma (Spinazzola, Blaustein, & van der Kolk, 2005). Treatments that are purely focused on trauma processing may be insufficient and additional problems such as emotion regulation difficulties, dissociation, and interpersonal problems may need to be addressed, too. Further, patients who have difficulty tolerating distress and managing feelings of anger and anxiety as well as those who are vulnerable to dissociation under stress and those who have difficulty maintaining a good therapeutic relationship may tolerate trauma-focused therapy less well than PTSD patients following type-I traumatic events (Levitt & Cloitre, 2005).

Cloitre and colleagues (2006) have developed a phase-based treatment consisting of a stabilization or skills-training phase (STAIR), in which emotion dysregulation and interpersonal problems are targeted, and a trauma-focused phase (MPE) consisting of prolonged imaginal exposure (Cloitre, Cohen, & Koenen, 2006). This STAIR/MPE treatment has been investigated in two randomized controlled trials (Cloitre et al., 2010; Cloitre, Koenen, Cohen, & Han, 2002). Results show that the treatment led to significant improvement in three specifically targeted problem domains (affect regulation problems, interpersonal skills deficits, and PTSD symptoms), and was more effective than (a) a wait-list control group, (b) imaginal exposure alone, and (c) STAIR alone. There is therefore promising evidence for STAIR/MPE as an evidence-based treatment of PTSD in this population.

A number of additional treatments of PTSD following type-II trauma have been suggested in the literature and are currently being used in clinical practice. Chard (2005) compared the effectiveness of cognitive processing therapy, for sexual abuse survivors with that of the minimal attention given to a wait-listed control group. It was found that cognitive processing therapy was more effective for reducing trauma-related symptoms than minimal attention, and the results were maintained for a year, which underlines the utility of a trauma-focused approach to treating PTSD in this group. Third, EMDR is an evidence-based treatment for PTSD following type-I traumas and has also been suggested to be used in type-II trauma survivors, either as a stand-alone treatment or in combination with stabilization techniques (e.g., Gelinas, 2003). However, no controlled study to date has investigated the efficacy of EMDR in this population. In a study of van der Kolk et al. (2007) the efficacy of EMDR, an SSRI (fluoxetine), and a pill placebo was investigated in a mixed trauma group suffering from PTSD. Whereas EMDR led to a significant and substantial reduction of PTSD symptoms in survivors of adult-onset trauma, the treatment did not lead to substantial reduction in symptomatology for survivors of childhood-onset trauma. In fact, this subgroup showed a significantly worse response to EMDR than to SSRI treatment.

Treatment Through the Internet

In the area of the Internet-based CBT treatments for PTSD six RCTs have been published (see Gallego & Emmelkamp, 2012). Results of the RCTs reveal that Internet-based CBT treatment for PTSD is more effective than no treatment and Internet-based supportive counseling, but Internet-based CBT treatment has not been compared with a traditional face-to-face CBT (but see Ruwaard et al., 2012).

Predictors of Treatment Outcome

Few predictors have been found to moderate treatment outcome in trauma-focused CBT. There is robust evidence that pretreatment severity is predictive of posttest levels of PTS symptoms (e.g., Foa, Riggs, Massie, and Yarczower, 1995; van Emmerik, Kamphuis, Noordhof, & Emmelkamp, 2011; van Minnen, Arntz, & Keijsers, 2002). Although it has been suggested that personality disorder may inhibit outcome, there is no evidence to support this (Clarke, Rizvi, & Resick, 2008; Feeny, Zoellner, & Foa, 2002). There is some evidence, however, that the personality traits openness and conscientiousness moderate reduction in PTS symptoms, such that patients with lower scores on these personality traits reported (slightly) more PTS symptoms after completing treatment (van Emmerik et al., 2011).

Concluding Remarks

Both trauma-focused CBT and EMDR can be considered empirically supported treatments for type I trauma. There is a clear need of treatment studies into type-II trauma. The few studies available suggest that trauma-focused CBT preceded by stabilization might be an effective treatment for this severe group of patients. Further, research is needed into the effects of trauma-focused CBT in patients with comorbid disorders. Preliminary results suggest that these treatments may also be effective in patients with schizophrenia and severe depression (Mueser et al., 2008) and in patients with substance use disorders (van Dam, Vedel, Ehring, & Emmelkamp, 2012), but further studies are needed before trauma-focused CBT can be considered an empirically supported treatment for patients with severe comorbid disorders as well.

DEPRESSION

A number of controlled outcome studies of the effectiveness of cognitive-behavioral interventions for depression have been reported. Before embarking on the task of reviewing these studies, a brief discussion of the major behavioral models of depression that have led to various treatment approaches is provided.

Behavioral Models

The operant-conditioning model is based on the assumption that depressive symptoms result from too low a rate of response-contingent reinforcement and that depression will be ameliorated when the rate of reinforcement for adaptive behavior is increased (Lewinsohn, 1975; Lewinsohn & Hoberman, 1982). According to Lewinsohn, when behavior decreases due to non-reinforcement, the other symptoms of depression such as low energy and low self-esteem will follow more or less automatically. Treatment approaches that are suggested by this formulation of depression include (a) reengagement of the depressed individual in constructive and rewarding activities, and (b) training in social skills to enhance the individual's capacity to receive social reinforcements resulting from social interactions. It has been suggested (e.g., Lewinsohn & Hoberman, 1982) that lack of social skill could be one of the antecedent conditions producing a low rate of positive reinforcement. Indeed, a number of studies have shown depressed individuals to be less socially skillful than controls (Dimidjian, Barrera, Martell, Munoz, & Lewinsohn, 2011). It should be pointed out, however, that an association between depressed mood and (lack of) social skills does not necessarily imply a causal relationship. Only prospective studies can answer the question of the direction of causality between depression on the one hand and social skills on the other. Results of most longitudinal studies investigating this issue were not consistent with the hypothesis that social skill deficits function as an antecedent to depression (Segrin, 2000). Although there is support for the covariation of reduced pleasant events and depressed mood, research directed at specifying the temporal relationship between response-contingent positive reinforcement and depression was less convincing (Dimidjian et al., 2011). Although it has been consistently found that daily mood ratings correlate with rate of pleasant activities, this finding does not necessarily imply that increasing pleasant-activity rate will improve mood (Manos, Kanter, & Busch, 2010).

Several researchers have stressed the co-occurrence of depression and marital distress (e.g., Beach, 2001). Depressed persons are characterized by an aversive interpersonal style to which others respond with negativity and rejection. A lower proportion of positive verbal behavior and a higher proportion of negative verbal and nonverbal behavior have characterized the interaction of depressed individuals with their partner. A substantial number of depressed patients presenting for treatment also experience marital distress, whereas in approximately half of the couples who have marital problems at least one of the spouses is depressed. These data suggest that depression and marital distress are closely linked. Furthermore, marital distress is an important precursor of depressive symptoms. In addition, persons who, after being treated for depression, return to distressed marriages are more likely to experience relapse. When patients are asked about the sequence of depression and marital distress most patients hold that marital distress preceded the depressive episode (Emmelkamp & Vedel, 2002). Results of the studies discussed above suggest that it might be important to enroll the partner in the treatment of depressed patients.

Behavioral Interventions

The major cognitive and behavioral approaches differ with respect to the role that they ascribe to the various factors in the etiology and functioning of depression, which leads to different emphases in the various therapeutic procedures based on these models. Cognitive therapies focus on changing patients' depressogenic cognitions and hence their depressed affect and behavior. Cognitive therapy aims to help patients identify the assumptions and schemas that support patterns of stereotypical negative thinking and to change specific errors in thinking (Chapter 11, this volume). Behavioral approaches, on the other hand, attempt to change the maladaptive behavior in order to increase positive reinforcement, which can be done by increasing activity level, enhancing social or relationship skills, and training in problem solving. Thus, although cognitive therapy and behavioral approaches share some elements, "they diverge on the point of cognition as a privileged causal factor in depression and as an essential therapeutic target" (Dimidjian et al., 2011, p. 15). Within behavior models of depression cognitions are seen as the consequence of depression, and hence it is assumed that these faulty cognitions will change as a result of the behavioral treatment.

Increasing pleasant activities. Lewinsohn (1975) has suggested increasing pleasant activities by means of homework assignments as one way of increasing positive reinforcement to the depressed person. A large number of studies have investigated whether this approach (activity scheduling) on its own could be successful in improving depression. Typically, activities that are rated as enjoyable but not engaged in during the last few weeks are given as homework assignments. In a meta-analysis (Cuijpers, van Straten, & Warmerdam, 2007a) on 16 RCTs with 780 subjects a large effect size was found between activity scheduling and control conditions at posttest ($d = 0.87$). In 10 studies included in this meta-analysis, cognitive therapy was compared to activity scheduling. The pooled effect size indicating the difference between these two types of treatment was 0.02, indicating that the difference between the effects of cognitive therapy and activity scheduling was nil. These results were retained at follow-up. Results were confirmed in

a recent meta-analysis of Mazzucchelli, Kane, and Rees, (2009).

Brief behavioral activation is a more recent variant of Lewinsohn's approach. Behavioral activation is a more idiographic and functional approach, giving more attention to the specific environmental contingencies maintaining a patient's depressed behavior. Brief behavioral activation encourages patients to keep active and engaged in life's activities, rather than leading inactive, withdrawn lifestyles. A central component of this approach is that patients learn to investigate how reinforcing activities influence their mood (LeJuez, Hopko, & Hopko, 2001). In this approach patients are asked to rate their life goals and values on a chart, after which patients create an activity hierarchy with 15 activities that are rated from "easiest" to "most difficult," which the patient has to perform from the easy to the more challenging tasks. A number of studies that have evaluated the effectiveness of brief behavioral activation, found this approach effective in depressed patients (Hopko, Lejuez, & Hopko, 2004) and in depressed patients with comorbid substance abuse (Daughters et al., 2008) and cancer (Hopko, Robertson, & Carvalho, 2009). An inpatient study conducted by Hopko and colleagues (2003) revealed that brief behavioral activation was substantially more effective than supportive psychotherapy ($d = 73$; Hopko, Lejuez, LePage, Hopko, & McNeil, 2003). Finally, Snarski et al. (2011) examined the effects of brief behavioral-activation treatment on depressive symptoms among older patients with mild to moderate cognitive impairment. Behavioral activation was associated with a reduction in depressive symptoms compared to treatment as usual. A number of reviews and meta-analyses revealed that behavioral activation is an empirically supported treatment for depression (Cuijpers et al., 2007a; Ekers, Richards, & Gilbody, 2008; Mazzucchelli, Kane, & Rees, 2009; Sturmey, 2009).

Social-skills training. Social skills training as a stand-alone treatment has been associated with decreases in depressive symptoms equivalent to other treatment packages (see Emmelkamp, 2004). Although these studies have shown social-skills training to lead to increased assertiveness and improved social performance, the relationship between improved social performance and reduction in depressed mood remains unclear. The studies conducted so far did not show that social-skills training per se was related to reduction of depression. Although social-skills training is still a component in a number of behavioral manuals for depression, interest in research as stand-alone treatment for depression has waned over the years (Kanter et al., 2010).

Rumination-Focused Therapies

Rumination is one of the key characteristics of depression (e.g. Nolen-Hoeksema, 2000; Papageorgiou & Wells, 2004). Several treatments for depression therefore include strategies that are aimed at directly targeting rumination, including rumination-focused cognitive-behavior therapy, and competitive memory training.

Rumination-focused cognitive-behavioural therapy. Watkins (2008) suggested that rumination is a mediator of treatment effects for depression, and developed an adaptation of CBT (Rumination-Focused Cognitive-Behavioural Therapy; RFCBT), specifically targeting rumination (Watkins et al., 2007). On a theoretical as well as technical level, RFCBT integrates two approaches. First, the basic behavior-analytic and contextual approach used in behavioral activation treatment is adapted to specifically focus on rumination as a dysfunctional coping and avoidance behavior respectively. Second, on the basis of basic experimental research (Watkins, 2008; Watkins et al., 2011) a distinction is made between dysfunctional rumination characterized by an abstract-evaluative and conceptual style of processing on the one hand and a more functional concrete-experiential and nonevaluative mode of processing on the other hand. In practice, RFBCT uses functional behavior analysis to help clients to evaluate the (un)helpfulness of rumination about negative self-experience and teaches clients to shift into the most effective style of thinking. Concreteness training was developed to increase specificity of processing in clients with depression: RFCBT uses experiential/imagery exercises and behavioral experiments to facilitate a more helpful concrete thinking style.

RFCBT was first investigated in a small series of clients with residual depression (Watkins et al., 2007). Generally, treatment led to a substantial reduction in depressed mood and in self-reported rumination as assessed by the Response Styles Questionnaire. A recent RCT investigated whether rumination-focused CBT provided added benefit to treatment as usual (TAU) in reducing residual symptoms of depression (Watkins et al., 2011). RFCBT plus TAU was more effective than TAU alone in reducing depressed mood and rumination. Moreover, change in rumination was found to be a mediator of the effects of treatment condition on reduction in depressive mood (Watkins et al., 2011).

Competitive memory training (COMET). Competitive memory training (COMET) for depressive rumination focuses on the relative retrievability and activation of positive and functional personal experiences (Maarsingh, Korrelboom, & Huijbrechts, 2010). COMET targets the amount of involvement the patient has with negative thoughts and emotions, rather than on the content of dysfunctional cognitions. It uses counter memories to reduce the negative effects of rumination. An incompatible emotional network is installed by clients by teaching them to become indifferent or to adopt an attitude of acceptance. Through repetitive activation in the therapy sessions it is hoped that the incompatible emotional network inhibits the depressive ruminative network.

In two out-patient samples, one with mixed diagnoses (Olij et al., 2006) and one with major depression (Maarsingh et al., 2010), COMET led to enhanced self-esteem and reduction in depressed mood, but these studies were uncontrolled. One controlled study with depressed elderly found COMET as add-on to care as usual more effective than care as usual alone in terms of reduction of depression and reduction of frequency of rumination (Ekkers et al., 2011).

Problem-Solving

There is now a large body of literature that demonstrates a relation between depression and a deficit in problem-solving (Chang, D'Zurilla, & Sanna, 2009; Chow & Chan, 2010; D'Zurilla, Chang, Nottingham, & Faccini, 1998; Lyubomirsky & Nolen-Hoeksema, 1995; Yeung, Lui, Ross, & Murrells, 2007). There is some evidence that training in problem-solving leads to improved mood in depressed individuals. In this treatment, the following phases can be distinguished: problem-orientation, problem-definition and formulation, generation of alternative solutions, decision making, and solution implementation and verification. In the largest study to date problem-solving therapy proved to be more effective in reducing depressive symptoms than no treatment control (Dowrick et al., 2000).

Mynors-Wallis, Gath, Day, and Baker (2000) found problem-solving therapy comparable to antidepressant drugs and superior to placebo (Mynors-Wallis et al., 2000). In a recent study with depressed cancer patients problem solving was as effective as behavioral activation (Hopko et al., 2011). Problem-solving therapy has also been found to be effective in elderly patients (Areán et al., 2010). In two meta-analyses, social problem-solving therapies for depression had a moderate effect size (Bell & D'Zurilla, 2009; Cuijpers et al., 2007b).

Spouse-Aided Therapy

Two forms of spouse-aided therapy have been evaluated. In cases with co-occurring depression and marital discord, conjoint *behavioral marital therapy* may be applied. Here, the emphasis is not only on the mood disorder, but also on the communication between the partners and problem solving. Generally, in the earlier phase of therapy, problems associated with depression that could hinder a successful application of marital therapy are dealt with. Examples of such problems are complicated grief or a low activity level in the depressed patient. Later on the focus of the therapy is shifted to training of communication skills in both spouses. To date, three controlled studies have shown that *conjoint behavioral marital therapy* in depressed, maritally distressed couples may be a good alternative to individual cognitive-behavior therapy (Beach & O'Leary, 1992; Bodenmann et al., 2008; Emanuels-Zuurveen & Emmelkamp, 1996; Jacobson, Dobson, Fruzetti, Schmaling, & Saluski, 1991). These studies suggest that with depressed, maritally distressed, couples, behavioral marital therapy seems to have an exclusive effect on the marital relationship, which is not found in individual cognitive-behavior therapy, while it is as effective as cognitive therapy in reducing depressed mood. Not surprisingly, behavioral marital therapy was hardly effective with depressed patients who did not experience marital problems. An abbreviated version of this program, five sessions of problem-focused treatment for couples, resulted in reducing the depressed partner's symptoms, and in reducing the nondepressed partner's levels of distress (Cohen, O'Leary, & Foran, 2010). In addition, treatment led to enhanced relationship satisfaction. Two thirds of the depressed patients (67%) improved and nearly half of them (47%) recovered at follow-up, compared to only 17%

improved and 8% recovered among patients in the waiting list control group.

Partner-assisted cognitive-behavior therapy for depression was developed by Emanuels-Zuurveen and Emmelkamp (1997) for depressed nonmaritally distressed couples and is based on Lewinsohn's and Beck's individual therapy of depression. During spouse-aided therapy, partners join all sessions. Treatment focuses on the depression and on ways both partners can deal more adequately with depression-related situations rather than on the marital relationship per se. Therefore, spouses are involved in devising reinforcing activities, in stimulating patients to engage in rewarding activities and to participate in role playing. Further, spouses are asked to attend to the dysfunctional thoughts of the patient and to discuss these with both patient and therapist. In addition, partners are actively involved in designing behavioral experiments to test (irrational) beliefs and are encouraged to take part in challenging the assumptions held by the patient. The results of partner-assisted cognitive-behavior therapy were comparable with those of individual cognitive-behavior therapy (Emanuels-Zuurveen & Emmelkamp, 1997). Both treatments led to statistically significant improvement on depressed mood, behavioral activity, and dysfunctional cognitions. However, none of the treatment formats affected relationship variables, which comes as no surprise, because couples were not maritally distressed prior to treatment. Thus, partner-assisted cognitive-behavior therapy was as effective as individual cognitive-behavior therapy.

Morbid Grief

When depression is caused by grief, alternative (behavioral) procedures may be indicated. Ramsay (1979) treated patients with pathological grief with a kind of imaginal prolonged exposure to bereavement cues and found this treatment to be effective in an uncontrolled series of 23 cases. Two controlled studies have been reported that both investigated the value of exposure in morbid grief (Mawson, Marks, Ramm, & Stern, 1981; Sireling, Cohen, & Marks, 1988). In both studies imaginal exposure (guided mourning) was found to be slightly superior to a treatment with anti-exposure instructions. Patients who had received anti-exposure instructions and who had been encouraged to undertake new activities and not to think about the loss (but to think about the future rather than to dwell on the past) improved markedly despite the continued avoidance of bereavement cues. In a study of Boelen, de Keijser, van den Hout, and van den Bout (2007) with suffererers of complicated grief, cognitive restructuring and exposure therapy were compared in a crossover design with supportive counseling. The combination of exposure and cognitive restructuring was more effective than supportive counseling. Exposure therapy proved to be more effective than cognitive restructuring. Finally, Shear, Frank, Houck, and Reynolds (2005) investigated the relative efficacy of cognitive-behavioral treatment (CBT) and interpersonal psychotherapy (IPT) for complicated grief: CBT was more effective than IPT.

Behavioral Therapy Versus Cognitive Therapy

A number of studies evaluated the relative efficacy of cognitive therapy with various forms of behavior therapy. In a number of reviews and meta-analyses behavior therapy was found to be as effective as cognitive therapy (Cuijpers et al., 2007a; Emmelkamp, 2004; Gloaguen, Cottraux, Cucherat, & Blackburn, 1998; Longmore & Worrell, 2007). Because a variety of depressed patients were involved in studies included in these meta-analyses (i.e., outpatients, inpatients, geriatric patients, and low-socioeconomic Puerto Rican women) and the results were quite consistent across these populations, the finding that both treatments are equally effective is quite robust.

Theoretically, one would expect that cognitive therapy and behavior therapy would have differential effects on cognitive and behavioral variables. Although a number of studies were designed to show that these treatments have specific effects on relevant targets, the results are rather negative. Generally, relevant behavioral and cognitive variables are changed as much by cognitive therapy as by behavior therapy (Emmelkamp, 2004; Longmore & Worell, 2007). Thus, effects of behavioral and cognitive programs appear to be "nonspecific," changing both behavioral and cognitive components, thus precluding conclusions with respect to the therapeutic processes responsible for the improvement. To complicate matters further, comparison of cognitive therapy with pharmacotherapy show that in most studies cognitions are changed as much by pharmacotherapy as by cognitive therapy (e.g., Garratt, Ingram, Rand, & Sawalani, 2007). Thus it seems that cognitive distortions act as symptoms of depression rather than as mediators of treatment outcome.

In sum, behavioral programs have shown statistically and clinically significant results in reduction of depression, change of thinking patterns, and improved social performance. Most studies were unable to show, however, that the target behavior directly addressed in the treatment modality was selectively affected. Rather, effects of behavioral programs were "nonspecific," changing both behavioral and cognitive components, thus precluding conclusions with respect to the therapeutic processes responsible for the improvement.

One major problem in interpreting the results of cognitive therapy for depression concerns the behavioral components included in the "cognitive" package (Beck, Rush, Shaw, & Emery, 1987). Cognitive therapy seeks to uncover dysfunctional depressogenic cognitions and to correct these cognitions by systematic "reality testing." Actually, this particular treatment approach is an amalgam of cognitive and behavioral interventions, including behavioral task assignments and assertiveness training. However, findings from a component analysis of this cognitive package suggest that the behavioral activation components alone worked as well as the full cognitive package (Jacobson et al., 1996). Also at 2-year follow-up the behavioral package did not result in more relapse than the full cognitive package (Gortner, Gollan, Dobson, & Jacobson, 1998).

Various pharmacological interventions have long been established as the standard of treatment for major depression. Although a number of studies have compared the effects of drug treatment with cognitive therapy (e.g., DeRubeis, Gelfand, Tang, & Simons, 1999), relatively few studies have compared behavioral procedures with drug treatment (see Emmelkamp, 2004). One study is of particular interest. Dimidjian et al. (2006) compared behavioral activation, cognitive therapy, and antidepressant medication in a randomized placebo-controlled design in adults with major depressive disorder ($N = 241$). Although all three treatments were equally effective in moderately depressed patients, among more severely depressed patients, behavioral activation was comparable to antidepressant medication, and both significantly outperformed cognitive therapy. Interestingly, behavioral activation was superior to medication and cognitive therapy in terms of less dropout and percentage of participants brought to remission. At 2-year follow-up both behavioral activation and cognitive therapy were as effective as the condition in which the patients had maintained their medication (Dobson et al., 2008).

Although a number of studies have evaluated the efficacy of Internet interventions for depression symptoms (see Gallego & Emmelkamp, 2012; Ruwaard et al., 2012), most of these programs contain both cognitive restructuring and behavioral assignments, thus precluding definite conclusions with respect to the feasibility of an Internet-based pure behavioral treatment. Nevertheless, there is some evidence that Internet-based broad-spectrum CBT programs are no more effective than Internet-based problem-solving therapy. One deficiency of the studies into Internet-based treatments for depression is the lack of formal diagnosis in most studies.

Concluding Remarks

There is now increased evidence that cognitive and behavioral approaches are effective in alleviating depression in mildly to moderately depressed individuals, but no single approach has been found to be consistently superior. Unfortunately, long-term follow-up studies are relatively rare. Only a few studies have addressed the issue of maintenance of treatment effects and generally, results are disappointing (Emmelkamp, 2004). In a study of Gortner et al. (1998), almost half of the patients who recovered by the end of treatment had suffered a relapse 2 years later. The principal finding of the present review is that a variety of cognitive-behavioral procedures are successful in improving depression, but one cannot conclude that the specific components of treatment were responsible for improvement. This finding suggests that common elements in these treatments are responsible for the improvements achieved. Such common elements are a clear rationale, highly structured therapy, homework assignments, and the training in skills (either cognitive or behavioral) that the patient can utilize in handling his or her problems.

Future research to identify the specific active ingredients of effective interventions should include component (e.g., Jacobson et al., 1996) and process analysis approaches. Future studies would enhance understanding of the processes by which various cognitive and behavioral interventions achieve clinically significant outcome when moderators and mediators would be studied. Results so far suggest that the results achieved are not specifically related to the specific intervention investigated, given that cognitions change as well as a result of behavioral activation as a result of cognitive therapy (e.g., Jacobson et al., 1996). In addition to establishing a firmer theoretical basis for these interventions, identifying potential moderators and mediators of change may help identify who is likely or unlikely to respond to particular interventions. Given the chronic nature of depression and the high chance of relapse, studies into the long-term effects (beyond 2 years) are needed. Finally, research into the association between neural and genetic factors that are related to depression may help to understand who will benefit from treatment and who will not.

ALCOHOL ABUSE

Alcohol dependence is characterized by either tolerance (need for markedly increased amounts of alcohol to achieve the desired effect) or alcohol withdrawal symptoms after cessation or reduction in drinking. Aversive conditioning has long been used in the treatment of alcoholism (Emmelkamp, 1986, 1994), but interest has waned in the past decades. In recent years the interest of clinicians and researchers has moved away from aversive conditioning methods to alternative cognitive-behavioral methods (Emmelkamp & Vedel, 2006).

Motivational Interviewing

Motivational interviewing is one of the most popular behavioral methods in the addiction field, although one might wonder what is exactly behavioral in this procedure. Motivational interviewing was developed by Miller (1983, 1996) and tries to influence the expectations and behavior of the substance abuser. This is achieved by an empathetic therapist who tries to help the patients to reach their own decisions with respect to the pros and cons of substance abuse, by giving advice, clarification, and feedback. Thus, rather than being coercive or confrontational, the therapist facilitates the patient to become aware of the necessity for behavioral change, and to convey the patient's responsibility in choosing whether and how to make changes. Motivational interviewing was found to be more effective than directive confrontational counseling (Miller, Benefield, & Tonigan, 1993). Although motivational interviewing originally was intended to be a prelude to treatment, it might also be used as a stand-alone treatment.

Motivational interviewing has now been evaluated in a number of controlled studies either as "appetizer" or as stand-alone treatment. As far as enhancement of motivation and prevention of dropout is concerned, this procedure is more effective than other treatments, but only in less severely dependent drinkers (see Emmelkamp & Vedel, 2006). Although motivational interviewing as stand-alone treatment was found to be as effective as cognitive-behavior therapy and the 12-step approach (Project MATCH Research Group, 1997a), results of meta-analyses reveal that the effect size of motivational interviewing is low to moderate ($d = 0.26$, Andréasson & Ōjehagen, 2003; $d = 0.41$, Hettema, Steele, & Miller, 2005). There is considerable variability in effects across studies, which may be related to different patient populations (e.g., alcohol dependence versus alcohol abuse; comorbidity versus no comorbidity), and heterogeneity in the implementation of motivational interviewing (Crits-Christoph et al., 2009).

Controlled Drinking

Although many practitioners in the addiction field hold that total abstinence is the only viable treatment goal, there is robust evidence that a substantial number of problem drinkers can learn and maintain a pattern of moderate and nonproblem drinking, even when the treatment focused on total abstinence. Controlled-drinking treatment programs typically involve self-monitoring of drinking, training in drinking rate control (e.g., expanding the time frame between drinks), goal setting, functional analysis of drinking behavior including identifying high-risk situations, and instructions about alternatives to alcohol abuse.

A series of studies have evaluated this particular approach, and this program is at least as effective as more traditional abstinence oriented programs (see Emmelkamp & Vedel, 2006). Most controlled-drinking clients achieved moderation of alcohol use, and most abstinence-oriented clients failed to abstain but nonetheless moderated their drinking. Walters (2000) included 17 studies in a meta-analysis and found that behavioral self-control programs were more effective than no-treatment and at least as effective as abstinence-oriented programs, especially at follow-ups of 1 year or longer. The follow-up findings are rather important because the proponents of the abstinence-oriented approach hold that the effects of controlled drinking programs are temporary. In addition, this meta-analysis does not support claims that abstinence-oriented programs achieve superior results to controlled-drinking programs in alcohol-dependent subjects rather than in problem drinkers. Further research is needed to investigate for which patients abstinence-oriented programs are better suited than controlled-drinking programs and vice versa.

Cue Exposure

Siegel (1983) suggested that drug cues may serve as conditioned stimuli for a compensatory response (opposite in direction to the unconditioned drug effect) that compensates for the impending unconditioned drug response. In alcoholics this compensatory response would probably be an aversive state and may be interpreted as craving. Since then, many addiction theories assume that craving plays a central role in the acquisition and maintenance of drug dependence and relapse (Tiffany & Conklin, 2000).

A few studies have investigated whether cue-exposure therapy could also be used as treatment for individuals, with controlled drinking rather than abstinence as their treatment goal. Studies from the United Kingdom (Heather et al., 2000) and from Australia (Dawe, Rees, Sitharthan, Mattick, & Heather, 2002) investigated whether moderation-oriented cue-exposure would be superior in effectiveness to the conventional method of training problem drinkers to moderate their consumption, which is known as behavioral self-control training. Results revealed that moderation-oriented cue-exposure was equally as effective as behavioral self-control training. It should be noted, however, that the generalizability of these findings applies to the population of problem drinkers with a mean level of dependence in the mild to moderate range. Severely dependent patients were not included in these studies. In sum, cue exposure may be effective in problem drinkers, but there is no evidence that cue exposure is effective as stand-alone treatment in severely alcohol dependent patients (Emmelkamp & Vedel, 2006).

Coping-Skills Training and Relapse Prevention

Based on cognitive-social learning theory a number of cognitive-behavioral treatments have been devised, including self-management programs, social-skills training, cognitive-restructuring, and problem solving. A central feature of these various methods is the development of coping skills to enable the patient to stop or control his or her drinking. These approaches are at least partly based on the assumption that alcoholism or problem drinking is a habitual, maladaptive way of coping with stress. Indeed, there is considerable evidence that relapse among alcoholics is related to high levels of stress, lack of coping resources, poor social support, and low self-efficacy (Ames & Roitzsch, 2000; Emmelkamp & Vedel, 2006).

In a now classic paper, Marlatt and Gordon (1980) reported that for alcoholics, 23% of relapses involved social-pressure situations such as being offered a drink, and in another 29% of the cases, frustrating situations in which the individual was unable to express anger preceded drinking behavior. According to the relapse-prevention model proposed by Marlatt and Witkiewitz (2010), relapse is likely to occur when at-risk individuals who lack adequate coping skills are confronted with high risk.

Techniques that are directed at relapse prevention include self-monitoring of craving and substance (ab)use, the identification of high-risk situations for relapse, strategies for coping with craving, and training in social skills (e.g., refusing a drink), problem solving to deal with future lapses and, more recently, emotion regulation skills. Such multimodal relapse-prevention programs were found to be more effective than no treatment at all (see Emmelkamp & Vedel, 2006). In the MATCH study, coping-skills training was compared with 12-step facilitation and motivational enhancement therapy. Results of the MATCH study found that all three treatment approaches were more or less equally effective (Project MATCH Research Group, 1997a, 1997b, 1998). The results of comparative evaluations with other interventions—that is, interactional group therapy (Ito, Donovan, & Hall, 1988; Kadden, Cooney, Getter, & Litt, 1989; Litt, Kadden, Cooney, & Kabela, 2003) and supportive therapy (O'Malley et al., 1996), are inconclusive.

In a meta-analysis by Irvin, Bowers, Dunn, and Wang (1999), relapse prevention in substance-abuse disorders resulted in a rather modest effect size ($d = 0.25$), which tended to decrease over time. Relapse prevention was most effective in alcohol-use disorders in contrast to drug use and smoking. Further, relapse prevention was found to have more effect on psychosocial functioning than on alcohol use. In the meta-analysis of Andréasson and Öjehagen (2003) cognitive-behavior therapy resulted in an effect size of $d = 0.73$.

Although it is generally assumed that the results of coping-skills training is mediated by a change in coping skills, this has hardly been investigated (Emmelkamp & Vedel, 2006; Litt, Kadden, Kabela-Cormier, 2009). In sum, coping-skills training has been found to be effective in a number of studies, but only a few studies have found support for a mediating role of adaptive coping in reducing drinking. Further studies are needed to determine which of the various components included in the treatment package (e.g., self-monitoring, the identification of high-risk situations, strategies for coping with craving, and training in problem solving) are the necessary ingredients for successful therapeutic outcome and prevention of relapse, and which components are redundant (DiClemente, 2007; Longabaugh et al., 2005).

Anticraving Medication and CBT

A number of controlled studies have evaluated the effects of anticraving medication in alcoholics (i.e., naltrexone and acamprosate), usually in combination with some form of counseling or psychotherapy. The effects of acamprosate and naltrexone relate to different aspects of drinking behavior, with acamprosate decreasing alcohol consumption and naltrexone stabilizing abstinence. In a meta-analysis, effect sizes for naltrexone and acamprosate were modest: $d = .28$ and $d = 0.26$, respectively (Berglund, 2005). In a large comparative study (the Combined Pharmacotherapies and Behavioral Interventions [COMBINE]), the effects of naltrexone and acamprosate were compared with the effects of CBT with or without medication. Results from the COMBINE study indicated that CBT was effective in reducing heavy drinking following treatment with or without the provision of pharmacotherapy (Anton et al., 2006; Donovan et al., 2008; LoCastro et al., 2009).

Drug Abuse

Multiple drugs used concurrently is the rule rather than the exception, especially in opioid users and crack cocaine users. In reading the following review of outcome studies, the reader should keep in mind that many opioid users and crack cocaine users often meet criteria for comorbid alcohol, cannabis, stimulant, and sedative dependence (Emmelkamp & Vedel, 2006).

Motivational Interviewing

More than 15 randomized controlled trials (RCTs) demonstrated that motivational interviewing had some effects in terms of enhanced motivation in drug-dependent populations, including cannabis-dependent adolescents, opiate-dependent adults, cocaine-dependent adults, amphetamine users, and polydrug users (Vedel & Emmelkamp, 2012). Most studies found that motivational interviewing led to a better adherence and increased motivation, but only a few studies found that motivational interviewing led to decreased drug use or abstinence. Two meta-analyses (Burke, Arkowitz, & Menchola, 2003; Hettema et al., 2005) analyzed data from clinical trials on the effects of motivational interviewing on substance abuse and health behavior. Motivational interviewing was equivalent to other active treatments and superior to no treatment and placebo controls for problems involving drug abuse. Motivational interviewing resulted in a medium effect size in studies with illicit drug use. Burke et al. (2003) found an investigator allegiance effect: Studies by the founder of motivational interviewing (W. R. Miller) resulted in better outcome than other studies.

Cue Exposure

In cue-exposure treatment of drug abusing patients, patients are repeatedly exposed to the sights, or smells of substances, such as the sight of white powder on a mirror, until the cravings elicited by these cues substantially weaken. In actual practice cue exposure is difficult to apply, because in advance generalization needs to be planned by identifying and sampling many conditioned stimuli (CS) from the start. After successful reductions in the strength of experienced craving, substance-abusing patients are assumed to be more able to resist drug use when confronted with these cues in daily life. In most treatment protocols, cue exposure is not used as a stand-alone treatment, but rather as an adjunct to a broader cognitive-behavioral treatment package.

Results of randomized controlled trials are inconclusive (Vedel & Emmelkamp, 2012). Treatments using cue exposure have yielded promising results in some studies with illicit drug users, but others have reported negative results.

Cue-exposure therapy is probably efficacious in selected patients with illicit drug use disorders, but only as part of a more comprehensive treatment program. Cue exposure has not been shown to be effective in opiate addicts so far.

Coping-Skills Training and Relapse Prevention

There are a number of studies with primarily cocaine-dependent patients that show favorable effects for CBT.

There is considerable evidence that relapse prevention-based CBT is effective in the treatment of cocaine use disorders; there is no evidence, however, that cognitive therapy is effective with these disorders. Results in other drug disorders than cocaine are inconclusive. In amphetamine users, studies found only small and on most measures nonsignificant differences between coping-skills training and other treatment approaches (for review see Vedel & Emmelkamp, 2012). In marijuana users, results are inconclusive. Although relapse prevention–based CBT was more effective than motivational interviewing (Marijuana Treatment Project Research Group, 2004) it was less effective than abstinence-based vouchers at follow-up (Budney, Moore, Rocha, & Higgins, 2006).

There is considerable evidence that in opioid dependence methadone maintenance treatment is effective in decreasing heroin use (see Emmelkamp & Vedel, 2006). There is, however, relatively little evidence available that CBT might enhance methadone maintenance treatment. Scherbaum et al. (2005) found that a 20-week group CBT program as add-on to methadone maintenance led to a significant difference in drug use at 6-month follow-up. In a study by Hayes at al. (2004) there was also some evidence that adding a particular variant of CBT, acceptance and commitment therapy, to methadone maintenance treatment resulted in better outcome than methadone maintenance treatment on its own. In a meta-analysis by Irvin et al. (1999), relapse prevention–based CBT in substance abuse disorders resulted in a rather modest effect size ($d = 0.25$), which tended to decrease over time. Relapse prevention was most effective in alcohol use disorders in contrast to drug use and smoking. In the meta-analysis of Dutra et al. (2008) the efficacy of CBT was compared to treatment as usual or inactive treatment. The CBT and relapse prevention effect sizes were in the low—moderate range: CBT ($d = 0.28$) and relapse prevention ($d = 0.32$). In contrast, contingency management produced a moderate to high effect size ($d = 0.58$).

There is consistent evidence that CBT and relapse prevention are more effective than inactive control conditions, but effect sizes are small. Results of CBT and relapse prevention with illicit drug users are generally comparable to those achieved with 12-step approaches.

Contingency Management and Community Reinforcement Approach

There is now considerable evidence that contingency management is particularly useful for drug abusers. Contingency management (CM) is based on operant conditioning. In CM the programs tangible reinforcers (vouchers) are provided when the desired behavior is shown, or withheld when the desired behavior does not occur. For example, biochemically verified abstinence from recent drug use is reinforced with vouchers exchangeable for retail items meeting a predetermined therapeutic goal. These vouchers are redeemable for goods and services, the value of the vouchers escalating with each successive drug-free specimen. In these programs various target behaviors have been used (e.g., drug abstinence, medication compliance, or attendance at therapy sessions).

The main advantage of vouchers is that they can be handed out immediately following the desired behavior. A number of programs also use punishment following positive drug tests, including suspension of employment with subsequent loss of income, removal from house facilities, and transportation to a shelter.

In some treatment protocols, voucher-based incentive is combined with an intensive behavioral treatment known as the *community reinforcement approach* (CRA) (Hunt & Azrin, 1973). CRA encourages involvement in rewarding, nondrug-related alternatives to illicit drug use and is directed to change a lifestyle of substance abuse into lifestyle that is more rewarding than substance abuse. Thus, the emphasis is not only on promoting abstinence of substance abuse using voucher-based incentive programs as described earlier, but on social activities that are incompatible with substance use as well. Community reinforcement may contribute to persistence of abstinence after discontinuation of vouchers.

CM procedures have been found to be effective in cocaine dependent patients (e.g., Ghitza et al., 2007; Petry, Alessi, Hanson, & Sierra, 2007), opioid dependent patients (e.g., Ghitza et al., 2007), metamphetamine dependence (e.g., Peck, Reback, Yang, Rotheram-Fuller, & Shoptaw, 2005; Peirce, Petry, & Stitzer, 2006; Rawson et al., 2006) and have also led to a reduced use of marijuana (e.g., Kadden et al., 2007). CM interventions appear to affect the behaviors they target, and they do not readily extend to other areas (Petry, Martin, & Simcic, 2005). There is robust evidence that it is not the delivery of the reinforcer per se, but the *contingent* reinforcement that is effective (Vedel & Emmelkamp, 2012). Further, higher density of reinforcement led to higher abstinence rates from cocaine (Ghitza et al., 2007). Taken together the results with respect to the contingency and density of reinforcers, support the general principles of operant behavior.

Reinforcement is usually contingent upon abstinence but CM techniques that reinforce completion of nondrug-related activities that are incompatible with drug use may be efficacious in treating substance dependence as well (e.g., Lewis & Petry, 2005). Sindelar, Elbel, and Petry (2007) tested the cost-effectiveness of contingency management in cocaine abuse comparing lower versus higher prices as reinforcement for abstinence. The higher pay-out prices were found to be cost-effective across all three outcome measures: average consecutive weeks abstaining, percentage completing a 12-week program, and percentage samples of drug-free urine.

Several meta-analyses have been conducted regarding the effectiveness of contingency management. In a meta-analysis by Lusier, Heil, Mongeon, Badger, and Higgins (2006) voucher-based reinforcement therapy generated significantly better outcomes than control conditions. The average effect size was 0.32 (small). More immediate voucher delivery resulted in an effect size that was approximately twice as high (0.37) as delayed delivery (0.19). Further greater monetary value of the voucher (> 16\$) resulted in a higher effect size (0.43) as compared to smaller monetary value < 5\$ (0.23). In a meta-analysis by

Schumacher et al. (2007) a series of four RCTs evaluating CM in Birmingham, Alabama were reanalyzed. Subjects were homeless cocaine users. CM was more effective than day treatment. At follow-up 6 months after treatment 55% of the CM group was abstinent as compared to 25% of the day-treatment group. In the meta-analysis of Prendergast et al. (2006) on the effectiveness of community reinforcement approaches in alcohol, tobacco, or illicit drugs the mean (weighted) effect size was $d = 0.42$ (medium); however, most studies did not involve illicit drug users. CM was more effective in the treatment of opiate use ($d = 0.65$) and cocaine use ($d = 0.66$) compared to multiple drugs ($d = 0.42$).

In a meta-analysis of Dutra et al. (2008) the efficacy of behavioral treatments were compared to control conditions including treatment as usual or inactive treatment for cannabis, cocaine, opiate, and polysubstance abuse and dependence. Thirty-four studies were included ($N = 2,340$), 16 studies on CM, of which two combined CM with cognitive-behavior therapy (CBT), 13 studies on CBT and 5 studies on relapse prevention. CM demonstrated the lowest dropout rates (29.4%), compared to CBT (35.3%), and CBT plus CM (44.5%). CM produced a moderate-high effect size ($d = 0.58$), compared to CBT ($d = 0.28$) and relapse prevention ($d = 0.32$), which effect sizes are in the low to moderate range.

In sum, community reinforcement approaches are probably the most effective interventions for illicit drug use disorders. Although there is some evidence that the combination of community reinforcement and CBT is slightly more effective than community reinforcement as stand-alone treatment, this is based on a few studies only.

Spouse-Aided Therapy

A growing number of studies have accumulated over the past 30 years supporting the use of behavioral couples therapy (BCT) for alcohol and drug use disorders (Emmelkamp & Vedel, 2006). Studies show that patients suffering from substance use disorders often have higher relationship distress (Emmelkamp & Vedel, 2002) and this relationship distress or interpersonal conflict is frequently associated with relapse (see also Chapter 15, this volume).

Actively involving a spouse or partner in treatment as an adjunctive therapeutic strategy can serve different purposes; a partner can be involved as a coach in the process of behavior change, disorder-specific relationship issues can be addressed (protecting the patient from the negative consequences of his/her problem behavior), or more general relationship functioning can be addressed. BCT in the treatment of substance use disorders combines all of these elements. BCT assumes that substance abuse and relationship functioning are reciprocal. In this view, substance abuse has a deteriorating effect on relationship functioning and high levels of relationship distress in combination with attempts by the partners to control substance use may cue craving, reinforce substance use, or trigger relapse (Powers, Vedel, & Emmelkamp, 2008).

A number of studies have evaluated the effects of BCT. In a meta-analysis (Powers, Vedel et al., 2008) 12 ($n = 754$) randomized-controlled BCT trials were included. BCT outperformed control conditions not only on frequency of use, but also on consequences of use, and relationship satisfaction. Further, there is some evidence that restoring marital satisfaction and reducing conflicts reduce the chance for relapse (Emmelkamp & Vedel, 2002).

Concluding Remarks

As noted before, many substance abusers are polydrug users, which hampers interpretation of studies into the effects of specific CBT treatment for specific substance abuse. Nevertheless, as reported in this chapter, across a large number of diverse studies, CBT for adult substance-use disorders resulted in small, but statistically significant, effect over care as usual and CBT was found as effective or more effective than other psychotherapies. The meta-analyses show effect sizes for CBT generally in the small to moderate range (e.g., Dutra et al., 2008; Irvin et al., 1999; Magill & Ray, 2007; Powers et al., 2008; Prendergast et al., 2006).

PERSONALITY DISORDERS

A number of outcome studies have been conducted, which evaluate the effects of (cognitive) behavior therapy in patients with personality disorders (PDs). In a number of controlled studies that have been conducted encouraging results have been achieved with (cognitive)-behavior therapy in chronically suicidal borderline patients and in patients with avoidant personality disorder. Few studies have involved antisocial PD. To date no RCT has focused on patients with schizotypal, schizoid, and paranoid PDs (but see Bartak et al., 2010).

The Anxious-Inhibited Cluster (Cluster C)

A number of studies have evaluated the effects of psychological treatments (i.e., psychodynamic and cognitive-behavioral therapies) with patients with Cluster C personality disorders. A study by Svartberg, Stiles, and Seltzer (2004) examined the effects of a 40-session short-term dynamic psychotherapy specifically designed for personality problems and comparing this to cognitive therapy. Fifty-one patients with Cluster C personality disorders were randomly allocated to receive weekly sessions of dynamic therapy (Malan's approach) or cognitive therapy (Beck's approach). Both groups improved and continued to improve after treatment until 2-year follow-up both in distress and in terms of avoidant personality profile (Millon's Clinical Multiaxial Inventory). Two years after treatment, 54% of the short-term dynamic psychotherapy patients and 42% of the cognitive therapy patients had recovered symptomatically, whereas approximately 40% of the patients in both groups had recovered in terms of interpersonal problems and personality functioning. With respect to interpersonal problems, effect sizes for both treatments were large (short-term dynamic psychotherapy: $d = 1.07$; cognitive therapy: $d = 1.29$). None of the differences between dynamic therapy and cognitive therapy were significant. Increases in insight, however, predicted improvement within the psychodynamic group, but not within the CBT group (Kallestad et al., 2010). Results were replicated in another RCT; also here short-term dynamic psychotherapy was found to be as effective as CBT (Muran, Safran, Samstag, & Winston, 2005).

Psychoeducation and problem solving has also been evaluated in a RCT with patients with PDs. Huband, McMurran, Evans, and Duggan (2007) compared problem solving therapy (N-87) to a waiting list control condition for patients suffering from mixed personality disorders. Problem-solving therapy led to significant improvement in problem solving as well as overall functioning, compared with the control condition. About half of the sample consisted of patients with Cluster C PDs.

Results were corroborated in a meta-analytic review of psychotherapy for individuals with Cluster C disorders. Cognitive-behavioral therapy, social skills training, and psychodynamic therapy resulted in clinically significant improvements (medium to large effects) and treatment gains were maintained up to follow-up periods of 3 years (Simon, 2009).

Avoidant Personality Disorder

A number of studies have evaluated the effects of psychological treatments with patients with avoidant PD. Although a number of studies into CBT with social phobia included patients with a comorbid avoidant PD, generally, the effects of treatment on the avoidant PD was not established. Further, comparisons between trials with social phobia rather than avoidant personality disorder as primary complaint are fraught with difficulty because of differences in selection criteria, and other characteristics. It is questionable whether patients with a primary diagnosis of social phobia with comorbid avoidant PD are comparable to patients with a primary diagnosis of avoidant PD. Therefore, we limit our discussion here to studies evaluating treatment for avoidant PD as the primary complaint.

Because patients with avoidant PD may misinterpret ambiguous social information and are inclined to infer rejection, they will avoid all kinds of social situations. A variety of cognitive and behavioral strategies can be used to challenge and refute negative expectations and inferences about social encounters, while behavioral exposure in vivo strategies may be used to help patients habituate to aversive social stimulation. Emmelkamp et al. (2006) compared the effectiveness of such a CBT with brief dynamic therapy in outpatients suffering from avoidant personality disorder. Treatment lasted 20 sessions. CBT in general operates from the assumption that adjustment is dependent on accurate information processing. Accordingly, it aims to identify and modify core dysfunctional beliefs that automatically organize biased perceptions of self, others, and the future. CBT in this study was based on the assumption that anxiety and avoidance in avoidant PD are related to individuals' maladaptive beliefs and related thought processes. The model emphasizes collaborative interactions between patient and therapist in conjunction with specific cognitive and behavioral techniques such as Socratic dialogue, monitoring of beliefs, analysis of the advantages/disadvantages of avoidance analysis, activity monitoring and scheduling, graded exposure assignments, behavioral experiments, and role-play (Beck, Freeman, & Davis, 2004; Emmelkamp et al., 1992).

Brief dynamic therapy was based on the assumption that anxiety and avoidance are related to individuals' unconscious psychodynamic conflicts, in addition to which shame plays a major role. Treatment was directed at defense restructuring and affect restructuring (Malan, 1979). However, a flexible approach was used. In a number of cases a more supportive attitude and technique was used to bolster threatened equilibrium and to relieve the consequences of unconscious conflict by means of methods such as suggestion, reassurance, and encouragement (Luborsky & Mark, 1991).

At posttest immediately after treatment the most favorable outcome was obtained from CBT: CBT was more effective than waiting-list control and brief dynamic therapy for all primary outcome measures. At 6-month follow-up, CBT was found to be significantly superior to brief dynamic therapy on most measures: only 9% of the CBT patients were still classified as having avoidant personality disorder, whereas 36% of the brief dynamic therapy patients still fulfilled the criteria.

The results of the Emmelkamp et al. (2006) study support earlier studies that evaluated behavioral treatments for patients classified as having avoidant PD (e.g., Renneberg, Goldstein, & Phillips, 1990). The behavioral treatments investigated in these studies included social skills training and in vivo exposure to social situations, but none looked at cognitive therapy. Whether cognitive therapy enhances the effects of behavior therapy deserves further study. Given the high prevalence of avoidant PD in the community (Torgersen, 2005), the persistence of avoidant PD (Shea et al., 2002), and the high-functional impairment related to avoidant PD (e.g., Skodol et al., 2002), the robust finding across a number of studies that (cognitive) behavioural treatments are effective with avoidant PD provides an important step forward for community mental health care.

Borderline Personality Disorder

Until 1990, the dominant idea was that borderline PD was essentially untreatable and that clinical management was the best one could do for these "highly dysfunctional and notoriously difficult patients." Several promising psychosocial interventions have been developed, some of which fared well in controlled research. To date, four alternative approaches to therapy with borderline PD have been manualized as well as subjected to controlled empirical studies. These are dialectical behaviour therapy (Linehan, 1993), schema-focused therapy (Young, Klosko, & Weishaar, 2003), transference-focused therapy (Clarkin, Yeomans, & Kernberg, 1999), and mentalization-based therapy (Bateman & Fonagy, 2004).

Dialectical Behavior Therapy (DBT)

DBT was specifically developed for chronically suicidal and severely dysfunctional borderline individuals (Linehan, 1993). Linehan considers emotional dysregulation at the core of the borderline pathology. Emotional dysregulation leads to a cascade of dysregulation in other domains: interpersonal dysregulation, cognitive dysregulation, and a dysregulated sense of self. The idea is that the patients do not learn to recognize, label, and modulate their (intense) emotional experiences and that they do not develop trust in their private experiences. DBT treatment strategies aim to enhance emotion regulation by increasing awareness and acceptance of the emotional experience, and by changing negative affect through new learning experiences (Linehan, 1993). Thus, the fundamental "dialectic" of DBT is between acceptance and change. A comprehensive DBT treatment package consists of (a) weekly individual outpatient DBT sessions, (b) a weekly DBT group skills training, (c) adjunctive telephone consultation, (d) supported by a consultation team, and (e) auxiliary treatments (e.g., pharmacotherapy).

To date, a number of controlled studies have demonstrated the effectiveness of this approach for borderline patients. In a landmark study in which patients with borderline PD who recently had engaged in parasuicidal behavior were randomly assigned to 1-year outpatient DBT or treatment as usual Linehan and colleagues (Linehan, Armstrong, Suarez, Allmon, & Heard, 1991; Linehan, Heard, & Armstrong, 1993) demonstrated efficacy for this form of therapy in reducing the frequency of parasuicidal behavior, and in retaining patients in therapy: DBT led to less dropout of treatment (16%). Further, after a year patients receiving DBT spent less time in the hospital than patients assigned to treatment as usual. However, DBT was not more effective than the control condition in terms of reduction of hopelessness, depressed mood, and suicidal ideation. At 1-year follow-up differences between DBT and treatment as usual were less pronounced, although patients treated with DBT continued to show superior outcomes on some measures.

The first replication study by an independent group, though only a small pilot study, provided further support for the efficacy of the DBT model (Koons et al., 2001). In female borderline patients (U.S. veterans) 6 months of DBT resulted in more improvement than controls in suicidal ideation, hopelessness, depression, and anger expression. The enhanced outcome on depression, hopelessness, and suicidal ideation in the Koons et al. (2001) study may be attributed to the fact that their patients were less severe in terms of suicidal behavior.

Linehan's DBT was developed as an outpatient treatment to prevent emergency room visits and hospital admissions. On the other hand, attempts have been made to adapt this treatment to a hospital setting for inpatients with borderline PD (Swenson, Sanderson, Dulit, & Linehan, 2001). Inpatient DBT treatment procedures include contingency management procedures, skills training including mindfulness training and coaching, behavioral analysis, structured response protocols to suicidal behaviors on the unit, and consultation team meetings for DBT staff. Bohus et al. (2004) compared DBT (3 months) in a hospital setting with outpatient care as usual. One month after treatment DBT patients improved significantly more than controls on self-mutilation, depression and anxiety, interpersonal functioning, social adjustment, and global psychopathology. Unfortunately, patients were not randomly assigned to conditions, which limits the conclusions that can be drawn with respect to the efficacy of inpatient DBT for borderline PD.

Roepke et al. (2011) tested the impact of a 12-week inpatient DBT program versus waiting-list control in a RCT. Patients treated with the DBT program showed significantly more improvement in self-concept, an enhancement in self-esteem, and reduction of psychopathological symptoms compared to patients on the waiting list; 75% of patients fulfilled criteria of clinical improvement as calculated by the RCI. This is the first study that demonstrated that relatively short-term DBT is able to improve identity disturbance in borderline PD patients.

In a study in Australia (Pasiencny & Connor, 2011) the clinical and cost effectiveness of providing DBT over care as usual was investigated. After 6 months of treatment the DBT group showed significantly greater reductions in suicidal/nonsuicidal self-injury, emergency department visits, psychiatric admissions, and bed days. Self-report measures were administered to a reduced sample of patients. Average treatment costs were significantly lower for those patients in DBT than those receiving TAU. Further prolonging DBT with another 6 months led to further clinical improvements.

Few studies have compared DBT with other bona fide manualized treatments for borderline PD. In one study (McMain et al., 2009) it was found that 1 year of dialectical behavior therapy was no more effective than intensive general psychiatric management for the treatment of suicidal patients with borderline personality disorder. Although both manualized treatments resulted in significant reductions in borderline symptoms, suicidal behavior, general distress, depression, anger, and health care utilization, and in improved interpersonal functioning, both treatments were equally effective across a range of outcomes.

Another RCT compared transference-focused therapy with DBT (Clarkin, Levy, Lenzenweger, & Kernberg, 2007). A third treatment condition, supportive treatment, was used as a control for attention and support. Male and female borderline PD patients were randomly assigned to one of these three treatment conditions for 1-year outpatient treatment. Results have been reported to 12 months. Suicidality and anger reduced in patients treated with TFP and DBT, but not in those treated with supportive treatment; all three treatments were effective in reducing depression and in improving global functioning and social adjustment. Thus, although DBT is generally found to be more effective than treatment as usual, superiority over other manualized treatments specifically developed for borderline PD has not been demonstrated.

DBT and substance abuse. It should be noted that individuals with substance dependence were excluded in a number of studies discussed earlier. Verheul et al. (2003) reported that standard DBT could be effectively applied with borderline patients with comorbid substance abuse in terms of lower levels of parasuicidal and impulsive behaviours. However, DBT was not more effective compared to treatment as usual in reducing substance use problems. At 6-month follow-up the benefits of DBT over care as usual persisted. There were still no differences between the treatment conditions for drug abuse, but patients who had received DBT drank less alcohol as compared to patients in the treatment as usual condition (van den Bosch, Verheul, Schippers, & van den Brink, 2002).

The standard DBT package has now been modified to treat patients with borderline PD and substance abuse (Linehan et al., 1999). Several modifications were added to standard DBT, including a dialectic stance on drug use that insists on total abstinence. However, in the case of a lapse into substance use, coping strategies from cognitive behavioral therapy are used to prevent lapses becoming full relapse, followed by a quick return to the original treatment goal of total abstinence. Further, treatment also involved transitional maintenance medication in the perspective of "replacing pills with skills" later on in the program. In a randomized controlled trial, patients with borderline PD and drug dependence who received this adjusted DBT program had significantly greater reduction in drug use at 16-month follow-up than control patients who had received treatment as usual. Further, DBT resulted in less attrition from treatment and better social adjustment as compared to the controls (Linehan et al., 1999).

Axelrod, Perepletchikova, Holtzman, and Sinha (2011) investigated whether the improvement in emotion regulation mediated reduction of substance abuse following DBT treatment. Improved emotion regulation, but not improved mood, explained the variance of decreased substance use frequency.

Although DBT is still the only treatment for borderline PD that was given the status of "empirically supported therapy" by the Division of Clinical Psychology of the American Psychological Association, there are a number of critical issues that deserve some comment. First of all, to date most studies have been conducted with relatively small samples, consisting primarily of parasuicidal females. Borderline PD is a heterogeneous condition with significant differences in individual symptom patterns. Some (e.g., Verheul et al., 2003) have suggested that DBT is particularly suited for the impulsive subtype of patients with borderline PD and that DBT is primarily a treatment for parasuicide. This is confirmed in a recent meta-analysis of DBT that revealed moderate effect sizes for treatment change in self-harm and suicidal behaviors (Kliem, Kroger, & Kosfelder, 2010).

It is questionable whether DBT is equally effective for patients who are primarily characterized by chronic feelings of emptiness and boredom, interpersonal instability, or identity disturbance. Another concern relates to the long-term effects of DBT. Few studies have investigated this issue and the observation that after 1 year, differences between DBT and treatment as usual tended to disappear (Linehan et al., 1993) does not seem optimistic. Further, DBT consists of many elements and research has not yet dismantled the essential elements of this approach, but research is in progress. Skills training is one of the four modes of DBT that is held to be an essential element in DBT treatment given the skills deficit underlying BPD. Soler et al. (2009) investigated whether skills training on its own was effective in patients with BPD in comparison with psychodynamic group therapy. Skills training led to less dropout and more improvement in depression, anxiety, and affect instability as compared to psychodynamic group therapy.

A final issue that deserves further study is whether DBT is easily implanted in routine clinical care. DBT is a highly sophisticated treatment program that requires intensive training and supervision. In fact, therapists in most studies were either trained by Linehan herself or by (former) collaborators of hers. Whether frontline mental health professionals outside academic research centers can effectively learn this treatment is questionable, although some uncontrolled studies in community mental health centres suggest that this may be feasible (e.g., Turner, 2000).

Systems Training for Emotional Predictability and Problem Solving

Another behavioral intervention is called *Systems Training for Emotional Predictability and Problem Solving* (STEPPS), which is a group treatment consisting of psychoeducation about borderline PD, emotion management skills training, and behavior management skills training, which elicits support of family and friends (e.g., Bos, van Wel, Appelo, & Verbraak, 2010). Thus far there have been two RCTs in adults with borderline PD (Blum et al., 2008; Bos et al., 2010) of STEPPS. In both studies STEPPS either as stand-alone (Bos et al., 2010) or as add-on to treatment as usual (Blum et al., 2008) resulted in improvements in borderline BPD symptoms compared with treatment as usual, but no differences were observed in self-damaging behaviors (Bos et al., 2010). In adolescents with borderline PD, however, STEPPS was not more effective than care as usual (Schuppert et al., 2009, in press).

Cognitive Therapy

Despite the fact that cognitive therapy has become rather popular among clinicians since the publication of *Cognitive Therapy of Personality Disorders* by Beck and Freeman (1990), only one RCT has been reported, involving a variant of CT rather than a straight Beckian approach. In the BOSCOT trial, 106 patients with borderline PD were randomly assigned to either cognitive therapy or treatment as usual (Davidson et al., 2006). Treatment lasted 12 months and patients attended on average 16 of the 30 sessions offered. Cognitive therapy was superior to treatment as usual in terms of a reduction of suicidal acts, state anxiety, and dysfunctional beliefs, but not in depressed mood. The clinically superior outcome, however, was not revealed in the quality of life as assessed with the EuroQol, and not in terms of cost-effectiveness (Palmer, 2006). Patients maintained this gain through a 6-year follow-up period, and the CBT group had fewer hospitalizations during follow-up, in comparison with the treatment as usual group (Davidson, Tyrer, Norrie, Palmer, & Tyrer, 2010).

Schema-focused therapy (SFT) was more recently developed for the treatment of borderline PD (Young et al., 2003) and only few studies have investigated this form of therapy as yet. Giesen-Bloo et al. (2006) reported on a randomized control trial (RCT) into the effects of schema-focused therapy with patients with borderline PD. In this study the effects of schema-focused therapy were compared with those of transference-focused therapy, a manualized psychodynamically oriented individual psychotherapy. Patients were treated for a maximum of 3 years. Effectiveness of treatment became apparent at 12 months and steadily increased. SFT was superior to transference-focused therapy on changes in borderline criteria, including parasuicide, general psychopathology, and change in pathogenic personality features. Additional advantages of SFT over transference-focused therapy were lower attrition and better cost-effectiveness. In another small RCT, 8 months of SFT was compared with care as usual for 32 patients with borderline PD. SFT resulted in significant reductions in BPD symptoms and global severity of symptoms (Farrell, Shaw, & Webber, 2009).

Common Ingredients

Given that now a number of psychological treatments have been found to have some empirical support in patients with borderline PD, it might be interesting to look at common and specific treatment strategies in these various approaches. Weinberg, Ronningstam, Goldblatt, Schechter, and Maltsberger (2011) compared these various approaches for borderline PD and found them to have several common strategies: clear treatment framework, attention to affect, focus on treatment relationship, an active therapist, and exploratory and change-oriented interventions. Ironically, it is rather funny to see that cognitive therapy (i.e., schema-focused therapy) has to focus on the past and psychodynamic therapy (i.e., transference-focused therapy and mentalization-based treatment) has to focus on the present to become empirically supported treatments for borderline PD.

Treatment for Antisocial Personality Disorder

In contrast to conduct disorder for which a few evidence-based interventions exist (e.g., van Manen, Prins, & Emmelkamp, 2004), there are no evidence-based interventions available for individuals with antisocial PD. Generally, clinicians are highly pessimistic about the results of psychological treatment of antisocial PD and psychopathy. Although this pessimism may be understandable for the treatment of true "psychopaths," a negative attitude with respect to possible outcome of psychological treatment of antisocial PD may not be totally justified.

Research into treatment of antisocial PD has been conducted in the context of the criminal justice system. Several studies have examined the effects of treatment for offenders and forensic psychiatric patients. Although it is likely that many of these patients met the criteria of antisocial PD (usually more than 70%), this was not formally established in most studies. The conclusions drawn from several reviews and meta-analytic studies on the effectiveness of treatment outcome studies in general were that treatment reduces recidivism rates (roughly estimated at about 10%) and that (cognitive) behavioral treatment is more effective in reducing recidivism (Allen, Mackenzie, & Hickman, 2001; Andrews & Bonta,

2010; Hanson, Bourgon, Hel, & Hodgson, 2009; Hollin, 1999) than psychodynamic and nondirective interventions. In general, there is some consensus that structured treatment, aimed at the alteration of cognitions and behaviors, is more effective in offender populations than less structured treatment.

There is some evidence that offenders with antisocial personality pathology benefit less from treatment (Hanson & Morton-Bourgon, 2005; Olver, Stockdale, & Wormith, 2011). In a recent study (Polaschek, 2011) investigating the effects of cognitive-behavioral rehabilitation, 112 medium- and high-risk prisoners who had received CBT were matched to 112 untreated men. Reconviction outcome data over an average of 3.5 years postrelease show that the CBT program led to significantly less violent recidivism compared to the untreated controls, but not all participants had antisocial PD. To date, only one RCT involved the effects of treatment for antisocial PD exclusively. In this study with males with antisocial PD in a community setting 6 months of care as usual, supplemented with CBT, was compared with care as usual alone (Davidson et al., 2009). Although the combined treatment (care as usual plus CBT) showed superior outcomes in terms of social functioning and problematic drinking, there were no significant differences between both conditions.

Effects of Treatment in Psychopaths

Although most workers in the field agree that true psychopaths are difficult to treat, a meta-analysis on the effectiveness of treatment of psychopathy (Salekin, 2002) suggests that intensive individual cognitive-behavioral, psychodynamic, and eclectic therapy for psychopathy were effective, not only in terms of a reduction in recidivism, but also in terms of a reduction of core psychopathic features (e.g., a decrease in lying, an increase in remorse and empathy), and improved relations with others. Treatment in the context of therapeutic communities where mental health professionals had little or no contact with patients was generally ineffective. Most studies reviewed, however, were of poor methodological quality, often including case studies, and lacking objective measures of criminal recidivism, which render the conclusions to be drawn from this meta-analysis inconclusive. Further, psychopathy was often loosely defined. Studies that used the more stringent criteria of Hare (2003) resulted in less positive outcome than studies using more lenient criteria.

SUMMARY AND CONCLUSIONS

Research on behavioral-based treatments for anxiety disorders has clearly and consistently shown the positive effects of interventions. The effects of exposure in vivo are now well established for agoraphobia, simple phobia, social phobia and obsessive-compulsive disorders. Similarly, trauma-focused therapy consisting of imaginal and in vivo exposure has also been found to be an empirically supported treatment. Further, in a number of these disorders, there is now robust evidence that these treatments can also be applied in virtual reality and through the Internet.

The progression of research into the behavioral and cognitive treatment of depression has supported conclusions of earlier reviews in this handbook that behavioral activation and problem-solving therapy are at least as effective as cognitive therapy (Emmelkamp, 1986, 1994, 2004). Also here, a number of studies have shown that mildly to moderate depressed individuals can be treated through the Internet. Nevertheless, there are still a number of important issues that need to be dealt with. For example, we have no idea why cognitive therapy, behavioral interventions as behavioral activation and problem-solving therapy, IPT and pharmacotherapy work equally well with depressed patients, although various researchers provide various theoretical explanations. Unfortunately, to date there is no evidence that either cognitive or behavioral theories explain the improvements achieved with these various treatment procedures.

Progress in the treatment of substance abuse and dependence is impressive. One area that has received relatively less attention is comorbidity. Most patients in substance abuse centers do have comorbid conditions such as depression, anxiety disorders (including PTSD), ADHD, and personalty disorders. There is a clear need for studies addressing the effectiveness of programs dealing with substance use and the other comorbid condition(s) concurrently.

Although behavior therapists have been productive in evaluating the efficacy of various techniques, relatively little attention has been devoted to the therapeutic process. Evidently, the once close relationship between theory and practice in (cognitive-) behavior therapy has changed considerably over the past decades. Today the dominant paradigm is the evidence-based treatment paradigm. This is a normative approach with an emphasis on group means rather than on individual cases. In the early days of behavior therapy the emphasis was on a more idiosyncratic approach: the individualized case formulation, firmly based in theory (Emmelkamp et al., 2010). In recent years, the claim for accountability of psychotherapy has hugely affected the current appraisal of the role of theory underlying effective interventions. In a major part of the field, the emphasis is now on demonstrating efficacy and effectiveness of specific procedures for specific *DSM-IV* disorders.

A number of current developments may turn out to be fruitful in the future. These include the suggestion to focus more on empirically supported principles of change rather than whole treatment packages (Rosen & Davison, 2003). In addition, there is an increasing recognition that many processes involved in the development and maintenance of emotional disorders appear to be transdiagnostic rather than disorder-specific (Harvey, Watkins, Mansell, & Shafran, 2004). Future treatments may therefore focus more on targeting relevant processes rather than being focused on distinct diagnostic categories. Although it remains to be tested whether these approaches result in more effective interventions, it appears that they may help to overcome some of the dichotomies between theory-based and evidence-based approaches in the current literature.

Finally, as noted in my last review for this handbook (Emmelkamp, 2004), it does seem that studies evaluating the outcome of behavioral techniques whose effects have already been established for the "average" patient are not likely to produce new knowledge. Studies investigating conditions leading to success or failure of these techniques are badly needed. The therapeutic relationship seems to be one area where future research efforts are needed. Presumably, results of such research programs may eventually lead to preventing failure in a substantial number of cases.

REFERENCES

Abramowitz, J. S. (1996). Variants of exposure and response prevention in the treatment of obsessive-compulsive disorder: A meta-analysis. *Behavior Therapy, 27,* 583–600.

Abramowitz, J. S., Foa, E. B., & Franklin, M. E. (2003). Exposure and ritual prevention for obsessive-compulsive disorder: Effects of intensive versus twice weekly sessions. *Journal of Consulting & Clinical Psychology, 71,* 394–398.

Allen, L. C., Mackenzie, D. L., & Hickman, L. J. (2001). The effectiveness of cognitive behavioral treatment for adult offenders: A methodological, quality based review. *International Journal of Offender Therapy and Comparative Criminology, 45,* 498–514.

American Psychiatric Association. (1994). *Diagnostic and statistical manual of mental disorders* (4th ed.). Washington, DC: Author.

Ames, S. C., & Roitzsch, J. C. (2000). The impact of minor stressful life events and social support on cravings: A study of inpatients receiving treatment for substance dependence. *Addictive Behaviors, 25,* 539–547.

Amir, N., Freshman, M., & Foa, E. B. (2000). Family distress and involvement in relatives of obsessive-compulsive disorder patients. *Journal of Anxiety Disorders, 14,* 209–217.

Anderson, R. A., & Rees, C. S. (2007). Group versus individual cognitive-behavioural treatment for obsessive-compulsive disorder: A controlled trial. *Behaviour Research & Therapy, 45,* 123–137.

Andréasson, S., & Öjehagen, A. (2003). Psychosocial treatment for alcohol dependence. In M. Berglund, E. Johnsson, & S. Thelander (Eds.), *Treatment of alcohol and drug abuse: An evidence-based review* (pp. 43–188). Weinheim, Germany: Wiley-VCH.

Andrews, D. A., & Bonta, J. (2010). Rehabilitating criminal justice policy and practice. *Psychology, Public Policy, and Law, 16,* 39–55.

Anton, R. F., O'Malley, S. S., Ciraulo, D. A., Cisler, R. A., Couper, D., Donovan, D. M., & Zweben, A. (2006). Combined pharmacotherapies and behavioral interventions for alcohol dependence: The COMBINE study. A randomized controlled trial. *JAMA, 295,* 2003–2017.

Antony, M. M., Ledley, D. R., Liss, A., & Swinson, R. P. (2006). Responses to symptom induction exercises in panic disorder. *Behaviour Research & Therapy, 44*(1), 85–98.

Areán, P. A., Raue, P., Mackin, R. S., Kanellopoulos, D., McCulloch, C., & Alexopoulos, G. S. (2010). Problem-solving therapy and supportive therapy in older adults with major depression and executive dysfunction. *American Journal of Psychiatry, 167,* 1391–1398.

Axelrod, S. R., Perepletchikova, F., Holtzman, K., & Sinha, R. (2011). Emotion regulation and substance use frequency in women with substance dependence and borderline personality disorder receiving dialectical behavior therapy. *American Journal of Drug and Alcohol Abuse, 37,* 37–42.

Ayala, E. S., Meuret, A. E., & Ritz, T. (2009). Treatments for blood-injury-injection phobia: A critical review of current evidence. *Journal of Psychiatric Research*, *43*, 1235–1242.

Bachofen, M., Nakagawa, A., Marks, I. M., Park, J. M., Greist, J. H., Baer, L.,...Dottl, S. L. (1999). Home self-assessment and self-treatment on obsessive-compulsive disorder using a manual and a computer-conducted telephone interview: Replication of a U.K.-U. S. study. *Journal of Clinical Psychiatry*, *60*, 545–549.

Bandelow, B., Seidler-Brandler, U., Becker, A., Wedekind, D., & Rüther, E. (2007). Meta-analysis of randomized controlled comparisons of psychopharmacological and psychological treatments for anxiety disorders. *World Journal of Biological Psychiatry*, *8*, 175–187.

Barlow, D. H., Gorman, J. M., Shear, M. K., & Woods, S. W. (2000). Cognitive-behavioral therapy, imipramine, or their combination for panic disorder: A randomized controlled trial. *JAMA*, *283*, 2529–2536.

Bartak, A., Andrea, H., Spreeuwenberg, M. D., Thunnissen, M., Ziegler, U. M., Dekker, J.,...Emmelkamp, P. M. G. (2010). Patients with cluster A personality disorders in psychotherapy: An effectiveness study. *Psychotherapy & Psychosomatic*, *80*, 88–99.

Basoglu, M., Lax, T., Kasvikis, Y, & Marks, I. M. (1988). Predictors of improvement in obsessive-compulsive disorder. *Journal of Anxiety Disorders*, *2*, 299–308.

Bateman, A. W., & Fonagy, P. (2004). *Psychotherapy for borderline PD: Mentalization based treatment*. Oxford, United Kingdom: Oxford University Press.

Beach, S. R. H. (2001). *Marital and family processes in depression*. Washington, DC: American Psychological Association.

Beach, S. R. H., & O'Leary, K. D. (1992). Treating depression in the context of marital discord: Outcome and predictors of response for marital therapy versus cognitive therapy. *Behavior Therapy*, *23*, 507–528.

Beck, A. T., Emery, G., & Greenberg, R. L. (1985). *Anxiety disorders and phobias: A cognitive perspective*. New York, NY: Basic Books.

Beck, A. T., & Freeman, A. (1990). *Cognitive therapy of personality disorders*. New York, NY: Guilford Press.

Beck, A. T., Freeman, A., & Davis, D. D. (2004). *Cognitive therapy of personality disorders*. New York, NY: Guilford Press.

Beck, A. T., Rush, A. J., Shaw, B. F., & Emery, F. (1987) *Cognitive therapy of depression*. New York, NY: Guilford Press.

Beck, A. T., Wright, F. D., Newman, C. S., & Liese, B. S. (1993). *Cognitive therapy of substance abuse*. New York, NY: Guilford Press.

Bell, A. C., & D'Zurilla, T. J. (2009). Problem-solving therapy for depression: A meta-analysis. *Clinical Psychology Review*, *29*, 348–353.

Belloch, A., Cabedo, E., & Carrio, C. (2008). Cognitive versus behavior therapy in the individual treatment of obsessive compulsive disorder: Changes in cognitions and clinically significant outcomes at posttreatment and one-year follow-up. *Behavioural and Cognitive Psychotherapy*, *36*, 521–540.

Berglund, M. (2005). A better widget? Three lessons for improving addiction treatment from a meta-analytical study. *Addiction*, *100*, 742–750.

Bisson, J. I., Ehlers, A., Matthews, R., Pilling, S., Richards, D., & Turner, S. (2007). Psychological treatments for chronic post-traumatic stress disorder. Systematic review and meta-analysis. *British Journal of Psychiatry*, *190*, 97–104.

Blum, N., St John, D., Pfohl, B., Stuart, S., McCormick, B., Allen, J., & Black, D. W. (2008). Systems training for emotional predictability and problem solving (STEPPS) for outpatients with borderline personality disorder: A randomized controlled trial and 1-year follow-up. *American Journal of Psychiatry*, *165*, 468–478.

Bodenmann, G., Plancherel, B., Beach, S. R. H., Widmer, K., Gabriel, B., Meuwly, N.,...Schramm, E. (2008). Effects of a coping-oriented couples therapy on depression: A randomized clinical trial. *Journal of Consulting and Clinical Psychology*, *76*, 944–954.

Boelen, P. A., de Keijser, J., van den Hout, M. A., & van den Bout, J. (2007). Treatment of complicated grief: A comparison between cognitive-behavioral therapy and supportive counseling. *Journal of Consulting and Clinical Psychology*, *75*, 277–284.

Boersma, K., Dekker, J., & Emmelkamp, P. M. G. (1976). Exposure and response prevention in the natural environment: A comparison with obsessive-compulsive patients. *Behaviour Research Therapy*, *14*(1), 19–24

Bögels, S. M., & Voncken, M. (2008). Social skills training versus cognitive therapy for social anxiety disorder characterized by fear of blushing, trembling, or sweating International *Journal of Cognitive Psychotherapy*, *1*, 138–150.

Bohus, M., Haaf, B., Simms, T., Limberger, M. F., Schmahl, C., Unckel, C.,...Linehan, M. M. (2004). Effectiveness of inpatient dialectical behavioral therapy for borderline PD: A controlled trial. *Behaviour Research and Therapy*, *42*, 487–499.

Borkovec, T. D., Alcaine, O. M., & Behar, E. (2004). Avoidance theory of worry and generalized anxiety disorder. In R. G. Heimberg, C. L. Turk, & D. S. Mennin (Eds.), *Generalized anxiety disorder: Advances in research and practice* (pp. 77–108). New York, NY: Guilford Press.

Borkovec, T. D., & Costello, E. (1993). Efficacy of applied relaxation and cognitive-behavioral therapy in the treatment of generalized anxiety disorder. *Journal of Consulting and Clinical Psychology*, *61*, 611–619.

Borkovec, T. D., Newman, M. G., Pincus, A. L., & Lytle, R. (2002). A component analysis of cognitive-behavioral therapy for generalized anxiety disorder and the role of interpersonal problems. *Journal of Consulting and Clinical Psychology*, *70*, 288–298.

Borkovec, T. D., Ray, W. J., & Stöber, J. (1998). Worry: A cognitive phenomenon intimately linked to affective, physiological, and interpersonal behavioral processes. *Cognitive Therapy and Research*, *22*, 561–576.

Bos, E. H., van Wel, E. B., Appelo, M. T., & Verbraak, M. J. P. M. (2010). A randomized controlled trial of a Dutch version of systems training for emotional predictability and problem solving for borderline personality disorder. *Journal of Nervous and Mental Disease*, *198*, 299–304.

Botella, C. Gallego, M. J., Garcia-Palacios, A., Guillen, V., Baños, R. M., Quero, S., & Alcañiz, M. (2010). An Internet-based self-help treatment for fear of public speaking: A controlled trial. *Cyberpsychology, Behavior & Social Networking*, *13*, 407–421.

Botella, C., Garcia-Palacios, A., Villa, H., Banos, R. M., Quero, S., Alcaniz, M., & Riva, G. (2007). Virtual reality exposure in the treatment of panic disorder and agoraphobia: A controlled study. *Clinical Psychology and Psychotherapy*, *14*, 164–175.

Bowen, R. C., D'Arcy, C., Keegan, D., & Stenhilsel, van A. (2000). A controlled trial of cognitive behavioral treatment of panic in alcoholic inpatients with comorbid panic disorder. *Addictive Behaviors*, *25*, 593–597.

Bradley, R., Greene, J., Russ, E., Dutra, L., & Westen, D. (2005). A multidimensional meta-analysis of psychotherapy for PTSD. *American Journal of Psychiatry*, *162*, 214–227.

Brady, A., & Raines, D. (2009). Dynamic hierarchies: A control system paradigm for exposure therapy. *Cognitive Behaviour Therapist*, *2*, 51–62.

Bruce, T. J., Spiegel, D. A., Gregg, S. F., & Nuzzarello, A. (1995). Predictors of alprazolam discontinuation with and without cognitive behavior therapy in panic disorder. *American Journal of Psychiatry*, *152*, 1156–1160.

Bryant, R. A., Moulds, M. L., Guthrie, R. M., Dang, S. T., Mastrodomenico, J., Nixon, R. D. V., . . . Creamer, M. (2008). A randomized controlled trial of exposure therapy and cognitive restructuring for posttraumatic stress disorder. *Journal of Consulting and Clinical Psychology*, *76*, 695–703.

Budney, A. J., Moore, B. A., Rocha, H. L., & Higgins, S. T. (2006). Clinical trial of abstinence-based vouchers and cognitive-behavioral therapy for cannabis dependence. *Journal of Consulting and Clinical Psychology*, *74*(2), 307–316.

Burke, B. L., Arkowitz, H., & Menchola, M. (2003). The efficacy of motivational interviewing: A meta-analysis of controlled clinical trials. *Journal of Consulting and Clinical Psychology*, *71*, 843–861.

Carlbring, P., Nilsson-Ihrfelt, E., Waara, J., Ceciclia, K., Buhrman, M., Kaldo, V., . . . Andersson, G. (2005). Treatment of panic disorder: Live therapy vs. self-help via the Internet. *Behaviour Research and Therapy*, *43*, 1321–1333.

Chambless, D. L., & Steketee, G. (1999). Expressed emotion and behavior therapy outcome: A prospective study with obsessive-compulsive and agoraphobic outpatients. *Journal of Consulting and Clinical Psychology*, *67*, 658–665.

Chang, E. C., D'Zurilla, T. J., & Sanna, L. J. (2009). Social problem solving as a mediator of the link between stress and psychological well-being in middle-adulthood. *Cognitive Therapy & Research*, *33*, 33–49.

Chard, K. (2005). An evaluation of cognitive processing therapy for the treatment of posttraumatic stress disorder related to childhood sexual abuse. *Journal of Consulting and Clinical Psychology*, *73*, 965–971.

Chow, S. K. Y., & Chan, W. C. (2010). Depression: Problem-solving appraisal and self-rated health among Hong Kong Chinese migrant women. *Nursing and Health Sciences*, *12*, 352–359.

Clark, D. M. (1986). A cognitive approach to panic. *Behaviour Research and Therapy*, *24*, 461–470.

Clark, D. M. (1999). Anxiety disorders: Why they persist and how to treat them. *Behaviour Research and Therapy*, *37*, S5–S27.

Clarke, S. B., Rizvi, S. L., & Resick, P. A. (2008). Borderline personality characteristics and treatment outcome in cognitive-behavioral treatments for PTSD in female rape victims. *Behavior Therapy*, *39*, 72–78.

Clarkin, J. F., Levy, K. N., Lenzenweger, M. F., & Kernberg, O. F. (2007). Evaluating three treatments for borderline personality disorder: A multiwave study. *American Journal of Psychiatry*, *164*, 922–928.

Clarkin, J. F., Yeomans, F. E., & Kernberg, O. F. (1999). *Psychotherapy for borderline personality*. New York, NY: Wiley.

Cloitre, M., Cohen, L. R., & Koenen, K. C. (2006). *Treating survivors of childhood abuse: Psychotherapy for the interrupted life*. New York, NY: Guilford Press.

Cloitre, M., Koenen, K. C., Cohen, L. R., & Han, H. (2002). Skills training in affective and interpersonal regulation followed by exposure: A phase-based treatment for PTSD related to childhood abuse. *Journal of Consulting and Clinical Psychology*, *70*, 1067–1074.

Cloitre, M., Stovall-McClough, K. C., Nooner, K., Zorbas, P., Cherry, S., Jackson, C. L., . . . Petkova,

E. (2010). Treatment for PTSD related to childhood abuse: A randomized controlled trial. *American Journal of Psychiatry, 167*, 915–924.

Cohen, S., O'Leary, K. D., & Foran, H. (2010). A randomized clinical trial of a brief, problem-focused couple therapy for depression. *Behavior Therapy, 41*, 433–446.

Cote, G., Gauthier, J. G., Laberge, B., & Cormier, H. J. (1994). Reduced therapist contact in the cognitive behavioral treatment of panic disorder. *Behavior Therapy, 25*, 123–145.

Cottraux, J., Note, I., Yao, S. N., Lafront, S., Note, B., Mollard, E., . . . Dartigues, J. F. (2001). A randomized controlled trial of cognitive therapy versus intensive behavior therapy in obsessive compulsive disorder. *Psychotherapy & Psychosomatics, 70*, 288–297.

Covin, R., Ouimet, A. J., Seeds, P. M., & Dozois, D. J. A. (2008). A meta-analysis of CBT for pathological worry among clients with GAD. *Journal of Anxiety Disorders, 22*, 108–116.

Craske, M. G. (1999). *Anxiety disorders: Psychological approaches to theory and treatment*. Boulder, CO: Westview Press.

Craske, M. G., & Barlow, D. H. (2006). *Mastery of your anxiety and panic: Therapist guide*. New York, NY: Oxford University Press.

Craske, M. G., & Barlow, D. H. (2007). Panic disorder and agoraphobia. In D. H. Barlow (Ed.), *Clinical handbook of psychological disorders* (pp. 1–52). New York, NY: Guilford Press.

Craske, M. G., Kircanski, K., Zelikowsky, M., Mystkowski, J., Chowdhury, N., & Baker, A. (2008). Optimizing inhibitory learning during exposure therapy. *Behaviour Research and Therapy, 46*, 5–27.

Craske, M. G., Rowe, M., Lewin, M., & Noriega-Dimitri, R. (1997). Interoceptive exposure versus breathing retraining within cognitive-behavioral therapy for panic disorder with agoraphobia. *British Journal of Clinical Psychology, 36*, 85–99.

Crits-Christoph, P., Gallop, R., Temes, C. M., Woody, G., Ball, S. A., Martino, S., & Carroll, K. M. (2009). The alliance in motivational enhancement therapy and counseling as usual for substance use problems. *Journal of Consulting and Clinical Psychology, 77*, 1125–1135.

Cuijpers, P., van Straten, A., & Warmerdam, L. (2007a). Behavioral activation treatments of depression: A meta-analysis. *Clinical Psychology Review, 27*, 318–326.

Cuijpers P., van Straten A., & Warmerdam L. (2007b). Problem solving therapies for depression: A meta-analysis. *European Psychiatry, 22*, 9–15.

Daughters, S. B., Braun, A. R., Sargeant, M., Reynolds, E. R., Hopko, D., Blanco, C., & Lejuez, C. W. (2008). Effectiveness of a brief behavioral treatment for inner-city illicit drug users with elevated depressive symptoms: The life enhancement treatment for substance use (LETS ACT!). *Journal of Clinical Psychiatry, 69*, 122–129.

Davidson, K., Norrie, J., Tyrer, P., Gumley, A., Tata, P., Murray, H., & Palmer, S. (2006). The effectiveness of cognitive behavior therapy for borderline personality disorder: Results from the borderline personality disorder study of cognitive therapy (BOSCOT) trial. *Journal of Personality Disorders, 20*, 450–465.

Davidson, K. M., Tyrer, P. T., Norrie, J., Palmer, S. J., & Tyrer, H. (2010). Cognitive therapy v. usual treatment for borderline personality disorder: Prospective 6-year follow-up. *British Journal of Psychiatry, 197*, 456–462.

Davidson, K., Tyrer, P., Tata, P., Cooke, D., Gumley, A., Ford, I., & Crawford, M. J. (2009). Cognitive behaviour therapy for violent men with antisocial personality disorder in the community: An exploratory randomized controlled trial. *Psychological Medicine, 39*, 569–577.

Dawe, S., Rees, V. W., Sitharthan, T., Mattick, R. P., & Heather, N. (2002). Efficacy of moderation-oriented cue-exposure for problem drinkers: A randomised controlled trial. *Journal of Consulting and Clinical Psychology, 70*, 1045–1050.

DeRubeis, R. J., Gelfand, L. A., Tang, T. Z., & Simons, A. D. (1999). Medications versus cognitive behavior therapy for severely depressed outpatients: Mega-analysis of four randomized comparisons. *American Journal of Psychiatry, 156*, 1007–1013.

DiClemente, C. C. (2007). Mechanisms, determinants and processes of change in the modification of drinking behavior. *Alcoholism: Clinical and Experimental Research, 31*, 13S–20S.

Diefenbach, G. J., Abramowitz, J. S., Norberg, M. M., & Tolin, D. F. (2007). Changes in quality of life following cognitive-behavioral therapy for obsessive-compulsive disorder. *Behaviour Research & Therapy, 45*, 3060–3068.

Dimidjian, S., Barrera, M., Martell, C., Munoz, R. F., & Lewinsohn, P. M. (2011). The origins and current status of behavioral activation treatments for depression. *Annual Review of Clinical Psychology, 7*, 1–38.

Dimidjian, S., Dobson, K. S., Kohlenberg, R. J., Gallop, R., Markley, D. K., Atkins, D. C., . . . Jacobson, N. S. (2006). Randomized trial of behavioral activation, cognitive therapy, and antidepressant medication in the acute treatment of adults with major depression. *Journal of Consulting and Clinical Psychology, 74*, 658–670.

Dobson, K. S., Hollon, S. D., Dimidjian, S., Schmaling, K. B., Kohlenberg, R. J., Gallop, R. J., . . . Jacobson, N. S. (2008). Randomized trial of behavioral activation, cognitive therapy, and antidepressant medication in the prevention of relapse and recurrence in major depression. *Journal of Consulting and Clinical Psychology, 76*, 468–477.

Donovan, D. M., Anton, R. F., Miller, W. R., Longabaugh, R., Hosking, D. J., Youngblood, M., & Combine Study Research Group. (2008). Combined pharmacotherapies and behavioral interventions for alcohol dependence (the COMBINE Study): Examination of post-treatment drinking outcomes. *Journal of Studies on Alcohol and Drugs, 69*, 5–13.

Dowrick C., Dunn G., Ayuso-Mateos, J. L., Dalgard, O. S., Page, H., Lehtinen, V.,...Wilkinson, G. (2000). Problem solving treatment and group psychoeducation for depression: Multicentre randomised controlled trial. *British Medical Journal, 321*, 1–6.

Dugas, M. J., Brillon, P., Savard, P., Turcotte, J., Gaudet, A., & Ladouceur, R. (2010). A randomized clinical trial of cognitive-behavioral therapy and applied relaxation for adults with generalized anxiety disorder. *Behavior Therapy, 41*, 46–58.

Dugas, M. J., Gagnon, F., Ladouceur, R., & Freeston, M. H. (1998). Generalized anxiety disorder: A preliminary test of a conceptual model. *Behaviour Research and Therapy, 36*, 215–226.

Dugas, M. J., Ladouceur, R., Leger, E., Freeston, M. H., Langlois, F., & Provencher, M. D. (2003). Group cognitive-behavioral therapy for generalized anxiety disorder: Treatment outcome and long-term follow-up. *Journal of Consulting and Clinical Psychology, 71*, 821–825.

Dugas, M. J., & Robichaud, M. (2006). *Cognitive-behavioral treatment for generalized anxiety disorder: From science to practice:* New York, NY: Routledge.

Dutra, L., Stathopoulou, G., Basden, S. L., Leyro, T. M., Powers, M. B., & Otto, M. W. (2008). A meta-analytic review of psychosocial interventions for substance use disorders. *American Journal of Psychiatry, 165*, 179–187.

D'Zurilla, T. J., Chang, E. C., Nottingham, E., & Faccini, L. (1998). Social problem-solving deficits and hopelessness, depression, and suicidal risk in college students and psychiatric inpatients. *Journal of Clinical Psychology, 54*, 1091–1107.

Eddy, K. T., Dutra, L., Bradley, R., & Westen, D. (2004). A multidimensional meta-analysis of psychotherapy and pharmacotherapy for obsessive-compulsive disorder. *Clinical Psychology Review, 24*, 2004.

Ehlers, A., & Margraf, J. (1989). The psychophysiological model of panic attacks. In P. M. G. Emmelkamp, W. Everaerd, F. Kraaimaat, & M. van Son (Eds.), *Fresh perspectives on anxiety* (pp. 1–29). Amsterdam, The Netherlands: Swets.

Ekers, D., Richards, D., & Gilbody, S. (2008). A meta-analysis of randomized trials of behavioural treatment of depression. *Psychological Medicine, 38*, 611–623.

Ekkers, W., Korrelboom, K., Huijbrechts, I., Smits, N., Cuijpers, P., & van der Gaag, M. (2011). Competitive memory training for treating depression and rumination in depressed older adults: A randomized controlled trial. *Behaviour Research and Therapy, 49*, 588–596.

Elofsson, U. O. E., von Scheele, B., Theorell, T., & Söndergaard, H. P. (2008). Physiological correlates of eye movement desensitization and reprocessing. *Journal of Anxiety Disorders, 22*, 622–634.

Emanuels-Zuurveen, L., & Emmelkamp, P. M. G. (1996). Individual behavioural-cognitive therapy vs. marital therapy for depression in martially distressed couples. *British Journal of Psychiatry, 169*, 181–188.

Emanuels-Zuurveen, L., & Emmelkamp, P. M. G. (1997). Spouse-aided therapy with depressed patients. *Behavior Modification, 21*, 62–77.

Emmelkamp, P. M. G. (1982). *Phobic and obsessive-compulsive disorders: Theory, research and practice*. New York, NY: Plenum Press.

Emmelkamp, P. M. G. (1986). Behavior therapy with adults. In A. Bergin & S. Garfield (Eds.), *Handbook of psychotherapy and behavior change* (3rd ed., pp. 385–442). New York, NY: Wiley.

Emmelkamp, P. M. G. (1994). Behavior therapy with adults. In A. Bergin & S. Garfield (Eds.), *Handbook of psychotherapy and behavior change* (4th ed.). New York, NY: Wiley.

Emmelkamp, P. M. G. (2004). Behavior therapy with adults. In M. J. Lambert (Ed.), *Bergin and Garfield's handbook of psychotherapy and behavior change* (5th ed., pp. 393–446). Hoboken, NJ: Wiley.

Emmelkamp, P. M. G. (2005). Technological innovations in clinical assessment and psychotherapy. *Psychotherapy & Psychosomatics, 74*, 336–343.

Emmelkamp, P. M. G., & Beens, H. (1991). Cognitive therapy with obsessive-compulsive disorder: A comparative evaluation. *Behaviour Research and Therapy, 29*, 293–300.

Emmelkamp, P. M. G., Benner, A., Kuipers, A., Feiertag, G. A., Koster, H. C., & van Apeldoorn, F. J. (2006). Comparison of brief dynamic and cognitive-behavioural therapies in avoidant personality disorder. *British Journal of Psychiatry, 189*, 60–64.

Emmelkamp, P. M. G., Bouman, T. K., & Blaauw, E. (1994). Individualized versus standardized therapy: A comparative evaluation in obsessive-compulsive disorder. *Clinical Psychology and Psychotherapy, 1*, 95–100.

Emmelkamp, P. M. G., de Haan, E., & Hoogduin, C.A.L. (1990). Marital adjustment and obsessive compulsive disorder. *British Journal of Psychiatry, 156*, 55–60.

Emmelkamp, P. M. G., Ehring, T., & Powers, M. B. (2010). Philosophy, psychology, causes, and treatments of mental disorders. In N. Kazantis, M. A. Reinecke, & A. Freeman (Eds.), *Cognitive and behavior theories in clinical practice* (pp. 1–27). New York, NY: Guilfiord Press.

Emmelkamp, P. M. G., & Felten, M. (1985). The process of exposure in vivo: Cognitive and physiological changes during treatment of acrophobia. *Behaviour Research and Therapy, 23*, 219–223.

Emmelkamp, P. M. G., Helm, M., van der Zanten, B., & Plochg, I. (1980). Contributions of self-instructional training to the effectiveness of exposure in vivo: A comparison with obsessive-compulsive patients. *Behaviour Research and Therapy, 18*, 61–66.

Emmelkamp, P. M. G., & Kamphuis, J. H. (2007). *Personality disorders*. Hove, United Kingdom: Psychology Press.

Emmelkamp, P. M. G., Kloek, J., & Blaauw, E. (1994). Obsessive-compulsive disorder. In P. Wilson (Ed.), *Relapse prevention* (pp. 213–234). New York, NY: Guilford Press.

Emmelkamp, P. M. G., Linden van den Heuvell, C. van. Rüphan, M., & Sanderman, R. (1989). Home-based treatment of OCD patients: Intersession interval and therapist involvement. *Behaviour Research & Therapy, 27*, 89–93.

Emmelkamp, P. M. G., & Powers, M. B. (2010). Agoraphobia. In J. Thomas & M. Hersen (Eds.), *Handbook of clinical psychology competencies* (pp. 723–758). New York, NY: Springer.

Emmelkamp, P. M. G., van Oppen, P., & van Balkom, A. (2002). Cognitive changes in patients with obsessive-compulsive rituals treated with exposure in vivo and response prevention. In R. O. Frost & G. Steketee (Eds.), *Cognitive approaches to obsessions and compulsions: Theory, assessment and treatment* (pp. 391–401). Oxford, United Kingdom: Elsevier Press.

Emmelkamp, P. M. G., & Vedel, E. (2002). Spouse-aided therapy. In M. Hersen & W. Sledge (Eds.), *The encyclopedia of psychotherapy*. New York, NY: Academic Press.

Emmelkamp, P. M. G., & Vedel, E. (2006). *Evidence based treatment for alcohol and drug abuse*. New York, NY: Taylor & Francis.

Emmelkamp, P. M. G., Visser, S., & Hoekstra, R. (1988). Cognitive therapy vs. exposure in the treatment of obsessive-compulsives. *Cognitive Therapy and Research, 12*, 103–114.

Expert Consensus Panel for Obsessive-Compulsive Disorder. (1997). Treatment of obsessive-compulsive disorder. *Journal of Clinical Psychiatry, 58*(Suppl. 4), 2–72.

Fanner, D., & Urquhart, C. (2008). Bibliotherapy for mental health service users Part 1: A systematic review. *Health Information and Libraries Journal, 25*, 237–252.

Farrell, J., Shaw, I. A., & Webber, M. A. (2009). A schema-focused approach to group psychotherapy for outpatients with borderline personality disorder: A randomized controlled trial. *Journal of*

Behavior Therapy and Experimental Psychiatry, 40, 317–328.

Fedoroff, I. C., & Taylor, S. (2001). Psychological and pharmacological treatments of social phobia: A meta-analysis. *Journal of Clinical Psychopharmacology, 21*, 311–324.

Feeny, N. C., Zoellner, L. A., & Foa, E. B. (2002). Treatment outcome for chronic PTSD among female assault victims with borderline personality characteristics: A preliminary examination. *Journal of Personality Disorders, 16*, 30–40.

Feske, U., & Chambless, D. L. (1995). Cognitive behavioral versus exposure only treatment for social phobia: A meta-analysis. *Behavior Therapy, 26*, 695–720.

Fisher, P. L. (2006). The efficacy of psychological treatments for generalized anxiety disorder. In G. C. L. Davey & E. Wells (Eds.), *Worry and its psychological disorders: Theory, assessment and treatment*. Chichester, United Kingdom: Wiley.

Fisher, P. L., & Wells, A. (2005). How effective are cognitive and behavioral treatments for obsessive-compulsive disorder? A clinical significance analysis. *Behaviour Research & Therapy, 43*, 1543–1558.

Foa, E. B., Hembree, E. A., Cahill, S. P., Rauch, S. A. M., Riggs, D. S., Feeny, N. C., & Yadin, E. (2005). Randomized trial of prolonged exposure for posttraumatic stress disorder with and without cognitive restructuring: Outcome at academic and community clinics. *Journal of Consulting and Clinical Psychology, 73*, 953–964.

Foa, E. B., Huppert, J. D., & Cahill, S. P. (2006). Emotional processing theory: An update. In B. O. Rothbaum (Ed.), *Pathological anxiety: Emotional processing in etiology and treatment* (pp. 3–24). New York, NY: Guilford Press.

Foa, E. B., & Kozak, M. J. (1986). Emotional processing of fear: Exposure to corrective information. *Psychological Bulletin, 99*, 20–35.

Foa, E. B., Liebowitz, M. R., Kozak, M. J., Davies, S. O., Campeas, R. E., ... Tu, X. (2005). Randomized, placebo-controlled trial of exposure and ritual prevention, clomipramine, and their combination in the treatment of obsessive-compulsive disorder A. *American Journal of Psychiatry, 162*, 151–161.

Foa, E. B., & Rauch, S. A. M. (2004). Cognitive changes during prolonged exposure versus prolonged exposure plus cognitive restructuring in female assault survivors with posttraumatic stress disorder. *Journal of Consulting and Clinical Psychology, 72*, 879–884.

Foa, E. B., Riggs, D. S., Massie, E. D., & Yarczower, M. (1995). The impact of fear activation and anger on the efficacy of exposure treatment for posttraumatic stress disorder. *Behavior Therapy, 26*, 487–499.

Foa, E. B., Steketee, G., Grayson, J. B., & Doppelt, H. G. (1983). Treatment of obsessive-compulsives: When do we fail? In E. B. Foa & P. M. G.

Emmelkamp (Eds.), *Failures in behavior therapy*. New York, NY: Wiley.

Franklin, M. E., Abramowitz, J. S., Kozak, M. J., Levitt, J. T., & Foa, E. B. (2000). Effectiveness of exposure and ritual prevention for obsessive-compulsive disorder: Randomized compared with nonrandomized samples. *Journal of Consulting and Clinical Psychology, 68*, 594–602.

Furukawa, T. A., Watanabe, N., & Churchill, R. (2007). Combined psychotherapy plus antidepressants for panic disorder with or without agoraphobia. *Cochrane Database of Systematic Reviews, 24*(1), CD004364.

Gallego, M. J., & Emmelkamp, P. M. G. (2012). Effectiveness of Internet psychological treatments in mental health disorders. In L. L'Abate & D. Kaisers (Eds.), *Handbook of technology in psychology, psychiatry, and neurology: Theory, research, and practice*. Hauppauge, NY: Nova.

Gallego, M. J., Emmelkamp, P. M. G., van der Kooij, M., & Mees, H. (2011). The effects of a Dutch version of an Internet-based treatment program for fear of public speaking: A controlled study. *International Journal of Clinical and Health Psychology, 11*, 459–472.

Garratt, G., Ingram, R. E., Rand, K. L., & Sawalani, G. (2007). Cognitive processes in cognitive therapy: Evaluation of the mechanisms of change in the treatment of depression. *Clinical Psychology: Science and Practice, 14*, 224–239.

Gelinas, D. J. (2003). Integrating EMDR into phase-oriented treatment for trauma. *Journal of Trauma and Dissociation, 4*, 91–135.

Ghitza, U. E., Epstein, D. H., Schmittner, J., Vahabzadeh, M., Lin, J. L., & Preston, K. L. (2007). Randomized trial of prize-based reinforcement density for simultaneous abstinence from cocaine and heroin. *Journal of Consulting and Clinical Psychology, 75*, 765–774.

Giesen-Bloo, J., van Dyck, R., Spinhoven, P., van Tilburg, W., Dirksen, C., van Asselt, T., . . . Arntz, A. (2006). Outpatient psychotherapy for borderline personality disorder: Randomized trial of schema-focused therapy vs transference-focused psychotherapy. *Archives of General Psychiatry, 63*, 649–658.

Gloaguen, V., Cottraux, J., Cucherat, M., & Blackburn, I. M. (1998). A meta-analysis of the effects of cognitive therapy in depressed patients. *Journal of Affective Disorders, 49*, 59–72.

Gloster, A. T., Wittchen, H. U., Einsle, F., Lang, T., Helbig-Lang, S., Fydrich, T., . . . Arolt, V. (2011). Psychological treatment for panic disorder with agoraphobia: A randomized controlled trial to examine the role of therapist-guided exposure in situ in CBT. *Journal of Consulting & Clinical Psychology, 79*, 3, 406–420.

Gortner, E. T., Gollan, J. K., Dobson, K. S., & Jacobson, N. S. (1998). Cognitive-behavioral treatment for depression: Relapse prevention. *Journal of Consulting and Clinical Psychology, 66*, 377–384.

Gosselin, P., Ladouceur, R., Morin, C. M., Dugas, M. J., & Baillargeon, L. (2006). Benzodiazepine discontinuation among adults with GAD: A randomized trial of cognitive-behavioral therapy. *Journal of Consulting and Clinical Psychology, 74*, 908–919.

Gould, R. A., Buckminster, S., Pollack, M. H., Otto, M. W., & Yap, L. (1997). Cognitive–behavioral and pharmacological treatment for social phobia: A meta-analysis. *Clinical Psychology: Science and Practice, 4*, 291–306.

Gould, R. A., Safren, S. A., Washington, D. O., & Otto, M. W. (2004). A meta-analytic review of cognitive-behavioral treatments. In R. G. Heimberg, C. A. Turk, & Menin, D. S. (Eds.), *Generalized anxiety disorder: Advances in research and practice*. New York, NY: Guilford Press.

Gunter, R. W., & Bodner, G. E. (2008). How eye movements affect unpleasant memories: Support for a working-memory account. *Behaviour Research and Therapy, 46*, 913–931.

Hanson, R. K., Bourgon, G., Helmus, L., & Hodgson, S. (2009). The principles of effective correctional treatment also apply to sexual offenders. *Criminal Justice and Behavior, 36*, 865–891.

Hanson, R. K., Morton-Bourgon, K. E. (2005). The characteristics of persistent sexual offenders: a meta-analysis of recidivism studies. *Journal of Consulting and Clinical Psychology, 73*, 1154–1163.

Hare, R. D. (2003). *Manual for the hare psychopathy checklist—Revised* (2nd ed.). Toronto, Canada: Multi-Health Systems.

Harvey, A. G., Watkins, E., Mansell, W., & Shafran, R. (2004). *Cognitive behavioural processes across psychological disorders*. Oxford, United Kingdom: Oxford University Press.

Hayes, S. A., Hope, D. A., & Heimberg, R. G. (2008). The pattern of subjective anxiety during in-session exposures over the course of cognitive-behavioral therapy for clients with social anxiety disorder. *Behavior Therapy, 39*, 286–299.

Hayes, S. C., Wilson, K. G., Gifford, E. V., Bissett, R., Piasecki, M., Batten, S. V., & Gregg, J. (2004). A preliminary report of twelve step facilitation and acceptance and commitment therapy with polysubstance abusing methadone maintained opiate addicts. *Behavior Therapy, 35*, 4, 667–688.

Heather, N., Brodie, J., Wale, S., Wilkinson, G., Luce, A., Webb, E., & McCarthy, S. (2000). A randomized controlled trial of moderation-oriented cue exposure. *Journal of Studies on Alcohol, 61*, 561–570.

Hecker, J. E., Losee, M. C., Roberson-Nay, R., & Maki, K. (2004). Mastery of your anxiety and panic and brief therapist contact in the treatment of panic disorder. *Journal of Anxiety Disorders, 18*, 111–126.

Herbert, J. D., Gaudiano, B. A., Rheingold, A. A., Myers, V. H., Dalrymple, K., & Nolan, E. M. (2006). Social skills training augments the effectiveness of cognitive behavioral group therapy for social anxiety disorder. *Behavior Therapy, 36*, 125–138.

Hettema, J., Steele, J., & Miller, W. R. (2005). Motivational interviewing. *Annual Reviews of Clinical Psychology, 1*, 91–111.

Himle, J. A., Van Etten, M. L., Janeck, A. S., & Fischer, D. J. (2006). Insight as a predictor of treatment outcome in behavioral group treatment for obsessive-compulsive disorder. *Cognitive Therapy & Research, 30*, 661–666.

Hofmann, S. G., & Smits, J. A. (2008). Cognitive-behavioral therapy for adult anxiety disorders: A meta-analysis of randomized placebo-controlled trials. *Journal of Clinical Psychiatry, 69*, 621–632.

Hohagen, F., Winkelmann, G., Rasche-Reuchle, H., Hand, I., Koenig, A., Muenschau, N., . . . Berger, M. (1998). Combination of behavior therapy with fluvoxamine in comparison with behaviour therapy and placebo: Results of a multicentre study. *British Journal of Psychiatry, 173*, 71–78.

Hollin, C. R. (1999). Treatment programs for offenders: Meta-analysis, "what works," and beyond. *International Journal of Law and Psychiatry, 22*, 361–372.

Hopko, D. R., Armento, M. E. A., Robertson, S. M. C., Carvalho, J. P., Ryba, M., Johanson, L., . . . Lejuez, C. W. (2011). Behavior activation and problem-solving therapy for depressed breast cancer patients: Randomized trial. *Journal of Consulting and Clinical Psychology, 79*, 834–849.

Hopko, D. R., Lejuez, C. W., & Hopko, S. D. (2004). Behavioral activation as an intervention for coexistent depressive and anxiety symptoms. *Clinical Case Studies, 3*, 37–48.

Hopko, D. R., Lejuez, C. W., LePage, J. P., Hopko, S. D., & McNeil, D.W. (2003). A brief behavioral activation treatment for depression. A randomized pilot trial within an inpatient psychiatric hospital. *Behavior Modification, 27*, 458–469.

Hopko, D. R., Robertson, R. C. M., & Carvalho, J. P. (2009). Sudden gains in depressed cancer patients treated with behavioral activation therapy. *Behavior Therapy, 40*, 346–356.

Hoyer, J., Beesdo, K., Gloster, A. T., Runge, J., Hofler, M., & Becker, E. S. (2009). Worry exposure versus applied relaxation in the treatment of generalized anxiety disorder. *Psychotherapy and Psychosomatics, 78*, 106–115.

Huband, N., McMurran, M., Evans, C., & Duggan, C. (2007). Social problem-solving plus psychoeducation for adults with personality disorder. *British Journal of Psychiatry, 190*, 307–313.

Hunsley, J., & Lee, C.M. (2007). Research-informed benchmarks for psychological treatments: Efficacy studies, effectiveness studies, and beyond. *Professional Psychology, Research & Practice, 38*, 21–33.

Hunt, G. M., & Azrin, N. H. (1973). A community-reinforcement approach to alcoholism. *Behaviour, Research and Therapy, 11*, 91–104.

Irvin, J. E., Bowers, C. A., Dunn, M. E., & Wang, M. C. (1999). Efficacy of relapse prevention: A meta-analytic review. *Journal of Consulting and Clinical Psychology, 67*, 563–570.

Ito, J. R., Donovan, D. M., & Hall, J. J. (1988). Relapse prevention in alcohol aftercare: Effects on drinking outcome, change process, and aftercare attendance. *British Journal of Addiction, 83*, 171–181.

Jacobson, N. S., Dobson, K., Fruzetti, A. E., Schmaling, K. B., & Salusky, S. (1991). Marital therapy as a treatment for depression. *Journal of Consulting and Clinical Psychology, 59*, 547–557.

Jacobson, N. S., Dobson, K., Truax, P. A., Addis, M. E., Koerner, K., Gollan, J. K., . . . Prince, S. E. (1996). A component analysis of cognitive-behavioral treatment for depression. *Journal of Consulting and Clinical Psychology, 64*, 295–304.

Jaurrieta, N., Jimenez-Murcia, S., Menchón, J. M., Del Pino Alonso, M., Segalas, S., Álvarez-Moya, E. M., . . . Vallejo, J. (2008). Individual versus group cognitive-behavioral treatment for obsessive-compulsive disorder: A controlled pilot study. *Psychotherapy Research, 18*, 604–614.

Johnstone, K. A., & Page, A. C. (2004). Attention to phobic stimuli during exposure: The effect of distraction on anxiety reduction, self-efficacy and perceived control. *Behaviour Research and Therapy, 42*, 249–275.

Kadden, R. M., Cooney, N. L., Getter, H., & Litt, M. D. (1989). Matching alcoholics to coping skills or interactional therapies: Posttreatment results. *Journal of Consulting and Clinical Psychology, 57*, 698–704.

Kadden, R. M., Litt, M. D., Kabela-Cormier, E., & Petry, N. M. (2007). Abstinence rates following behavioral treatments for marijuana dependence. *Addictive Behaviors, 32*(6), 1220–1236.

Kallestad, H., Valen, J., McCullough, L., Svartberg, M., Hoglend, P., & Stiles, T. C. (2010). The relationship between insight gained during therapy and long-term outcome in short-term dynamic psychotherapy and cognitive therapy for cluster C personality disorders. *Psychotherapy Research, 20*, 526–534.

Kanter, J. W., Manos, R. C., Bowe, W. M., Baruch, D. E., Busch, A. M., & Rusch, L. C. (2010). What is behavioral activation? A review of the empirical literature. *Clinical Psychology Review, 30*, 608–620.

Kasvikis, Y., & Marks, I. M. (1988). Clomipramine, self-exposure and therapist-accompanied exposure in obsessive-compulsive ritualizers: Two year follow-up. *Journal of Anxiety Disorders, 2*, 291–298.

Kingdon, D., Tyrer, P., Seivewright, N., Ferguson, B., & Murphy, S. (1996). The Nottingham study of neurotic disorders: Influence of cognitive therapists on outcome. *British Journal of Psychiatry, 169*, 93–97.

Kiropoulos, L. A., Klein, B., Austin, D. W., Gilson, K., Pier., C., Mitchell, J. & Ciechomski, L. (2008). Is Internet-based CBT for panic disorder and agoraphobia as effective as face-to-face CBT? *Journal of Anxiety Disorders, 22,* 1273–1284.

Kliem, S., Kroger, C., & Kosfelder, J. (2010). Dialectical behavior therapy for borderline personality disorder: A meta-analysis using mixed-effects modeling. *Journal of Consulting and Clinical Psychology, 78,* 936–951.

Klinger, E., Bouchard, S., Legeron, P., Roy, S., Lauer, F., Chemin, I., & Nugues, P. (2005). Virtual reality therapy versus cognitive behavior therapy for social phobia: A preliminary controlled study. *CyberPsychology & Behavior, 8,* 76–88.

Kobak, K. A., Greist, J. H., Jefferson, J. W., Katzelnick, D. J., & Henry, J. (1998). Behavioral versus pharmacological treatments of obsessive compulsive disorder: A meta-analysis. *Psychopharmacology, 136,* 205–216.

Koch, E. I., Spates, C. R., & Himle, J. A. (2004). Comparison of behavioral and cognitive-behavioral one-session exposure treatments for small animal phobias. *Behaviour Research and Therapy, 42,* 1483–1504.

Koons, C. R., Robins, C. J., Tweed, J. L., Lynch, T. R., Gonzalez, A. M., Morse, J. Q., & Bastian, L. A. (2001). Efficacy of dialectical behavior therapy in women veterans with borderline personality disorder. *Behavior Therapy, 32,* 371–390.

Kushner, M. G., Abrams, K., Thuras, P., Hanson, K. L., Brekke, M., & Sletten, S. (2005). A follow-up study of anxiety disorder and alcohol dependence in comorbid substance abuse treatment patients. *Alcoholism: Clinical and Experimental Research, 29,* 1432–1443.

Kushner, M. G., Sletten, S., Donahue, C., Thuras, P., Maurer, E., Schneider, A., . . . van Demark, J. (2009). Cognitive-behavioral therapy for panic disorder in patients being treated for alcohol dependence: Moderating effects of alcohol outcome expectancies. *Addictive Behaviors, 34,* 554–560.

Ladouceur, R., Dugas, M. J., Freeston, M. H., Léger, E., Gagnon, F., & Thibodeau, N. (2000). Efficacy of a new cognitive-behavioral treatment for generalized anxiety disorder: Evaluation in a controlled clinical trial. *Journal of Consulting and Clinical Psychology, 68,* 957–964.

Lange, A., Rietdijk, D., Hudcovicova, M., van de Ven, J., Schrieken, B., & Emmelkamp, P. M. G. (2003). Interapy: A controlled randomized trial of the standardized treatment of posttraumatic stress through the Internet. *Journal of Consulting and Clinical Psychology, 71,* 901–909.

Leichsenring, F., Salzer, S., Jaeger, U., Kächele, H., Kreische, R., Leweke, F., . . . Leibing, E. (2009). Short-term psychodynamic psychotherapy and cognitive-behavioral therapy in generalized anxiety disorder: A randomized, controlled trial. *American Journal of Psychiatry, 166,* 875–881.

Lejuez, C. W., Hopko, D. R., & Hopko, S. D. (2001). A brief behavioral activation treatment for depression: Treatment manual. *Behavior Modification, 25,* 255–286.

Levitt, J. T., & Cloitre, M. (2005). A clinician's guide to STAIR/MPE: Treatment for PTSD related to childhood abuse. *Cognitive and Behavioral Practice, 12,* 40–52.

Lewinsohn, P. M. (1975). The behavioral study and treatment of depression. In M. Hersen, R. M. Eisler, & P. M. Miller (Eds.), *Progress in behavior modification* (Vol. 1, pp. 19–65). New York, NY: Academic Press.

Lewinsohn, P. M., & Hoberman, H. M. (1982). Depression. In A. S. Bellack, M. Hersen, & A. E. Kazdin (Eds.), *International handbook of behavior modification and therapy* (pp. 397–431). New York, NY: Plenum Press.

Lewis, M. W., & Petry, N. M. (2005). Contingency management treatments that reinforce completion of goal-related activities: Participation in family activities and its association with outcomes. *Drug and Alcohol Dependence, 79,* 267–271.

Linehan, M. M. (1993). *Cognitive behavioural treatment of borderline personality disorder*. New York, NY: Guilford Press.

Linehan, M. M., Armstrong, H. E., Suarez, A., Allmon, D., & Heard, H. L. (1991). Cognitive-behavioural treatment of chronically parasuicidal borderline patients. *Archives of General Psychiatry, 48,* 1060–1064.

Linehan, M. M., Heard, H. L., & Armstrong, H. E. (1993). Naturalistic follow-up of a behavioural treatment for chronically parasuicidal borderline patients. *Archives of General Psychiatry, 50,* 971–974.

Linehan, M. M., Schmidt, H., Dimeff, L. A., Craft, J. C., Kanter, J., & Comtois, K. A. (1999). DBT for patients with borderline PD and drug dependence. *American Journal of Addictions, 8,* 279–292.

Litt, M. D., Kadden, R. M., Cooney, N. L., & Kabela, E. (2003). Coping skills and treatment outcomes in cognitive-behavioral and interactional group therapy for alcoholism. *Journal of Consulting and Clinical Psychology, 71,* 118–128.

Litt, M. D., Kadden, R. M., & Kabela-Cormier, E. (2009). Individualized assessment and treatment program for alcohol dependence: Results of an initial study to train coping skills. *Addiction, 104,* 1837–1848.

LoCastro, J., Youngblood, M. A., Cisler, R., Mattson, M. M., Zweben, A., & Anton, R. (2009). Alcohol treatment effects on secondary nondrinking outcomes and quality of life: The COMBINE Study. *Journal of Studies on Drugs and Alcohol, 70,* 186–196.

Longabaugh, R., Donovan, D. M., Karno, M. P., McCrady, B. S., Morgenstern, J., & Tonigan, J. S. (2005). Active ingredients: How and why evidence-based alcohol behavioral treatment interventions work. *Alcoholism: Clinical and Experimental Research, 29,* 235–247.

Longmore, R. J., & Worrell, M. (2007). Do we need to challenge thoughts in cognitive behavior therapy? *Clinical Psychology Review*, 27, 173–187.

Lovell, K., & Bee, P. (2011). Optimising treatment resources for OCD: A review of the evidence base for technology-enhanced delivery. *Journal of mental Health*, 20, 525–542.

Luborsky, L., & Mark, D. (1991). Short term supportive-expressive psychoanalytic psychotherapy. In P. Crits-Cristoph & J. P. Barber (Eds.), *Handbook of short-term dynamic psychotherapy* (pp. 110–136). New York, NY: Basic Books.

Lusier, J. P., Heil, S. H., Mongeon, J. A., Badger, G. J. & Higgins, S. T. (2006). A meta-analysis of voucher-based reinforcement therapy for substance use disorders. *Addiction*, 101, 192–203.

Lyubomirsky, S., & Nolen-Hoeksema, S. (1995). Effects of self-focused rumination on negative thinking and interpersonal problem-solving. *Journal of Personality and Social Psychology*, 69, 176–190.

Maarsingh, M., Korrelboom, C. W., & Huijbrechts, I. P. A. M. (2010). Competitive memory training (COMET) voor een negatief zelfbeeld als aanvullende behandeling bij depressieve patiënten; een pilot studie. (COMET for low self-esteem as add-on treatment for depressed patients; a pilot-study.) *Directieve Therapie*, 30, 94–113.

Magill, M., & Ray, L. A. (2007). Cognitive-behavioral treatment with adult alcohol and illicit drug users: A meta-analysis of randomized controlled trials. *Journal of Studies on Alcohol & Drugs*, 70, 516–527.

Malan, D. H. (1979). *Individual psychotherapy and the science of psychodynamics*. London, United Kingdom: Butterworth.

Manos, R. C., Kanter, J. W., & Busch, A. M. (2010). A critical review of assessment strategies to measure the behavioral activation model of depression. *Clinical Psychology Review*, 30, 547–561.

Marchand, M., Coutu M. F., Dupuis, G., Fleet, R., Borgeat, B., Todorov, C., & Mainguy, N. (2008). Treatment of panic disorder with agoraphobia: Randomized placebo-controlled trial of four psychosocial treatments combined with imipramine or placebo. *Cognitive Behavior Therapy*, 37, 146–159.

Marijuana Treatment Project Research Group. (2004). Brief treatments for cannabis dependence: Findings from a randomized multisite trial. *Journal of Consulting and Clinical Psychology*, 72, 455–466.

Marks, I. M. (1997). Behaviour therapy for obsessive-compulsive disorder: A decade of progress. *Canadian Journal of Psychiatry*, 42, 1021–1027.

Marks, I. M., Hodgson, R., & Rachman, S. (1975). Treatment of chronic obsessive-compulsive neurosis by in vivo exposure. *British Journal of Psychiatry*, 127, 349–364.

Marks, I. M., Lelliott, P., Basoglu, M., Noshirvani, H., Monteiro, W., Cohen, D., & Kasvikis, Y. (1988). Clomipramine, self-exposure and therapist-aided exposure for obsessive-compulsive rituals. *British Journal of Psychiatry*, 152, 522–534.

Marks, I., Lovell, K., Noshirvani, H., Livanou, M., & Thrasher, S. (1998). Treatment of posttraumatic stress disorder by exposure and/or cognitive restructuring: A controlled study. *Archives of General Psychiatry*, 55, 317–325.

Marks, I., Swinson, R. P., Basoglu, M., Kuch, K., Noshirvani, H., O'sullivan, G., & Wickwire, K. (1993). Alprazolam and exposure alone and combined in panic disorder with agoraphobia. A controlled study in London and Toronto. *British Journal of Psychiatry*, 162, 776–787.

Marlatt, G. A., & Gordon, J. R. (1980). Determinants of relapse: Implications for the maintenance of behavior change. In P. Davidson (Ed.), *Behavioral medicine: Changing health lifestyles*. New York, NY: Brunner/Mazel.

Marlatt, G. A., & Witkiewitz, K. (2010). Update on harm-reduction policy and intervention research. *Annual Review of Clinical Psychology*, 6, 591–606.

Marquenie, L., Schadé, A., van Balkom, A., Koeter, M., Frenken, S., van den Brink, W., & van Dyck, R. (2006). Comorbid phobic disorders do not influence outcome of alcohol dependence treatment. Results of a naturalistic follow-up study. *Alcohol & Alcoholism*, 41, 168–173.

Mataix-Cols, D., Marks, I. M., Greist, J. H., Kobak, K. A., & Baer, L. (2002). Obsessive-compulsive symptom dimensions as predictors of compliance with and response to behaviour therapy: Results from a controlled trial. *Psychotherapy & Psychosomatics*, 71, 255–262.

Mawson, D., Marks, I., Ramm, E., & Stern, R. S. (1981). Guided mourning for morbid grief: A controlled study. *British Journal of Psychiatry*, 138, 185–193.

Mazzucchelli, T., Kane, R., & Rees, C. (2009). Behavioral activation treatments for adults: A meta-analysis and review. *Clinical Psychology: Science and Practice*, 16, 383–411.

McDonagh, A., Friedman, M., McHugo, G., Ford, J., Sengupta, A., Mueser, K., . . . Descamps, M. (2005). Randomized trial of cognitive–behavioral therapy for chronic posttraumatic stress disorder in adult female survivors of childhood sexual abuse. *Journal of Consulting and Clinical Psychology*, 73, 515–524.

McEvoy, P.M., & Shand, F. (2008). The effect of comorbid substance use disorders on treatment outcome for anxiety disorders. *Journal of Anxiety Disorders*, 22, 1087–1098.

McLean, P. L., Whittal, M. L., & Thordarson, D. S. (2001). Cognitive versus behavior therapy in the group treatment of obsessive-compulsive disorder. *Journal of Consulting & Clinical Psychology*, 69, 205–214.

McMain, S. F., Links, P. S., Gnam, W. H., Cardish, R. J., Korman, L., & Streiner, D. L. (2009). A randomized trial of dialectical behavior therapy versus general psychiatric management for borderline personality disorder. *American Journal of Psychiatry, 166*, 1365–1374.

Meca, J., Alcazar, A., & Rodriguez, J. (2004). El tratamiento de la fobia social especifica y generalizada en Europa: Un estudio meta–analitico. *Anales de Psicologia, 4*, 55–68.

Mersch, P. P. A., Emmelkamp, P. M. G., & Lips, C. (1991). Social phobia: Individual response patterns and the long-term effects of behavioral and cognitive interventions. A follow-up study. *Behaviour Research and Therapy, 29*, 357–362.

Meyerbröker, K., & Emmelkamp, P. M. G. (2010). Virtual reality exposure therapy in anxiety disorders: A systematic review of process-and outcome studies. *Depression and Anxiety, 27*(10), 933–944.

Meyerbröker, K., Morina, N., Kerkhof, G., & Emmelkamp, P. M. G. (in press). Virtual reality exposure therapy does not provide any additional value in agoraphobic patients: A randomized controlled trial. *Psychotherapy & Psychosomatics*.

Meyerbröker, K., Powers, M., van Stegeren, A., & Emmelkamp, P. M. G. (2012). Does yohimbine hydrochloride facilitate fear extinction in virtual reality treatment of fear of flying? A randomized placebo-controlled trial. *Psychotherapy & Psychosomatics, 81*, 29–37.

Miller, W. R. (1983). Motivational interviewing with problem drinkers. *Behavioural Psychotherapy, 11*, 441–448.

Miller, W. R. (1996). Motivational interviewing: Research, practice and puzzles. *Addictive Behaviors, 21*, 835–842.

Miller, W. R., Benefield, G., & Tonigan, J. S. (1993). Enhancing motivation for change in problem drinking: A controlled comparison of two therapist styles. *Journal of Consulting and Clinical Psychology, 61*, 455–461.

Mitte, K. A. (2005a). Meta-analysis of the efficacy of psycho- and pharmacotherapy in panic disorder with and without agoraphobia. *Journal of Affective Disorders, 88*, 27–45.

Mitte, K. A. (2005b). Meta-analysis of cognitive–behavioral treatments for generalized anxiety disorder: A comparison with pharmacotherapy. *Psychological Bulletin, 131*, 785–795.

Moreno, P., Carrillo, G., & Meca, J. (2001). Effectiveness of cognitive-behavioural treatment in social phobia: A meta-analytic review. *Psychology in Spain, 5*, 17–25.

Morris, R. W., & Bouton, M. E. (2007). The effect of yohimbine on the extinction of conditioned fear: A role for context. *Behavioral Neuroscience, 121*, 501–514.

Mortberg, E., Clark, D. M., Sundin, O., & Wistedt, A. A. (2007). Intensive group cognitive therapy and individual cognitive therapy versus treatment as usual in social phobia: A randomized controlled trial. *Acta Psychiatrica Scandinavica, 115*, 142–154.

Moscovitch, D. A., Antony, M. M., & Swinson, R. P. (2009). Exposure-based treatments for anxiety disorders: Theory and process. In M. M. Antony & M. B. Stein (Eds.), *Oxford handbook of anxiety and related disorders* (pp. 461–475). New York, NY: Oxford University Press.

Mueser, K. T., Rosenberg, S. D., Xie, H., Jankowski, M. K., Bolton, E. E., Lu, W.,...Wolfe, R. (2008). A randomized controlled trial of cognitive-behavioral treatment for posttraumatic stress disorder in severe mental illness. *Journal of Consulting and Clinical Psychology, 76*, 259–271.

Muran, J. C., Safran, J. D., Samstag, L. W., & Winston, A. (2005). Evaluating an alliance-focused treatment for personality disorders. *Psychotherapy: Theory, Research, Practice, Training, 42*, 532–545.

Mynors-Wallis, L. M., Gath, D. H., Day, A., & Baker, F. (2000). Randomised controlled trial of problem solving treatment, antidepressant medication, and combined treatment for major depression in primary care. *British Medical Journal, 320*, 26–30.

Nakatani, E., Mataix-Cols. D., Micali, N., Turner, C., & Heyman, I. (2009). Outcomes of cognitive behaviour therapy for obsessive compulsive disorder in a clinical setting. *Child and Adolescent Mental Health, 14*, 133–139.

Newman, M. G., Castonguay, L. G., Borkovec, T. D., Fisher, A. J., Boswell, J. F., & Szkodny, L. E. (2011). A randomized controlled trial of cognitive-behavioral therapy for generalized anxiety disorder with integrated techniques from emotion-focused and interpersonal therapies. *Journal of Consulting and Clinical Psychology, 79*, 171–181.

Nolen-Hoeksema, S. (2000). The role of rumination in depressive disorders and mixed anxiety/depressive symptoms. *Journal of Abnormal Psychology, 109*, 504–511.

Norton, P. J., Hayes-Skelton, S. A., & Klenck, S. C. (2011). What happens in session does not stay in session: Changes within exposures predict subsequent improvement and dropout. *Journal of Anxiety Disorders, 25*, 654–660.

Obsessive Compulsive Cognitions Working Group. (1997). Cognitive assessment of obsessive-compulsive disorder. *Behaviour Research and Therapy, 35*, 667–681.

O'Connor, K. P., Aardema, F., Bouthillier, D., Fournier, S., Guay, S., Robillard, S.,...Pitre, D. (2005). Evaluation of an inference-based approach to treating obsessive-compulsive disorder. *Cognitive Behaviour Therapy, 34*(3), 148–163.

O'Connor, K., Freeston, M. H., Gareau, D., Careau, Y., Dufour, M. J., Aardema, F., & Todorov, C. (2005). Group versus individual treatment in obsessions without compulsions. *Clinical Psychology & Psychotherapy, 12*, 87–96.

Olij, R. J. B., Korrelboom, C. W., Huijbrechts, I. P. A. M., Jong de, M., Cloin, M., Maarsingh, M., &

Paumen, B. N. W. (2006). De module zelfbeeld in een groep: werkwijze en eerste bevindingen. (Treating low self-esteem in a group: procedure and first results). *Directieve Therapie*, *26*, 307–325.

Olver, M. E., Stockdale, K. C., & Wormith, S. (2011). A meta-analysis of predictors of offender treatment attrition and its relationship to recidivism. *Journal of Consulting and Clinical Psychology*, *79*, 6–21.

O'Malley, S. S., Jaffe, A. J., Chang, G., Rode, S., Schottenfeld, R. S., Meyer, R. E., & Rounsaville, B. (1996). Six-month follow-up of naltrexone and coping skills therapy for alcohol dependence. *Archives of General Psychiatry*, *53*, 217–224.

Orsillo, S. M., Roemer, L., Block Lerner, J., & Tull, M. T. (2004). Acceptance, mindfulness, and cognitive–behavioral therapy: Comparisons, contrasts, and application to anxiety. In S. C. Hayes, V. M. Follette, & M. M. Linehan (Eds.), *Mindfulness and acceptance: Expanding the cognitive–behavioral tradition* (pp. 66–95). New York, NY: Guilford Press.

Öst, L. G., Fellenius, J., & Sterner, K. (1991). Applied tension, exposure in vivo, and tension-only in the treatment of blood phobia. *Behavior Research and Therapy*, *29*, 561–574.

Öst, L.-G., Salkovskis, P., & Hellström, K. (1991). One-session therapist directed exposure vs. self-exposure in the treatment of spider phobia. *Behavior Therapy*, *22*, 407–422.

Öst, L. G., Thulin, U., & Ramnero, J. (2004). Cognitive behavior therapy vs. exposure in vivo in the treatment of panic disorder with agoraphobia. *Behaviour Research and Therapy*, *42*, 1105–1127. doi: 10.1016/j.brat.2003.07.004.

Otto, M. W., Pollack, M. H., & Sabatino, S. A. (1996). Maintenance of remission following cognitive behavior therapy for panic disorder: Possible deleterious effects of concurrent medication treatment. *Behavior Therapy*, *27*, 473–482.

Otto, M. W., Tolin, D. F., Simon, N. M., Pearlson, G. D., Basden, S., Meunier, S. A., . . . Pollack, M. H. (2010). Efficacy of d-cycloserine for enhancing response to cognitive-behavior therapy for panic disorder. *Biological Psychiatry*, *67*, 365–370.

Palmer, S. (2006, February). *Cost effectiveness of the BOSCOT trial*. Paper presented at the Annual Conference of the British and Irish Group for the Study of Personality Disorder, Nottingham, United Kingdom.

Papageorgiou, C., & Wells, A. (Eds.). (2004). *Depressive rumination. Nature, theory and treatment*. Chichester, United Kingdom: Wiley.

Pasiencny, N., & Connor, J. (2011). The effectiveness of dialectical behaviour therapy in routine public mental health settings: An Australian controlled trial. *Behavior Research & Therapy*, *49*, 4–10.

Paunovic, N., & Ost, L. G. (2001). Cognitive behavior therapy vs. exposure therapy in the treatment of PTSD in refugees. *Behavior Research and Therapy*, *39*, 1183–1197.

Peck, J. A., Reback, C. J., Yang, X., Rotheram-Fuller, E. & Shoptaw, S. (2005). Sustained reductions in drug use and depression symptoms from treatment for drug abuse in methamphetamine-dependent gay and bisexual men. *Journal of Urban Health*, *82*(Suppl. 1), 100–108.

Peirce, J. M., Petry, N. M., & Stitzer, M. L. (2006). Effects of lower-cost incentives on stimulant abstinence in methadone maintenance treatment: A national drug abuse treatment clinical trials network study. *Archives of General Psychiatry*, *63*, 201–208.

Peter, H., Brückner, E., Hand, I., Rohr, W., & Rufer, M. (2008). Treatment outcome of female agoraphobics 3–9 years after exposure in vivo: A comparison with healthy controls. *Journal of Behavior Therapy & Experimental Psychiatry*, *39*, 3–10.

Petry, N. M., Alessi, S. M., Hanson, T., & Sierra, S. (2007). Randomized trial of contingent prizes versus vouchers in cocaine-using methadone patients. *Journal of Consulting and Clinical Psychology*, *75*, 983–991.

Petry, N. M., Martin, B., & Simcic, F. (2005). Prize reinforcement contingency management for cocaine dependence: Integration with group therapy in a methadone clinic. *Journal of Consulting and Clinical Psychology*, *73*, 354–359.

Polaschek, D. L. L. (2011). High-intensity rehabilitation for violent offenders in New Zealand: Reconviction outcomes for high and medium-risk prisoners. *Journal of Interpersonal Violence*, *26*, 664–682.

Ponniah, K., & Hollon, S. D. (2007). Empirically supported psychological interventions for social phobia in adults: A qualitative review of randomized controlled trials. *Psychological Medicine*, 1–12.

Powers, M. B., & Emmelkamp, P. M. G. (2008). Virtual reality exposure therapy for anxiety disorders: A meta-analysis. *Journal of Anxiety Disorders*, *22*(3), pp. 561–569.

Powers M. B., & Emmelkamp, P. M. G. (2009). Dissemination of research findings. In D. C. S. Richard & S. K. Huprich (Eds.), *Clinical psychology: Assessment, treatment and research* (pp. 495–524). New York, NY: Academic Press.

Powers, M. B., Halpern, J. M., Ferenschak, M. P., Gillihan, S. J., & Foa, E. B. (2010). A meta-analytic review of prolonged exposure for posttraumatic stress disorder. *Clinical Psychology Review*, *30*, 635–641.

Powers, M. B., Sigmarsson, S. R., & Emmelkamp, P. M. G. (2008). A meta–analytic review of psychological treatments for social anxiety disorder. *International Journal of Cognitive Therapy*, *1*, 94–113.

Powers, M. B., Smits, J. A., Otto, M. W., Sanders, C., & Emmelkamp, P. M. G. (2009). Facilitation of fear extinction in phobic participants with a novel cognitive enhancer: A randomized placebo controlled trial of yohimbine augmentation. *Journal of Anxiety Disorders*, *23*, 350–356.

Powers, M. B., Vedel, E., & Emmelkamp, P. M. G. (2008). Behavioral couples therapy (BCT) for alcohol and drug use disorders: A meta-analysis *Clinical Psychology Review*, *28*, 952–962.

Prendergast, M., Podus, D., Finney, J., Greenwell, L. & Roll, J. (2006). Contingency management for treatment of substance use disorders: A meta-analysis. *Addiction*, *101*, 1546–1560.

Project MATCH Research Group. (1997a). Matching alcoholism treatments to client heterogeneity: Project MATCH posttreatment drinking outcomes. *Journal of Studies on Alcohol*, *58*, 7–29.

Project MATCH Research Group. (1997b). Project MATCH secondary a priori hypotheses. *Addiction*, *92*, 1671–1698.

Project MATCH Research Group. (1998). Matching alcoholism treatments to client heterogeneity: Project MATCH three-year drinking outcomes. *Journal of Studies on Alcohol*, *58*, 7–29.

Raes, A. K., Koster, E. H. W., Loeys, T., & De Raedt, R. (2011). Pathways to change in one-session exposure with and without cognitive intervention: An exploratory study in spider phobia. *Journal of Anxiety Disorders*, doi: 10.1016/j.janxdis.2011.06.003

Ramsay, R. (1979). Bereavement. In D. Sjödén, S. Bayes, & W. S. Dorkens (Eds.), *Trends in behavior therapy*. New York, NY: Academic Press.

Rawson, R. A., McCann, M. J., Flammino, F., Shoptaw, S., Miotto, K., Reiber, C., & Ling, W. (2006). A comparison of contingency management and cognitive—Behavioral approaches for stimulant-dependent individuals. *Addiction*, *101*, 267–274.

Renneberg, B., Goldstein, A. J., & Phillips, D. (1990). Intensive behavioral group treatment of avoidant personality disorder. *Behavior Therapy*, *21*, 363–377.

Resick, P., Galovski, T. E., O'Brien Uhlmansiek, M., Scher, C. D., Clum, G. A., & Young-Xu, Y. (2008). A randomized clinical trial to dismantle components of cognitive processing therapy for posttraumatic stress disorder in female victims of interpersonal violence. *Journal of Consulting and Clinical Psychology*, *76*, 243–258.

Resick, P. A., Nishith, P., Weaver, T. L., Astin, M. C., & Feuer, C. A. (2002). A comparison of cognitive processing therapy, prolonged exposure, and a waiting condition for the treatment of posttraumatic stress disorder in female rape victims. *Journal of Consulting and Clinical Psychology*, *70*, 867–879.

Ressler, K. J., Rothbaum, B. O., Tannenbaum, L., Anderson, P., Graap, K., Zimand, E., . . . Davis, M. (2004). Cognitive enhancers as adjuncts to psychotherapy use of d-cycloserine in phobic individuals to facilitate extinction of fear. *Archives of General Psychiatry*, *6*, 1136–114.

Ritz, T., Meuret, A. E., & Ayala, E. S. (2010). The psychophysiology of blood-injection-injury phobia: Looking beyond the diphasic response paradigm. *International Journal of Psychophysiology*, *78*, 50–67.

Robjant, K., & Fazel, M. (2010). The emerging evidence for narrative exposure therapy: A review. *Clinical Psychology Review*, *30*, 1030–1039.

Roepke, S., Schröder-Abé, M., Schütz, A., Jacob, G., Dams, A., Vater, A., . . . Lammers, C. H. (2011). Dialectic behavioural therapy has an impact on self-concept clarity and facets of self-esteem in women with borderline personality disorder. *Clinical Psychology and Psychotherapy*, *18*, 148–158.

Rollman, B. L., Belnap, B. H., & Mazumdar, S., Houck, P. R., Zhu, F., Gardner, W., . . . Shear, M.K. (2005). A randomized trial to improve the quality of treatment for panic and generalized anxiety disorders in primary care. *Archives of General Psychiatry*, *62*, 1332–1341.

Rosa-Alcazar, A. I., Sanchez-Meca, J., Gomez-Conesta, A., & Marin-Martinez, F. (2008). Psychological treatment of obsessive-compulsive disorder: A meta-analysis. *Clinical Psychology Review*, *28*, 1310–1325.

Rosen, G. M., & Davison, G. C. (2003). Psychology should list empirically supported principles of change (ESPs) and not credential trademarked therapies or other treatment packages. *Behavior Modification*, *27*, 300–312.

Rothbaum, B. O., & Shahar, F. (2000). Behavioral treatment of obsessive-compulsive disorder in a naturalistic setting. *Cognitive Behavioral Practice*, *7*, 262–270.

Rufer, M., Fricke, S., Moritz, S., Kloss, M., & Hand, I. (2006). Symptom dimensions in obsessive-compulsive disorder: Prediction of cognitive-behavior therapy outcome. *Acta Psychiatria Scandinavia*, *113*, 440–446.

Rufer, M., Hand, I., Alsleben, H., Braatz, A., Ortmann, J., Katenkamp, B., . . . Peter, H. (2005). Long-term course and outcome of obsessive-compulsive patients after cognitive-behavioral therapy in combination with either fluvoxamine or placebo: A 7-year follow-up of a randomized double-blind trial. *European Archives of Psychiatry and Clinical Neuroscience*, *255*, 121–128.

Rufer, M., Held, D., Cremer, J., Fricke, S., Moritz, S., Peter, H. & Hand, I. (2006). Dissociation as a predictor of cognitive behavior therapy outcome in patients with obsessive-compulsive disorder. *Psychotherapy & Psychosomatics*, *75*, 40–46.

Ruwaard, J., Lange, A., Schrieken, B., Dolan, C. V., & Emmelkamp, P.M.G. (2012). The effectiveness of online cognitive behavioral treatment in routine clinical practice. *PLoS One*, *7*(7), e40089. Epub July 5, 2012.

Salekin, R. T. (2002). Psychopathy and therapeutic pessimism. Clinical lore or clinical reality? *Clinical Psychology Review*, *22*, 79–112.

Sánchez-Meca, J., Rosa-Alcázar, A. I., Marin-Martínez, F., & Gómez-Conesa, A. (2010). Psychological treatment of panic disorder with or without agoraphobia: A meta-analysis. *Clinical Psychology Review*, *30*, 37–50.

Schadé, A., Marquenie, L. A., van Balkom, A. J., Koeter, M. W., de Beurs, E, van den Brink, W., & van Dyck, R. (2005). The effectiveness of anxiety treatment on alcohol-dependent patients with a comorbid phobic disorder: A randomized controlled trial. *Alcoholism Clinical & Experimental Research*, *29*, 794–800.

Scherbaum, N., Kluwig, J., Specka, M., Krause, D., Merget, B., Finkenbeiner T., & Gaspar, M. (2005). Group psychotherapy for opiate addicts in methadone maintenance treatment—A controlled trial. *European Addiction Research*, *11*, 163–171.

Schmidt, N. B., Woolaway-Bickel, K., Trakowski, J., Santiago, H., Storey, J., Koselka, M., & Cook, J. (2000). Dismantling cognitive-behavioral treatment for panic disorder: Questioning the utility of breathing retraining. *Journal of Consulting and Clinical Psychology*, *68*, 417–424.

Schneider, A. J., Mataix-Cols, D., Marks, I. M., & Bachofen, M. (2005). Internet-guided self-help with or without exposure therapy for phobic and panic disorders. *Psychotherapy & Psychosomatics*, *74*, 154–164.

Scholing, A., & Emmelkamp, P. M. G. (1993). Exposure with and without cognitive therapy for generalized social phobia: Effects of individual and group treatment. *Behaviour Research and Therapy*, *31*, 667–681.

Scholing, A., & Emmelkamp, P. M. G. (1996a). Treatment of generalized social phobia: Results at long-term follow-up. *Behaviour Research and Therapy*, *34*, 447–452.

Scholing, A., & Emmelkamp, P. M. G. (1996b). Treatment of fear of blushing, sweating, or trembling: Results at long-term follow-up. *Behavior Modification*, *20*, 338–356.

Schumacher, J. E., Milby, J. B., Wallace, D., Meehan, D., Kertesz, S., Vuchinich, R., . . . Usdan, S. (2007). Meta-Analysis of day treatment and contingency-management dismantling research: Birmingham homeless cocaine studies (1990–2006). *Journal of Consulting and Clinical Psychology*, *75*, 823–828.

Schuppert, H. M., Giesen-Bloo, J., van Gemert, T. G., Wiersema, H., Minderaa, R. B., Emmelkamp, P. M. G., & Nauta, M. H. (2009). Effectiveness of an emotion regulation group training for adolescents—A randomized controlled pilot study. *Clinical Psychology & Psychotherapy*, *16*, 467–478.

Schuppert, H. M., Timmerman, M. E., Bloo, J., van Gemert, T. G., Wiersema, H., Minderaa, R. B., . . . Nauta, M. H. (in press). Emotion Regulation Training for adolescents with borderline personality disorder traits: A randomized controlled trial. *Journal of the American Academy of Child and Adolescent Psychiatry*.

Segrin, C. (2000). Social skills deficits associated with depression. *Clinical Psychology Review*, *20*, 379–403.

Seidler, G. H., & Wagner, F. E. (2006). Comparing the efficacy of EMDR and trauma-focused cognitive behavioral therapy in the treatment of PTSD: A meta-analytic study. *Psychological Medicine*, *36*, 1515–1522.

Shapiro, F. (1995). *Eye movement desensitization and reprocessing: Basic principles, protocols, and procedures*. New York, NY: Guilford Press.

Shea, M. T., Stout, R., Gunderson, J., Morey, L. C., Grilo, C. M., McGlashan, T., . . . Keller, M. B. (2002). Short-term diagnostic stability of schizotypal, borderline, avoidant, and obsessive-compulsive personality disorders. *American Journal of Psychiatry*, *159*, 2036–2041.

Shear, K., Frank, E., Houck, P. R., & Reynolds, C. F. (2005). Treatment of complicated grief: A randomized controlled trial. *JAMA*, *293*, 2601–2608.

Siegel, S. (1983). Classical conditioning, drug tolerance, and drug dependence. In R. G. Smart, F. B. Glaser, Y. Israel, H. Kalant, R. E. Popham, & W. Schmidt (Eds.), *Research advances in alcohol and drug problems* (Vol. 7, pp. 207–246). New York, NY: Plenum Press.

Siegmund, A., Golfels, F., Finck, C., Halisch, A., Räth, D., Plag, J., & Ströhle, A. (2011). D-Cycloserine does not improve but might slightly speed up the outcome of in-vivo exposure therapy in patients with severe agoraphobia and panic disorder in a randomized double blind clinical trial. *Journal of Psychiatric Research*, *45*, 1042–1047.

Siev, J., & Chambless, D. L. (2007). Specificity of treatment effects: Cognitive therapy and relaxation for generalized anxiety and panic disorders. *Journal of Consulting and Clinical Psychology*, *75*, 513–522.

Simon, W. (2009). Follow-up psychotherapy outcome of patients with dependent, avoidant and obsessive—Compulsive personality disorders: A meta-analytic review. *International Journal of Psychiatry in Clinical Practice*, *13*, 153–165.

Simpson, H. B., Liebowitz, M. R., Foa, E. B., Kozak, M. J., Schmidt, A. B., . . . Campeas, R. (2004). Post-treatment effects of exposure therapy and clomipramine in obsessive-compulsive disorder. *Depression &. Anxiety*, *19*, 225–233.

Simpson, H., Maher, M. J., Wang, Y., Bao, Y., Foa, E. B., & Franklin, M. (2011). Patient adherence predicts outcome from cognitive behavioral therapy in obsessive-compulsive disorder. *Journal of Consulting and Clinical Psychology*, *79*, 247–252.

Sindelar, J., Elbel, B., & Petry, N. M. (2007). What do we get for our money? Cost-effectiveness of adding contingency management. *Addiction*, *102*, 309–316.

Sireling, L., Cohen, D., & Marks, I. (1988). Guided mourning for morbid grief: A controlled replication. *Behavior Therapy*, *19*, 121–132.

Skodol, A. E., Gunderson, J. G., McGlashan, T. H., Dyck, I. R., Stout, R. L., Bender, D. S.,...Oldham, J. M. (2002). Functional impairment in patients with schizotypal, borderline, avoidant, or obsessive-compulsive personality disorder. *American Journal of Psychiatry*, *159*, 276–283.

Snarski, M., Scogin, F., DiNapoli, E., Presnell, A., McAlpine, J., & Marcinak, J. (2011). The effects of behavioral activation therapy with inpatient geriatric psychiatry patients. *Behavior Therapy*, *42*, 100–108.

Soler, J., Pascual, J. C., Tiana, T., Cebria, A., Barrachina, J., Campins, M. J.,...Perez, V. (2009). Dialectical behaviour therapy skills training compared to standard group therapy in borderline personality disorder: A 3-month randomised controlled clinical trial. *Behaviour Research & Therapy*, *47*, 353–358.

Spiegel, D. A., & Bruce, T. J. (1997). Benzodiazepines and exposure-based cognitive behavior therapies for panic disorder: Conclusions from combined treatment trials. *American Journal of Psychiatry*, *154*(6), 773–781.

Spinazzola, J., Blaustein, M., & van der Kolk, B. A. (2005). Posttraumatic stress disorder treatment outcome research: The study of unrepresentative samples? *Journal of Traumatic Stress*, *18*, 425–436.

Stangier, U., Heidenreich, T., Peitz, M., Lauterbach, W., & Clark, D. M. (2003). Cognitive therapy for social phobia: Individual versus group treatment. *Behaviour Research and Therapy*, *41*, 991–1007.

Storch, E. A., Geffken, G. R., Merlo, L. J., Mann, D., Duke, D., & Munson, M. (2007). Family-based cognitive-behavioral therapy for pediatric obsessive–compulsive disorder: Comparison of intensive and weekly approaches, *Journal of the American Academy of Child and Adolescent Psychiatry*, *46*, 469–478.

Storch, E. A., Merlo, L. J., Lehmkuhl, H., Geffken, G. R., Jacob, M., Ricketts, E.,...Goodman, W. K. (2008). Cognitive behaviour therapy for obsessive-compulsive disorder: A non-randomized comparison of intensive and weekly approaches. *Journal of Anxiety Disorders*, *22*, 1146–1158.

Sturmey, P. (Ed). (2007). *Functional analysis in clinical treatment*. New York, NY: Academic Press.

Sturmey, P. (2009). Behavioral activation is an evidence-based treatment for depression. *Behavior Modification*, *33*, 818–829.

Svartberg, M., Stiles, T. C., & Seltzer, M. H.(2004). Randomized, controlled trial of the effectiveness of short-term dynamic psychotherapy and cognitive therapy for cluster C personality disorders. *American Journal of Psychiatry*, *161*, 810–817.

Swenson, C. R., Sanderson, C., Dulit, R. A., & Linehan, M. M. (2001). The application of DBT for patients with borderline PD on inpatient units. *Psychiatric Quarterly*, *72*, 307–324.

Taylor, J. E., & Harvey, S. T. (2010). A meta-analysis of the effects of psychotherapy with adults sexually abused in childhood. *Clinical Psychology Review*, *30*, 749–767.

Taylor, S. (1996). Meta–analysis of cognitive-behavioral treatments for social phobia. *Journal of Behavior Therapy and Experimental Psychiatry*, *27*, 1–9.

Tiffany, S. T., & Conklin, C. A. (2000). A cognitive processing model of alcohol craving and compulsive alcohol use. *Addiction*, *95*(Suppl.), S145–S153.

Titov, N., Andrews, G., Choi, I., Schwencke, G., & Johnston, L. (2009). Randomized controlled trial of web-based treatment social phobia without clinical guidance. *Australian and New Zealand Journal of Psychiatry*, *42*, 913–919.

Titov. N., Andrews, G., Choi, I., Schwencke, G. & Mahoney, A. (2008). Shyness 3: Randomized controlled trial of guided versus unguided Internet-based CBT for social phobia. *Australian and New Zealand Journal of Psychiatry*, *42*, 1030–1040.

Tolin, D. F., Hannan, S., Maltby, N., Diefenbach, G. J., Worhunsky, P., & Brady, R. E. (2007). A randomized controlled trial of self-directed versus therapist-directed cognitive-behavioral therapy for obsessive-compulsive disorder patients with prior medication trials. *Behavior Therapy*, *38*, 179–191.

Torgersen, S. (2005). Epidemiology. In J. M. Oldham, A. E. Skodol, & D. S. Bender (Eds.), *Textbook of personality disorders* (pp. 129–142). Washington, DC: American Psychiatric.

Tumur, I., Kaltenthaler, E., Ferriter, M., Beverley, C., & Parry, G. (2007). Computerised cognitive behaviour therapy for obsessive-compulsive disorder: A systematic review. *Psychotherapy & Psychosomatics*, *76*, 196–202.

Turner, R. M. (2000). Naturalistic evaluation of dialectical behavior therapy-oriented treatment for borderline personality disorder. *Cognitive and Behavioral Practice*, *7*, 413–419.

Turner, S. M., Beidel, D. C., Cooley-Quille, M. R. (1995). Two-year follow-up of social phobics treated with social effectivennes therapy. *Behaviour Research and Therapy*, *33*, 553–555.

Van Apeldoorn, F. J., Van Hout, W. J. P. J., Mersch, P. P. A., Huisman, M., Slaap, B., Hale, W. W.,...Den Boer, J. A. (2008). Is a combined therapy more effective than either CBT or SSRI alone? Results of a multicenter trial on panic disorder with or without agoraphobia. *Acta Psychiatrica Scandinavica*, *117*, 260–270.

van Balkom, A. J. L. M., de Haan, E., van Oppen, P., Spinhoven, P., Hoogduin, K. A. L.,...van

Dyck, R. (1998). Cognitive and behavioral therapies alone versus in combination with fluvoxamine in the treatment of obsessive compulsive disorder. *Journal of Nervous & Mental Disease, 186*, 492–499.

van Dam, D., Vedel, E., Ehring, T., & Emmelkamp, P. M. G. (2012). Psychological treatments for concurrent posttraumatic stress disorder and substance use disorder: A systematic review. *Clinical Psychology Review, 32*(3), 202–214.

van den Bosch, L. M. C., Verheul, R., Schippers, G. M., & van den Brink, W. (2002). Dialectical behavior therapy of borderline patients with and without substance use problems, implementation and long term effects, *Addictive Behaviors, 27*, 911–923.

van den Hout, M. A., Emmelkamp, P. M. G., Kraaykamp, J., & Griez, E. (1988). Behavioural treatment of obsessive-compulsives: Inpatient versus outpatient. *Behaviour Research and Therapy, 26*, 331–332.

van der Heiden, C., Muris, P., & van der Molen, H. T. (2012). Randomized controlled trial on the effectiveness of metacognitive therapy and intolerance-of-uncertainty therapy for generalized anxiety disorder. *Behaviour Research and Therapy, 50*, 100–109.

van der Kolk, B. A., Roth, S., Pelcovitz, D., Sunday, S., & Spinazzola, J. (2005). Disorders of extreme stress: The empirical foundation of a complex adaptation to trauma. *Journal of Traumatic Stress, 18*, 389–399.

van der Kolk, B. A., Spinazzola, J., Blaustein, M. E., Hopper, J. W., Hopper, E. K., Korn, D. L., & Simpson, W. B. (2007). A randomized clinical trial of eye movement desensitization and reprocessing (EMDR), fluoxetine, and pill placebo in the treatment of posttraumatic stress disorder: treatment effects and long-term maintenance. *Journal of Clinical Psychiatry, 68*, 37–46.

van Emmerik, A. A. P., Kamphuis, J. H., & Emmelkamp, P.M.G. (2008). Treating acute stress disorder and posttraumatic stress disorder with cognitive behavioral therapy or structured writing therapy: A randomized controlled trial. *Psychotherapy & Psychosomatics, 77*, 93–100.

van Emmerik, A. A. P., Kamphuis, J. H., Noordhof, A., & Emmelkamp, P. M. G. (2011). Catch me if you can: Do the five-factor model personality traits moderate dropout and acute treatment response in post-traumatic stress disorder patients? *Psychotherapy & Psychosomatics, 80*(6), 386–388.

van Etten, M. L., & Taylor, S. (1998). Comparative efficacy of treatments for post-traumatic stress disorder: A meta-analysis. *Clinical Psychology and Psychotherapy, 5*, 126–144.

van Hout, W. J. P. J., & Emmelkamp, P. M. G. (2002). Exposure in vivo. In M. Hersen & W. Sledge (Eds.), *The Encyclopedia of Psychotherapy*. New York, NY: Academic Press.

van Hout, W. J. P. J., Emmelkamp, P. M. G., & Scholing, A. (1994). The role of negative self-statements in agoraphobic situations: A process study of eight panic disorder patients with agoraphobia. *Behavior Modification, 18*, 389–410.

van Manen, T. G., Prins, P. J., & Emmelkamp, P. M. G. (2004). Reducing aggressive behavior in boys with a social cognitive group treatment: Results of a randomized, controlled trial. *Journal of the American Academy of Child and Adolescent Psychiatry, 43*, 1478–1487.

van Minnen, A., Arntz, A., & Keijsers, G. P. J. (2002). Prolonged exposure in patients with chronic PTSD: Predictors of treatment outcome and dropout. *Behaviour Research & Therapy, 40*, 439–457.

van Noppen, B. L., Pato, M. T., Marsland, R., & Rasmussen, S. A. (1998). A time-limited behavioral group treatment of obsessive-compulsive disorder. *Journal of Psychotherapy Practice and Research, 7*, 272–280.

van Oppen, P., van Balkom, A. J. L. M., De Haan, E., & van Dyck, R. (2005). Cognitive therapy and exposure in vivo alone and in combination with fluvoxamine in obsessive-compulsive disorder: A 5-year follow-up. *Journal of Clinical Psychiatry, 66*(11), 1415–1422.

van Oppen, P., van Balkom, A. J. L. M., Smit, J. H., Schuurmans, J., van Dyck, R., & Emmelkamp, P. M. G. (2010). What matters most in the treatment of obsessive-compulsive disorder: The therapy manual or the therapist. *Journal of Clinical Psychiatry, 71*, 1158–1167.

Vedel, E., & Emmelkamp, P. M. G. (2012). Illicit substance-related disorders. In P. Sturmey & M. Hersen (Eds.), *Handbook of evidence-based practice in clinical psychology* (Vol. II). Hoboken, NJ: Wiley.

Verheul, R., van den Bosch, L. M. C., Koeter, M. W. J., de Ridder, M. A. J., Stijnen, T., & van den Brink, W. (2003). DBT for women with borderline PD. *British Journal of Psychiatry, 182*, 135–140.

Visser, S., Hoekstra, R. J., & Emmelkamp, P. M. G. (1992). Long-term follow-up study on behavioural treatment of obsessive-compulsive disorders. In A. Ehlers, W. Fiegenbaum, I. Florin, & J. Margraf (Eds.), *Perspectives and promises of clinical psychology* (pp. 157–170). New York, NY: Plenum Press.

Wallach, H. S., Safir, M. P., & Bar-Zvi, M. (2009). Virtual reality cognitive behavior therapy for public speaking anxiety: A randomized clinical trial. *Behavior Modification, 33*, 314–338.

Walters, G. D. (2000). Behavioral self-control training for problem drinkers: A meta-analysis of randomized control studies. *Behavior Therapy, 31*, 135–149.

Watanabe, N., Churchill, R., & Furukawa, T. A. (2007). Combination of psychotherapies and benzodiazepines versus either therapy alone for panic disorder: A systematic review. *BMC-Psychiatry*, 7, 18.

Watkins, E. (2008). Constructive and unconstructive repetitive thought. *Psychological Bulletin, 134*, 163–206.

Watkins, E. R., Mullan, E., Wingrove, J., Rimes, J., Steiner, H., Bathurst, N., ... & Scott, J. (2011). Rumination-focused cognitive–behavioural therapy for residual depression: Phase II randomised controlled trial. *British Journal of Psychiatry, 1–6*. doi: 0.1192/bjp.bp.110.090282

Watkins, E. R., Scott, J., Wingrove, J., Rimes, K. A., Bathurst, N., Steiner, H.,...Malliaris, Y. (2007). Rumination-focused cognitive behavior therapy for residual depression: A case series. *Behaviour Research and Therapy*, 45, 2144–2154.

Weinberg, I., Ronningstam, E., Goldblatt, M. J., Schechter, M., & Maltsberger, J. T. (2011). Common factors in empirically supported treatments of borderline personality disorder. *Current Psychiatry Reports*, *13*(Suppl. 1), 60–68.

Wells, A. (2010). Metacognitive theory and therapy for worry and generalized anxiety disorder: Review and status. *Journal of Experimental Psychopathology*, *1*, 133–145.

Wells, A., Welford, M., King, P., Papageorgiou, C., Wisely, J., & Mendel, E. (2010). A pilot randomized trial of metacognitive therapy vs applied relaxation in the treatment of adults with generalized anxiety disorder. *Behaviour Research and Therapy*, *48*, 429–434.

Whittal, M. L., Robichaud, M., Thordarson, D. S., McLean, P. D. (2008). Group and individual treatment of obsessivecompulsive disorder using cognitive therapy and exposure plus response prevention: A 2-year follow-up of two randomized trials. *Journal of consulting & Clinical Psychology*, 76, 1003–1014.

Whittal, M. L., Thordarson, D. S., & McLean, P. D. (2005). Treatment of obsessive-compulsive disorder: Cognitive behavior therapy versus exposure and response prevention. *Behaviour Research and Therapy*, *43*, 1559–1576.

Yeung, S., Lui, M., Ross, F., & Murrells, T. (2007). Family carers in stroke care: Examining the relationship between problem-solving, depression and general health. *Journal of Clinical Nursing, 16*, 344–352.

Young, J. E., Klosko, J. S., & Weishaar, M. E. (2003). *Schema-focused therapy: A practitioner's guide*. New York, NY: Guilford Press.

Zlomke, K., & Davis, T. E. (2008). One-session treatment of specific phobias: A detailed description and review of treatment efficacy. *Behavior Therapy*, *39*, 207–223.

COGNITIVE AND COGNITIVE-BEHAVIORAL THERAPIES

STEVEN D. HOLLON AND AARON T. BECK

COGNITIVE AND COGNITIVE-BEHAVIORAL THERAPIES

The cognitive and cognitive-behavioral interventions are among the best supported and most widely practiced of the psychosocial interventions. These approaches are based on the notion that thinking plays a role in the etiology or maintenance of the psychological disorders and seek to reduce distress and to enhance coping by changing maladaptive beliefs and teaching new information-processing skills. The various approaches differ in the role they accord to cognitive change in their explanatory models and therefore use cognitive and behavioral strategies to different extents and for different reasons. Nonetheless, they all address the role of cognition in treatment and many refer to them under the general rubric of cognitive-behavior therapy (CBT).

It is useful to distinguish the underlying theory of disorder (*etiology*) from the theory of change that it implies (*process*) and each from the actual strategies used to bring about that change (*procedure*). The more cognitive approaches emphasize the role of meaning in their etiological models (*cognitive theory of disorder*) and conceptualize therapy as a process of testing the accuracy of existing beliefs (*cognitive theory of change*). The theorists who developed these approaches often were trained dynamically and incorporated behavioral procedures into their treatments in the service of testing the beliefs (Beck, 2005). The more behavioral approaches tend to use peripheral learning theories in their etiological models and conceptualize change in terms of operant or classical conditioning. The theorists who developed these approaches typically were trained behaviorally and incorporated cognitive strategies into their treatments to facilitate behavior change or to explain it after the fact (Barlow, 2002). Both use the same procedures but each tends to do so for different reasons and to different extents. For many of the disorders we review, there are more cognitive versions of CBT (usually called cognitive therapy or CT) that conceptualize change in terms of cognitive mechanisms and more behavioral versions of CBT that conceptualize change in terms of traditional conditioning models (see Chapter 10, this volume). We address throughout whether this distinction impacts outcome in any meaningful way.

That being said, few interventions have been as extensively tested and fewer still have done so well in those tests. CBT is at least as efficacious as other types of psychotherapy or medications and often more enduring in the treatment of the nonpsychotic disorders and can play an adjunctive role to medication in the treatment of psychotic disorders (Butler, Chapman, Forman, & Beck, 2006). Treatments can be characterized as being *efficacious* if they work better than their absence and as being *specific* if they work better than nonspecific controls or a credible alternative intervention (Chambless & Hollon, 1998). The qualifier *possibly* is added if the relevant support comes from a single study or if all the relevant studies come from a single research group. Although not included in the Chambless and Hollon criteria, we use the term *superior* to indicate a situation in which a given treatment outperforms all other viable alternative interventions.

Recent reviews indicate that CBT is the psychosocial intervention most likely to be found to be both *efficacious and specific* for a variety of disorders in both children (Kazdin & Weiss, 1998) and adults (DeRubeis & Crits-Christoph, 1998). CBT has outstripped the dynamic and humanistic interventions in terms of the amount and quality of the empirical support that it has garnered and is rivaled only by the more purely behavioral interventions or medications in that regard. CBT is the most widely practiced psychosocial intervention in the field today (Norcross, Karpiak, & Santoro, 2005) and along with interpersonal psychotherapy the only psychosocial interventions mandated for training in psychiatric residency programs (Weissman et al., 2006).

Perhaps the most exciting attribute of CBT is that it appears to produce an *enduring effect* that lasts beyond the end of treatment. This is something that cannot yet be said for any other intervention (except perhaps the more purely behavioral interventions) and may never be said for most. As effective as psychiatric medications are for many disorders, there is no evidence that they are anything more than *palliative*; that is, they suppress symptoms so long as they are taken, but do nothing to reduce risk for symptom return once their use is terminated (Hollon, Thase, & Markowitz, 2002). In fact, there are concerns that psychiatric medications may actually exacerbate underlying risk and worsen the long-term course of the disorder in a way that makes them difficult to discontinue (Whitaker, 2010). CBT on the other hand appears to reduce risk in a manner that is either *compensatory or curative* (Barber & DeRubeis, 1989) so that patients need not stay in treatment forever (Hollon, Stewart, & Strunk, 2006) or even *preventive* in a manner that can keep disorders from ever being expressed in the first place (Horowitz & Garber, 2006).

We plan to be illustrative rather than exhaustive in this chapter. We use existing reviews and meta-analyses to summarize the main findings in a literature so as to focus on key studies that illuminate important points. We first summarize the literature with respect to CBT in the treatment of depression before moving on to a discussion of its role in the treatment of the anxiety disorders. We follow with a review of CBT in the treatment of the eating disorders and a discussion of its role in the treatment of children and adolescence

(see also Chapter 14, this volume). We then turn our attention to CBT in the treatment of substance abuse before concluding with its role in the treatment of the personality disorders and schizophrenia. Other chapters in this handbook address the role of CBT in marital distress and behavioral medicine (Chapters 15 and 17, respectively). For each we ask whether CBT is *efficacious* and *specific* and if it has an *enduring* effect. We also ask whether it has specific benefits for different types of patients (*moderation*) and what is known about its underlying mechanisms of action (*mediation*).

DEPRESSION AND THE PREVENTION OF RELAPSE

Depression is the single most prevalent psychological disorder (American Psychiatric Association [APA], 1994). Unipolar depression is moderately heritable and about twice as common in women as in men whereas bipolar disorder is one of the most heritable of the psychiatric disorders and comparably distributed across the genders. More than three quarters of all patients will have multiple episodes (recurrent) and up to a quarter will have episodes that last for 2 or more years (chronic). Depression adversely affects work performance and interpersonal relations and is a leading cause of suicide (APA, 2003). Given its prevalence, its chronic or recurrent nature, and its capacity to undermine adaptive function, it is hardly surprising that depression is the fourth leading cause of disability worldwide (Murray & Lopez, 1997).

No disorder has received more attention from cognitive theorists than depression. Work in this area has played an integral role in the development of cognitive theory and given rise to a number of different interventions. These include cognitive therapy (Beck, Rush, Shaw, & Emery, 1979) and mindfulness-based cognitive therapy (Segal, Williams, & Teasdale, 2002), as well as efforts to incorporate cognitive principles into largely behavioral interventions (Lewinsohn, Munoz, Youngren, & Zeiss, 1986) and even more recent efforts to integrate these approaches with dynamic theory (McCullough, 2000). All show the impact of cognitive theory on practice.

The resultant interventions have done well in controlled trials. CBT is *efficacious and specific* in the treatment of unipolar depression and shows an *enduring effect* with respect to the prevention of subsequent relapse and recurrence

(Hollon & Ponniah, 2010). It also is *efficacious* as an adjunct to medication in the treatment of bipolar disorder. CBT is listed as a psychosocial treatment of choice (along with interpersonal psychotherapy and behavioral activation) for major depression by both the National Health Service in the United Kingdom (National Institute for Health and Clinical Excellence [NICE], 2010) and the APA (2010). The latter guideline does suggest that medications are to be preferred for more severe depression, a point to which we will return. The bulk of the empirical work in fully clinical populations has focused on CT, but other versions of CBT generally have done well with such patients when they have been tested.

Cognitive Therapy for Severe and Recurrent Depression

Cognitive therapy (CT) was the first of the cognitive-behavioral interventions and the progenitor of the approach. It takes its name from a *cognitive theory of disorder* that posits that people who are depressed hold inaccurate negative beliefs about themselves, their worlds, and their futures (the negative cognitive triad) and fall prey to systematic distortions in information-processing that leave them unable to correct these maladaptive beliefs (Beck, 2005). Their internal dialogues are filled with *negative automatic thoughts* that seem to arise unbidden and that are organized in accordance with depressogenic *core beliefs* and *underlying assumptions* that put them at risk for future depressions. These problematic beliefs and maladaptive information-processing proclivities are part of larger integrated knowledge structures called *schemas* that influence both the way that incoming information is processed and the resultant judgments that are formed. Schemas operate as latent predispositions (often laid down in childhood) that can lie dormant for years before being activated by some kind of stressful life event (Beck, 2008).

Patients in CT are taught to systematically evaluate their beliefs and to become aware of their information processing proclivities in the service of becoming less depressed and reducing subsequent risk (Beck et al., 1979). The approach relies heavily on the process of empirical disconfirmation; patients are taught to treat their beliefs as hypotheses and to gather additional information and conduct behavioral experiments to test their accuracy. In essence, patients are encouraged to act like scientists, withholding judgment about the validity of their beliefs until they have been examined in a systematic fashion. Behavioral procedures are incorporated but largely in the service of testing beliefs. Thus the approach adheres explicitly to a cognitive theory of change (*process*) while incorporating both behavioral and cognitive *procedures* in an integrated fashion.

The approach has been modified in recent years to deal more effectively with the kind of stable *core beliefs* that give rise to the maladaptive interpersonal behavioral propensities that are the hallmarks of long-standing personality disorders (Beck, Freeman, Davis, & Associates, 2004). Whereas the emphasis is kept on current life concerns with most patients, attention also is paid to childhood antecedents and the therapeutic relationship with patients whose depressions are superimposed on long-standing personality disorders (the "three-legged stool"). However, even in such instances patients are encouraged to test the accuracy of their beliefs by acting in ways that are inconsistent with the behavioral propensities (*compensatory strategies*) intended to protect them from what they think will happen if their beliefs are true. Thus, even when dealing with issues arising from childhood or the therapeutic relationship, the therapist integrates cognitive and behavioral strategies (*procedures*) within the context of a cognitive theory of change (*process*).

CT has fared well in comparisons to alternative interventions with respect to the reduction of acute distress. Most quantitative reviews find CT superior to no treatment or nonspecific treatment controls and at least as effective as alternative psychosocial or pharmacological interventions (Cuijpers, van Straten, Andersson, & van Oppen, 2008). Effect sizes tend to be large relative to minimal treatment controls ($ES = .80$), moderate with respect to nonspecific controls ($ES = .40$), and negligible with respect to alternative interventions including medications ($ES = .00$). Most patients show a good response with about a third showing complete remission. Studies suggest that its efficacy may even extend to inpatients (Bowers, 1990; Miller, Norman, Keitner, Bishop, & Dow, 1989). CT also appears to be *efficacious* (if not specific) in the treatment of bipolar depression (Lam, Hayward, Watkins, Wright, & Sham, 2005; Miklowitz et al., 2007; but see also Scott et al., 2006), although largely as an adjunct to medications (APA, 2002; NICE, 2006).

Although CT is clearly effective in the treatment of depression, questions remain regarding how it compares to pharmacotherapy for patients with more severe depressions. The National

Institute of Mental Health's Treatment of Depression Collaborative Research Program (NIMH TDCRP) found CT less efficacious than either medications or interpersonal psychotherapy (the latter at the level of a nonsignificant trend) and no better than pill-placebo on clinician ratings of change in the treatment of patients with more severe depressions (Elkin et al., 1995). These findings played into an a priori belief that severe depression is biological in nature and led early guidelines to conclude that it must be treated with medication (APA, 2000). This notion was reinforced when these findings were essentially replicated in a subsequent trial in which CT was less efficacious than either medications or a more purely behavioral approach called behavioral activation and no better than pill-placebo in the treatment of patients with more severe depressions (Dimidjian et al., 2006). As a consequence, some now conclude that medications are to be preferred over CBT (or any psychotherapy) in the treatment of patients with more severe depressions (APA, 2010).

However, such a conclusion is inconsistent with a meta-analysis aggregating across patient-level data that found that CT was as efficacious as medications in the treatment of such patients (DeRubeis, Gelfand, Tang, & Simons, 1999) and also is not consistent with other recent placebo-controlled trials. Jarrett and colleagues (1999) found CT as effective as a monoamine oxidase inhibitor and each superior to pill-placebo in the treatment of patients with atypical depression (Jarrett et al., 1999) and DeRubeis and colleagues (2005) found CT as efficacious as paroxetine pharmacotherapy (augmented for nonresponders) and superior to a pill-placebo in patients with more severe depression (DeRubeis et al., 2005). This latter study was designed to test the efficacy of CT in precisely the kind of patients for whom the APA guideline says that medications should be preferred. These findings are depicted in Figure 11.1.

We suspect that these differences in outcome across the various studies are a consequence of variability in therapist training and competence. In the NIMH TDCRP, CT was comparable to medication at the site that had more experienced cognitive therapists and no better than pill-placebo at the sites at which the cognitive therapists were less experienced in its use (Jacobson & Hollon, 1996). Similarly, CT was superior to medications at the site with the more experienced cognitive therapists (Pennsylvania) and less efficacious than medications at the site where the cognitive therapists were less experienced (Vanderbilt) in the study by DeRubeis and colleagues (2005). It became apparent early in that study that the less experienced therapists at Vanderbilt were having trouble keeping up with their more

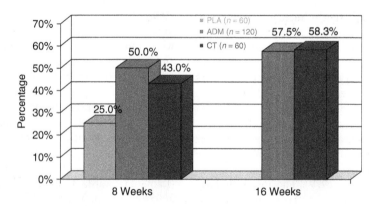

FIGURE 11.1 Cognitive therapy is as efficacious as antidepressant medications in the treatment of patients with moderate-to-severe depression: A placebo-controlled comparison. Response rates at 8 and 16 weeks (sans placebo) for antidepressant medication therapy pill-placebo (PLA; $n = 60$), antidepressant medications (ADM; $n = 120$), and cognitive therapy (CT; $n = 60$).

Source: Adapted from "Cognitive Therapy vs. Medications in the Treatment of Moderate to Severe Depression" by R. J. DeRubeis et al., 2005, *Archives of General Psychiatry*, 62, p. 413. Copyright 2005 by the American Medical Association. Reprinted by permission.

experienced counterparts at Pennsylvania. Therefore the less experienced therapists at Vanderbilt were provided with additional training and supervision from the Beck Institute in Philadelphia that improved both their rated competence and patient outcomes over the remainder of the trial (DeRubeis et al., 2005). Cognitive therapists in the Dimidjian study were no more experienced than the Vanderbilt therapists at the outset of their trial but received no such supplemental training (Coffman, Martell, Dimidjian, Gallop, & Hollon, 2007). Looking across these studies it would appear that when provided with adequate training and supervision cognitive therapists can do as well as medications even with more severely depressed patients.

Moreover, a recent study from New Zealand found CT superior to interpersonal psychotherapy in the treatment of patients with either more severe depression (Luty et al., 2007) or comorbid personality disorders (Joyce et al., 2007). These findings stand in direct contradiction to what was found in the NIMH TDCRP with respect to comparisons between the two psychosocial interventions in treatment of patients with more severe depressions. Medication doses are easier to standardize across settings but the efficacy of a psychosocial intervention appears to depend upon its quality of implementation and that can vary across sites and studies.

CT also appears to have an *enduring effect* that protects against symptom return following successful treatment. Depression tends to be an episodic disorder and even patients who respond to treatment are at considerable risk for future episodes. Although pharmacotherapy suppresses the reemergence of symptoms so long as it is taken, there is no indication that it does anything to reduce underlying risk (Hollon et al., 2002). Current practice calls for continuing patients on medications for at least 6 months following initial remission and maintaining patients with a history of recurrent or chronic depression on medications indefinitely (APA, 2010). Numerous studies have shown that patients treated to remission with CT are only about half as likely to relapse following treatment termination as patients treated to remission with medications (Hollon et al., 2006). The NIMH TDCRP is the sole exception and even in that study nonsignificant differences favored prior CT over the other interventions (Shea et al., 1992).

Figure 11.2 illustrates this effect. It follows the course of patients (all more severely depressed) who responded to treatment in the study by DeRubeis and colleagues described above across a subsequent 2-year interval (Hollon, DeRubeis, et al., 2005). Patients who responded to CT were allowed no more than an occasional booster session whereas patients who responded to medication were randomized to stay on continuation medication or withdrawn onto pill-placebo and followed for another year. At the end of that period all pills were discontinued and the patients were followed for another year. Patients who responded to CT were no more likely to relapse following treatment termination than medication responders continued on active medications and considerably less likely to relapse than medication responders switched to pill-placebo. This pattern was essentially replicated with respect to recurrence (the onset of new episodes) in the second year of the follow-up when all medications were withdrawn. These findings were essentially replicated in the follow-up to the Seattle study with CT showing the highest rate of sustained response (Dobson et al., 2008). In both studies, prior CT was as efficacious as continuation medications and superior to medication withdrawal. These findings strongly suggest that patients in CT learn something that reduces subsequent risk. In a recurrent disorder like depression this may be the single biggest advantage that CT has over medications (Hollon, 2011).

Although impressive these differences could be an artifact of differential retention brought about if higher risk patients require medications to get better. This is not a risk when patients are randomized to CT following initial response to medications. At least three studies have shown that patients treated with CT following initial response to medication are less likely to relapse or recur following subsequent treatment termination (Bockting et al., 2005; Fava, Rafanelli, Grandi, Conti, Belluardo, 1998; Paykel et al., 1999). Similar findings have been reported for mindfulness-based cognitive therapy (MBCT) that draws on meditation and acceptance to help patients learn to "float above" their depressive ruminations (Teasdale, Segal, & Williams, 1995). In MBCT, patients are trained to focus not so much on the content of thinking as on its process and to be aware of their thoughts without responding to them in an affective fashion. MBCT has been shown to have an enduring effect that reduces risk for relapse among patients first treated to remission with medications (Ma & Teasdale, 2004; Teasdale, Segal, Williams, Ridgeway, Soulsby,

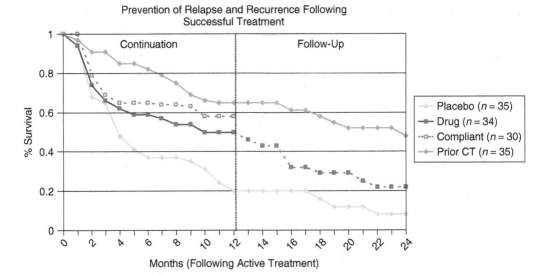

Prevention of Relapse and Recurrence Following Successful Treatment

FIGURE 11.2 Prior cognitive therapy has an enduring effect relative to prior medication treatment following treatment termination that is at least as efficacious as continuation medication. Cumulative proportion of treatment responders who survived without relapse during continuation (first 12 months) and recurrence during follow-up (second 12 months). Prior CT indicates patients had cognitive therapy during acute treatment; drug, continuation antidepressant medication (paroxetine plus possible augmentation); compliant, adherence to continuation medication (censoring patients who failed to adhere to continuation medication); and placebo, withdrawal onto pill-placebo.

Source: Adapted from "Prevention of Relapse Following Cognitive Therapy vs. Medications in Moderate to Severe Depression," by S. D. Hollon et al., 2005, *Archives of General Psychiatry*, *62*, p. 420. Copyright 2005 by the American Medical Association. Reprinted by permission.

& Lau, 2000). Curiously, this effect was found only among patients with three or more prior episodes. Subsequent studies have shown that adding MBCT prior to medication taper is at least as efficacious as maintenance medication in preventing subsequent relapse or recurrence (Kuyken et al., 2008) and that patients with unstable remissions were the ones most likely to benefit from MBCT (Segal et al., 2010). Given that meditation is widely accepted in the culture and can be provided in an economical group format, MBCT has generated considerable interest in the field.

Although there are no clear contraindications to combining CT and medications, we would recommend against doing so on a routine basis (see also Forand, DeRubeis, & Amsterdam in Chapter 18, this volume). Combining CT with medications appears to produce only a modest increment in efficacy (10%-15%) over either monotherapy alone and may interfere with CT's enduring effect. Findings from the two relevant studies in the literature go in opposite directions with one study finding an enduring effect for prior

CT regardless of whether it was provided with or without medication (Evans et al., 1992) and the other finding an enduring effect only when CT was provided alone (Simons et al., 1986). As we see in a later section there is evidence that combining CBT with medication wipes out its enduring effect in the treatment of panic disorder. It may be that patients attribute the gains they make to the medications or that having medications on board may afford little opportunity to learn to use CT skills to manage one's depression. This issue needs further exploration. For now we would recommend only adding medications in a sequential fashion (augmentation) for patients who do not respond to an initial course of CT.

Prognostic indices are patient characteristics that can be used to predict which patients will respond best to a given treatment, whereas *prescriptive indices* can be used to select the best treatment for a given patient (Fournier et al., 2009). Statisticians call the latter *moderation* and it is expressed analytically as a patient-by-treatment interaction (Kraemer, Wilson,

Fairburn, & Agras, 2002). As already described, severity appears to moderate response to treatment such that patients with more severe depressions tend to do less well in CT when treated by less experienced therapists than they do in medication treatment or other psychotherapies, whereas no such differences were apparent among patients with less severe depressions (Dimidjian et al., 2006; Elkin et al., 1989).

Severity also moderates the pharmacological effect of medications over and above pill-placebo (its "true" drug effect). Among patients with major depression, active medications separate from pill-placebo only among those patients with the most severe depressions (less than half of all patients) (see for example Fournier et al., 2010). What this means is that when patients with less severe depressions respond to medication treatment, they do so for largely psychological reasons. That being the case, it is hard to justify using antidepressant medications as a first-line treatment for patients with less severe depressions (Hollon, 2011). Psychosocial interventions also may work through largely nonspecific mechanisms with such patients (Driessen, Cuijpers, Hollon, & Dekker, 2010). Even so, CT would still be preferred since it has an *enduring effect* not found for medications (which also applies to less severe patients) and is free from problematic *side effects*.

The treatment guideline published by the APA (2010) also states that CT should be preferred over medications in the treatment of depressed patients with comorbid personality disorders, but this recommendation is based on a misreading of the findings from the NIMH TDCRP (Shea et al., 1990). In point of fact, patients with personality disorders in the Penn/Vandy study did better on medications than they did in CT, whereas patients without personality disorders showed the opposite pattern (Fournier et al., 2008). This is exactly opposite to what was recommended by the APA treatment guideline. On the other hand, a recent New Zealand study found that CT was superior to IPT in the treatment of patients with personality disorders (Joyce et al., 2007). Clearly, more work needs to be done before we can draw any conclusions regarding the prescriptive status of personality disorders with respect to CT.

There are indications that CT works through processes of change specified by theory. Therapist competence accounted for 15% of the variance in clinician rated outcome in the NIMH TDCRP after controlling for adherence and nonspecific facilitative conditions (Shaw et al., 1999). DeRubeis and colleagues found that adherence to CT early in treatment predicted subsequent response, whereas the quality of the nonspecific therapeutic alliance was more a consequence than a cause of symptom change (DeRubeis & Feeley, 1990; Feeley, DeRubeis, & Gelfand, 1999). Working from tapes generated in the Penn/Vandy study, Strunk and colleagues found that competence in early sessions predicted subsequent response (Strunk, Brotman, DeRubeis, & Hollon, 2010). Thus, CT appears to produce change through processes specified by theory (although Webb, DeRubeis, & Barber, 2010, found that this is not true for all implementations).

Change in cognition also appears to be the *mechanism of change* within patients. Early trials found that pharmacotherapy produced as much change in cognition as CT (e.g., Imber et al., 1990; Simons, Garfield, & Murphy, 1984), but specificity of change is not required with respect to mediation (Hollon, DeRubeis, & Evans, 1987). Patterns of covariation across time are more informative and studies that have examined the relation between change in beliefs and subsequent change in depression have found stronger relations in CT than in pharmacotherapy (see, for example, DeRubeis et al., 1990). Such a pattern is consistent with the notion that change in cognition mediates subsequent change in depression in CT.

Theory further suggests that it is the acquisition of cognitive skills and the ability to respond to one's negative beliefs is central to the prevention of subsequent episodes. Consistent with these predictions, Strunk and colleagues found that patients in CT who best mastered the cognitive skills taught in that approach were least likely to relapse following treatment termination (Strunk, DeRubeis, Chiu, & Alvarez, 2007). Teasdale and colleagues also reported that change in underlying cognitive propensities predicted freedom from subsequent relapse, although in their trial it was becoming less extreme that was beneficial and not simply becoming less negative (Teasdale et al., 2001). These findings are consistent with the notion that different aspects of cognitive change mediate different aspects of response to CT.

Finally, Tang and DeRubeis (1999) have observed that many patients treated with CT show "sudden gains" following some particular session that accounts for the bulk of the change they show across the course of treatment. These "sudden gains" occur at different times for different patients, but tend to be preceded by cognitive change and followed by improved ratings of the therapeutic alliance. In effect, it's as if the patient catches on to the notion that negative thinking and not some personality defect is the source of their discontent. Once patients come to that realization they seem to do a better job of managing their own affect and subsequent behavior. Patients who show these "sudden gains" not only get better faster they also have fewer relapses than patients who show a more gradual response (Tang, DeRubeis, Hollon, Amsterdam, & Shelton, 2007). Whereas work on treatment process suggests that change is most likely to occur when the therapist focuses on specific cognitive and behavioral strategies in a methodical fashion (like the tortoise), the phenomenon of "sudden gains" suggests that lasting change in the patients can occur in a rapid fashion once they grasp the cognitive model and its implications (like the hare). For a further discussion of sudden gains the reader should consult Lambert and Wampold (this volume) who observe that sudden gains are not limited to CBT and can be observed across other schools of psychotherapy and patient problems other than depression.

Other Cognitive Behavioral Approaches

Several approaches to depression treatment incorporate cognitive components into largely behavioral frameworks. These interventions generally are referred to as being cognitive behavioral in nature. For example, Lewinsohn and colleagues developed a psychoeducational approach for the prevention and treatment of depression that incorporates cognitive strategies into a more conventional behavioral framework (Lewinsohn et al., 1986). Initial trials with adults were supportive (Lewinsohn, Hoberman, & Clarke, 1989) and an early meta-analysis suggested that the magnitude of its effect approached that magnitude produced by individual CBT (Cuijpers, 1998). However, it has rarely been applied in fully clinical populations, although it has been used in the prevention and treatment of depression in children and adolescents, as discussed in a later section.

Problem-solving therapy (PST) was designed to offset the tendency of depressed patients to dismiss potential options out of hand by separating hypothesis generation (brainstorming) from response evaluation (selection). PST has done well in controlled trials in recruited adult populations (see, for example, Nezu & Perri, 1989), as well as suicidal adolescents (Lerner & Clum, 1990) and adult patients with a history of repeated suicide attempts (Salkovskis, Atha, & Storer, 1990). A simplified version of PST was found to be as effective as medication and superior to pill-placebo in one study in a primary care sample (Mynors-Wallis, Gath, Lloyd-Thomas, & Tomlison, 1995) and comparable to medications in a second (Mynors-Wallis, Gath, Day, & Baker, 2000). PST was less efficacious than medications in a pair of studies on patients with dysthymia but essentially compared only half "doses" of the psychosocial intervention (six sessions) against full doses of medication (J. E. Barrett et al., 2001; Williams et al., 2000).

Finally, a Cognitive Behavioral Analysis System for Psychotherapy (CBASP) is a blend of cognitive, behavioral, and dynamic-interpersonal components developed specifically for patients with chronic depression. It is predicated on the notion that such patients have difficulty learning from experience in problematic interpersonal relationships (McCullough, 2000). In its first major trial, the combination of CBASP plus medication proved almost half again as effective as either single modality alone (Keller et al., 2000). Temporal patterns of response over time suggested that medications worked early, whereas CBASP worked late with combined treatment doing both. This study generated considerable interest in the approach. However, a subsequent study by many of the same investigators found that adding CBASP did little to enhance response among patients who showed less than full response to medication monotherapy (Kocsis et al., 2009).

Summary

CT is *efficacious and specific* in the treatment of depression and the same is likely true for the more behavioral versions of CBT. CT has been tested extensively in clinical populations and appears to be as effective as medications with respect to the reduction of acute distress even among patients with more severe depression when implemented by experienced therapists. Moreover, CT has an *enduring* effect not found for medications, something that appears to be true for MBCT as well. In a recurrent disorder like depression any evidence of a preventive effect is most exciting. CT works through *processes* specified by theory to mobilize change in *mechanisms* related to beliefs and information processing proclivities. More behavioral versions of CBT have fared well in limited trials and as discussed in a subsequent section show promise in the prevention and treatment of depression among children and adolescents. CBASP showed initial promise but did not fare well in a subsequent replication in a largely refractory population.

ANXIETY DISORDERS

The various anxiety disorders are in aggregate the most prevalent of the psychiatric disorders (APA, 1994). CBT is the psychosocial treatment of choice for most of the discrete disorders along with more purely behavioral interventions and medication treatment. As was the case for the affective disorders, some versions of CBT adhere more to a cognitive theory of change and put an emphasis on testing the accuracy of beliefs and exploring idiosyncratic meaning systems whereas others emphasize peripheral explanatory constructs and spend more time teaching coping skills and repeating exposure exercises. In some instances one approach seems to offer some advantages over the other and in other instances it is hard to tell the two apart in terms of the outcomes they produce. That being said the application of the cognitive model has (along with behavior theory) revolutionized our understanding of the anxiety disorders and led to the development of a particularly powerful set of treatments.

Panic Disorder and Catastrophic Cognitions

Panic disorder involves the sudden and overwhelming experience of fear that seems to arise unbidden and can sometimes lead to the agoraphobic avoidance of situations in which help could not be obtained if such an attack were to occur (APA, 1994). Behavior theory views panic as a conditioned response to internal or external cues that is best extinguished via repeated exposure over the course of weeks or months. Biological models view panic as the consequence of a propensity for the neural centers underlying the stress response to discharge spontaneously and treat it with medications for an indefinite period of time. According to cognitive theory, people experience panic attacks when they misinterpret benign bodily sensations as signs of impending physical or mental catastrophe (Beck

& Emery, 1985; Clark, 1986). These catastrophic cognitions are seen as the necessary and sufficient cause of panic attacks (and by extension agoraphobia) and their disconfirmation is the primary treatment goal.

Cognitive behavioral interventions based on this model are both *efficacious and specific* in the treatment of panic disorder (DeRubeis & Crits-Christoph, 1998) and are listed as the treatment of choice for panic by the NICE (2007). Even psychiatric guidelines list CBT as the psychosocial treatment of choice and consider it to be at least as efficacious as medication (APA, 2009). Effect sizes are large relative to no treatment ($ES = .87$) and moderate with respect to nonspecific controls ($ES = .51$) and CBT is at least as efficacious as behavior therapy or medication treatment (Mitte, 2005a).

Theorists with a more behavioral orientation like Barlow emphasize repeated exposure to interioceptive cues and incorporate a broad range of coping strategies like relaxation training within an approach they call *panic control treatment* (PCT; Barlow & Cerny, 1988). Cognition is addressed in this approach but as only one of many coping tools. Conversely, more cognitively oriented theorists like Clark focus on the disconfirmation of the catastrophic beliefs and tend to discourage the use of coping skills that function as safety behaviors (CT; Clark & Salkovskis, 1991). Both use exposure to interioceptive cues but Barlow does so in the service of promoting classical extinction whereas Clark does so in the service of disconfirming catastrophic beliefs.

Early studies of generic cognitive interventions were unimpressive, but typically tested treatments that did not focus explicitly on catastrophic misinterpretations (see Hollon & Beck, 2004, for a review). Interventions focused specifically on catastrophic misinterpretations have been considerably more successful. Barlow and Lehman (1996) reviewed a dozen trials conducted through the mid-1990s and found that either PCT or CT eliminated panic in up to 80% of treated patients and typically were superior to various no treatment or nonspecific controls. Although the two approaches have not been compared directly, effect sizes produced by CT tend to be larger than those produced by PCT in comparisons to comparable controls (Siev & Chambless, 2007).

Two studies illustrate the efficacy of the cognitive behavioral interventions. Barlow and colleagues conducted a multisite placebo-controlled trial in which patients with panic disorder (with or without agoraphobia) were randomly assigned to 3 months of weekly acute treatment followed by 6 months of monthly maintenance treatment with either CBT or imipramine alone or in combination (Barlow, Gorman, Shear, & Woods, 2000). The study also included a fifth cell in which CBT was provided alone. Each monotherapy was superior to pill-placebo and combined treatment better still by the end of maintenance treatment. Imipramine produced the highest rates of response among treatment completers, but CBT was more enduring. As shown in Figure 11.3, patients who responded to CBT were less likely to relapse following treatment termination than patients who responded to imipramine. Adding medications to CBT interfered with its enduring effect as patients in the combined condition were more likely to relapse than patients treated with CBT alone. This has implications for the wisdom of combining CBT with medications.

In the other illustrative study, Clark and colleagues found CT focused on catastrophic misinterpretations superior to either imipramine pharmacotherapy or applied relaxation with each superior to a wait list control (Clark et al., 1994). Nearly 90% of the patients treated with CT were panic-free after 3 months of treatment versus only about 50% of the patients in the other two treatments and virtually none of the patients assigned to the wait-list control. CT also produced greater change in catastrophic cognitions than did the other conditions in a manner suggestive of *mediation*. Medications were continued for another 6 months and then withdrawn with patients in the psychosocial conditions receiving only a limited number of booster sessions between 3 and 6 months. All patients were then followed across the next 9 months. During the follow-up period, only 5% of the patients previously treated with CT relapsed, compared with 40% of patients withdrawn from medications. Patients who had the fewest catastrophic cognitions at the end of treatment were least likely to relapse following treatment termination. This suggests that CT not only has an *enduring effect* similar to that found in depression but also that it is *mediated* by change in cognition as specified by theory. The approach is so powerful that even a handful of sessions can be highly efficacious (Clark et al., 1999).

It remains to be determined whether either approach (CT or CBT) will prove to be superior to the other but both are *efficacious and specific* and both have *enduring effects* that extend beyond the end of treatment. Both also appear to be *mediated* by changes in catastrophic cognitions as specified by theory (Clark et al., 1994; Hofmann et al., 2007). There are few disorders for which the optimal treatment is so clear or theory has been so fully justified.

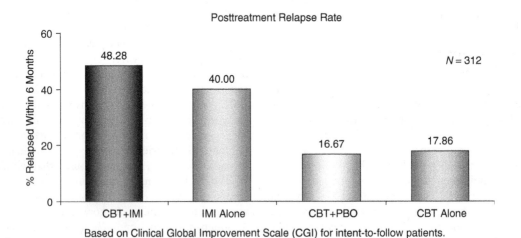

Based on Clinical Global Improvement Scale (CGI) for intent-to-follow patients.

FIGURE 11.3 Cognitive-behavior therapy has an enduring effect relative to medication following treatment termination unless combined with medication. Cognitive-behavior therapy (CBT), imipramine pharmacotherapy (IMI), and pill-placebo (PBO).

Source: Adapted from "Cognitive-Behavioral Therapy, Imipramine, or Their Combination for Panic Disorder: A Randomized Controlled Trial," by D. H. Barlow et al., 2000, *JAMA*, *283*, 2529–2536. Copyright 2000 by the American Medical Association. Reprinted by permission.

Hypochondriasis and Health Anxiety

Hypochondriasis is more often found in medical settings than it is in psychiatric clinics. These patients believe that they have a physical illness and take little comfort from medical reassurance. It has rarely been studied empirically and was long thought to be largely impervious to treatment. However, the cognitive model for panic was extended to this disorder in the early 1990s in a manner that allowed for the development of a promising cognitive approach (Warwick & Salkovskis, 1990). According to this theoretical extension, the central feature of hypochondriasis (subsequently renamed health anxiety) is an enduring tendency to misinterpret innocuous physical signs and symptoms as evidence of serious illness. These misinterpretations lead to considerable anxiety and repeated efforts to seek reassurance. According to this model, the primary difference between panic and hypochondriasis involves the imminence of the medical risk. Panic typically involves threats that could happen within the next several minutes like having a heart attack whereas hypochondriasis typically involves concerns about developing an illness like cancer over a period of months or years.

As might be expected, treatment for hypochondriasis is patterned closely after CT for panic. Patients are provided with a rationale that suggests that the problem is not a matter of health but rather health anxiety. They are encouraged to examine the evidence for and against their belief that their bodily sensations represent symptoms of some underlying disease and helped to construct more realistic interpretations. Behavioral experiments are used to induce innocuous "symptoms" via deliberately focusing on the body and efforts are made to prevent repeated body checking and reassurance seeking. Homework assignments are given after each session and patients are encouraged to keep a daily record of negative thoughts and rational responses.

This approach has been tested in a series of studies with clinical populations. In the first, CT was found to be superior to a wait-list control after 4 months of treatment with gains essentially maintained across a 3-month follow-up (Warwick, Clark, Cobb, & Salkovskis, 1996). Patients went from spending more than 50% of their time worried about their health to less than 15% and disease conviction dropped from nearly 70% to less than 10%. In a subsequent trial, CT was found to be somewhat better than a more purely behavioral stress-management condition

with each superior to a wait-list control (Clark et al., 1998). Yet a third study using a modified version of this approach (now called *CBT*) found the intervention superior to treatment-as-usual in a genitourinary medicine clinic (Seivewright et al. 2008).

Visser and Bouman (2001) found CT as described above as efficacious as exposure plus response prevention and each superior to a wait-list control with treatment gains maintained across a 7-month follow-up. This same group subsequently found that essentially the same clinical intervention (again called CBT) was at least as efficacious as paroxetine pharmacotherapy and superior to a pill-placebo control (Greeven et al., 2007). Barsky and Ahern (2004) developed a briefer six-session cognitive behavioral intervention that also was superior to a usual care control.

These studies suggest that CT/CBT is *efficacious* and quite possibly *specific* in the treatment of hypochondriasis (now called *health anxiety*). It is not easy to tell why the approach is sometimes referred to as CT in some studies and CBT in others since all but Barsky and Ahern cite the original treatment protocol developed by Warwick and Salkovskis (1990). What is clear is that CT/CBT has performed remarkably well in treating a disorder that has long been considered refractory and that it should be considered the current treatment of choice for health anxiety.

Generalized Anxiety Disorder and the Primacy of Worry

Generalized anxiety disorder (GAD) is a common mental disorder that is diagnosed about twice as often in women as in men (Kessler, Berglund, et al., 2005). Whereas pervasive arousal was once seen as the core of the disorder, it is now defined in terms of chronic worry (Brown, Barlow, & Liebowitz, 1994). This represents a problem for more purely behavioral approaches because there is no clear external referent for the disorder and interventions like exposure plus response prevention are of little use. Benzodiazepines induce dependence and lose potency with prolonged use and antidepressants are purely palliative and do nothing to reduce future risk. Traditional forms of psychotherapy have been unimpressive the few times they have been tested.

CBT is both *efficacious and specific* in the treatment of GAD. Comparisons to minimal treatment controls generate large effects (.87) and comparisons to nonspecific controls are at least moderate (.57) in size (Mitte, 2005b). CBT is one of two psychosocial interventions (along with the more purely behavioral applied relaxation) recommended as a first-line treatment for GAD by the NICE guidelines (NICE, 2011). It appears to be at least as efficacious as medications and quite possibly longer lasting, although direct comparisons are few and discontinuation designs have yet to be implemented. CBT is not addictive like the benzodiazepines and is free from the side effects found for antidepressants.

That being said, CBT has evolved to a considerable extent over time and has become increasingly cognitive in nature in a manner that reflects the new-found focus on worry. Early cognitive behavioral approaches that combined relaxation training or meditation with cognitive restructuring were superior to no treatment and nonspecific controls in a number of studies (see Borkovec & Ruscio, 2001, for a review) and more effective than either dynamic (Durham et al., 1994; Leichsenring et al., 2009) or nondirective therapy (Borkovec & Costello, 1993). Although these early versions of CBT were rarely superior to behavior therapy alone with respect to acute response, differences favoring the more cognitive versions sometimes emerged over extended follow-up periods (Salzer, Winkelbach, Leweke, Leibing, & Leichsenring, 2011). CBT appears to be *efficacious but not necessarily specific* with respect to the treatment of older adults (Stanley, Beck, et al., 2003; Stanley, Hopko, et al., 2003; Wetherell, Gatz, & Craske, 2003) and targeting interpersonal problems and emotional avoidance did little to enhance its efficacy (Newman et al., 2011).

With the change in emphasis in the disorder from arousal to worry, Ladouceur and colleagues dropped relaxation training entirely to focus more intensively on purely cognitive targets like the intolerance of uncertainty and cognitive avoidance (Ladouceur et al., 1999). This more intensive cognitive intervention was superior to a minimal treatment control with gains sustained over a 1-year follow-up regardless of whether it was provided in an individual (Ladouceur et al., 2000) or group format (Dugas et al., 2003). Recent trials suggest that this more intensive cognitive approach and an even more recent treatment that focuses on beliefs about uncontrollability each may be superior to and longer lasting than more purely behavioral relaxation approaches (Dugas et al., 2010; Wells et al., 2010).

Social Phobia and Self-Focused Attention

Social phobia involves an undue fear of evaluation by others and the accompanying desire to avoid situations in which such scrutiny is anticipated (APA, 1994). It is a surprisingly common disorder (with 12% lifetime prevalence) that when generalized can have quite a disruptive effect on functioning and quality of life (Kessler, Berglund, et al., 2005).

According to cognitive theory, persons with social phobia have an underlying belief that they are defective or inadequate in some way that will be exposed in social situations and lead to ridicule or censure from others (Beck & Emery, 1985). Cognitive and cognitive behavioral therapies based on this model and its more recent extensions represent the psychosocial treatment of choice for social phobia (Ponniah & Hollon, 2008). Behavioral exposure intended to offset the inhibiting effect of conditioned anxiety plus skills training can be said to be efficacious but not necessarily specific in the treatment of social phobia and pharmacological interventions (typically antidepressants) can suppress symptoms but have no enduring effects (Hollon & Beck, 2004).

Early studies combined generic cognitive restructuring with exposure to social situations. Heimberg and colleagues did some of the best early work in this literature, developing a cognitive behavioral group treatment (CBGT) that proved superior to supportive therapy with gains that were maintained across a 5-year follow-up (Heimberg, Salzman, Holt, & Blendell, 1993). A subsequent multisite trial (one of the most impressive in the literature) found CBGT comparable to phenelzine and each superior to either pill-placebo or supportive group therapy controls (Heimberg et al., 1998). Most importantly, 50% of the patients treated with phenelzine relapsed following treatment termination compared to only 17% of the patients treated with CBGT (Liebowitz et al., 1999). These findings indicate that CBGT is at least as efficacious as medication in the treatment of social phobia and quite possibly longer lasting. GCBT was comparable to medication and superior to pill-placebo in two subsequent trials that either did not (Davidson et al., 2004) or did find an advantage for combined treatment (Blanco et al., 2010). No follow-up has yet been reported for either study so we do not know whether adding medication undercut any enduring effect for CBT as occurs in the treatment of panic. There are indications that cognitive change *mediates* the effects of treatment (Hofmann, 2004).

One limitation of those earlier approaches is that a substantial proportion of patients continued to experience significant social difficulties even after completing treatment. In a major revision of cognitive theory, Clark and Wells (1995) proposed that people with social phobia selectively attend to internal images of themselves that are unduly negative and less flattering than they actually appear to others. In keeping with this revised cognitive model, Clark videotapes patients engaging in feared social interactions both with and without safety behaviors and then invites them to watch both tapes and rate themselves on various characteristics. Patients typically find that they appear more competent when they drop their safety behaviors (something of a revelation) and that their internal images of themselves are considerably more negative than how they actually come across. Clark argues that targeting self-focused attention and encouraging patients to drop their safety behaviors during exposure facilitates their capacity to learn from experience and hastens their response to treatment.

Moreover, patients show greater change in beliefs and reductions in anxiety when they drop their safety behaviors in exposure situations.

This modified approach to cognitive therapy (CT) typically is conducted in an individual format to facilitate the identification of idiosyncratic ideation that is used to guide more powerful video-assisted exposure exercises. Individual CT was superior to conventional group CBT in a German trial (Stangier, Heidenreich, Peitz, Lauterbach, & Clark, 2003) and superior to either group CBT or treatment as usual (including medications) in another trial conducted in Sweden (Mörtberg et al., 2007) with gains maintained for up to 5 years (Mörtberg, Clark, & Bejerota, 2011). This modified approach to CT was superior to either fluoxetine or pill-placebo in the first of two English studies (Clark et al., 2003) and, as shown in Figure 11.4, superior to exposure plus response prevention in a second (Clark et al., 2006). Finally, a recent multisite German trial found CT superior to IPT at each of two different sites including one with an allegiance to IPT (Stangier, Schramm, & Heidenreich, Berger, & Clark, 2011). Cognitive change appears to

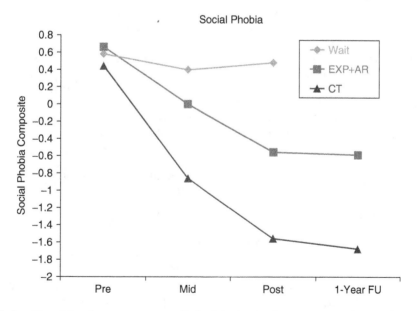

FIGURE 11.4 Cognitive therapy versus applied relaxation in the treatment of generalized social phobia. Social phobia composite scores at each assessment; Wait = wait-list control condition; EXP + AR = exposure plus applied relaxation; CT = cognitive therapy; Pre = pretreatment; Post = posttreatment; 1-Year FU = 1-year follow-up.

Source: From "Cognitive Therapy Versus Exposure and Applied Relaxation in Social Phobia: A Randomized Controlled Trial," by D. M. Clark et al., 2006, *Journal of Consulting and Clinical Psychology*, *74*, 568–578. Copyright 2006 by the American Psychological Association. Reprinted by permission.

mediate the effects of treatment, as specified by theory (Hoffart, Borge, Sexton, & Clark, 2009).

This is an impressive series of studies that clearly establishes this specialized form of CT as being both *efficacious and specific* and quite possibly *superior* to the major alternative interventions. This is not the first time that Clark has extended cognitive theory in a novel fashion and made treatment even more powerful as a consequence. He did much the same by targeting the disconfirmation of catastrophic cognitions in panic disorder. He uses a phenomenological approach to identify key etiological processes that he then targets with innovative clinical strategies refined in analogy studies so as to maximize impact before moving to controlled clinical trials (Clark, 2004). This is similar to the approach that Beck followed 50 years earlier to develop cognitive therapy for depression (Beck, 2005). Social phobia, like panic disorder, represents one of the clear triumphs of the cognitive model and the interventions it has inspired.

Specific Phobias and the Situational Misperception of Danger in Context

Specific phobias involve an intense fear of certain objects or situations and a corresponding desire to avoid being in their presence (APA, 1994). Specific phobias typically involve fears of bodily harm or danger and can be distinguished from social phobias that involve concerns about being evaluated negatively by others. Specific phobias are relatively common with a lifetime prevalence of 12.5% (Kessler, Berglund, et al., 2005). They are somewhat less likely to impair function than some of the other anxiety disorders (Kessler, Chiu, et al., 2005) but often go untreated and tend to persist over time (Stinson et al., 2007).

According to cognitive theory, individuals with specific phobias perceive greater danger or risk in the feared situation than do other people (Beck & Emery, 1985). Such individuals often have a "dual" belief system in that they recognize that their fears are unwarranted when they are not in the phobic situation, but become overwhelmed by thoughts of impending danger with visual or somatic images consistent with those beliefs as they approach the thing that they fear. By way of contrast, behavior theory suggests that phobias are established via traumatic conditioning and maintained by avoidance behaviors that protect them from extinction. Behavioral interventions such as systematic desensitization and especially

exposure plus response prevention are clearly efficacious and have long been considered the standard for treatment. Cognitive theorists also make use of exposure but do so to disconfirm the misperceptions of danger that fuel the fear and motivate the avoidance behaviors in phobic situations (Davis, Ollendick, & Öst, 2009).

Öst developed a single session approach to CBT called "one-session treatment" (OST) that combines graduated in vivo exposure, participant modeling, and reinforced practice into a coherent package that is targeted at disconfirming the patient's overestimation of danger (Öst, 1989). The approach has been found to be rapid and effective in the treatment of a variety of different specific phobias (Zlomke & Davis, 2008). For example, OST for spider phobia was superior to a wait list control in one study (Thorpe & Salkovskis, 1997) and a manual-based self-exposure treatment in another (Öst, Salkovskis, & Hellstrom, 1991). OST for claustrophobia was found to be superior to a wait-list control and did not differ from a full five sessions of exposure (Öst, Alm, Brandberg, & Brietholtz, 2001). Similarly, OST was as efficacious as five sessions of graduated exposure for fear of flying (Öst, Brandberg, & Alm, 1997). Finally, in a multiple baseline design, a patient with several different small animal phobias showed change in a particular phobia only when it was specifically targeted in treatment (Öst, 1987). OST appears to be *efficacious and specific* in the treatment of the specific phobias and may work more rapidly than more purely behavioral interventions like exposure and response prevention, the current standard of treatment.

Obsessive-Compulsive Disorder and Personal Responsibility

Obsessive compulsive disorder (OCD) is a condition characterized by recurrent intrusive thoughts (*obsessions*) followed by attempts to reduce or neutralize the anxiety or prevent a dreaded outcome associated with the obsessions through carrying out repetitive ritualistic behavioral or mental actions (*compulsions*). It often has a gradual onset starting in childhood or adolescence and tends to follow a chronic episodic course with exacerbations during periods of stress (APA, 1994). It affects approximately 1% to 3% of all adults and is one of the most impairing of the nonpsychotic mental health disorders (Kessler, Chiu, et al., 2005). Comorbidity with mood disorders is high and tends to complicate treatment (Storch et al., 2010).

The classic two-process behavioral model of OCD posits that obsessions are previously neutral internal stimuli that acquire their capacity to elicit anxiety by virtue of having been paired with inherently arousing stimuli (classical conditioning) whereas compulsions are negatively reinforced escape/avoidance behaviors (operant conditioning) that maintain the conditioned anxiety response by virtue of preventing extinction (Rachman, 1971). Behavior therapy for OCD involves prolonged exposure to the feared stimulus (obsession) to allow classical extinction to occur, and prevention of the escape/avoidance response (compulsion) to ensure that it does.

Behavioral *exposure plus response prevention* (ERP) is the oldest and best established of the empirically supported psychosocial interventions for OCD (APA, 2007a; NICE, 2005a). It has been found to be superior to its absence (*efficacy*) and nonspecific controls (*specificity*) in dozens of trials. It was more efficacious than medications in a direct comparison (Foa, Liebowitz, et al., 2005) and enhanced their efficacy when provided in combination (Tenneij, van Megen, Denys, & Westenberg, 2005). Most critically, ERP appears to have an *enduring effect* not found for medication following treatment termination (Simpson et al., 2004). This is an impressive record for any intervention.

That being said, it is no longer clear that ERP is purely behavioral in nature. Recent ERP protocols often include discussion of the patient's OCD-related beliefs along with the evidential disconfirmation provided by exposure assignments and often incorporate behavioral experiments in an explicit effort to test beliefs (McMillan & Lee, 2010). In effect, what was originally a largely behavioral intervention has morphed into one that is best described as being somewhat cognitive behavioral in nature. Some now conceptualize the differences between ERP and CBT as largely a matter of emphasis (Abramowitz, Taylor, & McKay, 2005). Many of the procedures are shared to at least some extent although each still adheres to somewhat different explanatory principles.

Contemporary cognitive theory with respect to OCD has taken this process even further and come to emphasize what it means to the patient to have had the obsessive intrusion rather than focus on the content of the obsession itself (Rachman, 2003). For example, the fact that a young mother has intrusive thoughts that she might kill her infant is not inherently problematic in itself unless she further assumes that this means that she really does want to kill her child or that she is a bad person for having such thoughts. In most instances the problematic interpretation underlying the intrusion (and leading to distress) is one of *personal responsibility* in the sense of being a danger to oneself or others for failing to engage in the compulsion (Salkovskis, 1999).

Given this formulation, the focus of this newer cognitive approach is to identify and change the interpretation of the intrusion rather than to dispute its accuracy (as in conventional CBT) or to simply extinguish the anxiety that it generates (as in ERP). As a consequence, this newer approach, called *integrative CBT*, employs a process of guided discovery to help the patient construct an alternative formulation to the obsessive concern ("It is not that I want to hurt my child but rather that I worry about what it means that I have that thought") and then engage in a series of experiments to test between the competing formulations. Exposure and response prevention are still used in integrative CBT but represents only one of several strategies designed to test the accuracy of the underlying beliefs. Thus integrative CBT is similar to approaches labeled cognitive therapy in the treatment of depression and social phobia.

Integrative CBT has been found to be superior to wait-list controls or stress management in the treatment of patients without overt compulsions for whom ERP alone could not be applied (Freeston et al., 1997; Whittal et al., 2010). The majority of the direct comparisons to ERP in patients with overt compulsions have found no differences between the two approaches (Cottraux et al., 2001; O'Connor et al., 2005; Vogel, Stiles, & Gotestam, 2004; Whittal, Thordarson, & McLean, 2005). When differences have emerged they tend to reflect problems in the implementation of the less efficacious modality. For example, McLean and colleagues (2001) found ERP superior to integrative CBT but implemented both modalities in a group format that precluded exploring the idiosyncratic meaning behind the obsessions. Conversely, van Oppen and colleagues (1995) found integrative CBT superior to ERP but implemented the latter in a less impactful self-guided format. It remains unclear whether either is superior to the other when each is adequately implemented.

Both compare favorably to medication treatment (de Haan et al., 1997; Foa, Liebowitz, et al., 2005; Jaurrieta et al., 2008; Sousa, Isolan, Oliveira, Manfro, & Cordioli, 2006; van Balkom et al., 1998) although only ERP has been tested in a design capable of detecting enduring effects (Simpson et al., 2004). ERP remains somewhat better established if only because it has been around longer and tested more often, but integrative CBT has done well in those trials in which it has been tested. Whether it has any advantage over ERP in patients other than those who lack overt compulsions remains to be determined but both are clearly *efficacious and specific* in the treatment of OCD.

PTSD and the Perception of Current Threat

Exposure to traumatic events can produce a clinical syndrome known as posttraumatic stress disorder (PTSD) that shares the symptoms of increased arousal and persistent avoidance with the other phobic disorders but also includes distinct symptoms such as flashbacks and intrusive recollections (APA, 1994). There is an emerging consensus that trauma-focused approaches like cognitive behavior therapy (TFCBT) and eye-movement desensitization and reprocessing (EMDR) represent the treatments of choice for PTSD (APA, 2004a; NICE, 2005b; Ponniah & Hollon, 2009). Each has been found to be superior to no treatment (demonstrating *efficacy*) and other therapies (suggesting *specificity*) (Bisson et al., 2007). Claims that all *bona fide* treatments are comparable in efficacy (Benish, Imel, & Wampold, 2008) rest on the selective exclusion of trials supporting the specificity of TFCBT and a failure to demonstrate the independent efficacy of the non-trauma-focused therapies (Ehlers, Bisson, et al., 2010). The latter is important since single-session debriefing applied in an unselective fashion can be iatrogenic (Bisson, Jenkins, Alexander, & Bannister, 1997; Mayou, Ehlers, & Hobbs, 2000).

TFCBT typically involves some combination of exposure to the traumatic memory (reliving in imagination or writing a trauma narrative) along with some effort to address the meaning of the traumatic event (cognitive restructuring). Just how this is done tends to vary across different types of TFCBT. More behavioral approaches like *prolonged exposure* (PE) rely on repeated instances of imaginal reliving in the service of habituation (Foa & Rothbaum, 1998). The goal is to facilitate the "emotional processing" of the trauma memory that incorporates

corrective information about the experience and the actual amount of danger it portends (Foa, 2011). Early efforts to deal with the meaning of the event in conjunction with PE were generic in nature and did little to enhance its efficacy (Foa et al., 1999; Foa, Hembree, et al., 2005; Marks, Lovell, Noshirvani, Livanou, & Thrasher, 1998). PE has outperformed both its absence (*efficacy*) (Foa, Rothbaum, Riggs, & Murdock, 1991) and nonspecific controls (*specificity*) (Schnurr et al., 2007).

More cognitive approaches like *cognitive processing therapy* (CPT) put a greater emphasis on reappraisal of the meaning of the traumatic memory and depend less on repeated exposure to the memory itself (Resick & Schnicke, 1993). CPT relies instead on narrative writing to explore the meaning of the traumatic event and Socratic questioning by the therapist to explore any erroneous conclusions embedded in its appraisal. This is a more sophisticated approach to cognitive restructuring that tends to be at least comparable to prolonged exposure when done in a competent fashion (Blanchard et al., 2003; Resick, Nishith, Weaver, Astin, & Feuer, 2002; Tarrier et al., 1999). A recent dismantling study found that cognitive restructuring was more efficacious than narrative writing and accounted for the bulk of the CPT treatment effect (Resick et al., 2008). As with prolonged exposure, CPT has demonstrated *efficacy* relative to its absence (Monson et al., 2006) and *specificity* relative to nonspecific controls (McDonagh et al., 2005).

In a major theoretical reformulation, Ehlers and Clark (2000) proposed that PTSD becomes persistent when individuals process trauma in a way that leads to a sense of serious *current* threat. The authors suggest that the paradox of PTSD is that memories for prior events create a state of current anxiety despite the fact that no such threat is actually impending. This sense of current threat is seen as a consequence of the combination of an excessively negative appraisal of the implications of the prior trauma and a disturbance of autobiographical memory characterized by poor elaboration and perceptual triggers. The problem is maintained by cognitive strategies like thought suppression and safety-seeking behaviors that reduce current distress at the expense of preventing reappraisal of the trauma memory or reprocessing the memory itself.

Their newly developed cognitive therapy for PTSD seeks to redress this problem by modifying excessively negative appraisals of the trauma, elaborating the trauma memories and discriminating triggers to reduce the frequency and vividness of reexperiencing, and dropping safety behaviors that interfere with putting the memory in perspective. Idiosyncratic appraisals are identified via imaginal reliving or narrative writing and corrected via the process of Socratic questioning and behavioral experiments that are then incorporated into the affective "hot spots." The reduction in reexperiencing is facilitated via updating the trauma memory and revisiting the site of the trauma to facilitate the discrimination of triggers. These triggers are identified and brought into the therapy process so that the patient can learn to differentiate "then" from "now." Finally, patients are encouraged to drop safety behaviors via the use of behavioral experiments that demonstrate the counterproductive nature of those misguided efforts at self-protection.

CT was found to be superior to both a self-help booklet and an assessment-only control in the treatment of motor vehicle accident survivors with recent onset PTSD with differential gains maintained through a 6-month follow-up (Ehlers et al., 2003). Patients in the brief self-help condition actually did worse than the assessment-only patients on some measures, reminiscent of the iatrogenic effect for single-session debriefing previously described. A subsequent trial found a 3-month course of CT superior to a wait-list control with gains again maintained across a 6-month follow-up (Ehlers, Clark, Hackmann, McManus, & Fennell, 2005). Attrition was minimal in both studies and the magnitude of the change was about twice what is typically reported in other controlled trials. A nonexperimental comparison suggested that a comparable amount of change could be accomplished with an intensive 1-week program (Ehlers, Clark, et al., 2010).

The approach was so successful in dealing with PTSD subsequent to a terrorist bombing in Omagh (Gillespie, Duffy, Hackmann, & Clark, 2002) that the government of Northern Ireland established a center for the treatment of trauma victims at which CT was found to be superior to a wait-list control in an applied setting (Duffy, Gillespie, & Clark, 2007). The approach still needs to be tested against nonspecific controls and alternative interventions (especially the established cognitive and behavioral approaches), but it is clearly *efficacious* (if not yet *specific*) and the magnitude of the change it produces in the absence of attrition is remarkable for this literature.

Summary

CBT appears to be the treatment of choice for the majority of the anxiety disorders. It is at least as efficacious as more purely behavioral interventions and longer lasting than medications. More traditional dynamic and humanistic psychotherapies have rarely been tested and not fared all that well when they have. Cognitive approaches that emphasize the disconfirmation of specific beliefs or the restructuring of underlying meaning systems look to be particularly promising in the treatment of panic, social phobia, and PTSD. It is not clear that such approaches provide any advantage over a more purely behavioral ERP in the treatment of OCD (other than for patients with obsessions only) but each is superior to other psychosocial interventions. GAD and health anxiety (hypochondriasis) are probably best approached with more cognitive versions of CBT and the treatment of specific phobias can be speeded along by using idiosyncratic beliefs to guide the process of exposure. CBT clearly is *efficacious and specific* in the treatment of the anxiety disorders and more *enduring* than medications. Approaches that adhere most closely to cognitive theory show particular promise in the treatment of several of the specific disorders.

EATING DISORDERS AND OBESITY

Aberrant beliefs regarding shape and weight play such a major role in the etiology of the eating disorders that CBT might be expected to be particularly efficacious in their treatment. CBT appears to be *efficacious and specific* with *enduring effects* in the treatment of bulimia nervosa and *possibly efficacious* in maintaining weight in the treatment of anorexia. CBT also appears to be *efficacious and specific* in the treatment of binge eating disorder. CBT appears to facilitate weight loss in obesity but has yet to be shown to be able to prevent subsequent weight regain.

Bulimia Nervosa and Transdiagnostic CBT

Bulimia nervosa is a disorder characterized by a chaotic eating pattern that consists of extreme dieting punctuated by episodes of binge eating and subsequent efforts to purge, typically via vomiting, laxative abuse, or fasting (APA, 1994). Self-esteem is often poor and associated psychopathology is common, particularly affective distress and substance abuse. Bulimia nervosa is about 10 times more common in women than in men and is most likely to emerge during adolescence although it can continue well into adulthood.

Although once believed to be refractory to treatment, bulimia nervosa responds to a number of different psychosocial or pharmacological approaches (Shapiro et al., 2007). CBT has been shown to be superior to minimal treatment and nonspecific controls to demonstrate both *efficacy and specificity* (Agras et al., 1989; Hsu et al., 2001; Sundgot-Borgen, Rosenvinge, Bahr, & Schneider, 2002; Wilfley et al., 1993). Moreover, it has been found to exceed the efficacy of other viable alternative interventions like more purely behavioral interventions or interpersonal psychotherapy (Agras et al., 2000; Cooper & Steere, 1995; Fairburn et al., 1991). It is at least as efficacious as medication treatment (Agras et al., 1992; Walsh et al., 1997) and considerably more *enduring* (Agras, Rossiter, et al., 1994). Change in self-efficacy beliefs and dietary restraint *mediate* the effects of treatment (Wilson, Fairburn, Agras, Walsh, & Kraemer, 2002). It is hard to find another disorder in which CBT is so clearly superior to its alternatives. Most treatment guidelines list it as the preferred intervention for bulimia nervosa (APA, 2006; NICE, 2004).

Cognitive theory posits that overvalued ideas concerning weight and shape and unrealistic beliefs about what one should and should not eat are at the core of bulimia nervosa (Fairburn, 1981). These beliefs lead the individuals to engage in excessive dietary restraint, which then puts them (most are female) at risk for loss of control binge eating, particularly under conditions of stress. Once a binge has occurred, the bulimic individual typically engages in some form of purge behavior in an effort to avoid gaining weight. Therapies based on this theory typically incorporate both behavioral and cognitive components, with the former emphasized in the early sessions and the latter coming increasingly into play as treatment proceeds. Behavioral components focus on establishing more regular eating patterns (including the prohibition of restrictive dieting and purge behaviors), whereas cognitive strategies are used to identify and change beliefs regarding food, weight, and body image, with attention to relapse prevention in later sessions. More purely behavioral approaches based on exposure plus response prevention interrupt the sequence of behaviors but do nothing to address the underlying beliefs and values (Fairburn, Jones, Peveler, Hope, & O'Connor, 1993). Similarly,

medications suppress cravings and make it easier to engage in restrictive dieting but also do nothing to redress the beliefs that drive the process (Agras, Telch, et al., 1994). Both result in short-term change but high rates of relapse following treatment termination. IPT addresses the relational issues that often contribute to excessive concerns about shape and weight but takes longer to produce its effects (Agras et al., 2000; Fairburn et al., 1991).

Fairburn and colleagues note that the same concerns about shape and weight that underlie bulimia nervosa are common to the other eating disorders (Fairburn, Cooper, & Shafran, 2003). They further note that patients move back and forth between the different diagnoses (with eating disorder not otherwise specified being the most common single diagnosis) and argue for a "transdiagnostic" approach to the disorders. They have reformulated their approach to apply to eating disorders broadly defined (now called *enhanced* CBT) and added modules to their basic approach to deal with more complex issues like mood intolerance or perfectionism. This results in two versions of the enhanced transdiagnostic approach (focused versus broad). The two approaches were compared to each other and each to a wait-list control in a sample that consisted of patients that met criteria for either bulimia nervosa or eating disorder not otherwise specified (Fairburn et al., 2009). Both versions of CBT were superior to the wait-list control with gains maintained across a 60-month follow-up. As shown in Figure 11.5, there were indications that the simpler focused approach could serve as the default option for less complicated patients, whereas the more complex broad treatment was better suited for patients with more complicated problems. As predicted, outcomes did not differ as a function of diagnostic status.

Thus, it appears that the *efficacy* of CBT and quite possibly its *enduring effect* extends beyond bulimia nervosa in a transdiagnostic fashion. Additional studies are needed to see if the same can be said for its *specificity* and *superiority* to other treatments, but it is clearly the case for the core disorder of bulimia nervosa. It is clear that CBT for bulimia nervosa (and possibly the other eating disorders) is one of the major success stories in the empirical literature.

Anorexia Nervosa and the Esthetics of Self-Denial

Anorexia nervosa involves a pervasive pattern of self-starvation to the point that weight-loss

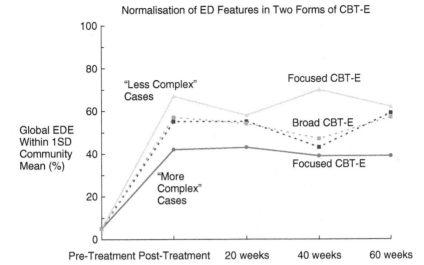

FIGURE 11.5 Normalization of eating disorders features in two forms of enhanced cognitive behavior therapy (CBT-E). Focused CBT-E = focused form of enhanced CBT; broad CBT-E = broad form of enhanced CBT; EDE = eating disorder examination.

Source: From "Transdiagnostic Cognitive Behavioral Therapy for Patients With Eating Disorders: A Two-Site Trial With 60-Week Follow-Up," by C. G. Fairburn et al., 2009, *American Journal of Psychiatry*, *166*, 311–319. Copyright 2009 by the American Psychiatric Association. Reprinted by permission.

can become life threatening (Wilson, Vitousek, & Loeb, 2000). Anorexia shares the same misguided beliefs about food and weight found in bulimia nervosa, but also involves the notion that exercising control over physiological desires is consistent with a higher ascetic ideal (Garner & Bemis, 1982). Treatment is complicated not only by the rigidity of the beliefs regarding the consequences of becoming fat, but also by the sense of accomplishment that accompanies the pursuit of thinness. Vitousek and colleagues encourage clinicians to recognize that their clients really do want to be thin and see its pursuit as a means of providing meaning and order to their lives (Vitousek, Watson, & Wilson, 1998). They recommend that the clinician first examine the functional utility of weight loss in a Socratic fashion that makes explicit use of experimental strategies and then explore the personal values and sense of ascetic ideal that underlies the pursuit of thinness. The importance of thinness is examined in relation to other life goals and considerable attention is paid to underlying concerns about self-worth and interpersonal relationships.

Pike and colleagues compared CBT based on these principles to nutritional counseling in preventing relapse in a sample of formerly anorexic patients who had successfully completed

inpatient treatment (Pike, Walsh, Vitousek, Wilson, & Bauer, 2003). As shown in Figure 11.6, patients treated with CBT were significantly less likely to relapse in the year following discharge from the hospital than patients treated with nutritional counseling. Given that nutritional counseling is a credible clinical intervention that controlled for time and contact, these findings speak not only to the *efficacy* but also the *possible specificity* of the intervention. Replication will be required before such a claim can be made but the initial results were impressive.

Efforts to treat underweight anorectic patients have been few and not particularly impressive (Bulik, Berkman, Brownley, Sedway, & Lohr, 2007). In the earliest RCT in this literature, pooled CBT and behavior therapy conditions improved nutritional functioning more than nonspecific supportive clinical management but the latter showed greater improvement in terms of drive for thinness (Channon, De Silva, Hemsley, & Perkins, 1989). In a more recent trial, nonspecific supportive clinical management outperformed IPT with CBT intermediate and not significantly different from either of the other two conditions (McIntosh et al., 2005). Whether the rather lackluster performance of CBT in these two trials reflects an inherent difficulty in treating

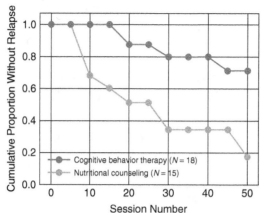

a The patients receiving cognitive behavior therapy remained in treatment significantly longer without relapsing (mean session = 43.79, SD + 2.9) than those receiving nutritional counseling (mean session = 27.21, SD = 5.9) (log-rank statistic = 8.39, p<0.004).

FIGURE 11.6 Cognitive behavior therapy versus nutritional counseling in the treatment of anorexia. Survival analysis of time to relapse for patients with anorexia nervosa who received 1-year posthospitalization treatment with cognitive behavior therapy or nutritional counseling.

Source: From "Cognitive Behavior Therapy in the Posthospitalization Treatment of Anorexia Nervosa," by K. M. Pike et al., 2003, *American Journal of Psychiatry*, *160*, 2046–2049. Copyright 2003 by the American Psychiatric Association. Reprinted by permission.

underweight patients or the use of a less powerful approach to CBT remains to be seen. At this time, inpatient management with intensive behavioral refeeding programs appears to represent the optimal treatment of seriously underweight patients with anorexia nervosa (APA, 2006; NICE, 2004).

Binge Eating Disorder and the Absence of Constraint

Binge eating disorder currently has provisional status in the psychiatric nomenclature and is likely to be listed as a disorder in the next revision (APA, 1994). Binge eating disorder is characterized by frequent and persistent episodes of excessive food intake accompanied by feelings of loss of control over eating and marked distress in the absence of restrictive dieting or efforts to purge. Dietary restriction appears to play little role in binge eating disorder but it does appear to share many of the same kinds of overvalued beliefs regarding shape and weight found in the other eating disorders (Wilson & Agras, 2001). CBT for binge eating disorder uses self-monitoring and self-control strategies to foster a regular pattern of moderate eating that is maintained via training in problem-solving and relapse prevention (Fairburn, 1995).

CBT and to a lesser extent IPT are the current treatments of choice for binge eating

disorder (APA, 2006; NICE, 2004). About half of all treated patients achieve remission and most show specific reductions in overvalued beliefs and associated affective distress (Wilson, 2011). CBT is more efficacious than behavioral weight loss in reducing binge frequency (being both *efficacious and specific* in that regard) but less efficacious in terms of producing weight loss (Brownley, Berkman, Sedway, Lohr, & Bulik, 2007). CBT also has been shown to be superior to antidepressant medications in the reduction of binge eating (Grilo, Masheb, & Wilson, 2005).

CBT has been adapted to a guided self-help format that shows great promise. In this approach patients are provided with a self-help manual based on the larger Fairburn model and provided only limited therapist contact. A recent RCT found that guided self-help CBT with a non-professional therapist was as efficacious as a full course of IPT with an experienced therapist and that each was superior to a behavioral weight-loss intervention in eliminating binge eating across the 2 years following treatment (Wilson, Wilfley, Agras, & Bryson, 2010). As shown in Figure 11.7 the lack of differences at posttreatment and the growing separation across the follow-up suggests a more *enduring* effect for both CBT and IPT. Two earlier trials also found CBT superior to behavioral weight-loss interventions with respect

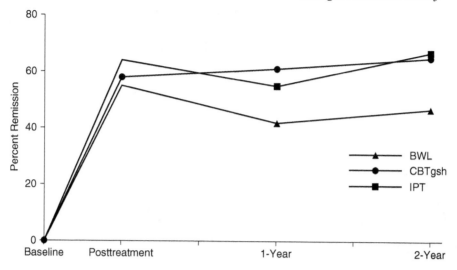

FIGURE 11.7 Self-guided CBT versus IPT in the treatment of binge eating disorder. Remission rates at posttreatment and 1- and 2-year follow-up. BWL indicates behavioral weight loss treatment; CBTgsh, guided self-help based on cognitive behavior therapy; and IPT, interpersonal psychotherapy.

Source: From "Psychological Treatments for Binge Eating Disorder," by G. T. Wilson et al., 2010, *Archives of General Psychiatry, 67*, 94–101. Copyright 2010 by the American Medical Association. Reprinted by permission.

to the reduction of binge eating regardless of whether comparisons were made between self-guided formats (Grilo & Masheb, 2005) or full treatment packages (Munsch et al., 2007). These findings in aggregate indicate that CBT is not only *efficacious and specific* in the treatment of binge eating disorder but also that a self-guided version might be a sufficient first-line treatment for at least some of these patients.

Obesity and the Impermanence of Weight Loss

There is considerable controversy as to whether it is possible to produce lasting weight loss through purely psychosocial means in people who are obese (Brownell, 2010). Many obese individuals will lose weight in standard behavioral programs, but the majority will regain most of the weight lost within a few years of treatment termination (Turk et al., 2009). Efforts directed at providing ongoing therapeutic support appear to delay weight regain, but their effects are modest and often do not persist (Svetkey et al., 2008; Wing, Tate, Gorin, Raynor, & Fava, 2006). Nonetheless, sustained weight loss remains a highly valued goal; since even modest weight loss on the order of 5% to 10% appears to confer significant health benefits if the weight is not regained (Knowler et al., 2009).

Cooper and Fairburn (2001) have suggested that the primary problem with existing weight loss programs is that they fail to take into account cognitive factors that lead to weight regain. They suggest that too many patients set unrealistic goals that are hard to meet and as a consequence abandon efforts that have produced more modest levels of weight loss. They recommend adopting an individualized approach that helps patients accept more limited weight loss goals and describe specific strategies for maintaining losses that have already been achieved. The authors developed a new form of CBT designed to address this concern (Cooper, Fairburn, & Hawker, 2003) and tested it in a randomized controlled comparison to a standard behavioral weight-loss intervention and a guided self-help approach (Cooper et al., 2010). As shown in Figure 11.8, both CBT and the behavioral intervention produced greater weight loss than guided self-help across the course of 44 weeks of treatment (demonstrating *efficacy* if not specificity) but virtually all of the weight lost was regained over the subsequent 3 years. Despite producing greater change in the kinds of cognitions specified by theory, CBT was no better at preventing weight regain than was behavior therapy. It is clear that the major problem in this field remains the inability of most patients to sustain the weight loss that they do

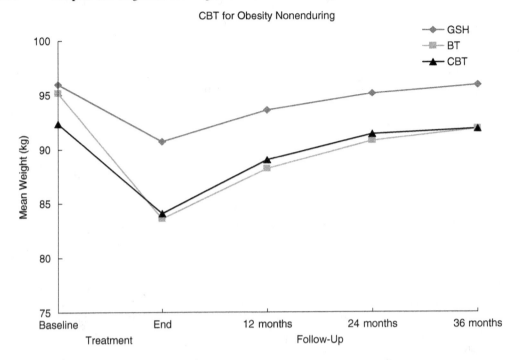

FIGURE 11.8   Cognitive behavior therapy and weight regain following successful treatment. Mean weight (kg) during treatment and 3-year follow-up in participants receiving either cognitive behavior therapy (CBT), behavior therapy (BT), or guided self-help (GSH).

Source: From "Testing a New Cognitive Behavioral Treatment for Obesity: A Randomized Controlled Trial With Three-Year Follow-Up," by Z. Cooper et al., 2010, *Behaviour Research and Therapy*, *48*, 706–713. Copyright 2010 by the Elsevier Publications. Reprinted by permission.

achieve and that at this time the inclusion of more cognitive components to treatment does nothing to redress that problem.

Summary

CBT is *efficacious and specific* and the treatment of choice for bulimia nervosa and in the spirit of a transdiagnostic approach eating disorders not otherwise specified as well. It is more efficacious than IPT or more traditional interventions and more enduring than either behavior therapy or medications. Anorexia nervosa remains problematic although one recent trial suggests that CBT may facilitate the maintenance of weight regain. CBT also appears to be *efficacious and specific* in the treatment of binge eating disorder (relative to either more purely behavioral or pharmacological interventions) and a cost-effective self-guided program may well facilitate the process of dissemination. With respect to obesity, CBT appears to be similar to more purely behavioral interventions in that it helps take weight off but that

most of that weight is regained within a few years of the end of treatment. It is clear that CBT is *efficacious and specific* and quite *possibly enduring* in the treatment of the eating disorders but that obesity remains a puzzle that has yet to be solved.

CHILD AND ADOLESCENT DISORDERS

Disorders of childhood and adolescence are divided into undercontrolled (externalizing) versus overcontrolled (internalizing) disorders (Kazdin & Weisz, 1998). Undercontrolled disorders typically involve behaviors that are problematic to others, such as aggression or hyperactivity, whereas overcontrolled disorders tend to involve personal distress. Much of the early work in the area focused on addressing deficits in cognitive mediation in the undercontrolled disorders using skills training approaches like problem-solving therapy and self-instructional training (Hollon & Beck, 2004). More recent work has focused on correcting distortions in existing beliefs that contribute to the overcontrolled disorders like depression and anxiety. As is seen there is considerable but not uniform support for CBT in the treatment of these disorders.

Depression in Children and Adolescents

CBT generally is thought to be *efficacious and specific* in the treatment of depression in children and adolescents and it along with IPT is one of two psychosocial treatments most often recommended (Birmaher, Brent, Work Group on Quality Issues, 2007; NICE, 2005c). Although CBT has performed well in several high-profile studies, there is reason to think that those recommendations may be premature and that the robustness of its effect in the treatment of children and adolescents has not yet been established.

In the most extensive and rigorous meta-analysis to date Weisz and colleagues found a relatively modest effect for the CBT (.35) less than half the size previously reported in the depression treatment literature for children and adolescents or adults (Weisz, McCarty, & Valerie, 2006). Moreover, these effects dissipated rapidly over time and had largely disappeared within a year. This was not the kind of performance that inspires confidence in the recommendations.

The modest size of this effect was largely a consequence of variability in the quality of CBT provided across the different trials. For example, Brent and colleagues used a version of CBT closely modeled on Beck's cognitive therapy and found it to be at least as efficacious as systematic behavioral family therapy and superior to nondirective supportive therapy in depressed and suicidal adolescents (Brent et al., 1997). The version of CBT used in that trial allows for considerable flexibility to deal with the idiosyncratic needs of the child but takes time to learn and requires considerable skill on the part of the therapist (Brent, 2006). By way of contrast, CBT was less efficacious than fluoxetine and did not separate from pill placebo in the Treatment of Adolescents with Depression Study (TADS; 2004). However, the particular version of CBT used in that trial was so overloaded with specific procedures each delivered at such a low "dose" that it was hard for therapists to conduct a coherent version of therapy (Hollon, Garber, & Shelton, 2005). We think TADS sacrificed the power of the intervention for the sake of disseminability.

Adding CBT did more to enhance response than simply switching pharmacological agents for depressed adolescents who failed to respond to an initial medication in the Treatment of SSRI-Resistant Depression in Adolescents (TORDIA) trial (Brent et al., 2008). The version of CBT implemented in that study was more similar to the cognitively sophisticated approach used by Brent in his earlier trial than the more behaviorally oriented approach first developed by Lewinsohn and adapted for use in TADS. Clarke and colleagues found only a weak effect for the more behaviorally oriented approach when added in combination to medication in a pediatric primary care clinic (Clarke et al., 2005). Melvin and colleagues found CBT comparable to combined treatment and superior to medication alone but unduly restricted their medication dosage (Melvin et al., 2006). Goodyer and colleagues found that combined treatment with CBT was no better than medication monotherapy but noted that attendance rates for CBT were quite low (Goodyer et al., 2007). Our sense is that the further treatment gets from the kind of fully integrated and clinically flexible approach used by Brent the less likely it is to be successful and the smaller its effects with clinically representative populations.

The bulk of the studies done with preadolescent children have been conducted in school-based settings with samples selected on the basis of self-reported (but not diagnosed) depression (Curry, 2001). With younger children we think it is appropriate to emphasize more behavioral components like activity scheduling and skills training. Although the mean effect size for studies that focused exclusively on children was somewhat larger than for those that focused exclusively on adolescents (.41 versus .33), neither was all that impressive, although at least one study found evidence of sustained response (Weisz, Thurber, Sweeney, Proffitt, & LeGagnoux, 1997). Again, the problem appears to be variability in the quality of the interventions, with some groups using more powerful and clinically representative approaches (Brent and Weisz) and others using over structured or insufficiently flexible versions of CBT that have a more limited impact.

That being said there are indications that CBT can be used to prevent the onset of depression in at-risk adolescents who are not currently in episode. Clarke and colleagues showed that a cognitive behavioral program could reduce risk relative to usual care in the adolescent offspring of parents with a history of depression (Clarke

Onset of Depressive Episodes

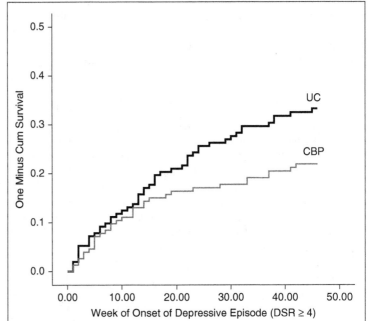

▸ The hazard of depression onset was significantly lower in CB than UC ($X^2 = 4.90$, p = 0.03; Hazard Ratio (HR) = 0.63, 95% CI: 0.40–0.98).

▸ 32.7% of adolescents in the UC control condition were diagnosed with a probable or definite MDE.

▸ 21.4% of youth in the CB program had a MDE.

FIGURE 11.9 Cognitive behavioral program prevents the onset of depression in at-risk adolescents. CBP = cognitive behavioral program; UC = usual care.

Source: From "Prevention of Depression in At-Risk Adolescents: A Randomized Controlled Trial," by J. Garber et al., 2009, *JAMA*, *301*, 2215–2224. Copyright 1997 by the American Medical Association. Reprinted by permission.

et al., 1995; Clarke et al., 2001). Garber and colleagues enhanced the cognitive restructuring component of this package and replicated these findings in a sample of at-risk adolescents, as shown in Figure 11.9 (Garber et al., 2009). Curiously, the cognitive behavioral program reduced rates of episode onset among at-risk adolescents whose parents were not currently depressed but not among adolescents whose parents were currently depressed. It remains unclear why parental depression should moderate the preventive effects, but this was consistent with the earlier Clark studies. This is one of the few instances of replication in the prevention literature (Horowitz & Garber, 2006) and it is reminiscent of the enduring effect found with CT for adults (Hollon et al., 2006).

Treatment of Anxiety Disorders in Children and Adolescents

CBT is *efficacious and specific* in the treatment of anxiety disorders in children and adults (Silverman, Pina, & Viswesvaran, 2008). Kendall and

colleagues developed an approach that combines cognitive restructuring with behavioral exposure and relaxation training to help children and adolescents deal with their fears. RCTs in samples with mixed anxiety disorder diagnoses have shown the approach to be superior to its absence whether provided to individuals (Barrett, Dadds, & Rapee, 1996; Kendall, 1994; Kendall et al., 1997) or in groups (Barrett, 1998; Silverman et al., 1999). Gains have been impressive (most who are treated no longer meet criteria for their respective anxiety disorders) and typically maintained over extended follow-up intervals (Barrett, Duffy, Dadds, & Rapee, 2001; Flannery-Schroeder & Kendall, 2000; Kendall & Southam-Gerow, 1996). Incorporating the family into treatment can enhance the efficacy the intervention (Kendall, Hudson, Gosch, Flannery-Schroeder, Suveg, 2008) and a developmentally appropriate version of the approach has been extended to children as young as 4 (Hirshfeld-Becker et al., 2010). Change in anxious self-statements *mediates* reductions in anxiety during CBT (Kendall & Treadwell, 2007).

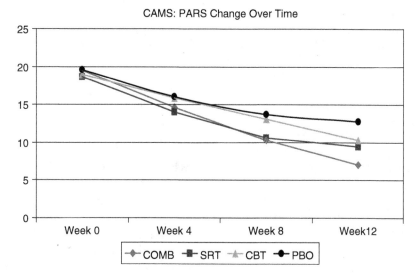

CAMS: PARS Change Over Time

FIGURE 11.10 Cognitive-behavioral therapy (CBT) and sertraline (SRT) alone and in combination (COMB) in the placebo (PBO) controlled treatment of childhood anxiety disorders. Scores on the Pediatric Anxiety Rating Scale during the 12-week study. Scores on the Pediatric Anxiety Rating Scale range from 0 to 30, with scores higher than 13 consistent with moderate levels of anxiety and a diagnosis of an anxiety disorder. The expected mean score is the mean of the sampling distribution of the mean.

Source: From "Cognitive Behavioral Therapy, Sertraline, or a Combination in Childhood Anxiety," by J. T. Walkup et al., 2008, *New England Journal of Medicine*, *359*, 1–14. Copyright 2008 by the American Medical Association. Reprinted by permission.

In perhaps the most impressive study in this literature, CBT was found to be as efficacious as sertraline with each monotherapy superior to pill-placebo and combined treatment better still in the treatment of children and adolescents with a variety of different anxiety disorders (Walkup et al., 2008). As shown in Figure 11.10, medication worked faster than CBT but overall response was virtually identical between the two monotherapies by the end of treatment. A somewhat different version of CBT that focused on social effectiveness training also was as efficacious as fluoxetine and superior to pill-placebo in the treatment of social phobia and superior to either in terms of enhancing social skills (Beidel et al., 2007) Taken in aggregate, these studies indicate that CBT is both *efficacious and specific* in the treatment of youth anxiety disorders and can enhance the efficacy of medications when added in combination. It will be interesting to see whether CBT is more enduring than medications as tends to be the case in the adult literature and whether that effect is retained when combined with medication.

The studies just described typically looked at children or adolescents (or both) with any of several different anxiety disorders (including

separation anxiety disorder, GAD, or social phobia) in various combinations depending on the specific study. CBT also appears to be efficacious in the treatment of a number of other specific childhood anxiety disorders. For example, intensive one-session treatment (OST) appears to be *efficacious and possibly specific* (relative to wait list and nonspecific controls respectively) in the treatment of specific phobias in children and adolescents as it is with adults (Ollendick et al., 2009). Exposure-based CBT also appears to be *efficacious and possibly specific* in the treatment of pediatric OCD (Barrett, Farrell, Pina, Peris, & Piacentini, 2008). Family-focused CBT was found to be superior to a wait-list control regardless of whether it was provided in an individual or group format (Barrett, Healy-Farrell, & March, 2004) and superior to pill-placebo and as efficacious as medications alone and enhanced their efficacy when added in combination in the Pediatric OCD Treatment Study (POTS; 2004). CBT also enhanced response among children and adolescents who showed only partial improvement to medications (Franklin et al., 2011). Finally, trauma-focused CBT appears to be *efficacious and specific* in the treatment of PTSD in children and adolescents (Silverman, Ortiz, et al., 2008). For example, Cohen and colleagues found TFCBT superior to child-centered or nonspecific therapy in a pair of studies (Cohen, Deblinger, Mannarino & Steer, 2004; Cohen, Mannarino, & Knudson, 2005), Ahrens and Rexford (2002) found CPT superior to a wait-list control in a sample of incarcerated male adolescents with PTSD, and Smith and colleagues found CT superior to a wait list control in a sample of children and adolescents exposed to a single traumatic event (Smith et al., 2007). These studies all suggest that interventions developed for adults can be *efficacious* (and in some instances specific) when extended with appropriate developmental modifications to the treatment of anxiety disorders in children and adolescents.

Aggression and Conduct Disorder

Aggression and conduct disorder have been linked to deficits and distortions in social information processing (Dodge, 2008). Several different cognitive behavioral interventions have tried to address these issues with some evidence of success (Eyberg, Nelson, & Boggs, 2008). Anger Control Training was an early cognitive-behavioral intervention designed to address disruptive behavior in elementary school age children that was found to be superior to wait-list controls in a pair of studies by independent research groups (Lochman, Coie, Underwood, & Terry, 1993; Robinson, Smith, & Miller, 2002). A Dutch group found a social cognitive group treatment based on the Dodge model superior to both social skills training and a wait list control (van Manen, Prins, & Emmelkamp, 2004). Dodge and colleagues found that a multimodal intervention program based on social cognitive principles (Fast Track) could prevent the onset of conduct disorder problems in high-risk children (Conduct Problems Prevention Research Group, 2007). This work not only suggests that cognitive processes play a role in the development of aggression and conduct disorders in children and adolescents but that cognitive behavioral interventions that address those processes can be play a role in its treatment and prevention.

Summary

CBT is *efficacious and specific* in the treatment of depression in children and adolescents but its overall impact is modest at best and not necessarily enduring. This appears to reflect variability in the clinical sophistication of the approaches used.

CBT is *efficacious and specific* in the treatment of several different types of anxiety disorders and is the psychosocial treatment of choice and at least as efficacious as medications. CBT is *efficacious and specific* in the treatment of aggression and conduct disorder and may have a preventive effect not found for interventions.

SUBSTANCE ABUSE AND THE PREVENTION OF RELAPSE

CBT for substance abuse disorders typically targets the dysfunctional thoughts that lead to substance use and the problematic behaviors involved at each step along the path. As with obesity, change often is easier to produce than it is to maintain and cognitive theorists have focused on the development of procedures designed to prevent relapse following successful treatment (Brownell, Marlatt, Lichtenstein, & Wilson, 1986). Relapse prevention (RP) focuses on helping patients learn to avoid "loss of control" with respect to substance use and has been widely adopted by the field (Marlatt & Gordon, 1985). Strategies used include discussing ambivalence, identifying emotional and environmental cues, exploring the decision chain leading to the resumption of use, and learning how not to let a brief "lapse" lead to a "loss of control" binge. Despite generating considerable enthusiasm in the addictions treatment community, the empirical evidence speaking to its efficacy is mixed at best and inconsistent across the various substance abuse domains.

Relapse Prevention in the Treatment of Alcohol Abuse

Few areas of research have been as heavily politicized as the treatment of alcohol abuse. Strong competing ideologies exist and disputes over their implications and the interpretation of the empirical trials have spilled into the popular press (Marlatt, 1983). Traditional disease models suggest that alcoholism is a progressive disorder and that abstinence is the only viable option. Conversely, social learning theory suggests that self-regulatory skills can be acquired at any point in that progression and that insistence on abstinence undermines self-control and increases risk for relapse. The current consensus is that there is some truth to each perspective. Many people can handle controlled drinking but those patients with the most severe and chronic problems or cognitive impairment may do best with abstinence (APA, 2007b).

Early studies indicated that CBT in general and RP in particular reduces the severity (if not the frequency) of relapses (Carroll, 1996). RP appears to produce a moderate sized effect ($ES = .37$) in the treatment of alcoholism (Irvin, Bowers, Dunn, & Wang, 1999). One trial found that less impaired patients do better with CBT than in supportive therapy (Jaffe et al., 1996). However, the largest and most visible study in the literature found no advantage for CBT relative to either a traditional 12-step approach or motivational interviewing and little evidence of moderation (Project MATCH Research Group, 1997). The general consensus at this time appears to be that CBT is *efficacious but not specific* in the treatment of alcohol abuse but that RP may hold special promise for relapse prevention.

Treatment of Drug Abuse

The same types of cognitive behavioral interventions used in the treatment of alcohol abuse also are used in the treatment of illicit drug use (APA, 2007b). A recent meta-analysis found 20 RCTs that tested various versions of CBT (including 5 for RP and 13 for generic CBT) and 14 that tested a more purely behavioral contingency management (CM) (Dutra et al., 2008). The combination of CBT and CM produced the largest effect ($d = 1.02$) whereas CM alone produced a moderate-sized effect ($d = .58$) and CBT or RP each alone produced small effects ($d = .28$ and $.32$ respectively). Although the bulk of the comparisons were made against standard care or other nonspecific conditions, a recent trial found CBT superior to IPT in the treatment of cocaine addiction (Carroll et al., 2004). Overall, these findings suggest that CBT is *efficacious and possibly specific* in the treatment of substance abuse disorders but perhaps not as efficacious as a more purely behavioral CM.

However, there is evidence that the effects of CBT may last over time. For example, patients treated with RP (adapted to emphasize abstinence) continued to improve following treatment termination whereas desipramine pharmacotherapy had only a short-lived effect that dissipated before the end of treatment (Carroll et al., 1994). In another study, 60% of patients treated with CBT provided clean toxicology screens 1 year after treatment (Rawson et al., 2002). These findings suggest that CBT may have enduring effects

that make it particularly suited to this population (McHugh, Hearon, & Otto, 2010).

Smoking Cessation and Subsequent Relapse

CBT appears to be *efficacious* with respect to smoking cessation but perhaps not as well established as more purely behavioral interventions (APA, 2007b). Six-month quit rates typically are 20% to 25% or about double what is found for control conditions and RP and related CBT strategies can reduce risk of subsequent relapse (Law & Tang, 1995). These interventions appear to prolong the duration of treatment effects and reduce the severity of relapses when they do occur (Carroll, 1996). CBT appears to be particularly helpful in the treatment of smokers with a history of affective distress (Brown et al., 2001). CBT adapted for the treatment of depression has been found to enhance treatment efficacy among patients with a history of depression when added to nicotine gum (Hall, Munoz, & Reus, 1994) or nortriptyline (Hall et al., 1998). These findings suggest that while behavior therapy may represent the current standard in the reduction of smoking behaviors, CBT targeted at both smoking and depression may be particularly useful for participants with a history of affective distress.

Summary

CBT is *efficacious and possibly specific* in the treatment of the various substance use disorders although perhaps not so efficacious as the more purely behavioral interventions. RP does appear to be particularly useful in the prevention of subsequent relapse and CBT focused on depression may enhance response among smokers with comorbid affective disorders.

Schema-Focused Therapy and the Treatment of Personality Disorders

Patients with characterological disorders are notoriously difficult to treat and patients with borderline personality disorder are perhaps the most challenging of all. Borderline personality disorder is marked by chronic instability as evidenced by emotional dysregulation, frequent and repeated instances of self-harm, impulsivity, and identity disturbance (APA, 1994). These patients relate to others (including their therapists) in an unpredictable and affectively labile fashion and their inability to tolerate negative affect is seen by some as the central deficit in the disorder (Linehan, 1993). Lifetime prevalence is estimated at up to 3% of the population but given the chronically dramatic nature of their symptoms they take up a disproportionate amount of time and energy in treatment settings.

Both psychodynamic psychotherapy and dialectic behavior therapy (DBT) have been recommended in the treatment of borderline personality disorder by the APA (2001). Both involve rather sophisticated therapeutic programs that go beyond simple individual psychotherapy. Psychodynamic psychotherapy provided in the context of a partial hospitalization program was found to be superior to general psychiatric treatment (Bateman & Fonagy, 1999) with gains maintained across an 18-month follow-up (Bateman & Fonagy, 2001). DBT combines individual psychotherapy with skills training in a group format and adds ongoing support groups for the therapists. DBT combines acceptance strategies adapted from Zen teaching with a variety of cognitive and behavioral techniques including assertion training, contingency management, cognitive modification, and exposure to emotional cues. DBT reduced the frequency of parasuicidal behaviors and days hospitalized relative to "treatment as usual" in the community in one study (Linehan, Armstrong, Suarez, Allmon, & Heard, 1991) and did the same with respect to community treatment by expert clinicians in yet another (Linehan et al., 2006). These findings have been replicated by other groups (Verheul et al., 2003) and maintained following treatment termination (Linehan, Heard, & Armstrong, 1993). DBT can be said to be *efficacious and specific* for borderline personality disorder and to have effects that likely are *enduring*.

As impressive as these findings are, DBT is at best a minimally cognitive intervention. It is best be classified as a "third wave" behavioral intervention (along with acceptance and commitment therapy and behavioral activation) and there is concern among its devotees that efforts to examine the accuracy of what patients believe risks invalidating their subjective experience, a process that is seen as contributing to the basic etiology of the disorder (Linehan, 1993). DBT often is described as a cognitive-behavioral intervention but if there is a distinction within behaviorism between the cognitive "second wave" and a more affect-focused "third wave" that incorporates acceptance and mindfulness training, then DBT is a better fit to the latter.

Cognitive therapy has been adapted for use with personality disordered patients by integrating attention to childhood antecedents and the therapeutic relationship into its ongoing focus on current life problems (the *"three-legged stool"*) (Beck et al., 2004). The resultant schema-focused therapy (SFT) further specifies specific patterns of thinking, feeling, and behavior that are distinctive to borderline personality disorder (Young, 1994). SFT uses all the traditional tools of cognitive therapy including cognitive restructuring and behavioral experiments to work through past traumas and facilitate better emotional regulation.

As shown in Figure 11.11, SFT was found to be superior to dynamic transference-focused psychotherapy in the treatment of patients with borderline personality disorder (Giesen-Bloo et al., 2006). Treatment consisted of twice-weekly sessions over a 3-year period in both conditions with the SFT based on a manualized approach (Young, Klosko, & Weishaar, 2003). Dynamic psychotherapy was associated with significant change over time in borderline symptoms and measures of underlying personality but SFT was superior to dynamic therapy in all of these respects. A subsequent follow-up found that treatment gains were maintained beyond the end of treatment such that SFT was more cost-effective than dynamic therapy (van Asselt et al., 2008). Subsequent comparisons have found SFT superior to Rogerian supportive therapy on at least

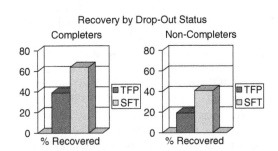

FIGURE 11.11   Schema-focused therapy is superior to dynamic psychotherapy in the treatment of borderline personality disorder. Recovery by drop-out status for transference-focused psychotherapy (TFP) and schema-focused therapy (SFT) patients.

Source: Adapted from "Outpatient Psychotherapy for Borderline Personality Disorder: Randomized Trial of Schema-Focused Therapy vs. Transference-Focused Psychotherapy," by J. Giesen-Bloo et al., 2006, *Archives of General Psychiatry*, *63*(6), 649–658. Copyright 2006 by the American Medical Association. Reprinted by permission.

some measures (Cottraux et al., 2009) and that it enhanced the efficacy of treatment-as-usual in a community setting when added in combination by nonexpert therapists (Davidson et al., 2006).

In aggregate, these studies indicate that both DBT and SFT are *efficacious and specific* (albeit only possibly so in the case of SFT) in the treatment of borderline personality disorder and quite possibly *superior* to other alternative interventions and with an *enduring* effect. This last is important since there is no specific pharmacological intervention for borderline personality disorder and the various medications used in its treatment do little more than provide transient symptom relief that lasts only so long as they are taken. DBT remains the more extensively tested of the two and has been impressive in those trials, but SFT appears to be a viable alternative that may merit direct comparisons.

Schizophrenia and Delusional Thinking

Schizophrenia is a debilitating condition that affects about one person in a hundred (APA, 1994). Its age of onset typically is in the late teens or early adulthood and it tends to follow a chronic or fluctuating course. Its cardinal feature is a loss of contact with reality as evidenced by hallucinations and delusions (positive symptoms) but its long-term sequelae like affective flattening, apathy, anhedonia, and asociality (negative symptoms) can be even more debilitating. Antipsychotic medications are the first-line treatment for the disorder but the majority of patients continue to experience residual symptoms (Lieberman et al., 2005) or experience intolerable adverse effects (Leucht, Pitschel-Walz, Abraham, & Kissling, 1999).

It has long been thought that delusions and hallucinations were impervious to logic or empirical disconfirmation but this may not be as true as was once believed. In the early 1950s Beck published a case study in which he used a forerunner of what would eventually become cognitive therapy in the successful treatment of a schizophrenic patient (Beck, 1952). Despite this initial success his work was largely ignored in the United States until the thread was picked up by investigators in England (Rathod, Phiri, & Kingdon, 2010). Starting in the decade of the 1990s, the approach first pioneered by Beck was adapted and shaped to fit by investigators in the United Kingdom and tested as an adjunct to medication treatment in a series of randomized controlled trials. A recent meta-analysis lists more than 30 such comparisons to treatment-as-usual in medicated patients and found that CBT had a modest-sized effect (with ds ranging from .35 to .45) on both positive and negative symptoms as well as general functioning and social anxiety (Wykes, Steel, Everitt, & Tarrier, 2008). It is clear that CBT is *efficacious* (and quite possibly *specific*) in the treatment of residual symptoms in schizophrenic patients and it is recommended as an adjunct to medications by guidelines in both the United States (APA, 2004b) and the United Kingdom (NICE, 2009).

Implicit in this approach is the notion that delusions represent an attempt to make sense out of troublesome or puzzling experiences and that patients with schizophrenia are not wholly impervious to reason or evidence (Beck & Rector, 2000). Efforts to confront the implausibility of the beliefs directly appear to be less effective than a gentler approach that examines the context in which the beliefs first developed and the quality of the evidence that provides their support. Strong efforts are made to engage the patient in the treatment process and feelings are elicited with great care. A rationale based on a diathesis-stress model is presented and careful attention is paid to normalizing symptoms and exploring possible alternative explanations for their emergence.

The treatment itself proceeds much as it does for depression but in a gentler and more leisurely fashion. Patients are encouraged to express their beliefs regarding the basis for their symptoms with the therapist suggesting (but not insisting on) possible alternative explanations that are more likely to conform to conventional notions of reality. The patient is invited to gather additional information and to run experiments so as to choose between the competing explanations. This is a striking departure from more purely behavioral interventions that systematically ignore "crazy talk" in the service of extinction (Liberman, Teigen, Patterson, & Baker, 1973). Patients often say that it is the first time that anyone gave their beliefs a respectful hearing and this seems to play a role in helping them consider alternative explanations to their delusional thinking.

The bulk of the studies have treated patients with chronic schizophrenia. Adding CBT to medications led to greater reductions in delusions and hallucinations than adding problem solving (Tarrier et al., 1993), supportive counseling (Tarrier et al., 1998), or routine care (Kuipers et al., 1997) and held up better over time (Kuipers et al., 1998; Pinto, La Pia, Mannella, Domenico,

& DeSimone, 1999; Sensky et al., 2000; Tarrier et al., 2000). Drury and colleagues extended this work to acutely ill inpatients and found that adding CBT shortened the time to recovery by about half relative to routine care (Drury, Birchwood, Cochrane, & MacMillian, 1996).

There are even indications that cognitive therapy can be used to help low-functioning chronic schizophrenic patients with neurocognitive impairment reconnect with life. These patients are among the most treatment-refractory individuals in the schizophrenia spectrum and incur 5 times the per-patient cost of the typical depressed patient due to the high level of services they command and lost productivity. In order to adapt CT for such patients, Beck and colleagues shifted the emphasis from the predominantly symptom-oriented approach that typifies the UK protocols to a person-oriented approach that highlights the interests and strengths of each patient (Beck, Rector, Stolar, & Grant, 2009). Treatment is focused on identifying and promoting concrete goals that improve the quality of life and facilitate reintegration into society. At its core is the notion that "defeatist" beliefs exacerbate the impact of neurocognitive impairment on basic life functions; in effect, patients give up trying to pursue goals in the face of the realistic obstacles that they face (Grant & Beck, 2009). The approach is explicitly recovery-oriented and treats functional outcomes as the primary target rather than an exclusive focus on symptom change.

As shown in Figure 11.12, a recent RCT found that the addition of this recovery-oriented approach to CT produced meaningful improvements in functional outcomes relative to standard treatment including medication and supportive counseling across 18 months of treatment (Grant, Huh, Perivoliotis, Stolar, & Beck, 2012). There was minimal change across time in global functioning in standard treatment whereas the addition of CT was associated with a moderate sized effect ($d = .56$). Significant changes also were observed on both positive symptoms and one negative symptom (avolition-apathy) with visible but nonsignificant improvement in other areas.

CBT appears to be *efficacious and specific* and quite possibly *enduring* as an adjunct to medications in the treatment of schizophrenia. This is one of the most exciting developments in the treatment of this chronic and debilitating disorder. Such patients often show residual positive and especially negative symptoms that need to be addressed. Moreover, indications that CT can be used to increase levels of motivation and global functioning in patients with neurocognitive impairment are most welcome. These studies suggest that CBT may have a useful adjunctive role to play in the treatment of schizophrenia that has been recognized in the UK but not yet in the United States.

CONCLUSIONS AND RECOMMENDATIONS

The cognitive and cognitive-behavioral interventions are *efficacious and specific* in the treatment of a variety of clinical disorders and often the psychosocial treatment of choice. They are at least as efficacious as medications for most nonpsychotic disorders and have an *enduring effect* that pharmacotherapy must be continued or maintained to match. In the several decades since they were first introduced they have garnered the most empirical support and become the most widely practiced approach to psychosocial treatment in the field. This is a very impressive record of success. With respect to specific areas of disorder, the following seven conclusions can be drawn:

1. CT is at least as efficacious as alternative interventions in the treatment of outpatient *depression* (along with medications only IPT and perhaps BA match its efficacy) and reduces risk following treatment termination (something that cannot be said for medications). It appears to be a useful adjunct to medications in the treatment of inpatient populations and possibly in the treatment of bipolar disorder as well. It appears to work through active ingredients specified by theory to modify the beliefs and behaviors targeted as its mechanism of change (especially with respect to its enduring effect). Other cognitive-behavioral approaches have shown promise in the treatment of children and adolescents, but have not been evaluated as extensively as in adult clinical populations.

2. Some of the most dramatic breakthroughs in the past few decades have come in the treatment of the *anxiety disorders*. CBT is efficacious and specific in the treatment of panic, health anxiety (hypochondriasis), GAD, social phobia, and PTSD. As for depression there are indications of an enduring effect not found for medications that lasts beyond the end of treatment. More purely behavioral interventions based on exposure plus

Negative Symptoms

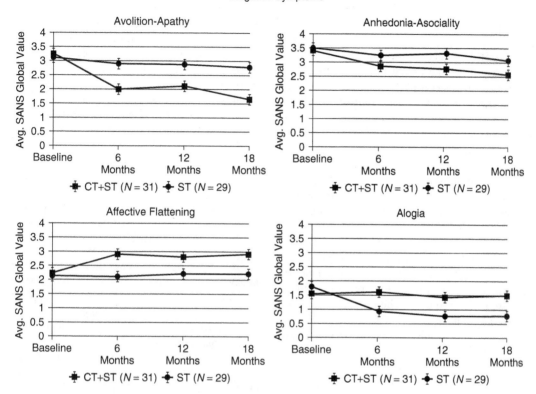

FIGURE 11.12 Cognitive behavioral therapy in the treatment of negative symptoms in chronic schizophrenia. The mean global scores for the avolition-apathy (A), anhedonia-asociality (B), affective flattening (C), and alogia (D) subscales of the Scale for the Assessment of Negative Symptoms (SANS) are shown. The values at baseline are raw means; the values at 6, 12, and 18 months are adjusted means (SEs) from the intent-to-treat hierarchical linear models. CT indicates cognitive therapy; ST, standard treatment. *$P = .01$ for the mean difference based on the hierarchical linear modeling interaction of treatment condition-assessment time.

Source: From "Cognitive Behavioral Therapy for Schizophrenia: An Empirical Review," by P. M. Grant et al. 2012, *Archives of General Psychiatry*, *69*, 121–127. Copyright 2012 by the American Medical Association. Reprinted by permission.

response prevention remain the standard of treatment for OCD and specific phobia, but they are now rivaled by sophisticated cognitive behavioral approaches that hold considerable promise. Some theorists emphasize cognitive mechanisms of change whereas others focus on more peripheral processes like extinction/habituation and each combines cognitive and behavioral strategies to different extents. Whether this distinction influences treatment outcomes remains unclear, but both do quite well relative to other types of treatment, and CBT is often the psychosocial treatment of choice.

3. CBT is efficacious and often specific in the treatment of the various *eating disorders* and

there is a growing recognition that the different disorders share a common set of beliefs regarding shape and weight that might best be approached in a transdiagnostic fashion. CBT has become the standard of treatment for bulimia nervosa and is more efficacious than IPT and more enduring than either behavior therapy or medications. Anorexia nervosa is still best treated by inpatient behavioral programs when patients are dangerously underweight but a sophisticated cognitive approach has been shown to be possibly efficacious in terms of maintaining weight gain following discharge from the hospital. CBT is efficacious and specific in the treatment of binge eating disorder and a self-help version may be more cost-effective than its primary rivals (IPT and behavioral weight loss programs). Only obesity continues to elude efforts to produce enduring change. As for behavioral weight loss programs, CBT can be used to help take weight off, but there is still no evidence that it does anything to forestall the eventual weight regain that often follows successful weight loss.

4. CBT is efficacious and specific in the treatment of *internalizing disorders in children and adolescents*. The magnitude of that effect is not all that impressive with respect to depression (something that may reflect the differences in the clinical sophistication of more cognitive versus more behavioral approaches), but CBT has emerged as the psychosocial treatment of choice for the treatment of anxiety disorders in youth and is at least as efficacious as medication treatment. The picture is more mixed with respect to the *externalizing disorders* although approaches based on cognitive behavioral principles have shown real promise in the treatment and prevention of aggression and conduct disorders. These issues are covered in greater detail in the chapter on the treatment of children and adolescents by Weisz and colleagues (see Chapter 14 this volume).

5. CBT is efficacious and possibly specific in the treatment of the various *substance use disorders* but perhaps not as efficacious as more purely behavioral interventions. Relapse prevention does appear to reduce risk for relapse among less severe problem drinkers and has been successfully adapted to an abstinence model in the treatment of drug abuse but is clearly no panacea. It is not clear that CBT adds to more purely behavioral strategies in the reduction of smoking, although it does appear to reduce risk for relapse among smokers who also are depressed.

6. DBT is efficacious and specific in the treatment of *borderline personality disorder* and has been shown to be superior to more traditional dynamic psychotherapy. Although DBT may be better classified as a *third wave* behavioral intervention, a more cognitive intervention named *schema-focused therapy* (SFT) also has been shown to be superior to dynamic psychotherapy in a recent RCT and can be considered possibly efficacious and specific pending replication. It will be interesting to see how the two interventions (DBT and SFT) compare to one another.

7. One of the most exciting and least heralded developments over the past few decades has been the emerging evidence that CT can be used as an adjunct to medications in the treatment of patients with *schizophrenia*. Although originally inspired by work done in the United States in the 1950s, the bulk of the work on positive symptoms since that time has been done in the United Kingdom and has only recently begun to generate interest elsewhere. Even more recent work done in the United States suggests that CT can be used to treat negative symptoms that undermine the quality of life in chronic patients that are largely unaddressed by medications.

On the whole, the cognitive and cognitive-behavioral interventions have generated powerful evidence of success in a large number of sophisticated trials in fully clinical populations. Negative findings are few and when they do occur tend to be a consequence of less than adequate implementation. CBT has been found to be *efficacious and specific* in the treatment of most of the nonpsychotic disorders in which it has been tested and often emerges (along with IPT in some instances and the more purely behavioral interventions) as the psychosocial treatment of choice. Moreover, it appears to have an *enduring effect* not found for medications that reduces risk for subsequent symptom return. This is perhaps its greatest advantage over medications and one that may be put in peril when provided in combination. Forand and colleagues argue in their chapter on combined treatment it may prove best for the nonpsychotic disorders to start with CBT alone and add in medications only for those patients who do not respond (see Chapter 18, this volume).

It is one thing to be efficacious in controlled research settings and another altogether to be effective when disseminated to the broader community. CBT is the current focus of the largest dissemination project that has ever been attempted with regard to mental health. The NHS in the United Kingdom has invested hundreds of millions of pounds to train several thousand additional therapists to provide CBT to the general populace (Clark et al., 2009). Initial findings indicate that the program is right on schedule with thousands of newly trained therapists treating hundreds of thousands of additional patients to remission of whom tens of thousands are getting off the public dole (Clark, 2011). This is most impressive.

Other important issues remain as well. For many disorders, the extent to which the underlying mechanisms of change are cognitive in nature remains unclear. Different theorists emphasize different mechanisms and adjust their interventions accordingly. For example, more cognitively oriented theorists like Clark or Ehlers use exposure to disconfirm their patients' worst fears whereas theorists like Barlow or Foa are more likely to rely on multiple exposures in the service of habituation. Similarly, Beck and colleagues spend more time mapping out the belief systems (cognitive conceptualizations) of their patients than do theorists like Jacobson or Linehan. Whether these differences in theory and implementation influence the quality or nature of the outcomes produced remains to be seen, but they are apparent, even if somewhat subtle.

It also remains unclear just how these processes are represented in the brain, but with the advent of imagining technologies questions can now be addressed empirically that could only be dreamed of in the past. All aspects of human experience from cognition to affect to behavior have an underlying neural representation and we can now ask questions as to how these processes develop and change at the neural level (Beck, 2008). We also can explore what changes during treatment and whether different kinds of interventions work through different neural mechanisms (DeRubeis, Siegel, & Hollon, 2008). Early indications suggest that medications work from the "bottom-up" in terms of affecting brain stem and limbic regions whereas CBT works from the "top down" through cortical mechanisms (Kennedy et al., 2007). This would be wholly consistent with work with infrahuman species that has demonstrated that the perception of control is processed through cortical regions, and that those cortical regions in turn send projections to the brain stem and limbic regions that inhibit the stress response when animals are exposed to trauma (Maier, Amat, Baratta, Paul, & Watkins, 2006). That this cortically mediated "learned resilience" protects against the generation of the stress response in subsequent traumatic situations only completes the analogy to the enduring effects produced by CBT.

Although important questions remain and interesting opportunities now exist to deepen our understanding as to how the various treatment interventions work (and why CBT has an enduring effect that other treatments lack), it appears that the cognitive and cognitive-behavioral interventions are *efficacious and often specific* in the treatment of a broad range of disorders. The growth in the quality and quantity of the empirical support for these approaches over the past quarter century has been impressive. In most instances, those studies have suggested that these approaches are at least as efficacious as the best available alternatives for the majority of the nonpsychotic disorders and useful adjuncts to medications for those disorders that are psychotic. Moreover, there are indications that these interventions produce an *enduring effect* that has yet to be found for most other psychosocial interventions and is clearly not found for medication treatment. Questions of mediation can now be addressed that could only be dreamed of in the past. The cognitive and cognitive-behavioral interventions have clearly come of age, including examination of treatment failure and its causes (Dimidjian & Hollon, 2011).

REFERENCES

Abramowitz, J. S., Taylor, S., & McKay, D. (2005). Potentials and limitations of cognitive treatments for obsessive-compulsive disorder. *Cognitive Behavior Therapy*, 34, 140–147. Retrieved from http://www.tandf.co.uk/journals/titles/16506073.asp

Agras, W. S., Rossiter, E., Arnow, B., Telch, C., Raeburn, S., Bruce, B., & Koran, L. M. (1994). One-year follow-up of psychosocial and pharmacologic treatments for bulimia nervosa. *Journal of Clinical Psychiatry*, 55, 179–183. Retrieved from http://www.psychiatrist.com

Agras, W. S., Rossiter, E. M., Arnow, B., Schneider, J. A., Telch, C. F., Raeburn, S. D., ... Koran, L. M. (1992). Pharmacological and cognitive-behavioral treatment for bulimia nervosa: A controlled comparison. *American Journal of Psychiatry*, 149, 82–87. Retrieved from http://www.ajp.psychiatryonline.org

Agras, W., Schneider, J., Arnow, B., Raeburn, S., & Telch, C. (1989). Cognitive behavioral and response-prevention treatments for bulimia nervosa. *Journal of Consulting and Clinical Psychology*, 57, 215–221. Retrieved from http://www.apa.org/pubs/journals/ccp/index.aspx

Agras, W. S., Telch, C. F., Arnow, B., Eldredge, K., Wilfley, D., Raeburn, S. D., ... Marnell, M. (1994). Weight loss, cognitive-behavioral, and desipramine treatments in binge eating disorder:

An additive design. *Behavior Therapy, 25*, 225–238. Retrieved from http://www.sciencedirect.com .proxy.library.vanderbilt.edu/science/journal

Agras, W. S., Walsh, T., Fairburn, C. G., Wilson, G. T., & Kraemer, H. C. (2000). A multicenter comparison of cognitive-behavioral therapy and interpersonal psychotherapy for bulimia nervosa. *Archives of General Psychiatry, 57*, 459–466. Retrieved from http://www.archgenpsychiatry.com

Ahrens, J., & Rexford, L. (2002). Cognitive processing therapy for incarcerated adolescents with PTSD. *Journal of Aggression, Maltreatment & Trauma, 6*, 201–216. Retrieved from http://www .tandf.co.uk/journals/WAMT

American Psychiatric Association. (1994). *Diagnostic and statistical manual of mental disorders* (4th ed. rev.). Washington, DC: American Psychiatric Association.

American Psychiatric Association (2000). Practice guideline for the treatment of patients with major depressive disorder (revision). *American Journal of Psychiatry, 157*(Suppl. 4), 1–45.

American Psychiatric Association. (2001). Practice guideline for the treatment of patients with borderline personality disorder. *American Journal of Psychiatry, 158*(Suppl. 10), 1–52. Retrieved from http://ajp.psychiatryonline.org

American Psychiatric Association. (2002). Practice guideline for the treatment of patients with bipolar disorder. *American Journal of Psychiatry, 159*(Suppl. 4), 1–50. Retrieved from http:// ajp.psychiatryonline.org

American Psychiatric Association. (2003). Practice guideline for the assessment and treatment of patients with suicidal behaviors. *American Journal of Psychiatry, 160*(Suppl. 11), 1–60. Retrieved from http://ajp.psychiatryonline.org

American Psychiatric Association. (2004a). Practice guideline for the treatment of patients with acute stress disorders and post-traumatic stress disorders. *American Journal of Psychiatry, 161*(Suppl. 11), 1–31. Retrieved from http:// ajp.psychiatryonline.org

American Psychiatric Association. (2004b). Practice guideline for the treatment of patients with schizophrenia (2nd ed.). *American Journal of Psychiatry, 161*(Suppl. 2), 1–56. Retrieved from http://ajp.psychiatryonline.org

American Psychiatric Association. (2006). Practice guideline for the treatment of patients with eating disorders (3rd ed.). *American Journal of Psychiatry, 163*(Suppl. 7), 1–54. Retrieved from http://ajp.psychiatryonline.org

American Psychiatric Association. (2007a). Practice guideline for the treatment of patients with obsessive compulsive disorders. *American Journal of Psychiatry, 164*(Suppl. 7), 1–53. Retrieved from http://ajp.psychiatryonline.org

American Psychiatric Association. (2007b). Practice guideline for the treatment of patients with substance use disorders (2nd ed.). *American Journal of Psychiatry, 164*(Suppl. 4), 1–124. Retrieved from http://ajp.psychiatryonline.org

American Psychiatric Association (2009). Practice guideline for the treatment of patients with panic disorder (2nd ed.). *American Journal of Psychiatry, 166*(Suppl. 2), 1–68. Retrieved from http://ajp.psychiatryonline.org

American Psychiatric Association. (2010). *Practice guideline for the treatment of patients with major depressive disorder* (3rd ed.). Washington, DC: Author. Retrieved from http://www .psychiatryonline.com/pracGuide/pracGuideTop ic_7.aspx

Barber, J. P., & DeRubeis, R. J. (1989). On second thought: Where the action is in cognitive therapy for depression. *Cognitive Therapy and Research, 13*, 441–457. Retrieved from http:// www.springerlink.com

Barlow, D. H. (2002). *Anxiety and its disorders: The nature and treatment of anxiety and panic* (2nd ed.). New York, NY: Guilford Press.

Barlow, D. H., & Cerny, J. A. (1988). *Psychological treatment of panic*. New York, NY: Guilford Press.

Barlow, D. H., Gorman, J. M., Shear, M. K., & Woods, S. W. (2000). Cognitive-behavioral therapy, imipramine, or their combination for panic disorder: A randomized controlled trial. *JAMA, 283*, 2529–2536. Retrieved from http://www.jama.com

Barlow, D. H., & Lehman, C. L. (1996). Advances in the psychosocial treatment of anxiety disorders. *Archives of General Psychiatry, 53*, 727–735. Retrieved from http://www .archgenpsychiatry.com

Barrett, J. E., Williams, J. W., Oxman, T. E., Frank, E., Katon, W., Sullivan, M., . . . Sengupta, A. S. (2001). Treatment of dysthymia and minor depression in primary care: A randomized trial in patients aged 18 to 59 years. *Journal of Family Practice, 50*, 405–412. Retrieved from http://www.go.galegroup.com

Barrett, P. M. (1998). An evaluation of cognitive-behavioral group treatments for childhood anxiety disorders. *Journal of Clinical Child Psychology, 27*, 459–468. Retrieved from http://www.tandfonline.com

Barrett, P. M., Dadds, M. R., & Rapee, R. M. (1996). Family treatment of childhood anxiety: A controlled trial. *Journal of Consulting and Clinical Psychology, 64*, 333–342. Retrieved from http://www.apa.org/pubs/journals/ccp/index.aspx

Barrett, P. M., Duffy, A. L., Dadds, M. R., & Rapee, R. M. (2001). Cognitive-behavioral treatment of anxiety disorders in children: Long-term (6-year) follow-up. *Journal of Consulting and Clinical Psychology, 69*, 135–141. doi: 10.1037//0022–006x.69.i.135

Barrett, P. M., Farrell, L., Pina, A. A., Peris, T. S., & Piacentini, J. (2008). Evidence-based psychosocial treatments for child and adolescent obsessive–compulsive disorder. *Journal of Clinical Child & Adolescent Psychology, 37*, 131–155. doi: 10.1080/15374410701817956

Barrett, P. M., Healy-Farrell, L. J., & March, J. S. (2004). Cognitive–behavioral family treatment of childhood obsessive–compulsive disorder: A controlled trial. *Journal of the American Academy of Child & Adolescent Psychiatry, 43*, 46–62. Retrieved from http://www.sciencedirect.com

Barsky, A. J., & Ahern, D. K. (2004). Cognitive behavior therapy for hypochondriasis: A randomized controlled trial. *JAMA, 291*, 1464–1470. Retrieved from http://www.jama.com

Bateman, A., & Fonagy, P. (1999). Effectiveness of partial hospitalization in the treatment of borderline personality disorder: A randomized controlled trial. *American Journal of Psychiatry, 156*, 1563–1569. Retrieved from http://ajp.psychiatryonline.org

Bateman, A., & Fonagy, P. (2001). Treatment of borderline personality disorder with psychoanalytically oriented partial hospitalization: An 18-month follow-up. *American Journal of Psychiatry, 158*, 36–42. Retrieved from http://ajp.psychiatryonline.org

Beck, A. T. (1952). Successful out-patient psychotherapy of a chronic schizophrenic with a delusion based on borrowed guilt. *Psychiatry, 15*, 205–212. Retrieved from http://www.ncbi.nlm.nih.gov/pnc/journals/901

Beck, A. T. (2005). The current state of cognitive therapy: A 40-year retrospective. *Archives of General Psychiatry, 62*, 953–959. Retrieved from http://www.archgenpsychiatry.com

Beck, A. T. (2008). The evolution of the cognitive model of depression and its neural correlates. *American Journal of Psychiatry, 165*, 969–977. Retrieved from http://ajp.psychiatryonline.org

Beck, A. T., & Emery, G. (1985). *Anxiety disorders and phobias: A cognitive perspective*. New York, NY: Basic Books.

Beck, A. T., Freeman, A., Davis, D. D., & Associates (2004). *Cognitive therapy of personality disorders* (2nd ed.). New York, NY: Guilford Press.

Beck, A. T., & Rector, N. A. (2000). Cognitive therapy of schizophrenia: A new therapy for the new millennium. *American Journal of Psychotherapy, 54*, 291–300. Retrieved from http://ajp.psychiatryonline.org

Beck, A. T., Rector, N. A., Stolar, N. M., & Grant, P. M. (2009). *Schizophrenia: Cognitive theory, research and therapy*. New York, NY: Guilford Press.

Beck, A. T., Rush, A. J., Shaw, B. F., & Emery, G. (1979). *Cognitive therapy of depression*. New York, NY: Guilford Press.

Beidel, D. C., Turner, S. M., Sallee, F. R., Ammerman, R. T., Crosby, L. A., & Pathak, S. (2007). SET-C versus fluoxetine in the treatment of childhood social phobia. *Journal of the American Academy of Child and Adolescent Psychiatry, 46*, 1622–32. Retrieved from http://www.sciencedirect.com

Benish, S. G., Imel, Z. E., & Wampold, B. E. (2008). The relative efficacy of *bona fide* psychotherapies for treating post-traumatic stress disorder: A meta-analysis of direct comparisons *Clinical Psychology Review, 28*, 746–758 doi: 10.1016/j.cpr.2007.10.005

Birmaher, B., Brent, D., & Work Group on Quality Issues. (2007). Practice parameters for the assessment and treatment of children and adolescents with depressive disorders. *Journal of the American Academy of Child and Adolescent Psychiatry, 46*, 1503–1526. doi: 10.1097/chi.0b013e318145ae1c

Bisson, J. I., Ehlers, A., Matthews, R., Pilling, S., Richards, D., & Turner, S. (2007). Psychological treatments for chronic post-traumatic stress disorder: Systematic review and meta-analysis. *British Journal of Psychiatry, 190*, 97–104. doi: 10.1192/bjp.bp.106.021402

Bisson, J. I., Jenkins, P. L., Alexander, J., & Bannister, C. (1997). Randomised controlled trial of psychological debriefing for victims of acute burn trauma. *British Journal of Psychiatry, 171*, 78–81. doi: 10.1192/bjp.171.1.78

Blanchard, E. B., Hickling, E. J., Devineni, T., Veazey, C. H., Galovski, T. E., Mundy, E., . . . Buckley, T. C. (2003). A controlled evaluation of cognitive behaviorial therapy for posttraumatic stress in motor vehicle accident survivors. *Behaviour Research and Therapy, 41*, 79–96. Retrieved from http://www.elsevier.com/locate/brat

Blanco, C., Heimberg, R. G., Schneier, F. R., Fresco, D. M., Chen, H., Turk, C. L., D., . . . Liebowitz, M. R. (2010). A placebo-controlled trial of phenelzine, cognitive behavioral group therapy, and their combination for social anxiety disorder. *Archives of General Psychiatry, 67*, 286–295. Retrieved from http:// www.archgenpsychiatry.com

Bockting, C. L. H., Schene, A. H., Spinhoven, P., Koeter, M. W. J., Wouters, L. F., Huyser, J., . . . the Delta Study Group (2005). Preventing relapse/recurrence in recurrent depression with cognitive therapy: A randomized controlled trial. *Journal of Consulting and Clinical Psychology, 73*, 647–657. doi: 10.1037/0022–006x.73.4.647

Borkovec, T. D., & Costello, E. (1993). Efficacy of applied relaxation and cognitive behavioral therapy in the treatment of generalized anxiety disorder. *Journal of Consulting and Clinical Psychology, 61*, 611–619. Retrieved from http://www.apa.org/pubs/journals/ccp/index.aspx

Borkovec, T. D., & Ruscio, A. M. (2001). Psychotherapy for generalized anxiety disorder. *Journal of*

Clinical Psychiatry, 62(Suppl. 11), 37–42. Retrieved from http://www.psychiatrist.com

Bowers, W. A. (1990). Treatment of depressed inpatients: Cognitive therapy plus medication, relaxation plus medication, and medication alone. *British Journal of Psychiatry, 156,* 73–78. doi: 10.1192/bjp.156.1.73

Brent, D. A. (2006), Glad for what TADS adds, but many TADS grads still sad. *Journal of the American Academy of Child and Adolescent Psychiatry, 45,* 1461–1464. Retrieved from http://www.sciencedirect.com

Brent, D. A., Emslie, G., Clarke, G., Wagner, K. D., Asarnow, J. R., Keller, M.,...Zelazny, J. (2008). Switching to another SSRI or to venlafaxine with or without cognitive behavioral therapy for adolescents with SSRI-resistant depression: The TORDIA randomized controlled trial. *JAMA, 299,* 901–913. Retrieved from http://www.jama.com

Brent, D. A., Holder, D., Kolko, K. J., Birmaher, B., Baugher, M., Roth, C.,...Johnson, B. A. (1997). A clinical psychotherapy trial for adolescent depression comparing cognitive, family, and supportive treatments. *Archives of General Psychiatry, 54,* 877–885. Retrieved from http://www.archgenpsychiatry.com

Brown, R. A., Kahler, C. W., Niaura, R., Abrams, D. B., Sales, S. D., Ramsey, S. E.,...Miller, I. W. (2001). Cognitive-behavioral treatment for depression in smoking cessation. *Journal of Consulting and Clinical Psychology, 69,* 471–480. doi: 10.1037//0022–006x.69.3.471

Brown, T. A., Barlow, D. H., & Liebowitz, M. R. (1994). The empirical basis of generalized anxiety disorder. *American Journal of Psychiatry, 15,* 1272–1280. Retrieved from http://ajp.psychiatryonline.org

Brownell, K. (2010). The humbling experience of treating obesity: Should we persist or desist? *Behaviour Research and Therapy, 48,* 717–719. doi: 10.1016/j.brat.2010.05.018

Brownell, K. D., Marlatt, G. A., Lichtenstein, E., & Wilson, G. T. (1986). Understanding and preventing relapse. *American Psychologist, 41,* 765–782. Retrieved from http://www.ft.csa.com

Brownley, K. A., Berkman, N. D., Sedway, J. A., Lohr, K. N., & Bulik, C. M. (2007). Binge eating disorder treatment: A systematic review of randomized controlled trials. *International Journal of Eating Disorders, 40,* 337–348. doi: 10.1002/eat

Bulik, C. M., Berkman, N. D., Brownley, K. A., Sedway, J. A., & Lohr, K. N. (2007). Anorexia nervosa treatment: A systematic review of randomized controlled trials. *International Journal of Eating Disorders, 40,* 310–320. doi: 10.1002/eat

Butler, A. C., Chapman, J. E., Forman, E. M., & Beck, A. T. (2006). The empirical status of cognitive-behavioral therapy: A review of meta-analyses. *Clinical Psychology Review, 26,* 17–31. doi: 10.1016/j.cpr.2005.07.003

Carroll, K. M. (1996). Relapse prevention as a psychosocial treatment: A review of controlled clinical trials. *Experimental and Clinical Psychopharmacology, 4,* 46–54. Retrieved from http://www.ft.csa.com

Carroll, K. M., Fenton, L. R., Ball, S. A., Nich, C., Frankforter, T. L., Shi, J., & Rounsaville, B. J. (2004). Efficacy of disulfiram and cognitive behavioral therapy in cocaine-dependent outpatients: A randomized placebo controlled trial. *Archives of General Psychiatry, 61,* 264–272. Retrieved from http://www.archgenpsychiatry.com

Carroll, K. M., Rounsaville, B. J., Nich, C., Gordon, L. T., Wirtz, P. W., & Gawin, F. (1994). One-year follow-up of psychotherapy and pharmacotherapy for cocaine dependence: Delayed emergence of psychotherapy effects. *Archives of General Psychiatry, 51,* 989–997. Retrieved from http://www.archgenpsychiatry.com

Chambless, D. L., & Hollon, S. D. (1998). Defining empirically supported therapies. *Journal of Consulting and Clinical Psychology, 66,* 7–18. Retrieved from http://www.apa.org/pubs/journals/ccp/index.aspx

Channon, S., De Silva, P., Hemsley, D., & Perkins, R. (1989). A controlled trial of cognitive-behavioural and behavioural treatment of anorexia nervosa. *Behaviour Research and Therapy, 27,* 529–535. Retrieved from http://www.els-cdn.com

Clark, D. M. (1986). A cognitive approach to panic. *Behaviour Research and Therapy, 24,* 461–470. Retrieved from http://www.els-cdn.com

Clark, D. M. (2004). Developing new treatments: On the interplay between theories, experimental science and clinical innovation. *Behaviour Research and Therapy, 42,* 1089–1104. doi: 10.1016/j.brat.2004.05.002

Clark, D. M. (2011). Implementing NICE guidelines for the psychological treatment of depression and anxiety disorders: The IAPT experience. *International Review of Psychiatry, 23,* 375–384. doi: 10.3109/09540261.2011.606803

Clark, D. M., Ehlers, A., Hackmann, A., McManus, F., Fennell, M., Grey, N.,...Wild, J. (2006). Cognitive therapy versus exposure and applied relaxation in social phobia: A randomized controlled trial. *Journal of Consulting and Clinical Psychology, 74,* 568–578. doi: 10.1037/0022–006x.74.3.568

Clark, D. M., Ehlers, A., McManus, F., Hackmann, A., Fennell, M. J. V., Campbell, H.,...Louis, B. (2003). Cognitive therapy versus fluoxetine in generalized social phobia: A randomized placebo-controlled trial. *Journal of Consulting and Clinical Psychology, 71,* 1058–1067. doi: 10.1037/0022–006x.71.6.1058

Clark, D. M., Layard, R., Smithies, R., Richards, D. A., Suckling, R., & Wright, B. (2009).

Improving access to psychological therapy: Initial evaluation of two UK demonstration sites. *Behaviour Research and Therapy, 47*, 910–920. doi: 10.1016/j.brat.2009.07.010

Clark, D. M., & Salkovskis, P. M. (1991). *Cognitive therapy with panic and hypochondriasis.* New York, NY: Pergamon Press.

Clark, D. M., Salkovskis, P. M., Hackmann, A., Middleton, H., Anastasiades, P., & Gelder, M. (1994). A comparison of cognitive therapy, applied relaxation and imipramine in the treatment of panic disorder. *British Journal of Psychiatry, 164*, 759–769. doi: 10.1192/bjp.164.6.759

Clark, D. M., Salkovskis, P. M., Hackmann, A., Wells, A., Fennell, M., Ludgate, J., . . . Gelder, M. (1998). Two psychological treatments for hypochondrias: A randomised controlled trial. *British Journal of Psychiatry, 173*, 218–225. doi: 10.1192/bjp.173.3.218

Clark, D. M., Salkovskis, P. M., Hackmann, A., Wells, A., Ludgate, J., & Gelder, M. (1999). Brief cognitive therapy for panic disorder: A randomized controlled trial. *Journal of Consulting and Clinical Psychology, 67*, 583–589. Retrieved from http://www.apa.org/pubs/journals/ccp/index.aspx

Clark, D. M., & Wells, A. (1995). A cognitive model of social phobia. In R. Heimberg, M. Liebowitz, D. A. Hope, & F. R. Schneier (Eds.), *Social phobia: Diagnosis, assessment, and treatment* (pp. 69–93). New York, NY: Guilford Press.

Clarke, G., Debar, L., Lynch, F., Powell, J., Gale, J., O'Connor, E., . . . Hertert, S. (2005). A randomized effectiveness trial of brief cognitive-behavioral therapy for depressed adolescents receiving antidepressant medication. *Journal of the American Academy of Child and Adolescent Psychiatry, 44*, 888–898. doi: 10.1097/01.chi.0000171904.23947.54

Clarke, G. N., Hawkins, W., Murphy, M., Sheeber, L. B., Lewinsohn, P. M., & Seeley, J. (1995). Targeted prevention of unipolar depressive disorder in an at-risk sample of high school adolescents: A randomized trial of a group cognitive intervention. *Journal of the American Academy of Child and Adolescent Psychiatry, 34*, 312–321. Retrieved from http://www.sciencedirect.com

Clarke, G. N., Hornbrook, M. C., Lynch, F., Polen, M., Gale, J., Beardslee, W. R., . . . Seeley, J. (2001). A randomized trial of a group cognitive intervention for preventing depression in offspring of depressed parents. *Archives of General Psychiatry, 58*, 1127–1134. Retrieved from http://www.archgenpsychiatry.com

Coffman, S., Martell, C. R., Dimidjian, S., Gallop, R., & Hollon, S. D. (2007). Extreme non-response in cognitive therapy: Can behavioral activation succeed where cognitive therapy fails? *Journal of Consulting and Clinical Psychology, 75*, 531–541. doi: 10.1037/0022-006x.75.4.531

Cohen, J. A., Deblinger, E., Mannarino, A. P., & Steer, R. A. (2004). A multisite randomized controlled study of sexually abused, multiply traumatized children with PTSD: Initial treatment outcome. *Journal of the American Academy of Child and Adolescent Psychiatry, 43*, 393–402. Retrieved from http://www.sciencedirect.com

Cohen, J. A., Mannarino, A. P., & Knudsen, K. (2005). Treating sexually abused children: 1 year follow-up of a randomized controlled trial. *Child Abuse & Neglect, 29*, 135–145. doi: 10.1016/j.chiabu.2004.12.005

Conduct Problems Prevention Research Group. (2007). The fast track randomized controlled trial to prevent externalizing psychiatric disorders: Findings from grades 3 to 9. *Journal of the American Academy of Child and Adolescent Psychiatry, 46*, 1250–1262. Retrieved from http://www.sciencedirect.com

Cooper, P., & Steere, J. (1995). A comparison of two psychological treatments for bulimia nervosa: Implications for models of maintenance. *Behaviour Research and Therapy, 33*, 875–885. Retrieved from http://www.els-cdn.com

Cooper, Z., Doll, H., Hawker, D., Byrne, S., Bonner, G., Eeley, E., . . . Fairburn, C. G. (2010). Testing a new cognitive behavioral treatment for obesity: A randomized controlled trial with three-year follow-up. *Behaviour Research and Therapy, 48*, 706–713. doi: 10.1016/j.brat.2010.03.008

Cooper, Z., & Fairburn, C. G. (2001). A new cognitive behavioural approach to the treatment of obesity. *Behaviour Research and Therapy, 39*, 499–511. Retrieved from http://www.els-cdn.com

Cooper, Z., Fairburn, C. G., & Hawker, D. M. (2003). *Cognitive-behavioral treatment of obesity: A clinician's guide.* New York, NY: Guilford Press.

Cottraux, J., Note, I., Boutitie, F., Milliery, M., Genouihlac, V., Yao, S. N., . . . Gueyffier, F. (2009). Cognitive therapy versus Rogerian supportive therapy in borderline personality disorder: Two-year follow-up of a controlled pilot study. *Psychotherapy and Psychosomatics, 78*, 307–316. doi: 10.1159/000229769

Cottraux, J., Note, I., Yao, S. N., Lafont, S., Note, B., Mollard, E., . . . Dartigues, J-F. (2001). A randomized controlled trial of cognitive therapy versus intensive behavior therapy in obsessive compulsive disorder. *Psychotherapy and Psychosomatics, 70*, 288–297. Retrieved from http://www.karger.com/journals/pps

Cuijpers, P. (1998). A psychoeducational approach to the treatment of depression: A meta-analysis of Lewinsohn's "Coping with Depression" course. *Behavior Therapy, 29*, 521–533. Retrieved from http://www.sciencedirect.com.proxy.library.vanderbilt.edu/science/journal

Cuijpers, P., van Straten, A., Andersson, G., & van Oppen, P. (2008). Psychotherapy for depression in adults: A meta-analysis of comparative outcome studies. *Journal of Consulting and Clinical Psychology*, 76, 909–922. doi: 10.1037/a0013075

Curry, J. F. (2001). Specific psychotherapies for childhood and adolescent depression. *Biological Psychiatry*, 49, 1091–1100. Retrieved from http://www.ac.el-cdn.com

Davidson, J. R., Foa, E. B., Huppert, J. D., Keefe, F. J., Franklin, M. E., Compton, J. S.,...Gadde, K. M. (2004). Fluoxetine, comprehensive cognitive behavioral therapy, and placebo in generalized social phobia. *Archives of General Psychiatry*, 61, 1005–1013. Retrieved from http://www.archgenpsychiatry.com

Davidson, K., Norrie, J., Tyrer, P., Gumley, A., Tata, P., Murray, H., & Palmer, S. (2006). The effectiveness of cognitive behavior therapy for borderline personality disorder: Results from the borderline personality disorder study of cognitive therapy (BOSCOT) trial. *Journal of Personality Disorders*, 20, 450–465. Retrieved from http://www.guilfordjournals.com

Davis, T. E. III, Ollendick, T. H., & Öst, L.-G. (2009). Intensive treatment of specific phobias in children and adolescents. *Cognitive and Behavioral Practice*, 16, 294–303. Retrieved from http://www.elsevier.com/locate/cabp

de Haan, E., van Oppen, P., van Balkom, A. J. Spinhoven, P., Hoogduin, K. A. L., & van Dyck, R. (1997). Prediction of outcome and early vs. late improvement in OCD patients treated with cognitive behaviour therapy and pharmacotherapy. *Acta Psychiatrica Scandinavia*, 96, 354–361. Retrieved from http://www.onlinelibrary.wiley.com

DeRubeis, R. J., & Crits-Christoph, P. (1998). Empirically supported individual and group psychological treatments for adult mental disorders. *Journal of Consulting and Clinical Psychology*, 66, 37–52. Retrieved from http://www.apa.org/pubs/journals/ccp/index.aspx

DeRubeis, R. J., Evans, M. D., Hollon, S. D., Garvey, M. J., Grove, W. M., & Tuason, V. B. (1990). How does cognitive therapy work? Cognitive change and symptom change in cognitive therapy and pharmacotherapy for depression. *Journal of Consulting and Clinical Psychology*, 58, 862–869. Retrieved from http://www.apa.org/pubs/journals/ccp/index.aspx

DeRubeis, R. J., & Feeley, M. (1990). Determinants of change in cognitive therapy for depression. *Cognitive Therapy and Research*, 14, 469–482. Retrieved from http://www.springerlink.com

DeRubeis, R. J., Gelfand, L. A., Tang, T. Z., & Simons, A. D. (1999). Medications versus cognitive behavioral therapy for severely depressed outpatients: Mega-analysis of four randomized comparisons. *American Journal of Psychiatry*, 156, 1007–1013. Retrieved from http://ajp.psychiatryonline.org

DeRubeis, R. J., Hollon, S. D., Amsterdam, J. D., Shelton, R. C., Young, P. R., Salomon, R. M.,...Gallop, R. (2005). Cognitive therapy vs. medications in the treatment of moderate to severe depression. *Archives of General Psychiatry*, 62, 409–416. Retrieved from http://www.archgenpsychiatry.com

DeRubeis, R. J., Seigle, G. J., & Hollon, S. D. (2008). Cognitive therapy versus medication for depression: Treatment outcomes and neural mechanisms. *Nature Reviews Neuroscience*, 9, 788–796. doi: 10.1038/nrn2345

Dimidjian, S., & Hollon, S. D. (2011). What can be learned when empirically supported treatments fail? Introduction. *Cognitive and Behavioral Practice*, 18, 303–305.

Dimidjian, S., Hollon, S. D., Dobson, K. S., Schmaling, K. B., Kohlenberg, R. J., Addis, M. E.,...Jacobson, N. S. (2006). Behavioral activation, cognitive therapy, and antidepressant medication in the acute treatment of major depression. *Journal of Consulting and Clinical Psychology*, 74, 658–670. doi: 10.1037/0022–006x.74.4.658

Dobson, K. S., Hollon, S. D., Dimidjian, S., Schmaling, K. B., Kohlenberg, R. J., Gallop, R. J.,...Jacobson, N. S. (2008). Randomized trial of behavioral activation, cognitive therapy, and antidepressant medication in the prevention of relapse and recurrence in major depression. *Journal of Consulting and Clinical Psychology*. 76, 468–477. doi: 10.1037/0022–006x.76.3.468

Dodge, K. A. (2008). Framing public policy and prevention of chronic violence in American youth. *American Psychologist*, 63, 573–590. doi: 10.1037/0003–066X.63.7.573

Driessen, E., Cuijpers, P., Hollon, S. D., & Dekker, J. J. M. (2010). Does pretreatment severity moderate the efficacy of psychological treatment of adult outpatient depression? A meta-analysis. *Journal of Consulting and Clinical Psychology*, 78, 668–680. doi: 10.1037/a0020570

Drury, V., Birchwood, M., Cochrane, R., & MacMillan, F. (1996). Cognitive therapy and recovery from acute psychosis: A controlled trial, I: Impact on psychotic symptoms. *British Journal of Psychiatry*, 169, 593–601. doi: 10.1192/bjp.169.5.593

Duffy, M., Gillespie, K., & Clark, D. M. (2007). Post-traumatic stress disorder in the context of terrorism and other civil conflict in Northern Ireland: Randomised controlled trial. *British Medical Journal*, 334, 1147–1150. doi: 10.1136/bmj.39021.846852.be

Dugas, M. J., Brillon, P., Savard, P., Turcotte, J., Gaudet, A., Ladouceur, R.,...Gervais, N. J. (2010) A randomized clinical trial of cognitive-behavioral therapy and applied relaxation for adults with generalized anxiety disorder. *Behavior Therapy*, 41, 46–58. Available online at www.sciencedirect.com

Dugas, M. J., Ladouceur, R., Léger, E., Freeston, M. H., Langlois, F., Provencher, M. D., & Boisvert,

J. (2003). Group cognitive–behavioral therapy for generalized anxiety disorder: Treatment outcome and long-term follow-up. *Journal of Consulting and Clinical Psychology*, 71, 821–825. doi: 10.1037/0022–006X.71.4.821

Durham, R. C., Murphy, T., Allan, T., Richard, K., Treliving, L. R., & Fenton, G. W. (1994). Cognitive therapy, analytic psychotherapy and anxiety management for generalised anxiety disorder. *British Journal of Psychiatry*, 165, 315–323. doi: 10.1192/bjp.165.3.315

Dutra, L., Stathopoulou, G., Basden, S. L., Leyro, M., Powers, M. B., & Otto, M. B. (2008). A meta-analytic review of psychosocial interventions for substance use disorders. *American Journal of Psychiatry*, 165, 179–187. Retrieved from http://ajp.psychiatryonline.org

Ehlers, A., Bisson, J., Clark, D. M., Creamer, M., Pilling, S., Richards, D., ... Yule, W. (2010). Do all psychological treatments really work the same in posttraumatic stress disorder? *Clinical Psychology Review*, 30, 269–276. doi:10.1016/j.cpr.2009.12.001

Ehlers, A., & Clark, D. M. (2000). A cognitive model of posttraumatic stress disorder. *Behaviour Research and Therapy*, 38, 319–345. Retrieved from http://www.elsevier.com/locate/brat

Ehlers, A., Clark, D. M., Hackmann, A., Grey, N., Liness, S., Wild, J., ... Waddington, L. (2010). Intensive cognitive therapy for PTSD: A feasibility study. *Behavioural and Cognitive Psychotherapy*, 38, 383–398. doi:10.1017/S1352465810000214

Ehlers, A., Clark, D. M., Hackmann, A., McManus, F., & Fennell, M. (2005). Cognitive therapy for posttraumatic stress disorder: Development and evaluation. *Behaviour Research and Therapy*, 43, 413–431. doi: 10.1016/j.brat.2004.03.006

Ehlers, A., Clark, D. M., Hackmann, A., McManus, F., Fennell, M., Herbert, C., & Mayou, R. (2003). A randomized controlled trial of cognitive therapy, a self-help booklet, and repeated assessments as early interventions for posttraumatic stress disorder. *Archives of General Psychiatry*, 60, 1024–1032. Retrieved from http://wwwarchgenpsychiatry.com

Elkin, I., Gibbons, R. D., Shea, T., Sotsky, S. M., Watkins, J. T., Pilkonis, P. A., & Hedeker, D. (1995). Initial severity and differential treatment outcome in the national institute of mental health treatment of depression collaborative research program. *Journal of Consulting and Clinical Psychology*, 63, 841–847. Retrieved from http://www.apa.org/pubs/journals/ccp/index.aspx

Elkin, I., Shea, M. T., Watkins, J. T., Imber, S. D., Sotsky, S. M., Collins, J. F., ... Parloff, M. B. (1989). NIMH treatment of depression collaborative research program: I. General effectiveness of treatments. *Archives of*

General Psychiatry, 46, 971–982. Retrieved from http://www.archgenpsychiatry.com

Evans, M. D., Hollon, S. D., DeRubeis, R. J., Piasecki, J. M., Grove, W. M., Garvey, M. J., & Tuason, V. B. (1992). Differential relapse following cognitive therapy and pharmacotherapy for depression. *Archives of General Psychiatry*, 49, 802–808. Retrieved from http://www.archgenpsychiatry.com

Eyberg, S. M., Nelson, M. M., & Boggs, S. R. (2008). Evidence-based psychosocial treatments for children and adolescents with disruptive behavior. *Journal of Clinical Child & Adolescent Psychology*, 37, 215–237. doi: 10.1080/15374410701820117

Fairburn, C. G. (1981). A cognitive behavioral approach to the treatment of bulimia. *Psychological Medicine*, 11, 707–711. doi: 10.1017/S0033291700041209

Fairburn, C. G. (1995). *Overcoming binge eating*. New York, NY: Guilford Press.

Fairburn, C. G., Cooper, Z., Doll, H. A., O'Connor, M. E., Bohn, K., Hawker, D. M., ... Palmer, R. L. (2009). Transdiagnostic cognitive behavioral therapy for patients with eating disorders: A two-site trial with 60-week followup. *American Journal of Psychiatry*, 166, 311–319. Retrieved from http://ajp.psychiatryonline.org

Fairburn, C. G., Cooper, Z., & Shafran, R. (2003). Cognitive behaviour therapy for eating disorders: A "transdiagnostic" theory and treatment. *Behaviour Research and Therapy*, 41, 509–528. doi: 10.1016/s0005–7967(02)00088–8

Fairburn, C. G., Jones, R., Peveler, R. C., Carr, S. J., Solomon, R. A., O'Connor, M. E., ... Hope, R. A. (1991). Three psychological treatments for bulimia nervosa: A comparative trial. *Archives of General Psychiatry*, 48, 463–469. Retrieved from http://www.archgenpsychiatry.com

Fairburn, C. G., Jones, R., Peveler, R. C., Hope, R. A., & O'Connor, M. (1993). Psychotherapy and bulimia nervosa: Long-term effects of interpersonal psychotherapy, behavior therapy and cognitive-behavior therapy. *Archives of General Psychiatry*, 50, 419–428. Retrieved from http://www.archgenpsychiatry.com

Fava, G. A., Rafanelli, C., Grandi, S., Conti, S., & Belluardo, P. (1998). Prevention of recurrent depression with cognitive behavioral therapy. *Archives of General Psychiatry*, 55, 816–820. Retrieved from http://www.archgenpsychiatry.com

Feeley, M., DeRubeis, R. J., & Gelfand, L. A. (1999). The temporal relation of adherence and alliance to symptom change in cognitive therapy for depression. *Journal of Consulting and Clinical Psychology*, 67, 578–582. Retrieved from http://www.apa.org/pubs/journals/ccp/index.aspx

Flannery-Schroeder, E. C., & Kendall, P. C. (2000). Group and individual cognitive-behavioral treatments for youth with anxiety disorders: A randomized clinical trial. *Cognitive Therapy and*

Research, *24*, 251–278. Retrieved from http://www.springerlink.com

Foa, E. B. (2011). Prolonged exposure therapy: Past, present, and future. *Depression and Anxiety*, *28*, 1043–1047. doi: 10.1002/da.20907

Foa, E. B., Dancu, C. V., Hembree, E. A., Jaycox, L. H., Meadows, E. A., & Street, G. P. (1999). Comparison of exposure therapy, stress inoculation training, and their combination for reducing posttraumatic stress disorder in female assault victims. *Journal of Consulting and Clinical Psychology*, *67*, 194–200. Retrieved from http://www.apa.org/pubs/journals/ccp/index.aspx

Foa, E. B., Hembree, E. A., Cahill, S. E., Rauch, S. A. M., Riggs, D. S., Feeny, N. C., & Yadin, E. (2005). Randomized trial of prolonged exposure for posttraumatic stress disorder with and without cognitive restructuring: Outcome at academic and community clinics. *Journal of Consulting and Clinical Psychology*, *73*, 953–964. doi: 10.1037/0022–006x.73.5.953

Foa, E. B., Liebowitz, M. R., Kozak, M. J., Davies, S., Campeas, R., Franklin, M. E., ... Tu, X. (2005). Randomized, placebo-controlled trial of exposure and ritual prevention, clomipramine, and their combination in the treatment of obsessive-compulsive disorder. *American Journal of Psychiatry*, *162*, 151–161. Retrieved from http://ajp.psychiatryonline.org

Foa, E. B., & Rothbaum, B. O. (1998). *Treating the trauma of rape*. New York, NY: Guilford Press.

Foa, E. B., Rothbaum, B., Riggs, D., & Murdock, T. (1991). Treatment of posttraumatic stress disorder in rape victims: A comparison between cognitive-behavioral procedures and counseling. *Journal of Consulting and Clinical Psychology*, *59*, 715–723. Retrieved from http://www.apa.org/pubs/journals/ccp/index.aspx

Fournier, J. C., DeRubeis, R. J., Hollon, S. D., Dimidjian, S., Amsterdam, J. D., Shelton, R. C., & Fawcett, J. (2010). Antidepressant drug effects and depression severity: A patient-level meta-analysis. *JAMA*, *303*, 47–53. doi: 10.1001/jama.2009.1943

Fournier, J. C., DeRubeis, R. J., Shelton, R. C., Gallop, R., Amsterdam, J. D., & Hollon, S. D. (2008). Antidepressant medications versus cognitive therapy in depressed patients with or without personality disorder. *British Journal of Psychiatry*, *192*, 124–129. doi: 10.1192/bjp.bp .107.037234

Fournier, J. C., DeRubeis, R. J., Shelton, R. C., Hollon, S. D., Amsterdam, J. D., & Gallop, R. (2009). Prediction of response to medication and cognitive therapy in the treatment of moderate to severe depression. *Journal of Consulting and Clinical Psychology*, *77*, 775–787. doi: 10.1037/a0015401

Franklin, M. E., Sapyta, J., Freeman, J. B., Khanna, M., Compton, S., Almirall, D., ... March, J. S. (2011). Cognitive behavior therapy augmentation of pharmacotherapy in pediatric obsessive-compulsive disorder: The pediatric OCD treatment study II (POTS II) Randomized Controlled Trial. *JAMA*, *306*, 1224–1232. Retrieved from http://www.jama.com

Freeston, M. H., Ladouceur, R., Gagnon, F., Thibodeau, N., Rheaume, J., Letarte, H., & Bujold, A. (1997). Cognitive-behavioral treatment of obsessive thoughts: A controlled study. *Journal of Consulting and Clinical Psychology*, *65*, 405–413. Retrieved from http://www.ft.csa.com

Garber, J., Clarke, G. N., Weersing, V. R., Beardslee, W. R., Brent, D. A., Gladstone, T. R. G., ... Iyengar, S. (2009). Prevention of depression in at-risk adolescents: A randomized controlled trial. *JAMA*, *301*, 2215–2224. Retrieved from http://www.jama.com

Garner, D. M., & Bemis, K. M. (1982). A cognitive-behavioral approach to anorexia nervosa. *Cognitive Therapy and Research*, *6*, 123–150. Retrieved from http://www.springerlink.com

Giesen-Bloo, J., van Dyck, R., Spinhoven, P., van Tilburg, W., Dirksen, C., van Asselt, T., ... Arntz, A. (2006). Outpatient psychotherapy for borderline personality disorder: randomized trial of schema-focused therapy vs transference-focused psychotherapy. *Archives of General Psychiatry*, *63*, 649–658. Retrieved from http://www.archgenpsychiatry.com

Gillespie, K., Duffy, M., Hackmann, A., & Clark, D. M. (2002). Community based cognitive therapy in the treatment of posttraumatic stress disorder following the Omagh bomb. *Behaviour Research and Therapy*, *40*, 345–357. Retrieved from http://www.elsevier.com/locate /brat

Goodyer, I. M., Dubicka, B., Wilkinson, P., Kelvin, R., Roberts, C., Byford, S., ... Harrington, R. (2007). A randomized controlled trial of SSRIs and routine specialist care with and without cognitive behavior therapy in adolescents with major depression. *BMJ*, *335*, 142–146. doi: 10.1136/bmj.39224.494340.55

Grant, P. M., & Beck, A. T. (2009). Defeatist beliefs as a mediator of cognitive impairment, negative symptoms, and functioning in schizophrenia. *Schizophrenia Bulletin*, *35*, 798–806. doi: 10.1093/schbul/sbn008

Grant, P. M., Huh, G. A., Perivoliotis, D., Stolar, N. M., & Beck, A. T. (2012). Randomized trial to evaluate the efficacy of cognitive therapy for low-functioning patients with schizophrenia. *Archives of General Psychiatry*, *69*, 121–127. Retrieved from http://www.archgenpsychiatry.com

Greeven, A., van Balkom, A. J. L. M., Visser, S., Merkelbach, J. W., van Rood, Y. R., van Dyck, R., ... Spinhoven, P. (2007). Cognitive behavior therapy and paroxetine in the treatment of hypochondriasis: A randomized controlled trial. *American Journal of Psychiatry*, *164*, 91–99. Retrieved from http://www.ajp.psychiatryonline.org

Grilo, C. M., & Masheb, R. M. (2005). A randomized controlled comparison of guided self-help cognitive behavioral therapy and behavioral weight loss for binge eating disorder. *Behaviour Research and Therapy*, *43*, 1509–1525. doi: 10.1016/j.brat.2004.11.010

Grilo, C. M., Masheb, R. M., & Wilson, G. T. (2005). Efficacy of cognitive behavioral therapy and fluoxetine for the treatment of binge eating disorder: a randomized double-blind placebo-controlled comparison. *Biological Psychiatry*, *57*, 301–309. doi: 10.1016/j.biopsych.2004.11.002

Hall, S. M., Munoz, R. F., & Reus, V. I. (1994). Cognitive-behavioral intervention increases abstinence rates for depressive-history smokers. *Journal of Consulting and Clinical Psychology*, *62*, 141–146. Retrieved from http://www.apa.org/pubs/journals/ccp/index.aspx

Hall, S. M., Reus, V. I., Munoz, R. F., Sees, K. L., Humfleet, G., Hartz, D. T., . . . Triffleman, E. (1998). Nortriptyline and cognitive-behavioral therapy in the treatment of cigarette smoking. *Archives of General Psychiatry*, *55*, 683–690. Retrieved from http://www.archgenpsychiatry.com

Heimberg, R. G., Liebowitz, M. R., Hope, D. A., Schneier, F. R., Holt, C. S., Welkowitz, L. A., . . . Klein, D. F. (1998). Cognitive behavioral group therapy vs phenelzine therapy for social phobia: 12-week outcome. *Archives of General Psychiatry*, *55*, 1133–1141. Retrieved from http://www.archgenpsychiatry.com

Heimberg, R. G., Salzman, D. G., Holt, C. S., & Blendell, K. A. (1993). Cognitive-behavioral group treatment for social phobia: Effectiveness at five-year follow-up. *Cognitive Therapy and Research*, *17*, 325–339. Retrieved from http://www.springerlink.com

Hirshfeld-Becker, D. R., Masek, B., Henin, A., Blakely, L. R., Pollock-Wurman, R. A., McQuade, J., . . . Biederman, J. (2010). Cognitive behavioral therapy for 4- to 7-year-old children with anxiety disorders: A randomized clinical trial. *Journal of Consulting and Clinical Psychology*, *78*, 498–510. doi: 10.1037/a0019055

Hoffart, A., Borge, F. M., Sexton, H., & Clark, D. M. (2009). Change processes in residential cognitive and interpersonal therapy for social phobia: A process outcome study. *Behavior Therapy*, *40*, 10–22. doi: 10.1016/j.beth.2007.12.003

Hofmann, S. G. (2004). Cognitive mediation of treatment change in social phobia. *Journal of Consulting and Clinical Psychology*, *72*, 392–399. doi: 10.1037/0022–006X.72.3.392

Hofmann, S. G., Meuret, A. E., Rosenfield, D., Suvak, M. K., Barlow, D. H., Gorman, J. M., . . . Woods, S. W. (2007). Preliminary evidence for cognitive mediation during cognitive-behavioral therapy of panic disorder. *Journal of Consulting and Clinical Psychology*, *75*, 374–379. doi: 10.1037/0022–006X.75.3.374

Hollon, S. D. (2011). Cognitive and behavior therapy in the treatment and prevention of depression. *Depression and Anxiety*, *28*, 263–266. doi: 10.1002/da.20797

Hollon, S. D., & Beck, A. T. (2004). Cognitive and cognitive behavioral therapies. In M. J. Lambert (Ed.), *Bergin and Garfield's handbook of psychotherapy and behavior change* (5th ed., pp. 447–492). Hoboken, NJ: Wiley.

Hollon, S. D., DeRubeis, R. J., & Evans, M. D. (1987). Causal mediation of change in treatment for depression: Discriminating between nonspecificity and noncausality. *Psychological Bulletin*, *102*, 139–149. Retrieved from http://www.ft.csa.com

Hollon, S. D., DeRubeis, R. J., Shelton, R. C., Amsterdam, J. D., Salomon, R. M., O'Reardon, J. P., . . . Gallop, R. (2005). Prevention of relapse following cognitive therapy versus medications in moderate to severe depression. *Archives of General Psychiatry*, *62*, 417–422. Retrieved from http://www.archgenpsychiatry.com

Hollon, S. D., Garber, J., & Shelton, R. C. (2005). Treatment of depression in adolescents with cognitive behavior therapy and medications: A commentary on the TADS Project. *Cognitive and Behavioral Practice*, *12*, 149–155. Retrieved from http://www.elsevier.com/locate/cabp

Hollon, S. D., & Ponniah, K. (2010). A review of empirically supported psychological therapies for mood disorders in adults. *Depression and Anxiety*, *27*, 891–932. doi: 10.1002/da.20741

Hollon, S. D., Stewart, M. O., & Strunk, D. (2006). Cognitive behavior therapy has enduring effects in the treatment of depression and anxiety. *Annual Review of Psychology*, *57*, 285–315. doi: 10.1146/annurev.psych.57.102904.190044

Hollon, S. D., Thase, M. E., & Markowitz, J. C. (2002). Treatment and prevention of depression. *Psychological Science in the Public Interest*, *3*, 39–77. doi: 10.1111/1529–1006.00008

Horowitz, J. L., & Garber, J. (2006). The prevention of depressive symptoms in children and adolescents: A metaanalytic review. *Journal of Consulting and Clinical Psychology*, *74*, 401–415. doi: 10.1037/0022–006x.74.3.401

Hsu, L. K., Rand, W., Sullivan, S., Liu, D. W., Mulliken, B., McDonagh, B., & Kaye, W. H. (2001). Cognitive therapy, nutritional therapy and their combination in the treatment of bulimia nervosa. *Psychological Medicine*, *31*, 871–879. doi: 10.1017/s003329170100410x

Imber, S. D., Pilkonis, P. A., Sotsky, S. M., Elkin, I., Watkins, J. T., Collins, J. F., . . . Glass, D. R.

(1990). Mode-specific effects among three treatments for depression. *Journal of Consulting and Clinical Psychology, 58,* 352–359. Retrieved from http://www.ft.csa.com

Irvin, J. E., Bowers, C. A., Dunn, M. E., & Wang, M. C. (1999). Efficacy and relapse prevention: A metaanalytic review. *Journal of Consulting and Clinical Psychology, 67,* 563–570. Retrieved from http://www.ft.csa.com

Jacobson, N. S., & Hollon, S. D. (1996). Prospects for future comparisons between drugs and psychotherapy: Lessons from the CBT-versus-pharmacotherapy exchange. *Journal of Consulting and Clinical Psychology, 64,* 104–108. Retrieved from http://www.ft.csa.com

Jaffe, A. J., Rounsaville, B. J., Chang, G., Schottenfeld, R. S., Meyer, R. E., & O'Malley, S. S. (1996). Naltrexone, relapse prevention, and supportive therapy with alcoholics: An analysis of patient treatment matching. *Journal of Consulting and Clinical Psychology, 64,* 1044–1053. Retrieved from http://www.ft.csa.com

Jarrett, R. B., Schaffer, M., McIntire, D., Witt-Browder, A., Kraft, D., & Risser, R. C. (1999). Treatment of atypical depression with cognitive therapy or phenelzine: A double-blind, placebo-controlled trial. *Archives of General Psychiatry, 56,* 431–437. Retrieved from http://www.archgenpsychiatry.com

Jaurrieta, N., Jimenez-Murcia, S., Menchón, J. M., del Pino Alonso, M., Segalàs, C., Álvarez- Moya, E. M., . . . Vallejo, J. (2008). Individual versus group cognitive-behavioral treatment for obsessive-compulsive disorder. *Psychotherapy Research, 18,* 604–614. doi: 10.1080/10503300802192141

Joyce, P. R., McKenzie, J. M., Carter, J. D., Rae, M. A., Luty, S. E., Frampton, C. M. A., & Mulder, R. T. (2007). Temperament, character and personality disorders as predictors of response to interpersonal psychotherapy and cognitive-behavior therapy for depression. *British Journal of Psychiatry, 190,* 503–508. doi: 10.1192/bjp.bp.106.024737

Kazdin, A. E., & Weisz, J. R. (1998). Identifying and developing empirically supported child and adolescent treatments. *Journal of Consulting and Clinical Psychology, 66,* 19–36. Retrieved from http://www.ft.csa.com

Keller, M. B., McCullough, J. P., Klein, D. N., Arnow, B., Dunner, D. L., Gelenberg, A. J., . . . Zajecka, J. (2000). A comparison of nefazodone, the cognitive behavioral-analysis system of psychotherapy, and their combination for the treatment of chronic depression. *New England Journal of Medicine, 342,* 1462–1470. Retrieved from http://www.proquest.umi.com

Kendall, P. C. (1994). Treating anxiety disorders in children: Results of a randomized clinical trial. *Journal of Consulting and Clinical Psychology, 62,* 100–110. Retrieved from http://www.ft.csa.com

Kendall, P. C., Flannery-Schroeder, E., Panichilli-Mindel, S. M., Southam-Gerow, M., Henin, A., & Warman, M. (1997). Therapy for youths with anxiety disorders: A second randomized clinical trial. *Journal of Consulting and Clinical Psychology, 65,* 366–380. Retrieved from http://www.ft.csa.com

Kendall, P. C., Hudson, J. L., Gosch, E., Flannery-Schroeder, E., & Suveg, C. (2008). Cognitive–behavioral therapy for anxiety disordered youth: A randomized clinical trial evaluating child and family modalities. *Journal of Consulting and Clinical Psychology, 76,* 282–297. doi: 10.1037/0022–006x.76.2.282

Kendall, P. C., & Southam-Gerow, M. A. (1996). Long-term follow-up of a cognitive-behavioral therapy for anxiety-disorder youth. *Journal of Consulting and Clinical Psychology, 64,* 724–730. Retrieved from http://www.ft.csa.com

Kendall, P. C., & Treadwell, K. R. H. (2007). The role of self-statements as a mediator in treatment for youth with anxiety disorders. *Journal of Consulting and Clinical Psychology, 75,* 380–389. doi: 10.1037/0022–006x.75.3.380

Kennedy, S. H., Konarski, J. Z., Segal, Z. V., Lau, M. A., Bieling, P. J., McIntyre, R. S., & Mayberg, H. S. (2007). Differences in brain glucose metabolism between responders to CBT and venlafaxine in a 16-week randomized controlled trial. *American Journal of Psychiatry, 164,* 778–788. Retrieved from http://ajp.psychiatryonline.org

Kessler, R. C., Berglund, P., Demler, O., Jin, R., Merikangas, K. R., & Walters, E. E. (2005). Lifetime prevalence and age-of-onset distributions of DSM-IV disorders in the national comorbidity survey replication. *Archives of General Psychiatry, 62,* 593–602. Retrieved from http://www.archgenpsychiatry.com

Kessler, R. C., Chiu, W. T., Demler, O., Merikangas, K. R., & Walters, E. E. (2005). Prevalence, severity, and comorbidity of 12-month DSM-IV disorders in the national comorbidity survey replication. *Archives of General Psychiatry, 62,* 617–627. Retrieved from http://www.archgenpsychiatry.com

Knowler, W. C., Fowler, S. E., Hamman, R. F., Christophi, C. A., Hoffman, H. J. Brenneman, A. T., . . . Diabetes Prevention Program Research Group (2009). 10-year follow-up of diabetes incidence and weight loss in the diabetes prevention program outcomes study. *Lancet, 374,* 1677–1686. doi: 10.1016/S0140–6736(09)61457–4

Kocsis, J. H., Gelenberg, A. J., Rothbaum, B. O., Klein, D. K., Trivedi, M. H., Manber, R., . . . for the REVAMP Investigators. (2009). Cognitive behavioral analysis system of psychotherapy and brief supportive psychotherapy for augmentation of antidepressant nonresponse in chronic depression: The REVAMP trial. *Archives of*

General Psychiatry, 66, 1178–1188. Retrieved from http://www.archgenpsychiatry.com

Kraemer, H. C., Wilson, G. T., Fairburn, C. G., & Agras, W. S. (2002). Mediators and moderators of treatment effects in randomized clinical trials. *Archives of General Psychiatry, 59*, 877–883. Retrieved from http://www.archgen psychiatry.com

Kuipers, E., Fowler, D., Garety, P., Chisholm, D., Freeman, D., Dunn, G., . . . Hadley, C. (1998). London-East Anglia randomised controlled trial of cognitive behaviour therapy for psychosis: III. Follow-up and economic evaluation at 18 months. *British Journal of Psychiatry, 173*, 61–68. doi: 10.1192/bjp.173.1.61

Kuipers, E., Garety, P., Fowler, D., Dunn, G., Bebbington, P., Freeman, D., & Hadley, C. (1997). The London-East Anglia randomised controlled trial of cognitive behaviour therapy for psychosis: Effects of the treatment phase. *British Journal of Psychiatry, 171*, 319–325. doi: 10.1192/bjp.171.4.319

Kuyken, W., Byford, S., Taylor, R. S., Watkins, E., Holden, E., White, K., . . . Teasdale, J. D. (2008). Mindfulness-based cognitive therapy to prevent relapse in recurrent depression. *Journal of Consulting and Clinical Psychology, 76*, 966–978. doi: 10.1037/a0013786

Ladouceur, R., Dugas, M. J., Freeston, M. H., Leger, E., Gagnon, F., & Thibodeau, N. (2000). Efficacy of a cognitive-behavioral treatment for generalized anxiety disorder: Evaluation in a controlled clinical trial. *Journal of Consulting and Clinical Psychology, 68*, 957–964. doi: 10.1037//0022–006x.68.6.957

Ladouceur, R., Dugas, M. J., Freeston, M. H., Rheaume, J., Blais, F., Gagnon, F., . . . Boisvert, J.-M. (1999). Specificity of generalized anxiety disorder symptoms and processes. *Behavior Therapy, 30*, 191–207. Available online at www.sciencedirect.com

Lam, D. H., Hayward, P., Watkins, E. R., Wright, K., & Sham, P. (2005). Relapse prevention in patients with bipolar disorder: Cognitive therapy outcome after 2 years. *American Journal of Psychiatry, 162*, 324–329. Retrieved from http://ajp.psychiatryonline.org

Law, M., & Tang, J. L. (1995). An analysis of the effectiveness of interventions intended to help people stop smoking. *Archives of Internal Medicine, 155*, 1933–1941. Retrieved from http://www.archinte.ama-assn.org

Leichsenring, F., Salzer, S., Jaeger, U., Kächele, H., Kreische, R., Leweke, F., . . . Leibing, E. (2009). Short-term psychodynamic psychotherapy and cognitive-behavioral therapy in generalized anxiety disorder: A randomized, controlled trial. *American Journal of Psychiatry, 166*, 875–881. Retrieved from http://www.ajp.psychiatryonline.org

Lerner, M. S., & Clum, G. A. (1990). Treatment of suicide ideators: A problem-solving approach. *Behavior Therapy, 21*, 403–411. Available online at www.sciencedirect.com

Leucht, S., Pitschel-Walz, G., Abraham, D., & Kissling, W. (1999). Efficacy and extrapyramidal side-effects of the new antipsychotics olanzapine, quetiapine, risperidone, and sertindole compared to conventional antipsychotics and placebo: A metaanalysis of randomized controlled trials. *Schizophrenia Research, 35*, 51–68. Retrieved from http://www.ac.els-cdn.com

Lewinsohn, P. M., Hoberman, H. M., & Clarke, G. N. (1989). The coping with depression course: Review and future directions. *Canadian Journal of Behavioural Science, 21*, 470–493. Retrieved from http://www.ft.csa.com

Lewinsohn, P. M., Munoz, R. F., Youngren, M. A., & Zeiss, A. M. (1986). *Control your depression*. Englewood Cliffs, NJ: Prentice-Hall.

Liberman, R. P., Teigen, J., Patterson, R., & Baker, V. (1973). Reducing delusional speech in chronic paranoid schizophrenics. *Journal of Applied Behavior Analysis, 6*, 57–64. Retrieved from http://www.ncbi.nlm.nih.gov/pmc/articles/PMC131080 6/pdf/jaba00063-0059.pdf

Lieberman, J. A., Stroup, T. S., McEvoy, J. P., Swartz, M. S., Rosenheck, R. A., Perkins, D. O., . . . Clinical Antipsychotic Trials of Intervention Effectiveness (CATIE) Investigators. (2005). Effectiveness of antipsychotic drugs in patients with chronic schizophrenia. *New England Journal of Medicine, 353*, 1209–1223. Retrieved from http://www.proquest.umi.com

Liebowitz, M. R., Heimberg, R. G., Schneier, F. R., Hope, D. A., Davies, S., Holt, C. S., . . . Klein, D. N. (1999). Cognitive-behavioral group therapy versus phenelzine in social phobia: Long-term outcome. *Depression and Anxiety, 10*, 89–98. Retrieved from http://www.onlinelibrary.wiley.com

Linehan, M. M. (1993). *Cognitive-behavioral treatment of borderline personality disorder*. New York, NY: Guilford Press.

Linehan, M. M., Armstrong, H. E., Suarez, A., Allmon, D., & Heard, H. L. (1991). Cognitive-behavioral treatment of chronically parasuicidal borderline patients. *Archives of General Psychiatry, 48*, 1060–1064. Retrieved from http://www.archgenpsychiatry.com

Linehan, M. M., Comtois, K. A., Murray, A. M., Brown, M. Z., Gallop, R. J., Heard, H. L., . . . Lindenboim, N. (2006). Two-year randomized controlled trial and follow-up of dialectical behavior therapy vs therapy by experts for suicidal behaviors and borderline personality disorder. *Archives of General Psychiatry, 62*, 1–10. Retrieved from http://www.archgenpsychiatry.com

Linehan, M. M., Heard, H. L., & Armstrong, H. E. (1993). Naturalistic follow-up of a behavioral treatment for chronically parasuicidal borderline patients. *Archives of General Psychiatry, 50,* 971–974. Retrieved from http://www.archgenpsychiatry.com

Lochman, J. E., Coie, J. D., Underwood, M. K., & Terry, R. (1993). Effectiveness of a social relations intervention program for aggressive and nonaggressive, rejected children. *Journal of Consulting and Clinical Psychology, 61,* 1053–1058. Retrieved from http://www.ft.csa.com

Luty, S. E., Carter, J. D., McKenzie, J. M., Rae, A. M., Frampton, C. M. A., Mulder, R. T., & Joyce, P. R. (2007). Randomised controlled trial of interpersonal psychotherapy and cognitive-behavioural therapy for depression. *British Journal of Psychiatry, 190,* 496–502. doi: 10.1192/bjp.bp.106.024729

Ma, S. H., & Teasdale, J. D. (2004). Mindfulness-based cognitive therapy for depression: Replication and exploration of differential relapse prevention effects. *Journal of Consulting and Clinical Psychology, 72,* 31–40. doi: 10.1037/0022–006x.72.1.31

Maier, S. F., Amat, J., Baratta, M. V., Paul, E., & Watkins, L. R. (2006). Behavioral control, the medial prefrontal cortex, and resilience. *Dialogues in Clinical Neuroscience, 8,* 353–373. Retrieved from http://www.dialogues-cns.org

Marks, I., Lovell, K., Noshirvani, H., Livanou, M., & Thrasher, S. (1998). Treatment of posttraumatic stress disorder by exposure and/or cognitive restructuring: A controlled study. *Archives of General Psychiatry, 55,* 317–325. Retrieved from http://www.archgenpsychiatry.com

Marlatt, G. A. (1983). The controlled-drinking controversy: A commentary. *American Psychologist, 38,* 1097–1110. Retrieved from http://www.ft.csa.com

Marlatt, A., & Gordon, J. (1985). *Relapse prevention: Maintenance strategies in the treatment of addictive behaviors.* New York, NY: Guilford Press.

Mayou, R. A., Ehlers, A., & Hobbs, M. (2000). Psychological debriefing for road traffic accident victims. *British Journal of Psychiatry, 176,* 589–593. doi: 10.1192/bjp.176.6.589

McCullough, J. P. (2000). *Treatment for chronic depression: Cognitive behavioral analysis system of psychotherapy.* New York, NY: Guilford Press.

McDonagh, A., Friedman, M., McHugo, G., Ford, J., Sengupta, A., Mueser, K., ... Descamps, M. (2005). Randomized trial of cognitive-behavioral therapy for chronic posttraumatic stress disorder in adult female survivors of childhood sexual abuse. *Journal of Consulting and Clinical Psychology, 73,* 515–524. doi: 10.1037/0022–006X.73.3.515

McHugh, R. K., Hearon, B. A., & Otto, M. W. (2010). Cognitive behavioral therapy for substance use disorders. *Psychiatric Clinics of North America, 33,* 511–525. doi: 10.1016/j.psc .2010.04.012

McIntosh, V., Jordan, J., Carter, F., Luty, S., McKenzie, J., Bulik, C., ... Joyce, P. R. (2005). Three psychotherapies for anorexia nervosa: A randomized controlled trial. *American Journal of Psychiatry, 162,* 741–747. Retrieved from http://www.ajp.psychiatryonline.org

McLean, P. D., Whittal, M. L., Thordarson, D. S., Taylor, S., Sochting, I., Koch, W. J., ... Anderson, K. W. (2001). Cognitive versus behavior therapy in the group treatment of obsessive-compulsive disorder. *Journal of Consulting and Clinical Psychology, 69,* 205–214. doi: 10.1037 //0022–006x.69.2.205

McMillan, D., & Lee, R. (2010). A systematic review of behavioral experiments vs exposure alone in the treatment of anxiety disorders: A case of exposure while wearing the emperor's new clothes? *Clinical Psychology Review, 30,* 467–478. doi: 10.1016/j.cpr.2010.01.003

Melvin, G. A., Tonge, B. J., King, N. J., Heyne, D., Gordon, M. S., & Klimkeit, E. (2006). A comparison of cognitive-behavioral therapy, sertraline, and their combination for adolescent depression. *Journal of the American Academy of Child and Adolescent Psychiatry, 45,* 1151–1161. doi: 10.1097/01.chi.0000233157.21925.71

Miklowitz, D. J., Otto, M. W., Frank, E., Reilly-Harrington, N. A., Wisniewski, S. R., Kogan, J. N., ... Sachs, G. S. (2007). Psychosocial treatments for bipolar depression: A 1-year randomized trial from the systematic treatment enhancement program. *Archives of General Psychiatry, 64,* 419–427. Retrieved from http://www .archgenpsychiatry.com

Miller, I. W., Norman, W. H., Keitner, G. I., Bishop, S. B., & Dow, M. G. (1989). Cognitive-behavioral treatment of depressed inpatients. *Behavior Therapy, 20,* 25–47. Retrieved from www.sciencedirect.com

Mitte, K. (2005a). A meta-analysis of the efficacy of psycho- and pharmacotherapy in panic disorder with and without agoraphobia. *Journal of Affective Disorders, 88,* 27–45. Retrieved from http://www.elsevier.com/locate/jad

Mitte, K. (2005b). Meta-analysis of cognitive-behavioral treatments for generalized anxiety disorder: A comparison with pharmacotherapy. *Psychological Bulletin, 131,* 785–795. doi: 10.1037/0033–2909.131.5.785

Monson, C. M., Schnurr, P. P., Resick, P. A., Friedman, M. J., Young-Xu, Y., & Stevens, S. P. (2006). Cognitive processing therapy for veterans with military-related posttraumatic stress disorder. *Journal of Consulting and Clinical Psychology, 74,* 898–907. doi: 10.1037/0022–006x.74.5.898

Mörtberg, E., Clark, D. M., & Bejerota, S. (2011). Intensive group cognitive therapy and individual cognitive therapy for social phobia: Sustained improvement at 5-year follow-up. *Journal of Anxiety Disorders, 25,* 994–1000. doi: 10.1016/j.janxdis.2011.06.007

Mörtberg, E., Clark, D. M., Sundin, O., & Aberg, W. A. (2007). Intensive group cognitive treatment and individual cognitive therapy vs treatment as usual in social phobia: A randomized controlled trial. *Acta Psychiatrica Scandinavica, 115,* 142–154. doi: 10.1111/j.1600–0447.2006.00839.x

Munsch, S., Biedert, E., Meyer, A., Michael, T., Schlup, B., Tuch, A., & Magraf, J. (2007). A randomized comparison of cognitive behavioral therapy and behavioral weight loss treatment for overweight individuals with binge eating disorder. *International Journal of Eating Disorders, 40,* 102–113. doi: 10.1002/eat.20350

Murray, C. J. L., & Lopez, A. D. (1997). Global mortality, disability, and the contribution of risk factors: Global burden of disease study. *Lancet, 349,* 1436–1442. Retrieved from http://www.ac.els-cdn.com

Mynors-Wallis, L. M., Gath, D. H., Day, A., & Baker, F. (2000). Randomized controlled trial of problem solving treatment, antidepressant medication, and combined treatment for major depression in primary care. *British Medical Journal, 320,* 26–30. doi: 10.1136/bmj.320.7226.26

Mynors-Wallis, L. M., Gath, D. H., Lloyd-Thomas, A. R., & Tomlinson, D. (1995). Randomised controlled trial comparing problem solving treatment with amitriptyline and placebo for major depression in primary care. *British Medical Journal, 310,* 441–445. Retrieved from http://bmj.bmjjournals.com/cgi/content/full/310/6977/441

National Institute for Health and Clinical Excellence. (2004). *Eating disorders—Core interventions in the treatment and management of anorexia nervosa, bulimia nervosa and related eating disorders.* NICE clinical guideline 9. Available from www.nice.org.uk/CG9

National Institute for Health and Clinical Excellence. (2005a). *Obsessive-compulsive disorder: Core interventions in the treatment of obsessive-compulsive disorder and body dysmorphic disorder.* NICE clinical guideline 31. Available from www.nice.org.uk/CG31

National Institute for Health and Clinical Excellence. (2005b). *Post-traumatic stress disorder (PTSD): The management of PTSD in adults and children in primary and secondary care.* NICE clinical guideline 26. Available from www.nice.org.uk/CG26

National Institute for Health and Clinical Excellence. (2005c). *Depression in children and young people: Identification and management in primary, community, and secondary care.* NICE clinical guideline 28. Available from www.nice.org.uk/CG28

National Institute for Health and Clinical Excellence. (2006). *Bipolar disorder: The management of bipolar disorder in adults, children and adolescents, in primary and secondary care.* NICE clinical guideline 38. Available from www.nice.org.uk/CG38

National Institute for Health and Clinical Excellence. (2007). *Anxiety: Management of anxiety (panic disorder, with or without agoraphobia, and generalized anxiety disorder) in adults in primary, secondary and community care.* NICE clinical guideline 22. Available from www.nice.org.uk/CG22

National Institute for Health and Clinical Excellence. (2009). *Schizophrenia: Core interventions in the treatment and management of schizophrenia in in adults in primary and secondary care.* NICE clinical guideline 82. Available from www.nice.org.uk/CG82

National Institute for Health and Clinical Excellence. (2010). *Depression: The treatment and management of depression in adults (updated edition).* NICE clinical guideline 90. Available from www.nice.org.uk/CG90

National Institute for Health and Clinical Excellence. (2011). *Generalised anxiety disorder in adults: Management in primary, secondary and community care.* NICE clinical guideline 113. Available from www.nice.org.uk/CG113

Newman, M. G., Castonguay, L. G., Borkovec, T. D., Fisher, A. J., Boswell, J. F., Szkodny, L. E., & Nordberg, S. S. (2011). A randomized controlled trial of cognitive-behavioral therapy for generalized anxiety disorder with integrated techniques from emotion-focused and interpersonal therapies. *Journal of Consulting and Clinical Psychology, 79,* 171–181. doi: 10.1037/a0022489

Nezu, A. M., & Perri, M. G. (1989). Social problem-solving therapy for unipolar depression: An initial dismantling investigation. *Journal of Consulting and Clinical Psychology, 57,* 408–413. Retrieved from http://www.apa.org/pubs/journals/ccp/index.aspx

Norcross, J. C., Karpiak, C. P., & Santoro, S. O. (2005). Clinical psychologists across the years: The division of clinical psychology from 1960 to 2003. *Journal of Clinical Psychology, 61,* 1467–1483. doi: 10.1002/jclp.20135

O'Connor, K. P., Aardema, F., Bouthillier, D., Fournier, S., Guay, S., Robillard, S., … Pitre, D. (2005). Evaluation of an inference-based approach to treating obsessive-compulsive disorder. *Cognitive Behavior Therapy, 34,* 148–163. Retrieved from http://www.tandf.co.uk/journals/titles/16506073.asp

Ollendick, T. H., Öst, L.-G., Reuterskiöld, L., Costa, N., Cederlund, R., Sirbu, C., … Jarrett, M. A. (2009). One-session treatment of specific phobias in youth: A randomized clinical trial in the United States and Sweden. *Journal of Consulting and Clinical Psychology, 77,* 504–516. doi: 10.1037/a0015158

Öst, L.-G. (1987). One-session treatments for a case of multiple simple phobias. *Scandinavian Journal of Behavior Therapy, 16,* 175–184. Retrieved from http://www.tandfonline.com/loi/sbeh19

Öst, L.-G. (1989). One-session treatment for specific phobias. *Behaviour Research and Therapy, 27,* 1–7. Retrieved from http://www.ac.els-cdn.com

Öst, L.-G., Alm, T., Brandberg, M., & Breitholtz, E. (2001). One vs. five sessions of exposure and five sessions of cognitive therapy in the treatment of claustrophobia. *Behaviour Research and Therapy,*

39, 167–183. Retrieved from http://www.ac.els-cdn.com

Öst, L.-G., Brandberg, M., & Alm, T. (1997). One versus five sessions of exposure in the treatment of flying phobia. *Behaviour Research and Therapy*, *35*, 987–996. Retrieved from http://www.ac.els-cdn.com

Öst, L.-G., Salkovskis, P., & Hellström, K. (1991). One-session therapist directed exposure vs. self-exposure in the treatment of spider phobia. *Behavior Therapy*, *22*, 407–422. Retrieved from www.sciencedirect.com

Paykel, E. S., Scott, J., Teasdale, J. D., Johnson, A. L., Garland, A., Moore, R., . . . Pope, M. (1999). Prevention of relapse in residual depression by cognitive therapy. *Archives of General Psychiatry*, *56*, 829–835. Retrieved from http://www.archgenpsychiatry.com

Pediatric OCD Treatment Study (POTS) Team. (2004). Cognitive-behavior therapy, sertraline, and their combination for children and adolescents with obsessive compulsive disorder: The pediatric OCD treatment study (POTS) randomized controlled trial. *JAMA*, *292*, 1969–1976. doi: 10.1001/jama.292.16.1969

Pike, K. M., Walsh, B. T., Vitousek, K., Wilson, G. T., & Bauer, J. (2003). Cognitive behavior therapy in the posthospitalization treatment of anorexia nervosa. *American Journal of Psychiatry*, *160*, 2046–2049. Retrieved from http://ajp.psychiatryonline.org

Pinto, A., La Pia, S., Mannella, R., Domenico, G., & DeSimone, L. (1999). Cognitive-behavioral therapy and clozapine for clients with treatment-refractory schizophrenia. *Psychiatric Services*, *50*, 901–904. Retrieved from http://www.ps.psychiatryonline.org

Ponniah, K., & Hollon, S. D. (2008). Empirically supported psychological interventions for social phobia in adults: A qualitative review of randomized controlled trials. *Psychological Medicine*, *38*, 3–14. doi: 10.1017/S0033291707000918

Ponniah, K., & Hollon, S. D. (2009). Empirically supported psychological treatments for adult acute stress disorder and posttraumatic stress disorder: A review. *Depression and Anxiety*, *26*, 1086–1109. doi: 10.1002/da.20635

Project MATCH Research Group. (1997). Matching alcoholism treatments to client heterogeneity: Project MATCH posttreatment drinking outcomes. *Journal of Studies on Alcohol*, *58*, 7–29. Retrieved from http://www.go.galegroup.com

Rachman, S. J. (1971). Obsessional ruminations. *Behaviour Research and Therapy*, *9*, 225–238. Retrieved from http://www.ac.els-cdn.com

Rachman, S. J. (2003). *The treatment of obsessions*. Oxford, United Kingdom: Oxford University Press.

Rathod, S., Phiri, P., & Kingdon, D. (2010). Cognitive behavioral therapy for schizophrenia. *Psychiatric Clinics of North America*, *33*, 527–536. doi: 10.1016/j.psc.2010.04.009

Rawson, R. A., Huber, A., McCann, M., Shoptaw, S., Farabee, D., Reiber, C., & Ling, W. (2002). A comparison of contingency management and cognitive-behavioral approaches during methadone maintenance treatment for cocaine dependence. *Archives of General Psychiatry*, *59*, 817–824. Retrieved from http://www.archgenpsychiatry.com

Resick, P. A., Galovski, T. E., Uhlmansiek, M. O., Scher, C. D., Clum, G. A., & Young-Xu, Y. (2008). A randomized clinical trial to dismantle components of cognitive processing therapy for posttraumatic stress disorder in female victims of interpersonal violence. *Journal of Consulting and Clinical Psychology*, *76*, 243–258. doi: 10.1037/0022–006x.76.2.243

Resick, P. A., Nishith, P., Weaver, T. L., Astin, M. C., & Feuer, C. A. (2002). A comparison of cognitive-processing therapy with prolonged exposure and a waiting condition for the treatment of chronic posttraumatic stress disorder in female rape victims. *Journal of Consulting and Clinical Psychology*, *70*, 867–879. doi: 10.1037//0022–006x.70.4.867

Resick, P. A., & Schnicke, M. K. (1993). *Cognitive processing therapy for rape victims: A treatment manual*. Newbury Park, CA: Sage.

Robinson, T., Smith, S. W., & Miller, M. (2002). Effect of a cognitive behavioral intervention on responses to anger by middle school students with chronic behavior problems. *Behavioral Disorders*, *27*, 256–271. Retrieved from http://www.go.galegroup.com

Salkovskis, P. M. (1999). Understanding and treating obsessive-compulsive disorder. *Behaviour Research and Therapy*, *37*(Suppl. 1), S29–S52. Retrieved from http://www.ac.els-cdn.com

Salkovskis, P. M., Atha, C., & Storer, D. (1990). Cognitive-behavioural problem solving in the treatment of patients who repeatedly attempt suicide: A controlled trial. *British Journal of Psychiatry*, *157*, 871–876. doi: 10.1192/bjp.157.6.871

Salzer, S., Winkelbach, C., Leweke, F., Leibing, E., & Leichsenring, F. (2011). Long-term effects of short-term psychodynamic psychotherapy and cognitive-behavioural therapy in generalized anxiety disorder: 12-month follow-up. *Canadian Journal of Psychiatry*, *56*, 503–508. Retrieved from http://www.publications.cpa-apc.org

Schnurr, P. P., Friedman, M. J., Engel, C. C., Foa, E. B., Shea, T., Chow, B. K., . . . Bernardy, N. (2007). Cognitive-behavioral therapy for posttraumatic stress disorder in women: A randomized controlled trial. *Journal of the American Medical Association*, *297*, 820–830. Retrieved from http://www.jama.com

Scott, J., Paykel, E., Morriss, R., Bentall, R., Kinderman, P., Johnson, T., . . . Hayhurst, H. (2006). Cognitive-behavioural therapy for severe and recurrent bipolar disorders. *British Journal of Psychiatry*, *188*, 313–320. doi: 10.1192/bjp.188.4.313

Segal, Z. S., Bieling, P., Young, T., MacQueen, G., Cooke, R., Martin, L.,...Levitan, R. D. (2010). Antidepressant monotherapy vs sequential pharmacotherapy and mindfulness-based cognitive therapy, or placebo, for relapse prophylaxis in recurrent depression. *Archives of General Psychiatry*, *67*, 1256–1264. Retrieved from http://www.archgenpsychiatry.com

Segal, Z. V., Williams, J. M. G., & Teasdale, J. D. (2002). *Mindfulness based cognitive therapy for depression—A new approach to preventing relapse*. New York, NY: Guilford Press.

Seivewright, H., Green, J., Salkovskis, P., Barrett, B., Nur, U., & Tyrer, P. (2008). Cognitive-behavioural therapy for health anxiety in a genitourinary medicine clinic: Randomised controlled trial. *British Journal of Psychiatry*, *193*, 332–337. doi: 10.1192/bjp.bp.108.052936

Sensky, T., Turkington, D., Kingdon, D., Scott, J. L., Scott, J., Siddle, R.,...Barnes, T. R. E. (2000). Cognitive-behavioural treatment for persistent symptoms in schizophrenia. *Archives of General Psychiatry*, *57*, 165–173. Retrieved from http://www.archgenpsychiatry.com

Shapiro, J. R., Berkman, N. D., Brownley, K. A., Sedway, J. A., Lohr, K. N., & Bulik, C. M. (2007). Bulimia nervosa treatment: A systematic review of randomized controlled trials. *International Journal of Eating Disorders*, *40*, 321–336. doi: 10.1002/eat

Shaw, B. F., Elkin, I., Yamaguchi, J., Olmsted, M., Vallis, T. M., Dobson, K. S.,...Imber, S. D. (1999). Therapist competence ratings in relation to clinical outcome in cognitive therapy of depression. *Journal of Consulting and Clinical Psychology*, *67*, 837–846. Retrieved from http://ft.csa.com

Shea, M. T., Elkin, I., Imber, S. D., Sotsky, S. M., Watkins, J. T., Collins, J. F.,...Parloff, M. B. (1992). Course of depressive symptoms over follow-up: Findings from the national institute of mental health treatment of depression collaborative research program. *Archives of General Psychiatry*, *49*, 782–787. Retrieved from http://www.archgenpsychiatry.com

Shea, M. T., Pilkonis, P. A., Beckham, E., Collins, J. F., Elkin, I., Sotsky, S. M., & Docherty, J. P. (1990). Personality disorders and treatment outcome in the NIMH Treatment of Depression Collaborative Research Program. *American Journal of Psychiatry*, *147*, 711–718. Retrieved from http://ajp.psychiatryonline.org

Siev, J., & Chambless, D. L. (2007). Specificity of treatment effects: Cognitive therapy and relaxation for generalized anxiety and panic disorders. *Journal of Consulting and Clinical Psychology*, *75*, 573–522. doi: 10.1037/0022–006x.75.4.513

Silverman, W. K., Kurtines, W. M., Ginsburg, G. S., Weems, C. F., Lumpkin, P. W., & Carmichael, D. H. (1999). Treating anxiety disorders in children with group cognitive-behavioral therapy: A randomized clinical trial. *Journal of Consulting and Clinical Psychology*, *67*, 995–1003. Retrieved from http://www.apa.org/pubs/journals/ccp/index.aspx

Silverman, W. K., Ortiz, C. D., Viswesvaran, C., Burns, B. J., Kolko, D. J., Putnam, F. W., & Amaya-Jackson, L. (2008). Evidence-based psychosocial treatments for children and adolescents exposed to traumatic events. *Journal of Clinical Child & Adolescent Psychology*, *37*, 156–183. doi: 10.1080/15374410701817907

Silverman, W. K., Pina, A. A., & Viswesvaran, C. (2008). Evidence-based psychosocial treatments for phobic and anxiety disorders in children and adolescents. *Journal of Clinical Child & Adolescent Psychology*, *37*, 105–130. doi: 10.1080/15374410701818293

Simons, A. D., Garfield, S. L., & Murphy, G. E. (1984). The process of change in cognitive therapy and pharmacotherapy for depression. *Archives of General Psychiatry*, *41*, 45–51. Retrieved from http://www.archgenpsychiatry.com

Simons, A. D., Murphy, G. E., Levine, J. L., & Wetzel, R. D. (1986). Cognitive therapy and pharmacotherapy for depression: Sustained improvement over one year. *Archives of General Psychiatry*, *43*, 43–48. Retrieved from http://www.archgenpsychiatry.com

Simpson, H. B., Liebowitz, M. R., Foa, E. B., Kozak, M. J., Schmidt, A. B., Rowan, V.,...Campeas, R. (2004). Post-treatment effects of exposure therapy and clomipramine in obsessive-compulsive disorder. *Depression and Anxiety*, *19*, 225–233. doi: 10.1002/da.20003

Smith, P., Yule, W., Perrin, S., Tranah, T., Dalgleish, T., & Clark, D. M. (2007). Cognitive-behavioral therapy for PTSD in children and adolescents: A preliminary randomized controlled trial. *Journal of the American Academy of Child and Adolescent Psychiatry*, *46*, 1051–1061. doi: 10.1097/chi.0b013e318067e288

Sousa, M. B., Isolan, L. R., Oliveira, R. R., Manfro, G. G., & Cordioli, A. V. (2006). A randomized clinical trial of cognitive-behavioral group therapy and sertraline in the treatment of obsessive-compulsive disorder. *Journal of Clinical Psychiatry*, *67*, 1133–1139. Retrieved from http://www.psychiatrist.com

Stangier, U., Heidenreich, T., Peitz, M., Lauterbach, W., & Clark, D. M. (2003). Cognitive therapy for social phobia: Individual versus group treatment. *Behaviour Research and Therapy*, *41*, 991–1007. doi:10.1016/S0005–7967(02)00176–6

Stangier, U., Schramm, E., Heidenreich, T., Berger, M., & Clark, D. M. (2011). Cognitive therapy vs interpersonal psychotherapy in social anxiety disorder: A randomized controlled trial. *Archives of General Psychiatry*, *68*, 692–700. Retrieved from http://www.archgenpsychiatry.com

Stanley, M. A., Beck, J. G., Novy, D. M., Averill, P. M., Swann, A. C., Diefenbach, G. J., & Hopko, D. R. (2003). Cognitive–behavioral treatment of late-life generalized anxiety disorder. *Journal of Consulting and Clinical Psychology*, 71, 309–319. doi: 10.1037/0022–006x.71.2.309

Stanley, M. A., Hopko, D. R., Diefenbach, G. J., Bourland, S. L., Rodriguez, H., & Wagener, P. (2003). Cognitive–behavior therapy for late-life generalized anxiety disorder in primary care: Preliminary findings. *American Journal of Geriatric Psychiatry*, 11, 92–96. Retrieved from http://www.ovidsp.tx.ovid.com

Stinson, F. S., Dawson, D. A., Chou, S. P., Smith, S., Goldstein, R. B., Ruan, W. J., & Grant, B. F. (2007). The epidemiology of DSM-IV specific phobia in the USA: Results from the national epidemiologic survey on alcohol and related conditions. *Psychological Medicine*, 37, 1047–1059. doi: 10.1017/s0033291707000086

Storch, E. A., Lewin, A. B., Farrell, L., Aldea, M. A., Reid, J., Geffken, G. R., & Murphy, T. K. (2010). Does cognitive-behavioral therapy response among adults with obsessive-compulsive disorder differ as a function of certain comorbidities? *Journal of Anxiety Disorders*, 24, 547–552. doi: 10.1016/j.janxdis.2010.03.013

Strunk, D. R., Brotman, M., DeRubeis, R. J., & Hollon, S. D. (2010). Therapist competence in cognitive therapy for depression: Predicting subsequent symptom change. *Journal of Consulting and Clinical Psychology*, 78, 429–437. doi: 10.1037/a0019631

Strunk, D. R., DeRubeis, R. J., Chiu, A. W., & Alvarez, J. (2007). Patients' competence in and performance of cognitive therapy skills: Relation to the reduction of relapse risk following treatment for depression. *Journal of Consulting and Clinical Psychology*, 75, 523–530. doi: 10.1037/0022–006x.75.4.523

Sundgot-Borgen, J., Rosenvinge, J. H., Bahr, R., & Schneider, L. S. (2002). The effect of exercise, cognitive therapy, and nutritional counseling in treating bulimia nervosa. *Medicine & Science in Sports & Exercise*, 34, 190–195. Retrieved from http://www.journals.lww.com/acsm-msse/pages/default.aspx

Svetkey, L. P., Stevens, V. J., Brantley, P. J., Appel, L. J., Hollis, J. F., Loria, C. M., . . . Weight Loss Maintenance Collaborative Research Group. (2008). Comparison of strategies for sustaining weight loss: The weight maintenance randomized controlled trial. *JAMA*, 299, 1139–1148. doi: 10.1001/jama.299.10.1139

Tang, T. Z., & DeRubeis, R. J. (1999). Sudden gains and critical sessions in cognitive-behavioral therapy for depression. *Journal of Consulting and Clinical Psychology*, 67, 894–904. Retrieved from http://www.apa.org/pubs/journals/ccp/index.aspx

Tang, T. Z., DeRubeis, R. J., Hollon, S. D., Amsterdam, J. D., & Shelton, R. C. (2007). Sudden gains in cognitive therapy of depression and relapse/recurrence. *Journal of Consulting and Clinical Psychology*, 75, 404–408. doi: 10.1037/0022–006x.75.3.404

Tarrier, N., Beckett, R., Harwood, S., Baker, A., Yusupoff, L., & Ugarteburu, I. (1993). A trial of two cognitive-behavioural methods of treating drug-resistant residual psychotic symptoms in schizophrenic patients: I. Outcome. *British Journal of Psychiatry*, 162, 524–532. doi: 10.1192/bjp.162.4.524

Tarrier, N., Kinney, C., McCarthy, E., Humphreys, L., Wittkowski, A., & Morris, J. (2000). Two-year follow-up of cognitive-behavioral therapy and supportive counseling in the treatment of persistent symptoms in chronic schizophrenia. *Journal of Consulting and Clinical Psychology*, 68, 917–922. Retrieved from http://www.apa.org/pubs/journals/ccp/index.aspx

Tarrier, N., Pilgrim, H., Sommerfield, C., Faragher, B., Reynolds, M., Graham, E., & Barrowclough, C. (1999). A randomized trial of cognitive therapy and imaginal exposure in the treatment of chronic posttraumatic stress disorder. *Journal of Consulting and Clinical Psychology*, 67, 13–18. Retrieved from http://www.apa.org/pubs/journals/ccp/index.aspx

Tarrier, N., Yusupoff, L., Kinney, C., McCarthy, E., Gledhill, A., Haddock, G., & Morris, J. (1998). A randomised controlled trial of intensive cognitive behaviour therapy for chronic schizophrenia. *British Medical Journal*, 317, 303–307. Retrieved from http://www.ncbi.nlm.nih.gov

Teasdale, J. D., Scott, J., Moore, R. G., Hayhurst, H., Pope, M., & Paykel, E. S. (2001). How does cognitive therapy prevent relapse in residual depression? Evidence from a controlled trial. *Journal of Consulting and Clinical Psychology*, 69, 347–357. doi: 10.10377/W22–006X.69.3.347

Teasdale, J. D., Segal, Z., & Williams, J. M. G. (1995). How does cognitive therapy prevent depressive relapse and why should attentional control (mindfulness) training help? *Behaviour Research and Therapy*, 33, 25–39. Retrieved from http://www.ac.els-cdn.com

Teasdale, J. D., Segal, Z., Williams, J. M. G., Ridgeway, V. A., Soulsby, J. M., & Lau, M. A. (2000). Prevention of relapse/recurrence in major depression by mindfulness-based cognitive therapy. *Journal of Consulting and Clinical Psychology*, 68, 615–623. doi: 10.1037//0022–006x.68.4.615

Tenneij, N. H., van Megen, H. J. G. M., Denys, D. A. J. P., & Westenberg, H. G. M. (2005). Behavior therapy augments response of patients with obsessive-compulsive disorder responding to drug treatment. *Journal of Clinical Psychiatry*, 66, 1169–1175. Retrieved from http://www.psychiatrist.com

Thorpe, S. J., & Salkovskis, P. M. (1997). The effect of one-session treatment for spider phobia on attentional bias and beliefs. *British Journal of Clinical Psychology, 36,* 225–241. Retrieved from http://www.proquest.umi.com

Treatment for Adolescents with Depression Study (TADS) Team. (2004). Fluoxetine, cognitive-behavioral therapy, and their combination for adolescents with depression: Treatment for Adolescents with Depression Study (TADS) randomized controlled trial. *JAMA, 292,* 807–820. Retrieved from http://www.jama.com

Turk, M. W., Yang, K., Hravnak, M., Sereika, S. M., Ewing, L. J., & Burke, L. E. (2009). Randomized clinical trials of weight loss maintenance: A review. *Journal of Cardiovascular Nursing, 24,* 58–80. doi: 10.1097/01.jcn.0000317471.58048.32

Van Asselt, A. D., Dirksen, C. D., Arntz, A., Giesen-Bloo, J. H., van Dyck, R., Spinhoven, P.,...Severens, J. L. (2008). Out-patient psychotherapy for borderline personality disorder: Cost-effectiveness of schema-focused therapy v. transference-focused psychotherapy. *British Journal of Psychiatry, 192,* 450–457. doi: 10.1192/bjp.bp.106.033597

van Balkom, A. J. L. M., de Haan, E., van Oppen, P. Spinhoven, P., Hoogduin, K. A., & van Dyck, R. (1998). Cognitive and behavioral therapies alone versus in combination with fluvoxamine in the treatment of obsessive compulsive disorder. *Journal of Nervous and Mental Disease, 186,* 492–499. Retrieved from http://www.ovidsp.tx.ovid.com

Van Manen, T. G., Prins, P. J., & Emmelkamp, P. M. (2004). Reducing aggressive behavior in boys with a social cognitive group treatment: Results of a randomized, controlled trial. *Journal of the American Academy of Child and Adolescent Psychiatry, 43,* 1478–1487. Retrieved from http://www.sciencedirect.com

van Oppen, P., de Haan, E., van Balkom, A., Spinhoven, P., Hoogduin, K., & van Dyck, R. (1995). Cognitive therapy and exposure in vivo in the treatment of obsessive compulsive disorder. *Behaviour Research and Therapy, 33,* 379–390. Retrieved from http://www.ac.els-cdn.com

Verheul, R., van den Bosch, M. C., Koeter, M. W. J., de Ridder, M. A. J., Stijnen, T., & van den Brink, W. (2003). Efficacy of dialectical behavior therapy: A Dutch randomised controlled trial. *British Journal of Psychiatry, 182,* 135–140. doi: 10.1192/bjp.02.184

Visser, S., & Bouman, T. K. (2001). The treatment of hypochondriasis: Exposure plus response prevention vs cognitive therapy. *Behaviour Research and Therapy, 39,* 423–442. Retrieved from http://www.elsevier.com/locate/brat

Vitousek, K., Watson, S., & Wilson, G. T. (1998). Enhancing motivation for change in treatment-resistant eating disorders. *Clinical Psychology Review, 18,* 391–420. Retrieved from http://www.ac.els-cdn.com

Vogel, P. A., Stiles, T. C., & Gotestam, K. G. (2004). Adding cognitive therapy elements to exposure therapy for obsessive compulsive disorder: A controlled study. *Behavioural and Cognitive Psychotherapy, 32,* 275–290. Retrieved from http://www.journals.cambridge.org/action/displayJournal?jid=BCP

Walkup, J. T., Albano, A. M., Piacentini, J., Birmaher, B., Compton, S. N., Sherrill, J. T.,...Kendall, P. C. (2008). Cognitive behavioral therapy, sertraline, or a combination in childhood anxiety. *New England Journal of Medicine, 359,* 1–14. doi: 10.1056/NEJMoa0804633

Walsh, B. T., Wilson, G. T., Loeb, K. L., Devlin, M. J., Pike, K. M., Roose, S. P.,...Waternaux, C. (1997). Medication and psychotherapy in the treatment of bulimia nervosa. *American Journal of Psychiatry, 154,* 523–531. Retrieved from http://ajp.psychiatryonline.org

Warwick, H. M. C., Clark, D. M., Cobb, A. M., & Salkovskis, P. M. (1996). A controlled trial of cognitive-behavioural treatment of hypochondriasis. *British Journal of Psychiatry, 169,* 189–195. doi: 10.1192/bjp.169.2.189

Warwick, H. M. C., & Salkovskis, P. M. (1990). Hypochondriasis. *Behaviour Research and Therapy, 28,* 105–117. Retrieved from http://www.ac.els-cdn.com

Webb, C. A., DeRubeis, R. J., & Barber, J. P. (2010). Therapist adherence/competence and treatment outcome: A meta-analytic review. *Journal of Consulting & Clinical Psychology, 78,* 200–211. doi: 10.1037/a0018912

Weissman, M. M., Verdeli, H., Gameroff, M. J., Bledsoe, S. E., Betts, K., Mufson, L.,...Wickramaratne, P. (2006). National survey of psychotherapy training in psychiatry, psychology, and social work. *Archives of General Psychiatry, 63,* 925–934. Retrieved from http://www.archgenpsychiatry.com

Weisz, J. R., McCarty, C. A., & Valeri, S. M. (2006). Effects of psychotherapy for depression in children and adolescents: A meta-analysis. *Psychological Bulletin, 132,* 132–149. doi: 10.1037/0033-2909.132.1.132

Weisz, J. R., Thurber, C. A., Sweeney, L., Proffitt, V. D., & LeGagnoux, G. L. (1997). Brief treatment of mild to moderate child depression using primary and secondary control enhancement training. *Journal of Consulting and Clinical Psychology, 65,* 703–707. Retrieved from http://www.apa.org/pubs/journals/ccp/index.aspx

Wells, A., Welford, M., King, P., Papageorgiou, Wisely, J., & Mendel, E. (2010) A pilot randomized trial of metacognitive therapy vs applied relaxation in the treatment of adults with generalized anxiety disorder. *Behaviour Research and Therapy*, *48*, 429–434. doi: 10.1016/j.brat.2009.11.013

Wetherell, J. L., Gatz, M., & Craske, M. G. (2003). Treatment of generalized anxiety disorder in older adults. *Journal of Consulting and Clinical Psychology*, *71*, 31–40. doi: 10.1037/0022–006x.71.1.31

Whitaker, R. (2010). *Anatomy of an epidemic: Magic bullets, psychiatric drugs, and the astonishing rise of mental illness in America*. New York, NY: Crown.

Whittal, M. L., Thordarson, D. S., & McLean, P. D. (2005). Treatment of obsessive-compulsive disorder: Cognitive behavior therapy vs. exposure and response prevention. *Behaviour Research and Therapy*, *43*, 1559–1576. doi: 10.1016/j.brat.2004.11.012

Whittal, M. L., Woody, S. R., McLean, P. D., Rachman, S. J., & Robichaud, M. (2010). Treatment of obsessions: A randomized controlled trial. *Behaviour Research and Therapy*, *48*, 295–303. doi: 10.1016/j.brat.2009.11.010

Wilfley, D. E., Agras, W. S., Telch, C. F., Rossiter, E. M., Schneider, J. A., Cole, A. G., . . . Raeburn, S. D. (1993). Group cognitive-behavioral therapy and group interpersonal psychotherapy for the non-purging bulimic individual: A controlled comparison. *Journal of Consulting and Clinical Psychology*, *61*, 296–305. Retrieved from http://www.apa.org/pubs/journals/ccp/index.aspx

Williams, J. W., Barrett, J., Oxman T., Frank, E., Katon, W., Sullivan, M., . . . Sengupta, A. (2000). Treatment of dysthymia and minor depression in primary care: A randomized controlled trial in older adults. *JAMA*, *284*, 1519–1526. Retrieved from http://www.jama.ama-assn.org

Wilson, G. T. (2011). Treatment of binge eating disorder. *Psychiatric Clinics of North America*, *34*, 773–783. doi: 10.1016/j.psc.2011.08.011

Wilson, G. T., & Agras, W. S. (2001). Practice guidelines for eating disorders. *Behavior Therapy*, *32*, 219–234. Retrieved from www.sciencedirect.com

Wilson, G. T., Fairburn, C. G., Agras, W. S., Walsh, B. T., & Kraemer, H. (2002). Cognitive–behavioral therapy for bulimia nervosa: Time course and mechanisms of change. *Journal of Consulting and Clinical Psychology*, *70*, 267–274. doi: 10.1037//0022–006x.70.2.267

Wilson, G. T., Vitousek, K. M., & Loeb, K. L. (2000). Stepped care treatment for eating disorders. *Journal of Consulting and Clinical Psychology*, *68*, 564–572. doi: 10.1037//0022–006X.68.4.564

Wilson, G. T., Wilfley, D. E., Agras, W. S., & Bryson, S. W. (2010). Psychological treatments for binge eating disorder. *Archives of General Psychiatry*, *67*, 94–101. Retrieved from http://www.archgenpsychiatry.com

Wing, R. R., Tate, D. F., Gorin, A. A., Raynor, H. A., & Fava, J. L. (2006). A self-regulation program for maintenance of weight loss. *New England Journal of Medicine*, *355*, 1563–1571. Retrieved from http://www.proquest.umi.com

Wykes, T., Steel, C., Everitt, B., & Tarrier, N. (2008). Cognitive behavior therapy for schizophrenia: Effect sizes, clinical models, and methodological rigor. *Schizophrenia Bulletin*, *34*(3), 523–537. doi: 10.1093/schbul/sbm114

Young, J. E. (1994). *Cognitive therapy for personality disorders: A schema-focused approach* (rev. ed.). Sarasota, FL: Professional Resource Press.

Young, J., Klosko, J., & Weishaar, M. (2003). *Schema therapy: A practitioner's guide*. New York, NY: Guilford Press.

Zlomke, K., & Davis, T. E. III. (2008). One-session treatment of specific phobias: A detailed description and review of treatment efficacy. *Behavior Therapy*, *39*, 207–223. Retrieved from http://www.elsevier.com/locate/bt

RESEARCH ON DYNAMIC THERAPIES

JACQUES P. BARBER, J. CHRISTOPHER MURAN, KEVIN S. MCCARTHY, AND JOHN R. KEEFE

Once psychoanalysis or psychodynamic therapy ruled the earth. Unlike the dinosaurs, it did not disappear but rather sprouted many variations and new offspring. Today those offspring have forgotten everything about their origins.

A chapter on dynamic therapy (DT) has been omitted from some editions of this handbook. Not including one may have been seen as somewhat consistent with the decrease in the place and importance of psychodynamic psychotherapies in academic psychology, especially in English-speaking countries. However, we think the under-representation of DT is unfortunate, as its main ideas are at the foundation of many forms of psychotherapy, including recently developed ones (e.g., Summers & Barber, 2009). Ignoring and neglecting the historical legacy and clinical wisdom of dynamic therapy may adversely impact clinical care (e.g., the role of emotions, implicit cognitions, and defenses). It is quite clear (e.g., Summers & Barber, 2009) that many forms of therapy evolved from psychoanalysis, including cognitive and humanistic therapies. Some of the important theorists behind these relatively newer approaches were trained as psychoanalysts (e.g., A. T. Beck, Fritz Perls, Albert Ellis) and for various reasons were dissatisfied with major aspects of psychoanalysis. Thus, these influential individuals went on to make improvements over psychoanalysis and developed their own version of therapy. In their attempts to define their new approach to treatment, they emphasized what was different from psychoanalysis and perhaps minimized what they took with them from those therapies (e.g., the importance of the therapeutic relationship and encouraging a more realistic view of the world). However, more relevant to the present volume is the awakening of psychodynamically oriented

researchers in the past two decades. Specifically, there has been an increase in empirical evidence for the efficacy of these DT for specific disorders as well as investigations on how and for whom DT might be helpful, as we will show.

Characteristics of DT

This chapter covers approaches to psychotherapy generally referred to as *psychodynamic* or *analytic*. DT—as well as cognitive-behavior therapy (CBT) for that matter—represents a family of therapies. As in all large families, the degrees of divergence and agreement vary quite a bit. Some members of the families are not even on speaking terms and sometimes even speak different languages. Thus, by necessity, this chapter presents a narrow representation of the psychodynamic family of therapies. Under this large umbrella, there are many approaches, which vary in their understanding of what is the nature of "disease" or "problem" (pathology) and on how to resolve or help deal with them. Most schools of therapy derive their view of pathology and intervention from a theory of human nature that includes, among others, a theory of personality and development. We hesitate to state a view of human nature that would be acceptable to all streams of DT. We would say that psychodynamics would involve recognizing that people are not always aware of the reasons for their behavior, that human motivations are to some extent rooted biologically, and that they are often driven by unknown motives.

Similarly, it would be wonderful if we could easily define what DT is and what it is not. There have been several attempts to characterize psychodynamic psychotherapy (e.g., Blagys & Hilsenroth, 2000); however, it would be almost impossible to find a set of necessary and sufficient conditions to define what is psychodynamic. Nevertheless, DT can be captured by the following characteristics: focus on unconscious processes; focus on affect, cognitions, wishes, fantasies and interpersonal relationships; lack of traditional homework; relatively less guidance, use of open-ended questions; use of interpretation and clarification; consideration of the transference and countertransference; and use of the therapeutic relationship to increase self-awareness, self-understanding, and exploration.

One of the questions we needed to address is whether interpersonal therapy (IPT; Klerman, Weissman, Rounsaville, & Chevron, 1984), popular in the treatment of depression, is a form of DT. IPT is similar to many DTs because it focuses on underlying schemas and repetitive scenarios involving loss and transition, and uses empathy, exploration of painful affects, and (rarely) transference interpretations. It differs in that it is highly focused and includes a significant educational component. In fact, there is research to suggest that in practice IPT is more like CBT than DT (e.g., Ablon & Jones, 2002). Our opinion is that depending on the training of the IPT therapists (e.g., their previous exposure to DT or the extent of their IPT training), the differences between IPT and DT can be elusive. Some meta-analyses of DT (e.g., Leichsenring 2001) included studies of IPT and showed that the overall meta-analytic results were unchanged if excluded. To be conservative, we decided not to include IPT as a form of DT therapy, mainly due to its explicit rejection of some critical dynamic concepts.

In this chapter we cover three general aspects of DT: its efficacy for symptom improvement; the therapeutic alliance and its role in DT; and processes of change, including mechanisms and outcome unique to DT and the correlates of DT techniques.

RESEARCH ON ADDRESSING THE EFFICACY OF DT

In the past two decades, there have been increasingly more studies examining the therapeutic

efficacy of DT (e.g., Shedler, 2010).[1] However, it seems that the number of meta-analyses has increased even more. The majority of these meta-analyses have focused on short-term DT (STDP) rather than long-term DT (LTDP) or psychoanalysis (for notable exceptions concerning possible LTDP superiority over controls and less intense treatments, see Leichsenring & Rabung, 2008, 2011; Smit et al., 2012). Briefly speaking, STDP differs from LTDP in that it generally: (a) takes place in a shorter, often time-limited format (usually at least 8 sessions, often 12 to 20, but sometimes up to 40 depending on the manual, disorder, etc.); (b) typically targets specific symptomatic versus global or structural change; and (c) does so by often identifying and working through a relatively specific dynamic-interpersonal focus conceptualized to underlie expressed psychopathology (e.g., a patient's core-conflictual relationship theme [CCRT] in Luborsky's [1984] supportive-expressive therapy [SE]).

Interventions in STDP are often classified as being on a continuum of "expressive" to "supportive" (Luborsky, 1984). Broadly, expressive (or interpretive) techniques such as transference and defense interpretations seek to augment patient insight and understanding of in-the-moment or repetitive interpersonal and intrapsychic patterns or conflicts. Insight or self-understanding may allow a patient to better tolerate distressing thoughts, affects, and fantasies that are defended against in a way that creates psychopathology; insight might also potentiate working through repetitive intrapsychic and interpersonal dynamics previously disavowed, misunderstood, or unknown. Supportive techniques are conceived both in terms of building the therapeutic alliance and of boosting client capacity to use extant healthy capabilities (e.g., adaptive defenses, social networks) when such a capacity may be compromised (see later in the chapter for a more extensive discussion on both the alliance and dynamic

---

[1] Due to space restrictions, our original chapter was sharply shortened as we approached our publication deadline. In particular, we had to cut our reference list by more than 50%. We also removed several additional meta-analyses that we had conducted in preparation for this chapter. For space reasons we were required to eliminate references of many studies and meta-analyses, of measures used, and of many theoretical manuals underpinning delivered treatments. We apologize in advance to researchers whose work we are not citing.

interventions). Expressive and supportive interventions are often thought to work synergistically to promote patient change. For example, supportive interventions may create a positive "holding" environment involving therapist and patient that serves as a uniquely safe interpersonal space for: (a) experiments in self-change (e.g., trying out diferent modes of relating through the therapist-patient interaction); (b) expressive exploration of thoughts, feelings, and fantasies; and (c) experiencing emotions and insights in an impactful way as a result of reduced defensivenss.

Generally, previous meta-analyses of DT reached one or more of the following four different conclusions: (1) DT outcome does not differ from alternative therapies (e.g., for DT across disorders, see Leichsenring, Rabung, & Leibing, 2004; for depression, see Leichsenring, 2001; for personality disorders, see Leichsenring & Leibing, 2003); (2) there are small ES differences in favor of DT (e.g., Anderson & Lambert, 1995, at follow-up in some analyses of DT); (3) there are small differences in favor of alternative treatments across disorders (e.g., Tolin, 2010, as compared to some CBTs, though including controls as DT treatments) or in depression specifically (e.g., Driessen et al., 2010 finding a small difference at termination but not follow-up); and (4) DT is significantly superior to control treatments (e.g., for DT across disorders, see Abbass, Hancock, Henderson, & Kisely, 2006; Leichsenring et al., 2004; for somatic conditions specifically, see Abbass, Kisely, & Kroenke, 2009).

In a representative and rigorous meta-analysis of patients with different disorders, Leichsenring et al. (2004) identified 17 well-conducted post-1970 studies of STDP, and found that STDPs yielded large pretreatment-posttreatment ESs for target problems ($d = 1.39$), general psychiatric symptoms ($d = .90$), and social functioning ($d = .80$). The ESs of STDP significantly exceeded those of waiting-list controls ($d = .27$) and treatments as usual ($d = .55$) for treatment of target problems. No significant differences were found between STDP and other forms of psychotherapy at either termination or follow-up.

Meta-analyses have also differed in their inclusion criteria; some of them included any study that mentioned DT while others were more selective. For example, a recent Cochrane review of STDP by Abbass et al. (2006) found 57 studies of STDP, but excluded 34 studies for various design issues, mostly because they did not have a control treatment group. They also excluded studies that had more than a 20% dropout rate. Nevertheless, their meta-analysis included 23 RCTs comprising 1,431 patients, and found moderate-to-large between-groups ES advantages for STDP over control groups on measures of general psychopathology, anxiety, and depression at termination, short-term and long-term follow-up.

Keeping in mind that there are few high-quality studies of DT (Gerber et al., 2011; see also Thoma et al., 2012, for a similar finding in the CBT literature), we considered different inclusion criteria with the wish to include only studies that had the potential to be high quality. We considered strictly following the criteria used by the task force of Division 12 of the American Psychological Association for designating psychotherapies as empirically supported (Task Force on Promotion and Dissemination of Psychological Procedures, 1995; Chambless & Hollon, 1998), as the most convincing evidence for the scientific world and for governmental agencies comes from RCTs. We recognized that these criteria are controversial (e.g., Westen, Novonty, & Thompson-Brenner, 2004) and that RCTs have unique drawbacks in psychotherapy research. Those drawbacks may be more pronounced for the study of DT, which may for example require on the part of the patient a certain amount of psychological mindedness and willingness to introspect to have a chance of working (cf. Barber, 2009). Because manualized DTs seldom include session-by-session guidelines, we included studies where manualization was not definite and to test whether manualization makes a difference.

Methodology for the Meta-Analysis

The inconsistency of results across existing meta-analyses could have been the result of inconsistencies on whether the analysis focused on a specific disorder or not, or whether they included only RCTs or any outcome study. As a way to address those issues and to be consistent with recent trends, we focused on addressing the question of whether DT is effective for the treatment of specific disorders or disorder groups. This resulted in a series of separate meta-analyses for the following disorder groups: depression, anxiety disorders, and personality disorders.

Study Inclusion Criteria

The primary sample of DT studies reviewed and meta-analyzed was taken from the Gerber et al. (2011) quality-based review of RCTs of DT. We used the same terms to search for more recent publications. In addition, we reexamined past reviews and meta-analyses for studies missed in the aforementioned searches and contacted experts in the field for citations for recently completed studies.

To be included, a study had to be an RCT comparing individual DT for adults to either a control condition (e.g., TAU, wait list) or alternative non-DT intervention (e.g., CBT, pharmacotherapy). However, we did include mentalization-based treatment (MBT; Bateman & Fonagy, 2006)—which includes group therapy—as it is a state-of-the-art, well-defined DT for borderline personality disorder and does include a strong individual component. For similar reasons, we included dialectical-behavioral therapy (DBT) as a comparison treatment despite it consisting of both individual and group therapies. We excluded studies that had an eclectic treatment incorporating dynamic ideas. We also did not include studies comparing combined DT and pharmacotherapy (e.g., SSRI) to another combined group using a different therapy (e.g., CBT + SSRI).

Statistical Analyses

Calculations of weighted mean effect size (ES), heterogeneity, and moderator analyses were conducted using Comprehensive Meta-Analysis, version 2.2.046 (Borenstein et al., 2005); a priori, it was decided to conduct our meta-analyses using a random-effects model for a more stringent and generalizable test of the efficacy of DT. For our ES measure, we used Hedge's g—similar to the traditional Cohen's d, but corrected for upward bias (Hedges, 1981). Both g and d are ES statistics standardized by standard deviations units, wherein a g/d of 1.00 indicates that the difference between two means is one (pooled) standard deviation unit large. Values of 0.20, 0.50, and 0.80 are considered small, medium, and large effects, respectively, in social science research, although these conventions apply only to between-group ESs (Cohen, 1992).

Between-groups ESs using outcome scores on continuous measures were meta-analyzed. In the event of incomplete reporting of scores, ESs were imputed or estimated from available data and reported statistical tests as per Lipsey and Wilson (2001). For overall analyses, ESs calculated from scores were chosen over ESs calculated from binary outcomes (e.g., remission) if available, except as noted. When relevant data or tests were not available, attempts were made to contact corresponding authors.[2] Meta-analyses were performed for outcomes at termination, and—when at least three relevant studies with data were available—at short-term follow-up (3 to 9 months posttermination) and long-term follow-up (> 9 months posttermination) periods.

So as to not violate independence when comparing DT to multiple active treatments within the same study (e.g., behavioral therapy and cognitive therapy in Gallagher & Thompson, 1982), data from active treatment groups were collapsed and used to calculate overall ESs and variance as per formulas in the Cochrane Handbook for Systematic Reviews of Interventions (2011). Similarly, when multiple bona fide DTs were performed within the same study (e.g., transference-focused therapy and manualized dynamic-supportive therapy in Clarkin, Levy, Lenzenweger, & Kernberg, 2007), data from these groups were collapsed using the same methodology.

However, for one meta-analysis (depression), we had a sample of studies that allowed us to explore whether DT was differently efficacious from medication and/or alternative psychotherapies. Because it would be invalid to include the same study twice, as it would violate ES-independence criteria for meta-analysis, we included in a particular moderation analysis only the between-groups ES for the treatment type as the focus of that moderation.

Heterogeneity of ESs was examined using the Q statistic and the I^2 index (Higgins & Thompson, 2002). Significant Q statistics indicate that the observed range of ES is significantly larger than what would otherwise be expected based on within-study variances; the I^2 index is a quantification of this heterogeneity, with 25%, 50%, and 75% reflecting respectively low, medium, and high heterogeneity. Robustness of meta-analytic results was also examined by performing a sensitivity analysis to see if a given result relied on the ES of a single study.

---

[2] Notably, we did receive data from the Clarkin et al. (2007) study of dynamic and DBT treatment of BPD. They sent us estimated pre- and post scores based on the hierarchical linear models they ran to analyze their three treatment groups—as they were the best data available for this study, we used these score estimates in our meta-analyses.

Regardless of observed heterogeneity for a given meta-analysis, exploratory analyses were conducted to assess for moderators of ES. Moderators are categorical (e.g., manualization status) or continuous (e.g., quality score) characteristics of studies, used to predict outcome (i.e., ES). Categorical moderators were assessed using an analysis of variance (ANOVA) of mixed-effects models for each variable hypothesized to influence the ES. Meta-regression analyses using a maximum-likelihood model were conducted to assess the effects of continuous moderators, including an index of study quality scores using the Randomized Controlled Trial Psychotherapy Quality Rating Scale (RCT-PQRS; Kocsis et al., 2010). When describing included studies, we reported both total quality scores (ranging from 0 to 48) and subjective Item 25 "omnibus" study quality rating (1 to 7; 1 being extremely poor, 7 being exceptionally good). Gerber et al. (2011) demarcate a total score of 24 as the minimum for an adequate quality study. If RCT-PQRS scores were not available from Gerber et al. (2011), studies were instead scored by two independent graduate students who attained excellent agreement ($ICC = .97$). With the exception of some comparisons in our depression meta-analysis, all moderator analyses should be considered highly exploratory due to low ($n < 10$) study sample size (see guidelines from Higgins & Green, 2011). Low study sample size may mean that there is not enough data for the moderation to be generalized, may not have enough power to find an extant effect, and can lead to biased results due to heightened effects of between-study characteristic confounds and nonrandom clustering of study characteristics. However, we performed moderator analyses in the interests of synthesizing a preliminary picture of the current state of the literature and to perhaps direct future research questions and analyses. Descriptions of precise moderator findings have sometimes been truncated for space reasons, but we always reported on moderators if significant at least at trend level ($p < .10$).

Publication bias was assessed by examination of publication bias funnel plots and Duval and Tweedie's (2000) trim-and-fill procedure. When asymmetry was evident in the funnel plot, we applied Duval and Tweedie's trim-and-fill procedure to provide an adjusted ES estimate that corrects for the number and assumed location of the missing studies.

Mood Disorders

Reflecting the variety of DTs and STDPs, studies reporting on DT for unipolar depression have used different forms of therapy. From a dynamic perspective, the essential issues in depression are loss and guilt over loss, along with low self-esteem and failures in the attempt to restore self-esteem (Freud, 1917). Treatment generally involves: (a) encouraging greater activity in the patient and instillation of hope; (b) identification of major losses, anger, conflict over anger, guilt, as well as the cycle of self-esteem restoration; and (c) proactive attempt to understand vulnerability in situations and change in response and behavior to prevent recurrence (e.g., Busch, Rudden, & Shapiro, 2004; Summers & Barber, 2009).

There have been two previous meta-analyses focusing on STDP for depression. Leichsenring (2001) meta-analyzed seven studies comparing STDP to CBT, finding no significant differences between them in either outcome scores or rates of remission/response. The most recent meta-analysis (Driessen et al., 2010) included a larger sample of 23 studies: 10 of them were not RCTs, and covered both individual and group therapy for depression. Using data from 13 RCTs, unlike Leichsenring the authors found that STDP was more effective than control groups ($d = 0.80$) but less effective than alternative treatments ($d = -0.35$) at termination, though this difference was not found at follow-up. Driessen et al. did not find significant moderators apart from an advantage of individual over group therapies using uncontrolled ES.

In our meta-analysis, we have tended to be inclusive rather than exclusive. However, we excluded studies where DT was delivered in combination with other treatments. We also sought to explore moderators not investigated by previous meta-analyses—such as type of alternative treatments, impact of study quality, and addition of pharmacotherapy. Our preferred outcome measure (if available) was the Hamilton Rating Scale for Depression (HRSD).

Controlled Comparisons

The comparison of DT for depression to control conditions (two "treatment as usuals" [TAUs], one wait list, and one pill-placebo) suggested a moderate controlled ES (study $n = 4$, subject $n = 303$, $g = 0.457$ [0.097 to 0.818], $p = 0.013$, fail-safe N of 12). Heterogeneity was found at a trend level ($Q = 6.794$, $I^2 = 55.846$, $p = 0.079$).

Although we did not find any significant categorical moderators, there was a trend indicating that better study quality was associated with smaller controlled ES (slope $= -0.0368$, total model $p = 0.079$; see Cuijpers, van Straten, Bohlmeijer, Hollon, Andersson, 2010, for a similar finding in the depression literature overall). As patient population varied highly between studies (e.g., severity, duration, comorbidity), our findings should be interpreted cautiously.

Active Treatment Comparisons

At termination, DT and alternative treatments did not differ (study $n = 11$, subject $n = 830$, $g = -0.115$ [-0.257 to 0.026], $p = .110$), with no significant heterogeneity among ESs. This result was sensitive to the removal of Cooper et al. (2003), which results in an estimate of a small ES benefit to using alternative treatments over DT (study $n = 10$, subject $n = 696$, $g = -0.161$ [-0.315 to -0.007], $p = 0.040$). Conversely, checking for publication bias via trim and fill suggested the existence of unpublished studies favoring DT, raising the ES estimate to a still-insignificant $g = -0.096$. We did not find any evidence that DT had significantly different between-groups ESs when compared against antidepressants versus alternative therapies ($Q = 0.232$, $p = 0.630$), when compared against CBT versus non-CBT treatments ($Q = 1.032$, $p = 0.310$), or even when compared against CBT *or* antidepressants versus remaining alternative treatments ($Q = 0.785$, $p = 0.376$). Total quality score (slope $= -0.0100$, *ns*), manualization of DT ($Q = 0.093$, $p = 0.760$), whether or not the depressed population was geriatric ($Q = 0.857$, $p = 0.355$), and number of sessions of DT (slope $= 0.00128$, *ns*) were also not significant moderators of ES. At termination, DT and alternative therapies for depression—including CBTs and antidepressants—likely effect similar overall outcomes. Any overall difference, if extant but undetected, is likely to be of small ES.

DT was also not significantly different from alternative treatments at short-term follow-up (study $n = 6$, subject $n = 496$, mean $FU = 4.29$ months, $g = -0.122$ [-0.524 to 0.280], $p = 0.553$), with no evidence of publication bias or that the result was due to including any single study. However, unlike termination, ESs at short-term follow-up did have significant heterogeneity ($Q = 14.732$, $I^2 = 66.061$, $p = 0.012$). In an exploratory moderator analysis comparing alternative treatment types ($Q = 5.447$, $p = 0.020$),

we found that at short-term follow-up DT performed significantly worse against CBTs (study $n = 4$, subject $n = 299$, $g = -0.380$ [-0.756 to -0.004], $p = 0.048$) than when compared to non-CBT treatments (study $n = 2$, subject $n = 57$, $g = 0.530$ [-0.103 to 1.163], $p = 0.101$). Some dynamic therapists anticipate symptoms return around termination, and this bounce in symptoms may be an expectable reaction in DT. Also, at short-term follow-up, we found a significant moderation ($Q = 6.660$, $p = 0.010$) suggesting that DT was inferior to alternative treatments for geriatric (study $n = 2$, subject $n = 96$ $g = -0.853$ [-1.484 to -0.222], $p = 0.008$) but not nongeriatric patient populations (study $n = 4$, subject $n = 400$, $g = 0.086$ [-0.247 to 0.419], $p = 0.611$). It is possible that older patients may benefit more from concrete, direct interventions for depression because the concerns leading to their depression may be more grounded in actual experience associated with aging (e.g., loss of support, declining physical health) than in internal conflict. Because all geriatric studies used CBTs as their comparison therapies, it is difficult to disambiguate whether the geriatric patient population or use of CBTs (or perhaps both or neither) was the primary reason for DT diminished performance among these studies. However, in both DT and CBT, geriatric depressed patients improve less than other patients. Among only studies in which DT was compared to a CBT, DT performed significantly worse than CBTs ($Q = 4.922$, $p = 0.027$) in geriatric studies ($g = -0.625$ and -1.096) than in nongeriatric studies ($g = -0.157$ and -0.149). This finding is consistent with the interpretation that the moderation showing diminished comparative efficacy for DT against CBTs may in fact be driven by diminished DT efficacy for geriatric patients rather than a superiority of CBTs per se.

Finally, DT did not differ from alternative treatments at long-term follow-up (study $n = 5$, subject $n = 487$, mean $FU = 23$ months, $g = -0.205$ [-0.546 to 0.136], $p = 0.239$), again with no evidence of publication bias or single-study sensitivity. As at short-term follow-up, ESs at long-term follow-up displayed significant heterogeneity ($Q = 9.772$, $I^2 = 59.068$, $p = 0.044$). No moderators were significant, notably including geriatric patient population. Furthermore, at long-term follow-up, *all* alternative treatments investigated were CBTs (with the exception of the supportive therapy group from Cooper et al. [2003], which does not differ notably in ES from the study's CBT group). Thus, the use of CBT vs. non-CBT comparison therapies cannot explain observed ES heterogeneity at this time point.

Combined DT + Pharmacotherapy Versus Pharmacotherapy

Using remission rates as the common outcome variable, we found a moderate ES advantage at termination (study $n = 3$, subject $n = 295$, $g = 0.470$ [0.036 to 0.904], $p = 0.034$) of combined DT and antidepressant treatment over antidepressants alone, with no indication of publication bias (see Cuijpers, Dekker, Hollon, & Andersson, 2009; de Maat et al., 2008 for similar findings). There was, however, significant heterogeneity among the three studies ($Q = 6.649$, $I^2 = 69.919$, $p = 0.036$). No moderators were significant.

Conclusions: The Efficacy of DT for Depression

Despite limiting our meta-analysis to only RCTs and individual DT, our results converge with those of Driessen et al. (2010). We found that DTs are as therapeutically effective as alternative treatments (both psychosocial and pharmacological) in the treatment of depression at the end of active treatment and at short- and long-term follow-up. DT was also found to be more effective than control conditions. We further found that combined DT and pharmacotherapy may be more efficacious than pharmacotherapy alone, a finding that has not often been confirmed in the literature.

Some versions of DTs for depression may meet criteria for being *probably efficacious* as defined by APA Division 12 "empirically supported treatments" criteria (e.g., brief dynamic interpersonal therapy, parent-infant psychodynamic therapy [Cooper et al., 2003]). Conversely, no one specific version of DT for depression meets full, formal APA Division 12 criteria to be designated a well-established EST because there has not been a replication by a *separate* research group of any effective, manualized form of DT for depression (Chambless & Hollon, 1998; Connolly Gibbons, Crits-Christoph & Hearon, 2008). However, it is not always clear just how different from each other various versions of DT for depression actually are in theory and practice—in many instances, the manuals appear largely convergent. This raises the interesting question as to how to decide that a specific treatment has been replicated in order to meet Division 12 criteria. Regardless of DT's official status as an EST or not, readers need to keep in mind that few treatments have been shown to be more effective than other active treatments for depression (Cuijpers, van Straten, Andersson, & van Oppen, 2008). In light of the strong trend in the meta-analytic literature of equivalence for depression between major therapeutic models, future investigations might pay specific attention to which specific depressed patients might be best suited for DT versus other therapies (see Barber & Muenz, 1996; Barber et al., 2012).

Anxiety Disorders

Though DT is widely used to treat anxiety disorders (e.g., Goisman, Warshaw, & Keller, 1999), the empirical literature supporting its effectiveness is nascent but growing (see Slavin-Mulford & Hilsenroth, 2012, for a review including naturalistic and quasi-experimental empirical evidence). The question of whether DT is efficacious for the treatment of anxiety disorder is one of the most important areas of research in terms of addressing the specific versus common hypothesis of psychological change (cf. Castonguay & Grosse Holtfort, 2005; Schut & Castonguay, 2001). Many CBT researchers may agree that nonspecific (common) factors could explain positive results in depression, but they would argue that the specific aspects of CBT for anxiety disorders are responsible for the greater rate of improvement for those disorders (cf. Chambless, 2002; Chambless & Ollendick, 2001).

Dynamic conceptualizations of the etiology, maintenance, and treatment of anxiety symptoms do often differ dramatically from those commonly described in the CBT traditions, and propose different specific mechanisms of change. DT for anxiety disorder is well-exemplified by manualized panic-focused psychodynamic psychotherapy (PFPP; Busch, Milrod, Singer, & Aronson, 2011). PFPP posits that panic attacks arise from specific unconscious conflicts, most commonly conflicts of dependency and attachment (e.g., panic as a way to indirectly express a need for care without requiring direct acknowledgment of surrounding conflicts) or feelings of anger (e.g., panic as an aggressive means of coercing attention or as a fearful reaction to the anger felt toward essential figures). Guilt about dependent and angry wishes is also frequently a contributor, with panic acting as a means of unconscious punishment. Treatment involves interpreting the emotional significance of panic, the psychological meaning of specific symptoms and panic triggers, identifying the relevant intrapsychic conflicts alluded to above, and increasing the understanding of inner experiences related to panic and their underlying dynamics. As in many DTs, this would entail working through repetitive conflicts surrounding the psychological meanings of panic through demonstration that the same conflicts may be emerging in multiple settings, including in the transference.

To date there has never been a meta-analysis synthesizing the literature on the effects of DT in the controlled treatment of anxiety disorders. Due to the paucity of studies, we have decided to focus on anxiety disorders in general. So as to include multiple anxiety disorders in the same meta-analysis, we used the author-identified primary outcome measure when available to calculate ESs. When primary outcome was not explicitly indicated, the judgment of the meta-analysis authors was used to select outcome measures for analysis based on the specific psychopathology of the disorder in question. Regarding the construct of general anxiety, the clinician-based Hamilton Rating Scale for Anxiety (HRSA) was our preferred outcome measure.

Controlled Comparisons

Keeping in mind the very small number of studies analyzed, DT was superior to control conditions with a large estimated controlled ES (study $n = 3$, subject $n = 105$, $g = 0.775$ [0.381 to 1.168], $p < 0.001$, fail-safe $N = 10$). Two studies used a minimal treatment control (Alstrom et al., 1984a, 1984b; providing study assessments, psychoeducation, and recommendation/instruction for self-exposure but no ongoing treatment), while one used a wait-list control (Brom, Kleber, & Defares, 1989). There was no significant heterogeneity among ESs, nor was there single-study sensitivity. A trim-and-fill check for publication bias suggested adjustment downward to $g = 0.630$ (0.313 to 0.946). Given the quality of those studies, their date of publication (none after 1990), and their small sample sizes, replication of controlled ES for DT against controls is needed, especially against active controls.

Active Treatment Comparisons

DT for anxiety disorders did not have significantly different outcomes compared to alternative treatments (study $n = 8$, subject $n = 390$, $g = 0.083$ [−0.247 to 0.413], $p = 0.622$). This result was insensitive to the removal of any single study

from the meta-analysis, and there was no indication of publication bias. A significant level of heterogeneity among study outcomes was found ($Q = 17.544$, $I^2 = 60.101$, $p = 0.014$). As several DT treatment protocols contained explicit references to minor exposure elements (e.g., a recommendation to self-expose and then discuss in SE therapy for GAD), we were curious as to whether the inclusion of such a stipulation in the treatment protocol moderated ESs. However, whether a DT used such a minor exposure element (Alstrom et al., 1984a, 1984b; Crits-Christoph et al., 2005; Leichsenring et al., 2009) did not significantly moderate ESs ($Q = 0.084$, $p = 0.772$). It remains possible, however, that in commonly delivered DT there are elements of exposure (cf. Lambert & Ogles, 2004). It is also possible that commonly delivered CBTs include elements of DT such as interpretations of unconscious wishes and defenses. A single moderator was significant: DT for disorders *other than* GAD was more comparatively efficacious than DT for GAD ($Q = 5.370$, $p = 0.020$). More specifically, we found a small ES benefit to using DT over alternative treatments when treating anxiety disorders other than GAD (study $n = 4$, subject $n = 203$, $g = 0.364$ [0.008 to 0.720], $p = 0.045$), whereas DT for GAD was not significantly different from alternative treatments (study $n = 4$, subject $n = 187$, $g = -0.238$ [−0.602 to 0.126], $p = 0.199$).

At short-term follow-up, equivalence between DT and alternative treatments was maintained (study $n = 6$, subject $n = 304$, average $FU = 6.16$ months, $g = -0.154$ [−0.691 to 0.383], $p = 0.573$), a finding that was also insensitive to removing any single study. This result may need to be interpreted cautiously, as a high level of heterogeneity was found among ESs ($Q = 25.087$, $I^2 = 80.070$, $p < 0.001$). In addition, a trim-and-fill check for publication bias imputed the existence of studies to the right of the estimated ES, raising the estimate to an insignificant $g = 0.182$. Using exploratory moderator analysis we found some suggestion that, by follow-up, DT for GAD may be significantly less effective than alternative treatments ($Q = 5.310$, $p = 0.021$). At short-term follow-up, DT for GAD was moderately worse than alternative treatments (study $n = 3$, subject $n = 159$, $g = -0.601$ [−1.125 to −0.077], $p = 0.025$), while there was no significant difference between DT and other therapies when treating other anxiety disorders (study $n = 3$, subject $n = 145$, $g = 0.275$

[−0.255 to 0.805], $p = 0.309$). This follow-up result, however, was dependent on our inclusion of Durham et al. (1994), which was unbalanced to the detriment of DT (i.e., no manual or even theoretical formulation was used for DT but were for the CBT conditions). Replication using another manualized DT would help elucidate to what extent our moderator analysis reflects a "true" disadvantage of DT for GAD, or merely bias due to differences in treatment fidelity. No other moderator was found to be significant.

Conclusions: The Efficacy of DT for Anxiety Disorders

Despite common beliefs to the contrary (cf. Chambless, 2002; Tolin, 2010), the evidence from RCTs suggests that DT is largely neither better nor worse for treatment of anxiety disorders than are other active treatments (predominantly CBTs), a finding carried into short-term follow-up. We also found evidence that DT may have a medium-to-large ES advantage over minimal-to-no treatment controls on primary outcome, although among a small number of older studies.

One limitation to our meta-analysis is that these results are—with the exception of the GAD moderation analysis—collapsed across disorders (see Table 12.2), and notably included no controlled studies of obsessive-compulsive disorder. With the current studies available, it is not possible to further disambiguate the relative effects of DT for different anxiety disorders. Another limitation is the low quality of some studies included in the meta-analysis (e.g., both Alstrom studies; Pierloot & Vinck, 1978), though study quality did not moderate ESs. Furthermore, several studies had pilot-level sample sizes. Nevertheless, our meta-analysis introduces the possibility that DT for anxiety disorders may be as efficacious as alternative treatments. Several large scale DT RCTs are currently underway (investigating panic disorder and social phobia), and their results will be published over the next few years. Future research into the effects of DT for specific anxiety disorders is warranted, especially for GAD.

Personality Disorders (PD)

It is always difficult to provide a summary statement about the essence of DT for any disorder, but even more so for PD due to the diversity of PDs and of forms of DT. Following Magnavita (1997), one could say that DT for PD generally entails the identification of maladaptive, recurring

patterns of thinking, perceiving, and behavioral and emotional responding, and the restructuring of these patterns, primarily through linking the current and transference patterns to early relational disruptions of attachment and trauma. For example, Kernberg's transference-focused psychotherapy (TFP) for borderline personality disorder (BPD) proposes that the symptomatology of BPD (e.g., flip-flopping "split" perceptions of relationships as being all-good or all-bad, intolerable feelings of emptiness) emerges from pervasively unintegrated self-object representations (Clarkin et al., 2006). Accordingly, the primary mechanism of treatment in TFP is the gradual elucidation and integration of these split-off self-object representations as they emerge in the transference. In an attempt to integrate these disparate and polarized self-object representations, the therapist brings these representations into conscious conflict with another when otherwise they would pass without recognition of their mutual incoherence. Therapists further seek to analyze both what triggers the emergence of particular representations and what defensive roles the separation and switching between "good" and "bad" representations serves. This is thought to help the patient improve their reality testing, ability to mentalize the thoughts and feelings of others (see Bateman & Fonagy, 2006), interpersonal stability, and sense of internal coherence and wholeness.

Prior synthesis of the clinical literature via meta-analysis indicates that psychotherapy is generally efficacious in the treatment of PD (Perry, Banon, & Ianni, 1999). Leichsenring and Leibing's (2003) meta-analysis was the first to examine the specific efficacy of DT in the treatment of PD, as compared to the efficacy of CBT. Based on 15 studies (6 controlled, 9 naturalistic), they reported large within-groups (or uncontrolled) ESs for both overall change ($d = 1.46$) and specific measures of personality pathology ($d = 1.56$ from the subset of 6 studies that reported personality pathology scores). The uncontrolled ES for DT was not significantly different than the one calculated for CBT ($d = 1.00$ from a sample of ten studies). Notably, all ESs were calculated using data from the furthest point available from termination (average 78 weeks for DT and 13 weeks for CBT), perhaps explaining why the ES for DT was arithmetically (but not significantly) larger than the one found for CBT. From those results, they inferred that DT (and, to a lesser extent, CBT) can cause long-term, sustained change in psychopathology. More recently, Abbass, Town, and Driessen (2011) meta-analyzed a small number of controlled and uncontrolled studies examining DT for patients with depression and co-morbid personality pathology, finding both large within-group ESs and no significant differences in efficacy compared to other investigated treatments.

In the current meta-analysis, we focused on between-groups ES estimates for PD treatment, averaging together ESs from patient-reported and/or observer-reported measures of psychopathology within the study. We refer to this composite ES as "general outcome." Assessing general outcome across measures allows for the inclusion of more studies within the meta-analysis. However, there is broad disagreement as to what precisely constitutes change within a given PD, never mind across PDs. As such, we also performed a secondary set of meta-analyses for both between-groups and controlled ESs for improvement in specific psychopathology construct for which at least three studies could contribute an ES (e.g., three controlled studies used a variant of the Inventory for Interpersonal Problems [IIP; Horowitz, Rosenberg, Baer, Ureño, & Villaseñor, 1988]).

Controlled Comparisons

At termination, DT for PD was more effective than controls for general outcome (study $n = 7$, subject $n = 452$, $g = 0.593$ [0.258 to 0.918], $p = 0.001$, fail-safe $N = 52$). Control conditions included two enhanced TAUs (Bateman & Fonagy, 2009; Doering et al., 2010), two TAUs (Bateman & Fonagy, 1999; Gregory et al., 2008), and three wait-list controls (Abbass, Sheldon, Gyra, & Kalpin, 2008; Emmelkamp et al., 2006; Winston et al., 1994). Though this comparison showed moderate heterogeneity ($Q = 15.903$, $I^2 = 62.272$, $p = 0.014$)—as to be expected from including different intensities of control treatments—there was no evidence of publication bias or that the result was driven by any single study.

The heterogeneity of control conditions used should caution against overinterpretation of the precise magnitude of the controlled effect size. However, we could not meaningfully test moderator effects of using active controls versus inactive controls *or* testing for borderline personality disorder (BPD) patients versus other PD patients because all BPD studies used an active control and all others used an inactive control.

Furthermore, we could not examine the effects of manualization as only one study in this comparison (Emmelkamp et al., 2006) did not qualify as manualized; this study—comparing DT versus a wait-list for avoidant PD treatment—had the lowest controlled ES ($g = -0.030$). No moderators were significant, though future explorations of moderators (e.g., number of therapy sessions) might be better served using samples with the same types of control treatments (e.g., only versus wait-list).

Active Treatment Comparisons

DT did not differ from alternative therapies for PD in terms of general outcome (study $n = 7$, subject $n = 528$, $g = -0.145$ [-0.342 to 0.052], $p = 0.150$). This ES estimate was not impacted by significant heterogeneity or indication of publication bias, nor did any one study drive this finding. As only one study was unmanualized (Emmelkamp et al., 2006; though see footnote 4), it was not possible to investigate whether manualization affected ES. No moderators were significant. In particular, we did not find significant moderation for whether the study concerned the treatment of BPD ($Q = 0.093$, $p = 0.761$) or a primary Cluster-C disorder. ($Q = 0.152$, $p = 0.696$).

In terms of short-term follow-up, there was again no significant difference in general outcome between DT and alternative treatments (study $n = 5$, subject $n = 381$, average $FU = 6$ months, $g = -0.056$ [-0.367 to 0.255], $p = 0.723$). There was a trend toward heterogeneity among ESs at follow-up ($Q = 7.784$, $p < 0.100$, $I^2 = 48.616$), though there was no indication of publication bias. The result was not single-study sensitive. Again, only Emmelkamp et al. (2006) was not manualized, though it did have the lowest ES ($g = -0.658$). Exploratory meta-regression suggested a trend of a significant, positive relation between number of dynamic sessions and between-groups ES (slope $= 0.04395$, total model $p < 0.100$).

Secondary Analyses: Specific Treatment Outcomes of DT for PD

In a secondary set of analyses, we performed meta-analyses for both between-groups and controlled ESs for improvement in any specific psychopathology construct for which at least three studies could contribute an ES (e.g., three controlled studies used a variant of the IIP). Six constructs were identified: personality pathology (e.g., STIPO, PDQ); general symptomatology (e.g., SCL-90); global functioning (measured by the GAF); interpersonal problems (measured by the IIP); depression (measured by the BDI); and suicidality (e.g., rates of patients attempting suicide). All six constructs had enough studies contributing data to perform preliminary meta-analyses for controlled outcome. However, only three constructs (general symptomatology, personality pathology, and interpersonal problems) had enough studies to meta-analyze DT compared to other active therapies.

We found no significant differences between DT and other therapies on measures of personality pathology (study $n = 6$, $g = -0.108$ [-0.357 to 0.140], $p = 0.392$), general symptomatology (study $n = 4$, $g = -0.078$ [-0.291 to 0.136], $p = 0.476$), and interpersonal problems (study $n = 4$, $g = 0.019$ [-0.194 to 0.232], $p = 0.861$). For controlled ES, DT had a significant advantage over control treatments on measures of general symptomatology (study $n = 5$, $g = 0.565$ [0.135 to 0.994], $p = 0.010$), suicidality (study $n = 4$, $g = 0.649$ [0.394 to 0.904], $p = 0.000$), global functioning (study $n = 3$, $g = 0.579$ [0.204 to 0.955], $p = 0.002$), interpersonal problems ($n = 3$, $g = 1.245$ [0.463 to 2.028], $p = 0.002$), personality pathology ($n = 3$, $g = 0.311$ [0.015 to 0.607], $p = 0.040$), and a trend toward an advantage in treating depressive symptomatology (study $n = 4$, $g = 0.645$ [-0.060 to 1.349], $p = 0.073$). It is possible that the controlled ES for personality pathology outcome may be somewhat underestimated at treatment termination relative to follow up, as both Bateman and Fonagy (1999 for original study, 2008 for follow-up report) and Gregory et al. (2008 for original, 2010 for follow-up) report long-term follow-up between-groups ESs for personality pathology that are substantially larger than our estimate here ($d = 1.80$ and $d = 1.31$, respectively).

Conclusions: The Efficacy of DT for PD

Among the small number of RCTs of DT for PDs, DT is superior to control conditions, but not different than alternative treatments in terms of general psychopathological outcome at termination and short-term FU. We did not find any indication from exploratory moderator analysis that DT showed significantly different between-groups ESs when treating either BPD or Cluster-C PDs. It may behoove future dynamic trials of PD treatments to use more active controls to better assess the efficacy of DT treatment and examine whether benefits of DT over active

controls is maintained after termination (for evidence that this may be true, see follow-up reports Bateman & Fonagy, 2008; Gregory et al., 2010).

Given the nature of DT (its goals and processes), there may be the expectation that DT would do well with and perhaps better than other types of psychotherapy with personality pathology and interpersonal relations. However, we found that overall equivalence between DT and other treatments for PD is the rule when specifically examining personality pathology, general symptomatology, and interpersonal problems. It seems that the Dodo Bird verdict (Luborsky, Rosenthal, et al., 2002) applies to existing controlled studies of PD up to short-term follow-up. We further showed superiority of DT over controls in the domains of general symptomatology, suicidality, global functioning, interpersonal problems, personality pathology, and—less definitively—depressive symptoms. With regard to controlled effect, DT may have the strongest evidence base in the domain of PD treatment.

In fact, DT's first full "EST" has come from the treatment of personality pathology: TFP has recently been designated a *well-established* treatment for BPD by APA Division 12 (2012). Mentalization-based treatment has also been determined to be *probably efficacious* for BPD (APA Division 12, 2012) for exhibiting clear superiority to both a strong TAU and a manualized enhanced TAU in two RCTs, one RCT showing large ES advantages over TAU over 5 years after treatment. Several individual manualized variants of DT might also be considered at least *probably efficacious* for the treatment of PDs as per APA criteria (Chambless & Hollon, 1998): Vaillant McCullough's STDP (Svartberg et al., 2004 for Cluster-C), brief relational therapy (Muran et al., 2005 for Cluster C), intensive STDP (Abbass et al., 2008; Winston et al., 1994 for general PD), brief adaptive psychotherapy (Muran et al., 2005, Winston et al., 1994 for general PD and Cluster C), psychodynamic psychiatric management (McMain et al., 2009/2012, for BPD), and manualized dynamic-supportive therapy (Clarkin et al., 2007, for BPD, though less preferable to TFP on measures of suicidality).

Unambiguously, DTs should be considered viable and efficacious treatments for personality pathology. Especially in consideration of the dearth of well-studied, efficacious treatments for PDs compared to other disorders, replications and extensions of several DT treatments for PDs are highly warranted. Clearly, there is a need to

TABLE 12.1 Description of DT RCTs of Mood Disorders (Depressive Dxs)

Study	Depression Type	Dynamic Therapy Groups	Comparison Groups	Follow-Up Period (mos.)	Primary Outcome Findings	Total/Overall Quality Score	Outcome Measure
Barber et al. (2012)	Chronic MDD	20 sessions SE, MAN (n = 51)	ADP (n = 55), PL (n = 50)	None	SE = ADP = PL	43/6	HRSD
Barkham et al. (1999)	Subsyndromal, dysthymia, mild MDD	2 weekly sessions then 1 session 3 months later VBDIT, MAN (n = 54)	VBCBT (n = 62)	12	VBDIT = VBCBT FU: Long-term FU: VBDIT < VBCBT	29/4	BDI
Burnand, Andreoli, Kolatte, Venturini, and Rosset (2002)	MDD	82 inpatient days of DIT + ADP, UNMAN (n = 35)	ADP (n = 39)	None	DIT + ADM > ADM	27/4	HRSD
Cooper, Murray, Wilson, and Romaniuk (2003)	Postpartum	10 sessions PIPT, MAN (n = 45)	CBT (n = 42), NDC (n = 47), TAU (n = 50)	4, 13, and 55	Termination: PIPT = CBT, NDC on scores but PIPT > CBT, NDC on remission; PIPT > TAU Short-term FU: PIPT = CBT, NDC, TAU Long-term FU: maintained	37/5	EPDS
de Jonghe, Kool, van Aalst, Dekker, and Peen (2001)	MDD with or without dysthymia	8 weekly and 8 sessions every 2 weeks DST + ADP, UNMAN (n = 72)	ADP (n = 57)	None	DST + AD > AD	35/6	HRSD
Gallagher and Thompson (1982)	Geriatric MDD	16 sessions over 12 weeks BRT, UNMAN (n = 10)	CT (n = 10), BT (n = 10)	1.5, 3, 6, and 12	Termination: BRT = BT, CT Short- and long-term FU: maintained	27/4	HRSD
Gallagher-Thompson and Steffen (1994)	Geriatric major, minor, or intermittent depressive disorder	16–20 sessions BDT, UNMAN (n = 30)	CBT (n = 36)	3	BDT = CBT	27/6	RDC improvement or remission
Hersen, Bellack, Himmelhoch, and Thase (1984)	MDD	12 sessions BDT + PL (undefined), UNMAN (n = 22)	SST + PL (n = 25), ADP (n = 14)	None	BDT + PL = SST + PL, AD	31/4	HRSD

Study	Diagnosis	Treatment	Comparison	Sessions/FU	Results	Score	Measure
Maina, Forner, and Bogetto (2005)	Dysthymia, minor depressive disorder, or adjustment disorder with depressed mood	Avg. 20 sessions BDT, UNMAN (n = 10)	SP (n = 10), WLC (n = 10)	6	BDT, SP > Wait list Short-term FU: BDT > SP	22/3	HRSD
Maina, Rosso, and Bogetto (2009)	First-episode MDD	Avg. 18.3 sessions BDT + ADP, UNMAN (n = 41)	ADP (n = 51)	6, 28, 48, but only for remitters	Termination: BDT + AD = AD Short-term FU: BDT + AD > AD Long-term FU: maintained	38.5/5.5	HRSD
Salminen et al. (2008)	MDD	16 sessions BDT, UNMAN (n = 26)	ADP (n = 25)	None	BDT = AD	28/5	HRSD
Shapiro et al. (1994)	Mild, moderate, and severe MDD	8 or 16 sessions of BDIT, MAN (n = 57)	8 or 16 sessions of CBT (n = 59)	3.75 and 12	Termination: BDIT < CBT on BDI but not on other measures of depression and symptoms Short-term FU: maintained Long-term FU: 8-session BDIT < 8-session CBT, 16-session CBT, and 16-session BDIT	35/7	BDI
Thompson, Gallagher, and Breckenridge (1987)	MDD	16–20 sessions BDT, UNMAN (n = 24 before wait-list integration, 30 post)	BT (n = 30 post wait-list), CT (n = 31 post wait list, DTC (n = 19)	12 and 24	Termination: BDT = CT, BT Long-term FU: maintained	18/4	HRSD, RDC remission at FU
Thyme et al. (2007)	Dysthymia or subsyndromal depression	Avg. 21 sessions BDT, UNMAN (n = 21)	AT (n = 18)	3	Termination: BDT = AT Short-term FU: Maintained	17/3	HRSD
Vitriol, Ballesteros, Florenzano, Weil, and Benadof (2009)	MDD with childhood trauma	Avg. 12 sessions BDT, UNMAN (n = 44)	Enhanced TAU (n = 43)	3	Termination: BDT > TAU Short-term FU: Maintained	27/4	HRSD

ADP = Antidepressant Drug Protocol, AT = Art Therapy, BDI = Beck Depression Inventory, BDIT = Brief Dynamic-Interpersonal Therapy, BDT = Brief Dynamic Therapy, BRT = Brief Relational Therapy BT = Behavioral Therapy, CBT = Cognitive Behavioral Therapy, CT = Cognitive Therapy, EPDS = Edinburgh Postnatal Depression Scale GAD = Generalized Anxiety Disorder, HRSD = Hamilton Rating Scale for Depression, MAN = Manualized Therapy, MDD = Major Depressive Disorder, NDC = Nondirected Counseling, PC = Psychodynamically Informed Counseling, PIPT = Parent-Infant Psychodynamic Therapy, PL = Placebo, SE = Supportive-Expressive Therapy, SP = Manualized Supportive Psychotherapy, SST = Social Skills Training, TAU = Treatment as Usual, UNMAN = Unmanualized Therapy, VBCBT = Very Brief CBT, VBDIT = Very Brief Dynamic-Interpersonal Therapy, WLC = Wait List Control

TABLE 12.2 Description of DT RCTs for Anxiety Disorders

Study	Disorder	Dynamic Therapy Groups	Comparison Groups	Follow-Up Period (mos.)	Primary Findings	Total/Overall Quality Score	Outcome Measure
Alstrom, Norlund, Persson, Harding, and Ljungqvist (1984a)	Agoraphobia	Avg. 8.5 sessions DST, UNMAN (n = 14 at T, 13 at FU)	PE (n = 11 at T, 9 at FU); AR (n = 17 at T and FU); BTC (n = 19 at T, 12 at FU)	9	Termination: DST = PE; DST > AR & BTC Short-term FU: DST > PE, AR, & BTC	19/3	AIPS global rating
Alstrom, Norlund, Persson, Harding, and Ljungqvist (1984b)	Specific social phobia	Avg. 9.4 sessions DST, UNMAN (n = 16 at T, 13 at FU)	PE (n = 7 at T and FU); AR (n = 9 at T, 6 at FU); BTC (n = 10 at T, 8 at FU)	9	Termination: DST < PE; DST > AR & BTC Short-term FU: maintained	19/3	AIPS global rating
Brom, Kleber, and Defares (1989)	PTSD	Avg. 18.8 sessions TBDT, MAN (n = 26)	TD (n = 28); BHT (n = 26); WLC (n = 20)	3	Termination: TBDT = BHT, TD; TFDT > WLC Short-term FU: maintained	23/5	Combined: TSS + IES
Crits-Cristoph, Gibbons, Narducci, Schamberger, and Gallop (2005)	GAD	16 sessions SE therapy adapted to GAD, MAN (n = 14)	SP (n = 14)	None	SE = SP on scores, SE > SP on remission	35.5/5	HAM-a
Durham et al. (1994)	Chronic GAD	8 or 16 sessions of an unspecified model, UNMAN (n = 29)	8 sessions CT (n = 20); 16 session CT (n = 15); AMT (n = 16)	6	Termination: DT <AMT, CT-8 and CT-16 Short-term FU: maintained	29/5	HAM-a for Termination, STAI-T (Form Y) for FU

Leichsenring et al. (2009)	GAD	30 sessions SE for GAD, MAN (n = 28)	CBT (n = 29)	6	Termination: SE = CBT on primary outcome, some secondary Short-term FU: maintained	38/6	HAM-a
Milrod, Leon, Busch, et al. (2007)	Panic disorder with and without agoraphobia	24 sessions PFPP, MAN (n = 26)	AR (n = 23)	None	PFPP > AR	42/6	PDSS
Pierloot and Vinck (1978)	General anxiety	Avg. 19.77 sessions FDT, UNMAN (n = 9)	SD (n = 13)	Mean of 3.95 months	Termination: FDT < SD Short-term FU: FDT = SD	8/2	Combined: PSS-a + TMAS + STAI-T

AIPS = Alstrom Interview of Phobic Symptoms, AMT = Anxiety Management Training, AR = Applied Relaxation, BTC = Basal Therapy Control, BHT = Behavioral Hypnotherapy, CT = Cognitive Therapy, CBT = Cognitive-Behavioral Therapy, DST = Dynamic Supportive Therapy, FDT = Focal Dynamic Therapy, GAD = Generalized Anxiety Disorder, HAM-a = Hamilton Anxiety Rating Scale, MAN = Manualized Therapy, PDSS = Panic Disorder Severity Scale, PE = Prolonged Exposure, PFPP = Panic Focused Psychodynamic Psychotherapy PSS-a = Psychiatric Status Schedule-Anxiety Subsection (PTSD) = Post-Traumatic Stress Disorder, SD = Systematic Desensitization, SE = Supportive-Expressive Therapy (SP = Manualized Supportive Psychotherapy, STAI-T = State-Trait Anxiety Inventory (Trait), TBDT = Trauma-Based Dynamic Therapy, TD = Trauma Desensitization, TSS = Trauma Symptoms Scale, TMAS = Taylor Manifest Anxiety Scale, UNMAN = Unmanualized Therapy, WLC = Wait-List Control

TABLE 12.3 Description of DT RCTs for Personality Disorders

Study	Disorder	Dynamic Therapy Groups	Comparison Groups	Follow-Up Period (mos.)	Primary Findings	Total/ Overall Quality Score	Outcome Measures
Abbass et al. (2008)	Mixed PD	Avg. 27.7 sessions ISTDP, MAN (*n* = 14)	WLC (*n* = 13)	None	ISTDP > WLC	27/5	BSI-GSI, GAF-Symptoms, GAF-Social-occupational, IIP-64
Bateman and Fonagy (1999)	BPD	18 months of partial hospitalization MBT, MAN (*n* = 19)	TAU (*n* = 19)	6, 12, 18, 60	MBT > TAU Short-term FU: maintained Long-term FU: maintained	29.5/6	BDI, GAF (Long-term FU Only), IIP-Circumflex, Parasuicidal composite, SAS, SCL-90-R, ZRS (Long-term FU Only)
Bateman and Fonagy (2009)	BPD	78 individual/78 group sessions MBT, MAN (*n* = 71)	Enhanced TAU (*n* = 63)	None	MBT > Enhanced TAU	45/7	BDI, GAF, IIP-Circumflex, Parasuicidal composite, SCL-90-R
Clarkin et al. (2007)	BPD	102 sessions TFP, MAN (*n* = 23); at least 52 sessions SP, MAN (*n* = 22)	DBT (*n* = 17)	None	TFP = DBT, SP	26/4	AIAQ, BIS-II, BAI, BDI-II, GAF, OAS-M, SAS
Doering et al. (2010)	BPD	102 sessions TFP, MAN (*n* = 52)	CETC (*n* = 52)	None	TFP > CETC	32/5	BDI, BSI-GSI, GAF, Parasuicidal composite, STIPO

Study	Disorder	Treatment	Comparison	FU	Results		Measures
Emmelkamp et al. (2006)	Avoidant PD	20 session BDT (multiple manuals, including both Malan, 1979 and Luborsky, 1984), UNMAN[3] (n = 22, 25 at short-term FU)	CBT (n = 18, 22 at Short-term FU), WLC (n = 16)	6	Termination: BDT < CBT; BDT = WLC Short-term FU: maintained	24/5	AS, LWASQ, PDBQ-Avoidant, SPAI
Giesen-Bloo et al. (2006)	BPD	Avg. 231 sessions (for "completers"[4]) TFP, MAN but poor adherence[5] (n = 42)	SFT (n = 44)	N	TFP < SFT	42/7	BPDSI, General psychopathology factor score
Gregory et al. (2008)	BPD and substance abuse/ dependence	52 sessions DDT, MAN (n = 15, 11 at Long-term FU)	TAU (n = 15, 13 at Long-term FU)	18	Termination: DDT > TAU Long-term FU: maintained	31/5	BDI, BEST, DES, Parasuicidal Composite, SPS
Hellerstein et al. (1998)	Mixed PD, Cluster C and PD-NOS	30–40 sessions STDP, MAN (n = 14)	SP (n = 12 at termination, 10 at Short-term FU)	6	STDP = SP	30/5	IIP, SCL-90-R, TCS
McMain et al. (2009/2012)	BPD	Avg. 31 sessions PPCM, MAN (n = 90)	DBT (n = 90)	6, 12, 18, 24	Termination: PPCM = DBT Short-term FU: maintained Long-term FU: maintained	44/7	BDI, IIP-64, MRSSE (Parasuicidality), SCL-90-R, STAEI, ZRS

(continued)

[3] Both despite and in part because of the citing of several disparate DT manuals and texts, we did not consider the therapy in Emmelkamp et al., 2006 to be manualized. It is unclear that a specific formulation of DT for the treatment of avoidant PD was used, especially in comparison to the use of Beck's schema-focused CBT for PD in the comparison treatment.

[4] Though Giesen-Bloo et al. (2006) chose 3 years as the analysis period for their study, the supermajority of patients (>80%) in both the TFP and SFT groups had not terminated with their therapist in this window (see Levy, Meehan, & Yeomans, 2012 for discussion).

[5] Though Giesen-Bloo et al. (2006) ostensibly investigated manualized DT of TFP, Yeomans (2007) claims that TFP therapists were neither properly trained nor supervised in TFP. Indeed, the published level of adherence to TFP was remarkably low, while the adherence to SFT was very high, though the original study authors counterclaimed this did not affect TFP treatment efficacy (Giesen-Bloo & Arntz, 2007).

TABLE 12.3 *(Continued)*

Study	Disorder	Dynamic Therapy Groups	Comparison Groups	Follow-Up Period (mos.)	Overall Findings	Total/Overall Quality Score	Outcome Measures
Muran, Safran, Samstag, and Winston (2005)	Cluster C & PD-NOS	30 sessions BAP, MAN (n = 22); 30 sessions BRT, MAN (n = 33)	CBT (n = 29)	6	Termination: BAP = BRT = CBT Short-term FU: maintained	40/5	GAS, IIP, SCL-90-R, TCS (patient and therapist),WISPI
Svartberg, Stiles, and Seltzer (2004)	Cluster C PD	40 sessions STDP, MAN (n = 25 at Termination, 22 at short-term FU, 23 at long-term FU)	CBT (n = 25 at Termination, 24 at Short-term FU, 21 at Long-term FU)	6, 12, 24	Termination: STDP = CBT Short-term FU: maintained Long-term FU: maintained	38/6	IIP, MCMI, SCL-90-R
Winston et al. (1994)	Mixed PD, primarily Cluster C	Avg. 40.3 sessions of ISTDP, MAN (n = 25); BAP, MAN (n = 30)	WLC (n = 26)	None	ISTDP + BAP > WLC	22/3	SAS, SCL-90-R, TCS

AIAQ = Anger, Irritability, and Assault Questionnaire, AS = Avoidance Scale, BAP = Brief Adaptive Psychotherapy, BDI = Beck Depression Inventory, BEST = Borderline Evaluation of Severity over Time (BIS-II = Barratt Impulsiveness Scale-II, BPD = Borderline Personality Disorder, BPDSI = Borderline Personality Disorder Severity Index, BRT = Brief Relational Therapy, BSI-GSI = Brief Symptom Inventory—Global Severity Index, CBT = Cognitive-Behavioral Therapy, CETC = Community Expert Treatment Control, DBT = Dialectical-Behavioral Therapy, DDT = Dynamic-Deconstructive Therapy, DES = Dissociative Experiences Scale, GAF = Global Assessment of Functioning, GAS = Global Assessment Scale, IIP = Inventory of Interpersonal Problems, IPDE = International Personality Disorder Examination, ISTDP = Intensive Short-Term Dynamic Psychotherapy LWASQ = Lehrer Woolfolk Anxiety Symptoms Questionnaire, MAN = Manualized, MCMI = Millon Clinical Multiaxial Inventory, MBT = Mentalization-Based Treatment, MRSSE = Medical Risk of Suicide and Self-Injurious Episodes, OAS-M = Overt Aggression Scale-Modified, PDBQ = Personality Disorder Belief, Questionnaire, PPCM = Psychodynamic Psychiatric Case Management, SAS = Social Adjustment Scale, SCL-90-R = Symptom Checklist-90-Revised, SFT = Schema-Focused Therapy, SP = Manualized Supportive Psychotherapy, SPS = Social Provisions Scale, SPAI = Social Phobia Anxiety Inventory, STAEI = State-Trait Anger Expression Inventory, STDP = Short-Term Dynamic Psychotherapy, STIPO = Structured Interview for Personality Organization, TAU = Treatment as Usual, TCS = Target Complaints Scale, TFP = Transference-Focused Psychotherapy, UNMAN = Unmanualized, WISPI = Wisconsin Personality Inventory, WLC = Wait-List Control, ZRS = Zanarini Rating Scale for Borderline Personality Criteria encourage the replication of important findings by independent researchers. However, the lack of incentives to replicate outcome studies needs to be addressed by the field.

THE EFFICACY OF DT AND "WHAT WORKS FOR WHOM"

As described earlier, there has been a notable increase in the quality (Gerber et al., 2011) and number of RCTs addressing DT efficacy. Our three meta-analyses for specific disorders are consistent with the overall conclusion that in RCTs, DT has been shown to be as effective as alternative therapies at termination and follow-up and superior to control conditions (e.g., TAU, wait-list controls).

Overall, we were particularly cautious not to overexclude studies in a manner favorable to DT. We included studies of nonmanualized DT. Pointedly, we did not include studies in which a "stripped-down" DT-like condition was unambiguously used as a control.[5] However, we did not thoroughly screen for more subtle straw-man or "intent-to-fail" DT conditions. Such "intent-to-fail" DT conditions might include versions of DT in which therapists are artificially restricted such as by being specifically forbidden to discuss relevant symptoms (e.g., eating disorder behavior in Garner et al., 1993). We might also consider as being intent-to-fail studies where it is not evident that the investigators drew upon empirical or theoretical literature describing psychodynamics or DT for the target condition (e.g., Durham et al., 1994; Emmelkamp et al., 2006).

---

[5]An example would be the manualized control therapy (titled "emotion-focused psychotherapy" but not to be confused with Les Greenberg's humanistic-experiential therapy) from the Shear, Houck, Greeno, & Masters (2001) study of panic disorder. The therapy was devised to represent nonprescriptive, nonspecific therapy that might be provided in the community to panic patients. Active components included supportive listening, problem solving, and general identification and discussion of emotions. Despite Shear et al. (2001) explicitly stating that the therapy was "not a psychoanalytic therapy," it was included in the Tolin (2010) meta-analysis of CBT vs. other therapies as a bona fide DT, which it clearly is not. Another illustrative example would be Linehan et al., 2006, which compared DBT to an enhanced TAU condition wherein TAU therapists identified their primary orientation as dynamic or eclectic. Nevertheless, Smit et al., 2012, included this as a valid long-term DT condition in their meta-analysis.

Past meta-analytic investigations have suggested that rigorously and systematically filtering for "intent-to-fail" treatments tends to yield findings of no significant differences between treatments (Benish, Imel, & Wampold, 2008, for PTSD; Wampold, Minami, Baskin, & Tierney, 2002, for depression). Engaging in such a process for DT—that is, meta-analyzing only DT studies systematically selected as bona fide (see Wampold et al., 1997, for a description of what might constitute a bona fide therapy)—might be a topic worthy of future study. However, the problem is who decides what is a bona fide DT.

Notably, none of the meta-analyses we performed found DT to be significantly inferior or superior to alternative treatments at either termination or follow-up. In addition, DT was always found to be superior to combined control conditions. Interestingly, despite the fact that we did not exclude what may be relatively poor studies of DT (e.g., Durham et al., 1994; Giesen-Bloo et al., 2006 as argued by Levy, Meehan, & Yeomans, 2012), we found little evidence that DT was inferior to alternative treatments for any disorder group. There were some exceptions from moderation analyses (see our earlier discussions of depression treatment follow-up and DT for GAD treatment); however, they must be considered exploratory due to the small number of studies analyzed (Higgins & Green, 2011).

Our exploratory moderator analysis did not reveal consistent moderators of between-groups ES across disorders. For example, we did not find a consistent relation of between-groups ESs and quality score or number of sessions of DT perhaps because of the limited statistical power of our samples. A more omnibus (folding across disorders) meta-analysis might be necessary to elucidate the effects of specific moderators in DT given the number of available studies. Also of note is that we did not find a consistent relation between DT manualization and between-groups ES, perhaps because manualization is common in RCTs (for an RCT of manualized vs. unmanualized DT for PD, see Vinnars, Barber, Noren, Gallop, & Weinryb, 2005). However, we point out that assessing fidelity is not a panacea. For example, whether fidelity is assessed or not does not guarantee that the treatment delivered did not include interventions from another treatment (e.g., Ablon & Jones, 1998; McCarthy & Barber, 2009), that investigator allegiance did not impact treatment delivery, or that there is no variability in the delivery of the therapy for a specific intervention. Merely knowing that adherence was assessed does not suffice, and the field will need to assess ways of integrating the data from adherence with outcome to decide how to evaluate the outcome of any RCT. This is a complex question as there is some evidence that adherent delivery of a treatment is not associated with outcome (Webb, DeRubeis, & Barber, 2010).

Investigator allegiance, which was not explored in our meta-analysis, may explain some of the variance in treatment outcomes, especially in trials of lower methodological quality (see Munder, Gerger, Trelle, & Barth, 2011, for a recent meta-analysis showing this relation). Allegiance could be especially relevant when the counterallegiance therapy is unmanualized but the allegiance-syntonic therapy is. In this situation, the unmanualized counterallegiance therapy may be more likely to be a "stripped-down," unrigorous, and/or unrepresentative version of that therapy, unformulated to the disorder in question. Thus, any future meta-analytic investigations of manualization may need to be examined through the lens of imbalance in manualization and in the context of allegiance. As is obvious from Tables 12.1 through 12.3, many different exemplars of DT were used in these analyses. Though all DTs share important characteristics, there nevertheless remain significant theoretical and implementation differences between many of these treatments (e.g., primacy of interpretation of the transference relationship in TFP versus more circumspect transference interpretations in MBT). The few RCTs that have directly compared different models of DT mostly involved PD patients and have reported mixed findings. One such study investigating BPD treatment (Clarkin et al., 2007) compared two forms of manualized DTs (TFP versus manualized dynamic-supportive therapy), and the results were mostly equivocal with the notable exceptions of suicidality and some secondary outcome measures (e.g., reflective functioning) in favor of TFP. Conversely, Muran et al. (2005) did report results suggesting that BRT may be somewhat superior to BAP in the treatment of Cluster-C personality disorders and PD-NOS. It is entirely possible that differences in the effectiveness of DTs exist for different disorders and patient types. However, due to the small sample of studies, heterogeneous comparison conditions, and differences in specific disorders treated, we cannot meaningfully contribute to the question of whether or not certain bona fide dynamic treatments are better than others in the treatment of psychopathology.

Including a wide range of DT could be conceived to both increase and harm generalizability of the meta-analytic results in different ways. On the one hand, that we included several DT exemplars might indicate that the "average" DT performed in an RCT is equivalent to alternative treatments, a finding which may or may not extend to delivery of DT by experts in the field. This might also imply that the characteristics shared amongst DTs are in some way therapeutically sound, or at the very least not counterproductive to treatment. On the other hand, meta-analyzing several DTs at once makes it difficult to determine whether certain DTs drive our findings more than others. By that same token, it may be also problematic to collapse all comparison treatments into "alternative therapies" (see Siev & Chambless, 2007, suggesting differential effectiveness of different CBTs) or control treatments (ranging from wait-list controls to intensity-matched, manualized TAUs). The limited size of the evidence base necessarily restricted our methodological rigor, as not enough comparisons are available to meta-analyze within a disorder group in such a granular way.

Importantly, meta-analyzing at the level of diagnostic entities is unlikely to lead to the identification of relevant differences in treatment efficacy for clinical subpopulations (Beutler, 2002). "Fit" between the patient and the therapist, the therapeutic relationship, and the therapy itself may together account for more of the variance in outcomes than the treatment model alone, considered apart from "fit" (cf. Beutler, 2009). In other words, the question of "what works for whom" is relevant not only on the level of treatment type and disorder, but also regarding characteristics of patients, therapists, the therapeutic relationship, and their interrelationship (see Norcross, 2011 for meta-analytic reviews on many related topics; Muran & Barber, 2010 and later in this chapter regarding the therapeutic alliance specifically).

Barber et al. (2012) reported secondary analyses from an urban, disadvantaged, chronically depressed RCT sample suggesting that SE therapy may be specifically efficacious for minority males and White females. In a unique study that further illustrates this principle of "fit," Heinonen, Lindfors, Laaksonen, and Knekt (2012) found an interaction influencing treatment outcome between the personality of a therapist and the therapy they were practicing in an RCT treating a mixed-disorder sample. Whereas more extroverted and interpersonally active therapists tended to effect better outcomes in both short-term therapies investigated (a DT and problem-solving therapy), more introverted, cautious, and nonintrusive therapists effected better outcomes in the long-term DT condition. Different implementations of the same therapeutic model (e.g., which techniques are actually used, to what degree they are used, use of proscribed counter-theory interventions) could also have differential impact on patient change (e.g., Høglend et al., 2008, found that use of transference interpretations is perhaps most important for patients with more severe deficits in object relations; see also McCarthy, 2009).

In the context of "what works for whom," it is possible that DT may be able to help fill treatment gaps, both by developing efficacious treatments that are tolerable to different patients and that may be specifically efficacious for particular patients. For instance, Milrod, Leon, Barber, Markowitz, and Graf (2007) found that DT may be *more* efficacious for patients with Cluster-C personality pathology than for patients without, a counterintuitive finding (awaiting replication) considering many view personality pathology as an obstacle to treatment. Clinically speaking, enhanced DT efficacy for panic and PD comorbid patients may be highly relevant because 20% to 50% of panic patients may qualify for a PD (e.g., Massion et al., 2002; Milrod, Leon, Busch, et al., 2007; Ozkan & Altindaq, 2005). Similarly, using data from the NIMH TDCRP depression RCT (Elkin et al., 1989), Barber and Muenz (1996) have shown that depressed patients with comorbid obsessive-compulsive PD had better outcomes with IPT than cognitive therapy (CT), while patients with comorbid avoidant PD (APD) did better with CT than IPT. This could be understood as an instance of anticomplementarity. Patients with more obsessive personalities may be best served by a therapy (IPT) that challenges them to explore their inner lives and interpersonal relationships on a feeling level rather than a thinking level, while patients with more avoidant personalities may do best in a more directive therapy (CT) that challenges them to actively break out of their passive or retreating patterns (see also Liebowitz, Stone, & Turkat, 1986). On the other hand, overly aggressive behavior on the part of DT therapists—as represented by both the concentration of interpretations delivered and by disaffiliative patient-therapist interactions surrounding and during interpretation—may be sometimes deleterious to outcome in APD patients (Schut et al., 2005), suggesting possible

limits or complications to anticomplementarity. In terms of matching among dynamic treatments, data suggest that more introjective (i.e., ruminative, preoccupied with self-definition) patients improve more in longer-term, explorative psychoanalysis, while more anaclitic (i.e., strongly emotionally dependent, concerned with relatedness) patients improve more in more active and shorter DT (Blatt, 1992; Blatt & Shahar, 2004). Although these possible treatment recommendations certainly behoove replication, they nevertheless illustrate the manifest need for deeper analysis of trial data.

Overall, these findings suggest that therapy-patient "match" may be highly relevant to treatment planning. Certainly, meta-analyses such as ours are helpful in demonstrating fairly robustly the repeated, controlled efficacy for DT across multiple disparate studies. Indeed, we have shown that current RCT data indicate that—with a few tenuous exceptions—DT is likely equivalent to alternative therapies and superior to control conditions in the treatment of many forms of psychopathology. However, there is also a need to study for whom and under what circumstances different effective therapies—including DT—may be most efficacious. This challenge is perhaps a way to fruitfully engage practitioners of different theoretical backgrounds in collaborative endeavor with researchers.

Like many psychotherapy researchers, we postulate that understanding the process of therapy will increase our ability to develop further our treatments, to make them more effective, and to perhaps individualize them better for the needs of specific individuals. We now turn to the research on those processes and begin our survey by examining a construct that has attained paramount importance in psychotherapy research, the therapeutic alliance.

THE THERAPEUTIC ALLIANCE IN DT

Alliance Construct

The therapeutic alliance was first a psychodynamic construct, before it became a transtheoretical formulation (Bordin, 1979), an integrative variable (Wolfe & Goldfried, 1988), and a common factor (Wampold, 2001). The history of the construct dates back to Freud's early suggestion of the importance of making a "collaborator" of the patient in the therapeutic process, but was brought to prominence by the ego psychological tradition with its emphasis on the reality-oriented adaptation of the ego to the environment. A number of ego psychologists (Bibring, 1937; Greenson, 1967; Sterba, 1934; Zetzel, 1956) developed the alliance construct to counteract a perceived overemphasis on transference in many object relational approaches and to provide theoretical justification for greater technical flexibility. By highlighting the critical importance of the real, human aspects of the therapeutic relationship, the construct provided grounds for departing from the idealized therapist stance of abstinence and neutrality. In general, it highlighted the importance of the therapist being supportive and the patient identifying with the therapist and adapting to the therapist view of the treatment process.

Over the years, many dynamic theorists have grappled with questions of how to conceptualize the alliance and transferential aspects of the therapeutic relationship and whether the alliance construct is meaningful and useful (Brenner, 1979; Dickes, 1975; Hanly, 1992; Kanzer, 1975; Lacan, 1973; Langs, 1976). For example, criticisms have ranged from suggesting the alliance construct can lead to leaving transferential aspects unanalyzed to promoting conformity to the therapist's desires. Interestingly, the alliance construct has not received much attention from the interpersonal tradition. This is probably due to the tradition's more flexible approach to the therapist's position and recognition of the therapist's ultimate embeddedness in the interpersonal field and irreducible subjectivity. This perspective has been more radically advanced by contemporary relational analysts, who have promoted an intersubjective and social constructivist take on the therapeutic relationship (e.g., Aron, 1996; Mitchell, 1988, 1993). From a relational take, Safran and Muran (2000, 2006) have argued that developing the alliance and resolving alliance ruptures are not prerequisite to change, but rather the very essence of the change process.

Alliance Research

Beginning in the 1970s, the alliance construct became the focus of the psychotherapy research community. This was due in large part to two major contributions: (1) Luborsky's (1976) development of the Penn Helping Alliance Questionnaire (HAq), which yielded measures of Perceived Helpfulness (Type I: to what extent the patient perceived the therapist to be helpful) and Collaboration or Bonding (Type II: to what degree the patient and therapist were working together); and (2) Bordin's reformulation that defined the alliance as comprised of three interdependent dimensions—Agreement on Tasks, Agreement on Goals, and the Affective Bond—which became the basis for the development of the Working Alliance Inventory (WAI; Horvath & Greenberg, 1989). These contributions spurred a proliferation of research on the alliance, as well as further measurement development. They also (Bordin's conceptualization especially) contributed to the growing interest in psychotherapy integration and the understanding of common factors that has been evident in the field since the 1980s (e.g., Goldfried, 1980).

With the development of so many alliance measures, both Hatcher (2010) and Horvath (2006) have argued that there has been a cost in the loss of definitional precision: The variety of measures has brought a variety of idiosyncratic definitions of the alliance construct and arguably a great deal of confusion about its meaning. In addition to the HAq and the WAI, other measures most often used include the Vanderbilt Psychotherapy Process Scale (VPPS; O'Malley, Suh, & Strupp, 1983) and the California Psychotherapy Alliance Scales (CALPAS; Gaston & Marmar, 1994). The VPPS has subscales measuring Patient Psychic Distress, Patient Participation, Patient Hostility, Patient Exploration, Patient Dependency, Therapist Warmth and Friendliness, Therapist Exploration, and Negative Therapist Attitude.

According to Horvath, Del Re, Flückiger, and Symonds's (2011) recent meta-analysis, two thirds of the studies conducted regarding the alliance-outcome relationship involved these four "core" measures, which shared less than 50% of the variance. Arguably, the confusion comes from the emphasis of patient versus therapist contributions, the relation between alliance and technical intervention, and the relation between alliance and outcome. The HAq was especially criticized for conflating the quality of the relationship with outcome by its measure of Type I alliance, Perceived Helpfulness (Barber & Crits-Christoph, 1996) and was revised to address this criticism by removing several items (Luborsky et al., 1996). Trying to disentangle the alliance from these relationships, however, may be impossible: To illustrate, although the WAI emphasizes purposeful collaboration and does not include any items regarding patient or therapist contribution (unlike the CALPAS and VPPS), its emphasis on agreement on tasks and goals does suggest that technique and outcome are inherent to its conceptualization of the alliance. Nevertheless, we review the research regarding these relationships.

Alliance and Outcome
Survey

There are now several meta-analyses on the predictive relationship between therapeutic alliance and treatment outcome in psychotherapy (e.g., Horvath & Symonds, 1991; Martin, Garske, & Davis, 2000). The most recent (Horvath et al., 2011) surveyed studies up to 2009 and supported previous efforts demonstrating a consistent but modest relationship, with no apparent significant difference among treatment orientations. In an update of this effort, we examined this relationship in only psychodynamically oriented treatments, with a significant expressive component; we removed two studies that used only premature termination as a criterion variable, and we added four studies published since 2009 and up through 2011 ($N = 36$: Cailhol et al., 2009; Hendriksen et al., 2010; Muran et al., 2009; Owen & Hilsenroth, 2011; contact the authors for the complete list of studies). Our reanalysis yielded a medium ES of $r = .284$ (95% CI .25–32, p < .001) for the alliance-outcome relationship in DTs that was statistically significant. Thus we found no significant difference from the Horvath et al. (2011) result of $r = .275$ ($N = 190$) for all treatments. There is also ample evidence in DTs that weakened alliances are correlated with unilateral termination (e.g., Muran et al., 2009; Tryon & Kane, 1993).

Early Gains

There have been some noteworthy challenges to the interpretation of the alliance-outcome correlation. A number of studies have examined the relationship between early treatment gains and alliance with some finding the former carries the predictive load. In other words, it has been suggested that the alliance itself could simply be a product of earlier changes in symptoms. Several studies have failed to demonstrate that the alliance predicts subsequent symptom change when controlling for early treatment gains (Barber et al., 1999; Barber et al., 2001; DeRubeis & Feeley, 1990; Feeley, DeRubeis, & Gelfand, 1999; Strunk, Brotman, & DeRubeis,

2010). Several other studies, however, have still found that the alliance is predictive of outcome above and beyond the impact of early gains (e.g., Barber, Connolly, Crits-Christoph, Gladis, & Siqueland, 2000; Brottman, 2004; Constantino, Arnow, Blasey & Agras, 2005; Gaston et al., 1991; Klein, Schwartz, et al., 2003; Strauss et al., 2006). The lack of convergence in the literature reflects the complexity of the alliance construct and the need for further research in this regard.

Alliance and Contributing Factors

Regardless of specific theoretical slant, the alliance is essentially a construct developed to understand the interaction of two people (i.e., the patient and the therapist) in the therapy context. As such, the alliance subsumes a pair of individuals' life histories, expectations, personality constellations, interpersonal and attachment styles, ways of organizing experience, and worldviews. These factors represent an important set of variables related to the development of the therapeutic alliance.

Patient Factors

Research has identified several important patient factors that contribute to the formation of a strong alliance. For example, patient preconceptions and expectations regarding improvement have been found to be associated with the quality of the alliance such that positive expectations are linked to stronger alliances and better overall treatment outcomes (Messer & Wolitzky, 2010; Watson & Kaloogerakos, 2010).

Patient personality has also been associated to the alliance: Open, agreeable, extraverted, conscientious personality traits are associated with strong alliance, whereas the presence of personality pathology strongly predicts poor early alliance (see Sharpless, Muran, & Barber, 2010). In fact, research suggests that people with personality disorders pose the most difficulty for establishing and maintaining the therapeutic alliance (for a review, see Bender, 2005). In particular, patients with borderline, narcissistic, antisocial, and paranoid personality features are likely to have troubled interpersonal attitudes and behaviors that will complicate, but not necessarily compromise the development of the therapeutic alliance.

Patients' interpersonal functioning, object relations, and attachment style have also been associated with the alliance (see Sharpless et al., 2010, for a review). Patients with affiliative styles are more likely to manifest strong alliances than patients who are more anxious, avoidant, uncomfortable with interpersonal exchanges, and fearful of interpersonal closeness. However, there is also some evidence that poor alliances can improve with patients that have a history of interpersonal problems or those who present interpersonal challenges (see Benjamin & Critchfield, 2010, for a review). Piper, Ogrodniczuk, and Joyce (2004) identified the quality of object relations as a moderator of the alliance-outcome relation in short-term individual therapy. Diener and Monroe's (2011) meta-analysis indicated a positive relationship between patients' attachment security and the therapeutic alliance.

Therapist Factors

Similar to the findings on patient variables, some therapist factors have been identified as facilitators of the alliance, whereas other qualities may impede positive alliance development. Research has generally focused on therapist attachment, personality traits, and factors that comprise technical skill and ability. Some of these variables are relatively stable, core characteristics of the therapist's person (e.g., attachment, personality), whereas other factors appear to be conducive to therapist training or remediation (e.g., technical skills).

In their review of the research, Ackerman and Hilsenroth (2003) identified several key personal qualities that support the development of a positive alliance, including professional demeanor, friendliness, empathy, flexibility, honesty, trustworthiness, confidence, genuineness, alertness and warmth. On the other hand, therapists who are perceived by patients as rigid, uncertain, exploitive, overly critical, distant, aloof, and/or distracted tend to experience negative alliances (Ackerman & Hilsenroth, 2001). More recent research on therapist contributions to the alliance has demonstrated a predictive relation of such personality traits as agreeableness, conscientiousness, and congruence (see Chapman et al., 2009; Hersoug, Høglend, Havik, von der Lippe, & Monsen, 2009; Nissen-Lie, Monsen, & Rønnestad, 2010; Taber, Leibert, & Agaskar, 2011). There are also a few studies suggesting that therapists' attachment security (i.e., low-attachment anxiety, low-attachment avoidance, greater comfort with closeness, strong interpersonal relations) predicts alliance (e.g., Black, Hardy, Turpin, & Parry, 2005; Schauenburg et al., 2010). And in a recent meta-analysis of 53 studies addressing

the relevance of therapist racial/ethnic identity, there was no indication that therapist-patient match in this regard has implications for the therapeutic alliance or treatment success (Cabral & Smith, 2011).

Finally, there is research indicating that specific therapist factors such as therapist skills and abilities (as opposed to the aforementioned, nonspecific trait-based factors) make considerable contributions to the alliance. Techniques such as the appropriate use of silence, mindfulness, apposite transference interpretation, countertransference and self-disclosure contribute to a strong alliance (see Crits-Christoph, Barber, & Kurcias, 1993; Davis & Hayes, 2011; Hayes, Gelso, & Hummel, 2011), whereas misdiagnosis, poor case conceptualization, and excessive or mechanical use of technique have been associated with negative alliance (Hersoug et al., 2009; see Sharpless et al., 2010). With regard to ability, there is growing evidence demonstrating that therapists' individual differences predict alliance quality and treatment success, that some therapists are better at developing alliances, as well as achieving better outcomes (see Baldwin, Wampold, & Imel, 2007; Luborsky et al., 1986; Najavits & Strupp, 1994; Wampold, 2001).

Alliance Ruptures and Resolution: Postsession Analysis
Across-Treatment Evaluations

Although there is much research supporting that a strong and improving alliance predicts a positive treatment outcome (as cited earlier), there is also a growing body of research examining alliance patterns across the course of treatment and demonstrating patterns of deterioration or rupture and in cases of good outcome rupture resolution. This research was initially informed by the work of Mann (1973) and Gelso and Carter (1994), who suggested that there are identifiable patterns of alliance development: specifically, an initial high alliance when patients become mobilized and hopeful, a middle phase of low alliance when patients feel ambivalent about therapy, and then (if this phase is successfully negotiated) a high alliance indicating a working through.

Testing this perspective, Golden and Robbins (1990) analyzed two successful therapy cases and found that patients' alliance ratings increased, dropped, and then increased again during the course of the therapy, despite the fact that therapists exhibited a fair amount of warmth and friendliness and high levels of exploration consistently throughout both treatments. Patton, Kivlighan, and Multon (1997) videotaped 16 patients and six therapists over two semesters. Analysis indicated that a quadratic high-low-high pattern of alliance development was present and related to improved outcome. Although a significant linear increase across sessions was also observed, it was found to be unrelated to client outcome. In a later study Kivlighan and Shaughnessy (2000) used cluster analysis to examine patterns of alliance development in 79 therapist-patient dyads across four counseling sessions. They found three distinct patterns of alliance development: stable alliance, linear alliance growth, and quadratic alliance growth. The quadratic pattern of alliance development was associated with greater improvement compared to other patterns of alliance development.

Stiles and colleagues (2004) initially sought to replicate Kivlighan and Shaughnessy's (2000) findings that a U-shape (high-low-high) alliance pattern was predictive of good outcome. When they were unable to replicate this finding, they shifted their focus from the global alliance pattern to the examination of discrete high-low-high, or V-shape rupture-repair episodes. In a sample of 79 cases (mixed dynamic and cognitive-behavioral), they identified rupture-repair episodes in 17 (21.5%) of the cases and found that these cases evidenced larger gains than the rest of the sample. Strauss et al. (2006) replicated this predictive relationship to outcome in a sample of CT cases, finding rupture-repair sequences in 14/25 (56%) of the cases examined. In contrast, although Stevens, Muran, Safran, Gorman, and Winston (2007) also found 22/44 (50%) cases (mixed dynamic and cognitive-behavioral) with rupture-repair episodes, they did not find a relationship between these and outcome. In a recent meta-analysis of these three studies (Safran, Muran, & Eubanks-Carter, 2011), the aggregated correlation of rupture-repair episodes to treatment outcome indicated a medium effect of .24 (95% CI .09–39, $p > .01$) that was statistically significant.

In-Session Evaluations

In contrast to the efforts mentioned above that examined patterns of postsession alliance ratings for evidence of rupture and resolution, there are a number of studies that have examined in-session evidence of ruptures and resolution. For example, Muran et al. (2009) in a clinical trial of 128 PD

patients comparing a cognitive with a dynamic and an alliance-focused treatment asked patients and therapists to complete a postsession questionnaire (PSQ; Muran, Safran, Samstag, & Winston, 1992), which included a self-report measure of the alliance (WAI-12; Tracey & Kokotovic, 1989), as well as self-report indices measuring the occurrence of ruptures, rupture intensity, and the extent to which ruptures were resolved. They found that ruptures occurred frequently in the first six sessions of the three therapy treatments: Ruptures were reported by 37% of patients and 56% of therapists. Ruptures were also found to negatively predict outcome, and failure to resolve these ruptures predicted dropout. Eames and Roth (2000) also administered the WAI items and the rupture indices from the PSQ after Sessions 2 through 5 to 11 therapists and 30 of their patients receiving treatment as usual at outpatient clinics in the United Kingdom. Similar to Muran et al. (2009), they found that therapists reported ruptures more often, reporting them in 43% of sessions, while patients reported them in 19%.

Sommerfeld, Orbach, Zim, and Mikulincer (2008) examined the difference between patient-report and observer-ratings of ruptures. In a study of 151 sessions from five patients in DT, patients completed PSQs and reported ruptures in 42% of the sessions. Based on transcripts, judges identified confrontation and withdrawal ruptures using Harper's coding system (1989a, 1989b): Rupture markers were identified by observers in 77% of sessions. Eubanks-Carter, Muran, and Safran (2010) developed an observer-based coding system (not requiring transcription) the Rupture Resolution Rating System (3RS) and compared it to patient-rated PSQs in a sample of 48 sessions from early treatment of 20 cases. They found patients reported ruptures in 35% of sessions, observers detected withdrawal rupture markers in every session, and confrontation rupture markers in 75% of sessions. Colli and Lingiardi (2009) developed a transcript-based method for assessing alliance ruptures and resolution, the Collaborative Interaction Scale (CIS), and applied it to a sample of 32 sessions from 16 patients receiving either cognitive or dynamic psychotherapy. They found significant correlations between negative therapist interventions (e.g., showing hostility) and patient rupture markers and between positive therapist interventions (e.g., focusing on the here and now of the relationship) and collaborative patient processes (e.g., talking about feelings or thoughts).

In sum, these studies of in-session events suggest that alliance ruptures are quite prevalent, however measured. They demonstrate that (a) patients report ruptures in 19% to 42% of sessions, (b) therapists report them in 43% to 56% of sessions, and (c) third-party raters observe ruptures anywhere from 41% to 100% of sessions. In studies that examined postsession alliance ratings across treatment to identify the prevalence of rupture-repair sequences, patients reported such sequences in 22% to 56% of cases, suggesting these are fairly common events that deserve more intensive study of what they entail.

Alliance Rupture Resolution: Task Analyses

Several researchers have employed the task analytic paradigm (Rice & Greenberg, 1984), which blends qualitative and quantitative methods to study rupture resolution as a process of change. Although they did not identify their method as task analysis, one of the earliest studies of ruptures and resolution, conducted by Foreman and Marmar (1985), employed an approach that is consistent with task analysis. They selected six cases of short-term dynamic therapy in which the early alliance was rated as poor by observers; in half of these cases, the alliance remained weak and outcome was poor, while in the other half, the alliance improved and good outcome was achieved. They found that addressing and drawing links among the patient's defenses, guilt and expectation of punishment, and problematic feelings in relation to the therapist most strongly differentiated between good and poor outcome cases. Exploration of problematic feelings in the patient's other relationships did not differentiate the two groups.

Safran, Muran, and colleagues built upon Foreman and Marmar's study by undertaking a more intensive examination of the process of rupture resolution in a series of small-scale studies following the task analytic paradigm (Safran, Crocker, McMain, & Murray, 1990; Safran & Muran, 1996; Safran, Muran, & Samstag, 1994). They compared matched resolution and nonresolution sessions from seven different cases, pulled from a pool of more than 29 cases, based on selection criteria from patient-rated PSQs, and then applied various measures of psychotherapy process to the transcribed sessions to operationalize multiple dimensions (that is, interpersonal behavior, emotional involvement, and vocal quality) of each patient and therapist position in the resolution process. They then conducted a series of lag one sequential analyses and tested the significance of transitional probabilities in order to confirm the hypothesized sequences and demonstrate a difference between resolution and nonresolution sessions.

The result of their task analysis was a stage-process model, which is comprised of four interactions involving patient and therapist: (1) *Attending to the Rupture Marker*, (2) *Exploring the Rupture Experience*, (3) *Exploring the Avoidance*, and (4) *Emergence of Wish/Need*. They observed that the type of rupture marker (withdrawal or confrontation) dictated differences in the resolution process. For example, the common progression in the resolution of withdrawal ruptures consists of moving through increasingly clearer articulations of discontent to self-assertion, in which the need for agency is realized. The progression in the resolution of confrontation ruptures consists of moving through feelings of anger, to feelings of disappointment and hurt over having been failed by the therapist, to contacting vulnerability and the wish to be nurtured. Typical avoidant operations that emerge, regardless of rupture type, concern anxieties resulting from the fear of being too aggressive or too vulnerable associated with the expectation of retaliation or rejection by the therapist. In short, the result demonstrated evidence supporting the significance for the therapist and the patient to participate in a collaborative inquiry about the rupture event, including patient expression of negative feelings and therapist nondefensiveness.

Building on the work of Safran and Muran (1996), three additional studies have developed similar rupture resolution procedures using the task analytic paradigm. Agnew, Harper, Shapiro, and Barkham (1994) tested a psychodynamic-interpersonal model of resolution of confrontation ruptures using one good outcome case of eight-session psychodynamic-interpersonal therapy from the Sheffield study of treatment for depression. One rupture and one resolution session were selected based on changes in postsession, patient rated alliance scores. Confrontation rupture markers in these sessions were identified using Harper's coding system for identifying confrontation ruptures (Harper, 1989a). Similar to Safran and Muran's (1996) model, Agnew et al. (1994) begin the resolution process with the therapist acknowledging the rupture, and then exploring the rupture collaboratively with the patient to reach a shared understanding. However, whereas Safran and Muran's (1996) model depicts resolution as a progression toward clarification of the patient's underlying wish or need, Agnew et al. (1994) place greater focus on linking the alliance rupture to situations outside of therapy and discussing new ways to handle those situations.

Bennett, Parry, and Ryle (2006) used task analysis to examine rupture resolution in cognitive analytic therapy (CAT; Ryle, 1997) for BPD. The task analysis was performed using six cases, four with good outcome and two with poor. Rupture sessions were selected based on deviations in postsession, patient-rated alliance scores. Based on a qualitative analysis by experienced CAT clinicians, a total of 107 ruptures from 82 sessions across the six cases were observed, and evidence for resolution was examined, from which a rational model of rupture resolution was developed. Consistent with Safran and Muran's (1996) research, Bennett et al. (2006) found that in good outcome cases, therapists recognized and focused attention on the majority of ruptures, while in poor outcome cases they usually failed to notice or draw attention to the alliance threat. Bennett et al. also stressed a collaborative, nondefensive stance on the part of the therapist. However, in contrast to Safran and Muran's (1996) focus on the immediate process and progressive clarification of the patient's underlying needs, Bennett et al. placed greater emphasis on linking the rupture to a preestablished case formulation and to the patient's other relationships.

Similarly, Aspland, Llewelyn, Hardy, Barkham, and Stiles (2008) used task analysis to refine a preliminary model of rupture resolution in CBT. They examined ruptures (confrontation and withdrawal) and resolution in two good outcome cases of CBT for depression from the Second Sheffield Psychotherapy Project (Shapiro et al., 1994). Cases were identified based on changes in postsession, patient-rated alliance scores. For each of the two cases, a rupture session and a resolution session were selected. Two experienced clinicians examined transcripts of the sessions and identified confrontation and withdrawal markers following Harper's (1994) and Safran and Muran's (2000) descriptions of these types of ruptures. The judges also identified markers of resolution, which was defined as reengagement in the task of therapy. Aspland et al. observed that most ruptures appeared to arise from unvoiced disagreements about the tasks and goals of therapy, which led to negative complementary interactions in which the therapist focused on the task and the patient withdrew. Resolution occurred when therapists shifted their focus from the therapy task to issues that were salient for the patient. Consistent with Safran and Muran, Aspland et al. (2008) emphasized the therapist's collaborative stance. However, in contrast to Safran and Muran (2000), as well as Agnew et al. (1994) and Bennett et al. (2006), Aspland et al.'s (2008) final resolution model did not include any overt recognition or discussion of the rupture itself.

Alliance Ruptures: Qualitative Studies

Although there is growing evidence to support the importance of recognizing and addressing ruptures in the therapeutic alliance, there are also a number of qualitative studies demonstrating the difficulties of doing so for therapists in practice. To begin with, patients are not always able or willing to reveal when they are uncomfortable or disagree with their therapist. Rennie (1994) found in a study of 14 patients that their deference to their therapists played a significant role in therapeutic interactions. He found a number of factors to be associated with patient deference, including fear of criticizing the therapist, need to meet the therapists perceived expectations, acceptance of the therapist's limitations, fear of threatening the therapist's self-esteem, and a sense of indebtedness to the therapist among others. If, as these findings suggest, patients believe protecting their therapists is the best way to maintain the relationship, it is understandable that they would be reluctant to talk openly with them about their concerns regarding treatment. It is thus critical for therapists to be able to pick up on cues that the alliance is in trouble and address them in a way that allows the patient to participate without undue anxiety.

Unfortunately, research conducted by Hill and colleagues has shown that even experienced therapists may have considerable difficulty recognizing such moments. Regan and Hill (1992) asked 24 patients and therapists to report on thoughts or feelings that they were unable to express in treatment, and they found that most things left unsaid by both patients and therapists were negative. In addition, they found therapists were only aware of 17% of the things patients left unsaid. Taking a different tack, Rhodes,

Hill, Thompson, and Elliott (1994), asked 19 therapists and therapists-in-training to recall events from their own treatment and found that although some of the patients were able to talk openly about their negative feelings towards the therapist, patients who felt uncomfortable addressing misunderstanding events were able to conceal them from their therapists and the misunderstandings remained unaddressed, often leading to termination.

Hill, Thompson, Cogar, and Denman (1993) extended the investigation into patient covert processes (reactions to in-session events) to include things left unsaid and secrets in a sample of 26 patients. As in their previous studies, they found that therapists were often unaware of patients' unexpressed reactions. They also found that patients were particularly likely to hide negative feelings and that even experienced, long-term therapists were only able to guess when patients had hidden negative feelings 45% of the time. Furthermore, 65% of the patients in the study left something unsaid (most often negative), and only 27% of the therapists were accurate in their guesses about what their patients were withholding. In a later study, Hill, Nutt-Williams, Heaton, Thompson, and Rhodes (1996) conducted an analysis of 11 therapists' recollections of impasse events that had ended in termination and also found that patients did not reveal their dissatisfaction until they quit therapy. Moreover, therapists reported that they became aware of patients' dissatisfaction only with the announcement of termination and were often taken by surprise.

Even if therapists do become aware of their patients' reservations, it may prove quite difficult to address them in a way that is beneficial to the treatment. A number of studies have suggested that therapists' awareness of patients' negative reactions can be detrimental to outcome (e.g., Fuller & Hill, 1985; Martin, Martin, Meyer, & Slemon, 1986; Martin, Martin, & Slemon, 1987). There is empirical evidence to support various interpretations of this type of finding. One is that therapists may increase their adherence to their preferred treatment model in a rigid fashion, rather than responding flexibly to a perceived rupture in the alliance. Another is that therapists may respond to patients' negative feelings by expressing their own negative feelings in a defensive fashion.

Piper, Azim, Joyce, and McCallum (1991) found an inverse relationship between the proportion of transference interpretations and both alliance and outcome for 64 patients with a history of high-quality object relations. Examining the findings, they hypothesized that increased concentration of transference interpretations may have been an attempt to repair a weakened alliance. They observed an alternating pattern of silences and transference interpretations and found that the inverse relationship between transference interpretations and alliance strengthened over the course of the treatment. This suggests that the patients and therapists may have been engaged in a vicious cycle in which therapists intensified their transference interpretations in a counterproductive attempt to remedy the situation, as the alliance continued to weaken. In a later study, Piper et al. (1999) compared a sample of 22 dropouts with 22 matched completers on pretherapy and therapy process variables. In addition to assessing patient hostility and patient and therapist exploration and focus on transference, they examined the last session prior to drop out for typical patterns. Qualitative analysis of the therapeutic process indicated that sessions typically started with patients expressing dissatisfaction or disappointment with treatment and therapists responding with transference interpretations. As the patients continued to withdraw or express resistance, therapists often continued to focus on transference issues. Sessions often ended with patients agreeing to continue treatment at the recommendation of the therapist, but never returning.

Hill et al. (2003) interviewed 13 experienced therapists about their experiences working with patient expressions of anger. Therapists reported having significantly more difficulty handling overt or asserted expressions of anger. They tended to experience anxiety (e.g., feeling incompetent) and anger at the patient when faced with such expressions and to challenge patients, which resulted in further negative interactions.

The findings in these studies are consistent with those of the Vanderbilt II study conducted by Strupp and his colleagues (Henry, Schacht, Strupp, Butler, & Binder, 1993; Henry, Strupp, Butler, Schacht, & Binder 1993). In this study, a group of experienced therapists ($N = 16$) treated a cohort of patients and were subsequently given a year of intensive training in a manualized form of psychodynamic treatment. The training paid special attention to helping therapists detect and manage maladaptive interpersonal patterns as they are enacted in the therapeutic relationship. Following their training, the therapists treated a second cohort of patients. Evaluation of the differences in the therapeutic process and outcome showed that therapists were, in fact, able to shift their work to correspond more closely with the treatment manual. At the same time, however, the researchers found that rather than being able to treat their patients more skillfully, therapists displayed more hostile behaviors (medium effect that approached statistical significance) and complex communications, such as those that can be seen as both helpful and critical (large significant effect): Both forms of interpersonal behavior have been shown to be related to poor outcome in previous research (Henry, Schacht & Strupp, 1986, 1990). The results of this study suggest that, even when trained to recognize negative process, therapists may respond with counterhostility or defensiveness.

In contrast, several studies suggest that when therapists *are* able to respond nondefensively, attend directly to the alliance, adjust their behavior and address rifts as they occur, the alliance improves. For example, Lansford (1986) looked at six short-term therapy cases, identifying weakening and repairs in the alliance. Independent raters were able to predict outcome by observing excerpts showing weakening and repair of the alliance even though these segments made up a small proportion of the therapy (as little as 8%). Analysis showed that segments when therapists and patients took direct action to repair weakened alliances were followed by the highest levels of patient alliance ratings and the degree of success in addressing weaknesses was predictive of outcome. And the aforementioned studies by Foreman and Marmar (1985) and by Rhodes et al. (1994) yielded similar results, supporting the importance of addressing ruptures directly and nondefensively.

Alliance-Focused Training: Clinical Trials

The research reviewed thus far demonstrates both the importance of addressing ruptures and the difficulties for therapists to do so. The findings of the Vanderbilt studies mentioned earlier, for example, demonstrated how difficult it can be to train therapists to resolve alliance ruptures. Accordingly, therapists may sometimes adhere to manuals in a rigid fashion that interferes with their normally supportive style (Henry, Strupp, et al., 1993), and there was little outcome benefit as a result of such training (Bien et al.,

2000). Similarly, Castonguay, Goldfried, Wiser, Raue, and Hayes' (1996) study of cognitive therapy for depression, and Piper and colleagues' (Piper, Azim, Joyce, & McCallum, 1991; Piper, Ogrodniczuk, et al., 1999) and Schut et al.'s (2005) studies of psychodynamic therapy have found evidence that some therapists attempt to resolve ruptures by increasing their adherence to a theoretical model (e.g., challenging distorted cognitions in cognitive therapy or making transference interpretations in dynamic therapy). These studies found that this rigid adherence in the context of a rupture is linked to poor outcome and premature termination.

Nevertheless, there is also more recent research demonstrating that training therapists in manualized approaches that emphasize the development of an alliance and abilities to resolve ruptures may actually have a beneficial impact on treatment. For example, Hilsenroth, Ackerman, Clemence, Strassle, and Handler (2002) examined the effect of providing structured training in short-term dynamic psychotherapy to 13 graduate student clinicians treating 34 outpatients, who were then compared to a matched group of 15 student clinicians and another 34 outpatients. The training included a focus on a therapeutic model of assessment, which sought to incorporate collaborative goal setting, the development of a therapeutic bond into the assessment phase of treatment, and intensive instruction in SE techniques. Analysis of alliance ratings made after the third or fourth session of therapy found that the structured training was associated with higher alliance scores as rated by patients and by therapists than a standard supervision condition.

For another example, Bambling, King, Raue, Schweitzer, and Lambert (2006) evaluated the impact of two alliance-focused supervision conditions (alliance skill-focused and alliance process-focused supervision) versus a no-supervision condition in a brief eight-session treatment of 127 patients with major depression. In the skill-focused supervision, therapists were given explicit advice and guidance concerning the kinds of behaviors and interventions likely to enhance alliance. In the process-focused supervision, the therapists were trained to monitor implicit client feedback, changes in client anxiety level, flow of exchanges, resistance, and perceived dynamics in the relationship with the therapist. Eight sessions of supervision were provided, including one pretreatment. The results indicated a significant benefit of both supervision conditions over the no-supervision condition on working alliance, symptom change, and treatment retention, but no differences were found between supervision conditions.

In a pilot study, Crits-Christoph and colleagues (2006) found support for training therapists in alliance-fostering therapy, a 16-session treatment for depression that combines psychodynamic-interpersonal interventions with alliance-focused techniques such as responding to ruptures directly by encouraging patients to express their underlying feelings and the interpersonal issues connected to them. Crits-Christoph et al. found that the training resulted in increases in alliance scores that were moderate to large in size but not statistically significant, as well as small improvements in depressive symptoms and larger improvements in quality of life.

The largest studies that have tested the effectiveness of an alliance-focused treatment have been conducted by Safran, Muran, and colleagues, who developed a short-term, alliance-focused psychotherapy treatment informed by their findings from task analytic work: Brief Relational Therapy (BRT; Safran & Muran, 2000). By closely attending to ruptures, therapists and patients in BRT work collaboratively to identify the patient's core relational processes and to explore in the session with new ways of relating. The emphasis in BRT is on helping the patient to develop a generalizable skill of awareness through the use of metacommunication by which the therapist explicitly draws the patient's attention to ruptures emerging in their interactions that represent markers of core relational processes. One study compared BRT with CBT and STDT in a sample of 128 patients with Cluster C PDs and PD NOS (Muran, Safran, Samstag, & Winston, 2005). This study found that BRT was as effective as CBT and STDP with regard to statistical and clinical significance, and was more successful than the other two treatments with respect to retention. In another study of 18 patients with PD who were identified as at risk for treatment failure from a sample of 60 patients, Safran, Muran, Samstag, and Winston (2005) reported additional evidence that BRT successfully keeps challenging patients engaged in treatment. While Safran, Muran, and colleagues continue to investigate the effectiveness of BRT, they are also exploring ways to integrate relational, alliance-focused principles into standard cognitive therapy. Currently, an NIMH-funded study led by Muran and Safran (Muran, Safran, Gorman, Eubanks-Carter, & Banthin, 2008) is underway to see if integrating

rupture resolution training into CBT training improves therapy process and outcome.

Similar efforts to integrate rupture resolution (largely informed by dynamic principles) into CT have been conducted by Castonguay and colleagues. In an effort to improve cognitive therapists' ability to respond to alliance ruptures, Castonguay developed Integrative CT for Depression (ICT; Castonguay, 1996), which primarily integrates Safran and Muran's rupture resolution strategies (Safran & Muran, 1996; Safran & Segal, 1990) into traditional CT. When ruptures are identified, the therapist breaks from the cognitive therapy protocol and addresses the rupture by inviting the patient to explore the rupture, empathizing with the patient's emotional reaction, and reducing the patient's anger or dissatisfaction by validating negative feelings or criticisms and taking at least partial responsibility for the rupture. In a pilot study ($N = 11$), Castonguay et al. (2004) found that patient symptom improvement was greater in ICT than a wait-list condition, and compared favorably to previous findings for cognitive therapy. In a randomized trial comparing ICT to CT ($N = 11$), Constantino et al. (2008) found that ICT patients had greater improvement on depression and global symptoms and more clinically significant change than CT patients. ICT also yielded better patient-rated alliance quality and therapist empathy, and there was a trend toward better patient retention in ICT than in CT. A similar effort to integrate rupture resolution strategies into CT for GAD was undertaken by Newman, Castonguay, Borkovec, Fisher, and Nordberg (2008). The study ($N = 18$) found that the integrative treatment significantly decreased GAD symptoms, yielding a higher ES than the average ES of CT for GAD in the treatment literature. Participants also showed clinically significant improvements in GAD symptoms and interpersonal problems with continued gains at 1-year follow-up.

In a meta-analysis that examined the impact of rupture resolution training or supervision on patient outcome in the eight studies mentioned above (Bambling et al., 2006; Bein et al., 2000; Castonguay et al., 2004; Constantino et al., 2008; Crits-Christoph et al., 2006; Hilsenroth et al., 2002; Muran et al., 2005; Newman et al., 2008), Safran, Muran, and Eubanks-Carter (2011) calculated pre-post and group contrast ESs and found a large pre-post r for the rupture resolution training of .65 (95% CI .46 − .78, p < .001) and a small between-group ES of .15 (95% CI .04 − .26, p < .01), in both cases indicating a statistically significant effect. Adding to the promise of alliance-focused training suggested by this meta-analysis is the body of research by Lambert and colleagues (Lambert et al., 2003) examining the impact of providing therapists feedback and clinical support when risk for treatment failure is indicated. A poor therapeutic alliance is one of the risk factors and triggers a clinical support tool primarily informed by principles defined by Safran and Muran (2000). In a recent meta-analysis of six major studies ($N = 6,151$) conducted by Shimokawa, Lambert, and Smart (2010), they found feedback interventions were effective in preventing treatment failure.

PSYCHODYNAMIC CHANGE MECHANISMS AND OUTCOMES

Studies of psychotherapy effectiveness often place symptom change as the ultimate measure of improvement, but many DT patients, practitioners, and researchers have a different perspective about what type of change is expected from therapy. Symptoms are believed to be a product of an unconscious conflict or ambivalence (e.g., a socially unacceptable desire; an unprocessed traumatic event) acquired from early relational experiences. A symptom has the function of expressing that unconscious conflict in a consciously painful but socially acceptable way (e.g., feeling panic instead of anger; dissociating important feelings and memories of a trauma). These conflicts make up part of an individual's personality, and as such personality change is often a goal in DT. Additionally, because these symptoms often repeat earlier interpersonal experiences, discovering new ways of perceiving and relating to others is viewed as a good outcome in DT. Five unique ways in which DT seeks to help patients are: (1) fostering insight into unconscious conflict; (2) increasing the use of adaptive psychological defenses; (3) decreasing rigidity in interpersonal perceptions and behaviors; (4) improving the quality of patients' mental representations of relationships; and (5) increasing their comprehension of their own and others' mental states. These unique DT mechanisms may be outcomes in themselves or mediators by which DT affects symptom change.

Insight

Insight, or self-understanding, is the awareness a person has into his or her motivations, expectations, and behaviors. Self-understanding has been defined in many ways but has long been considered the cardinal goal of DT (Messer & McWilliams, 2007). Insight is thought to be instilled through the therapist's interpretation of similarities between the patient's past and present experiences (e.g., Strachey, 1934) or through the processing of the shared relationship between patient and therapist (e.g., Hirsch, 1998). Frequently, insight is sudden and accompanied by a sensation of discovery, or an "aha" moment (Elliott et al., 1994), although it may develop slowly over treatment (e.g., Jones, Parke, & Pulos, 1992). Insight may affect symptoms by making them feel more manageable through the development of an explanation or narrative as to why those symptoms occur. Alternately, self-understanding may free the individual to act in new ways by providing an emotional release (Freud, 1917/1958) or by triggering a reappraisal of the usefulness of symptom behaviors. Self-understanding may occur at an intellectual or emotional level (Gibbons, Crits-Christoph, Barber, & Schamberg, 2007). Intellectual insight is the cognitive recognition of the origin or purpose of symptoms. Emotional insight refers to the experience of the conflict at a new or different level. Often emotional insight can be a different sensation of an old memory or familiar experience, a corrective emotional experience (Alexander & French, 1946; Sharpless & Barber, 2012), or a sense of mastery over a previously puzzling experience (Grenyer & Luborsky, 1996; Weiss, Sampson, & Mount Zion Psychotherapy Research Group, 1986). Insight has been measured by therapist judgment (e.g., Graff & Luborsky, 1977); observer judgment from interview (e.g., Johansson et al., 2010), session content (e.g., Grenyer & Luborsky, 1996; Messer & McWilliams, 2007), or patient-generated stimulus material (e.g., Falk & Hill, 1995); and patient self-report (e.g., Connolly et al., 1999).

Many studies show that insight increases over the course of DT (e.g., Connolly et al., 1999; Gibbons et al., 2009; Grande, Rudolf, Oberbracht, & Pauli-Magnus, 2003; Kivlighan, Multon, & Patton, 2000; for an exception, see Crits-Christoph et al., 2003). Increases in insight over treatment have been associated with symptom change in DT (Grande et al., 2003; Grenyer & Luborsky, 1996; Johansson et al., 2010; Kivlighan et al., 2000; Gibbons et al., 2009; for exceptions, see Connolly et al., 1999; Crits-Christoph et al., 2003). Some preliminary evidence suggests that changes in self-understanding precede symptom improvement (e.g., Grande et al., 2003; Kivlighan et al., 2000). Interestingly, changes in insight may be unique to DT, as self-understanding does not change in other treatments, nor is it correlated with symptom change (Connolly et al., 1999; Crits-Christoph et al., 2003; Gibbons et al., 2009; for an exception, see Hoffart, Versland, & Sexton, 2002). However, greater insight may not explain the initial development of symptoms, as seen by the lack of relation to symptom level prior to therapy (Connolly et al., 1999). People who are generally happy and higher-functioning may have little reason to delve into why they act and feel the way they do. Finally, although theorists believe that greater pretreatment insight will predict success in DT (Messer & McWilliams, 2007), the few studies examining this relation are equivocal (e.g., Cromer & Hilsenroth, 2010). Initial insight level is related to treatment retention (Cromer & Hilsenroth, 2010), which may be one partial route through which insight affects change in DT. Overall, insight is strongly implicated in the process of change in DT, and greater precision in the definition and measurement of insight may increase our ability to detect who will benefit most from DT.

Defense Style

Psychological defenses are normative and universal mechanisms by which individuals protect themselves against anxiety arising from unconscious conflict. These mechanisms permit the expression of unacceptable feelings or behavior by the transformation of experience (e.g., denial, or refusal to admit an unpleasant experience happened). Defenses differ from coping mechanisms in that their focus is on managing the internal world of the individual, whereas coping mechanisms are patterns of handling problems in the external world (Cramer, 1998; although see Kramer, 2010). Defenses vary in their levels of maturity, which represents their developmental appearance as well as their effectiveness in managing conflict (e.g., Cramer, 1991; Vaillant, 1992). Less mature defenses are seen in children and in individuals with severe mental illness. They distort perception to reduce anxiety but in doing so lead to strong inappropriate reactions or withdrawal (e.g., splitting, or when something with multiple characteristics is seen as entirely bad or good). Mature defenses are seen in healthy adults and both express and inhibit conflict at the same time (e.g., sublimation, or turning strong desires into socially acceptable products like art or financial success). The type and frequency of defenses used are thought to constitute an individual's personality. A defensive style that employs immature defenses or that uses more mature defenses too rigidly can impair the ability to perceive and interact with the world. DT works to increase the maturity and flexibility of defense use by pointing out the function of defenses and encouraging the use of more adaptive defenses (e.g., Summers & Barber, 2009). Measurement of defenses has been well reviewed elsewhere (Davidson & MacGregor, 1998; Perry & Ianni, 1998) and includes interview measures, projective testing, and self-report instruments. These measures describe the typical defenses employed by an individual as well as an overall maturity level of the person's defense style.

Many studies have demonstrated the decrease in the use of immature defenses over therapy (Akkerman, Carr, & Lewin, 1992; Kneepkens & Oakley, 1996; Roy, Perry, Luborsky, & Banon, 2009), as well as the increase in the use of more mature defenses (e.g., Bond & Perry, 2004; Johansen, Krebs, Svartberg, Stiles, & Holen, 2011, Kramer, Despland, Michel, Drapeau, & de Roten, 2010; Roy et al., 2009). Changes in the maturity of defensive functioning have been related to changes in symptom level (e.g., Akkerman et al., 1992; Bond & Perry, 2004; Johansen et al., 2011; Kneepkens & Oakley, 1996). The most change in defenses may come after the reduction of acute symptoms (Hersoug, Sexton, & Høglend, 2002), and so the temporal relation of defenses and symptom change requires further investigation. Furthermore, changes in defensive style may not be unique to DT, as these changes are present and are related to symptom change in other treatments (e.g., Coleman, Cole, & Wuest, 2010; Johansen et al., 2011). Pretreatment use of maladaptive defenses has been consistently linked with greater symptom levels and psychopathology (e.g., Kramer, 2010; for a review, see Bond, 2004). Possessing greater adaptive defenses at the beginning of treatment also predicted a better response to DT (e.g., Bond & Perry, 2004) and other treatments (Muris & Merckelbach, 1996). Defenses may be uniquely addressed by DT, but may be common to change processes in multiple forms of treatment. Further work needs to examine what factors in therapy create changes in defense style.

Relationship Rigidity

In psychodynamic theory, individuals have characteristic patterns of motivations, expectations, and reactions in their interactions with others that are learned from childhood experiences.

These patterns are used later in life to interpret interpersonal information and guide behavior in new relationships (Blatt, Auerbach, & Levy, 1997; Bowlby, 1988; Freud, 1912/1958). The application of these central interpersonal patterns to new relationships is called *transference* and is generally thought to be found in all individuals to some degree. Less healthy individuals apply their relationship patterns more rigidly, adapt less to the demands of their current relationships, and experience poorer relationships and greater symptoms as a result (e.g., Kiesler, 1996). Dynamic therapists help make patients aware of their relationship patterns, perhaps through increasing insight, so that patients can more flexibly respond in their interpersonal relationships (e.g., Summers & Barber, 2009). Divergent methods have been used to estimate relationship rigidity (for a review, see McCarthy, Gibbons, & Barber, 2008), including amplitude (i.e., the distinctiveness of a single interpersonal theme in a profile of interpersonal themes; Gurtman & Balakrishnan, 1998), pervasiveness (i.e., the frequency of a person's central relationship pattern in a sample of narratives; Crits-Christoph & Luborsky, 1998), dispersion (i.e., the spread of a distribution of interpersonal themes; Cierpka et al., 1998; Slonim, Shefler, Gvirsman, & Tishby, 2011), and profile correlation (i.e., the covariance the interpersonal themes among a patient's relationships; McCarthy et al., 2008).

Rigidity has been shown to decrease in response to DT (Crits-Christoph & Luborsky, 1998; Gross, Stasch, Schmal, Hillenbrand, & Cierpka, 2007; Salzer et al., 2010; Slonim et al., 2011; Tishby, Raitchick, & Shefler, 2007; for exceptions, see Lunnen, Ogles, Anderson, & Barnes, 2006; Weinryb, Wilczek, Barber, Gustavsson, & Asberg, 2004). However, changes in rigidity do not appear to relate to changes in symptoms over the same period (Gross et al., 2007; Lunnen et al., 2006; Staats, May, Herrmann, Kersting, & Konig, 1998; Wilczek et al., 2004; for exceptions, see Crits-Christoph & Luborsky, 1998; Slonim et al., 2011). No studies appear to compare how rigidity might change in different psychotherapies (although see Ruiz et al., 2004) so it remains unclear whether DT uniquely affects relationship rigidity. Levels of relationship rigidity may be independent of psychiatric symptoms, as the concurrent relation observed in the literature has been equivocal (e.g., Slonim et al., 2011; for a review, see McCarthy et al., 2008). Differences in operationalization may account for the mixed findings in the role

of rigidity in DT (McCarthy et al., 2008). Furthermore, it is often unclear whether rigidity is measured across relationships (i.e., how similar is a person perceiving and acting in each of their relationships), within relationships (i.e., how similar is a person perceiving and acting in the same relationship), or both across and within, which may have implications for how widespread and distressing a person's interpersonal problems are (Foltz, Barber, Weinryb, Morse, & Chittams, 1999). Finally, interpersonal rigidity may share a curvilinear relation with symptoms (McCarthy et al., 2008; Slonim et al., 2011), as individuals who are either too inflexible or too inconsistent in their relationships may experience more problems. Greater definition and study of rigidity may bring clarity as the concept is brought more in line with how it is experienced and worked through by DT patients and therapists.

Quality of Object Relations (QOR)

Object relations refers to the cognitive and affective representations that individuals have of their relationships and interpersonal life. Creating a schema of relationships is a developmental process that involves several tasks: populating the representation with objects (persons) derived from actual relationships; storing and organizing episodic and emotional information about these relationships; and integrating the conflicting demands within and among these relationships. These mental representations differ in quality depending on the early experiences of the person and his or her ability to resolve specific developmental challenges. Having internal representations of relationships allows for the belief that one's own and others' personalities are stable and enduring, for soothing one's self without the direct assistance of others, and for goal-directed interactions with others. The presumed product of good QOR is long-standing, satisfying interpersonal relationships in the real world and satisfying, comforting memories of relationships past, as well as the ability to form a strong emotional bond with the therapist in DT and to examine and grow from the strains that emerge in that relationship. Measurement of QOR has been well reviewed (Huprich & Greenberg, 2003) and includes clinician interview about relationships, projective testing, and self-report. Whereas most assessment tools describe life-long patterns of QOR, some instruments focus more on the derivatives of object relations, like current interpersonal functioning (Connolly et al., 1999; Piper et al., 1991).

QOR has been shown to change across DT in multiple studies (e.g., Blatt et al., 1996; Lindgren, Werbart, & Philips, 2010; Porcerelli et al., 2006; Vermote et al., 2010). Changes in QOR overtreatment have been associated with symptom improvement as well (Blatt, Stayner, Auerbach, & Behrends, 1996; Vermote et al., 2010). Change in QOR in other treatments has not been investigated and so remains an open research question. The majority of work on QOR has been as a predictor of suitability or likelihood of success in DT. Better pretreatement QOR has been shown to be associated with greater improvement in symptoms and functioning after DT (e.g., Piper, Joyce, McCallum, & Azim, 1998; Piper, McCallum, Joyce, Rosie, & Ogrodniczuk, 2001; Van et al., 2008; but see Høglend et al., 2006; Joyce, Ogrodniczuk, Piper & Sheptycki, 2010). Pretreatment QOR is not related to outcome in supportive therapy (Piper et al., 1998, 2001; but see Joyce et al., 2010), providing partial evidence for the specificity of QOR in moderating the effectiveness of DT. Better pretreatment QOR has also been linked to better alliances across therapy (e.g., Hersoug, Monsen, Havik & Høglend, 2002; Goldman & Anderson, 2007; Van et al., 2008), which may provide the platform for the work of DT (cf. Piper, Ogrodniczuk, & Joyce, 2004). In addition, QOR moderates the relation between DT interventions and outcome, although it remains unclear how this relation works (e.g., Connolly et al., 1999; Høglend et al., 2006; Piper et al., 2004). Higher levels of QOR have been related to better psychological functioning and can distinguish between clinical and nonclinical samples (e.g., Porcerelli, Huprich, & Markova, 2010).

Reflective Functioning

Perhaps the newest change factor to emerge in the dynamic theory is mentalization, or reflective functioning (RF; Fonagy & Bateman, 2006). Grounded in attachment theory (Bowlby, 1988) and theory of mind (Baron-Cohen, Leslie, & Frith, 1985), RF is the ability to comprehend one's own and other's mental states and to use that information to explain and guide relationship behavior. It is considered to be a developmental achievement that occurs through the empathic mirroring behavior of early caregivers and a lack of disruptive traumatic experiences. Individuals with a high degree of RF are able to contemplate their own and other's cognitive and affective states, distinguish between the implicit and explicit intentions possible in behavior, and understand how relational interactions change and develop over time. The concept of RF was initially developed to explain the experiences of patients with BPD but has been expanded to understand other conditions as well (Fonagy, Bateman, & Bateman, 2011).

Measurement of mentalization has largely used the Reflective Functioning Scale (RFS; Fonagy, Target, Steele, & Steele, 1998), which is coded from clinical interviews (e.g., Harpaz-Rotem & Blatt, 2005; Main, Goldwyn, & Hesse, 2002) or narratives told by patients in psychotherapy (e.g., Karlsson & Kermott, 2006). One study showed a medium-size correspondence when the RFS was applied to different assessment methods (Lowyck et al., 2009). Additional scales to assess disorder-specific mentalization have been added to the RFS (Rudden, Milrod, Target, Ackerman, & Graf, 2006; Taubner, Kessler, Buchheim, Kachele, & Staun, 2011). Other instruments rate RF from individuals' responses to videotaped social interactions (e.g., Arntz & Veen, 2001).

RF has been shown to increase over DT in one study of BPD (Levy et al., 2006), but not in studies of other disorders (Karlsson & Kermott, 2006; Rudden et al., 2006; Vermote et al., 2010). Panic-specific RF did change over the course of treatment for Panic Disorder (Rudden et al., 2006), suggesting that mentalization may have adaptations to particular types of psychopathology. RF did not increase in CBT (Karlsson & Kermott, 2006; Levy et al., 2006) and significantly decreased in a study of interpersonal psychotherapy (Karlsson & Kermott, 2006). Only one study correlated change in RF with change in symptoms and found no association (Vermote et al., 2010). Lower RF prior to therapy was associated with greater symptoms or more severe diagnoses in some studies (e.g., Bazin et al., 2009; Bouchard et al., 2008; Fonagy et al., 1996; Sharp et al., 2011) but not others (e.g., MacBeth, Gumley, Schwannauer, & Fisher, 2011; Fischer-Kern et al., 2010; Taubner et al., 2011). Similarly, pretreatment RF predicted treatment response in one study (Muller, Kaufbold, Overbeck, & Grabhorn, 2006) but not in another (Taubner et al., 2011). The theory and study of RF is still in its infancy, and few definitive conclusions can be drawn about its relation to process and outcome in DT. However, future studies will need to take note of the specific population being examined, as qualitative differences may exist in mentalization by disorder. Additionally, mentalization-based DT includes interventions and a therapeutic stance that may differ from other types of DT (Fonagy & Bateman, 2006), and so RF may be expected to change more in this form of DT compared to other forms.

TECHNIQUE USE IN DT

The two major types of DT techniques are supportive and expressive (Luborsky, 1984; Piper, Joyce, McCallum, Azim, & Ogrodniczuk, 2001). Supportive techniques include many of the common factors like warmth and empathy but also include ego-strengthening interventions more unique to DT like boundary setting, gratification, and bolstering adaptive defenses. Expressive or interpretative interventions are designed to uncover or "express" the unconscious conflict behind a patient's symptoms. These interventions include exploration of affect and interpersonal themes (i.e., encouraging patients to generate affective and relationship material through free association or selectively focusing the patient's attention on these themes), clarification (i.e., drawing a patient's attention to knowledge they already possess but in a new light), and interpretation (i.e., making meaningful connections between past and present relationship experiences, especially involving the therapist).

The use of DT techniques in a session or segment of a session is often assessed for either a single class of interventions (e.g., transference interpretations) or for DT intervention use on average. Measurement of psychodynamic techniques can be accomplished with frequency counts (e.g., Connolly et al., 1999), percentage of total intervention use in a session (e.g., Piper, Joyce, McCallum, & Azim, 1993), or average subscale scores from intervention measures (e.g., Hilsenroth, Blagys, Ackerman, Bonge, & Blais, 2005; McCarthy & Barber, 2009). A specific type of intervention measure is an adherence scale (e.g., Barber & Crits-Christoph, 1996; Klein, Milrod, & Busch, 1999), which measures the degree to which a therapist followed the principles and techniques set out in a therapy manual. Adherence is often used as a manipulation check to ensure that the treatment was delivered (e.g., Spinhoven, Giesen-Bloo, van Dyck, Kooiman, & Arntz, 2007) but is only infrequently studied in relation to DT process and outcome. Adherence and technique use are not synonymous (adherence is a subset of technique use), but we will not

consider them separately here due to the limited number of process studies that examine the effects of DT techniques.

Expressive interventions, when measured together on average, have demonstrated an equivocal relation with treatment outcome (for no relation, see Barber et al., 1996; DeFife, Hilsenroth, & Gold, 2008; Ogrodniczuk & Piper, 1999; Ogrodniczuk, Piper, Joyce, & McCallum, 2000; Owen & Hilsenroth, 2011; for a favorable relation, see Ablon & Jones, 1998; Luborsky, McLellan, Woody, O'Brien, & Auerbach, 1985; Hilsenroth et al., 2005; Hendriksen et al., 2011; for an unfavorable relation, see Barber et al., 2008). Investigations of individual expressive techniques provide some additional detail to the ambiguity of these findings. Exploration of affect has been consistently linked to more positive outcomes (for a meta-analysis, see Diener, Hilsenroth, & Weinberger, 2007). A recent study of graduate trainees conducting DT for anxiety disorders also showed a moderate-size but nonsignificant effect of emotional exploration on outcome (Slavin-Mulford, Hilsenroth, Weinberger, & Gold, 2011). Exploration of interpersonal themes has been linked to outcome on a fairly consistent basis (Gaston et al., 1998; Klein, Milrod, Busch, Levy, & Shapiro, 2003; Slavin-Mulford et al., 2011).

Interpretation and clarification are perhaps the most studied of the expressive interventions, and in contrast to other expressive interventions, are often found to be related to worse therapeutic outcomes (e.g., Høglend et al., 2006; Ryum, Stiles, Svartberg, & McCullough, 2010; Schut et al., 2005; for a review, see Høglend, 2004). It is probable that interpretation and outcome share a small-size negative linear relation, although these studies have been too diverse in their methodology and reporting of their results to compare quantitatively. One obvious explanation of this negative association might be that interpretation has a deleterious effect on patients, although this account is contradicted by the efficacy data for DT as well as by clinical observation. A more subtle understanding of the negative relation between interpretation and outcome has been titled the "high risk-high gain" phenomenon (Gabbard et al., 1994). Targeted and sparing use of interpretations may lead to better outcome, but frequent use of interpretation may destabilize the patient's defense structure and therefore might increase symptoms. This explanation is based on observed helpfulness of interpretation in many cases and the long-standing belief among dynamic theorists that interpretations can be overwhelming for certain patients (Strachey, 1934). Some studies of the immediate in-session climate associated with interpretation support this account. For instance, interpretations are more related to symptom improvement when followed by emotion processing (McCullough et al., 1991; Milbrath et al., 1999). At the same time, interpretative work has a high probability of being perceived as disaffiliative (Coady, 1991; Klein, Schwartz, et al., 2003; Schut et al., 2005) and may lead to alliance ruptures and poor outcome if not handled correctly by therapists. A final explanation of the negative relation between interpretation and symptoms might be that patients unlikely to improve may receive or pull for more interpretations from their therapists (Høglend, 2004).

Supportive interventions have largely been measured in aggregate as opposed to singly (e.g., Barber, Crits-Christoph, & Luborsky, 1996) or in relation to the expressive interventions in DT sessions (e.g., Hendriksen et al., 2011). Surprisingly, there has consistently been no result when supportive interventions were correlated with outcome (Barber et al., 1996, 2008; Hersoug et al., 2005; Milbrath et al., 1999; Ogrodniczuk et al., 2000). The lack of more thorough investigation of supportive techniques might be due to the greater emphasis placed on expressive techniques in DT theory or due to the tendency to overlook supportive interventions in favor of the therapeutic alliance.

Moderators of DT Technique Use and Outcome

The relation between technique use and outcome in DT has proved quite complex, although in the absence of other factors, it can be recommended that more affective and interpersonal exploration be used but only sparing interpretation. While initially contradictory to psychodynamic theory, the complexity of the association between DT interventions and outcome has caused dynamic theorists and researchers to look for how the process of therapy might influence the relation of technique use and outcome and how different methodologies might produce different findings.

Level of Intervention Use

Psychodynamic theorists have long postulated the powerful but potentially destabilizing nature of their interventions (Strachey, 1934). Paired with the mixed findings of DT technique and

outcome, researchers have moved to examine not only a "more is better" linear relation to DT technique use and outcome, in which greater levels of technique predict greater improvement, but also a "just right" curvilinear approach, in which a more moderate level of technique use may be associated with better outcome than very low or very high levels. Piper and colleagues (1991) were perhaps the first to examine this hypothesis empirically, and they found a positively accelerating function of interpretation use and outcome. Low and moderate levels of interpretation were both related to favorable outcome whereas higher levels of interpretation were related to rapidly worsening outcome. However, Ogrodniczuk and Piper (1999) were unable to replicate this finding. In designing his experimental study of transference interpretations, Høglend (personal communication 02/15/10), chose not to assign patients to receive a "high" level of transference interpretation because he and his colleagues thought such a condition would be counterindicated. In the DT arm of a randomized trial for cocaine dependence, Barber and colleagues (2008) observed that very high and low levels of psychodynamic interventions, but not moderate levels, were related to greater drug abstinence, the opposite of the "just right" hypothesis. However, the process of DT for substance use disorders may differ from the treatment of other disorders due to the tendency of many substance dependent patients to use externalizing behaviors (e.g., blaming, substance intake) to manage their own emotional reactions rather than verbalizing their problems more directly. To date, McCarthy (2009) presented the only study to confirm the "just right" hypothesis, in which patients with depression who received a moderate amount of DT interventions improved more compared to patients receiving very low or very high levels.

Therapeutic Alliance

DT techniques are often assumed to influence outcome through the therapeutic alliance, but exactly how this relationship works has been a matter of continued discussion (see prior section on the alliance in DT for more on the complexity of this relationship). For instance, early theorists thought that the alliance represented the rational side of the patient's unconscious and that the interventions of the therapist recognized by the unconscious and responded to with an increased alliance (Greenson, 1965). In support of this idea, technique use at one time point in therapy is often associated with higher levels of alliance at a later point (e.g., Gaston, Thompson, Gallagher, Cournoyer, & Gagnon, 1998; Patton, Kivilighan, & Multon, 1997). Alliance has also been studied as a distinct factor against which technique competes to explain the variance in outcome (e.g., Barber et al., 1996; Ogrodniczuk et al., 2000). Still others have investigated how the alliance is fostered differently in different treatments (e.g., Spinhoven et al., 2007).

However, many psychodynamic thinkers and researchers believe that alliance provides a context for technique use, such that greater levels of alliance permit DT techniques to be more effective (Gaston et al., 1998). Recent studies have observed an interaction of DT interventions and alliance (Ryum et al., 2010; Owen & Hilsenroth, 2011), and with closer examination the driving factor in the interaction of technique and alliance appears to be the negative effect on outcome of expressive techniques in the context of lower alliances. Outcome is moderate with lower technique use regardless of the alliance level (poor or strong), and is equivalent or slightly better when both a strong alliance and high levels of technique are present. Similarly, Barber and others (2008) found moderate drug abstinence in cocaine-dependent individuals with little differential effect of adherence to expressive technique at lower levels of alliance. At higher levels of alliance, greater adherence predicted slightly greater abstinence than more moderate adherence levels. Adherence was modeled curvilinearly in this study, and nominal adherence was related to the most abstinence at high levels of alliance, compared to both moderate and very high adherence. In contrast to these studies, Høglend and colleagues (2011) found that patients with higher alliances evidenced better outcomes when minimal interpretations were offered whereas patients with lower alliances benefited more from higher (moderate) levels of transference interpretation, although these findings were further qualified by the pretreatment QOR of the patient. At this point, there are simply too few studies examining the interaction of alliance and technique together to draw strong conclusions. Detecting interaction effects often requires large samples and good variability in both factors examined (McClelland & Judd, 1993), and few studies in psychotherapy research have those advantages.

Competence. Competency is how well a therapist employs DT techniques with a given patient and progress of the therapy. Competence is typically judged by individuals with recognized expertise in psychotherapy practice. Some factors entering into a judgment of a therapist's competence are: (a) the ability to formulate patient's personality organization or symptom constellation; (b) the accurate assessment of the patient's need at the moment of intervention, including the patient's receptivity to intervention; (c) the choice of a specific intervention for a given problem, including its appropriateness for the problem; (d) the comparison of the chosen intervention to other potential interventions not selected, especially techniques proscribed for DT; and (e) the execution of the intervention. Holistic judgments are common over a certain period of observation, although competence is often measured for multiple classes of interventions. Greater competence necessitates some use of DT techniques, although the correlation found between DT technique use or adherence to a DT manual may be modest (Barber, Sharpless, Klostermann, & McCarthy, 2007).

Competency has been shown to be related to alliance (Despland et al., 2009), however, the relation between global competence in DT and outcome has been equivocal. In a study of patients with depression a positive relation between competence in expressive techniques and subsequent symptom improvement was found (Barber et al., 1996). Similarly, a positive relation between competency and outcome was observed in very brief (four-session) DT, but only for those patients whose alliances improved over the four sessions (Despland et al., 2009). In a study of psychodynamic treatment for cocaine-dependent individuals, no relation was observed (Barber et al., 2008). Finally, competence was associated with worse outcomes in a study of short-term anxiety-provoking psychotherapy (Svartberg & Stiles, 1994). Clearly more work is needed to understand why the intuitive relation between competence and outcome is not always observed and to investigate the conditions under which competence is related to improvement. One possibility is the breadth of judgments required to assess competence reduces not only reliability of competency estimates, but compounds the problem by multiple unreliabilities across dimensions. When dimensions of competency are examined singly, a clearer picture may emerge.

Accuracy of Interpretations

One dimension of competency in DT is how accurate a therapist's interpretations are to the unconscious conflict of the patient. Accuracy has been defined as the extent to which the interpretations keep with a patient's formulation, or the theoretical understanding of the patient's problems given his or her unique history. Researchers have used experienced therapists' formulations of their patients (e.g., Piper et al., 1993) or observer-derived formulations (e.g., Luborsky & Crits-Christoph, 1998; Curtis, Silberschatz, Sampson, & Weiss, 1994) as the criterion to compare the accuracy of their subsequent interpretations. There has been a strong positive correlation between accuracy and subsequent outcome (Andruszna, Luborsky, Pham, & Tang, 2006; Crits-Christoph, Cooper, & Luborsky, 1988; Norville, Sampson, & Weiss, 1996; Silberschatz, Fretter, & Curtis, 1986) or alliance (Crits-Christoph et al., 1988; Stigler, de Roten, Drapeau, & Despland, 2007). One interesting new finding is that when outside judges formulate a patient's typical interpersonal problems, greater correspondence of interventions leads to better outcome in IPT but deleterious outcomes in CBT, providing partial evidence that interpersonal-focused psychotherapies may work in a unique and specific way through relationships (Crits-Christoph, Gibbons, Temes, Elkin, & Gallop, 2010).

Despite the evidence for the efficacy of DT, the process of how DT affects change in patients remains unsettled. The relation of technique use to outcome is complex, although interpersonal and affective exploration appear to be generally helpful as well as the sparing use of accurate interpretation. Supportive techniques may provide a necessary backdrop for the development of the alliance and delivery of other techniques. DT techniques may produce the most change with individuals with good pretreatment QOR and high alliances. Much more exciting work into the process of DT remains to be done, including examining how DT techniques relate not just to symptom change but also to change mechanisms and outcomes specific to DT; how complex and curvilinear relations might exist among process variables in DT; and how we might tailor DT for the benefit of different individuals.

REFERENCES

*Asterisk indicates works used in meta-analysis.

Abbass, A. A., Hancock, J. T., Henderson, J., & Kisely, S. R. (2006). Short-term psychodynamic psychotherapies for common mental disorders. *Cochrane Database of Systematic Reviews, 18*(4), CD004687.

Abbass, A., Kisely, S., & Kroenke, K. (2009). Short-term psychodynamic psychotherapy for somatic disorders: Systematic review of meta-analysis of clinical trials. *Psychotherapy and Psychosomatics, 78*(5), 265–274.

*Abbass, A., Sheldon, A., Gyra, J., & Kalpin, A. (2008). Intensive short-term dynamic psychotherapy for DSM-IV personality disorders: A randomized controlled trial. *Journal of Nervous and Mental Disease, 196*(3), 211–216.

Abbass, A., Town, J., & Driessen, E. (2011). The efficacy of short-term psychodynamic psychotherapy for depressive disorders with comorbid personality disorder. *Psychiatry, 74*(1), 58–71.

Ablon, J., & Jones, E. E. (1998). How expert clinicians' prototypes of an ideal treatment correlate with outcome in psychodynamic and cognitive-behavioral therapy. *Psychotherapy Research, 8*(1), 71–83.

Ablon, J. S., & Jones, E. E. (2002). Validity of controlled clinical trials of psychotherapy: Findings from the NIMH Treatment of Depression Collaborative Research Program. *American Journal of Psychiatry, 159*, 775–783.

Ackerman, S. J., & Hilsenroth, M. J. (2001). *A review of therapist characteristics and technique negatively impacting the therapeutic alliance.* Psychotherapy: Theory, Research, Practice, Training, 171–185.

Ackerman, S., & Hilsenroth, M. (2003), A review of therapist characteristics and techniques positively impacting the therapeutic alliance. *Clinical Psychology Review, 23*, 1–33.

Agnew, R. M., Harper, H., Shapiro, D. A., & Barkham, M. (1994). Resolving a challenge to the therapeutic relationship: A single-case study. *British Journal of Medical Psychology, 67*, 155–170.

Akkerman, K., Carr, V., & Lewin, T. (1992). Changes in ego defenses with recovery from depression. *Journal of Nervous and Mental Disease, 180*(10), 634–638.

Alexander, F., & French, T. M. (1946). *Psychoanalytic therapy; principles and application.* Oxford, United Kingdom: Ronald Press.

*Alstrom, J. E., Norlund, C. L., Persson, G., Harding, M., & Ljungqvist, C. (1984a). Effects of four treatment methods on agoraphobic women not suitable for insight-oriented psychotherapy. *Acta Psychiatrica Scandinavica, 70*(1), 1–17.

*Alstrom, J. E., Norlund, C. L., Persson, G., Harding, M., & Ljungqvist, C. (1984b). Effects of four treatment methods on social phobic patients not suitable for insight-oriented psychotherapy. *Acta Psychiatrica Scandinavica, 70*(2), 97–110.

American Psychological Association Division 12. (2012). Website on research-supported psychological treatments. Retrieved from http://www.div12.org/PsychologicalTreatments/index.html

Anderson, E. M., & Lambert, M. J. (1995). Short-term dynamically oriented psychotherapy: A review and meta-analysis. *Clinical Psychology Review*, *15*(6), 503–514.

Andrusyna, T. P., Luborsky, L., Pham, T., & Tang, T. Z. (2006). The mechanisms of sudden gains in supportive–expressive therapy for depression. *Psychotherapy Research*, *16*(5), 526–536.

Arntz, A., & Veen, G. (2001). Evaluations of others by borderline patients. *Journal of Nervous and Mental Disease*, *189*, 513–521.

Aron, L. (1996). *A meeting of minds: Mutuality in psychoanalysis*. Relational perspectives book series (Vol. 4). Hillsdale, NJ: Analytic Press.

Aspland, H., Llewelyn, S., Hardy, G. E., Barkham, M., & Stiles, W. (2008). Alliance ruptures and rupture resolution in cognitive-behavior therapy: A preliminary task analysis. *Psychotherapy Research*, *18*, 699–710.

Baldwin, S. A., Wampold, B. E., & Imel, Z. E. (2007). Untangling the alliance-outcome correlation: Exploring the relative importance of therapist and patient variability in the alliance. *Journal of Consulting and Clinical Psychology*, *75*, 842–852.

Bambling, M., King, R., Raue, P., Schweitzer, R., & Lambert, W., (2006). Clinical supervision: Its influence on client-rated working alliance and client symptom reduction in the brief treatment of major depression. *Psychotherapy Research*, *16*(3), 317–331.

Barber, J. P. (2009). Towards a working through of some core conflicts in psychotherapy research. *Psychotherapy Research*, *19*, 1–12. doi: 10.1080/10503300802609680

Barber, J. P., Barrett, M. S. Gallop, R., Rynn, M., & Rickels, K. (2012). Short-Term Dynamic Therapy vs. pharmacotherapy for major depressive disorder. *Journal of Clinical Psychiatry*, *73*(1), 66–73. 10.4088/JCP.11m06831

Barber, J. P., Connolly, M. B., Crits-Christoph, P., Gladis, L., & Siqueland, L. (2000). Alliance predicts patients' outcome beyond in-treatment change in symptoms. *Journal of Consulting and Clinical Psychology*, *68*(6), 1027–1032.

Barber, J. P., & Crits-Christoph, P. (1996). Development of a therapist adherence/competence rating scale for supportive-expressive dynamic psychotherapy: A preliminary report. *Psychotherapy Research*, *6*(2), 81–94.

Barber, J. P., Crits-Christoph, P., & Luborsky, L. (1996). Effects of therapist adherence and competence on patient outcome in brief dynamic therapy. *Journal of Consulting and Clinical Psychology*, *64*(3), 619–622. doi: 10.1037/0022–006X.64.3.619

Barber, J. P., Luborsky, L., Crits-Christoph, P., Thase, M. E., Wiess, R., Frank, A., . . . Gallop, R. (1999). Therapeutic alliance as a predictor of outcome in treatment of cocaine dependence. *Psychotherapy Research*, *9*(1), 54–73.

Barber, J. P., Luborsky, L., Gallop, R., Crits-Christoph, P., Weiss, R. D., Thase, M. E., . . . Siqueland, L. (2001). Therapeutic alliance as a predictor of outcome and retention in the National Institute on Drug Abuse Collaborative Cocaine Treatment Study. *Journal of Consulting and Clinical Psychology*, *69*, 119–124.

Barber, J. P., & Muenz, L. R. (1996). The role of avoidance and obsessiveness in matching patients to cognitive and interpersonal psychotherapy: Empirical findings from the treatment for depression collaborative research program. *Journal of Consulting and Clinical Psychology*, *64*, 951–958. doi: 10.1037/0022–006X.64.5.951

Barber, J. P., Robert, G., Crits-Christoph, P., Barrett, M. S., Klostermann, S., McCarthy, K. S., & Sharpless, B. A. (2008). The role of the alliance and techniques in predicting outcome of supportive-expressive dynamic therapy for cocaine dependence. *Psychoanalytic Psychology*, *25*(3), 461–482.

Barber, J. P., Sharpless, B. A., Klostermann, S., & McCarthy, K. S. (2007). Assessing intervention competence and its relation to therapy outcome: A selected review derived from the outcome literature. *Professional Psychology: Research and Practice*, *38*(5), 493–500.

*Barkham, M., Shapiro, D. A., Hardy, G. E., & Rees, A. (1999). Psychotherapy in two-plus-one sessions: Outcomes of a randomized controlled trial of cognitive–behavioral and psychodynamic–interpersonal therapy for subsyndromal depression. *Journal of Consulting and Clinical Psychology*, *67*(2), 201–211. doi: 10.1037/0022–006X.67.2.201

Baron-Cohen, S., Leslie, A., & Frith, U. (1985). Does the autistic child have a "theory of mind?" *Cognition*, *21*, 37–46.

*Bateman A. W., & Fonagy P. (1999). Effectiveness of partial hospitalization in the treatment of borderline personality disorder: A randomized controlled trial. *American Journal of Psychiatry*, *156*(10), 1563–1569.

Bateman A. W., & Fonagy P. (2006). *Mentalization based treatment for borderline personality disorder: a practical guide*. Oxford, United Kingdom: Oxford University Press.

Bateman, A. W., & Fonagy, P. (2008). 8-year follow-up of patients treated for borderline personality disorder: Mentalization-based treatment versus treatment as usual. *American Journal of Psychiatry*, *165*(5), 631–638.

*Bateman A. W., & Fonagy P. (2009). Randomized controlled trial of outpatient mentalization-based treatment versus structured clinical management for borderline personality disorder. *American Journal of Psychiatry*, *166*(12), 1355–1364. doi: 10.1176/appi.ajp.2009.09040539

Bazin, N., Brunet-Gouet, E., Bourdet, C., Kayser, N., Falissard, B., Hardy-Baylé, M.-C., & Passerieux, C. (2009). Quantitative assessment of attribution of intentions to others in schizophrenia using an ecological video-based task: A comparison with manic and depressed patients. *Psychiatry Research*, 167, 28–35.

Bender, D. S. (2005). The therapeutic alliance in the treatment of personality disorders. *Journal of Psychiatric Practice*, 11(2), 73–87.

Benish, S. G., Imel, Z. E., & Wampold, B. E. (2008). The relative efficacy of bona fide psychotherapies for treating post-traumatic stress disorder: A meta-analysis of direct comparison. *Clinical Psychology Review*, 28, 746–758.

Benjamin, L. S., & Critchfield, K. L. (2010). An interpersonal perspective on therapy alliances and techniques. In J. C. Muran & J. P. Barber (Eds.), *The therapeutic alliance: An evidence-based guide to practice* (pp. 123–149). New York, NY: Guilford Press.

Bennett, D., Parry, G., & Ryle, A. (2006). Resolving threats to the therapeutic alliance in cognitive analytic therapy of borderline personality disorder: A task analysis. *Psychology and Psychotherapy: Theory, Research, and Practice*, 79, 395–418.

Beutler, L. E. (2002). The dodo bird is extinct. *Clinical Psychology: Science & Practice*, 9, 30–34.

Beutler, L. E. (2009). Making science matter in clinical practice: Redefining psychotherapy. *Clinical Psychology: Science and Practice*, 16(3), 301–317.

Bibring, E. (1937). Symposium on the theory of the therapeutic results of psychoanalysis. *International Journal of Psychoanalysis*, 18, 170–189.

Bien, E., Anderson, T., Strupp, H., Henry, W., Schacht, T., Binder, J., & Butler, S. (2000). The effects of training in time-limited dynamic psychotherapy: Changes in therapeutic outcome. *Psychotherapy Research*, 10(2), 119–132.

Black, S., Hardy, G., Turpin, G., & Parry, G. (2005). Self-reported attachment styles and therapeutic orientation of therapists and their relationship with reported general alliance quality and problems in therapy. *Psychology and Psychotherapy: Theory, Research and Practice*, 78(3), 363–377.

Blagys, M., & Hilsenroth, M. (2000). Distinctive features of short-term psychodynamic-interpersonal psychotherapy: An empirical review of the comparative psychotherapy process literature. *Clinical Psychology: Science and Practice*, 7, 167–188.

Blatt, S. J. (1992). The differential effect of psychotherapy and psychoanalysis with anaclitic and introjective patients: The Menninger psychotherapy research project revisited. *Journal of the American Psychoanalytic Association*, 40(3), 691–724.

Blatt, S. J., Auerbach, J. S., & Levy, K. N. (1997). Mental representations in personality development, psychopathology, and the therapeutic process. *Review of General Psychology*, 1(4), 351–374.

Blatt, S. J., & Shahar, G. (2004). Psychoanalysis—With whom, for what, and how? Comparisons with psychotherapy. *Journal of the American Psychoanalytic Association*, 52(2), 393–447.

Blatt, S. J., Stayner, D. A., Auerbach, J. S., & Behrends, R. S. (1996). Change in object and self-representations in long-term, intensive, inpatient treatment of seriously disturbed adolescents and young adults. *Psychiatry*, 59, 82–107.

Bond, M. (2004). Empirical studies of defense style: Relationships with psychopathology and change. *Harvard Review of Psychiatry*, 12, 263–278.

Bond, M., & Perry, J. C. (2004). Long-term changes in defense styles with psychodynamic psychotherapy for depressive, anxiety, and personality disorders. *American Journal of Psychiatry*, 161, 1665–1671.

Bordin, E. (1979). The generalizability of the psychoanalytic concept of the working alliance. *Psychotherapy: Theory, Research, and Practice*, 16, 252–260.

Borenstein, M., Hedges, L., Higgins, J., & Rothstein, H. (2005). *Comprehensive Meta-Analysis (Version 2)*. Englewood, NJ: Biostat.

Bouchard, M.-A., Target, M., Lecours, S., Fonagy, P., Tremblay, L.-M., Schachter, A., & Stein, H. (2008). Mentalization in adult attachment narratives: Reflective functioning, mental states, and affect elaboration compared. *Psychoanalytic Psychology*, 25, 47–66.

Bowlby, J. (1988). *A secure base*. New York, NY: Basic Books.

Brenner, C. (1979). Working alliance, therapeutic alliance, and transference. *Journal of the American Psychoanalytic Association*, 27, 136–158.

*Brom, D., Kleber, R. J., & Defares, P. B. (1989). Brief psychotherapy for posttraumatic stress disorders. *Journal of Consulting and Clinical Psychology*, 57(5), 607–612.

Brottman, M. A. (2004). *Therapeutic alliance and adherence in cognitive therapy for depression*. Unpublished doctoral dissertation, University of Pennsylvania, Philadelphia.

Burnand, Y., Andreoli, A., Kolatte, E., Venturini, A., & Rosset, N. (2002). Psychodynamic psychotherapy and clomipramine in the treatment of major depression. *Psychiatric Services*, 53(5), 585–590. doi: 10.1176/appi.ps.53.5.585

Busch, F. N., Milrod, B. L., Singer, M. B., & Aronson, A. C. (2011). *Manual of panic focused psychodynamic psychotherapy—eXtended range* (2nd ed.). New York, NY: Routledge.

Busch, F. N., Rudden, M., & Shapiro, T. (2004). *Psychodynamic treatment of depression* (1st ed.). Arlington, VA: American Psychiatric.

Cabral, R. R., & Smith, T. B. (2011). Racial/ethnic matching of clients and therapists in mental health services: A meta-analytic review of preferences, perceptions, and outcomes. *Journal of Counseling Psychology*, 58(4), 537–554.

Cailhol, L., Rodgers, R., Burnand, Y., Brunet, A., Damsa, C., & Andreoli, A. (2009). Therapeutic alliance in short-term supportive and psychodynamic psychotherapies: A necessary but not sufficient condition for outcome? *Psychiatry Research*, 170, 229–233.

Castonguay, L. G. (1996). *Integrative cognitive therapy for depression treatment manual*. Unpublished manuscript, Pennsylvania State University.

Castonguay, L. G., Goldfried, M. R., Wiser, S. L., Raue, P. J. & Hayes, A. M. (1996). Predicting the effect of cognitive therapy for depression: A study of unique and common factors. *Journal of Consulting and Clinical Psychology, 64*, 497–504.

Castonguay, L. G., & Grosse Holtfort, M. (2005). Change in psychotherapy: A plea for no more "non-specific" and false dichotomy. *Clinical Psychology: Science and Practice, 12*, 198–201.

Castonguay, L. G., Schut, A. J., Aikins, D., Constantino, M. J., Lawrenceau, J. P., Bologh, L., & Burns, D. D. (2004). Repairing alliance ruptures in cognitive therapy: a preliminary investigation of an integrative therapy for depression. *Journal of Psychotherapy Integration, 14*, 4–20.

Chambless, D. L. (2002). Beware the dodo bird: The dangers of overgeneralization. *Clinical Psychology: Science & Practice, 9*(1), 13–16.

Chambless, D. L., & Hollon, S. D. (1998). Defining empirically supported therapies. *Journal of Consulting and Clinical Psychology, 66*(1), 7–18.

Chambless, D. L., & Ollendick, T. H. (2001). Empirically supported psychological interventions: Controversies and evidence. *Annual Review of Psychology, 52*, 685–716.

Chapman, B. P., Talbot, N., Tatman, A. W., & Britton, P. C. (2009). Personality traits and the working alliance in psychotherapy trainees: An organizing role for the five factor model? *Journal of Social and Clinical Psychology, 28*(5), 577–596.

Cierpka, M., Strack, M., Benninghoven, D., Staats, H., Dahlbender, R., Pokorny, D., ... Albani, C. (1998). Stereotypical relationship patterns and psychopathology. *Psychotherapy and Psychosomatics, 67*, 241–248.

*Clarkin, J. F., Levy, K. M., Lenzenweger, M. F., & Kernberg, O. F. (2007). Evaluating three treatments for borderline personality disorder: A multiwave study. *American Journal of Psychiatry, 164*(6), 922–928.

Clarkin, J. F., Yeomans F. E., & Kernberg O. F. (2006). *Psychotherapy for borderline personality disorder focusing on object relations*. Washington, DC: American Psychiatric.

Coady, N. F. (1991). The association between complex types of therapist interventions and outcomes in psychodynamic psychotherapy. *Research on Social Work Practice, 1*(3), 257–277.

Cohen, J. (1992). A power primer. *Psychological Bulletin, 112*(1), 155–159.

Coleman, D., Cole, D., & Wuest, L. (2010). Cognitive and psychodynamic mechanisms of change in treated and untreated depression. *Journal of Clinical Psychology, 66*(3), 215–228.

Colli, A., & Lingiardi, V. (2009). The collaborative interactions scale: A new transcript-based method for the assessment of therapeutic alliance ruptures and resolutions in psychotherapy. *Psychotherapy Research, 19*, 718–734.

Connolly, M. B., Crits-Christoph, P., Shelton, R. C., Hollon, S., Kurtz, J., Barber, J. P., & Thase, M. E. (1999). The reliability and validity of a measure of self-understanding of interpersonal patterns. *Journal of Counseling Psychology, 46*(4), 472–482.

Connolly Gibbons, M. B., Crits-Christoph, P., & Hearon, B. (2008). The empirical status of psychodynamic therapies. *Annual Review of Clinical Psychology, 4*, 93–108.

Constantino, M. J., Arnow, B. A., Blasey, C. & Agras, W. S. (2005). The association between patient characteristics and the therapeutic alliance in cognitive-behavioral and interpersonal therapy for bulimia nervosa. *Journal of Consulting & Clinical Psychology, 73*, 203–211.

Constantino, M. J., Marnell, M. E., Haile, A. J., Kanther-Sista, S. N., Wolman, K., Zappert, L., & Arnow, B. A. (2008). Integrative cognitive therapy for depression: A randomized pilot comparison. *Psychotherapy: Theory, Research, Practice, Training, 45*, 122–134.

Cooper, P. J., Murray, L., Wilson, A., & Romaniuk, H. (2003). Controlled trial of the short- and long-term effect of psychological treatment of postpartum depression. 1. Impact on maternal mood. *British Journal of Psychiatry, 182*(5), 412–419. doi: 10.1192/bjp.182.5.412

Cramer, P. (1991). *The development of defense mechanisms: Theory, research and assessment*. New York, NY: Springer-Verlag.

Cramer, P. (1998). Coping and defense mechanisms: What's the difference? *Journal of Personality, 66*(6), 919–946.

Crits-Christoph, P., Barber, J. P., & Kurcias, J. S. (1993). The accuracy of therapists' interpretations and the development of the therapeutic alliance. *Psychotherapy Research, 3*, 25–35.

Crits-Christoph, P., Cooper, A., & Luborsky, L. (1988). The accuracy of therapists' interpretations and the outcome of dynamic psychotherapy. *Journal of Consulting and Clinical Psychology, 56*(4), 490–495.

Crits-Christoph, P., Gibbons, M. B. C., Barber, J. P., Gallop, R., Beck, A. T., Mercer, D., & Frank, A. (2003). Mediators of outcome of psychosocial treatments for cocaine dependence. *Journal of Consulting and Clinical Psychology, 71*, 918–925.

Crits-Christoph, P., Gibbons, M. B., Crits-Christoph, K., Narducci, J., Schamberger, M., & Gallop, R. (2006). Can therapists be trained to improve their alliances? A preliminary study of alliance-fostering psychotherapy. *Psychotherapy Research, 16*, 268–281.

*Crits-Christoph, P., Gibbons, M. B. C., Narducci, J., Schamberger, M., & Gallop, R. (2005). Interpersonal problems and the outcome of interpersonally oriented psychodynamic treatment of GAD.

Psychotherapy: Theory, Research, Practice, Training, 42(2), 211–224. doi: 10.1037/0033–3204.42.2.211

Crits-Christoph, P., Gibbons, M. B. C., Temes, C. M., Elkin, I., & Gallop, R. (2010). Interpersonal accuracy of interventions and the outcome of cognitive and interpersonal therapies for depression. *Journal of Consulting and Clinical Psychology, 78*(3), 420–428.

Crits-Christoph, P., & Luborsky, L. (1998). Changes in CCRT pervasiveness during psychotherapy. In L. Luborsky & P. Crits-Christoph (Eds.), *Understanding transference: The core conflictual relationship theme method* (2nd ed., pp. 151–163). Washington, DC: American Psychological Association.

Cromer, T. D., & Hilsenroth, M. J. (2010). Patient personality and outcome in short-term psychodynamic psychotherapy. *Journal of Nervous and Mental Disease, 198*, 59–66.

Cuijpers, P., Dekker, J., Hollon, S. D., & Andersson, G. (2009). Adding psychotherapy to pharmacotherapy in the treatment of depressive disorder in adults: A meta-analysis. *Journal of Clinical Psychiatry, 70*(9), 1219–1229.

Cuijpers, P., van Straten, A., Andersson, G., & van Oppen, P. (2008). Psychotherapy for depression in adults: A meta-analysis of comparative outcome studies. *Journal of Consulting and Clinical Psychology, 76*(6), 909–922.

Cuijpers, P., van Straten, A., Bohlmeijer, E., Hollon, S. D., & Andersson, G. (2010). The effects of psychotherapy for adult depression are overrated: A meta-analysis of study quality and effect size. *Psychological Medicine, 40*(2), 211–223.

Curtis, J., Silberschatz, G., Sampson, H., & Weiss, J. (1994). The plan formulation method. *Psychotherapy Research, 4*, 197–207.

Davidson, K., & MacGregor, M. W. (1998). A critical appraisal of self-report defense mechanism measures. *Journal of Personality, 66*(6), 965–992.

Davis, D. M., & Hayes, J. A. (2011). What are the benefits of mindfulness? A practice review of psychotherapy-related research. *Psychotherapy, 48*(2), 198–208.

DeFife, J. A., Hilsenroth, M. J., & Gold, J. R. (2008). Patient ratings of psychodynamic psychotherapy session activities and their relation to outcome. *Journal of Nervous & Mental Disease, 196*(7), 538–547.

*de Jonghe, F., Kool, S., van Aalst, G., Dekker, J., & Peen, J. (2001). Combining psychotherapy and antidepressants in the treatment of depression. *Journal of Affective Disorders, 64*(2–3), 217–229. doi: 10.1016/S0165–0327(00)00259–7

de Maat, S., Dekker, J., Schoevers, R., van Aalst, G., Gijsbers-van Wijk, C., Hendriksen, M., . . . de Jonghe, F. (2008). Short Psychodynamic Supportive Psychotherapy, antidepressants, and their combination in the treatment of major depression: A mega-analysis based on three randomized clinical trials. *Depression and Anxiety, 25*(7), 565–574. doi: 10.1002/da.20305

DeRubeis, R., & Feeley, M. (1990). Determinants of change in cognitive therapy for depression. *Cognitive Therapy and Research, 14*, 469–482.

Despland, J.-N., de Roten, Y., Drapeau, M., Currat, T., Beretta, V., & Kramer, U. (2009). The role of alliance in the relationship between therapist competence and outcome in brief psychodynamic psychotherapy. *Journal of Nervous & Mental Disease, 197*(5), 362–367.

Dickes, R. (1975). Technical considerations of the therapeutic and working alliance. *International Journal of Psychoanalytic Psychotherapy, 4*, 1–24.

Diener, M. J., Hilsenroth, M. J., & Weinberger, J. (2007). Therapist affect focus and patient outcomes in psychodynamic psychotherapy: A meta-analysis. *American Journal of Psychiatry, 164*, 936–941.

Diener, M. J., & Monroe, J. M. (2011). The relationship between adult attachment style and therapeutic alliance in individual psychotherapy: A meta-analytic review. *Psychotherapy, 48*, 237–248.

*Doering, S., Hörz, S., Rentrop, M., Fischer-Kern, M., Schuster, P., Benecke, C., . . . Buchheim, P. (2010). Transference-focused psychotherapy v. treatment by community psychotherapists for borderline personality disorder: Randomised controlled trial. *British Journal of Psychiatry, 196*(5), 389–395.

Driessen, E., Cuijpers, P., de Maat, S. C. M., Abbass, A. A., de Jonghe F., & Dekker, J. J. M. (2010). The efficacy of short-term psychodynamic psychotherapy for depression: a meta-analysis. *Clinical Psychology Review, 30*(1), 25–36.

*Durham, R. C., Murphy, T., Allan, T., Richard, K., Treliving, L. R., & Fenton, G. W. (1994). Cognitive therapy, analytic psychotherapy and anxiety management training for generalised anxiety disorder. *British Journal of Psychiatry, 165*(3), 315–323. doi: 10.1192/bjp.165.3.315

Duval, S., & Tweedie, R. (2000). Trim and fill: A simple funnel-plot-based method of testing and adjusting for publication bias in meta-analysis. *Biometrics, 56*, 2, 455–463.

Eames, V., & Roth, A. (2000). Patient attachment orientation and the early working alliance: A study of patient and therapist reports of alliance quality and ruptures. *Psychotherapy Research, 10*, 421–434.

Elkin, I., Shea, M. T., Watkin, J. T., Imber, S. D., Sotsky, S. M., Collins, J. F., . . . Partoff, M. B. (1989). NIMH treatment of depression collaborative research program: General effectiveness of treatments. *Archives of General Psychiatry, 46*, 971–982.

Elliott, R., Shapiro, D. A., Firth-Cozens, J., Stiles, W. B., Hardy, G. E., Llewelyn, S. P., & Margison, F. R. (1994). Comprehensive process analysis of insight events in cognitive-behavioral and psychodynamic-interpersonal psychotherapies. *Journal of Counseling Psychology, 41*, 449–463.

*Emmelkamp, P. M. G., Benner, A., Kuipers, A., Feiertag, G. A., Koster, H. C., & van Apeldoorn, F. J. (2006). Comparison of brief dynamic and cognitive-behavioural therapies in avoidant personality disorder. *British Journal of Psychiatry*, *189*(1), 60–64. doi: 10.1192/bjp.bp.105.012153

Eubanks-Carter, C., Muran, J. C., & Safran, J. D. (2010). Alliance ruptures and resolution. In J. C. Muran & J. P. Barber (Eds.), *The therapeutic alliance: An evidence-based approach to practice and training* (pp. 74–96). New York, NY: Guilford Press.

Falk, D., & Hill, C. E. (1995). The effectiveness of dream interpretation groups for women undergoing a divorce transition. *Dreaming*, *5*, 29–42.

Feeley, M., DeRubeis, R. J., & Gelfand, L. A. (1999). The temporal relation of adherence and alliance to symptom change in cognitive therapy for depression. *Journal of Consulting and Clinical Psychology*, *67*(4), 578–582.

Fischer-Kern, M., Buchheim, A., Horz, S., Schuster, P., Doering, S., Kapusta, N. D.,...Fonagy, P. (2010). The relationship between personality organization, reflective functioning, and psychiatric classification in borderline personality disorder. *Psychoanalytic Psychology*, *27*, 395–409.

Foltz, C., Barber, J. P., Weinryb, R. M., Morse, J. Q., & Chittams, J. (1999). Consistency of themes across interpersonal relationships. *Journal of Social and Clinical Psychology*, *18*(2), 204–222.

Fonagy, P., & Bateman, A. W. (2006). Mechanisms of change in mentalization-based treatment of BPD. *Journal of Clinical Psychology*, *62*, 411–430.

Fonagy, P., Bateman, A., & Bateman, A. (2011). The widening scope of mentalization: A discussion. *Psychology and Psychotherapy: Theory, Research and Practice*, *84*, 98–110.

Fonagy, P., Leigh, T., Steele, M., Steele, H., Kennedy, R., Mattoon, G., & Gerber, A. (1996). The relation of attachment status, psychiatric classification, and response to psychotherapy. *Journal of Consulting and Clinical Psychology*, *64*, 22–31.

Fonagy, P., Target, M., Steele, H., & Steele, M. (1998). *Reflective functioning manual (Version 5)*. London, United Kingdom: University College London Psychoanalysis Unit.

Foreman, S. A., & Marmar, C. R. (1985). Therapist actions that address initially poor therapeutic alliances in psychotherapy. *American Journal of Psychiatry*, *142*(8), 922–926.

Freud, S. (1958a). Mourning and melancholia. In J. Strachey (Ed. and Trans.), *The standard edition of the complete psychological works of Sigmund Freud* (Vol. 14, pp. 237–258). London, United Kingdom: Hogarth Press. (Original work published 1917)

Freud, S. (1958b). The dynamics of transference. In J. Strachey (Ed. & Trans.), *The standard edition of the complete psychological works of Sigmund Freud* (Vol. 1, pp. 295–301). London, United Kingdom: Hogarth Press. (Original work published 1912)

Fuller, F., & Hill, C. E. (1985). Counselor and helpee perceptions of counselor intentions in relation to outcome in a single counseling session. *Journal of Counseling Psychology*, *32*, 329–338.

Gabbard, G. O., Horwitz, L., Allen, J. G., Frieswyk, S., Newsom, G., Colson, D. B., & Coyne, L. (1994). Transference interpretation in the psychotherapy of borderline patients: A high-risk, high-gain phenomenon. *Harvard Review of Psychiatry*, *2*(2), 59–69

*Gallagher, D. E., & Thompson, L. W. (1982). Treatment of major depressive disorder in older adult outpatients with brief psychotherapies. *Psychotherapy: Theory, Research & Practice*, *19*(4), 482–490. doi: 10.1037/h0088461

*Gallagher-Thompson, D. & Steffen, A. M. (1994). Comparative effects of cognitive-behavioral and brief psychodynamic psychotherapies for depressed family caregivers. *Journal of Consulting and Clinical Psychology*, *62*(3), 543–549.

Garner, D. M., Rockert, W., Davis, R., Garner, M. V., Olmstead M. P., & Eagle, M. (1993). Comparison of cognitive-behavioral and supportive-expressive therapy for bulimia nervosa. *American Journal of Psychiatry*, *150*(1), 37–46.

Gaston, L., & Marmar, C. (1994). The California Psychotherapy Alliance Scales. In A. O. Horvath & L. S. Greenberg (Eds.), *The working alliance: Theory, research, & practice* (pp. 85–108). New York, NY: Wiley.

Gaston, L., Marmar, C., Thompson, L., & Gallagher, D. (1991). Alliance prediction beyond in-treatment symptomatic change as psychotherapy progresses. *Psychotherapy Research*, *1*, 104–112.

Gaston, L., Thompson, L., Gallagher, D., Cournoyer, L., & Gagnon, R. (1998). Alliance, technique, and their interactions in predicting outcome of behavioral, cognitive, and brief dynamic therapy. *Psychotherapy Research*, *8*(2), 190–209.

Gelso, C. J., & Carter, J. A. (1994). Components of the psychotherapy relationship: Their interaction and unfolding during treatment. *Journal of Counseling Psychology*, *41*, 296–30.

Gerber, A. J., Kocsis, J. H., Milrod, B. L., Roose, S. P., Barber, J. P., Thase, M. E.,...Leon, A. C. (2011). A quality-based review of randomized controlled trials of psychodynamic psychotherapy. *American Journal of Psychiatry*, *168*(1), 19–28.

Gibbons, M. B., Crits-Christoph, P., Barber, J. P., & Schamberg, M. (2007). Insight in psychotherapy: A review of empirical literature. In L. G. Castonguay & C. E. Hill (Eds.), *Insight in psychotherapy* (pp. 143–166). Washington, DC: APA. doi: 10.1037/11532–007

Gibbons, M. B. C., Crits-Christoph, P., Barber, J. P., Stirman, S. W., Gallop, R., Goldstein, L. A., & Ring-Kurtz, S. (2009). Unique and common mechanisms of change across cognitive and dynamic psychotherapies. *Journal of Consulting and Clinical Psychology*, *77*, 801–813.

Giesen-Bloo, J., & Arntz, A. (2007). Questions concerning the randomized trial of schema-focused therapy vs. transference-focused therapy—Reply. *Archives of General Psychiatry, 64*(5), 610–611.

*Giesen-Bloo, J., van Dyck, R., Spinhoven, P., van Tilburg, W., Dirksen, C., van Asselt, T., . . . Arntz, A. (2006). Outpatient psychotherapy for borderline personality disorder: Randomized trial of schema-focused therapy vs transference-focused psychotherapy. *Archives of General Psychiatry, 63*(6), 649–658. doi: 10.1001/archpsyc.63.6.649

Goisman, R. M., Warshaw, M. G., & Keller, M. B. (1999). Psychosocial treatment prescriptions for generalized anxiety disorder, panic disorder, and social phobia, 1991–1996. *American Journal of Psychiatry, 156*(11), 1819–1821.

Golden, B. R., & Robbins, S. B. (1990). The working alliance within time-limited therapy. *Professional Psychology: Research and Practice, 21,* 476–481.

Goldfried, M. R. (1980). Toward the delineation of therapeutic change principles. *American Psychologist, 35,* 991–999.

Goldman, G. A., & Anderson, T. (2007). Quality of object relations and security of attachment as predictors of early therapeutic alliance. *Journal of Counseling Psychology, 54*(2), 111–117.

Graff, H., & Luborsky, L. (1977). Long-term trends in transference and resistance: A report on a quantitative-analytic method applied to four psychoanalyses. *Journal of the American Psychoanalytic Association, 25,* 471–490.

Grande, T., Rudolf, G., Oberbracht, C., & Pauli-Magnus, C. (2003). Progressive changes in patients' lives after psychotherapy: Which treatment effects support them? *Psychotherapy Research, 13,* 43–58.

Greenson, R. R. (1965). The working alliance and the transference neurosis. *Psychoanalytic Quarterly, 34,* 155–179.

Greenson, R. R. (1967). *Technique and practice of psychoanalysis.* New York, NY: International University Press.

Gregory, R. J., DeLucia-Deranja, E., & Mogle, J. A. (2010). Dynamic deconstructive psychotherapy versus optimized community care for borderline personaity disorder co-occuring with alcohol use disorders: A 30-month follow-up. *Journal of Nervous and Mental Disease, 198*(4), 292–298.

*Gregory, R. J., Chlebowski, S., Kang, D., Remen, A. L., Soderberg, M. G., Stepkovitch, J., & Virk, S. (2008). A controlled trial of psychodynamic psychotherapy for co-occurring borderline personality disorder and alcohol use disorder. *Psychotherapy: Theory, Research, Practice, Training, 45*(1), 28–41. doi: 10.1037/0033-3204.45.1.28

Grenyer, B. F. S., & Luborsky, L. (1996). Dynamic change in psychotherapy: Mastery of interpersonal conflicts. *Journal of Consulting and Clinical Psychology, 64,* 411–416.

Gross, S., Stasch, M., Schmal, H., Hillenbrand, E., & Cierpka, M. (2007). Changes in the mental representations of relational behavior in depressive patients. *Psychotherapy Research, 17*(5), 522–534.

Gurtman, M. B., & Balakrishnan, J. D. (1998). Circular measurement redux: The analysis and interpretation of interpersonal circle profiles. *Clinical Psychology: Science and Practice, 5*(3), 344–360.

Hanly, C. (1992). *The problem of truth in applied psychoanalysis. The Guilford psychoanalysis series.* New York, NY: Guilford Press.

Harpaz-Rotem, I., & Blatt, S. J. (2005). Changes in representations of self-designated significant other in long-term intensive inpatient treatment of seriously disturbed adolescents and young adults. *Psychiatry, 68,* 266–282.

Harper, H. (1989a). *Coding Guide I: Identification of confrontation challenges in exploratory therapy.* Sheffield, England: University of Sheffield.

Harper, H. (1989b). *Coding Guide II: Identification of withdrawal challenges in exploratory therapy.* Sheffield, England: University of Sheffield.

Harper, H. (1994). *The resolution of client confrontation challenges in exploratory psychotherapy: Developing the new paradigm in psychotherapy research.* Unpublished doctoral dissertation, University of Sheffield.

Hatcher, R. L. (2010). Alliance theory and measurement. In J. C. Muran & J. P. Barber (Eds.), *The therapeutic alliance: An evidence-based approach to practice and training* (pp. 7–28). New York, NY: Guilford Press.

Hayes, J. A., Gelso, C. J., & Hummel, A. M. (2011). Managing countertransference. *Psychotherapy, 48*(1), 88–97.

Hedges, L. V. (1981). Distribution theory for Glass's estimator of effect size and related estimators. *Journal of Educational Statistics, 6*(2), 107–128.

Heinonen, E., Lindfors, O., Laaksonen, M. A., & Knekt, P. (2012). Therapists' professional and personal characteristics as predictors of outcome in short- and long-term psychotherapy. *Journal of Affective Disorders, 138*(3), 301–12.

*Hellerstein, D. J., Rosenthal, R. N., Pinsker, H., Samstag, L. W., Muran, J. C., & Winston, A. (1998). A randomized prospective study comparing supportive and dynamic therapies: Outcome and alliance. *Journal of Psychotherapy Practice & Research, 7*(4), 261–271.

Hendriksen, M., Van, R., Peen, J., Oudejans, S., Schoevers, R., & Dekker, J. (2010). Psychometric properties of the Helping Alliance Questionnaire-I in psychodynamic psychotherapy for major depression. *Psychotherapy Research, 20,* 589–598.

Hendriksen, M., Van, H. L., Schoevers, R. A., de Jonghe, F. E. R. E. R., Gijsbers van Wijk, C. M. T., Peen, J., & Dekker, J. M. (2011). Therapist judgment of defense styles and therapeutic technique related to outcome in psychodynamic psychotherapy for depression. *Psychotherapy and Psychosomatics, 80,* 377–379.

Henry, W. P., Schacht, T. E., & Strupp, H. H. (1986). Structural analysis of social behavior: Application to a study of interpersonal process in differential psychotherapeutic outcome. *Journal of Consulting and Clinical Psychology, 54*, 27–31.

Henry, W. P., Schacht, T. E., & Strupp, H. H. (1990). Patient and therapist introject, interpersonal process, and differential psychotherapy outcome. *Journal of Consulting and Clinical Psychology, 58*, 768–774.

Henry, W. P., Schacht, T. E., Strupp, H. H., Butler, S. F., & Binder, J. L. (1993a). Effects of training in time-limited dynamic psychotherapy: Mediators of therapists' responses to training. *Journal of Consulting and Clinical Psychology, 61*, 441–447.

Henry, W. P., Strupp, H. H., Butler, S. F., Schacht, T. E., & Binder, J. L. (1993b). Effects of training in time-limited dynamic psychotherapy: Changes in therapist behavior. *Journal of Consulting and Clinical Psychology, 61*, 434–440.

*Hersen, M., Bellack, A. S., Himmelhoch, J. M., & Thase, M. E. (1984). Effects of social skill training, amitriptyline, and psychotherapy in unipolar depressed women. *Behavior Therapy, 15*(1), 21–40. doi: 10.1016/S0005–7894(84)80039–8

Hersoug, A. G., Bogwald, K.-P., & Høglend, P. (2005). Changes of defensive functioning. Does interpretation contribute to change? *Clinical Psychology and Psychotherapy, 12*, 288–296.

Hersoug, A. G., Høglend, P., Havik, O., von der Lippe, A., & Monsen, J. (2009). Therapist characteristics influencing the quality of alliance in long-term psychotherapy. *Clinical Psychology & Psychotherapy, 16*(2), 100–110.

Hersoug, A. G., Monsen, J. T., Havik, O. E., & Høglend, P. (2002a). Quality of early working alliance in psychotherapy: Diagnoses, relationship and intrapsychic variables as Predictors. *Psychotherapy and Psychosomatic, 71*, 18–27.

Hersoug, A. G., Sexton, H. C., & Høglend, P. (2002b). Contribution of defensive functioning to the quality of working alliance and psychotherapy outcome. *American Journal of Psychotherapy, 56*(4), 539–554.

Higgins, J. P. T., & Green, S. (Eds.). (2011). *Cochrane handbook for systematic reviews of interventions*. Retrieved from www.cochrane-handbook.org

Higgins, J. P., & Thompson, S. G. (2002). Quantifying heterogeneity in meta-analysis. *Statistics in Medicine, 21*(11), 1539–1558.

Hill, C. E., Kellems, I. S., Kolchakian, M. R., Wonnell, T. L., Davis, T. L., & Nakayama, E. Y. (2003). The therapist experience of being the target of hostile versus suspected-unasserted client anger: Factors associated with resolution. *Psychotherapy Research, 13*(4), 475–491.

Hill, C. E., Nutt-Williams, E., Heaton, K. J., Thompson, B. J., & Rhodes, R. H. (1996). Therapist retrospective recall of impasses in long-term psychotherapy: A qualitative analysis. *Journal of Counseling Psychology, 43*, 207–217.

Hill, C. E., Thompson, B. J., Cogar, M. C., & Denman, D. W. (1993). Beneath the surface of long-term therapy: Therapist and client report of their own and each other's covert processes. *Journal of Counseling Psychology, 40*, 278–287.

Hilsenroth, M. J., Ackerman, S. J., Clemence, A. J., Strassle, C. G., & Handler, L. (2002). Effect of structured clinician training on patient and therapist perspectives of alliance early in psychotherapy. *Psychotherapy: Theory/Research/Practice/Training, 39*, 309–323.

Hilsenroth, M. J., Blagys, M. D. Ackerman, S. J., Bonge, D. R., & Blais, M. A. (2005). Measuring psychodynamic-interpersonal and cognitive-behavioral techniques: Development of the comparative psychotherapy process scale. *Psychotherapy: Theory, Research, Practice, Training, 42*(3), 340–356.

Hirsch, I. (1998). The concept of enactment and theoretical convergence. *Psychoanalytic Dialogues, 4*, 171–192.

Hoffart, A., Versland, S., & Sexton, H. (2002). Self-understanding, empathy, guided discovery, and schema belief in schema-focused cognitive therapy of personality problems: A process-outcome. *Cognitive Therapy and Research, 26*, 199–219.

Høglend, P. (2004). Analysis of transference in psychodynamic psychotherapy: a review of empirical research. *Canadian Journal of Psychoanalysis, 12*(2), 280–300.

Høglend, P., Amlo, S., Marble, A., Bogwald, K.-P., Sorbye, O., Sjaastad, M. C., & Heyerdahl, O. (2006). Analysis of the patient-therapist relationship in dynamic psychotherapy: An experimental study of transference interpretations. *American Journal of Psychiatry, 163*, 1739–1746.

Høglend, P., Bøgwald, K. P., Amlo, S., Marble, A., Ulberg, R., Sjaastad, M. C., . . . Johansson P. (2008). Transference interpretations in dynamic psychotherapy: Do they really yield sustained effects? *American Journal of Psychiatry, 165*(6), 763–771.

Høglend, P., Hersoug, A. G., Bogwald, K.-P., Amlo, S., Marble, A., Sorbye, O., . . . Crits-Christoph, P. (2011). Effects of transference work in the context of therapeutic alliance and quality of object relations. *Journal of Consulting and Clinical Psychology, 79*(5), 697–706.

Horowitz, L. M., Rosenberg, S. E., Baer, B. A., Ureño, G., & Villaseñor, V. S. (1988). Inventory of interpersonal problems: Psychometric properties and clinical applications. *Journal of Consulting and Clinical Psychology, 56*(6), 885–892.

Horvath, A. O. (2006). The alliance in context: Accomplishments, challenges, and future directions. *Psychotherapy: Theory, Research, Practice, Training, 43*, 258–263.

Horvath, A. O., Del Re, A. C., Flückiger, C., & Symonds, D. (2011). Alliance in individual psychotherapy. In J. Norcross (Ed.), *Psychotherapy relationships that work: Evidence-based responsiveness* (pp. 25–69). New York, NY: Oxford University Press.

Horvath, A. O., & Greenberg, L. S. (1989). Development and validation of the working alliance inventory. *Journal of Counseling Psychology, 36,* 223–233.

Horvath, A. O., & Symonds, B. D. (1991). Relation between working alliance and outcome in psychotherapy: A meta-analysis. *Journal of Counseling Psychology, 38,* 139–149.

Huprich, S. K., & Greenberg, R. P. (2003). Advances in the assessment of object relations in the 1990s. *Clinical Psychology Review, 23,* 665–698.

Johansen, P., Krebs, T. S., Svartberg, M., Stiles, & Holen, A. (2011). Change in defense mechanisms during short-term dynamic and cognitive therapy in patients with cluster C personality disorders. *Journal of Nervous & Mental Disease, 199*(9), 712–715.

Johansson, P., Høglend, P., Ulberg, R., Amlo, S., Marble, A., Bogwald, K.-P., & Heyerdahl, O. (2010). The mediating role of insight for long-term improvements in psychodynamic therapy. *Journal of Consulting and Clinical Psychology, 78,* 438–448.

Jones, E. E., Parke, L. A., & Pulos, S. M. (1992). How therapy is conducted in the private consulting room: A multidimensional description of brief psychodynamic treatments. *Psychotherapy Research, 2*(1), 16–30.

Joyce, A. S., McCallum, M., Piper, W. E., & Ogrodniczuk, J. S. (2000). Role behavior expectancies and alliance change in short-term individual psychotherapy. *Journal of Psychotherapy Practice & Research, 9*(4), 213–225.

Joyce, A. S., Ogrodniczuk, J. S., Piper, W. E., & Sheptycki, A. R. (2010). Interpersonal predictors of outcome following short-term group therapy for complicated grief: A replication. *Clinical Psychology and Psychotherapy, 17,* 122–135.

Kanzer, M. (1975). The therapeutic and working alliances: An assessment. *International Journal of Psychoanalytic Psychotherapy, 4,* 48–68.

Karlsson, R., & Kermott, A. (2006). Reflective-functioning during the process in brief psychotherapies. *Psychotherapy: Theory, Research, Practice, Training, 43,* 65–84.

Kiesler, D. J. (1996). *Contemporary interpersonal theory and research: Personality, psychopathology, and psychotherapy.* Oxford, United Kingdom: Wiley.

Kivlighan, D. M., Multon, K. D., & Patton, M. J. (2000). Insight and symptom reduction in time-limited psychoanalytic counseling. *Journal of Counseling Psychology, 47,* 50–58.

Kivlighan, D. M., & Shaughnessy, P. (2000). Patterns of working alliance development: A typology of client's working alliance ratings. *Journal of Counseling Psychology, 47,* 362–371.

Klein, C., Milrod, B., & Busch, F. (1999). *Interactive process assessment.* (Rater manual. Unpublished manuscript). Weill Cornell Medical College.

Klein, C., Milrod, B., Busch F., Levy, K., & Shapiro, T. (2003a). A preliminary study of clinical process in relation to outcome in psychodynamic psychotherapy for panic disorder. *Psychoanalytic Inquiry, 23*(2), 308–331.

Klein, D. N., Schwartz, J. E., Santiago, N. J., Vivian, D., Vocisano, C., Castonguay, L. G., . . . Keller, M. B. (2003b). Therapeutic alliance in depression treatment: Controlling for prior change and patient characteristics. *Journal of Consulting and Clinical Psychology, 71*(6), 997–1006.

Klerman, G., Weissman, M., Rounsaville, B., & Chevron, E. . (1984). *Interpersonal Psychotherapy of Depression.* New York, NY: Basic Books.

Kneepkens, R. G., & Oakley, L. D. (1996). Rapid improvement in the defense style of hospitalized depressed adults. *Journal of Nervous and Mental Disease, 184,* 358–361.

Kocsis, J. H., Gerber, A. J., Milrod, B., Roose, S. P., Barber, J., Thase, M. E., . . . Leon, A. C. (2010). A new scale for assessing the quality of randomized controlled trials of psychotherapy. *Comprehensive Psychiatry, 51*(3), 319–324.

Kramer, U. (2010). Coping and defence mechanisms: What's the difference?—Second act. *Psychology and Psychotherapy: Theory, Research and Practice, 83,* 207–221.

Kramer, U., Despland, J.-N., Michel, L., Drapeau, M., & de Roten, Y. (2010). Change in defense mechanisms and coping over the course of short-term dynamic psychotherapy for adjustment disorder. *Journal of Clinical Psychology, 66*(12), 1232–1241.

Lacan, J. (1973). *The four fundamental concepts of psychoanalysis.* London, United Kingdom: Penguin.

Lambert, M. J., & Ogles, B. M. (2004). The efficacy and effectiveness of psychotherapy. In M. J. Lambert (Ed.), *Bergin and Garfield's handbook of psychotherapy and behavior change* (5th ed., pp. 139–193). Hoboken, NJ: Wiley.

Lambert, M. J., Whipple, J. L., Hawkins, E. J., Vermeersch, D. A., Nielsen, S. L., & Smart, D. W. (2003). Is it time for clinicians to routinely track patient outcome? A meta-analysis. *Clinical Psychology: Science and Practice, 10,* 288–301.

Langs, R. (1976). *The bipersonal field.* New York, NY: Aronson.

Lansford, E. (1986). Weakenings and repairs of the working alliance in short-term psychotherapy. *Professional Psychology: Research and Practice, 17,* 364–366.

Leichsenring, F. (2001). Comparative effects of short-term psychodynamic psychotherapy and cognitive-behavioral therapy in depression: A meta-analytic approach. *Clinical Psychology Review, 21*(3), 401–419.

Leichsenring, F., & Leibing, E. (2003). The effectiveness of psychodynamic therapy and cognitive behavior therapy in the treatment of personality disorders: A meta-analysis. *American Journal of Psychiatry, 160*(7), 1223–1232.

Leichsenring, F., & Rabung, S. (2008). Effectiveness of long-term psychodynamic psychotherapy: A meta-analysis. *Journal of the American Medical Association, 300*(13), 1551–1565.

Leichsenring, F., & Rabung, S. (2011). Long-term psychodynamic psychotherapy in complex mental disorders: Update of a meta-analysis. *British Journal of Psychiatry, 199*(1), 15–22.

Leichsenring, F., Rabung, S., & Leibing, E. (2004). The efficacy of short-term psychodynamic psychotherapy in specific psychiatric disorders. *Archives of General Psychiatry, 61*(12), 1208–1216.

*Leichsenring, F., Salzer, S., Jaeger, U., Kächele, H., Kreische, R., Leweke, F.,…Leibing, E. (2009). Short-term psychodynamic psychotherapy and cognitive-behavioral therapy in generalized anxiety disorder: a randomized, controlled trial. *American Journal of Psychiatry, 166*(8), 875–881. doi: 10.1176/appi.ajp.2009.09030441

Levy, K. N., Meehan, K. B., Kelly, K. M., Reynoso, J. S., Weber, M., Clarkin, J. F., & Kernberg, O. F. (2006). Change in attachment patterns and reflective functioning in a randomized control trial of transference-focused psychotherapy for borderline personality disorder. *Journal of Consulting and Clinical Psychology, 74*, 1027–1040.

Levy, K. N., Meehan, K. B., & Yeomans, F. E. (2012). An update and overview of the empirical evidence for transference-focused psychotherapy and other psychotherapies for borderline personality disorder. In R. A. Levy, J. S. Ablon, & H. Kächele (Eds.), *Psychodynamic psychotherapy research: Evidence-based practice and practice-based evidence* (pp. 139–167). New York, NY: Springer.

Liebowitz, M. R., Stone, M. H., & Turkat, I. R. (1986). *Treatment of personality disorders*. In A. J. Frances & R. E. Hales (Eds.), *Psychiatry Update: The American Psychiatric Association Annual Review* (Vol. 5, pp. 356–393). Washington, DC: American Psychiatric Association.

Lindgren, A., Werbart, A., & Philips, B. (2010). Long-term outcome and post-treatment effects of psychoanalytic psychotherapy with young adults. *Psychology and Psychotherapy: Theory, Research and Practice, 83*(1), 27–43.

Linehan, M. M., Comtois, K. A., Murray, A. M., Brown, M. Z., Gallop, R. J., & Heard, H. L. (2006). Two-year randomized controlled trial and follow-up of dialectical behavioral therapy vs. therapy by exerts for suicidal behaviors and personality disorder. *Archives of General Psychiatry, 63*, 767–766.

Lipsey, M. W., & Wilson, D. B. (2001). *Practical meta-analysis. Applied social research methods series* (Vol. 49). Thousand Oaks, CA: SAGE.

Lowyck, B., Vermote, R., Luyten, P., Franssen, M., Verhaest, Y., Vertommen, H., & Peuskens, J. (2009). Comparison of reflective functioning as measured on the adult attachment interview and the object relations inventory in patients with a personality disorder: A preliminary study. *Journal of the American Psychoanalytic Association, 57*, 1469–1472.

Luborsky, L. (1976). Helping alliances in psychotherapy. In J. L. Cleghhorn (Ed.), *Successful psychotherapy* (pp. 92–116). New York, NY: Brunner/Mazel.

Luborsky, L. (1984). *Principles of psychoanalytic therapy*. New York, NY: Basic Books.

Luborsky, L., Barber, J. P., Siqueland, L., Johnson, S., Najavits, L. M., Frank, A., & Daley, D. (1996). The revised helping alliance questionnaire (HAQ-II): Psychometric properties. *Journal of Psychotherapy Practice and Research, 5*, 260–271.

Luborsky, L. & Crits-Christoph, P. (1998). *Understanding transference: The core conflictual relationship theme method*. (2nd ed., pp. 151–163). Washington, DC: American Psychological Association.

Luborsky, L., Crits-Christoph, P., McLellan, A. T., Woody, G., Piper, W., Liberman, B.,…Pilkonis, P. (1986). Do therapists vary much in their success? Findings from four outcome studies. *American Journal of Orthopsychiatry, 56*(4), 501–512.

Luborsky, L., McLellan, A. T., Woody, G. E., O'Brien, C. P., & Auerbach, A. (1985). Therapist success and its determinants. *Archives of General Psychiatry, 42*(6), 602–611.

Luborsky, L., Rosenthal, R., Diguer, L., Adrusyna, T. P., Berman, J. S., Levitt, J. T.,…Krause, E. D. (2002). The Dodo bird verdict is alive and well—mostly. *Clinical Psychology: Science and Practice, 9*(1), 2–12.

Lunnen, K. M., Ogles, B. M., Anderson, T. M., & Barnes, D. L. (2006). A comparison of CCRT pervasiveness and symptomatic improvement in brief therapy. *Psychology and Psychotherapy: Theory, Research and Practice, 79*, 289–302.

MacBeth, A., Gumley, A., Schwannauer, M., & Fisher, R. (2011). Attachment states of mind, mentalization and their correlates in a first episode psychosis sample. *Psychology and Psychotherapy: Theory, Research and Practice, 84*, 42–57.

Magnavita, J. J. (1997). *Restructuring personality disorders: A short-term dynamic approach*. New York, NY: Guilford Press.

Main, M., Goldwyn, R., & Hesse, E. (2002). *Adult attachment classification system manual* (in Draft: Version 7.1). Unpublished manuscript, University of California at Berkeley.

*Maina, G., Forner, F., & Bogetto, F. (2005). Randomized controlled trial comparing brief dynamic and supportive therapy with waiting list condition in minor depressive disorders. *Psychotherapy and Psychosomatics, 74*(1), 43–50. doi: 10.1159/000082026

*Maina, G., Rosso, G., & Bogetto, F. (2009). Brief dynamic therapy combined with pharmacotherapy in the treatment of major depressive disorder: Long-term results. *Journal of Affective Disorders, 114*, 200–207.

Malan, D. H. (1979). *Individual psychotherapy and the science of psychotherapy*. London, United Kingdom: Butterworth.

Mann, J. (1973). *Time-limited psychotherapy*. Cambridge, MA: Harvard University Press.

Martin, D. J., Garske, J. P., & Davis, M. K. (2000). Relation of the therapeutic alliance with outcome and other variables: A meta-analytic review. *Journal of Consulting & Clinical Psychology*, *68*, 438–450.

Martin, J., Martin, W., Meyer, M., & Slemon, A. (1986). Empirical investigation of the cognitive mediational paradigm for research in counseling. *Journal of Counseling Psychology*, *33*, 115–123.

Martin, J., Martin, W., & Slemon, A. (1987). Cognitive mediation in person-centered and rational–emotive therapy. *Journal of Counseling Psychology*, *34*, 251–260.

Massion, A. O., Dyck, I. R., Shea, M. T., Phillips, K. A., Warshaw, M. G., & Keller, M. B. (2002). Personality disorders and time to remission in generalized anxiety disorder, social phobia, and panic disorder. *Archives of General Psychiatry*, *59*(5), 434–440.

McCarthy, K. S. (2009). *Specific, common, and unintended factors in psychotherapy: Descriptive and correlational approaches to what creates change* (Doctoral Dissertation). Retrieved from publicly accessible Penn Dissertations (Paper 62).

McCarthy, K. S., & Barber, J. P. (2009). The multitheoretical list of therapeutic interventions (MULTI): Initial report. *Psychotherapy Research*, *19*(1), 96–113.

McCarthy, K. S., Gibbons, M. B. C., & Barber, J. P. (2008). The relation of rigidity across relationships with symptoms and functioning: An investigation with the revised central relationship questionnaire. *Journal of Counseling Psychology*, *55*(3), 346–358.

McClelland, G. H., & Judd, C. M. (1993). Statistical difficulties of detecting interactions and moderator effects. *Psychological Bulletin*, *114*, 376–390.

McCullough, L., Winston, H. A., Farber, B. A., Porter, F., Pollack, J., Laikin, M., Vingiano, W., & Trujillo, M. (1991). The relationship of patient-therapist interaction to the outcome in brief dynamic psychotherapy. *Psychotherapy: Theory, Practice, Research, Training*, *28*, 525–533.

*McMain, S. F., Guimon, T., Streiner, D. L., Cardish, R. J., & Links, P. S. (2012). Dialectical behavior therapy compared with general psychiatric management for borderline personality disorder: Clinical outcomes and functioning over a 2-year follow-up. *American Journal of Psychiatry*, *169*(6), 650–661.

*McMain, S. F., Links, P. S., Gnam, W. H., Guimond, T., Cardish, R. J., Korman, L., & Streiner, D. L. (2009). A randomized trial of dialectical behavior therapy versus general psychiatric management for borderline personality disorder. *American Journal of Psychiatry*, *166*(12), 1365–1374. doi: 10.1176/appi.ajp.2009.09010039

Messer, S. B., & McWilliams, N. (2007). Insight in psychodynamic therapy: Theory and assessment. In L. G. Castonguay & C. Hill (Eds.), *Insight in psychotherapy* (pp. 9–29). Washington, DC: American Psychological Association.

Messer, S. B., & Wolitzky, D. L. (2010). A psychodynamic perspective on the therapeutic alliance. In J. C. Muran & J. P. Barber (Eds.), *The therapeutic alliance: An evidence-based guide to practice* (pp. 97–122). New York, NY: Guilford Press.

Milbrath, C., Bond, M., Cooper, S., Znoj, H. J., Horowitz, M. J., & Perry, J. C. (1999). Sequential consequences of therapists' interventions. *Journal of Psychotherapy Practice and Research*, *8*(1), 40–54.

Milrod, B., Leon, A., Barber J. P., Markowitz, J., & Graf, E. (2007a). Do comorbid personality disorders moderate panic-focused psychotherapy? An exploratory examination of the American Psychiatric Association practice guideline. *Journal of Clinical Psychiatry*, *68*(6), 885–891.

*Milrod, B., Leon, A. C., Busch, F., Rudden, M., Schwalberg, M., Clarkin, J., . . . & Shear, M. K. (2007b). A randomized controlled clinical trial of psychoanalytic psychotherapy for panic disorder. *American Journal of Psychiatry*, *164*(2), 265–272.

Mitchell, S. A. (1988). *Relational concepts in psychoanalysis*. Cambridge, MA: Harvard University Press.

Mitchell, S. A. (1993). *Hope and dread in psychoanalysis*. New York, NY: Basic Books.

Muller, C., Kaufhold, J., Overbeck, G., & Grabhorn, R. (2006). The importance of reflective functioning to the diagnosis of psychic structure. *Psychology and Psychotherapy: Theory, Research and Practice*, *79*, 485–494.

Munder, T., Gerger, H., Trelle, S., & Barth, J. (2011). Testing the allegiance bias hypothesis: A meta-analysis. *Psychotherapy Research*, *21*(6), 670–684.

Muran, J. C., & Barber, J. P. (2010). *The therapeutic alliance: An evidence-based guide to practice*. New York, NY: Guilford Press.

Muran J. C., & Safran, J. D. (2002). A relational approach to psychotherapy: Resolving ruptures in the therapeutic alliance. In F. W. Kaslow (Ed.), *Comprehensive handbook of psychotherapy* (pp. 253–281). Hoboken, NJ: Wiley.

Muran, J. C., Safran, J. D., Gorman, B. S., Eubanks-Carter, C., & Banthin, D. (2008, June). Identifying ruptures & their resolution from postsession self-report measures. In J. C. Muran (Chair), *Recent developments in rupture resolution research*. Panel conducted at the annual meeting of the Society for Psychotherapy Research, Barcelona, Spain.

Muran, J. C., Safran, J. D., Gorman, B. S., Samstag, L. W., Eubanks-Carter, C., & Winston, A. (2009). The relationship of early alliance ruptures and their resolution to process and outcome in three time-limited psychotherapies for personality disorders. *Psychotherapy: Theory, Research, Practice, Training*, *46*, 233–248.

Muran, J. C., Safran, J. D., Samstag, L. W., & Winston, A. (1992). *Patient and therapist postsession questionnaires, Version 1992*. Beth Israel Medical Center, New York.

*Muran, J. C., Safran, J. D., Samstag, L. W., & Winston, A. (2005). Evaluating an alliance-focused treatment for personality disorders. *Psychotherapy: Theory, Research, Practice, Training, 42*, 532–545.

Muris, P., & Merckelbach, H. (1996). Defence style and behaviour therapy outcome in a specific phobia. *Psychological Medicine, 26*, 635–639.

Najavits, L. M., & Strupp, H. H. (1994). Differences in the effectiveness of psychodynamic therapists: a process-outcome study. *Psychotherapy, 31*, 114–123.

Newman, M. G., Castonguay, L. G., Borkovec, T. D., Fisher, A. J., & Nordberg, S. S. (2008). An open trial of integrative therapy for generalized anxiety disorder. *Psychotherapy: Theory, Research, Practice, Training, 45*, 135–147.

Nissen-Lie, H. A., Monsen, J. T., & Rønnestad, M. H. (2010). Therapist predictors of early patient-rated working alliance: A multilevel approach. *Psychotherapy Research, 20*(6), 627–646.

Norcross, J. C. (Ed.). (2011). *Psychotherapy relationships that work: Evidence-based responsiveness* (2nd ed.). New York, NY: Oxford University Press.

Norville, R., Sampson, H., & Weiss, J. (1996). Accurate interpretations and brief psychotherapy outcome. *Psychotherapy Research, 6*(1), 16–29.

Ogrodniczuk, J. S., & Piper, W. E. (1999). Use of transference interpretations in dynamically oriented individual psychotherapy for patients with personality disorders. *Journal of Personality Disorders, 297–311*.

Ogrodniczuk, J. S., Piper, W. E., Joyce, A. S., & McCallum, M. (2000). Different perspectives of the therapeutic alliance and therapist technique in 2 forms of dynamically oriented psychotherapy. *Canadian Journal of Psychiatry, 45*, 452–458.

O'Malley, S. S., Suh, C. S., & Strupp, H. H. (1983). The Vanderbilt psychotherapy process scale: A report on the scale development and a process-outcome study. *Journal of Consulting and Clinical Psychology, 51*(4), 581–586.

Owen, J., & Hilsenroth, M. J. (2011). Interaction between alliance and technique in predicting patient outcome during psychodynamic psychotherapy. *Journal of Nervous and Mental Disease, 199*(6), 384–389.

Ozkan, M., & Altindaq, A. (2005). Comorbid personality disorders in subjects with panic disorder: Do personality disorders increase clinical severity? *Comprehensive Psychiatry, 46*(1), 20–26.

Patton, M. J., Kivlighan, D. M., & Multon, K. D. (1997). The Missouri psychoanalytic counseling research project: Relation of changes in counseling process to client outcomes. *Journal of Counseling Psychology, 44*(2), 189–208.

Perry, J. C., Banon, E., & Ianni, F. (1999). Effectiveness of psychotherapy for personality disorders. *American Journal of Psychiatry, 156*(9), 1312–1321.

Perry, J. C., & Ianni, F. F. (1998). Observer-rated measures of defense mechanisms. *Journal of Personality, 66*(6), 993–1024.

*Pierloot, R. & Vinck, A. (1978). Differential outcome of short-term dynamic psychotherapy and systematic desensitization in the treatment of anxious outpatients: A preliminary report. *Psychologica Belgica, 18*(1), 87–98.

Piper, W. E., Azim, H. F., Joyce, A. S., & McCallum, M. (1991). Transference interpretations, therapeutic alliance, and outcome in short-term individual psychotherapy. *Archive of General Psychiatry, 48*(10), 946–953.

Piper, W. E., Azim, H. F., McCallum, M., & Joyce, A. S. (1990). Patient suitability and outcome in short-term individual psychotherapy. *Journal of Consulting and Clinical Psychology, 58*(4), 475–481. doi: 10.1037/0022–006X.58.4.475

Piper, W. E., Joyce, A. S., McCallum, M., & Azim, H. F. (1993). Concentration and correspondence of transference interpretations in short-term psychotherapy. *Journal of Consulting and Clinical Psychology, 61*(4), 586–595.

Piper, W. E., Joyce, A. S., McCallum, M., & Azim, H. F. (1998). Interpretive and supportive forms of psychotherapy and patient personality variables. *Journal of Consulting and Clinical Psychology, 66*(3), 558–567.

Piper, W. E., McCallum, M., Joyce, A. S., Rosie, J. S., & Ogrodniczuk, J. S. (2001). Patient personality and time-limited group psychotherapy for complicated grief. *International Journal of Group Psychotherapy, 51*(4) 525–552.

Piper, W. E., Ogrodniczuk, J. S., & Joyce, A. S. (2004). Quality of object relations as a moderator of the relationship between pattern of alliance and outcome in short-term individual psychotherapy. *Journal of Personality Assessment, 83*(3), 345–356.

Piper, W. E., Ogrodniczuk, J. S., Joyce, A. S., McCallum, M., Rosie, J. S., O'Kelly, J. G., & Steinberg, P. I. (1999). Prediction of dropping out in time-limited, interpretive individual psychotherapy. *Psychotherapy, 36*, 114–122.

Porcerelli, J. H., Huprich, S. K., & Markova, T. (2010). Mental representations in women with panic disorder: An urban African-American sample. *Journal of Nervous & Mental Disease, 198*(2), 144–149.

Porcerelli, J. H., Shahar, G., Blatt, S. J., Ford, R. Q., Mezza, J. A., & Greenlee, L. M. (2006). Social cognition and object relations scale: Convergent validity and changes following intensive inpatient treatment. *Personality and Individual Differences, 41*, 407–417.

Regan, A. M., & Hill, C. E. (1992). An investigation of what clients and counselors do not say in brief therapy. *Journal of Counseling Psychology, 39*, 168–174.

Rennie, D. (1994). Clients' deference in psychotherapy. *Journal of Counseling Psychology, 41,* 427–437.

Rhodes, R., Hill, C., Thompson, B., & Elliott, R. (1994). Client retrospective recall of resolved and unresolved misunderstanding events. *Counseling Psychology, 41,* 473–483.

Rice, L. N., & Greenberg, L. S. (1984). *Patterns of change: Intensive analysis of psychotherapy process.* New York, NY: Guilford Press.

Roy, C. A., Perry, J. C., Luborsky, L., & Banon, E. (2009). Changes in defensive functioning in completed psychoanalyses: The Penn psychoanalytic treatment collection. *Journal of the American Psychoanalytic Association, 57,* 399–415.

Rudden, M., Milrod, B., Target, M., Ackerman, S., & Graf, E. (2006). Reflective functioning in panic disorder patients: A pilot study. *Journal of the American Psychoanalytic Association, 54,* 1339–1343.

Ruiz, M. A., Pincus, A. L., Borkovec, T. D., Echemendia, R. J., Castonguay, L. G., & Ragusea, S. A. (2004). Validity of the inventory of interpersonal problems for predicting treatment outcome: An investigation with the Pennsylvania practice research network. *Journal of Personality Assessment, 83*(3), 213–222.

Ryle, A. (1997). *Cognitive analytic therapy and borderline personality disorder: The model and the method.* Chichester, United Kingdom: Wiley.

Ryum, T., Stiles, T. C., Svartberg, M., & McCullough, L. (2010). The role of transference work, the therapeutic alliance, and their interaction in reducing interpersonal problems among psychotherapy patients with cluster c personality disorders. *Psychotherapy: Theory, Research, Practice, Training, 47*(4), 442–453.

Safran, J. D., Crocker, P., McMain, S., & Murray, P. (1990). Therapeutic alliance rupture as a therapy event for empirical investigation. *Psychotherapy: Theory, Research, and Practice, 27,* 154–165.

Safran, J. D., & Muran, J. C. (1996). The resolution of ruptures in the therapeutic alliance. *Journal of Consulting and Clinical Psychology, 64,* 447–458.

Safran, J. D., & Muran, J. C. (2000). *Negotiating the therapeutic alliance: A relational treatment guide.* New York, NY: Guilford Press.

Safran, J. D., & Muran, J. C. (2006). Has the concept of the therapeutic alliance outlived its usefulness? *Psychotherapy: Theory, Research, Practice, Training, 43,* 286–291.

Safran, J. D., Muran, J. C., & Eubanks-Carter, C. (2011). Repairing alliance ruptures. *Psychotherapy, 48*(1), 80–87.

Safran, J. D., Muran, J. C., & Samstag, L. W. (1994). Resolving therapeutic alliance ruptures: a task analytic investigation. In A. O. Horvath & L. S. Greenberg (Eds.), *The working alliance: Theory, research, and practice* (pp. 225–255). New York, NY: Wiley.

Safran, J. D., Muran, J. C., Samstag, L. W., & Winston, A. (2005). Evaluating alliance-focused intervention for potential treatment failures: A feasibility study and descriptive analysis. *Psychotherapy: Theory, Research, Practice, Training, 42,* 512–531.

Safran, J. D., & Segal, Z. V. (1990). *Interpersonal process in cognitive therapy.* New York, NY: Basic Books.

*Salminen, J. K., Karlsson, H., Hietala, J., Kajander, J., Aalto, S., Markkula, J., . . . Toikka, T. (2008). Short-term psychodynamic psychotherapy and fluoxetine in major depressive disorder: A randomized comparative study. *Psychotherapy and Psychosomatics, 77*(6), 351–357. doi: 10.1159/000151388

Salzer, S., Leibing, E., Thorsten, J., Rudolf, G., Brockmann, J., Eckert, J., & Leichsenring, F. (2010). Patterns of interpersonal problems and their improvement in depressive and anxious patients treated with psychoanalytic therapy. *Bulletin of the Menninger Clinic, 74*(4), 283–300.

Schauenburg, H., Buchheim, A., Beckh, K., Nolte, T., Brenk-Franz, K., Leichsenring, F., . . . Dinger, U. (2010). The influence of psychodynamically oriented therapists' attachment representations on outcome and alliance in inpatient psychotherapy. *Psychotherapy Research, 20*(2), 193–202.

Schut, A. J., & Castonguay, L. G. (2001). Reviving Freud's vision of a psychoanalytic science: Implications for clinical training and education. *Psychotherapy: Theory, Research, Practice, Training, 38*(1), 40–49.

Schut, A. J., Castonguay, L. G., Flanagan, K. M., Yamasaki, A. S., Barber, J. P., Bedics, J. D., & Smith, T. L. (2005). Therapist interpretation, patient-therapist interpersonal process, and outcome in psychodynamic psychotherapy, for avoidant personality disorder. *Psychotherapy: Theory, Research, Practice, Training, 42*(4), 494–511.

*Shapiro, D. A., Barkham, M., Rees, A. A., Hardy, G. E., Reynolds, S., & Startup, M. (1994). Effects of treatment duration and severity of depression on the effectiveness of cognitive-behavioral and psychodynamic-interpersonal psychotherapy. *Journal of Consulting and Clinical Psychology, 62*(3), 522–534. doi: 10.1037/0022–006X.62.3.522

Sharp, C., Pane, H., Ha, C., Venta, A., Patel, A. B., Sturek, J., & Fonagy, P. (2011). Theory of mind and emotion regulation difficulties in adolescents with borderline traits. *Journal of the American Academy of Child and Adolescent Psychiatry, 50,* 563–573.

Sharpless, B. A., & Barber, J. P. (2012). Corrective emotional experiences from a psychodynamic perspective. In L. G. Castonguay & C. Hill (Eds.), *Transformation in psychotherapy: Corrective experiences across cognitive behavioral, humanistic, and psychodynamic approaches.* Washington, DC: American Psychological Association.

Sharpless, B. A., Muran, J. C., & Barber, J. P. (2010). Coda: Recommendations for practice and training.

In J. C. Muran & J. P. Barber (Eds.), *The therapeutic alliance: An evidence based approach to practice* (pp. 341–354). New York, NY: Guilford Press.

Shear, M. K., Houck, P., Greeno, C., & Masters, S. (2001). Emotion-focused psychotherapy for patients with panic disorder. *American Journal of Psychiatry, 158*(12), 1993–1998.

Shedler, J. (2010). The efficacy of psychodynamic psychotherapy. *American Psychologist, 65*(2), 98–109.

Shimokawa, K., Lambert, M. J., & Smart, D. W. (2010). Enhancing treatment outcome of patients at risk of treatment failure: Meta-analytic and mega-analytic review of a psychotherapy quality assurance system. *Journal of Consulting and Clinical Psychology, 78*(3), 298–311.

Siev, J., & Chambless, D. L. (2007). Specificity of treatment effects: Cognitive therapy and relaxation for generalized anxiety and panic disorders. *Journal of Consulting and Clinical Psychology, 75*(4), 513–522.

Silberschatz, G., Fretter, P. B., & Curtis, J. T. (1986). How do interpretations influence the process of psychotherapy? *Journal of Consulting and Clinical Psychology, 54*(5), 646–652.

Slavin-Mulford, J., & Hilsenroth M. J. (2012). Evidence-based psychodynamic treatments for anxiety disorders: A review. In J. F. Rosenbaum (Series Ed.), R. A. Levy, A. S. Ablon, & H. Kächele (Eds.), *Psychodyanmic psychotherapy research: Evidence-based practice and practice-based evidence* (pp. 117–138). New York, NY: Humana Press.

Slavin-Mulford, J., Hilsenroth, M., Weinberger, J., & Gold, J. (2011). Therapeutic interventions related to outcome in psychodynamic psychotherapy for anxiety disorder patients. *Journal of Nervous and Mental Disease, 199*(4), 214–221.

Slonim, D. A., Shefler, G., Gvirsman, S. D., & Tishby, O. (2011). Changes in rigidity and symptoms among adolescents in psychodynamic psychotherapy. *Psychotherapy Research, 21*, 685–697.

Smit, Y., Huibers, M. J. H., Ioannidis, J. P. A., van Dyck, R., van Tilburg, W., & Arntz, A. (2012). The effectiveness of long-term psychoanalytic psychotherapy—A meta-analysis of randomized controlled trials. *Clinical Psychology Review, 32*(2), 81–92.

Sommerfeld, E., Orbach, I., Zim, S., & Mikulincer, M. (2008). An in-session exploration of ruptures in working alliance and their associations with clients' core conflictual relationship themes, alliance-related discourse, and clients' postsession evaluation. *Psychotherapy Research, 18*, 377–388.

Spinhoven, P., Giesen-Bloo, J., van Dyck, R., Kooiman, K., & Arntz, A. (2007). The therapeutic alliance in schema-focused therapy and transference-focused psychotherapy for borderline personality disorder. *Journal of Consulting and Clinical Psychology, 75*(1), 104–111.

Staats, H., May, M., Herrmann, C., Kersting, A., & Konig, K. (1998). Different patterns of change in narratives of men and women during analytical group psychotherapy. *International Journal of Group Psychotherapy, 48*(3), 363–380.

Sterba, R. E. (1934). The fate of the ego in analytic therapy. *International Journal of Psychoanalysis, 115*, 117–126.

Stevens, C. L. Muran, J. C., Safran, J. D., Gorman, B. S., & Winston, A. (2007). Levels and patterns of the therapeutic alliance in brief psychotherapy. *American Journal of Psychotherapy, 61*, 109–129.

Stigler, M., de Roten, Y., Drapeau, M., & Despland, J. N. (2007). Process research in psychodynamic psychotherapy: A combined measure of accuracy and conflictuality of interpretations. *Swiss Archives of Neurology and Psychiatry, 58*, 225–232.

Stiles, W. B., Glick, M. J., Osatuke, K., Hardy, G. E., Shapiro, D. A., Agnew-Davies, R.,…Barkham, M. (2004). Patterns of alliance development and the rupture-repair hypothesis: Are productive relationships *U*-shaped or *V*-shaped? *Journal of Counseling Psychology, 51*, 81–92.

Strachey, J. (1934). The nature of the therapeutic action of psycho-analysis. *International Journal of Psycho-Analysis, 15*, 127–159.

Strauss, J. L., Hayes, A. M., Johnson, S. L., Newman, C. F., Brown, G. K., Barber, J. P.,…Beck, A. T. (2006). Early alliance, alliance ruptures, and symptom change in a nonrandomized trial of cognitive therapy for avoidant and obsessive-compulsive personality disorders. *Journal of Consulting and Clinical Psychology, 74*, 337–345.

Strunk, D. R., Brotman, M. A., & DeRubeis, R. J. (2010). The process of change in cognitive therapy for depression: Predictors of early inter-session symptom gains. *Behaviour Research and Therapy, 48*(7), 599–606.

Summers, R. J., & Barber, J. P. (2009). *Dynamic psychotherapy: A guide to evidence-based practice.* New York, NY: Guilford Press.

Svartberg, M., & Stiles, T. (1994). Therapeutic alliance, therapist competence, and client change in short-term anxiety-provoking psychotherapy. *Psychotherapy Research, 4*, 20–33.

*Svartberg, M., Stiles, T. C., & Seltzer, M. H. (2004). Randomized, controlled trial of the effectiveness of short-term dynamic psychotherapy and cognitive therapy for cluster C personality disorders. *American Journal of Psychiatry, 161*(5), 810–817. doi: 10.1176/appi.ajp.161.5.810

Taber, B. J., Leibert, T. W., & Agaskar, V. R. (2011). Relationships among client–therapist personality congruence, working alliance, and therapeutic outcome. *Psychotherapy, 48*(4), 376–380.

Task Force on Promotion and Dissemination of Psychological Procedures. (1995). Training in and dissemination of empirically validated treatments: Report and recommendations. *Clinical Psychologist, 48*(1), 3–23.

Taubner, S., Kessler, H., Buchheim, A., Kachele, H., & Staun, L. (2011). The role of mentalization in the psychoanalytic treatment of chronic depression. *Psychiatry, 74,* 49–57.

Thoma, N. C., McKay, D., Gerber, A. J., Milrod, B. L., Edwards, A. R., & Kocsis, J. H. (2012). A quality-based review of randomized controlled trials of cognitive-behavioral therapy for depression: An assessment and metaregression. *American Journal of Psychiatry, 169*(1), 22–30.

*Thompson, L. W., Gallagher, D., & Breckenridge, J. S. (1987). Comparative effectiveness of psychotherapies for depressed elders. *Journal of Consulting and Clinical Psychology, 55*(3), 385–390. doi: 10.1037/0022–006X.55.3.385

*Thyme, K. E., Sundin, E. C., Stahlberg, G., Lindstrom, B., Eklof, H., & Wiberg, B. (2007). The outcome of short-term psychodynamic art therapy compared to short-term psychodynamic verbal therapy for depressed women. *Psychoanalytic Psychotherapy, 21*(3), 250–264. doi: 10.1080/02668730701535610

Tishby, O., Raitchick, I., & Shefler, G. (2007). Changes in interpersonal conflicts among adolescents during psychodynamic therapy. *Psychotherapy Research, 17*(3), 297–304.

Tolin, D. F. (2010). Is cognitive-behavioral therapy more effective than other therapies?: A meta-analytic review. *Clinical Psychology Review, 30*(6), 710–720.

Tracey, T. J., & Kokotovic, A. M. (1989). Factor structure of the working alliance inventory. trials. *Psychological Bulletin, 130*(4), 631–663.

Tryon, G. S., & Kane, A. S. (1993). Relationship of working alliance to mutual and unilateral termination. *Journal of Counseling Psychology, 40,* 33–36.

Vaillant, G. (1992). *Ego mechanisms of defense: A guide for clinicians and researchers.* Washington DC: American Psychiatric Press.

Van, H. L., Hendriksen, M., Schoevers, R. A., Peen, J., Abraham, R. A., & Dekker, J. (2008). Predictive value of object relations for therapeutic alliance and outcome in psychotherapy for depression: An exploratory study. *Journal of Nervous & Mental Disease, 196*(9), 655–662.

Vermote, R., Lowyck, B., Luyten, P., Vertommen, H., Corveleyn, J., Verhaest, Y., & Peuskens, J. (2010). Process and outcome in psychodynamic hospitalization-based treatment for patients with a personality disorder. *Journal of Nervous & Mental Disease, 198*(2), 110–115.

Vinnars, B., Barber, J. P., Noren, K., Gallop, R., & Weinryb, R. M. (2005). Manualized supportive-expressive psychotherapy versus nonmanualized community-delivered psychodynamic therapy for patients with personality disorders: Bridging efficacy and effectiveness. *American Journal of Psychiatry, 162*(10), 1933–1940.

*Vitriol, V. G., Ballesteros, S. T., Florenzano, R. U., Weil, K. P., & Benadof, D. F. (2009). Evaluation of an outpatient intervention for women with severe depression and a history of childhood trauma. *Psychiatric Services, 60*(7), 936–942. doi: 10.1176/appi.ps.60.7.936

Wampold, B. E. (2001). *The great psychotherapy debate: Models, methods, and findings.* Mahwah, NJ: Erlbaum.

Wampold, B., Minami, T., Baskin, T., & Tierney, S. (2002). A meta-(re)analysis of the effects of cognitive therapy versus "other therapies" for depression. *Journal of Affective Disorders, 68,* 159–165.

Wampold, B. E., Mondin, G. W., Moody, M., Stich, F., Benson, K., & Ahn, H. (1997). A meta-analysis of outcome studies comparing bona fide psychotherapies: Empirically, "All must have prizes" *Psychological Bulletin, 122,* 203–215.

Watson, J. C., & Kalogerakos, F. (2010). The therapeutic alliance in humanistic psychotherapy. In J. C. Muran & J. P. Barber (eds.), *The therapeutic alliance: An evidence-based guide to practice* (pp. 191–209). New York, NY: Guilford Press.

Webb, C. A., DeRubeis, R. J., & Barber, J. P. (2010). Therapist adherence/competence and treatment outcome: A meta-analytic review. *Journal of Consulting and Clinical Psychology, 78,* 200–211.

Weiss, J., Sampson, H., & Mount Zion Psychotherapy Research Group. (1986). *The psychoanalytic process: Theory, clinical observation, empirical research.* New York, NY: Guilford Press.

Westen, D., Novonty, C. M., & Thompson-Brenner, H. (2004). The empirical status of empirically supported psychotherapies: Assumptions, findings, and reporting in controlled clinical trials. *Psychological Bulletin, 130*(4), 631–663.

Wilczek, A. Weinryb, R. M., Barber, J. P., Gustavsson, J. P., & Asberg, M. (2004). Change in the core conflictual relationship theme after long-term dynamic psychotherapy. *Psychotherapy Research, 14*(1), 107–125.

*Winston, A., Laikin, M., Pollack, J., Samstag, L. W., McCullough, L., & Muran, J. C. (1994). Short-term psychotherapy of personality disorders. *American Journal of Psychiatry, 151*(2), 190–194.

Wolfe, B. E., & Goldfried, M. R. (1988). Research on psychotherapy integration: Recommendations and conclusions from an NIMH workshop. *Journal of Consulting and Clinical Psychology, 56,* 448–451.

Yeomans, F. (2007). Questions concerning the randomized trial of schema-focused therapy vs transference-focused psychotherapy. *Archives of General Psychiatry, 64*(5), 609–610.

Zetzel, E. R. (1956). Current concepts of transference. *International Journal of Psychoanalysis, 37,* 369–437.

CHAPTER 13

RESEARCH ON HUMANISTIC-EXPERIENTIAL PSYCHOTHERAPIES

ROBERT ELLIOTT, LESLIE S. GREENBERG, JEANNE WATSON, LADISLAV TIMULAK, AND ELIZABETH FREIRE

This review covers approaches to psychotherapy generally referred to as *humanistic* or *experiential*. These therapies are part of the main tradition of humanistic psychology (see Cain & Seeman, 2002), with major subapproaches being person-centered therapy (PCT; e.g., Rogers, 1961), gestalt (e.g., Perls, Hefferline & Goodman, 1951), emotion-focused (EFT, also known as process-experiential; Greenberg, Rice, & Elliott, 1993), existential (e.g., Yalom, 1980), psychodrama (J. Moreno & Moreno, 1959), focusing-oriented (Gendlin, 1996), expressive (Daldrup, Beutler, Engle, & Greenberg, 1988), and body-oriented (Kepner, 1993). In addition, humanistic-experiential psychotherapies (HEPs) are often used as generic relationship control conditions by researchers from other theoretical orientations under store-brand labels such as *supportive* or *nondirective*.

Although these approaches have varied somewhat in technique and conception over the course of their historical development, in their contemporary expressions they nevertheless share several distinctive theoretical assumptions. Most important among these is the centrality of a genuinely empathic and prizing *therapeutic relationship*. In the HEPs, the therapeutic relationship

is seen as potentially curative. Each person's subjective experience is of central importance, and, in an effort to grasp this experience, the therapist attempts to enter empathically into the client's world in a way that goes beyond usual relationships or the subject-object dichotomy. Being allowed to share another person's world is viewed as a privilege, and all HEPs reject the idea that the relationship between the client and the therapist can be reduced to an unconscious repetition of previous attachments. Rather, they generally share the view that an authentic but boundaried relationship with the therapist provides the client with a new, emotionally validating experience.

HEPs also share a focus on promoting in-therapy client *experiencing*, defined as the holistic process of immediate, ongoing awareness that includes perceiving, sensing, feeling, thinking, and wanting/intending. Thus, methods that deepen or stimulate client emotional experiencing are used within the context of an empathic facilitative relationship. Commitment to a phenomenological approach flows directly from this central interest in experiencing. People are viewed as meaning-creating, symbolizing agents, whose subjective experience is an essential aspect of their humanity. In addition, the experiential-humanistic view of functioning emphasizes the operation of an integrative, formative tendency, oriented toward survival, growth, and the creation of meaning. Moreover, all HEPs are united by the general principle that people are wiser than their intellect alone. Internal tacit experiencing is seen as an important guide to conscious experience,

We acknowledge the contributions of the many colleagues who sent us information on their research; we ask them to continue sending omitted or new studies. The outcome meta-analysis was supported in part by a grant to Robert Elliott and Elizabeth Freire from the British Association for the Person-Centred Approach.

fundamentally adaptive, and potentially available to awareness when the person turns attention internally within the context of a supportive interpersonal relationship. Interpersonal safety and support are thus viewed as key elements in enhancing the amount of attention available for self-awareness and exploration. HEPs are also consistently *person-centered*. This involves genuine concern and respect for each person. The person is viewed holistically, neither as a symptom-driven case nor as a diagnosis.

Recent developments in the HEPs include a revival of research on person-centered therapy (PCT) and continued study of focusing-oriented (Gendlin, 1996) and emotion-focused approaches (Greenberg et al., 1993). Like gestalt therapy, these newer approaches use experiments in directed awareness to help focus and concentrate attention on unformed experience and to intensify its vividness. For example, focusing-oriented therapy emphasizes the creation of new meaning by focusing awareness on bodily feelings, while EFT integrates person-centered and gestalt therapy traditions, emphasizing both the relationship and the process of reflection on aroused emotions to create new meaning. In practice, these and other *process-guiding* contemporary approaches strive to maintain a creative tension between the person-centered emphasis on creating a genuinely empathic and prizing therapeutic relationship, and a more active, task-focused process-facilitating style of engagement that promotes deeper experiencing and consequent meaning creation. Although coming from a different tradition, "third generation" cognitive-behavioral therapy (CBT), such as mindfulness-based cognitive therapy (Segal, Williams, & Teasdale, 2001), acceptance and commitment therapy (Hayes, Strosahl, & Wilson, 1999), and compassion-focused therapy (Gilbert, 2009) have expanded to have much in common with HEPs.

A continuing key point of contention within the humanistic-experiential psychotherapies, however, is the degree to which therapists should act as process-experts by offering ways clients can work more productively on particular types of problems ("process guiding"). All HEPs are process-guiding to a certain extent, but EFT and gestalt are more so, while PCT and so-called supportive or nondirective therapies attempt to minimize process guiding.

In this chapter we focus on research published since our previous reviews (Elliott, Greenberg, & Lietaer, 2004; Greenberg, Elliott, & Lietaer, 1994), which covered research published between 1978 and 2001, plus additional earlier research on HEP outcome that we have been able to track down. A key element of the chapter is a meta-analysis of nearly 200 HEP outcome studies (through 2008) and a survey of the use of the approach with different client groups. In addition, we offer a meta-synthesis of qualitative research on these therapies (cf. Timulak, 2007), and provide a narrative review of recent quantitative research on change processes in HEPs. Finally, we once again apply the criteria for designating psychotherapies as empirically supported, originally proposed by the Society of Clinical Psychology (Division 12, American Psychological Association; see Task Force on Promotion and Dissemination of Psychological Procedures, 1995) and subsequently modified by Chambless and Hollon (1998). We realize that these criteria are controversial (e.g., Elliott, 1998), but use them here because they are the clearest such guidelines available and are widely recognized.

Because of space limitations and the increasing amount and range of research this survey is not exhaustive. In particular, we have not reviewed research on the therapeutic alliance, child psychotherapy, and on measure development (but see Cooper, Watson, & Hölldampf, 2010, for reviews of these topics). In addition, we have chosen not to review research on the growing number of related integrative approaches, such as emotion-focused psychodynamic approaches (e.g., Fosha, 2000), motivational interviewing (Lundahl, Kunz, Brownell, Tollefson, & Burke, 2010), and "third wave" CBT (e.g., Gilbert, 2009; Hayes et al., 1999; Segal et al., 2001).

As noted in our previous review (Elliott et al., 2004), although clear progress has taken place in the past 20 years, including increasing numbers of studies on specific client populations, additional programmatic empirical research on humanistic-experiential therapies is still needed.

ARE HUMANISTIC-EXPERIENTIAL THERAPIES EFFECTIVE? A META-ANALYSIS

In North America and Europe, economic pressures on mental health services and scientific-political trends toward treatment standardization have led to the development of guidelines calling for certain psychological treatments to be officially recognized as effective, reimbursed by insurance, and actively promoted in training courses, at the expense of other treatments (e.g., Task Force on Promotion and Dissemination of Psychological Procedures, 1995; Meyer, Richter, Grawe, von Schulenburg & Schulte, 1991; National Collaborating Centre for Mental Health, 2009). To date, these guidelines have not been kind to the HEPs, and have in effect enshrined widely shared preconceptions about the perceived ineffectiveness of these approaches as supposed scientific fact and health care policy. Although research on HEPs has rapidly expanded over the past 20 years (see previous reviews in Cain & Seeman, 2002; Cooper et al., 2010; Elliott et al., 2004), they continue to be overlooked or dismissed, as in the NICE Guidelines for Depression and Schizophrenia (National Collaborating Centre for Mental Health, 2009, 2010).

Understandably, humanistic-experiential therapists (e.g., Bohart, O'Hara, & Leitner, 1998; Schneider, 1998) have responded to these challenges with alarm. Although philosophical assumptions and methods of the evidence-based practice movement have been and continue to be challenged, our strategy here is to look instead at the existing research evidence, which has sometimes been neglected in the controversy. In fact, as we show, a substantial and rapidly growing body of research data supports the effectiveness of HEPs.

We report here the latest of a continuing series of meta-analytic reviews of HEP quantitative outcome research, substantially updating earlier reports (Elliott, 1996, 2002; Elliott et al., 2004; Greenberg et al., 1994). The present analysis includes more than 5 times the number of studies analyzed in Greenberg et al.'s (1994) original review, from 35 to 195, including 77 studies not included in our most recent review (Elliott et al., 2004). Eleven of these studies were published prior to 1970; 25 came from the 1970s; 36 from the 1980s; 63 from the 1990s; and 60 from the first decade of the 2000s. These studies offer evidence for a revival of outcome research on HEPs. We have included all the studies we could locate and analyze through 2008 (unfortunately, the accelerating pace of the research has currently outstripped our ability to keep up with it beyond that date).

At this point, the analysis includes pre-post effect size data from 199 different samples of clients seen in some form of HEP, drawing from 186 studies (involving a total of 14,206 clients). In terms of controlled studies with wait-list or no-treatment conditions, there are 62 comparisons, from 59 studies (involving 2,149 therapy clients and 1,988 controls); 31 of these were randomized control trials (RCTs). As for comparative studies, in which HEPs were compared to other treatments, there are 135 comparisons, derived from 108 samples of clients in HEP in 100 different studies, 82 of these RCTs ($n = 6,271$ HEP clients, 7,214 clients in non-HEP therapies). Finally, there are 9 comparisons between more versus less process-guiding HEPs (7 studies, 264 clients).

The pre-post therapy samples were categorized into six clusters: (1) 74 involved person-centered therapy (PCT) in a relatively pure form; (2) 33 focused on generic versions of HEP most commonly referred to as *supportive* or *nondirective*; (3) 34 studies examined task-focused, integrative emotion-focused therapies (EFT, also known as *process-experiential*), including emotionally focused therapy for couples (EFT-C); (4) new in this review, we analyzed 10 studies of existentially oriented supportive-expressive group therapy for medical populations (e.g., cancer); (5) finally, 43 samples of clients received other HEPs (gestalt therapy, psychodrama, focusing-oriented, encounter, or integrative); and (6) five got treatments that mixed HEP with some other kind of treatment such as medication or advice. The average length of therapy was 20 sessions (sd: 21, range 2–124); the average number of clients studied was 70 (sd: 240; range 5– 2,742). For the pre-post effects sample, *researcher* theoretical allegiances were most commonly pro-HEP (65%), while for comparative studies this figure was only 31%.

For each study, characteristics of the treatments, clients, therapists or the studies were rated to estimate the contribution of these features to effect size. For example, internal validity was coded, with one group pre-post uncontrolled open clinical trials rated as "0"; one group wait list own control designs as "1"; two group non-randomized designs as "2"; and two group randomized controlled trials (RCTs), given a "3" rating.

Standardized pre-post differences (d) were used for effect size (ES) calculations using standard estimation procedures (e.g., Smith, Glass, & Miller, 1980) and D/STAT (Johnson, 1989). ESs were calculated for each subscale of each outcome measure used, then averaged across subscales within measures for each of three assessment periods: posttherapy, early follow-up (less than a year), and late follow-up (a year or longer). For *pre-post effect sizes*, measure effects were first averaged, then across the three assessment periods to yield an overall value for each treatment in each study. In addition, standard corrections for small sample bias and inverse error (based on sample-size) weighting formulas (Hunter & Schmidt, 1990) were applied to these ESs in order to obtain more precise estimates of overall effect. Analyses of *controlled and comparative effect sizes* compared mean overall pre-post effects between control or comparative treatment conditions, with positive values assigned where the HEP treatment showed a larger amount of change. In addition, random-effects significance testing (Wilson & Lipsey, 2001), using the *Comprehensive Meta Analysis* software package was combined with equivalence analyses (Rogers, Howard, & Vessey, 1993) for key comparisons, using .4 sd, as previously proposed by Elliott, Stiles, and Shapiro (1993), as a demarcation between a small and a medium effect size This is useful for defining the minimum clinically interesting difference, relevant to individual clinical practitioners, who see small numbers of clients at one time. Next, we analyzed for heterogeneity of effects using Cochrane's Q, which tests for whether the overall effect estimate is compromised by significant between-study variability. Finally, we estimated the proportion of the between study variation due to true variability as opposed to random error by using the I^2 statistic (Higgins, Thompson, Deeks, & Altman, 2003). (Higgins et al. [2003] recommend interpreting I^2 values of 25%, 50%, and 75% respectively as small, medium, and large.)

In addition, when examining particular client populations (e.g., depression), we applied the Chambless and Hollon (1998) revised criteria for designating level of empirical support. According to their formulation, studies are generally expected to meet certain quality criteria: (a) reasonable sample size ($n > 25$ per group); (b) use of treatment manual or adherence checks; (c) a specific client population defined by reliable, valid inclusion criteria; (d) use of reliable, valid outcome measures, including measurement of targeted client difficulties; and (e) appropriate data analysis (e.g., direct comparisons, evaluation of all outcome measures). The three levels of efficacy are defined as:

1. *Possibly efficacious*: One controlled study in absence of conflicting evidence.
2. *Efficacious*: In at least two independent research settings, the treatment is either

(a) superior to no treatment or another treatment, or (b) equivalent to an established treatment using studies of reasonable size ($n > 25$ per group). With conflicting evidence, the preponderance of the well-controlled studies supports the treatment.

3. *Efficacious and specific*: In at least two independent research settings, the treatment must have been shown to be statistically significant and superior either (a) to a non–bona fide treatment (e.g., a "placebo") or (b) to an alternative bona fide treatment. With conflicting evidence, the preponderance of the well-controlled studies supports the treatment.

Total Pre-Post Change in Humanistic-Experiential Therapies

Table 13.1 summarizes pre-post effects for all studies for which these could be calculated. The unweighted average pre-post effect (d), across the 199 treatment samples and assessment periods, was .96. This exceeds the .8 standard cited by Cohen (1988) as a large effect size. The data clearly indicate that clients maintained or perhaps even increased their immediate posttreatment gains ($d = .95$) over the posttherapy period, with slightly larger effects obtained at early (1–11 months; 1.05) and late (12+ months; 1.11) follow-ups. Weighting effects by inverse error (a function of sample size) produced a virtually identical overall mean ES of .93 (95% confidence interval: .86 to 1.00).

CONTROLLED STUDIES ON THE EFFECTIVENESS OF HUMANISTIC-EXPERIENTIAL THERAPIES

Pre-post effects do not tell us whether clients in HEPs fared better than untreated clients, and thus make it difficult to infer that therapy was responsible for changes made by clients. They have also been reported to produce generally larger effects than control group comparisons (Lipsey & Wilson, 1993). Therefore, we examined control-referenced effect sizes (differences between pre-post ESs) in the 62 treated groups in which HEPs were compared to wait-list or no-treatment controls. The unweighted mean controlled effect size for these studies (Table 13.1) was also large, .81, a value only slightly less than

TABLE 13.1 Summary of Overall Pre-Post Change, Controlled and Comparative Effect Sizes

	n	m	sd
Pre-Post Change ES (mean g)			
By assessment point:			
Post	181	.95	.61
Early follow-up (1–11 mos.)	77	1.05	.65
Late follow-up (12+ mos)	52	1.11	.68
Overall (mES):			
Unweighted	199	.96	.61
Weighted (d_w)	199	.93	.04[a]
Controlled ES (vs. untreated clients)[b]			
Unweighted mean difference	62	.81	.62
Unweighted m diff, RCTs only	*31*	*.81*	*.68*
Experiential mean pre-post ES	59	1.01	.68
Control mean pre-post ES	53	.19	.32
Weighted	62	.76	.06
Weighted m diff, RCTs only	*31*	*.76*	*.10[a]*
Comparative ES (vs. other treatments)[b]			
Unweighted mean difference	135	−.02	.53
Unweighted m diff, RCTs only	*113*	*−.02*	*.53*
Experiential mean pre-post ES	124	.98	.62
Comparative treatment mean pre-post ES	124	1.02	.69
Weighted mean difference	135	.01	.03[a]
Weighted m diff, RCTs only	*113*	*−.01*	*.04[a]*
Comparative ES (more vs. less process-guiding experiential)[b]			
Unweighted	9	.33	.51
Weighted by n	9	.14	.18[a]

Note: Hedge's g used (corrects for small sample bias). Weighted effects used inverse variance based on *n* of clients in humanistic-experiential therapy conditions.
[a]Standard error of the mean given for weighted effects.
[b]Mean difference in change ESs for conditions compared, except where these are unavailable; positive values indicate pro-HEP or pro-process guiding results.

the mean pre-post effect of .96. In contrast, the average pre-post effect for the 53 untreated conditions (the number for which data were available) was .19, only a fifth the size of the effect for clients in HEPs. The weighted effect (d_w) was .76 (CI: .64 to .88) and moderately heterogeneous ($Q = 162.8; p < .001; I^2 = 62\%$). The same unweighted and weighted results held when only the 31 randomized studies were analyzed. From this pattern of results, three conclusions can be drawn: (1) there is a strong causal relationship between HEP and client change; (2) the controlled effects are highly consistent with the pre-post effects, and suggest that about 80% of the pre-post gains reported for clients in HEPs can be attributed to the therapy (including both client and therapist within-therapy factors), as opposed to external or nontherapy factors; (3) these results hold,

regardless of whether RCT designs are used or not, thus supporting the internal validity of the nonrandomized controlled studies, as well as the much larger body of one-group pre-post studies.

Comparative Outcome Research on Humanistic-Experiential Versus Other Therapies

While impressive, the pre-post and controlled effect-size analyses reported do not address the issue of comparative treatment effectiveness, which is central to continuing discussions about mental health policy, the effectiveness of HEPs and the sources of their effects. For this, we analyzed 135 comparisons between HEPs and other therapies. The average unweighted difference in pre-post effects was −.02, indicating no overall difference (see Table 13.1). Weighting by inverse error produced comparable but moderately heterogeneous results ($d_w = .01$; CI: $-.05$ to $.07$; $Q = 305.1$, $p < .001$; $I^2 = 56\%$). Once again, analyzing only the 113 randomized effects produced nearly identical results (see Table 13.1). In 81 (60%) of the comparisons, pre-post change in clients in HEPs vs. non-HEP, *non-HEP*s were within .4 standard deviation of each other, a value proposed as the minimum clinically interesting difference in effects (Elliott et al., 1993). The heterogeneity in comparative effect sizes was evidenced by the fact that in 28 comparisons (21%) clients in the non-HEP treatment did substantially better (comparative effect size $< -.4$ sd) than clients in HEP, while HEP clients did substantially better ($>.4$ sd) in the remaining 26 (19%) comparisons.

Particularly noteworthy recent mixed sample outcome studies are the two studies by Stiles and colleagues (2006, 2008) comparing person-centered, CBT, and psychodynamic therapies in primary care settings, with very large naturalistic U.K. samples (Stiles, Barkham, Mellor-Clark, & Connell, 2008; Stiles, Barkham, Twigg, Mellor-Clark, & Cooper, 2006). In both studies, the studies approximated RCTs in spite of the lack of randomization, because clients in all three treatments were statistically identical at pre- and posttest yet showed large amounts of pre-post change.

Equivalence Analysis

Applying random effects model significance testing (Wilson & Lipsey, 2001) and equivalence analysis to this and other treatment comparisons made it possible to demonstrate statistical equivalence between HEPs and non-HEPs. These analyses are summarized in Table 13.2, with equivalence analyses given in the "95% Confidence Interval," "Different from 0," and "Different from 1.41" columns. If the "Different from 0" column is "No" and the "Different from 1.41" column is "Yes," it means that the confidence interval includes zero but neither +.4 or −.4, indicating that the mean comparative effect demonstrated statistical equivalence. In addition, because of the large sample sizes for most of the equivalence analyses, we adopted the following conventions for interpreting the practical or clinical implications of these and later results: "Equivalent": within .1 sd of zero (greater than −.1 and less than .1); "Trivially Different": between .1 and .2 sd from zero; "Equivocal": between .2 and .4 sd from zero; "Clinically Better/Worse": at least .4 sd from zero.

In the case of the overall comparison between HEPs and non-HEPs, not only was the obtained .01 value within the specified "equivalent" range, but this practical equivalence was also supported

TABLE 13.2   Overall Comparisons Between HEPs and non-HEPs

	n	d_w	SE	95% CI	Diff: 0	Diff: <1.41	Result[a]
Whole Data set							
HEP vs. non-HEP	135	.01	.03	−.05 to .07	No	Yes	Equivalent
HEP vs. CBT	76	−.13	.04	−.21 to −.06	Yes	Yes	Trivially worse
		(−.03)[b]		(−.11 to .05)	(No)		(Equivalent)
HEP vs. non-CBT other therapies	59	.17	.05	.08 to .27	Yes	Yes	Trivially better
		(.06)		(−.04 to .16)	(No)		(Equivalent)
RCTs only							
HEP vs. non-HEP	113	−.01	.04	−.09 to .07	No	Yes	Equivalent
HEP vs. CBT	65	−.14	.05	−.24 to −.05	Yes	Yes	Trivially worse
		(−.02)		(−.11 to .08)	(No)		(Equivalent)
HEP vs. non-CBT other therapies	48	.15	.06	.04 to .27	Yes	Yes	Trivially better
		(.04)		(−.08 to .17)	(No)		(Equivalent)

Note. d_w: weighted comparative effect size (difference between therapies weighted by inverse variance); SE: standard error for the comparative effect sizes, random effects model; 95%CI: 95% confidential interval; Diff: 0: mES statistically significantly different from zero; Diff: <1.41 : mES statistically significantly smaller than minimum clinical practical value of .4 sd. HEP: humanistic-experiential psychotherapy; CBT: cognitive-behavioral therapy.

[a]"Result" refers to the practice implications of obtained value of mES: "Equivalent": within .1 sd of zero (greater than −.1 and less than .1); "Trivially (worse/better)": between .1 and .2 sd from zero; "Equivocally (worse/better)": between .2 and .4 sd from zero; "Clinically worse/better": at least .4 sd from zero.

[b]Values in parenthesized italics are results of analyses controlling for researcher allegiance, performed when uncontrolled differences had been obtained.

statistically by its confidence interval including zero but not −.4 or .4 sd. In other words, on the basis of this sample, it can be concluded that HEPs are in general, equivalent to other treatments in their effectiveness. This result has been a consistent result of our earlier meta-analyses (e.g., Elliott et al., 2004) and appears to be quite stable at this point. Nevertheless, this consistent near-zero figure conceals statistically significant variability in effects, as indicated by a Cochrane's Q of 305.15 ($p < 0.001$); in addition, the estimated proportion of true between study variability (I^2) was 56%, considered to be a medium-size value. This means that examination of possible moderators of comparative outcome effects is called for (Lipsey & Wilson, 2001).

HEPs Versus Cognitive-Behavioral Therapies (CBTs)

A significant center of controversy involves widely held assumptions to the effect that HEPs are inferior to cognitive-behavioral treatments. The comparative studies analyzed above did not exclusively use CBT (76 out of 135 comparisons). Therefore, it can be argued that the effects of the CBT were watered down by the inclusion of comparisons involving other types of therapy (most often "treatment as usual," psychodynamic, or integrative).

To clarify this issue, we undertook a series of further equivalence analyses (see Table 13.2). These analyses indicated that, for the subsample of 59 comparisons analyzed here, HEPs showed slightly larger pre-post effects than non-CBT treatments, an advantage of .17 sd, statistically significant but trivial for clinical purposes: it would take at least 10 clients receiving HEP rather than a non-CBT therapy for one additional client to benefit (cf. Furukawa, 1999). By the same token, 76 studies comparing HEPs to CBT revealed a comparable but opposite mean difference of −.13, in favor of CBT. This effect was statistically significant but also too trivial to serve as a guide for individual practitioners, although when considered from an epidemiological point of view it could be seen as meaningful. Next, we examined the 113 randomized comparisons separately in order to see if these findings held up when only RCTs were analyzed (see Table 13.2): The results were virtually identical.

Of considerable importance to practitioners and policy makers is the fact that statistically controlling for researcher allegiance or bias diminishes the small differences that have been reported. There was, in fact, a relatively high rate of negative researcher allegiance (44%) in these studies, and also a large negative correlation ($r = -.49$; $n = 135$; $p < .001$) between researcher allegiance and comparative effect size. Therefore, we ran additional analyses statistically controlling for researcher allegiance, by removing variance in comparative ESs due to this variable. When this was done (see Table 13.2, values in italics), these statistically significant but trivially small treatment differences disappeared. Thus, these data support the claim that HEPs have been found to be practically and statistically equivalent to CBT in effectiveness. Researcher allegiance in comparative outcome studies continues to confound the interpretation of differences found between treatments generally (e.g., Luborsky et al., 1999).

CBT Versus HEP Subtypes

In this meta-analysis, our larger sample enabled us to examine our data more closely than in previous meta-analyses, in order to see if we could understand better the statistically significant but trivially small advantage of CBT over HEPs. In order to do this, we looked at the four types of PCE therapy for which there were at least two comparative studies: PCT, supportive treatments, EFT, and other HEPs. The results of these analyses are given in Table 13.3, which reveal:

1. *Supportive therapies* appeared to be equivocally less effective than CBT (total sample: $n = 37$; $d_w = -.27$; CI: −.4 to −.13; RCTs: $n = 35$; $d_w = -.25$; CI: −.4 to −.11). As Table 13.3 indicates, the confidence intervals for these differences fall below zero (it is statistically significantly worse than CBT) and at the minimum clinically interesting value of −.4. Furthermore, these values are moderately inconsistent, with statistically significant Q values and I^2 of around 40%, indicating further within group differences needing to be explored. Further investigation of the supportive therapies revealed them to be watered down, typically non–bona fide versions of PCE therapies, commonly used by CBT researchers, especially in the United States; in fact, when researcher allegiance was controlled for, the weighted effect dropped to −.01 (CI: −.16 to .13). We have included these here as part of our inclusive search strategy, because they meet our inclusion criteria and because they have been widely researched.

TABLE 13.3   Equivalence Analysis: Comparisons Between CBT and Type of HEP

	n	d_w	SE	95% CI	Diff: 0	Diff: <∣.4∣	Result[a]
PCT vs. CBT	22	−.06	.02	−.11 to −.01	Yes	Yes	Equivalent
	(17)	*(−.10)*	*(.06)*	*(−.23 to −.02)*			*(Trivially worse)*
Supportive vs. CBT	37	−.27	.07	−.41 to −.13	Yes	No	Equivocally worse
	(35)	*(−.25)*		*(−.40 to −.11)*			
EFT vs. CBT	6	.53	.2	.13 to .93	Yes	No	Clinically better
	(5)	*(.51)*	*(.23)*	*(.06 to .97)*			
Other HEP vs. CBT	10	−.17	.10	−.37 to .03	No	Yes	Trivially worse
	(7)	*(.06)*	*(.12)*	*(−.30 to .18)*			*(Equivalent)*
Low process-guiding vs. CBT	59	−.16	.04	−.23 to −.08	Yes	Yes	Trivially worse
	(52)	*(−.19)*	*(.05)*	*(−.29 to −.09)*			
High process-guiding vs. CBT	17	.04	.12	−.2 to .27	No	Yes	Equivalent
	(13)	*(.12)*	*(.13)*	*(−.15 to .38)*			*(Trivially better)*
More vs. less Process-guiding	9	.14	.18	−.21 to .5	No	No	Trivially better
	(8)	*(.08)*	*(.19)*	*(−.30 to .44)*			*(Equivalent)*

Note: For table column abbreviations, see notes for Table 13.2. HEP: humanistic-experiential; CBT: cognitive-behavioral therapy; PCT: person-centered therapy; EFT: emotion-focused therapy. Low process-guiding: PCT + Supportive; high process-guiding: EFT + other experiential + supportive-expressive group.

[a] "Equivalent": within .1 sd of zero (greater than −.1 and less than .1); "Trivially (worse/better)": between .1 and .2 sd from zero; "Equivocally (worse/better)": between .2 and .4 sd from zero; "Clinically worse/better": at least .4 sd from zero.
[b] Values in parenthesized italics are results of analyses of randomized studies.

2. The supportive subgroup of HEPs appeared to be responsible for the small ("trivial") advantage of CBT over the remaining HEPs. When the supportive treatments were removed, the result was a relatively consistent equivalence finding for the total sample ($n = 39$; mES = −.06; $Q = 48.1$, p > .1; $I^2 = 21\%$) and for RCTs ($n = 30$; mES = −.03; $Q = 39.6$, $p > .05$; $I^2 = 27\%$).

3. *PCT* appeared to be consistently, statistically, and practically equivalent in effectiveness to CBT (22 studies, including 17 RCTs, with effect sizes of −.06 and −.1 respectively and Q's with $p > .5$), even without controlling for researcher allegiance.

4. Although based on only six studies (5 RCTs), *EFT* for individuals or couples appeared to be statistically and clinically more effective than CBT, with an effect size of .53 (.51 for the RCTs). However, controlling for researcher allegiance lowered the weighted effect to an equivocal, nonsignificant .21 (CI: −.19 to .61.)

5. *Other HEPs* were trivially worse than CBT overall (10 studies; ES = −.17; $Q = 6$, $p > .5$) but equivalent for the RCT subset (7 studies, ES = −.06). (This was a consistent finding with Q's having $p > .5$, and remained even after controlling for researcher allegiance.)

High Versus Low Process-Guiding Humanistic-Experiential Therapies

As noted earlier, HEPs such as gestalt, EFT, and focusing encourage the therapist to act as a process expert or guide by offering the client different ways of working in the session at different times. This stand has sometimes proven to be controversial (e.g., Brodley, 1990), so it is useful to examine what our meta-analytic data have to say about this issue. As shown in Table 13.3, in general, HEPs low on process-guiding (i.e., PCT and supportive therapies) were trivially worse than CBT for the whole sample ($n = 59$; mES: −.16) and for RCTs ($n = 52$, mES: −.19), while high process-guiding therapies (EFT, other HEP) were equivalent to CBT for the total sample ($n = 17$; mES = .04) and trivially better for RCTs ($n = 13$, mES = .12). On the other hand, in the nine comparisons (eight randomized) where more process guiding therapies (e.g., EFT, gestalt) were compared directly to less process guiding therapies (most commonly PCT), the comparative effect sizes for the more process-guiding approaches was only trivially better (and equivalent for RCTs) and not particularly consistent (total sample: mES = .14; CI: −.21 to .5; $Q = 16.9$, $p < .05$; $I^2 = 53\%$; RCTs: mES = .08; CI: −.3 to .44; $Q = 14.3$, $p < .05$; $I^2 = 51\%$.). It is worth noting that process-guiding exists along a continuum, so that different studies have compared pairs of

HEPs at different points on the spectrum, making it difficult to integrate the results. Researcher allegiance effects also likely play a role here. Clearly, more research is needed to explore this key issue.

OUTCOME FOR DIFFERENT CLIENT PROBLEMS: DIFFERENTIAL TREATMENT EFFECTS

Investigation of HEPs for specific client presenting problems or disorders has blossomed over the past 20 years. The three lines of evidence (pre-post, controlled, and comparative studies) are summarized in Table 13.4 for six commonly studied relatively coherent types of client problem, evaluated both relative to zero and for bench-marking purposes to the whole sample. In brief, the largest amount of evidence and the strongest support for HEPs have been found for depression, relationship problems, coping with chronic medical problems (e.g., HIV, cancer), habitual self-damaging behaviors (substance misuse, eating disorders), and psychosis. There is also considerable, but more mixed, evidence supporting the application of these approaches with anxiety. In this section, we provide meta-analytic evidence, summarize key recent studies, and evaluate the status of HEPs as empirically supported treatments for these six particular client problems.

Depression

There are more studies of depression in our data set than any other client presenting problem, with the strongest evidence provided by pre-post and comparative treatment studies. We found 34 samples of clients (from 27 studies; $n = 1,287$ clients) for whom pre-post effects could be calculated, most commonly PCT (10 samples), supportive (9 samples), or EFT (8 samples). The weighted mean pre-post effect size across these 34 samples was large ($d_w = 1.23$, CI: 1.0 to 1.45).

On the other hand, the eight controlled comparisons with no treatment or waitlist controls provided a somewhat weaker but still statistically significant weighted effect in the small to medium range (weighted controlled ES: .42; 95% confidence interval: .06 to .78), including two outliers (Maynard, 1993; Tyson & Range, 1987), the only two negative controlled effects in the data set as a whole, both small sample studies using non–bona fide group interventions.

The 37 HEP versus non-HEP comparisons (from 23 studies, $n = 755$ and 1,261 respectively; most commonly CBT) support an equivalence conclusion (mean comparative d_w: −.02; CI: −.16 to .13). In fact, substantial (>|.4|) positive and negative comparative results were evenly balanced (positive: 8; negative: 10; neutral: 19).

Four of the comparisons between more and less process guiding HEPs involved depressed clients. These studies showed a consistent, reliable and clinically significant advantage for more process guiding approaches like EFT (Goldman, Greenberg, & Angus, 2006; Greenberg &

TABLE 13.4 Effect Size by Selected Client Problems/Disorders

Problem/Disorder	Pre-Post ES		Controlled ES		Comparative ES	
	n	$d_w \pm$ 95% CI	n	$d_w \pm$ 95% CI	n	$d_w \pm$ 95% CI
Depression Relationship/interpersonal/ trauma	34	$1.23 \pm .23^*(+)$	8	$.42 \pm .36^*(=)$	37	$-.02 \pm .15(=)$
Anxiety	20	$.94 \pm .22^*(=)$	4	$.50 \pm .34^*(=)$	19	$-.39 \pm .16^*(-)$
Medical/physical	25	$.57 \pm .27^*(-)$	6	$.52 \pm .34^*(=)$	24	$-.00 \pm .11(=)$
Psychosis	6	$1.08 \pm .17^*(=)$	—	—	6	$.39 \pm .29^*(+)$
Habit/substance misuse	13	$.65 \pm .26^*(-)$	2	$.55 \pm .39^*(=)$	10	$.07 \pm .23(=)$
Total sample (used for bench-marking)	201	$.93 \pm .08^*$	62	$.76 \pm .12^*$	135	$.01 \pm .06$

Note: $^*p < .05$ in null hypothesis test against ES = 0; ns refer to number of client samples (pre-post ESs) or comparisons with other conditions (controlled and comparative ESs). Benchmarking results vs. total sample: (=): confidence interval includes benchmark value; (+): confidence interval is above bench-mark value; (−): confidence interval is below benchmark.

Watson, 1998) or gestalt therapy (Beutler et al., 1991; Tyson & Range, 1987), with a weighted comparative ES of .44 (confidence interval: .10 to .78).

Two clusters of evidence on depression are worth noting: First, there are three well-designed RCTs testing EFT for depression (Goldman et al., 2006; Greenberg & Watson, 1998; Watson, Gordon, Stermac, Kalogerakos, & Steckley, 2001) comparing EFT to other therapies in the treatment of major depressive disorder, using medium-size samples and conducted by two different research teams. In particular, Goldman et al. (2006) found that EFT had significantly better outcomes (including very low relapse rates) when compared to PCT. Watson et al. (2003) found equivalent, and on some measures better, results than CBT. Second, there are four well-designed RCTs of PCT for perinatal depression with medium to large sample sizes that either show superiority to treatment as usual (Holden, Sagovsky, & Cox, 1989; Morrell et al., 2009; Wickberg & Hwang, 1996), or no difference in comparison to CBT (Cooper, Murray, Wilson, & Romaniuk, 2003) or short-term psychodynamic therapy (Cooper et al., 2003; Morrell et al., 2009). Both of these clusters of well-controlled studies meet Chambless and Hollon's (1998) criteria for *efficacious and specific* treatments.

Key new studies since our last review include the Cooper et al. (2003) and Morrell et al. (2009) studies with perinatal depression, mentioned above, and two studies by Mohr and colleagues on depression in a medical population (Mohr, et al., 2005; Mohr, Boudewyn, Goodkin, Bostrom, & Epstein 2001), to be discussed later. The other substantial study is Stice, Burton, Bearman, and Rohde (2006; Stice, Rohde, Gau, & Wade, 2010), in which adolescents with mild to moderate depression were randomized to one of four conditions: supportive group therapy versus CBT group therapy versus CBT bibliotherapy versus controls. Participants seen in supportive therapy showed benefits comparable to those in CBT out to 2-year follow-ups and did much better than control group clients.

Relationship and Interpersonal Difficulties

Of all client-presenting problems, HEPs appear to be most consistently effective for clients presenting with either specific unresolved relationship issues or more general interpersonal difficulties. The largest number of the 24 studies included in our meta-analysis addressed specific relationship problems, generally within the context of couples therapy (10 studies, e.g., Denton, Burleson, Clark, Rodriguez, & Hobbs, 2000). However, there were also smaller clusters of studies on general interpersonal difficulties, generally treated individually (six studies, e.g., Grawe, Caspar, & Ambühl, 1990); and specific emotional injuries, treated either individually or in couples (five studies, e.g., Greenberg, Warwar, & Malcolm, 2010; Makinen & Johnson, 2006). Finally, we found three studies that focused on posttrauma difficulties or formally diagnosed PTSD, with some (e.g., Szapocznik et al., 2004) including substantial portions of clients with this diagnosis. The strongest evidence was for EFT-C (emotion- or emotionally focused therapy for couples), developed by Greenberg and Johnson (1988). We found 23 samples of clients (from 21 studies; $n = 467$ clients) for whom pre-post effects could be calculated, most commonly EFT-C (10 samples), EFT for individuals (6 samples), PCT (3 samples), and other HEP (4 samples). The weighted mean pre-post effect size across these 23 samples was large but quite variable ($d_w = 1.27$, CI: .96 to 1.58; $Q = 96.9$, $p < .001$; $I^2 = 77\%$). Effects were somewhat (but not significantly) larger for therapies delivered in couple or family format ($n = 13$; $d_w = 1.50$, CI: 1.11 to 1.90) versus being carried out individually ($n = 10$; $d_w = .97$, CI: .53 to 1.41).

The 11 controlled comparisons (7 of them RCTs, 7 studies on EFT-C) with no treatment or waitlist controls provided a very large weighted effect ($d_w = 1.39$; CI: .99 to 1.79), with all controlled effects being substantial and positive.

There were 15 controlled comparisons (from 13 studies) of clients seen in HEPs ($n = 250$) versus non-HEPs ($n = 327$), most commonly CBT or psychoeducational interventions. The overall weighted effect was moderately heterogeneous but points to the superiority of HEPs over non-HEPs for relational difficulties (comparative $d_w = .34$; CI: .07 to .62; $Q = 39.1$, $p < .001$; $I^2 = 64\%$). Seven of the 15 comparative effects were substantial (>1.4|) and positive, with no substantial effects favoring the alternative treatment. For the eight comparisons involving EFT (both couples and individual), the weighted effect ($d_w = .69$; CI: .32 to 1.06) was significantly larger than for the five comparisons involving PCT ($d_w = -.08$; CI: −.30 to .13). Both forms of EFT appeared to be highly effective: EFT for couples for addressing relational injuries (3 studies; d_w = .88; CI: −.16 to 1.92), and EFT for individuals with unresolved interpersonal issues or abuse suffered by individuals (5 studies; d_w = .62; CI: .26 to .97). In addition, whether the non-HEP was CBT or psychoeducation made relatively little difference: versus CBT the weighted effect was .34 (6 studies; CI: −.15 to .83); the value for comparisons with psychoeducation was .51 (n = 4; CI: −.10 to 1.13).

EFT for couples has long been included in lists of empirically supported treatments for marital distress (e.g., Baucom, Mueser, Shoham, & Daiuto, 1998); however, our meta-analytic data indicate that EFT for individuals is *efficacious and specific* for unresolved relationship issues, including emotional injuries (Greenberg, Warwar, & Malcolm, 2008; Souliere, 1995) such as unresolved abuse survivor issues (Paivio et al., 2001; Paivio, Jarry, Chagigiorgis, Hall, & Ralston, 2010).

Four recent studies not in our meta-analysis support and extend the results reported here. Two of these underscore and develop the results already reported: Greenberg, Warwar, and Malcolm (2010) offered promising results for an EFT couples approach specific to emotional injury and forgiveness. Paivio and associates (2010) extended earlier results with EFT for individuals who had experienced childhood abuse (62% met criteria for PTSD), finding that EFT with empty chair work produced better outcomes but more dropouts than EFT without chair work. Two other recent pilot studies opened up new areas for working with relational difficulties but were at the same time consistent with the overall findings for this client population: In an initial uncontrolled study, McLean and colleagues (2008) provided promising evidence that EFT-C can help couples improve their relationship and reduce psychological distress in the face of advanced breast cancer. Also, in a newly located study, Miller (1999) found that a PCT group was as effective as a social learning theory-based CBT group for reducing dating violence in at-risk young people with histories of observing domestic violence or committing dating violence themselves. (See anxiety section next for discussion of the evidence on PTSD.)

Anxiety

Research on HEPs for anxiety, most commonly the application of supportive therapies with panic/agoraphobia or generalized anxiety disorder, is much more mixed than is the case for depression, but is strongest for pre-post and controlled studies. We found 20 samples of clients (n = 19 studies, 305 clients) for whom pre-post effects could be calculated, mostly supportive (8 samples of clients), PCT (6 samples), and other HEP (5 samples), carried out in studies where there was a negative researcher allegiance (14 samples). Anxiety disorders studied included panic/agoraphobia (6 samples), generalized anxiety disorder (6 samples), phobias (usually chronic or complex; 6 samples), and mixed anxiety (2 samples). The weighted mean pre-post effect size for the 20 sets of anxious clients was .94 (CI: .73 to 1.16), quite near the benchmark for the entire sample of pre-post effects (see Table 13.4). Although the confidence intervals all overlapped, pre-post effects varied significantly across type of HEP (Q = 8.17; p < .05), with effects for supportive treatments somewhat smaller (d_w = .66; CI: .40 to .92) than for PCT (d_w = 1.0; CI: .71 to 1.28) or other HEP (d_w = 1.41; CI: .84 to 1.97).

There were only four controlled studies, all with relatively small samples (< 25); these showed a controlled effect size of .5 (CI: .17 to .83) a medium effect size slightly but not statistically significantly less than the bench-mark value of .76 for the entire sample.

Of the six client population clusters we are reviewing for comparative effects in this chapter, HEPs fared most poorly with anxiety problems, with a mean comparative effect size of −.39 (CI: −.55 to −.23) across 19 comparisons with non-HEP. This is consistently, moderately and significantly in favor of the non-HEPs, almost all some form of CBT. Nine of the 18 comparative effects with CBT substantially favored CBT (<−.4), with none favoring an HEP. In comparisons with CBT, there was very little variation (d_w = −.42 to −.36) across type of HEP (supportive, PCT, other).

Applying the Chambless and Hollon (1998) criteria to specific types of anxiety disorder, the picture is clearest for *generalized anxiety disorder*, where six of nine comparisons substantially favored CBT, including studies by two independent research teams (Bond, Wingrove, Curran, & Lader, 2002; Borkovec et al., 1987; Borkovec & Costello, 1993; Borkovec & Mathews, 1988); the other three comparisons showed equivocal results (Blowers, Cobb, & Mathews, 1987; Borkovec & Mathews, 1988; Stanley, Beck, & Glassco, 1996). Here, the preponderance of the evidence, both in terms of overall effect size ($d_w = -.44$) and numbers of studies and independent research teams, clearly favors CBT. The picture for *panic/agoraphobia* was somewhat more complicated: Two of the 6 comparisons favored CBT over HEP (from independent research teams: Beck, Sokol, Clark, Berchick, & Wright, 1992; Shear, Houck, Grenno, & Masters, 2001), with one comparison favoring medication over HEP (Shear et al., 2001), and three having equivocal results (Craske, Maidenberg, & Bystritsky, 1995; Shear, Pilkonis, Cloitre, & Leon, 1994; Teusch, Böhme, & Gastpar, 1997). Nevertheless, the weighted effect for panic/agoraphobia was $-.39$ (CI: $-.75$ to $-.04$). Thus, it can be said that for panic that the preponderance of the evidence somewhat favors CBT over HEP. Finally, for the three comparative studies of phobia, either complex or chronic phobia (Grawe, 1976; Johnson, 1977) or social phobia (Cottraux et al., 2000) all reported equivocal comparative effects ($d_w = -.15$).

At the same time, we found substantial pre-post effects for the great majority of anxiety studies, indicating that HEPs for anxiety meet Chambless and Hollon's (1998) criteria as *possibly efficacious*, while also suggesting that CBT may be somewhat more *specific and efficacious*. This apparent moderate CBT advantage is likely due to two possible factors. To begin with, it is likely to be due in part to researcher allegiance effects: When allegiance-controlled effects were analyzed, the difference, though still statistically significant, shrank to $-.21$ (CI: $-.38$ to $-.05$). In addition, it now seems likely to us that anxiety disorders may respond somewhat better to more structured treatments that include a psychoeducation component, such as CBT, as opposed to the predominantly nondirective forms of HEPs that have so far been studied. Interestingly, two recent studies of GAD point to potential benefits from adding forms of HEP to CBT: Newman et al. (2011) combined either supportive-nondirective therapy or interpersonal emotion processing therapy to CBT on a session-by-session basis; they reported no significant differences at post or follow-up but large pre-post effects for the two treatments combined ($d = 1.86$). In addition, Westra and Dozois (2006) found that adding three sessions of motivational interviewing (adapted for anxiety) prepared clients better for subsequent CBT and was associated with better treatment response and posttherapy maintenance of gains.

In our clinical experience, clients with significant anxiety difficulties frequently have a problem with the lack of structure of typical nondirective therapies, often asking directly for expert guidance. For this reason, several of the authors of this chapter are currently conducting studies on the effectiveness of EFT with generalized anxiety (Watson, Timulak) or social anxiety (Elliott); Elliott and Rodgers (2010) have reported promising initial results from their study in progress comparing PCT and EFT to each other and to published CBT outcome benchmarks. For now, our advice for humanistic-experiential therapists is to discuss the issue with clients, to consider adding process guiding elements to their therapy, or to provide information about the role of trauma or emotional processes in panic attacks (e.g., Wolfe & Sigl, 1998).

Finally, it is worth noting that although there is good evidence that HEPs, especially EFT, are effective with relational/interpersonal difficulties and even the long term sequelae of childhood trauma reviewed in the previous section, there is little research on PTSD per se. Further, the results reviewed here for other anxiety disorders are not encouraging as a basis for extrapolating to PTSD. It is particularly difficult to generalize from these various studies examined here to full blown or nonrelationally focused PTSD, especially PTSD due to combat (e.g., Ragsdale, Cox, Finn, & Eisler, 1996). Further research on HEPs for PTSD is urgently needed.

Coping With Chronic Medical Conditions

The use of HEPs to help clients coping with chronic or life-threatening medical illnesses has burgeoned in the past 20 years, with studies more than tripling since our 2004 review. Our 2008 meta-analysis sample turned up 29 studies ($n = 1145$ clients). The most common form of HEP studied was supportive-expressive group therapy, an existential-experiential treatment developed by Spiegel, Bloom, and Yalom (1981), which was the subject of 12 studies in our meta-analysis. Person-centered and supportive therapies were each examined in seven studies. Coping with a broad range of medical conditions has now been investigated, the most common being cancer, both early stage/remitted (7 studies) and late stage/metastatic (7 studies); however, autoimmune disorders such as lupus, MS, and rheumatoid arthritis are now being investigated

(5 studies), and the meta-analysis also includes two studies each for gastrointestinal problems (IBS, colitis, Crohn's), HIV-positive status, and pain (back- and head-ache) as well as four studies of other conditions (kidney, vitiligo, cardiac rehabilitation, sleep problems). Of the studies, 17 (59%) were carried out by researchers with a favorable researcher allegiance, and 17 were in a group format (see also the review by Burlingame et al., this volume, examining group psychotherapy). The overall weighted mean pre-post effect size across the 25 samples for which pre-post effects could be calculated was medium in size but highly inconsistent ($d_w = .57$, CI: .3 to .84; $Q = 195.1$, $p < .001$; $I^2 = 88\%$). Statistically significant pre-post effects (d_w) were found for autoimmune conditions (.68; CI: .08 to 1.29), early stage cancer (.55; CI: .28 to .83), early/late cancer combined (.62; CI: .18 to 1.05), and other medical conditions (.42; CI: .09 to .75).

There were six controlled studies versus no treatment/wait list, on diverse client populations (early stage cancer, cardiac, kidney, vitiligo); overall, these showed a fairly consistent medium effect size of .52 (CI: .19 to .86; $Q = 7.5$, NA; $I^2 = 33\%$), although the effects for the three older studies of early/remitted cancer were smaller and not statistically significant ($d_w = .36$; Dircks, Grimm, Tausch, & Wittern, 1982; Katonah, 1991; van der Pompe, Duivenvoorden, Antoni, Visser, & Heijnen, 1997).

There were 19 comparative studies, including 24 comparisons to non-HEPs. All but three comparisons were randomized (88%) and all but two used bona fide treatments (92%). The most common HEPs were PCT (9 comparisons), supportive (7 studies) and supportive-expressive groups (7 studies); HEPs were most often applied to helping clients cope with autoimmune disorders (7 studies), cancer early/remitted or late/metastatic (4 studies each), HIV positive status (3 studies). The most common non-HEPs were CBT (11 studies) and treatment as usual (8 studies). Researcher allegiances were roughly evenly divided (pro: 42%; con: 46%; neutral 13%).

The overall comparative effect was a clear and highly consistent equivalence finding ($d_w = -.00$; CI: −.11 to .10; $Q = 27.7$, NS; $I^2 = 17\%$). Only three comparisons substantially (>.4) favored non-HEPs therapies, two of these from the same study (Machado, Azevedo, Capanema, Neto & Cerceau, 2007; Mohr et al., 2001). Twenty effects were within .4 of each other, while one effect favored an HEP (Spiegel et al., 1981).

Furthermore, there were no differences in comparative effects between PCT, supportive, and supportive-expressive group therapies (between groups $Q = 1.85$, NS). However, there was a trend for comparisons with CBT ($d_w = -.13$; CI: −.29 to .02) to be slightly larger than comparisons with other non-HEP treatments ($d_w = .07$; CI: −.07 to .21; between groups $Q = 3.47$; $p = .06$). Furthermore, there were clear differences between different medical conditions ($Q = 15.4$, $p < .01$), with the strongest comparative effects for coping with advanced cancer ($d_w = .28$; CI: .10 to .47). HEPs appeared to do less well with autoimmune conditions when compared to non-HEPs ($d_w = -.22$; CI: −.44 to .01, $p = .06$), as illustrated particularly in the two studies of Mohr and colleagues (2001, 2005) on clients with MS and depression.

Given the diversity of medical conditions and treatments studies, it is difficult to apply the Chambless and Hollon (1998) criteria to this set of studies. Nevertheless, from these data, it appears that HEPs are *efficacious* treatments for helping clients cope with a variety of medical conditions, based on (a) their superiority to no treatment control conditions; and (b) their general equivalence to an established treatment (CBT).

However, a word of caution is in order: A recent search turned up at least 20 more studies on HEPs on this topic, about half of them on cancer, with the rest on a variety other medical conditions, especially cancer, HIV, chronic pain, rheumatoid arthritis, and so on. This is certainly an indicator of the vitality of this area of research on HEPs; but there is a strong possibility that these additional studies will modify the conclusions that can be made about HEP for medically ill populations. This is particularly true for supportive-expressive group therapy for cancer, which has been the subject of intense scientific scrutiny over the past 10 years, including a recent failure to replicate by the originator of the approach (Spiegel et al., 2007) and a large Canadian multicenter trial on the use of supportive-expressive group therapy to improve quality of life for women with metastatic breast cancer, which failed to show a benefit over a no treatment/usual care control (Bordeleau et al., 2003). This led a recent Cochrane review (Edwards, Hulbert-Williams, & Neal, 2008) to conclude, "There is insufficient evidence to advocate that group psychological therapies (either cognitive behavioural or supportive-expressive) should be made available to all women diagnosed with metastatic breast cancer."

The reviewers did, however, note that there was some positive evidence on psychological (as opposed to medical) outcome variables, especially in the short term. For now, the search continues for promising client subpopulations (e.g., estrogen-negative breast cancer; Spiegel et al., 2007) and target variables (e.g., fear of disease progression, relationship variables, treatment decision making). It is also worth noting that the new comparative outcome data appear to support our main conclusion of outcome equivalence between HEP and CBT for coping with breast cancer. However, the main issue here appears to be whether *any* psychosocial treatment—CBT or supportive-expressive group therapy included—can improve survival rates and psychological adjustment with breast cancer, either early stage or metastatic. We hope that further research now in progress will clarify this important issue.

Psychosis

The use of HEPs for clients diagnosed with psychosis, including schizophrenia, has become controversial, particularly in the United Kingdom, where the latest version of the Department of Health's treatment guidelines (National Collaborating Centre for Mental Health [NICE], 2010) effectively banned the practice via the following negative recommendation: "Do not routinely offer counselling and supportive psychotherapy (as specific interventions) to people with schizophrenia" (p. 290). This proclamation has had the effect of wiping out a United Kingdom tradition of offering person-centered counseling to individuals living with psychotic processes, documented by Traynor, Elliott, and Cooper (2011), and marked by the recent advances, including the addition of special methods for making psychological contact with clients when they are in psychotic states (Dekeyser, Prouty, & Elliott, 2008).

The full NICE 2010 guideline includes extensive documentation from the evidence survey on which the recommendation was supposedly based. Thus, it was not difficult for us to carry out a quick, rough analysis of the evidence from the nine studies comparing the supportive treatments (defined in the document as person-centered in orientation) to CBT in the NICE 2010 evidence survey (see Appendix 16D): Contrary to the strongly negative guideline, the data reported in the evidence survey instead point to a trivially small superiority for CBT over supportive counseling: mean $d = -.19$; mean relative risk ratio $= 1.08$. In addition, these overall mean effects were characterized by large standard deviations (.59, .32 respectively), indicating substantial heterogeneity. In fact, there are many instances in the NICE data summary where supportive treatments actually did substantially better than CBT (e.g., Tarrier et al., 2000, at 19-month follow-up). Two possible interpretations of these data appear to fit the evidence better than that drawn by the NICE committee: First, supportive treatments are almost as effective as CBT, even without the benefit of recent focused treatment development efforts and even when carried out by researchers with an anti-HEP theoretical allegiance. Second, more conservatively, the data are too inconsistent to warrant any overall conclusions at the present moment.

Although the committee defined supportive counseling as person-centered, the NICE 2010 evidence base is a mixture of different approaches, not all of them HEPs. Nevertheless, our meta-analysis data set does contain six studies (mostly RCTs) of patients with schizophrenic or psychotic diagnoses for which pre-post effect sizes could be calculated (Coons & Peacock, 1970; Dekeyser et al., 2008; Eckert & Wuchner, 1996; Serok & Zemet, 1983; Tarrier et al., 1998; Teusch, 1990), involving a total of 209 clients seen in treatments explicitly labeled as nondirective, gestalt, or PCT, including a promising recent form of PCT called pre-therapy. Clients were seen in both inpatient and outpatient settings and in a mixture of individual and group formats and evaluated on a range of measures, including symptom and life functioning ratings. The weighted pre-post effect size for these six studies was 1.08 (CI: .51 to 1.65). Although uncontrolled, these effects nevertheless demonstrate very large pre-post effect sizes with this chronic and severely distressed clinical population.

Second, although there were no studies comparing an HEP to a no-treatment or wait-list control condition, we did locate five comparative treatment RCTs (Coons, 1970; Dekeyser, 2008; Serok, Rabin, & Spitz, 1984; Serok & Zemet, 1983; Tarrier et al., 1998), providing six comparisons to non-HEPs and a total of 170 patients (75 in HEP). The HEPs were explicitly labeled as nondirective, gestalt, or pre-therapy; the non-HEPs were most commonly labeled as *treatment as usual*, but one study each involved CBT or exercise. The mean comparative effect size across the six comparisons was .39, in favor of HEP (CI: .10 to .67). This is a moderately large, fairly consistent controlled effect size that supports the effectiveness of HEP versus standard care for clients with schizophrenia or other psychotic diagnoses, and contrasts strongly with results of the studies reviewed by the NICE review committee.

Probably the safest conclusion here is that, based on existing evidence, HEPs appear to be, in Chambless and Hollon's (1998) terms, *possibly efficacious*. In other words, they are promising but require further development and outcome research, especially in light of developments in both the HEP approaches (e.g., new pre-therapy and process-guiding treatments, see Traynor et al., 2011) and in CBT (the advent of new person- or acceptance-based forms of CBT for schizophrenia, e.g., Chadwick, 2006).

Habitual Self-Damaging Activities

Recurrent self-damaging activities such as substance misuse and eating disorders are the subject of an emerging body of evidence using a wide variety of HEPs, including 13 studies already in our meta-analysis, with 15 samples (total $n = 413$) of clients focusing on recurrent, self-damaging habit difficulties, predominantly substance misuse (11 samples of clients) and eating difficulties (3 samples). (There was also one study on Tourette syndrome; Wilhelm et al., 2003.) The weighted pre-post effect was .65 (CI: .39 to .90). Effects were comparable for substance misuse ($d_w = .68$; CI: .36 to .99) and eating difficulties ($d_w = .62$; CI: .12 to 1.11).

There were two controlled studies of substance misuse (Sellman, Sullivan, Dore, Adamson, & MacEwan, 2001; Washington, 2001) versus no treatment or wait-list controls, with a weighted effect of .55 (CI: .17 to .93). Nine studies (7 RCTs, 10 comparisons of clients) compared a range of HEPs (supportive and other HEP were most common) to other treatments, most often CBT (6 studies). The weighted comparative effect was .07 (CI: −.15 to .30), indicating that HEPs and non-HEPs for habit difficulties were equivalent in effectiveness. For the six comparisons with CBT, the value was −.03 (CI: −.41 to .35), an equivalence finding in terms of effect size but including the 1.41 boundary. Six of the comparisons involved treatments for substance misuse; the weighted effect for these comparisons was .16 (CI: −.05 to .38). Finally, there were three comparisons between HEPs and CBT for substance misuse ($d_w = .16$; CI: −.27 to .60). Seven

of the 10 comparative effects were relatively small (<1.41). However, two studies—both on alcohol problems—produced effects that substantially (>.4) favored HEPs (Jacobs & Bangert, 2005; Wetzel et al., 2004). The one study on Tourette syndrome (Wilhelm et al., 2003) yielded a very strongly negative comparative effect (<−.8) for a comparison between supportive therapy and CBT.

Overall, the preponderance of the current evidence, including both controlled and comparative treatment lines of evidence, indicates that HEPs meet the Chambless–Hollon standards as an *efficacious* treatments for substance misuse (i.e., problems with alcohol and cocaine): Consistent with our meta-analysis, they have been shown to be superior to no treatment controls (two good-size, independent RCTs: Sellman et al., 2001; Washington, 2001); at the same time, the comparative treatment evidence (two independent $n > 25$ studies) indicates that they are either equivalent or superior to an already established treatment, CBT (Washington, 2001; Wetzel et al., 2004). The evidence on the use of HEPs for eating difficulties, however, remains equivocal at this point: there are only two small studies of overeating (Holstein, 1990; Kenardy, Mensch, Bowen, Green, & Walton, 2002), with equivocal, no difference results. As for Tourette syndrome, supportive therapy might be inferior to CBT (specifically, habit reversal), but so far there is only a single, negative researcher allegiance, small n study (Wilhelm et al., 2003).

Our meta-analysis missed at least one noteworthy recent study of an HEP for eating difficulties, a good-size German-language RCT by Schutzmann, Schutzmann & Eckert (2010), in which person-centered therapy had better results than guided self-help for bulimia. In addition, an EFT group treatment on a sample of 12 bulimic clients was associated with statistically significant decreases in the frequency of binge episodes, improvements in eating disorder related psychopathology, depression, alexithymia, emotion regulation, self-esteem, general psychiatric distress, and self-efficacy (Wnuk, 2009).

A more significant omission is that we have not to date included research on motivational interviewing (also known as motivational enhancement therapy, Miller & Rollnick, 2002), described as a directive form of client-centered therapy, adapted for clients who engage in patterns of self-damaging activity such as excessive drinking. This approach is often quite brief

(<3 sessions) and mixes PCT with significant information and feedback, making it difficult to categorize in spite of its clear roots in HEP and its large evidence base. Fortunately, a recent meta-analysis by Lundahl et al. (2010) provides up-to-date, comprehensive coverage of 119 controlled and comparative studies of motivational interviewing for a variety of habitual self-damaging activities (about 80% substance misuse), including 35 wait-list controlled studies, with an overall mean effect of .32 (CI: .22 to .42); 42 comparisons with nonspecific treatment as usual ($d_w = .24$; CI: .17 to .31); and 39 comparisons with specific evidence-based alternative treatments (primarily 12-step or CBT; $d_w = .09$; CI: −.01 to .18). These results are roughly comparable to ours, especially for the comparative studies.

QUALITATIVE OUTCOMES IN HUMANISTIC-EXPERIENTIAL PSYCHOTHERAPIES

The increased use of qualitative methods in the field of psychology generally, and for psychotherapy research specifically (see McLeod, this volume) has produced enough findings examining outcome to allow for a "meta-analytic" style of review (see Timulak, 2009). Timulak and Creaner (2010) recently conducted a qualitative meta-synthesis of qualitative studies on HEPs, covering outcome descriptions from 106 clients participating in a variety of HEPs (such as EFT and PCT). The data collection method most typically used was a posttherapy (follow-up) interview, such as the client change interview (Elliott, Slatick, & Urman, 2001).

Timulak and Creaner (2010) reported 11 categories that offered a comprehensive conceptualization of the outcomes reported by clients in individual HEPs (see Table 13.5). They found that many of the qualitative outcomes in the original studies corresponded with humanistic-experiential theories of therapy outcome. For instance, healthier emotional experiencing, empowerment, resilience, and increased self-awareness are traditionally emphasized as potential outcomes of HEPs (cf. Greenberg, 2010). It is interesting to note that the clients in these therapies also reported outcomes that are likely to be shared with other approaches to therapy such as mastery of symptoms (CBT) or improved interpersonal functioning and insight (psychodynamic approaches).

Two findings are, however, of particular interest. One of them is increased self-compassion. Though it resonates with the traditional concept of self-acceptance (cf. Rogers, 1961), it also captures the uniquely, warm, emotional quality of this type of self-relating. The other interesting finding is that of appreciating vulnerability as an outcome of therapy. This finding stands in quite the opposite position to the mainstream focus on symptom relief. Though unexpected, it is fully compatible with HEP theories, which place an emphasis on authentic being. Authentic being is not necessarily free of suffering and pain. However, clients apparently still appreciate that overcoming the avoidance cutting them off from fulfilling their needs in life is worth the risk of pain and suffering. The finding that some clients prefer settling for no change rather than risking pain, however, illustrates that this process may not be that straightforward or always pursued by clients in therapy (cf. Lipkin, 1954). What is interesting is that only two of the reviewed studies included negative outcomes of therapy. These included nonresolution of the problem(s) that led clients to seek therapy, feeling overwhelmed, feeling harmed by the therapist, disappointment over not being understood by the therapist, and, interestingly, fear of changing and a consequent increase in emotional restriction thereby preventing change.

Timulak and Creaner's (2010) qualitative meta-synthesis of outcomes in HEPs is one of the first of its kind, so it may be too early to draw firm conclusions from it. However, an independently conducted qualitative meta-synthesis by Elliott and colleagues (Elliott, 2002a) that also included unpublished studies, as well as recent case studies that also included qualitative assessment of outcome (e.g., Stephen, Elliott, & Macleod, 2011) draw very similar conclusions.

QUALITATIVE PROCESS RESEARCH ON HUMANISTIC-EXPERIENTIAL PSYCHOTHERAPIES

For this review we looked for qualitative research on HEPs and included all process studies identified by searching PsychInfo using combination of the key words "humanistic/experiential/client-centered/emotion-focused therapy" with "qualitative process research" (we also included some studies referenced in the selected studies). We

TABLE 13.5 Qualitative Outcomes/Effects Reported in Timulak and Creaner (2010) Qualitative Meta-Synthesis

Main Meta-Category	Meta-Categories	Primary Studies Findings
A. Appreciating experiences of self	1. Smoother and healthier emotional experiencing	Hopefulness (Klein & Elliott, 2006), peace and stability (Klein & Elliott, 2006), emotional well-being, greater sense of energy (Klein & Elliott, 2006); calmer, at peace (Elliott, 2002; Lipkin, 1954); improved mood, optimism (Elliott et al., 1990); general openness to own feelings (Elliott et al., 1990); ability to express and contain feelings (Dale, Allen, & Measor, 1998); feeling more free and easy, more light and lively (Lipkin, 1954) (4/8; i.e., 4 out of 8 studies on individual therapy)
	2. Appreciating vulnerability	Permission to feel the pain (Rodgers, 2002); transparency (dropping barriers and defenses) (Rodgers, 2002); honest with self (Elliott, 2002; Rodgers, 2002); open to change (Elliott, 2002); awareness of being old, process of grieving, grieving is undoing problematic anger/anxiety (Elliott, 2002); self-acceptance of existential isolation (Dale et al., 1998) more tolerant of difficulties and setbacks (Elliott et al., 2009) (4/8)
	3. Experience of self-compassion	Self-esteem, self-care (Klein & Elliott, 2006), improved self-esteem (Elliott et al., 1990); engagement with self (experiencing support from within) (Rodgers, 2002); valuing self (Dale et al., 1998) (4/8)
	4. Experience of resilience	Restructuring (recycling the bad things) (Rodgers, 2002); insight first painful then feeling better (Lipkin, 1954) (2/8)
	5. Feeling empowered	Self-confident, strength within (Klein & Elliott, 2006; Lipkin, 1954; Rodgers, 2002); General sense of well-being: health, energy, activities (Klein & Elliott, 2006), newfound or improved abilities to act (Klein & Elliott, 2006); improved general day-to-day coping (Dale et al., 1998); giving self credit for accomplishments, try new things, reading (Elliott, 2002); improved ability to cope (Elliott et al., 1990); preparing to take action to deal with problems (Elliott et al., 1990); specific wishes/attitudes strengthened (Elliott et al., 1990); being able to make decision, gaining control over life (Lipkin, 1954; Rodgers, 2002; Timulak, Belicova, & Miler., 2010); able to stand up for self, more initiative instead of fear of doing things (Lipkin, 1954) (7/8)
	6. Mastering symptoms	Can cross bridges, can fly (Elliott et al., 2009); symptoms went one by one, sudden relief (Lipkin, 1954) (2/8)
	7. Enjoying change in circumstances	Improved nonrelationship aspects of life independent of therapy (Elliott et al., 1990; Elliott, 2002) (2/8)

(continued)

TABLE 13.5 *(Continued)*

Main Meta-Category	Meta-Categories	Primary Studies Findings
B. Appreciating experience of self in relationship with others	1. Feeling supported	Feeling respected by children, seeking support group (Klein & Elliott, 2006). Note: Reported changes in others' view of self (Elliott et al., 1990); people tell me I am a nicer person (Elliott et al., 2009). In many studies attributions to therapy/therapist as providers of support (3/8)
	2. Enjoying interpersonal encounters	Better interpersonal functioning (all, romantic, family) (Klein & Elliott, 2006); reordering relationships (Dale et al., 1998); being able to cope with reactions of others (Timulak et al., 2010); increased independence/assertion (Elliott et al., 1990); increased positive openness (Elliott et al., 1990); improved relationships (Elliott et al., 1990); better relationship with my spouse, more tolerant (Elliott et al., 2009) (5/8)
C. Changed view of self/others	1. Self-insight and self-awareness	Development of meaning and understanding of abuse, learning from therapy (Dale et al., 1998; Lipkin, 1954); more aware and true to myself (Klein & Elliott, 2006); realizations about self (Elliott et al., 1990); enlightened (problem fitting in like a glove), better understanding self (I am not in the dark, I can do something about it), seeing patterns (Lipkin, 1954) (4/8)
	2. Changed view of others	See other viewpoints (Klein & Elliott, 2006); being more interested in others (Timulak et al., 2010); changes in client views and attitudes toward others (Elliott et al., 1990); accepting parent faults (Timulak et al., 2010) (3/8)

Note: From "Qualitative Meta-Analysis of Outcomes of Person-Centred/Experiential Therapies," by L. Timulak & M. Creaner, 2010, in M. Cooper, J. C. Watson, & D. Hölledampf (Eds.), *Person-centred and experiential psychotherapies wor*, Ross-on-Wye, United Kingdom: PCCS Books, pp. 75–76. Copyright Ladislav Timulak and Mary Creaner, 2010. Adapted with permission.

located 22 studies on HEPs that included a relevant qualitative research element. (We did not include studies that focused solely on the therapists' opinions about or experiences of therapy, e.g., Geller & Greenberg, 2002, studies that used traditional content analysis, e.g., Lietaer, 1992, or studies that used exclusively nominal scales with preset categories, e.g., Nicolo et al., 2008.)

Client General In-Session Experiences of Therapy

Qualitative studies of psychotherapy often focus on client experiences of therapy, either in general or in particular aspects (client-identified significant events studies are discussed separately). A landmark in research on client experiences was the work of Rennie (1990, 1992, 1994a, 1994b), who interviewed 14 clients of predominantly humanistic (person-centered and Gestalt) therapists about one of their recent therapy sessions. The interview (Interpersonal Process Recall, IPR; Elliott, 1986) was assisted by a recording of the session and clients were encouraged to stop the tape at any point where they remembered something meaningful happening; they were asked to describe the recalled experience. Clients' accounts were then analyzed using a version of grounded theory analysis (Rennie, Phillips, & Quartaro, 1988). Rennie documented many interesting phenomena, including showing how clients in the therapy session were engaged in a twofold process of pursuing personal meaning for themselves while also monitoring the therapist. Clients evaluated therapist interventions in terms of their compatibility with client plans or strategies for the session. The clients were also deferential toward the therapists (they did not confront them with criticism) and preferred to tolerate therapist shortcomings rather than challenge them. Most of the findings reported by Rennie have since been replicated by others, for example, Moerman and McLeod (2006), who used the IPR method with six clients who took part in person-centered counseling for alcohol-related problems.

A variation of Rennie's method was used by Watson and Rennie (1994), who investigated client experiences during evocative unfolding, an EFT intervention. Using IPR, eight clients with interpersonal problems were interviewed about their experiences during unfolding interventions. The authors reported that during this intervention clients were involved in creating a symbolic representation of their experiencing of the puzzling situation, reflectively examining their own experience and achieving new realizations that led to revision of self-concepts and understandings. These processes were either helpful and flowing, with the interaction between the client and the therapist being collaborative, or else they were hindering, in which case the flow was interrupted and the client felt confused by the therapist. The authors also noted that the intervention led to more new realizations and revisions of the self-concept when accompanied by client emotional experiencing along with curiosity and interest in recalling and re-examining disturbing material.

Client Retrospective Experiences of Helpful and Hindering Aspects of Therapy

Several recent studies of HEPs used client interviews given at the end of therapy to study helpful aspects of therapy (Knox, 2008; Lillie, 2002; Meyers, 2000; Rodgers, 2002; Schnellbacher & Leijssen, 2009). Overall, research on client experiences of helpful aspects of HEPs studies underscores the central importance of the relational qualities offered by the therapist, not only for client perceived safety in the relationship but also for the client perceived personal change. These studies show that therapist empathic skills may play a central role in fostering the development of insight and a new self-understanding in clients, and that clients appreciate having a space

devoted to tracking their own experiencing and expression of feelings. Additionally, clients appear to be reflective and to intentionally follow their own agenda, an observation still not adequately stressed in the theoretical literature. These studies also show that therapist misattunement (either from active misunderstanding or superficial interaction) may threaten the therapeutic work, and that this misattunement may not be pointed out to the therapist (cf. Rhodes, Hill, Thompson, & Elliott, 1994), although it can be tolerated by at least some clients.

Research on Helpful and Hindering Events

Helpful and hindering significant events studies represent a unique genre of research often using mixed methods. Significant events research focuses on the most helpful or hindering client-identified events in therapy sessions, which are subsequently studied in-depth by using the client descriptions to locate the event on the session recording. The recording of the event is then played back for the client and therapist in order to learn about their experience of the event (Elliott, 1985; Timulak, 2007, 2010). Given that the events are chosen by the client (as opposed to the researcher or the therapist), this type of research fits well with the humanistic-experiential paradigm, which gives voice to the client's felt experience.

Studies of helpful and hindering events (Grafanaki & McLeod, 1999, 2002; Timulak, Belicova, & Miler, 2010; Timulak & Elliott, 2003; Timulak & Lietaer, 2001), like those on client perceived outcomes and retrospective experiences just reviewed, show the importance of both fostering client safety in therapy and also its potential fragility. They also show that therapist skills at facilitating relational, empathic, and experiential processing can help the client to bear emotional pain, bring new awareness and insight, and help bring about a new sense of empowerment. These in-session events may thus be memorable experiences that can lead to a lasting impact. In these studies clients typically experienced the quality of relationship as a mutual encounter that had an enduring impact. For some it improved the therapeutic relationship and for others it was a moment of personal change. In general, the therapist's skillful clarification, guidance, compassionate presence, interpersonal affirmation, and awareness-promoting communication of empathic understanding contributed to helpful impacts, but sometimes private inner work by the client played an important role as well. In hindering events client vulnerability and occasionally therapist anxieties played role.

Qualitative Change Process Case Studies

Several qualitative studies examined processes perceived by clients to bring about change in HEPs. The most typical strategy for this kind of research was the intensive case study (for instance, Elliott's, 2002 Hermeneutic Single Case Efficacy Design), which collects a mixture of quantitative and qualitative process and outcome data from several sources while also offering a qualitative analysis of causal links between the therapy outcome and therapeutic processes. By means of this analysis Stephen, Elliott, and Macleod (2011) captured the connections between an improvement of a client with social phobia and her participation in PCT, while Elliott (2002) reported on the change processes in EFT for a client diagnosed with bipolar disorder. The studies identified, for instance, the importance of client experience of connection on a human level, increase in awareness of their own needs, support offered, and credit attributed to the therapist for bringing the client to experiences that the client would normally have avoided.

Several studies have analyzed HEP cases using the Assimilation of Problematic Experiences protocol (Stiles, 2002). Assimilation analysis tracks clients on a 7-stage stage model, in which the main foci of therapy are analyzed on a continuum ranging from being *warded-off*, through *insight into their nature* until they are *mastered*. The method uses the Assimilation of Problematic Experiences Scale (APES) as a qualitative framework for understanding the change process in therapy. APES was applied to three cases of EFT for depression (Brinegar, Salvi, & Stiles, 2008; Honos-Webb, Stiles, Greenberg, & Goldman, 1998; Honos-Webb, Surko, Stiles, & Greenberg, 1999) and one case of PCT for depression (Osatuke, Glick, Stiles, Shapiro, & Barkham, 2005). The studies highlighted several interesting findings. For instance, a comparison of a successful versus an unsuccessful case (Honos-Webb et al., 1998) not only revealed more advanced assimilation of problematic issues in the successful case, but also showed that the successful case sustained a clear focus of therapy, while the unsuccessful one did not. The same successful case was re-analyzed by a somewhat

different team (Brinegar et al., 2008) who found that the change (assimilation of problematic experiences) could be conceptualized as assimilation of two important empowering voices.

Another assimilation analysis of successful EFT (Honos-Webb et al., 1999) and PCT (Osatuke et al., 2005) cases showed a major change process to be the clients' gradual recognition of their own needs and the empowerment they experienced from standing up for self. Although assimilation analysis focuses on client change processes, careful reading of these cases along with the comments of the researchers (e.g., Osatuke et al., 2005) indicates that therapist affirmation of the client's previously disowned needs often played a crucial role in the change process.

Interestingly, one of the successful EFT cases analyzed using an APES framework (Brinegar et al., 2008; Honos-Webb et al., 1998) was also analyzed using the innovative moments coding system framework (Gonçalves, Mendes, Ribeiro, Angus, & Greenberg, 2010). This analysis, though using a different conceptual framework, converged with the assimilation analysis, reporting that the client's protest moments, in which she reclaimed her needs, allowed her to create a distance from significant others by whom she felt let down.

It is obvious that various theoretical frameworks such as assimilation of problematic experiences or similar theory-laden studies (e.g., Stinckens, Lietaer, & Leijssen's [2002] study on resolution of inner criticism) can be used to illustrate changes clients undergo in therapy. These changes might, however, just be accompanying epiphenomena that correspond with progress in therapy, but may not necessarily capture the core causal processes in change. Indeed, the more open-ended Hermeneutic Single Case Efficacy Design studies had greater difficulty in identifying clear, unambiguous links. Regardless of this, it seems that all of the reported case studies and the change processes tracked in them suggest that change comes via (a) the therapist responding to the client's core hurt/pain; (b) mobilization of the client's previously obscured unmet needs (typically to be respected, close, or secure); (c) the therapist offering compassion and affirmation to those unmet needs, as well as the client's self-compassion or protective anger/determination. These observations, reported by a variety of teams, are in line with recent work on change processes using a task analytic approach (e.g., Pascual-Leone & Greenberg, 2007).

Limitations of Qualitative Research on Humanistic-Experiential Therapies

Qualitative research on HEPs gives voice to client (and therapist) experiences of therapy and also provides a flexible framework that can facilitate studying the complexity of therapeutic change processes. Nevertheless, it is useful to be aware that these studies were conducted with clients with unrelated presenting issues, such as mood and anxiety disorders, and alcohol misuse, and may thus represent different underlying change processes. Also, there seems to be a lack of qualitative studies that use HEP theoretical frameworks for interpreting change processes and client experiences. For instance, the richness of APES studies (which use a rather trans-theoretical framework) illustrates how theoretically informed investigations of HEPs might look. As qualitative research is still a relatively recent development, the quality of studies reviewed here varied widely. Further attention needs to be devoted to raising standards in this area of research (cf. Elliott, Fischer, & Rennie, 1999; Chapter 3, this volume).

QUANTITATIVE PROCESS RESEARCH ON HUMANISTIC-EXPERIENTIAL PSYCHOTHERAPY

Research on the process of change is foundational to HEP approaches, as research clinicians within this approach have tried to specify the therapist and client processes that contribute to successful outcomes. Historically the focus of this research agenda has been on general therapeutic relationship conditions or attitudes as delineated by Rogers (1959) and on client experiencing (Gendlin, 1981). This has changed over time to a more differentiated focus on therapist interventions and techniques and client processes that are related to change in psychotherapy.

Process-Outcome Research on the Therapeutic Relationship

Since Rogers (1957) first articulated his hypothesis about the necessary and sufficient conditions of therapeutic change, much evidence has accumulated. Recent comprehensive reviews collected in Norcross (2011)'s *Psychotherapy Relationships That Work* provide an up-to-date summary of the broad base of evidence supporting these therapist relational conditions, including Elliott, Bohart, Watson, and Greenberg (2011) on empathy; Farber and Doolin (2011) on positive regard and affirmation; Kolden, Klein, Wang, and Austin (2011) on congruence/genuineness, and Horvath, Del Re, Flückiger, and Symonds (2011) on the therapeutic alliance generally. Subsequently, the task force on the therapeutic relationship designated therapist empathy as "demonstrably effective"; positive regard as "probably effective"; and congruence/genuineness as "promising but insufficient research to judge" (Norcross & Wampold, 2011, p. 424).

The research collected and meta-analyzed in the Norcross (2011) review volume comes from a broad range of therapies, mostly not from the HEP tradition. For example, only 8 out of 59 (14%) of the studies reviewed by Elliott et al.'s (2011) empathy-outcome meta-analysis focused on HEPs. The mean weighted correlation for these eight studies was .26, statistically significant, highly consistent ($I^2 = 9\%$) and in line with the overall value of .30 for the entire sample of 59 studies. HEPs are grouped under "other treatments" in the Farber and Doolin (2011) and Kolden et al. (2011) reviews of positive regard and genuineness respectively, but appear to comprise only a tiny proportion of the studies reviewed.

Moreover, several methodological weaknesses have been identified in this body of quantitative process-outcome research on the impact of the relationship conditions on outcome. In an earlier, unsystematic review, Sachse and Elliott (2002) noted that the facilitative conditions did not yield consistent results for all clients and client problems, as some clients seem to benefit and others not. Other methodological problems are failure to assess clients for incongruence (as originally proposed by Rogers, 1957); poor sampling methods; small sample sizes; different rating perspectives; inadequate levels of the therapeutic conditions; restricted range of measurement of the relationship conditions; possible nonlinear effects; low measurement reliability; and inconsistencies in the experience levels of the therapists (Watson, Greenberg, & Lietaer, 2010). Notwithstanding these methodological problems, the accumulated evidence to date points to a moderately strong relationship between the therapeutic conditions and outcome, although the relationship may be somewhat more complex than initially thought.

Among others, Lambert and Barley (2002) attributed the decline of research on the relationship conditions to the ascendancy of the therapeutic alliance construct. Nevertheless, the links between outcome, therapist empathy, and the working alliance are some of the most highly evidence-based findings in the psychotherapy research literature (Elliott et al., 2011; Horvath et al., 2011; Lambert, 2005). In an attempt to distinguish the two constructs Watson and Geller (2005) examined relationships among clients' ratings of the Barrett-Lennard Relationship Inventory (BLRI; Barrett-Lennard, 1962), psychotherapy outcome, and the working alliance in CBT and EFT. Overall, client reports of therapist positive regard, unconditionality, empathy, and congruence on the BLRI correlated .72 with clients' self-reports of the working alliance, pointing to the possibility of conceptual overlap. Nevertheless, client ratings of the four relationship conditions were predictive of treatment outcome on a wide range of outcome measures. The impact of the relationship conditions on outcome appeared to be mediated by therapeutic alliance for three out of four outcome measures, consistent with a model of the relationship conditions as instrumental in facilitating formation of a therapeutic bond and agreement on goals and tasks. There were no significant differences on client ratings between CBT and EFT therapists on therapist empathy, unconditionality, and congruence, but clients in EFT reported feeling more highly regarded by their therapists than clients in CBT.

Subsequently, McMullen and Watson (2005) examined differences between therapist and client behaviors in high and low alliance sessions in EFT and CBT. They found that in contrast to EFT therapists, CBT therapists taught more and asked more directive questions, while EFT therapists offered more support. However, therapists in both CBT and EFT provided more support during low-alliance than high alliance sessions. Interestingly, clients in EFT were rated as expressing more disagreement with therapist responses, and showing greater "resistance" in low-alliance sessions than clients in CBT.

However, process-outcome research supporting the role of therapist-offered relational conditions does not tell us what mediates the relation between therapist relational conditions and outcome. In order to address this question, Watson and her team have been investigating the role of the facilitative conditions and specifically empathy in the change process. Building on Barrett-Lennard's (1997) suggestion that therapist empathy leads to increased self-empathy, Steckley and Watson (Steckley, 2006; Steckley & Watson, 2000) examined this hypothesis in clients who were treated for major depression with either CBT or EFT. They found that client ratings of therapist empathy predicted improvements in client posttherapy attachment styles, as clients became less insecure and more self-accepting and protective of themselves. These changes were also associated with positive outcomes, accounting for moderate to large amounts of variance (42% to 70%). A subsequent study showed that empathy was an active ingredient of change. Watson and Prosser (2007) examined the complex relationship between empathy, affect regulation, and outcome using path analysis, reporting that the effect of therapist empathy on outcome was mediated by changes in clients' affect regulation. These more recent studies continue to provide additional evidence and support for the role of the clients' experience of the therapeutic relationship in promoting positive outcomes in psychotherapy.

Research on Specific Therapeutic Tasks

Research on specific therapeutic tasks continues to be a fruitful line of inquiry for understanding the relationship between tasks and client processing during sessions, and also for deepening our understanding of the steps necessary for facilitating client change in therapy.

Two-Chair Dialogue for Conflict Splits

Intensive analyses of the client change processes in the two-chair dialogue task in EFT and Gestalt therapies, originally led to the development of a model of the essential components of resolution of splits (Greenberg, 1979, 1983) that subsequently received empirical validation (Greenberg & Webster, 1982; Sicoli & Halberg, 1998; Whelton & Greenberg; 2000). More recently, Shahar and colleagues (2011) examined the efficacy of two-chair dialogue task at times of stress with nine clients who were judged to be self-critical. The intervention was associated with clients becoming significantly more compassionate and reassuring toward themselves, and to significant reductions in self-criticism and symptoms of depression and anxiety. Effect sizes were medium to large, with most clients exhibiting only low and nonclinical levels of symptoms at the end of therapy, and maintaining these gains over a 6-month follow-up period.

Empty Chair Dialogue for Unfinished Business

The empty chair task has been found to be more effective in resolving unfinished business than empathy using measures of both in-session process and session outcome (Greenberg & Foerster, 1996). Clients rated by observers as resolving their unfinished business reported significantly greater improvement in symptom distress, interpersonal problems, target complaints, affiliation toward self, and degree of unfinished business (Greenberg & Malcolm, 2002). More recently in a study of the resolution of interpersonal, emotional injuries, EFT was found to be more emotionally arousing than a psychoeducational treatment. However, the reported in-session emotional arousal did not relate directly to outcome in either group. The authors suggested that this finding probably reflects the fact that emotional arousal may signal different processes at different times (Greenberg et al., 2008). For example, emotional arousal at one point in therapy may be a sign of distress and at another point a sign that the client is actively working through distress (Greenberg & Watson, 2006; Kennedy-Moore & Watson, 1999).

Paivio et al.'s (2010) recent study comparing two forms of EFT for trauma is also relevant here: In one condition ("imaginal confrontation"), clients were required to use empty chair work, that is, to speak directly to the perpetrator of their abuse or important nonprotective others in the empty chair. In the other condition ("empathic exploration"), clients instead spoke to the therapist *about* the perpetrator/nonprotective other. Clients in both forms of EFT showed substantial pre-post gains. Clients using empty chair, showed more pre-post change; however, they also dropped out at a higher rate (20% versus 7%), suggesting that it may not be a good idea to require all clients to use this highly evocative therapeutic task.

Interpersonal Forgiveness

Research on specific therapeutic tasks has occurred within the context of couples therapy as well as individual therapy. Meneses and Greenberg (2011) explored how forgiveness unfolds in EFT for couples (EFT-C), using eight cases where women felt their partners had betrayed them. Forgiveness was defined as a process involving the reduction in negative feelings and the giving out of undeserved compassion. A task analysis was performed to rigorously track the steps leading to forgiveness using videotapes of therapy sessions. A comparison of those who forgave to those who did not yielded a model of the process of forgiveness in EFT for couples, from which a process rating system was developed. Five essential components of the model were found to distinguish between those who forgave and those who did not: (a) first, the injurer offered nondefensive acceptance of responsibility for the emotional injury; they then (b) expressed shame or empathic distress and (c) offered a heartfelt apology; (d) this was followed by the injured partner showing a shift in their view of the other; and (e) the injurer expressing acceptance of forgiveness, and relief or contrition.

In a further study, Woldarsky (2011) related the in-session process during the interpersonal forgiveness task to outcome, based on data from 33 couples who received emotion-focused couples therapy for an emotional injury (a betrayal) (Greenberg et al., 2010). The results showed that expressed shame accounted for 33% of the outcome variance in posttherapy forgiveness; the addition of acceptance explained an additional 9%, while in-session forgiveness explained another 8%, with the final regression model accounting for 50% of the outcome variance. These findings lend support to the couples' forgiveness model (Meneses & Greenberg, 2011). In addition, the therapeutic process was found to be more relevant to whether the injured partners forgave their partners than the degree of distress a couple was experiencing at the start of treatment.

Modeling Client Emotional Processing

Emotional processing of global distress is a generic task in EFT, in that clients often enter therapy with strong or partially blocked but undifferentiated feelings (i.e., feeling "upset" or "bad"). For this reason, Pascual-Leone and Greenberg (2007) carried out a task analysis on the emotional processing steps involved in clients' resolution of global distress, defined as an unprocessed emotion with high arousal and low meaningfulness, beginning with a rational-empirical model. The model hypothesized that in processing their emotions clients would move from a state of global distress through fear, shame, and aggressive anger to the articulation of needs and negative self-evaluations; then they would move on to assertive anger, self-soothing, hurt, and grief as states indicating more advanced processing (Pascual-Leone & Greenberg, 2007). The model was tested using a sample of 34 clients.

Results showed that the model of emotional processing predicted in-session outcomes and that distinct emotions emerged moment-by-moment in predicted sequential patterns.

Intermediate components in the form of personal evaluation and reevaluation predicted in-session outcomes. Experiences of fear/shame and statements of negative evaluation about the self (i.e., feeling worthless, frail, or unlovable) were present in both good and poor outcome cases and could not be predicted by in-session outcome. However, a heartfelt statement expressing an existential need to feel valuable, lovable, safe, or alive did predict and often preceded good within-session outcome (as measured by the Client Experiencing Scale).

In a subsequent study (Pascual-Leone, 2009) univariate and bootstrapping statistical methods were used to examine how dynamic emotional shifts accumulate moment-by-moment to produce in-session gains in emotional processing. It was found that effective emotional processing was simultaneously associated with steady improvement and increased emotional range. Good events were shown to occur in a "two-steps-forward, one-step-backward" fashion, and it was found that there were increasingly shorter emotional collapses in helpful in-session events, as compared to unhelpful in-session events where the opposite was true.

Research on Client Processes

In HEP theories of personality change (Gendlin, 1970; Greenberg & Van Balen, 1998; Rogers, 1959), depth of experiential self-exploration is seen as one of the pillars of psychotherapy process and change. During the past 50 years much research has been done on the relationship between experiential depth and outcome. Within this context several instruments have been constructed to measure levels of experiential depth, the first ones being Rogers' *Process Scale* (Rogers, Walker, & Rablen, 1960) and Truax's *Tentative scale for the measurement of depth of intrapersonal exploration* (1962; Truax & Carkhuff, 1967). Subsequently, the *Client Experiencing Scale* (Klein, Mathieu, Gendlin, & Kiesler, 1969/1983; Klein, Mathieu-Coughlan, & Kiesler, 1986) was developed, followed by Toukmanian's *Levels of client perceptual processing scale* (1986, 1992; Toukmanian & Gordon, 2004) and Sachse's *Processing Mode Scale* (1992a; Sachse & Maus, 1991). Although there are some differences between these scales, they all describe and measure the level of clients' involvement in an experiential process of self-exploration.

Depth of Experiencing and Outcome

Ratings of client depth of experiencing have been related to good outcome consistently in HEPs (Elliott et al., 2004; Hendricks, 2002). Moreover, clients' emotional processing in the session has been found to be beneficial across a range of other therapeutic approaches, including CBT and psychodynamic (Giyaur, Sharf, & Hilsenroth, 2005; Godfrey, Chalder, Risdale, Seed, & Ogden, 2007; Leahy, 2002). Research on depth of experiencing in therapy has found a consistent relationship between client experiencing during therapy and outcome: the higher the experiencing level, the better the therapy outcome (Elliott et al., 2004; Purton, 2004). Although the association between experiencing level and outcome is clear and consistent, it is not perfect, suggesting that other factors play a role in fruitful therapy process. In addition, it is simplistic to hold a linear view of the stages of the experiencing scale (i.e., "the higher the score, the better the process quality of the exploration process"). Recent investigations of psychotherapy change process (Angus & McLeod, 2004; Watson, Goldman, & Greenberg, 2007) emphasize that *all* narrative modalities, representing the full range of the client experiencing scale, are important and serve useful functions for clients in exploring their problems.

Rogers' process view (1961), however, also predicted that there would be an *increase* of experiencing level throughout the course of successful therapy. Unfortunately, this has not been confirmed in most studies, possibly due to methodological issues such as sampling problems. Researchers typically measure experiencing levels at the beginning, middle, and end phases of therapy, but randomly select segments within and across sessions. Noting this practice, Rice and Greenberg (1984) originally suggested that as a result key events of the psychotherapy process were not being investigated. As an alternative sampling method they selected segments that were linked to clients' problematic issues. Subsequently, Goldman, Greenberg, and Pos (2005) found that an increase in client levels of experiencing from early to late in therapy was a stronger predictor of outcome than the working alliance.

Like the early observations of Rogers (1959) and Gendlin (1970), several studies have revealed significant differences in the manner in which good and poor outcome clients refer to their emotional experience during the session, across different therapeutic approaches (Pos, Greenberg, Goldman, & Korman, 2003; Watson & Bedard, 2006). Watson and Bedard (2006) found that good outcome clients in both EFT and CBT for depression, began, continued, and ended therapy at higher modal and peak experiencing levels during the session than did clients with poor outcome. Good outcome clients engaged in deeper exploration, referred to their emotions more frequently, were more internally focused, and examined and reflected upon their experience to create new meaning and resolve their problems in personally meaningful ways. In contrast, clients with poorer outcomes were not as engaged in processing their emotional experience, nor did they reflect on or pose questions about their experience during the session, to examine it and try to understand the origins and implications of their experience more fully. As a result, poor outcome clients did not report important shifts in perspective or feeling during the session. These findings suggest that processing one's bodily felt experience and deepening this in therapy may well be a core ingredient of change in psychotherapy regardless of approach. However, an alternative interpretation is that clients who enter therapy with these skills do better in short term therapy than those who do not enter with these skills. Thus these skills may be an indicator of clients' readiness or capacity to engage in short term therapy.

Depth of Experiencing, Emotional Expression and Processing, and Outcome

Therapy researchers have begun to examine the relationship between clients' levels of emotional arousal and outcome. Process-outcome research on EFT for depression has shown that both higher emotional arousal at mid-treatment, coupled with reflection on the aroused emotion (Warwar & Greenberg, 2000) and deeper emotional processing late in therapy (Pos et al., 2003), predicted good treatment outcomes. High emotional arousal plus high reflection on aroused emotion distinguished good and poor outcome cases, indicating the importance of combining arousal and meaning construction (Missirlian, Toukmanian, Warwar, & Greenberg, 2005; Warwar, 2003). EFT thus appears to work by enhancing a particular type of emotional processing: first helping the client experience, then accept, and finally make sense of their emotions.

Warwar (2003) examined mid-therapy emotional arousal as well as experiencing in early, middle, and late phases of therapy. In this study clients who had higher emotional arousal at mid-therapy were found to have changed more at the end of therapy. Furthermore, client ability to use internal experience to make meaning as measured by the Client Experiencing Scale, particularly in the late phase of treatment, added to the outcome variance over and above middle phase emotional arousal. Thus, this study showed that the combination of emotional arousal and experiencing was a better predictor of outcome than either index alone.

It is important to note this study measured *expressed* as opposed to *experienced* emotion. In a study examining in-session client reports of *experienced* emotional intensity, Warwar, Greenberg, and Perepeluk (2003) found that client reports of in-session experienced emotion were not related to positive therapeutic change. A discrepancy was observed between clients' reports of in-session *experienced* emotions and the emotions that were actually *expressed* based on arousal ratings of videotaped therapy segments. For example, one client reported that she had experienced intense emotional pain in a session; however, her level of expressed emotional arousal was judged to be very low based on observer ratings of emotional arousal from videotaped therapy segments.

Pos et al. (2003) suggested that emotional processing late in therapy mediates between early emotional processing and outcome. Here emotional processing was defined as depth of experiencing during emotion episodes. Emotion episodes (Greenberg & Korman, 1993) are in-session segments in which clients express or talk about having experienced an emotion in relation to a real or imagined situation. The Client Experiencing Scale was used to rate only those in-session episodes that were emotionally laden. They found that client early capacity for emotional processing did not guarantee good outcome, nor did entering therapy without this capacity guarantee poor outcome. Thus, early emotional processing skill did not appear as critical as the ability to acquire or increase depth of emotional processing throughout therapy. In this study late emotional processing independently added 21% to the explained variance in reduction in symptoms, over and above early alliance and emotional processing.

Pos, Greenberg, and Warwar (2010) measured emotional processing and the alliance across three phases of therapy (beginning, working, and termination) for 74 clients who each received EFT for depression. Using path analysis, a model of the role of the alliance and emotional processing across different phases of therapy and how they relate to and predict improvement in depression and other symptoms, self-esteem, and interpersonal problems at the end of treatment, was proposed and tested. Both therapeutic alliance and emotional processing significantly increased across phases of therapy. After controlling for both the alliance and client emotional processing at the beginning of therapy, client level of experiencing during the working phase was found to directly and best predict reductions in depressive and general symptoms, as well as gains in self-esteem. Within working and termination phases of therapy, the alliance significantly contributed to emotional processing and indirectly contributed to outcome. In addition, the alliance, measured after session one, also directly predicted outcome, and client therapy process at the beginning of treatment predicted reductions in interpersonal problems. These findings suggest that although the EFT theory of change was supported, the quality of client emotional processing at the beginning of therapy may constrain their success in a short-term HEP and in particular resolution of interpersonal problems.

In another study of relations among the alliance, frequency of aroused emotional expression, and outcome, in EFT for depression, Carryer and Greenberg (2010) found that the expression of high versus low emotional arousal correlated with different types of outcome. Moderate frequency of heightened emotional arousal was found to add significantly to outcome variance predicted by the working alliance. The majority of process research studies have focused on a direct linear relationship between process and outcome; however, this study showed that a rate of 25% for moderate-to-high emotional expression predicted best outcomes. Lower rates, indicating lack of emotional involvement, represented an extension of the generally accepted relationship between low levels of expressed emotional arousal and poor outcome, while higher rates, indicating excessive amounts of highly aroused emotion, were related to poor outcome. This suggests that having the client achieve an intense and full level of emotional expression is predictive of good outcome, as long as the client does not maintain this level of emotional expression for too long a time or too often. In addition, frequency of reaching only minimal or

marginal level of arousal was found to predict poor outcome. Thus, emotional expression that does not attain a heightened level of emotional arousal, or that reflects an inability to express full arousal and possibly indicates interruption of arousal, appears undesirable, rather than a lesser but still desirable goal. This complex relationship offers a challenge to therapists in managing levels of arousal and possibly selecting clients for EFT.

In an intensive examination of four poor and four good outcome cases, however, Greenberg, Auszra, and Herrmann (2007) did not find a significant relationship between the frequency of higher levels of expressed emotional arousal measured over the whole course of treatment and outcome. They measured both aroused emotional expression and productivity of the expressed emotion, and concluded that productivity of aroused emotional expression was more important to therapeutic outcome than arousal alone.

The measure of productive emotional arousal used in the earlier study was further developed and its predictive validity was tested on a sample of 74 clients from the York depression studies (Auszra, Greenberg, & Herrmann, 2007). Emotional productivity was defined as a state of being in contact with and aware of a presently activated emotion, where contact and awareness were defined as involving the following necessary features: (a) attending to nonverbal aspects of experience; (b) symbolization in words; (c) congruence, matching between content and manner of expression; (d) acceptance, non-negative evaluation; (e) agency, not experiencing self as a victim of emotion but responsible for it; (f) regulation, not being overwhelmed; and (g) differentiation, being in a process of developing more specific meanings. Emotional productivity was found to increase from the beginning to the working and the termination phases of treatment. Working phase emotional productivity was found to predict 66% of treatment outcome variance, over and above variance accounted for by beginning phase emotional productivity, session four working alliance, and high expressed emotional arousal in the working phase. These results suggest that productive processing of emotion may be the best predictor of outcome of all process variables studied thus far.

In studies of EFT for trauma (Paivio & Pascual Leone, 2010) good client process, early in therapy, has been found to be particularly important because it sets the course for therapy and allows maximum time to explore and process emotion related to traumatic memories (Paivio et al., 2001). One practical implication of this research is the importance of facilitating clients' emotional engagement with painful memories early in therapy. A study of EFT for trauma found that therapist competence in facilitating imaginal confrontation using empty chair work, predicted better client processing. Moreover, when adult survivors of childhood abuse engaged in empty chair work, it contributed to the reduction of interpersonal problems, a contribution independent of therapeutic alliance (Paivio, Holowaty, & Hall, 2004). These important findings are consistent with those found in research on EFT for depression, which showed deeper levels of emotional experiencing had a curative effect over and above the alliance (Pos et al., 2003). Emotional processes have also been studied in the two controlled studies on resolving emotional injuries and interpersonal difficulties. Emotional arousal during imagined contact with a significant other was a process factor that distinguished EFT from a psycho-educational treatment and was related to outcome (Greenberg et al., 2008; Greenberg & Malcolm, 2002; Paivio & Greenberg, 1995).

Extending this line of inquiry, Watson, McMullen, Prosser, and Bedard (2011) recently examined relationships among client affect regulation, in-session emotional processing, working alliance, and outcome in 66 clients who received either CBT or EFT for depression. They found that client initial level of affect regulation predicted their emotional processing during early and working phases of therapy. Moreover, the quality of client emotional processing in the session mediated the relationship between client level of affect regulation at the beginning of therapy and at termination; and client level of affect regulation at the end of therapy mediated the relationship between client level of emotional processing in therapy and final outcome, independently of the working alliance. These studies demonstrate the importance of client emotional processing in the session and suggest important ways that it can be facilitated by specific therapist interventions, for example, by facilitating client symbolization, acceptance, owning, regulation, and differentiation of key emotions.

Finally, recent content analysis studies of client experiences of helpful factors in therapy (Dierick & Lietaer, 2008; Vanaerschot & Lietaer, 2010) have shown that processes referring to depth of experiential self-exploration have a central place among the therapeutic ingredients mentioned by clients as helpful and that these processes discriminate between "very good" and "rather poor" sessions. In content analysis studies done by Vanaerschot and Lietaer (2007, 2010) 20% to 40% of helpful factor descriptions mentioned by clients could be put under the following three categories: stimulation and deepening of self-exploration; focusing on and exploring more deeply; and intensively living through and experiencing fully.

Therapist Interventions and Client Experiencing

Several studies have investigated the role of therapist interventions in facilitating client productive engagement in the session. While the Experiencing Scale (Klein et al., 1986) has mainly been used to investigate client process in psychotherapy, Sachse has focused on the *interaction* between therapist and client. To do so he constructed two parallel scales, respectively for "the processing modes" (PM) of the client and the "processing proposals" (PP) of the therapist (Purton, 2004; Sachse, 1990, 1992b; Sachse & Elliott, 2002; Takens, 2008). In a series of empirical studies (Sachse, 1992a; Sachse & Maus, 1991; Sachse & Elliott, 2002; Sachse & Takens, 2004) showed the impact of therapist proposals on the depth of clients' exploration process. Similar to Rogers' (1961) and Gendlin's (1981) early observations about variations in client process, Sachse emphasized that the results of these micro-analytic studies suggest that the manner in which therapists respond to their clients can exert a significant influence on client exploration processes. As some clients may find it quite difficult to clarify, check, and modify their own feelings, needs, goals, and convictions, therapists can offer active assistance to support client processing efforts.

Adams and Greenberg (1996) looked at whether therapist experiencing had an impact on client level of processing. They found that therapist statements that were high in experiencing influenced level of client experiencing and that depth of therapist experiential focus predicted outcome. More specifically, if the client was externally focused and the therapist made an intervention that was targeted toward internal experience, the client was more likely to move to a deeper level of experiencing. This study replicates Sachse's (1990) earlier research and highlights the importance of the therapist's role in deepening emotional processes. Given that client experiencing predicts outcome, and that therapist depth of experiential focus influenced client experiencing and predicted outcome, a path to outcome was established that suggests that therapist depth of experiential focus influences client depth of experiencing, which in turn relates to positive outcome.

A series of studies carried out by Toukmanian and coworkers also examined the impact of therapist interventions, including attunement, tentativeness, and meaning exploration, on client level of cognitive and emotional processing in the session. They found that therapist empathy, attunement, and exploration were each associated with higher levels of client experiencing and client perceptual processing (Gordon & Toukmanian, 2002), and that therapist empathy was best predicted by therapist attunement (Macaulay, Toukmanian, & Gordon, 2007). Moreover, complexity of client manner of processing over the course of therapy predicted reduction in depression at post treatment (Toukmanian, Jadaa, & Armstrong, 2010).

Narrative processes. Studies led by Angus on client narrative sequences in EFT have revealed interesting patterns associated with good outcomes (Angus, Levitt, & Hardtke, 1999), with unique processing patterns associated with good treatment outcomes (Angus, et al., 1999; Angus, Lewin, Bouffard, & Rotondi-Trevisan, 2004). Lewin (2001) found that therapists in good outcome in EFT cases were twice as likely to help clients shift to internal/emotion-focused and reflexive narrative modes than therapists of clients with poor outcome. Additionally, good outcome depressed clients initiated more shifts to emotion-focused and reflexive discourse than poor outcome clients. Clients with good outcome in brief HEP, spent significantly more time engaged in reflexive and emotion-focused discourse than did poor outcome clients. These findings provide empirical support for the importance of emotion and reflexive processes in the treatment of depression.

Moreover high emotional arousal plus high reflection on aroused emotion distinguished good and poor outcome cases, indicating the importance of combining arousal and meaning construction (Missirlian et al., 2005; Warwar, 2003). More recently, Boritz, Angus, Monette, and Hollis-Walker (2008) and Boritz, Angus, Monette, Hollis-Walker, and Warwar (2011) investigated the relationship of expressed emotional arousal and specific autobiographical memory in the context of early, middle, and late

phase sessions drawn from the York I Depression Study (Greenberg & Watson, 1998). Hierarchical Linear Modeling analyses established that there was a significant increase in the specificity of autobiographical memories from early to late phase therapy sessions and that treatment outcome was predicted by a combination of high narrative specificity plus expressed arousal in late phase sessions. However, neither expressed emotional arousal nor narrative specificity alone was associated with complete recovery at treatment termination. Specifically, Boritz et al. (2010) found that recovered clients were significantly more able to emotionally express their feelings in the context of telling specific autobiographical memory narratives than clients who remained depressed at treatment termination.

Client Postsession Change and Outcome

A recent study by Watson, Schein, and McMullen (2010) examined the relationship of client-reported postsession change to determine whether it predicted outcome over and above the therapeutic alliance in a study of 66 clients treated with EFT or CBT for depression. An updated measure of client postsession change was used, the Client Task-Specific Changes-Revised scale. The measure showed high internal consistency. Factor analyses showed that the measure comprised two factors, conceptualized as Behavior Change and Awareness/Understanding. Client postsession scores increased over the course of psychotherapy and predicted change in depression at the end of therapy over and above the therapeutic alliance, explaining an additional 13% of the variance in outcome on the BDI.

CONCLUSIONS

In this latest review of research on humanistic-experiential psychotherapies, we have once again emphasized outcome research, but have also looked at qualitative studies of client experiences of outcome and helpful factors, as well as quantitative investigations of change processes.

Humanistic-Experiential Psychotherapies as Evidence-Based Treatments

Current mental health politics urgently require continuing collection, integration, and dissemination of information about the rapidly expanding body of accumulated outcome evidence, to help deal with challenges to HEPs in several countries, including the United States, United Kingdom, Germany, and the Netherlands (to mention only those with which we are most familiar). HEP outcome research has grown rapidly, with half of the existing studies appearing in the past 10 years. This has allowed us to pursue increasingly sophisticated analysis strategies and to break down the evidence by client subpopulation and type of HEP. We believe that these analyses go a long way toward meeting the demands implicit in the criteria put forward by various national guideline development groups (e.g., APA Division 12 Task Force on Empirically Supported Treatments in the United States; National Institute for Clinical Excellence [NICE] in the United Kingdom).

Looking at our entire data set of roughly 200 outcome studies, we see that evidence for the effectiveness of HEPs comes from three separate lines of evidence and supports the following conclusions:

First, overall, HEPs are associated with large *pre-post* client change. These client changes are maintained over early (<12 months) and late (a year or more) follow-ups.

Second, in *controlled studies*, clients in HEPs generally show large gains relative to clients who receive no therapy, regardless of whether studies are randomized or not. This allows the causal inference that HEP, in general, causes client change; or rather, speaking from the client's perspective, we can say that clients use HEP to cause themselves to change.

Third, in *comparative outcome* studies, HEPs in general are statistically and clinically equivalent in effectiveness to other therapies, regardless of whether studies are randomized or not.

Fourth, overall, CBT appears to have a trivial advantage over HEPs. However, this effect seems to be due to non–bona fide treatments usually labeled by researchers as *supportive* (or sometimes *nondirective*), which are generally less effective than CBT. These therapies are typically delivered when there is a negative researcher allegiance and in non–bona fide versions, and appear to be the mediator for the substantial researcher allegiance effect that we found. When the supportive treatments are removed from the sample, or when researcher allegiance is controlled for statistically, HEPs appear to be equivalent to CBT in their effectiveness.

Going beyond these general conclusions, we have argued that the existing research is now

more than sufficient to warrant varying positive valuations of HEP in six important client populations: depression, relationship/interpersonal problems, anxiety, coping with chronic medical conditions, psychosis, and substance misuse, even using the fairly strict criteria put forward by Chambless and Hollon (1998; the successor to the APA Division 12 Criteria).

For *depression*, HEPs have been extensively researched, to the point where the claim of empirical support as *efficacious and specific* (i.e., superior to a placebo or active treatment) can be supported for them in general (using meta-analytic data), and more specifically for EFT for mild to moderate depression (e.g., Goldman et al., 2006; Watson et al., 2003), and PCT for perinatal depression (e.g., Cooper et al., 2003; Holden et al., 1989).

For *relationship and interpersonal problems* EFT clearly meets criteria as an *efficacious and specific* treatment. These include current relationship problems among couples, where EFT for couples has long been recognized as an empirically supported treatment (e.g., Baucom et al., 1998). In our review here, however, we have also highlighted the use of EFT in both couples and individual formats for emotional injuries, including childhood abuse trauma (e.g., Greenberg et al., 2008; Paivio et al., 2010). It is important to note, however, that these studies do not focus on PTSD.

For helping clients cope psychologically with *chronic medical conditions* in general based on the meta-analytic data, it now appears that HEPs meet criteria as *efficacious* treatments, based either on their superiority to no treatment control conditions or on their equivalence to an established treatment (CBT). Supportive therapy, PCT, and supportive-expressive group therapy have been used with a wide variety of chronic and disabling medical conditions, including most commonly early and late stage cancer, and autoimmune disorders (e.g., lupus, MS), but also gastrointestinal problems (e.g., IBS), HIV, chronic pain and others. To date, the strongest pre-post and comparative effects have been found for cancer; however, recently reported large studies (e.g., Bordeleau et al., 2003; Spiegel et al., 2007) have shown weaker effects and point to the continuing need for further research.

For habitual self-damaging activities, our analysis indicates that HEPs (primarily supportive and other HEPs) meet the criteria for being *efficacious* treatments for substance misuse. (The sample was too small and the results too equivocal to properly assess the evidence for eating disorders.) These results are comparable for those of a closely related treatment for substance misuse, Motivational Interviewing (Lundahl et al., 2010).

For *anxiety* problems overall, the existing evidence is mixed, but sufficient to warrant a general continuing verdict of *possibly efficacious* (at least one study shows "equivalence" to an established treatment) for panic, generalized anxiety and phobia (see Borkovec & Mathews, 1988; Shear et al., 1994). However, the available evidence on treatment of panic and generalized anxiety (but not phobia) also suggests that HEPs may be *less efficacious* than CBT. Although this is likely to reflect researcher allegiance effects, it is also possible that the supportive, person-centered and other HEPs used so far are less effective than CBT for these client subpopulations, and that a more process-guiding approach is needed, as indicated by evidence now emerging from ongoing research (e.g., Elliott & Rodgers, 2010).

For *psychotic* conditions such as schizophrenia, we continue to recommend a cautious verdict of *possibly efficacious*, in spite of a recent UK guideline contra-indicating humanistic counseling for clients with this condition (National Collaborating Centre for Mental Health, 2010). In fact, the comparative evidence we have reviewed points to the possibility that HEPs may be *more* effective than the other therapies to which they have been compared; however, the number and sample size of the existing studies is relatively small, so we have preferred to err in the direction of caution here rather than going for a stronger conclusion.

Key Change Processes in Humanistic-Experiential Psychotherapies

Our review of quantitative and qualitative change process research on HEPs shows that researchers continue to refine their understanding of the therapist and client processes that bring about change in therapy. This research uses all four of the change process research paradigms defined by Elliott (2010), including quantitative process-outcome, qualitative helpful factors, significant events, and sequential process approaches, in the context of both group and individual case studies. Over time, the research has moved beyond global therapist facilitative processes such as empathy, positive regard, genuineness, and collaboration to more specific within-session change processes.

Qualitative change process research, for example, reveals the complexity of clients' experiences of therapy. Clients have their own agendas, may be ambivalent about change, and may have doubts about the therapist, all of which can significantly affect the outcomes of therapy. In successful therapy, the therapist is seen as reaching out to the client in a way that promotes the client's sense of safety, but that also responds to the client's emotional pain and unmet needs with compassionate and authentic presence. These needs are affirmed by the therapist, thus facilitating the development of self-compassion and self-acceptance as well as self-empowerment grounded in awareness of key emotions and unmet needs. All this interweaves with the collaborative development of a personally meaningful client narrative (Angus & Greenberg, 2011).

Furthermore, the use of task analysis to model sequences of particular client and therapist performances has led to the development of additional models of processes in individual and couples therapy and has broadened the range of therapist behaviors and types of interventions that have been shown to facilitate good outcome. Sequential and process-outcome research on client experiencing has been extended to look at clients' cognitive and emotional processing during the session as well as the quality of their narratives in order to identify productive client processes in HEPs.

The recent quantitative change process research reviewed here has involved continuing work on central therapeutic processes such as client experiencing, emotional expression, and elements of narrative, but has added a new set of important variables, including emotion episodes, emotional productivity and differentiation, affect regulation, innovative moments, and autobiographical memory specificity. These new variables and their associated process measures are providing more fine-grained tools for understanding how client change occurs. These conceptual and research tools are generating new, more precise maps of the change process. Thus, we can see more precise answers emerging to key questions about productive therapy process:

Question 1: When is client emotional expression most likely to lead to good outcome? Answer: When it is grounded in specific autobiographical memories, accompanied by deeper levels of experiencing, and becomes more regulated and differentiated as it is explored (research by Greenberg, Angus, Pascual-Leone, and colleagues).

Question 2: What is the most productive sequence of narrative exploration in therapy? Answer: Description of external events, leading to initial self-reflection, leading to access to internal experiences, leading to self-reflection on broader meaning (research by Angus and colleagues).

Question 3: How do problematic or painful client experiences get assimilated? Answer: Via an extended sequence over time starting from warded off or painful awareness, then to problem clarification and insight, and finally to working through and mastery (research by Stiles and colleagues).

Question 4: How do new narratives emerge and become established in client's lives? Answer: By a spiraling movement between action and reflection, starting with attempts to change the problem, leading to reflection on the nature of the old problematic narrative, followed by active protest or working against the problem, then to emerging re-conceptualization of self and the process of change, and finally to carrying out the change in one's life (research by Gonçalves and colleagues).

The many ways in which these different lines of theory development and research run parallel to and complement one another are plain to be seen and point to the possibility of a larger synthesis with many useful clinical implications.

Recommendations for Research, Practice, and Training

It is our view that the research reviewed here has important scientific and practical implications.

First, while the field of humanistic-experiential therapy research has made substantial progress during the past 10 years, more research is clearly needed, particularly with client populations where clear recommendations are not yet possible, such as different types of anxiety, psychosis, particular medical conditions, and eating disorders, and others. At the same time, more research on well-studied client problems such as depression are also needed, in order to bolster or upgrade the existing evidence, which runs the risk of becoming obsolete as standards for research evidence shift over time (e.g., requiring larger samples, RCTs, intent-to-treat analyses, and more sophisticated meta-analysis techniques).

Second, from a health care policy point of view, the available outcome data clearly support the proposition that HEPs are empirically supported by multiple lines of scientific evidence, including "gold standard" RCTs and recent large RCT-equivalent practice-based studies in the UK (e.g., Stiles et al., 2006, 2008). This body of research suggests that the lists of empirically supported or evidence-based psychotherapies that have been constructed in various countries—the NICE Guidelines in the United Kingdom or the list of empirically supported treatments in the United States, for example—need to be updated with the type of evidence we have reviewed. HEPs should be offered to clients in national health service contexts and other mental health settings, and paid for by health insurance, especially for the well-evidenced client populations highlighted.

Third, there is an important lesson to be learned from the negative results we have identified for supportive therapies. For those of us in the HEP tradition, the moral of this story is that we do not need to be afraid of quantitative outcome research, including RCTs. Naturally, there are many problems and limitations with RCTs, just as there are with all research methods. If, however, we insist as a matter of principle on conscientiously objecting to quantitative outcome research in general and RCTs in particular, then we create a situation in which we let others define our reality by constructing watered-down versions of what we do as a representation of our practice. If we continue to let this happen, then we are going to be in worse trouble than we already are. For this reason, it is imperative that as humanistic-experiential therapists we do our own outcome research—including RCTs—on bona fide versions of our therapies. It is also essential for us to train more HEP researchers.

Fourth, as for the specific research implications of our review, it certainly seems to us to illustrate the value of using a wide range of research methods, qualitative and quantitative, group and single case, to address questions of therapeutic change, effectiveness and efficacy. At the same time, it is worth noting that our data indicate that the current emphasis on randomization in controlled and comparative outcome studies is misplaced: In fact, we found that randomization made no difference whatsoever in our meta-analysis. Although randomization is a useful research tool, nonrandomized studies also need to be given significant weight in integrating research findings.

Fifth, it now appears to us that research alone will not suffice; the development of treatment guidelines in various countries has in our experience become increasingly politicized, with powerful interest groups dominating the committees charged with reviewing the evidence. These groups determine what counts as evidence, what evidence is reviewed, and how that evidence is interpreted as a basis for formulating treatment guidelines. This is often portrayed as an objective, neutral process of making straightforward inferences from research evidence to the real world of practice. According to Bayesian statistics (e.g., Lynch, 2010), however, this is an instance of the logical fallacy of the "transposed conditional" (Siegfried, 2010): The famous "null hypothesis" against which we test our results only evaluates the likelihood of hypothetical inference from practice (the "real world") to our research results, not in the opposite direction, from our results to practice, which is the inference that we want to make. Inference from evidence to practice only becomes possible when we factor in our prior expectations, that is, our researcher and reviewer theoretical allegiances. This means that it is critically important who reviews the research evidence and what their prior expectations or allegiances are. And that means that the guideline development committees that review research evidence will only produce valid and fair guidelines if they contain a balanced representation of researchers with varied theoretical allegiances. The implication for the HEPs is that they need to put pressure on guideline development bodies for proper representation.

Finally, we conclude as we did in our previous review (Elliott et al., 2004), with training implications: The neglect of HEPs in training programs and treatment guidelines is no longer warranted. Humanistic-experiential therapies should generally be offered in postgraduate programs and internships, especially as treatments for depression, relationship problems, and substance misuse, and also to help people cope with chronic medical problems, and possibly to support clients with psychotic processes, anxiety disorders, and eating difficulties. Like CBT, HEPs are evidence-based for a wide range of client presenting problems. In fact, we argue that the education of psychotherapists is incomplete and unscientific without a greater emphasis on these approaches, to the ultimate detriment of clients.

REFERENCES

*References marked with an asterisk indicate studies newly added or updated in the meta-analysis.

Adams, K. E., & Greenberg, L. S. (1996, June). *Therapists' influence on depressed clients' therapeutic experiencing and outcome*. Paper presented at the 43rd Annual convention of the Society for Psychotherapeutic Research, St. Amelia, Florida.

*Altenhoefer, A., Schwab, R., Schulz, W., & Eckert, J., (2007). Effectiveness of time limited client-centered psychotherapy in the treatment of patients with adjustment disorders. *Psychotherapeut, 52*, 24–34

Angus, L., & Greenberg, L. (2011). *Working with narrative in emotion-focused therapy: Changing stories, healing lives*. Washington DC: American Psychological Association.

Angus, L. E., Lewin, J., Bouffard, B., & Rotondi-Trevisan, D. (2004). "What's the story?" working with narrative in experiential psychotherapy. In L. E. Angus & J. McLeod (Eds.), *The handbook of narrative and psychotherapy: Practice, theory and research*. Thousand Oaks, CA: Sage.

Angus, L., Levitt, H., & Hardtke, K. (1999). The narrative processes coding system: Research applications and implications for psychotherapeutic practice. *Journal of Clinical Psychology, 55*, 1255–1270.

Angus, L., & McLeod, J. (2004). *The handbook of narrative and psychotherapy*. London, United Kingdom: Sage.

Auszra, L., Greenberg, L. S., & Herrmann, I. (2007, July). *Emotional productivity in experiential therapy for depression*. Symposium in Lisbon, Portugal.

Barrett-Lennard, G. (1962). Dimensions of therapist response as causal factors in therapeutic change. *Psychological Monographs: General and Applied, 76*(43), 1–36. doi: 10.1037/h0093918

Barrett-Lennard, G. (1997). The recovery of empathy: toward others and self. In Bohart A. C., Greenberg L. S. (Eds.), *Empathy reconsidered: New directions in psychotherapy*. Washington, DC: American Psychological Association.

*Barrowclough, C., King, P., Colville, J., Russell, E., Burns, A., & Tarrier, N. (2001). A randomized trial of the effectiveness of cognitive-behavioral therapy and supportive counselling for anxiety symptoms in older adults. *Journal of Consulting and Clinical Psychology, 69*, 756–762.

Baucom, D. H., Mueser, K. T., Shoham, V., & Daiuto, A. D. (1998). Empirically supported couple and family interventions for marital distress and adult mental health problems. *Journal of Consulting and Clinical Psychology, 66*, 53–88.

*Beck, A. T., Sokol, L., Clark, D. A., Berchick, R., & Wright, F. (1992). A crossover study of focused cognitive therapy for panic disorder. *American Journal of Psychiatry, 149*, 778–783.

Beutler, L. E., Engle, D., Mohr, D., Daldrup, R. J., Bergan, J., Meredith, K., & Merry, W. (1991). Predictors of differential response to cognitive, experiential, and self-directed psychotherapeutic procedures. *Journal of Consulting and Clinical Psychology*, *59*, 333–340.

*Blowers, C., Cobb, J., & Mathews, A. (1987). Generalised anxiety: A controlled treatment study. *Behaviour Research and Therapy*, *25*, 493–502.

Bohart, A. C., O'Hara, M. & Leitner, L. M. (1998). Empirically violated treatments: Disenfranchisement of humanistic and other psychotherapies. *Psychotherapy Research*, *8*, 141–157.

*Bond, A. J., Wingrove, J., Curran, H. V., & Lader, M. H. (2002). Treatment of generalized anxiety disorder with a short course of psychological therapy, combined with buspirone or placebo. *Journal of Affective Disorders*, *72*, 267–271.

Bordeleau, L., Szalai, J. P., Ennis, M., Leszcz, M., Speca, M., Sela, R., . . . Goodwin, P. J. (2003). Quality of life in a randomized trial of group psychosocial support in metastatic breast cancer: Overall effects of the intervention and an exploration of missing data. *Journal of Clinical Oncology*, *21*, 1944–1951. doi: 10.1200/jco.2003.04.080

Boritz, T. Z., Angus, L., Monette, G., & Hollis-Walker, L. (2008). An empirical analysis of autobiographical memory specificity subtypes in brief emotion-focused and client-centered treatments of depression. *Psychotherapy Research*, *18*, 584–593. doi: 10.1080/10503300802123245

Boritz, T. Z., Angus, L., Monette, G., Hollis-Walker, L., & Warwar, S. (2011). Narrative and emotion integration in psychotherapy: Investigating the relationship between autobiographical memory specificity and expressed emotional arousal in brief emotion-focused and client-centred treatments of depression. *Psychotherapy Research*, *21*, 16–26. doi: 10.1080/10503307.2010.504240

Borkovec, R., & Costello, E. (1993). Efficacy of applied relaxation and cognitive-behavioral therapy in the treatment of generalized anxiety disorder. *Journal of Consulting and Clinical Psychology*, *61*, 611–619.

Borkovec, T. D., & Mathews, A. (1988). Treatment of nonphobic anxiety disorders: A comparison of nondirective, cognitive, and coping desensitization therapy. *Journal of Consulting and Clinical Psychology*, *56*, 877–884.

*Borkovec, T. D., Mathews, A. M., Chambers, A., Ebrahimi, S., Lytle, R., & Nelson, R. (1987). The effects of relaxation training with cognitive or nondirective therapy and the role of relaxation-induced anxiety in the treatment of generalized anxiety. *Journal of Consulting and Clinical Psychology*, *55*, 883–888.

Brinegar, M. G., Salvi, L. M., & Stiles, W. B. (2008). The case of Lisa and the assimilation model: The interrelatedness of problematic voices. *Psychotherapy Research*, *18*, 657–66.

Brodley, B. T. (1990). Client-centered and experiential: Two different therapies. In G. Lietaer, J. Rombauts, & R. Van Balen (Eds.), *Client-centered and experiential psychotherapy towards the nineties* (pp. 87–107). Leuven, Belgium: Leuven University Press.

Cain, D., & Seeman, J. (Eds.). (2002). *Humanistic psychotherapies: Handbook of research and practice*. Washington, DC: APA.

Carryer, J. R., & Greenberg, L. S. (2010). Optimal levels of emotional arousal in experiential therapy of depression. *Journal of Consulting and Clinical Psychology*, *78*, 190–199. doi: 10.1037/a0018401

Chadwick, P. D. J. (2006). *Person-based cognitive therapy for distressing psychosis*. West Sussex, United Kingdom: Wiley.

Chambless, D. L., & Hollon, S. D. (1998). Defining empirically supported therapies. *Journal of Consulting and Clinical Psychology*, *66*, 7–18.

*Classen, C., Butler, L., Koopman, C., Miller, E., DiMiceli, S., Giese-Davis, J., . . . Spiegel, D. (2001). Supportive-expressive group therapy and distress in patients with metastatic breast cancer. *Archives of General Psychiatry*, *58*, 494–501.

Cohen, J. (1988). *Statistical power analysis for the behavioral sciences* (2nd ed.). Hillsdale, NJ: Erlbaum.

*Coons, W. H., & Peacock, M. A. (1970). Interpersonal interaction and personality change in group psychotherapy. *Canadian Psychiatric Association Journal*, *15*, 347–355.

*Cooper, M. (2004). *Counselling in schools project: Evaluation report*. Glasgow, United Kingdom: Counselling Unit, University of Strathclyde.

*Cooper, M. (2006). *Counselling in schools project phase II: Evaluation report*. Glasgow, United Kingdom: Counselling Unit, University of Strathclyde.

Cooper, M., Watson, J. C., & Hölldampf, D. (Eds.). (2010). *Person-centred and experiential therapies work: A review of the research on counselling, psychotherapy and related practices*. Ross-on-Wye, United Kingdom: PCCS Books.

*Cooper, P. J., Murray, L., Wilson, A., & Romaniuk, H. (2003). Controlled trial of the short- and long-term effect of psychological treatment of postpartum depression. *British Journal of Psychiatry*, *182*, 412–419.

*Cornelius-White, J. H. D. (2003). The effectiveness of a brief, nondirective person-centered practice. *Person-Centered Journal*, *10*, 31–38.

*Cottraux, J., Note, I., Albuisson, E., Yao, S. N., Note, B., Mollard, E., . . . Coudert, A. J. (2000). Cognitive behavior therapy versus supportive therapy in social phobia: A randomized controlled trial. *Psychotherapy and Psychosomatics*, *69*, 137–146.

*Cowen, E. L., & Combs, A. W. (1950). Follow-up study of 32 cases treated by nondirective therapy. *Journal of Abnormal Social Psychology*, *45*, 232–258.

*Craske, M. G., Maidenberg, E., & Bystritsky, A. (1995). Brief cognitive-behavioral versus nondirective therapy for panic disorder. *Journal of Behaviour Therapy & Experimental Psychiatry*, *26*, 113–120.

Daldrup, R., Beutler, L., Engle, D., & Greenberg, L. (1988). *Focused expressive therapy: Freeing the over-controlled patient*. London, United Kingdom: Cassell.

Dale, P., Allen, J., & Measor, L. (1998). Counselling adults who were abused as children: Clients' perceptions of efficacy, client-counsellor communication, and dissatisfaction. *British Journal of Guidance and Counselling*, *26*, 141–157.

*Dekeyser, M., Prouty, G., & Elliott, R. (2008). Pre-therapy process and outcome: A review of research instruments and findings. *Person-Centered and Experiential Psychotherapies*, *7*, 37–55.

*Denton, W. H., Burleson, B. R., Clark, T. E., Rodriguez, C. P., & Hobbs, B. V. (2000). A randomized trial of emotion-focused therapy for couples in a training clinic. *Journal of Marital and Family Therapy*, *26*, 65–78.

*Dessaules, A., Johnson, S. M., & Denton, W. (2003). Emotion-focused therapy for couples in the treatment of depression: A pilot study. *American Journal of Family Therapy*, *31*, 345–353.

*Diamond, G. S., Reis, B. F., Diamond, G. M., Siqueland, L., & Isaacs, L. (2002). Attachment-based family therapy for depressed adolescents: A treatment development study. *Journal of the American Academy of Child & Adolescent Psychiatry*, *41*, 1190–1196.

Dierick, P., & Lietaer, G. (2008). Client perception of therapeutic factors in group psychotherapy and growth groups: An empirically-based hierarchical model. *International Journal of Group Psychotherapy*, *58*, 203–230. doi: 10.1521/ijgp.2008.58.2.203

Dircks, P., Grimm, F., Tausch, A-M., & Wittern, J-O. (1982). Förderung der seelischen Lebensqualität von Krebspatienten durch personenzentrierte Gruppengespräche. *Zeitschrift für Klinische Psychologie*, *9*, 241–251.

*Dobkin, P. L., Da Costa, D., Joseph, L., Fortin, P. R., Edworthy, S., Barr, S., . . . Clarke, A. E. (2002). Counterbalancing patient demands with evidence: Results from a pan-Canadian randomized clinical trial of brief supportive-expressive group psychotherapy for women with systemic lupus erythematosus. *Annals of Behavioral Medicine*, *24*, 88–99.

*Dodge, W. (2003). A comparison between a convergent and an integrated approach to the treatment of oppositionally defiant adolescents with family therapy. Unpublished doctoral dissertation. San Francisco, California, Saybrook Graduate School.

Eckert, J., & Wuchner, M. (1996). Long-term development of borderline personality disorder. In R. Hutterer, G. Pawlowsky, P. E. Schmid, & R. Stipsits (Eds.), *Client-centered and experiential psychotherapy. A paradigm in motion* (pp. 213–233). Frankfurt, Germany: Peter Lang.

Edwards, A. G., Hulbert-Williams, N., & Neal, R. D. (2008). Psychological interventions for women with metastatic breast cancer. *Cochrane Database Systematic Reviews*, (3), CD004253. doi: 10.1002/14651858.CD004253.pub3

Elliott, R. (1985). Helpful and nonhelpful events in brief counseling interviews: An empirical taxonomy. *Journal of Counseling Psychology*, *32*, 307–322.

Elliott, R. (1986). Interpersonal process recall (IPR) as a psychotherapy process research method. In L. S. Greenberg & W. M. Pinsof (Eds.), *The psychotherapeutic process: A research handbook* (pp. 249–286). New York, NY: Guilford Press.

Elliott, R. (1996). Are client-centered/experiential therapies effective? A meta-analysis of outcome research. In U. Esser, H. Pabst, G-W Speierer (Eds.), *The power of the Person-Centered-Approach: New challenges-perspectives-answers* (pp. 125–138). Köln, Germany: GwG Verlag.

Elliott, R. (1998). Editor's introduction: A guide to the empirically-supported treatments controversy. *Psychotherapy Research*, *8*, 115–125.

Elliott, R. (2002). Research on the effectiveness of humanistic therapies: A meta-analysis. In D. Cain & J. Seeman (Eds.), *Humanistic psychotherapies: Handbook of research and practice* (pp. 57–81). Washington, DC: APA.

Elliott, R. (2002a). Hermeneutic single case efficacy design. *Psychotherapy Research*, *12*, 1–20.

Elliott, R. (2002b). Render unto Ceasar: Quantitative and qualitative knowing in research on humanistic therapies. *Person-Centered and Experiential Psychotherapies*, *1*, 102–117.

Elliott, R. (2010). Psychotherapy change process research: Realizing the promise. *Psychotherapy Research*, *20*, 123–135.

Elliott, R., Bohart, A. C., Watson, J. C., & Greenberg, L. S. (2011). Empathy. In J. Norcross (Ed.), *Psychotherapy relationships that work* (2nd ed., pp. 132–152). New York, NY: Oxford University Press.

Elliott, R., Clark, C., Kemeny, V., Wexler, M. M., Mack, C., & Brinkerhoff, L. J. (1990). The impact of experiential therapy on depression: The first ten cases. In G. Lietaer, J. Rombauts, & R. Van Balen (Eds.), *Client-centered and experiential psychotherapy in the nineties* (pp. 549–578). Leuven, Belgium: Katholieke Universiteit Leuven.

Elliott, R., Fischer, C. T., & Rennie, D. L. (1999). Evolving guidelines for publication of qualitative research studies in psychology and related fields. *British Journal of Clinical Psychology*, *38*, 215–229.

Elliott, R., Greenberg, L. S., & Lietaer, G. (2004). Research on experiential psychotherapies. In M. J. Lambert (Ed.), *Bergin & Garfield's handbook of psychotherapy and behaviour change* (5th ed., pp. 493–540). Hoboken, NJ: Wiley.

Elliott, R., Partyka, R., Wagner, J., Alperin, R., Dobrenski. R., Messer, S. B., . . . Castonguay, L.

G. (2009). An adjudicated hermeneutic single-case efficacy design of experiential therapy for panic/phobia. *Psychotherapy Research, 19*, 543–557.

Elliott, R., & Rodgers, B. (2010, March). *Person-centred/experiential approaches to social anxiety: Initial outcome results.* Paper presented at conference of the UK Chapter of the Society for Psychotherapy Research, Ravenscar, United Kingdom.

Elliott, R., Slatick, E., & Urman, M. (2001). Qualitative change process research on psychotherapy: Alternative strategies. In J. Frommer & D. L. Rennie (Eds.), *Qualitative psychotherapy research: Methods and methodology* (pp. 69–111). Lengerich, Germany: Pabst Science.

Elliott, R., Stiles, W. B., & Shapiro, D. A. (1993). Are some psychotherapies more equivalent than others? In T. R. Giles (Ed.), *Handbook of effective psychotherapy* (pp. 455–479). New York, NY: Plenum Press.

*Esplen, M. J., Hunter, J., Leszcz, M., Warner, E., Narod, S., Metcalfe, K.,...Wong, J. (2004). A multicenter study of supportive-expressive group therapy for women with BRCA1/BRCA2 mutations. *Cancer, 101*, 2327–2340.

Farber, B. A., & Doolin, E. M. (2011). Positive regard and affirmation. In J. Norcross (Ed.), *Psychotherapy relationships that work* (2nd ed., pp. 168–186). New York, NY: Oxford University Press.

Fosha, D. (2000). *The transforming power of affect: A model of accelerated change.* New York, NY: Basic Books.

*Foulds, M. L., & Hannigan, P. S.(1976). Effects of Gestalt marathon workshops on measured self-actualization: A replication and follow-up study. *Journal of Counseling Psychology, 23*, 60–65.

*Foulds, M. L., & Hannigan, P. S. (1977). Gestalt workshops and measured changes in self-actualization: Replication and refinement study. *Journal of College Student Personnel, 18*, 200–205.

*Friedli, K., King, M. B., Lloyd, M., & Horder, J. (1997). Randomized controlled assessment of non-directive psychotherapy versus routine general-practitioner care. *Lancet, 350*, 1662–1665.

*Freire, E. S., Hough, M., & Cooper, M. (2008). *Person-centred counselling in schools: An evaluation.* Internal report, Counselling Unit, University of Strathclyde, Glasgow, United Kingdom.

Furukawa, T.A. (1999). From effect size into number needed to treat. *Lancet, 353*, 1680.

Geller, S. M., & Greenberg, L. S. (2002). Therapeutic presence: Therapists' experience of presence in the psychotherapy encounter. *Person-Centered and Experiential Psychotherapies, 1*, 71–86.

Gendlin, E. T. (1970). A theory of personality change. In J. T. Hart & T. M. Tomlinson (Eds.), *New directions in client-centered therapy* (pp. 129–173). Boston, MA: Houghton Mifflin.

Gendlin, E. T. (1981). *Focusing.* New York, NY: Bantam Books.

Gendlin, E. T. (1996). *Focusing-oriented psychotherapy: A manual of the experiential method.* New York, NY: Guilford Press.

*Gibbard, I., & Hanley, T. (2008). A five-year evaluation of the effectiveness of person-centred counselling in routine clinical practice in primary care. *Counselling & Psychotherapy Research, 8*, 215–222

Giese-Davis, J., Koopman, C., Butler, L. D., Classen, C., Cordova, M., Fobair, P.,...Spiegel, D. (2002). Change in emotion-regulation strategy for women with metastatic breast cancer following supportive-expressive group therapy. *Journal of Consulting and Clinical Psychology, 70*, 916–925.

Gilbert, P. (2009). *The compassionate mind.* London, United Kingdom: Constable & Robinson.

Giyaur, K., Sharf, J., & Hilsenroth, M. J. (2005). The capacity for dynamic process scale (CDPS) and patient engagement in opiate addiction treatment. *Journal of Nervous and Mental Disease, 193*(12), 833–838. doi: 10.1097/01.nmd.0000188978.50765.39

Godfrey, E., Chalder, T., Risdale, L., Seed, P., & Ogden, J. (2007). Investigating the active ingredients of cognitive behavioural therapy and counselling for patients with chronic fatigue in primary care: Developing a new process measure to assess treatment fidelity and predict outcome. *British Journal of Clinical Psychology, 46*, 253–272.

Goldman, R. N., Greenberg, L. S., & Angus, L. (2006). The effects of adding emotion-focused interventions to the client-centered relationship conditions in the treatment of depression. *Psychotherapy Research, 16*, 537–549.

Goldman, R. N., Greenberg, L. S., & Pos, A. E. (2005). Depth of emotional experience and outcome. *Psychotherapy Research, 15*, 248–260.

Gonçalves, M., Mendes, I., Ribeiro, A., Angus, L., & Greenberg, L. (2010). Innovative moments and change in emotion-focused therapy: The case of Lisa. *Journal of Constructivist Psychology, 23*, 267–294.

*Goodwin, P. J., Leszcz, M., Ennis, M., Koopmans, J., Vincent, L., Guther, H.,...Hunter, J. (2001). The effect of group psychosocial support on survival in metastatic breast cancer. *New England Journal of Medicine, 345*, 1719–1726.

Gordon, K. M., & Toukmanian, S. G. (2002). Is how it is said important? the association between quality of therapist interventions and client processing. *Counselling & Psychotherapy Research, 2*, 88–98. doi: 10.1080/14733140212331384867

Grafanaki, S., & McLeod, J. (1999). Narrative processes in the construction of helpful and hindering events in experiential psychotherapy. *Psychotherapy Research, 9*, 289–303.

Grafanaki, S., & McLeod, J. (2002). Experiential congruence: Qualitative analysis of client and counselor narrative accounts of significant events in time-limited person-centred therapy. *Counselling and Psychotherapy Research, 2,* 20–32.

Grawe, K., (1976). *Differentielle Psychotherapie I: Indikation und spezifische Wirkung von Verhaltenstherapie und Gesprächspsychotherapie: Eine Untersuchung an phobischen Patienten.* Bern, Switzerland: Hans Huber.

Grawe, K., Caspar, F., & Ambühl, H. (1990). Differentielle Psychotherapieforschung: Vier Therapieformen im Vergleich. *Zeitschrift für Klinische Psychologie, 19,* 287–376.

Greenberg, L. S. (1979). Resolving splits: The two-chair technique. *Psychotherapy: Theory, Research and Practice, 16,* 310–318.

Greenberg, L. S. (1983). Toward a task analysis of conflict resolution in gestalt therapy. *Psychotherapy: Theory, Research and Practice, 20,* 190–201.

Greenberg, L. S. (2010). *Emotion-focused therapy.* Washington, DC: American Psychological Association.

Greenberg, L. S., Auszra, L., & Herrmann, I. R. (2007). The relationship among emotional productivity, emotional arousal and outcome in experiential therapy of depression. *Psychotherapy Research, 17,* 482–482–493. doi: 10.1080/10503300600977800

Greenberg, L. S., Elliott, R., & Lietaer, G. (1994). Research on humanistic and experiential psychotherapies. In A. E. Bergin & S. L. Garfield (Eds.), *Handbook of psychotherapy and behaviour change* (4th ed., pp. 509–539). New York, NY: Wiley.

Greenberg, L. S., & Foerster, F. (1996). Resolving unfinished business: The process of change. *Journal of Consulting and Clinical Psychology, 64,* 439–446.

Greenberg, L. S. & Johnson, S. M (1988). *Emotionally focused therapy for couples.* New York, NY: Guilford Press.

Greenberg, L. S., & Korman, L. M. (1993). Assimilating emotion into psychotherapy integration. *Journal of Psychotherapy Integration, 3,* 249–265.

Greenberg, L. S., & Malcolm, W. (2002). Resolving unfinished business: Relating process to outcome. *Journal of Consulting and Clinical Psychology, 70,* 406–416.

Greenberg, L. S., Rice, L. N., & Elliott, R. (1993). *Facilitating emotional change: The moment-by-moment process.* New York, NY: Guilford Press.

Greenberg, L. S., & Van Balen, R. (1998). The theory of experience-centered therapies. In L. S. Greenberg, J. C. Watson, & G. Lietaer (Eds.), *Handbook of experiential psychotherapy* (pp. 28–57). New York, NY: Guilford Press.

*Greenberg, L. J., Warwar, S. H., & Malcolm, W. M. (2008). Differential effects of emotion-focused therapy and psychoeducation in facilitating forgiveness and letting go of emotional injuries. *Journal of Counseling Psychology, 55,* 185–185–196. doi: 10.1037/0022–0167.55.2.185

*Greenberg, L., Warwar, S., & Malcolm, W. (2010). Emotion-focused couples therapy and the facilitation of forgiveness. *Journal of Marital and Family Therapy, 36*(1), 28–42. doi:10.1111/j.1752–0606.2009.00185.x

Greenberg, L. S., & Watson, J. (1998). Experiential therapy of depression: Differential effects of client-centered relationship conditions and process experiential interventions. *Psychotherapy Research, 8,* 210–224.

Greenberg, L. S., & Watson, J. C. (2006). *Emotion-focused therapy for depression.* Washington, DC: American Psychological Association. doi: 10.1037/11286–000

Greenberg, L. S., & Webster, M. (1982). Resolving decisional conflict by means of two-chair dialogue: Relating process to outcome. *Journal of Counseling Psychology, 29,* 468–477.

Hayes, S. C., Strosahl, K. D., & Wilson, K. G. (1999). *Acceptance and commitment therapy: An experiential approach to behavior change.* New York, NY: Guilford Press.

Hener, T., Weisenberg, M., & Har-Even, D. (1996). Supportive versus cognitive-behavioral intervention programs in achieving adjustment to home peritoneal kidney dialysis. *Journal of Consulting and Clinical Psychology, 64,* 731–741.

Hendricks, M. (2002). Focusing-oriented/experiential psychotherapy. In D. Cain & J. Seeman (Eds.), *Humanistic psychotherapies: Handbook of research and practice* (pp. 221–251). Washington, DC: American Psychological Association.

Higgins, J. P. T., Thompson, S. G., Deeks, J. J., & Altman, D. G. (2003). Measuring inconsistency in meta-analyses, *British Journal of Medicine, 327,* 557–560.

Holden, J. M., Sagovsky, R., & Cox, J. L. (1989). Counselling in a general practice setting: Controlled study of health visitor intervention in treatment of postnatal depression. *British Medical Journal, 298,* 223–226.

Holstein, B. E. (1990, August). *The use of focusing in combination with a cognitive-behavioral weight loss program.* Paper presented at American Psychological Association meeting, Boston, Massachusetts.

Honos-Webb, L., Stiles, W. B., Greenberg, L. S., & Goldman, R. N. (1998) Assimilation analysis of process-experiential psychotherapy: A comparison of two cases. *Psychotherapy Research, 8,* 264–286.

Honos-Webb, L. Surko, M., Stiles, W. B. & Greenberg, L. S. (1999). Assimilation of voices in psychotherapy: The case of Jan. *Journal of Counseling Psychology, 46,* 448–460.

Horvath, A., Del Re, A. C., Flückiger, C., & Symonds, D. (2011). Alliance in individual psychotherapy. In J. Norcross (Ed.), *Psychotherapy relationships that work* (2nd ed., pp. 25–91). New York, NY: Oxford University Press.

Hunter, J. E., & Schmidt, F. L. (1990). *Methods of meta-analysis*. Newbury Park, CA: Sage.

*Jacobs, S., & Bangert, M. (2005). Effekte und Prozessmerkmale der klientenzentrierten Gesprächspsychotherapie bei Alkoholismus. *Gesprächspsychotherapie und Personzentrierte Beratung, 2,* 97–107.

Johnson, B. T. (1989). *D/STAT: Software for the meta-analytic review of research literatures*. Hillsdale, NJ: Erlbaum.

Johnson, W. R. (1977). The use of a snake phobia paradigm and nonverbal behavior change in assessing treatment outcome: "The empty chair" versus systematic desensitization (Doctoral dissertation, Georgia State University, 1976). *Dissertation Abstracts International, 37,* 4146B. (University Microfilms No. 77–2933)

*Kaplan, S., & Kozin, F. (1981). A controlled study of group counseling in rheumatoid arthritis. *Journal of Rheumatology, 8,* 91–99.

Katonah, D. G. (1991). *Focusing and cancer: A psychological tool as an adjunct treatment for adaptive recovery*. Unpublished dissertation, Illinois School of Professional Psychology, Chicago, IL. Available online at www.focusing.org/adjunct_treatment.html

*Kenardy, J., Mensch, M., Bowen, K., Green, B., & Walton, J. (2002). Group therapy for binge eating in type 2 diabetes: A randomized trial. *Diabetic Medicine, 19,* 234–239.

Kennedy-Moore, E., & Watson, J. C. (1999). *Expressing emotion: Myths, realities and therapeutic strategies*. New York, NY: Guilford Press.

Kepner, J. (1993). *Body process: Working with the body in psychotherapy*. San Francisco, CA: Jossey-Bass.

*Kissane, D. W., Grabsch, B., Clarke, D. M., Smith, G. C., Love, A. W., Bloch, S., ... Yuelin, L. (2007). Supportive-expressive group therapy for women with metastatic breast cancer: Survival and psychosocial outcome from a randomized controlled trial. *Psycho-Oncology, 16,* 277–286.

Klein, M. H., Mathieu-Coughlan, P. L., Kiesler, D. J., & Gendlin, E. T. (1969/1983). *The experiencing scale: A research and training manual*. Madison: University of Wisconsin.

Klein, M. H., Mathieu-Coughlan, P. L., & Kiesler, D. J. (1986). The experiencing scales. In L. S. Greenberg & W. M. Pinsof (Eds.), *The psychotherapeutic process: A research handbook* (pp. 21–71). New York, NY: Guilford Press.

*Klein, M. J., & Elliott, R. (2006). Client accounts of personal change in process-experiential psychotherapy: A methodologically pluralistic approach. *Psychotherapy Research, 16,* 91–105.

*Klontz, B. T., Wolf, E. M., & Bivens, A. (2000). The effectiveness of a multimodal brief group experiential psychotherapy approach. *International Journal of Action Methods: Psychodrama, Skill-Training, and Role Playing, 53,* 119–135.

Knox, R. (2008) Clients' experiences of relational depth in person-centred counselling. *Counselling & Psychotherapy Research, 8,* 182–188.

Kolden, G. G., Klein, M. H., Wang, C-C., & Austin, S. B. (2011). Congruence/genuineness. In J. Norcross (Ed.), *Psychotherapy relationships that work* (2nd ed., pp. 187–202). New York, NY: Oxford University Press.

Lambert, M. J. (2005). Early response in psychotherapy: Further evidence for the importance of common factors rather than "placebo effects." *Journal of Clinical Psychology, 61*(7), 855–869.

Lambert, M. J., & Barley, D. E. (2002). *Research summary on the therapeutic relationship and psychotherapy outcome*. In J. Norcross (Ed.), *Psychotherapy relationships that work* (pp. 17–36). New York, NY: Oxford University Press.

Leahy, R. L. (2002). A model of emotional schemas. *Cognitive and Behavioral Practice, 9,* 177–190. doi: 10.1016/S1077-7229(02)80048-7

Lewin, J. K. (2001). *Both sides of the coin: Comparative analyses of narrative process patterns in poor and good outcome dyads engaged in brief experiential psychotherapy for depression*. Unpublished master's thesis, York University Toronto, Ontario, Canada.

Lietaer, G. (1992). Helping and hindering processes in client-centered/experiential psychotherapy: A content analysis of client and therapist postsession perceptions. In S. G. Toukmanian & D. L. Rennie (Eds.), *Psychotherapy process research: Paradigmatic and narrative approaches* (pp. 134–162). Newbury Park, CA: Sage.

Lillie, N. (2002). Women, alcohol, self-concept and self-esteem: A qualitative study of the experience of person-centred counselling. *Counselling & Psychotherapy Research, 2,* 99–107.

Lipkin, S. (1954). Clients' feelings and attitudes in relation to the outcome of client-centered therapy. *Psychological Monographs, 68,* 1–30.

Lipsey, M. W., & Wilson, D. B. (1993). The efficacy of psychological, educational, and behavioral treatment: Confirmation from meta-analysis. *American Psychologist, 48,* 1181–1209.

Lipsey, M. W., & Wilson, D. B. (2001). *Practical meta-analysis*. Thousand Oaks, CA: Sage .

Luborsky, L., Diguer, L., Seligman, D. A., Rosenthal, R., Krause, E. D., Johnson, S., ... Schweizer, E. (1999). The researcher's own therapy allegiances: A "wild card" in comparisons of treatment efficacy. *Clinical Psychology: Science and Practice, 6,* 95–106.

Lundahl, B. W., Kunz, C., Brownell, C., Tollefson, D., & Burke, B. L. (2010). A meta-analysis of motivational interviewing: Twenty-five years of empirical studies. *Research on Social Work Practice, 20,* 137–160.

Lynch, S. (2010). *Introduction to applied bayesian statistics and estimation for social scientists*. New York, NY: Springer.

Macaulay, H. L., Toukmanian, S. G., & Gordon, K. M. (2007). Attunement as the core of therapist-expressed empathy. *Canadian Journal of Counselling*, *41*, 244–244-254. Retrieved from http://search.proquest.com/docview/621941204?accountid=14771

*Machado, L. A. C., Azevedo, D. C., Capanema, M. B., Neto, T. N., & Cerceau, D. M. (2007). Client-centered therapy vs exercise therapy for chronic low back pain: A pilot randomized controlled trial in Brazil. *Pain Medicine*, *8*, 251–258.

*Maisiak, R., Austin, J. S., West, S. G., & Heck, L. (1996). The effect of person-centered counselling on the psychological status of persons with systemic lupus erythematosus or rheumatoid arthritis: A randomized, controlled trial. *Arthritis Care and Research*, *9*, 60–66.

*Makinen, J. A., & Johnson, S. M. (2006). Resolving attachment injuries in couples using emotionally focused therapy: Steps toward forgiveness and reconciliation. *Journal of Consulting and Clinical Psychology*, *74*, 1055–1064.

*Manne, S. L., Rubin, S., Edelson, M., Rosenblum, N., Bergman, C., Hernandez, E.,... Winkel, G. (2007). Coping and communication-enhancing intervention versus supportive counseling for women diagnosed with gynecological cancers. *Journal of consulting and Clinical Psychology*, *75*, 615–628.

*Martinez, M. (2002). Effectiveness of operationalized gestalt therapy role-playing in the treatment of phobic behaviors. *Gestalt Review*, *6*, 148–167.

*Maunder, R. G., & Esplen, M. J. (2001). Supportive-expressive group psychotherapy for persons with inflammatory bowel disease. *Canandian Journal of Psychiatry*, *46*, 622–626.

*Maynard, C. K. (1993). Comparison of effectiveness of group interventions for depression in women. *Archives of Psychiatric Nursing*, *7*, 277–283.

McLean, L. M., Jones, J. M., Rydall, A. C., Walsh, A., Esplen, M. J., Zimmermann, C., & Rodin, G. M. (2008). A couples intervention for patients facing advanced cancer and their spouse caregivers: Outcomes of a pilot study. *Psycho-Oncology*, *17*, 1152–1156. doi: 10.1002/pon.1319

McMullen, E., & Watson, J. C. (2005). An examination of therapist and client behaviour in high and low alliance sessions in cognitive-behavioural therapy and process experiential therapy. *Psychotherapy: Theory, Research, Practice, and Training*, *42*, 297–310.

*McNamara, K., & Horan, J. J. (1986). Experimental construct validity in the evaluation of cognitive and behavioral treatments for depression. *Journal of Counseling Psychology*, *33*, 23–30.

Meneses, C. W., & Greenberg, L. S. (2011), The construction of a model of the process of couples' forgiveness in emotion-focused therapy for couples.

Journal of Marital and Family Therapy, *37*, 491–502. doi: 10.1111/j.1752–0606.2011.00234.x

Meyer, A. E., Richter, R., Grawe, K., von Schulenburg, J.-M., & Schulte, B. (1991). *Forschungsgutachten zu Fragen eines Psychotherapeutengesetzes*. Hamburg, Germany: Universitaetskrankenhaus Eppendorf.

Meyers, S. (2000). Empathic listening: Reports on the experience of being heard. *Journal of Humanistic Psychology*, *40*, 148–173.

Miller, J. R. (1999). A social learning perspective toward the prevention of dating violence: An evaluation of a group counseling model (violence prevention). *Dissertation Abstracts International*, *60*, 3018B.

Miller, W. R., & Rollnick, S. (2002). *Motivational interviewing: Preparing people for change* (2nd ed.). New York, NY: Guilford Press.

Missirlian, T. M., Toukmanian, S. G., Warwar, S. H., & Greenberg, L. S. (2005). Emotional arousal, client perceptual processing, and the working alliance in experiential psychotherapy for depression. *Journal of Consulting and Clinical Psychology*, *73*, 801–871.

Moerman, M., & McLeod, J. (2006). Person-centered counseling for alcohol-related problems: The client's experience of self in the therapeutic relationship. *Person-Centered and Experiential Psychotherapies*, *5*, 21–35.

*Mohr, D. C., Boudewyn, A. C., Goodkin, D. E., Bostrom, A., & Epstein, L. (2001). Comparative outcomes for individual cognitive-behavior therapy, supportive-expressive group psychotherapy, and sertraline for the treatment of depression in multiple sclerosis. *Journal of Consulting and Clinical Psychology*, *69*, 942–949.

*Mohr, D. C., Classen, C., & Barrera, M. J. (2004). The relationship between social support, depression and treatment for depression in people with multiple sclerosis. *Psychological Medicine*, *34*, 533–541.

*Mohr, D. C., Hart, S. L., Julian, L., Catledge, C., Honos-Webb, L., Vella, L., & Tasch, E. T. (2005). Telephone-administered psychotherapy for depression. *Archives of General Psychiatry*, *62*, 1007–1014.

*Moorey, S., Greer, S., Bliss, J., & Law, M. (1998). A comparison of adjuvant psychological therapy and supportive counselling in patients with cancer. *Psycho-Oncology*, *7*, 218–228.

*Moran, M., Watson, C. G., Brown, J., White, C., & Jacobs, L. (1978). Systems releasing action therapy with alcoholics: An experimental evaluation. *Journal of Clinical Psychology*, *34*, 769–774.

*Moreno, J. L., & Moreno, Z.T. (1959). *Foundations of psychotherapy*. Beacon, NY: Beacon House.

*Morrell, C. J., Slade, P., Warner, R., Paley, G., Dixon, S., Walters, S. J.,... Nicholl, J. (2009). Clinical effectiveness of health visitor training in psychologically informed approaches for depression in postnatal women: Pragmatic cluster randomised trial in primary care. *British Medical Journal*, *338*, a3045.

*Müller-Hofer, B., Geiser, C., Juchli, E., & Laireiter, A-R. (2003). Kleintenzentrierte Körperpsychotherapie (GFK-Methode)—Ergebnisse einer Praxisevaluation [Client-centered body therapy: An effectiveness study]. *Psychotherapie Forum, 11,* 1–13.

National Collaborating Centre for Mental Health. (2009). *Depression: The treatment and management of depression in adults (update)* (NICE clinical guideline 90). London, United Kingdom: National Institute for Clinical Excellence. Available from www.nice.org.uk/CG90

National Collaborating Centre for Mental Health [NICE]. (2010). *Schizophrenia core interventions in the treatment and management of schizophrenia in adults in primary and secondary care* (updated edition). Leicester and London, United Kingdom: British Psychological Society & Royal College of Psychiatrists.

Newman, M. G., Castonguay, L. G., Borkovec, T. D., Fisher, A. J., Boswell, J. F., Szkodny, L. E., & Nordberg, S. S. (2011). A randomized controlled trial of cognitive-behavioral therapy for generalized anxiety disorder with integrated techniques from emotion-focused and interpersonal therapies. *Journal of Consulting and Clinical Psychology, 79,* 171–181. doi: 10.1037/a0022489

Nicolo, G., Dimaggio, G., Procacci, M., Semerari, A., Carcione, A., & Pedone, R. (2008). How states of mind change in psychotherapy: An intensive case analysis of Lisa's case using the grid of problematic states. *Psychotherapy Research, 18,* 645–656.

Norcross, J. (Ed.). (2011). *Psychotherapy relationships that work.* New York, NY: Oxford University Press.

Norcross, J. C., & Wampold, B. E. (2011). Evidence-based therapy relationships: Research conclusions and clinical practices. In J. Norcross (Ed.), *Psychotherapy relationships that work* (2nd ed., pp. 423–430). New York, NY: Oxford University Press.

*O'Brien, M., Harris, J., King, R., & O'Brien, T. (2008). Supportive-expressive group therapy for women with metastatic breast cancer: Improving access for Australian women through use of teleconference. *Counselling and Psychotherapy Research, 8,* 28–35.

Osatuke, K., Glick, M. J., Stiles, W. B., Shapiro, D. A., & Barkham, M. (2005). Temporal patterns of improvement in client-centred therapy and cognitive-behaviour therapy. *Counselling Psychology Quarterly, 18,* 95–108.

Paivio, S. C., & Greenberg, L. S. (1995). Resolving "unfinished business": Efficacy of experiential therapy using empty chair dialogue. *Journal of Consulting and Clinical Psychology, 63,* 419–425.

Paivio, S. C., Hall, I. E., Holowaty, K. A. M., Jellis, J. B., & Tran, N. (2001). Imaginal confrontation for resolving child abuse issues. *Psychotherapy Research, 11,* 433–453.

Paivio, S. C., Holowaty, K. A. M., & Hall, I. E. (2004). The influence of therapist adherence and competence on client reprocessing of child abuse memories. *Psychotherapy: Theory, Research, Practice, Training, 41,* 56–58.

Paivio, S. C., Jarry, J. L., Chagigiorgis, H., Hall, I., & Ralston, M. (2010). Efficacy of two versions of emotion-focused therapy for resolving child abuse trauma. *Psychotherapy Research,* 353–366.

Paivio, S. C., & Pascual-Leone, A. (2010). *Emotion-focused therapy for complex trauma: An integrative approach.* Washington, DC: American Psychological Association.

*Papadopoulos, L., Walker, C., & Anthis, L. (2004). Living with vitiligo: A controlled investigation into the effects of group cognitive-behavioural and person-centred therapies. *Dermatology and Psychosomatics, 5,* 172–177.

Pascual-Leone, A. (2009). Dynamic emotional processing in experiential therapy: Two steps forward, one step back. *Journal of Consulting and Clinical Psychology, 77*(1), 113–126. doi:10.1037/a0014488

Pascual-Leone, A., & Greenberg, L. S. (2007). Emotional processing in experiential therapy: Why "the only way out is through." *Journal of Consulting and Clinical Psychology, 75*(6), 875–887.

Perls, F. S., Hefferline, R. F., & Goodman, P. (1951). *Gestalt therapy.* New York, NY: Julian Press.

*Pintér, G. (1993a). A szemelykozpontu pszichoterapia hatekonysaganak vizsgalata I. *Psychiatria Hungarica, 8*(2), 139–152.

*Pintér, G. (1993b). A szemelykozpontu pszichoterapia hatekonysaganak vizsgalata II. *Psychiatria Hungarica, 8*(4), 279–292.

Pos, A. E., Greenberg, L. S., Goldman, R. N., & Korman, L. M. (2003). Emotional processing during experiential treatment of depression. *Journal of Consulting and Clinical Psychology, 71,* 1007–1016.

Pos, A. E., Greenberg, L. S., & Warwar, S. (2010). Testing a model of change for experiential treatment of depression. *Journal of Consulting and Cliinical Psychology, 77,* 1055–1066.

Purton, C. (2004). *Person-centred therapy. The focusing-oriented approach.* Basingstoke, United Kingdom: Palgrave Macmillan.

Ragsdale, K. G., Cox, R. D., Finn, P., & Eisler, R. M. (1996). Effectiveness of short-term specialized inpatient treatment for war-related posttraumatic stress disorder: A role for adventure-based counseling and psychodrama. *Journal of Traumatic Stress, 9,* 269–283.

Rennie, D. L. (1990). Toward a representation of the client's experience of the psychotherapy hour. In G. Lietaer, J. Rombauts, & R. Van Balen (Eds.), *Client-centered and experiential therapy in the nineties* (pp. 155–172). Leuven, Belgium: Leuven University Press.

Rennie, D. L. (1992). Qualitative analysis of the client's experience of psychotherapy: The unfolding of reflexivity. In S. Toukmanian & D. Rennie (Eds.), *Psychotherapy process research: Paradigmatic and narrative approaches* (pp. 211–233). Newbury Park, CA: Sage.

Rennie, D. (1994a). Client's deference in psychotherapy. *Journal of Counseling Psychology, 41*, 427–437.

Rennie, D. (1994b). Clients' accounts of resistance in counselling: A qualitative analysis. *Canadian Journal of Counselling, 28*(1), 1994b, 43–57.

Rennie, D. L., Phillips, J. R., & Quartaro, G. K. (1988). Grounded theory: A promising approach to conceptualization in psychology? *Canadian Psychology, 29*, 139–150.

Rhodes, R. H., Hill, C. E., Thompson, B. J., & Elliott, R. (1994). Client retrospective recall of resolved and unresolved misunderstanding events. *Journal of Counseling Psychology, 41*, 473–483.

Rice, L. N., & Greenberg, L.S. (1984). *Patterns of change. Intensive analysis of psychotherapy process*. New York, NY: Guilford Press.

Rodgers, B. (2002). Investigation into the client at the heart of therapy. *Counselling and Psychotherapy Research, 2*, 185–193.

Rogers, C. R. (1957). The necessary and sufficient conditions of therapeutic personality change. *Journal of Consulting Psychology, 21*, 95–103.

Rogers, C. R. (1959). A theory of therapy, personality and interpersonal relationships as developed in the client-centered framework. In S. Koch (Ed.), *Psychology: A study of science. Vol. III, Formulations of the person and the social context* (pp. 184–256). New York, NY: McGraw Hill.

Rogers, C. R. (1961) *On becoming a person: A therapist's view of psychotherapy*. London, United Kingdom: Constable.

*Rogers, C. R., & Dymond, R. F. (1954). (Eds.). *Psychotherapy and personality change*. Chicago, IL: University of Chicago Press.

Rogers, C. R., Walker, A., & Rablen, R. (1960). Development of a scale to measure process changes in psychotherapy. *Journal of Clinical Psychology, 16*, 79–85.

Rogers, J. L., Howard, K. I., & Vessey, J. T. (1993). Using significance tests to evaluate equivalence between two experimental groups. *Psychological Bulletin, 113*, 553–565.

Sachse, R. (1990). Concrete interventions are crucial: The influence of the therapist's processing proposals on the client's interpersonal exploration in client-centered therapy. In G. Lietaer, J. Rombauts, & R. Van Balen (Eds.), *Client-centered and experiential psychotherapy in the Nineties* (pp. 295–308). Leuven, Belgium: Leuven University Press.

Sachse, R. (1992a). *Zielorientierte Gesprächspsychotherapie*. Göttingen, Germany: Hogrefe.

Sachse, R. (1992b). Differential effects of processing proposals and content references on the explication process of clients with different starting conditions. *Psychotherapy Research, 2*, 235–251.

Sachse, R., & Elliott, R. (2002). Process-outcome research on humanistic therapy variables. In D. J. Cain & J. Seeman (Eds.), Humanistic psychotherapies. *Handbook of research and practice* (pp. 83–116). Washington, DC: APA Books.

Sachse, R., & Maus, C. (1991). *Zielorientiertes Handeln in der Gesprächspsychotherapie*. Stuttgart, Germany: Kohlhammer.

Sachse, R., & Takens, R.J. (2004). *Klärungsprozesse in der Psychotherapie*. Göttingen, Germany: Hogrefe.

Schneider, K. J. (1998). Toward a science of the heart: Romanticism and the revival of psychology. *American Psychologist, 53*, 277–289.

Schnellbacher, J., & Leijssen, M. (2009). The significance of therapist genuineness from the client's perspective. *Journal of Humanistic Psychology, 49*, 207–228.

Schutzmann, K., Schutzmann, M., & Eckert, J. (2010). Wirksamkeit von ambulanter Gesprachspsychotherapie bei Bulimia nervosa: Ergebnisse einer randomisiert-kontrollierten Studie [The efficacy of outpatient client-centered psychotherapy for bulimia nervosa: results of a randomised controlled trial]. *Psychotherapie, Psychosomatik, medizinische Psychologie, 60*, 52–63. doi: 10.1055/s-0029-1234134

Segal, Z. V., Williams, J. M. G., & Teasdale, J. D. (2001). *Mindfulness-based cognitive therapy for depression: A new approach to preventing relapse*. New York, NY: Guilford Press.

*Sellman, J. D., Sullivan, P. F., Dore, G. M., Adamson, S. J., & MacEwan, I. (2001). A randomized controlled trial of motivational enhancement therapy (MET) for mild to moderate alcohol dependence. *Journal of Studies on Alcohol, 62*, 389–396.

*Serok, S., & Levi, N. (1993). Application of gestalt therapy with long-term prison inmates in Israel. *Gestalt Journal, 16*, 105–127.

Serok, S., Rabin, C., & Spitz, Y. (1984). Intensive gestalt group therapy with schizophrenics. *International Journal of Group Psychotherapy, 34*, 431–450.

Serok, S., & Zemet, R. M. (1983). An experiment of gestalt group therapy with hospitalized schizophrenics. *Psychotherapy: Theory, Research & Practice, 20*, 417–424.

*Shaffer, C. S., Shapiro, J., Sank, L. I., & Coghlan, D. J. (1981). Positive changes in depression, anxiety, and assertion following individual and group cognitive behavior therapy intervention. *Cognitive Therapy and Research, 5*(2), 149–157.

Shahar, B., Carlin, E. R., Engle, D. E., Hegde, J., Szepsenwol, O., & Arkowitz, H. (2011), A pilot investigation of emotion-focused two-chair dialogue intervention for self-criticism. *Clinical Psychology & Psychotherapy*. doi: 10.1002/cpp.762

*Shear, K. M., Houck, P., Grenno, C., & Masters, S. (2001). Emotion-focused psychotherapy for patients with panic disorder. *American Journal of Psychiatry, 158*, 1993–1998.

Shear, K. M., Pilkonis, P. A., Cloitre, M., & Leon, A. C. (1994). Cognitive behavioral treatment compared with nonprescriptive treatment of panic disorder. *Archives of General Psychiatry*, *51*, 395–401.

Sicoli, L. A., & Hallberg, E. T. (1998). An analysis of client performance in the two-chair method. *Canadian Journal of Counselling*, *32*, 151–162.

Siegfried, T. (2010, March 27). Odds are, it's wrong: Science fails to face the shortcomings of statistics. *Science News*, 26–29.

Smith, M. L., Glass, G. V., & Miller, T. I. (1980). *The benefits of psychotherapy*. Baltimore, MD: Johns Hopkins University Press.

*Souliere, M. (1995). The differential effects of the empty chair dialogue and cognitive restructuring on the resolution of lingering angry feelings. (Doctoral dissertation, University of Ottawa, 1994). *Dissertation Abstracts International*, *56*, 2342B. (University Microfilms No. AAT NN95979)

Spiegel, D., Bloom, J. R., & Yalom, I. (1981). Group support for patients with metastatic cancer. *Archives of General Psychiatry*, *38*, 527–533.

Spiegel, D., Butler, L. D., Giese-Davis, J., Koopman, C., Miller, E., DiMiceli, S., . . . Kraemer, H. C. (2007). Effects of supportive-expressive group therapy on survival of patients with metastatic breast cancer: A randomized prospective trial. *Cancer*, *110*, 1130–1138. doi: 10.1002/cncr.22890

*Spiegel, D., Morrow, G. R., Classen, C., Raubertas, R., Stott, P. B., Mudaliar, N., . . . Riggs, G. (1999). Group psychotherapy for recently diagnosed breast cancer patients: A multicenter feasibility study. *Psycho-Oncology*, *8*, 482–493.

*Stanley, M. A., Beck, J. G., & Glassco, J. D. (1996). Treatment of generalized anxiety in older adults: A preliminary comparison of cognitive-behavioral and supportive approaches. *Behavior Therapy*, *27*, 565–581.

Steckley, P. L. (2006). An examination of the relationship between clients' attachment experiences, their internal working models of self and others, and therapists' empathy in the outcome of process-experiential and cognitive-behavioural therapies. *Dissertation Abstracts International*, *67*, 2055B.

Steckley, P., & Watson, J. C. (2000, June). *Client attachment styles and psychotherapy outcome in cognitive behavioural and process-experiential psychotherapy*. Paper presented at the 31st Annual Meeting of the Society for Psychotherapy Research Conference, Chicago, Illinois.

Stephen, S., Elliott, R. & Macleod, R. (2011). Person-centred therapy with a client experiencing social anxiety difficulties: A hermeneutic single case efficacy design. *Counselling & Psychotherapy Research*, *11*, 55–66.

*Stice, E., Burton, E., Bearman, S. K., & Rohde, P. (2006). Randomized trial of brief depression prevention program: An elusive search for a psychosocial placebo control condition. *Behaviour Research and Therapy*, *45*, 863–876.

Stice, E., Rohde, P., Gau, J. M., & Wade, E. (2010). Efficacy trial of a brief cognitive-behavioral depression prevention program for high-risk adolescents: Effects at 1- and 2-year follow-up. *Journal of Consulting and Clinical Psychology*, *78*, 856–867.

Stiles, W. B. (2002). Assimilation of problematic experiences. In J. C. Norcross (Ed.), *Psychotherapy relationships that work: Therapist contributions and responsiveness to patients* (pp. 357–365). New York, NY: Oxford University Press.

*Stiles, W. B., Barkham, M., Mellor-Clark, J., & Connell, J. (2008). Effectiveness of cognitive-Behavioural, person-centred, and psychodynamic therapies as practiced in UK primary care routine practice: replication in a larger sample. *Psychological Medicine*, *38*, 677–688.

*Stiles, W. B., Barkham, M., Twigg, E., Mellor-Clark, J. & Cooper, M. (2006). Effectiveness of cognitive-behavioural, person-centred and psychodynamic therapies as practiced in UK national health service settings. *Psychological Medicine*, *36*, 555–566.

Stinckens, N., Lietaer, G., & Leijssen, M. (2002). The inner critic on the move: Analysis of the change process in a case of short-term client-centred/experiential therapy. *Counselling & Psychotherapy Research*, *2*, 40–54.

*Svartberg, M., Seltzer, M. H., Choi, K., & Stiles, T. C. (2001). Cognitive change before, during, and after short-term dynamic and nondirective psychotherapies: A preliminary growth modeling study. *Psychotherapy Research*, *11*, 201–219.

*Svartberg, M., Seltzer, M. H., & Stiles, T. C. (1998). The effects of common and specific factors in short-term anxiety-provoking psychotherapy: A pilot process-outcome study. *The Journal of Nervous and Mental Disease*, *186*, 691–696.

*Szapocznik, J., Feaster, D. J., Mitrani, V. B., Prado, G., Smith, L., Robinson-Batista, C., . . . Robbins, M. S. (2004). Structural ecosystems therapy for HIV-Seropositive African American women: Effects on psychological distress, family hassles, and family support. *Journal of Consulting and Clinical Psychology*, *72*, 288–303.

*Szekely, B., Botwin, D., Eidelman, B. H. Becker, M., Elman, N., & Schemm, R. (1985). Nonpharmacological treatment of menstrual headache: Relaxation-biofeedback behavior therapy and person-centered insight therapy. *Headache*, *26*, 86–92.

Takens, R. J. (2008). Diepgang in het exploratieproces: analyse van de therapeutische interactie. In G. Lietaer, G. Vanaerschot, H. Snijders, & R. J. Takens (Eds.), *Handboek gesprekstherapie. De persoonsgerichte experiëntiële benadering* (pp. 181–203). Utrecht, The Netherlands: De Tijdstroom.

Tarrier, N., Kinney, C., McCarthy, E., Humphreys, L., Wittkowski, A., & Morris, J. (2000). Two-year follow-up of cognitive-behavioral therapy and supportive counseling in the treatment of persistent symptoms in chronic schizophrenia. *Journal of Consulting and Clinical Psychology, 68*, 917–922.

Tarrier, N., Yusupoff, L., Kinney, C., McCarthy, E., Gledhill, A., & Morris, J. (1998). A randomised controlled trial of intensive cognitive behaviour therapy for chronic schizophrenia. *British Medical Journal, 317*, 303–307.

Task Force on Promotion and Dissemination of Psychological Procedures. (1995). Training in and dissemination of empirically-validated psychological treatments: Report and recommendations. *Clinical Psychologist, 48*, 3–23.

Teusch, L. (1990). Positive effects and limitations of client-centered therapy with schizophrenic patients. In G. Lietaer, J. Rombauts, & R. Van Balen (Eds.), *Client-centered and experiential psychotherapy in the nineties* (pp. 637–644). Leuven, Belgium: Leuven University Press.

*Teusch, L., Böhme, H., Finke, J., Gastpar, M., & Skerra, B. (2003). Antidepressant medication and the assimilation of problematic experiences in psychotherapy. *Psychotherapy Research, 13*, 307–322.

Teusch, L., Böhme, H., & Gastpar, M. (1997). The benefit of an insight-oriented and experiential approach on panic and agoraphobia symptoms. *Psychotherapy & Psychosomatics, 66*, 293–301.

Timulak, L. (2007). Identifying core categories of client-identified impact of helpful events in psychotherapy: A qualitative meta-analysis. *Psychotherapy Research, 17*, 310–320.

Timulak, L. (2009). Qualitative meta-analysis: A tool for reviewing qualitative research findings in psychotherapy. *Psychotherapy Research, 19*, 591–600.

Timulak, L. (2010). Significant events in psychotherapy: An update of research findings. *Psychology and Psychotherapy, 83*, 421–447.

Timulak, L., Belicova, A., & Miler, M. (2010). Client identified significant events in a successful therapy case: The link between the significant events and outcome. *Counselling Psychology Quarterly, 23*, 371–386.

Timulak, L., & Creaner, M. (2010). Qualitative meta-analysis of outcomes of person-centred/experiential therapies. In M. Cooper, J. C. Watson, & D. Holledampf (Eds.), *Person-centred and experiential psychotherapies work*. Ross-on-Wye, United Kingdom: PCCS Books.

Timulak, L., & Elliott, R. (2003). Empowerment events in process-experiential psychotherapy of depression: A qualitative analysis. *Psychotherapy Research, 13*, 443–460.

Timulak, L., & Lietaer, G. (2001). Moments of empowerment: A qualitative analysis of positively experienced episodes in brief person-centred counseling. *Counselling & Psychotherapy Research, 1*, 62–73.

Toukmanian, S. G. (1986). A measure of client perceptual processing. In L. Greenberg & W. Pinsof (Eds.), *The psychotherapeutic process: A research handbook* (pp. 107–130). New York, NY: Guilford Press.

Toukmanian, S. G. (1992). Studying the client's perceptual process and their outcomes in psychotherapy. In S. G. Toukmanian & D. L. Rennie, (Eds.), *Psychotherapy process research: paradigmatic and narrative approaches* (pp. 77–107). Newbury Park, CA: Sage.

Toukmanian, S. G., & Gordon, K. M. (2004). *The levels of client perceptual processing (LCPP): A training manual*. Department of Psychology, York University, Toronto.

Toukmanian, S. G., Jadaa, D., & Armstrong, M. S. (2010). Change processes in clients' self-perceptions in experiential psychotherapy. *Person-Centered and Experiential Psychotherapies, 9*, 37–51. doi: 10.1080/14779757.2010.9688503

Traynor, W., Elliott, R., & Cooper, M. (2011). Helpful factors and outcomes in person-centered therapy with clients who experience psychotic processes: Therapists' perspectives. *Person-Centered and Experiential Psychotherapies, 10*, 89–104.

*Truax, C. B. (1962). *A tentative scale for the measurement of depth of intrapersonal exploration*. Wisconsin Psychiatric Institute, University of Wisconsin.

Truax, C. B., & Carkhuff, R. R. (1967). *Towards effective counseling and psychotherapy: Training and practice*. Chicago, IL: Aldine.

*Turner, R. M. (2000). Naturalistic evaluation of dialectical behavior therapy-oriented treatment for borderline personality disorder. *Cognitive and Behavioral Practice, 7*, 413–419.

*Tyson, G. M., & Range, L. M. (1987). Gestalt dialogues as a treatment for mild depression: Time works just as well. *Journal of Clinical Psychology, 43*, 227–231.

Vanaerschot, G., & Lietaer, G. (2007). Therapeutic ingredients in helping session episodes with observer-rated low and high empathic attunements: A content analysis of client and therapist postsession perceptions in three cases. *Psychotherapy Research, 17*, 338–338–352. doi: 10.1080/10503300600650910.

Vanaerschot, G., & Lietaer, G. (2010). Client and therapist postsession perceptions of therapeutic ingredients in helping episodes. A study based on three cases. *Person-Centered & Experiential Psychotherapies, 9*, 205–219. doi: 10.1080/14779757.2010.9689067.

van der Pompe, G., Duivenvoorden, H. J., Antoni, M. H., Visser, A., & Heijnen, C. J. (1997). Effectiveness of a short-term group psychotherapy program on endocrine and immune function in breast cancer patients: An exploratory study. *Journal of Psychosomatic Research, 42*, 453–466.

*Walker, J. G., Johnson, S., Manion, I., & Cloutier, P. (1996). Emotionally focused marital intervention for couples with chronically ill children. *Journal of Consulting and Clinical Psychology, 64*, 1029–1036.

Warwar, S. H. (2003). *Relating emotional processes to outcome in experiential psychotherapy of depression.* Unpublished doctoral dissertation, York University, Toronto, Canada.

Warwar, S. H., & Greenberg, L. S. (2000, June). *Catharsis is not enough: Changes in emotional processing related to psychotherapy outcome.* Paper presented at the International Society for Psychotherapy Research Annual Meeting. Chicago, Illinois.

Warwar, S. H., Greenberg, L. S., & Perepeluk, D. (2003). *Reported in-session emotional experience in therapy.* Paper presented at the annual meeting of the International Society for Psychotherapy Research. Weimar, Germany.

*Washington, O. (1999). Effects of cognitive and experiential group therapy on self-efficacy and perceptions of employability of chemically dependent women. *Issues in Mental Health Nursing, 20*, 181–198.

Washington, O. G. M. (2001). Using brief therapeutic interventions to create change in self-efficacy and personal control of chemically dependent women. *Archives of Psychiatric Nursing, 15*, 32–40.

Watson, J. C., & Bedard, D. L. (2006). Clients' emotional processing in psychotherapy: A comparison between cognitive-behavioral and process-experiential therapies. *Journal of Consulting and Clinical Psychology, 74*, 152–152–159. doi: 10.1037/0022–006X.74.1.152

Watson, J. C., & Geller, S. (2005). An examination of the relations among empathy, unconditional acceptance, positive regard and congruence in both cognitive-behavioral and process-experiential psychotherapy. *Psychotherapy Research, 15*, 25–33.

*Watson, J. C., Goldman, R. N., & Greenberg, L. S. (2007). *Case-studies in the experiential treatment of depression: A comparison of good and bad outcome.* Washington, DC: APA Books.

Watson, J. C., Gordon, L. B., Stermac, L., Kalogerakos, F., & Steckley, P. (2003). Comparing the effectiveness of process-experiential with cognitive-behavioral psychotherapy in the treatment of depression. *Journal of Consulting and Clinical Psychology, 71*, 773–781.

Watson, J. C., Greenberg, L. S., & Lietaer, G. (2010). Relating process to outcome in person-centered and experiential psychotherapies: The role of the relationship conditions and clients' experiencing. In M. Cooper, J. C. Watson & D. Hölldampf (Eds.), *Person-centred and experiential therapies work: A review of the research on counseling, psychotherapy and related practices* (pp. 132–163). Ross-on-Wye, United Kingdom: PCCS Books.

Watson, J. C., McMullen, E. J., Prosser, M. C., & Bedard, D. L. (2011). An examination of the relationships among clients' affect regulation, in-session emotional processing, the working alliance, and outcome. *Psychotherapy Research, 21*, 86–86–96. doi: 10.1080/10503307.2010.518637

Watson, J. C., & Prosser, M. (2007, July). *The relationship of affect regulation to outcome in the treatment of depression.* Paper presented to the 22nd Annual Conference of the Society for the Exploration of Psychotherapy Integration, Lisbon, Portugal.

Watson, J., & Rennie, D. (1994). Qualitative analysis of clients' subjective experience of significant moments during the exploration of problematic reactions. *Journal of Counseling Psychology, 41*, 500–509.

Watson, J. C., Schein, J., & McMullen, E. (2010). An examination of clients' in-session changes and their relationship to the working alliance and outcome. *Psychotherapy Research, 4*, 1–10. doi: 10.1080/10503300903311285

*Weston, T. (2005). *The clinical effectiveness of the person-centred psychotherapies: A preliminary inquiry including literature review, CORE-OM questionnaires, client session recordings and client feedback.* Unpublished Masters dissertation. University of East Anglia.

*Weston, T. (2008). *The clinical effectiveness of person-centred psychotherapies: The impact of the therapeutic relationship.* Unpublished draft doctoral dissertation, University of East Anglia.

Westra, H. A., & Dozois, D. J. A. (2006). Preparing clients for cognitive behavioral therapy: A randomized pilot study of motivational interviewing for anxiety. *Cognitive Therapy and Research, 30*, 481–498.

*Wetzel, H., Szegedi, A., Scheurich, A., Lörch, B., Singer, P., Schläfke, D., . . . Hautzinger, M. (2004). Combination treatment with nefazodone and cognitive-behavioral therapy for relapse prevention in alcohol-dependent men: A randomized controlled study. *Journal of Clinical Psychiatry, 65*, 1406–1413.

Whelton, W. J., & Greenberg, L. S. (2000). The self as a singular multiplicity: A process experiential perspective. In J. Muran (Ed.), *The self in psychotherapy.* Washington, DC: American Psychological Association.

*Wickberg, B., & Hwang, C. P. (1996). Counselling of postnatal depression: A controlled study on a population based Swedish sample. *Journal of Affective Disorders, 39*, 209–216.

*Wilhelm, S., Deckersbach, T., Coffey, B. J., Bohne, A., Peterson, A. L., & Baer, L. (2003). Habit reversal versus supportive psychotherapy for Tourette's disorder: A randomized controlled trial. *American Journal of Psychiatry, 160*, 1175–1177.

Wilson, D. B., & Lipsey, M. W. (2001). *Practical meta-analysis.* Thousand Oaks, CA: Sage.

*Wilson, G. L. (1990). Psychotherapy with depressed incarcerated felons: A comparative evaluation of treatments. *Psychological Reports, 67*, 1027–1041.

Wnuk, S. (2009). *Treatment development and evaluation of emotion-focused group therapy for women with symptoms of bulimia nervosa*. Unpublished Doctoral Dissertation, York University, Toronto, Canada.

Woldarsky, C. (2011). *Forgiveness in emotion-focused couples therapy: Relating process to outcome*. Unpublished PhD dissertation, York University, Toronto, Canada.

Wolfe, B., & Sigl, P. (1998). Experiential psychotherapy of the anxiety disorders. In L. S. Greenberg, J. C. Watson, & G. Lietaer (Eds.), *Handbook of experiential psychotherapy* (pp. 272–294). New York, NY: Guilford Press.

Yalom, I. D. (1980). *Existential psychotherapy*. New York, NY: Basic Books.

PART IV

RESEARCH
ON APPLICATIONS
IN SPECIAL GROUPS
AND SETTINGS

●

CHAPTER 14

PSYCHOTHERAPY FOR CHILDREN AND ADOLESCENTS

JOHN R. WEISZ, MEI YI NG, CHRISTOPHER RUTT, NANCY LAU, AND SARA MASLAND

Efforts to help children and adolescents (henceforth "youth") overcome behavioral and emotional problems are certainly as old as parenthood, but help in the form of psychotherapy may be traced back only about a century (Freedheim, Freudenberger, & Kessler, 1992). The work of Sigmund Freud (1856–1939) was pivotal, including his notion that even young children can be appropriate candidates for therapy. Classic steps in the birth of psychotherapy for young people included Freud's consultation with the father of "Little Hans" and his psychoanalysis of his own daughter, Anna (1895–1982), who became a prominent child analyst in her own right.

The rapid growth of youth psychotherapy was fueled by Freud's intellectual heirs and by models and methods very different from those of psychoanalysis, including an approach called "behaviorism." Mary Cover Jones (1924a, 1924b), for example, used modeling and "direct conditioning" to help a 2-year-old boy overcome his fear of a white rabbit, thus helping launch a behavioral revolution in therapy. Psychoanalytic and behavioral therapies for young people developed alongside other treatments sparked by the grand theories of psychology and the humanistic tradition. Later Beck and colleagues helped develop *cognitive therapy* (e.g., Beck, 1970), and Meichenbaum and colleagues (e.g., Meichenbaum & Goodman, 1971) helped launch *cognitive-behavioral therapy* (CBT) for children. By the late 20th century, youth psychotherapy had mushroomed dramatically. Indeed, Kazdin

(2000) identified 551 different named therapies used with children and adolescents. Even this large number greatly underestimates the array of approaches used in practice, with hundreds of thousands of practitioners eclectically blending their different training backgrounds and theoretical orientations to form distinctive approaches unlike those of any other practitioner.

In this chapter we describe the field of youth psychotherapy that has grown up over the past century, emphasizing what research has shown and what remains to be learned. We begin by noting some of the factors that make psychotherapy different with youths than with adults. We describe strategies for studying youth psychotherapy and its effects, including meta-analytic approaches to synthesizing findings across multiple studies. In a section on evidence-based youth psychotherapies, we note how these are defined and identify the treatments identified as evidence-based in a recent series of systematic reviews. This is followed by a section on understanding how, with whom, and under what conditions the evidence-based therapies work—which requires a focus on the study of mediation and moderation. This is followed by a discussion of family factors in youth psychotherapy and efforts to test youth therapies with various population groups that are at special risk. We then view the field from the perspective of a friendly critic, noting limitations of current approaches and suggesting a series of strategies for strengthening youth treatments.

Psychotherapy With Youths Versus Adults: Some Key Differences

Although adult and youth psychotherapy have overlapping ancestry and are similar in many ways, important differences warrant attention. First, most treatment of boys and girls is prompted by parents, teachers, or other adults. It is adults who typically seek professional help, initiate the youth therapy, identify some or all of the referral concerns and treatment goals, pay the bills (or obtain the insurance coverage), and make the final decision as to how long therapy will last. Young people do participate as the "patients," but the concerns they identify may not agree with those of their parents or other adults, and evidence suggest that they exert less influence than these adults on the focus and direction of therapy (Hawley & Weisz, 2003; Yeh & Weisz, 2001). With the impetus for youth psychotherapy coming mainly from adults, and adults influencing the goals of that therapy more than the youths, perhaps it is not surprising that youngsters often begin therapy with relatively low motivation for treatment. This can mean that a large component of youth therapy is engagement—that is, efforts by the therapist to build rapport, motivation, and a good therapeutic alliance with the young person.

Youth and adult psychotherapy also differ in the information sources available to therapists for planning treatment and tracking how it is going. Therapists working with young people almost invariably deal with information from their young patient as well as adults in the youngster's life—parents and teachers, for example. These different informants typically do not show very high concordance in the youth problems and strengths they report (Achenbach, McConaughy, & Howell, 1987; De Los Reyes, Goodman, Kliewer, & Reid-Quiñones, 2010; Richters, 1992). The accuracy of youth self-reports is limited by constraints on self-awareness and expressive and language ability. The accuracy of adult reports may be limited by lack of opportunity to observe youths in multiple settings, the effects of parents' own life stresses or mental health problems (see e.g., Kazdin & Weisz, 1998), and even by undetected agendas (e.g., high problem levels reported by adults who are desperate for help, or low levels reported by those who fear child protective services). Additionally, adults' reports of youths' behavior and reasons for referral can reflect the values, standards, practices, and social ideals of their cultural reference group (see Weisz, McCarty, Eastman, Chaiyasit, & Suwanlert, 1997). In sum, because youth therapy involves multiple stakeholders, each with different motivations, perceptions, and goals, assessing treatment needs, progress, and outcomes via information from these different stakeholders can magnify complexity in a way that appears less likely with adults.

Finally, boys and girls, much more than adults, are dependent on—and thus captives of—their externally engineered environments. Their family, neighborhood, and school contexts are largely selected and shaped by others, and in fact the "pathology" being treated may sometimes reside less in the youth than in the environment, which the youngster can neither escape nor alter significantly. The powerful impact of such factors as who lives in the home, how these people interact, what financial resources they have, and whether outside agencies (e.g., for child protection) are involved, may limit the impact of interventions that focus on the youth as solo or primary participant, highlighting a need to involve key members of the youth's social context in intervention (see, e.g., Henggeler, Schoenwald, Borduin, Rowland, & Cunningham, 1998), and sometimes making case management as salient as psychotherapy.

Studying the Effects of Youth Psychotherapy

Given the differences noted between youth and adult psychotherapy, it should be no surprise that separate treatments—albeit heavily influenced by adult approaches—have evolved for young people, together with a separate body of treatment outcome research. In contrast to the acceleration of youth psychotherapy practice over the past century, research tests of youth therapies took shape quite slowly, and only after a rough start. In 1952, Eysenck published a classic review of adult psychotherapy studies, raising serious doubts about whether therapy was effective. A few years later, Levitt (1957, 1963) reviewed treatment outcome research that included young people and concluded that rates of improvement in the youth samples were about the same with or without treatment. The studies available for those landmark reviews were irregular in quality. Treatment outcome research has grown more rigorous since those early days, treatments have evolved, and the number of youth outcome studies has increased dramatically, particularly in recent decades (see Silverman & Hinshaw, 2008;

Weisz & Kazdin, 2010). The focus of youth treatment research has also sharpened over time, with a shift from studies of unspecified "treatment" for often vaguely specified youth problems to tests of specific, well-documented therapies for specific problems and disorders.

The benefit derived from youth treatment is often assessed in randomized controlled trials (RCTs), and these RCTs are often pooled and synthesized in meta-analyses (see later). Multiple baseline designs, ABAB (sometimes called *reversal*) designs, and other single-subject approaches are useful, as well. These approaches (well described in Barlow, Nock, & Hersen, 2009; Kazdin, 2011) have been used in a variety of youth treatment situations—such as programs for attention-deficit/hyperactivity disorder (ADHD; see, e.g., Pelham et al., 2010), studies where an entire classroom needs to receive an intervention (see, e.g., Wurtele & Drabman, 1984), and cases (sometimes involving rare conditions) where only one or two youngsters will be treated (e.g., McGrath, Dorsett, Calhoun, & Drabman, 1987; Tarnowski, Rosen, McGrath, & Drabman, 1987). These alternative outcome assessment designs have generated a rich body of outcome data and some useful meta-analyses, for example on treatment approaches for disruptive behavior (Chen & Ma, 2007), autism spectrum disorders (Campbell, 2003), and social skill deficits (Mathur, Kavale, Quinn, Forness, & Rutherford, 1998). However, meta-analyses in the field have most often focused on RCTs.

Meta-Analytic Findings

Among meta-analyses of the RCTs, a few have synthesized findings from particularly broad arrays of youth treatments and forms of dysfunction. In four particularly broad-based meta-analyses, encompassing more than 350 outcome studies, the meta-analysts imposed few limits on the types of treated problems or types of intervention that would be included. In the earliest of the four, Casey and Berman (1985) focused on studies with children age 12 and younger. Weisz, Weiss, Alicke, and Klotz (1987) included studies with 4- to 18-year-olds. Kazdin, Bass, Ayers, and Rodgers (1990) synthesized findings of studies with 4- to 18-year-olds. And Weisz, Weiss, Han, Granger, and Morton (1995) included studies spanning ages 2 to 18. Mean effect sizes found in these four meta-analyses are shown in Figure 14.1, with a comparison to two widely cited meta-analyses of predominantly

adult psychotherapy (Shapiro & Shapiro, 1982; Smith & Glass, 1977). As the figure shows, the youth treatment effect sizes in Casey and Berman (1985), Weisz et al. (1987), Kazdin et al. (1990), and Weisz et al. (1995) fall roughly within the range of what has been found for adult therapy, and on average within the range of what Cohen (1988) suggests as benchmarks for medium (i.e., .5) to large (.8) effects. The last bar on the right in Figure 14.1 is discussed later in this chapter.

In addition to overall mean effects, two other youth meta-analytic findings sharpen the picture. First, findings (in Weisz et al., 1987; Weisz et al., 1995) indicate that effects measured immediately after treatment are quite similar to effects measured at follow-up assessments, averaging 5 to 6 months after treatment termination. This suggests that youth treatment benefit may have reasonable holding power. Second, findings on treatment specificity have shown that effects are larger for the specific problems targeted in treatment than for related problems that were not specifically addressed (Weisz et al., 1995, p. 460). This suggests that the tested therapies are not merely producing global "feeling better all over" effects, but instead are rather precise in impacting the forms of dysfunction they are designed to treat.

Although these findings suggest certain strengths of youth psychotherapies, meta-analysis can also be used to highlight challenges and critical questions for the field—for example, identifying problems and disorders for which youth treatment effects are modest, suggesting a need to strengthen interventions. Psychotherapies for youth depression, for example, appear to show more modest effects, on average, than treatments for a number of other youth problems and disorders (see Weisz, McCarty, & Valeri, 2006). Meta-analysis has also been used to evaluate the benefits of "evidence-based" psychotherapies, to which we now turn.

Identifying "Evidence-Based Psychotherapies"

As evidence accumulated over time showing beneficial effects of well-documented (typically manual-guided) psychotherapies for youths, adults, couples, and families, efforts were launched to identify the specific therapies sufficiently well-supported to be considered "empirically validated" or "evidence-based." Various task forces and review teams were formed—notably the APA Division 12 Task Force on Promotion

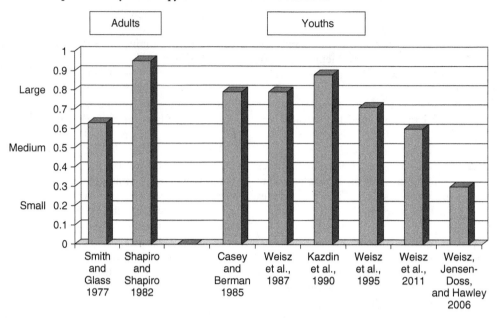

FIGURE 14.1 Mean effect sizes found in two broad-based meta-analyses of adult psychotherapy effects (Shapiro & Shapiro, 1982; Smith & Glass, 1977); four broad-based meta-analyses of youth psychotherapy effects (Casey & Berman, 1985; Kazdin et al., 1990; Weisz et al., 1987; Weisz et al., 1995); and the Weisz, Jensen-Doss, and Hawley (2006) meta-analysis of RCTs comparing evidence-based youth psychotherapies to usual care. (Reprinted with permission from John R. Weisz.)

and Dissemination of Psychological Procedures, led by Dianne Chambless (see e.g., Chambless et al., 1998)—to distill the evidence from outcome studies and identify therapies that reached threshold for different levels of empirical support. Building on this work, experts in youth psychotherapy have conducted systematic literature reviews, in some cases including meta-analytic findings, to compile reports on evidence-based psychotherapies (EBPs) for young people (see Lonigan, Elbert, & Johnson, 1998; Silverman & Hinshaw, 2008). In the most recent report, edited by Silverman and Hinshaw (2008), reviewers identified psychotherapies that met criteria for status as *well-established* (e.g., two good group-design experiments by different research teams in two different settings, showing the treatment to be "superior to pill, psychological placebo, or another treatment"), *probably efficacious* (e.g., "at least two good experiments showing the treatment is superior . . . to a wait-list control group"), *possibly efficacious* (e.g., "At least one 'good' study showing the treatment to be efficacious in the absence of conflicting evidence"), or *experimental* ("not yet tested in trials meeting task force criteria").

The reviewers in this 2008 report identified dozens of youth psychotherapies as either *well-established* or *probably efficacious*, spanning problem areas including early autism, anorexia nervosa, depression, anxiety disorders, ADHD, disruptive behavior problems and disorders, and substance abuse. Taken together, the reviews report a bumper crop of tested treatments, with more abundant lists in some treatment domains (e.g., conduct problems and anxiety) and more limited options in others (e.g., autism and eating disorders). Table 14.1 shows the treatments identified by the reviewers in the Silverman–Hinshaw (2008) special issue at the two highest levels of empirical support for various youth mental health problems and disorders.

Specific Evidence-Based Treatments Identified as "Well-Established" and "Probably Efficacious"

As Table 14.1 shows, interventions for several forms of youth dysfunction were been rated *probably efficacious* or *well-established* by the reviewers. For purposes of this chapter, we refer to these

TABLE 14.1 Youth Psychotherapies Identified as "Well-Established" or "Probably Efficacious"[1,2]

Problem/Disorder Category	Well-Established Therapies	Probably Efficacious Therapies
Early autism (Rogers & Vismara, 2008)	Lovaas model: Intensive behavioral intervention	Pivotal response treatment
Eating disorders in adolescence (Keel & Haedt, 2008)	Family therapy for anorexia nervosa	None
Depression (David-Ferdon & Kaslow, 2008)	CBT for children CBT for adolescents Interpersonal psychotherapy for adolescents	Behavior therapy for children
Phobic and anxiety disorders (Silverman, Pina, & Viswesvaran, 2008)	None	Group CBT Group CBT for social phobia Group CBT with parents Individual CBT Social effectiveness training for social phobia
Obsessive-compulsive disorder (Barrett, Farrell, Pina, Peris, & Piacentini, 2008)	None	Individual exposure-based CBT
Youths exposed to traumatic events (Silverman, Ortiz, et al., 2008)	Trauma-focused CBT	School-based group CBT
Attention-deficit/hyperactivity disorder (Pelham & Fabiano, 2008)	Behavioral classroom management Behavioral parent training Intensive peer-focused Behavioral interventions in recreational settings	None
Disruptive behavior (Eyberg, Nelson, & Boggs, 2008)	Parent management training Oregon model	Anger control training Group assertive training Helping the noncompliant child Incredible years parent training Incredible years child training Multidimensional treatment foster care Multisystemic therapy Parent–child interaction therapy Positive parenting program-standard Positive parenting program-enhanced Problem-solving skills training (PSST) PSST + practice PSST + parent management training Rational-emotive mental health program

(continued)

TABLE 14.1 *(Continued)*

Problem/Disorder Category	Well-Established Therapies	Probably Efficacious Therapies
Adolescent substance abuse (Waldron & Turner, 2008)	Functional family therapy Group CBT Individual CBT Multidimensional family therapy	Behavioral family therapy Brief strategic family therapy Multisystemic therapy

[1]From "Evidence-Based Psychosocial Treatments for Children and Adolescents: A Ten-Year Update." *Journal of Clinical Child and Adolescent Psychology*, *37*, 1–262.
[2]This table shows classifications for broad forms of psychotherapy (e.g., cognitive-behavioral therapy [CBT]); some reports in the special issue of the journal also classified specific treatment subtypes (e.g., group CBT for children, individual adolescent CBT plus parent/family component), which are not included in the table, given space limitations.

interventions in Table 14.1 as *evidence-based psychotherapies* (EBPs) for youth.

Autism

The only autism treatment rated as a well-established EBP in the review by Rogers and Vismara (2008) was Ivar Lovaas's model of early intensive behavioral intervention (EIBI; Lovaas, 1987; Smith, 2010), which involves individual discreet trials training (30 hours/week or more) to build, then scaffold, an array of specific core skills in such domains as language, self-help, and social interaction. Therapists provide treatment and train parents to conduct the intervention at home. Pivotal Response Training (PRT; Koegel, Koegel, Vernon, & Brookman-Frazee, 2010), rated probably efficacious, uses core skills of the Lovaas model but with an expanded emphasis on intervention in the child's natural environment and finding ways to boost motivation for learning (e.g., by using activities the youngster chooses and by identifying natural reinforcers). The treatment focuses on teaching communication, self-help, and academic, recreational, and social skills; parent training is a key component in reaching these goals.

Eating Disorders

Only one treatment for eating disorders was identified as an EBP by Keel and Haedt (2008). This was family therapy for anorexia nervosa, in particular the Maudsley model (Lock, Le Grange, Agras, & Dare, 2001). This model focuses on (a) "refeeding the client," a process in which family members work to return the young client to more normal eating behavior; (b) negotiating improved relationships in areas that impact eating behavior [e.g., if the family uses deceit to avoid conflict *and* the youth hides bingeing through deceit, then therapy focuses on alternatives to deceit]; and (c) termination, which includes ways of sustaining healthy intrafamily relationships, appropriate boundaries, and increased youth autonomy. Keel and Haedt (2008) found no EBPs for bulimia nervosa in adolescents, but they noted that CBT (e.g., addressing distorted cognitions about body shape and size, using behavioral procedures to structure healthy eating habits, and using behavioral exposure to build resistance to triggers that spark cycles of binge-ing and overcompensation) is a well-established treatment for bulimia in samples of young adults and older adolescents. A challenge in the eating domain is the array of different forms that eating disorders can take. Symptomatic of the problem is the fact that the most prevalent of all the eating disorder categories is "not otherwise specified." Thus, even with effective treatments established for anorexia and bulimia, significant work will remain to encompass the full spectrum of dysfunctional eating behavior.

Depression

David-Ferdon and Kaslow (2008) placed two broad approaches to depression treatment—that is, Interpersonal Psychotherapy for Adolescents (IPT-A; Mufson, Weissman, Moreau, & Garfinkel, 1999) and CBT—within the upper two categories of empirical support. IPT-A focuses therapeutic attention on interpersonal issues that are common among adolescents, such as changes in the parent–teen relationship as roles shift; the intervention is designed to help adolescents deal with their difficulties in relation to role transitions and disputes, grief, and interpersonal deficits; an important goal is to help the adolescents develop effective strategies for addressing the difficulties. Although CBT has varied in specific contents across various treatment trials, it typically includes such core components as identifying and scheduling mood-elevating activities, identifying and modifying inappropriately negative cognitions, relaxation training, and learning and practicing problem-solving skills. An approach deemed "behavior therapy" was included among the probably efficacious EBPs for youths (e.g., Kahn, Kehle, Jenson, & Clark, 1990); the contents resembled CBT in most respects.

Anxiety Disorders

For phobic and anxiety disorders in youth (reviewed by Silverman, Pina, & Viswesvaran, 2008), the most extensively tested psychotherapies are the CBTs, which blend graduated exposure to feared stimuli with identification and modification of distorted cognitions that can stimulate and sustain unreasonable fears. Several forms of CBT were rated as EBPs. These included individual youth CBT, group CBT, and group CBT with parents. Silverman, Pina, et al. (2008) also classified Social Effectiveness Therapy for Children (Beidel, Turner, & Morris, 2000) as an EBP. This treatment, designed for social phobia, includes group sessions for the youngsters in treatment, in vivo exposure sessions (including practice interacting with nonanxious peers), and work with parents to help them reward their children's progress toward less anxious behavior in social situations.

In a complementary review, focused only on obsessive-compulsive disorder (OCD), Barrett, Farrell, Pina, Peris, and Piacentini (2008) identified a single EBP: individual exposure-based CBT. The core component is exposure and response prevention (ERP): Youths are repeatedly exposed to stimuli that trigger obsessive fears with the mandate not to engage in the compulsive behavior typically prompted by those fears. Over time, across repeated exposures, obsession-prompted anxiety is thought to dissipate via autonomic habituation. Cognition is considered central, as well, as the youths learn that feared consequences of refraining from the compulsive rituals do not actually materialize.

Finally, focusing on treatment of youths exposed to traumatic events, Silverman, Ortiz, et al. (2008) identified trauma-focused CBT (TF-CBT; Cohen, Mannarino, & Deblinger, 2010) as an EBP. This treatment, designed for youngsters who have experienced sexual abuse and other forms of maltreatment, uses core components of CBT for anxiety, but with important additions tailored to fit the situations in which youngsters

have experienced trauma. These include safety planning (to reduce future environmental risk) and the use of a "trauma narrative," in which young people describe, in writing, their traumatic experiences. The narrative is first created in draft form, then read repeatedly in the presence of the therapist, as a form of exposure therapy. Distorted cognitions are addressed by modifying parts of the narrative—for example, by altering inappropriate self-blaming statements. Caregivers participate in the process, including by joining therapist and youth at later readings of the narrative and offering support for the youth's courage in sharing the story. Silverman, Ortiz, et al. (2008) also identified school-based group CBT (Kataoka et al., 2003; Stein et al., 2003) as an EBP. This treatment, designed for youths who have experienced trauma via exposure to community violence, includes psychoeducation, cognitive and coping skills training, social skills training, and graduated exposures in the form of writing and/or drawing activities.

Attention-Deficit/Hyperactivity Disorder

Pelham and Fabiano (2008) identified three treatments for ADHD as well-established. One was behavioral parent training, in which parents are taught a set of techniques (e.g., clear instructions, differential attention for desired versus undesired behavior, use of praise and reward, time-out) for effective behavior management. A second was behavioral contingency management in classrooms. The third was intensive peer-focused behavioral interventions in recreational settings (e.g., summer day camps). The model program of this type is Pelham's Summer Treatment Program (Pelham et al., 2010), in which youngsters are immersed in sports, academic, and social skill-building activities, all within the context of carefully-structured behavioral contingencies, and complemented by behavioral training and consultation with caregivers. Significantly, Pelham and Fabiano (2008) did not find empirical support for cognitive-behavioral or nonbehavioral treatments for ADHD youths.

Conduct-Related Problems and Disorders (Disruptive Behaviors)

In their review focused on disruptive behavior, Eyberg, Nelson, and Boggs (2008) identified a remarkable 16 EBPs. These included behavioral parent-training programs, some emphasizing parent management training (Forgatch & Patterson,

2010; Kazdin, 2010), some emphasizing real-time coaching during parent–child interaction sessions (e.g., McMahon & Forehand, 2003; Zisser & Eyberg, 2010), and one involving parent training at different levels of intensity delivered within a public health dissemination framework (Sanders & Murphy-Brennan, 2010). A video-guided approach developed by Webster-Stratton and colleagues (e.g., Webster-Stratton & Reid, 2010) includes programs for behavioral training with parents in groups and problem-solving and social skills training with children (ages 3 to 8) in groups; in these programs, shown to be beneficial independently and in combination, participants view and discuss video clips illustrating effective and ineffective strategies and apply what they learn to their own behavior. Other EBPs for conduct problems include cognitive and behavioral training programs to enhance anger management (Lochman, Boxmeyer, Powell, Barry, & Pardini, 2010), problem-solving skill (Kazdin, 2010), and appropriately assertive social behavior (Huey & Rank, 1984), as well as a school-based program, based on rational-emotive theory, designed to reduce disruptive and disobedient behavior by helping youths learn to make accurate cognitive appraisals of self and social situations (Block, 1978).

Finally, two EBPs blend behavioral training for caregivers with methods for engaging others in the youth's social system. These include the extensively studied Multisystemic Therapy (MST; Henggeler & Schaeffer, 2010), developed originally for delinquent youths but extended to treatment of other forms of youth dysfunction (e.g., sexual offending, suicidal behavior), and Multidimensional Treatment Foster Care (MTFC; Smith & Chamberlain, 2010), designed to provide effective foster care for disruptive youths in the child welfare system. Both MST and MTFC are discussed in greater detail later in this chapter.

Adolescent Substance Abuse

EBPs for adolescent substance abuse have focused most heavily on alcohol and marijuana use. For these and other substances, Waldron and Turner (2008) identified three EBPs that use a blend of behavioral methods, family systems perspectives, and outreach to systems outside the family. One of these, functional family therapy (FFT; Alexander & Parsons, 1982; Sexton, 2010), combines reliance on core behavioral techniques and a family systems orientation in an effort to

establish new patterns of family interaction, and therapists work with external systems such as schools and probation departments to maximize generalization in the community. In addition, both individual and group CBT approaches (see Waldron & Kaminer, 2004) were identified as EBPs. In general, these combine an emphasis on identifying and modifying distorted cognitions with an emphasis on behavioral coping skills needed to avoid substance use (e.g., coping with cravings, refusal in the face of social pressure, avoiding situations where substance use might be likely).

Understanding How, With Whom, and Under What Conditions Treatments Work

Identifying youth EBPs can be useful in a number of ways. The process can prompt detailed reviews of the evidence base, nudging experts in the field into periodic self-study and encouraging a kind of "taking stock" of what has been learned about how to help youths and families deal with dysfunction in various forms. Identifying efficacious treatments can also serve as a springboard, encouraging an understanding of the treatments that goes deeper than just finding out that they "work." Logical next questions can include, for example, *how* (i.e., through what processes) the treatments work, *with whom* they work, and *under what conditions* they work—questions to which we turn next (see also Chapter 2, this volume, for an overview of mediators and moderators).

Mediators and Mechanisms of Change

Ultimately, understanding *how* a treatment works requires identifying *mechanisms of change* (also known as *mechanisms of action*), the specific processes through which the treatment produces outcomes. A sound understanding of these mechanisms could help treatment developers strengthen the active ingredients of psychotherapy and reduce or eliminate inactive components, thereby increasing efficacy, efficiency, and cost-effectiveness of the therapy (Kraemer, Wilson, Fairburn, & Agras, 2002). A useful first step in identifying change mechanisms is testing whether a particular variable is a *mediator* of treatment outcome in a RCT, that is, an intermediate variable evident during treatment that statistically accounts for the treatment-outcome relationship

(Kazdin, 2007; Kraemer et al., 2002; Weersing & Weisz, 2002b).

Moderators of Treatment Outcome

In addition, researchers try to understand *with whom* treatments work and *under what conditions* they work, by studying *moderators* of treatment outcome. In the context of an RCT, a moderator is a variable present prior to randomization that interacts with treatment condition; that is, the effects of that treatment on outcome depend on the level of the moderator (Kraemer et al., 2002). Identifying treatment moderators can inform efforts to establish the boundaries of treatment benefit. For example, identifying client characteristics that moderate treatment effects can help investigators learn which groups benefit most, and least, from various treatments (Kraemer et al., 2002), and this information can be used to guide decisions about which treatments to employ with which groups, so as to optimize the effects of psychotherapy.

Mediators and Moderators Identified in Studies of Evidence-Based Psychotherapies

In the following sections, we review examples of findings on mediators and moderators of youth EBPs derived from treatment outcome studies. We focused only on those treatments identified as well-established and probably efficacious psychotherapies, as discussed in the previous section and shown in Table 14.1, and on treatment rather than prevention studies (i.e., the sample has to have elevated symptoms of a disorder to be recruited into the treatment study). Because a larger number of moderators have been identified in individual trials of youth therapies, we focused on the most robust ones, and where possible those that reach significance in meta-analyses. We limited our review of moderators to meta-analyses of randomized trials when available; otherwise, we extended our review of moderators to meta-analyses that include both randomized and nonrandomized trials and to individual RCTs. In the meta-analyses reviewed, we focused on moderators of between-group (treatment versus control) effect sizes rather than moderators of pre- to posttreatment effect sizes because the former type of moderator is conceptually similar to moderators in an individual RCT, whereas the latter type of moderator is more similar to predictors in an individual RCT.

Mediators and Moderators of EBPs for Autism

We did not find any research examining mediation of the effects of EIBI or PRT. The absence of studies examining mediation of EBPs for autism may be due in part to the small number of RCTs in this area and to the fact that the low prevalence rate of the condition makes it difficult to obtain the large study samples needed for properly-powered mediation testing. Two promising candidates—social initiations (i.e., behaviors aimed at seeking help, attention, or social interaction) and peer social avoidance—were identified by Rogers and Vismara (2008) as targets for future research on mediation in autism treatment.

Several moderators of EIBI or similar early behavioral treatments have been identified. Consistent with expectations, several characteristics of the treatment including higher treatment intensity, longer treatment duration, and the presence of a parent training component were associated with significantly larger between-group effect sizes in a meta-analysis that included randomized and nonrandomized trials (Makrygianni & Reed, 2010). Only one characteristic of the sample emerged as a significant moderator in the same meta-analysis; higher baseline adaptive functioning was associated with larger between-group effect sizes. Interestingly, higher baseline intellectual and language abilities did not moderate treatment effects (Makrygianni & Reed, 2010). The association between younger age and larger treatment effects approached significance (Makrygianni & Reed, 2010); the failure to reach significance may have been due to a ceiling effect because a mean sample age of 54 months or younger at baseline was an inclusion criterion in this meta-analysis. Makrygianni and Reed (2010) observed that studies with mean child age of 35 months or younger and treatment intensity of more than 25 weeks seemed to have larger pre-post effect sizes, but they did not subject this observation to a statistical test. We did not find any studies examining moderators of PRT, but research (Sherer & Schreibman, 2005) on behavioral profiles of responders and nonresponders to PRT may point to promising candidate moderators for future study. Clinical practice implications are limited thus far, given the small number of significant findings, but EIBI moderator evidence does suggest that better treatment outcomes for early intervention are associated with higher treatment intensity and longer duration, plus inclusion of parent training.

Mediators and Moderators of EBPs for Eating Disorders

A recent study (Le Grange et al., 2012) tested six candidate mediators of the effects of family therapy, compared to adolescent-focused therapy, on rates of remission among adolescents with anorexia nervosa. None of the candidates—changes in weight, restraint in eating, depressive symptoms, self-esteem, self-efficacy, and parent self-efficacy after 4 weeks of treatment—were significant treatment mediators. The mediators were tested separately in two subgroups based on a median split of the adolescents' baseline severity of eating-related obsessions and compulsions (because this was a significant moderator), which may have limited the power to detect significant mediation, according to Le Grange and colleagues (2012).

We found a few moderators of family therapy effects for adolescent anorexia in individual RCTs, but not in meta-analyses. Eating- and weight-related obsessions and compulsions were significant moderators of treatment outcome in two RCTs. Adolescents with more severe obsessions and compulsions benefited more from a year-long course of family therapy compared to adolescent-focused therapy of the same duration (Le Grange et al., 2012), and compared to a shorter 6-month course of family therapy (Lock, Agras, Bryson, & Kraemer, 2005), even though the treatments worked equally well for the whole sample. Adolescents with more severe eating disorder symptoms also benefited more from year-long family therapy than adolescent-focused therapy (Le Grange et al., 2012). Interestingly, other measures of baseline psychopathology (e.g., body mass index, comorbidity, internalizing symptoms) did not moderate treatment effects (Le Grange et al., 2012; Lock et al., 2005). These findings imply that adolescents with more severe psychopathology specific to eating disorders would respond best to a year-long course of family therapy, but that those with milder eating disorder psychopathology may respond well to family therapy (year-long or 6-month) or adolescent-focused therapy.

There are mixed findings on whether intact family status and parental Expressed Emotion (EE; Hooley & Parker, 2006)—critical, hostile, and emotionally overinvolved attitudes toward the patient by close family members—moderate family therapy outcomes for adolescent anorexia nervosa. Adolescents from nonintact families benefited more from the year-long course than the 6-month course of family therapy in one study (Lock et al., 2005), but benefited equally from family therapy and adolescent-focused therapy when both treatments lasted a year. This suggests that adolescents from nonintact families may simply need longer treatment, regardless of whether the treatment was focused on the family or on the adolescent. In addition, adolescents whose mothers displayed higher levels of *critical* EE (i.e., made three or more criticisms in a structured interview) responded significantly better to separated family therapy (i.e., adolescent and parents seen separately) than to conjoint family therapy (i.e., adolescent and parents seen together), whereas adolescents whose mothers displayed lower levels of critical EE (i.e., fewer than three criticisms) responded equally well to both kinds of family therapy at posttreatment and at 5-year follow-up (Eisler et al., 2000; Eisler, Simic, Russell, & Dare, 2007). The authors suggested that maternal criticism during treatment sessions may trigger feelings of guilt and blame, thereby attenuating treatment effects. However, EE did not significantly moderate outcome when family therapy was compared to adolescent-focused therapy in another RCT, possibly because separated family therapy targets the reduction of parental criticism whereas adolescent-focused therapy targets increases in the adolescent's autonomy (Le Grange et al., 2012). Implications for clinical practice with high EE families are to conduct separate therapy sessions for adolescents and parents and to make reduction of parental criticism a focus of treatment.

Mediators and Moderators of EBPs for Depression

Several RCTs have found cognitive variables to be significant mediators of CBT for youth depression. Explanatory style mediated outcomes for youths with elevated depressive symptoms, whereby shifts to less pessimistic (Jaycox, Reivich, Gilham, & Seligman, 1994) or more optimistic (Yu & Seligman, 2002) attributional patterns were associated with reduced depressive symptoms. In addition, reductions in negative cognitions mediated reductions in depressive symptoms among depressed adolescents (Ackerson, Scogin, McKendree-Smith, & Lyman, 1998; Kaufman, Rohde, Seeley, Clarke, & Stice, 2005; Stice, Rohde, Seeley, & Gau, 2010). However, findings are not consistent between and even within studies. Ackerson et al. (1998) found that reductions in negative cognitions as assessed by the Dysfunctional Attitudes Scale (DAS; Weissman, 1979) but not by the Automatic Thoughts Questionnaire (ATQ; Hollon & Kendall, 1980) mediated outcome. Conversely, Kaufman et al. (2005) showed the opposite pattern of results—the ATQ but not the DAS mediated outcome. To explain their findings, Kaufman et al. (2005) suggested that their version of CBT may have been able to change cognitions only at the level of negative automatic thoughts as measured by the ATQ, and that more intensive CBT may be required to change more entrenched core beliefs as measured by the DAS. However, Ackerson et al.'s (1998) version of CBT, cognitive bibliotherapy, was unlikely to be more intensive than Kaufman et al.'s (2005) in-person group CBT. Evidently, more research is needed to clarify these mixed findings.

Several other variables have been tested as potential mediators in the context of CBT for adolescent depression. Increased frequency of engaging in pleasant activities was a significant mediator in one RCT (Stice et al., 2010) of group CBT for adolescents recruited for treatment from high schools due to their elevated depressive symptoms, but not in another RCT (Kaufman et al., 2005) of group CBT for adolescents with diagnoses of major depression and comorbid conduct disorder referred for treatment by the juvenile justice system. These findings provide preliminary evidence that mediators may differ according to severity and comorbidity of the sample, as well as referral source, but of course any two studies will differ along so many dimensions that ferreting out the cause of different findings is essentially educated speculation. Other candidate mediators—frequency of engaging in relaxation, social problem solving, and youth–therapist alliance—were also not found to mediate treatment outcome in the sample with major depression and comorbid conduct disorder (Kaufman et al., 2005). Finally, readiness to change mediated treatment outcome in the Treatment for Adolescents with Depression Study (Lewis et al., 2009), with adolescents receiving CBT or combination treatment of CBT and fluoxetine displaying the greatest increase in readiness to change.

To summarize, there is some evidence that shifts in explanatory style may mediate CBT effects for *child* depression, mixed evidence that change in negative cognitions and engagement in pleasant activities are mediators of CBT effects for *adolescent* depression, and limited evidence

that readiness to change is a mediator of CBT effects for adolescent depression. Future research will be needed to determine which of these findings can be replicated, to clarify inconsistencies, and also to demonstrate temporal precedence of the mediators relative to change in depression levels. In the only study that documented the temporal relations of the mediators and outcome (Stice et al., 2010), fewer than 10% of youths showed a meaningful change (defined as 0.33 SD) in each of the two mediators (ATQ and engagement in pleasant activities) *before* a meaningful reduction in depressive symptoms. This raises a question as to whether change in cognitions and engagement in pleasant activities operate as true mechanisms of change in depression treatment, a question that warrants attention in future research (see our discussion of future research on mechanisms of change, below; see also discussion of mediation in Chapter 9, this volume). Future research will also be needed to help identify mediators of change in the context of IPT-A for adolescents and of behavior therapy for children; we have not identified any mediation research with these EBPs.

Moderators identified from meta-analyses of RCTs of psychotherapy for youth depression that included EBPs as well as non-EBPs include informant (i.e., who reports on the depression; Weisz, McCarty, et al., 2006) and depression severity at baseline (Watanabe, Hunot, Omori, Churchill, & Furukawa, 2007). Larger treatment effects were associated with youth-report than parent-report measures (see our later section on informant effects), and with higher baseline severity compared to lower baseline severity, possibly because youths with more severe psychopathology have more room for improvement. Youth age was a significant moderator in one of the meta-analyses (Watanabe et al., 2007), with larger effects obtained for adolescents than for children, but not in the other (Weisz, McCarty, et al., 2006). The positive finding, though not evident in both meta-analyses, is consistent with the idea that adolescents' more advanced cognitive level makes them better able than children to grasp concepts discussed in therapy.

Mediators and Moderators of EBPs for Phobic and Anxiety Disorders

Reductions in youths' anxious self-statements and improvements in the ratio of positive self-statements to the sum of positive and anxious self-statements (their "states of mind ratio") mediated youth-reported symptom reduction in two RCTs (Kendall & Treadwell, 2007; Treadwell & Kendall, 1996) of individual CBT for youth anxiety. Positive self-statements and depressive self-statements, by contrast, were not found to mediate treatment outcome (Kendall & Treadwell, 2007; Treadwell & Kendall, 1996). Another research team (Lau, Chan, Li, & Au, 2010) has replicated the mediating effects of anxious self-statements on outcome in group CBT for youth anxiety; this team also demonstrated that improvement in the youths' ability to cope with fear-inducing situations, as perceived by youths and by parents, mediated treatment-induced symptom reduction.

As with CBT for youth depression, future research will need to demonstrate temporal precedence for the above mediators of individual CBT and group CBT, relative to changes in youth anxiety symptoms, to be considered true mechanisms of change. Future research will also be needed to identify mediators associated with other EBPs for phobic and anxiety disorders (i.e., group CBT for social phobia, group CBT with parents, and social effectiveness training for social phobia).

Studies conducted in North America had larger effects than studies conducted elsewhere, but there appeared to be no other moderators of treatment outcome according to a meta-analysis of randomized and nonrandomized trials of psychosocial treatments for youth anxiety (Silverman, Pina, et al., 2008). Another meta-analysis (James, Soler, & Weatherall, 2005) that included only RCTs of CBT compared to a wait-list or attention control detected no heterogeneity among the 13 studies, suggesting that there were no robust moderators of CBT for youth anxiety. These findings suggest that more work needs to be done on adapting CBT for youth anxiety to cultures and treatment contexts outside North America, but otherwise, research has not yet found marked differences in anxiety treatment response between different groups of youths.

Mediators and Moderators of EBPs for Obsessive-Compulsive Disorder

As best we can determine, no mediators or moderators have been identified for individual exposure-based CBT to date. This gap in the evidence-base has been attributed to small sample sizes and the low power of treatment outcome studies of psychotherapy in this area (Barrett et al., 2008). Comorbid tic disorder was found to be a moderator of the effects of sertraline treatment, but not of CBT. Because youths with comorbid tic disorder did not respond well to medication alone in the Pediatric OCD Treatment Study (POTS), CBT alone or combined with medication has been recommended as a first-line treatment for these youths (March et al., 2007).

Mediators and Moderators of EBPs for Youths Exposed to Traumatic Events

We have not found good evidence for any mediators of TF-CBT or of school-based group CBT. A review by Cohen et al. (2010), creators of TF-CBT, suggests that potential candidates for a mediation role in TF-CBT might include parent emotional distress, parent support, and abuse-related attributions and perceptions of the youth (e.g., youths believing they are responsible for the abuse, perceiving that others do not believe their accounts of abuse, or feeling different from their peers; see Cohen & Mannarino, 2000).

We did not find any meta-analyses of CBT for youths exposed to traumatic events, and RCTs did not report significant moderators. One meta-analysis (Silverman, Ortiz, et al., 2008) that included both EBPs and non-EBPs for youths exposed to trauma suggested that treatment orientation, type of trauma, and parent involvement were moderators of treatments; differences between effect sizes at each level of the moderators were compared but not subjected to significance testing. As expected, CBT interventions performed better than non-CBT interventions, but surprisingly, youth-only interventions performed better than those with parent involvement (Silverman, Ortiz, et al., 2008). In addition, interventions for sexual abuse had relatively large effects on posttraumatic and depression symptom outcomes and relatively small effects on externalizing symptoms, compared to interventions for other types of trauma (Silverman, Ortiz, et al., 2008). The authors speculated that internalizing symptoms may be more severe in sexually abused youths, leading to a treatment focus on reducing internalizing symptoms among these youths, whereas the treatment focus may be on reducing externalizing symptoms among youths with other kinds of trauma such as physical abuse. Future research should confirm if the above findings are statistically significant (i.e., not merely due to chance), and if so, probe the underlying processes that explain these moderation effects.

Mediators and Moderators of EBPs for Attention-Deficit/Hyperactivity Disorder

The Multimodal Treatment Study of Children with ADHD (MTA; MTA Cooperative Group, 1999a), the largest RCT of ADHD treatments to date, compared behavioral treatment (i.e., behavioral parent training, summer treatment program, and teacher consultation emphasizing behavioral classroom management), medication management (methylphenidate, Ritalin), a combination of behavioral treatment plus medication, and regular community care. Youths receiving combination treatment or medication only did better than those receiving behavioral treatment only or community care. The superior effects of the combination treatment on youth social skills relative to community care were mediated by reductions in negative/ineffective discipline by parents (Hinshaw et al., 2000). Although both combination and behavioral treatments improved discipline, improved discipline was associated with improved youth social skills for the combination treatment only. It is possible that reduced behavior problems due to stimulant medication caused parents to use less harsh discipline, resulting in improved self-regulation by their children. It is also possible that improved social skills, driven by medication, caused parents to use less harsh discipline because temporal relationships between mediator and outcome could not be distinguished. Furthermore, a third variable could have driven improvements in both discipline and social skills (Hinshaw et al., 2000). It is noteworthy that other parent variables (i.e., attendance at behavioral treatment sessions, positive involvement, deficient monitoring) were not mediators of behavioral or combination treatment effects (Hinshaw et al., 2000; MTA Cooperative Group, 1999b).

Publication year was a moderator of outcome in a meta-analysis (Fabiano et al., 2009) of behavioral treatments for ADHD, with more recent publications associated with *smaller* effects, but various participant and family characteristics were not. The publication year finding is puzzling, in that treatments might be expected to become *more* effective with improved understanding of ADHD and intervention effects over the years. In another meta-analysis (Corcoran & Dattalo, 2006) of behavioral and cognitive-behavioral interventions for ADHD with parent involvement, two-parent households and older youths were associated with larger treatment effects.

Finally, the MTA study identified a moderator that has noteworthy implications—youngsters with comorbid anxiety disorder benefited more from behavioral treatment than did those with no anxiety disorder. The anxious youths showed outcomes comparable to those of the medication management group and superior to those of the community care group (MTA Cooperative Group, 1999b). Thus, Hinshaw (2007) has suggested that behavior therapy alone may potentially be a suitable first-line treatment for the subgroup of youths with ADHD who have comorbid anxiety.

Mediators and Moderators of EBPs for Disruptive Behavior Problems

Research on mediators of EBPs for disruptive behavior problems is especially rich compared to other problem areas. This reflects, in part, the fact that treatment in this area has been such a priority for the field, generating so much treatment development and intervention testing.

Most mediators identified across the various EBPs for disruptive behavior are some aspect of parent/caregiver practices and skills. This is consistent with expectations given that the parent or caregiver is seen as the principal change agent in most EBPs for disruptive behavior and is taught parenting skills in a number of domains, such as close monitoring of the youth, and preventing the youth from associating with deviant peers. For example, in MST, improved family and peer functioning were found to mediate reductions in delinquent behavior (Huey, Henggeler, Brondino, & Pickrel, 2000). In addition, caregivers' improved ability to follow through with disciplinary action and decreased concern about youths' negative peer relationships partially accounted for the superiority of MST over usual care in the treatment of juvenile sex offenders (Henggeler et al., 2009). Similarly, in MTFC, improvement in caregivers' family management skills (e.g., adult–youth relationship, supervision, discipline) and reduction in youths' relationships with deviant peers mediated treatment effects on the subsequent antisocial behavior of adolescent boys who were severe offenders (Eddy & Chamberlain, 2000). In addition, decreases in harsh, critical, and ineffective parenting practices accounted for reductions in youth externalizing symptoms in a study (Beauchaine, Webster-Stratton, & Reid, 2005) that pooled data from six RCTs of the Incredible Years (IY) treatment program in which participants received various combinations of child, parent, and/or teacher training. Interestingly, other aspects of parenting and peer relationships (i.e., caregiver monitoring, parent–youth communication, and peer delinquent behaviors and conventional activities) were not mediators in the Henggeler et al. (2009) study of sex offender treatment, suggesting that just which aspects of parenting need to be altered to generate youth behavior change may depend on the specific EBP or the condition being treated.

Youth-focused variables have also been shown to mediate outcomes of EBPs for disruptive behavior problems, but these mediators seem to be specific to the particular EBP or sample. Homework completion—a measure of engagement in school—mediated the effects of MTFC on the number of days offending girls spent in locked settings (Leve & Chamberlain, 2007). In addition, changes in boys' hostile attributions, reduced expectations that aggression would result in favorable outcomes, and increased internal locus of control, among other changes, accounted for improvements in school behavior, delinquency, and substance use among youths receiving anger control training (Lochman & Wells, 2002). This is not surprising given the emphasis in this treatment program on individual changes in the youths themselves.

It is encouraging that multiple studies by different research teams have converged on the conclusion that parenting practices and relationships with deviant peers mediate the effects of EBPs on disruptive behavior among youths. Indeed, this may be the most robust finding on any mediator of any EBP for youths. Evidence on youth-focused mediators are more limited and more in need of replication. As with EBPs for depression and anxiety, RCTs of EBPs for disruptive behavior will need to include multiple assessments of both mediators and outcomes during and after therapy to establish identified mediators as true mechanisms of change (see our later section on this topic).

Several moderators of behavioral parent training were identified in a meta-analysis (Lundahl, Risser, & Lovejoy, 2006) that included randomized and nonrandomized controlled trials. Youths from nonintact and economically disadvantaged families made smaller treatment gains than those not in these subgroups. It is probable that single and economically disadvantaged parents have less time and energy to attend all therapy sessions, to practice the parenting skills learned during therapy at home, and to monitor and regulate their children's peer associations. Lundahl et al. (2006) examined moderators of outcome within the group of studies with economically disadvantaged samples and found that individual parent training was more helpful than group parent training, suggesting that close individual attention may be especially helpful with economically disadvantaged families. Interestingly, treatments that involved only parents were associated with better outcomes in parent behavior and perceptions than were treatments that involved both parents and their children. An explanation proposed by Lundahl et al. (2006) is that parents may be more likely to see themselves as the primary agents of change and take more responsibility for effecting change when they are the sole recipients of treatment. In addition, studies with samples including clinically significant disruptive behavior problems showed larger treatment effects, possibly because there was more room for improvement in those samples.

Mediators and Moderators of EBPs for Adolescent Substance Abuse

Mirroring the mediation research on EBPs for ADHD and disruptive behavior problems, a change in parenting practices was a significant mediator of an EBP for adolescent substance abuse. MDFT improved parental monitoring of adolescents' daily activities and peers relative to peer group intervention, thereby increasing abstinence from substance use during a 12-month period following baseline assessment (Henderson, Rowe, Dakof, Hawes, & Liddle, 2009). Interestingly, improved parental monitoring mediated treatment effects only when the outcome was proportion of youths who were abstinent and not frequency of substance use, leading Henderson and colleagues (2009) to suggest that parental monitoring may prevent substance use, but not reduce substance use among adolescents who continue using substances after treatment. Improved parent-adolescent relationship quality, although associated with greater abstinence, was observed in both MDFT and peer group intervention conditions and thus was not a treatment mediator (Henderson et al., 2009). We do not know of any published mediation studies for other EBPs of adolescent substance abuse, but Waldron and Turner (2008) have suggested several candidates to examine, including family variables in FFT and MST, coping skills in individual and group

CBT, and therapeutic alliance for all treatment approaches.

We found several individual RCTs, but no meta-analyses, that identified moderators of EBPs for adolescent substance abuse. MDFT outperformed two alternative treatments (individual CBT and enhanced treatment as usual) for adolescents with more severe baseline substance use and comorbidity, but performed similarly to the alternative treatments for adolescents who had less severe baseline substance use and comorbidity (Henderson, Dakof, Greenbaum, & Liddle, 2010). The authors suggested that common factors of good psychotherapy (e.g., strategies to engage adolescents, sufficient duration and intensity) may be adequately therapeutic for adolescents with less psychopathology, whereas MDFT's specific focus on changing a greater number of documented risk factors, particularly family interactions, may be especially beneficial to adolescents with more psychopathology. Gender appears to moderate the effects of CBT on substance use, but findings are mixed on the direction of moderation, with one RCT favoring boys (Kaminer, Burleson, & Goldberger, 2002) and another favoring girls (Kaminer, Burleson, & Burke, 2008). The first RCT tested group CBT against a group psychoeducation control whereas the second RCT tested an aftercare intervention that included CBT and motivational enhancement therapy delivered either in-person or through the phone against a no aftercare control group *after* all participants completed group CBT. The discrepancy on the direction of moderation could reflect different processes involved in the initiation versus maintenance of behavior change (Kaminer et al., 2008), the use of different intervention approaches, or the presence of motivational enhancement therapy in the one instance. In other findings, several personality and temperament variables have been shown to moderate the effects of group CBT, including sensation seeking, anxiety sensitivity, hopelessness (Conrod, Stewart, Comeau, & Maclean, 2006) and rhythmicity (Burleson & Kaminer, 2008). These are early days for research on moderation in substance abuse treatment, but as future studies document which of these specific findings can be replicated, treatment may be optimized for substance-using adolescents by first screening them for personality/temperament variables and then matching them to treatments that have been documented to be more beneficial for individuals with their particular personality/temperament type.

Therapeutic Alliance and Other Relationship Variables

Notably absent from our review of mediators of youth EBPs are therapeutic alliance and other therapeutic relationship variables, which have been hypothesized to be key mechanisms of change in youth psychotherapy (Karver, Handelsman, Fields, & Bickman, 2005, 2006; Shirk & Karver, 2003). Unfortunately, we have only identified one youth RCT that has tested alliance as a mediator, and it found therapeutic alliance not to be a significant mediator (Kaufman et al., 2005; see our section on mediators and moderators of EBPs for depression). This dearth of research on alliance as a mediator is disappointing given the substantial number of studies that have examined the association between alliance and outcome in youths, as well as the intuitive belief by many that youngsters who see their therapist as understanding them and collaborating with them will have better outcomes. Evidence for this belief, via appropriate mediation testing, is absent thus far.

A meta-analysis (Karver et al., 2006) documented significant associations between a number of different therapeutic relationship variables (e.g., counselor interpersonal skills, therapist direct influence skills, youth affect toward therapist) and outcome. More recently, another meta-analysis (McLeod, 2011) with an exclusive focus on therapeutic alliance (rather than the broader construct of therapeutic relationship) and outcome in youth psychotherapies found a small but significant association ($r = 0.14$), with roughly equal associations for the alliance between youth and therapist (youth–therapist alliance) and the alliance between parent and therapist (parent–therapist alliance). This alliance–outcome association from 38 youth psychotherapy studies is half of that found in a meta-analysis of 190 adult psychotherapy studies ($r = 0.275$, Horvath, Del Re, Flückiger, & Symonds, 2011). Why is the alliance–outcome association so much weaker in youth psychotherapies than in adult psychotherapies? McLeod (2011) suggested that the moderators identified in his meta-analysis may provide clues to explain the smaller association in youth psychotherapies. Two of these moderators—therapeutic orientation and informant—may be especially pertinent to this question. Smaller alliance–outcome associations emerged for family-based or systemic therapies compared to individual-based youth or parent therapies and for youth- or observer-report compared to parent-report measures of alliance. Because family-based and systemic therapies are more common among youth than adult clients, the smaller alliance–outcome association of these therapies may have brought down the mean association across youth psychotherapies. It is also intriguing that the alliance–outcome association differed by informant but not by the specific client–therapist alliance (youth–therapist versus parent–therapist alliance) assessed. McLeod (2011) argued that the parent's perception of therapeutic alliance may be especially important for youth psychotherapy outcome because parents are the ones who seek treatment, consent to treatment, and physically bring the youth to treatment; moreover, youths may not be able to rate alliance as accurately as can adults due to their lower level of cognitive development (see our later section on this topic).

Even though the alliance-outcome association is small in youth psychotherapies, it is nevertheless reliably larger than zero. One potentially useful next step will be to test therapeutic alliance and other therapeutic relationship variables as mediators of treatment outcome in future youth psychotherapy studies.

Summary of Research on Mediators and Moderators of Evidence-Based Psychotherapies

To summarize the mediation evidence presented in the previous sections, mediators of EBPs for youths with depression, anxiety and phobic disorders, disruptive behavior problems, or substance abuse have been identified; a mediator of a medication-EBP combination treatment for ADHD has been identified; and no mediators of EBPs for youths with autism, eating disorders, OCD, or trauma have been identified, to our knowledge. Therapeutic alliance and relationship variables are promising candidates for future testing. Among the identified mediators, empirical support appears to be strongest for parenting skills and practices in the context of EBPs for disruptive behavior problems; evidence is also substantial for cognitive variables in the context of CBT for youth depression. More research will be needed to establish these mediators as true mechanisms of change (see our later section on this topic).

The evidence base on moderators of EBPs for youths is larger than that on mediators. Moderators were identified in relation to EBPs for every youth disorder except OCD (confirming significance tests are also needed for EBPs for trauma). A number of parent and family variables, including parent involvement in youth-focused treatments, youth involvement in parent-focused treatments, maternal EE, single- versus two-parent households, and parent versus youth as informant, emerged as moderators across several different disorders and treatment orientations.

Not surprisingly, a number of the findings on mediation and moderation concern family factors, a topic that warrants detailed attention in its own right. So, we focus now on the role of family factors in youth psychotherapy.

Family Factors in Youth Psychotherapy

As noted earlier, youth psychotherapy typically involves caregivers, and often other family members as well, and in a variety of roles—for example, referring the youth for treatment; identifying reasons for referral; providing information on the youth's current functioning and response to treatment; participating in the therapy; and collaborating in decisions about treatment content, structure, and termination. In some psychotherapy programs—such as Barkley's (1997) *Defiant Children* and Kazdin's (2010) *Parent Management Training* for disruptive, disobedient, and aggressive youngsters—caregivers are the primary participants in sessions with the therapist, learning skills to use with their children at home. In the context of such treatment programs, it is no surprise to find that parent–therapist alliance, like youth–therapist alliance, predicts treatment outcomes for young people (e.g., Kazdin, Whitley, & Marciano, 2006), and that youth outcomes are also predicted by the extent to which caregivers learn and use the new parenting skills therapy is designed to convey (Zisser & Eyberg, 2010). The full range of family factors relevant to youth psychotherapy is extensive and beyond the scope of this chapter (but see Chapter 15 in this volume for further elaboration). However, we offer here two examples of family factors that may warrant increased attention in future research.

Expressed Emotion

The home environment is a source of important protections from psychological distress and potential risk factors for poor psychological functioning. Of these risk factors, EE may be particularly relevant to the understanding of how psychological disorders develop and are maintained among both youths and adults. EE has been found to predict treatment outcome and relapse for a broad range of disorders (Hooley, 2007). Earlier in this chapter we noted the role of EE as a moderator of anorexia nervosa treatment effects (Eisler et al., 2000; Eisler et al., 2007). In addition, Asarnow, Goldstein, Tompson, and Guthrie (1993) found that youths with mood disorders were significantly more likely to maintain symptom reductions one year after inpatient treatment when returning home to live with a low rather than high EE mother. A correlation has been shown between critical EE and externalizing problems for children in first grade, and the critical EE of mothers of preschool children has been shown to longitudinally predict ADHD at grade three, even when accounting for both preschool behavior problems and maternal stress (Peris & Baker, 2000).

Although such findings are intriguing, further research is needed to clarify the association between EE and treatment process and outcome for children and adolescents. There has been considerable research on EE in children and adolescents, but questions remain regarding how the construct—originally developed for research on adult psychopathology—should be operationalized for youths. For example, McCarty and Weisz (2002) found that when using the Five Minute Speech Sample (FMSS; Magana et al., 1986) to assess EE, the emotional overinvolvement (EOI) facet has little connection to youth psychopathology, and positive comments made by the parent, which partially comprise EOI, have *negative* associations with youth psychopathology. These findings stand in direct conflict with predictions based on traditional conceptualization of EE, suggesting a need for a developmentally sensitive conceptualization of, and research on, EE. Consistent with traditional conceptualizations, however, McCarty and Weisz (2002) did find that *critical* EE was positively associated with symptoms of youth psychopathology.

Given that critical EE may well be the most important facet of EE for youth, based on research to date, it makes sense for future research to examine the role of perceived criticism (PC) in youth psychotherapy outcome and relapse. The study of EE within the adult literature naturally gave rise to the study of PC. Although critical expressed emotion is a measure of how much criticism is expressed by a relevant family member (e.g., a parent or a spouse) toward a specific patient or individual, it does not necessarily measure how much criticism "gets through" to

the patient. *Perceived* criticism may be a better indicator of how much criticism gets through to a patient, and even of how much criticism is perceived regardless of the actual content or the intent of the speaker. Hooley and Teasdale (1989) found that perceived criticism, which is much easier to assess than EE, is a powerful predictor of treatment relapse in its own right, has strong test–retest reliability, and yields ratings independent of illness severity. As further research is done on these constructs, it will be useful to investigate the impact of criticism and perceived criticism in their own right, controlling for the patient behavior that may, in some cases, prompt the criticism (i.e., higher levels of criticism might, in some cases, reflect higher levels of youth psychopathology, which are linked to more of the behavior that parents and others find objectionable, and thus criticize). Level of parental criticism could in principle be studied as a possible moderator of treatment outcome and as a candidate mediator (i.e., improved youth functioning might be mediated in part by reductions in parental criticism). Despite evidence that EE is important for predicting outcome and relapse in both youths and adults and that PC is a powerful predictor of adult outcome, we know of no research examining PC in the context of youth psychotherapy.

The Challenge of Different Perspectives

Going beyond the attitudes and behavior of caregivers, we focus next on the fact that different family members differ from one another in their perception of events and behavior, and how these differences impact youth psychotherapy processes and outcomes. Informant discrepancies in the reports of various family members on youth behavior, functioning, and psychopathology have been among the most consistent findings in youth clinical research (Achenbach et al., 1987; De Los Reyes, Goodman, et al., 2010; De Los Reyes & Kazdin, 2005; Richters, 1992; Weisz & Weiss, 1991). As suggested by Weisz et al. (1997), the study of youth psychopathology "is inevitably the study of two phenomena: the behavior of the child, and the lens through which adults view child behavior" (p. 569). Different adults inevitably view the young person's behavior through different lenses, and these differ from the lenses used by the youth.

The complications associated with informant discrepancies are apparent in a variety of studies using community samples. For example, in a study of female caregiver–youth dyads, discrepant reports of parental monitoring predicted increased levels of youth-reported delinquent behaviors after a period of 2 years (De Los Reyes, Goodman, et al., 2010). In other community samples, disagreement between adolescents and parents has been shown to predict a variety of undesirable future outcomes, including drug abuse, police and judicial contact, expulsion from school, job loss, deliberate self-harm, and suicidal ideation/attempts (Ferdinand, van der Ende, & Verhulst, 2004, 2006).

Although some of these findings are open to multiple interpretations (e.g., youth–caregiver discrepancy might reflect youth–caregiver discord, parental inattention, or even success by the youth in concealing behavior), the associations with adverse outcomes do raise the question of whether caregiver–youth discrepancy has consequences for the process or outcome of psychotherapy. Clinicians who work with young people routinely face the challenge of determining the appropriate problems to address in therapy when youth and caregiver perspectives disagree. Prior studies have illustrated how challenging the task can be. In a sample of clinic-referred youths and their parents, Yeh and Weisz (2001) obtained information separately from the youths and their parents regarding what problems needed to be targeted in treatment. Some 63% of the youth-parent pairs failed to agree on a single specific target problem, and 36% failed to agree on even a single broad category (e.g., aggressive behavior, anxiety/depression). Extending these findings to include the perspectives of therapists, Hawley and Weisz (2003) found that 76% of parent-youth-therapist triads failed to agree on a single target problem and 44% failed to reach consensus on even one general problem category.

One common explanation for a lack of agreement between youths and parents in the treatment context is that discrepancies result in part from differing perspectives (Achenbach et al., 1987; Forehand, Frame, Wierson, Armistead, & Kempton, 1991). According to this view, externalizing problems are readily observable by parents whereas internalizing problems (e.g., worry or sad feelings) are less outwardly observable and thus more likely to be detected by the youth, who experiences the internalizing distress, than the parent. Consistent with this view, Weisz and Weiss (1991) provided evidence that externalizing problems were more commonly the basis of youth clinic referrals by parents than internalizing problems were. But as these authors noted, there are additional reasons why externalizing problems might be referred more often than internalizing problems (e.g., externalizing behavior is more disruptive at home and school and more likely to be distressing to others in the youth's world). An additional factor may be relevant: language fluency.

Disagreement as to what problems a youth has, or which problems warrant treatment, could affect treatment process and outcome. In a study of youth outpatient clinic treatment, Brookman-Frazee, Haine, Gabayan, and Garland (2008) found a positive association between caregiver–youth agreement on treatment goals, on the one hand, and number of sessions attended, on the other. In another study of outpatient treatment, level of caregiver–youth agreement in reports of youth psychopathology and interpersonal problems was positively associated with level of caregiver involvement in the treatment process (Israel, Thomsen, Langeveld, & Stormark, 2007). It will be useful, in future research, to explore the extent to which caregiver–youth agreement/disagreement is a predictor of treatment outcome, and also important to explore methods of reducing discrepancies before dropout occurs.

De Los Reyes, Alfano, and Beidel (2010a) have stressed the potential information value of informant discrepancies in psychotherapy. In a study investigating discordant reports among parent–youth dyads on measures of youth social phobia symptoms, parent-youth discrepancies at pretreatment significantly predicted discrepancies at posttreatment. This relation was found to be moderated by treatment responder status in that significant relations were found only for treatment non-responders. De Los Reyes, Alfano, et al. (2010) argued that this stability in measures of informant discrepancies across time suggests that discordant reports may serve as tools for evaluating youths' response to treatment. Repeated measures of caregiver-youth agreement during the course of therapy, these authors' believe, may shed light on how well youths are responding to treatment. Thus, informant discrepancies, rather than being "measurement error," may provide information that can enrich our understanding of youth psychotherapy process and outcome (De Los Reyes, 2011; De Los Reyes & Kazdin, 2005).

Testing the Reach of Psychotherapies Across Population Groups

One way to test the strength and "reach" of youth EBPs is to examine the breadth of their impact across a range of population groups and risk conditions. We turn now to research addressing that agenda, with four groups of special interest.

Ethnic Minority Populations

The percentage of youths in the United States who are ethnic minorities was 43% in 2008, and this percentage continues to grow (Pollard & Mather, 2009). The prevalence of psychological disorders among ethnic minority groups in the United States is about the same as that of the general population (21%; U.S. Department of Health and Human Services, 2001), and the most recent statistics available suggest that about 13% of ethnic minority youths receive mental health services each year (Stagman & Cooper, 2010, estimate that 31% of European-American youths receive services). Although a large percentage of youths receiving mental health services belong to ethnic minority groups, some of the reports on treatment process and outcome for these youths have not been encouraging. For example, a U.S. Department of Health and Human Services document (DHHS, 2001) reported that only a small number of ethnic minorities had participated in psychotherapy RCTs, and that none of the studies had assessed the efficacy of the treatment by ethnicity or race. Chambless and colleagues (1996), in their review of treatments meeting EBP criteria, stated "We know of no psychotherapy treatment research that meets basic criteria important for demonstrating treatment efficacy for ethnic minority populations..." (Chambless et al., 1996). Additionally, some research had found ethnic minority youths more likely than European-Americans to drop out of treatment (Kazdin & Whitley, 2003) and significantly less likely to show clinical improvement when treated for depression (Weersing & Weisz, 2002a).

A more hopeful note was sounded by Huey and Polo (2008), in a selective review of youth treatment outcome studies from 1960 through 2006, in which at least 75% of participants in each study were ethnic minorities. Using the levels-of-support criteria we outlined earlier (see Silverman & Hinshaw, 2008), Huey and Polo (2008) found no "well-established" treatments, but they identified multiple treatments that were "probably efficacious" and "possibly efficacious" for minority youths, encompassing a range of conditions including anxiety, ADHD, depression, disruptive conduct, substance use, posttraumatic stress, and suicide risk, with CBT as the best-documented effective treatment for anxiety

disorders, depression, and trauma-related disorders. Adding a meta-analysis of 25 studies, Huey and Polo (2008) found a mean pre-post treatment effect size for minority youths averaging .44, just below Cohen's (1988) benchmark for a medium effect (as compared to control participants receiving no treatment, placebo, or treatment-as-usual).

Some in the field believe that assessing the effects of existing EBPs with minority youths is insufficient, and that, instead, EBPs should be structured specifically for, or at least tailored to fit ethnic minority populations. There is considerable interest in treatments that are sensitive to cultural values and norms (Sue, Fujino, Hu, Takeuchi, & Zane, 1991), and it is possible that treatments developed with European-American samples "may not take into account the language, values, customs, child-rearing traditions, expectancies for child and parent behavior, and distinctive stressors and resources associated with different cultural groups" (Weisz, Huey, & Weersing, 1998, p. 70). The intuitive appeal of these ideas notwithstanding, when Huey and Polo (2008) reviewed the small collection of RCTs that compared culturally adapted and tailored treatments to standard EBPs, they found no significant differences in treatment outcomes with minority youths. The one form of cultural adjustment for which some supportive evidence has been found is therapist–patient ethnic match, which has been found to be associated with superior treatment perseverance (e.g., reduced rates of dropout after initial treatment session; Yeh, Eastman, & Cheung, 1994) and superior treatment outcome (e.g., 33% improvement in level of symptom reduction on the Child Behavior Checklist; Halliday-Boykins, Shoenwald, & Letourneu, 2005).

It is clear that research on psychotherapy effects with ethnic minority populations has begun in earnest, but it has *only* begun. We look forward to reviewing an ever-richer base of information on this topic in the years ahead.

War-Exposed Youths

As we learn more about the best ways to make treatment responsive to ethnic and cultural variation, we are likely to learn more, as a field, about ways to help some of the world's youth who are most in need of support: youths exposed to armed conflict in low-resource and war-torn countries. These youths have experienced stressors such as military assault, sexual trauma, conscription as "child soldiers," and diverse sequelae of involuntary displacement (e.g., life in refugee camps, failure to understand the local language and culture, separation from family members) that can put them at risk for significant disorder and dysfunction. UNICEF (1996) reported that wars in the past decade had hampered normal child development, subjecting an estimated 20 million youths to homelessness, 6 million to physical injury and disability, and 1 million to parental separation. Research has shown that war-exposed youths are at increased risk for substance abuse, depression, anxiety, conduct problems, posttraumatic stress, and suicidal ideation (Lustig et al., 2004; Shaw, 2003).

Can the current array of therapies make a difference for youths exposed to armed conflict? The modest evidence base to date is somewhat encouraging. Bolton et al. (2007) tested a group interpersonal therapy (IPT) intervention for depression among adolescent Ugandan war refugees. IPT was compared to a creative play treatment program and to a waitlist control group. Compared to the other two interventions, IPT was more successful in significantly reducing depression symptoms (but not anxiety or conduct problems) for girls; boys also benefited from IPT but symptom reductions were nonsignificant. In the IPT condition at posttreatment, 37.1% of adolescents met criteria for recovery and 29.1% for remission, as compared to 12.4% recovery and 6.7% remission in the creative play condition, and 13.5% recovery and 8.9% remission in the control condition. The authors suggest the treatment may have been less effective for boys due to their being less open to discussing emotional problems in a group. Another contributing factor is the group IPT intervention has been shown to be less effective for youths with comorbid anxiety disorders and boys in the sample had more symptoms of posttraumatic stress disorder (PTSD) than girls. RCTs have also been conducted as large-scale school-based interventions. Tol, Komproe, Susanty, Jordans, and de Jong (2008) tested a trauma-focused group intervention for PTSD symptoms among youths in Indonesia exposed to political violence. The treatment included group CBT along with structured play activities and performing arts exercises. Compared to a waitlist control, the CBT group experienced a significantly larger decrease in PTSD symptoms (but not depression or anxiety symptoms). Jordans et al. (2010) tested a classroom-based intervention broadly designed to improve psychosocial functioning and general well-being

among adolescents in civil war–affected Nepal experiencing psychosocial stress. The intervention consisted of CBT, structured play activities, performing arts exercises, and narrative exposure techniques. Compared to a wait-list control, the treatment group experienced significantly larger improvements in general functioning, general psychological functioning, and significantly greater reduction in depression symptoms and anxiety symptoms. PTSD symptoms decreased and feelings of hope increased to a significant and comparable degree in both groups. Jordans et al.'s (2010) CBT program was a broad intervention to improve general well-being, whereas the Tol et al. (2008) CBT program was a trauma-focused intervention for youths who had experienced at least one violent event and PTSD symptoms. Given these differences in scope, objectives, and sample, it is difficult to interpret the difference in outcomes between the two studies.

Layne et al. (2008) assessed the effectiveness of components of a manualized treatment protocol known as trauma and grief component therapy (TGCT) for war-exposed Bosnian adolescents experiencing PTSD, depression, or grief symptoms along with impairment in functioning. TGCT has been widely disseminated in war-torn Bosnia as part of a UNICEF mental health program. Students were randomized to one of two treatment conditions, each consisting of components of TGCT: (1) trauma- and grief-centered therapy along with psychoeducation and social skills training (treatment condition), and (2) psychoeducation and social skills training only (active comparison group). Both TGCT treatment groups experienced a significant decrease in PTSD and depression symptoms; only the treatment condition involving trauma- and grief-centered therapy along with psychoeducation and social skills training showed a significant decrease in grief symptoms.

Dybdahl (2001) tested a psychosocial intervention for mother–youth refugee pairs internally displaced within Bosnia. The intervention consisted of parent discussion groups centered around trauma-processing and improving mother–youth interactions. As compared to a control group (receiving medical care only), the treatment group (who received the psychosocial intervention along with medical care) showed significantly more improvement in mothers' PTSD hyperarousal symptoms and youngsters' weight gain and psychosocial functioning (youths' PSTD symptoms were not explicitly assessed).

These studies illustrate that it is feasible to deliver structured psychotherapy interventions derived from the RCT evidence base to war-exposed youths even in very remote and under-resourced regions, and that measurable psychological benefit may result, at least for some groups on some dimensions of psychological functioning. Perhaps these early findings will be a springboard for work with other war-exposed and refugee populations whose need for support, and effective coping skills, is so profound. Longer-term follow-up evaluations appear to be missing, but these are obviously needed.

Youths in the Juvenile Justice System

More than 90,000 youths are detained in residential juvenile justice facilities, or adult jails or prisons, in the United States each year (Snyder & Sickmund, 2006; National Evaluation and Technical Assistance Center, 2010), and many more were involved with police and the court system. About 67% of adjudicated youths are housed in facilities that screen for mental health needs (Snyder & Sickmund, 2006), providing some limited data on psychopathology prevalence for this population. There have also been numerous studies of mental health problems and disorders in juvenile justice facilities, although the results have been inconsistent across studies, and the U.S. Department of Justice considers the information from extant studies to be insufficient to guide policy decisions (Teplin et al., 2006). Teplin and colleagues (Teplin et al., 2006) have assessed the prevalence of psychiatric disorders within the juvenile justice system using random sampling of detainees and empirically supported measures of psychopathology, including the Diagnostic Interview Schedule for Children (DISC) Version 2.3 (Shaffer et al., 1996). These investigators have found that the most common disorders among juvenile justice-involved youth relate to substance use and conduct-related disorders. Additionally, more than 25% of females and 20% of males meet criteria for at least one affective disorder, and comorbidity is substantial (Teplin et al., 2006).

One ostensible objective of the U.S. juvenile justice system is rehabilitation, and treatment for mental health problems is widely viewed as essential. It is disappointing that empirical support for many of the interventions used is mixed or absent, and it is possible that some of the most popular interventions may well be ineffective or harmful. The Blueprints for Violence Prevention project of the Center for the Study and Prevention of Violence, at the University of Colorado (see e.g., Mihalic, Fagan, Irwin, Ballard, & Elliott, 2002), has evaluated more than 900 programs aimed at rehabilitating youths. Supporting evidence for most of these was found to be either disappointing or entirely lacking. Examples include *Scared Straight*, a program using shock probation (the program actually appears to *increase* crime rates), youth boot camps, gun buy-back programs, peer counseling, summer job programs for at-risk youth, neighborhood watch programs, and home detention and monitoring programs. Blueprints did identify 11 treatment programs showing substantial evidence of effectiveness. Arguably the strongest evidence supports MST (Glisson et al., 2010; Henggeler & Schaeffer, 2010; Schoenwald, 2010), a coordinated array of interventions targeting multiple systems in youths' lives, including immediate and extended family, neighborhood, peer networks, and school. Across the various trials, MST has been shown to increase parenting skills, improve family relations, expand positive social resources such as number of non-delinquent friends, improve grades and vocational skills, and boost engagement in positive activities and social support networks. MST trials have shown reductions of up to 70% in rates of re-arrest and reductions of up to 64% in out-of-home placements. MST has proven more effective than a variety of "usual care" alternatives to which youths are typically assigned, including probation services, child welfare services, and individual outpatient therapy (Weisz, Kuppens, Eckshtain, Ugueto, Hawley, & Jensen-Doss, 2012). Unfortunately, a number of the practices found to be ineffective, or even harmful, continue to be widely used.

Most research on youths in the juvenile justice system has focused mainly on boys, or has neglected to explore potential gender differences. This is understandable in the light of the much higher rates of adjudication among boys, higher rates of conduct disorder in boys (Teplin et al., 2006), and generally more violent nature of crimes by boys relative to crimes by girls. However, the proportion of violent crimes perpetrated by girls is rising, particularly assault (Snyder & Sickmund, 2006), and more girls than boys commit status offenses (e.g., truancy, running away from home). These nuanced gender differences highlight the need for research that specifically addresses how adjudicated boys and girls differ and how treatments may be tailored to fit the differences. Some evidence suggests that female delinquents have higher rates of psychological dysfunction than male delinquents, and may also have experienced more abuse, neglect, and family history of mental illness (McCabe, Lansing, Garland, & Hough, 2002; Teplin et al., 2006). There does appear to be a need for research on effective strategies for tailoring treatments to the distinctive histories and current profiles of girls in the juvenile justice system.

Youths in the Child-Welfare System

Like youths involved in juvenile justice, youngsters caught up in the child welfare system often have complex needs. The maltreatment that causes youngsters to be removed from their homes and the stressful and confusing process of foster placement—indeed, often a series of placements—can be potent risk factors for mental disorder. The youths may live with total strangers, and in unfamiliar settings, with frequent changes making it difficult to form stable friendships or even school placements. Complicating the picture, the child welfare system is a secondary service sector, meaning it is not specifically designed for treatment of mental health problems, despite the fact that entry into the system is a common precursor to mental health services (see Garland, Hough, Landsverk, & Brown, 2001; Garland, Hough, McCabe, et al., 2001; Garland, Landsverk, Hough, & Ellis-Macleod, 1996), particularly for youths who have experienced physical or sexual abuse (Garland et al., 1996).

As with the juvenile justice population, successful interventions for child welfare youths have tended to employ strategies in multiple domains, and to involve multiple caregivers and community supports. A special adaptation of MST, Multisystemic Therapy-Child for Child Abuse and Neglect (MST-CAN) has proven effective in at least one randomized effectiveness trial (e.g., Swenson, Schaeffer, Henggeler, Faldowski, & Mayhew, 2010). MST-CAN includes the standard components of MST and integrates safety planning, anger management for parents, and additional emphasis on family problem-solving and communication. MST-CAN, when used in a community mental health treatment setting, is significantly more effective than enhanced outpatient treatment (EOT) in reducing youth psychopathology, youth out-of-home placements (e.g., hospitalizations), and youth placement changes. MST-CAN is also significantly more effective than EOT in improving parent functioning, as reflected in reduced psychological distress and fewer instances of violent discipline or other forms of maltreatment.

Another beneficial approach, this one growing out of four decades of research on development and treatment of antisocial behavior (see e.g., Forgatch & Patterson, 2010), is MTFC (Smith & Chamberlain, 2010). MTFC was developed in the mid-1980s to provide a community-based alternative to incarceration and placement of delinquent boys in residential group care settings; it has since been adapted for use with delinquent girls, and with youths referred from mental health and child welfare systems due to serious emotional and mental health problems. Intervention within MTFC involves working with youths, biological parents, and MTFC-trained foster parents using a combination of multilevel interventions that take place in family, community, and school contexts. Each youth is placed in an MTFC home for 6 to 9 months, where a comprehensive individually tailored behavior management program and case management are provided, together with close supervision and frequent reinforcement for learning and using positive adaptive social skills. Caregivers receive weekly family therapy guided by the Oregon Parent Management Training model (see Forgatch & Patterson, 2010); this includes effective parenting techniques, such as limit-setting, close monitoring of the youth's whereabouts, behavior, and peer associations, and reinforcement of the youth for prosocial and adaptive behavior.

Published trials have shown that MTFC is more effective in reducing delinquent behavior in boys (Chamberlain & Reid, 1998) and girls (Chamberlain, Leve, & DeGarmo, 2007) than standard group care. Importantly, the effects for girls included reduced pregnancy rates; at 24 months postbaseline, the rate was 27% for MTFC girls versus 46% for group care girls. Other trials have shown beneficial effects of MTFC in reducing severe mental health problems in youths from a mental hospital (Chamberlain & Reid, 1991) and the child welfare system (Chamberlain, Moreland, & Reid, 1992). More evidence on the nature, strength, and moderators of these effects will be useful in the years ahead, but given its success in the trials to date, MTFC is spreading fast as a resource for child welfare leaders who seek evidence-based approaches.

Young people involved in the child welfare system who have histories of maltreatment are at increased risk for PTSD, and may need specialty services for PTSD. Several relevant treatments are available, but the evidence appears strongest for TF-CBT (Cohen et al., 2010). TF-CBT has been shown to be effective for children as young as 3 (Sheeringa, Weems, Cohen, Amaya-Jackson, & Guthrie, 2011). This treatment integrates traditional CBT techniques with components specifically targeting trauma-related symptoms; one such component involves the creation and repeated reading of a trauma narrative—a form of exposure designed to reduce arousal and distress over time. Other components include parent training, safety planning, graduated exposure to nonthreatening trauma reminders (e.g., to safe playgrounds, if a traumatic event on a playground has prevented the youngster from enjoying playgrounds ever since), and joint parent–youth sessions designed to enhance communication and foster adaptive discussion about the abuse. RCTs have shown TF-CBT to be more effective in reducing PTSD symptoms than waitlist control groups, "supportive therapy," and "child-centered therapy" (see review in Cohen et al., 2010). This treatment approach was designated "well-established" in the Silverman et al. (2008) review of evidence-based treatments for youths exposed to trauma (see Table 14.1).

As we have seen, there are tested treatments available for youngsters in the child welfare system. A particular challenge for this group may be the broad array of mental health and behavioral challenges that can arise, and the fact that the profile may be quite different from one youth to another within the system. Chavira, Accurso, Garland, & Hough (2010) argue that evidence-based treatments for CW-involved youths should be sensitive to this diversity of profiles, equipped to address aggression and antisocial behavior, scholastic difficulties, socioeconomic disadvantage, and even suicidal behavior, as up to 33% of child welfare-involved youth report suicidal thoughts, threats, or attempts (Hukkanen, Souranger, & Bergroth, 2003).

Evidence-Based Psychotherapies and Everyday Youth Mental Health Care

At the heart of so much of the research on EBPs for youth is the implicit aim of improving care for the many youths who struggle with mental health problems, most of whom will never be participants in a treatment trial. It is worthwhile, from time to time, to take stock of how well we are doing, as a field, in pursuing this aim, and

what the associated challenges and opportunities for improvement may be.

Limited Success in Dissemination

There certainly is extensive publicity for EBPs, within prominent journals (e.g., the special issue of *Journal of Clinical Child and Adolescent Psychology*, noted previously) and through government entities (e.g., the Office of the Surgeon General [1999, 2004], the President's New Freedom Commission on Mental Health [2003], and the National Registry of Effective Programs and Practices, operated through the Substance Abuse and Mental Health Services Administration [SAMHSA]). Despite the publicity, not to mention the replicated scientific support for the numerous EBPs noted in Table 14.1, most of the tested treatments are currently "practiced" largely in treatment studies and have not made their way into most everyday clinical care. Some EBPs that focus on improving behavior management skills for caregivers of delinquent or aggressive youth (e.g., MST, MTFC, and Triple P) have active dissemination programs and have made inroads, but penetration is relatively low even for these programs, and most everyday clinical service programs show very low levels, if any, of EBP components (see Brookman-Frazee, Haine, Baker-Ericzen, Zoffness, & Garland, 2010; Garland et al., 2010; Southam-Gerow et al., 2010; Weisz et al., 2009). There is also some evidence from surveys of training directors that emphasis on EBPs may not actually be growing in training programs, at least within North American doctoral programs and internship sites in clinical psychology (Woody, Weisz, & McLean, 2005). Complementing these data from North America, a U.K. survey published in 2006 by the Association for Child and Adolescent Mental Health (see http://www.acamh.org.uk/POOLED/articles/bf_eventart/view.asp?Q=bf_eventart_213513) found that CBT was the dominant approach of only 20% of practitioner respondents, despite very substantial government pressure favoring CBT. Although the data available to us from North America and the United Kingdom are patchy, and certainly do not cover all practice or training sites, they do suggest that the EBPs emerging from five decades of research are not making their way into training or practice very quickly. Why not? Why wouldn't professionals who chose careers to help young people be eager to adopt practices that have been tested and shown to work?

Dissemination Challenges

Research in practice settings and with practitioner partners has suggested several challenges to dissemination of EBPs (Weisz, 2004; Weisz, Sandler, Durlak, & Anton, 2005; Weisz, Ugueto, Herren, Afienko, & Rutt, 2011). One is the fact that most of these treatments (see Table 14.1) have been designed for single problems or disorders (or homogeneous clusters—e.g., a few depressive disorders). For practitioners, whose caseloads tend to include a broad array of disorders, and whose cases tend to show marked comorbidity, learning one or two single-disorder EBPs may not be perceived as valuable enough to warrant the time and cost. An additional concern for some practitioners is that EBPs tend to ask a lot of therapists–e.g., learning a detailed manual (often a very lengthy one), preparing in advance for each session to an extent that would be rare in everyday practice, working from an agenda rather than letting the session flow freely, and coming up with creative ways to make the manualized, agenda-guided content engaging and motivating for the youth. None of these challenges is insurmountable, but each may require attention in efforts to disseminate EBPs, and perhaps in the very development of EBPs, a theme to which we turn next.

EBP Development and Testing Conditions Have Differed From the Conditions of Everyday Practice

The shape of EBPs, and particularly the degree to which they are compatible with the conditions of everyday practice, may have a lot to do with the conditions under which they are developed and tested. These conditions have tended to differ markedly from the conditions of actual clinical practice (Weisz, Jensen-Doss, & Hawley, 2005; Weisz & Gray, 2008). This may have limited our ability to extrapolate from the research findings to everyday youth clinical care. It may also have slowed the pace of dissemination to some degree, in part by raising practitioner concern over whether the treatments that look so promising in research are really equipped for prime time in real-world clinical practice. Youths referred to clinical care settings may differ from those recruited for efficacy trials in diverse ways, including severity and family adversity (Hammen, Rudolph, Weisz, Burge, & Rao, 1999; Southam-Gerow, Weisz, & Kendall, 2003). Staff clinicians in clinics tend to differ from research therapists in RCTs in their background and training,

daily work, clientele, and professional goals (see Palinkas et al., 2008; Weisz & Addis, 2006). In addition, clinical practice and research settings tend to differ in numerous ways that could affect youth treatment outcomes and prospects for dissemination. In practice settings, for example, a variety of time, productivity, financial, and other work pressures prevail that can make it hard to optimize the treatment environment in ways that are common in RCTs (Weisz & Addis, 2006). Such differences between the youths, therapists, and contexts of typical research and those of typical clinical care suggest that there is a significant gap between research and practice.

That gap might be addressed, of course, by research that examines the performance of treatment programs in real-world clinical care contexts. However, such research has been relatively rare, to date. In our own review of youth RCTs (Weisz, Jensen-Doss, & Hawley, 2005), we found that most studies took place in settings created for research (e.g., university labs and lab clinics, rooms in a school set aside for the study), with treatment provided to youths who were recruited (e.g., through ads), and with treatment provided not by practicing clinicians but rather by graduate students or others dependent on the researcher for their employment and income. Across the RCTs, only 13% of the youth samples were clinically-referred, treatment-seeking youth; only 19% of the studies used any practitioner as therapist (we only required that at least one practitioner be included among the study therapists); and in only 4% of the studies was treatment provided in a clinical service setting separate from the research program. Combining the three dimensions, we found that only 1% of the RCTs included clinically referred youths, at least one practicing clinician, and some treatment in a service setting. In sum, the literature provided little information about how EBPs might fare in fully representative clinical care conditions.

The evidence base is also limited in terms of a related question: Do EBPs produce better outcomes than the treatments youths would otherwise receive in usual clinical care? In some respects, this is the most basic question many in clinical practice might ask. Training and building competence in a typical manual-guided EBP can be quite costly, in both money and time, and may be challenging for clinicians who are managing the demands of a practice career (and it is unclear how many EBPs an individual therapist will need to be trained in). Thus, it is reasonable for practitioners, clinic directors, policy makers, and funders to ask whether shifting from usual treatment practices to EBPs will lead to better youth outcomes than current practices do. Youth treatment research has not emphasized the kinds of studies that could answer that question—that is, RCTs in which youths with significant mental health problems or disorders are randomly assigned to a specific EBP or to usual clinical care. However, a limited pool of such studies can be found, and we turn to those studies next.

Can EBPs Produce Better Outcomes Than Usual Clinical Care?

When our research group (Weisz, Jensen-Doss, & Hawley, 2006) set out to identify these studies and synthesize their findings within a meta-analysis, we were not at all sure what the studies would show. Although proponents of EBPs have suggested that they should be used in preference to usual clinical care, a number of authors have expressed concerns about EBPs and their manuals that raise questions about whether they would even be as effective as usual care. Various writers have raised concerns that EBPs (a) have been developed mainly with relatively simple cases, even subclinical youths, and may not work well with the more challenging cases often seen in usual care; (b) have been structured for single disorders or problems and may not fare well with co-occurring problems and comorbidity, which are common in usual care; (c) are so rigidly manualized that they make it hard for therapists to individualize treatment to fit distinctive client needs, including those of minority clients, or adjust to unexpected events in client's lives; and (d) are lacking in the flexibility needed for building rapport and a strong therapeutic relationship (Addis & Krasnow, 2000; Addis & Waltz, 2002; Bernal & Scharron-Del-Rio, 2001; Garfield, 1996; Gray-Little & Kaplan, 2000; Hall, 2001; Havik & VandenBos, 1996; Strupp & Anderson, 1997; Sue, 2003; Westen, Novotny, & Thompson-Brenner, 2004a, 2004b). The concerns raise questions about whether EBPs have the characteristics needed to outperform, or even match, the performance of usual clinical care when the two are pitted against one another in fair comparisons.

Our search yielded 32 methodologically acceptable RCTs (23 published articles, 9 dissertations) that had directly compared usual care to EBPs (identified through reviews explicitly structured to determine which treatments qualified as evidence-based). The 32 studies spanned 1973 to 2004; mean sample age ranged from 6 to 17 years; about three quarters of the EBPs were specific behavioral or CBT interventions, and most of the remainder were systems-oriented approaches such as multisystemic therapy. On average, the EBPs did outperform usual care. The mean posttreatment effect size was .30, falling between conventional cutoffs for "small" and "medium," and markedly lower than mean effects found in prior meta-analyses (see Figure 14.1). The superiority of the EBPs was not reduced by high levels of youth severity or by inclusion of minority youths, thus providing no support for at least two of the concerns raised by critics of these treatments. To put the findings into context, a mean effect of .30 translates into a probability of 58% (slightly better than the chance expectancy of 50%) that a randomly selected youth receiving an EBP would be better off after treatment than a randomly selected youth receiving usual care. A more pessimistic picture was presented in a reanalysis of the Weisz et al. (2006) meta-analysis studies by Spielmans, Gatlin, and McFall (2010); controlling for factors that they believed might bias study findings in favor of EBPs, Spielmans et al. (2010) concluded that EBPs did not significantly outperform usual care (see Ougrin & Latif [2011] for a similar conclusion regarding therapy *engagement* in six RCTs comparing usual care to a specific manualized (or replicable) psychotherapy for treatment of youth self-harm). One conclusion on which all the meta-analysis authors would likely agree is that outcomes have been quite variable across studies, with a number of studies showing the outcomes of usual care to be similar or superior to the EBP outcomes to which they were compared. This variability is shown in Figure 14.2.

Some Implications of the EBP Versus Usual Care Findings for Stakeholders in Youth Mental Health Care

The EBP versus usual care meta-analysis by Weisz et al. (2006), the reanalysis by Spielmans et al. (2010), and the therapy engagement meta-analysis by Ougrin and Latif (2011) are certainly not definitive, given the modest sample of studies included. However, the findings do suggest implications for future research and a question related to treatment adoption by various stakeholders in youth mental health. The question: What kind

EBP Versus Usual Care Effect Sizes

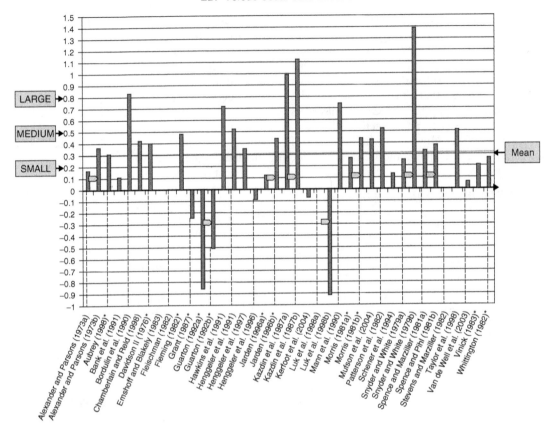

FIGURE 14.2 Effect sizes of individual studies comparing evidence-based psychotherapies to usual care, in a meta-analysis by Weisz, Jensen-Doss, and Hawley (2006). Horizontal bar at .30 shows mean effect size across the full study set. (Reprinted with permission from John R. Weisz.)

of evidence on "evidence-based psychotherapies" should be used when policy makers, clinical administrators, practitioners, and consumers of youth mental health care decide whether to shift from usual clinical practices to tested treatments? Because such a decision is a weighty one for most providers, encompassing the cost of care and the question of which forms of help will really help young people most, it seems important to know whether the evidence shows that a shift to the new treatment is likely to lead to better outcomes than simply retaining the intervention status quo. The meta-analytic findings shown in Figure 14.2 indicate that a number of treatments officially designated "evidence-based" may not meet that standard. Figure 14.2 suggests that we cannot safely assume that all EBPs are superior to what clinicians are doing routinely in usual care. Even studies testing EBPs of the same name (e.g.,

anger management and problem-solving skills) showed very different effects depending on (a) the specific treatment procedures used, and (b) to what form of usual care the EBPs were compared. From a clinical policy perspective, a case could be made that whether a specific form of usual care should be replaced with a particular EBP may need to depend on (a) not just the generic form of the EBP (e.g., anger management training) but the specific protocol, and (b) what form(s) of usual care prevail in the setting in question. Priority for changing current practices might best be given to the specific EBPs that outperform the kinds of usual care that prevail in the service setting where a change is contemplated. We consider other implications of the EBP versus usual care comparisons as we turn to a discussion of strategies for strengthening our tested treatments.

Strategies for Strengthening Youth Psychotherapies

Several strategies for building stronger treatments are suggested by the evidence reviewed thus far, including, but not limited to, the meta-analytic findings shown in Figure 14.2.

Learning From Usual Care

One possibility suggested by Figure 14.2 is that some of the interventions now regarded as usual care may have genuine potential as effective treatments. Those forms of usual care that outperform current EBPs may turn out to be interventions that warrant documenting in written protocols and testing in their own right. Some of these might eventually make their way into future lists of EBPs. For this to be feasible, however, investigators will need to shift from treating usual care as a mere "control condition" to regarding it as a set of interventions worth documenting and studying in their own right. In general, the studies cited in Figure 14.2 provided good documentation of the EBPs but poor documentation of the contents and procedures of the usual care conditions to which the EBPs were compared. In most cases we were unable to determine, with any precision, what "usual care" actually consisted of. This problem needs to be solved if we are to maximize the hypothesis-generating potential of EBP versus usual care research. Methods are now available for documenting the contents of usual care, through a standardized clinician checklist (Weersing, Weisz, & Donenberg, 2002) and through a system for observer coding of intervention sessions (McLeod & Weisz, 2005, 2010). The checklist has been used to describe usual care for a variety of youth problems and conditions (Weersing et al., 2002), and the observational coding system has been used to document characteristics of usual care in treatment of youth disruptive disorders (Brookman-Frazee et al., 2010; Garland et al., 2010) and depressive and anxiety disorders (Southam-Gerow et al., 2010; Weisz et al., 2009). In the next generation of youth treatment studies, these methods and others could be used to characterize those patterns of usual care that show evidence of benefit and might thus become candidates for testing in their own right.

Enriching Our Understanding of What Makes Treatments Work

Whatever the collection of EBPs looks like at any particular time, there is much to be gained by enriching our understanding of what makes these treatments work—that is, what the specific change processes are through which treatment benefit is generated. This knowledge can be used to strengthen the "punch" of treatments while shrinking or eliminating less essential components, thus enhancing both the potency and efficiency of intervention. One approach to this goal is mediation testing, ideally leading to identification of true mechanisms of change, but as our earlier review showed, surprisingly few mediators have been replicated in youth psychotherapy research. There are myriad plausible reasons for the elusiveness of replicated mediators, some of which may be addressed only by changing the way RCTs are designed, with assessment of multiple candidate mediators and outcomes at pretreatment, posttreatment, and at several occasions during treatment (Kazdin, 2007). Because frequent assessments with multiple measures are resource- and time-intensive, it may be wise to identify the most promising candidate mediators from existing RCT datasets with less-than-ideal assessment schedules for testing in future RCTs with enriched assessment schedules. Reviews (Chu & Harrison, 2007; Weersing & Weisz, 2002b) have found that researchers have often collected data on potential mediators but without then conducting formal tests of mediation. We encourage researchers to include such formal tests and to consider four strategies that could markedly enhance our understanding.

Boosting power to detect mediation. Because youth psychotherapy outcome studies rarely have very large sample sizes, it is imperative that researchers choose statistical methods with the highest power to detect hypothesized mediation effects (and with reasonable Type I error rates). Baron and Kenny's (1986) causal-steps method, used in 71% of the mediation tests published in the *Journal of Consulting and Clinical Psychology* and the *Journal of Applied Psychology* from 2000 to 2003, actually has very low power, according to Fritz and MacKinnon (2007). These authors recommended that researchers use, instead, one of the following more amply powered methods: (a) bias-corrected bootstrapping (a kind of resampling method), (b) joint significance testing, or (c) PRODCLIN asymmetric confidence-intervals testing (but see Fritz, Taylor, & MacKinnon, 2012 for conditions under which bias-corrected bootstrapping is likely to produce inflated Type I errors). An additional advantage of the recommended mediation tests is that the statistical code to conduct some of these tests with various software programs (e.g., SPSS, SAS, R) has been made freely available by mediation methodologists.[1]

Testing for mediation in the absence of a treatment main effect. Identifying a significant treatment condition main effect is a necessary step in Baron and Kenny's (1986) causal-steps test of mediation. However, mediation can occur in the absence of a main effect of treatment.[2] This is because a main effect (*total effect*) may be the sum total of several effects, including the *direct effect* of the treatment on the outcome and *indirect effects* of the treatment on the outcome through one or more mediators; if the direct and indirect effects are in opposite directions, they may sum to zero, resulting in a nonsignificant main effect (Hayes, 2009; MacKinnon, Fairchild, & Fritz, 2007). Mediation testing in the absence of significant main effects is particularly pertinent to more recent RCTs that have compared a target treatment to usual care or to an alternative treatment (rather than to a waitlist control) and found no significant treatment effects. The target therapy may lead to improved outcomes through increasing one hypothesized mediator, and the alternative treatment may lead to similarly improved outcomes through a second mediator. In such cases it would be unfortunate to miss out on the discovery of two mediators that could illuminate how two different treatments work because there was no main effect of treatment. Therefore, several mediation researchers have recommended testing for mediation even when main effects are nonsignificant (see e.g., Hayes, 2009). Fortunately, the three methods recommended in the previous paragraph allow tests of mediation whether main effects are significant or not.

Testing for moderated mediation or mediated moderation. For youth psychotherapy in general, change processes are likely to be too complex to be captured by a simple model involving one mediator. The strength or direction of the mediation relationship may be different in each treatment condition of an RCT or at each level of a moderator. These more complex models are examples of *moderated mediation* (Muller, Judd, & Yzerbyt, 2005), also termed *conditional indirect effects* (Preacher, Rucker, & Hayes 2007). Moderated mediation models make sense in that two different therapy protocols may have different effects on the mediator and also on how the mediator relates to outcome (Kraemer et al., 2002). On the other hand, *mediated moderation* occurs only when there is overall moderation of treatment effects and when a mediation relationship accounts for the moderation (Muller et al., 2005), that is, the mediator is an intermediate variable between the interaction (of the treatment and moderator) and the outcome (MacKinnon, Fairchild, et al., 2007). In a special case of mediated moderation, the *mediated baseline by treatment moderation*, the moderator is a baseline variable and the mediator is the change in that same variable during treatment (MacKinnon, Fairchild, et al., 2007). For example, in an RCT of parent training, if families high on harsh parenting at baseline (i.e., the moderator) showed greater improvement in youth externalizing symptom outcomes than families low on harsh parenting at baseline, relative to control, and change in harsh parenting mediated treatment effects, then the mediation would be accounting for the moderation. The mediated baseline by treatment moderation model is common in prevention research (MacKinnon, Fairchild, et al., 2007) and could be useful to youth psychotherapy researchers.

Identifying true mechanisms of change. Eventually it will be important to move beyond mere mediation to identify processes that operate as true mechanisms of change. Kazdin (2007) has proposed that although demonstrating statistical mediation is a first step in this process, for the mediator to qualify as a change mechanism requires (a) strong associations between the treatment and the mediator and between the mediator and change in outcome, (b) specificity of the mediator such that other candidate variables are shown not to mediate treatment outcome, (c) consistency of the mediation effect across studies, (d) experimental manipulation of the mediator in subsequent studies to confirm that the relation between mediator and outcome is causal and in the expected direction, (e) temporal precedence of the mediator in relation to treatment

---

[1]For bias-corrected bootstrapping see Preacher and Hayes (2004, 2008; see also http://quantpsy.org/medn.htm and http://www.afhayes.com/spss-sas-and-mplus-macros-and-code.html). For PRODCLIN see MacKinnon, Fritz, Williams, and Lockwood (2007; see also http://www.public.asu.edu/~davidpm/ripl/Prodclin/).

[2]Some researchers (e.g., Holmbeck, 1997) prefer to use the term *mediation* only when significant main effects are present and the term *indirect effects* when significant main effects are absent. Others (e.g., Kraemer et al., 2002) use the term mediation whether a significant main effect is present or not.

outcome, (f) a dose–response relationship in which enhancement of the mediator is associated with enhanced outcome, and (g) plausibility or coherence of how the mediator brings about therapeutic change and how relevant findings fit into the evidence base. As best we can determine, no true mechanism of change has yet been established according to these criteria, either in youth or adult psychotherapy. Indeed, satisfying all these criteria may well require marked improvements in measurement technology (e.g., to capture the precise timing of change in mediators and outcomes). Nonetheless, identifying change mechanisms is an important long-term aspiration for the field.

Understanding and Supporting Treatment Fidelity: Therapist Adherence and Competence

Regardless of the prior evidence supporting a particular treatment, its impact going forward is likely to depend significantly on how therapists deliver it. This brings us to the need for quality control in youth therapy. The development and testing of quality control standards, embodied within *treatment fidelity* measures, lags well behind the development and dissemination of evidence-based treatment protocols. Treatment fidelity includes two components: (1) *adherence*, defined as the degree to which a therapist follows the content and procedures of a manualized treatment protocol, and (2) *competence*, defined as the skillfulness with which a therapist conducts treatment (Waltz, Addis, Koerner, & Jacobson, 1993). In research trials, it is important that the treatment procedures used be a faithful representation of the treatment protocol that is ostensibly being evaluated, so that findings will indeed reflect on that specific protocol. In clinical practice, accurately representing the intervention provided to patients is a matter of professional ethics. However, in both research and clinical practice, there are surprisingly few quality control standards in place to ensure that treatments are carried out as they were intended to be delivered.

Treatment fidelity, although often discussed in our field, has remained surprisingly understudied to date. Kazdin et al. (1990) reviewed youth psychotherapy outcome studies published between 1970 and 1989 and found that 19.3% of the studies reported assessment of treatment fidelity. Perepletchikova, Treat, and Kazdin (2007) developed a measure, the Implementation of Treatment Integrity Procedures Scale (ITIPS),

to determine the degree to which RCTs assess treatment fidelity. The 22-item measure taps treatment integrity assessment (adherence and competence) via direct and indirect methods, psychometric properties of the treatment integrity measures used, a protocol to determine whether treatments delivered were an accurate representation of the intended treatment, the training of treatment integrity raters and evaluation of interrater reliability, and report of treatment integrity protocol implementation. A review of 147 youth and adult psychotherapy research articles published between 2000 and 2004 (Perepletchikova et al., 2007) revealed that only 3.5% of the RCTs included what the authors considered adequate assessment of treatment fidelity.

Measuring adherence. Therapist adherence has been studied more frequently and extensively than therapist competence. However, there is no commonly accepted measurement methodology. Adherence measures differ widely in a variety of important dimensions (Waltz et al., 1993), such as the criterion against which the therapist's performance is measured, complexity of the ratings scheme and level of expertise required to make ratings, sources of information (e.g., audiotapes, videotapes, therapist- or client-report on checklists and questionnaires), and unit of analyses (e.g., complete treatment session, randomly selected segments). Additionally, most adherence measures have been developed by researchers and only used for a single study or cluster of related studies conducted by a single research group, and thus may not be particularly transportable.

Direct methods of assessment, such as ratings of videotaped treatment sessions by an independent team of trained raters, certainly provide greater potential for objectivity than ratings by therapists, supervisors, or clients. However, feasibility of implementation is an important issue in treatment fidelity assessment, and observational coding systems are costly and time-consuming. Thus, Schoenwald, Henggeler, Brondino, and Rowland (2000) recommended the use of simple, brief, user-friendly measures that can be implemented in everyday clinical care settings and can be shown to be associated with treatment outcomes. Few such measures exist, but the MST treatment fidelity literature is headed in this direction.

Henggeler, Borduin, Schoenwald, Huey, and Chapman (2006) developed the 28-item MST Adherence Measure-Revised (TAM-R) rated on a 5-point Likert scale, to assess in-session therapist adherence. The TAM-R is completed separately by youths, caregivers, and therapists to rate level of adherence of treatment sessions. Examples of measure items are "the therapist tried to understand how the family's problems all fit together" (consistent with MST Principle 1, which states that the goal of assessment is to contextualize problems within a broader conceptual framework) and "the therapist recommended that family members do specific things to solve their problems" (consistent with MST Principle 4, which states that treatment should be present-focused and target specific problems for intervention). In a study assessing MST for juvenile offenders, Schoenwald, Chapman, Sheidow, and Carter (2009) found that parent-reported ratings of therapist adherence using the TAM-R predicted reduced rates of long-term criminal offenses. Similarly, Schoenwald and colleagues (2000) found that parent-reported ratings of therapist adherence using the TAM (Henggeler & Borduin, 1992) predicted reduced rates of criminal offenses, drug use, antisocial behavior problems, and improvements in family relationships. Ratings of youths, caregivers, and therapists have not been found to correlate very highly with one another, and we have not seen assessments of whether these informant reports are associated with external observer ratings; assessing these associations, to address the important question of measure validity, will be a valuable direction for future research.

Measuring competence. Youth psychotherapy fidelity research has mainly focused on therapist adherence. Competence assessments share the complexities noted earlier for adherence measurement (e.g., varied measurement modalities, sources of information, units of analyses), with the added challenge of operationalizing the construct of therapist competence. Additionally, raters are required to have a high level of expertise in order to assess quality of treatment delivery, and the subjectivity of such ratings could lead to low interrater reliability. Sburlati, Schniering, Lyneham, and Rapee (2011) proposed a model for conceptualizing therapist competencies in working with youngsters who have anxiety and depressive disorders; the model includes generic therapist competencies (general skills that are valued in therapists regardless of treatment orientation) and specific cognitive-behavioral therapy technique competencies, taking into account social, cognitive, and emotional developmental stages. It seems clear that operationalizing and

measuring competence in the delivery of youth treatments remains a significant challenge for the field.

Future directions for the study of treatment fidelity. As we have seen, adherence assessment methods have been developed and implemented in a number of youth therapy studies, and in multiple forms. Competence assessment has lagged behind, and significant work on the measure development front will be needed in the days ahead. For both forms of fidelity assessment, practical feasibility will be a key issue. In a recent review, Schoenwald and colleagues (2011) identified several challenges to implementation of fidelity measures, including financial and professional burdens and the ability to fit data collection and measurement seamlessly into clinic routines and protocol. Although observational coding systems are more objective and rigorous in their methodology, they may not be either practical or feasible in most treatment research or clinical practice (e.g., due to high cost, high level of expertise required, and time requirements). It seems clear that if fidelity assessment is to become a routine part of clinical research, and to be feasible for clinical practice, what will be needed are brief, user-friendly treatment fidelity measures that are low-cost and efficient while retaining psychometric integrity and validity. This may be a tall order, requiring some of our best minds.

Improving Our Use of Technology

Many youths who need effective mental health services cannot access them because of their geographic location or limited family resources. To address these and other barriers to care, some researchers are capitalizing on modern technological advances to increase the accessibility and cost-effectiveness of psychosocial treatments. In some cases, this involves a shift away from traditional forms of face-to-face therapist-patient talk therapy. Preliminary research on the use of computer-based and computer-assisted treatments for internalizing disorders and eating disorders in adults has been promising, but less research has been conducted with young people.

Camp Cope-A-Lot is a computer-assisted, animated treatment for youth anxiety disorders, based on the Coping Cat program (see Table 14.1; see Kendall and Hedtke, 2006). The young patient navigates through session activities and videos on the computer, interacting with animated figures, and with the therapist acting as a coach to guide the youngster through the program. One RCT comparing this computer-assisted treatment to standard individual CBT and a computer-based academic learning control condition showed that greater gains were made in both CBT conditions than the computer control condition (Kendall, Khanna, Edson, Cummings, & Harris, 2011). Although comparable gains were made in the two CBT conditions, youth participants reported greater treatment satisfaction with Camp Cope-a-Lot than with standard CBT.

Cognitive bias modification (CBM) interventions have also been used to treat youth anxiety disorders. The rationale is that youths with anxiety disorders, compared to nonanxious controls, have been found to show a bias toward automatic attention to threat. CBM is designed to target biased automatic cognitive/attentional processes by shaping disengagement from threatening stimuli and an attentional shift toward neutral stimuli. In the very first study of CBM for youth anxiety disorders, Rozenman, Weersing, and Amir (2011) used an attention dot probe task to treat 16 anxious youths. Youths completed the attention dot probe task on a computer. First, a fixation cross appeared on the computer screen for 500 ms. It was then replaced by two faces, one above the other, depicting the same person with either a neutral or disgust facial expression. After the presentation of the faces for 500 ms, a probe (the letter "E" or "F") appeared where one of the two faces used to be, and participants indicated the probe letter by pressing the "E" or "F" key on the computer keyboard. The probe appeared behind the neutral face for 80% of the trials; this tilt toward the neutral face was designed to create attentional disengagement from the threatening stimuli and increase attention to the neutral stimuli. In an open trial of this treatment approach, Rozenman and colleagues (2011) found that youths experienced a significant reduction in anxiety and depression symptoms at posttreatment, with 12 of the 16 youths no longer meeting *DSM-IV* criteria for an anxiety disorder diagnosis. These intriguing findings point to the potential value of a full RCT testing the CBM method against an appropriate control or comparison condition.

Merry and colleagues (see Fleming, Dixon, Frampton, & Merry, 2011; Merry et al., 2012) developed a self-help computer program (SPARX) for youth depression. SPARX is a video game in which youths customize an avatar and navigate through a 3-D fantasy world with challenges and puzzles that teach them CBT skills such as problem solving, coping with negative thoughts, and relaxation techniques. SPARX was tested against a wait-list control group in a randomized trial focused on adolescents who had been excluded from mainstream education and who had significant symptoms of depression (Fleming et al., 2011); those treated with SPARX showed significantly greater symptom reduction on core depression measures, but not on all measures of psychological functioning. In a second RCT (Merry et al., 2012), a "noninferiority trial" with adolescents who were seeking help for depression, SPARX showed similar outcomes to an active treatment-as-usual comparison group, suggesting that the efficient, low-cost computerized approach to CBT was no less effective than significantly more costly treatment involving primarily individual face-to-face counseling delivered by trained clinicians.

Technology may also prove helpful in therapist training. Kendall and Khanna (2008) developed a computer-based therapist training program for CBT for youth anxiety disorders. The program, called *CBT4CBT*, is a DVD that walks the therapist, step-by-step, through the same content as the print version of the therapist treatment manual, with quizzes included to check for understanding. The program also contains other helpful supplements, such as therapist notes/tips for each treatment session, and various audio-visual stimuli (e.g., exposure videos) for the therapist to use in-session. Kendall et al. (2011) conducted one RCT evaluating a CBT4CBT training group as compared to a manual-based training group and a waitlist control group; Trainees in the CBT4CBT and manual-based training groups (versus the wait-list control) showed similarly high levels of treatment knowledge and program satisfaction.

Future directions for technology-assisted and technology-based treatments for youth psychopathology are almost certainly more extensive than any of us can now imagine. As the reach of computer games, smartphone applications, and Internet sites spreads, and the forms of electronic communication diversify, opportunities to reach young people in new ways will continue to expand. There can be little doubt that we are on the verge of a massive mushrooming of RCTs testing new ways to deliver interventions to young people through the emerging technological advances that have so captured youth attention and interest.

Guiding Treatment Through Ongoing Feedback on Youth Treatment Response

One burgeoning field of research that has the potential to complement and improve therapy is the provision of feedback on youth treatment response to clinicians (and supervisors) throughout the course of therapy. Recent work with adult therapy has shown that providing feedback to clinicians can result in improved therapy success rates and reduced deterioration in client functioning (Anker, Duncan, & Sparks, 2009; Lambert et al., 2002). Relatively few studies have focused explicitly on youth treatment, but initial findings have shown an association between the use of routine feedback and improved therapeutic relationships and therapy outcome (Bickman, Breda, deAndrade, & Kelley, 2010; Stein, Kogan, Hutchison, Magee, & Sobero, 2010).

In a recent meta-analysis by Shimokawa, Lambert, and Smart (2010), data from six major studies employing a psychotherapy feedback system for adult therapy (i.e., Outcome Questionnaire-45) were reanalyzed in an effort to determine the effects of progress feedback on clinical outcomes. Feedback interventions were broken into three distinct categories—patient progress feedback to clinicians only, patient progress feedback to clinicians and patients, and patient progress feedback to clinicians plus additional clinical support tools. Results indicated that the use of all three forms of feedback intervention were associated with enhanced treatment outcomes.

In recent work on the youth therapy front, Chorpita, Weisz, and colleagues (Chorpita et al., 2010; Weisz et al., 2011) have developed strategies for generating ongoing, frequent feedback on youth patient progress during treatment via two brief, psychometrically sound measures, displayed within an Internet-based system. One of the measures, the Brief Problem Checklist (Chorpita et al., 2010) is a 12-item method for obtaining weekly youth and caregiver reports on severity of the youth's internalizing and externalizing problems. The other measure, Youth Top Problems (Weisz et al., 2011), is a 3-item idiographic consumer-driven method through which youths and caregivers identify, at pretreatment, the three most important problems for which the youth needs help in treatment, and then rate the severity of these problems weekly thereafter. Weekly ratings on these two measures are displayed within a web-based system that provides quick access to those making treatment plans and adjusting those plans throughout an episode of care. The system provides the kind of frequent updates on the youth's response to treatment that can guide ongoing treatment planning and supervision. The approach used to integrate this information with a manual-guided treatment program is described next.

Restructuring Evidence-Based Psychotherapies to Fit Clinical Practice Needs

Discussion of feedback systems connects in an interesting way to the theme of restructuring EBPs to fit the conditions of clinical practice. As we have seen (and as shown in Table 14.1), more than five decades of research have produced a rich array of EBPs, and a rich body of information on the groups with which and the conditions under which these treatments work. As we have also seen, most of these EBPs have been developed and tested under carefully arranged conditions that are appropriate for experimental tests but not very representative of the clientele, clinicians, or conditions of everyday clinical practice; and when EBPs are pitted against usual clinical care in randomized trials, their relative benefit is modest on average, and variable, such that a number of the EBPs show effects that are similar to or weaker than usual care. We have noted some of the challenges that may limit the effectiveness of many EBPs in everyday practice conditions. Among the challenges, (a) most EBPs are designed for single disorders or homogenous clusters (e.g., two depressive disorders), but most practitioners carry quite diverse caseloads, limiting the value of any single-disorder protocol; (b) the single-disorder focus of most EBPs also conflicts with the fact that most referred youths have comorbid disorders and co-occurring problems; (c) most EBPs are ballistic, designed for sustained focus on one goal or objective throughout treatment, but youths in treatment often show change in patterns of dysfunction and treatment needs during episodes of care. To address these needs, some investigators are moving toward restructured treatments that provide broader and more flexible coverage of problems and disorders while retaining the core components of the EBPs that have been developed and tested so carefully over the decades.

Our own effort in this regard is illustrative; it has developed as part of the work of the Research

Network on Youth Mental Health (see Schoenwald, Kelleher, Weisz, & the Research Network on Youth Mental Health, 2008), which set out to address challenges like those noted above. One result was an integrative modular approach to delivering the components of EBPs for depressive, anxiety, and conduct-related problems and disorders (Chorpita & Weisz, 2009; Weisz & Chorpita, 2011. The modules of this treatment protocol, called MATCH (for *Modular Approach to Therapy for Children* ... [Chorpita & Weisz, 2009]), were brief summaries of treatment elements commonly included in CBT for depression, CBT for anxiety, and behavioral parent training for disruptive conduct (see Chorpita & Daleiden, 2009; Chorpita, Daleiden, & Weisz, 2005). These modules are shown in Figure 14.3. By encompassing multiple broad domains of psychopathology, the modular treatment addresses the concern that practitioners typically carry broad caseloads, and that referred youths tend to have multiple

co-occurring disorders and problems. The multiproblem focus of MATCH also makes it possible to address the flux in treatment needs and problems that youths in treatment often show during episodes of care. As a youth's treatment needs shift, therapists are able to respond by navigating across the modules shown in Figure 14.3, to shift the focus of treatment as needed.

Navigating across modules appropriately, however, requires an ongoing flow of feedback on the youth's current functioning and response to treatment. This need for ongoing, timely feedback—ideally, weekly—has led us to develop the two brief, psychometrically sound measures described above—Brief Problem Checklist (Chorpita et al., 2010) and Youth Top Problems (Weisz et al., 2011)—and to build a Web-based system for displaying information from these measures, obtained from youths and caregivers each week. Weekly ratings on these two measures are displayed within an Internet-based system for

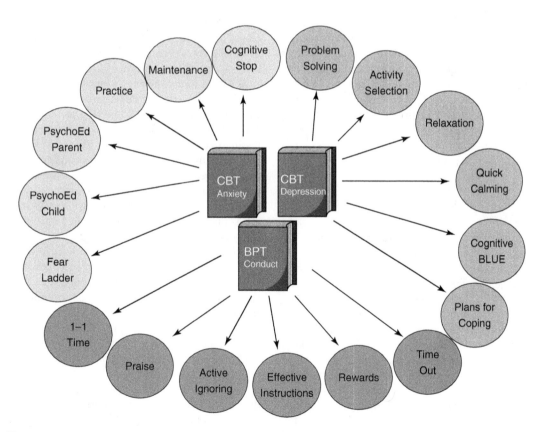

FIGURE 14.3 Design of *Modular Approach to Therapy with Children* (Chorpita & Weisz, 2009), showing some of the modules derived from three forms of evidence-based psychotherapy—that is, CBT for depression- and anxiety-related problems and disorders, and behavioral parent training (BPT) for conduct-related problems and disorders. (Reprinted with permission from John R. Weisz.)

ease of access. The weekly updates help guide decisions as to whether shifts in treatment focus are needed and which modules may be most appropriate for the next steps of treatment.

We have tested the MATCH modular approach in one completed randomized effectiveness trial (Weisz et al., 2012). Community practitioners from 10 different outpatient service settings participated. These were randomly assigned to three conditions: *Standard manual treatment* (therapists used standard separate manuals for CBT for depression, CBT for anxiety, and behavioral parent training for conduct problems); *modular treatment* (i.e., the MATCH manual, integrating the elements of the three separate treatments); and usual care. Outcomes were assessed in this study through the weekly BPC and TPA measures as well as through standardized diagnostic assessment at pre- and posttreatment. Our analyses showed that MATCH produced significantly steeper trajectories of improvement than usual care and standard treatment on multiple BPC and TPA measures. Youths treated with MATCH also had significantly fewer diagnoses than usual care youths at post-treatment. In contrast, outcomes of standard manual treatment did not differ significantly from usual care. These findings suggest that a modular redesign of EBPs that integrates core elements of EBPs for multiple forms of dysfunction may be an effective approach to adapting EBPs for everyday clinical care. Two other randomized effectiveness trials of MATCH are now underway.

Designing and Testing Treatments With Their Ultimate Deployment in Mind

Our effort to design EBPs for use in clinical care contexts is but one of a number of examples in the youth intervention literature (see, for example, Henggeler & Schaeffer, 2010; Smith & Chamberlain, 2010). These illustrate a broader approach to thinking about treatment development that has been identified in prior work (e.g., Weisz, 2004) as the *deployment-focused model* of treatment development and testing. This model reflects the basic idea that it makes sense to build and test interventions with the clientele and clinicians, and in the contexts for which those interventions are ultimately intended. Despite examples to the contrary, most EBPs have not been developed and tested in this manner, and it is possible that this fact may have contributed to some of what we saw in Figures 14.1 and 14.2. The growing body

of research in implementation science (Fixsen, Naoom, Blasé, Friedman, & Wallace, 2005) strongly suggests that any practices—including EBPs—risk a loss of potency when moved into contexts and conditions that are new and different from those where they were previously used and tested. Successful implementation usually requires considerably more than simply relocating the intervention; multiple steps of intervention adaptation, intervener selection and coaching, and often even recipient and organizational preparation may be required (Fixsen et al., 2005). The modest mean effect size for EBP versus usual care comparison, shown in Figure 14.1, and the fact that a number of EBPs did not outperform usual care, as shown in Figure 14.2, might be seen as highlighting the challenges of implementation.

This challenge may be particularly serious in those cases where the implementation context differs most from the context in which development and testing took place. The research lab development and series of efficacy trials through which most youth EBPs have been developed and tested have not exposed these therapies to the full array of factors present in the clientele, clinicians, and service clinic context of real-world clinical care. This might not be a major problem for psychotropics or other interventions that operate through the biological system. But for psychosocial interventions, a sequence of development and testing that bypasses those clinical context factors that may impact treatment process and outcome could leave the resulting therapies poorly prepared for real-world treatment conditions. As a result, the treatments that fare well in efficacy trials may not look so strong when placed in everyday care contexts and compared to the usual care that takes place in those conditions.

A relatively common pattern in youth therapy research has been for investigators to use carefully controlled efficacy designs to build and provide the evidence base for their treatment protocols, with the idea that effectiveness tests in representative clinical care settings will come later, when the intervention procedures have been perfected. Although this last step has not actually happened with EBPs, to date, the concept does acknowledge the value of assessing how well treatments fare in real-world treatment contexts. It is possible, though, that even when that last step is taken, the differences between treatment within efficacy research and treatment in actual practice are too numerous and too pronounced to be bridged as simply the final step after a series of efficacy studies. The number of dimensions along which treatment must be adjusted to span the lab-to-clinic gap may make the task of moving efficacy-tested treatments into everyday clinical care so complex that the task really needs to be a part of the treatment development process. Indeed, the very real-world factors that efficacy trial researchers might view as a nuisance or "noise" (e.g., youth comorbidity, parent pathology, family stressors that produce no-shows and dropouts, therapists with heavy caseloads) and thus attempt to avoid (e.g., by recruiting and screening cases, applying exclusion criteria, adding incentives for therapy attendance, hiring their own therapists), may in fact be precisely the kinds of factors that need to be understood and addressed if psychotherapy treatment protocols are to be created that fit well into clinical practice. EBPs that are stymied by these real-world factors may not fare so well in practice, no matter how strong they look in efficacy trials.

A closely related point is that implementing EBPs in practice settings may require interventions in those settings to address obstacles to effective use of the treatments. For example, treatments that call for weekly installments of skill-building with youths or parents may require new family engagement procedures (e.g., Nock & Kazdin, 2005) to generate faithful attendance. Or interventions that do not fit smoothly into the standard procedures of a clinic (e.g., assessment or supervision requirements that differ from the clinic routine) may only be possible if paired with organizational problem solving. Putting EBPs into the real-world settings for which they are ultimately intended could be the best way to identify, construct, and test the setting-focused interventions needed to make the target treatments succeed.

A Deployment-Focused Model of Treatment Development and Testing

Following this reasoning, we have proposed a shift from the traditional sequential efficacy trials model to a *deployment-focused model* of treatment development and testing (Weisz, 2004; Weisz, Jensen, & McLeod, 2005). This model includes a series of steps designed to (a) place the process of building treatments and testing their effects within the contexts for which they are ultimately intended, and (b) construe this process as ongoing and sequential, not as a single final step. A primary aim of the model is to create a process through which the treatment characteristics needed for success in real-world clinical application can be identified and built into the intervention as a natural part of the scientific process. A testable premise underlying the model is that the potential of an EBP to be beneficial in a practice context is most likely to be realized if the treatment has been adapted to practice conditions as a part of its development and testing. The model is consistent with findings in implementation science (Fixsen et al., 2005) that when interventions that succeed in one setting are moved to a very different setting, it is common for such efforts to struggle, and often fail initially. Some are ultimately successful, after multiple steps of intervention adaptation. The proposed deployment-focused model is a way of making that adaptation process a natural part of treatment development and testing, with the objective of creating treatments that are ready for prime time in clinical practice.

SUMMARY AND CONCLUSIONS

Youth psychotherapy has evolved over the past century from an art to a science, from a rich collection of principles and procedures built on the grand theories of the early 1900s to an empirically guided enterprise in which claims of effectiveness are tested scientifically. One result of this transition is an array of youth interventions that have met criteria for the status of "evidence-based psychotherapies," and a growing body of evidence on the processes through which these therapies work, and on the boundaries within which they work. As we learn more about how to implement these interventions in various settings and with various populations, we also need to monitor their goodness of fit to representative clinical care clients and conditions, and their effectiveness relative to the usual care that prevails in everyday treatment. Evidence indicates that our current collection of youth EBPs does improve on usual care, on average, but only modestly so, and not in every comparison. This suggests, in turn, that the agenda for future research might profitably include investigating strategies for strengthening EBPs, expanding their potential to benefit the youths and families who seek treatment in everyday clinical care.

REFERENCES

Achenbach, T. M., McConaughy, S. H., & Howell, C.T. (1987). Child/adolescent behavioral and emotional problems: Implications of cross-informant correlations for situational specificity. *Psychological Bulletin, 101,* 213–232.

Ackerson, J., Scogin, F., McKendree-Smith, N., & Lyman, R. D. (1998). Cognitive bibliotherapy for mild and moderate adolescent depressive symptomatology. *Journal of Consulting and Clinical Psychology, 66,* 685–690.

Addis, M. E., & Krasnow, A. D. (2000). A national survey of practicing psychologists' attitudes toward psychotherapy treatment manuals. *Journal of Consulting and Clinical Psychology, 68,* 331–339.

Addis, M. E., & Waltz, J. (2002). Implicit and untested assumptions about the role of psychotherapy treatment manuals in evidence based mental health practice. *Clinical Psychology: Science and Practice, 9,* 435–438.

Alexander, J. F., & Parsons, B. V. (1982). *Functional family therapy: Principles and procedures.* Monterey, CA: Brooks/Cole.

Anker, M. G., Duncan, B. L., & Sparks, J. A. (2009). Using client feedback to improve couple therapy outcomes: A randomized clinical trial in a naturalistic setting. *Journal of Consulting and Clinical Psychology, 77,* 693–704.

Asarnow, J. R., Goldstein, M. J., Tompson, M., & Guthrie, D. (1993). One-year outcomes of depressive disorders in child psychiatric inpatients: Evaluation of the prognostic power of a brief measure of expressed emotion. *Journal of Child Psychology and Psychiatry, 34,* 129–137.

Barkley, R. (1997). *Defiant children* (2nd ed.). New York, NY: Guilford Press.

Barlow, D. H., Nock, M. K., & Hersen, M. (2009). *Single case experimental designs: Strategies for studying behavior change* (3rd ed.). Boston, MA: Allyn & Bacon.

Baron, R. M., & Kenny, D. A. (1986). The moderator-mediator variable distinction in social psychological research: Conceptual, strategic, and statistical considerations. *Journal of Personality and Social Psychology, 51,* 1173–1182.

Barrett, P. M., Farrell, L., Pina, A. A., Peris, T. S., & Piacentini, J. (2008). Evidence-based psychosocial treatments for child and adolescent obsessive-compulsive disorders. *Journal of Child and Adolescent Clinical Psychology, 37,* 131–155.

Beauchaine, T. P., Webster-Stratton, C., & Reid, M. J. (2005). Mediators, moderators, and predictors of 1-year outcomes among children treated for early-onset conduct problems: A latent growth curve analysis. *Journal of Consulting and Clinical Psychology, 73,* 371–388.

Beck, A. T. (1970). Cognitive therapy: Nature and relation to behavior therapy. *Behavior Therapy, 1,* 184.

Bernal, G., & Scharron-Del-Rio, M. R. (2001). Are empirically supported treatments valid for ethnic minorities? Toward an alternative approach for treatment research. *Cultural Diversity and Ethnic Minority Psychology, 7,* 328–342.

Bickman, L., Breda, C., deAndrade, A. R. V., & Kelley, S. D. (2010). *CFIT evaluation report: The effects of CFIT on clinician behavior and youth mental health outcomes.* Nashville, TN: Center for Evaluation and Program Improvement.

Beidel, D. C., Turner, S. M., & Morris, T. L. (2000). Behavioral treatment of childhood social phobia. *Journal of Consulting and Clinical Psychology, 68,* 1072–1080.

Block, J. (1978). Effects of a rational-emotive mental health program on poorly achieving, disruptive high school students. *Journal of Counseling Psychology, 25,* 61–65.

Bolton, P., Bass, J., Betancourt, T., Speelman, L., Onyango, G., Clougherty, K., . . . Verdeli, H. (2007). Interventions for depression symptoms among adolescent survivors of war and displacement in Northern Uganda: A randomized controlled trial. *Journal of the American Medical Association, 298,* 519–527.

Brookman-Frazee, L., Haine, R. A., Baker-Ericzen, M., Zoffness, R., & Garland, A. F. (2010). Factors associated with use of evidence-based practice strategies in usual care youth psychotherapy. *Administration & Policy in Mental Health & Mental Health Services Research, 37,* 254–269.

Brookman-Frazee, L., Haine, R. A., Gabayan, E. N., & Garland, A. F. (2008). Predicting frequency of treatment visits in community-based youth psychotherapy. *Psychological Services, 5,* 126–138.

Burleson, J. A., & Kaminer, Y. (2008). Does temperament moderate treatment response in adolescent substance use disorders? *Substance Abuse, 29,* 89–95.

Campbell, J. M. (2003). Efficacy of behavioral interventions for reducing problem behavior in persons with autism: A quantitative synthesis of single-subject research. *Research in Developmental Disabilities, 24,* 120–138.

Casey, R. J., & Berman, J. S. (1985). The outcome of psychotherapy with children. *Psychological Bulletin, 98,* 388–400.

Chamberlain, P., Moreland, S., & Reid, K. (1992). Enhanced services and stipends for foster parents: Effects on retention rates and outcomes for children. *Child Welfare, 5,* 387–401.

Chamberlain, P., & Reid, J. B. (1991). Using a specialized foster care community treatment model for children and adolescents leaving the state mental hospital. *Journal of Community Psychology, 19,* 266–276.

Chamberlain, P., & Reid, J. B. (1998). Comparison of two community alternatives to incarceration for chronic juvenile offenders. *Journal of Consulting and Clinical Psychology, 66,* 624–633.

Chamberlain, P., Leve, L. D., & DeGarmo, D. S. (2007). Multidimensional Treatment Foster Care for girls in the juvenile justice system: A 2-year follow-up of a randomized clinical trial. *Journal of Consulting and Clinical Psychology*, 75, 187–193.

Chambless, D. L., Baker, M. J., Baucom, D. H., Beutler, L. E., Calhoun, K. S., Crits-Christoph, P., ... Woody, S. R. (1998). Update on empirically validated therapies II. *Clinical Psychologist*, 51, 3–16.

Chambless, D. L., Sanderson, W. C., Shoham V., Johnson, S. B., Pope, K. S., Crits-Cristoph, P., ... McCurry, S. (1996). An update on empirically validated therapies. *Clinical Psychologist*, 49, 5–18.

Chavira, D. A., Accurso, E. C., Garland, A. F., & Hough, R. (2010). Suicidal behavior among youth in five public sectors of care. *Child and Adolescent Mental Health*, 15, 44–51.

Chen, C., & Ma, H. (2007). Effects of treatment on disruptive behaviors: A quantitative synthesis of single-subject researches using the PEM approach. *Behavior Analyst Today*, 8, 380–397.

Chorpita, B. F., & Daleiden, E. L. (2009). Mapping evidence-based treatments for children and adolescents: Application of the distillation and matching model to 615 treatments from 322 randomized trials. *Journal of Consulting and Clinical Psychology*, 77, 566–579.

Chorpita, B. F., Daleiden, E. L., & Weisz, J. R. (2005). Identifying and selecting the common elements of evidence based interventions: A distillation and matching model. *Mental Health Services Research*, 7, 5–20.

Chorpita, B. F., Reise, S., Weisz, J. R., Grubbs, K., Becker, K. D., Krull, J. L., & the Research Network on Youth Mental Health. (2010). Evaluation of the brief problem checklist: Child and caregiver interviews to measure clinical progress. *Journal of Consulting and Clinical Psychology*, 78, 526–536.

Chorpita, B. F., & Weisz, J. R. (2009). *Modular approach to therapy for children with anxiety, depression, trauma, or conduct problems (MATCH-ADC)*. Satellite Beach, FL: PracticeWise.

Chu, B. C., & Harrison, T. L. (2007). Disorder-specific effects of CBT for anxious and depressed youth: A meta-analysis of candidate mediators of change. *Clinical Child and Family Psychology Review*, 20, 352–372.

Cohen, J. (1988). *Statistical power analysis for the behavioral sciences* (2nd ed.). Hillsdale, NJ: Erlbaum.

Cohen, J. A., & Mannarino, A. P. (2000). Predictors of treatment outcome in sexually abused children. *Child Abuse & Neglect*, 24, 983–994.

Cohen, J. A., Mannarino, A. P., & Deblinger, E. (2010). Trauma-focused cognitive-behavioral therapy for traumatized children. In J. R. Weisz & A. E. Kazdin (Eds.), *Evidence-based psychotherapies for children and adolescents* (2nd ed., pp. 295–311). New York, NY: Guilford Press.

Conrod, P. J., Stewart, S. H., Comeau, N., & Maclean, A. M. (2006). Efficacy of cognitive-behavioral interventions targeting personality risk factors for youth alcohol misuse. *Journal of Child and Adolescent Clinical Psychology*, 35, 550–563.

Corcoran, J., & Dattalo, P. (2006). Parent involvement in treatment for ADHD: A meta-analysis of the published studies. *Research on Social Work Practice*, 16, 561–570.

David-Ferdon, C., & Kaslow, N. J. (2008). Evidence-based psychosocial treatments for child and adolescent depression. *Journal of Child and Adolescent Clinical Psychology*, 37, 62–104.

De Los Reyes, A. (2011). Special section: More than measurement error: discovering meaning behind informant discrepancies in clinical assessments of children and adolescents. *Journal of Clinical Child and Adolescent Psychology*, 40, 1–9.

De Los Reyes, A., Alfano, C. A., & Beidel, D. C. (2010a). The relations among measurements of informant discrepancies within a multisite trial of treatments for childhood social phobia. *Journal of Abnormal Child Psychology*, 38, 395–404.

De Los Reyes, A., Goodman, K. L., Kliewer, W., & Reid-Quiñones, K. (2010b). The longitudinal consistency of mother–child reporting discrepancies of parental monitoring and their ability to predict child delinquent behaviors two years later. *Journal of Youth and Adolescence*, 39, 1417–1430.

De Los Reyes, A., & Kazdin, A. E. (2005). Informant discrepancies in the assessment of childhood psychopathology: A critical review, theoretical framework, and recommendations for further study. *Psychological Bulletin*, 131, 483–509.

Dybdahl, R. (2001). Children and mothers in war: An outcome study of a psychosocial intervention program. *Child Development*, 71, 1214–1230.

Eddy, J. M., & Chamberlain, P. (2000). Family management and deviant peer association as mediators of the impact of treatment condition on youth antisocial behavior. *Journal of Consulting and Clinical Psychology*, 68, 857–863.

Eisler, I., Dare, C., Hodes, M., Russell, G., Dodge, E., & Le Grange, D. (2000). Family therapy for adolescent anorexia nervosa: The results of a controlled comparison of two family interventions. *Journal of Child Psychology and Psychiatry and Allied Disciplines*, 41, 727–736.

Eisler, I., Simic, M., Russell, G. F. M., & Dare, C. (2007). A randomized controlled treatment trial of two forms of family therapy in adolescent anorexia nervosa: A 5-year follow-up. *Journal of Child Psychology and Psychiatry*, 48, 552–560.

Eyberg, S. M., Nelson, M. M., & Boggs, S. R. (2008). Evidence-based psychosocial treatments for children and adolescents with disruptive behavior. *Journal of Child and Adolescent Clinical Psychology*, 37, 215–237.

Eysenck, H. J. (1952). The effects of psychotherapy: An evaluation. *Journal of Consulting Psychology*, 16, 319–324.

Fabiano, G. A., Pelham, W. E., Coles, E. K., Gnagy, E. M., Chronis-Tuscano, A., & O'Connor, B. C. (2009). A meta-analysis of behavioral treatments for attention-deficit/hyperactivity disorder. *Clinical Psychology Review, 29*, 129–140.

Ferdinand, R. F., van der Ende, J., & Verhulst, F. C. (2004). Parent–adolescent disagreement regarding psychopathology in adolescents from the general population as a risk factor for adverse outcome. *Journal of Abnormal Psychology, 113*, 198–206.

Ferdinand, R. F., van der Ende, J., & Verhulst, F. C. (2006). Prognostic value of parent–adolescent disagreement in a referred sample. *European child & adolescent psychiatry, 15*, 156–62.

Fixsen, D. D., Naoom, S. F., Blasé, K. A., Friedman, R. M., & Wallace, F. (2005). *Implementation research: A synthesis of the literature* (FMHI Publication No. 231). Tampa, FLP University of South Florida, Luis de la Parte Florida Mental Health Institute, National Implementation Research Network.

Fleming, T., Dixon, R., Frampton, C., & Merry, S. (2011). Pragmatic randomised controlled trial of computerized CBT (SPARX) for depression among adolescents alienated from mainstream education. *Behavioural and Cognitive Psychotherapy*. doi:10.1017/S1352465811000695

Forehand, R., Frame, C. L., Wierson, M., Armistead, L., & Kempton, T. (1991). Assessment of incarcerated juvenile delinquents: Agreement across raters and approaches to psychopathology. *Journal of Psychopathology and Behavioral Assessment, 13*, 17–25.

Forgatch, M. S., & Patterson, G. R. (2010). Parent management training—Oregon model: An intervention for antisocial behavior in children and adolescents. In J. R. Weisz & A. E. Kazdin (Eds.), *Evidence-based psychotherapies for children and adolescents* (2nd ed., pp. 159–177). New York, NY: Guilford Press.

Freedheim, D. K., Freudenberger, H. J., & Kessler, J. W. (1992). *History of psychotherapy: A century of change*. Washington, DC: American Psychological Association.

Fritz, M. S., & MacKinnon, D. P. (2007). Required sample size to detect the mediated effect. *Psychological Science, 18*, 233–239.

Fritz, M. S., Taylor, A. B., & MacKinnon, D. P. (2012). Explanation of two anomalous results in statistical mediation analysis. *Multivariate Behavioral Research, 47*, 61–87.

Garfield, S. L. (1996). Some problems associated with "validated" forms of psychotherapy. *Clinical Psychology: Science and Practice, 3*, 218–229.

Garland, A. F., Brookman-Frazee, L., Hurlburt, M., Accurso, E., Zoffness, R., Haine-Schlagel, R., & Ganger W. (2010). Mental health care for children with disruptive behavior problems: A view inside therapists' offices. *Psychiatric Services, 61*, 788–795.

Garland, A. F., Hough, R. L., Landsverk, J. A., & Brown, S. A. (2001a). Multi-sector complexity of systems of care for youth with mental health needs. *Children's Services: Social Policy, Research, and Practice, 4*, 123–140.

Garland, A. F., Hough, R. L., McCabe, K. M., Yeh, M., Wood, P. A., & Aarons, G. A. (2001b). Prevalence of psychiatric disorders in youths across five sectors of care. *Journal of the American Academy of Child and Adolescent Psychiatry, 40*, 409–418.

Garland, A. F., Landsverk, J. A., Hough, R. L., & Ellis-Macleod, E. (1996). Type of maltreatment as a predictor of mental health service use for children in foster care. *Child Abuse and Neglect, 20*, 675–688.

Glisson, C., Schoenwald, S. K., Hemmelgarn, A., Green, P., Dukes, D., Armstrong, K. S., & Chapman, J. E. (2010). Randomized trial of MST and ARC in a two-level evidence-based treatment implementation strategy. *Journal of Consulting Psychology, 78*, 537–550.

Gray-Little, B., & Kaplan, D. (2000). Race and ethnicity in psychotherapy research. In C. R. Snyder & R. E. Ingram (Eds.), *Handbook of psychological change: Psychotherapy processes & practices for the 21st century* (pp. 591–613). New York, NY: Wiley.

Hall, G. C. N. (2001). Psychotherapy research with ethnic minorities: Empirical, ethical, and conceptual issues. *Journal of Consulting and Clinical Psychology, 69*, 502–510.

Halliday-Boykins, C. A., Schoenwald, S. K., & Letourneau, E. J. (2005). Caregiver–therapist ethnic similarity predicts youth outcomes from an empirically based treatment. *Journal of Consulting and Clinical Psychology, 73*, 808–818.

Hammen, C., Rudolph, K., Weisz, J. R., Burge, D., & Rao, U. (1999). The context of depression in clinic-referred youth: Neglected areas in treatment. *Journal of the American Academy of Child and Adolescent Psychiatry, 38*, 64–71.

Havik, O. E., & VandenBos, G. R. (1996). Limitations of manualized psychotherapy for everyday clinical practice. *Clinical Psychology: Science and Practice, 3*, 264–267.

Hawley, K. M., & Weisz, J. R. (2003). Child, parent, and therapist (dis)agreement on target problems in outpatient therapy: The therapist's dilemma and its implications. *Journal of Consulting and Clinical Psychology, 71*, 62–70.

Hayes, A. F. (2009). Beyond Baron and Kenny: Statistical mediation analysis in the new millennium. *Communication Monographs, 76*, 408–420.

Henderson, C. E., Dakof, G. A., Greenbaum, P. E., & Liddle, H. A. (2010). Effectiveness of multidimensional family therapy with higher severity substance-abusing adolescents: Report from two randomized controlled trials. *Journal of Consulting and Clinical Psychology, 78*, 885–897.

Henderson, C. E., Rowe, C. L., Dakof, G. A., Hawes, S. W., & Liddle, H. A. (2009). Parenting practices as mediators of treatment effects in an early-intervention trial of multidimensional family therapy. *American Journal of Drug and Alcohol Abuse, 35,* 220–226.

Henggeler, S. W., & Borduin, C. M. (1992). *Mutiltisystemic therapy adherence scales*. Unpublished instrument. Department of Psychiatry and Behavioral Sciences, Medical University of South Carolina.

Henggeler, S. W., Borduin, C. M., Schoenwald, S. K., Huey, S. J., & Chapman, J. E. (2006). MST therapist adherence measure–Revised (TAM–R). Charleston: Medical University of South Carolina, Family Services Research Center.

Henggeler, S. W., Letourneau, E. J., Chapman, J. E., Borduin, C. M., Schewe, P. A., & McCart, M. R. (2009). Mediators of change for multisystemic therapy with juvenile sexual offenders. *Journal of Consulting and Clinical Psychology, 77,* 451–462.

Henggeler, S. W., & Schaeffer, C. (2010). Treating serious antisocial behavior using Multisystemic Therapy. In J. R. Weisz & A. E. Kazdin (Eds.), *Evidence-based psychotherapies for children and adolescents* (2nd ed., pp. 259–276). New York, NY: Guilford Press.

Henggeler, S. W., Schoenwald, S. K., Borduin, C. M., Rowland, M. D., & Cunningham, P. B. (1998). *Multisystemic treatment of antisocial behavior in children and adolescents*. New York, NY: Guilford Press.

Holmbeck, G. N. (1997). Toward terminological, conceptual, and statistical clarity in the study of mediators and moderators: Examples from the child-clinical and pediatric psychology literatures. *Journal of Consulting and Clinical Psychology, 65,* 599–610.

Hinshaw, S. P. (2007). Moderators and mediators of treatment outcome for youth outcome for youth with ADHD: Understanding for whom and how interventions work. *Journal of Pediatric Psychology, 32,* 664–675.

Hinshaw, S. P., Owens, E. B., Wells, K. C., Kraemer, H. C., Abikoff, H. B., Arnold, L. E., . . . Wigal, T. (2000). Family processes and treatment outcome in the MTA: Negative/ineffective parenting practices in relation to multimodal treatment. *Journal of Abnormal Child Psychology, 28,* 555–568.

Hollon, S., & Kendall, P. (1980). Cognitive self-statements in depression: Development of an automatic thoughts questionnaire. *Cognitive Therapy and Research, 4,* 383–397.

Hooley, J. M. (2007). Expressed emotion and relapse of psychopathology. *Annual Review of Clinical Psychology, 3,* 329–352.

Hooley, J. M., & Parker, H. A. (2006). Measuring expressed emotion: An evaluation of the shortcuts. *Journal of Family Psychology, 20,* 386–396.

Hooley, J. M., & Teasdale, J. D. (1989). Predictors of relapse in unipolar depressives: Expressed emotion, marital distress, and perceived criticism. *Journal of Abnormal Psychology, 98,* 229–235.

Horvath, A. O., Del Re, A. C., Flückiger, C., & Symonds, D. (2011). Alliance in individual therapy. *Psychotherapy, 48,* 9–16.

Huey, S. J. Jr., Henggeler, S. W., Brondino, M. J., & Pickrel, S. G. (2000). Mechanisms of change in multisystemic therapy: Reducing delinquent behavior through therapist adherence and improved family and peer functioning. *Journal of Consulting and Clinical Psychology, 68,* 451–467.

Huey, S. J. Jr., & Polo, A. J. (2008). Evidence-based psychosocial treatments for ethnic minority youth. *Journal of Clinical Child and Adolescent Psychology, 37,* 262–301.

Huey, W. C., & Rank, R. C. (1984). Effects of counselor and peer-led group assertive training on black-adolescent aggression. *Journal of Counseling Psychology, 31,* 95–98.

Hukkanen, R., Souranger, A., & Bergroth, L. (2003). Suicidal ideation and behavior in children's homes. *Nordic Journal of Psychiatry, 57,* 131–137.

Israel, P., Thomsen, P. H., Langeveld, J. H., & Stormark, K. M. (2007). Parent–youth discrepancy in the assessment and treatment of youth in usual clinical care setting: Consequences to parent involvement. *European Child & Adolescent Psychiatry, 16,* 138–148.

Jaycox, L., Reivich, K., Gillham, J. E. & Seligman, M. E. P. (1994). Prevention of depressive symptoms in school children. *Behavioral Research and Therapy, 32,* 801–816.

James, A. A. C. J., Soler, A., & Weatherall, R. R. W. (2005). Cognitive behavioural therapy for anxiety disorder in children and adolescents. *Cochrane Database of Systematic Reviews,* (4). doi: 10.1002/14651858.CD004690.pub2.

Jones, M. C. (1924a). A laboratory study of fear: The case of Peter. *Pedagogical Seminary, 31,* 308–315.

Jones, M. C. (1924b). The elimination of children's fears. *Journal of Experimental Psychology, 7,* 382–390.

Jordans, M. J. D., Komproe, I. H., Tol, W. A., Kohrt, B. A., Luitel, N. P., Macy, R. D., & De Jong, J. T. V. M. (2010). Evaluation of a classroom-based psychosocial intervention in conflict-afflicted Nepal: A cluster randomized controlled trial. *Journal of Child Psychology and Psychiatry, 51,* 818–826.

Kahn, J., Kehle, T., Jenson, W., & Clark, E. (1990). Comparison of cognitive-behavioral, relaxation, and self-modeling interventions for depression among middle-school students. *School Psychology Review, 19,* 196–211.

Kaminer, Y., Burleson, J. A., & Burke, R. (2008). Efficacy of outpatient aftercare for adolescents with alcohol use disorders: A randomized controlled study. *Journal of the American Academy of Child and Adolescent Psychiatry, 47,* 1405–1412.

Kaminer, Y., Burleson, J. A., & Goldberger, R. (2002). Cognitive behavioral coping skills and psychoeducation therapies for adolescent substance abuse. *Journal of Nervous and Mental Disease, 190,* 737–745.

Karver, M. S., Handelsman, J. B., Fields, S., & Bickman, L. (2005). A theoretical model of common process factors in youth and family therapy. *Mental Health Services Research, 7,* 35–51.

Karver, M. S., Handelsman, J. B., Fields, S., & Bickman, L. (2006). Meta-analysis of therapeutic relationship variables in youth and family therapy: The evidence for different relationship variables in the child and adolescent treatment outcome literature. *Clinical Psychology Review, 26,* 50–65.

Kataoka, S. H., Stein, B. D., Jaycox, L. H., Wong, M., Escudero, P., Tu, W., . . . Fink, A. (2003). A school-based mental health program for traumatized Latino immigrant children. *Journal of the American Academy of Child and Adolescent Psychiatry, 42,* 311–318.

Kaufman, N. K., Rohde, P., Seeley, J. R., Clarke, G. N., & Stice, E. (2005). Potential mediators of cognitive-behavioral therapy for adolescents with co-morbid major depression and conduct disorder. *Journal of Consulting and Clinical Psychology, 73,* 38–46.

Kazdin, A. E. (2000). *Psychotherapy for children and adolescents: Directions for research and practice.* New York, NY: Oxford University Press.

Kazdin, A. E. (2007). Mediators and mechanisms of change in psychotherapy research. *Annual Review of Clinical Psychology, 3,* 1–27.

Kazdin, A. E. (2010). Problem-solving skills training and parent management training for oppositional defiant disorder and conduct disorder. In J. R. Weisz & A. E. Kazdin (Eds.), *Evidence-based psychotherapies for children and adolescents* (2nd ed., pp. 211–226). New York, NY: Guilford Press.

Kazdin, A. E. (2011). *Single-case research designs: Methods for clinical and applied settings.* Oxford, United Kingdom: Oxford University Press.

Kazdin, A. E., Bass, D., Ayers, W. A., & Rodgers, A. (1990). Empirical and clinical focus of child and adolescent psychotherapy research. *Journal of Consulting & Clinical Psychology, 58,* 729–740.

Kazdin, A. E., & Weisz, J. R. (1998). Identifying and developing empirically supported child and adolescent treatments. *Journal of Consulting and Clinical Psychology, 66,* 19–36.

Kazdin, A. E., & Whitley, M. K. (2003). Treatment of parental stress to enhance therapeutic change among children referred for aggressive and antisocial behavior. *Journal of Consulting & Clinical Psychology, 71,* 504–515.

Kazdin, A. E., Whitley, M., & Marciano, P. L. (2006). Child–therapist and parent–therapist alliance and therapeutic change in the treatment of children referred for oppositional, aggressive, and antisocial behavior. *Journal of Child Psychology and Psychiatry, 47,* 436–445.

Keel, P. K., & Haedt, A. (2008). Evidence-based psychosocial treatments for eating problems and eating disorders. *Journal of Child and Adolescent Clinical Psychology, 37,* 39–61.

Kendall, P. C., & Hedtke, K. (2006). *Cognitive-behavioral therapy for anxious children: Therapist manual* (3rd ed.). Ardmore, PA: Workbook. Available from http://workbookpublishing.com

Kendall, P. C., & Khanna, M. S. (2008). *Camp cope-a-lot: The coping cat DVD* [DVD]. Ardmore, PA: Workbook. Available from http://workbookpublishing.com

Kendall, P. C., Khanna, M. S., Edson, A., Cummings, C., & Harris, M. S. (2011). Computers and psychosocial treatment for child anxiety: Recent advances and ongoing efforts. *Depression and Anxiety, 28,* 58–66.

Kendall, P. C., & Treadwell, K. H. (2007). The role of self-statements as a mediator in treatment for youth with anxiety disorders. *Journal of Consulting and Clinical Psychology, 75,* 380–389.

Koegel, R. L., Koegel, L. K., Vernon, T. W., & Brookman-Frazee, L. I. (2010). Empirically supported pivotal response treatment for children with autism spectrum disorders. In J. R. Weisz & A. E. Kazdin (Eds.), *Evidence-based psychotherapies for children and adolescents* (2nd ed., pp. 327–344). New York, NY: Guilford Press.

Kraemer, H. C., Wilson, G. T., Fairburn, C. G., & Agras, W. S. (2002). Mediators and moderators of treatment effects in randomized clinical trials. *Archives of General Psychiatry, 59,* 877–883.

Lambert, M. J., Whipple, J. L., Vermeersch, D. A., Smart, D. W., Hawkins, E. J., Nielsen, S. L. & Goates, M. (2002). Enhancing psychotherapy outcomes via providing feedback on client progress: A replication. *Clinical Psychology & Psychotherapy, 9,* 91–103.

Lau, W.-Y., Chan, C. K.-Y., Li, J. C.-H., & Au, T. K.-F. (2010). Effectiveness of group cognitive-behavioral treatment for childhood anxiety in community clinics. *Behaviour Research and Therapy, 48,* 1067–1077.

Layne, C. M., Saltzman, W. R., Poppleton, L., Burlingame, G. M., Pasalic, A., Durakovic, E., . . . Pynoos, R. S. (2008). Effectiveness of a school-based group psychotherapy program for war-exposed adolescents: A randomized controlled trial. *Journal of the American Academy of Child and Adolescent Psychiatry, 47,* 1048–1062.

Le Grange, D., Lock, J., Agras, W. S., Moye, A., Bryson, S. W., Jo, B., & Kraemer, H. C. (2012). Moderators and mediators of remission in family-based treatment and adolescent focused therapy for anorexia nervosa. *Behaviour Research and Therapy, 50,* 85–92.

Leve, L. D., & Chamberlain, P. (2007). A randomized evaluation of multidimensional treatment foster care: Effects on school attendance and homework completion in juvenile justice girls. *Research on Social Work Practice, 17,* 657–663.

Levitt, E. E. (1957). The results of psychotherapy with children: An evaluation. *Journal of Consulting Psychology, 21,* 189–196.

Levitt, E. E. (1963). Psychotherapy with children: A further evaluation. *Behaviour Research and Therapy, 60,* 326–329.

Lewis, C. C., Simons, A. D., Silva, S. G., Rohde, P., Small, D. M., Murakami, J. L., . . . March, J. S. (2009). The role of readiness to change in response to treatment of adolescent depression. *Journal of Consulting and Clinical Psychology, 77,* 422–428.

Lochman, J. E., Boxmeyer, C. L., Powell, N. P., Barry, T. D., & Pardini, D. A. (2010). Anger control training for aggressive youth. In J. R. Weisz & A. E. Kazdin (Eds.), *Evidence-based psychotherapies for children and adolescents* (2nd ed., pp. 227–242). New York, NY: Guilford Press.

Lochman, J. E., & Wells, K. C. (2002). Contextual social-cognitive mediators and child outcome: A test of the theoretical model in the coping power program. *Development and Psychopathology, 14,* 971–993.

Lock, J., Agras, W. S., Bryson, S., & Kraemer, H. (2005). A comparison of short- and long-term family therapy for adolescent anorexia nervosa. *Journal of the American Academy of Child and Adolescent Psychiatry, 44,* 632–639.

Lock, J., Le Grange, D., Agras, W. S., & Dare, C. (2001). *A treatment manual for anorexia nervosa: A family-based approach.* New York, NY: Guilford Press.

Lonigan, C. J., Elbert, J. C., & Johnson, S. B. (1998). Empirically supported psychosocial interventions for children: An overview. *Journal of Clinical Child Psychology, 27,* 138–145.

Lovaas, O. I. (1987). Behavioral treatment and normal educational and intellectual functioning in young autistic children. *Journal of Consulting and Clinical Psychology, 55,* 3–9.

Lundahl, B., Risser, H. J., & Lovejoy, M. C. (2006). A meta-analysis of parent training: Moderators and follow-up effects. *Clinical Psychology Review, 26,* 86–104.

Lustig, S. L., Kia-Keating, M., Knight, W. G., Geltman, P., Ellis, H., Kinzie, J. D., . . . Saxe, G. N. (2004). Review of child and adolescent refugee mental health. *Journal of the American Academy of Child & Adolescent Psychiatry, 43,* 24–36.

MacKinnon, D. P., Fairchild, A. J., & Fritz, M. S. (2007). Mediation analysis. *Annual Review of Psychology, 58,* 593–614.

MacKinnon, D. P., Fritz, M. S., Williams, J., & Lockwood, C. M. (2007). Distribution of the product confidence limits for the indirect effect: Program PRODCLIN. *Behavior Research Methods, 39,* 348–389.

Magana, A. B., Goldstein, M. J., Karno, M., Miklowitz, D. J., Jenkins, J., & Falloon, R. H. (1986). A brief method for assessing expressed emotion in relatives of psychiatric patients. *Psychiatry Research, 17,* 203–212.

Makrygianni, M. K., & Reed, P. (2010). A meta-analytic review of the effectiveness of behavioural early intervention programs for children with autistic spectrum disorders. *Research in Autism Spectrum Disorders, 4,* 577–593.

March, J. S., Franklin, M. E., Leonard, H., Garcia, A., Moore, P., Freeman, J., & Foa, E. (2007). Tics moderate treatment outcome with sertraline but not cognitive–behavior therapy in pediatric obsessive-compulsive disorder. *Biological Psychiatry, 61,* 344–347.

Mathur, S. R., Kavale, K. A., Quinn, M. M., Forness, S. R., & Rutherford, R. B. Jr. (1998). Social skills interventions with students with emotional and behavioral problems: A quantitative synthesis of single-subject research. *Behavioral Disorders, 23,* 193–201.

McCabe, K. M., Lansing, A. E., Garland, A., & Hough, R. (2002). Gender differences in psychopathology, functional impairment, and familial risk factors among adjudicated delinquents. *Journal of the American Academy of Child and Adolescent Psychiatry, 34,* 1221–1229.

McCarty, C. A., & Weisz, J. R. (2002). Correlates of expressed emotion in mothers of clinically-referred youth: An examination of the five-minute speech sample. *Journal of Child Psychology and Psychiatry, 43,* 759–768.

McGrath, M. L., Dorsett, P. G., Calhoun, M. E., & Drabman, R. S. (1987). "Beat-the-buzzer": A method for decreasing parent–child morning conflicts. *Child and Family Behavior Therapy, 9(3–4),* 35–48.

McLeod, B. D. (2011). Relation of the alliance with outcomes in youth psychotherapy: A meta-analysis. *Clinical Psychology Review, 31,* 603–616.

McLeod, B. D., & Weisz, J. R. (2005). The therapy process observational coding system—Alliance scale: Measure characteristics and prediction of outcome in usual clinical practice. *Journal of Consulting and Clinical Psychology, 73,* 323–333.

McLeod, B. D., & Weisz, J. R. (2010). Therapy process observational coding system for child psychotherapy strategies scale. *Journal of Clinical Child and Adolescent Psychology, 39,* 436–443.

McMahon, R. J., & Forehand, R. (2003). *Helping the noncompliant child: Family based treatment for oppositional behavior* (2nd ed.). New York, NY: Guilford Press.

Meichenbaum, D., & Goodman, S. (1971). Training impulsive children to talk to themselves: A means of developing self-control. *Journal of Abnormal Psychology, 77,* 115–126.

Merry, S. N., Stasiak, K., Shepherd, M., Frampton, C., Fleming, T., & Lucassen, M. F. G. (2012). The effectiveness of SPARX, a computerized self help intervention for adolescents seeking help for depression: randomized controlled noninferiority trial. *British Medical Journal, 344,* 1–16. doi: 10.1136/bmj.e2598

Mihalic, S., Fagan, A., Irwin, K., Ballard, D., & Elliott, D. (2002). *Blueprints for violence prevention replications: Factors for implementation success.* Boulder, CO: Center for the Study and Prevention of Violence.

MTA Cooperative Group. (1999a). A 14-month randomized clinical trial of treatment strategies for attention-deficit/hyperactivity disorder. *Archives of General Psychiatry, 56,* 1073–1086.

MTA Cooperative Group. (1999b). Moderators and mediators of treatment response for children with attention-deficit/hyperactivity disorder. *Archives of General Psychiatry, 56,* 1088–1096.

Mufson, L. H., Weissman, M. M., Moreau, D., & Garfinkel, R. (1999). Efficacy of interpersonal therapy for depressed adolescents. *Archives of General Psychiatry, 56,* 573–579.

Muller, D., Judd, C. M., & Yzerbyt, V. Y. (2005). When moderation is mediated and mediation is moderated. *Journal of Personality and Social Psychology, 89,* 852–863.

National Evaluation and Technical Assistance Center. (2010). *Fact sheet: Juvenile justice facilities.* Washington, DC: NETAC.

Nock, M. K., & Kazdin, A. E. (2005). Randomized controlled trial of a brief intervention for increasing participation in parent management training. *Journal of Consulting & Clinical Psychology, 73,* 872–879.

Office of the Surgeon General. (1999). Mental health: A report of the surgeon general. Rockville, MD: U.S. Department of Health and Human Services.

Office of the Surgeon General. (2004). Report of the surgeon general's conferences on children's mental health: A national action agenda. Rockville, MD: U.S. Department of Health and Human Services.

Ougrin, D., & Latif, S. (2011). Specific psychological treatment versus treatment as usual in adolescents with self-harm: Systematic review and meta-analysis. *Crisis: The Journal of Crisis Intervention and Suicide Prevention, 32,* 74–80.

Palinkas, L. A., Aarons, G. A., Hoagwood, K. E., Chorpita, B. F., Landsverk, J., Weisz, J. R., & the Research Network on Youth Mental Health. (2008). An ethnographic study of implementation of evidence-based practice in child mental health: First steps. *Psychiatric Services, 59,* 738–746.

Pelham, W. E., & Fabiano, G. A. (2008). Evidence-based psychosocial treatments for attention-deficit/hyperactivity disorder. *Journal of Clinical Child and Adolescent Psychology, 37,* 184–214.

Pelham, W. E., Gnagy, E. M., Greiner, A. R., Waschbusch, D. A., Fabiano, G. A., & Burrows-MacLean, L. (2010). Summer treatment programs for attention-deficit/hyperactivity disorder. In J. R. Weisz & A. E. Kazdin (Eds.), *Evidence-based psychotherapies for children and adolescents* (2nd ed., pp. 277–292). New York, NY: Guilford Press.

Perepletchikova, F., Treat, T. A., & Kazdin, A. E. (2007). Treatment integrity in psychotherapy research: analysis of the studies and examination of the associated factors. *Journal of Consulting and Clinical Psychology, 75,* 829–841.

Peris, T. S., & Baker, B. L. (2000). Applications of the expressed emotion construct to young children with externalizing behavior: Stability and prediction over time. *Journal of Child Psychology and Psychiatry, 41,* 457–462.

Pollard, K., & Mather, M. (2009). *U.S. Hispanic and Asian population growth levels off.* Retrieved from the Population Reference Bureau website, www.prb.org/Articles/2009/hispanicasiall.aspx.

Preacher, K. J., & Hayes, A. F. (2004). SPSS and SAS procedures for estimating indirect effects in simple mediation models. *Behavior Research Methods, Instruments, and Computers, 36,* 717–731.

Preacher, K. J., & Hayes, A. F. (2008). Asymptotic and resampling strategies for assessing and comparing indirect effects in multiple mediator models. *Behavior Research Methods, 40,* 879–891.

Preacher, K. J., Rucker, D. D., & Hayes, A. F. (2007). Addressing moderated mediation hypotheses: theory, methods, and prescriptions. *Multivariate Behavioral Research, 42,* 185–227.

President's New Freedom Commission on Mental Health. (2003). *Achieving the promise: Transforming mental health care in America.* Final Report. DHHS Pub. No. SMA-03-3832: Rockville, MD.

Richters, J. E. (1992). Depressed mothers as informants about their children: A critical review of the evidence for distortion. *Psychological Bulletin, 112,* 485–499.

Rogers, S. J., & Vismara, L. A. (2008). Evidence-based comprehensive treatments for early autism. *Journal of Child and Adolescent Clinical Psychology, 37,* 8–38.

Rozenman, M., Weersing, V. R., & Amir, N. (2011). A case series of attention modification in clinically anxious youths. *Behaviour Research and Therapy, 49,* 324–330.

Sanders, M. R., & Murphy-Brennan, M. (2010). The international dissemination of the triple P— Positive parenting program. In J. R. Weisz & A. E. Kazdin (Eds.), *Evidence-based psychotherapies for children and adolescents* (2nd ed., pp. 519–537). New York, NY: Guilford Press.

Sburlati, E. S., Schniering, C. A., Lyneham, H. J., & Rapee, R. M. (2011). A model of therapist competencies for the empirically supported cognitive behavior treatment of child and adolescent anxiety and depressive disorders. *Clinical Child and Family Psychology Review, 14,* 89–109.

Schoenwald, S. K. (2010). From policy pinball to purposeful partnership: The policy contexts of Multisystemic Therapy transport and dissemination. In J. R. Weisz & A. E. Kazdin (Eds.), *Evidence-based psychotherapies for children and adolescents* (2nd ed., pp. 538–553). New York, NY: Guilford Press.

Schoenwald, S. K., Chapman, J. E., Sheidow, A. J., & Carter, R. E. (2009). Long-term youth criminal outcomes in MST transport: The impact of therapist adherence and organizational climate and structure. *Journal of Clinical Child & Adolescent Psychology, 38,* 91–105.

Schoenwald, S. K., Garland, A. F., Chapman, J. E., Frazier, S. L., Sheidow, A. J., & Southam-Gerow, M. A. (2011). Toward the effective and efficient measurement of implementation fidelity. *Administration and Policy in Mental Health and Mental Health Services Research, 38,* 32–43.

Schoenwald, S. K., Henggeler, S. W., Brondino, M. J., & Rowland, M. D. (2000). Multisystemic therapy: monitoring treatment fidelity. *Family Process, 39,* 83–103.

Schoenwald, S. K., Kelleher, K., Weisz, J. R., & the Research Network on Youth Mental Health. (2008). Building bridges to evidence-based practice: The MacArthur foundation child system and treatment enhancement projects (Child STEPs). *Administration and Policy in Mental Health and Mental Health Services Research, 35,* 66–72.

Sexton, T. L. (2010). *Functional family therapy in clinical practice: An evidence-based treatment model for working with troubled adolescents.* New York, NY: Routledge.

Shaffer, D., Fisher, P., Dulcan, M., Davies, M., Piacentini, J., Schwab-Stone, M. E., ... Regier, D. A. (1996). The NIMG diagnostic interview schedule for children version 2.3 (DISC-2.3): Description, acceptability, prevalence rates, and performance in the MECA study. *Journal of the American Academy of Child and Adolescent Psychiatry, 35,* 865–877.

Shapiro, D. A., & Shapiro, D. (1982). Meta-analysis of comparative therapy outcome studies: A replication and refinement. *Psychological Bulletin, 92,* 581–604.

Shaw, J. A. (2003). Children exposed to war/terrorism. *Clinical Child and Family Psychology Review, 6,* 237–246.

Sheeringa, M. S., Weems, C. F., Cohen, J. A., Amaya-Jackson, L., & Guthrie, D. (2011). Trauma-focused cognitive behavioral therapy for posttraumatic stress disorder in three-through six year-old children: A randomized trial. *Journal of Child Psychology and Psychiatry, 52,* 853–860.

Sherer, M. R., & Schreibman, L. (2005). Individual behavioral profiles and predictors of treatment effectiveness for children with autism. *Journal of Consulting and Clinical Psychology, 73,* 525–538.

Shimokawa, K., Lambert, M. J., & Smart, D. W. (2010). Enhancing treatment outcome of patients at risk of treatment failure: Meta-analytic and mega-analytic review of a psychotherapy quality assurance system. *Journal of Consulting and Clinical Psychology, 78,* 298–311.

Shirk, S. R., & Karver, M. (2003). Prediction of treatment outcome from relationship variables in child and adolescent therapy: A meta-analytic review. *Journal of Consulting and Clinical Psychology, 71,* 452–464.

Silverman, W. K., & Hinshaw, S. P. (2008). The second special issue on evidence-based psychosocial treatments for children and adolescents: A 10-year update. *Journal of Child and Adolescent Clinical Psychology, 37,* 1–7.

Silverman, W. K., Ortiz, C. D., Viswesvaran, C., Burns, B. J., Kolko, D. J., Putman, F. W., & Amaya-Jackson, L. (2008a). Evidence-based psychosocial treatments for children and adolescents exposed to traumatic events. *Journal of Child and Adolescent Clinical Psychology, 37,* 156–183.

Silverman, W. K., Pina, A. A., & Viswesvaran, C. (2008b). Evidence-based psychosocial treatments for phobic and anxiety disorders in children and adolescents. *Journal of Child and Adolescent Clinical Psychology, 37,* 105–130.

Smith, T. (2010). Early and intensive behavioral intervention in autism. In J. R. Weisz & A. E. Kazdin (Eds.), *Evidence-based psychotherapies for children and adolescents* (2nd ed., pp. 312–326). New York, NY: Guilford Press.

Smith, D. K., & Chamberlain, P. (2010). Multidimensional treatment foster care for adolescents: Processes and outcomes. In J. R. Weisz & A. E. Kazdin (Eds.), *Evidence-based psychotherapies for children and adolescents* (2nd ed., pp. 243–258). New York, NY: Guilford Press.

Smith, M. L., & Glass, G. V. (1977). Meta-analysis of psychotherapy outcome studies. *American Psychologist, 32,* 752–760.

Snyder, H. N., & Sickmund, M. (2006). *Juvenile offenders and victims: 2006 national report.* Pittsburgh, PA: National Center for Juvenile Justice.

Southam-Gerow, M. A., Weisz, J. R., Chu, B. C., McLeod, B. D., Gordis, E. B., & Connor-Smith, J. K. (2010). Does CBT for youth anxiety outperform usual care in community clinics? An initial effectiveness test. *Journal of the American Academy of Child & Adolescent Psychiatry, 49,* 1043–1052.

Southam-Gerow, M. A., Weisz, J. R., & Kendall, P. C. (2003). Youth with anxiety disorders in research and service clinics: Examining client differences and similarities. *Journal of Clinical Child and Adolescent Psychology, 32,* 375–385.

Spielmans, G. I., Gatlin, E. T., & McFall, J. P. (2010). The efficacy of evidence-based psychotherapies versus usual care for youths: Controlling confounds in a meta-reanalysis. *Psychotherapy Research, 20,* 234–246.

Stagman, S., & Cooper, J. L. (2010). *Children's mental health: What every policymaker should know.* New York, NY: National Center for Children in Poverty, Columbia University Mailman School of Public Health.

Stein, B. D., Jaycox, L. H., Kataoka, S. H., Wong, M., Tu, W., Elliott, M. N., & Fink, A. (2003). A mental health intervention for schoolchildren exposed to violence. *Journal of the American Medical Association, 290,* 603–611.

Stein, B. D., Kogan, J. N., Hutchison, S. L., Magee, E. A., & Sorbero, M. J. (2010). Use of outcomes information in child mental health treatment: Results from a pilot study. *Psychiatric Services, 61,* 1211–1216.

Stice, E., Rohde, P., Seeley, J. R., & Gau, J. M. (2010). Testing mediators of intervention effects in randomized controlled trials: An evaluation of three depression prevention programs. *Journal of Consulting and Clinical Psychology, 78,* 273–280.

Strupp, H. H., & Anderson, T. (1997). On the limitations of therapy manuals. *Clinical Psychology: Science and Practice, 4,* 76–82.

Sue, S. (2003). In defense of cultural competency in psychotherapy and treatment. *American Psychologist, 58,* 964–970.

Sue, S., Fujino, D. C., Hu, L. T., Takeuchi, D. T., & Zane, N. W. S. (1991). Community mental health services for ethnic minority groups: A test of the cultural responsiveness hypothesis. *Journal of Consulting & Clinical Psychology, 59,* 533–540.

Swenson, C. C., Schaeffer, C. M., Henggeler, S. W., Faldowski, R., & Mayhew, A. M. (2010). Multisystemic Therapy for Child Abuse and Neglect: A randomized effectiveness trial. *Journal of Family Psychology, 24,* 497–507.

Tarnowski, K. J., Rosén, L. A., McGrath, M. L., & Drabman, R. S. (1987). A modified habit reversal procedure in a recalcitrant case of trichotillomania. *Journal of Behavior Therapy and Experimental Psychiatry, 18,* 157–163.

Teplin, L. A., Abram, K. M., McClelland, G. M., Mericle, A. A., Dulcan, M. K., & Washburn, J. J. (2006). *Psychiatric disorders of youth in detention.* Washington, DC: U.S. Department of Justice.

Tol, W. A., Komproe, I. H., Susanty, D., Jordans, M. J. D., & de Jong, J. T. V. M. (2008). School-based mental health intervention for children affected by political violence in Indonesia: A cluster randomized trial. *Journal of the American Medical Association, 300,* 655–662.

Treadwell, K. H., & Kendall, P. C. (1996). Self-talk in youth with anxiety disorders: States of mind, content specificity. *Journal of Consulting and Clinical Psychology, 64,* 941–950.

UNICEF. (1996). *The state of the world's children.* New York, NY: Oxford University Press.

U.S. Department of Health and Human Services. (2001). *Mental health: Culture, race, and ethnicity–A supplement to Mental Health: A Report of the Surgeon General.* Rockville, MD: U.S. Department of Health and Human Services, Public Health Service, Office of the Surgeon General.

Waldron, H. B., & Kaminer, Y. (2004). On the learning curve: The emerging evidence supporting cognitive-behavioral therapies for adolescent substance abuse. *Addiction, 99*(Suppl. 2), 93–105.

Waldron, H. B., & Turner, C. W. (2008). Evidence-based psychosocial treatments for adolescent substance abuse. *Journal of Child and Adolescent Clinical Psychology, 37,* 238–261.

Waltz, J., Addis, M. E., Koerner, K. & Jacobson, N. S. (1993). Testing the integrity of a psychotherapy protocol: Assessment of adherence and competence. *Journal of Consulting and Clinical Psychology, 61,* 620–630.

Watanabe, N., Hunot, V., Omori, I. M., Churchill, R., & Furukawa, T. A. (2007). Psychotherapy for depression among children and adolescents: A systematic review. *Acta Psychiatrica Scandinavica, 116,* 84–95.

Webster-Stratton, C. & Reid, M. J. (2010). The incredible years parents, teachers, and children's training series: A multifaceted treatment approach for young children with conduct problems. In J. R. Weisz & A. E. Kazdin (Eds.), *Evidence-based psychotherapies for children and adolescents* (2nd ed., pp. 194–210). New York, NY: Guilford Press.

Weersing, V. R., & Weisz, J. R. (2002a). Community clinic treatment of depressed youth: Benchmarking usual care against CBT clinical trials. *Journal of Consulting and Clinical Psychology, 70,* 299–310.

Weersing, V. R., & Weisz, J. R. (2002b). Mechanisms of action in youth psychotherapy. *Journal of Child Psychology and Psychiatry, 43,* 3–29.

Weersing, V. R., Weisz, J. R., & Donenberg, G. R. (2002). Development of the therapy procedures checklist: A therapist-report measure of technique use in child and adolescent treatment. *Journal of Clinical Child and Adolescent Psychology, 31,* 168–180.

Weissman, A. (1979). The dysfunctional attitude scale: A validation study (Doctoral dissertation, University of Pennsylvania, 1979). *Dissertation Abstracts International, 40,* 1389–1390b.

Weisz, J. R. (2004). *Psychotherapy for children and adolescents: Evidence-based treatments and case examples.* Cambridge, United Kingdom: Cambridge University Press.

Weisz, J. R., & Addis, M. E. (2006). The research–practice tango and other choreographic challenges: Using and testing evidence-based psychotherapies in clinical care settings. In C. D. Goodheart, A. E. Kazdin, & R. J. Sternberg (Eds.), *Evidence-based psychotherapy: Where practice and research meet* (pp. 179–206). Washington, DC: American Psychological Association.

Weisz, J. R., & Chorpita, B. F. (2011). Mod squad for youth psychotherapy: Restructuring evidence-based treatment for clinical practice. In P.C. Kendall (Ed.), *Child and adolescent therapy: Cognitive-behavioral procedures* (4th ed., pp. 379–397). New York, NY: Guilford Press.

Weisz, J. R., Chorpita, B. F., Frye, A., Ng, M. Y., Lau, N., Bearman, S. K., . . . the Research Network on Youth Mental Health (2011a). Youth top problems: Using idiographic, consumer-guided assessment to identify treatment needs and track change during psychotherapy. *Journal of Consulting and Clinical Psychology, 79*, 369–380.

Weisz, J. R., Chorpita, B. F., Palinkas, L. A., Schoenwald, S. K., Miranda, J., Bearman, S. K., . . . the Research Network on Youth Mental Health. (2012a). Testing standard and modular designs for psychotherapy treating depression, anxiety, and conduct problems in youth: A randomized effectiveness trial. *Archives of General Psychiatry, 69*, 274–282.

Weisz, J. R., & Gray, J. S. (2008). Evidence-based psychotherapies for children and adolescents: Data from the present and a model for the future. *Child and Adolescent Mental Health, 13*, 54–65.

Weisz, J. R., Huey, S. J., & Weersing, V. R. (1998). Psychotherapy outcome research with children and adolescents: The state of the art. *Advances in Clinical Child Psychology, 20*, 49–91.

Weisz, J. R., Jensen-Doss, A. J., & Hawley, K. M. (2005). Youth psychotherapy outcome research: A review and critique of the evidence base. *Annual Review of Psychology, 56*, 337–363.

Weisz, J. R., Jensen-Doss, A., & Hawley, K. M. (2006). Evidence-based youth psychotherapies versus usual clinical care: A meta-analysis of direct comparisons. *American Psychologist, 61*, 671–689.

Weisz, J. R., Jensen, A. L., & McLeod, B. D. (2005b). Milestones and methods in the development and dissemination of child and adolescent psychotherapies: Review, commentary, and a new deployment-focused model. In E. D. Hibbs & P. S. Jensen (Eds.), *Psychosocial treatments for child and adolescent disorders: Empirically based strategies for clinical practice* (2nd ed., pp. 9–39). Washington, DC: American Psychological Association.

Weisz, J. R., & Kazdin, A. E. (Eds.). (2010). *Evidence-based psychotherapies for children and adolescents* (2nd ed.). New York, NY: Guilford Press.

Weisz, J. R., Kuppens, S., Eckshtain, D., Ugueto, A. M., Hawley, K. M., & Jensen-Doss, A. (2012b). Do evidence-based youth psychotherapies outperform usual care? A multilevel meta-analysis. Submitted for publication.

Weisz, J. R., McCarty, C. A., Eastman, K. L., Suwanlert, S., & Chaiyasit, W. (1997). Developmental psychopathology and culture: Ten lessons from Thailand. In S. S. Luthar, J. Burack, D. Cicchetti, & J. R. Weisz (Eds.), *Developmental psychopathology: Perspectives on adjustment, risk, and disorder* (pp. 568–592). Cambridge, United Kingdom: Cambridge University Press.

Weisz, J. R., McCarty, C. A., & Valeri, S. M. (2006b). Effects of psychotherapy for depression in children and adolescents: A meta-analysis. *Psychological Bulletin, 132*, 132–149.

Weisz, J. R., Sandler, I. N., Durlak, J. A., & Anton, B. S. (2005c). Promoting and protecting youth mental health through evidence-based prevention and treatment. *American Psychologist, 60*, 628–648.

Weisz, J. R., Southam-Gerow, M. A., Gordis, E. B., Connor-Smith, J. K., Chu, B. C., Langer, D. A., . . . Weiss, B. (2009). Cognitive-behavioral therapy versus usual clinical care for youth depression: An initial test of transportability to community clinics and clinicians. *Journal of Consulting and Clinical Psychology, 77*, 383–396.

Weisz, J. R., Ugueto, A. M., Herren, J., Afienko, S. R., & Rutt, C. (2011b). Kernels vs. ears, and other questions for a science of treatment dissemination. *Clinical Psychology: Science and Practice, 18*, 41–46.

Weisz, J. R., & Weiss, B. (1991). Studying the "referability" of child clinical problems. *Journal of Consulting and Clinical Psychology, 59*, 266–273.

Weisz, J. R., Weiss, B., Alicke, M. D., & Klotz, M. L. (1987). Effectiveness of psychotherapy with children and adolescents: A meta-analysis for clinicians. *Journal of Consulting & Clinical Psychology, 55*, 542–549.

Weisz, J. R., Weiss, B., Han, S. S., Granger, D. A., & Morton, T. (1995). Effects of psychotherapy with children and adolescents revisited: A meta-analysis of treatment outcome studies. *Psychological Bulletin, 117*, 450–468.

Westen, D., Novotny, C. M., & Thompson-Brenner, H. (2004a). The empirical status of empirically supported therapies: Assumptions, findings, and reporting in controlled trials. *Psychological Bulletin, 130*, 631–663.

Westen, D., Novotny, C. M., & Thompson-Brenner, H. (2004b). The next generation of psychotherapy research: Reply to Ablon and Marci (2004), Goldfried and Eubanks-Carter (2004), and Haaga (2004). *Psychological Bulletin, 130*, 677–683

Woody, S. R., Weisz, J. R., & McLean, C. (2005). Empirically supported treatments: 10 years later. *Clinical Psychologist, 58*, 5–11.

Wurtele, S. K., & Drabman, R. S. (1984). "Beat the buzzer" for classroom dawdling: A one-year trial. *Behavior Therapy, 15*, 403–409.

Yeh, M., Eastman, K., & Cheung, M. K. (1994). Children and adolescents in community health centers: Does the ethnicity or the language of the therapist matter? *Journal of Community Psychology, 22,* 153–163.

Yeh, M., & Weisz, J. R. (2001). Why are we here at the clinic? Parent–child (dis)agreement on referral problems. *Journal of Consulting and Clinical Psychology, 71,* 62–70.

Yu, D. L., & Seligman, M. E. P. (2002). Preventing depressive symptoms in Chinese children. *Prevention and Treatment, 5*(1). Article 9, posted May 8, 2002.

Zisser, A., & Eyberg, S. M. (2010). Parent–child interaction therapy and the treatment of disruptive behavior disorders. In J. R. Weisz & A. E. Kazdin (Eds.), *Evidence-based psychotherapies for children and adolescents* (2nd ed., pp. 179–193). New York, NY: Guilford Press.

CHAPTER 15

THE EFFECTIVENESS OF COUPLE AND FAMILY-BASED CLINICAL INTERVENTIONS

THOMAS L. SEXTON, CORINNE DATCHI, LAUREN EVANS, JULIE LAFOLLETTE, AND LAUREN WRIGHT

The evolution of couple and family therapy (CFT) illustrates the dynamic interaction between theory, practice, and research. CFT research has produced a robust body of constantly evolving and clinically relevant findings that can guide practice. The field has moved away from reductionist approaches that simplify complex clinical phenomena and moved toward research methods capable of capturing the unique interplay between client-presenting problems, therapeutic factors, demographic diversity, and model-specific process to outcome variations. (Seedall, Sprenkle, & Lebow, 2011; Sexton et al., 2007). This is illustrated by the evolution of clinical practices from "schools" of therapy to specific, systematic, and well-articulated clinical models. These models are therapeutic "maps" that guide practice with specific clinical foci (Alexander, Holtzworth-Monroe, & Jameson, 1994; Sexton & Alexander, 2003). Many of these models are built on long-standing research programs (Lebow, 1999), and they are often translated into practice by way of clinical manuals that constitute systematic and clinically responsive guides (Sexton, Alexander, & Mease, 2004). As researchers have come to accept the importance of specificity, they have also recognized the critical role of varied research methods. Randomized clinical trials (RCTs) have provided a valuable tool to validate absolute and relative efficacy (Kazdin, 2006). Currently, alternative scientific approaches are necessary to answer more clinically rich questions (Sexton, McEnery, & Wilson, 2011; Sexton & Turner, 2010). The extant scientific literature on CFT

models demonstrates what Liddle, Bray, Levant, and Santisteban (2002) call the emergence of "family intervention science," a growing body of outcome and process studies that meet the highest standards of research methodology.

Research reviews are helpful tools for bringing science and practice together. Reviews guide researchers by identifying areas that require further development, by assisting practitioners in synthesizing emerging CFT findings, and by translating scientific knowledge into practical clinical guidance. In this chapter, we present a systematic and comprehensive review of the CFT clinical research published since the last edition of this handbook (2004). Our goal is to focus on high-quality, CFT-specific interventions that are designed to address the unique clinical challenges of actual couple and family clients across diverse clinical settings. The methodology of our review is intended to provide both scientific and clinical utility, thus building a bridge between CFT research and practice. Our review focuses on clinical interventions and examines outcomes attached to specific clients, in specific contexts, and under specific conditions. We hope to offer the reader a measure of confidence in identifying effective CFT practices.

The past three editions of the *Handbook of Psychotherapy and Behavior Change* (1978, 1986, 2004) have chronicled the evolution of CFT intervention research. The next section aims to provide a brief summary of the information contained in these three editions, linking past and present findings and promoting an understanding about how the CFT knowledge base has evolved over the past 30 years. The following section describes the scope and methodology of this review, presents the results of our analysis, and determines the level of evidence that supports the effectiveness of CFT. We are interested in the general modality of CFT along with its specific interventions. We seek to answer questions about the problems that CFT practices address, the context in which the interventions work, and the strength of their outcomes. We conclude this chapter with a number of observations, conclusions, and recommendations for the next era of CFT research.

THE CONTEXT: EVOLUTION OF CFT RESEARCH

CFT research has made significant progress since its initial examination of broad questions. It advanced to the study of theories and models; then it developed to the present-day investigation of comprehensive, specific, and well-articulated treatment programs with increasingly diverse outcomes and contexts. It has produced evidence for the existence of common CFT change mechanisms, and it has also shown that specific programs have differing degrees of efficacy depending on the clinical problem they address. The reviews published in the past three editions of this handbook found that therapist and client factors moderated treatment outcome; it was recommended that practitioners and researchers keep this in mind as they apply research findings to real-life clinical practice.

The first review by Gurman and Kniskern (1991) identified more than 200 relevant studies of couple and family treatments. The authors found that broad CFT practices (e.g., CT and FT) were efficacious and that family therapy was often as effective, and potentially more effective, than many individual treatments for problems attributed to family conflict. Furthermore, it appeared that both behavioral and nonbehavioral treatments produced outcomes that were superior to no-treatment controls in about two thirds of the studies. In these studies, therapists who provided little structure in early sessions were found to have more negative outcomes, while those who were more structured and could demonstrate a mastery of technical skills seemed better able to prevent the worsening of family interactions. For example, those who employed highly supportive and relational skills had more positive outcomes in general (Gurman & Kniskern, 1991).

Gurman, Kniskern, and Pinsof (1986) used the results of 47 overlapping reviews of the couple and family literature published between 1970 and 1984. The primary focus was on 15 schools of practice. Interestingly, of the 15 "schools," only 6 had moderate-to-strong evidence of efficacy in the treatment of at least one clinical problem. When they were tested, the evidence suggested that the directive approaches were more successful than the less directive methods. This review also revealed that few "schools" of couple and family therapy had been empirically tested.

In the fourth edition of the handbook, Alexander et al. (1994) based their conclusions on the examination of previously published quantitative, qualitative, and meta-analytic reviews of couple and family therapy. They found that family treatments were a viable, and perhaps a preferred, vehicle for change when compared to no treatment and alternative treatments. "Pragmatic" therapeutic approaches, those that relied on behavioral methods, had positive outcomes, while the more global therapeutic interventions that lacked specificity were without strong research support. Alexander et al. (1994) suggested that future researchers focus on identifiable, well-articulated, and systematic models of CFT. Alexander et al. (1994) also recommended that researchers specify the clinical problems under investigation, the therapist characteristics that influence outcomes, and the change mechanisms that facilitate positive outcomes.

Sexton, Alexander, and Mease (2004) did a systematic review of 82 studies and 7 meta-analyses. They found a surprising lack of research concerning the majority of contemporary couple therapy (CT) approaches. Of those with evidence, it was clear that CT enhanced general marital satisfaction for approximately 40% of the treated couples. However, improvements were not sustained at follow-ups that occurred more than 6 months posttreatment. Despite these modest outcomes, the treated couples were better off than their nontreated peers. There was some evidence to suggest that CT was effective for women experiencing depression, but it was not more effective than individual therapy overall. As an adjunctive treatment for adults with alcohol and drug problems, CT seemed to improve outcomes, particularly at posttreatment. It appeared to be superior to individual therapy alone in approximately half of the studies included in the review, but its superiority was not maintained at follow-up periods that occurred 1 year later. Concerning specific intervention programs, there was evidence to suggest that a limited number of CT models, specifically behavioral couple therapy (BCT) and emotionally focused couple therapy (EFCT), could be considered empirically supported treatments (EST).

Sexton, Alexander, and Mease (2004) found that family therapy (FT) had been applied to the treatment of a wide variety of client disorders, yet most FT interventions did not meet criteria for being empirically supported. FT had a therapeutic impact on externalizing behavior problems including conduct disorders and substance abuse. Positive outcomes were mostly attributed to systematic treatment programs with a large body of outcome and process studies, such as functional family therapy (FFT) and multisystemic therapy (MST). Sexton, Ridley, and Kliner (2004) also identified a set of common change mechanisms that may contribute to the success of family therapy. Treatment effects appeared to be mediated by the therapist's ability to work through therapeutic impasses and by the therapist's ability to help families shift blame (i.e., the family's perception of who is causing the problem) from the identified client to the relational system. Other important mediators of change included the reduction of negativity within therapy sessions, improved family communication, therapist-family alliance, and the systematic structuring of treatment sessions.

The Current Review

This chapter, like the previous ones, focuses on clinical intervention research in couple and family therapy (CFT) and aims to build on the knowledge produced by the past three reviews. We present information about the overall effectiveness of CFT practices and level of specificity in regard to treatment outcomes, problems addressed, client characteristics, and contextual factors. We systematically sampled and rated studies of couple and family therapy interventions published between 2003 and 2010. First, we considered the depth and breadth of the CFT research literature. To conduct our first analyses, we rated characteristics of the interventions (i.e., type, focus, specificity), the variety of client characteristics (e.g. the demographic diversity of the sample), the types of clinical problems, and the strength of the outcomes. Second, we analyzed the effectiveness of specific CFT interventions. The results of the analysis helped us identify practices that were effective overall as well as practices that were effective in the treatment of particular groups of clients with specific problems.

Review and Rating Procedures

Our rating scale was constructed with specific categories in seven critical domains of assessment: interventions, clinical problems, strength of outcomes, client characteristics, clinical contexts, quality of the studies, and the strength of the evidence. These domains are those suggested by Sexton et al. (2011) for a level-of-evidence approach to the classification of couple and family therapy. Categories were selected to reflect the complexity of clinical practice and to facilitate treatment decisions about what works for whom and under what circumstances. Nominal categories were necessary to reflect client variables (e.g., clinical problem, type of client) and treatment context. However, for variables such as specificity, outcome strength, and study quality, each item of the scale was rated using a Likert scale that ranged from low to high, with higher numbers representing more comprehensive and specific interventions, more culturally diverse samples, and more rigorous designs. Our method for rating the strength of the study outcomes is based on that used by the Agency for Healthcare Research and Equality and the Effective Health-Care Program (AHRQ; Owens et al., 2010). The ratings were completed by a four-member rating team that trained together until they reached agreement on sample articles. The team met regularly to clarify and confirm rating decisions. Studies of CFT practices received ratings in seven different areas, which we define in the following paragraphs.

Interventions are the purposeful clinical activities of the therapist delivered to a client in a clinical context for the purpose of improving the client's personal and interactional functioning. Included in the broadest category are general modalities that, despite their lack of specificity, do represent a way of providing therapy (e.g., couple therapy or family therapy). On the other end of the spectrum are systematic intervention programs or models of practice (Alexander et al., 1994; Chambless & Hollon, 1998). Interventions also vary according to their type (skill-building, curricular, or therapeutic approach), specificity (manualized versus theory-based versus general practice), the populations they target (e.g., children, adolescents, families, couples), and the clinical problems they are designed to address. We rated CFT practices as either interventions or intervention programs. Interventions were defined as a single technique or a set of techniques that are designed to produce a particular outcome. Treatment programs were defined as comprehensive, specific, and systematic treatment approaches that target clinically meaningful syndromes or situations. Programs also have a coherent conceptual framework that includes the specific interventions and therapist qualities necessary to carry them out; such a framework is often presented in a treatment manual. Treatment manuals, clinical supervision, the measurement of treatment adherence, or a combination all suggest high treatment integrity, which was reflected in the coding of specificity.

Clinical outcomes represent the effectiveness of a CFT intervention for general and specific client concerns. They vary with respect to their target and strength, and they are often influenced by parameters (e.g., socioeconomic status). Type of outcome measure was also rated due to the fact that while there was a significant overlap between the client problem under investigation (e.g., substance abuse) and the outcome being measured (e.g., frequency of alcohol use), the two were often not exactly the same. Particularly for the couple therapy research, relationship satisfaction was often measured as an outcome even if relationship dissatisfaction was not the focus of treatment.

The *strength of research* is based on its type and methodological rigor and diversity of outcome measures. We rated the type of study (outcome, process, process to outcome, meta-analysis) and the type of outcome (iatrogenic effects: -1; no evidence of therapeutic effects: 0; as successful as alternative treatments: 1; mixed results: 2; or statistically significant outcomes: 3). We also coded the type of comparison group included in the study, the use of random assignment, the size of the sample, the assessment of treatment fidelity, and the use of multiple instruments and multiple perspectives (e.g., parent and teacher's report) to measure outcomes. Our method, while not based on a quantitative measure like effect size, follows the current guidelines set by AHRQ (Owens et al., 2010) and provides a clinically relevant measure of the degree to which one might have confidence that the outcomes could be realized in a clinical setting.

Understanding the characteristics of the *clients* that participate in clinical research helps researchers and practitioners make judgments about the generalizability of research findings. Interventions and research findings are specific to clients' demographic profiles. Of particular interest is the cultural diversity of the population for which intervention programs have been found to be effective. For each study we rated the age and diversity of the client(s).

Common therapeutic processes or intervention-specific factors are those variables that may have an impact on outcome and that signal the need for clinical adaptation or future research investigating how the intervention works differently in different contexts with different parameters.

The *context* of CFT research is important in determining the potential generalizability of the findings. Studies conducted in a broad range of contexts provide evidence that CFT is a viable approach across multiple settings. In addition, these studies further support the clinical utility of specific interventions with promising outcomes in diverse contexts. Consequently, we categorically coded the context of each of the studies for which contextual information was available.

The *quality of the research* determines both researchers' and clinicians' confidence in the strength of general trends and in the findings of individual studies. Studies that follow rigorous methodological standards, that use relevant comparison groups, random assignment, adherence measures, and diverse outcomes result in a high degree of confidence that the findings are very likely to be accurate and applicable to the larger population under investigation.

Review Methodology

The sample of couple and family therapy studies was identified by searching three major databases of the psychological literature: PsycInfo, PsycArticles, and Family Studies Abstracts. Only articles published since 2003 in peer-reviewed journals were considered. The peer-review process involves rigorous standards that guide the evaluation of manuscripts, and thus constitutes a measure of quality assurance as it relates to the inclusion of couple and family therapy studies in the sample. The following keywords were used in combination with the terms *family therapy/intervention*, *parenting program*, and *couple therapy/intervention* to locate relevant research. All abstracts were read carefully to determine whether the retrieved articles were studies concerning the moderators, mechanisms, or outcomes of couple and family therapy models, interventions, or techniques. Studies using qualitative data, and among them descriptive case reports, were excluded as they provided anecdotal rather than empirical evidence about the processes and effectiveness of systemic treatments. Publications in a language other than English were not included in the review. Meta-analyses of CFT research were considered separately from individual studies of clinical practices as the strength of their outcomes depends largely on the rigor of the studies selected and because they had variable outcome and clinical problems contained in the same study.

Our review is organized into two sections. First, we examine couple and family intervention studies to answer a variety of questions about CFT treatment approaches with research evidence: What are these interventions? Who are the clients for whom they have been tested? What are the clinical problems for which they have been evaluated? What are the range and strength of outcomes? What is the quality of the studies that make up the research base? These questions are important because they call attention to the growing breadth and diversity of CFT research and its increasing influence in clinical practice. In addition, answering these questions makes it possible to highlight trends in the literature, specifically the particular clinical activities, clients, problems, and contexts that have been the focus of CFT research. The second section of this review focuses on the effectiveness of couple and family therapy interventions and identifies those interventions that have positive outcomes, the clinical problems that effective CFT approaches target successfully, and the clinical contexts in which these treatments work. In addition, evidence about general and model-specific change mechanisms and delivery parameters are, when available, given attention, as it is important information that may guide the successful delivery of effective clinical interventions in clinical settings.

For the purpose of this review, skill-training parenting programs are considered a subset of family-focused intervention, whereas findings about couple-based programs are presented separately. Although family, parenting, and couple-based interventions belong to the same general CFT domain, they involve distinct clinical activities, goals, theories, and research that explain the interactional processes of intimate relationships. Despite their differences, both parenting programs and traditional family therapy are concerned about the characteristics of the family environment, such as parent–child interactions and family communication. Though they differ in their approach to treatment, parenting programs and family therapy share a similar focus, and for this reason are examined together.

Range of Research Evidence in Couple and Family Therapy

In the current review of the CFT research, we identified 13 meta-analysis and 249 individual intervention studies. The majority of the individual studies (205 or 82.3% of the sample) addressed family therapy or parenting programs, and 44 studies concerned couple therapy (17.7%).

Family interventions. Of the 205, 167 (81.46%) investigated systematic intervention programs while 38 (18.54%) were focused on broad and general interventions and treatment modalities. Family interventions were much more likely to be less specific (7.89% highly specific) as compared to comprehensive intervention programs, which were rated very specific (82.63%). The majority of family-focused interventions and programs treated the family conjointly (40.5%), or the parents (30.2%), or a combination of parents, youth, and family over the course of treatment (19.0%). Of these, 83 (66.2%) were family therapy or family-focused interventions while 42 (33.8%) were parent-focused.

The studies investigated the process and outcome of 124 specific interventions or intervention programs, which targeted 26 clinical problems. Of the 26 different clinical problems, the primary issues under investigation in the studies included youth behavior problems (40.0%), general mental health (3.4%), parenting (4.4%), family relationships (3.9%), and schizophrenic symptoms (3.4%). The vast majority of family therapy studies were outcome studies (174/84.9%); few (31/15.1%) were process or process-to-outcome studies that considered either change mechanisms or client and service delivery parameters. Thirty-nine percent of the studies investigated family therapy, 30.7% psychoeducational interventions, and 24.9% group-oriented family work. Twenty-two (10.7%) studies looked at a single intervention program (i.e., multisystemic therapy), 9 (4.4%) focused on multidimensional family therapy, 5 (2.4%) on functional family therapy, 15 (7.3%) on family-focused cognitive-behavioral therapy, 9 on parent–child interaction therapy (4.4%), and 11 (5.4%) on the parenting program called *Triple P Positive Parenting*.

These family-intervention studies have produced findings that are mostly applicable to non-Hispanic, White families. 15.6% of the studies ($n = 32$) of both interventions and intervention programs failed to specify the racial and ethnic composition of their samples. The studies were equally divided between single ethnic groups (43.4%) and mixed ethnic participant groups (41.0%). Similarly, 43.6% of the intervention and programs studied reported information indicating that their samples were homogeneous with regard to culture and sexuality (i.e., 47.4% of interventions and 65.4% of therapeutic models). African American, Latino, or Asian clients were represented in the family-focused literature with 41.2% of studies including one or more of these populations.

Couple therapy. Of the 44 couple therapy articles reviewed, 12 (27.3%) did not specify which conjoint therapy was investigated; 5 (4.5%) were studies of integrative, group-based, couple-focused interventions, and 4 (9%) were studies of brief psychoeducational couple therapy, congruence couple therapy, systemic couple therapy, coping-oriented couple therapy, and systemic constructivist couple therapy. The majority of the research (59.1% or 26 studies) focused on manualized treatment models: 22 studies looked at the implementation and parameters of behavioral couple therapy or one of its variants (i.e., integrative behavioral couple therapy, alcohol behavioral couple therapy, brief behavioral couple therapy); 3 studies were concerned about EFT and its adaptation, and 1 investigated the effectiveness of domestic violence focused couple treatment (DVFCT). In sum, most of the couple therapy research focused on identifiable interventions and therapeutic models that varied in levels of specificity: 59.1% of all studies investigated programs that were rated as highly specific; they followed a well-delineated protocol, were based on well-defined principles, and involved the use of adherence measures; 22.7% of the studies looked at interventions that were considered specific because they involved a coherent, theory-based group of techniques.

Couple therapy research has produced findings that are mostly applicable to non-Hispanic, White, heterosexual relationships: 27.3% of the studies ($n = 12$) failed to specify the racial and ethnic composition of their samples. These represent 44.4% and 15.4% of the research on couple interventions and manualized therapy models respectively; 56.8% of the studies reported information indicating that their samples were homogeneous with regard to culture and sexuality (i.e., 44.4% of interventions and 65.4% of therapeutic models). African American, Latino, Asian, and homosexual couples are largely underrepresented with only 15.9% of all studies including more than one ethnic and sexual group.

The majority of the couple therapy research looked at the impact of couple-based interventions and models for the treatment of relationship dissatisfaction (43.2%) independent of, or in relation to, general mental health (13.6%), anxiety (2.3%), and substance abuse (27.3%) problems in one of the partners. Among studies of therapeutic models, a large proportion (46.2%) investigated the role of conjoint therapy in the treatment of substance addictions. It is also noticeable that intimate partner violence (19.2%), infidelity (11.5%), and depression (7.7%) were three important clinical problems addressed by couple therapy models. Attention to the clinical issues of depression and relationship dissatisfaction was even more prominent among studies of couple-based interventions (33.3% and 61.1% respectively).

Most of the couple therapy research was conducted in two types of contexts: academic, including university-based training clinics ($n = 14$, 31.8%), and outpatient ($n = 7$, 15.9%), which comprises community-based mental health agencies and private practice. A few studies occurred in residential facilities ($n = 4$, 9%). It is noteworthy that the majority of the research on manualized treatment models such as behavioral couple therapy took place in university settings ($n = 10$, 38.46%). Few studies ($n = 5$; 19.2%) looked at the implementation of comprehensive and systematic CT models in outpatient or residential sites. By contrast, a large percentage of couple intervention studies ($n = 7$; 38.9%) occurred in community-based clinics or private practice. See Table 15.1.

Quality of the Studies

The quality of a study determines the degree of confidence that the field might have in the findings of CFT research. The majority of family therapy and parent training studies had large sample sizes (greater than 50 families 68.8%), involved comparison groups (77.6%), and random assignment (72.2%), and monitored and assessed therapists' adherence to the treatment protocol (64.4%). Outcome measurement was particularly relevant to the domain of couple and family therapy with 88.3% of the studies measuring outcome from multiple perspectives with multiple measures (see Table 15.1). A significant

TABLE 15.1 Study Characteristics

	General Approaches						Intervention Programs						Family Therapy		Couple Therapy	
	Couple Therapy		Family Therapy		Total		Couple Therapy		Family Therapy		Total					
	N	%	N	%	N	%	N	%	N	%	N	%	N	%	N	%
	18	40.91	38	18.54	56	100	26	59.09	167	81.46	193	100.00	205	100	44	100
Specificity																
Highly specific	0	0	3	7.89	3	5.36	26	100.00	138	82.63	164	84.97	141	68.78	26	59.09
Specific	10	55.56	22	57.89	32	57.14	0	0.00	24	14.37	24	12.44	46	22.44	10	22.73
Nonspecific	7	38.89	13	34.21	20	35.71	0	0.00	5	2.99	5	2.59	18	8.78	7	15.91
Unclear	1	5.56	0	0	1	1.79	0	0.00	0	0	0	0.00	0	0.00	1	2.27
Strength of study																
Comparison group (yes)	6	33.33	25	65.79	31	55.36	20	76.92	134	80.24	154	79.79	159	77.56	26	59.09
Random assignment (yes)	5	27.78	22	57.89	27	48.21	18	69.23	126	75.45	144	74.61	148	72.20	23	52.27
Treatment fidelity (yes)	5	27.78	9	23.68	14	25.00	15	57.69	123	73.65	138	71.50	132	64.39	20	45.45
Sample size																
<20	2	11.11	4	10.53	6	10.71	4	15.38	16	9.58	20	10.36	20	9.76	6	13.64
20–50	4	22.22	8	21.05	12	21.43	3	11.54	36	21.56	39	20.21	44	21.46	7	15.91
51–99	2	11.11	12	31.58	14	25.00	4	15.38	45	26.95	49	25.39	57	27.80	6	13.64
100+	10	55.56	14	36.84	24	42.86	15	57.69	70	41.92	85	44.04	84	40.98	25	56.82
Measures																
Single measure, single perspective	1	5.56	2	5.26	3	5.36	1	3.85	3	1.80	4	2.07	5	2.44	2	4.55
Multiple measures, single perspective	4	22.22	5	13.16	9	16.07	0	0.00	10	5.99	10	5.18	15	7.32	4	9.09
Single measure, multiple perspectives	4	22.22	1	2.63	5	8.93	4	15.38	2	1.20	6	3.11	3	1.46	8	18.18
Multiple measures and perspectives	9	50.00	30	78.95	39	69.64	20	76.92	151	90.42	171	88.60	181	88.29	29	65.91
Missing	0	0.00	0	0.00	0	0.00	1	3.85	1	0.60	2	1.04	1	0.49	1	2.27

(continued)

TABLE 15.1 *(Continued)*

Domain of measurement	General Approaches						Intervention Programs						Family Therapy		Couple Therapy	
	Couple Therapy		Family Therapy		Total		Couple Therapy		Family Therapy		Total					
	N	%	N	%	N	%	N	%	N	%	N	%	N	%	N	%
General mental health	7	38.89	6	15.79	13	23.21	3	11.54	24	14.37	27	13.99	30	14.63	10	22.73
Anxiety	1	5.56	0	0.00	1	1.79	0	0.00	10	5.99	10	5.18	10	4.88	1	2.27
Depression	8	44.44	2	5.26	10	17.86	2	7.69	14	8.38	16	8.29	16	7.80	10	22.73
Relationship satisfaction	17	94.44	0	0.00	17	30.36	15	57.69	3	1.80	18	9.33	3	1.46	32	72.73
OCD	2	11.11	1	2.63	3	5.36	0	0.00	4	2.40	4	2.07	5	2.44	2	4.55
Behavior problem	0	0.00	10	26.32	10	17.86	2	7.69	88	52.69	90	46.63	88	42.93	2	4.55
Substance use	0	0.00	3	7.89	3	5.36	11	42.31	20	11.98	31	16.06	23	11.22	11	25.00
Parenting	0	0.00	4	10.53	4	7.14	1	3.85	35	20.96	36	18.65	39	19.02	1	2.27
Bipolar	0	0.00	3	7.89	3	5.36	0	0.00	9	5.39	9	4.66	12	5.85	0	0.00
Family relationships	0	0.00	6	15.79	6	10.71	0	0.00	14	8.38	14	7.25	20	9.76	0	0.00
Medical issues	0	0.00	4	10.53	4	7.14	0	0.00	6	3.59	6	3.11	10	4.88	0	0.00
Parent–child conflict	0	0.00	1	2.63	1	1.79	0	0.00	10	5.99	10	5.18	11	5.37	0	0.00
Other	3	16.68	13	34.19	16	28.59	4	15.39	24	14.39	28	14.53	37	18.08	7	15.91
Client																
Couple	18	100.00	0	0.00	18	32.14	26	100.00	1	0.60	27	13.99	1	0.49	44	100
Family	0	0.00	21	55.26	21	37.50	0	0.00	62	37.13	62	32.12	83	40.49	0	0
Youth and parents separately	0	0.00	1	2.63	1	1.79	0	0.00	13	7.78	13	6.74	14	6.83	0	0
Parents	0	0.00	11	28.95	11	19.64	0	0.00	51	30.54	51	26.42	62	30.24	0	0
Family and adolescents themselves	0	0.00	0	0.00	0	0.00	0	0.00	4	2.40	4	2.07	4	1.95	0	0
Parents/youth separate and family	0	0.00	4	10.53	4	7.14	0	0.00	35	20.96	35	18.13	39	19.02	0	0
Adults	0	0.00	1	2.63	1	1.79	0	0.00	1	0.60	1	0.52	2	0.98	0	0

	n	%	n	%	n	%	n	%	n	%	n	%	n	%	n	%
Diversity																
Not specified	8	44.44	5	13.16	13.00	23.21	4	15.38	27	16.17	31	16.06	32	15.61	12	27.27
Homogeneous	8	44.44	18	47.37	26.00	46.43	17	65.38	71	42.51	88	45.60	89	43.41	25	56.81
More than one ethnic group	2	11.11	15	39.47	17.00	30.36	5	19.23	69	41.32	74	38.34	84	40.98	7	15.90
Type of study																
Outcome	13	72.22	33	86.84	46	82.14	22	84.61	141	84.43	163	84.46	174	84.88	35	85.36
Process to outcome	5	27.77	5	13.16	10	17.86	1	7.69	21	12.57	22	11.40	26	12.68	6	14.63
Process	0	0.00	0	0.00	0	0.00	1	3.84	5	2.99	6	3.11	5	2.44	1	2.43
Correlational	0	0.00	0	0.00	0	0.00	2	7.69	0	0.00	2	1.04	0	0.00	2	4.87
Treatment type																
Therapy	15	83.33	13	34.21	28	50	23	88.46	67	40.12	90	46.63	80	39.02	38	86.36
Psychoeducational	3	16.67	24	63.15	27	48.21	3	11.54	94	56.29	97	50.26	118	57.56	6	13.64
Both	0	0	1	2.63	1	1.79	0	0	6	3.59	6	3.11	7	3.41	0	0.00
Context																
Outpatient/community setting	7	38.89	22	57.89	29	51.8	4	15.39	118	70.67	122	63.22	140	68.31	11	25
University training clinic	4	22.22	8	21.05	12	21.43	10	38.46	37	22.16	47	24.35	45	21.95	14	31.82
Inpatient setting	3	16.67	7	18.42	10	17.85	1	3.85	6	3.6	7	3.63	13	6.34	4	9.09
Multiple settings	0	0	1	2.63	1	1.79	2	7.69	4	2.4	6	3.11	5	2.45	2	4.55
Not specified	4	22.22	0	0	4	7.14	9	34.62	2	1.2	11	5.7	2	0.98	13	29.55

part of the couple therapy research adhered to the criteria for establishing the quality of evidence. Specifically, 59.1% of all studies involved a comparison group, but this percentage was greater (76.9%) when only studies of therapeutic models were considered. For further insight into the quality of evidence in these studies, 52.3% (69.2% of couple-based model research) used random assignment, and 45.5% (57.7% of couple-based model research) monitored treatment adherence. The majority of the studies (70.4%) reported a sample size greater than 50, with 56.8% having more than 100 couple participants. Last, the majority of the research (65.9%) gathered outcome data from multiple perspectives with multiple measures (see Table 15.1).

A comparison of family and couple therapy research shows notable differences between these two domains as it relates to the quality of the studies: There were relatively more family studies with relevant comparison groups (77.56% versus 59.1% for couple therapy), random assignment (72.2% versus 52.3%), and specific measures of treatment fidelity (64.4% versus 45.45%). In addition, family therapy research was more likely to consider multiple perspectives (88.3% versus 65.9%) and to use multiple instruments to measure the effects of interventions.

EFFECTIVENESS OF FAMILY-BASED INTERVENTIONS

Previous reviews produced strong evidence to conclude that couple and family interventions are efficacious for a range of clinical problems (Gurman, 1971, 1973, 1975; Gurman & Kniskern 1981, 1991; Gurman, Kniskern, & Pinsof, 1986). Pinsof and Wynne (1995) found that family therapy produced positive results for a wide variety of specific clinical problems and that some interventions were more effective than individual or standard treatments for a number of disorders. Shadish and colleagues (Shadish, Ragsdale, Glaser, & Montgomery, 1995) found a weighted mean effect size for FT of $d = .47$. Although this effect size is lower than reported findings for group and individual therapy, it still suggests that those receiving family-based interventions fared better than those receiving no treatment at all. In general, FT interventions have done well in comparison to other treatment modalities across different presenting problems and divergent schools of FT approaches (Sexton, Alexander, et al., 2004). Sexton, Alexander, et al. (2004) found

that specific approaches were not only increasingly prevalent but also more successful than broad and nonspecific approaches for a wide range of client problems, particularly for schizophrenia and adolescent conduct disorders. However, at the time of that review, only a few types of FT had undergone substantial research regarding their outcomes and mechanisms of change. Overall, these earlier reviews suggested that FT demonstrated better results than treatment-as-usual groups, but few studies compared the relative effectiveness of different types of FT.

Family-Based Clinical Interventions

In this review, evidence for the efficacy of these interventions and programs come from both meta-analytic and specific clinical studies. Table 15.2 provides a summary of the meta-analytic results. Table 15.3 provides a summary of the family-based intervention programs, and Table 15.4 focuses on the couple-based intervention programs. Of the 205 studies of FT and parenting programs, 46% reported significant and positive outcomes, 43.4% reported mixed results that depended on either the specific outcome measures or moderating variables, and 10.2% found that FT interventions were equally successful as the alternative treatment in the study. Only 4.3% ($n = 9$) reported no outcome, and there were no studies in which the outcomes were, on average, iatrogenic. It is clear that FT and parenting programs are effective, but that success often depends on the specific outcomes and moderators of change. The analysis below focuses on these intervention programs that received the vast majority of the research attention, the contexts in which they were performed, the strength of the outcomes, and the unique innovations, adaptations, and features tested. Because it is not possible to draw conclusions about the effectiveness of an intervention from a single evaluation, we decided to limit the following description of programs that were considered in multiple studies.

Parent skills training interventions are directed at altering the skills of the parent(s) in order to improve the functioning of the youth. Parenting programs are certainly family-focused in that the ultimate aim is to change the way in which a family functions by altering the behavior of parents. Parenting programs tend to be skills-focused; they help parents build effective strategies for managing and supervising their

TABLE 15.2 Meta-Analytic Results for Outcome Studies of Family Therapy and Couple Therapy

Author(s) (Year)	Family Therapy, Couple Therapy, or Both	Intervention	Mean Effect Size (Cohen's d) (95% Confidence Interval)	Number of Studies	Heterogeneity (Q if not otherwise specified)	Principle Outcomes	Quality
Smit, Verdurmen, Monshouwer, and Smit (2008)	Family therapy	Family interventions	0.25* (95% CI: 0.12, 0.37)	5[a]	8.23	Frequency of alcohol use	Every included study: $N > 20$; Comparison group; Meta-analysis accounted for: Potential moderators (coded by consensus)
Bakermans-Kranenburg, van Ijzendoorn, and Juffer (2003)	Family therapy	Sensitivity and attachment interventions	0.44* (90% CI: 0.35, 0.52)	70	281.59*	Parental sensitivity	Meta-analysis accounted for: Potential moderators ($\kappa = 0.95$); Study quality
Reyno and McGrath (2006)[b]	Family therapy	Parenting skills training	None provided	18	None provided	Youth problem behavior	Every included study: $N > 20$; Meta-analysis accounted for: Potential moderators (no mention of interrater reliability)
McCart, Priester, Davies, and Azen (2006)	Family therapy	Behavioral parent training (BPT) versus cognitive-behavioral therapy (CBT)	0.40* (95% CI: 0.34, 0.47)	71 ($N = 30$ BPT, 41 CBT)	None provided	Youth problem behavior	Every included study: Comparison group; Meta-analysis accounted for: Potential moderators ($\kappa = 0.87$); Study quality; Potential variations within broad treatment type (e.g., type of family-based intervention)

(*continued*)

TABLE 15.2 (Continued)

Author(s) (Year)	Family Therapy, Couple Therapy, or Both	Intervention	Mean Effect Size (Cohen's d) (95% Confidence Interval)	Number of Studies	Heterogeneity (Q if not otherwise specified)	Principle Outcomes	Quality
Farrington and Welsh (2003)	Family therapy	Family-based prevention	0.22* (95% CI: 0.18, 0.27)	40	None provided	Youth problem behavior	Every included study: N > 20; Comparison group; Meta-analysis accounted for: Potential variations within broad treatment type (e.g., type of family-based intervention)
Nowak and Heinrichs (2008)	Family therapy	Triple P positive parenting	0.35* (95% CI: 0.22, 0.49)	55	None provided	Youth problem behavior Parenting	Every included study: N > 20; Meta-analysis accounted for: Potential moderators (coded by consensus); Study quality
Thomas and Zimmer-Gembeck (2007)	Family therapy	Triple P positive parenting (triple p) and parent–child interaction therapy (PCIT)	None provided	24 (N = 13 PCIT, 11 Triple P)	Not applicable	Youth problem behavior Parenting	Meta-analysis accounted for: Potential moderators (coded by consensus); Study quality; Potential variations within broad treatment type (e.g. type of family-based intervention)
Dretzke et al. (2009)[h]	Family therapy	Parenting programs	None provided	24[i]	None provided	Youth problem behavior	Every included study: Comparison group; Meta-analysis accounted for: Study quality

	Therapy category	Intervention	Effect size	N (studies)	Mean age	Outcomes	Every included study
Curtis, Ronan, and Borduin (2004)	Family therapy	Multisystemic treatment (MST)	0.55	7	11.73*	Youth problem behavior	Every included study: Comparison group; Meta-analysis accounted for: Potential moderators (no mention of interrater reliability)
Lundahl, Risser, and Lovejoy (2006)	Family therapy	Parent training programs	None included	83	Not applicable	Youth problem behavior, Parenting	Every included study: Comparison group; Meta-analysis accounted for: Study quality, Potential moderators (average intra-class correlation = 0.95, $\kappa = 0.89$)
Barbato and D'Avanzo (2008)	Couple therapy	Couple therapy	Not applicable	4[f]	None provided	Depression, Relationship distress	Every included study:Comparison group
Friedlander, Escudero, Heatherington, and Diamond (2011)	Both	Couple and family therapy	0.54* (95% CI: 0.41, 0.70)[g]	24 (N = 17 Family, 7 Couple)	None provided	Therapeutic alliance	Every included study: N > 20
Powers, Vedel, and Emmelkamp (2008)	Couple therapy	Behavioral couples therapy (BCT)	0.54* (95% CI: 0.37, 0.71)	12	None provided	Substance use, Relationship satisfaction	Every included study: Comparison group N > 20; Meta-analysis accounted for: Potential moderators (no mention of interrater reliability)

Note. *indicates $p < 0.05$. [a] There were 18 individual studies included in the meta-analysis, but only 5 had outcomes that could be converted into Cohen's *d*. [b] Moderators were found by correlating potential moderators to treatment outcome. [c] As measured by a standardized correlation between study quality and effect size. [d] Mean age of participants in CBT studies ($M = 11.28$) was significantly higher than the mean age of participants in BPT studies ($M = 5.44$); consequently, authors only directly compared studies with youth age 6 to 12. Resulting mean ages were 8.50 for BPT and 9.68 for CBT. [e] Moderators analyzed using a regression analysis. Estimated effect sizes were derived from controlled comparisons. Standard deviations were not provided for this analysis. [f] Only four (of a total of eight) studies were used to compute standardized mean difference (SMD) effect sizes analyzing the comparative efficacy of couple therapy over individual psychotherapy for depression and relationship distress. [g] Original effect sizes were correlation coefficients, but they were converted into Cohen's *d*. [h] Standardized mean difference (SMD) effect sizes were calculated rather than Cohen's *d*. [i] 57 studies included in the review, but only 24 had sufficient statistical information regarding child behavior.

TABLE 15.3 Study Information for Family Therapy Interventions*

Intervention Title	Author(s) (Year)	Problem(s) Addressed	Context(s)	Quality of Studies[a] (0–5)	Strength of Outcomes	Description Outcomes in Words
Behavioral parent training (N = 15)	Chacko et al. (2008)	Hyperactivity	University setting	2	2	Mixed results—significance depends on outcome measure
	Chacko, Wymbs, Wymbs, Pelham, et al. (2009)	Hyperactivity	University setting	4	3	Statistically significant results showing that treatment is successful
	Hawes and Dadds (2005)	Behavior problem	Outpatient home-based	3	2	Mixed results—significance depends on moderating variable
	Hayes, Matthews, Copley and Welsh (2008)	Parenting	Hospital	3	3	Statistically significant results showing that treatment is successful
	Morawska and Sanders (2009)	Behavior and general mental health	Community-based mental health agency	5	2	Mixed results—significance depends on outcome measure
	DeGarmo and Forgatch (2005)	Behavior problem	Community-based mental health agency	5	2	Mixed results—significance depends on moderating variable
	Fossum et al. (2009)	Behavior problem	Outpatient clinic-based, university setting	5	2	Significance depends on moderating variable and on outcome measure
	Hutchings et al. (2007)	Behavior problem	Community settings	5	2	Mixed results—significance depends on outcome measure
	Hutchings, Lane, and Kelly (2004)	Behavior problem	Outpatient clinic-based, outpatient home-based	3	3	Statistically significant results showing that treatment is successful
	Gross et al. (2008)	Parent–child conflict	Community settings	5	2	Mixed results—significance depends on moderating variable

Treatment	Study	Disorder/problem	Setting			Results
	Weiskop, Richdale, and Matthews (2005)	Developmental disorders	University setting	5	3	Statistically significant results showing that treatment is successful
	Hunter, Steele, and Steele (2008)	Medical issues	University setting	2	2	Mixed results—significance depends on moderating variable
	Webster-Stratton, Reid, and Hammond (2004)	Behavior problem	University setting	4	1	As successful as alternative treatment, no group differences
	Lavigne et al. (2008)	Behavior problem	Primary care practice	5	2	Mixed results—significance depends on moderating variable
	Yaruss, Coleman, and Hammer (2006)	Speech disorders	Outpatient clinic-based	4	3	Statistically significant results showing that treatment is successful
Family cognitive behavioral therapy (FCBT) (N = 15)	Barrett, Farrell, Dadds, & Boulter (2005)	OCD	University setting	5	2	Mixed results—results depend on moderating variable and as successful as alternative treatment
	Barrett, Healy-Farrell, and March (2004)	OCD	University setting	5	1	As successful as alternative treatment, no group differences
	Sellwood, Wittkowski, Tarrier, and Barrowclough (2007)	Schizophrenia	Hospital	3	3	Statistically significant results showing that treatment is successful
	O'Leary, Barrett, and Fjermestad (2009)	OCD	Community settings	2	3	Statistically significant results showing that treatment is successful
	Suveg et al. (2009)	Anxiety	Training clinic	5	1	As successful as alternative treatment, no group differences
	Puleo and Kendall (2011)	Anxiety, developmental disorders	Outpatient home-based	4	3	Statistically significant results showing that treatment is successful

(continued)

TABLE 15.3 *(Continued)*

Intervention Title	Author(s) (Year)	Problem(s) Addressed	Context(s)	Quality of Studies[a] (0–5)	Strength of Outcomes	Description Outcomes in Words
	Leong, Cobham, Groot, and McDermott (2009)	Anxiety	Training clinic	5	1	As successful as alternative treatment, no group differences
	Freeman et al. (2008)	OCD	University setting	5	3	Statistically significant results showing that treatment is successful
	Kendall, Hudson, Gosch, Schroeder, and Suveg (2008)	Anxiety	Outpatient clinic-based	5	2	Mixed results—significance depends on moderating variable
	Khanna and Kendall (2009)	Anxiety	University setting	5	2	Mixed results—significance depends on outcome measure
	Montero, Masanet, Bellver, and Lacruz (2006)	Schizophrenia	Outpatient home-based, inpatient setting	4	2	Mixed results—significance depends on outcome measure and as successful as alternative treatment
	Storch, Geffken, Merlo, Mann, Duke, Munson, Adkins, Grabill, Murphy, and Goodman (2007)	OCD	University setting	2	1	As successful as alternative treatment, no group differences
	Bodden et al. (2008)	Anxiety	Community-based mental health agency	5	2	Significance depends on moderating variable and on outcome measure
	Compas et al. (2010)	Behavior problem, general mental health	University setting	4	2	Mixed results—significance depends on moderating variable

	Study	Problem	Setting			Results
Family therapy (N = 7)	Storch et al. (2010)	OCD	Outpatient clinic-based	3	2	Mixed results—significance depends on outcome measure
	Escudero, Friedlander, Varela, and Aascal (2008)	Family relationships	University setting	2	2	Mixed results—significance depends on outcome measure
	Friedlander, Lambert, Escudero, and Cragun (2008)	Family relationships	Community-based mental health agency	3	2	Mixed results—significance depends on moderating variable
	Graves, Shelton, and Kaslow (2009)	Behavior problem	Community-based mental health agency	2	2	Mixed results—significance depends on outcome measure
	Hogue, Dauber, Stambaugh, Cecero, and Liddle (2006)	Substance abuse, behavior problem	Community-based mental health agency	5	2	Mixed results—significance depends on moderating variable
	Johnson, Ketring, Rohacs, and Brewer (2006)	Family relationships	Outpatient home-based	2	2	Mixed results—significance depends on moderating variable
	Miller et al. (2008)	Bipolar	Inpatient setting	4	2	Mixed results—significance depends on moderating variable
	French et al. (2008)	Substance abuse	University setting	4	2	Significance depends on moderating variable and on outcome measure
Functional Family Therapy (FFT) (N = 5)	Breuk et al. (2006)	Behavior problem	Outpatient clinic-based	1	0	No evidence
	Flicker, Waldron, Turner, Brody, and Hops (2008)	Substance abuse	University setting	5	2	Mixed results—significance depends on moderating variable
	Robbins, Alexander, Newell, and Turner (1996)	Family relationships	University setting	3	2	Mixed results—significance depends on moderating variable
	Sexton and Turner (2010)	Behavior problem	Community settings	3	2	Mixed results—significance depends on moderating variable

(continued)

TABLE 15.3 *(Continued)*

Intervention Title	Author(s) (Year)	Problem(s) Addressed	Context(s)	Quality of Studies[a] (0–5)	Strength of Outcomes	Description Outcomes in Words
	Slesnick, Bartle-Haring, and Gangamma (2006)	Sexual or physical or verbal abuse	Outpatient clinic-based, outpatient home-based	5	3	Statistically significant results showing that treatment is successful
Incredible Years parenting program (*N* = 7)	Bywater, Hutchings, Linck, Whitaker, et al. (2010)	Behavior problem, depression	Community settings	5	3	Statistically significant results showing that treatment is successful
	Foster, Olchowski, and Webster-Stratton (2007)	Behavior problem	Mixed setting(s)	5	3	Statistically significant results showing that treatment is successful
	Gardner, Burton, and Klimes (2006)	Behavior problem	Community-based mental health agency, community settings	5	3	Statistically significant results showing that treatment is successful
	Hartman, Stage, and Webster-Stratton (2003)	Hyperactivity	Outpatient clinic-based	2	3	Statistically significant results showing that treatment is successful
	Larsson et al. (2009)	Behavior problem	Outpatient clinic-based	5	2	Mixed results—significance depends on outcome measure
	McIntyre (2008)	Parent–child conflict, behavior problem	University setting	5	2	Mixed results—significance depends on outcome measure
	Reid, Webster-Stratton, and Baydar (2004)	Behavior problem	Community settings	2	2	Mixed results—significance depends on moderating variable
Triple P Positive Parenting (Triple P) (*N* = 11)	Matsumoto, Sofronoff, and Sanders (2010)	Behavior problem, parenting	Community settings	3	3	Statistically significant results showing that treatment is successful

Study	Problem focus	Setting			Results
Bodenmann, Cina, Ledermann, and Sanders (2008)	Parenting, behavior problem	University setting	5	2	Significance depends on moderating variable and on outcome measure
Prinz, Sanders, Shapiro, Whitaker, and Lutzker (2009)	Sexual or physical or verbal abuse	Community settings	2	3	Statistically significant results showing that treatment is successful
Sanders, Bor, and Morawska (2007)	Behavior problem, parenting	Community settings	1	1	As successful as alternative treatment, no group differences
Sanders et al. (2004)	Behavior problem, parenting	Community-based mental health agency	5	3	Statistically significant results showing that treatment is successful
Wiggins, Sofronoff, and Sanders (2009)	Parent–child relationship, parenting	Community-based mental health agency	4	3	Statistically significant results showing that treatment is successful
Morawska and Sanders (2006)	Parenting, behavior problem	Outpatient home-based	5	2	Mixed results—significance depends on moderating variable
Markie-Dadds and Sanders (2006)	Behavior problem	Outpatient home-based	4	2	Mixed results—significance depends on outcome measure
Plant and Sanders (2007)	Behavior problem	Community-based mental health agency, outpatient home-based	1	2	Mixed results—significance depends on outcome measure
Roberts, Mazzucchelli, Studman, and Sanders (2006)	Behavior problem	Community-based mental health agency	5	2	Mixed results—significance depends on moderating variable
Turner, Richards, and Sanders (2007)	Behavior problem	Community-based mental health agency	4	2	Mixed results—significance depends on outcome measure
Multidimensional Family Therapy (MDFT) (N = 9)					
Hogue, Henderson, Dauber et al. (2008)	Substance abuse, behavior problem	Inpatient setting	5	2	Mixed results—significance depends on moderating variable

(continued)

TABLE 15.3 (Continued)

Intervention Title	Author(s) (Year)	Problem(s) Addressed	Context(s)	Quality of Studies[a] (0–5)	Strength of Outcomes	Description Outcomes in Words
	Hogue, Liddle, Dauber, and Samullis (2004)	Substance abuse, behavior problem	Outpatient clinic-based	5	2	Mixed results—significance depends on moderating variable
	Hogue, Liddle, Singer, and Leckrone (2005)	Substance abuse, behavior problem	Outpatient home-based, community settings	5	1	As successful as alternative treatment, no group differences
	Liddle, Dakof, Turner, Henderson, and Greenbaum (2008)	Substance abuse, behavior problem	University setting	5	2	Mixed results—significance depends on outcome measure
	Liddle, Rowe, Dakof, Ungaro, and Henderson (2004)	Substance abuse, behavior problem	Outpatient clinic-based, outpatient home-based	5	3	Statistically significant results showing that treatment is successful
	Liddle et al. (2006)	Substance abuse	Outpatient clinic-based	3	2	Mixed results—significance depends on outcome measure
	Liddle, Rowe, Dakof, Henderson, and Greenbaum (2009)	Substance abuse, behavior problem	Community-based mental health agency	5	3	Statistically significant results showing that treatment is successful
	Robbins et al. (2006)	Substance abuse	Outpatient clinic-based	5	3	Statistically significant results showing that treatment is successful
	Shelef, Diamond, Diamond, and Liddle (2005)	Substance abuse	Outpatient clinic-based	5	2	Mixed results—significance depends on outcome measure
Multisystemic Therapy (MST) (N = 22)	Curtis, Ronan, Heiblum, and Crellin (2009)	Behavior problem	Outpatient home-based, community setting	3	1	As successful as alternative treatment, no group differences

Study	Problem	Setting			Results
Ellis, Naar-King, Cunningham, and Secord (2006)	Medical issues	Hospital, outpatient home-based	3	3	Statistically significant results showing that treatment is successful
Ellis, Naar-King, Templin, Frey, and Cunningham (2007)	Medical issues	Outpatient home-based, community settings	5	3	Statistically significant results showing that treatment is successful
Ellis et al. (2004)	Medical issues	Outpatient home-based, community settings	5	3	Statistically significant results showing that treatment is successful
Ellis, Yopp, et al. (2007)	Medical issues	Outpatient home-based, community settings	5	2	Mixed results—significance depends on moderating variable
Grimbos and Granic (2009)	Behavior problem	Hospital	2	2	Mixed results—significance depends on moderating variable
Halliday-Boykins, Schoenwald, and Letourneau (2005)	Behavior problem, general mental health	Outpatient home-based, community settings	3	2	Mixed results—significance depends on moderating variable
Henggeler, Letourneau, Chapman, Borduin et al. (2009)	Deviant sexual behaviors, behavior problem	Outpatient home-based, community settings	5	2	Mixed results—significance depends on moderating variable
Huey et al. (2004)	Suicide, depression	Outpatient home-based	5	2	Mixed results—significance depends on moderating variable
Huey et al. (2005)	Suicide	Outpatient home-based	5	2	Mixed results—significance depends on moderating variable
Letourneau et al. (2009)	Deviant sexual behaviors, behavior problem	Outpatient home-based, community settings	5	3	Statistically significant results showing that treatment is successful

(continued)

TABLE 15.3 (*Continued*)

Intervention Title	Author(s) (Year)	Problem(s) Addressed	Context(s)	Quality of Studies[a] (0–5)	Strength of Outcomes	Description Outcomes in Words
	MacDonell, Ellis, Naar-King, and Cunningham (2010)	Medical issues	Outpatient home-based, community settings	5	2	Mixed results—significance depends on moderating variable
	Ogden and Amlund Hagen (2009)	Behavior problem	Outpatient clinic-based	5	0	No evidence
	Ogden and Halliday-Boykins (2004)	Behavior and general mental health	Community-based mental health agency	5	3	Statistically significant results showing that treatment is successful
	Rowland et al. (2005)	Behavior and general mental health	Mixed setting(s)	2	3	Statistically significant results showing that treatment is successful
	Schoenwald, Chapman, Sheidow, and Carter (2009)	Behavior problem	Outpatient services, including private practice	4	2	Mixed results—significance depends on moderating variable
	Schoenwald, Sheidow, and Chapman (2009)	Behavior problem	Missing	4	2	Mixed results—significance depends on moderating variable
	Schoenwald, Sheidow, and Letourneau (2004)	Behavior problem	Community settings	5	2	Mixed results—significance depends on moderating variable
	Stambaugh et al. (2007)	Behavior problem	Missing	3	2	Mixed results—significance depends on outcome measure
	Timmons-Mitchell, Bender, Kishna, and Mitchell (2006)	Behavior problem	Community settings	5	3	Statistically significant results showing that treatment is successful

Treatment	Study	Presenting problem	Setting			Results
	Tolman, Mueller, Daleiden, Stumpf, and Pestle (2008)	Behavior and general mental health	Community-based mental health agency	1	3	Statistically significant results showing that treatment is successful
	Sundell et al. (2008)	Behavior and general mental health	Community-based mental health agency	5	1	As successful as alternative treatment, no group differences
Parent–child Interaction Therapy (PCIT) (N = 9)	Nixon, Sweeney, Erickson, and Touyz (2004)	Behavior problem	Outpatient clinic-based	5	1	As successful as alternative treatment, no group differences
	Solomon, Ono, Timmer, and Goodlin-Jones (2008)	Developmental disorders	University setting	4	3	Statistically significant results showing that treatment is successful
	Timmer, Urquiza, Zebell, and McGrath (2005)	Sexual or physical or verbal abuse	Outpatient clinic-based	5	2	Mixed results—significance depends on moderating variable
	Timmer, Ware, Urquiza, and Zebell (2010)	Behavior problem, physical or sexual or verbal abuse	Community-based mental health agency	4	1	As successful as alternative treatment, no group differences
	Timmer, Zebell, Culver, and Urquiza (2010)	Behavior problem	Outpatient clinic-based, outpatient home-based	4	1	As successful as alternative treatment, no group differences
	Werba, Eyberg, Boggs, and Algina (2006)	Behavior problem	Outpatient clinic-based	5	2	Mixed results—significance depends on moderating variable
	Chase and Eyberg (2008)	Behavior problem	University setting	5	2	Mixed results—significance depends on outcome measure

(continued)

TABLE 15.3 (*Continued*)

Intervention Title	Author(s) (Year)	Problem(s) Addressed	Context(s)	Quality of Studies[a] (0–5)	Strength of Outcomes	Description Outcomes in Words
	Matos, Bauermeister, and Bernal (2009)	Hyperactivity	University setting	5	3	Statistically significant results showing that treatment is successful
	Chaffin et al. (2004)	Physical or sexual abuse	University setting	5	2	Mixed results—significance depends on outcome measure
Parent Management Training (PMT) ($N = 6$)	Chamberlain, Price, Reid, and Landsverk (2008)	Behavior problem, general mental health	Community settings, outpatient home-based	4	2	Mixed results—significance depends on moderating variable
	DeGarmo, Patterson, and Forgatch (2004)	Behavior problem	Outpatient services, including private practice	5	2	Mixed results—significance depends on moderating variable
	Kazdin and Whitley (2003)	Behavior problem	Outpatient clinic-based	5	2	Mixed results—significance depends on outcome measure
	Martinez and Eddy (2005)	Behavior problem	Outpatient services, including private practice	5	2	Mixed results—significance depends on moderating variable
	Forgatch, DeGarmo, and Beldavs (2005)	Behavior problem	Outpatient services, including private practice	5	2	Mixed results—significance depends on moderating variable
	Ogden and Hagen (2008)	Behavior problem	Outpatient services, including private practice	5	3	Statistically significant results showing that treatment is successful

Note. *Not all family studies are included in this table; only the studies in our sample that addressed the interventions listed in the table were included. [a]Sum of random assignment, comparison group, treatment adherence, and strength of outcome measures.

TABLE 15.4 Study Information for Couple Therapy Interventions*

Intervention Title	Author(s) (Year)	Problem(s) Addressed	Context	Quality of Studies[a] (0–5)	Strength of Outcomes (0–3)	Description of Outcome
Alcohol Behavioral Couple Therapy (ABCT) ($N = 4$)	Epstein et al. (2007)	Substance abuse	Does not specify	3	2	Significance depends on moderator variable and on outcome measure
	McCrady, Epstein, Cook, Jensen, and Hildebrandt, (2009)	Substance abuse	University setting	5	2	Significance depends on moderator variable and on outcome measure
	Hildebrandt et al. (2010)	Substance abuse	Does not specify	5	2	Mixed results—significant results depend on moderator variable
	McCrady, Epstein, and Kahler (2004)	Substance abuse	Does not specify	5	Not applicable	Not applicable
Behavioral Couple Therapy (BCT) ($N = 10$)	Fals-Stewart, Lam, and Kelley (2009)	Substance abuse, intimate partner violence	Outpatient clinic-based	4	1	As successful as alternative treatment, no group differences
	O'Farrell, Murphy, Stephan, Fals-Stewart, & Murphy (2004)	Intimate partner violence	Mixed setting	3	Not applicable	Not applicable
	Schumm, O'Farrell, Murphy, & Fals-Stewart (2009)	Intimate partner violence, substance abuse	Mixed setting	3	Not applicable	Not applicable
	Simpson, Atkins, Gattis, and Christensen (2008)	Intimate partner violence	University setting	4	2	Mixed results—significant results depend on outcome measure
	Vedel, Emmelkamp, and Schippers (2008)	Substance abuse	Community-based mental health center	4	2	Mixed results—significant results depend on outcome measure
	Walitzer and Dermen (2004)	Substance abuse	University setting	5	1	As successful as alternative treatment, no group differences

(continued)

TABLE 15.4 *(Continued)*

Intervention Title	Author(s) (Year)	Problem(s) Addressed	Context	Quality of Studies[a] (0–5)	Strength of Outcomes (0–3)	Description of Outcome
	Fals-Stewart and Lam (2008)	Substance abuse, couple relationship dissatisfaction	Outpatient clinic-based	5	2	Mixed results—significant results depend on outcome measure
	Gattis, Simpson, and Christensen (2008)	Family relationships, couple relationship dissatisfaction	University setting	5	3	Statistically significant results showing that treatment is successful
	Fals-Stewart, Birchler, and Kelley (2006)	Substance abuse	Does not specify	5	3	Statistically significant results showing that treatment is successful
	Fals-Stewart et al. (2009)	Substance abuse	Outpatient clinic-based	4	2	Mixed results—significant results depend on outcome measure
Couple therapy (*N* = 12)	Lundblad and Hansson (2005)	General mental health	Outpatient clinic-based	3	3	Statistically significant results showing that treatment is successful
	Reese, Toland, Slone, and Norsworthy (2010)	Couple relationship dissatisfaction, OCD	Training clinic	4	3	Statistically significant results showing that treatment is successful
	Rowe, Doss, Hsueh, Libet, and Mitchell (2011)	Anxiety, depression, intimate partner violence	Outpatient clinic-based	1	2	Mixed results—significant results depend on moderator variable
	Tambling and Johnson (2008)	Couple relationship dissatisfaction, general mental health	University setting	2	2	Mixed results—significant results depend on moderator variable
	Tilden, Gude, Sexton, Finset, and Hoffart (2010)	Couple relationship dissatisfaction, depression	Inpatient setting	1	3	Statistically significant results showing that treatment is successful

Reference	Target problem	Setting			Result
	Tilden, Gude, and Hoffart (2010)	Couple relationship dissatisfaction, depression	Inpatient setting	1	3	Statistically significant results showing that treatment is successful
	Tilden, Gude, Hoffart, and Sexton (2010)	Couple relationship dissatisfaction, depression	Inpatient setting	1	3	Statistically significant results showing that treatment is successful
	Isakson et al. (2006)	General mental health	University setting	1	2	Mixed results—significant results depend on moderator variable
	Anker et al. (2010)	Couple relationship dissatisfaction	Community-based mental health center	2	3	Statistically significant results showing that treatment is successful
	Atkins et al. (2010)	Infidelity	Community-based mental health center	1	3	Statistically significant results showing that treatment is successful
	Schulz, Cowan, and Cowan (2006)	Couple relationship dissatisfaction	Does not specify	4	3	Statistically significant results showing that treatment is successful
	Kirby and Baucom (2007)	General mental health, couple relationship dissatisfaction	Outpatient clinic-based	2	2	Mixed results—significant results depend on outcome measure
Integrative behavioral couple therapy (IBCT) and traditional behavioral couple therapy (N = 8)	Anker et al. (2009)	Couple relationship dissatisfaction	Community-based mental health center	2	3	Statistically significant results showing that treatment is successful
	Atkins, Dimidjian, Bedics, and Christensen (2009)	Depression, couple relationship dissatisfaction	Does not specify	2	0	No evidence
	Atkins, Berns, et al. (2005)	Infidelity	Does not specify	2	3	Statistically significant results showing that treatment is successful

(continued)

613

TABLE 15.4 *(Continued)*

Intervention Title	Author(s) (Year)	Problem(s) Addressed	Context	Quality of Studies[a] (0–5)	Strength of Outcomes (0–3)	Description of Outcome
	Baucom et al. (2009)	Couple relationship dissatisfaction	University setting	1	Not applicable	Not applicable
	Atkins, Eldridge, et al. (2005)	Infidelity	Does not specify	1	3	Statistically significant results showing that treatment is successful
	Christensen et al. (2006)	General mental health, couple relationship dissatisfaction	University setting	5	Not applicable	Not applicable
	Christensen et al. (2010)	Couple relationship dissatisfaction	University setting	5	Not applicable	Not applicable
	Christensen et al. (2004)	General mental health, couple relationship dissatisfaction	University setting	5	1	As successful as alternative treatment, no group differences
Emotionally focused therapy (EFT) (N = 3)	Greenberg, Warwar, and Malcolm (2010)	Infidelity	University setting	4	3	Statistically significant results showing that treatment is successful
	Dessaulles (2003)	Depression	University setting	3	1	As successful as alternative treatment, no group differences
	McLean et al. (2008)	Medical issues	Hospital	2	2	Mixed results—significant results depend on outcome measure
Other	Gordon, Baucom, and Snyder (2004)	Infidelity	Does not specify	3	2	Mixed results—significant results depend on moderator variable

Study	Problem addressed	Setting		[a]	Results
Lee and Rovers (2008)	Pathological gambling	Does not specify	3	2	Mixed results—significant results depend on outcome measure
Bodenmann et al. (2008)	Depression	Outpatient services, including private practice	5	1	As successful as alternative treatment, no group differences
Stith, Rosen, McCollum, and Thomsen (2004)	Intimate partner violence	Does not specify	5	Not applicable	Not applicable
Kelley and Fals-Stewart (2007)	Behavior and general mental health, subance abuse, relationship dissatisfaction	Does not specify	2	3	Statistically significant results showing that treatment is successful
Reid and Woolley (2006)	Couple relationship dissatisfaction	University setting	2	3	Statistically significant results showing that treatment is successful

Note. *Not all couple studies are included in this table; only the studies in our sample that addressed the interventions listed in the table were included. [a]Sum of random assignment, comparison group, treatment adherence, and strength of outcome measures.

children, and thus indirectly impact the behaviors of children. The earliest reviews of family-intervention research pointed out that parenting programs were the first specific models for changing youth behavior. Family-therapy interventions were general and nonspecific. Over time, research has shown that parenting-skills training was most effective for younger children (preadolescents). In our review, the majority of meta-analytic and individual studies focused on four comprehensive skills training programs and a broad general category of parent-skills training studies.

Meta analysis. The meta-analytic studies of parent skills training suggest an average effect size of .44 when including all types of comparison groups and outcome measures. An effect size of .44 indicates that approximately 60% of those in the parent training intervention group were successful, while only 40% of those in the comparison group improved. For example, two meta-analyses focused on a specific parenting program, Triple P Positive Parenting. Nowak and Heinrichs (2008) found Triple P to significantly increase parenting skills and reduce child problem behavior when compared to no treatment controls ($ES = .35$). For youth problem behavior, the magnitude of the effect appeared to be dependent on the type of outcome measure; maternal reports yielded larger effects ($ES = 0.42$) than independent observational measures ($ES = .18$). This corresponds to 71% improvement in the intervention group as measured by maternal report compared to only 59% improvement in the intervention group as measured by independent observers. Additionally, it is important to note that not all of the included studies were randomized controlled trials, and the effect size for the randomized controlled trials ($ES = .44$) was significantly higher than that of the nonrandomized controlled trails ($ES = .10$). With regard to the Triple P program, the individual approach to treatment ($ES = .43$) was found to be more effective than the group ($ES = .20$) and self-administered approaches ($ES = .23$), which indicates that about 72% of the individual intervention group improved compared to only 60% of the group intervention group and 62% of the self-administered intervention group.

Thomas and Zimmer-Gembeck (2007) compared Triple P and parent–child interaction therapy (PCIT) and found both programs to be effective compared to wait-list and to no treatment. Both treatments improved children's behavior as measured by parent-reports when compared to wait-list control groups; concerning

PCIT, an effect size of 1.45 translates to approximately 80% improvement for the intervention group and only 20% improvement for the wait-list control group. Similarly, an effect size of 0.69 for Triple P translates to about 66% improvement for the intervention group and 34% improvement for the wait-list control group.

Individual studies. Four comprehensive parenting programs and one general approach account for the majority of parenting interventions in individual studies; they represent 17.6% of all family studies. There were 31 studies of specific parenting intervention programs; of these, 12 (38.7%) had positive and significant outcomes, 15 (48.4%) had mixed results, and 4 (12.9%) had outcomes no different than the comparison group. When compared to the general parent training intervention models in this review, 50% of these specific approaches have positive and statistically significant outcomes. These programs, the problems for which they are designed, the strength of the outcomes, and the clients are briefly described below.

• *Parent child interaction training* (PCIT) is a family-based parenting program for young children between 2 and 7 years of age (Timmer, Ware, Urquiza, & Zebell, 2010). PCIT targets child behavior problems and is delivered in a manualized form. Based on social learning and attachment theories, PCIT posits that by coaching parents and teaching them new ways of interacting with their children, they become a more functional agent of change in improving their child's behavior. In the PCIT studies that were reviewed, most focused on the efficacy of PCIT on different populations, specifically those with autism or those that were victims of interpersonal violence. The research also investigated how the addition of an in-home component improved outcome. There were nine PCIT studies that addressed a variety of child problems including hyperactivity and other externalizing behaviors, sexual acting out, and developmental issues. Of these nine studies, three (33%) reported significant and positive outcomes; three (33%) had mixed results dependent on which problem was the target of treatment; and three produced outcomes that were equal to the alternative treatment that differed along one dimension for two of the studies and was a wait list for one of them. The strongest effects occurred when PCIT targeted problem behaviors related to developmental disorders and hyperactivity; the weakest results occurred when the intervention was used to treat general behavior problems, verbal aggression, and sexual aggression. Half of the studies took place in outpatient or home settings while the other half occurred in university settings. The average study quality index was 4.5, indicating strong methodological rigor for the studies of PCIT. All of the studies measured outcomes with multiple instruments and from multiple perspectives.

- *Triple P positive parenting program* is a manualized intervention for children and younger adolescents that is delivered in individual, group, and family settings. Triple P is used to both treat and prevent emotional and behavioral problems from developing in children by changing the aspects of the family environment that may be reinforcing problem behaviors (Nowak & Heinrichs, 2008; Sanders, 1999). Most of the studies featuring Triple P were designed to evaluate the extent to which the program helps to minimize externalizing behaviors at termination and follow-up. Nine studies of Triple P were identified. Half used multiple assessments and perspectives to measure outcomes, and the other half used only one assessment instrument (usually parent-focused). The majority of the studies took place in outpatient mental health settings (seven out of nine). Four (44%) found significant positive outcomes; two (22.2%) reported mixed results that presumably depended on client factors; and one (11.1%) found positive effects that were no greater than the comparison group. Three of the studies investigated which modality of treatment delivery (group versus individual) was most effective.

- *Incredible years parent training* (IYPT) is a curriculum-based parenting intervention program focused on improving youth behavior problems and parent–child conflict. It is most often delivered in community and agency settings. As a psychosocial approach to treatment, IYPT aims to reduce conduct disorders in young children by increasing parental competencies (Webster-Stratton, 1984, 1994). There is some evidence to suggest that IYPT is efficacious in treating a diverse range of child behavioral issues across varied familial conditions (Bywater et al., 2010; Larsson et al., 2009; McIntyre, 2008). In addition, IYPT has been shown to be a low-cost solution for improving child behavior (Bywater et al.,

2010; Foster, Olchowski, & Webster-Stratton, 2007). There were seven studies of IYPT that focused on child behavior problems, depression, hyperactivity, and parent–child problems. In four (57.4%) of these studies, the program produced statistically significant positive outcomes; the other three (42.8%) studies suggested that the success of IYPT depended on client factors and outcome measures.

- *Parent management training* (PMT) is a manualized, parent-training program focused on behavior problems in children (DeGarmo & Forgatch, 2005). Although studies of PMT have varied across age of youth and severity of externalizing problems, PMT typically strives to improve behavior management through psychoeducational initiatives with caregivers that focus on core parental processes (Chamberlain, Price, Reid, & Landsverk, 2008; DeGarmo & Forgatch, 2005; Forgatch, DeGarmo, & Beldavs, 2005). Of the six studies of PMT, five (83.3%) had mixed results indicating that the efficacy of the program was restricted by certain client characteristics and that it was not constant across all outcome measures. Only one (16.7%) study found the intervention to have a positive and statistically significant impact on the problem. Strongest effects were for general behavior problems, and the weakest were for mental health problems. It is likely that the range of client problems in these studies was diverse and that PMT might not work equally as well with the entire range of youth problems.

- General *parent training* (PT) describes a group of nonspecific interventions that are oriented toward the development of parenting skills and the management of child and adolescent behavior (Fossum, Mørch, Handegård, Drugli, & Larsson, 2009; Gross, Shaw, & Moilanen 2008; Hutchings et al., 2007; Hutchings, Lane, & Kelly, 2004). The target of these PT studies is exclusively child behavior problems, hyperactivity, and youth developmental disorders. Three of the six (50%) studies found that PT had mixed results and that outcomes varied with different client variables. Another three (50%) found that PT had a statistically and clinically important impact with stronger results (positive and significant) found for general child behavior problems and developmental disabilities. The majority of studies were conducted in clinical and home-based settings. All studies involved the use of multiple measures and multiple perspectives.

Family Therapy Interventions

In the former editions of the handbook, it was found that a number of specific family therapy programs were effective and that the research on these models was robust. In the last review (Sexton et al., 2003), comprehensive treatment programs were a growing area of research. Sexton and colleagues (2003) identified four family-based intervention models that had significant research evidence from meta-analytic, qualitative, and individual clinical studies: functional family therapy (Alexander, Pugh, Parsons, & Sexton, 2000; Sexton & Alexander, 2003; Sexton & Turner, 2010), multisystemic therapy (Henggeler, Schoenwald, Borduin, Rowland, & Cunningham, 1998), brief structural strategic therapy (Szapocznik et al., 2002) for youth behavior and drug abuse problems, family psychoeducational approaches for schizophrenia treatment, and behavioral family systems therapy (Robin, 2003) for eating disorders. They concluded that family therapy models had effects substantial enough to suggest they should be the primary treatment options for child and youth behavior problems, substance use/abuse, eating disorders, and the management of schizophrenia. Surprisingly, this review identified few meta-analyses of specific family therapy models.

Meta-Analysis

Only two meta-analyses included systematic family therapy interventions, both focusing on the same model, that is, multisystemic therapy (MST). Farrington and Welsh (2003) did a meta-analysis of controlled outcome studies regarding the efficacy of differing types of family-based programs designed to prevent delinquency and antisocial child behavior. Overall, the programs were successful in reducing behavioral problems, but the type of intervention, which was intimately tied to treatment setting in the authors' analysis, significantly moderated treatment outcome. The most effective types of programs used were specific intervention models: MST (6) and behavioral parent training (10) were the most effective with effect sizes of .41 and .40 respectively, corresponding to 60% improvement in the treatment groups versus 40% improvement in the control groups; the least effective interventions were those based in schools (7) and in the community or at home (8), with effect sizes of .07 and

.18 respectively. Home visits and interventions based in day care or preschool were moderately effective ($ES = .24 - .26$), indicating that 56% of the intervention groups improved versus 44% of the control groups. Curtis, Ronan, and Borduin (2004) performed a meta-analysis of controlled outcome studies regarding the effectiveness of multisystemic therapy (MST) for antisocial youth. The mean effect size ($ES = .55$) demonstrated that MST significantly improved youth functioning to the extent that 63% improved in the treatment groups compared to 37% of the treatment as usual groups. Additionally, the mean effect size in efficacy studies where therapists were graduate students ($ES = .81$) was significantly higher than the mean effect size for effectiveness studies conducted in community-based settings with professional clinicians ($ES = .26$) (when compared to treatment as usual).

Individual Studies

Approximately 50% of the FT studies focused on five types of interventions: four were systematic intervention programs and one was general family therapy. Twenty studies reported positive and significant outcomes (35.7%), 24 (42.8%) had mixed results, and three (5.6%) found no significant differences as it relates to the comparative effectiveness of FT programs. These programs, the problems they targeted, the strength of the outcomes, and the clients they served are briefly described below.

- *Multisystemic therapy* (Henggeler et al., 1998) is one of the most studied comprehensive family-based interventions. MST is a well-established program developed to treat youth with serious antisocial behaviors. MST targets multiple problem areas in the home and in the community that surrounds the youth. Specifically, MST strives to empower caregivers to increase protective factors (e.g., monitoring, supervision, discipline) in an effort to minimize youth's destructive behavior (Ellis, Naar-King, Templin, Frey, & Cunningham, 2007; Henggeler et al., 2009). MST research has moved beyond simple effectiveness studies to the examination of specific mediators and moderators of client outcome. Caregiver mental health status, behaviors, and demographic factors have all been examined as potential moderators and mediators of therapeutic outcomes for at-risk youth struggling with a variety of health and behavioral issues (Ellis, Naar-King, et al.,

2007; Grimbos & Granic, 2009; Henggeler et al., 2009; MacDonell, Ellis, Naar-King, & Cunningham, 2010). Twenty-two studies of MST were identified; they focused on a wide range of clinical problems including youth behavior problems and general mental health, deviant sexual behavior, medical issues, suicide, and depression. Of these 22 studies, 8 (36.4%) found MST to be successful; two (9.1%) showed that it was no more successful than the alternative treatment; 11 (50%) produced mixed results that were dependent on the outcome measures or the client variables; and one (4.5%) had no quantitative evidence. The variation in outcomes was evident across client clinical problems. Eight studies found positive effects for youth behavior problems, medical problems, general mental health, and youth sexual behavior problems. However, other studies found contradictory evidence with regard to the effectiveness of MST for behavior problems and substance abuse. All of the MST studies took place in hospitals and outpatient or community settings. In addition, MST has been the focus of research in diverse cultures and geographic locations to provide evidence of transportability (Curtis, Ronan, Heiblum, & Crellin, 2009). The outcomes of the MST studies varied in strength and types, and the MST research had an average quality index score of 4.1, indicating that the studies in this review were of high methodological quality.

- *Functional family therapy* (FFT) is a long-standing family therapy intervention program for youth with behavior, substance use, and family relational problems (Alexander & Sexton, 2002; Sexton et al., 2004; Sexton & Turner, 2010). FFT is frequently implemented in juvenile justice and community mental health center settings. In addition to its well-established efficacy in treating a diverse range of adolescent behavioral problems (Flicker, Waldron, Turner, Brody, & Hops, 2008; Slesnick & Prestopnik, 2005), evidence suggests that successful outcomes in FFT are largely dependent on therapist adherence to the treatment model, with lower adherence predicting greater recidivism rates among adjudicated youth (Sexton & Turner, 2010). The five FFT studies included in this review looked at the effect of treatment on youth behavior problems, family relationship problems, substance use, and sexually deviant youth behavior.

Of these studies, one (20%) found no significant outcome, three (60%) showed that FFT had significant positive effects depending on client or measurement factors, and one (20%) produced evidence that FFT was significantly more successful than treatment as usual. The strongest effect was found in studies that investigated the impact of treatment on substance use and family relational functioning. Half of the research was based in community settings and the other half in university clinics. The studies of FFT had an average quality index score of 3.4 indicating that they were of high methodological quality. This score was lower than the ones obtained for other FT models; it reflects a scientific shift from randomized control trials to community-based effectiveness studies that take into consideration the complexity of practice. Because FFT is a mature and long-standing evidence-based program, this shift is to be expected; it corresponds to a new focus of attention and to the investigation of contextual factors that moderate the effect of treatment.

- *Multidimensional family therapy* (MDFT; Liddle, 1995) is a model primarily focused on substance abusing youth and their families. Recognized as a "best practice" in drug abuse prevention and intervention (National Institute on Drug Abuse; NIDA, 1999), MDFT is a multisystem, manualized, phasic approach that targets multiple risk and protective factors across diverse social domains of adolescent and family functioning (Liddle, Rowe, Dakof, Ungaro, & Henderson, 2004). In recent years, MDFT research has expanded the focus of its investigations to various therapeutic factors that impact treatment success. Evidence suggests that therapist adherence and alliance building are both significant predictors of therapeutic outcomes for MDFT (Hogue et al., 2006; Hogue et al., 2008). Specific change mechanisms are also being explored as mediators of treatment outcome. A process-outcome study found that family focus in treatment (versus adolescent focus) was a significant predictor of treatment success (Hogue, Liddle, Dauber, & Samuolis, 2004). Of the nine MDFT studies in this review, all occurred in community settings including one study in an inpatient hospital. All of these studies used diverse outcome measures and gathered data from multiple perspectives, and they also measured treatment fidelity. The outcomes of the studies were varied. In one study, MDFT was found to be equal but not superior to a treatment alternative that differed along only one dimension. Five studies showed that the effectiveness of MDFT was moderated by the specific type of outcome, and three that the MDFT model had significantly more positive results compared to the alternative treatments, regardless of the outcome measures or the client characteristics. The average study quality index score was 4.9. Although impressive, this score most likely reflects the fact that MDFT has in the last decade undergone extensive randomized clinical trials to validate its efficacy.

- *Cognitive behavioral family therapy* is an individual therapy approach implemented with families. In general, family-based CBT (CBT-FT) strives to incorporate parents into an established cognitive behavioral treatment for youth in order to improve outcomes via parent training or support (Freeman et al., 2008; Kendall, Hudson, Gosch, Flannery-Schroeder, & Suveg, 2008). Studies typically focus on the relative efficacy of CBT-FT compared to individual and supportive treatments in randomized control trials (Freeman et al., 2008; Kendall et al., 2008). The problems that this general approach targets were quite different from those addressed by the other family interventions; the majority of studies looked at the effectiveness of cognitive behavioral family therapy (CBT-FT) with a wide range of individually oriented symptoms including obsessive-compulsive disorders in youth, depression, and anxiety. There were a significant number of CBT-FT studies (*n* = 20). Nineteen of these investigated the effects of CBT-FT alone; one study considered CBT-FT integrated with a nonspecific attachment-based intervention. The majority of these studies were conducted in university settings rather than community-based agencies. Of the 19 studies of CBT-FT alone, one (5%) found no evidence of an effect; seven (37%) found that the intervention had significantly positive outcomes; four (21%) indicated that CBT-FT was not more successful than the alternative treatment; and one study found significant results that depended on client and contextual variables. Studies of CFT-FT were of high quality. The strength of the outcomes ranged from low (1) to moderate (2.25). Studies investigating CBT family therapy with depression received low outcome ratings, while studies of

anxiety received moderate ratings. Like other studies of family therapy models, CBT-FT research involved the use of multiple measures and perspectives. The quality index score for CBT-FT studies was relatively high at 4.2.

General family therapy studies were those that investigated family therapy as a modality rather than a specific and comprehensive intervention program. There were eight different individual studies, seven of which focused on family therapy and one that compared FT to an alternative intervention. Of these, the majority focused on changes in family relationships. A smaller number of studies aimed at understanding the impact of FT on youth behavior problems, substance use problems, and general mental health problems. The vast majority of studies were in community settings. Few of the studies measured treatment fidelity (only two of eight studies). The average study quality index score was 2.14. Five (62%) studies indicated mixed results that were a function of client characteristics and outcome measures. Three studies found FT to be successful (37%). FT was most successful with eating disorders while it had mixed results with behavior problems, substance use problems, bipolar disorders, and general family relationships.

Clinical Problems for Which FT Is Effective

In this review, a range of clinical problems was the focus of FT studies. These problems were similar to those identified in the previous review (Sexton et al., 2004) where children and youth substance use and abuse, behavior problems, serious mental illness, and other mental health problems were symptoms that could be successfully reduced through CFT intervention programs.

Child and Youth Behavior Problems

The majority of the studies (75 or 33.8%) investigated the effects of family and parenting programs on clinical problems related to child and youth behavior problems. Twenty-five (33.3%) reported positive and significant outcomes; 35 (46.7%) found mixed results; 11 (15.6%) showed that FT and parenting interventions produced outcomes that were equal to another comparable treatment; and four (5.3%) produced no evidence of success. Both meta-analytic and individual studies support the effectiveness of FT and parenting programs with a broad range of child and youth behavior problems. Dretzke et al. (2009)

conducted a meta-analysis of controlled studies of parenting programs for children with conduct problems. They found that all the programs significantly decreased problematic behavior in youth from both the perspective of parents and independent raters. However, the strength of the outcome depended on the relationship of the raters to the youth. Parents reported more significantly positive outcomes (parent: $d = .67$) when compared to outcomes assessed by independent raters ($d = .44$). Farrington and Welsh (2003) found that family-based programs were generally successful in reducing problem behavior, but type of intervention, which was intrinsically tied to treatment setting in the authors' analysis, significantly moderated treatment outcome. The most effective types of programs were specific intervention models (MST, 6; $d = .41$) and behavioral parent training (10; $d = .40$), while the least effective interventions, all nonspecific parent skills training, were those based in schools (7; $d = .07$) and home/community-based (8; $d = .18$). Home visiting and day care/preschool-based interventions were only somewhat effective ($d = .24 - .26$).

Three meta-analyses focused on specific interventions programs. For example, in a meta-analysis of two different specific intervention models, McCart, Priester, Davies, and Azen (2006) looked at outcomes of 71 randomized controlled trials of behavior parenting training compared to cognitive-behavior therapy for anti-social youth. Results indicated both programs had a strongly positive effect size (.40). These outcomes did decrease post treatment ($ES = .40$) to follow-up ($ES = .22$) for both the behavior parent training studies and the cognitive-behavior therapy studies. Farrington and Welsh (2003) studied the impact of different general and specific treatment programs and modalities for preventing future delinquency and antisocial child behaviors. Overall, the programs were successful in reducing problem behavior, but type of intervention (and its context) significantly moderated treatment outcome.

A number of studies considered the impact of specific interventions. Two of these were studies of general parent training and its impact on various changes in youth behavior. These focused on effectiveness, client variables that mediate outcome, and delivery methods that may impact outcome. Lundahl, Risser, and Lovejoy (2006) did a meta-analysis of controlled studies of parent training programs. In general, parenting

training programs were found to be moderately effective. Parent training was least effective for economically disadvantaged families (.24 versus .54 for high SES). The good outcomes occurred across delivery modalities; individual ($ES = .69$), self-directed ($ES = .51$), and group approaches ($ES = 0.34$).

Curtis et al. (2004) did a unique analysis in that it only looked at specific treatment programs, such as MST, applied in various settings. The intent was to identify any within-setting superiority for programs. This approach creates strong support for the model if results are strong and persist over contexts. The mean effect size ($d = .55$) demonstrated that MST significantly improved youth functioning regardless of setting. Additionally, the mean effect size for the efficacy studies with graduate students as therapists ($ES = .81$) was significantly higher than the mean effect size for the effectiveness studies with community therapists ($ES = .26$). The authors pointed out that the efficacy trials conducted with graduate students were supervised by the creators of the intervention, which explains the disparity between the effect sizes found in the efficacy studies and the more complex effectiveness studies that used community therapists. These finding reinforce the emerging trend that clinical outcomes are lower in the complex community setting. Reyno and McGrath (2006) indicate that some variables (e.g., severity of youth's behavioral symptoms) are moderately correlated with treatment outcome. The largest correlation was found between low family income and treatment outcome ($r = 0.52$).

Youth Substance Use/Abuse Problems

Both meta-analytic and individual clinical studies indicated that family intervention programs could be successful with youth substance use/abuse problems. Of the 23 individual studies that analyzed the effect of an FT intervention on substance abuse, nine (39.1%) had significant and positive outcomes, 13 (56.5%) had mixed outcomes, and one (4.3%) found the FT interventions to be no more successful than the comparison group. These results are consistent with the single meta-analysis (Smit, Verdurmen, Monshouwer, & Smit, 2008) that investigated the effect of family-based interventions, including family therapy, family psychoeducation, and parenting skills training, on alcohol consumption in participating youth. Results from the five relevant controlled studies suggest that family-focused interventions are effective ($ES = 0.25$)

in reducing youths' frequency of alcohol use. No differences were found due to client ethnicity.

Youth Bipolar, Depressive Disorder, and General Medical Conditions

Bipolar disorder is often viewed as an individually based clinical problem. However, this review found 12 individual studies investigating the role of parenting and family interventions with this disorder. Of these studies, six (50%) found significant and positive outcomes, five (41.6%) had mixed results and only one had outcomes equal to the alternative treatment. This would indicate that FT and parenting interventions are promising interventions for what is often viewed as an individual problem. Youth depression is also a clinical problem that is often viewed as an individual clinical issue. Of the nine studies of family and parenting interventions directed at youth depression, three (33.3%) were successful, three (33.3%) reported mixed results, two had outcomes no different than the alternative, and only one had no evidence of effectiveness. General medical conditions of youth are an area of increasing focus in the family intervention literature. Of the 12 studies (5.9%) in this area, all were either significantly positive (50%) or had mixed results (50%). These outcomes would indicate that family interventions are a promising intervention category for medically-based problems for youth.

The Effectiveness of Couples Therapy Interventions and Programs

Couple-based clinical interventions are intervention programs targeting the couple relationship in an attempt to improve relationship satisfaction and a variety of individual clinical symptoms that might be experienced by one member of the couple. Sexton and colleagues (2004) noted that the effectiveness of couple therapy had been tested for a relatively limited number of problems. They suggested that this had allowed the field to investigate and refine a small number of well-defined comprehensive treatment models; however, at the same time, it might also have restricted the use of couple therapy (CT) as a primary intervention model for many of the diverse problems experienced in clinical practice.

The last review (Sexton et al., 2004) evaluated the overall effectiveness of CT based on three meta-analytic reviews and 14 individual clinical studies. One of these meta-analyses (Shadish, Ragsdale, Glaser, & Montogomery, 1995) looked at 71 CT studies and produced an average effect size of .60. This result was confirmed by Dunn and Schwebel (1995), who found an effect size of .79 at termination and .52 at follow-up. This result seemed stable across outcome and context. It was noted that despite these effects, only about half of the treated couples experienced positive change (Christensen & Heavey, 1999). These meta-analyses reviewed the studies of three systematic treatment models: behavioral marital/couple therapy had an effect size of .78, emotionally focused couple therapy .87, and cognitive behavioral therapy (CBT) .54. Couple therapy appeared to be effective for depression, sexual disorders, and alcohol and drug problems experienced by one or both partners. The strongest moderators and mediators of outcomes were the therapeutic alliance and reduction in negative communication and blame.

Our review focuses on couple-based interventions and comprehensive programs; it highlights these areas of couple therapy practice that were investigated in meta-analyses and individual studies. Table 15.2 summarizes information derived from the meta-analyses of couple therapy, and Table 15.4 presents data obtained from the review of individual studies. The majority of studies were devoted to three systematic intervention programs in which both the efficacy of the program and the variables that may improve outcomes were studied.

Meta-Analyses

Two meta-analyses of couple therapy (CT) interventions were identified in our review (Barbato & D'Avanzo, 2008; Powers, Vedel, & Emmelkamp, 2008). Barbato and D'Avanzo (2008) reviewed eight randomized controlled trials of couple therapy and evaluated the relative effectiveness of CT compared to individual therapy and psychopharmacotherapy. Their meta-analysis showed that CT had a significant positive effect on relationship satisfaction ($d = .94$), but was not more effective than individual therapy in the treatment of depression. In other words, there was no evidence that reduction in relationship distress was associated with fewer mood symptoms. Using the findings of 12 controlled trials of behavioral couple therapy (BCT) for alcohol and substance use disorders, Powers et al. (2008) compared the outcomes of BCT to alternative treatment modalities (i.e., psychoeducation, individual and group therapy). The results of this meta-analysis showed that BCT was superior to the control conditions for alcohol and substance-related problems overall; it produced greater reduction in frequency of substance use ($d = .36$) along with fewer consequences ($d = .52$) and greater relationship satisfaction ($d = .58$). This meta-analysis also revealed that the relative efficacy of BCT was a function of time and outcome. Although BCT outperformed other conditions on measures of relationship satisfaction at both termination and follow-up, its positive effects on frequency and consequences of use were not greater than those of alternative treatments at termination. However, significant between-group differences were found at follow-up 3 months later, suggesting that relationship outcomes are an important factor in the reduction of problem drinking and substance use over time.

- *Individual studies*. As noted earlier, we included those general and specific programs that included the most studies. Of the 44 studies of couple therapy published since 2003, 12 (27.3%) looked at the outcomes of couple therapy as a modality of treatment, 10 of which were couple-based interventions and two of which were group-based interventions. The majority, 23 or 52.3%, were studies of intervention programs (behavioral couple therapy) and its variations. Specifically, 10 (22.7%) investigated the effects of BCT; seven (15.9%) compared integrative behavioral couple therapy (IBCT) to traditional BCT; and five (11.36%) examined the efficacy of BCT programs for alcohol and substance-related problems (alcohol behavioral couple therapy and Learning Sobriety Together). Many of the studies (22 or 50%) focused on general approaches to helping couples and individual partners with specific clinical problems.

- *Behavioral couple therapy* (BCT) is a well-established therapeutic program based on theories of learning and conditioning that has been and continues to be the focus of much effectiveness research. The outcome of this research has informed new developments of the BCT model in that it addresses concerns about posttreatment relapse and response to the needs of specific populations. Traditional and brief versions of BCT have been tested in conjunction with individual therapy and 12-step group counseling in the treatment of substance abuse (Fals-Stewart, Birchler, & Kelley, 2006; Fals-Stewart & Lam, 2008; Kelley & Fals-Stewart, 2007). In this review, we identified 10 studies of traditional BCT. Two (20%)

of these studies found that the variations of the BCT program produced significantly positive outcomes for substance abuse problems and relationship satisfaction. Four (40%) reported mixed results, meaning that the effectiveness of the intervention depended on the problem being addressed; for example, BCT was found to be most successful for relationship satisfaction. Last, two (20%) of the studies showed that the outcomes of BCT were not greater than those of the comparison group. Two (20%) of the studies did not have quantitative outcome data. Research on BCT was primarily conducted in academic and community-based outpatient settings.

- *Behavioral couple therapy for drug abuse and alcohol* (BCTD, ABCT, and Learning Sobriety Together) is a specific variation of BCT focused on couples with alcohol and substance use disorders. BCTD is an adaptation of ABCT for drug abusers (Epstein et al., 2007) and Learning Sobriety Together (Kelley & Fals-Stewart, 2007) is a program that integrates behavioral couple therapy and individual counseling in the treatment of adult alcoholism. We identified five studies of BCT for alcohol and substance use, two of which also examined the predictive role of abstinence during treatment (Hildebrandt, McCrady, Epstein, Cook, & Jensen, 2010) and the association between parents' drinking outcomes and children's functioning (Kelley & Fals-Stewart, 2007). Four of the studies (Epstein et al., 2007; Hildebrandt et al., 2010; Kelley & Fals-Stewart, 2007; McCrady, Epstein, & Kahler, 2004) produced significant results showing that BCT programs for alcohol and drug use helped to enhance relationship satisfaction and promote sobriety. In addition, the findings of Kelley and Fals-Stewart (2007) suggest that BCT may have a distal positive effect on preadolescent externalizing behaviors. McCrady et al. (2004) compared the outcomes of ABCT to two enhanced versions of the same treatment (i.e., ABCT followed by Alcoholic Anonymous and booster sessions and ABCT followed by posttreatment aftercare sessions). They found ABCT, regardless of its format, produced positive outcomes that persisted over time; however, there was no evidence of between-group differences in relationship satisfaction and drinking abstinence.

- *Integrative behavioral couple therapy* (IBCT) is a specific intervention model that is a variation of BCT. IBCT emphasizes both behaviors and emotions in the restructuring of less punishing and more rewarding couple interactions. In addition to teaching problem solving and communication skills, IBCT aims to increase partners' emotional understanding and acceptance. We identified seven studies of IBCT, three of which compared the outcomes of IBCT to traditional BCT (Christensen et al., 2004; Christensen, Atkins, Yi, Baucom, & George, 2006; Christensen, Atkins, Baucom, & Yi, 2010). The results of these three studies confirmed the overall effectiveness of both programs and indicated that between-group differences were moderated by gender and client severity of distress or level of functioning. However, IBCT was found to be superior to TBCT as it relates to the percentage of couples maintaining gains at follow up. Although the goal of these studies was to determine what clients with what problems benefited the most from treatments, their findings confirmed the overall success of IBCT and BCT for issues of relationship satisfaction and general mental health with the exception of depression. All IBCT studies were conducted in university settings.

- *General couple therapy* is a broad category of interventions that was not defined or identified in the studies. There were 12 studies of general couple therapy: eight (66.7%) reported significant positive outcomes of CT for relationship satisfaction, depression, OCD, and general mental health. One (8.3%) study produced mixed findings about the effects of CT on anxiety and depression, yet found a significant positive effect of CT on relationship satisfaction. Three (25%) studies had mixed results that depended on within-treatment therapeutic processes.

Clinical Problems for Which CT Is Effective

As was the case in the previous review, there was a relatively narrow range of clinical problems investigated in the CT research. These problem areas are similar to those identified in the last review with the exception of an increased focus on treating infidelity in couple relationships.

- *Relationship satisfaction*. The majority of general CT studies (11 or 25%) investigated the impact of CT on relationship satisfaction. Of these 11 studies, 7 (63.63%) found that CT

produced significantly positive outcomes; 3 (27.3%) showed that CT's effects on relationship satisfaction were moderated by clients' initial level of distress.

- *Alcohol and substance use/abuse* was a common topic of CT research with 12 studies (27.3%) investigating the effectiveness of various behavioral couple therapy programs. (See section on behavioral couple therapy for alcohol and drug use.)

- *Infidelity* was the topic of five (11.4%) studies. CT is particularly successful in the treatment of intimate partner violence with four of these studies (80%) reporting significant positive outcomes.

- *Intimate partner violence*. Two studies of BCT looked at the impact of treatment on physical aggression associated with substance use, but found no evidence of a significant, positive effect. The results provided preliminary evidence that DVCFT helped to reduce physical aggression and increase relationship satisfaction.

- *General mental health and depression* were the focus of five (11.4%) studies. The research produced little evidence that CT was effective in the treatment of mental health issues with only one study yielding statistically significant outcomes. Likewise, CT appears to have a limited impact on depression with only one study yielding significant positive results and three reporting mixed results.

Moderators and Mediators of CFT Interventions

The field of couple and family therapy has long been involved in research focusing on the mediators and predictors of change. Identifying which therapeutic processes and parameters improve outcomes is important to guide clinicians in their use of interventions. In the previous review, Sexton et al. (2004) found that research had provided supporting evidence for a number of common change mechanisms such as reduction of negativity, problem redefinition, impasse resolution, therapeutic alliance, improved behavioral competency, and treatment adherence. In this review, three major domains of mediators and moderators were the target of clinical research: alliance, model-specific fidelity, and specific client factors. Interestingly, the majority of the research on therapeutic processes occurred in the field of family therapy.

- *Therapeutic alliance*. The therapeutic alliance is a core relational process that has been the focus of many couple and family therapy studies (Sexton et al., 2004). It is all the more important to consider given its role in promoting positive family interactions. Current meta-analytic research (Friedlander, Escudero, Heatherington, & Diamond, 2011) suggests that the alliance is significantly related to outcomes in both couple and family therapy (CFT), but may account for more variability in outcomes in couple therapy. Friedlander et al. (2011) reviewed 24 process-outcome studies of the therapeutic alliance in CFT. Seven of these studies focused on couple therapy and yielded an average weighted effect size (r) of .37 compared to .26 for family therapy.
- *Model-specific fidelity and adherence*. Evidence suggests that therapist adherence and the therapeutic alliance are both significant predictors of treatment outcomes for the MDFT model (Hogue et al., 2006; Hogue et al., 2008). One of the most dramatic investigations of the importance of model specific adherence was a study of FFT (Sexton & Turner, 2010). In this study, when FFT was implemented in a community-based setting, it had successful outcomes only when community-based therapists demonstrated high levels of model specific adherence. In addition, it was found that adherence in FFT was most important in working with clients who presented high risks such as peer group influence and within family negativity.
- *Client factors* moderate the effects of treatment. Identifying client factors make it possible to determine which youth, families, and couples might benefit the most from a specific therapy intervention. For example, Reyno and McGrath (2006) showed that some variables (e.g., severity of youth's behavioral symptoms) were moderately correlated with treatment outcomes meaning that as the initial problem severity grows outcomes decrease. The largest correlation was found between low family income and treatment outcome ($r = 0.52$). In contrast, Lundahl et al. (2006) found that parent training was least effective for economically disadvantaged families ($d = .24$ for low SES vs. $d = 54$ for high SES). In addition, parent training was shown to be more effective for clients with higher symptom severity, with a correlation of .40 in Reyno and McGrath and Cohen's d values of 0.52 for clinical cases

versus .31 for nonclinical cases in Lundahl et al.'s (2006) study. Studies of behavioral couple therapy (Atkins, Berns, et al., 2005; Baucom, Atkins, Simpson, & Christensen, 2009) have shown that the couple's level of initial distress and sexual satisfaction, number of years married, type of influence strategies, and degree of emotional arousal were significant predictors of treatment response.

CFT has a long tradition of studies of the mediators and moderators that may improve the successful outcome. Understanding mediators and moderators helps clinicians know what works about interventions, what challenges there are to using the interventions, and what to emphasize clinically that might help improve outcome. In the previous handbook review, a number of common change mechanisms were found to have significant research support including: redefining negativity, impasse resolution, alliance, improved behavioral competency, and treatment adherence. In this review, three major domains of mediators and moderators were the target of clinical research: alliance, model specific fidelity, and specific client factors. Interestingly, the majority of research looks at relational process that might impact outcome concentrated in the FT area.

- *Therapeutic alliance*. The role of the therapeutic alliance was a commonly studied moderator of therapeutic outcome in FT (Sexton et al., 2004). The therapeutic alliance is particularly important given the relational focus of the interventions themselves and the role that alliance plays in successful family interactions. Current meta-analytic research suggests that alliance is a factor in the outcomes of both couple and family therapy but to different degrees. Friedlander et al. (2011) did one of the first meta-analysis of studies investigating the relationship between outcome and therapeutic alliance in both family therapy and couple therapy. In this review, alliance was significantly related to outcome for both types of therapy, but alliance had a stronger relationship to outcome for couple therapy than family therapy.
- *Model specific fidelity and adherence*. Evidence suggests that therapist adherence and alliance building are both significant predictors of therapeutic outcomes with the MDFT model (Hogue et al., 2006; Hogue et al., 2008). One of the most dramatic studies of the importance of model specific adherence was evidenced

in FFT. Sexton & Turner (2010) found that when FFT is moved to a community-based setting with community-based therapists, the program only has success when it is done with high model-specific adherence. In addition, this study found that while important, adherence in FFT was most evident with those high-risk cases (high peer-group influence and within-family negativity).

- *Client factors* are those variables that may mediate or moderate the outcome of treatment. Client factors may help determine which youth, families, and couples might be most treatable. For example, Reyno and McGrath (2006) found that some variables (e.g., severity of youth's behavioral symptoms) were moderately correlated with treatment outcome. The largest correlation was found between low family income and treatment outcome ($r = 0.52$), though in the meta-analysis conducted by Lundahl et al. (2006), parent training was least effective for economically disadvantaged families (.24 for low SES versus .54 for high SES). These families benefited more from individually delivered parent training compared to group delivery. In this same meta-analysis, treatment was more effective for those clients with higher severity ($d = .52$ clinical, $d = .31$ nonclinical, $d = .22$ mixed). There was no significant difference based on who was the target of the intervention (parent only, parent and child, etc.). In behavioral couple therapy, the level of client distress was significantly related to outcome. Similarly, studies of BCT found that the level of depression, relationship distress, and infidelity status all had a significant impact on response to treatment (Atkins, Berns, et al., 2005; Atkins, Eldridge, Baucom, & Christensen, 2005; Atkins, Marín, Lo, Klann, & Hahlweg, 2010; Baucom et al., 2009). It is noteworthy that the majority of IBCT studies (four or 57.14%) focused on patterns of change and predictors of client response to treatment (Atkins, Berns, et al., 2005; Atkins, Eldridge, et al., 2005; Atkins et al., 2010; Baucom et al., 2009).

TRENDS, ISSUES, AND THE CURRENT STATE OF CFT RESEARCH AND PRACTICE

Research reviews serve an important function in providing a link between science and practice.

The series of CFT research reviews in previous editions of the handbook chronicle the extensive body of knowledge regarding CFT clinical interventions and their outcomes. The results of our review indicate that CFT intervention programs are based on high-quality studies that, at least for the FT interventions, were conducted in community-based settings with diverse clients. They also addressed a wide range of clinical problems with strong evidence of effectiveness. Adding the 249 CFT studies and 13 meta-analyses we identified to those reported in the previous publications of the handbook means that the cumulated body of CFT research now extends over more than 30 years and is comprised of hundreds of studies that involved thousands of clients. CFT intervention research is broad in scope and forms a strong and comprehensive knowledge base that can help answer many clinical questions with confidence.

Despite the impressive outcomes and strong findings in the research literature, the gap between research and practice remains. Critics of the research literature often cite its lack of clinical relevance and comprehensiveness. These criticisms raise a central question: Is the research base supporting CFT comprehensive enough to be a credible source of information for clinicians who face complex and diverse clients with co-morbid clinical problems in community settings? These trends may help to determine whether the research is comprehensive and relevant to clinical practice. In addition, our analysis of the empirical findings highlights new directions for the next generation of CFT research, which we discuss next; it also helps to establish the clinical credibility of the CFT knowledge base. Finally, this analysis helps to answer the question, "Is CFT comprehensive and clinically useful?"

THE STATE OF COUPLE AND FAMILY INTERVENTION RESEARCH LITERATURE

In the past decade, it appears that CFT research has focused more on therapeutic programs than individual clinical interventions. This trend in the research literature is similar to that in the clinical field where the emphasis has moved from broad and nonspecific theoretical and modality-based questions ("Does CFT work?") to highly specific, comprehensive, and integrated clinical models of practice (Sexton et al., 2004). The current generation of comprehensive CFS treatment programs is highly specific as demonstrated by the use of clinical manuals and protocols in clinical practice. Unlike general models, specific ones most often target specific clinical problems and populations; they are not designed to be all things to all clients. This scientific focus on systematic and comprehensive therapeutic programs is a trend that is more pronounced in the field of family therapy (FT) research (80% of the FT studies focused versus 59.1% of the CT research). This is consistent with the trend identified by Sexton et al. (2004), and likely results from the widespread success of various systematic treatment models for specific problems. Most of the CFT research is focused on family therapy with far fewer studies aimed at investigating couple therapy. This is no surprise and is consistent with the continued development and evolution of intervention programs in the CFT area.

In the studies we reviewed, there was a remarkable lack of attention to the relational and clinical mechanisms of change and very few systematic studies of the common core factors that may unify and cut across all intervention models. Instead, CFT research continues to focus on the outcomes of CFT interventions and programs (approximately 85% of the studies). Few studies (12.68% and 14.6% respectively) examine the mediating influence of common and specific change mechanisms. This would suggest that both family and couple interventions research has more to say about program outcomes than therapeutic mechanisms and processes. This trend is unfortunate because just as we suggested a decade ago, we still know relatively little about why intervention programs work. Given the lively, and at times contentious, debate in the literature with regard to the primacy of common factors versus specific models, this finding is quite a surprise (Seedall et al., 2011; Sexton, Ridley, & Kliner, 2004). In fact, we found only one study investigating the efficacy of the common factor approach advocated so strongly by many in the field (Anker, Owen, Duncan, & Sparks, 2010). It is unlikely that mechanisms and common factors are not of great interest. Instead, the trend may represent the complexity of doing systematic and high-quality process studies of mechanisms of change. Such work requires both highly specific and well-defined interventions as well as complex research strategies to study the mediation effects of change mechanisms.

Similarly, the range of clinical outcomes and clinical problems represented in both the CT and FT literature clusters on a relatively small subset of clinical issues. For example, the studies of family treatment most commonly focused on behavior problems, one of the most common reasons for referrals to outpatient settings. This is not surprising given the significant psychological and economic impact of these problems on individual families and communities. We found a growing number of studies investigating the effects of family therapy on medical issues; we also identified a significant number of studies examining the outcomes of couple therapy for what are often viewed as individual clinical problems (e.g., depression). This may represent an emerging trend in both research and clinical practice, with more attention being paid to the role of systemic treatments in primary care settings.

Of the family therapy studies, many evaluated the effects of family-focused interventions on a diverse range of clients. Half of the FT research looked at the outcomes of family therapy with one specific ethnic group (e.g., Hispanic adolescents) while the other half involved multicultural samples with different ethnic groups being represented. By contrast, couple therapy research included participants that were predominantly non-Hispanic, White, and heterosexual. Only a small percentage of the studies (15%) were deemed demographically diverse. There might be several explanations for this limited cultural diversity in couple therapy research: As noted previously, a large proportion of the CT studies occurred in university settings that are not equally accessible to different cultural communities. In addition, CT research may be more concerned about establishing the relevance of couple-based interventions for specific clinical problems, hence its focus on the interaction between interpersonal variables and individual psychopathology as it relates to treatment outcomes. It may also be more concerned about the development, adaptation, refinement, and testing of new comprehensive and systematic intervention models.

It is noticeable that the CFT studies adhered to rigorous standards and that they were very strong methodologically. They had relevant comparison groups; they used random assignment; they had large sample sizes; and they measured fidelity in a systematic way. These are the hallmarks of studies with high methodological quality (Sexton et al., 2011). The high-quality studies we reviewed consistently used multiple methods and multiple perspectives to measure outcomes over time. In addition, some of the CFT research involves the use of the most complex statistical and methodological approaches available.

Is the CFT research literature comprehensive? As one might expect, the answer is: It depends. Based on our review, the CFT literature is methodologically sound, clinically specific, and community based. However, the literature is narrow in focus; studies are not representative of the diverse problems confronted by various clients in different clinical settings. In addition, they focus on specific and comprehensive programs rather than the general approaches and individual techniques that are often the intervention of choice in clinical practice. This does not mean that the research literature is not inclusive of nonspecific techniques and interventions, but instead suggests that it is concerned about highlighting the availability of programs designed for specific clinical problems that have the potential to improve the outcomes of clinical practice.

A Challenge for the Next Generation of CFT Research and Practice

The trends and limitations noted above also provide guidance for the next generation of CFT research as it relates to the enhancement and testing of sophisticated models of clinical practice. Our final remarks highlight areas of further developments; they are not only intended to guide the work of researchers who study CFT practice, but also to inform clinicians in their use of CFT interventions.

Expand the Range of Treatment Programs and Interventions Studied

A limited number of highly visible CFT programs are the objects of investigations. There is no question that specific and comprehensive programs like multisystemic therapy (the most studied of the family therapy interventions) and behavioral couple therapy (the most studied CT program) are helpful. The long-standing research activities associated with these two therapeutic approaches illustrate how an intervention can be evaluated systematically and rigorously with different clients and how mechanisms and predictors of change can be identified. This information can then be used to further develop the intervention and improve its outcomes. It is striking to note that we know so little about the effectiveness of various CFT intervention programs that do exist and that are used in clinical practice. We know even less about single techniques and clinical interventions. As a result, it is difficult to

draw conclusions about the value of specific vs. common therapeutic approaches. Expanding the research base will not only expand our knowledge of what works, but also increase the clinical relevance of research and show clinicians the diversity of practical choices that are available.

Broaden the Range of Clinical Problems Studied

There are good reasons why certain clinical problems have been and continue to be the focus of CFT research. On one hand, these are the problems for which some of the most studied intervention programs were designed (e.g., adolescent behavior and substance abuse problems). On the other hand, the emerging data suggest that CFT may be applicable to many more problems, including those that have been the domain of individual therapy approaches such as depression and anxiety. To move the field forward, researchers need to broaden the range of clinical problems they look at when investigating the effectiveness of CFT. Broadening and specifying the outcomes of CFT will become even more important in the future as practice guidelines emerge and instruct training and funding for community-based clinical services. Without a broad base of outcomes, CFT may find itself on the sidelines of the continued evolution of health care.

Expand CFT Research Beyond the Study of Outcomes

The CFT field needs to move beyond the study of outcomes. We have established that some programs like MST and BCT work; however, we don't know why they work. To date, some of the most studied programs have little, if any, change mechanism research. Two steps need to occur for this to happen. First, the techniques common to CFT need specific definitions (i.e., in research terms, clear operational definitions) so that they can be studied, implemented, and transported to diverse sites in a reliable and systematic manner. Far too many studies continue to address nonspecific family or couple therapy without describing what those interventions really look like. To advance the debate over common versus model-specific elements of therapeutic programs, it is essential that we specify the "common factors" of CFT, the outcome of those factors, and the conceptual and theoretical mechanisms by which they might work. Increased specificity will make it possible to investigate the therapeutic processes of CFT. Likewise, it is important that research on major clinical intervention programs like MST and BCT focus on change mechanisms, that is, "how" and "why" positive outcomes occur in these highly specific and comprehensive approaches. Without change mechanism research, program developers do not have evidence-based information regarding the specific components of the program and how they work to produce specific outcomes. With the exception of the systematic work of Friedlander and colleagues (2011), this goal has not been realized.

Study the Variables That May Increase the Efficacy of CFT When Implemented in Community Settings

One of the most promising trends for the translation of research into practice is the study of factors that may improve outcomes in community settings. For example, both Sexton and Turner (2010) and Liddle et al. (2004) found model adherence to be directly related to successful community outcomes. In a unique study, Hogue and colleagues (2008) found a curvilinear relationship between adherence and outcome: When therapists gained experience, adherence appeared to hinder rather than improve outcomes. This finding highlights the need for translational research to study the ways in which programs can be better applied and adapted in clinical settings. The work of Lambert (2010) and Bickman, Kelley, Breda, de Andrade, and Riemer (2011) illustrates ways in which brief measures of therapeutic processes can be combined with advanced computer technology to give practitioners instant access to data regarding proximal outcomes and core therapeutic mechanisms. The ongoing measurement of process and outcome in clinical practice serves as real time feedback that mental health providers may use to make evidence-informed decisions about the delivery and adaptation of their interventions. These feedback systems assist clinicians in becoming local scientists responsible for monitoring the effectiveness of their interventions; they promote the integration of science and practice at the level of the therapist (Stricker, 2007). These feedback systems may represent the next and maybe the most exciting chapter of CFT research.

Adopt and Use Systemic Treatments When Available

The evidence in this and other reviews suggests that systematic treatment programs with a strong record of successful outcomes should be the first line of interventions used in community mental health settings. Some practitioners may disregard research as a source of clinical guidance because not all clinical problems have been investigated and shown to be influenced by specific treatment approaches. There will always be gaps in the research literature, and research will most likely never answer all the complex questions of clinical practice. It is not possible to put each problem and each client and contextual factor in a simple formula that tells clinicians what to do. In other words, the professional wisdom of mental health providers is a crucial element of bringing creativity and art to the practice of the most specific and systematic intervention program. As noted by Sexton and van Dam (2010), these programs provide a clinical structure within which therapists can be creative. It may well be that this structure actually supports and enhances clinicians' creativity, and thus should be considered as the basis for exercising individual expertise.

Adopt the Emerging Methods for Systematic Review and Treatment Guidelines

New methods are now being used to produce treatment guidelines that are intended to influence practice. These methods go well beyond the current tools used for research reviews like the one in this chapter. They have developed from the growing realization in medicine, psychology, and education, among other fields, that research evidence is an essential part of practice. These emerging methods are likely to help move forward many of the current debates about the role of empirical evidence in clinical practice. The field of health care provides an example: As policy makers become increasingly savvy in utilizing comparative effectiveness studies, systematic reviews, and treatment guidelines that translate research into practice, the AHRQ (Owens et al., 2010), the Institute of Medicine (IOM) (Berg et al., 2011; McNeil et al., 2008), and the U.S. Preventive Services Task Force (USPSTF) (AHRQ, 2011) are leading a movement to set standards for the systematic review of research. The aim of this movement is to promote the accuracy and transparency of scientific reviews in order to facilitate well-informed decisions. Reviews are clear judgments about the strength of the evidence that supports specific treatment programs. They must include the participation of key stakeholders including clients from diverse disciplines and fields of expertise. They also involve rating the evidence according to its precision, directness, potential bias, and consistency. Systematic reviews can then be translated into practice guidelines that consist of specific treatment recommendations. Guidelines should also say something about the strength of the evidence and thus the level of confidence that clinicians may have in each recommendation. This approach is critical and does answer many of the criticisms of integrating research into practice.

Do More Comparative Effectiveness Trials

There are surprisingly few studies in which treatments are compared to one another. Comparative effectiveness trials are particularly absent from programs of research that focus on the most specific and comprehensive treatment models. The exception is the comparison of PCIT and Triple P noted above. However, comparative effectiveness trials would produce crucial knowledge about the specific uses of intervention programs; they would also provide developers with what seems to be needed information for further program development and refinement.

Using Diverse Research Methods

The evidence summarized in this review continues to be based on what is called the *gold standard* of clinical intervention research: randomized clinical trials (RCTs). There is no question that RCTs provide methodologically strong results that increase the validity and reliability of the findings. However, as noted by Sexton, Kinser, and Hanes (2008), it may be time to go beyond a single standard and to expand the range of methods used to produce evidence. Using alternative research methods does not mean sacrificing methodological soundness and rigor. There are alternative methods that produce valid and reliable findings and that are particularly helpful to capture the subtleties of clinical practice. Because RCTs are expensive and complex, they can be a disincentive for researchers interested in studying a particular technique. In fact, it is possible that the dearth of research on therapeutic techniques results because of the perceived need to use RCTs. Sexton et al. (2011) suggested that once the effectiveness of a program is well-established, diverse research methods with nonrandomized comparison groups, correlational designs, and lower levels of methodological power are particularly suited for the study of parameters associated with the delivery of treatment, client characteristics, and type of clinical settings. It

is our view in this chapter that the adoption of methodologically sound yet diverse methods will help to expand the focus of CFT research and increase its clinical utility.

REFERENCES

Alexander, J. F., Holtzworth-Monroe, A., & Jameson, P. B. (1994). The process and outcome of marital and family therapy: Research, review, and evaluation. In A. E. Bergin & S. L. Garfield (Eds.), *Handbook of psychotherapy and behavior change* (4th ed., pp. 595–630). Oxford, United Kingdom: Wiley.

Alexander, J. F., Pugh, C., Parsons, B., & Sexton, T. L. (2000). Functional family therapy. In D. Elliot (Series Ed.), *Blueprints for violence prevention* (2nd ed.). Golden, CO: Venture.

Alexander, J. F., & Sexton, T. L. (2002). Functional family therapy: A model for treating high-risk, acting-out youth. In J. Lebow (Ed.), *Comprehensive handbook of psychotherapy, Vol. IV: Integrative/Eclectic*. Hoboken, NJ: Wiley.

Anker, M. G., Duncan, B. L., & Sparks, J. A. (2009). Using client feedback to improve couple therapy outcomes: A randomized clinical trial in a naturalistic setting. *Journal of Consulting and Clinical Psychology*, 77, 693–704. doi: 10.1037/0003-066x.61.4.271

Anker, M. G., Owen, J., Duncan, B. L., & Sparks, J. A. (2010). The alliance in couple therapy: Partner influence, early change, and alliance patterns in a naturalistic sample. *Journal of Consulting and Clinical Psychology*, 78(5), 635–645. doi: 10.1037/h0085885.

Atkins, D. C., Berns, S. B., George, W. H., Doss, B. D., Gattis, K., & Christensen, A. (2005). Prediction of response to treatment in a randomized clinical trial of marital therapy. *Journal of Consulting and Clinical Psychology*, 73(5), 893–903. doi: 10.1146/annurev.psych.50.1.165

Atkins, D. C., Dimidjian, S., Bedics, J. D., & Christensen, A. (2009). Couple discord and depression in couples during couple therapy and in depressed individuals during depression treatment. *Journal of Consulting and Clinical Psychology*, 77, 1089–1099. doi: 10.1037/0893-3200.17.4.557

Atkins, D. C., Eldridge, K. A., Baucom, D. H., & Christensen, A. (2005). Infidelity and behavioral couple therapy: Optimism in the face of betrayal. *Journal of Consulting and Clinical Psychology*, 73(1), 144–150. doi: 10.1037/0022–006x.68.5.774

Atkins, D. C., Marín, R. A., Lo, T. T. Y., Klann, N., & Hahlweg, K. (2010). Outcomes of couples with infidelity in a community-based sample of couple therapy. *Journal of Family Psychology*, 24(2), 212–216.

Bakermans-Kranenburg, M. J., van IJzendoorn, M. H., & Juffer, F. (2003). Less is more: Meta-analyses of sensitivity and attachment interventions in early childhood. *Psychological Bulletin, 129*, 195–215. doi: 10.1037/0033–2909.129.2.195

Barbato, A., & D'Avanzo, B. (2008). Efficacy of couple therapy as a treatment for depression: A meta-analysis. *Psychiatric Quarterly, 79*(2), 121–121–132. doi: 10.1007/s11126–008–9068–0

Barrett, P., Farrell, L., Dadds, M., & Boulter, N. (2005). Cognitive-behavioral family treatment of childhood obsessive-compulsive disorder: Long-term follow-up and predictors of outcome. *Journal of the American Academy of Child & Adolescent Psychiatry, 44*, 1005–1014. doi: 10.1097/01.chi.0000172555.26349.94

Barrett, P., Healy-Farrell, L., & March, J. S. (2004). Cognitive-behavioral family treatment of childhood obsessive-compulsive disorder: A controlled trial. *Journal of the American Academy of Child & Adolescent Psychiatry, 43*, 46–62. doi: 10.1097/00004583-200401000-00014

Baucom, B. R., Atkins, D. C., Simpson, L. E., & Christensen, A. (2009). Prediction of response to treatment in a randomized clinical trial of couple therapy: A 2-year follow-up. *Journal of Consulting and Clinical Psychology, 77*(1), 160–173.

Berg, A. O., Morton, S. C., Berlin, J. A., Bhandari, M., Corbie-Smith, G., Dickerson, K., & Wallace, P. (2011). Report brief from the Committee on Standards for Systematic Reviews of Comparative Effectiveness Research: Finding what works in health care: Standards for systematic review. *Institute of Medicine*. Retrieved from http://www.iom.edu/Reports/2011/Finding-What-Works-in-Health-Care-Standards-for-Systematic-Reviews.aspx

Bickman, L., Kelley, S. D., Breda, C., de Andrade, A. R., & Riemer, M. (2011). Effects of routine feedback to clinicians on mental health outcomes: Results of a randomized trial. *Psychiatric Services, 62*(12), 1423–1429.

Bodden, D. H. M., Bögels, S. M., Nauta, M. H., De Haan, E., Riingrose, J., Appelboom, C., . . . Appelboom-Geerts, K. C. M. M. J. (2008). Child versus family cognitive-behavioral therapy in clinically anxious youth: An efficacy and partial effectiveness study. *Journal of the American Academy of Child & Adolescent Psychiatry, 47*, 1384–1394.

Bodenmann, G., Cina, A., Ledermann, T., & Sanders, M. R. (2008). The efficacy of the Triple P-Positive Parenting Program in improving parenting and child behavior: A comparison with two other treatment conditions. *Behaviour Research and Therapy, 46*, 411–427. doi: 10.1037/1040-3590.5.2.137

Breuk, R. E., Sexton, T. L., Van Dam, A., Disse, C., Doreleijers, T. A. H., Slot, W. N., & Rowland, M. K. (2006). The implementation and the cultural adjustment of functional family therapy in a Dutch psychiatric day-treatment center. *Journal of Marital and Family Therapy, 32*, 515–529. doi: 10.1111/j.1752-0606.2006.tb01625.x

Bywater, T., Hutchings, J., Linck, P., Whitaker, C., Daley, D., Yeo, S. T., & Edwards, R. T. (2010). Incredible years parent training support for foster carers in Wales: A multi-centre feasibility study. *Child: Care, Health and Development, 37*(2), 233–243.

Chacko, A., Wymbs, B. T., Flammer-Rivera, L. M., Pelham, W. E., Walker, K. S., Arnold, F. W., . . . Herbst, L. (2008). A pilot study of the feasibility and efficacy of the Strategies to Enhance Positive Parenting (STEPP) program for single mothers of children with ADHD. *Journal of Attention Disorders, 12*, 270–280. doi: 10.1177/1087054707306119

Chacko, A., Wymbs, B. T., Wymbs, F. A., Pelham, W. E., Swanger-Gagne, M. S., Girio, E., . . . O'Connor, B. (2009). Enhancing traditional behavioral parent training for single mothers of children with ADHD. *Journal of Clinical Child and Adolescent Psychology, 38*, 206–218. doi: 10.1207/s15374424jccp3403_5

Chaffin, M., Silovsky, J. F., Funderburk, B., Valle, L. A., Brestan, E. V., Balachova, T., . . . Bonner, B. L. (2004). Parent–child interaction therapy with physically abusive parents: Efficacy for reducing future abuse reports. *Journal of Consulting and Clinical Psychology, 72*, 500–510. doi: 10.1037/0022-006x.72.3.500

Chamberlain, P., Price, J., Reid, J., & Landsverk, J. (2008). Cascading implementation of a foster and kinship parent intervention. *Child Welfare: Journal of Policy, Practice, and Program, 87*(5), 27–48. doi: 10.1007/s10802–005–3571–7

Chambless, D. L., & Hollon, S. D. (1998). Defining empirically supported therapies. *Journal of Consulting and Clinical Psychology, 66*(1), 7–18.

Chase, R. M., & Eyberg, S. M. (2008). Clinical presentation and treatment outcome for children with comorbid externalizing and internalizing symptoms. *Journal of Anxiety Disorders, 22*, 273–282. doi:10.1016/j.janxdis.[[mkup]]2007[[mkup]].03.006

Christensen, A., Atkins, D. C., Baucom, B., & Yi, J. (2010). Marital status and satisfaction five years following a randomized clinical trial comparing traditional versus integrative behavioral couple therapy. *Journal of Consulting and Clinical Psychology, 78*(2), 225–235.

Christensen, A., Atkins, D. C., Berns, S., Wheeler, J., Baucom, D. H., & Simpson, L. E. (2004). Traditional versus integrative behavioral couple therapy for significantly and chronically distressed married couples. *Journal of Consulting and Clinical Psychology, 72*(2), 176–191.

Christensen, A., Atkins, D. C., Yi, J., Baucom, D. H., & George, W. H. (2006). Couple and individual adjustment for 2 years following a randomized clinical trial comparing traditional versus integrative behavioral couple therapy. *Journal of Consulting and Clinical Psychology, 74*(6), 1180–1191.

Christensen, A., & Heavey, C. L. (1999). Interventions for couples. *Annual Review of Psychology, 50*(0066–4308, 0066–4308), 165–190. doi: 10.1146/annurev.psych.50.1.165

Compas, B. E., Champion, J. E., Forehand, R., Cole, D. A., Reeslund, K. L., Fear, J., . . . Roberts, L. (2010). Coping and parenting: Mediators of 12-month outcomes of a family group cognitive–behavioral preventive intervention with families of depressed parents. *Journal of Consulting and Clinical Psychology, 78*, 623–634. doi: 10.1001/jama.2009.788

Curtis, N. M., Ronan, K. R., & Borduin, C. M. (2004). Multisystemic treatment: A meta-analysis of outcome studies. *Journal of Family Psychology, 18*(3), 411–419. doi: 10.1037/0893–3200.18.3.411

Curtis, N. M., Ronan, K. R., Heiblum, N., & Crellin, K. (2009). Dissemination and effectiveness of multisystemic treatment in New Zealand: A benchmarking study. *Journal of Family Psychology, 23*(2), 119–129.

DeGarmo, D. S., & Forgatch, M. S. (2005). Early development of delinquency within divorced families: Evaluating a randomized preventive intervention trial. *Developmental Science, 8*(3), 229–229–239. doi: 10.1111/j.1467–7687.[[mkup]]2005[[mkup]].00412.x

DeGarmo, D. S., Patterson, G. R., & Forgatch, M. S. (2004). How do outcomes in a specified parent training intervention maintain or wane over time? *Prevention Science, 5*, 73–89. doi: 10.1023/B:PREV.0000023078.30191.e0

Dessaulles, A., Johnson, S. M., & Denton, W. H. (2003). Emotion-focused therapy for couples in the treatment of depression: A pilot study. *American Journal of Family Therapy, 31*, 345–353. doi: 10.1111/j.1752-0606.1997.tb00239.x

Dretzke, J., Davenport, C., Frew, E., Barlow, J., Stewart-Brown, S., Bayliss, S., . . . Hyde, C. (2009). The clinical effectiveness of different parenting programmes for children with conduct problems: A systematic review of randomised controlled trials. *Child and Adolescent Psychiatry and Mental Health, 3.* doi: 10.1186/1753–2000-3-7

Dunn, R. L., & Schwebel, A. I. (1995). Meta-analytic review of marital therapy outcome research. *Journal of Family Psychology, 9*(1), 58–68. doi: 10.1037/0003–066x.48.12.1181

Ellis, D. A., Naar-King, S., Cunningham, P. B., & Secord, E. (2006). Use of multisystemic therapy to improve antiretroviral adherence and health outcomes in HIV-infected pediatric patients: Evaluation of a pilot program. *AIDS Patient Care and STDs, 20*, 112–121. doi: 10.1089/apc.2006.20.112

Ellis, D. A., Naar-King, S., Frey, M., Templin, T., Rowland, M., & Greger, N. (2004). Use of multisystemic therapy to improve regimen adherence among adolescents with type 1 diabetes in poor metabolic control: A pilot investigation. *Journal of Clinical Psychology in Medical Settings, 11*(4), 315–324.

Ellis, D. A., Naar-King, S., Templin, T., Frey, M. A., & Cunningham, P. B. (2007). Improving health outcomes among youth with poorly controlled type I diabetes: The role of treatment fidelity in a randomized clinical trial of multisystemic therapy. *Journal of Family Psychology, 21*(3), 363–371. doi: 10.1037/0893–3200.21.3.363

Ellis, D. A., Yopp, J., Templin, T., Naar-King, S., Frey, M. A., Cunningham, P. B., . . . Niec, L. N. (2007). Family mediators and moderators of treatment outcomes among youths with poorly controlled type 1 diabetes: Results from a randomized controlled trial. *Journal of Pediatric Psychology, 32*, 194–205. doi: 10.1093/jpepsy/jsj116

Epstein, E. E., McCrady, B. S., Morgan, T. J., Cook, S. M., Kugler, G., & Ziedonis, D. (2007). Couples treatment for drug-dependent males: Preliminary efficacy of a stand alone outpatient model. *Addictive Disorders & Their Treatment, 6*(1), 21–37.

Escudero, V., Friedlander, M. L., Varela, N., & Abascal, A. (2008). Observing the therapeutic alliance in family therapy: Associations with participants' perceptions and therapeutic outcomes. *Journal of Family Therapy, 30*, 194–214. doi: 10.1111/j.1467-6427.2008.00425.x

Fals-Stewart, W., Birchler, G. R., & Kelley, M. L. (2006). Learning sobriety together: A randomized clinical trial examining behavioral couples therapy with alcoholic female patients. *Journal of Consulting and Clinical Psychology, 74*(3), 579–591. doi: 10.1037/0022–006x.74.3.579

Fals-Stewart, W., & Lam, W. K. K. (2008). Brief behavioral couples therapy for drug abuse: A randomized clinical trial examining clinical efficacy and cost-effectiveness. *Families, Systems, & Health, 26*(4), 377–392.

Fals-Stewart, W., Lam, W., & Kelley, M. L. (2009). Learning sobriety together: Behavioural couples therapy for alcoholism and drug abuse. *Journal of Family Therapy, 31*(2), 115–125.

Farrington, D. P., & Welsh, B. C. (2003). Family-based prevention of offending: A meta-analysis. *Australian and New Zealand Journal of Criminology, 36*, 127–151. doi:10.1375/acri.36.2.127

Flicker, S. M., Waldron, H. B., Turner, C. W., Brody, J. L., & Hops, H. (2008). Ethnic matching and treatment outcome with Hispanic and Anglo substance-abusing adolescents in family therapy. *Journal of Family Psychology, 22*(3), 439–447. doi: 10.1037/0893–3200.22.3.439

Forgatch, M. S., DeGarmo, D. S., & Beldavs, Z. G. (2005). An efficacious theory-based intervention for stepfamilies. *Behavior Therapy, 36*(4), 357–365.

Fossum, S., Mørch, W.-T., Handegård, B. H., Drugli, M. B., & Larsson, B. (2009). Parent training for young Norwegian children with ODD and CD problems: Predictors and mediators of treatment outcome. *Scandinavian Journal of Psychology, 50*(2), 173–181. doi: 10.1111/j.1467–9450.2008.00700.x

Foster, E. M., Olchowski, A. E., & Webster-Stratton, C. H. (2007). Is stacking intervention components cost-effective? An analysis of the incredible years program. *Journal of the American Academy of Child & Adolescent Psychiatry, 46*(11), 1414–1424. doi: 10.1001/archpsyc.62.6.593

Freeman, J. B., Garcia, A. M., Coyne, L., Ale, C., Przeworski, A., Himle, M.,...Leonard, H. L. (2008). Early childhood OCD: Preliminary findings from a family-based cognitive-behavioral approach. *Journal of the American Academy of Child & Adolescent Psychiatry, 47*(5), 593–602. doi: 10.1097/CHI.0b013e31816765f9

French, M. T., Zavala, S. K., McCollister, K. E., Waldron, H. B., Turner, C. W., & Ozechowski, T. J. (2008). Cost-effectiveness analysis of four interventions for adolescents with a substance use disorder. *Journal of Substance Abuse Treatment, 34,* 272–281. doi: 10.1016/j.jsat.2007.04.008

Friedlander, M. L., Escudero, V., Heatherington, L., & Diamond, G. M. (2011). Alliance in couple and family therapy. *Psychotherapy, 48*(1), 25–33. doi: 10.1037/a0022060

Friedlander, M. L., Lambert, J. E., Escudero, V., & Cragun, C. (2008). How do therapists enhance family alliances? Sequential analyses of therapist-client behavior in two contrasting cases. *Psychotherapy: Theory, Research, Practice, Training, 45*(1), 75–87.

Gardner, F., Burton, J., & Klimes, I. (2006). Randomised controlled trial of a parenting intervention in the voluntary sector for reducing child conduct problems: Outcomes and mechanisms of change. *Journal of Child Psychology and Psychiatry, 47,* 1123–1132. doi: 10.1111/j.1469-7610.2006.01668.x

Gattis, K. S., Simpson, L. E., & Christensen, A. (2008). What about the kids? Parenting and child adjustment in the context of couple therapy. *Journal of Family Psychology, 22,* 833–842. doi: 10.1146/annurev.psych.50.1.165

Gordon, K. C., Baucom, D. H., & Snyder, D. K. (2004). An integrative intervention for promoting recovery from extramarital affairs. *Journal of Marital and Family Therapy, 30,* 213–231. doi: 10.1037//0022-006x.68.5.774

Graves, K. N., Shelton, T. L., & Kaslow, N. J. (2009). Utilization of individual versus family therapy among adolescents with severe emotional disturbance. *American Journal of Family Therapy, 37,* 227–238. doi: 10.1080/01926180802403328

Greenberg, L., Warwar, S., & Malcolm, W. (2010). Emotion-focused couples therapy and the facilitation of forgiveness. *Journal of Marital and Family Therapy, 36,* 28–42. doi: 10.1037/h0029382.

Grimbos, T., & Granic, I. (2009). Changes in maternal depression are associated with MST outcomes for adolescents with co-occurring externalizing and internalizing problems. *Journal of Adolescence, 32*(6), 1415–1423. doi: 10.1016/j.adolescence.2009.05.004

Gross, H., Shaw, D., & Moilanen, K. (2008). Reciprocal associations between boy's externalizing problems and mother's depressive symptoms. *Journal of Abnormal Child Psychology, 36,* 693–709.

Gurman, A. S. (1971). Group marital therapy: Clinical and empirical implications for outcome research. *International Journal of Psychotherapy, 21,* 174–189.

Gurman, A. S. (1973). The effects of effectiveness of marital therapy: A review of outcome research. *Family Process, 12,* 45–54.

Gurman, A. S. (1975). Couples' facilitative communication skill as a dimension of marital therapy outcome. *Journal of Marriage and Family Counseling, 1,* 163–174.

Gurman, A. S. & Kniskern, D. P. (Eds.). (1981). *Handbook of family therapy.* New York, NY: Brunner/Mazel.

Gurman, A. S., & Kniskern, D. P. (1986). Commentary: Individual marital therapy: Have reports of your death been somewhat exaggerated? *Family Process, 25*(1), 51–62. doi: 10.1111/j.1545-5300.1986.00051.x

Gurman, A. S., & Kniskern, D. P. (Eds.). (1991). *Handbook of family therapy* (Vol. 2). Philadelphia, PA: Brunner/Mazel.

Gurman, A., Kniskern, D., & Pinsof, W. M. (1986). Process and outcome research in family and marital therapy. In A.Bergin & S. Garfield (Eds.), *The handbook of psychotherapy and behavior change* (Vol. 3, pp. 550–649). New York, NY: Wiley.

Halliday-Boykins, C. A., Schoenwald, S. K., & Letourneau, E. J. (2005). Caregiver-therapist ethnic similarity predicts youth outcomes from an empirically based treatment. *Journal of Consulting and Clinical Psychology, 73,* 808–818. doi: 10.1037/0022-006x.73.5.808

Hartman, R. R., Stage, S. A., & Webster-Stratton, C. (2003). A growth curve analysis of parent training outcomes: Examining the influence of child risk factors (inattention, impulsivity, and hyperactivity problems), parental and family risk factors. *Journal of Child Psychology and Psychiatry, 44,* 388–398. doi: 10.1111/1469-7610.00129

Hawes, D. J., & Dadds, M. R. (2005). The Treatment of Conduct Problems in Children With Callous-Unemotional Traits. *Journal of Consulting and Clinical Psychology, 73,* 737–741. doi: 10.1037/0022-006x.73.4.737

Hayes, L., Matthews, J., Copley, A., & Welsh, D. (2008). A randomized controlled trial of a mother-infant or toddler parenting program: Demonstrating effectiveness in practice. *Journal of Pediatric Psychology, 33,* 473–486. doi: 10.1093/jpepsy/jsm085

Henggeler, S. W., Letourneau, E. J., Chapman, J. E., Borduin, C. M., Schewe, P. A., & McCart, M. R. (2009). Mediators of change for multisystemic therapy with juvenile sexual offenders. *Journal of Consulting and Clinical Psychology, 77*(3), 451–462. doi: 10.1037/a0013971

Henggeler, S. W., Schoenwald, S. K., Borduin, C. M., Rowland, M. D., & Cunningham, P. B. (1998). *Multisystemic treatment of antisocial behavior in children and adolescents.* New York, NY: Guilford Press.

Hildebrandt, T., McCrady, B., Epstein, E., Cook, S., & Jensen, N. (2010). When should clinicians switch treatments? An application of signal detection theory to two treatments for women with alcohol use disorders. *Behaviour Research and Therapy, 48*(6), 524–530. doi: 10.1046/j.1359–6357.2003.00586.x

Hogue, A., Dauber, S., Stambaugh, L. F., Cecero, J. J., & Liddle, H. A. (2006). Early therapeutic alliance and treatment outcome in individual and family therapy for adolescent behavior problems. *Journal of Consulting and Clinical Psychology, 74*(1), 121–129. doi: 10.1037/0022–006x.74.1.121

Hogue, A., Henderson, C. E., Dauber, S., Barajas, P. C., Fried, A., & Liddle, H. A. (2008). Treatment adherence, competence, and outcome in individual and family therapy for adolescent behavior problems. *Journal of Consulting and Clinical Psychology, 76*(4), 544–555. doi: 10.1037/0022–006x.76.4.544

Hogue, A., Liddle, H. A., Dauber, S., & Samuolis, J. (2004). Linking session focus to treatment outcome in evidence-based treatments for adolescent substance abuse. *Psychotherapy: Theory, Research, Practice, Training, 41*(2), 83–96. doi: 10.1037/0033–3204.41.2.83

Hogue, A., Liddle, H. A., Singer, A., & Leckrone, J. (2005). Intervention fidelity in family-based prevention counseling for adolescent problem behaviors. *Journal of Community Psychology, 33*, 191–211. doi: 10.1002/jcop.20031

Huey, S. J., Henggeler, S. W., Rowland, M. D., Halliday-Boykins, C. A., Cunningham, P. B., & Pickrel, S. G. (2005). Predictors of treatment response for suicidal youth referred for emergency psychiatric hospitalization. *Journal of Clinical Child and Adolescent Psychology, 34*, 582–589. doi: 10.1207/s15374424jccp3403_13

Huey, S. J., Henggeler, S. W., Rowland, M. D., Halliday-Boykins, C. A., Cunningham, P. B., Pickrel, S. G., & Edwards, J. (2004). Multisystemic therapy effects on attempted suicide by youths presenting psychiatric emergencies. *Journal of the American Academy of Child & Adolescent Psychiatry, 43*, 183–190. doi: 10.1097/00004583-200402000-00014

Hunter, H. L., Steele, R. G., & Steele, M. M. (2008). Family-based treatment for pediatric overweight: Parental weight loss as a predictor of children's treatment success. *Children's Health Care, 37*, 112–125. doi: 10.1080/02739610802006510

Hutchings, J., Gardner, F., Bywater, T., Daley, D., Whitaker, C., Jones, K., ... Edwards, R. T. (2007). Parenting intervention in sure start services for children at risk of developing conduct disorder: Pragmatic randomised controlled trial. *BMJ: British Medical Journal, 334*(7595), 678–678. doi: 10.1136/bmj.39126.620799.55

Hutchings, J., Lane, E., & Kelly, J. (2004). Comparison of two treatments for children with severely disruptive behaviours: A four-year follow-up. *Behavioural and Cognitive Psychotherapy, 32*(1), 15–30. doi: 10.1017/s1352465804001018

Isakson, R. L., Hawkins, E. J., Harmon, S. C., Slade, K., Martinez, J. S., & Lambert, M. J. (2006). Assessing couple therapy as a treatment for individual distress: When is referral to couple therapy contraindicated? *Contemporary Family Therapy: An International Journal, 28*, 313–322. doi: 10.1002/jclp.1056

Johnson, L. N., Ketring, S. A., Rohacs, J., & Brewer, A. L. (2006). Attachment and the therapeutic alliance in family therapy. *American Journal of Family Therapy, 34*, 205–218. doi: 10.1080/01926180500358022

Kazdin, A. E. (2006). Arbitrary metrics: Implications for identifying evidence-based treatments. *American Psychologist, 61*(1), 42–49.

Kazdin, A. E., & Whitley, M. K. (2003). Treatment of parental stress to enhance therapeutic change among children referred for aggressive and antisocial behavior. *Journal of Consulting and Clinical Psychology, 71*, 504–515. doi: 10.1037/0022–006x.71.3.504

Kelley, M. L., & Fals-Stewart, W. (2007). Treating paternal alcoholism with learning sobriety together: Effects on adolescents versus preadolescents. *Journal of Family Psychology, 21*(3), 435–444. doi: 10.2307/350547

Kendall, P. C., Hudson, J. L., Gosch, E., Flannery-Schroeder, E., & Suveg, C. (2008). Cognitive-behavioral therapy for anxiety disordered youth: A randomized clinical trial evaluating child and family modalities. *Journal of Consulting and Clinical Psychology, 76*(2), 282–297. doi: 10.1037/0022–006x.76.2.282

Khanna, M. S., & Kendall, P. C. (2009). Exploring the role of parent training in the treatment of childhood anxiety. *Journal of Consulting and Clinical Psychology, 77*, 981–986. doi: 10.1037/a0016920

Kirby, J. S., & Baucom, D. H. (2007). Integrating dialectical behavior therapy and cognitive-behavioral couple therapy: A couples skills group for emotion dysregulation. *Cognitive and Behavioral Practice, 14*, 394–405. doi: 10.1037/0022–006x.59.3.458

Lambert, M. J. (2010). *Using progress feedback to inform treatment: Conceptual issues and initial findings.* Washington, DC: American Psychological Association. doi:10.1037/12141–005

Larsson, B., Fossum, S., Clifford, G., Drugli, M. B., Handegård, B. H., & Mørch, W. (2009). Treatment of oppositional defiant and conduct problems in young Norwegian children: Results of a randomized controlled trial. *European Child & Adolescent Psychiatry, 18*(1), 42–52. doi: 10.1007/s00787–008–0702-z

Lavigne, J. V., LeBailly, S. A., Gouze, K. R., Cicchetti, C., Pochyly, J., Arend, R., ... Binns, H. J.

(2008). Treating oppositional defiant disorder in primary care: A comparison of three models. *Journal of Pediatric Psychology, 33*(5), 449–461. doi: 10.1093/jpepsy/jsm074

Lebow, J. L. (1999). Building a science of couple relationships: Comments on two articles by Gottman and Levenson. *Family Process, 38*(2), 167–173. doi: 10.1111/j.1545–5300.1999.00167.x

Lee, B. K., & Rovers, M. (2008). "Bringing torn lives together again": Effects of the first Congruence Couple Therapy training application to clients in pathological gambling. *International Gambling Studies, 8,* 113–129. doi: 10.1016/s0740-5472(98)00076-2

Leong, J., Cobham, V. E., de Groot, J., & McDermott, B. (2009). Comparing different modes of delivery: A pilot evaluation of a family-focused, cognitive-behavioral intervention for anxiety-disordered children. *European Child & Adolescent Psychiatry, 18,* 231–239. doi: 10.1007/s00787-008-0723-7

Letourneau, E. J., Henggeler, S. W., Borduin, C. M., Schewe, P. A., McCart, M. R., Chapman, J. E., & Saldana, L. (2009). Multisystemic therapy for juvenile sexual offenders: 1-year results from a randomized effectiveness trial. *Journal of Family Psychology, 23,* 89–102. doi: 10.1037/a0014352

Liddle, H. A. (1995). Conceptual and clinical dimensions of a multidimensional, multisystems engagement strategy in family-based adolescent treatment (Special issue: Adolescent Psychotherapy). *Psychotherapy: Theory, Research, and Practice, 32,* 39–58.

Liddle, H. A., Bray, J. H., Levant, R. F., & Santisteban, D. A. (2002). *Family psychology intervention science: An emerging area of science and practice.* Washington, DC: American Psychological Association.

Liddle, H. A., Dakof, G. A., Turner, R. M., Henderson, C. E., & Greenbaum, P. E. (2008). Treating adolescent drug abuse: A randomized trial comparing multidimensional family therapy and cognitive behavior therapy. *Addiction, 103,* 1660–1670. doi: 10.1111/j.1360-0443.2008.02274.x

Liddle, H. A., Rowe, C. L., Dakof, G. A., Henderson, C. E., & Greenbaum, P. E. (2009). Multidimensional family therapy for young adolescent substance abuse: Twelve-month outcomes of a randomized controlled trial. *Journal of Consulting and Clinical Psychology, 77*(1), 12–25. doi: 10.1037/a0014160

Liddle, H. A., Rowe, C. L., Dakof, G. A., Ungaro, R. A., & Henderson, C. E. (2004). Early intervention for adolescent substance abuse: pretreatment to posttreatment outcomes of a randomized clinical trial comparing multidimensional family therapy and peer group treatment. *Journal of Psychoactive Drugs, 36*(1), 49–63.

Liddle, H. A., Rowe, C. L., Gonzalez, A., Henderson, C. E., Dakof, G. A., & Greenbaum, P. E. (2006). Changing provider practices, program environment, and improving outcomes by transporting multidimensional family therapy to an adolescent drug treatment setting. *American Journal on Addictions, 15,* 102–112. doi: 10.1080/10550490601003698

Lundblad, A.-M., & Hansson, K. (2005). Outcomes in couple therapy: Reduced psychiatric symptoms and improved sense of coherence. *Nordic Journal of Psychiatry, 59*(5), 374–380. doi: 10.1016/0277-9536(93)90033-z

Lundahl, B., Risser, H. J., & Lovejoy, M. C. (2006). A meta-analysis of parent training: Moderators and follow-up effects. *Clinical Psychology Review, 26*(1), 86–104. doi: 10.1016/j.cpr.2005.07.004

MacDonell, K., Ellis, D., Naar-King, S., & Cunningham, P. (2010). Predictors of home-based obesity treatment efficacy for African American youth. *Children's Health Care, 39*(1), 1–14. doi: 10.1080/02739610903455087

Markie-Dadds, C., & Sanders, M. R. (2006). Self-directed Triple P (Positive Parenting Program) for mothers with children at risk of developing conduct problems. *Behavioural and Cognitive Psychotherapy, 34,* 259–275. doi: 10.1017/s1352465806002797

Martinez, C. R., & Eddy, J. M. (2005). Effects of culturally adapted parent management training on Latino youth behavioral health outcomes. *Journal of Consulting and Clinical Psychology, 73,* 841–851. doi: 10.1037/0022-006x.73.5.841

Matos, M., Bauermeister, J. J., & Bernal, G. (2009). Parent–child interaction therapy for Puerto Rican preschool children with ADHD and behavior problems: A pilot efficacy study. *Family Process, 48,* 232–252. doi: 10.1111/j.1545-5300.2009 .01279.x

Matsumoto, Y., Sofronoff, K., & Sanders, M. R. (2010). Investigation of the effectiveness and social validity of the Triple P Positive Parenting Program in Japanese society. *Journal of Family Psychology, 24,* 87–91. doi: 10.1037/a0018181

McCart, M. R., Priester, P. E., Davies, W. H., & Azen, R. (2006). Differential effectiveness of behavioral parent-training and cognitive-behavioral therapy for antisocial youth: A meta-analysis. *Journal of Abnormal Child Psychology: An Official Publication of the International Society for Research in Child and Adolescent Psychopathology, 34*(4), 527–543. doi: 10.1007/s10802–006–9031–1

McCrady, B. S., Epstein, E. E., Cook, S., Jensen, N., & Hildebrandt, T. (2009). A randomized trial of individual and couple behavioral alcohol treatment for women. *Journal of Consulting and Clinical Psychology, 77,* 243–256. doi:10.1037/a0014686

McCrady, B. S., Epstein, E. E., & Kahler, C. W. (2004). Alcoholics anonymous and relapse prevention as maintenance strategies after conjoint behavioral alcohol treatment for men: 18-month outcomes. *Journal of Consulting and Clinical Psychology, 72*(5), 870–878. doi: 10.1037/0033–2909.101.1.147

McIntyre, L. L. (2008). Adapting Webster-Stratton's incredible years parent training for children with developmental delay: Findings from a treatment group only study. *Journal of Intellectual Disability*

Research, 52(12), 1176–1192. doi: 10.1111/j.1365-2788.2008.01108.x

McLean, L. M., Jones, J. M., Rydall, A. C., Walsh, A., Esplen, M. J., Zimmermann, C., & Rodin, G. M. (2008). A couples intervention for patients facing advanced cancer and their spouse caregivers: Outcomes of a pilot study. *Psycho-Oncology, 17*, 1152–1156. doi: 10.1002/pon.1319

McNeil, B. J., Sox, H. C., Daniels, A., Dickerson, K., Galvin, R. S., Goldman, D. P., ... Steele, G. D. (2008). Report brief from the committee on reviewing evidence to identify highly effective clinical services: Systematic review: The central link between evidence and clinical decision making. *Institute of Medicine*.

Miller, I. W., Keitner, G. I., Ryan, C. E., Uebelacker, L. A., Johnson, S. L., & Solomon, D. A. (2008). Family treatment for bipolar disorder: Family impairment by treatment interactions. *Journal of Clinical Psychiatry, 69*, 732–740. doi: 10.4088/JCP.v69n0506

Montero, I., Masanet, M. J., Bellver, F., & Lacruz, M. (2006). The long-term outcome of 2 family intervention strategies in schizophrenia. *Comprehensive Psychiatry, 47*, 362–367. doi: 10.1016/j.comppsych.2006.02.001

Morawska, A., & Sanders, M. R. (2006). Self-administered behavioural family intervention for parents of toddlers: Effectiveness and dissemination. *Behaviour Research and Therapy, 44*, 1839–1848. doi: 10.1016/j.brat.2005.11.015

Morawska, A., & Sanders, M. (2009). An evaluation of a behavioural parenting intervention for parents of gifted children. *Behaviour Research and Therapy, 47*, 463–470. doi: 10.1037/1040-3590.5.2.137

National Institute on Drug Abuse (NIDA). (1999). *Principles of drug addiction treatment: A research-based guide* (2nd ed.). Retrieved from https://www.drugabuse.gov/sites/default/files/podat_0.pdf

Nixon, R. D. V., Sweeney, L., Erickson, D. B., & Touyz, S. W. (2004). Parent–child interaction therapy: One- and two-year follow-up of standard and abbreviated treatments for oppositional preschoolers. *Journal of Abnormal Child Psychology: An official publication of the International Society for Research in Child and Adolescent Psychopathology, 32*, 263–271. doi: 10.1023/b:jacp.0000026140.60558.05

Nowak, C., & Heinrichs, N. (2008). A comprehensive meta-analysis of triple p-positive parenting program using hierarchical linear modeling: Effectiveness and moderating variables. *Clinical Child and Family Psychology Review, 11*(3), 114–144. doi: 10.1097/00004703-200010000-00006

O'Farrell, T. J., Murphy, C. M., Stephan, S. H., Fals-Stewart, W., & Murphy, M. (2004). Partner violence before and after couples-based alcoholism treatment for male alcoholic patients: The role of treatment involvement and abstinence. *Journal of Consulting and Clinical Psychology, 72*(2), 202–217.

O'Leary, E. M. M., Barrett, P., & Fjermestad, K. W. (2009). Cognitive-behavioral family treatment for childhood obsessive-compulsive disorder: A 7-year follow-up study. *Journal of Anxiety Disorders, 23*, 973–978. doi: 10.1016/j.janxdis.2009.06.009

Ogden, T., & Amlund Hagen, K. (2009). What works for whom? Gender differences in intake characteristics and treatment outcomes following multisystemic therapy. *Journal of Adolescence, 32*, 1425–1435. doi: 10.1037/0893-3200.18.3.411

Ogden, T., & Hagen, K. A. (2008). Treatment effectiveness of parent management training in Norway: A randomized controlled trial of children with conduct problems. *Journal of Consulting and Clinical Psychology, 76*, 607–621. doi: 10.1037/0022-006x.76.4.607

Ogden, T., & Halliday-Boykins, C. A. (2004). Multisystemic treatment of antisocial adolescents in Norway: Replication of clinical outcomes outside of the US. *Child and Adolescent Mental Health, 9*, 77–83. doi: 10.1111/j.1475-3588.2004.00085.x

Owens, D. K., Lohr, K. N., Atkins, D., Treadwell, J. R., Reston, J. T., Bass, E. B., ... Helfand, M. (2010). AHRQ series paper 5: Grading the strength of a body of evidence when comparing medical interventions—Agency for Healthcare Research and Equality and the Effective Health-Care Program. *Journal of Clinical Epistomology, 63*, 513–523. doi: 10.1016/j.jclinepi.2009.03.009

Pinsof, W. M., & Wynne, L. C. (1995). The efficacy of marital and family therapy: An empirical overview, conclusions, and recommendations. *Journal of Marital and Family Therapy, 21*(4), 585–613. doi: 10.1111/j.1752-0606.1995.tb00179.x

Plant, K. M., & Sanders, M. R. (2007). Reducing problem behavior during care-giving in families of preschool-aged children with developmental disabilities. *Research in Developmental Disabilities, 28*, 362–385. doi: 10.1016/j.ridd.2006.02.009

Powers, M. B., Vedel, E., & Emmelkamp, P. M. G. (2008). Behavioral couples therapy (BCT) for alcohol and drug use disorders: A meta-analysis. *Clinical Psychology Review, 28*(6), 952–962. doi: 10.1016/j.cpr.2008.02.002

Prinz, R. J., Sanders, M. R., Shapiro, C. J., Whitaker, D. J., & Lutzker, J. R. (2009). Population-based prevention of child maltreatment: The U.S. Triple P system population trial. *Prevention Science, 10*, 1–12. doi: 10.1007/s11121-009-0123-3

Puleo, C. M., & Kendall, P. C. (2011). Anxiety disorders in typically developing youth: Autism spectrum symptoms as a predictor of cognitive-behavioral treatment. *Journal of Autism and Developmental Disorders, 41*, 275–286. doi: 10.1007/s10803-010-1047-2

Reid, M. J., Webster-Stratton, C., & Baydar, N. (2004). Halting the development of conduct problems in Head Start children: The effects of parent training. *Journal of Clinical Child and Adolescent Psychology, 33*, 279–291. doi: 10.1207/s15374424jccp3302_10

Reid, R. C., & Woolley, S. R. (2006). Using emotionally focused therapy for couples to resolve attachment ruptures created by hypersexual behavior. *Sexual Addiction & Compulsivity, 13*, 219–239. doi: 10.1111/j.1752-0606.2004.tb01235.x

Reese, R. J., Toland, M. D., Slone, N. C., & Norsworthy, L. A. (2010). Effect of client feedback on couple psychotherapy outcomes. *Psychotherapy: Theory, Research, Practice, Training, 47*(4), 616–630.

Reyno, S. M., & McGrath, P. J. (2006). Predictors of parent training efficacy for child externalizing behavior problem: A meta-analytic review. *Journal of Child Psychology and Psychiatry, 47*(1), 99–111. doi: 10.1111/j.1469-7610.2005.01544.x

Roberts, C., Mazzucchelli, T., Studman, L., & Sanders, M. R. (2006). Behavioral family intervention for children with developmental disabilities and behavioral problems. *Journal of Clinical Child and Adolescent Psychology, 35*, 180–193. doi: 10.1207/s15374424jccp3502_2

Robin, A. L. (2003). *Behavioral family systems therapy for adolescents with anorexia nervosa*. In A. E. Kazdin & J. R. Weisz (Eds.), *Evidence-based psychotherapies for children and adolescents* (pp. 358–373). New York, NY: Guilford Press.

Robbins, M. S., Alexander, J. F., Newell, R. M., & Turner, C. W. (1996). The immediate effect of reframing on client attitude in family therapy. *Journal of Family Psychology, 10*, 28–34. doi: 10.1037/0893-3200.10.1.28

Robbins, M. S., Liddle, H. A., Turner, C. W., Dakof, G. A., Alexander, J. F., & Kogan, S. M. (2006). Adolescent and parent therapeutic alliances as predictors of dropout in multidimensional family therapy. *Journal of Family Psychology, 20*, 108–116. doi: 10.1037/0893-3200.20.1.108

Rowe, L. S., Doss, B. D., Hsueh, A. C., Libet, J., & Mitchell, A. E. (2011). Coexisting difficulties and couple therapy outcomes: Psychopathology and intimate partner violence. *Journal of Family Psychology, 25*, 455–458. doi:10.1037/a0023696

Rowland, M. D., Halliday-Boykins, C. A., Henggeler, S. W., Cunningham, P. B., Lee, T. G., Kruesi, M. J. P., & Shapiro, S. B. (2005). A randomized trial of multisystemic therapy with Hawaii's Felix class youths. *Journal of Emotional and Behavioral Disorders, 13*, 13–23. doi: 10.1177/10634266050130010201

Sanders, M. R. (1999). Triple P–Positive Parenting Program: Towards an empirically validated multilevel parenting and family support strategy for the prevention of behavior and emotional problems in children. *Clinical Child and Family Psychology Review, 2*, 71–90.

Sanders, M. R., Bor, W., & Morawska, A. (2007). Maintenance of treatment gains: A comparison of enhanced, standard, and self-directed triple P-positive parenting program. *Journal of Abnormal Child Psychology: An official publication of the International Society for Research in Child and Adolescent Psychopathology, 35*, 983–998. doi: 10.1007/s10802-007-9148-x

Sanders, M. R., Pidgeon, A. M., Gravestock, F., Connors, M. D., Brown, S., & Young, R. W. (2004). Does parental attributional retraining and anger management enhance the effects of the Triple P-Positive Parenting Program with parents at risk of child maltreatment? *Behavior Therapy, 35*, 513–535. doi: 10.1016/s0005-7894(04)80030-3

Schoenwald, S. K., Chapman, J. E., Sheidow, A. J., & Carter, R. E. (2009). Long-term youth criminal outcomes in MST transport: The impact of therapist adherence and organizational climate and structure. *Journal of Clinical Child and Adolescent Psychology, 38*, 91–105. doi: 10.1080/15374410802575388

Schoenwald, S. K., Sheidow, A. J., & Chapman, J. E. (2009). Clinical supervision in treatment transport: Effects on adherence and outcomes. *Journal of Consulting and Clinical Psychology, 77*, 410–421. doi: 10.1037/a0013788

Schoenwald, S. K., Sheidow, A. J., & Letourneau, E. J. (2004). Toward effective quality assurance in evidence-based practice: Links between expert consultation, therapist fidelity, and child outcomes. *Journal of Clinical Child and Adolescent Psychology, 33*, 94–104. doi: 10.1207/s15374424jccp3301_10

Schulz, M. S., Cowan, C. P., & Cowan, P. A. (2006). Promoting healthy beginnings: A randomized controlled trial of a preventive intervention to preserve marital quality during the transition to parenthood. *Journal of Consulting and Clinical Psychology, 74*, 20–31. doi: 10.1037/0022-3514.64.5.794

Schumm, J. A., O'Farrell, T. J., Murphy, C. M., & Fals-Stewart, W. (2009). Partner violence before and after couples-based alcoholism treatment for female alcoholic patients. *Journal of Consulting and Clinical Psychology, 77*, 1136–1146.

Seedall, R. B., Sprenkle, D. H., & Lebow, J. L. (2011). Review of common factors in couple and family therapy: The overlooked foundation for effective practice. *Journal of Marital and Family Therapy, 37*(3), 374–375. doi: 10.1111/j.1752-0606.2011.00241_5.x

Sellwood, W., Wittkowski, A., Tarrier, N., & Barrowclough, C. (2007). Needs-based cognitive-behavioural family intervention for patients suffering from schizophrenia: 5-year follow-up of a randomized controlled effectiveness trial. *Acta Psychiatrica Scandinavica, 116*, 447–452. doi: 10.1111/j.1600-0447.2007.01097.x

Sexton, T. L., & Alexander, J. F. (2003). Functional family therapy: A mature clinical model for working with at-risk adolescents and their families. In T. L. Sexton, G. R. Weeks, & M. S. Robbins (Eds.), *Handbook of family therapy* (pp. 371–400). New York, NY: Brunner-Routledge.

Sexton, T. L., Alexander, J. F., & Mease, A. L. (2004). Levels of evidence for the models and mechanisms of therapeutic change in family and couple therapy.

In M. J. Lambert (Ed.), *Bergin and Garfield's handbook of psychotherapy and behavior change* (5th ed., pp. 590–646). Hoboken, NJ: Wiley.

Sexton, T. L., Coop-Gordon, K., Gurman, A. S., Lebow, J. L., Holtzworth-Munroe, A., & Johnson, S. (2007). *Report of the task force for evidence-based treatments in couple and family psychology.* Washington, DC: American Psychological Association.

Sexton, T. L., & van Dam, A. E. (2010). Creativity within the structure: Clinical expertise and evidence-based treatments. *Journal of Contemporary Psychotherapy, 40*(3), 175–180.

Sexton, T. L., Kinser, J. C., & Hanes, C. W. (2008). Beyond a single standard: Levels of evidence approach for evaluating marriage and family therapy research and practice. *Journal of Family Therapy, 30*(4), 386–398.

Sexton, T. L., McEnery, A. M., & Wilson, L. R. (2011). *Family research: Understanding families, family-based clinical interventions, and clinically useful outcomes.* New York, NY: Routledge/Taylor & Francis.

Sexton, T. L., Ridley, C. R., & Kliner, A., (2004). Beyond common factors: Multilevel-process models of therapeutic change in marriage and family therapy. *Journal of Marital and Family Therapy, 30*(2), 1–12.

Sexton, T. L., & Turner, C. T. (2010). The effectiveness of functional family therapy for youth with behavioral problems in a community practice setting. *Journal of Family Psychology, 24*(3), 339–348.

Shadish, W. R., Ragsdale, K., Glaser, R. R., & Montgomery, L. M. (1995). The efficacy and effectiveness of marital and family therapy: A perspective from meta-analysis. *Journal of Marital and Family Therapy, 21*(4), 345–360. doi: 10.1111/j.1752-0606.1995.tb00170.x

Shelef, K., Diamond, G. M., Diamond, G. S., & Liddle, H. A. (2005). Adolescent and parent alliance and treatment outcome in multidimensional family therapy. *Journal of Consulting and Clinical Psychology, 73*, 689–698. doi: 10.1037/0022-006x.73.4.689

Simpson, L. E., Atkins, D. C., Gattis, K. S., & Christensen, A. (2008). Low-level relationship aggression and couple therapy outcomes. *Journal of Family Psychology, 22*, 102–111. doi: 10.1037/08933200.19.1.98

Slesnick, N., Bartle-Haring, S., & Gangamma, R. (2006). Predictors of substance use and family therapy outcome among physically and sexually abused runaway adolescents. *Journal of Marital and Family Therapy, 32*, 261–281. doi: 10.1111/j.1752-0606.2006.tb01606.x

Slesnick, N., & Prestopnik, J. L. (2005). Ecologically based family therapy outcome with substance abusing runaway adolescents. *Journal of Adolescence, 28*(2), 277–298.

Smit, E., Verdurmen, J., Monshouwer, K., & Smit, F. (2008). Family interventions and their effect on adolescent alcohol use in general populations: A meta-analysis of randomized controlled trials. *Drug and Alcohol Dependence, 97*(3), 195–206. doi: 10.1016/j.drugalcdep.2008.03.032

Solomon, M., Ono, M., Timmer, S., & Goodlin-Jones, B. (2008). The effectiveness of parent–child interaction therapy for families of children on the autism spectrum. *Journal of Autism and Developmental Disorders, 38*, 1767–1776. doi: 10.1007/s10803-008-0567-5

Stambaugh, L. F., Mustillo, S. A., Burns, B. J., Stephens, R. L., Baxter, B., Edwards, D., & DeKraai, M. (2007). Outcomes from wraparound and multisystemic therapy in a center for mental health services system-of-care demonstration site. *Journal of Emotional and Behavioral Disorders, 15*, 143–155. doi: 10.1177/10634266070150030201

Stith, S. M., Rosen, K. H., McCollum, E. E., & Thomsen, C. J. (2004). Treating intimate partner violence within intact couple relationships: Outcomes of multi-couple versus individual couple therapy. *Journal of Marital and Family Therapy, 30*, 305–318. doi: 10.1037/0033-2909.126.5.651

Storch, E. A., Geffken, G. R., Merlo, L. J., Mann, G., Duke, D., Munson, M., ... Goodman, W. K. (2007). Family-based cognitive-behavioral therapy for pediatric obsessive-compulsive disorder: Comparison of intensive and weekly approaches. *Journal of the American Academy of Child & Adolescent Psychiatry, 46*, 469–478. doi: 10.1097/chi.0b013e31803062e7

Storch, E. A., Lehmkuhl, H. D., Ricketts, E., Geffken, G. R., Marien, W., & Murphy, T. K. (2010). An open trial of intensive family based cognitive-behavioral therapy in youth with obsessive-compulsive disorder who are medication partial responders or nonresponders. *Journal of Clinical Child and Adolescent Psychology, 39*, 260–268. doi: 10.1097/01.chi.0000246065.93200.al

Stricker, G. (2007). The local clinical scientist. In S. G. Hofmann & J. Weinberger (Eds.), *The Art of Psychotherapy* (pp. 85–99). New York, NY: Routledge/Taylor & Francis.

Sundell, K., Hansson, K., Löfholm, C. A., Olsson, T., Gustle, L.-H., & Kadesjö, C. (2008). The transportability of multisystemic therapy to Sweden: Short-term results from a randomized trial of conduct-disordered youths. *Journal of Family Psychology, 22*, 550–560. doi:10.1037/a0012790

Suveg, C., Hudson, J. L., Brewer, G., Flannery-Schroeder, E., Gosch, E., & Kendall, P. C. (2009). Cognitive-behavioral therapy for anxiety-disordered youth: Secondary outcomes from a randomized clinical trial evaluating child and family modalities. *Journal of Anxiety Disorders, 23*, 341–349. doi: 10.1016/j.janxdis.2009.01.003

Szapocznik, J., Robbins, M. S., Mitrani, V. B., Santisteban, D. A., Hervis, O., & Williams, R. A. (2002). Brief strategic family therapy with behavior problem Hispanic youth. In J. Lebow (Ed.), *Integrative and eclectic psychotherapies*. Vol. 4 in F. W. Kaslow (Ed.), *Comprehensive handbook of psychotherapy* (pp. 83–109). Hoboken, NJ: Wiley.

Tambling, R. B., & Johnson, L. N. (2008). The relationship between stages of change and outcome in couple therapy. *American Journal of Family Therapy*, *36*, 229–241. doi: 10.1037/0003-066x.47.9.1102

Thomas, R., & Zimmer-Gembeck, M. J. (2007). Behavioral outcomes of parent–child interaction therapy and triple p-positive parenting program: A review and meta-analysis. *Journal of Abnormal Child Psychology: An official publication of the International Society for Research in Child and Adolescent Psychopathology*, *35*(3), 475–495. doi: 10.1037/0022–006x.66.1.7

Tilden, T., Gude, T., & Hoffart, A. (2010). The course of dyadic adjustment and depressive symptoms during and after couples therapy: A prospective follow-up study of inpatient treatment. *Journal of Marital and Family Therapy*, *36*, 43–58. doi: 10.1146/annurev.psych.50.1.165

Tilden, T., Gude, T., Hoffart, A., & Sexton, H. (2010). Individual distress and dyadic adjustment over a three-year follow-up period in couple therapy: A bi-directional relationship? *Journal of Family Therapy*, *32*, 119–141. doi: 10.1146/annurev.psych.50.1.165

Tilden, T., Gude, T., Sexton, H., Finset, A., & Hoffart, A. (2010). The associations between intensive residential couple therapy and change in a three-year follow-up period. *Contemporary Family Therapy: An International Journal*, *32*, 69–85. doi: 10.1146/annurev.psych.50.1.165

Timmer, S. G., Urquiza, A. J., Zebell, N. M., & McGrath, J. M. (2005). Parent–child interaction therapy: Application to maltreating parent–child dyads. *Child Abuse & Neglect*, *29*, 825–842.

Timmer, S. G., Ware, L. M., Urquiza, A. J., & Zebell, N. M. (2010). The effectiveness of parent–child interaction therapy for victims of interparental violence. *Violence and Victims*, *25*(4), 486–486–503. doi: 10.1891/0886–6708.25.4.486

Timmer, S. G., Zebell, N. M., Culver, M. A., & Urquiza, A. J. (2010). Efficacy of adjunct in-home coaching to improve outcomes in parent–child interaction therapy. *Research on Social Work Practice*, *20*, 36–45. doi:10.1177/1049731509332842

Timmons-Mitchell, J., Bender, M. B., Kishna, M. A., & Mitchell, C. C. (2006). An independent effectiveness trial of multisystemic therapy with juvenile justice youth. *Journal of Clinical Child and Adolescent Psychology*, *35*, 227–236. doi: 10.1207/s15374424jccp3502_6

Tolman, R. T., Mueller, C. W., Daleiden, E. L., Stumpf, R. E., & Pestle, S. L. (2008). Outcomes from multisystemic therapy in a statewide system of care. *Journal of Child and Family Studies*, *17*, 894–908. doi: 10.1007/s10826-008-9197-y

Turner, K. M. T., Richards, M., & Sanders, M. R. (2007). Randomised clinical trial of a group parent education programme for Australian indigenous families. *Journal of Paediatrics and Child Health*, *43*, 429–437. doi: 10.1111/j.1440-1754.2007.01053.x

U.S. Preventive Services Task Force ([USPSTF], 2011). About the USPSTF. Retrieved from http://www.uspreventiveservicestaskforce.org/index.html

Vedel, E., Emmelkamp, P. M. G., & Schippers, G. M. (2008). Individual cognitive-behavioral therapy and behavioral couples therapy in alcohol use disorder: A comparative evaluation in community-based addiction treatment centers. *Psychotherapy and Psychosomatics*, *77*, 280–288. doi:10.1159/000140087

Walitzer, K. S., & Dermen, K. H. (2004). Alcohol-focused spouse involvement and behavioral couples therapy: Evaluation of enhancements to drinking reduction treatment for male problem drinkers. *Journal of Consulting and Clinical Psychology*, *72*, 944–955. doi: 10.1037/0022-006x.58.3.304

Webster-Stratton, C. (1984). Randomized trial of two parent-training programs for families with conduct-disordered children. *Journal of Consulting and Clinical Psychology*, *52*(4), 666–678. doi: 10.1080/15374418009532938

Webster-Stratton, C. (1994). Advancing videotape parent training: A comparison study. *Journal of Consulting and Clinical Psychology*, *62*(3), 583–593.

Webster-Stratton, C., Reid, M. J., & Hammond, M. (2004). Treating Children With Early-Onset Conduct Problems: Intervention Outcomes for Parent, Child, and Teacher Training. *Journal of Clinical Child and Adolescent Psychology*, *33*, 105–124. doi: 10.1207/s15374424jccp3301_11

Weiskop, S., Richdale, A., & Matthews, J. (2005). Behavioural treatment to reduce sleep problems in children with autism or Fragile X syndrome. *Developmental Medicine & Child Neurology*, *47*, 94–104. doi: 10.1017/s0012162205000186

Werba, B. E., Eyberg, S. M., Boggs, S. R., & Algina, J. (2006). Predicting outcome in parent–child interaction therapy: Success and attrition. *Behavior Modification*, *30*, 618–646. doi: 10.1037/h0079571.1995-10840-00110.1037/h0079571

Wiggins, T. L., Sofronoff, K., & Sanders, M. R. (2009). Pathways Triple P-Positive Parenting Program: Effects on parent-child relationships and child behavior problems. *Family Process*, *48*(4), 517–530.

Yaruss, J. S., Coleman, C., & Hammer, D. (2006). Treating preschool children who stutter: Description and preliminary evaluation of a family-focused treatment approach. *Language, Speech, and Hearing Services in Schools*, *37*, 118–136. doi: 10.1044/0161-1461(2006/014)

CHAPTER 16

CHANGE MECHANISMS AND EFFECTIVENESS OF SMALL GROUP TREATMENTS

GARY M. BURLINGAME, BERNHARD STRAUSS, AND ANTHONY S. JOYCE

We had two aims in the revision of our corresponding chapter from the last handbook (Burlingame, MacKenzie, & Strauss, 2004): (1) provide the best evidence-based recommendations for using specific group approaches to treat specific patient populations; and (2) highlight factors other than the treatment model that may explain additional outcome variance. Today's group treatments are guided by structured protocols that have been submitted to rigorous empirical scrutiny. The typical research study identifies a particular disorder and then articulates specific group interventions that are proposed to lead to desired effects (e.g., reduction in depression). Indeed, in our previous review we criticized some areas of the group literature for lack of clarity in the desired effects and the interventions intended to produce these effects (e.g., groups for the elderly). Consequently, the bulk of the current chapter summarizes evidence about specific group interventions that lead to specific effects for specific patient populations. However, it is clear that study authors continue to struggle with outcome variance that is *not* explained by specific group interventions based on a theoretical model. We believe insufficient attention is given to well-known and measurable group properties and processes, which account for some part of this unexplained treatment variance.

There is a distinct difference in the group treatments reviewed in this chapter from those covered in past handbook chapters. Earlier group research was conducted by investigators who held group treatment as a major part of their professional identity. They were conversant with the group dynamic and process literature, built these properties into their protocols, and often tested them as mechanisms of change that were independent of the theoretical model guiding treatment. In contrast, most of the randomized clinical trials (RCTs) summarized in this chapter appear to be conducted by investigators who are specialists in either a particular psychiatric or medical disorder (e.g., depression) or theoretical orientation (cognitive-behavior therapy; CBT) with the research being an extension of one or both of these identities. Stated differently, being a group clinician or specialist in group dynamics does not seem to be a core part of the identity of the investigators producing recent group treatment research.

The state of the current literature and our own appreciation of the group dynamic literature led us to a choice point: criticize nearly all RCTs for not explicitly incorporating group properties, or present a heuristic to assist future investigations. Our fundamental objective is to use empirical knowledge regarding group properties to increase the effectiveness of group treatments. Hence, we provide a general model of evidence-based group properties later in the chapter and select a few properties to illustrate their relationship to patient outcomes. We urge both researchers and clinicians to become familiar with this part of the evidence-based group literature. We end with a discussion of a small but growing movement that uses sound measures of these properties to assist the clinician to maximize outcome in group treatment: *practice-based group treatment*.

CONCEPTUALIZING GROUP TREATMENTS

In 2004 (Burlingame et al., 2004), we introduced a model that identified the main sources that empirically explain patient improvement in group treatment (Figure 16.1). This model subsequently spawned new research and evidence-based summaries; given its apparent heuristic value, we reintroduce it with refinements as an organizational framework. An abbreviated summary follows and the interested reader is directed to our previous summary for more detail. The model begins with a general conclusion drawn from the research literature—group treatment facilitates client improvement—represented by the *therapeutic outcomes of group treatment* element. Below, we explore five sources of potential effects on these outcomes.

The first source—*formal change theory*—captures the mechanisms of change as tested by efficacy or effectiveness studies. Group formal change theories overlap with the general psychotherapy literature (e.g., psychodynamic, interpersonal, cognitive-behavioral, humanistic) but also include support, skills training, and psychoeducational groups. Information related to

theories of change is the most prevalent in the literature and thus makes up the bulk of our review. The second source—*principles of small group process*—reflect group mechanisms of change that have been empirically linked to outcome and reflect the confluence of theory and research from the clinical and nonclinical group literatures (e.g., social psychology). In short, the therapeutic environment of the group is a potent source of change that is *independent* of formal change theory. We introduce a more detailed model of group process later to guide research and practice.

A third source is the *patient*. Typical patient factors considered by recent group RCTs are those related to the disorder (e.g., pretreatment severity of depressive symptoms). However, our model's intent is to highlight *group format* characteristics that predict improvement or deterioration. For instance, interactions between patient personality characteristics (e.g., attachment style, maturity of interpersonal relations) in conjunction with type of group approach have been recently studied as predictors of benefit. The fourth source—*group structural factors*—takes into consideration logistical features of group such as dose (number and length of sessions), intensity of sessions (weekly, monthly, and bi-monthly), group size, setting, and cultural factors. Structural features can affect the size and durability of treatment effects, for example, studies of booster sessions and varying dosage are emerging as important.

The interconnection of all four sources is up to the *group leader*, who determines how these sources are integrated, whether the group is used as a vehicle of change or if individual therapy is conducted in a group setting without regard for group dynamic factors. In 2004 we documented excellent examples of how to modify interventions created for individual therapy to fit a group format (cf. Wilfley, Frank, Welch, Spurrell, & Rounsaville, 1998), noting that neglect of such considerations can actually lower effectiveness (Burlingame et al., 2004).

The complexity of group treatment emerges when these five sources interact. Structural properties can interact with small group process (e.g., increased size can decrease member interaction and cohesion), formal change strategies may compete with group process principles (e.g., in-depth individual exploration versus shared floor-time), and patient characteristics may interact with group processes (e.g., insecurely attached clients respond differently to cohesion). In short,

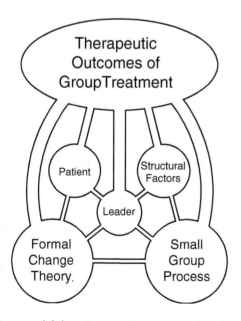

FIGURE 16.1 Forces that govern the therapeutic outcomes of group psychology.

the group is comprised of multiple interactive parts and these multifaceted relationships change over time.

CHAPTER ORGANIZATION AND REVIEW APPROACH

This review includes studies from virtually every continent. It is encouraging that recent studies have begun to transfer group protocols developed in Europe, North America, or Australia to new cultures; likewise, new protocols being developed in Asia hold promise for Western application. The typical group continues to be time-limited (10 to 20 sessions) and of a diagnostically homogenous composition, but there is an increase in long-term (1 to 2 years) psychodynamically oriented groups with diagnostically heterogeneous membership. We see the increase in published research on these groups as a positive development because it examines actual clinical practice in many parts of the world.

The efficacy and effectiveness literature is presented first and is organized by five sections: (1) disorders where group is the *primary* or sole treatment (mood, social phobia, panic, obsessive compulsive and eating disorders); (2) disorders where group is an adjunctive to other treatments (substance and posttraumatic stress disorders); (3) groups offered in hospital/medical settings (cancer, pain/somatoform, inpatient); (4) groups for severe mental illness (schizophrenia and personality disorders); and, (5) studies comparing the differential efficacy of the group versus individual formats. We end this section with promising developments organized by the five sources noted in Figure 16.1. The second major section describes a model to assist the reader in understanding group mechanisms of change based on the group dynamic literature. We then select four mechanisms from this model to illustrate how robust empirical evidence can guide group practice and hopefully strengthen the effects described in the efficacy section. We end our chapter with a framework—practice-based group treatment (PBGT)—to illustrate how one might integrate the evidence-based protocols described in the efficacy section with measures of process to empirically guide group practice.

The studies reviewed in the efficacy section were located through a computer search of PsycInfo, Medline, PubMed, ERIC, and Google Scholar using the search terms group psychotherapy, counseling, treatment, and therapy producing thousands of abstracts. Each was carefully read and accepted for inclusion using the following criteria: published between January 2000 and June 2011; clinical populations; randomized clinical trials (RCTs) or effectiveness studies; and methodologically rigorous. Topics with sufficient research (> 5 studies) were supplemented with meta-analytic findings when available.

EVIDENCE FOR EFFICACY AND EFFECTIVENESS OF GROUP TREATMENT

Our primary interest in this section is to offer evidence-based recommendations to guide clinical practice. In doing so, we summarized the best efficacy and effectiveness studies that we could find in Tables 16.1 to 16.3. Efficacy studies are often fewer in number and provide an upper limit of the improvement one might expect when using a particular group treatment. Effectiveness studies are included to provide an estimate of pre–postimprovement one might see in daily clinical practice.

The studies in Tables 16.1 to 16.3 are classified across three domains; study and sample characteristics as well as the outcomes targeted for change. The study characteristics section begins with the percentage of studies employing a randomized clinical trial (%RCT) because experimental rigor rules out many confounds. Disorders employing a higher percentage of RCTs (e.g., adult substance abuse) may claim greater rigor and causal inference than those that primarily employ pre-post effectiveness designs (e.g., bipolar). We then note the percent of studies that use a conservative intent-to-treat (%ITT) versus completer analyses, which is especially important when there is either high or differential rates of attrition; the range of percent of attrition (%Attr) follows immediately thereafter. Finally, an indicator of durability of outcomes is reflected by the presence of and length of follow-up assessment.

The increased number of RCTs allowed us to identify several important sample characteristics including sample size in active (A) and control (C) conditions, which is important because smaller samples are more susceptible to confounds. We also list average age and gender ranges because both can moderate treatment effects. Finally, we identify the primary and secondary effects or outcomes targeted by treatment, indicating the number of studies studying each effect. This is critical since it affects how one would communicate the expected benefits of treatment to a prospective patient.

Group as Primary
Mood Disorders

In 2004, we concluded that group treatment produced reliable improvement over wait-list controls; that cognitive-behavioral group therapy (CBGT) had the most convincing randomized clinical trial (RCT) support; that there was little support for differential efficacy based on the theoretical model guiding treatment; and that individual and group formats produced equivalent effects (Burlingame et al., 2004). These findings were replicated and extended in 17 new studies listed in Table 16.1. Two meta-analyses (McDermut, Miller, & Brown, 2001; Oei & Dingle, 2008, summarizing pre-2000 studies) yielded 28 unique RCTs, with group therapy producing large effects (1.03 and 1.10, respectively) relative to untreated controls. With some variation, the aggregate results from 14 studies showed equivalence between individual and group formats (see below). The most recent literature clustered around two distinct diagnostic groupings (Table 16.1).

Ten studies focused on *major depressive disorder* (MDD) with primary effects including depression (the Beck Depression Inventory—BDI—was employed in eight studies) and cognitive measures [dysfunctional attitudes (6) and automatic thoughts (3)]; quality of life (QoL) was the most studied secondary effect (3). Groups were closed, lasted between 10 and 12 sessions, and had CBGT as the primary model (8) although behavioral activation (Porter, Spates, & Smitham, 2004) and Eastern philosophy models (Hsiao et al., 2007) were also tested. Five teams extended CBGT models that were shown to be efficacious in past research to new populations (e.g., depressed treatment-resistant medication patients; Enns, Cox, & Pidlubny, 2002; Hsiao et al., 2007; Matsunaga et al., 2010; Porter et al., 2004; Wong, 2008). All studies reported statistically significant superiority for the active compared to control conditions on measures of depression and depressive thinking. Enns et al. (2002) found that higher levels of pretreatment self-criticism predicted less BDI improvement. Three teams explored the change process of CBGT groups. Swan and colleagues (2009) explored change on a quality of life measured with 212 MDD patients, finding that posttreatment

QoL change was explained by both pretreatment levels of depression and QoL (21%) as well as by posttreatment change in depression (40%). Despite these high percentages, they concluded that QoL was not an epiphenomenon of depression and that QoL changes cannot be solely explained by reductions in depression.

Oei and colleagues (Furlong & Oei, 2002; Kwon & Oei, 2003; Oei, Bullbeck, & Campbell, 2006) conducted a series of studies to better understand changes in depression and cognition over the course of CBGT. The findings, in summary, called into question the cognitive component as a primary change agent, leading the authors to explore alternative explanations (e.g., group as positive reinforcement). Kelly, Roberts, and Ciesla (2005) noted sudden gains for more than 40% of CBGT members, with early gains (Sessions 1 to 5) being related to greater improvement; sudden gains were unrelated to cognitive change, suggesting another mechanism of action (e.g., common factors). Unfortunately none of these studies could empirically link any aspect of group treatment to changes in depression.

Seven studies focused on *bipolar disorder* (BD) with only two using RCT designs. Most (5) tested psychoeducational groups (PEG) on diverse effects including recurrence and length of manic/depressive episodes (3), depression (5), mania (2), medication compliance (2), and general functioning (2). PEG length varied widely, from 4 sessions in an open inpatient group to 21 sessions in an outpatient setting. Patients ranged from mild or euthymic to acute and requiring hospitalization. In short, there was little coherence in the treatments offered, patients served, and effects studied. The strongest effects came from the RCTs. Colom and colleagues (2003) showed that PEG led to a reduced number of recurrences and hospitalizations, with gains maintained at 5 years (Colom et al., 2009); patients with more than seven previous episodes, however, did not show the same improvement (Colom et al., 2010). Simon and colleagues (2005) tested a multicomponent systemic care management program (e.g., telephone monitoring, feedback to treatment team) that included a two-phase PEG (disease management for five sessions followed by biweekly maintenance sessions) for 212 patients versus 229 TAU controls. More than half completed both phases (59% and 52%, respectively) leading to fewer manic episodes, less intense symptoms, and more medication management visits; gains were maintained

TABLE 16.1 Group as Primary Efficacy and Effectiveness Research

| | Study Characteristics | | | | Sample Characteristics | | | | | |
| | | | | | | | Range Average Age | % Females | Effects Related to Different Outcome Criteria |
Study	%RCT	%ITT	%Attr	Follow-Up	A	C			
MOOD DISORDERS									
Major Depressive Disorder: Enns et al., 2002; Furlong and Oei, 2002; Hsiao et al., 2007; Kelly et al., 2005; Kwon and Oei, 2003; Matsunaga et al., 2010; Oei et al., 2006; Porter et al., 2004; Swan et al., 2009; Wong., 2008	20	20	8–26	3–12 m	12–176	13–159	36–45	44–100	Depressed mood (9), cognitive (7), quality of life/well-being (4), general distress/functioning (3), anxiety (1)
Bipolar Disorder: Castle et al., 2007; Colom et al., 2003, 2009; de Andres et al., 2006; Michalak, Yatham, Wan, and Lam, 2005; Patelis-Siotis et al., 2001; Pollack et al., 2001; Simon et al., 2005, 2006	22	22	15–41	6–60m	9–212	60–229	34–44	57–82	Depression (5), episode recurrence/length (3), mania (2), medication compliance (2), general symptoms (2)
SOCIAL PHOBIA									
CBGT: adults: Ashbaugh et al., 2007; Borgeat et al., 2009; Delsignore, 2008; Fogler et al., 2007; Gaston et al., 2006; Gruber et al., 2001; Herbert et al., 2005; Hofman, 2004; Hofman and Suvak, 2005; Hofman et al., 2006; Kingsep et al., 2003; Marom et al., 2009; McEvoy, 2007; McEvoy et al., 2009; McEvoy and Perini, 2009; Mörtberg et al., 2005, 2006; Moscovitch et al., 2005; Rapee et al., 2007; Rosser et al., 2004; Stangier et al., 2003; Van Ingen and Novicki, 2009	45	23	0–48	2–12m	17–219	17–84	21–39	33–60	Social phobia symptoms (20), depression (9), general anxiety (2), general psychopathology (2)
CBGT: children and adolescents: Baer and Garland, 2005; Gallagher et al., 2002; Garcia-Lopez et al., 2006; Hayward et al., 2000; Joormann and Unnewehr, 2002; Liber et al., 2008	83	16	0–43	3w.–5yrs	6–127	6–65	8–16	40–100	Social phobia symptoms (6), depression (3)

PANIC

Austin et al., 2008, Bohni et al., 2009; Clerkin et al., 2008; Erickson, 2003; Erickson et al., 2007; Galassi et al., 2007; Norton, 2008; Oei and Boschen, 2009; Otto et al., 2000; Roberge et al., 2008, Rosenberg and Hougaard, 2005; Rufer et al., 2010; Sharp et al., 2004	38	23	0–42	0–24m	18–396	??	33–43	56–79	General anxiety (11), panic (9), depression (8), functioning (6), bodily sensation (2)

OCD

Effectiveness: Braga et al., 2005; Cordioli et al., 2002; Fenger et al., 2007; Himle et al., 2001; Meier et al., 2006	0	20	6–28	3–49m	24–89	None	29–40	Not Reported	Y-BOCS (5) depression (2), functioning (2) anxiety (1)
Comparative studies: Aigner et al., 2004; Anderson & Rees 2007; Cordioli et al., 2003; Fineberg et al., 2005; Jaurrieta, Jiminez-Murcia, Alonso, et al., 2008; Jaurrieta, Jimenez-Murcia, Menchón, et al., 2008; McLean, 2001; Sousa et al., 2006	86	43	14	1–24m	17–55	17–55	32–40	Not Reported	Y-BOCS (7) depression (5) anxiety (4), functioning (3), QOL (3)

(continued)

TABLE 16.1 *(Continued)*

Study	Study Characteristics				Sample Characteristics				Effects Related to Different Outcome Criteria
	%RCT	%ITT	%Attr	Follow-Up	A	C	Range Average Age	% Females	
EATING DISORDERS									
Bulimia Nervosa (BN)									
Bailer et al., 2004; Bogh et al., 2005; Chen et al., 2003; Jacobi et al., 2002; Leung et al., 2000; Nevonen & Broberg, 2006; Openshaw et al., 2004; Peterson et al., 2004; Shapiro et al., 2010	44	67	3–42	3–54m	19–109	16–82	21–28	97–100	BN symptoms (4); B&P frequency (2); eating-related cognitions (2). Comparative studies demonstrated equivalence of effects (see text)
Binge Eating Disorder (BED)									
Ashton et al., 2009; Duchesne et al., 2007; Friederich et al., 2007; Gollings and Paxton, 2006; Gorin et al., 2003; Kenardy et al., 2002; Munsch et al., 2007; Nauta et al., 2000, 2001; Paxton et al., 2007; Peterson et al., 2001; Renjilian et al., 2001; Safer et al., 2010; Schlup et al., 2009; Shapiro et al., 2007; Shelley-Ummenhofer and MacMillan, 2007; Tasca, Ritchie, et al., 2006, Tasca, Balfour, et al., 2007; Telch et al., 2000, 2001; Wilfley et al., 2002	76	90	0–41	1–12 m	11–253	9–51	21–58	76–100	BE symptoms (11); depression (9); BE frequency (7); abstinence (5); eating-related attitudes/concerns (4); self-esteem (3); mood regulation (3); emotional eating (3); weight (1)

at the 2-year follow-up (Simon, Ludman, Bauer, Unutzer, & Operskalski, 2006) but no differences on depression were noted between PEG and TAU. These results are promising given that medication compliance is likely linked to reduced frequency and intensity of recurrences. The two RCTs underscore the relapse prevention potential of PEG, but additional rigorous research is needed before we can move our evaluation from promising to efficacious.

Social Phobia. In 2004 we detailed "compelling evidence" for the efficacy of a single model —CBGT—developed by Heimberg and Becker (2002) (Burlingame et al., 2004). This model, along with two similar group approaches (Clark & Wells, 1995; Rapee & Heimberg, 1997), was the focus of 28 outcome studies published over the past decade (Table 16.1). A recent meta-analysis (Powers, Sigmarsson, & Emmelkamp, 2008) summarizing a portion of these studies estimated identical effectiveness for group ($d = .68$) and individual treatments ($d = .69$). The typical group was closed, and consisted of 5 to 10 patients who participated in weekly sessions of varying duration (90 to 240 min.). Patients were between 30 and 40 years old with equal gender representation.

Overall, the effects of CBGT have been confirmed related to primary outcomes of social phobia symptoms (commonly based on the Liebowitz Social Anxiety Scale) as well as on depression and several secondary outcomes (e.g., general anxiety, perfectionism, post-event processing; Ashbaugh et al., 2007; McEvoy, Mahoney, Perini, & Kingsep, 2009). A subset of studies looked at the effectiveness of successfully transferring manualized CBGT from a research setting to private practice or community clinics (e.g., Gaston, Abbot, Rapee, & Neary, 2006; Marom, Gilboa-Schechtman, Aderka, Weizman, & Hermesh, 2009; McEvoy, et al., 2007, 2009). Other studies summarized in Table 16.1 revealed CBGT to be effective for specific populations (Kingsep, Nathan, & Castle, 2003, Van Ingen & Novicki, 2009), other settings (e.g., intensive treatment, Mörtberg et al., 2005, 2006), combined with adjuncts (e.g., antidepressants; Rosser, Erskine, & Crino, 2004) or showed effects of CBGT depending on other variables (e.g., prior treatment; depression; Delsignore, 2008; Fogler, Tompson, Steketee, Hofmann, 2007; Marom et al., 2009). We found nine other studies testing the differential effects of CBGT with other treatments (e.g., exposure therapy, self-help groups with and without therapist assistance, individual CBT) or in combination with other interventions (e.g., social skills training or attention training), most (8) were RCTs. Many of the studies that were located defied easy classification other than being on social anxiety and involving group. Although all studies are related to the CBGT manuals, the literature reveals a general lack of cohesion or focus on systematic programmatic research. One study (Stangier, Heidenreich, Peitz, Lauterbach, & Clark, 2003) found individual more effective than group; however, the manual was not modified for the group setting, an omission shown to lower group effectiveness (Burlingame et al., 2004).

In view of recent epidemiological studies showing that social phobia/anxiety is common (lifetime prevalence 4% to 14%) and begins early (11 to 13 years), it is not surprising that recent research included children and adolescents. A Cochrane Review for anxiety disorders in children and adolescents (James, Soler, & Weatherall, 2005) showed a remission rate of 56% for CBT versus 28% for different control conditions, and observed that individual, family, and group formats produced similar results (cf. Garcia-Lopez et al., 2006; Silverman, Pina, & Viswesvaran, 2008). Six recent studies tested CBGT for children and adolescents aged 8 to 16 years (Table 16.1). Most (5) were RCTs, although sample sizes were relatively small. All six studies indicated positive effects of the active treatment on primary (social anxiety) as well as secondary outcomes (depression, $n = 3$). Social anxiety was usually assessed with the Social Phobia and Anxiety Inventory or the Anxiety Disorders Interview Schedule for Children. There were positive effects of CBGT on social anxiety in a community-based setting (Baer & Garland, 2005) and in non-English–speaking countries (Joormann & Unnewehr, 2002). One study supported the equivalence of the individual and the group formats (Liber et al., 2008).

In summary, although there is increasing evidence supporting CBGT as an efficacious treatment for social phobia, not all patients benefit. One study examined whether the active ingredients of CBT were responsible for improvement: Rapee, Abbot, Baillie, and Gaton (2007) showed that self-help groups were more effective in reducing social phobia symptoms than wait lists and that self-help groups augmented with minimal therapist assistance produced gains similar to CBGT. This does not nullify the effects of the high-quality CBGT but encourages future research to explore mechanisms of change.

The past decade of research has put group treatment of social phobia on an even stronger foundation—particularly CBGT. It must be said that for many patients this has not proved to be sufficient. Recent studies have attempted to refine and supplement this already effective treatment by augmenting it with other interventions (e.g., acceptance and commitment therapy), by transferring it from laboratory to naturalistic settings and extending it to adolescents with both remedial and prevention goals. Moreover, there is some evidence for the additive value of several interventions (e.g., exposure, social skills training, self-help groups, and relaxation training). Research is still needed regarding alternative approaches for patients who do not benefit from CBGT. Knijnik, Kapczinski, Chachamovich, Margis, and Eizirik (2004) have systematically tested a manualized psychodynamic approach that may prove useful. The handful of studies with adolescents is promising but more comparisons would clarify potential preventive and economic value.

Panic Disorder

In 2004, we noted CBGT as the dominant model for treating panic disorder and of the 13 new studies included (Table 16.1), all used CBGT (Burlingame et al., 2004). Approximately 40% were RCTs with the average patient being a female of 30 to 40 years of age who had suffered for 6 to 15 years with panic disorder and a comorbid anxiety or depressive disorder. The typical study had between 20 and 50 subjects; general anxiety and panic symptoms were the primary outcomes, depression, and general functioning served as secondary effects. The Mobility Inventory for Agoraphobia and the Beck Anxiety Inventory were the most frequently used measures (5 and 4 studies, respectively) with the dominant models being Barlow and colleagues' panic control treatment and Clark's cognitive therapy (Barlow, Craske, Cerny, & Klosko, 1989; Clark, 1986). Most patients were on medication (SSRI and tricyclic), which, when combined with CBGT, has been shown to produce the greatest and most durable changes (Roy-Byrne, Craske, & Stein, 2006). The primary focus across studies was the clinical application and refinement of CBGT.

The largest group of studies focused on naturalistic open trials, testing the feasibility and effectiveness of transferring CBGT protocols from RCTs into clinical practice (Austin, Sumbundu, Lykke & Oestrich, 2008; Galassi, Quercioli, Charismas, Niccolai, & Barciulli 2007;

Oei & Boschen, 2009; Rosenberg & Hougaard, 2005; Rufer et al., 2010); all tended to have weak methodologies and pre- to posteffect sizes were smaller compared to previous RCTs (.12 – .69). Oei and Boschen's (2009) large retrospective study of routine clinical practice in Australia is noteworthy for its sample size ($n = 396$); the study demonstrated variability of outcome by domain in pre–post comparisons with general anxiety posting higher gains ($d = .64$) than panic or depression ($d = .32 – .55$ and $d = .12 – .69$, respectively).

A second group of studies investigated how change takes place in CBGT. In an RCT, Bohni, Spindler, Arendt, Hougaard, and Rosenberg (2009) tested for differential improvement when a 12-session CBGT group was offered weekly over 12 weeks or in a massed 3-week protocol (4-hour daily sessions in Week 1, two 2-hour sessions in Week 2, one 2-hour session in Week 3). Both posted equivalent results with moderate to large pre–post effects ($d = .67 – 1.47$). Clerkin, Teachman, and Smith-Janik (2008) studied sudden gains in CBGT, noting that those occurring in Session 2 or after (20% of members) were associated with better improvement by termination; this agrees with sudden gains in individual CBT for panic disorder (Tang, DeRubeis, Hollon, Amsterdam, & Shelton, 2007).

Obsessive-Compulsive Disorder (OCD)

In 2004 (Burlingame et al., 2004) we noted exposure and response prevention (ERP) as the dominant treatment but expressed caution since it was supported by only a single RCT (Fals-Stewart, Marks, & Schafer, 1993). The past decade produced six RCTs and four pre-post studies (Table 16.1); the Yale-Brown Obsessive Compulsive Scale (YBOCS) continues to be the primary outcome scale, making direct effect size comparisons possible; secondary outcomes include depression, anxiety, general functioning and QoL. CBT protocols that include ERP emerged and reflect the majority of protocols tested. The average patient was in his or her late 30s, suffering from chronic OCD (average duration 17 years) with high co-morbidity (anxiety and depressive disorders), treated in a group lasting an average of 12 sessions (range = 7–20).

With one exception (Himle et al., 2001), most *pre-post studies* involved small samples (Table 16.1). Pre-post effect sizes reflecting improvement on the YBOCS vary between 0.91 (Fenger, Mortensen, Rasmussen, & Lau, 2007) and 1.74 (Cordioli et al., 2002); changes in anxiety and depression measures were moderate. A low withdrawal rate (6%, Cordioli et al., 2002) suggests high acceptance of CGBT. In the study by Braga, Cordioli, Niederauer, and Manfro (2005), 35% of the sample relapsed at the 1-year follow-up. The strongest predictors for not relapsing were rapid improvement and full remission (YBOCS < 9) by the end of treatment; onset age, comorbidity, initial symptom severity, and intensity of obsessions were unrelated to relapse. In a Danish study of CBGT effectiveness (Fenger et al., 2007), a pregroup session to develop individualized treatment goals was added. Smaller effect sizes were explained by higher levels of comorbidity. In a German study (Meier, Fricke, Moritz, Hand, & Rufer, 2006), it was noted that comorbid dependent personality disorder was a risk factor for worse outcome. The largest open trial (Himle et al., 2001) experimentally contrasted the dose (7– versus 12-session) of an earlier group ERP model (Krone, Himle, & Nesse, 1991). No differences on the YBOCS or depression measures were found, and they surmised that 12-week patients simply paced themselves slower than 7-week patients.

The past decade also saw a number of *comparative studies*. Two teams (Anderson & Rees, 2007; Jaurrieta, Jiminez-Murcia, Alonso, et al., 2008; Jaurrieta, Jiminez-Murcia, Murchón, et al., 2008) tested the differential efficacy of group (G) versus individual (I) formats, replicating the equivalence finding of Fals-Stewart et al. (1993). CBGT was also compared to wait-list control, ERP and medication. Cordioli et al. (2003) reported similar gains on the YBOCS as Anderson and Rees (2007) for a 12-session CBGT ($ES = 1.3$). Modest improvement was found for quality of life but none found for anxiety. McLean, Whittal, Thordarson, and Taylor (2001) examined the differential efficacy of ERP against a contemporary CBGT protocol. Both ERP and CBGT outperformed the wait-list control on the YBOCS ($ES = 1.6$ versus 1.0, respectively) and when differences in medication use were controlled, ERP proved superior to CBGT. Surprisingly, both active treatments posted equivalent improvement on only one of three cognitive measures, suggesting ERP and CBGT produced identical cognitive gains; a 2-year follow-up supported these findings (Whittal, Robichaud, Thordarson, & McLean, 2008). Aigner, Demal, Zitterl, Bach, and Lenz (2004), in a nonrandomized comparative study, examined the effectiveness of CBGT with and without medication (SSRI). Although both conditions caused improvement on the YBOCS, CBGT plus medication led to more improvement

than medication alone. Finally, Sousa, Isolan, Oliveira, Manfro, and Cordioli (2006) studied the differential gains for a 12-session CBGT and sertraline. Both CBGT and sertraline posted reliable pre–postimprovement on YBOCS ($ES = 1.6$ and 1.2, respectively), anxiety, depression, general functioning, and QoL measures. When complete remission was used as the outcome criterion, CBGT was more effective and demonstrated greater gains in clinician-rated general functioning.

The comparative RCT of Fineberg, Hughes, Gale, and Roberts (2005) tested if CBGT effects could be attributed to the active ingredients or the nonspecific effects of participating in a group. Following Fals-Stewart et al. (1993), they used a relaxation therapy (RT) as a placebo attention condition to compare the effects of treatment on OCD symptoms, depression, anxiety, adjustment, and general functioning measures. CBGT interventions were contrasted with progressive muscle relaxation, imagery, meditation, reflexology, aromatherapy, and breathing interventions in the RT group. No differences were found on any outcome measure or in attitudes toward treatment although there was a higher dropout rate for RT; patients with a more recent history of OCD responded better to CBGT.

There is now ample evidence for the efficacy of ERP and CBGT when compared to waitlist control—a different conclusion from our last review. Indeed, a recent meta-analysis of 13 studies (Jonsson & Hougaard, 2008) produced an average effect size of 1.1 on the YBOCS for both treatments when compared to wait-list controls. Interestingly, a few investigators have argued for *group ERP* and *individual CBT* (McLean et al., 2001; Whittal et al., 2008) although the collective evidence does not support a differential preference. The findings of the single placebo attention group study, while intriguing, have been criticized for a high differential dropout (Jonsson & Hougaard, 2008). Similarly, the paucity of comparisons with medications makes conclusions about differential effects impossible to draw at this time. Nearly every study noted the power of group dynamics in increasing attendance and involvement relative to alternate treatments (but without offering a specific estimate of this effect), and they also highlighted the economic advantage of group treatments.

Eating Disorders (EDs)

Research on group therapy for EDs has burgeoned since our last review, especially regarding binge-eating disorder (BED) (Table 16.1). We previously concluded that there was strong evidence for the effectiveness of CBGT for *bulimia nervosa* (BN). Recent studies have reinforced this conclusion, addressed mechanisms of change, and expanded treatment to areas of patient functioning beyond ED. Despite a high rate of dropout, CBGT had consistent effects on BN symptoms and frequency of bingeing and purging (BAP) in intent-to-treat analyses. Three pre-post studies examined refinements of CBGT (Leung, Waller, & Thomas, 2000; Shapiro et al., 2010); one included controls (Peterson et al., 2004). Refinements included variations of session frequency or contracting for abstinence from purging (Peterson et al. 2004; found no effects for either), and the use of nightly text messaging as a means of monitoring BAP (Shapiro et al. 2010, report positive effects). These studies offered initial tests of key principles of CBT theory, that is, the association of core beliefs, attitudinal distortions, or behavioral monitoring to recovery from BN.

Three comparative studies, all employing RCT designs, ITT analyses, and follow-up, tested for differential efficacy by comparing CBGT with guided self-help (Bailer et al., 2004), individual therapy (Chen et al., 2003), or with fluoxetine or combined treatment (Jacobi, Dahme, & Dittmann, 2002). Equivalence across conditions was the rule regardless of post-treatment outcome measure. However, Bailer et al. (2004) observed higher remission rates for CBGT at 1-year follow-up, Chen et al. (2003) recorded larger effects for group therapy on impulsivity and state anxiety by 3- and 6-month follow-up, and Jacobi et al. (2002) found that CBGT alone resulted in greater abstinence than combined treatment at post-treatment and follow-up. These studies provide evidence for maintenance of benefits from CBGT for BN.

Three studies examined the effectiveness of CBGT incorporating elements of psychodynamic and psycho-educational models (Bogh, Hagedorn, Rokkedal, & Valbak, 2005) or interpersonal therapy (IPT; Nevonen & Broberg, 2006; Openshaw, Waller, & Sperlinger, 2004). Dropout rates were low (~12%), perhaps due to a more relational focus in group sessions. Effects were evident on ED and general symptoms, with rates of remission/recovery ranging between 21% and 58%. Bogh et al. (2005) noted that early reductions in BN behaviors were predictive of better outcome. Openshaw et al. (2004) reported

reliable change of 28% to 45% on ED symptoms and depression but lower rates of recovery from BN and no effect for anxiety. The effectiveness of integrated group treatments for BN appears promising; more controlled and comparative trials are needed.

Most research focused on BED with CBGT as the dominant model. These studies demonstrated strong rigor, with RCT designs, ITT analyses, follow-up, and attention to power and clinical significance. Thirteen studies compared CBGT against alternative approaches and with related conditions (e.g., subclinical BED, body dissatisfaction and disordered eating). Dropout rates varied considerably around an average of 20% and did not differ between treatments. Alternative modes of delivery such as video (Peterson et al., 2001), CD-ROM (Shapiro et al., 2007), or the Internet (Gollings & Paxton, 2006; Paxton, McLean, Gollings, Faulkner, & Wertheim, 2007) proved equivalent to CBGT with both outperforming controls, though Paxton et al. (2007) noted larger effects for group on ED-related attitudes, depression, and self-esteem. Gorin, Le Grange, and Stone (2003) found no additional benefit when spouses were involved in group sessions. Three studies examined CBGT versus a behavioral weight control group (Munsch et al., 2007; Nauta, Hospers, & Jansen, 2001; Nauta, Hospers, Kok, & Jansen, 2000); consistently, the latter was more effective for weight loss but the former had larger, more comprehensive effects on ED symptoms and behaviors. Finally, four studies compared CBGT against IPT (Wilfley et al., 2002), psychodynamic (Tasca, Balfour, Ritchie, & Bassada, 2007; Tasca, Ritchie, et al., 2006), or nondirective groups (Kenardy, Mensch, Bowen, Green & Walton, 2002). Equivalent effects on BE behaviors, BED-specific and general symptoms, self-esteem and social functioning were common findings. Kenardy et al. (2002) reported greater effects for CBGT on BE at 3-month follow-up; patients in the "nonprescriptive" group had shown relapse. Tasca, Ritchie, et al. (2006) reported mode-specific differential effects, with the dynamic-interpersonal group superior on depression and CBGT superior on attitudes and susceptibility to hunger.

Two studies reported positive effects for adaptations of CBGT (Ashton, Drerup, Windover, & Heinberg, 2009; Duchesne et al., 2007). Three studies addressed protocol refinements (Friederich et al., 2007; Schlup, Munsch,

Meyer, Margraf, & Wilhelm, 2009; Shelley-Ummenhofer & MacMillan, 2007), with clear findings, that is, twice-weekly sessions were less effective, and booster sessions were associated with continued improvement over follow-up. Further studies of modifications of CBGT for BED are expected and necessary before clinical recommendations become possible.

Group as Adjunct
Substance-Related Disorders

Burlingame et al. (2004) saw limited support for the effectiveness of group treatment with substance related disorders since formal change theories did *not* sufficiently explain variations in outcome. We located six studies testing the comparative efficacy of group treatments, three studies that compared group and individual formats, and seven studies concerning group treatments for adolescents (Table 16.2). Among the comparative studies, groups varied from very short (1 to 5 sessions, Tross et al., 2008) to relatively long interventions (26 sessions, Litt Kadden, Cooney, & Kabela, 2003). Almost all groups were closed with a few studies treating only males (Easton et al., 2007) or only females (Tross et al., 2008), but most had mixed gender with females in the minority (30% to 50%). The mean age of the participants varied between 38 and 45 years. The primary outcome was substance-related (i.e., substance use and related problems, abstinence, and urinalysis); secondary effects included mood, violent behavior, and HIV risk behavior (Table 16.2).

One study contrasted CBGT with interactional groups (Litt et al., 2003), yielding equivalence on abstinence rates and improved coping skills, and raising the question of specific versus nonspecific effects explaining outcomes. The other comparative studies tested *specific group programs for specific populations*. Weiss et al. (2007, 2009) contrasted an integrated group (IG) therapy for patients with dual diagnosis (bipolar disorder, substance abuse) with group counseling and reported a moderate advantage for IG on substance-use outcomes. Easton et al. (2007) conducted a RCT with CBGT designed for domestic-violence offenders. CBGT was superior to a 12-step group control only on substance use at the end of treatment but differences disappeared at follow-up. Similarly, a study comparing contingency management (CM) with a 12-step control in patients with HIV infection showed

early advantages for CM, which also disappeared at follow-up (Petry, Weinstock, Alessi, Lewis, & Dieckhaus, 2010). Although most protocols produced positive results compared to *no treatment*, effect sizes were small to moderate when specific group programs were compared to other control conditions ($d = 0.3-0.7$; e.g., Liddle, Rowe, Dakof, Henderson, & Greenbaum, 2009; Petry et al., 2010), supporting our previous conclusions.

As with social phobia, *group treatments for adolescent substance abuse* emerged as a promising intervention (Waldron & Turner, 2008). The typical adolescent study treated a high proportion of males (75% to 80%) with an average age of 15 years. Most had multiple substance abuse problems (illicit drugs, mainly marijuana), and less commonly alcohol dependency, alcohol/drug related problems, and/or behavioral problems/delinquency. Groups were primarily closed, ranged between 8 and 20 sessions (usually weekly), and tested a wide array of interventions including feedback and motivational interviewing (Smith, Hall, Williams, An, & Gotman, 2006), psychoeducation (Burleson & Kaminer, 2005), social learning (Battjes et al., 2004) and CBGT components (Dennis et al., 2004; Liddle et al., 2004, 2009). Some multimodal approaches embedded individual and/or family sessions into the program (Dennis et al., 2004; Smith et al., 2006).

Five studies compared family-based group interventions, with two showing advantages for a multidimensional family therapy compared to peer group treatment on primary outcomes of substance abuse, substance use problems, and delinquency (Liddle et al., 2004, 2009) and three finding few significant differences between approaches (Battjes et al., 2004; French et al., 2008; Smith et al., 2006). The only nonrandomized study of a group based on social learning theory reported positive effects on marijuana abuse, but not alcohol abuse and delinquency (Battjes et al., 2004).

Collectively, groups for substance abuse (and comorbid disorders) postmoderate positive effects for both adolescents and adults. There are minor differences in effectiveness between specific formal change theories and these often disappear over time. Accordingly, several studies explored factors that might explain additional variance. A family history of alcohol abuse, specific combinations of gender and ethnicity (e.g., female and non-Caucasian) and social anxiety appear to be hindering factors (Book, Thomas, Dempsey,

TABLE 16.2 Group as Adjunct Efficacy and Effectiveness Research

Study	Study Characteristics				Sample Characteristics				Effects Related to Different Outcome Criteria
	%RCT	%ITT	%Attr	Follow-Up	A	C	Range Average Age	% Females	
SUBSTANCE ABUSE									
Comparative studies with adult patients: Easton et al., 2007; Litt et al., 2003; Petry et al., 2010; Tross et al., 2008; Weiss et al., 2007, 2009	100	50	9–38	3–18m	31–247	30–262	38–35	0–100	Criteria of substance abuse (use, abstinence, urinalysis) (4), mood/coping (2), violent episodes (1), HIV risk behavior (1), unprotected sex occasion (1)
Studies comparing individual vs. group treatment: Panas et al., 2003; John et al., 2003; Sobell et al., 2009	67	0	11–21	12m	143–2471	144–3919	41	28–31	Criteria of substance abuse (2), treatment completion and goal achievement (1)
Group treatments for adolescent substance abuse: Battjes et al., 2004; Burleson and Kaminer, 2005; Dennis et al., 2004; French et al., 2008; Liddle et al., 2004, 2009; Smith et al., 2006	86	14	8–29	6–12m	35–194	30–58	13–16	24–79	Criteria of substance abuse (5), delinquency (1), internalized stress (1), reducing risks in family, peers (1), self-efficacy (1)

TRAUMA/PTSD

Amaro et al., 2007; Bradley and Follingstad, 2003; Chard, 2005; Classen et al., 2011; Cloitre and Koenen, 2001; Creamer et al., 2002; Donovan et al., 2001; Dorrepal et al., 2010; Falsetti et al., 2001; Gatz et al., 2007; Ginzburg et al., 2009; Gorey, Richter, and Snider, 2001; Hébert and Bergeron, 2007; Kibler and Lyons, 2008; Kreidler, 2005; Lau and Kristensen, 2007; Layne et al., 2001; Lundqvist et al., 2009; Lundqvist and Öjehagen, 2001; Lundqvist et al., 2006; Möller and Steel, 2002; Morrison and Treliving, 2002; Mueser et al., 2007; Rieckert and Möller, 2000; Ruzek et al., 2001; Ryan et al., 2005; Saltzman et al., 2001; Schnurr et al., 2003; Sharpe et al., 2001; Sikkema et al., 2004, 2007, 2008; Spiegel et al., 2004; Toussaint et al., 2007; Vaa et al., 2002; Wallis, 2002; Westwood et al., 2010; Zlotnick et al., 2003	32	29	0–41	2–60m	12–181	11–177	12–55	0–100	Trauma symptoms (21), depression (16), general psychiatric symptoms (13), PTSD diagnosis (6), self-esteem (6), anger (5), anxiety (5), coping/avoidance (5), guilt (4), assertiveness (3), social function (3), alcohol/drug severity (2), HIV risk behavior (2), grief (2), GPA (2)

Randall, & Randall, 2009; LaBrie, Feres, Kenney, & Lac, 2009; McNeese-Smith et al., 2009), while higher motivation (Litt et al., 2003), social reinforcement (Lash, Burden, Monteleone, & Lehmann, 2004), music therapy (Dingle, Gleadhill, & Baker, 2008), PTSD symptom reduction (Hien et al., 2010), and contingency management (Ledgerwood, Alessi, Hanson, Godley, & Petry, 2008) enhance adherence and outcome.

Trauma-Related Disorders

Interest in group treatment of trauma has flourished since our last review. Studies usually highlighted one of four approaches, that is, support/process-oriented, psychodynamic, CBGT, or more recent *integrated* models (e.g., Gatz et al., 2007), and varied in methodological rigor. Three themes are evident in this literature. First, it is now accepted that trauma experience covaries with substance use and other activities, which increase HIV risk, encouraging the incorporation of a trauma focus into rehabilitation and prevention programs. Second, the importance of a clear group structure in trauma treatment has been acknowledged. Third, a distinction between "trauma-focused" and "present-focused" groups has been raised by psychodynamic (Spiegel, Classen, Thurston, & Butler, 2004) and CBT practitioners (Schnurr et al., 2003) alike. "Trauma-focused" groups are concerned with the past trauma itself while "present-focused" groups are concerned with present circumstances and residual consequences. Apart from minor differential effects, the primary finding in comparative studies has been equivalence. It remains unclear if this distinction is important, that is, whether different patients or trauma experiences necessarily imply the use of a "trauma-focused" or "present-focused" group approach.

Support/process groups were evaluated in three uncontrolled studies involving female patients, but with minimal assessment of trauma symptoms. These groups recorded few dropouts (< 16%). Effects on depression and other symptoms, guilt feelings, and self-esteem were observed, but more consistent evaluations of outcome are needed. Comorbidity with eating disorders limited the effect of a problem-solving support group (Harper, Richter, & Gorey, 2009). A large uncontrolled study involved the Center for Victims of Torture (CVT) of Minneapolis offering 10-week support/process groups to 4,000 Sierra Leonean refugees in Guyanese camps. Leaders were native paraprofessionals trained by the CVT team. Benefits on PTSD symptoms, social support, and daily functioning were seen at follow-up 1, 3, 6, and 12 months after intake (Stepakoff et al., 2006).

Psychodynamic groups were often used to treat female survivors of child sexual abuse (CSA), and less often for male survivors (Morrison & Treliving, 2002; Sharpe, Selley, Low, & Hall, 2001). Three studies involved RCTs (Ginzburg et al., 2009; Lau & Kristensen, 2007; Spiegel et al., 2004). Most groups were of moderate length (24 to 36 sessions), but 1- (Lau & Kristensen, 2007) and 2-year models (Lundqvist et al., 2006; 2009; Lundqvist & Öjehagen, 2001) appeared. Effects on general psychiatric and trauma-specific symptoms, social functioning, and assertiveness were reported. Follow-up evaluations occurred in 40% of studies; maintenance of post-therapy gains was not always evident (Sharpe et al., 2001). Cloitre and Koenen (2001) reported benefits for a 12-week interpersonal-dynamic group but noted that groups having even a single member diagnosed with borderline personality disorder had poorer outcomes. Kreidler (2005) evaluated a 50-session dynamic group for survivors with or without chronic mental illness (CMI); all patients showed improvement on trauma symptoms, distress, and depression, but most CMI patients remained in the dysfunctional range. Lau and Kristensen (2007) reported positive effects for survivors in either a 12-month analytic group or a 5-month systemic group (solution-focused, with psychoeducation); effect sizes on global and social functioning, distress, and quality of life were larger for the more structured, briefer group. Finally, no differential effects were observed when dynamically oriented "trauma-focused" and "present-focused" groups were compared (Ginzburg et al., 2009; Spiegel et al., 2004), and both outperformed wait-list controls.

The majority of studies featured CBGT. A trauma-focus was often paired with cognitive restructuring (e.g., Classen et al., 2011) but not consistently (e.g., Ruzek et al., 2001); the latter study reported no effects of treatment, suggesting trauma-focused groups are insufficient without a cognitive component. Skills training was standard in present-focused groups. Both approaches used 10 to 20 session formats and often incorporated psychoeducation and attention to group process. Methodological rigor was high with some studies being state-of-the-art (Classen et al., 2011; Schnurr et al., 2003). Target populations were heterogeneous (female CSA survivors, e.g.,

Classen et al., 2011; male veterans with chronic PTSD, e.g., Kibler & Lyons, 2008). Studies provided strong evidence for effectiveness on trauma symptoms, depression and remission of PTSD (e.g., Chard, 2005). Secondary outcomes (anger, dissociation, anxiety, guilt) also improved. CBGT lowered HIV-related risk behavior with a "present-focused" (Classen et al., 2011) being more effective than a trauma-focused (Sikkema et al., 2008) group approach.

Integrated treatments for co-occurring trauma and substance abuse (SA) melded CBT skills-training, psychoeducation, psychodynamic, and interpersonal-process group techniques, often within residential or day treatment programs. Research included multisite studies (Women, Co-occurring Disorders and Violence Study; Giard et al., 2005) and evaluations of mental health systems-level effects (Morrissey et al., 2005). The Seeking Safety (Najavits, Weiss, Shaw, & Muenz, 1998) and Trauma Recovery and Empowerment (TREM; Harris, 1998) programs were evaluated for women with a history of trauma and SA (Amaro et al., 2007; Gatz et al., 2007; Toussaint, VanDeMark, Bornemann, & Graeber, 2007; Zlotnick, Najavits, Rohsenow, & Johnson, 2003), while the Transcend program (Donovan, Padin-Rivera, & Kowaliw, 2001) was evaluated for male veterans with co-occurring PTSD and SA. All programs impacted positively on trauma symptoms or the PTSD diagnosis (Toussaint et al., 2007). However, three studies observed no incremental effects for SA severity relative to TAU (Amaro et al., 2007; Gatz et al., 2007; Toussaint et al., 2007), though Amaro et al. (2007) reported greater abstinence at 6- and 12-month follow-up. Two studies also reported long-term effects for SA (Zlotnick et al., 2003; Donovan et al., 2001). Finally, two comparative studies (Creamer, Forbes, Biddle, & Elliott, 2002; Ryan, Nitsun, Gilbert, & Mason, 2005) and two effectiveness studies (Vaa, Enger, & Sexton, 2002; Westwood, McLean, Cave, Borgen, Slakov, 2010) showed promising results when CBT and psychodynamic techniques were combined. Integrated models show definite promise for the treatment of trauma and related conditions.

Groups Within Medical Settings
Breast Cancer

In 2004, we concluded that a variety of group treatments had small to moderate effects for cancer patients on anxiety, depression and psychological distress, and that phase of disease was a critical consideration (Burlingame et al., 2004). We noted smaller effects for educational interventions, mixed effects on survival and a link between therapist experience and improvement. Twenty-three studies were located testing breast cancer treatments for different phases of the illness (Table 16.3).

Eight of nine studies employed a RCT design using an inert control group to test the efficacy of *supportive expressive group therapy* (SEGT) that typically consisted of 6 to 10 women participating in 90-minute weekly sessions for at least 1 year. The format was slow open (e.g., members added as space becomes available) with a supportive environment to confront problems, express emotions, strengthen relationships and find life meaning. The inert control primarily (88%) involved a self-directed educational intervention that included access to various media regarding relaxation and nutrition. SEGT attrition ranged from 8% to 38% and few studies (4) tested power a priori (range .89–.99). ITT analysis was used by half, with five primary effects: distress, quality of life, survival, coping, and pain.

Psychological distress, assessed most frequently (4) by the Profile of Mood States (POMS; McNair, Lorr, & Droppleman, 1992), was improved in four studies (Bordelau et al., 2003; Goodwin et al., 2001; Kissane et al., 2007; O'Brien, Harris, King, & O'Brien, 2008). Classen et al. (2001) noted a marked increase in POMS distress shortly before death, when these individuals were excluded, SEGT showed more improvement than controls. The sole *primary breast cancer* study (Classen et al., 2008) used an abbreviated SEGT protocol (12 weeks) and found no differences suggesting that it may be ineffective, too short, or that primary breast cancer women are insufficiently distressed for treatment to have an effect.

Mixed findings resulted on the same QoL measure (EORTC QoL C-30) with Kissane et al. (2007) reporting an increased QoL for SEGT and Bordelau et al. (2003) finding no effect. Two studies (Giese-Davis et al., 2002; Kissane et al., 2007) supported SEGT's effect on adjustment to cancer on distinct measures, while Classen et al. (2008) failed to find an effect with primary breast cancer patients. SEGT's effect on QoL is unclear but there are three studies treating metastatic patients supporting SEGT's effect on adjustment to the disease. Three new studies tested the *survival* advantage of SEGT (Goodwin et al., 2001; Kissane et al., 2007; Spiegel et al., 2007) and the collective results from 514 women is that there is

TABLE 16.3 Efficacy and Effectiveness Research for Groups With Medical, Hospital, and Seriously Mentally Ill Patients

Study	Study Characteristics				Sample Characteristics				Effects Related to Different Outcome Criteria
	%RCT	%ITT	%Attr	Follow-Up	A	C	Range Average Age	% Females	
BREAST CANCER									
Supportive-expressive group therapy									
Bordeleau et al. 2003; Butler et al., 2009; Classen et al., 2001, 2008; Giese-Davis et al. 2002; Goodwin et al., 2001; Kissane et al., 2007; O'Brien et al., 2008; Spiegel et al., 2007	89	44	8–24	12–24m	56–178	41–179	48–54	100	Distress (6), quality of life (4), survival (4), coping (5), pain (4)
Cognitive-behavior therapy									
Antoni et al., 2006; Cohen and Fried, 2007; Dolbeault et al., 2009; Hunter et al., 2009	75	50	15–29	2–9m	17–102	37–107	50–56	100	Distress (4), quality of life (2), coping (2), physical (1)
Psychoeducational groups									
Fukui et al., 2000; Heiney et al., 2003; Helgeson et al., 2001; Hosaka et al., 2001; Sherman, et al., 2010	60	20	3–32	2–6m	25–116	25–77	53–54	100	Distress (4), quality of life (3), social support (1) physical (1)
Related studies									
Andersen et al., 2004; Bultz et al., 2000; Kissane et al., 2003; Lane and Viney 2005; Manne et al., 2005, 2007	83	??	0–35	3–12m	15–154	19–149	46–51	100	Distress (5), family functioning (3) support (2) coping/adjustment (2), physical (1)

656

PERSONALITY DISORDERS

Outpatient

Reference								Outcomes
Ben-Porath et al., 2004; Blum et al., 2002, 2008; Bos et al., 2010, 2011; Farrell et al., 2009; Gratz and Gunderson, 2006; Harned et al., 2008; Harvey et al., 2010; Huband et al., 2007; Kliem et al., 2010; Koons et al., 2001; Linehan et al., 2002, 2006; McMain et al., 2009; McQuillan et al., 2005; Turner, 2000; van den Bosch et al., 2002; Verheul et al., 2003	78	0–39	4–12m	10–90	10–90	22–37	51–100	Suicide ideation/attempts (6), self-harm (6), general psychiatric symptoms (4), depression (4), negative affect/emotion regulation (4), global function (3), quality of life (2), hopelessness (2), admissions (2), drug use (2)

Day Treatment

Reference								Outcomes
Bateman and Fonagy, 2001, 2003, 2008; Davies and Campling, 2003; Hulbert and Thomas, 2007; Karterud et al., 2003; Petersen et al., 2008; Reisch et al., 2001; Warren et al., 2004	33	16–38	3–96m	22–1244	19–60	27–49	47–100	Suicide attempts (4), self-harm (4), general psychiatric symptoms (3), depression (2), social function (2), hospital admissions (2), quality of life (2), medication usage (2)

Inpatient

Reference								Outcomes
Chiesa and Fonagy, 2000, 2003; Chiesa et al., 2003, 2004, 2006	0	47–58	6–72m	40–47	49	32–35	65–79	Social function (5), global function (5), general psychiatric symptoms (4), clinical indicators (4)

(continued)

TABLE 16.3 Efficacy and Effectiveness Research for Groups With Medical, Hospital, and Seriously Mentally Ill Patients

Study	Study Characteristics				Sample Characteristics				Effects Related to Different Outcome Criteria
	%RCT	%ITT	%Attr	Follow-Up	A	C	Range Average Age	% Females	

SCHIZOPHRENIA

Cognitive-behavioral group therapy (CBGT):
Barrowclough et al., 2006; Bechdolf et al., 2005, 2010; Borras et al. 2009; Granholm et al., 2006, 2007, 2008, 2009; Halperin et al., 2000; Kingsep et al., 2003; Klingberg et al., 2010; Knight et al., 2006; McCay et al., 2006; Patterson et al., 2006; Roberts et al., 2010

%RCT 80; %ITT 40; %Attr 3–51; Follow-Up 0–12m; A 7–124; C 20–116; Range Average Age 26–41; % Females 19–54

Effects Related to Different Outcome Criteria: Psychopathological symptoms/patient functioning (6), self-esteem (3), social anxiety (2), service utilization (2), social/living skills (3), QoL (3), neuropsychological functioning (1), social cognition (1)

Psychoeducation:
Bäuml et al., 2007; Burlingame et al., 2007; Chien & Wong 2007; Haller et al., 2009

%RCT 50; %ITT 25; %Attr 8–53; Follow-Up 0–84m; A 24–44; C 24–28; Range Average Age 31–43; % Females 30–66

Effects Related to Different Outcome Criteria: Psychopathological symptoms/patient functioning (3), service utilization (2), family burden/functioning (1), QoL (1)

Multifamily groups (MFG):
Chien and Chan, 2004; Dyck et al., 2002; Hazel et al., 2004; McDonell et al., 2003, 2006

%RCT 100; %ITT 60; %Attr 2–25; Follow-Up 0–12m; A 32–55; C 31–51; Range Average Age 32–38; % Females 22–41

Effects Related to Different Outcome Criteria: Service utilization (3), family burden/functioning (2), psychopathological symptoms/patient functioning (1)

CBCBGT = Cognitive Behavioral Group Therapy, MFG = Multifamily Group, PEG = Psychoeducational Group, SEGT = Supportive Expressive Group Treatment *no* evidence for this effect. The research team that replicated Spiegel, Kraemer, Bloom, and Gottheil's (1989) survival effect (Fawzy et al., 1993) used a shorter intervention with a different cancer population, and survival benefits were not maintained at 10-year follow-up (Fawzy, Canada, & Fawzy, 2003). In short, SEGT does *not* improve survival and there are alternative explanations for past findings to explain the discrepancies (Coyne, Hanisch, & Palmer, 2007).

A woman's *coping with her illness* (measured with the Impact of Event Scale; IES; or the POMS) is enhanced by SEGT (Classen et al., 2001; Giese-Davis et al., 2002; Kissane et al., 2007; O'Brien, et al., 2008). There were, however, no effects on the IES with primary breast cancer patients (Classen et al., 2008). Three studies addressed effects of SEGT on *pain management*. Although all patients in Goodwin et al.'s (2001) study reported pain worsening as cancer progressed, SEGT patients reported *less* worsening than controls. Butler and colleagues (2009) found a similar effect (only when they eliminated assessments proximal to death), no effect was found with primary breast cancer patients (Classen et al., 2008). SEGT's small effect on pain requires one to think in terms of *less* worsening rather than absolute reductions.

Three rigorous studies tested *CBGT* with early stage (I–II) breast cancer women between 50 and 56 years of age, participating in a closed group lasting 6 to 10 sessions. The unanimity of findings across eight self- and rater-completed measures supports CBGT's efficacy in reducing psychological distress. There were mixed effects on QoL (Cohen & Fried, 2007; Dolbeault et al., 2009), but improved coping and reduced stress (Antoni et al., 2006; Cohen & Fried, 2007).

Five studies tested *psychoeducational groups* (PEG) with four using a model originating with F. Fawzy and Fawzy (1994) with several modifications (e.g., PEG provided via telephone conference call, Heiney et al., 2003). All but two (Hosaka et al., 2001, and Sherman, Heard, & Cavanagh, 2010) used a RCT design, with attrition ranging from 8% to 32%. A closed format (six to eight sessions) was used for women, age 26 to 65, with early breast cancer. Primary effects included distress, QoL, and social support. Uniform results across studies were shown for psychological distress (Fukui et al., 2000; Heiney et al., 2003; Hosaka et al. 2001). Helgeson, Cohen, Shulz, and Yasko's study (2001) is noteworthy because peer support groups facilitated by poorly trained leaders led to suboptimal effects. Fukui et al. (2000) found no effects for depression and anxiety but reported improvement on two QoL measures, as did Heiney et al. (2003) and Sherman et al. (2010). The uniform findings on psychological distress suggests PEG's efficacy on this variable. There is promising but less definitive support for improvement in QoL.

Eight *related studies* extend the above findings. Andersen and colleagues (2004) conducted a RCT for early breast cancer with a two-phase 26-session group intervention. The 4-month intensive phase includes 18 weekly sessions focusing on psychosocial interventions (relaxation, coping, social support) and health strategies (diet, exercise, adherence); the maintenance phase involved monthly sessions. The intensive phase led to reduced distress, improved immune functioning, better coping and health behavior, and reduced risk of disease recurrence and death (Andersen et al., 2007, 2008). Two explanations for improvement were offered: (1) those with the greatest reduction in distress and physical symptoms practiced relaxation more frequently, highlighting the link between daily stress and health, and (2) higher levels of group cohesion were related to change on psychological, behavioral, and physical health measures. Kissane et al.'s (2003) 20-session cognitive-existential group for early stage breast cancer reduced anxiety and improved family functioning; experienced psychologists emerged as more effective leaders. Lane and Viney's (2005) eight-session personal construct group with a similar population resulted in greater improvement on anxiety, death anxiety, depression, and hope measures. Two teams (Bultz, Speca, Brasher, Geggie & Page, 2003; Manne et al., 2005) studied PEGS for partners of breast cancer patients and showed improvement on psychological distress, depression, well-being, and marital satisfaction.

The results from all 23 studies (Table 16.3) did not vary by analysis and compared to our last review, studies were more rigorous, better powered, and produced more conclusive findings. The most reliable effect for SEGT, CBT, and PEG was improved emotional distress; what is less clear are the conditions when this effect is *not* realized, although it may be related to the patient's initial level of distress. Both SEGT and CBT produced reliable increases in coping with the illness, which was not seen in PEG. SEGT groups may have an edge in improving life adjustment, although it is more costly. Finally, there is virtually no support for the conclusion that these group treatments extend life.

Promising developments include the moderator analysis by Manne et al. (2005) who showed greater benefit on depression for women with greater impairment and unsupportive partners. There was a single study (Antoni et al., 2006) that experimentally separated the effect of information from group effects finding group produced more improvement on psychological distress ($d = .33$ to .74) and coping ($d = .55$) than information dissemination alone. Kissane et al.'s (2003) link between experience and outcomes underscores our previous conclusion and the protocol modifications based on culture are a promising step toward accommodating diversity (e.g., Dolbeault et al., 2009; Fukui, et al., 2000; Hosaka et al., 2001). Finally, several studies (e.g., Bulz et al., 2000; Heiney et al., 2003; Lane & Viney, 2005) noted group processes as an important component, but the size of effect associated with these processes is unknown.

Pain and Somatoform Disorders

Systematic reviews summarizing behavioral treatment for chronic pain concluded that study methodology was poor (only 25% of studies reached a threshold for high quality, e.g., van Tulder et al., 2001). In contrast to individual psychotherapy (mostly CBT), research on group treatment in this area is limited but shows potential.

RCTs dealing with irritable bowel syndrome all indicate that CBGT is effective in reducing pain and psychological symptoms, as well as increasing quality of life (Blanchard et al., 2006). CBGT is provided to patients with heterogeneous chronic pain symptoms (e.g., White, Beecham, & Kirkwood, 2008) or specific pain (e.g., myofascial, Bogart et al., 2007; low-back, Lamb et al., 2010) with positive effects on pain intensity, functional impairment, depression and anxiety. CBGT in primary care also appears to be cost-effective (Lamb et al., 2010). On the other hand, a recent meta-analysis on CBT techniques for distress and pain in cancer patients concluded that individual was more effective than group treatment, both for pain ($d = .61$ versus $d = .20$) and distress ($d = .48$ versus $d = -.06$). As innovative manualized group treatments for pain emerge (e.g., Nickel, Ademmer, Egle, 2010), we expect an increase of studies in the future.

Inpatient Groups

In European health care systems, group therapy has always been a primary treatment for psychotherapy inpatients. Groups are usually delivered to mixed populations comprising affective, anxiety, eating and personality disorders. The only systematic summary available in our last review was a meta-analysis by Burlingame, Fuhriman, and Mosier (2003), concluding that outpatient group ($ES = 0.55$) outperformed inpatient group therapy ($ES = 0.20$) when both were compared to waitlist controls. One limitation of this conclusion was that it rested on only 6 inpatient studies.

In a more recent meta-analysis, Kösters, Burlingame, Nachtigall, and Strauss (2006) estimated the effectiveness of inpatient group therapy based on 24 controlled and 46 effectiveness studies published between 1980 and 2005. Beneficial effects for inpatient group emerged in controlled studies ($d = 0.31$) as well as effectiveness studies ($d = 0.59$). Greater improvement was exhibited in patients with affective and anxiety disorders compared to samples of mixed, psychosomatic, PTSD or schizophrenic disorders.

We did not locate any RCTs that were not included in the Kösters et al. (2006) meta-analytic review. Instead, effectiveness studies suggested that greater attendance in inpatient group psychotherapy can improve inpatient outcomes (Page & Hooke, 2009) and that CBGT might be related to a reduction in readmissions as well as improvement in patients' personal and work satisfaction (Veltro et al., 2008). Other studies have focused on process-outcome questions (e.g., Dinger & Schauenburg, 2010), or on the influence of specific patient characteristics on outcome (e.g., attachment, Strauss et al., 2006; alexithymia, Spitzer, Siebel-Jürges, Barnow, Grabe, & Freyberger, 2005).

Groups for Severe Mental Illness
Schizophrenia

In 2004 (Burlingame et al., 2004) we described a large number of studies testing the efficacy of one of four models for group treatment of schizophrenia: social skills (SS), psychoeducation (PEG), cognitive-information processing and cognitive-behavioral therapy (CBGT), as well as multi-family groups (MFG). Over the past decade, 27 new studies either tested modifications to the above models or introduced innovative approaches (e.g., Motivational Group

Interventions, Beebe et al., 2010; Adventure- and Recreation-Based Group Intervention, e.g., Voruganti et al., 2006; Group Programs Teaching Metacognitive Strategies, Roncone et al., 2004).

Table 16.3 summarizes 24 studies testing differential effects of CBT approaches with a wide array of specific interventions (e.g., social skills training, cognitive therapy, functional adaptation skills-training and cognitive restructuring), along with PEG and MFG studies. Groups are typically closed with the number of sessions (8 to 45) and treatment duration (2 to 24 months) varying widely. Samples are heterogeneous on age and gender and consist predominantly of outpatient populations; inpatient studies are primarily from European settings (e.g., Klingberg et al., 2010).

There was a sizeable increase in CBGT studies (Lawrence, Bradshaw, & Mairs, 2006). In contrast to our previous review, where most studies used the UCLA-Social and Independent Living Skills program or integrated psychological therapy, recent CBGT studies were much more heterogeneous with regard to treatment components, target populations, and outcomes. The majority were RCTs comparing CBGT with standard care or other active treatments (e.g., psychoeducation, social-skills training). Psychopathological symptoms were assessed as primary or secondary outcomes in most (10) studies, but these did not always change following CBGT (e.g., Barrowclaugh et al., 2006; Bechdolf, Köhn, Knost, Pukrop, & Klosterkötter, 2005). Other effects included self-esteem (Barrowclough et al., 2006; Borras et al., 2009; Knight, Wykes, & Hayward, 2006), social anxiety (Halperin, Nathan, Drummond, & Castle 2000; Kingsep et al., 2003) and cognition and coping (McCay et al., 2006; Roberts, Penn, Labate, Margolis, & Sterne, 2010), functional adaptation and skills training (Granholm et al., 2007; Patterson et al., 2006), and quality of life (Bechdolf et al., 2010; Kingsep et al., 2003; Klingberg et al., 2010).

Granholm et al. (2006, 2007, 2008, 2009) describe a series of studies for older persons (> 50 years) with schizophrenia, showing positive results for social and living skills as well as neuropsychological functioning. One study (Klingberg et al., 2010) focused on relapse prevention and reduction of rehospitalizations using a complex CBGT program. CBGT successfully lengthened time-to-relapse compared to standard care but did not reduce rehospitalizations.

The four studies testing PEGs commonly used patient symptoms and/or functioning and parameters of service utilization (reduced rehospitalizations/total days in hospital) as primary outcomes in pre–poststudies or studies comparing PEG with standard care. Chien and Wong (2007) found that a PEG targeting family members reduced family burden and also improved patient functioning and reduced rehospitalization rates. Bäuml, Pitschel-Walz, Volz, Engel, and Kissling (2007) examined the 7-year follow-up outcomes for the Munich Psychosis Information Project Study and noted higher survival rates as well as lower rates of rehospitalization and hospital days for the PEG when compared to the control group. This study is noteworthy since recent evidence suggests a 25-year reduction in expected life span for this clinical population (Parks, Svendsen, Singer, & Foti, 2006). Similarly, Haller et al. (2009) found that PEGs decreased psychotic symptoms and improved QoL. Finally, Burlingame et al. (2007) found that intense training of nurses in running PEGs was unrelated to symptom improvement, failing to replicate earlier work (Burlingame, Fuhriman, Paul, & Ogles, 1989).

We previously concluded that *multi-family groups* (MFG) à la McFarlane, Link, Dushay, Marcial, and Crilly (1995) produced equivalent improvement in symptoms, social and vocational functioning as well as treatment compliance when compared to single family therapies. Consequently, MFG may be a more cost-efficient treatment with respect to primary outcomes and relapse rates, a vexing challenge with this population. Interestingly, the number of new MFG studies over the past decade decreased, with only five new studies found. All were RCTs comparing MFG with standard care (4) or PEG (1); results were mixed. Two (Dyck, Hendryx, Short, Voss, & McFarlane 2002; McDonell, Short, Berry, & Dyck, 2003, report a decrease in rehospitalizations with a third (McDonell, Short, Hazel, Berry, & Dyck, 2006) reporting a parallel increase in outpatient service which partially offset cost-efficiency. As per previous research, patients in MFG groups did not differ in symptom reduction with one exception (Chien & Chan, 2004). Thus, while MFG produced comparable symptom and functioning improvement, it appears to have an advantage for stress reduction, improved family functioning and reduced rates of rehospitalization (Hazel et al., 2004; McDonell, Short, Berry, & Dyck, 2003).

Group treatment for schizophrenia has good to excellent support. CBGT was dominant and shown to be effective across a wide range of outcomes. MFG and PE studies have decreased in number; the disappearance of traditional verbal therapies for schizophrenics continues (Burlingame et al., 2004).

Personality Disorders

Group interventions for patients diagnosed with personality disorders (PDs) was an active area of research since our last review. Studies consistently targeted Borderline PD (BPD) and central problems of the disorder: suicidality, parasuicidality, depression, hopelessness, and hospitalization. Studies at each *level of care* primarily tested the effectiveness of "treatment packages" comprising multiple interventions. The outpatient orientation is uniformly cognitive-behavioral (CBT); day treatment/residential and inpatient programs combined CBT and psychodynamic approaches.

Outpatient dialectical behavior therapy (DBT) received more attention than any other approach; studies were frequently RCTs. DBT uses a skills-training group (2.5 hours/week for the usual year of treatment) that complements twice-weekly individual therapy and telephone coaching to address emotion regulation, distress tolerance, and interpersonal behavior. A dismantling study did not find the group component effective when added to ongoing, non-DBT individual therapy (Koerner & Linehan, 2000), but a recent RCT found a DBT group alone more effective than a dynamic group on retention, psychiatric symptoms, lability, and anger (Soler et al., 2009). Further study is needed to establish if skills training can be effective on its own, and if the three DBT components function synergistically.

Two lines of evidence supported DBT's effectiveness with BPD. First, a RCT of DBT versus community treatment by experts (CTBE) offered a highly credible control that accounted for multiple therapist, treatment, and contextual factors (Linehan et al., 2006). Both DBT and CTBE had effects on depressive symptoms, but DBT also impacted suicide attempts, crisis or inpatient service use, and drop out. Second, a meta-analysis (Kliem, Kröger, & Kosfelder, 2010), four RCTs (Koons et al., 2001; McMain et al., 2009; Turner, 2000; Verheul et al., 2003), and two pre–poststudies (Ben-Porath, Peterson, & Smee, 2004; McQuillan et al., 2005) conducted by *independent* researchers also supported DBT's efficacy. Consistent effects on suicidal ideation, self-harm, or problematic

emotional states were demonstrated. The Kliem et al. (2010) meta-analysis highlighted effects on suicidal and self-harm behaviors but noted these are reduced when the comparison treatment is also BPD-specific. McMain et al. (2009) showed that DBT versus psychiatric management conducted in line with practice guidelines (American Psychological Association [APA], 2001) had equivalent effects for a majority of clinical outcomes. Verheul et al. (2003) observed that DBT was especially effective for patients with a history of more frequent self-harm.

The efficacy of DBT for BPD with comorbid SA was shown in two of three RCTs (Harned et al., 2008; Linehan et al., 2002; van den Bosch, Verheul, Schippers, & van den Brink, 2002) although a third of patients failed to complete DBT. Recent adaptations include DBT for adolescent (Fleischhaker et al., 2011), community mental health center (Comtois, Elwood, Holdcraft, Smith, & Simpson, 2007), and inpatient groups (Bohus et al., 2004; Kleindienst et al., 2008; Kröger et al., 2006).

Systems Training for Emotional Predictability and Problem-Solving (STEPPS) was introduced in a pre-post study of the 20-week group for 52 BPD patients (Blum, Pfohl, St. John, Monahan, & Black, 2002). STEPPS consists of CBGT emphasizing skills training for emotion and behavior management and a PEG for key members of the patient's support network. The study noted a decline in BPD symptoms. Four rigorous trials (Blum et al., 2008; Bos, van Wel, Appelo, & Berbraak, 2010, 2011; Harvey, Black, & Blum, 2010) showed strong effects on BPD symptoms, global functioning and QoL. Bos et al. (2011) showed that STEPPS benefited patients with either a "subsyndromal" or full BPD diagnosis; deterioration was noted for 20% of TAU but only 4% of STEPPS patients. Later studies used STEPPS as a *primary* treatment, reflecting confidence in the model, but a higher dropout rate (21% to 36%) than TAU (11% to 26%) is an issue.

Small-scale RCTs of *other treatments* for PDs tested schema-focused (Farrell, Shaw, & Webber, 2009), acceptance-based (Gratz & Gunderson, 2006), and problem-solving group therapy (Huband, McMurran, Evans, & Duggan, 2007). These studies recruited samples with a high proportion of male BPD patients and reported positive effects on BPD symptoms.

Several *day treatment* models for PDs have been tested. The 18-month *Mentalization-Based*

Day Treatment (MBDT; Bateman & Fonagy, 1999) was compared to TAU for 38 severe BPD patients and proved superior on self-harm, suicide attempts, health services use, and medication use. Results were maintained at 18-month and 8-year follow up (Bateman & Fonagy, 2001, 2008). MBDT was associated with reductions in emergency room visits and admissions relative to TAU, with the savings offsetting the costs of MBDT itself (Bateman & Fonagy, 2003). All MBDT patients attended a weekly maintenance group after discharge, but only a third of TAU patients sought similar therapy.

Four pre-post and two naturalistic clinical trials (Peterson et al., 2008; Warren, Evans, Dolan, & Norton, 2004) evaluated traditional day treatment (DT) programs. Samples involved a range of PDs with BPD predominant. Karterud et al. (2003) is notable for recruiting 8 DT programs and over 1,200 patients. Programs reflected a cognitive orientation (Reisch, Thommen, Tschacher, & Hirsbrunner, 2001) or, more commonly, a package of cognitive, dynamic, and process groups. These studies used a diverse array of outcome measures, but demonstrated substantial effects on psychiatric symptoms, hospital admissions, social functioning and QoL.

Inpatient settings also featured applications of group treatment. The Cassel Hospital study targeted a mixed PD sample (predominantly BPD). Using a naturalistic trial design, a one-stage, 12-month analytically-informed inpatient milieu, plus twice-weekly individual therapy, was contrasted with a two-stage "step-down" program involving 6 months of inpatient treatment followed by 12 to 18 months of outpatient dynamic group therapy and 6 months of outreach nursing (Chiesa & Fonagy, 2000, 2003). Premature terminations were frequent in both inpatient groups (47%) but the rate of early dropout was higher for the one-stage program. Both programs outperformed TAU (medication and case management in the community) on measures of social functioning, global functioning, psychiatric symptoms, and clinical indicators. There was greater benefit in the two-stage program with differences maintained at 24-month follow-up. Twice as many two-stage patients showed reliable and clinically significant change at 24 (Chiesa, Fonagy, Holmes, & Drahorad, 2004) and 72-month follow-up (Chiesa, Fonagy, & Holmes, 2006). Costs were offset by reduced health and social service use in the year after treatment termination (Chiesa, Fonagy, Holmes, Drahorad, &

Harrison-Hall, 2002). The outpatient group appeared to help patients make the transition to the community while the one-stage program had regressive effects following discharge.

Two studies (Leirvåg, Pedersen, & Karterud, 2010; Wilberg et al., 2003) evaluated different outpatient groups following intensive DT. The step-down approach for severe PDs makes clinical sense—it appears to be critical to the success of MBDT—but there remain issues with patient compliance and retention and as yet no definitive picture regarding treatment effects.

Group Versus Individual

The comparative effectiveness of the group versus individual format was extensively reviewed. We concluded that the collective evidence would "strongly support the no difference conclusion in the aggregate but is weak with respect to format by diagnosis interactions" (Burlingame et al., 2004, p. 652). During the past 10 years, several meta-analyses have been published that dealt with *specific diagnoses*. In addition, we found 23 single studies comparing the two formats related to a wide variety of target problems.

The "no difference conclusion" is more or less confirmed for mood disorders (Baines, Joseph, & Jindal, 2004; Cuijpers, van Straten, Andersson, & van Oppen, 2008; Lockwood, Page, & Conroy-Hiller, 2004a; Roselló, Bernal, & Rivera-Medina, 2008), panic disorders (Sharp et al., 2004), personality disorders (Arnevik et al., 2009; Kelly, Nur, Tyrer, & Casey, 2009), schizophrenia (Lockwood, Page, & Conroy-Hiller, 2004b), and eating disorders (Chen et al., 2003; Nevonen & Broberg, 2006). Exceptions occur including Nevonen and Broberg's (2006) finding at 1-year follow-up that effects on most measures were larger for individual. Renjilian et al. (2001) reported that CBGT was more effective than individual CBT for weight loss in BED patients, but the formats proved equivalent regarding symptom improvement; patient preference for either treatment had no impact. Equivalence was also shown for substance related disorders: One study (Panas, Caspi, Fournier, & McCarty, 2003) used archival data ($n > 7,000$ cases) and showed an increased likelihood of treatment completion and goal achievement for patients treated "heavily" in groups (i.e. > 2/3 of sessions in groups). Of course this finding was not based on random assignment. John, Veltrup, Driessen, Wetterling, & Dilling (2003) tested a motivational intervention provided as individual counseling or as a 2-week group program and noted differences, but these disappeared at 12-month follow-up with equivalence on the primary outcome of abstinence. The Sobell, Sobell, and Agrawal (2009) study randomly assigned alcohol and drug dependent patients to short-term individual versus group treatment (4 sessions) with equivalent outcomes but an economic advantage for group (41.4% less therapist time).

The picture is less clear with social phobia, where reviewers come to contradictory conclusions noting advantages of individual therapy on effect sizes and attrition rates (Aderka, 2009; Stangier et al., 2003) or equivalence (Powers et al., 2008). Similarly, contradictory results were found for trauma-related disorders (advantages of individual treatment for political prisoners suffering from PTSD, Salo, Punamäi, Qouta, & Sarraj, 2008; equivalence or economic advantages of group treatment for childhood sexual abuse survivors, Ryan et al., 2005; McCrone et al., 2005).

Among the OCD studies, format equivalence has been shown on YBOCS and depression measures (Anderson & Rees, 2007; Jaurrieta, Jiminez-Murcia, Alonso, et al., 2008; Jaurrieta, Jiminez-Murcia, Murchón, et al., 2008; O'Leary, Barrett, & Fjermestad, 2009). Interestingly, in one study superior outcomes for individual were reported in the completer analysis but equivalence in the ITT analyses, underscoring the importance of both types of analysis (Jaurrieta, Jiminez-Murcia, Alonso, et al., 2008; Jaurrieta, Jiminez-Murcia, Murchón, et al., 2008). A recent study (Belloch et al., 2011) showed comparable effects on depression and tendencies to worry. Individual treatment was more effective than group treatment in decreasing dysfunctional beliefs and the use of suppression as a thought control strategy. Nevertheless, coupling these findings with Fals-Stewart et al. (1993), we find sufficient evidence to conclude format equivalence. O'Connor and colleagues (2005) findings contradict this conclusion but their results are based on nine group members, liberally analyzed (i.e., completer-analysis) with a high refusal rate. Most studies calculated the economic advantage of group at a 3:1 to 5:1 savings (cf. Jonsson & Hougaard, 2008).

From the remaining studies, the majority support the equivalence hypothesis (Bastien et al., 2004; Rose, O'Brien, & Rose, 2009; Shechtman, 2004; Turner-Stokes et al., 2003). One study indicates an advantage for group (related to coping with HIV infections; Heckman et al., 2011) while another supports the individual format in a mixed clinical sample (Bachar, Canetti, Yonah, & Bonne, 2004), but economic advantages for group are constant.

Two teams went beyond the prosaic acknowledgement of the group's cost-effectiveness by employing distinct methods to estimate cost and effectiveness. Otto Pollack, and Maki (2000) compared group, individual, and psychopharmacology costs for patients treated for panic disorder. Absolute costs ranked group lowest ($523) followed by individual ($1,357) and medication ($2,305). Using clinician ratings, group was found to be most cost effective ($246), followed by medication and individual therapy ($447 and $565, respectively). Roberge, Marchand, Reinharz, and Savard (2008) compared 14-session individual and group treatments with a brief 7-session individual CBT that did not include in vivo exposure for patients with panic disorder, on a composite index made up of six panic, anxiety, and depression measures. Absolute costs ranked the brief approach as lowest ($154) followed by group and standard individual therapy ($249 and $376, respectively). However, when cost-effectiveness was included in the equation, group was more effective and somewhat less costly while the brief individual therapy was less costly and slightly less effective.

General Conclusions Regarding Effectiveness

We have summarized more than 250 studies that estimated the efficacy and/or effectiveness of group therapy for 12 disorders/patient populations (Tables 16.1 to 16.3). Taken together, the last decade of research demonstrated greater rigor and continued to provide clear support for group treatment with good or excellent evidence for most disorders reviewed (panic, social phobia, OCD, eating disorders, substance abuse, trauma-related disorders, breast cancer, schizophrenia, and personality disorders) and promising for others (mood, pain/somatoform, inpatient). Comparisons of different models often produced equivalent outcomes and, when differences were shown, they were small; thus, the clinician has choice. Although there may be some disorders where the individual format seems more promising (e.g., specific trauma-related disorders), format equivalence is convincingly supported, as are the economic advantages. Indeed, there are now empirically derived cost-effectiveness estimates supporting group over individual treatment.

Several new trends emerged. There is an increasing number of dismantling studies testing whether theorized treatment mechanisms indeed explain change (e.g., mood, social phobia, and OCD). In some instances they did not, leading investigators to explain change by common effects, that is, group properties and processes. Once again, the bulk of research tested the efficacy of specific formal change theories, predominantly CBT, but also interpersonal (breast cancer), psychodynamic (personality, eating disorders), and integrated models. Protocols were tested for their feasibility and transportability into clinical practice (e.g., social phobia and panic), providing the clinician with an empirical gauge on their likely impact. We saw an increased focus on groups for relapse prevention in populations that suffer from high relapse rates (e.g., bipolar and schizophrenia), as well as models transferred to adolescent populations to attenuate or prevent an illness (e.g., social phobia and substance). Several studies refined past efficacious protocols to see if a more intense yet smaller dose led to similar outcomes; results were mixed. Patient change is now a topic of study with sudden gains showing different patterns by disorder (e.g., MDD, panic, social phobia). This has relevance for practitioners who track patient change using sensitive outcome measures.

Despite these positive developments, improvements are needed. Greater consistency in the outcomes assessed would increase comparability across studies. We attempt to highlight this challenge in the effects column of the tables because, fundamentally, clarity regarding expected effects is what the practitioner and client need. Fortunately, with some disorders (YBOCS in OCD, LSAS in social phobia), standard measures of outcome have been established that facilitate the aggregation of results. Methodologically, most studies are still using liberal completer analyses. We read several studies where results were reversed when ITT analyses were applied. As we noted last time, only a few teams addressed within-group dependency effects and power, both of which are essential to derive unambiguous conclusions. Baldwin, Murray, and Shadish (2005; Baldwin, Stice, & Rohde, 2008) have empirically demonstrated that a small (.05) level of group dependency and/or not analytically nesting members within groups leads to a predictable inflation of Type I error. This means our group studies may be declaring significant effects when none exists. Given that these effects were unaddressed in most studies, the above effectiveness conclusions are likely inflated; we just don't know how much.

Promising Developments

There have been several noteworthy developments over the past decade. Some advance research noted in our last review while others reflect new developments. We briefly summarize this research by the five sources in Figure 16.1.

Formal Change Theories: Treatment Integration

An interesting trend is the integration of heretofore "competing" approaches (e.g., CBGT + dynamic or IPT) for the treatment of certain disorders (e.g., trauma and ED). Clinicians treating these disorders are dealing with complex conditions and integrating multiple treatments is an attempt to address several effects. In a related manner, evidence-based treatment models shown efficacious for specific disorders are being applied to new disorders. For example, DBT, originally developed to treat BPD, is increasingly and successfully applied to BED (e.g., Safer, Robinson, & Jo, 2010; Telch, Agras, & Linehan, 2000, 2001), shifting the theory behind treatment from distorted beliefs/attitudes to emotion regulation.

Structure: Mixed Group Composition

A reality for many clinicians is the difficulty composing diagnostically homogeneous groups. Previously, we noted a single RCT that targeted a diagnostically heterogeneous group and praised it on clinical relevance. Several studies have advanced this cause by examining the effects of *mixed diagnosis* (MD) groups for mood and anxiety (Lorentzen, Ruud, Baldwin, & Hoglend, 2011; McEvoy & Nathan, 2007; Rief, TrenKamp, Auer, & Fichter, 2000), anxiety and posttraumatic stress (Dunn et al., 2007), mixed anxiety (social phobia, generalized, OCD and panic) and co-occurring disorders (trauma and substance use). Results were invariably positive; for example, Norton and Hope (2005), and Norton and Whittal (2004) showed that patients suffering from either social phobia (48%) or panic disorder (42%) had equivalent improvement in general anxiety ($d = 1.06$). Similar results were posted by Erickson, Janeck, and Tallman (2007), Lumpkin, Silverman, Weems, Markham, and Kurtines (2002) and van Ingen et al. (2009). Lorentzen and colleagues showed no differential benefit between short- and long-term analytic group treatment, although results were moderated by the presence of a personality disorder. Studies of group interventions for *mixed eating disorder* (MED) samples have also encompassed all levels of care (outpatient, day treatment, inpatient) and were weighted more toward evaluative than hypothesis-driven research (Newns, Bell, & Thomas, 2003; Rø, Martinsen, Hoffart, & Rosenvinge, 2003). Generally, studies integrated CBGT with other approaches for mixed ED with promising results. However, only two provided a control condition (Crafti, 2002; Kong, 2005), making causal inferences premature.

Patient Characteristics: Focus on Attachment Styles

As in other treatment formats, constructs from attachment theory play an increasing role in the group literature (Markin & Marmarosh, 2010; Strauss, 2012). Existing studies provide evidence that attachment functions as a predictor of outcome in group psychotherapy (e.g., Strauss et al., 2006) and as a mediator/moderator of cohesion, group climate (e.g., Kirchmann et al., 2009), interpersonal perceptions (Mallinckrodt & Chen, 2004), and self-disclosure (Shechtman & Rybko, 2004). There are an increasing number of studies focusing on attachment *to the therapy group* using measures of group avoidance and group dependency (e.g., Marmarosh et al., 2006). Studies from social psychology addressing the relationship between attachment and processes in nonclinical groups have been recently reviewed (Mikulincer & Shaver, 2007).

Leader: "Virtual Leaders" and Online Groups

Research is now evaluating the augmentation of existing group treatments through technology, that is, online modes of delivery. Group treatment has been combined and contrasted with both asynchronous (e.g., email from therapist) and synchronous contact (e.g., real time). The most thorough testing of *asynchronous therapy* was conducted by a Swedish team that developed a nine-module web-delivered program (ICBT) for social phobia. The first RCT tested ICBT combined with two live exposure group sessions. Large improvements in social phobia symptoms resulted, compared to a waitlist control ($ES = .87$); however, nearly half failed to attend both exposure sessions (Andersson et al., 2006). ICBT was then tested without group exposure and produced similar results (Carlbring, Furmark, Steczko, Ekselius, & Andersson 2006), calling into question the value of group exposure. Next, ICBT was tested with and without a 10-minute weekly

telephone call to increase module completion (Carlbring, et al., 2007). A large average effect size on social phobia symptoms resulted when compared to waitlist ($ES = .95$, range .39–1.3); 93% completed all modules. Next, ICBT was tested with and without a five-session group exposure (Tillfors et al., 2008) with both conditions producing similar improvements ($ES = 1$); definitive conclusions are difficult because nearly 40% failed to attend a single exposure session. Finally, ICBT for panic disorder was contrasted with traditional CBGT (Bergström et al., 2010) with equivalent outcomes and costs favouring ICBT over traditional CBGT at a 1:4 ratio.

Synchronous online treatment was examined in a naturalistic study (Golkaramnay, Bauer, Haug, Wolf, & Kordy, 2007) using real-time chat rooms composed of 8 to 10 members lasting 12 to 15 weeks following inpatient care. Low dropout (9%) and high attendance rates (85%) with small gains on symptom distress and well-being resulted ($ES = .27–.32$). Subsequent research confirmed that treatment gains were maintained (Haug, Sedway, & Kordy, 2008; Haug, Strauss, Gallas, & Kordy, 2008) and recent research (Bauer, Wolf, Haug, & Kordy, 2011) found lower relapse rates compared to controls. Other studies focused on PTSD (Morland et al., 2010), depression (Houston, Cooper, & Ford, 2002), or body dissatisfaction and disordered eating (Heinicke, Paxton, McLean, & Wertheim, 2007); all of these posted reliable improvements. Lieberman, Wizlenberg, Golant, and Di Minno (2005) examined heterogeneous versus homogeneous internet support groups for patients suffering from Parkinson's disease, showing homogenous groups were significantly more committed and posted better depression outcomes. A Dutch study compared *asynchronous and synchronous* treatment (Blankers, Koeter, & Schippers, 2011) using a three-arm RCT to test a self-guided ICBT approach that included motivational interviewing (MI) for problematic alcohol drinkers. Using the same manual, the self-guided ICBT was compared to a synchronous seven-session 40-minute chat group or waitlist control. All groups showed a reduction in alcohol consumption and the two active treatments outperformed the waitlist but at 6-month follow-up the synchronous condition showed a greater reduction in consumption; effect sizes were modest. We see this study as an exciting advancement for online treatment and encourage future research to explore differential outcomes of online approaches.

Small Group Process: Attempts to Integrate Relationship Constructs

One of the more exciting developments over the past decade is the conceptual clarity that has resulted from studies of the therapeutic relationship in groups. Previously, we offered a set of instruments "as a 'beginning' process assessment battery" (Burlingame et al., 2004, p. 679) to address the lack of conceptual and measurement clarity regarding the therapeutic relationship in groups. Our measurement proposal was tested and refined in a series of studies from Europe and North America. The first study (Johnson, Burlingame, Davies, & Gleave, 2005) estimated the conceptual and empirical overlap of four commonly used cohesion, climate, working alliance and empathy measures by having 662 members of 111 counseling center and personal growth groups complete a copy of each. A 2-dimensional model resulted with the *quality* of relationship defined by three factors (*positive bond*, *positive work*, and *negative relationship*) and the *structure* of relationship defined by two commonly accepted facets (*member-to-member* and *member-to-leader*). Bormann and Strauss (2007) replicated and extended the Johnson et al. (2005) model by collecting identical data from members of 67 inpatient psychodynamic groups drawn from 15 German and Swiss hospitals. The three factors of the quality dimension were replicated but a third structure factor emerged (member-to-group). Next, a Norwegian team (Bakali, Baldwin, & Lorentzen, 2009) replicated the Bormann and Strauss (2007) model with members from 1- and 2-year outpatient analytic groups, and found that strong member-leader structure eclipsed member-member and member-group structures in the early sessions of the group.

The robust factor structure from four distinct group populations (personal growth, counseling center, outpatient analytic and inpatient psychodynamic) and countries was sufficiently promising to develop a 40-item Group Questionnaire (GQ) using two criteria: (1) empirical fit with the aforementioned model and (2) content linked to specific group interventions to address relationship problems (cf. Burlingame, McClendon, & Alonso, 2011). Krogel (2009) replicated the model using the GQ with 485 members drawn from three group populations (personal growth, counseling center, and state psychiatric hospital), finding that 30 items were sufficient. A recent study replicated Krogel's (2009) work with 438 inpatient psychodynamic group members and demonstrated good criterion validity with well-known German relationship measures studies (Bormann, Burlingame & Strauss, 2011). Finally, Thayer (2012) replicated Krogel's factor analysis with 219 group members drawn from 65 groups conducted at four U.S. university counseling centers and demonstrated good criterion validity with the original measures used by Johnson et al. (2005), to create the GQ. Most recently, the GQ subscales have been linked to leader interventions, providing clinicians with evidence-based action steps to improve the therapeutic relationship in groups (Burlingame et al., 2011).

UNDERSTANDING GROUP-LEVEL MECHANISMS OF CHANGE

After reviewing group effectiveness across 12 disorders and populations we've offered conclusions regarding specific outcomes being causally linked to specific models. In other cases, outcomes were linked to unspecified group properties by study authors. Defining these unspecified group properties has been a challenge for past reviewers. To illustrate, we've noted that cohesion, a ubiquitous group property, is assessed by no fewer than 23 measures (Burlingame et al., 2011). This lack of clarity has led some to introduce new group properties and discard old ill-defined ones (Hornsey, Dwyer, Oei, & Dingle, 2009). Our previous response (Burlingame et al., 2004) was to highlight research programs that carefully defined and tested these group properties. While useful, such research tends to be highly specific and takes decades to develop. Conclusions are often too narrow for clinicians to apply broadly in their practice. In this section we provide an alternative.

The organizational scheme shown in Figure 16.2 is an expansion of the small group process and structure domains found in Figure 16.1. It identifies distinct group properties and processes that have been extensively studied (Burlingame, Strauss, Bormann, & Johnson, 2008). Indeed, entire chapters have been devoted to summarizing the research on single components such as cohesion (cf. Burlingame et al., 2011). The model is based on Berne's (1966) analogy that knowledge of group dynamics for a group leader is as essential as knowledge of physiology for a physician. Living organisms are composed of anatomical form and physiological functions.

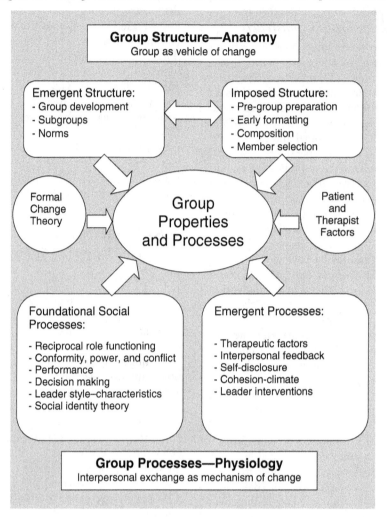

FIGURE 16.2 Group structure—Anatomy.

Anatomical structure often sets limits on physiological function. Likewise, our model identifies the form (structure) and function (processes) of small groups. We believe it is essential for group leaders to be knowledgeable about group form and function. Too many RCTs end with authors speculating that unaccounted for outcome variance might be explained by group properties. While we acknowledged the likelihood that many group investigators do not come from a group dynamic identity, we believe future progress *must* include measures of well-known group properties to at least rule them in or out as potential mechanisms of change. Such research would also positively impact clinical practice; see Burlingame et al. (2008) for more detailed description.

Anatomy of a Group—Structure

In our model, anatomy refers to the form of a group (Figure 16.2) and relates to leader actions that create the group—*imposed structure*. Similarly, member actions can also affect form—*emergent structure*. The components of *imposed structure* range from (a) how a leader selects (b) and prepares group members before and in (c) early group sessions to (d) how they compose the group. Pregroup preparation and structure have sufficient empirical depth to produce evidence-based guidelines; the interested reader is referred to past handbook chapters. Expertise in group dynamics is not required to recognize that all groups develop a unique "personality." *Emergent structure* describes how this personality is formed with three constructs: development, subgroups, and norms. Most theories of group development describe it as an emergent property of closed groups that reflects temporal patterns of work and climate. Norms are formal and informal rules that develop in the first sessions while subgroups form more gradually over time. We highlight a single component of each type of structure.

Imposed Structure — Composition

The impact of group composition has been a presence in the clinical literature for decades. The accepted principle that "the therapist strives for maximum heterogeneity in the clients' conflict areas and pattern of coping, and at the same time strives for homogeneity of the clients' degree of vulnerability and capacity to tolerate anxiety" (Yalom & Leszcz, 2005, pp. 272–273) is counterbalanced by limited empirical findings over the past decade. Two meta-analyses (Ang & Hughes, 2001; Burlingame, Fuhriman, & Mosier, 2003) identified heterogeneous group composition, based on problem focus or gender, respectively, as more effective. The former summarized 18 studies of social-skills groups for antisocial youth and found mixed groups (combined anti- and prosocial youth) produced more improvement at posttreatment ($d = .70$ versus .55) and follow-up ($d = .46$ versus .30). Similarly, Burlingame et al. (2003) concluded that mixed-gender groups were more effective than single-gender groups, relative to wait-list controls ($d = .66$ versus .40). Shechtman, Goldberg, and Cariani (2008) varied the ethnic composition of counselor trainee groups in Israel and found that Arab students in ethnically heterogeneous groups demonstrated greater engagement, more disclosure, and less regret after disclosure than their Arab counterparts in homogeneous groups.

In counterpoint, three studies demonstrated greater effectiveness for homogeneous groups. The Burlingame et al. (2003) meta-analysis identified groups homogeneous for problem focus as more effective than heterogeneous groups, relative to wait-list controls ($d = .56$ versus .25) and in terms of pre-post change ($d = .82$ versus .42). In Lieberman et al.'s (2005) aforementioned study of online support groups for Parkinson's disorder patients, homogeneous groups demonstrated greater improvement than heterogeneous groups on depression and symptom severity. Greenfield et al. (2008) demonstrated greater effectiveness for a women-only group treatment for substance abuse (Women's Recovery Group) relative to a mixed-gender treatment (Group Drug Counseling), but only among women having greater symptom severity.

More complex composition effects based on the *proportional* representation of certain patient variables were also studied. Wade and Goldman (2006) examined the gender composition of 2-week, 6-hour groups aimed at promoting forgiveness of actions by others that members felt were harmful (e.g., relationship break-up, abuse). As the proportion of men in the group increased, women showed greater declines in the desire for revenge while men became less empathic towards their offender. We highlighted Piper and colleagues' work on composition in our last chapter because they had identified an interaction between an aptitude (quality of object relations — QOR) reflecting interpersonal maturity and type of treatment (interpretive versus supportive groups; Piper, McCallum, Joyce, Rosie, & Ogrodniczuk, 2001). More recently, Piper, Ogrodniczuk, Joyce, Weideman, and Rosie (2007) composed groups using the QOR variable; homogeneous groups were predicted to outperform heterogeneous groups but this was not supported. Instead, the proportion of high-QOR patients predicted better outcomes for all members, regardless of a member's QOR or the treatment approach. These studies raise the intriguing question of the optimal proportion (men, high-QOR patients) needed to maximize outcomes.

The diversity of findings regarding composition suggests that there is no simple rule to follow, requiring group leaders to be conversant with relevant research findings. Gender provides a good example: For certain topics (e.g., shared traumatic experience, gender-specific issues), homogeneity can be a boon, but for others (e.g., relational problems with the opposite gender) heterogeneity would be preferred. Patients' needs and deficits and the group's purpose and focus are important elements of the context, and there are likely additional parameters that require consideration in order to facilitate composition effects.

Emergent Structure — Group Development

Group development posits that closed groups pass through recognizable temporal stages that affect work and emotional climate. Recent reviews (Johnson, Burlingame, Strauss, & Bormann, 2008; McClendon & Burlingame, 2011b) argue that our empirical knowledge rests upon use of MacKenzie's Group Climate Questionnaire (GCQ; MacKenzie, 1983) and this trend continued over the past decade. Two studies tested MacKenzie's (1994) stage model of group development with the GCQ in CBGT versus IPT groups for inpatients with eating disorders (Tasca, Balfour, et al., 2006) or social phobia (Bonsaksen, Borge, Sexton, et al., 2011). The Engagement subscale captures affective group bonds and is commonly regarded as an indicator of cohesion. Both studies documented a linear increase in CBGT but a fluctuating (Tasca, Balfour, et al., 2006) or linear decline (Bonsaksen et al., 2011) in the interpersonal-dynamic group. Tasca, Balfour, et al. (2006) suggest the fluctuations captured an alliance rupture-repair cycle while Bonsaksen et al. (2011) ascribed the decline to a focal shift from intra- to extra-group relationships. The high-low-high pattern described by MacKenzie (1994) was not supported. The Conflict subscale reflects the level of distrust, anger, and friction in the group with a low-high-low sequence expected. Tasca, Balfour, et al. (2006) reported a linear decrease in both groups; Bonsaksen et al. (2011) found support for the phasic pattern in both groups but only after the removal of extreme outlier scores (7.5% of the sample). The Avoidance subscale reflects members' efforts to conform to perceived expectations. Tasca, Balfour, et al. (2006) reported stability throughout the IPT and a linear decrease in CBGT; Bonsaksen et al. (2011) found no temporal changes in either group. Finally, both studies found that linear growth in Engagement, a group-level effect, was associated with individual-level treatment outcome (see also Ogrodniczuk & Piper, 2003; Ryum, Hagen, Nordahl, Vogul, & Stiles, 2009).

These studies, while limited in number, agree with past research (cf. Johnson et al., 2008; McClendon & Burlingame, 2011) and suggest that characteristics of the patient (diagnosis), treatment approach (focus on skills-training versus interpersonal process), setting (outpatient, inpatient), and possibly culture (North American versus Scandinavian) may influence patterns of group development in complex ways. In turn, there is evidence that group climate can mediate the impact of therapist intentions and interventions on eventual outcome (Kivlighan & Tarrant, 2001). Attention to moderators of the group developmental sequence and the impact on outcome are worthy aims for further research and critical for practitioners to be aware of to effectively harness group-level mechanisms.

Physiology of a Group—Emergent and Foundational Processes

Physiology reflects *function* and we've argued that group *function* is best articulated by considering *member interaction* as a primary mechanism of change (Burlingame et al., 2008). The five components in *emergent processes* describe empirically tested member/leader interactions (interpersonal feedback, self-disclosure, leader interventions) or byproducts (cohesion and therapeutic factors) that have been linked to outcome. The six *foundational social processes* reflect social and organizational psychology principles that have relevance to group treatment. We highlight a few relevant findings to raise reader awareness.

Emergent Processes—Cohesion

As noted earlier, greater clarity has been achieved in measuring the group therapeutic relationship, but what about the relationship between cohesion and outcome? Heretofore, two challenges with the construct of cohesion have created active debate on what we can conclude: (1) some studies empirically link cohesion with outcome while others do not, and (2) the sheer number of measures makes it impossible to know what is meant when a writer uses the construct. We believe the findings of a recent meta-analysis address both challenges (Burlingame et al., 2011).

A weighted and significant aggregate correlation between cohesion and outcome of $r = .25$ (95% confidence range of .17–.32; a medium effect) was estimated from 40 studies published between 1969 and 2009. A high level of heterogeneity was present, necessitating a moderator analysis; five moderators were detected. Interpersonal groups posted the highest relationship ($r = .58$) followed by psychodynamic ($r = .25$) and CBT ($r = .18$); but all coefficients were significant. Groups with five to nine members posted a stronger relationship ($r = .35$) than smaller or larger groups ($r = .16$), groups of more than 12 sessions posted a stronger relationship ($r = .36$) than those of 12 or fewer sessions ($r = .18$), and groups emphasizing member interaction, irrespective of orientation, posted a higher cohesion-outcome relationship than those with a problem-specific focus ($r = .38$ and $r = .21$, respectively). Finally, groups composed of younger members had a higher cohesion-outcome relationship ($r = -.63$). Interestingly, the cohesion-outcome relationship varied by measure (.04–.58) but most defined cohesion by the positive bond between the member and group. The overall conclusion is that cohesion predicts outcome across the most common theoretical orientations and that the size of this relationship varies by measure; further, moderators may exist that suggest specific leader actions (e.g., group size and member interaction).

Foundational Social Psychological Processes

The last component attends to the impressive array of studies conducted by social and organizational psychologists. The components delineated represent a subset of the available basic science and field research studies that focus upon small group functioning. We encourage group clinicians to become acquainted with the foundational theories and findings by consulting excellent textbooks (e.g., Forsyth, 2010). In these texts, constructs such as entitativity (Yzerbyt, Corneille, & Judd, 2004) capture member perception of "groupness," a potential barometer for when a therapist should increase the importance given to group properties in their treatment groups.

Emergent social psychological processes such as conformity, power, and the management of conflict are relevant to clinical groups. For example, ample direction is available in models related to conflict development, escalation and resolution (e.g., Lewicki, Saunders, & Barry, 2006). All groups, including treatment groups, have specific goals and there is an impressive literature on group performance and decision making that has not been translated to the field of psychotherapy. For example, some social psychology studies give guidance on increasing member involvement to reduce social loafing (DeMatteo, Eby, & Sundstrom, 1998). The organizational psychology literature provides a wide range of theories and research on leader style such as situational leadership theory (Hersey, Blanchard, & Johnson, 2001). This theory assumes that an effective leader must display at least four different leadership styles as groups move though different phases, that is, directing, coaching, supporting, or delegating. The theory fits well with models of process-related leadership in groups. Finally, how and to what extent members identify with their group (social identity theory) is a critical consideration regarding emergent structure and group process. It is still an incompletely answered question about which factors (e.g., categorization, identification) transform group membership into a social (group-related) identity. As we have stated elsewhere (Fuhriman & Burlingame, 1994), there is an enormous potential for improving our conceptual and empirical understanding of clinical groups in the theories and empirical literature of social and organizational psychology.

Becoming an Evidence-Based Group Practitioner

We end by sharing our view of an evidence-based group leader. Our context is important; we operate in an era of accountability with evidence-based practice (EBP) being a fundamental component of contemporary mental health care worldwide (McClendon & Burlingame, 2011a). This context can generate substantial clinician resistance since it can be experienced as interfering with professional autonomy. As Kobos and Lescsz (2012) pointed out, three vectors of evidence-based practice have been articulated:

1. The use of empirically supported therapies (ESTs; APA, 2006).
2. Practice-based evidence and the acquisition of ongoing data regarding patients in treatment via standardized measures.
3. The use of clinical practice guidelines.

Several sections of this chapter report on RCTs that test group ESTs for specific disorders, revealing a solid foundation of support. Two major initiatives of the American Group Psychotherapy Association (AGPA) during the past decade specifically addressed the latter two vectors; namely the revision of the AGPA CORE Battery (Burlingame et al., 2006; Strauss, Burlingame, & Bormann, 2008) and the publication of clinical practice guidelines (CPGs) that synthesize the best available research evidence, coupled with clinical expert consensus (Bernard et al., 2008). Each is briefly described.

In the early 1980s, the AGPA sponsored the development and dissemination of a CORE Battery consisting of outcome instruments commonly used in group research and shown to be sensitive to change. The aim of the CORE was to assist practitioner-members in evaluating the effectiveness of their groups and to augment clinical perception (MacKenzie & Dies, 1982). A task force to expand and revise the CORE was created in 2003 and produced a revised CORE Battery consisting of three types of measures: (1) group selection and principles for starting a group, (2) group-level processes, and (3) outcomes. The measures were selected by an international task force based on their psychometric soundness and ability to assist group leaders *at all stages* of their

TABLE 16.4   Summary of Measures and Handouts in CORE-R (Strauss et al., 2008)

Section	Material/Method

Group selection and pregroup preparation	Handouts for group leaders and members
	    Presenting group therapy to clients
	    How to get the most out of group therapy
	    Information regarding group therapy
	    Group confidentiality agreement
	
	Methods for group selection
	    Group Therapy Questionnaire (GTQ)
	    Group Selection Questionnaire (GSQ)

Process measures	Primary assessment tools:
	Group Questionnaire*
	Working Alliance Inventory (WAI)
	Other assessment tools:
	    Empathy Scale (ES)
	    The Group Climate Questionnaire-Short Form (GCQ-S)
	    Therapeutic Factors Inventory Cohesiveness Scale (TFI)
	    Cohesion to the Therapist Scale (CTS)
	    Critical Incidents Questionnaire (CI)

Outcome measures	Primary assessment tools:
	    Outcome Questionnaire-45 (OQ-45)
	    Youth Outcome Questionnaire (Y-OQ)
	Other assessment tools:
	    Inventory of Interpersonal Problems (IIP-32)
	    Group Evaluation Scale (GES)
	    Rosenberg Self-Esteem Scale (SES)
	    Target Complaints Scale (TCS)

* Not included in the CORE-R manual but derived from recommended measures (see promising development section on group process).

TABLE 16.5   Key Domains of Practice Guidelines for Group Psychotherapy (Kobos & Leszcz, 2008)

1. Creating Successful Therapy Groups (client referrals, administrative collaboration)
2. Therapeutic Factors and Therapeutic Mechanisms (change mechanisms, group cohesion)
3. Selection of Clients (inclusion/exclusion, composition of groups, instruments)
4. Preparation and Pregroup Training (objectives, methods, procedures, impact and benefits)
5. Group Development (models, developmental stages)
6. Group Process (social system, group as a whole, subgroups and splits, roles)
7. Therapist Interventions (different functions, transparency)
8. Reducing Adverse Outcomes and the Ethical Practice of Group Psychotherapy
9. Concurrent Therapies
10. Termination of Group Psychotherapy

group work. Table 16.4 provides an overview of the recommended material and methods for each section. A very recent application of these recommendations in clinical practice is provided by Jensen and colleagues (2012).

AGPA also impaneled a Science to Service task force composed of notable group practitioners, educators, and researchers to develop evidence-based Clinical Practice Guidelines (CPG; Klein, 2008; Leszcz & Kobos, 2008). A

FIGURE 16.3   Resources support evidence-based group treatment.

working assumption of the CPGs is that the principles reflect evidence-based factors accounting for patient change in group therapy. The CPGs were written to supplement clinician judgment rather than to supplant it. Their aim is to serve as a guide to the practice of effective, ethical and clinically sound group treatment. Table 16.5 summarizes the 10 key domains of the CPGs.

In 2008, the *Journal of Clinical Psychology* published a special issue on evidence-based group treatment. The caricature in Figure 16.3 was used to describe the key components of an evidenced based group clinician (Burlingame & Beecher, 2008) including the use of: (a) a research supported protocol (EST), which make up the bulk of this chapter; (b) practice guidelines which are described in both Figure 16.2 and Table 16.5; (c) practice-based assessment or using measures summarized in Table 16.4 to guide practice; and (d) multicultural competence, evidenced in part by the growing number of group protocols that have been tested with different cultures and ethnic groups. There is much more to effective group treatment than simply applying an EST to a group of patients with the "same disorder." We see promising advances in the past decade in all four areas and encourage group leaders to inform their practice with these bodies of evidence.

REFERENCES

Aderka, I. M. (2009). Factors affecting treatment efficacy in social phobia: The use of video feedback and individual vs. group formats. *Journal of Anxiety Disorders, 23*, 12–17.

Aigner, M., Demal, U., Zitterl, W., Bach, M., & Lenz, G. (2004) Verhaltenstherapeuti sche Gruppentherapie fur Zwangsstorungen. *Verhaltenstherapie, 14*, 7–14.

Amaro, H., Dai, J., Arévalo, S., Acevedo, A., Matsumoto, A., Nieves, R., & Prado, G. (2007). Effects of integrated trauma treatment on outcomes in a racially/ethnically diverse sample of women in urban community-based substance abuse treatment. *Journal of Urban Health: Bulletin of the New York Academy of Medicine, 84*, 508–522.

American Psychiatric Association. (2001). Practice guideline for the treatment of patients with Borderline Personality Disorder. *American Journal of Psychiatry, 158*(Oct. suppl.).

American Psychological Association. (2006). Evidence-based practice in psychotherapy. *American Psychologist, 61*, 271–285.

Andersen, B., Farrar, W., Golden-Kreutz, D. M., Glaser, R., Emery, C., Crespin, T.,...Carson, W. (2004). Psychological, behavioral, and immune changes after a psychological intervention. *Journal of Clinical Oncology, 22*, 3670–3580.

Andersen, B. L., Farrar, W. B., Golden-Kreutz, D., Emery, C. F., Glaser, R., Crespin, T., & Carson III, W. E. (2007). Distress reduction from a psychological intervention contributes to improved health for cancer patients. *Brain, Behavior, and Immunity, 21*(7), 953–961.

Andersen, B. L., Hae-Chung, Y., Farrar, W. B., Golden-Kreutz, D. M., Emery, C. F., Thornton, L. M., . . . Carson III, W. E. (2008). Psychologic intervention improves survival for breast cancer patients. *Cancer, 113*(12), 3450–3458.

Anderson, R. A., & Rees, C. S. (2007). Group versus individual cognitive-behavioural treatment for obsessive-compulsive disorder. *Behaviour Research and Therapy, 45*(1), 123–137.

Andersson, G., Carlbring, P., Holström, A., Sparthan, E., Furmark, T., Nilsson-Ihrfelt, E., . . . Ekselius, L. (2006). Internet-based self-help with therapist feedback and in vivo group exposure for social phobia. *Journal of Consulting and Clinical Psychology, 74*(4), 677–686.

Ang, R. P., & Hughes, J. N. (2001). Differential benefits of skills training with antisocial youth based on group composition: A meta-analytic investigation. *School Psychology Review, 31*, 164–185.

Antoni, M., Wimberly, S., Lechner, S., Kazi, A., Sifre, T., Urcuyo, K., . . . Carver, C. (2006). Reduction cancer-specific thought intrusions and anxiety symptoms with a stress management intervention among women undergoing treatment for breast cancer. *American Journal of Psychiatry, 163*(10), 1791–1797.

Arnevik, E., Wilberg, T., Urnes, Ø., Johansen, M., Monsen, J. T., & Karterud, S. (2009). Psychotherapy for personality disorders: Short-term day hospital psychotherapy versus outpatient individual therapy—A randomized controlled study. *European Psychiatry, 24*, 71–78.

Ashbaugh, A., Antony, M. M., Liss, A., Summerfeldt, L. J., McCabe, R. E., & Swinson, R. P. (2007). Changes in perfectionism following cognitive-behavioral treatment for social phobia. *Depression and Anxiety, 24*, 169–177.

Ashton K., Drerup, M., Windover, A., & Heinberg, L. (2009). Brief, four-session group CBT reduces binge eating behaviors among bariatric surgery candidates. *Surgery for Obesity & Related Diseases, 5,* 257–62.

Austin, S., Sumbundu, A., Lykke, J., & Oestrich, I. (2008). Treating panic symptoms within everyday clinical settings: The feasibility of a group cognitive behavioural intervention. *Nordic Journal of Psychiatry, 62*(4), 287–293.

Bachar, E., Canetti, L., Yonah, I., & Bonne, O. (2004). Group versus individual supportive-expressive psychotherapy for chronic, symptomatically stabilized outpatients. *Psychotherapy Research, 14*(2), 244–251.

Baer, S., & Garland, J. (2005). Pilot study of community-based cognitive behavioural group therapy for adolescents with social phobia. *Journal of the American Academy of Child and Adolescent Psychiatry, 44*, 258–264.

Bailer, U., de Zwaan, M., Leisch, F., Strnad, A., Lennkh-Wolfsberg, C., El-Giamal, N., . . . Kasper, S. (2004). Guided self-help versus cognitive-behavioral group therapy in the treatment of bulimia nervosa. *International Journal of Eating Disorders, 35*, 522–537.

Baines, L. S., Joseph, J. T., & Jindal, R. M. (2004). Prospective randomized study of individual and group psychotherapy versus controls in recipients of renal transplants. *Kidney International, 65*, 1937–1942.

Bakali, J., Baldwin, S., & Lorentzen, S. (2009). Modeling group process constructs at three stages in group psychotherapy. *Psychotherapy Research, 19*, 332–343.

Baldwin, S., Murray, D., & Shadish, W. (2005). Empirically supported treatments or type I errors? *Journal of Consulting and Clinical Psychology, 73*(5), 924–935.

Baldwin, S., Stice, E., & Rohde, P. (2008). Statistical analysis of group-administered intervention data. *Psychotherapy Research, 18*(4), 365–376.

Barlow, D. H., Craske, M. G., Cerny, J. A., & Klosko, J. S. (1989). Behavioral treatment of panic disorder. *Behavior Therapy, 20*(2), 261–282.

Barrowclough, C., Haddock, G., Lobban, F., Jones, F., Siddle, R., Roberts, C., & Gregg, L. (2006). Group cognitive-behavioural therapy for schizophrenia. *British Journal of Psychiatry, 189*, 527– 532.

Bastien, C. H., Morin, C. M., Oullet, M.-C., Blais, F. C., & Bouchard, S. (2004). Cognitive-behavioral therapy for insomnia: Comparison of individual therapy, group therapy, and telephone consultations. *Journal of Consulting and Clinical Psychology, 72*, 653–659.

Bateman, A., & Fonagy, P. (1999). The effectiveness of partial hospitalization in the treatment of borderline personality disorder. *American Journal of Psychiatry, 156*, 1563–1569.

Bateman, A., & Fonagy, P. (2001). Treatment of borderline personality disorder with psychoanalytically oriented partial hospitalization. *American Journal of Psychiatry, 158*, 36–42.

Bateman, A., & Fonagy, P. (2003). Health service utilization costs for borderline personality disorder patients treated with psychoanalytically oriented partial hospitalization versus general psychiatric care. *American Journal of Psychiatry,160*, 169–171.

Bateman, A., & Fonagy, P. (2008). 8-year follow-up of patients treated for borderline personality disorder. *American Journal of Psychiatry, 165*, 631–638.

Battjes, R. J., Gordon, M. S., O'Grady, K. E., Kinlock, T. W., Katz, E. C., & Sears, E. A. (2004). Evaluation of a group-based substance abuse treatment program for adolescents. *Journal of Substance Abuse Treatment, 20*, 123–134.

Bauer, S., Wolf, M., Haug, S., & Kordy, H. (2011). The effectiveness of internet chat groups in the relapse prevention after inpatient psychotherapy. *Psychotherapy Research, 21*, 219–226.

Bäuml, J., Pitschel-Walz, G., Volz, A., Engel, R. R., & Kissling, W. (2007). Psychoeducation in schizophrenia. *Journal of Clinical Psychiatry, 68*, 854–861.

Bechdolf, A., Köhn, D., Knost, B., Pukrop, R., & Klosterkötter, J. (2005). A randomized comparison of group cognitive-behavioural therapy and group psychoeducation in acute patients with schizophrenia. *Acta Psychiatrica Scandinavia, 112*, 173–179.

Bechdolf, A., Knost, B., Nelson, B., Schneider, N., Veith, V., Yung, A. R., & Pukrop, R. (2010). Randomized comparison of group cognitive behaviour therapy and group psychoeducation in acute patients with schizophrenia. *Australian and New Zealand Journal of Psychiatry, 44*, 144–150.

Beebe, L. H., Smith K., Burk, R., Dessieux, O., Velligan, D., Tavakoli, A., & Tennison, C. (2010). Effects of a motivational group intervention on exercise self-efficacy and outcome expectations for exercise in schizophrenia spectrum disorders. *Journal of the American Psychiatric Nurses Association, 16*, 105–113.

Belloch, A., Cabedo, E., Carrió, C., Fernández-Alvarez, H., García, F., & Larsson, C. (2011). Group versus individual cognitive treatment for obsessive-compulsive disorder: Changes in non-OCD symptoms and cognitions at post-treatment and one-year follow-up. *Psychiatry Research, 187*, 174–179.

Ben-Porath, D. D., Peterson, G. A., & Smee, J. (2004). Treatment of individuals with borderline personality disorder using dialectical behavior therapy in a community mental health setting. *Cognitive and Behavioral Practice, 11*, 424–434.

Bergström, J., Andersson, G., Ljótsson, B., Rück, C., Andréewitch, S., Karlsson, A., & Lindefors, N. (2010). Internet-versus group-administered cognitive behavior therapy for panic disorder in a psychiatric setting. *BMC Psychiatry, 10*, ArtID 54.

Bernard, H., Burlingame, G., Flores, P., Greene, L., Joyce, A., Kobos, J., . . . Feirman, D. (2008). Clinical practice guidelines for group psychotherapy. *International Journal of Group Psychotherapy, 58*(4), 455–542.

Berne, E. (1966). *Principles of group treatment*. Oxford, United Kingdom: Oxford University Press.

Blanchard, E. B., Lackner, J. M., Gusmano, R., Gudelski, G. D., Sanders, K., Keefer, L., & Krasner, S. (2006). Prediction of treatment outcome among patients with irritable bowel syndrome treated with group cognitive therapy. *Behaviour Research and Therapy, 44*, 317–337.

Blankers, M., Koeter, M. W. J., & Schippers, G. M. (2011). Internet therapy versus internet self-help versus no treatment for problematic alcohol use. *Journal of Consulting and Clinical Psychology, 79*(3), 330–341.

Blum, N., Pfohl, B., St. John, D., Monahan, P., & Black, D. W. (2002). STEPPS: A cognitive behavioral systems based group treatment for outpatients with borderline personality disorder. *Comprehensive Psychiatry, 43*, 301–310.

Blum, N., St. John, D., Pfohl, B., Stuart, S., McCormick, B., Allen, J., . . . Black, D. W. (2008). Systems training for emotional predictability and problem solving (STEPPS) for outpatients with borderline personality disorder. *American Journal of Psychiatry, 165*, 468–478.

Bogart, R. K., McDaniel, R. J., Dunn, W. J., Hunter, C., Peterson, A. L., & Wright, E. F. (2007). Efficacy of group cognitive behavior therapy for the treatment of myofascial pain. *Military medicine, 172*, 169–174.

Bogh, E., Hagedorn, R., Rokkedal, K., & Valbak, K. (2005). A 4-year follow-up on bulimia nervosa. *European Eating Disorders Review, 13*, 48–53.

Bohni, M., Spindler, H., Arendt, M., Hougaard, E., & Rosenberg N. (2009). A randomized study of massed three-week cognitive behavioural therapy schedule for panic disorder. *ACTA Psychiattrica Scandinavica, 120*, 187–195.

Bohus, M., Haaf, B., Simms, T., Limberger, M. F., Schmahl, C., Unckel, C., . . . Linehan, M. M. (2004). Effectiveness of inpatient Dialectical Behavioral Therapy for Borderline Personality Disorder. *Behavior Research and Therapy, 42*, 387–499.

Bonsaksen, T., Anners, L., Borge, F-M., Sexton, H., & Hoffart, A. (2011). Group climate development in cognitive and interpersonal group therapy for social phobia. *Group Dynamics: Theory, Research, and Practice, 15*, 32–48.

Book, S. W., Thomas, S. E., Dempsey, J. P., Randall, P. K., & Randall, C. L. (2009). Social anxiety impacts willingness to participate in addiction treatment. *Addictive Behaviors, 34*, 474–476.

Bordeleau, L., Szalai, J., Ennis, M., Leszcz, M., Speca, M., Sela, R., . . . Goodwin, P. (2003). Quality of life in a randomized trial of group psychosocial support in metastatic breast cancer. *Journal of Clinical Oncology, 21*(10), 1944–1951.

Borgeat, F., Stankovic, M., Khazaal, Y., Weber Rouget, B., Baumann, M.-C., Riquier, F., . . . Bondolfi, G. (2009). Does the form or the amount of exposure make a difference in the cognitive-behavioral therapy treatment social phobia. *Journal of Nervous and Mental Disease, 197*, 507–513.

Bormann, B., & Strauss, B. (2007) Gruppenklima, Kohäsion, Allianz und Empathie als Komponenten der therapeutischen Beziehung in Gruppenpsychotherapien—Überprüfung eines

Mehrebenen-Modells. [Group climate, cohesion, alliance and empathy as components of therapeutic relationships in group treatments] *Gruppenpsychotherapie und Gruppendynamik, 43,* 1–20.

Bormann, B., Burlingame, G., & Strauss, B (2011). Der Gruppenfragenbogen (GQ-D): Instrument zur Messung von therapeutischen Beziehungen in der Gruppenpsychotherapie. [The Group questionnaire (GQ-D): *An instrument to measure therapeutic relationships in group therapy]* Psychotherapeut, *56,* 297–309.

Borras, L., Boucherie, M., Mohr, S., Lecomte, T., Perroud, N., & Huguelet, P. (2009). Increasing self-esteem. *European Psychiatry, 24,* 307–316.

Bos, E. H., van Wel, E. B., Appelo, M. T., & Verbraak, M. J. P. M. (2010). A randomized controlled trial of a Dutch version of systems training for emotional predictability and problem solving for borderline personality disorder. *Journal of Nervous and Mental Disease, 198,* 299–304.

Bos, E. H., van Wel, E. B., Appelo, M. T., & Verbraak, M. J. P. M. (2011). Effectiveness of systems training for emotional predictability and problem solving (STEPPS) for borderline personality disorder in a "real-world" sample. *Psychotherapy and Psychosomatics, 80,* 173–181.

Bradley, R. G., & Follingstad, D. R. (2003). Group therapy for incarcerated women who experienced interpersonal violence. *Journal of Traumatic Stress, 16,* 337–340.

Braga, D. T., Cordioli, A. V., Niederauer, K. K., & Manfro, G. G. (2005). Cognitive-behavioral group therapy for obsessive-compulsive disorder. *Acta Psychiatrica Scandinavica, 112*(3), 180–186.

Bultz, B., Speca, M., Brasher, P., Geggie, P. & Page, S. (2000). A randomized controlled trial of a brief psychoeducational support group for partners of early stage breast cancer. *Psycho-Oncology, 9,* 303–313.

Burleson, J. A., & Kaminer, Y. (2005). Self-efficacy as a predictor of treatment outcome in adolescent substance use disorders. *Addictive Behaviors, 30,* 1751–1764.

Burlingame, G. M., & Beecher, M. E. (2008). New directions and resources in group psychotherapy: Introduction to the issue. *Journal of Clinical Psychology, 64*(11), 1197–1205.

Burlingame, G. M., Earnshaw, D., Ridge, N. W., Matsumo, J., Bulkley, C., Lee, J., & Hwang, A. D., (2007). Psycho-educational group treatment for the severely and persistently mentally ill. *International Journal of Group Psychotherapy, 57,* 178–218.

Burlingame, G. M., Fuhriman, A., & Mosier, J. (2003). The differential effectiveness of group psychotherapy: A meta-analytic perspective. *Group Dynamics: Theory, Research, and Practice, 7,* 3–12.

Burlingame, G. M., Fuhriman, A., Paul, S., & Ogles, B. M. (1989). Implementing a time-limited therapy program. *Psychotherapy: Theory, Research, Practice, Training, 26,* 303–313.

Burlingame, G. M., MacKenzie, K. R., & Strauss, B. (2004). Small group treatment: Evidence for effectiveness and mechanisms of change. In M. J. Lambert (Ed.), *Bergin & Garfield's handbook of psychotherapy and behavior change* (5th ed., pp. 647–696). Hoboken, NJ: Wiley.

Burlingame, G., McClendon, D., & Alonso, J (2011). Cohesion in group psychotherapy. In J. C. Norcross (Ed.), *A Guide to Psychotherapy Relationships that Work* (2nd ed.). Oxford, United Kingdom: Oxford University Press.

Burlingame, G., Strauss, B., Borman, B., & Johnson, J. (2008). Are there common change mechanisms for all small group treatments? A conceptual model for change mechanisms inherent in small groups. *Gruppenpsychotherapie und Gruppendynamik, 44*(3), 177–241.

Burlingame, G. M., Strauss, B., Joyce, A., MacNair-Semands, R., MacKenzie, K. R., Ogrodniczuk, J., & Taylor, S. M. (2006). *CORE Battery—Revised: An Assessment Tool Kit for Promoting Optimal Group Selection, Process and Outcome.* New York, NY: AGPA.

Butler, L., Koopman, C., Neri, E., Giese-Davis, J., Palesh, O., Thorne-Yocam, K., . . . Spiegel, D. (2009). Effects of supportive-expressive group therapy on pain in women with metastatic breast cancer. *Health Psychology, 28*(5), 579–587.

Carlbring, P., Furmark, T., Steczko, J., Ekselius, L., & Andersson, G. (2006). An open study of Internet-based bibliotherapy with minimal therapist contact via email for social phobia. *Clinical Psychologist, 10*(1), 30–38.

Carlbring, P., Gunnarsdóttir, M., Hedensjö, L., Andersson, G., Ekselius, L., & Furmark, T. (2007). Treatment of social phobia. *British Journal of Psychiatry, 190,* 122–128.

Castle, D., Berk, M., Berk, L., Lauder, S., Chamberlain, J., & Gilbert, M. (2007). Pilot of group intervention for bipolar disorder. *International Journal of Psychiatry in Clinical Practice, 11*(4), 279–284.

Chard, K. M. (2005). An evaluation of cognitive processing therapy for the treatment of posttraumatic stress disorder related to childhood sexual abuse. *Journal of Consulting and Clinical Psychology, 73,* 965–971.

Chen, E., Touyz, S. W., Beumont, P. J., Fairburn, C. G., Griffiths, R., Butow, P., . . . Basten, C. (2003). Comparison of group and individual cognitive-behavioral therapy for patients with bulimia nervosa. *International Journal of Eating Disorders, 33,* 241–254.

Chien, W.-T., & Chan, S. W. T. (2004). One-year follow-up of a multiple-family-group intervention for Chinese families of patients with schizophrenia. *Psychiatric Services, 55,* 1276–1284.

Chien, W.-T., & Wong, K. F. (2007). A family psychoeducation group program for Chinese people with schizophrenia in Hong Kong. *Psychiatric Services, 58,* 1003–1006.

Chiesa, M., & Fonagy, P. (2000). Cassel personality disorder study. *British Journal of Psychiatry, 176,* 485–491.

Chiesa, M., & Fonagy, P. (2002). From the therapeutic community to the community. *Therapeutic Communities, 23,* 247–259.

Chiesa, M., & Fonagy, P. (2003). Psychosocial treatment for severe personality disorder: 36-month follow-up. *British Journal of Psychiatry, 183,* 356–362.

Chiesa, M., Fonagy, P., & Holmes, J. (2003). When less is more. *International Journal of Psychoanalysis, 84,* 637–650.

Chiesa, M., Fonagy, P., & Holmes, J. (2006). Six-year follow-up of three treatment programs to personality disorder. *Journal of Personality Disorders, 20,* 493–509.

Chiesa, M., Fonagy, P., Holmes, J., & Drahorad, C. (2004). Residential versus community treatment of personality disorders. *American Journal of Psychiatry, 161,* 1463–1470.

Chiesa, M., Fonagy, P., Holmes, J., Drahorad, C., & Harrison-Hall, A. (2002). Health service use costs by personality disorder following specialist and non-specialist treatment. *Journal of Personality Disorders, 16,* 160–173.

Clark, D. M. (1986). A cognitive approach to panic. *Behavior Research and Therapy, 24*(4), 461–470.

Clark, D. M., & Wells, A. (1995). A cognitive model of social phobia. In R. G. Heimberg, M. Liebowitz, D. Hope, & F. Schneier (Eds.), *Social phobia: Diagnosis, assessment, and treatment* (pp. 69–93). New York, NY: Guilford Press.

Classen, C., Butler, L., Koopman, C., Miller, E., DiMiceli, S., Giese-Davis, J.,...Spiegel, D. (2001). Supportive-expressive group therapy and distress in patients with metastatic breast cancer. *Archives of General Psychiatry, 58*(5), 494–501.

Classen, C. C., Cavanaugh, C. E., Kaupp, J. W., Aggarwal, R., Palesh, O. G., Koopman, C.,...Spiegel, D. (2011). A comparison of trauma-focused and present-focused group therapy for survivors of childhood sexual abuse. *Psychological Trauma: Theory, Research, Practice, and Policy, 3,* 84–93.

Classen, C., Kraemer, H., Blasey, C., Giese-Davis, J., Koopman, C., Gronskaya Palesh, O., & Spiegel, D. (2008). Supportive-expressive group therapy for primary breast cancer patients. *Psycho-Oncology, 17*(5), 438–447.

Clerkin, E., Teachman, B., & Smith-Janik, S. (2008). Sudden gains in group cognitive-behavioral therapy for panic disorder. *Behavior Research and Therapy, 46,* 1244–1250.

Cloitre, M., & Koenen, K. C. (2001). The impact of borderline personality disorder on process group

outcome among women with posttraumatic stress disorder related to childhood abuse. *International Journal of Group Psychotherapy, 51,* 379–398.

Cohen, M., & Fried, G. (2007). Comparing relaxation training and cognitive-behavioral group therapy for women with breast cancer. *Research on Social Work Practice, 17,* 313–323.

Colom, F., Reinares, M., Pacchiarotti, I., Popovic, D., Mazzarini, L., Martínez-Arán, A.,...Vieta, E. (2010). Has number of previous episodes any effect on response to group psychoeducation in bipolar patients? *Acta Neuropsychiatrica, 22,* 50–53.

Colom, F., Vieta, E., Martinez-Arán, A., Reinares, M., Goikolea, J., Benabarre, A.,...Corominas, J. (2003). A randomized trial on the efficacy of group psychoeducation in the prophylaxis of recurrences in bipolar patients whose disease is in remission. *Archives of General Psychiatry, 60*(4), 402–407.

Colom, F., Vieta, E., Sánchez-Moreno, J., Palomino-Otiniano, M., Reinares, M., Goikolea, J. M.,...Martínez-Arán, A. (2009). Group psychoeducation for stabilised bipolar disorders. *British Journal of Psychiatry, 194,* 260–265.

Comtois, K. A., Elwood, L. M., Holdcraft, L. C., Smith, W. R., & Simpson, T. L. (2007). Effectiveness of dialectical behavior therapy in a community mental health setting. *Cognitive and Behavioral Practice, 14,* 406–414.

Cordioli, A., Heldt, E., Bochi, D. B., Margis, R., de Sousa, M. B., Tonello, J. F.,...Kapczinski, F. (2002). Cognitive-behavioral group therapy in obsessive-compulsive disorder. *Revista Brasiliera de Psiquiatra,* 113–120.

Cordioli, A., Heldt, E., Bochi, D. B., Margis, R., de Sousa, M. B., Tonello, J. F.,...Kapczinski, F. (2003). Cognitive-Behavioral Group Therapy in Obsessive-Compulsive Disorder. *Psychotherapy and Psychosomatics, 72,* 211–216.

Coyne, J., Hanisch, L., & Palmer, S. (2007). Psychotherapy does not promote survival (Kissane et al., 2007): Now what? *Psycho-Oncology, 16,* 1050–1052.

Crafti, N. A. (2002). Integrating cognitive-behavioural and interpersonal approaches in a group program for the eating disorders. *Behaviour Change, 19,* 22–38.

Creamer, M., Forbes, D., Biddle, D., & Elliott, P. (2002). Inpatient versus day hospital treatment for chronic, combat-related posttraumatic stress disorder. *Journal of Nervous and Mental Disease, 190,* 183–189.

Cuijpers, P., van Straten, A., Andersson, G., & van Oppen, P. (2008). Psychotherapy for depression in adults: A meta-analysis of comparative outcome studies. *Journal of Consulting and Clinical Psychology, 76*(6), 909–922.

Davies, S., & Campling, P. (2003). Therapeutic community treatment for personality disorder: Service use and mortality over 3 years' follow-up. *British Journal of Psychiatry, 182,* 24–27.

de Andres, R. D., Aillon, N., Bardiot, M., Bourgeois, P., Mertel, S., Nerfin, F., . . . Aubry, J. (2006). Impact of the life goals group therapy program for bipolar patients: An open study. *Journal of Affective Disorders, 93,* 253–257.

Delsignore, A. (2008). Does prior psychotherapy experience affect the course of cognitive-behavioural therapy for social anxiety disorders? *Canadian Journal of Psychiatry, 53,* 509–516.

DeMatteo, J. S., Eby, L. T., & Sundstrom, E. (1998). Team-based rewards: Current empirical evidence and directions for future research. *Research in Organizational Behavior, 20,* 141–183.

Dennis, M., Godley, S. H., Diamond, G., Tims, F. M., Babor, T., Donaldson, J., . . . Funk, R. (2004). The cannabis youth treatment (CYT) study. *Journal of Substance Abuse Treatment, 27,* 197–213.

Dinger, U., & Schauenburg, H. (2010). Effects of individual cohesion and patient interpersonal style on outcome in psychodynamically oriented inpatient group psychotherapy. *Psychotherapy Research, 20,* 22–29.

Dingle, G. A., Gleadhill, L., & Baker, F. A. (2008). Can music therapy engage patients in group cognitive behavior therapy for substance abuse treatment? *Drug and Alcohol Review, 27,* 190–196.

Dolbeault, S., Cayrou, S., Bredart, A., Viala, A. L., Desclaux, P., Saltel, P., . . . Dickes, P. (2009). The effectiveness of a psycho-educational group after early-stage breast cancer treatment. *Psycho-Oncology, 18,* 647–656.

Donovan, B., Padin-Rivera, E., & Kowaliw, S. (2001). "Transcend." Initial outcomes from a Posttraumatic Stress Disorder/substance abuse treatment program. *Journal of Traumatic Stress, 14,* 757–772.

Dorrepal, E., Thomaes, K., Smit, J. H., van Balkom, A. J. L. M., van Dyck, R., Veltman, K. J., & Draijer, N. (2010). Stabilizing group treatment for complex posttraumatic stress disorder related to childhood abuse based on psycho-education and cognitive behavioral therapy. *Child Abuse & Neglect, 34,* 284–288.

Duchesne, M., Appolinario, J. C., Range, B. P., Fandino, J., Moya, T., & Freitas S. R. (2007). The use of a manual-driven group cognitive behavior therapy in a Brazilian sample of obese individuals with binge-eating disorder. *Revista Brasileira de Psiquiatria, 29,* 23–25.

Dunn, N., Rehm, L., Schillaci, J., Souchek, J., Mehta, P., Ashton, C., . . . Hamilton, J. (2007). A randomized trial of self-management and psychoeducational group therapies for comorbid chronic posttraumatic stress disorder and depressive disorder. *Journal of Traumatic Stress, 20*(3), 221–237.

Dyck, D. G., Hendryx, M. S., Short, R. A., Voss, W. D., & McFarlane, W. R. (2002). Service use among patients with schizophrenia in psychoeducational multiple-family group treatment. *Psychiatric Services, 53,* 749–754.

Easton, C. J., Mandel, D. L., Hunkele, K. A., Nich, C., Rounsaville, B. J., & Carroll, K. M. (2007). A cognitive behavioral therapy for alcohol-dependent domestic violence offenders. *The American Journal on Addictions, 16,* 24–31.

Enns, M. W., Cox, B. J., & Pidlubny, S. R. (2002). Group cognitive behavior therapy for residual depression. *Cognitive Behavior Therapy, 31*(1), 31–40.

Erickson, D. H. (2003). Group cognitive behavioural therapy for heterogeneous anxiety disorders. *Cognitive Behaviour Therapy, 32*(4), 179–186.

Erickson, D. H., Janeck, A. S., & Tallman, K. (2007). A cognitive-behavioral group for patients with various anxiety disorders. *Psychiatric Services, 58*(9), 1205–1211.

Falsetti, S. A., Resnick, H. S., Davis, J., & Gallagher, N. G. (2001). Treatment of posttraumatic stress disorder with comorbid panic attacks. *Group Dynamics: Theory, Research, and Practice, 5,* 252–260.

Fals-Stewart, W., Marks, W., & Schafer, J. (1993). A comparison of behavioral group therapy and individual behavior therapy in treating obsessive compulsive disorder. *Journal of Nervous and Mental Disorders, 181,* 189–193.

Farrell, J. M., Shaw, I. A., & Webber, M. A. (2009). A schema-focused approach to group psychotherapy for outpatients with borderline personality disorder. *Journal of Behavior Therapy and Experimental Psychiatry, 40,* 317–328.

Fawzy, F. I., Canada A. L., & Fawzy R. N. (2003). Malignant melanoma. *Archives of General Psychiatry, 60,* 100–103.

Fawzy, F. I., & Fawzy, W. (1994). A structured psychoeducational intervention for cancer patients. *General Hospital Psychiatry, 16*(3), 149–192.

Fawzy, F. I., Fawzy, N. W., Hyun, C. S., Elashoff, R., Guthrie, D., Fahey, J. L., & Morton, D. L. (1993). Malignant melanoma. *Archives of General Psychiatry, 50*(9), 681–689.

Fenger, M. M., Mortensen, E. L., Rasmussen, J., & Lau, M. (2007). Group therapy with OCD *Nordic Psychology,* 332–346.

Fineberg, N., Hughes, A., Gale, T., & Roberts, A. (2005). Group cognitive behaviour therapy in obsessive-compulsive disorder. *International Journal of Psychiatry in Clinical Practice, 9,* 257–263.

Fleischhaker, C., Böhme, R., Sixt, B., Brück, C., Schneider, C., & Schulz, E. (2011). Dialectical behavioral therapy for adolescents (DBT-A). *Child and Adolescent Psychiatry and Mental Health, 5,* 3.

Fogler, J. M., Tompson, M. C., Steketee, G., & Hofmann, S. G. (2007). Influence of expressed emotion and perceived criticism on cognitive-behavioral therapy for social phobia. *Behaviour Research and Therapy, 45*, 235–249.

Forsyth, D. R. (2010). *Group dynamics* (5th ed.). Belmont, CA: Wadsworth.

French, M. T., Zavala, S. K., McCollister, K. E., Waldron, H. B., Turner, C. W., & Ozechowski, C. J. (2008). Cost-effectiveness analysis of four interventions for adolescents with a substance use disorder. *Journal of Substance Abuse Treatment, 34*, 272–281.

Friederich, H. C., Schild, S., Wild, B., de Zwaan, M., Quenter, A., Herzog, W., & Zipfel, S. (2007). Treatment outcome in people with subthreshold compared with full-syndrome binge eating disorder. *Obesity, 15*, 283–287.

Fuhriman, A., & Burlingame, G. M. (Eds.). (1994). *Handbook of group psychotherapy: An empirical and clinical synthesis*. New York, NY: Wiley.

Fukui, S., Kugaya, A., Okamura, H., Kamiya, M., Koike, M., Nakanishi, T., . . . Uchitomi, Y. (2000). A psychosocial group intervention for Japanese women with primary breast carcinoma. *Cancer, 89*(5), 1026–1036.

Furlong, M., & Oei, T. (2002). Changes to automatic thoughts and dysfunctional attitudes in group CBT for depression. *Behavioral and Cognitive Psychotherapy, 30*(3), 351–360.

Galassi, F., Quercioli, S., Charismas, D., Niccolai, V., & Barciulli, E. (2007). Cognitive-behavioral group treatment for panic disorder with agoraphobia. *Journal of Clinical Psychology, 63*, 409–416.

Gallagher, H. M., Rabian, B. A., & McCloskey, M. S. (2002). A brief group cognitive-behavioral intervention for social phobia in childhood. *Anxiety Disorders, 18*, 459–479.

Garcia-Lopez, L.-J., Olivares, J., Beidel, D., Albano, A.-M., Turner, S., & Rosa, A. I. (2006). Efficacy of three treatment protocols for adolescents with social anxiety disorder. *Anxiety Disorders, 20*, 175–191.

Gaston, J. E., Abbot, M. J., Rapee, R. M., & Neary, S. A. (2006). Do empirically supported treatments generalize to private practice? *British Journal of Clinical Psychology, 45*, 33–48.

Gatz, M., Brown, V., Hennigan, K., Rechberger, E., O'Keefe, M., Rose, T., & Bjelajac, P. (2007). Effectiveness of an integrated, trauma-informed approach to treating women with co-occurring disorders and histories of trauma. *Journal of Community Psychology, 35*, 863–878.

Giard, J., Hennigan, K., Huntington, N., Vogel, W., Rinehart, D., Mazelis, R., . . . Veysey, B. M. (2005). Development and implementation of a multisite evaluation for the women, co-occurring disorders and violence study. *Journal of Community Psychology, 33*, 411–427.

Giese-Davis, J., Koopman, C., Butler, L., Classen, C., Cordova, M., Fobair, P., . . . Spiegel, D. (2002). Change in emotion-regulation strategy for women with metastatic breast cancer following supportive-expressive group therapy. *Journal of Consulting and Clinical Psychology, 70*(4), 916–925.

Ginzburg, K., Butler, L. D., Giese-Davis, J., Cavanaugh, C. E., Neri, E., Koopman, C., . . . Spiegel, D. (2009). Shame, guilt, and post-traumatic stress disorder in adult survivors of childhood sexual abuse at risk for human immunodeficiency virus. *Journal of Nervous and Mental Disease, 197*, 536–542.

Golkaramnay, V., Bauer, S., Haug, S., Wolf, M., & Kordy, H. (2007). The exploration of the effectiveness of group therapy through an Internet chat as aftercare. *Psychotherapy and Psychosomatics, 76*(4), 219–225.

Gollings, E. K. & Paxton, S. J. (2006). Comparison of Internet and face-to-face delivery of a group body image and disordered eating intervention for women. *Eating Disorders: The Journal of Treatment & Prevention, 14*, 1–15.

Goodwin, P., Leszcz, M., Ennis, M., Koopmans, J., Vincent, L., Guther, H., . . . Hunter, J. (2001). The effect of group psychosocial support on survival in metastatic breast cancer. *New England Journal of Medicine, 345*(24), 1719–1726.

Gorey, K. M., Richter, N. L., & Snider, E. (2001). Guilt, isolation and hopelessness among female survivors of childhood sexual abuse: Effectiveness of group work intervention. *Child Abuse & Neglect, 25*, 347–355.

Gorin, A. A., Le Grange, D., & Stone, A. A. (2003). Effectiveness of spouse involvement in cognitive behavioral therapy for binge eating disorder. *International Journal of Eating Disorders, 33*, 421–433.

Granholm, E., Auslander, L. A., Gottlieb, J. D., McQuaid, J. R., & McClure, W. R. (2006). Therapeutic factors contributing to change in cognitive-behavioral group therapy for older persons with schizophrenia. *Journal of Contemporary Psychotherapy, 36*, 31–41.

Granholm, E., Ben-Zeev, D., & Link, P. C. (2009). Social disinterest attitudes and Group Cognitive-Behavioral Social Skills Training for functional disability in schizophrenia. *Schizophrenia Bulletin, 35*, 874–883.

Granholm, E., McQuaid, J. R., Link, P. C., Fish S., Patterson, T., & Jeste, D. V. (2008). Neuropsychological predictors of functional outcome in Cognitive Behavioral Social Skills Training for older people with schizophrenia. *Schizophrenia Research, 100*, 133–143.

Granholm, E., McQuaid, J. R., McClure, W. R., Link, P. C., Perivoliotis, D., Gottlieb, J. D., . . . Jeste, D. V. (2007). Randomized controlled trial of cognitive behavioral social skills training for older people with schizophrenia. *Journal of Clinical Psychiatry, 68*, 730–737.

Gratz, K. L., & Gunderson, J. G. (2006). Preliminary data on an acceptance-based emotion regulation group intervention for deliberate self-harm among women with borderline personality disorder. *Behavior Therapy, 37*, 25–35.

Greenfield, S. F., Sharpe Potter, J., Lincoln, M. F., Popuch, R. E., Kuper, L., & Gallop, R. J. (2008). High psychiatric symptom severity is a moderator of substance abuse treatment outcomes among women in single vs. mixed gender group treatment. *American Journal of Drug and Alcohol Abuse, 34*, 594–602.

Gruber, K., Moran, P. J., Roth, W. T., & Taylor, C. B. (2001). Computer-assisted cognitive behavioral group therapy for social phobia. *Behavior Therapy, 32*, 155–165.

Haller, C., Andres, K., Hofer, A., Hummer, M., Gutweniger, S., Kemmler, G., ... Meise, U. (2009). Psychoedukative und bewältigungsorientierte Gruppentherapie für SchizophreniepatientInnen. *Neuropsychiatrie, 23*, 174–183.

Halperin, S., Nathan, P., Drummond, P., & Castle, D. (2000). A cognitive–behavioural, group-based intervention for social anxiety in schizophrenia. *Australian and New Zealand Journal of Psychiatry, 34*, 809–813.

Harned, M. S., Chapman, A. L., Dexter-Mazza, E. T., Murray, A., Comtois, K. A., & Linehan, M. M. (2008). Treating co-occurring axis I disorders in recurrently suicidal women with borderline personality disorder. *Journal of Consulting and Clinical Psychology, 76*, 1068–1075.

Harper, K., Richter, N. L., & Gorey, K. M. (2009). Group work with female survivors of childhood sexual abuse. *Eating Behaviors, 10*, 45–48.

Harris, M. (1998). *Trauma recovery and empowerment.* New York, NY: Free Press.

Harvey, R., Black, D. W., & Blum, N. (2010). Systems training for emotional predictability and problem solving (STEPPS) in the United Kingdom. *Journal of Contemporary Psychotherapy, 40*, 225–232.

Haug, S., Sedway, J., & Kordy, H. (2008). Group processes and process evaluations in a new treatment setting. *International Journal of Group Psychotherapy, 58*(1), 35–53.

Haug, S., Strauss, B., Gallas, C., & Kordy, H. (2008). New prospects for process research in group therapy. *Psychotherapy Research, 18*(1), 88–96.

Hayward, C., Varady, S., Albano, A. M., Thienemann, M., Henderson, L., & Schatzberg, A. F. (2000). Cognitive-behavioral group therapy for social phobia in female adolescents. *Journal of the American Academy of Child and Adolescent Psychiatry, 39*, 721–726.

Hazel, N. A., McDonell, M. G., Short, R. A., Berry, M. C., Voss, W. D., Rodgers, M. L., & Dyck, D. G. (2004). Impact of multiple-family groups for outpatients with schizophrenia on caregivers' distress and resources. *Psychiatric Services, 55*, 35–41.

Hébert, M., & Bergeron, M. (2007). Efficacy of a group intervention for adult women survivors of sexual abuse. *Journal of Child Sexual Abuse, 16*, 37–61.

Heckman, T. G., Sikkema, K. J., Hansen, N., Kochman, A., Heh, V., & Neufeld, S. (2011). A randomized clinical trial of a coping improvement group intervention for HIV-infected older adults. *Journal of Behavioral Medicine, 34*, 102–111.

Heimberg, R. G., & Becker, R. E. (2002). *Cognitive-behavioral group therapy for social phobia.* New York, NY: Guilford Press.

Heiney, S., McWayne, J., Hurley, T., Lamb, L., Bryant, L., Butler, W., & Godder, K. (2003). Efficacy of therapeutic group by telephone for women with breast cancer. *Cancer Nursing, 26*(6), 439–447.

Heinicke, B. E., Paxton, S. J., McLean, S. A., & Wertheim, E. H. (2007). Internet-delivered targeted group intervention for body dissatisfaction and disordered eating in adolescent girls. *Journal of Abnormal Child Psychology, 35*(3), 379–391.

Helgeson, V., Cohen, S., Schulz, R., & Yasko, J. (2001). Long-term effects of educational and peer discussion group interventions on adjustment to breast cancer. *Health Psychology, 20*(5), 387–392.

Herbert, J. D., Gaudiano, B. A., Rheingold, A. A., Myers, V. H., Dalrymple, K., & Nolan, E. M. (2005). Social skills training augments the effectiveness of cognitive behavioral group therapy for social anxiety disorder. *Behavior Therapy, 36*, 125–138.

Hersey, P., Blanchard, K. J. H., & Johnson, D. E. (2001). *Management of organizational behavior: Leading human resources* (8th ed.). Upper Saddle River, NJ: Prentice Hall.

Hien, D. A., Jiang, H., Campbell, A. N. C., Hu, M., Miele, G. M., Cohen, L. R., ... Nunes, E. V. (2010). Do treatment improvements in PTSD severity affect substance use outcomes? *American Journal of Psychiatry, 167*, 95–101.

Himle, J. A., Rassi, S., Haghighatgou, H., Krone, K. P., Nesse, R. M., & Abelson, J. (2001). Group behavioral therapy of obsessive-compulsive disorder. *Depression and Anxiety, 13*, 161–165.

Hofman, S. G. (2004). Cognitive mediation of treatment change in social phobia. *Journal of Consulting and Clinical Psychology, 72*, 392–399.

Hofman, S. G., Schulz, S. M., Meuret, A. E., Moscovitch, D. A. & Suvak, M. (2006). Sudden gains during therapy of social phobia. *Journal of Consulting and Clinical Psychology, 74*, 687–697.

Hofman, S. G., & Suvak, M. (2005). Treatment attrition during group therapy for social phobia. *Journal of Anxiety Disorders, 20*, 961–972.

Hornsey, M., Dwyer, L., Oei, T., & Dingle, G. A. (2009). Group processes and outcomes in group therapy: Is it time to let go of cohesiveness? *International Journal of Group Psychotherapy, 59*(2), 267–278.

Hosaka, T., Sugiyama, Y., Hirai, K., Okuyama, T., Sugawara, Y., & Nakamura, Y. (2001). Effects of a modified group intervention with early-stage breast cancer patients. *General Hospital Psychiatry, 23*(3), 145–151.

Houston, T., Cooper, L., & Ford, D. (2002). Internet support groups for depression. *American Journal of Psychiatry, 159*(12), 2062–2068.

Hsiao, F-H., Yang, T-T., Chen, C-C., Tsai, S-Y., Wang, K-C., Lai, W-M.,...Chang, W-Y. (2007). The comparison of effectiveness of two modalities of mental health nurse follow-up programmes for female outpatients with depression in Taipei, Taiwan. *Journal of Clinical Nursing, 16*, 1141–1150.

Huband, N., McMurran, M., Evans, C., & Duggan, C. (2007). Social problem-solving plus psychoeducation for adults with personality disorder. *British Journal of Psychiatry, 190*, 307–313.

Hulbert, C., & Thomas, R. (2007). Public sector group treatment for severe personality disorder: A 12-month follow-up study. *Australasian Psychiatry, 15*, 226–231.

Hunter, M., Coventry, S., Hamed, H., Fentiman, I., & Grunfeld, E. (2009). Evaluation of a group cognitive behavioral intervention for women suffering from menopausal symptoms following breast cancer treatment. *Psycho-Oncology, 18*(5), 560–563.

Jacobi, C., Dahme, B., & Dittmann, R. (2002). Cognitive-behavioural, fluoxetine and combined treatment for bulimia nervosa. *European Eating Disorders Review, 10*, 179–198.

James, A., Soler, A., & Weatherall, R. (2005). Cognitive behavioural therapy for anxiety disorders in children and adolescents. *Cochrane Database of Systematic Reviews*, Art. No. CD004690.

Jaurrieta, N., Jimenez-Murcia, S., Alonso, P., Granero, R., Segalas, C., Labad, J., & Menchon, J. M. (2008). Individual versus group cognitive behavioral treatment for obsessive-compulsive disorder: Follow-up. *Psychiatry and Clinical Neurosciences, 62*, 697–704.

Jaurrieta, N., Jimenez-Murcia, S., Menchón, J., Alonso, M., Segalas, C., Álvarez-Moya, E. M.,...Vallejo, J. (2008). Individual versus group cognitive-behavioral treatment for obsessive-compulsive disorder. *Psychotherapy Research, 18*, 604–614.

Jensen, D., Abbott, K., Beecher, M., Griner, D., Golightly, T., Cannon, J. (2012). Taking the pulse of the group: The utilization of practice-based evidence in group psychotherapy, *Professional Psychology: Research and Practice*. Advance online publication. doi: 10.1037/a0029033

John, U., Veltrup, C., Driessen, M., Wetterling, T., & Dilling, H. (2003). Motivational intervention. *Alcohol and Alcoholism, 38*, 26–269.

Johnson, J. E., Burlingame, G. M., Olsen, J., Davies, D. R., & Gleave, R. L. (2005). Group climate, cohesion, alliance, and empathy in group psychotherapy. *Journal of Counseling Psychology, 52*(3), 310–321.

Johnson, J. E., Burlingame, G. M., Strauss, B., & Bormann, B. (2008). Die therapeutischen beziehungen in der gruppenpsychotherapie. *Gruppenpsychotherapie und Gruppendynamik, 44*, 52–89.

Jonsson, H., & Hougaard, E. (2008). Group cognitive behavioural therapy for obsessive-compulsive disorder. *Acta Pscyciatrica Scandinavica, 119*, 98–106.

Joormann, J., & Unnewehr, S. (2002). Eine kontrollierte Studie zur Wirksamkeit einer kognitiv-verhaltenstherapeutischen Gruppentherapie bei Kindern und Jugendlichen mit Sozialer Phobie. *Zeitschrift für Klinische Psychologie und Psychotherapie, 31*(4), 284–290.

Karterud, S., Pedersen, G., Bjordal, E., Brabrand, J., Friis, S., Haaseth, Ø.,...Urnes, Ø. (2003). Day treatment of patients with personality disorders. *Journal of Personality Disorders, 17*, 243–262.

Kelly, B. D., Nur, U. A., Tyrer, P., & Casey, P. (2009). Impact of severity of personality disorder on the outcome of depression. *European Psychiatry, 24*, 322–326.

Kelly, M., Roberts, J., & Ciesla, J. (2005). Sudden gains in cognitive behavioral treatment for depression. *Behavioral Research and Therapy, 43*, 703–714.

Kenardy, J., Mensch, M., Bowen, K., Green, B., & Walton, J. (2002). Group therapy for binge eating in Type 2 diabetes. *Diabetic Medicine, 19*, 234–239.

Kibler, J. L., & Lyons, J. A. (2008). Brief cognition-focused group therapy for depressive symptoms in chronic Posttraumatic Stress Disorder. *Journal of Psychological Trauma, 7*, 122–138.

Kingsep P., Nathan, P., & Castle, D. (2003). Cognitive-behavioural group treatment for social anxiety in schizophrenia. *Schizophrenia Research, 63*, 121–129.

Kirchmann, H., Mestel, R., Schreiber-Willnow, K., Mattke, D., Seidler, K., & Strauss, B. (2009). Associations among attachment characteristics, patients' assessment of therapeutic factors, and treatment outcome following inpatient psychodynamic group psychotherapy. *Psychotherapy Research, 19*(2), 234–248.

Kissane, D., Bloch, S., Smith, G., Miach, P., Clarke, D., Ikin, J.,...McKenzie, D. (2003). Cognitive-existential group psychotherapy for women with primary breast cancer. *Psycho-Oncology, 12*(6), 532–546.

Kissane, D., Grabsch, B., Clarke, D., Smith, G., Love, A., Bloch, S.,...Li, Y. (2007). Supportive-expressive group therapy for women with metastatic breast cancer. *Psycho-Oncology, 16*(4), 277–286.

Kivlighan, D. M., & Tarrant, J. M. (2001). Does group climate mediate the group leadership-group member outcome relationship? *Group Dynamics, 5*, 220–234. doi: 10.1037//1089-2699.5.3.220

Klein, R. H. (2008). Toward evidence-based practices in group psychotherapy. *International Journal of Group Psychotherapy, 58*, 441–454.

Kleindienst, N., Limberger, M. F., Schmahl, C., Steil, R., Ebner-Priemer, U. W., & Bohus, M. (2008). Do improvements after inpatient dialectical behavioral therapy persist in the long term? *Journal of Nervous and Mental Disease, 196,* 847–851.

Kliem, S., Kröger, C., & Kosfelder, J. (2010). Dialectical behavior therapy for borderline personality disorder. *Journal of Consulting and Clinical Psychology, 78,* 936–951.

Klingberg, S., Wittorf, A., Fischer, A., Jakob-Deters K., Buchkremer, G., & Wiedemann, G. (2010). Evaluation of a cognitive behaviourally oriented service for relapse prevention in schizophrenia. *Acta Psychiatrica Scandinavica, 121,* 340–350.

Knight, M. T. D., Wykes, T., & Hayward, P. (2006). Group treatment of perceived stigma and self-esteem in schizophrenia. *Behavioural and Cognitive Psychotherapy, 34,* 305–318.

Knijnik, D. Z., Kapczinski, F., Chachamovich, E., Margis, R., & Eizirik, C. L. (2004). Psychodynamic group treatment for generalized social phobia. *Revista Brasileira de Psiquiatria, 26,* 77–81.

Kobos, J. C., & Leszcz, M. (2012). Using the evidence: Contemporary group psychotherapy and the American group psychotherapy association's (AGPA) clinical practice guidelines. In B. Strauss & D. Mattke (Eds.), *Gruppenpsychotherapie—Ein Lehrbuch für die Praxis* [Group Psychotherapy—A Textbook for practioners] (in press). Heidelberg, Germany: Springer.

Koerner, K., & Linehan, M. M. (2000). Research on dialectical behavior therapy for patients with borderline personality disorder. *Psychiatric Clinics of North America, 23,* 151–167.

Kong, S. (2005). Day treatment programme for patients with eating disorders. *Journal of Advanced Nursing, 51,* 5–14.

Koons, C. R., Robins, C. J., Tweed, J. L., Lynch, T. R., Gonzalez, A. M., Morse, J. Q., . . . Bastian, L. A. (2001). Efficacy of dialectical behavior therapy in women veterans with borderline personality disorder. *Behavior Therapy, 32,* 371–390.

Kösters, M., Burlingame, G. M., Nachtigall, C., & Strauss, B. (2006). A meta-analytic review of the effectiveness of inpatient group psychotherapy. *Group Dynamics: Theory, Research and Practice, 10,* 146–163.

Kreidler, M. (2005). Group therapy for survivors of childhood sexual abuse who have chronic mental illness. *Archives of Psychiatric Nursing, 19,* 176–183.

Krogel, J. (2009). *The group questionnaire: A new measure of the group relationship*. Unpublished doctoral dissertation. Brigham Young University, Provo, Utah.

Kröger, C., Schweiger, U., Sipos, V., Arnold, R., Kahl, K. G., Schunert, T., . . . Reinecker, H. (2006). Effectiveness of dialectical behavior therapy for borderline personality disorder in an inpatient setting. *Behaviour Research and Therapy, 44,* 1211–1217.

Krone, K., Himle J., & Nesse, R. (1991). A standardized behavioral group treatment program for obsessive compulsive disorder. *Behaviour Research and Therapy, 29,* 627–631.

Kwon, S., & Oei, T. (2003). Cognitive change processes in a group cognitive behavior therapy of depression. *Journal of Behavior Therapy and Experimental Psychiatry, 34*(1), 73–85.

LaBrie, J. W., Feres, N., Kenney, S. R., & Lac, A. (2009). Family history of alcohol abuse moderates effectiveness of a group motivational enhancement intervention in college women. *Addictive Behaviors, 34,* 415–420.

Lamb, S. E., Hansen, Z., Lall, R., Castelnuovo, E., Withers, E. J., Nichols, V., . . . Underwood, M. R. (2010). Group cognitive behavioural treatment for low-back pain in primary care. *Lancet, 375,* 916–923.

Lane, L., & Viney, L. (2005). The effects of personal construct group therapy on breast cancer survivors. *Journal of Consulting and Clinical Psychology, 73*(2), 284–292.

Lash, S. J., Burden, J. L., Monteleone, B. R., & Lehmann, L. P. (2004). Social reinforcement of substance abuse treatment aftercare participation. *Addictive Behaviors, 29,* 337–342.

Lau, M., & Kristensen, E. (2007). Outcome of systemic and analytic group psychotherapy for adult women with history of intrafamilial childhood sexual abuse. *Acta Psychiatrica Scandinavica, 116,* 96–104.

Lawrence, R., Bradshaw, T., & Mairs, H. (2006). Group cognitive behavioural therapy for schizophrenia. *Journal of Psychiatric and Mental Health Nursing, 13,* 673–681.

Layne, C. M., Saltzman, W. R., Savjak, N., Popović, T., Mušić, M., Djapo, N., . . . Houston, R. (2001). Trauma/grief-focused group psychotherapy. *Group Dynamics: Theory, Research, and Practice, 5,* 277–290.

Ledgerwood, D. M., Alessi, S. M., Hanson, T., Godley, M. D., & Petry, N. M. (2008). Contingency management for attendance to group substance abuse treatment administered by clinicians in community clinics. *Journal of Applied Behavior Analysis, 41,* 517–526.

Leirvåg, H., Pedersen, G., & Karterud, S. (2010). Long-term continuation treatment after short-term day treatment of female patients with severe personality disorders. *Nordic Journal of Psychiatry, 64,* 115–122.

Leszcz, M., & Kobos, J. C. (2008). Evidence-based group psychotherapy. *Journal of Clinical Psychology: In Session, 64,* 1238–1260.

Leung, N., Waller, G., & Thomas, G. (2000). Outcome of group cognitive-behavior therapy for bulimia nervosa. *Behaviour Research & Therapy, 38,* 145–156.

Lewicki, R. J., Saunders, D. M., & Barry, B. (2006). *Negotiation* (5th ed.). New York, NY: McGraw-Hill.

Liber, J. M., Van Widenfelt, B. M., Utens, E. M. W. J., Ferdinand, R. F., Van der Leeden, A. J. M., Van Gastel, W., & Treffers, P. D. A. (2008). No differences between group versus individual treatment of childhood anxiety disorders in a randomised clinical trial. *Journal of Child Psychology and Psychiatry, 49*, 886–893.

Liddle, H. A., Rowe, C. L., Dakof, G. A., Henderson, C. E., & Greenbaum, P. E. (2009). Multidimensional family therapy for young adolescent substance abuse. *Journal of Consulting and Clinical Psychology, 77*, 12–25.

Liddle, H. A., Rowe, C. L., Dakof, G. A., Ungaro, R. A., & Henderson, C. E. (2004). Early intervention for adolescent substance abuse. *Journal of Psychoactive Drugs, 36*, 49–63.

Lieberman, M. A., Wizlenberg, A., Golant, M., & Di Minno, M. (2005). The impact of group composition on Internet support groups. *Group Dynamics: Theory, Research, and Practice, 9*(4), 239–250.

Linehan, M. M., Comtois, K. A., Murray, A. M., Brown, M. Z., Gallop, R. J., Heard, H. L., . . . Lindenboim, N. (2006). Two-year randomized controlled trial and follow-up of dialectical behavior therapy vs therapy by experts for suicidal behaviors and borderline personality disorder. *Archives of General Psychiatry, 63*, 757–766.

Linehan, M. M., Dimeff, L. A., Reynolds, S. K., Comtois, K. A., Welch, S. S., Heagerty, P., & Kivlahan, D. R. (2002). Dialectical behavior therapy versus comprehensive validation therapy plus 12-step for the treatment of opioid dependent women meeting criteria for borderline personality disorder. *Drug and Alcohol Dependence, 67*, 13–26.

Litt, M. D., Kadden, R. M., Cooney, N. L., & Kabela, E. (2003). Coping skills and treatment outcomes in cognitive-behavioral and interactional group therapy for alcoholism. *Journal of Consulting and Clinical Psychology, 71*, 118–128.

Lockwood, C., Page, T., & Conroy-Hiller, T. (2004a). Comparing the effectiveness of cognitive behaviour therapy using individual or group therapy in the treatment of depression. *JBI Reports, 2*, 185–206.

Lockwood, C., Page, T., & Conroy-Hiller, T. (2004b). Effectiveness of individual therapy and group therapy in the treatment of schizophrenia. *JBI Reports, 2*, 309–338.

Lorentzen, S., Rudd, T., Baldwin, S., & Hoglend, P. (2011). Randomized trial on the effectiveness of short- and long-term psychodynamic psychotherapy during a 3-year follow-up. Paper presented at the annual conference of the Society for Psychotherapy Research, Bern, Switzerland.

Lumpkin, P. W., Silverman, W. K., Weems, C. F., Markham, M. R., & Kurtines, W. M. (2002). Treating a heterogeneous set of anxiety disorders in youths with group cognitive behavior therapy. *Behavior Therapy, 33*, 163–177.

Lundqvist, G., Hansson, K., & Svedin, C. G. (2009). Group therapy for women sexually abused as children. *Psychoanalytic Social Work, 16*, 158–175.

Lundqvist, G., & Öjehagen, A. (2001). Childhood sexual abuse. *European Psychiatry, 16*, 64–67.

Lundqvist, G., Svedin, C. G., Hansson, K., & Broman, I. (2006). Group therapy for women sexually abused as children. *Journal of Interpersonal Violence, 21*, 1665–1677.

MacKenzie, K. R. (1983). The clinical application of a group climate measure. In R. R. Dies & K. R. MacKenzie (Eds.), *Advances in group psychotherapy: Integrating research and practice* (pp. 159–170). Madison, CT: International Universities Press.

MacKenzie, K. R. (1994). Group development. In A. Fuhriman & G. M. Burlingame (Eds.), *Handbook of group psychotherapy: An empirical and clinical synthesis* (pp. 159–170). New York, NY: Wiley.

MacKenzie, K. R., & Dies, R. R. (1982). *CORE battery: Clinical outcome results*. New York, NY: American Group Psychotherapy.

Mallinckrodt, B., & Chen, E. C. (2004). Attachment and interpersonal impact perceptions of group members. *Psychotherapy Research, 14*, 210–230.

Manne, S., Ostroff, J., & Winkel, G. (2007). Social-cognitive processes as moderators of a couple-focused group intervention for women with early stage breast cancer. *Health Psychology, 26*(6), 735–744.

Manne, S. L., Ostroff, J. S., Winkel, G., Fox, K., Grana, G., Miller, E., Ross, S. & Frazier, T. (2005). Couple-focused group intervention for women with early stage breast cancer. *Journal of Consulting and Clinical Psychology, 73*(4), 634–646.

Markin, R. D., & Marmarosh, C. (2010). Application of adult attachment theory to group member transference and the group therapy process. *Psychotherapy: Theory, Research, Practice, Training, 47*(1), 111–121.

Marmarosh, C., Franz, V., Koloi, M., Majors, R., Rahimi, A., Ronguillo, J., . . . Zimmer, K. (2006). Therapists' group attachments and patients' perceptions of group therapy treatment. *International Journal of Group Psychotherapy, 56*, 325–338.

Marom, S., Gilboa-Schechtman, E., Aderka, I. M., Weizman, A., & Hermesh, H. (2009). Impact of depression on treatment effectiveness and gains maintenance in social phobia. *Depression and Anxiety, 26*, 289–300.

Matsunaga, M., Okamoto, Y., Suzuki, S., Kinoshita, A., Yoshimura, S., Yoshino, A., . . . Yamawaki, S. (2010). Psychosocial functioning in patients with treatment-resistant depression after group cognitive behavioral therapy. *BMC Psychiatry, 10*, ArtID 22.

McCay, E., Beanlands H., Leszcz, M., Goering, P., Seeman, M. V., Ryan, K., . . . Vishnevsky, T. (2006). A group intervention to promote healthy self-concepts and guide recovery in first episode schizophrenia. *Psychiatric Rehabilitation Journal, 30*, 105–111.

McClendon, D., & Burlingame, G. (2011a). Group climate: Construct in search of clarity. In R. Conyne (Ed.), *Oxford handbook of group counseling*. Oxford, United Kingdom: Oxford University Press.

McClendon, D., & Burlingame, G. M. (2011b). Has the magic of psychotherapy disappeared? Integrating evidence-based practice into therapist awareness and development. In R. H. Klein, H. S. Bernard, & V. L. Schermer (Eds.), *On becoming a psychotherapist* (pp. 190–211). Oxford, United Kingdom: Oxford University Press.

McCrone, P., Weeramanthari, T., Knapp, M., Rushton, A., Trowll, J., Miles, G., & Kolvin, I. (2005). Cost-effectiveness of individual versus group psychotherapy for sexually abused girls. *Child and Adolescent Mental Health, 10*, 26–31.

McDermut, W., Miller, I., & Brown, R. (2001). The efficacy of group psychotherapy for depression. *Clinical Psychology: Science and Practice, 8*(1), 98–116.

McDonell, M. G., Short, R. A., Berry, C. M., & Dyck, D. G. (2003). Burden in schizophrenia caregivers. *Family process, 42*, 91–103.

McDonell, M. G., Short, R. A., Hazel, N. A., Berry, C. M., & Dyck, D. G. (2006). Multiple-Family Group Treatment of outpatients with schizophrenia. *Family Process, 45*, 359–373.

McEvoy, P. M. (2007). Effectiveness of cognitive behavioural group therapy for social phobia in a community clinic. *Behaviour Research and Therapy, 45*, 3030–3040.

McEvoy, P. M., Mahoney, A., Perini, S. J., & Kingsep, P. (2009). Changes in post-event processing and metacognitions during cognitive behavioral group therapy for social phobia. *Journal of Anxiety Disorders, 23*, 617–623.

McEvoy, P. M., & Nathan, P. (2007). Effectiveness of cognitive behavior therapy for diagnostically heterogeneous groups. *Journal of Consulting and Clinical Psychology, 75*(2), 344–350.

McEvoy, P. M., & Perini, S. J. (2009). Cognitive behavioral group therapy for social phobia with or without attention training. *Journal of Anxiety Disorders, 23*, 519–528.

McFarlane, W. R., Link, B., Dushay, R., Marcial, J., & Crilly, J. (1995). Psychoeducational multiple family groups: Four-year relapse outcome in schizophrenia. *Family Process, 34*(2), 127–144.

McLean, P., Whittal, M., Thordarson, D., & Taylor, S. (2001). Cognitive versus behavior therapy in the group treatment of obsessive-compulsive disorder. *Journal of Consulting and Clinical Psychology, 69*(2), 205–214.

McMain, S. F., Links, P. S., Gnam, W. H., Guimond, T., Cardish, R. J., Korman, L., & Streiner, D. L. (2009). A randomized trial of dialectical behavior therapy versus general psychiatric management for borderline personality disorder. *American Journal of Psychiatry, 166*, 1365–1374.

McNair, D. M., Lorr, M., & Droppleman, L. F. (1992). *The Profile of Mood States*. San Diego, CA: Educational and Industrial Testing Service.

McNeese-Smith, D. K., Wickman, M., Nyamanthi, A., Kehoe, P., Earvolino-Ramirez, M., Robertson, S., . . . Obert, J. (2009). Gender and ethnicity group differences among substance abuse treatment clients insured under managed care. *Journal of Addictions Nursing, 20*, 185–202.

McQuillan, A., Nicastro, R., Guenot, F., Girard, M., Lissner, C., & Ferrero, F. (2005). Intensive dialectical behavior therapy for outpatients with borderline personality disorder who are in crisis. *Psychiatric Services, 56*, 193–197.

Meier, S., Fricke, S., Moritz, S., Hand, I., & Rufer, M. (2006). Ambulate verhaltenstherapeutische Gruppentherapie bei Zwangsstorungen ein effectiver Behandlungsansatz? *Verhaltenstherapie, 16*, 173–182.

Michalak, E., Yatham, L., Wan, D., & Lam, R. (2005). Perceived quality of life in patients with bipolar disorder. *Canadian Journal of Psychiatry, 50*(2), 95–100.

Mikulincer, M., & Shaver, P. R. (2007). Attachment, group-related processes and psychotherapy. *International Journal of Group Psychotherapy, 57*, 233–245.

Möller, A. T., & Steel, H. R. (2002). Clinically significant change after cognitive restructuring for adult survivors of childhood sexual abuse. *Journal of Rational-Emotive & Cognitive-Behavior Therapy, 20*, 4964.

Morland, L., Greene, C., Rosen, C., Foy, D., Reilly, P., Shore, J., . . . Frueh, C. (2010). Telemedicine for anger management therapy in a rural population of combat veterans with posttraumatic stress disorder. *Journal of Clinical Psychiatry, 71*(7), 855–863.

Morrison, A., & Treliving, L. (2002). Evaluation of outcome in a dynamically orientated group for adult males who have been sexually abused in childhood. *British Journal of Psychotherapy, 19*, 59–75.

Morrissey, J. P., Ellis, A. R., Gatz, M., Amaro, H., Reed, B. G., Savage, A., . . . Banks, S. (2005). Outcomes for women with co-occurring disorders and trauma. *Journal of Substance Abuse Treatment, 28*, 121–133.

Mörtberg, E., Berglund, G., & Sundin, Ö. (2005). Intensive cognitive behavioural group treatment for social phobia. *Cognitive Behaviour Therapy, 34*(1), 41–49.

Mörtberg, E., Karlsson, A., Fyring, C., & Sundin, Ö. (2006). Intensive cognitive behavioral group treatment (CBGT) of social phobia. *Anxiety Disorders, 20,* 646–660.

Moscovitch, D. A., Hofmann, S. G., Suvak, M. K., & In-Albon, T. (2005). Mediation of changes in anxiety and depression during treatment of social phobia. *Journal of Consulting and Clinical Psychology, 73,* 945–952.

Mueser, K. T., Bolton, E., Carty, P. C., Bradley, M. J., Ahlgren, K. F., DiStaso, D. R.,...Liddell, C. (2007). The trauma recovery group. *Community Mental Health Journal, 43,* 281–304.

Munsch, S., Biedert, E., Meyer, A., Michael, T., Schlup, B., Tuch, A., & Margraf, J. (2007). A randomized comparison of cognitive behavioral therapy and behavioral weight loss treatment for overweight individuals with binge eating disorder. *International Journal of Eating Disorders, 40,* 102–113.

Najavits, L., Weiss, R., Shaw, S., & Muenz, L. (1998). Seeking safety. *Journal of Traumatic Stress, 22,* 437–456.

Nauta, H., Hospers, H., & Jansen, A. (2001). One-year follow-up effects of two obesity treatments on psychological well-being and weight. *British Journal of Health Psychology, 6,* 271–284.

Nauta, H., Hospers, H., Kok, G., & Jansen, A. (2000). A comparison between a cognitive and a behavioral treatment for obese binge eaters and obese non-binge eaters. *Behavior Therapy, 31,* 441–461.

Nevonen, L., & Broberg, A. G. (2006). A comparison of sequenced individual and group psychotherapy for patients with bulimia nervosa. *International Journal of Eating Disorders, 39,* 117–127.

Newns, K., Bell, L., & Thomas, S. (2003). The impact of a self-esteem group for people with eating disorders. *Clinical Psychology & Psychotherapy, 10,* 64–68.

Nickel, R., Ademmer, K., & Egle, U. T. (2010). Manualized psychodynamic-interactional group therapy for the treatment of somatoform disorders. *Bulletin of the Menninger Clinic, 74,* 219–237.

Norton, P. J. (2008). An open trial of a transdiagnostic cognitive-behavioral group therapy for anxiety disorder. *Behavior Therapy, 39,* 242–250.

Norton, P. J., & Hope, D. A. (2005). Preliminary evaluation of a broad-spectrum cognitive-behavioral group therapy for anxiety. *Journal of Behavior Therapy and Experimental Psychiatry, 36*(2), 79–97.

Norton, P. J., & Whittal, M. L. (2004). Thematic similarity and clinical outcome in obsessive-compulsive disorder group treatment. *Depression and Anxiety, 20*(4), 195–197.

O'Brien, M., Harris, J., King, R., & O'Brien, T. (2008). Supportive-expressive group therapy for women with metastatic breast cancer. *Counseling and Psychotherapy Research, 8*(1), 28–35.

O'Connor, K., Freeston, M., Gareau, D., Careau, Y., Dufour, M., Aasrdema, F., & Todorov, C. (2005). Group versus individual treatment in obsessions without compulsions. *Clinical Psychology and Psychotherapy, 12,* 87–96

Oei, P. S., & Boschen, M. (2009). Clinical effectiveness of a cognitive behavioral group treatment program for anxiety disorders. *Journal of Anxiety Disorder, 23,* 950–957.

Oei, T., Bullbeck, K., & Campbell, J. (2006). Cognitive change process during group cognitive behavior therapy for depression. *Journal of Affective Disorders, 92*(2–3), 231–241.

Oei, T., & Dingle, G. (2008). The effectiveness of group cognitive behaviour therapy for unipolar depressive disorders. *Journal of Affective Disorders, 107*(1–3), 5–21.

Ogrodniczuk, J., & Piper, W. (2003). The effect of group climate on outcome in two forms of short-term group therapy. *Group Dynamics: Theory, Research, and Practice, 7,* 64–76.

O'Leary, E. M. M., Barrett, P., & Fjermestad, K. W. (2009). Cognitive-behavioral family treatment for childhood obsessive-compulsive disorder: A 7-year follow-up study. *Journal of Anxiety Disorders, 23,* 973–978.

Openshaw, C., Waller, G., & Sperlinger, D. (2004). Group cognitive-behavior therapy for bulimia nervosa. *International Journal of Eating Disorders, 36,* 363–375.

Otto, M., Pollack, M., & Maki, K. (2000). Empirically supported treatments for panic disorder. *Journal of Consulting and Clinical Psychology, 68*(4), 556–563.

Page, A. C., & Hooke, G. R. (2009). Increased attendance in inpatient group psychotherapy improves patient outcomes. *Psychiatric Services, 60,* 426–428.

Panas, L., Caspi, Y., Fournier, E., & McCarty, D. (2003). Performance measures for outpatient substance abuse services. *Journal of Substance Abuse Treatment, 25,* 271–278.

Parks, J., Svendsen, D., Singer, P., & Foti, M. E. (2006). *Morbidity and mortality in people with serious mental illness.* Technical Report. Alexandria, VA: NASMHPD.

Patelis-Siotis, I., Young, L., Robb, J., Marriott, M., Bieling, P., Cox, L., & Joffe, R. (2001). Group cognitive behavioral therapy for bipolar disorder. *Journal of Affective Disorders, 65*(2), 145–153.

Patterson, T. L., Mausbach, B. T., McKibbin, C., Goldman, S., Bucardo, J., & Jeste, D. V. (2006). Functional adaptation skills training (FAST): A randomized trial of a psychosocial intervention for middle-aged and older patients with chronic psychotic disorders. *Schizophrenia Research, 86,* 291–299.

Paxton, S., McLean, S. A., Gollings, E. K., Faulkner, C., & Wertheim, E. H. (2007). Comparison of face-to-face and internet interventions for body image and eating problems in adult women. *International Journal of Eating Disorders, 40,* 692–704.

Petersen, B., Toft, J., Christensen, N. B., Foldager, L., Munk-Jörgensen, P., Lien, K., & Valbak, K. (2008). Outcome of a psychotherapeutic programme for patients with severe personality disorders. *Nordic Journal of Psychiatry, 62,* 450–456.

Peterson, C. B., Mitchell, J. E., Engbloom, S., Nugent, S., Pederson Mussell, M., Crow, S. J., & Thuras P. (2001). Self-help versus therapist-led group cognitive-behavioral treatment of binge eating disorder at follow-up. *International Journal of Eating Disorders, 30,* 363–374.

Peterson, C. B., Wimmer, S., Ackard, D. M., Crosby, R., Cavanagh, L. C., Engbloom, S., & Mitchell, J. E. (2004). Changes in body image during cognitive-behavioral treatment in women with bulimia nervosa. *Body Image, 2,* 139–153.

Petry, N. M., Weinstock, J., Alessi, S. M., Lewis, M. W., & Dieckhaus, K. (2010). Group-based randomized trial of contingencies for health and abstinence in HIV patients. *Journal of Consulting and Clinical Psychology, 78,* 89–97.

Piper, W. E., McCallum, M., Joyce, A. S., Rosie, J. S., & Ogrodniczuk, J. S. (2001). Patient personality and time-limited group psychotherapy for complicated grief. *International Journal of Group Psychotherapy, 51,* 525–552.

Piper, W. E., Ogrodniczuk, J. S., Joyce, A. S., Weideman, R., & Rosie, J. S. (2007). Group composition and group therapy for complicated grief. *Journal of Consulting and Clinical Psychology, 75,* 116–125.

Pollack, L. E., Harvin, S., & Cramer, R. D. (2001). Inpatient group therapies for people with bipolar disorder. *Journal of the American Psychiatric Nurses Association, 7,* 179–187.

Porter, J. F., Spates, C. R., & Smitham, S. (2004). Behavioral activation group therapy in public mental health settings. *Professional Psychology: Research and Practice, 35*(3), 297–301.

Powers, M. B., Sigmarsson, S. R., & Emmelkamp, P. M. G. (2008). A meta-analytic review of psychological treatments for social anxiety disorder. *International Journal of Cognitive Therapy, 1,* 94–113.

Rapee, R. M., Abbot, M. J., Baillie, A. J., & Gaton, J. E. (2007). Treatment of social phobia through pure self-help and therapist-augmented self-help. *British Journal of Psychiatry, 191,* 246–252.

Rapee, R. M., & Heimberg, R. G. (1997). A cognitive-behavioural model of anxiety in social phobia. *Behaviour Research and Therapy, 35,* 741–756.

Reisch, T., Thommen, M., Tschacher, W., & Hirsbrunner, H. P. (2001). Outcomes of a cognitive-behavioral day treatment program for a heterogeneous patient group. *Psychiatric Services, 52,* 970–972.

Renjilian, D. A., Perri, M. G., Nezu, A. M., McKelvey, W. F., Shermer, R. L., & Anton, S. D. (2001). Individual versus group therapy for obesity. *Journal of Consulting & Clinical Psychology, 69,* 717–721.

Rieckert, J., & Möller, A. T. (2000). Rational-emotive behavior therapy in the treatment of adult victims of childhood sexual abuse. *Journal of Rational-Emotive & Cognitive-Behavioral Therapy, 18,* 87–101.

Rief, W., TrenKamp, S., Auer, C., & Fichter, M. (2000). Cognitive behavior therapy in panic disorder and comoribid major depression. *Psychotherapy and Psychosomatics, 69,* 70–78.

Rø, O., Martinsen, E. W., Hoffart, A., & Rosenvinge, J. H. (2003). Short-term follow-up of severe bulimia nervosa after inpatient treatment. *European Eating Disorders Review, 11,* 405–417.

Roberge, P., Marchand, A., Reinharz, D., & Savard, P. (2008). Cognitive-behavioral treatment for panic disorder with agoraphobia. *Behavior Modification, 32,* 333–351.

Roberts, D. L., Penn, D. L., Labate, D., Margolis, S. A., & Sterne, A. (2010). Transportability and feasibility of social cognition and interaction training (SCIT) in community settings. *Behavioural and Cognitive Psychotherapy, 38,* 35–47.

Roncone, R., Mazza, M., Frangou, I., de Risio, A., Ussorio, D., Tozzini, C., & Massimo, C. (2004). Rehabilitation of theory of mind deficit in schizophrenia. *Neuropsychological Rehabilitation, 14,* 421–435.

Rose, J., O'Brien, A., & Rose, D. (2009). Group and individual cognitive behavioural interventions for anger. *Advances in Mental Health and Learning Disabilities, 3,* 45–50.

Roselló, J., Bernal, G., & Rivera-Medina, C. (2008). Individual and group CBT and IPT for Puerto Rican adolescents with depressive symptoms. *Cultural Diversity and Ethnic Minority Psychology, 14,* 234–245.

Rosenberg N. K., & Hougaard, E. (2005). Cognitive-behavioural group treatment of panic disorder and agoraphobia in a psychiatric setting. *Nordic Journal of Psychiatry, 59,* 109–204.

Rosser, S., Erskine, A., & Crino, R. (2004). Pre-existing antidepressants and the outcome of group cognitive behaviour therapy for social phobia. *Australian and New Zealand Journal of Psychiatry, 38,* 233–239.

Roy-Byrne, P. P., Craske, M. G., & Stein, M. B. (2006). Panic disorder. *Lancet, 368*(9540), 1023–1032.

Rufer, M., Albrecht, R., Schmidt, O., Zaum, J., Schnyder, U., Hand, I., & Mueller-Pfeiffer, C. (2010). Changes in quality of life following cognitive-behavioral group therapy for panic disorder. *European Psychiatry, 25*(1), 8–14.

Ruzek, J. I., Riney, S. J., Leskin, G., Drescher, K. D., Foy, D. W., & Gusman, F. D. (2001). Do posttraumatic stress disorder symptoms worsen during trauma focus group treatment? *Military Medicine, 166,* 989–902.

Ryan, M., Nitsun, M., Gilbert, L., & Mason, H. (2005). A prospective study of the effectiveness of group and individual psychotherapy for women CSA survivors. *Psychology and Psychotherapy: Theory, Research and Practice, 78,* 465–479.

Ryum, T., Hagen, R., Nordahl, H. M., Vogel, P. A., & Stiles, T. C. (2009). Perceived group climate as a predictor of long-term outcome in a randomized controlled trial of cognitive-behavioral group therapy for patients with comorbid psychiatric disorders. *Behavioral and Cognitive Psychotherapy, 11,* 1–14.

Safer, D. L., Robinson, A. H., & Jo, B. (2010). Outcome from a randomized controlled trial of group therapy for binge eating disorder. *Behavior Therapy, 41,* 106–120.

Salo, J., Punamäki, R.-L., Qouta, S., & El Sarraj, E. (2008). Individual and group treatment and self and other representations predicting posttraumatic recovery among former political prisoners. *Traumatology, 14,* 45–61.

Saltzman, W. R., Layne, C. M., Pynoos, R. S., Steinberg, A. M., & Aisenberg, E. (2001). Trauma- and grief-focused intervention for adolescents exposed to community violence. *Group Dynamics: Theory, Research, and Practice, 5,* 291–303.

Schlup, B., Munsch, S., Meyer, A. H., Margraf, J., & Wilhelm, F. H. (2009). The efficacy of a short version of a cognitive-behavioral treatment followed by booster sessions for binge eating disorder. *Behaviour Research and Therapy, 47,* 628–635.

Schnurr, P. P., Friedman, M. J., Foy, D. W., Shea, M. T., Hsieh, F. Y., Lavori, P. W., . . . Bernardy, N. C. (2003). Randomized trial of trauma-focused group therapy for posttraumatic stress disorder. *Archives of General Psychiatry, 60,* 481–489.

Shapiro, J. R., Bauer, S., Andrews, E., Pisetsky, E., Bulik-Sullivan, B., Hamer, R., & Bulik, C. M. (2010). Mobile therapy. *International Journal of Eating Disorders, 43,* 513–519.

Shapiro, J. R., Reba-Harrelson, L., Dymek-Valentine, M., Woolson, S. L., Hamer, R. M., & Bulik, C. M. (2007). Feasibility and acceptability of CD-ROM-based cognitive-behavioural treatment for binge-eating disorder. *European Eating Disorders Review, 15,* 175–184.

Sharp, D. M., Power, K. G., & Swanson, V. (2004). A comparison of the efficacy and acceptability of group versus individual cognitive behaviour therapy in the treatment of panic disorder and agoraphobia in primary care. *Clinical Psychology and Psychotherapy, 11,* 73–82.

Sharpe, J., Selley, C., Low, L., & Hall, Z. (2001). Group analytic therapy for male survivors of childhood sexual abuse. *Group Analysis, 34,* 195–208.

Shechtman, Z. (2004). Client behavior and therapist helping skills in individual and group treatment of aggressive boys. *Journal of Counseling Psychology, 51,* 463–472.

Shechtman, Z., Goldberg, A., & Cariani, R. (2008). Arab and Israeli counseling trainees: A comparison of ethnically homogeneous and heterogeneous groups. *Group Dynamics: Theory, Research, and Practice, 12,* 85–95.

Shechtman, Z., & Rybko, J. (2004). Attachment style and observed initial self-disclosure as explanatory variables of group functioning. *Group Dynamics: Theory, Research, and Practice, 8,* 207–220.

Shelley-Ummenhofer, J. & MacMillan, P. D. (2007). Cognitive-behavioural treatment for women who binge eat. *Canadian Journal of Dietetic Practice & Research, 68,* 139–142.

Sherman, K. A., Heard, G., & Cavanagh, K. L. (2010). Psychological effects and mediators of a group multi-component program for breast cancer survivors. *Journal of Behavioral Medicine, 33*(5), 378–391.

Sikkema, K. J., Hansen, N. B., Kochman, A., Tarakeshwar, N., Neufeld, S., Meade, C. S., & Fox, A. M. (2007). Outcomes from a group intervention for coping with HIV/AIDS and childhood sexual abuse. *AIDS and Behavior, 11,* 49–60.

Sikkema, K. J., Hansen, N. B., Tarakeshwar, N., Kochman, A., Tate, D. C., & Lee, R. S. (2004). The clinical significance of change in trauma-related symptoms following a pilot group intervention for coping with HIV-AIDS and childhood sexual trauma. *AIDS and Behavior, 8,* 277–291.

Sikkema, K. J., Wilson, P. A., Hansen, N. B., Kochman, A., Neufeld, S., Ghebremichael, M. S., & Kershaw, T. (2008). Effects of a coping intervention on transmission risk behavior among people living with HIV/AIDS and a history of childhood sexual abuse. *Journal of Acquired Immune Deficiency Syndrome, 47,* 506–513.

Silverman, W. K., Pina, A. A., & Viswesvaran, C. (2008). Evidence-based psychosocial treatments for phobias and anxiety disorders in children and adolescents. *Journal of Clinical Child & Adolescent Psychology, 37,* 105–130.

Simon, G., Ludman, E., Bauer, M., Unutzer, J., & Operskalski, B. (2006). Long-term effectiveness and cost of a systematic care program for bipolar disorder. *Archives of General Psychiatry, 63,* 500–508.

Simon, G., Ludman, E., Unutzer, J., Bauer, M., Operskalski, B., & Rutter, C. (2005). Randomized trial of a population-based care program for people with bipolar disorder. *Psychological Medicine, 35,* 13–24.

Smith, D. C., Hall, J. A., Williams, J. K., An, H., & Gotman, N. (2006). Comparative efficacy of family and group treatment for adolescent substance abuse. *The American Journal on Addictions, 15,* 131–136.

Sobell, L. C., Sobell, M. B., & Agrawal, S. (2009). Randomized controlled trial of a cognitive–behavioral motivational intervention in a group versus individual format for substance use disorders. *Psychology of Addictive Behaviors, 23,* 672–683.

Soler, J., Pascual, J. C., Tiana, T., Cebrià, A., Barrachina, J., Campins, M. J., . . . Pérez, V. (2009). Dialectical behavior therapy skills training compared to standard group therapy in borderline personality disorder. *Behaviour Research and Therapy, 47,* 353–358.

Sousa, M. B., Isolan, L. R., Oliveira, R. R., Manfro, G. G., & Cordioli, A. V. (2006). A randomized clinical trial of cognitive-behavioral group therapy and sertraline in the treatment of obsessive - compulsive disorder. *Journal of Clinical Psychiatry*, *67*(7), 1133–1199.

Spiegel, D., Butler, L., Giese-Davis, J., Koopman, C., Miller, E., DiMiceli, S.,…Kraemer, H. (2007). Effects of supportive-expressive group therapy on survival of patients with metastatic breast cancer. *Cancer*, *110*(5), 1130–1138.

Spiegel, D., Classen, C., Thurston, E., & Butler, L. (2004). Trauma-focused versus present-focused models of group therapy for women sexually abused in childhood. In L. J. Koenig, L. S. Doll, A. O'Leary, & W. Pequegnot, W. (Eds.), *From child sexual abuse to adult sexual risk: Trauma, revictimization, and intervention* (pp. 251–268). Washington, DC: American Psychological Association Press.

Spiegel, D., Kraemer, H. C., Bloom, J. R., & Gottheil, E. (1989). Effect of psychosocial treatment on survival of patients with metastatic breast cancer. *Lancet*, *334*(8668), 888–891.

Spitzer, C., Siebel-Jürges, U., Barnow, S., Grabe, H. J., & Freyberger, H. J. (2005). Alexithymia and interpersonal problems. *Psychotherapy and Psychosomatics*, *74*, 240–246.

Stangier, U., Heidenreich, T., Peitz, M., Lauterbach, W., & Clark, D. M. (2003). Cognitive therapy for social phobia. *Behaviour Research and Therapy*, *41*, 991–1007.

Stepakoff, S., Hubbard, J., Katoh, M., Falk, E., Mikulu, J-B., Nkhoma, P. & Omagwa, Y. (2006). Trauma healing in refugee camps in Guinea. *American Psychologist*, *61*, 921–932.

Strauss, B. (2012). The group as a secure base—Attachment theoretical reflections on group psychotherapy. In B. Strauss, D. Mattke (Eds.), *Group Psychotherapy—A Textbook for Practicioners* (in German). Heidelberg, Germany: Springer.

Strauss, B., Burlingame, G. M., & Bormann, B. (2008). Using the CORE-R battery in group psychotherapy. *Journal of Clinical Psychology: In Session*, *64*, 1225–1237.

Strauss, B., Kirchmann, H., Eckert, J., Lobo-Drost, A., Marquet, A., Papenhausen, R.,…Höger, D. (2006). Attachment characteristics and treatment outcome following inpatient psychotherapy: Results of a multisite study. *Psychotherapy Research*, *16*(5), 579–594.

Swan, A., Watson, H. J., & Nathan, P. R. (2009). Quality of life in depression. *Clinical Psychology and Psychotherapy*, *16*, 485–496.

Tang, T., DeRubeis, R., Hollon, St., Amsterdam, J., & Shelton, R. (2007) *Journal of Consulting and Clinical Psychology*, *75*(3), 404–408.

Tasca, G. A., Balfour, L., Ritchie, K., & Bissada, H. (2006). Developmental changes in group climate in two forms of group therapy for binge-eating disorder. *Psychotherapy Research*, *16*, 499–514.

Tasca, G., Balfour, L., Ritchie, K., & Bissada, H. (2007). Change in attachment anxiety is associated with improved depression among women with binge eating disorder. *Psychotherapy: Theory, Research, Practice, Training*, *44*, 423–433.

Tasca, G. A., Ritchie, K., Conrad, G., Balfour, L., Gayton, J., Daigle, V., & Bissada, H. (2006). Attachment scales predict outcome in a randomized controlled trial of two group therapies for Binge Eating Disorder. *Psychotherapy Research*, *16*, 106–121.

Telch, C. F., Agras, W. S., & Linehan, M. M. (2000). Group dialectical behavior therapy for binge-eating disorder. *Behavior Therapy*, *31*, 569–582.

Telch, C. F., Agras, W. S., & Linehan, M. M. (2001). Dialectical behavior therapy for binge eating disorder. *Journal of Consulting & Clinical Psychology*, *69*, 1061–1065.

Thayer, S. (2012). *The validity of the group questionnaire: Construct clarity or drift*. Unpublished doctoral dissertation. Brigham Young University, Utah.

Tillfors, M., Carlbring, P., Furmark, T., Lewenhaupt, S., Spak, M., Eriksson, A.,…Andersson, G. (2008). Treating university students with social phobia and public speaking fears. *Depression and Anxiety*, *25*(8), 708–717.

Toussaint, D. W., VanDeMark, N. R., Bornemann, A., & Graeber, C. J. (2007). Modifications to the Trauma Recovery and Empowerment Model (TREM) for substance-abusing women with histories of violence. *Journal of Community Psychology*, *35*, 879–894.

Tross, S., Campbell, A. N. C., Cohen, L. R., Calsyn, D., Pavlicova, M., Miele, G.,…Nunes, E. V. (2008). Effectiveness of HIV/STD sexual risk reduction groups for women in substance abuse treatment programs: Results of a NIDA clinical trials network trial. *Journal of Acquired Immune Deficiency Syndromes*, *15*, 581–589.

Turner, R. M. (2000). Naturalistic evaluation of dialectical behavior therapy-oriented treatment for borderline personality disorder. *Cognitive and Behavioral Practice*, *7*, 413–419.

Turner-Stokes, L., Erkeller-Yuksel, F., Miles, A., Pincus, T., Shipley, M., & Pearce, S. (2003). Outpatient cognitive behavioral pain management programs. *Archives of Physical Medicine and Rehabilitation*, *84*, 781–788.

Vaa, G., Egner, R., & Sexton, H. (2002). Sexually abused women after multimodal group therapy: A long-term follow-up study. *Nordic Journal of Psychiatry*, *56*, 215–221.

Van den Bosch, L. M. C., Verheul, R., Schippers, G. M., & van den Brink, W. (2002). Dialectical behavior therapy of borderline patients with and without substance use problems. *Addictive Behaviors*, *27*, 911–923.

Van Ingen, D. J., & Novicki, D. J. (2009). An effectiveness study of group therapy for anxiety disorders. *International Journal of Group Psychotherapy, 59,* 243–251.

van Tulder, M. W., Ostelo, R., Vlaeyen, J. W. S., Linton, S. J., Morley, S. J., & Assendelft, W. J. J. (2001). Behavioral treatment for chronic low back pain, a systematic review within the framework of the Cochrane back review group. *SPINE, 26,* 270–281.

Veltro, F., Vendittelli, N., Oricchio, I., Addona, F., Avino, C., Figliolia, G., & Morosini, P. (2008). Effectiveness and efficiency of cognitive-behavioral group therapy for inpatients: 4-year follow-up study. *Journal of Psychiatric Practice, 14,* 281–288.

Verheul, R., van den Bosch, L. M. C., Koeter, M. W. J., de Ridder, M. A. J., Stijnen, T., & van den Brink, W. (2003). Dialectical behaviour therapy for women with borderline personality disorder. *British Journal of Psychiatry, 182,* 135–140.

Voruganti, L. N. P., Whatham, J., Bard, E., Parker, G., Babbey, C., Ryan, J., . . . MacCrimmon, D. (2006). Going beyond: An adventure- and recreation-based group intervention promotes well-being and weight loss in schizophrenia. *Canadian Journal of Psychiatry, 51*(9), 575–580.

Wade, N. J., & Goldman, D. B. (2006). Sex, group composition, and the efficacy of group interventions to promote forgiveness. *Group Dynamics: Theory, Research, and Practice, 10,* 297–308.

Waldron, H. B., & Turner, C. W. (2008). Evidence-based psychosocial treatments for adolescent substance abuse. *Journal of Clinical Child and Adolescent Psychology, 37,* 238–261.

Wallis, D. A. N. (2002). Reduction of trauma symptoms following group therapy. *Australian and New Zealand Journal of Psychiatry, 36,* 67–74.

Warren, F., Evans, C., Dolan, B., & Norton, K. (2004). Impulsivity and self-damaging behaviour in severe personality disorder. *Therapeutic Communities, 25,* 55–71.

Weiss, R. D., Griffin, M., Jaffee, E., Bender, R. E., Graff, F. S., Gallop, R., & Fitzmaurice, G. M. (2009). A "community-friendly" version of integrated group therapy for patients with bipolar disorder and substance dependence. *Drug and Alcohol Dependence, 106,* 212–219.

Weiss, R. D., Griffin, M. L., Kolozdiej, M. E., Greenfield, S. F., Najavits, L. M., Daley, D. C., . . . Hennen, J. A. (2007). A randomized trial of integrated group therapy versus group drug counseling for patients with bipolar disorder and substance dependence. *American Journal of Psychiatry, 164,* 100–107.

Westwood, M. J., McLean, H., Cave, D., Borgen, W., & Slakov, P. (2010). Coming home: A group-based approach for assisting military veterans in transition. *Journal for Specialists in Group Work, 35,* 44–68.

White, D. C., Beecham, R., & Kirkwood, K. (2008). The vocational continuum. *Journal of Occupational Rehabilitation, 18,* 307–317.

Whittal, M. L., Robichaud, M., Thordarson, D. S., & McLean, P. D. (2008). Group and individual treatment of obsessive-compulsive disorder using cognitive therapy and exposure plus response prevention. *Journal of Consulting and Clinical Psychology, 76*(6), 1003–1004.

Wilberg, T., Karterud, S., Pedersen, G., Urnes, Ø., Irion, T., Brabrand, J., . . . Stubbhaug, B. (2003). Out-patient group psychotherapy following day treatment of patients with personality disorders. *Journal of Personality Disorders, 17,* 510–521.

Wilfley, D. E., Frank, M., Welch, R., Spurrell, E., & Rounsaville, B. (1998). Adapting interpersonal psychotherapy to a group format (IPT-G) for binge eating disorder: Toward a model for adapting empirically supported treatments. *Psychotherapy Research, 8*(4), 379–391.

Wilfley, D. E., Welch, R. R., Stein, R. I., Spurrell, E. B., Cohen, L. R., Saelens, B. E., . . . Matt, G. E. (2002). A randomized comparison of group cognitive-behavioral therapy and group interpersonal psychotherapy for the treatment of overweight individuals with binge-eating disorder. *Archives of General Psychiatry, 59,* 713–721.

Wong, D. F. K. (2008). Cognitive and health-related outcomes of group cognitive behavioural treatment for people with depressive symptoms in Hong Kong. *Australian and New Zealand Journal of Psychiatry, 42,* 702–711.

Yalom, I. D., & Leszcz, M. (2005). *The theory and practice of group psychotherapy* (5th ed.). New York, NY: Basic Books.

Yzerbyt, V., Corneille, O., & Judd, C. M. (2004). *The psychology of group perception: Perceived variability, entitativity, and essentialism*. London, United Kingdom: Psychology Press.

Zlotnick, C., Najavits, L. M., Rohsenow, D. J., & Johnson, D. M. (2003). A cognitive-behavioral treatment for incarcerated women with substance abuse disorder and posttraumatic stress disorder. *Journal of Substance Abuse Treatment, 25,* 99–105.

CHAPTER 17

BEHAVIORAL MEDICINE AND CLINICAL HEALTH PSYCHOLOGY

TIMOTHY W. SMITH AND PAULA G. WILLIAMS

INTRODUCTION

Since their formal beginnings in the 1970s, the related fields of behavioral medicine and health psychology have grown substantially and evolved. In many ways, their emergence was a necessary response to changing patterns of health. By the latter half of the 20th century, advances in public health and medicine (e.g., improved sanitation, hygiene, and nutrition; development of vaccines and antibiotics) had produced a dramatic reduction in morbidity and mortality from infectious disease in the United States and other industrialized nations, where previously they had been the leading causes of death. In these nations, infectious diseases were replaced by cardiovascular disease (e.g., coronary heart disease, stroke), cancer, chronic pulmonary disease, and diabetes as leading causes of death in adulthood.

These noncommunicable, chronic diseases differ from the previously predominant infectious diseases in several ways that involve major roles for behavioral science in biomedical research and health care (Fisher et al., 2011). Specific modifiable behaviors (e.g., smoking, high dietary intake of calories and fat, physical inactivity) strongly increase the risk for the initial development of these chronic conditions and influence their course, making behavioral processes key targets in prevention and treatment. Hence, the development of a scientific understanding of the determinants and modification of these behavioral risk factors has become a pressing priority. Also, these chronic diseases can have a profound impact on psychological and behavioral functioning or quality of life, broadly defined (e.g., emotional adjustment, social and vocational functioning, disability). As a result, management of these health outcomes and related effects of chronic disease (e.g., physical symptoms and distress) is an important component of efforts to reduce the burden of these conditions. Management of these consequences of chronic disease goes beyond biomedical treatments of the underlying physical condition, to include psychosocial approaches specifically targeting these emotional and behavioral outcomes, as adjuncts to traditional medical care. Finally, for several of these conditions, physiological effects of stress, negative emotion, and other psychosocial factors seem to play a direct role—independent of health behavior risk factors—in their development and course, creating a potential role for related psychological interventions in treatment of the underlying disease process.

The rapid expansion and evolution of health psychology and behavioral medicine is evident in the chapters on the topic appearing in prior versions of this handbook, and in the somewhat distinct focus of this, the fourth such chapter. Pomerleau and Rodin (1986) provided an overview of these still-emerging fields, focusing on areas of basic research (e.g., psychobiology of stress and disease) and applied research (e.g., adherence with medical regimens, coping with stressful medical procedures) that became important elements of the foundation of these fields. They also reviewed a smaller number of topics in emerging research on interventions (e.g., smoking cessation). Blanchard (1994) focused more specifically on intervention research, in which mostly individual and small group behavioral and cognitive-behavioral approaches targeted specific conditions (e.g., hypertension, chronic pain, insomnia) or risk factors for important diseases (e.g., obesity, smoking). This review provided clear evidence—from a rapidly growing number of increasingly methodologically rigorous intervention studies—that such treatments could produce clinically meaningful changes in risk factors, reduce the severity of several chronic medical conditions, and lessen their impact on functioning, making them useful additions to traditional approaches to medical care and prevention in many instances.

Creer, Holroyd, Glasgow, and Smith (2004) provided an updated review of many of these same intervention topics that included much additional evidence of clinically meaningful effects, but noted that the field had expanded so rapidly that a comprehensive review was no longer feasible. They also broadened their focus beyond the chronic diseases and conditions in industrialized nations to include more global or world health issues, such as the burden of infectious diseases (i.e., HIV, tuberculosis) in less developed nations. This global focus made clear that much of the potential impact of behavioral medicine and health psychology lies in their role in public health, policy, and various population-level interventions, as well as the more traditional individual and small group-level approaches.

In this chapter, after a brief overview of the conceptual foundations of these closely related fields we, too, provide a necessarily condensed and selective update of the empirical status of intervention research and applications in behavioral medicine and health psychology, focusing almost exclusively on adults. As a guide to a more thorough coverage of the field for interested readers, we cite qualitative and quantitative reviews of many specific topics. Consistent with the overall focus of the handbook, we primarily review intervention issues, covering other topics to the extent that they are needed to appreciate the current state and future directions of these fields. Although we heartily endorse the view of Creer and colleagues (2004) that health psychology and behavioral medicine have much to offer efforts to address the burdens of infectious illness in developing and less industrialized nations of the world, we focus primarily on intervention issues in the United States and other industrialized countries. However, it is important to note that 60% of

deaths worldwide are due to noncommunicable chronic diseases, and 80% of those deaths occur in the developing world (Alwan et al., 2010). Hence, the issues we address are highly relevant in both industrialized and developing nations. Further, as we discuss in closing, in the coming years the health agendas in industrialized and developing nations are expected to converge further, and we discuss the implications of these trends for health psychology and behavioral medicine.

Given the primary focus of this handbook on services delivered to individuals and small groups, we emphasize similar approaches to the modification of health relevant behavior and the treatment or management of chronic disease, as opposed to more broadly focused large-group, population-level, policy, or public health intervention approaches. Hence, in a departure from prior editions of the handbook, our chapter title specifically refers to behavioral medicine and *clinical* health psychology, to designate our greater focus on the delivery of psychological services in medical settings and psychological consultation or collaboration with traditional health care providers. The rapidly evolving nature of medical care in the United States and other industrialized nations poses both major opportunities and daunting challenges for these central aspects of behavioral medicine and clinical health psychology.

However, just as the psychotherapy and behavior change research community has increasingly recognized the need to expand the portfolio of mental health services beyond traditional interventions for emotional distress and disorders delivered to individuals and small groups to include more population-based, preventive, and public health strategies (Kazdin & Blase, 2011), we also discuss the larger-group and population-based approaches that are a central focus in more broadly defined behavioral medicine and health psychology. These aspects of behavioral medicine and health psychology face an equally far-reaching set of opportunities and challenges. Indeed, these two trends in the field—refinement of individual and small group approaches and their integration into evolving models of medical care, and the development and dissemination of more large-group and population-focused strategies primarily addressing health behavior change—represent an evolving distinction within these fields. These two segments of behavioral medicine and health psychology involve different training requirements (e.g., traditional psychological approaches, transposed to health care settings and medical populations versus organizational, community, policy, and public health approaches to behavior change) and sets of likely collaborators (e.g., primary medical care providers and medical specialists versus health educators, practitioners in community and public health, policy makers).

DEFINITIONS, CONTENT, AND CONCEPTUAL FOUNDATIONS

The terms *health psychology* and *behavioral medicine* are sometimes distinguished quite carefully (Pomerleau & Rodin, 1986), and at other times are used interchangeably (Creer et al., 2004). Initially, the two fields were distinguished in part by a more explicit inclusion of biomedical science and clinical medicine within the description of behavioral medicine. Also, early in its emergence, behavioral medicine was more closely based in operant and classical learning theory approaches to psychological aspects of the development and management of disease (Pomerleau & Brady, 1979; Surwit, Williams, & Shapiro, 1982). That is, *behavioral* medicine was explicitly associated with behaviorism in early definitions, in part to distinguish it from the psychoanalytic perspective that had previously characterized one of its main historical predecessors—*psychosomatic medicine*. In contrast, health psychology reflected a broader array of conceptual perspectives on psychological processes, based in social, clinical, developmental, experimental, physiological, and personality psychology (Stone, Cohen, & Adler, 1979). Soon, behavioral medicine also came to include a greater variety of conceptual approaches and traditions regarding the behavioral, psychological, and social-environmental aspects of disease (Gentry, 1984), as did psychosomatic medicine (cf. Novak et al., 2007).

Currently, both behavioral medicine and health psychology involve the development and integration of behavioral, psychosocial, and biomedical research in an effort to understand health and illness, and the application of the resulting knowledge in efforts to prevent and treat physical illness. The distinction between health psychology and behavioral medicine now lies mostly in matters of professional identify and training, rather than their overall mission or conceptual orientation. Health psychology is conducted largely—but not exclusively—by psychologists, whereas behavioral medicine involves a greater

variety of professionals, including psychologists, physicians, epidemiologists, sociologists, nurses, and others. In this way, behavioral medicine is the broader, more inclusive field, of which health psychology is a subfield. Clinical health psychology, in turn, is the subfield within health psychology that involves research and applied services regarding the prevention, management, and treatment of physical illness. Whereas health psychology broadly defined includes large-group and population-based approaches to prevention and health behavior change, clinical health psychology focuses more specifically on applications with individuals and small groups, often for those with well-established unhealthy behavior or existing physical illness or other medical conditions.

Both health psychology and behavioral medicine comprise three general, interrelated topics. *Stress and disease*—or *psychosomatics*—is perhaps the oldest, and concerns the direct psychobiological effects of stress, negative emotion, and related processes on the pathophysiology of disease. Within this topic, researchers examine the associations of psychosocial risk factors (e.g., social isolation, job stress, chronic anger, depression) with the development and course of disease (Everson-Rose & Clark, 2010). Other studies examine the physiological mechanisms (e.g., alterations in neuroendocrine, cardiovascular, or immune system responses) that link psychosocial inputs and disease outcomes (Lovallo, 2010). Animal studies of this topic manipulate levels of environmental stress in ways that are not possible with human participants to examine effects on disease processes and underlying physiological mechanisms (Nation, Schneiderman, & McCabe, 2010). Results of such efforts guide the development and evaluation of interventions that target stress, negative emotion, and related factors in order to alter the development and course of disease (Schneiderman, Antoni, Penedo, & Ironson, 2010).

The second major topic—*health behavior and prevention*—examines the association of daily habits (e.g., smoking, diet, physical activity) with the development and course of disease (Kaplan, 2010), as well as the determinants of these behaviors (Schwarzer, 2011). This information then guides the development, evaluation, and implementation of interventions intended to promote healthier lifestyles. The third topic—*psychosocial aspects of medical illness and medical care*—examines the impact of physical illness and related medical care on a variety of aspects of functioning, including emotional adjustment, physical distress, social and vocational roles, and general levels of functional activity versus disability (Stanton, Revenson, & Tennen, 2007). This general topic also includes behavioral aspects of medical treatment (e.g., adherence with medical regimens), and the process of health care utilization (e.g., patient-provider communication, seeking health services; Baldwin, Kellerman, & Christensen, 2010). Research in this third area guides the development, evaluation, and implementation of adjunctive psychological and behavioral treatments for medical conditions (Schneiderman et al., 2010).

These topics are clearly overlapping. For example, exercise may be prescribed for recovering heart patients not only because of its direct physiological effects in reducing the risk of recurrent coronary events, but also because exercise is sometimes useful both in managing the depressive symptoms that often accompany coronary disease and in helping the patients to return to work and prior levels of functional activity (Stein, 2012). Across all three topics, treatment research of various types tests the efficacy and effectiveness of the resulting interventions as potential additions to standard medical and surgical approaches to prevention and disease management (Oldenburg, Absetz, & Chan, 2010).

The Biopsychosocial Model

Since their inception, health psychology and behavioral medicine have been strongly tied to the biopsychosocial model (Suls, Luger, & Martin, 2010). Traditional medicine is based on the biomedical model of disease, in which biological processes are seen as providing a sufficient basis for understanding, treating, and preventing disease. The success of this model is readily apparent in dramatic improvements in health and advances in medical treatment over the last century. Yet, many authors over many decades have deemed the biomedical approach to be incomplete, given its neglect of the role of psychological, social, and cultural factors in disease etiology and medical treatment (Suls et al., 2010). As a response to these perceived limitations, Engel (1977) proposed the biopsychosocial model (see Figure 17.1). Rather than reducing disease to basic biological causes and focusing only on biologically based treatments, the biopsychosocial model describes health and illness as the result of reciprocal influences among hierarchically arranged levels of analysis (von Bertalanffy, 1968). These levels

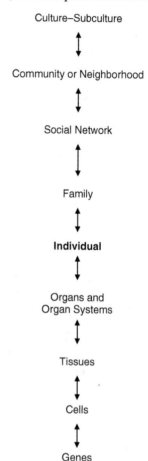

FIGURE 17.1 Systems hierarchy in the biopsychosocial model (based on Engel, 1977).

range from the lower or more basic levels of the traditional biomedical model (i.e., biochemical processes, genes, cells, tissues, and organ systems) to the level of the behaving individual and on to higher levels of interpersonal, social, and broader environmental and cultural levels. In traditional scientific approaches, each level of analysis is understood through its own models and methods. However, in the biopsychosocial framework, each system or level influences and is influenced by the adjacent levels. In this view, any specific disease process (e.g., atherosclerosis in the coronary arteries) cannot be fully understood through a given level of analysis (e.g., molecular biology of inflammation; tissue pathology). It also must be considered at the multiple levels above and below in the hierarchy.

The implications for research, medical care, and the prevention of disease are clear. To understand the contributing factors for any given disease or medical condition, multilevel, integrative research is needed. Similarly, for an optimal approach to prevention, treatment, and management, opportunities at multiple levels must be explored. In discussing the applied implications of his model for clinical care, Engel (1980) suggested that "while the bench scientist can with relative impunity single out and isolate for sequential study components of an organized whole, the physician does so at the risk of neglect of, if not injury to, the object of study" (p. 536). Hence, the biopsychosocial model directs health care providers toward a multilevel, integrative approach to the evaluation and treatment of individual patients.

This framework also clearly suggests that regardless of whether they are biological or behavioral in focus, individual-based approaches to a given medical problem are incomplete; they should be augmented by broader social, organizational, community, and cultural level strategies for prevention and management. Leading causes of death (e.g., cardiovascular disease, cancer) will be best understood, prevented, and managed if each of these levels of analysis are considered and addressed. Although it is typically not feasible to address all levels of analysis in providing care to individual patients, a comprehensive medical, public health, and policy approach to the challenges posed by any given disease must consider the full range of levels of analysis. Consideration of these multiple levels also makes clear that a comprehensive, biopsychosocial model includes not only treatment of existing disease, but the prevention and reduction of disease risk well before its clinical onset.

Perspectives on the Individual and Behavior

As described previously, the behavioral perspective was the main psychological conceptual view during the formative years of behavioral medicine (Pomerleau & Brady, 1979; Surwit et al., 1982), and remains an important, but less dominant perspective today. Many interventions currently in use in the field are based on operant and classical learning models, both in prevention efforts and in the management of chronic illness and other medical problems. Paralleling trends in clinical psychology, behavioral medicine soon incorporated the cognitive-behavioral perspective (Wilson, 1980), most notably social learning theory (Bandura, 1977) and related perspectives

emerging in the 1970s (Beck, 1976; Mahoney, 1977; Meichenbaum, 1977).

A major influence in all areas of health psychology and behavioral medicine has been the stress and coping model developed by Lazarus and his colleagues (Cohen & Lazarus, 1979; Lazarus, 1966; Lazarus & Folkman, 1984). Articulation of the role in stress of primary appraisal (i.e., judgments about potential for threat, harm, or loss) and secondary appraisal (i.e., judgments about opportunities for preventing or moderating the potential negative outcome) and emotion-focused coping (i.e., efforts to reduce the negative affect in response to stress) and problem-focused coping (i.e., efforts to reduce the demands of the stressor) produced a clear set of testable hypotheses and potential targets for interventions for stress-related problems. Given that stress plays a central role in all three of the major issues or topics in behavioral medicine and health psychology described previously (i.e., health behavior and prevention, stress and disease, psychosocial aspects of medical illness and medical care), this general perspective is a cornerstone in the foundation of these fields. The cognitive-behavioral perspective provided an important extension of the stress and coping paradigm, in describing an array of interventions easily adapted to focus on modification of the key concepts of appraisal and coping.

Personality characteristics are increasingly recognized as important influences on stress and disease, health behavior, and the impact of medical illness and aspects of medical care on emotional adjustment and functional activity (Smith, 2006a). For example, personality characteristics influence exposure to various sources of stress (e.g., interpersonal conflict), the magnitude of emotional and physiological stress responses, emotional and physiological recovery after stress exposure, and stress-related restorative processes (e.g., sleep quality; Williams, Smith, Gunn, & Uchino, 2011). Current theory and research in behavioral medicine and health psychology utilizes traditional trait approaches to personality, as well as social-cognitive and interpersonal perspectives to address these issues. Social psychological perspectives on individual behavior are also prominent, especially those perspectives that emphasize individuals' attitudes and beliefs about health relevant behavior (Kiviniemi & Rothman, 2010) and internal representations or "cognitive models" of the nature of specific medical conditions and related treatments (Leventhal, Breland, Mora, & Leventhal, 2010).

The Social Context

In each of the three main research topics in behavioral medicine and health psychology, social relationships are a central consideration. The availability and quality of personal relationships (i.e., social support and integration versus isolation) is an important predictor of the development and course of serious disease (Holt-Lunstad, Smith, & Layton, 2010; Lett et al., 2005), and a variety of psychobiological mechanisms have been identified as potentially underlying such associations (Uchino, 2006). The quality of marriage and similar close relationships is a similarly important influence on the development and course of disease (e.g., De Vogli, Chandola, & Marmot, 2007; Rohrbaugh, Shoham, & Coyne, 2006; Smith, Uchino, Berg, & Florsheim, 2012), and on adaptation to chronic medical conditions (Hagedoorn, Sanderman, Bolks, Tuinstra, & Coyne, 2008; Leonard, Cano, & Johansen, 2006). Couple-based interventions have been found to be useful in addressing a variety of behavioral risk reduction efforts and the management of several chronic diseases (Martire, Schulz, Helgeson, Small, & Saghafi, 2010; Shields, Finley, Chawla, & Meadows, 2012).

Broader features or levels of social context are an important component of the biopsychosocial model. For example, effective health behavior change programs have been developed for delivery in schools (Katz, 2009), worksites (Goetzel & Ozminkowski, 2008), and churches (Campbell et al., 2007). Characteristics of neighborhoods and the built environment (e.g., socioeconomic level, cohesion, safety, "walk-ability" and conduciveness to physical activity) have robust influences on health (Diez-Roux & Mair, 2010). Socioeconomic status (SES) has a strong, inverse relationship with the development and course of virtually all major causes of morbidity and mortality (Matthews & Gallo, 2010). Low SES is also associated with smaller declines in major causes of morbidity and mortality in recent years, due primarily to slower decreases in behavioral risks, less access to effective procedures for early detection, and less access to improved treatments (Byers, 2010). Public policy and environmental-level interventions (e.g., prohibition on smoking in public places) can clearly have effects on health behavior and the development and course of chronic disease (Brownson, Haire-Joshu, & Luke, 2006; Fisher et al., 2010). Hence, multiple levels of social—environmental context are the focus of current research and interventions in behavioral medicine and health psychology.

Methodological Considerations

In recent years, behavioral medicine and health psychology have responded to the growing influence of the evidence based medicine movement (Spring et al., 2005), which calls for the development and use of a sound research base as a guide to medical care (Sackett, Rosenberg, Gray, Haynes, & Richardson, 1996). In this perspective, a hierarchy of evidence informs clinical practice, with randomized clinical trials (RCTs) and systematic reviews of multiple RCTs as the top two tiers of evidence. This has involved adopting accepted, rigorous standards for conducting and reporting both RCTs (Altman et al., 2001) and systematic reviews of literatures where multiple trials have been conducted (Higgins & Green, 2011). Many previous RCTs in behavioral medicine and health psychology had been designed, analyzed, and/or reported in ways that fell short of these commendable, more recent standards (Davidson et al., 2003; Davidson, Trudeau, Ockene, Orleans, & Kalpan, 2004; Spring, Pagato, Knatterud, Kozak, & Hedeker, 2007), as had many systematic reviews and meta-analyses (Coyne, Thombs, & Hagendoorn, 2010). As a result, the impact of much of the prior intervention research in the field has been reduced somewhat by this recent history of new and rising methodological standards. At the same time, issues surrounding appropriate endpoints or health outcomes for intervention research have been also been evolving in important ways.

In some cases, behavioral endpoints (e.g., smoking cessation, physical activity levels) have always been straightforward in intervention research, as have some intermediate biologic endpoints (e.g., weight loss, blood pressure reductions), although the methods used to measure the endpoints and draw conclusions about the clinical implications of observed treatment effects have been a matter of considerable discussion (Smith, 2011). However, because traditional medical research typically emphasizes objective indicators of disease-specific morbidity and mortality (i.e., evidence of myocardial infarction in ECG changes and cardiac enzyme elevations; survivorship in advanced cancer) in evaluating medical and surgical interventions, demonstrations of effects of behavioral interventions on these "hard" medical outcomes has been an important source of evidence in the field. Indeed, the field as a whole has periodically been criticized by traditional medical researchers for the lack of consistent effects of psychological intervention on these endpoints (Relman & Angell, 2002).

Although objectively assessed morbidity and mortality continue to be outcomes of paramount importance in intervention research, medical research and policy as a whole has expanded to emphasize a broader view of health outcomes. Specifically, emerging definitions of health include behavioral and subjective endpoints. Levels of functional activity versus disability, physical symptoms (e.g., pain, fatigue), emotional adjustment, and social functioning in personal relationships and vocational or academic roles have long been important outcomes in behavioral medicine and health psychology intervention research. But interest in these behavioral outcomes and subjective reports has been increasing in recent years in the biomedical and health care research community.

For example, in 2004 the National Institutes of Health established the Patient Reported Outcomes Measurement Information System (PROMIS; www.nihpromis.org), and expanded the program in 2010. The goal of this initiative is the development and dissemination of patient-reported measures of physical, mental, and social well-being. Traditional measurement issues (i.e., reliability, validity) are a major focus of current and planned PROMIS research, but the mission is broader. One goal is to develop measures that provide standardized, comparable information across a variety of domains and medical conditions. Flexibility in measurement use and applicability to a wide range of demographic groups is also a major focus. In this way the impact of a variety of medical conditions can be compared, as can variations in their impact across segments of the population. Importantly, standardized and broadly applicable measures will facilitate more precise, integrated, and comparative evaluations of a wide variety of interventions.

The increased emphasis on patient reported outcomes is also evident in the recently established Patient-Centered Outcomes Research Institute (P-CORI: www.pcori.org). This independent, nonprofit institute was established by the United States Congress in 2010, through the Patient Protection and Affordable Care Act. Its mission is to develop and disseminate information to inform health care decisions, specifically information based on empirical evidence about the effectiveness, benefits, and harms of treatment

options patients and providers are considering, and the ways in which those outcomes differ for specific types of patients. In addition to information about survival or longevity and other objective biomedical outcomes for morbidity in various conditions (e.g., blood pressure, plasma lipid levels, blood glucose levels), the P-CORI mission specifically includes patient functioning (i.e., activity versus disability), symptoms, and health-related quality of life (H-QOL). Hence, classes of outcomes that have historically been seen as "soft" and providing weak evidence regarding the effects of interventions in behavioral medicine and health psychology are increasingly seen as important—for evaluations of clinical efficacy and effectiveness, for patients and providers choosing among treatment options, and as a guide to policy decisions regarding health care spending.

Outcomes that capture morbidity, mortality, and H-QOL have an important role not only in evaluating the effects of specific interventions, but also in comparing the relative benefits of various interventions. An increasingly common outcome index is the quality adjusted life year (QALY), which essentially weights each year of life by the H-QOL during that year (Kaplan & Groessl, 2002). QALYs can be used to compare not only a variety of intervention outcomes, but also can evaluate their cost-effectiveness by quantifying the cost associated with each QALY produced by that intervention (Kaplan & Groessl, 2002). It is possible that this growing emphasis on broader assessments of health outcomes will make the value of interventions in behavioral medicine and health psychology more apparent. They have the potential to influence not only mortality, but also directly improve components of H-QOL and do so at relatively low cost.

In addition to efforts to implement new standards for design, analysis, and reporting of RCTs, the choice of appropriate comparison or control conditions has received increased attention in behavioral medicine and clinical health psychology intervention research (Freedland, Mohr, Davidson, & Schwartz, 2011). The magnitude and meaning of the observed intervention effect depend, in large part, on the nature of the comparison or control conditions, and different comparison conditions are appropriate for specific questions. For example, comparisons to usual medical or surgical care are often used in initial evaluations of the efficacy of an adjunctive behavioral or psychological intervention, but can be faulted for failure to control for expectancies and

TABLE 17.1   The RE-AIM Framework (Glasgow, Vogt, & Boles, 1999)

Reach	Proportion of the target population participating in the intervention
Efficacy	Success rate if intervention is implemented as intended in guidelines
Adoption	Proportion of settings, practices, and health care plans adopting the intervention
Implementation	Extent to which intervention is implemented as intended in real-world settings
Maintenance	Extent to which intervention program is sustained over time

other nonspecific factors. Variations in comparison conditions across multiple RCTs evaluating a given intervention can complicate systematic reviews and meta-analyses, the highest form of evidence in the EBM perspective.

Relative to prior reviews of the efficacy of interventions in behavioral medicine and health psychology (e.g., Blanchard, 1994), it is clear that methodological standards for the RCTs have been raised. However, facilitating an expansion of the research base demonstrating efficacy is not the only challenge for current intervention research. Enhancing the external validity of intervention trials and producing stronger evidence of effectiveness of interventions in representative health care settings is an increasingly important concern (Glasgow, 2008; Glasgow & Emmons, 2007).

In terms of impact on population health, intervention efficacy and effectiveness are critical concerns, but so is the number of individuals reached by a given intervention (Abrams et al., 1996). Even a highly efficacious intervention will have limited impact on population health if high costs or restricted access means it reaches a limited number of people who might otherwise benefit. Conversely, an intervention with relatively modest efficacy (i.e., a small treatment effect size) can have a substantial impact on population health if it reaches a very large portion of that population. This concept has been expanded in the RE-AIM (Reach, Efficacy, Adoption, Implementation, Maintenance) framework of Glasgow and colleagues, which has been applied to both prevention-oriented health behavior change interventions (Glasgow, Vogt, & Boles, 1999) and chronic illness management (Glasgow, McKay, Piette, & Reynolds, 2001). In this expanded perspective (see Table 17.1), the health impact of a given intervention is the product of its reach and efficacy (i.e., Impact = Reach × Efficacy), but other critical determinants of health impact are the extent to which the intervention is adopted in health services, the consistency and fidelity with which it is implemented in those

settings, and the maintenance of that implementation. The RE-AIM model defines the important issue of intervention *effectiveness* as Efficacy × Implementation.

From this perspective, some issues in maximizing the potential health impact of behavioral medicine and health psychology interventions are largely new topics for research. Specifically the process of *dissemination* of research findings from RCTs of intervention efficacy, effectiveness studies, and systematic reviews, and the processes of intervention adoption and implementation are increasingly the focus of research in their own right (Kerner, Rimer, & Emmons, 2005; McHugh & Barlow, 2011). This emerging focus on translational science in the field recognizes that, "the behaviors in need of change are not just those of our patients, but also those of our main professional partners" including health care providers and policy makers (Spring, 2011, p. 1).

PREVENTION AND HEALTH BEHAVIOR CHANGE

Smoking, levels of physical activity and fitness, dietary intake of calories and fat, and related levels of adiposity (i.e., overweight) are strongly related—individually and in combination—to cardiovascular disease (CVD) morbidity and mortality, cancer morbidity and mortality, diabetes, and all-cause mortality (Lee, Sui, Artero, et al., 2011; Lee, Sui, & Blair, 2009; Lee, Sui, Hooker, Herbert, & Blair, 2011). A substantial proportion of the decreases in morbidity and mortality associated with CVD and cancer in recent decades are attributable to population decreases in unhealthy behaviors (Byers, 2010; Ford & Capewell, 2011). Despite this progress, some estimates suggest that approximately 80% of CVD and diabetes, and 40% of cancers are still due to poor diet, physical inactivity, and tobacco use (Fisher et al., 2011; Spring, 2011). Further, has been suggested that type 2 diabetes could be largely eliminated through population-based changes in excess adiposity, moderate diet, and physical activity (Schulz & Hu, 2005). Yet in the United States spending on related prevention efforts is 5% or less of total health care expenditures (McGinnis, Williams-Russo, & Knickman, 2002; Satcher, 2006). Relative to the costs of treating these chronic health conditions, efforts to prevent them through the modification of related behaviors are highly cost-effective (Gordon, Graves, Hawkes, & Eaken, 2007).

Conceptual Models

Prominent models conceptualize health behavior change as a multiphase process, in which different points in the change process pose distinct challenges and require distinct intervention elements. This view is most formally represented in the Stages of Change Model, also known as the *Trans-Theoretical Model* (SOC/TTM; J. O. Prochaska, DiClemente, & Norcross, 1992). In this view, individuals pass sequentially through precontemplation, contemplation, preparation, action, and maintenance stages, perhaps multiple times in the event of relapse and renewed change attempts. In theory, different types of interventions are effective at different stages, creating a stage-by-intervention-type matching prediction regarding optimal change; interventions tailored or matched to the individual's specific location along the multistage process will be more effective than unmatched interventions. This tailoring or matching prediction has been supported in some research (Johnson et al., 2008; Krebs, Prochaska, & Rossi, 2010), as have other elements of the model (Hall & Rossi, 2008). However, the stages are often difficult to distinguish empirically (Herzog, 2008; Weinstein, Rothman, & Sutton, 1998), and matched or tailored interventions are often no more effective—or only slightly more effective—than nonmatched interventions (Armitage, 2009; Noar, Benac, & Harris, 2007).

The earliest point in the process of health behavior change is the primary focus of another influential model and related technique—motivational interviewing (Miller & Rose, 2009). This approach to patient interviews regarding potential health behavior change involves empathy, acceptance, and collaboration rather than the directive and problem-focused style that characterizes most medical encounters. The motivational interviewing (MI) approach also attempts to evoke and reinforce the patient's spontaneous and self-initiated "change talk." Motivational interviewing is often implemented in brief contacts with patients in primary medical care, and has been found to have positive effects on efforts to modify smoking, diet, exercise, and the control of chronic disease (e.g., diabetes) (Lundahl & Burke, 2009; Martin & McNeil, 2009). However, RCTs on motivational interviewing have been criticized as methodologically limited, and producing small effect sizes (Knight, McGowan, Dickens, & Bundy, 2006). Many health behavior change attempts result in initial success but subsequent failure (Brandon, Vidrine, & Litvin, 2007), leading to the common practice of incorporating relapse prevention training as a component of interventions (Hendershot, Witkiewitz, George, & Marlatt, 2011). The approach is understandably widely used, but it has been difficult to demonstrate its independent efficacy (Agboola, McNeill, Coleman, & Bee, 2010).

Finally, in an effort to maximize health impact while minimizing costs, stepped care approaches have been developed in which low cost, largely self-guided health behavior change interventions are attempted initially, reserving professionally—delivered small group and individual treatments for cases where the less involved and costly "steps" fail to produce desired results (Abrams et al., 1996). The initial, low intensity and low cost steps have greater reach (Glasgow et al., 1999), and therefore have the potential to have important population impact. The higher efficacy but more intensive and costly approaches can be reserved for individuals who experience difficulty achieving or maintaining desired changes. Large group, organizational, and public policy interventions have the greatest potential reach. Given the remarkable prevalence of nearly all of the major behavioral risk factors, these approaches are a major focus of more broadly defined behavioral medicine and health psychology.

Smoking

After decades of steady reductions in the prevalence of smoking in the United States and some other industrialized nations, this progress has slowed in recent years. Currently, approximately 20% of adults in the United States smoke, and this behavior remains the leading cause of preventable death. The most common reason for attempting to quit smoking is a concern about health (McCaul et al., 2006), and for smokers there is no other behavior change that will provide as great a potential health benefit. Yet, most cessation attempts result in failure. Hence, smoking cessation is a major challenge in current behavioral medicine and clinical health psychology.

For individual and small-group based approaches to smoking cessation, the major treatments currently in use are multicomponent interventions, often combining pharmacologic and behavioral interventions. Major meta-analyses indicate that CBT for smoking cessation (e.g., problem solving, skills training, stress management) is modestly effective, producing a 40% to 60% increase in the odds of maintained cessation (Fiore et al., 2008; Lancaster & Stead, 2005). However, it is important to note that given that as many as 90% or more of unaided quit attempts result in failure within 6 to 12 months, even in the most successful interventions the majority of smokers relapse within the typical follow-up periods. Given the design of the individual trials, it is difficult to identify the most effective elements of CBT. In most of the individual RCTs the experimental control of nonspecific factors is minimal. To address these limitations, RCTs are needed to test specific components and packages, while controlling nonspecific factors and evaluating hypotheses regarding the mechanisms contributing to change (Bricker, 2010).

Meta-analytic reviews and major RCTs have demonstrated the efficacy of nicotine replacement therapy in both longer-acting (e.g., nicotine patches) and shorter-acting (e.g., nicotine gum) forms, and the efficacy of buproprion (i.e., Zyban, Wellbutron) and varenicline (i.e., Chantix) (Baker et al., 2011; Fiore et al., 2008; Fiore & Baker, 2011; Stead, Perera, Bullen, Mant, & Lancaster, 2008). These pharmacological treatments provide improved outcomes over CBT alone, and hence the combination of CBT or similar counseling approaches with pharmacological treatment is currently considered the standard of care (Fiore et al., 2008), although even the strongest effects of medication demonstrated in these reviews indicate that most treated smokers do not maintain cessation. It is possible that pharmacologic treatment may be even more effective if initiated well before the smoker's "quit date" (Baker et al., 2011).

Many smokers have considered smoking cessation but have not made a serious attempt to quit, or have failed in previous attempts. As a result, at any given time a large number of smokers are characterized by a low level of motivation for cessation. Motivational interviewing would seem to be a useful approach in this scenario, but to date there is little evidence that it produces a significant, independent effect on cessation (Bricker, 2010; Hettema, Steele, & Miller, 2005). Given that many smokers relapse after an initially successful quit attempt, relapse prevention is a common element of CBT approaches to smoking cessation. However, the evidence from RCTs specifically evaluating the effects of relapse prevention training indicates that it has little or no additional benefit (Lancaster, Hajek, Stead, West, & Jarvis, 2006). Research on the SOC/TTM approach in which specific interventions are matched to the smoker's stage along the continuum of change described previously has produced evidence of small improvements in cessation and abstinence (Noar et al., 2007), but some RCTs based on the model have not found evidence of the predicted benefits of matching (e.g., Aveyard, Massey, Parsons, Manasecki, & Griffin, 2009). This pattern of findings has led to the conclusion that the model is largely unsupported in this important health behavior domain (e.g., Bricker, 2010; West, 2005).

Despite the limited evidence in support of the SOC/TTM predictions regarding the effects of matching specific interventions to phases of the change process on smoking cessation and abstinence, it is clear that different sets of multifaceted challenges are prominent at different points in the smoking cessation process—motivating smokers to seriously consider quitting, preparing for cessation, the actual process of cessation, and maintaining abstinence and managing brief lapses and more prolonged relapses. Further, it is apparent that within each of these phases, the multiple challenges likely require multiple intervention approaches (Baker et al., 2011). Thus, process approaches warrant additional research, though perhaps should be expanded beyond the traditional stages of change framework. However, even in the absence of clear and specific evidence from RCTs, the current status of the evidence on the psychobiology of nicotine dependence and addiction and related behavioral research on addictive behavior suggests that it is appropriate to select and combine approaches to address these specific sets of challenges (Baker et al., 2011). Hence, this emerging expansion of the standard of care recognizes the value of combined pharmacologic and CBT treatments that should also reflect the differing challenges at various points in the process of smoking cessation.

Several environmental and policy-level approaches to smoking have been found effective in reducing smoking and lowering related health care costs, including raising taxes on tobacco, reducing smoke exposure (i.e., "secondhand" smoke) by prohibiting smoking in public places, bans on tobacco advertising and sponsorships, regulation of packaging and warning labels, promoting public awareness, increasing access to smoking cessation through expanded insurance coverage and public funding, and decreasing tobacco sales to minors through increased penalties for illegal sales (Cummings, Fong, & Borland, 2009). Policy-based changes in health care systems have also been found to be effective, including improved tracking of smoking status in health records, and increasing health care professionals' frequency and consistency of asking about smoking status and providing encouragement to quit (Curry, Keller, Orleans, & Fiore, 2008). Specific guidelines have been developed for health care providers for addressing smoking among their patients (Fiore & Baker, 2011). These guidelines involve regular inquires about the patient's smoking status and readiness to pursue smoking cessation, motivational interventions for those low in readiness, and specific pharmacological and behavioral interventions for those smoking patients who are ready to proceed.

Obesity and Weight Loss

Obesity defined as a body mass index (BMI) greater than 30 kg/m^2 has been associated with a host of negative health outcomes including coronary heart disease (Bogers et al., 2007), type 2 diabetes (Guh et al., 2009), some forms of cancer (Renehan, Tyson, Egger, Heller, & Zwahlen, 2008), and mortality related to these and other conditions (Whitlock et al., 2009). Importantly, recent prevalence estimates indicate that more than 30% of adults are obese (Flegal, Carroll, Ogden, & Curtin, 2010). Prevalence rates have more than doubled since the late 1970s, and even though this dramatic increase has slowed in recent years for children, adolescents, and adults (Flegal, Carroll, Kit, & Ogden, 2012; Ogden, Carroll, Kit, & Flegal, 2012), medical experts now consider obesity to be "epidemic" (Stein & Colditz, 2004). Not surprisingly then, behavioral approaches to weight loss continue to be a major focus of clinical health psychology and behavioral medicine.

A recent review of behavioral treatments for obesity concluded that, on average, intervention studies report a 10% decrease in body weight—enough for improvements in health—but that maintaining weight loss continues to be challenging (Butryn, Webb, & Wadden, 2011). Using in-person, Internet, or telephone contact between patients and providers to prolong engagement in interventions, encouraging high amounts of physical activity, or combining lifestyle behavior change with pharmacotherapy have shown promise in preventing weight regain (Butryn et al., 2011). For example, a recent randomized controlled trial demonstrated the efficacy of combined naltrexone/bupropion therapy as an adjunct to intensive behavior modification for obesity, with the drug intervention producing a 9% reduction in body weight compared to 5% among controls (Wadden et al., 2011). In another recent RCT, two behavioral interventions, one delivered with in-person support and the other delivered remotely, without face-to-face contact between participants and weight-loss coaches, resulted in clinically significant weight loss averaging more than 10 pounds over a period of 24 months, compared to only approximately 2 pounds in a comparison group (Appel et al., 2011). Other RCTs of web-based intervention have found that greater weight loss is observed among those with higher levels of website utilization (Bennett et al., 2010). Another recent RCT examined the efficacy and cost-effectiveness of a cognitive-behavioral weight management program in the form of written materials and basic web access, complemented by an interactive website and brief telephone/email coaching. Participants (1,755 overweight) were randomized to one of three conditions with increasing intervention intensity. Participants experienced significant weight loss, increased physical activity, and decreased blood pressure across conditions. Cost-effectiveness ratios were $900 to $1,100/quality-adjusted life year for the two lower intensity interventions and $1,900/quality-adjusted life year for the higher intensity intervention (web intervention plus coaching). The cost recovery analyses indicated that the costs of treatment were matched by savings in health care expenditures after 3 years for the two lower intensity interventions and after 6 years for the other intervention (Hersey et al., 2012). A recent meta-analysis indicated that the addition of motivational interviewing to weight loss intervention resulted in a small (3 pounds) additional weight loss in obese and overweight individuals (Armstrong et al., 2011). Collectively, these studies highlight the importance of adequate and continued support, which can be in varying modalities and that this increased support is cost-effective in the long run.

Promoting increases in physical activity is central to prevention of obesity, weight loss among obese individuals, and in maintenance of weight loss. In a recent review, Goldberg and King (2007) report that to prevent age-related weight gain generally, levels of vigorous physical activity above the usually recommended 30 minutes daily (e.g., to 45 to 60 minutes daily) may be necessary. For weight loss, physical activity interventions alone usually produce only modest results (e.g., 3 to 6 pounds), suggesting that for obese individuals significant weight loss also requires dietary change. Goldberg and King (2007) also note that current research suggests that high levels of physical activity (e.g., 40 to 90 minutes daily) may be necessary for weight loss maintenance.

Meta-analysis of psychobehavioral interventions in preventing weight gains or reducing weight among U.S. multiethnic and minority adults has indicated that multicomponent (versus single component) lifestyle interventions were efficacious and suggested that incorporation of individual sessions, family involvement, and problem-solving strategies are useful (Seo & Sa, 2008). Beyond traditional individually delivered weight loss intervention, recent research has also focused on environmental approaches to healthy eating (Story, Kapingst, Robinson-O'Brien, & Glanz, 2008) and worksite weight-loss intervention (Anderson et al., 2009). Given the dramatic recent increases in childhood obesity and the robust association of childhood and adolescent obesity with obesity in adulthood, it is clear that intervention efforts targeting weight loss in children are essential. Approaches with at least preliminary evidence of success in producing meaningful and sustained weight loss include school-based interventions (Katz, 2009), family-based approaches (Epstein, Paluch, Roemmich, & Beecher, 2007), and environmental and policy approaches (Brennan, Castro, Brownson, Claus, & Orleans, 2011).

Exercise and Physical Activity

Physical activity level and sedentary behavior are risk factors for the development of many chronic illnesses and negative health conditions including obesity, hypertension, type 2 diabetes,

and coronary heart disease. Interestingly, recent research suggests that sedentary behavior may be a distinct risk factor, independent of commonly used measures of physical activity, for a variety of adverse health outcomes in adults (Thorpe, Owen, Neuhaus, & Dunstan, 2011). The "dose" of physical activity that is needed continues to be debated; however, recent research has emphasized that even light activity improves health in sedentary individuals and that recommending small, gradual increases in activity helps to mitigate the incidence of adverse events and improve adherence to physical activity regimens (Powell, Paluch, & Blair, 2011). Given the role of physical activity and sedentary behavior in development of chronic illness, interventions focused on increasing activity levels and exercise behavior continue to be central to clinical health psychology and behavioral medicine. For example, current evidence supports the effectiveness of increasing physical activity in the prevention and treatment of obesity (Goldberg & King, 2007) and in the management of type 2 diabetes (Umpierre et al., 2011). Exercise has sustained beneficial effects on depression (Conn, 2010; Hoffman et al., 2011), and a recent meta-analysis of randomized controlled trials concluded that exercise is effective in reducing depressive symptoms in individuals with chronic illness, particularly those with mild-to-moderate depression (Herring, Puetz, O'Connor, & Dishman, 2012). Exercise has also been found to improve various aspects of cognitive functioning, including attention, processing speed, executive functioning, and memory (Smith, Blumenthal et al., 2010).

Given the evidence that declining physical activity and increases in sedentary behavior in the population over recent decades derive largely from environmental factors (Brownson, Boehmer, & Luke, 2005) interventions have increasingly moved beyond individually delivered approaches. Examples include worksite interventions (Abraham & Graham-Rower, 2009) and ecological approaches (e.g., increasing the "walkability" of communities and access to recreation sites) to increase physical activity (Sallis et al., 2006). Further, given the dramatic increase in childhood obesity and the success of adult-focused diabetes prevention efforts focused on increasing physical activity (Diabetes Prevention Program Research Group, 2002), school-based exercise programs have been the focus of recent RCTs demonstrating improvement in body composition, fitness, and insulin sensitivity in children (Carrel et al., 2005). However, maintenance of such benefits over prolonged school vacations can be problematic (Carrel et al., 2007).

Prevention of HIV Infection

HIV continues to be a major public health burden, with incidence rates in the United States ranging from 47,800 to 56,000 over the years 2006 to 2009 (Prejean et al., 2011), making preventive intervention a continued focus of clinical health psychology and behavioral medicine. HIV prevention efforts have involved a combination of behavioral (e.g., condom use, reduction in presex alcohol and drug use, reduction in needle-sharing among drug users), biomedical (e.g., antiretroviral medications to reduce transmission), and structural (i.e., social, economic, political) intervention strategies; many of these interventions have been found effective in reducing HIV risk behaviors by 25% to 50% (see Rotheram-Borus, Swendeman, & Chovnick, 2009). Although a variety of interventions have proven useful and cost-effective, inadequate funding, imperfect targeting strategies, and a problematic policy environment have been barriers to the widespread implementation of these life-saving interventions (Holtgrave & Curran, 2006).

Given these issues, HIV prevention efforts have increasingly focused on targeted interventions for high-risk groups. Groups at particular risk include young men who have sex with men, the only group that continues to show an increase in HIV infection, and African American men and women who have an estimated HIV incidence rate 7 times that of whites (Prejean et al., 2011). In a recent review of prevention efforts in young men who have sex with men, Mustanski, Newcomb, Du Bois, Garcia, and Grov (2011) suggest that Internet-based interventions, integration of biomedical and behavioral approaches, and interventions that take advantage of community and network factors are particularly promising. African American women also represent a high-risk target group. A recent meta-analysis indicated that interventions that used gender- or culture-specific materials, used female deliverers, addressed empowerment issues, provided skills training in condom use and negotiation of safer sex, and used role-playing to teach negotiation skills were particularly efficacious in HIV prevention in this risk group (Crepaz et al., 2009). Individuals who already have a

sexually transmitted disease are at higher risk for additional STDs as well as HIV infection; a recent meta-analysis confirmed that targeting prevention efforts toward patients at STD clinics is effective and should be a high public health priority (Scott-Sheldon, Fielder, & Carey, 2010).

Multiple Risk Factor Change and Comorbid Emotional Distress

Many individuals are characterized by more than one unhealthy behavior; smokers often are relatively sedentary, as are many individuals who consume a diet too high in calories, refined sugars, and saturated fat. The scope of this problem is even greater, if emotional difficulties such as depression are included in the definition of multiple risks. This creates the need for effective approaches to multiple risk behavior change interventions (J. J. Prochaska, Nigg, Spring, Velicer, & Prochaska, 2010; J. J. Prochaska & Prochaska, 2009). As seen in the preceding discussion of interventions for obesity and weight loss, the targeting of multiple behaviors (e.g., diet and exercise) is standard in many instances. Yet, RCTs of multiple health behavior change approaches are a relatively new development in the field. In many cases, the issue poses minimal difficulties. For example, treatment of other behavioral risks (e.g., diet, sun exposure) does not appear to interfere with the effectiveness of smoking cessation (J. J. Prochaska, Velicer, Prochaska, Delucchi, & Hall, 2006). Other combinations of risks poses more complicated challenges. For example, many smokers express the concern that smoking cessation will lead to weight gain, and weight gain can lead to failure to achieve and maintain abstinence. Combined treatments for smoking cessation and weight management can increase abstinence and reduce weight gain initially, but these benefits are often not maintained (Spring et al., 2009), indicating the need for additional treatment methods.

In weight loss efforts, comorbid depression is a common concern (Fabricatore & Wadden, 2006). Obesity and depression have a robust concurrent association, perhaps reflecting a bidirectional pattern of influence over time (Atlantis & Baker, 2008; Markowitz, Friedman, & Arent, 2008). The prospective association in which depression predicts weight gain over time is somewhat stronger than the role of initial adiposity in later depression (Atlantis & Baker, 2008; Gariepy, Wang, Lesage, & Schmitz, 2010; Patten,

Williams, Lavorato, Khaled, & Bulloch, 2011). Attrition from clinical weight loss trials has been found to be related to depression at baseline and poor early weight loss (Fabricatore et al., 2009). In an RCT aimed at addressing co-occurring depression, women with comorbid obesity and depression were randomized to behavioral weight loss or behavioral weight loss combined with cognitive-behavioral depression management. Women in both groups demonstrated significant weight loss and reduction in levels of depression (Linde et al., 2011). The failure to find added benefit of specific depression treatment may reflect common elements across these two interventions. Both included behavioral activation, problem-solving training, social support, and cognitive restructuring. Hence, the weight loss only condition may have included useful treatment elements for addressing depression. High levels of stress have a modest but significant prospective association with increasing adiposity (Wardle, Chida, Gibson, Whitaker, & Steptoe, 2011). Hence, the effects of stress reduction as an adjunctive treatment in weight loss programs among patients experiencing high levels of stress or related emotion regulation difficulties is a potentially important topic for future intervention research. Given the prevalence of both depression and obesity in the general population, the efficacy and effectiveness of approaches to weight loss among depressed persons is an important topic for further research.

The co-occurrence of smoking and depression is also common and poses similar challenges (Aubin, Rollema, Svensson, & Winterer, 2012; Hall & Prochaska, 2009). Traditional cessation programs can be successfully adapted for use with depressed smokers (Hall et al., 2006), and smoking cessation does not appear to increase depression or other emotional symptoms (Bolan, West, & Gunnell, 2011), even among initially depressed smokers (J. J. Prochaska, Hall, Tsoh, et al., 2008). However, rates of successful cessation and maintained abstinence are often lower in depressed smokers (Hall & Prochaska, 2009). Preliminary evidence suggests that the addition of CBT for depression may be a useful addition to cessation treatments for individuals prone to depression (Kapson & Haaga, 2010). Further, physical activity may facilitate abstinence after smoking cessation (J. J. Prochaska, Hall, Humfleet, et al., 2008), especially in light of the fact that exercise can have beneficial effects on depression (Blumenthal, 2011).

PSYCHOLOGICAL INTERVENTIONS IN CHRONIC MEDICAL ILLNESS AND MEDICAL CARE

Chronic medical illness poses a multifaceted adaptive challenge for patients and their families. The physical symptoms and distress (i.e., pain) stemming from these illnesses can be burdensome, and they often are the cause of serious reductions in functional activity across a variety of roles and domains (Stanton, Revenson, & Tennen, 2007). Depression and other emotional difficulties are much more common among persons with chronic medical illness, given these stressors (Smith, 2010a). Patients must also adhere to often complex medical regimens, and the extent to which they do so has important effects on health outcomes (Cramer, Benedict, Muszbek, Keskinaslan, & Khan, 2008; Gehi, Ali, Na, & Whooley, 2007). Yet, even in conditions like cardiovascular disease where the value of medications is quite substantial, as little as 50% of prescribed medications are taken (Baroletti & Dell'Orfano, 2010). In the same health care settings in which psychologists provide services to individuals with chronic medical illness, they are increasingly called to manage other presenting complaints and problems where traditional medical approaches are not optimal (e.g., sleep disturbance, somatoform disorders). In what follows here, we review intervention research findings on both the most common medical illnesses, and complaints that often are presented in medical settings.

Approaches to adjunctive psychosocial care vary somewhat across specific illness and presenting problems, but several are broadly applicable. Cognitive-behavioral interventions for stress, pain, sleep, somatic complaints, and emotional adjustment are widely used, as are supportive-expressive therapies. Rehabilitation often includes operant and exposure-based treatments for progressively increasing functional activities and reducing avoidance of feared activities. Couple and family approaches are less commonly used, but have considerable potential given that the patient's degree of adaption to chronic illness affects and is affected by family members. Exercise interventions have broad applicability. They can improve functional activity, but in some conditions are useful in treating the underlying disease and in improving emotional adjustment (Herring et al., 2012).

Cardiovascular Disease

Cardiovascular disease is the leading cause of death in the United States, as it is in many industrialized nations. One of these conditions, essential hypertension is a contributing cause of the other two primary cardiovascular diseases—coronary heart disease and stroke—but also increases risk of other serious illness (e.g., renal disease).

Hypertension

Behavior changes involving diet, exercise, and weight loss are standard aspects of the medical management of essential hypertension, both as an initial intervention for mild levels and as an adjunct to pharmacologic treatment. This is particularly true in the case of overweight individuals, as adiposity is a common contributing factor in essential hypertension. Clinical trials have demonstrated the efficacy and effectiveness of the Dietary Approaches to Stop Hypertension (DASH) and DASH-low sodium diets in preventing and treating hypertension (Appel et al., 2006). Compared to a typical U.S. diet, the DASH diet is low in saturated fat, red meat, and refined sugars, and high in intake of fruits, vegetables, and low fat dairy products, with a substantial portion of the diet including whole grain, fish, poultry, and nuts. Adherence to DASH diet has been found to reduce blood pressure by a clinically meaningful 5 to 10 mmHg among high-risk individuals, and risk of CHD and stroke by as much as 20% (Fung et al., 2008).

These important reductions in blood pressure can be augmented when the DASH diet is accompanied by exercise and weight loss interventions. For example, combining the DASH diet with an exercise program and a reduction in caloric intake intended to produce weight loss improves both standard clinic-based measurements of blood pressure and levels of the more prognostic indicator of ambulatory blood pressure for overweight hypertensives (Blumenthal, Babyak, Hinderliter, et al., 2010). This combined intervention was also more effective in altering other markers of vascular, cardiac, and metabolic risk including pulse wave velocity (i.e., arterial stiffness), left ventricular mass, insulin insensitivity or glucose regulation, and plasma cholesterol and triglycerides (Blumenthal, Babyak, Sherwood, et al., 2010; Blumenthal, Babyak, Hinderliter, et al., 2010). Hence, the combined dietary, exercise, and weight loss intervention has broad health benefits, especially among overweight persons. The exercise and weight loss also reduce depressive symptoms among hypertensives, especially among those with higher initial levels of depression (Smith, Blumenthal, Babyak, et al., 2007). Attenuated nocturnal decreases (i.e., "dipping") in blood pressure are an independent risk factor for cardiovascular disease, more common among African Americans than whites. In this regard, it is important to note preliminary evidence that the DASH diet can improve nocturnal blood pressure dipping among African Americans (Prather, Blumenthal, Hinderliter, & Sherwood, 2011).

Chronic stress is associated with increased risk of high blood pressure and the development of diagnosed hypertension (Sparrenberger et al., 2009), providing the rationale for various stress management and relaxation therapies as adjuncts to traditional approaches to the management of hypertension. A meta-analysis of 25 trials including a total of more than 1,000 patients found small but significant reductions (SBP −5.5 mmHg; DBP −3.5 mmHg) in blood pressure (Dickinson et al., 2008). Although even small blood pressure reductions can be clinically meaningful, methodological weaknesses of some the individual trials (e.g., small sample sizes, failure to control nonspecific factors) raise concerns about the reproducibility of this result. As a result, exercise, dietary, and weight loss interventions have stronger support as treatments for hypertension, compared to stress management.

Coronary Heart Disease

The standard medical management of coronary heart disease (CHD) has included behavioral interventions for many years. Adherence to diet, exercise, and smoking cessation recommendations for CHD patients is associated with a 40% to 50% reduction in recurrent cardiac events (e.g., additional myocardial infarction, death) within the first 6 months after hospitalization for acute coronary syndrome (Chow et al., 2010). Among smokers who develop acute coronary disease, between 30% and 50% quit without formal smoking cessation intervention. However, interventions for smoking cessation produce added benefits among these patients, increasing the chances of successful cessation by 60% (Barth, Critchley, & Bengel, 2008) with associated reductions in risk of future cardiac events following successful cessation. However, quit rates are far from satisfactory, suggesting the need for more effective interventions and more consistent implementation of effective approaches. Meta-analyses have consistently demonstrated that exercise-based cardiac rehabilitation reduces recurrent cardiac events and all-cause mortality by approximately 20% (Taylor et al., 2004), although improvements in access, implementation, and adherence are needed.

The effects of psychological stress and negative emotion on the development and course of coronary heart disease (CHD) are well-established, with extensive evidence accumulating from animal models, human epidemiological research, and clinical studies of CHD patient populations (Williams, 2008). Specific forms of stress linked to CHD include work stress (Eller et al., 2009) and stress in personal close relationships (De Vogli et al., 2007; Matthews & Gump, 2002; Orth-Gomer et al., 2000; Rohrbaugh et al., 2006; Smith et al., 2012). Further, psychological stress and negative emotion are associated with increased CHD risk across the full time course of the disease, from the development and progression of asymptomatic atherosclerosis, to the emergence of cardiac events, and the course of established CHD (Bhattacharyya & Steptoe, 2007; Williams, 2008). Given the important historical role played by the Type A behavior pattern in this research area, a major aspect of this evidence concerns the association of anger and hostility—key unhealthy elements of the broader Type A pattern—with the development and course of CHD (Chida & Steptoe, 2009). However, in recent years extensive evidence has accumulated indicating that depression and anxiety are also risk factors for the development of CHD among initially healthy persons, and for increased risk among patients with disease (Nicholson, Kuper, & Hemingway, 2006; Rutledge, Reiss, Linke, Greenberg, & Mills, 2006; Smith, 2010a; Suls & Bunde, 2005). These associations with CHD provide the foundation for a variety of studies of the effectiveness of stress management and interventions for negative affective symptoms and conditions.

The potential value of such approaches was initially demonstrated in the Recurrent Coronary Prevention Project (RCPP), in which group therapy intended to reduce Type A behavior among CHD patients not only successfully modified this behavioral endpoint, but also resulted in a significant and nearly 50% reduction in subsequent coronary events (15% in comparison condition versus 8% in treatment condition; Friedman et al., 1986). A recent meta-analysis of RCTs of stress management and similar psychosocial interventions for patients with CHD found evidence of a significant reduction of more than 40% in recurrent coronary events for 2 years after treatment and a 27% reduction in all-cause mortality over the same follow-up period (Linden, Phillips, & Leclerc, 2007). These benefits were limited to men, however, with no effect on prognosis among women. Further, interventions were significantly more effective when initiated 2 months or more after the initial coronary event rather than closer in time to hospitalization, and the interventions were significantly more effective if they also reduced indications of emotional distress (Linden et al., 2007).

Subsequent studies have confirmed the general effectiveness of these interventions. In a randomized controlled trial of cognitive-behavioral stress management in a sample of more than 350 CHD patients, the intervention produced a significant reduction in risk of recurrent cardiovascular events. Specifically, 47% of patients receiving usual care experienced a recurrent cardiovascular event over an average of 8 years of follow-up, compared to 36% of the patients receiving CBT (Gulliksson et al., 2011). Importantly, a recent RCT of cognitive-behavioral stress management for women with CHD (Orth-Gomer et al., 2009) found that over a 7-year follow-up women in the treatment group had a 3-times smaller risk of death than those in the control (i.e., 7% mortality versus 20%). Thus, the CBT approach was successfully adapted for women with CHD in this case. Given the considerable attention to the study of anger and CHD (Chida & Steptoe, 2009) and the availability of empirically supported anger treatments (Smith & Traupman, 2012), it is surprising that few studies have directly examined the benefits of such interventions among CHD patients. One small RCT did find that CBT for anger and hostility produced a significant reduction in recurrent coronary events and a related savings in health care costs (Davidson, Gidron, Mostofsky, & Trudeau, 2007). Stress management interventions have also been found to alter biomarkers of CHD severity (e.g., reductions in stress-induced cardiac ischemia, increases in flow-mediated arterial dilation), illustrating plausible mechanisms underlying the effect of psychosocial interventions on coronary outcomes (Blumenthal, Sherwood et al., 2005). However, it is important to note that other systematic reviews of the topic (Whalley et al., 2011) have not reached the same positive conclusions as those of Linden et al. (2007).

In another historically important behavioral approach to the treatment of coronary disease, Ornish and colleagues (1990, 1998) have examined the effects among CHD patients of a comprehensive lifestyle change program involving a low-fat, whole foods diet (i.e., whole grains, fruits, vegetables), moderate exercise, stress management, and attendance at regular support group meetings. Early RCTs of the program demonstrated significant effects on the coronary risk factors, extent of coronary artery disease, other indicators of underlying disease severity, and coronary events (e.g., Gould et al., 1995; Ornish et al., 1990, 1998). Subsequent research has demonstrated additional beneficial effects on coronary outcomes, various aspects of quality of life, and related health care costs (for reviews, see Vizza, 2012; Weidner & Kendel, 2010).

The extensive evidence of an association between depression and the course of CHD has prompted efforts to examine the benefits of related treatments. The most notable effort was the multicenter Enhancing Recovery in Coronary Heart Disease (ENRICHD) (Berkman et al., 2003). ENRICHD enrolled more than 2,000 CHD patients selected primarily for elevated levels of depression, but also for social isolation, a related and significant psychosocial risk for poor cardiac outcomes. In comparison to the control condition, the CBT-based intervention produced small but significant improvements in depression and social isolation, but no effects on the primary combined outcomes of death and recurrent coronary events (Berkman et al., 2003). Secondary subgroup analyses indicated that there were beneficial effects on the primary outcome for white men (Schneiderman et al., 2004) and those patients who had received at least some of the CBT intervention in group as opposed to only individual sessions (Saab et al., 2009).

CBT for depression has been found to be effective for CHD patients experiencing depression following coronary artery bypass graft surgery (CABG) (Freedland et al., 2009). Also among depressed post-CABG patients, telephone-based collaborative care that includes psychoeducation and supportive counseling for depression was found to be effective in reducing negative mood symptoms, improving HQOL, and levels of physical functioning (Rollman et al., 2009). Davidson et al. (2010) randomized depressed acute coronary syndrome patients to usual care or an enhanced depression care condition in which patients self-selected into either pharmacotherapy or problem-solving therapy, followed by stepped care for continuing depression. The treatment group showed significantly better depression outcomes and a significant reduction in adverse cardiac events, although the latter outcome should be considered preliminary given the small number of events. To date, studies evaluating the effects of pharmacotherapy for depression in CHD patients have found mixed evidence of effects on depression, and no evidence of improved cardiac outcomes (for a review, see Kop & Plumoff, 2012).

As noted above, exercise is effective for CHD improving prognosis for patients, and it has also been found to improve depression. Hence, exercise seems promising as a potential treatment for depressed CHD patients (Blumenthal, 2011; Smith 2006b). However, it is important to note that the supporting evidence is indirect and preliminary, and such exercise interventions for depression in CHD patients would need to address the fact that depression predicts failure to complete exercise-based cardiac rehabilitation (Casey, Hughes, Waechter, Josephson, & Rosneck, 2008).

Given the high prevalence of depression in various CHD patient groups and its association with adverse events and mortality in this population, the American Heart Association has endorsed screening and increased availability of depression management for CHD patients (Lichtman et al., 2008). However, to date there are no empirical demonstrations that such procedures result in improved care or cardiac outcomes (Thombs et al., 2008). Nonetheless, depression is a direct contributor to poor HQOL, and can interfere with other behavioral interventions with well-established benefits for CHD patients, such as exercise (Casey et al., 2008) and smoking cessation (Thorndike et al., 2008). Hence, depression treatment should be a regular focus in the clinical management of CHD, but one whose effect is not as strong as would be hoped.

The mixed results of interventions for depression in CHD raise the important question as to whether the interventions have the optimal focus. Specifically, in health populations and in CHD populations, depressive symptoms and disorders overlap considerably with other negative affective symptoms and disorders related to adverse cardiac outcomes (Smith 2010a; Suls & Bunde, 2005). In addition to further attention to the unique versus independent associations of these interrelated psychosocial risk factors with the course of CHD, intervention research should explore the value of treatments that address common rather than unique features of various negative affective problems (e.g., Wilamowska et al., 2010). Negative affective characteristics also are closely related to difficulties in close relationships (e.g., high conflict, low support) known to influence the development and course of CHD (e.g., Matthews & Gump, 2002; Rohrbaugh et al., 2006). As a result, intervention research for CHD patients might also usefully explore the potential benefits of empirically supported treatments for relationship difficulties generally (Lebow, Chambers, Christensen, & Johnson, 2012) and in the specific context of health problems (Shields et al., 2012).

Stroke

The rehabilitation and management of stroke patients has traditionally been the purview of rehabilitation psychologists and neuropsychologists, rather than clinical health psychologists, and as a result is somewhat beyond our present scope. However, in addition to cognitive rehabilitation and physical therapy, it should be noted that many of the behavioral interventions described for hypertension and CHD are core elements of the medical management of these patients (review Caplan, 2010). Further, depression is common among stroke patients, and is more frequent among patients with more severe strokes, greater physical disability, and greater cognitive impairments (Hackett & Anderson, 2005). Psychological therapies (i.e., counseling, psychotherapy) are at least somewhat effective for preventing depression after strokes, but pharmacological therapies are not (Hackett, Anderson, House, & Halteh, 2008). However, among stroke patients who have already developed significant levels of depression, the opposite seems to be true; pharmacological therapies are at least somewhat useful, but psychological therapies are not (Hackett, Anderson, House, & Xia, 2008).

Cancer

Psychosocial interventions in cancer have targeted the emotional distress that often accompanies the disease, quality of life generally, and side effects of cancer treatment, such as fatigue. The effect of psychosocial treatments on survival among cancer patients has a controversial history in the field.

CBT and related therapies (e.g., problem-solving training) for depression and general emotional distress in cancer patients reduces distress, improves social support, and improves health behavior (e.g., diet, smoking) (Andersen et al., 2004; Antoni et al., 2009; Nezu, Nezu, Felgoise, McClure, & Houts, 2003). CBT is also effective specifically among depressed cancer patients (Hopko et al., 2008). Psychotherapy has been found to be effective for reducing depressive symptoms among incurable cancer patients (Akechi, Okuyama, Onishi, Morita, & Furukawa, 2008). Coping and communication interventions are also effective in reducing depression relative to usual care control conditions, as is supportive counseling (Manne et al., 2007). Mindfulness-based stress reduction has been found to reduce levels of depression and anxiety, and to increase energy, physical functioning, and role functioning (Lengacher et al., 2009). Some meta-analyses of mindfulness-based approaches have demonstrated positive effects on indicators of psychological adjustment (Ledesma & Kumano, 2009), but others have reached more cautious conclusions (Edwards, Hulbert-Williams, & Neal, 2008).

Across multiple interventions and specific cancer populations, psychosocial interventions are effective in reducing emotional distress, but the effect size is up to 3 times larger among patients preselected for elevated signs of distress, as compared to unselected patients (Linden & Girgis, 2011). Despite these generally consistent results, some reviews have concluded that the overall evidence of benefits from adjunctive psychosocial treatments in cancer is limited by methodological features of many individual RCTs (Coyne, Lepore, & Palmer, 2006). Further, to date there is no strong evidence that screening for depression or distress in cancer patient populations by itself results in improved overall outcomes for emotional adjustment (Meijer et al., 2011; Palmer, Van Scheppinger, & Coyne, 2011). Some evidence suggests that screening for unmet psychosocial needs rather than depression specifically may be a more efficient approach to the identification of cancer patients who would benefit from the treatments described above (van Scheppingen et al., 2011). Thus, the best means for identification of patients most likely to benefit from specific psychosocial treatments is an important topic for research.

Medical treatments for cancer, although often highly effective, frequently have major side effects that are themselves a detriment to

H-QOL. Fatigue is the most common example. Meta-analyses of RCTs have demonstrated that exercise and other psychosocial treatments are effective in reducing fatigue in cancer patients (Cramp & Daniel, 2008; Kangas, Bovbjerg, & Montgomery, 2008). Of the nonexercise treatments, both supportive-expressive therapy and CBT show promise. Notably, fatigue and its seeming opposite physical or emotional symptoms (e.g., vigor) actually function as separate outcomes; when both fatigue and vigor or positive affect are measured independently, treatment effects on one are not necessarily accompanied by parallel changes on the other. In this regard, it is important to note that a combined CBT and hypnosis intervention reduced the fatigue accompanying radiation therapy in breast cancer patients (Montgomery et al., 2009), and reduced negative affect while increasing positive affect (Schnur et al., 2009).

In basic research on animal models of cancer progression and in human clinical studies of recurrence and survival, there is considerable evidence that stress, negative emotion, and other psychosocial risk factors can contribute to the course of some forms of the disease (Antoni et al., 2006; Chida, Hamer, Wardle, & Steptoe, 2008). Further, in animal research and human clinical studies, plausible psychobiologic mechanisms underlying these effects have been identified (Antoni et al., 2006). These observations have raised the question as to whether psychosocial treatments known to effect emotional adjustment, side effects, and H-QOL generally might also have beneficial effects on the course of the illness. An early study reported that supportive-expressive group therapy for women with advanced, metastatic breast cancer not only had beneficial effects on psychosocial functioning but also resulted in increased survival (Spiegel, Bloom, Kraemer, & Gottheil, 1989). Similar results were reported by other investigators for other forms of cancer (Fawzy et al., 1993). However, meta-analyses and related critiques have called these findings into serious question (Coyne, Stefanek, & Palmer, 2007; Edwards et al., 2008). Even though subsequent RCTs evaluating CBT have reported positive effects on cancer survival (Andersen et al., 2008) and on multiple biologic pathways that could alter the course of cancer progression (Antoni et al., 2009; Antoni et al., 2012), the evidence of effects on the course of cancer is not sufficient to support using these interventions as treatments of the disease, per

se (Stefanek, Palmer, Thombs, & Coyne, 2009). Rather, their other, better-documented effects on important aspects of H-QOL provide a more appropriate rationale.

Diabetes

Diabetes is a group of diseases marked by high levels of blood glucose resulting from defects in insulin production, insulin action, or both. Type 1 diabetes, previously called *insulin-dependent diabetes mellitus* or *juvenile-onset diabetes*, develops when the body's immune system destroys insulin-producing pancreatic beta cells. To survive, people with type 1 diabetes must have insulin delivered by injection or a pump. This form of diabetes usually strikes children and young adults, although disease onset can occur at any age. Type 2 diabetes, previously called *non–insulin-dependent diabetes mellitus* or *adult-onset diabetes*, accounts for the vast majority of all diagnosed cases of diabetes. It is characterized by insulin resistance, and as the need for insulin rises the pancreas gradually loses its ability to produce it. Type 2 diabetes is associated with older age, obesity, family history of diabetes, history of gestational diabetes, impaired glucose metabolism, physical inactivity, and race/ethnicity. African Americans, Hispanic/Latino Americans, American Indians, and some Asian Americans and Native Hawaiians or other Pacific Islanders are at particularly high risk for type 2 diabetes and its complications. With an adult prevalence of 20.7 million that has increased in recent years (Cowie et al., 2010) and the continued emphasis on behavior change in disease management, a focus on type 2 diabetes continues to be a key part of clinical health psychology and behavioral medicine intervention science.

In addition to medical intervention (e.g., insulin), diabetes management typically involves multicomponent lifestyle changes including regular blood glucose monitoring, weight loss/dietary changes, and exercise. Stress management has also proven to be beneficial (Surwit et al., 2002). Given the active role of patients in monitoring blood glucose and adjusting self-administered insulin, adherences to this demanding medical regimen and overall self-management is an important challenge. Further, because modest weight loss and exercise changes have been demonstrated to significantly reduce the incidence of diabetes (Diabetes Prevention Program Research Group, 2002), behavioral medicine intervention to prevent the onset of type 2 diabetes has become a priority (see Schulz & Hu, 2005).

Given the prevalence of type 2 diabetes, intervention efforts have increasingly focused on integrated care strategies that reach large numbers of primary care patients. For example, in a recent RCT targeting type 2 diabetes and depression, integrated care managers collaborated with physicians to offer education and guideline-based treatment recommendations and to monitor adherence and clinical status. Compared to usual care, this intervention increased the percentage of patients meeting treatment goals for diabetic control (i.e., HbA1C < 7%; 61% in intervention group versus 36% in usual care) and depression (59% scoring in nondepressed range in intervention group versus 31% in usual care) (Bogner, Morales, de Vries, & Capolla, 2012).

The issue of depression in diabetes care is increasingly important. Meta-analyses have demonstrated that depression predicts the development of Type 2 diabetes (Knol et al., 2006), and depression and related psychosocial risk factors predict poor glucose control and prognosis in diabetes (Chida & Hamer, 2008). Some evidence suggests a bidirectional association between depression and diabetes (Golden et al., 2008), although in some studies self-report scales assessing emotional distress specifically related to diabetes rather than scales measuring depression are stronger predictors of impaired glucose regulation (Fisher et al., 2010). Depression is also associated with poor adherence to medical treatment regimens in diabetes (Gonzalez et al., 2008). A variety of psychosocial interventions have been found to be effective in treating depression in diabetes, although effects on metabolic control (i.e., glucose regulation) are not demonstrated consistently (Van der Feltz-Cornelis, Nuygen, et al., 2010). Despite a lack of clear effects on glucose regulation, collaborative care for depression in diabetes is cost-effective in reducing both depression and overall health care costs (Simon et al., 2007)

Although group-based patient education interventions reach more patients and have some demonstrated efficacy (Deakin, McShane, Cade, & Williams, 2005), individual approaches have been found to be more effective than group-delivered education (Sperl-Hillen et al., 2011). Utilizing available technology, patient-centered, computer-assisted self-management intervention appears effective in improving diabetes self-management outcomes and increases in

perceived autonomy and competence are mechanisms of change in this approach (Williams, Lynch, & Glasgow, 2007). Beyond individually focused intervention, adding a brief, family-based intervention targeting negative and/or inaccurate illness perceptions to usual care results in improvements in HbA1C levels in patients with poorly controlled type 2 diabetes (Keogh et al., 2011). Review of trials of various dietary approaches and diet plus exercise interventions for treatment of type 2 diabetes indicated that adoption of regular exercise is a good way to promote better glycemic control (Nield et al., 2007).

The metabolic syndrome (MetS) is a collection of biomedical risk factors (i.e., elevated blood glucose/insulin resistance; elevated cholesterol and triglycerides, high blood pressure; abdominal adiposity) that although falling short of the criteria for diabetes, is a strong risk factor for the development of type 2 diabetes, as well as atherosclerotic cardiovascular disease (Eckel, Grundy, & Zimmet, 2005). Modification of diet and physical activity are mainstays of the treatment of MetS, and are effective, especially if they produce weight loss. However, maintenance is difficult (Magkos Yannakoulia, Chan, & Mantzoros, 2009). Psychosocial factors (e.g., depression, chronic stress) increase risk for MetS (Goldbacher & Matthews, 2007), but little research has examined the effects of related interventions on this "prediabetic" condition.

HIV/AIDS

Introduced in 1996, highly active antiretroviral therapy (HAART) produced a marked decrease in AIDS related morbidity and mortality. As a result HIV has become much more of a chronic disease similar to others reviewed here. The related impact on psychosocial functioning has become a major focus of current care in HIV, much more so than in the pre-HAART era when acute illness issues were more central. However, the medication regimen that made this change possible is complex and demanding, with notable side effects. Even with a simplified dosing, lifelong adherence is often highly challenging, especially in light of the fact that a very high level of adherence is required to produce maximum effectiveness. Psychosocial factors such as life stress and depression can disrupt adherence to HAART (Bottonari, Safran, McQuaid, Hsiao, & Roberts, 2010; Gonzalez, Batchelder, Psaros, & Safren, 2011). One RCT of a multi-component intervention addressing barriers to adherence, supporting the patients' autonomy in meeting these challenges, and promoting social support and network involvement demonstrated important improvements in adherence (Koenig et al., 2008). In another recent RCT, CBT focused on reducing depression and improving adherence with the medical regimen had beneficial effects in both cases, both after treatment and during a prolonged follow-up period (Safren et al., 2009).

Given the serious nature of the disease and the demands of related treatment, psychosocial issues are an important focus of patient care. The ways in which individuals cope with HIV-related stressors is important. Direct action and positive reappraisal are associated with better outcomes, across emotional adjustment, health behavior, and physical symptoms and medical outcomes (Moskowitz, Hult, Bussolari, & Acree, 2009). In contrast, behavioral disengagement and coping through use of drugs and alcohol are associated with worse outcomes across domains. Hence, CBT and related interventions may be more effective to the extent that they enhance the former and reduce the latter forms of coping.

In meta-analyses of prospective studies, psychosocial factors have been found to predict the course of HIV (Chida & Vedhara, 2009), and psychobiologic mechanisms potentially contributing to these effects of chronic stress and negative emotion on the course of HIV have been described (Cole, 2008). These findings raise the question as to whether psychosocial interventions can alter the underlying immunologic condition. In some studies of persons with HIV, CBT, relaxation therapies, and other interventions (e.g., tai-chi) have been found to improve immune functioning relative to control conditions (e.g., McCain et al., 2008). However, meta-analyses have concluded that stress management has beneficial effects on emotional adjustment and H-QOL, but not immune functioning, although the latter finding is inconclusive given methodological limitations of the available studies (Scott-Sheldon, Kalichman, Carey, & Fielder, 2008). Further, the literature on stress management in HIV has been criticized as too focused on mindfulness-based approaches to the exclusion of other promising treatments, characterized by short follow-ups that raise concerns about the maintenance of treatment effects, and also a lack of specific attention to HIV-related stressors (Brown & Vanable, 2008).

Chronic Pain

The prevalence of chronic pain is estimated to be between 15% and 20% of adults in the United States and similar industrialized nations (Turk, Wilson & Cahana, 2011). Musculoskeletal pain (e.g., chronic low back pain), headache, rheumatoid and osteoarthritis, fibromyalgia, and chronic fatigue syndrome are the most common types of chronic pain problems. A growing variety of interventions have been developed to treat chronic pain (Jensen, 2011; Turk et al., 2011), and several have been evaluated in multiple RTCs. Chronic pain treatments have the obvious goal of reducing pain, but also improving levels of functional activity (versus disability), improving H-QOL, and reducing the depression that often accompanies chronic pain. Behavioral approaches emphasize the operant strategies for the reduction of reinforcement for pain behavior, the shaping of functional (i.e., "nonpain") behavior, and graded exposure to activities that are sources of fear of further injury or pain. Cognitive-behavioral approaches address maladaptive thoughts and coping strategies (e.g., catastrophizing), whereas relaxation and stress management approaches reduce emotional and physiological arousal that can exacerbate pain. These approaches are often combined in multicomponent interventions, including comprehensive pain rehabilitation programs that combine psychosocial treatments with rehabilitation-oriented physical therapy.

In a meta-analysis of 22 studies of chronic low back pain, psychosocial treatments were found to have positive effects on pain levels, pain-related interference in daily activities, H-QOL, and depression. CBT and self-regulation approaches were found to be particularly effective, and comprehensive, multidisciplinary programs had the additional benefit of improved rates of return to work (Hoffman, Papas, Chatkoff, & Kerns, 2007). However, it is important to note that others have suggested that the conclusions of this meta-analysis should be qualified by the limitations of several of the studies included and the review processes (Coyne et al., 2010). More recently developed acceptance-based treatments (i.e., acceptance and commitment therapy, mindfulness-based stress reduction) for chronic pain have been evaluated in multiple RCTs, and a meta-analysis indicated significant, albeit small to medium effects relative to control conditions for both pain and depression (Veehof, Oskam, Scheurs, & Bohlmeijer, 2011). The benefits of these various psychosocial treatments for chronic pain demonstrated in efficacy-focused RCTs are also evident in effectiveness studies in practice settings (e.g., Morley, Williams, & Hussain, 2008). Chronic pain is often associated with poor sleep, and a preliminary RCT of CBT for insomnia among patients with chronic neck or back pain demonstrated significant improvements in sleep and the degree to which pain interfered with the patients' daily activities (Jungquist et al., 2010).

Both tension headaches and migraine headaches have been the subject of multiple RCTs, most often evaluating the effects of various forms of biofeedback, CBT, stress management, relaxation therapies, and multicomponent approaches. Quantitative and qualitative reviews indicate the effectiveness of most of these treatment modalities (Holroyd, Martin, & Nash, 2006; Nestoric & Martin, 2007; Nestoric, Rief, & Martin, 2008; Sun-Edelstein & Mauskop, 2011). These therapies are often found to be superior to comparison conditions that provide controls for nonspecific factors (D'souza, Lumley, Kraft, & Dooley, 2008). The evidence has been sufficiently compelling as to warrant the inclusion of these psychological therapies in established clinical guidelines for headache care.

A meta-analysis of psychosocial interventions for rheumatoid arthritis and osteoarthritis found significant effects on pain, emotional adjustment (i.e., reduced anxiety and depression), functional activity, and biological outcomes (i.e., joint swelling on physical exam) (Dixon, Keefe, Scipio, Perri, & Abernethy, 2007). CBT was by far the most common treatment among the available studies. A RCT found that mindfulness-based stress reduction had modest, delayed effects in improving emotional adjustment in rheumatoid arthritis but no effects on disease activity (Pradhan et al., 2007). However, another recent RCT comparing CBT, mindfulness meditation, and a patient education control for rheumatoid arthritis suggested mindfulness interventions may be useful in some contexts. Specifically, CBT was more effective than mediation and education in reducing pain and biologic evidence of systemic inflammation (i.e., IL-6 levels) (Zautra et al., 2008). However, among patients with a history of recurrent depression, mindfulness meditation was superior to CBT in reducing emotional adjustment and joint tenderness. A recent meta-analysis for psychosocial treatments for fibromyalgia indicated an overall beneficial effect on short-term reductions in pain, and somewhat larger effect on

longer term reductions in pain, improved sleep, lower depression, increases in functional activity, and reduced catastrophizing (Glombiewski et al., 2010).

Although symptoms of fatigue are the primary focus in treatments of chronic fatigue syndrome, chronic pain complaints are a common and distressing clinical feature. Cognitive-behavioral stress management has been found to reduce stress, mood disturbance, and physical symptoms in chronic fatigue patients (Lopez et al., 2011), and a recent meta-analysis found that both CBT and graded physical exercise were effective, although CBT was somewhat better when chronic fatigue was accompanied by symptoms of anxiety and depression, as is common (Castell, Kazantzis, & Moss-Morris 2011).

Patients seeking treatment for chest pain are often found to be free of clinical indications of CHD. Despite the lack of evidence of serious heart disease, noncardiac chest pain remains a distressing problem. Both cognitive-behavioral coping skills training and sertraline have been found effective in reducing pain in a placebo-controlled RCT (Keefe et al., 2011). The combination of CBT and pharmacotherapy may be particularly useful, as it reduced pain, anxiety, and catastrophizing.

Other treatment-delivery modalities have been found to be useful in managing chronic pain. For example, telephone-based CBT for chronic widespread pain produced significant and sustained improvement in overall functioning (McBeth et al., 2012). A telephone-based self-management intervention also produced reductions in pain among osteoarthritis patients (Allen et al., 2010). Internet-based interventions have also been evaluated. For example, an Internet-based intervention for headache demonstrated significant reductions in headache activity (i.e., frequency, duration) and related limitations in functional activity (Devineni & Blanchard, 2005). A recent meta-analysis found overall small but significant reductions in pain for Internet-based treatments of chronic pain (Macea, Gajos, Calil, & Fregni, 2010).

Organ Transplantation

Solid organ transplantation has become increasingly common in medical intervention for a variety of conditions including liver and kidney disease and cystic fibrosis (i.e., lung transplantation). Behavioral medicine issues relevant for the psychologist involved in organ transplantation programs include pretransplant assessment, adherence following transplant, prevention of alcohol and drug use, and adjustment/quality of life. Psychosocial evaluation to determine eligibility for organ transplantation typical includes psychiatric history; history and current use of alcohol, nicotine, and other substances; past and current adherence to medical regimens; cognitive capacity, especially related to understanding of post-transplant medical and self-care requirements; and social support system, especially relevant to post-transplant care (see Dew & DiMartini, 2011). The critical issues regarding eligibility vary somewhat with the specific organ. Behavioral medicine interventions that have been shown to be beneficial in patients following organ transplantation include educational-behavioral interventions to improve medication adherence (DeGeest et al., 2006), group and individual psychotherapy for reduction of depressive symptoms (Baines, Joseph, & Jindal, 2004), and mindfulness-based stress reduction (Gross et al., 2010).

Gastrointestinal Disorders

Although clinical health psychologists and behavioral medicine practitioners may encounter patients with a variety of gastrointestinal disturbances, irritable bowel syndrome (IBS) is among the most prevalent. IBS is characterized by abdominal pain and abnormal bowel habits (i.e., diarrhea or constipation), as well as general physical weakness in the absence of abnormal morphological, histological, or inflammatory markers. The main diagnostic Rome III criteria, established by international professional organizations, are based on exclusion criteria and the occurrence and rate of symptoms. Because the pathophysiology and causes of IBS are poorly understood, treatment approaches are mainly focused on symptom management to maintain everyday functioning and improving quality of life for persons with IBS; thus, biopsychosocial interventions are central to disease management. The mainstay of medical intervention is pharmacological treatment with antispasmodics and antidiarrheals for diarrhea, prokinetics and high-fiber diets for constipation, and supportive therapy with low-dose antidepressants to normalize gastrointestinal motility (Grundmann & Yoon, 2010). Behavioral medicine interventions include lifestyle and

dietary changes and psychotherapy. Additional alternative medicine therapies include herbal therapies and acupuncture.

In recent RCTs focused on behavioral intervention for IBS, a manualized CBT-based self-management program was effective in reducing subjective IBS symptom severity at the end of treatment (2 months), and 3 and 6 months posttreatment (Moss-Morris, McAlpine, Didsbury, & Spence, 2009). The addition of relaxation training to enhanced medical care (treatment as usual plus two counseling sessions) has resulted in significant improvement in subjective functional impairment (Lahmann et al., 2010). A small RCT demonstrated that a brief (5-week) CBT-based Internet intervention with limited therapist email resulted in significant symptom reduction and improved quality of life in IBS patients compared to a wait-list control group (Hunt, Moshier, & Milonova, 2009). Both Internet-delivered (Ljótsson et al., 2010) and in-person mindfulness group intervention (Gaylord et al., 2011) have been found to reduce IBS symptoms and improved quality of life in randomized controlled trials.

Multiple Sclerosis

Historically, neurological disease has not been a major focus in behavioral medicine and clinical health psychology. However, recent research on multiple sclerosis (MS) indicates the considerable potential for important contributions to patient care. For example, fatigue is a common and often debilitating symptom in MS. In a RCT comparing the efficacy of CBT for fatigue, relaxation therapy, and a usual care control, van Kessel et al. (2008) found that both CBT and relaxation were beneficial, but CBT was more so. Both treatments produced sustained benefits. Depression is also common in MS, and CBT delivered via the telephone has been found to reduce depression (Mohr et al., 2005) and improve H-QOL in depressed MS patients (Cosio, Jin, Siddique, & Mohr, 2011).

Sleep Disturbance and Insomnia

Poor sleep is associated with increased health care use, work absenteeism, and reduced work productivity (Daley et al., 2009), along with a growing list of adverse health outcomes, including impaired immune functioning (Lange, Perras, Fehm, & Born, 2003), susceptibility to infectious illness (Cohen, Doyle, Alper, Janicki-Deverts, & Turner, 2009), metabolic syndrome (Hall et al.,

2008; Jennings, Muldoon, Hall, Buysee, & Manuck, 2007), inflammation (Irwin et al., 2008; Mills et al., 2007), coronary artery disease (King et al., 2008), all-cause mortality (Dew et al., 2003; Gallicchio & Kalesan, 2009), as well as obesity and diabetes (see Pack & Pien, 2011). Thus, whereas insomnia is considered a mental health disorder, poor sleep generally is central to health and is, therefore, a target for intervention among clinical health psychologists and behavioral medicine practitioners. Indeed, behavioral sleep medicine is now a specific subspecialty with its own certification process from the American Board of Sleep Medicine.

To date, intervention research has largely focused on the treatment of insomnia. For many years, the treatment of choice has been cognitive behavioral therapy for insomnia (CBT-I) a multicomponent treatment that includes stimulus control, sleep restriction, sleep hygiene, paradoxical intention, relaxation therapy, and cognitive restructuring (Morin & Espie, 2003). More recently, variations and extensions of this treatment have been tested (see Bootzin & Epstein, 2011). For example, it has been shown that adding intensive sleep retraining (ISR) to stimulus control intervention results in superior treatment outcomes (Harris, Lack, Kemp, Wright, & Bootzin, 2012). ISR is a brief (25 hours in a sleep lab) behavioral conditioning intervention in which patients are awakened after a few consecutive minutes of each sleep stage, measured by electroencephalograph (EEG), thereby inducing acute sleep deprivation and repeatedly exposing patients to sleep onset.

It is important to note, however, that much of the insomnia intervention research has not focused on chronic illness. Further, research linking poor sleep to adverse health outcomes is not specific to insomnia. Thus, an important recent direction for health psychology and behavioral medicine is the improvement of sleep both as a preventive effort, as well as in the management of chronic illnesses with associated sleep difficulties. For example, CBT-I has been successfully applied to patients with comorbid osteoarthritis and insomnia resulting in improved sleep and decreased pain (Vitiello, Rybarczyk, Von Korff, & Stepanski, 2009). Exercise training has been shown to be effective in improving objective indicators of obstructive sleep apnea, as well as improvements in sleep (Kline et al., 2011). An RCT is underway to investigate the effectiveness of mindfulness-based stress management and

CBT in improving sleep among cancer patients (Garland, Carlson, Antle, Samuels, & Campbell, 2011). Increasing evidence for the role of sleep and circadian rhythm disturbance in the development of mood disorders (Harvey, 2011) suggest that sleep intervention may also prove useful in treating co-occurring chronic illness and mood disorder, especially depression.

Somatoform Disorders

The somatoform disorders are relevant to clinical health psychology and behavioral medicine because patients with these disorders often first present in medical settings and this can have profound effects on health care service provision; relationships between physicians and patients are often strained in such cases, and the quality, cost, and outcome of medical care can suffer (see Williams, Smith, & Jordan, 2010). In the current diagnostic system, the somatoform disorders include hypochondriasis, somatization disorder, somatoform pain disorder, body dysmorphic disorder, and conversion disorder, though there will likely be changes in the future revision of the *DSM*. The shared focus of these diagnoses is a dysfunction in the perception of the body. Beyond the *DSM*, hypochondriasis and somatization disorder are included in the category of *medically unexplained symptoms* (Brown, 2007). Medically unexplained symptoms refer to conditions patients present to medical care that are subsequently judged as not having an identifiable physical basis. Hence, somatoform disorders are relatively extreme and persistent versions of such symptoms. Recent research has also focused on illness behavior (e.g., avoidance of physical activity) in the maintenance and chronicity of the somatoform disorders (Witthoft & Hiller, 2010).

Although there is some variation across the somatoform disorders, the most common and well-supported intervention is cognitive behavioral therapy (CBT). A CBT approach for hypochondriasis, for example, targets both inaccurate and catastrophic cognitions about the meaning of physical sensations and the amplification of symptoms. Cognitive restructuring involves the monitoring of illness-related thoughts and reappraisal of somatic experiences, and is often combined with relaxation training and desensitization (Stuart, Noyes, Starcevic, & Barski, 2008). Randomized clinical trials generally demonstrate that CBT produces reductions in symptoms of hypochondriasis and health anxiety, other types of emotional distress (e.g., anxiety, depressive symptoms), functional disability levels, and even health care utilization (e.g., Barsky & Ahern, 2004; Greeven et al., 2007). The general CBT approach produces similar benefits for patients with somatization disorder (Allen, Woolfolk, Escobar, Gara, & Hamer, 2006). Indeed, a recent review of randomized controlled trials found that the CBT model has broad applicability and effectiveness for somatoform disorders (Kroenke, 2007). Recent systematic reviews also indicate that collaborative care and mental health consultation produce improvements in patient functioning and well-being, and reductions in health care utilization and related costs (Van der Feltz-Cornelis, Van Os, Van Marwijk, & Leentjens, 2010). Effective consultations typically involve documentation of the somatoform disorder, recommendations for a conservative approach to future medical diagnostic and treatment procedures, and the use of regularly scheduled health care visits, rather than "on demand" use of medical services.

Caregiver Stress

Stress management has been a long-standing, key component of clinical health psychology and behavioral medicine intervention across many health foci. However, one particular type of stress has emerged as so significant as to provoke a substantial intervention literature: caregiver stress. Individuals who care for others through chronic, debilitating illness, such as Alzheimer's disease, experience such significant stress that intervention science has begun to target this population specifically. For example, coping skills training can reduce caregiver burden (Elliott, Burgio, & DeCoster, 2010).

A prominent evidence-based intervention for caregivers of dementia patients is the Resources for Enhancing Alzheimer's Caregiver Health (REACH) II program (Belle et al., 2006). In this randomized controlled trial, caregivers received education on dementia and caregiving, skills training focused on increasing pleasant events or relaxation techniques, physical environment safety instruction, guidance and encouragement in caregiver physical self-care, skills for accessing social support, and written "behavioral prescriptions" for managing various activities of daily living (ADL) and independent ADL in patients, and common behavior problems. Results from the clinical trial showed significantly greater improvements in quality of life and depression

in the intervention group. These results were true for African American, Caucasian, and Hispanic samples. The REACH II program has recently been modified for use in other contexts, with demonstrated positive effects on caregiver subjective burden, social support, caregiver frustration, depression, caregiver health, care recipient behavior problems, and mood (Burgio et al., 2009; Nichols, Martindale-Adams, Burns, Graney, & Zuber, 2011).

Another recently reported longitudinal, randomized controlled trial examined the effects of the Tailored Caregiver Assessment and Referral (TCARE®) protocol, a care management process designed to help family caregivers with care planning and assess caregiver outcomes. Caregivers in the intervention group utilized a greater number of support services, had lower stress burden, and reduced depressive symptoms than caregivers in the control group (Kwak, Montgomery, Kosloski, & Lang, 2011). A pilot randomized trial evaluated the effectiveness of a mindfulness meditation intervention in relation to two comparison groups: an education class based on Powerful Tools for Caregivers serving as an active control group and a respite-only group serving as a pragmatic control in caregivers of close relatives with dementia. Both mindfulness and education interventions decreased the self-rated caregiver stress compared to the respite-only control (Oken et al., 2010). A randomized controlled trial is underway to evaluate the effectiveness of mindfulness-based stress reduction for caregivers (Whitebird et al., 2011).

Recent research on the determinants and consequences of caregiving stress may lead to further refinements in these interventions. For example, in some cases caregiving is associated with reduced distress and improved well-being (Brown et al., 2009), raising questions regarding potential moderators of the effects of caregiving or "active ingredients" in its unhealthy effects. Some evidence suggests that witnessing suffering of loved ones, rather than caregiving, per se is unhealthy (Monin & Schulz, 2009). If supported in future research, such findings could lead to more precisely targeted interventions.

CONCLUSIONS AND EMERGING ISSUES

The intervention research findings reviewed here demonstrate that behavioral medicine and clinical health psychology continue to make considerable progress in the reduction of behavioral risk factors for disease, in the management of chronic medical conditions that are the leading sources of morbidity and health care expenditures, and in the management of other distressing and costly problems patients often present in medical care settings. Several issues will shape the agenda for future intervention research and the implementation of those research findings in the delivery of health services.

Implications for Intervention Research

In earlier reviews of intervention research in behavioral medicine and clinical health psychology (e.g., Blanchard, 1994; Smith, Kendall, & Keefe, 2002) the vast majority of studies were RCTs of the efficacy of well-defined interventions for specific behavioral risk factors or medical conditions. This type of intervention research will continue to be important, in part because much of the earlier intervention research in the field did not meet the more recently articulated standards for the design, analysis and reporting of RCTs. The field has quickly evolved to meet these standards much more routinely, but the "second generation" of larger, higher quality RCTs of intervention efficacy will continue to be an essential part of the research portfolio in the field going forward.

With increasing emphasis on evidence-based practice in medical care and related aspects of health policy, this second generation of RCTs in clinical health psychology must take full advantage of various approaches to documenting the clinical significance of intervention effects. In addition to commonly reported information about effect sizes, consistent reporting of the percentage of patients with clinically meaningful improvements is important (e.g., Thieme, Turk, & Flor, 2007). For some outcomes and medical problems, this may require additional research to establish the optimal criteria for such improvements. Increasing use of common metrics across specific medical problems (e.g., quality-adjusted life years) will facilitate clinically meaningful and policy-relevant comparisons. In addition, the effects of various interventions of health care utilization and related health care costs will be increasingly important. When the endpoints of trials include outcomes that are relatively low in frequency (e.g., prevention of recurrent cardiac events among patients with

CHD), multisite trials that have been rare in behavioral medicine and clinical health psychology but more common in other medical treatment research will be needed. Even though the ENRICHD trial (Berkman et al., 2003) produced null results on the primary endpoint, the experience gained by the researchers involved in the trial will be an invaluable asset in future efforts of this type.

However, other kinds of intervention studies that are familiar to psychotherapy and behavior change researchers are also needed. Person by treatment interactional or moderational designs are needed to address the important challenge of matching specific types of clinical problems and patients with specific types of treatments. Dismantling designs will be useful for identifying the critical elements within the widely used multicomponent interventions. In several cases, treatments have been evaluated with inadequate control of non-specific factors, resulting in the need for critical considerations of appropriate comparison conditions in future research (Freedland, Mohr, Davidson, & Schwartz, 2011).

A small but growing literature in behavioral medicine and clinical health psychology addresses mechanisms of change in interventions, and results to date suggest that this comparatively understudied issue is also important. For example, reductions in catastrophizing mediate therapeutic improvement not only in CBT for chronic pain, but also other forms of pain treatment that do not directly address this cognitive process (Burns, Day, & Thorn, 2012; Smeets, Vtaeyen, Kester, & Knottnerus, 2006). The quality of the therapeutic alliance predicts therapeutic outcomes in adjunctive psychological treatments for MS patients (Beckner, Vella, Howard, & Mohr, 2007; Howard, Turner, Okin, & Mohr, 2006). Also, group cohesion and rapport in group-based psychosocial treatments for cancer patients similarly predict therapeutic outcomes (Andersen, Shelby, & Golden-Kreutz, 2007; Schnur & Montgomery, 2010). Additional research on mechanisms of change and intervention processes could help refine the development and delivery of interventions, and identify key competences to be emphasized in training. To date, much of the behavioral and cognitive-behavioral intervention research in behavioral medicine and clinical health psychology has implicitly emphasized the high-fidelity delivery of manualized therapies; a broader intervention research agenda could be a very valuable addition.

As noted previously, for interventions found to be efficacious in closely controlled RCTs, research on their effectiveness when delivered in representative health care settings will be important (Glasgow, 2008; Glasgow & Emmons, 2007). Finally, research on the dissemination and uptake of evidence-based practices in health care will be an increasingly important focus in the field (Kerner et al., 2005; McHugh & Barlow, 2011). In such efforts, traditional intervention researchers may find value in collaborative efforts with health services researchers. For effectiveness and dissemination research, the RE-AIM framework as applied to health behavior change (Glasgow et al., 1999) and chronic illness management (Glasgow et al., 2001) articulates several specific research topics to address these issues.

Behavioral Medicine and Clinical Health Psychology in Medical Care

In some emerging models, clinical health psychology and behavioral medicine services are delivered as an integral component of medical care. Rather than providing separate services in distinct settings, clinical health psychologists work in direct collaboration with other health care professionals. In these new roles, psychologists often provide both typical services for mental health problems (e.g., anxiety, depression) that patients present in those medical settings, as well as services more directly related to the medical issues (e.g., behavioral risk reduction, adjunctive treatments for chronic disease). Hence, these recent care models cross traditional boundaries between clinical and counseling psychology on the one hand, and health psychology and behavioral medicine on the other.

Much of this change and the related opportunities involve the expanding role of psychological services in primary medical care. Four formal medical specializations provide primary care (i.e., general internal medicine, family practice, pediatrics, and obstetrics-gynecology). In addition, primary medical care is provided by nurse practitioners and physician assistants who practice in collaboration with primary care physicians. Primary medical care in the United States currently faces a variety of challenges, especially problems with access and staffing, but also managing the growing burden of chronic medical illness (Bodenheimer & Phan, 2010). The concept of the *patient-centered medical home* is considered a valuable new model for more effective and

efficient primary medical care (Landon, Gill, Antonelli, & Rich, 2010), in which team-based, coordinated care under the direction of a primary care physician is the foundation for providing both acute and chronic care, addressing the needs of the "whole person" from childhood through end-of-life issues (Strange et al., 2010).

Over the past decade, psychologists have articulated the potential value of primary medical care as a setting for the provision of psychological services, proposing the development of the new field or specialty of primary care psychology (Frank, McDaniel, Bray, & Heldring, 2004; Haas, 2004). This emerging role for psychologists fits quite well with descriptions of the patient-centered medical home (McDaniel & Fogerty, 2009). The behavioral risk reduction interventions reviewed here could routinely be delivered in this context, as could adjunctive treatments for the management of chronic illness and interventions for common psychological problems presenting in primary care (i.e., mood and anxiety disorders, insomnia, somatoform disorders). The common comorbidity of depression and chronic medical illness is a prototypical example of the need for such integrative services (Smith, 2010b). In addition to direct psychological treatment of such conditions, there is substantial evidence of improved outcomes for depression and somatoform disorders when mental health consultations are readily available (Van der Feltz-Cornelis, Van Os, et al., 2010). Hence, after emerging as distinct new fields several decades ago, clinical health psychology and behavioral medicine may be poised to become a more common element of multifaceted, comprehensive health care, in which traditional distinctions between mental health services and behavioral medicine/clinical health psychology services are blurred as they are both increasingly delivered in the context of primary medical settings.

To the extent that the patient-centered medical home does come to include the full life span, other roles are available for psychologists. For example, stress, anxiety, and low social support during pregnancy increase the risk of preterm births and low birth weight, which in turn often have negative long-term consequences for the child's emotional, social, and educational functioning (Dunkel Schetter, 2011; Lobel et al., 2008). Group-based provision of comprehensive psychosocial care for high-risk expectant mothers has been found to reduce preterm birth and low birth weight, and to improve a variety of aspects of psychosocial functioning among such women (Ickovics et al., 2007, 2011).

In terms of end-of-life care, an emerging psychosocial topic among terminal patients involves end-of-life planning discussions, which are sometimes seen as a potential stressor for patients and their families, and passively or intentionally avoided by health care providers as a result. However, such discussions are generally well tolerated by patients and their caregivers, and are associated with less aggressive medical care as patients approach death and earlier referral to hospice care (Wright et al., 2008). Less aggressive medical care, in turn, has been found to be associated with higher patient quality of life in the days and weeks preceding death, and with less emotional distress among their caregivers (Wright et al., 2008). Hence, consultation-liaison interventions surrounding these issues could be a useful element of expanded roles of clinical health psychologists in the patient-centered medical home. Similarly, bereavement is normal, but it does pose a health risk (Stroebe, Schut, & Stroebe, 2007). Although psychological interventions have no demonstrable beneficial effects in cases of normal bereavement (Stroebe, Schut, & Stroebe, 2005), a meta-analysis demonstrated that bereavement therapy was useful for people with more severe and prolonged reactions (Currier, Neimeyer, & Berman, 2008). Hence, primary care psychology as a component of the patient-centered medical home has the potential to make useful additions to care across the life span. The possibilities for integration of psychology in primary medical care are increasingly recognized as important challenges and opportunities for a broad range of psychological researchers and service providers (Bray, 2010; Goodheart, 2011). As psychologists transition into these roles, issues of the general and unique training needs for this interdisciplinary environment will require further attention (France et al., 2008), as will the empirical evaluation of the effects of various training models for psychologists on health services outcomes.

Technology and Changing Models of Service Delivery

In health behavior change and chronic illness management, research has at least initially demonstrated the value of a range of options for delivery of behavioral interventions, from traditional one-on-one and small group approaches, to interactive computer and telephone delivery, to alterations in health system practices (Glasgow et al., 2001). Telephone and Internet-delivery models can be useful in meeting the needs of rural populations with limited access to behavioral health professionals, as well as the needs of patients whose chronic medical conditions pose mobility and transportation challenges. Examples of the efficacy of telephone interventions include challenging and specialized populations such as MS patients (Mohr, Hart, & Vella, 2007) and transplant candidates (Blumenthal et al., 2006). Computer-based interventions have been developed and evaluated in an even greater variety of applications (for reviews, see Bennett & Glasgow, 2009; Strecher, 2007), including CBT for gastrointestinal conditions (Hunt et al., 2009), management of diabetes (Glasgow et al., 2005), and bereavement support (van der Houwen, Schut, van den Bout, Stroebe, & Stroebe, 2010). Telephone interventions have the potential to address many problems with health care access, but still require real-time availability of health care providers. In contrast, computer-based approaches also can address access problems, but also have tremendous potential as large-scale interventions that can have important effects on population levels of behavior change and chronic illness management due to the their dramatically greater reach. In this way, computer-based interventions can be a "first step of choice" in stepped care approaches to many specific problems.

Changing Demographics

In the United States and other industrialized nations, increasing ethnic and racial diversity poses a variety of challenges. In terms of the leading sources of morbidity and mortality, several ethnic and racial minority groups are at increased risk of CVD, for example. They often have increased levels of modifiable risk factors, yet are underserved in terms of various prevention resources (Stuart-Shor, Berra, Kamau, & Kumanyika, 2012). Racial and ethnic minority status is an essential aspect of external validity considerations in effectiveness research. There is also a great need for culturally and linguistically tailored community-based interventions. Initial efforts in culturally enhanced or tailored health behavior change interventions indicate major potential benefits (Barrera, Castro, Strycker, & Tolbert, 2012).

In many industrialized nations, the average age of the population is increasing. Chronic illness is more prevalent among older adults, as are the related burdens. Hence, health behavior change and chronic disease management will increasingly need to incorporate the concepts, methods, and knowledge base from adult development and aging research (Aldwin, Park, & Spiro, 2007). However, some chronic diseases of middle and later adulthood, such as CHD, often have their beginnings in pathophysiological changes evident in childhood and adolescence (Charakida, Deanfield, & Halcox, 2009). Further, the health behaviors (e.g., excessive dietary intake of calories and saturated fat, physical inactivity, smoking) that are major sources of these same chronic diseases among middle-aged and older adults are first apparent—and most easily modified—in childhood and adolescence (Wilson, St. George, & Zarrett, 2010). Similarly, exposure to psychosocial stressors during childhood and adolescence (e.g., low childhood SES, severe family stressors) can influence risk for chronic diseases of aging (Cohen, Janicki-Deverts, Chen, & Matthews, 2010; Miller, Chen, & Parker, 2011). Thus, it is possible that health behavior and psychosocial risk reduction efforts for the prevention of adult chronic disease could usefully incorporate a broader set of child and adolescent prevention approaches (Smith, Orleans, & Jenkins, 2004).

Changing Emphases in Medical Care and Future World Health Perspectives

In the United States, the Department of Health and Human Services has sponsored the development and revision of the *Healthy People* initiatives for the past three decades, the most recent version being *Healthy People 2020*. The overarching goals of the initiative and the foundation health measures that are tracked to evaluate progress include not only longer lives and a reduction in preventable causes of death, but also higher quality lives free of limitations in functional activity and threats to well-being, broadly but specifically defined (see www.healthypeople.gov/2020/topicsobjectives2020). These goals and progress benchmarks make clear that the perspectives and approaches of behavioral medicine and health psychology converge closely with national priorities for the foreseeable future.

The primary current health challenges for more and less developed countries differ, with nonindustrialized nations facing greater relative overall burdens and death rates from perinatal conditions (i.e., prematurity, birth trauma, infections) and various infectious diseases (e.g., lower

respiratory infections, tuberculosis, HIV/AIDS), compared to the proportionally greater burdens and death rates associated with cardiovascular disease (i.e., ischemic heart disease and cerebrovascular disease) and cancer in industrialized nations (Oldenburg, de Courten, & Frean, 2010). However, projections suggest a trend toward convergence over the next 25 to 30 years, in which the burden of perinatal and infections disease other than HIV/AIDS falls worldwide while deaths and overall burdens from cardiovascular disease, tobacco-related conditions, obesity related conditions, and HIV/AIDS rise (Mathers & Loncar, 2006). These trends suggest that across the globe the current prevention perspective in health psychology and behavioral medicine focusing on smoking, diet, physical activity, and sexually transmitted infections will only increase in importance, as will the need for psychosocial adjunctive treatments for cardiovascular and other chronic conditions. Hence, within the industrialized nations—and increasingly beyond them—the need for research and intervention services in health psychology and behavioral medicine is likely to grow.

Concluding Thoughts

In the years since the last edition of this handbook, intervention research in behavioral medicine and clinical health psychology has expanded considerably—increasing not only in amount, but also in quality and the range of applications. Yet, during the same period, the standards for intervention research have been raised substantially, to the point where the status of the evidence base is promising but quite modest in some areas (Oldenburg, Absetz, et al., 2010). This underscores the need for continued efforts in methodologically rigorous RCTs and systematic reviews, but with an even greater emphasis on the degree of clinically meaningful change, broadly comparable outcome metrics, and effects on health care utilization and costs. However, there is also a need for an expanded view of intervention research that includes a greater investment in research on effectiveness, applications to diverse populations and health disparities, intervention process and mechanisms of change, dissemination, and implementation. Behavioral medicine and health psychology have always been multidisciplinary endeavors; this expanded intervention research agenda seems to require additional partnerships in health services research, health care policy, and other areas.

At a time when health care costs in the United States and elsewhere are rising to levels that pose unsustainable economic burdens, health psychology, and behavioral medicine face both daunting challenges and major opportunities in the prevention and management of disease, by contributing to more effective and efficient medical care. These challenges and opportunities lie in two distinct areas. The first challenges involve a growing divergence in its focus on two very different forms of intervention and intervention research. Research and applications in behavioral medicine and health psychology must retain and enhance its active focus on traditional clinical models of individual and small-group based approaches, because these interventions have the potential to provide improved care and much needed reductions in health care spending (Belar & Deardooff, 2009). However, intervention research must also continue to address the challenges posed by the need for much broader population-based approaches that dramatically extend the reach of evidence based interventions for health behavior change and the management of chronic illness, with even greater possibilities for efficiencies in care. This growing divergence of intervention missions has the potential to alter traditional conceptualizations of the structure of the field, as it becomes more closely related to public health on the one hand, and more closely linked to an expanded multidisciplinary approach to clinical health care, on the other.

In the second challenge, research and applications regarding the more traditional individual and small group approaches in behavioral medicine and clinical health psychology must address the rapidly changing economic, policy, and practice environment in health care. If behavioral medicine and clinical health psychology can firmly establish a substantial role in evolving systems of primary medical care while maintaining their more long-standing role in some specialized medical applications (e.g., pain treatment, oncology), their place among the intervention sciences and health care professions will continue to grow and evolve.

REFERENCES

Abraham, C., & Graham-Rower, E. (2009). Are worksite interventions effective in increasing physical activity? A systematic review and meta-analysis. *Health Psychology Review, 3,* 108–144.

Abrams, D. B., Orleans, C. T., Niaura, R., Goldstein, M., Prochaska, J., & Velicer, W. (1996). Integrating individual and public health perspectives for treatment of tobacco dependence under managed care. A combined stepped care and matching model. *Annals of Behavioral Medicine, 18,* 290–304.

Agboola, S., McNeill, A., Coleman, T., & Bee, J. L. (2010). A systematic review of the effectiveness of smoking relapse prevention interventions for abstinent smokers. *Addiction, 105,* 1362–1380.

Akechi, T., Okuyama, T., Onishi, J., Morita, T., & Furukawa, T. A. (2008). Psychotherapy for depression among incurable cancer patients. *Cochrane Database of Systematic Reviews (2),* CD005537.

Aldwin, C. M., Park, C. L., & Spiro, A. (Eds). (2007). *Handbook of health psychology and aging.* New York, NY: Guilford Press.

Allen, K. D., Oddone, E. Z., Coffman, C. J., Datta, S. K., Juntilla, K. A., Lindquist, J. H., . . . Bosworth, H. B. (2010). Telephone-based self-management of osteoarthritis: A randomized trial. *Annals of Internal Medicine, 153,* 570–579.

Allen, L. A., Woolfolk, R. L., Escobar, J. I., Gara, M. A., & Hamer, R. M. (2006). Cognitive-behavioral therapy for somatization disorder: A randomized controlled trial. *Archives of Internal Medicine, 166,* 1512–1518.

Altman, D. G., Schulz, K. F., Moher, D., Egger, D., Davidoff, F., & Elbourne, D. (2001). The revised CONSORT statement for reporting randomized trials: Explanation and elaboration. *Annals of Internal Medicine, 134,* 663–694.

Alwan, A., MacLean, D. R., Riley, L. M., d'Espaignet, E. T., Mathers, C. D., Stevens, G. A., & Bettcher, D. (2010). Monitoring and surveillance of chronic non-communicable diseases: Progress and capacity in high-burden countries. *Lancet, 376,* 1861–1868.

Andersen, B. L., Farrar, W. B., Golden-Kreutz, D. M., Glaser, R., Emery, C. F., Crespin, T. R., . . . Carson, W. E. (2004). Psychological, behavioral, and immune changes after a psychological intervention: A clinical trial. *Journal of Clinical Oncology, 22,* 3570–3580.

Andersen, B. L., Shelby, R. A., & Golden-Kreutz, D. M. (2007). RCT of a psychological intervention for patients with cancer: I. Mechanisms of change. *Journal of Consulting and Clinical Psychology, 75,* 927–938. doi: 10.1037/0022–006X.75.6.927

Andersen, B. L., Yang, H., Farrar, W., Golden-Kreutz, D., Emery, C., Thornton, L., . . . Carson, W. (2008). Psychologic intervention improves survival for breast cancer patients: A randomized clinical trial. *Cancer, 113,* 3450 3458.

Anderson, L., Quinn, T., Glanz, K., Ramirez, G., Kahwati, L., Johnson, D. B., . . . Katz, D. L. (2009). The effectiveness of worksite nutrition and physical activity interventions for controlling employee overweight and obesity. *American Journal of Preventive Medicine, 37,* 340–357.

Antoni, M. H., Lechner, S., Diaz, A., Vargas, S., Holley, H., Phillips, K., . . . Blomberg, B. (2009). Cognitive behavioral stress management effects on psychosocial and physiological adaptation in women undergoing treatment for breast cancer. *Brain, Behavior, and Immunity, 23,* 580–591.

Antoni, M., Lutgendorf, S. K., Blomberg, B., Carver, C. S., Lechner, S., Diaz, A. . . . Cole, S. W. (2012). Cognitive-behavioral stress management reverses anxiety-related leukocyte transcriptional dynamics. *Biological Psychiatry, 71,* 366–372.

Antoni, M. H., Lutgendorf, S., Cole, S., Dhabhar, F., Sephton, S., McDonald, P., . . . Sood, A. (2006). The influence of biobehavioral factors on tumor biology: Pathways and mechanisms. *Nature Reviews Cancer, 6,* 240–248.

Appel, L. J., Brands, M. W., Daniels, S. R., Karanja, N., Elmer, P. J., & Sacks, F. (2006). Dietary approaches to prevent and treat hypertension. *Hypertension, 47,* 296–308.

Appel, L. J., Clark, J. M., Yeh, H. C., Wang, N. Y., Coughlin, J. W., Daumit, G., . . . Brancati, F. L. (2011). Comparative effectiveness of weight-loss interventions in clinical practice. *New England Journal of Medicine, 365,* 1959–1968.

Armitage, C. J. (2009). Is there utility in the transtheoretical model? *British Journal of Health Psychology, 14,* 195–210.

Armstrong, M. J., Mottershead, T. A., Ronksley, P. E., Sigal, R. J., Campbell, T. S., & Hemmelgarn, B. R. (2011). Motivational interviewing to improve weight loss in overweight and/or obese patients: A systematic review and meta-analysis of randomized controlled trials. *Obesity Reviews, 12,* 709–723.

Atlantis, E., & Baker, M. (2008). Obesity effects on depression: Systematic review of epidemiological studies. *International Journal of Obesity, 32,* 881–891.

Aubin, H., Rollema, H., Svensson, T., & Winterer, G. (2012). Smoking, quitting, and psychiatric disease. *A review. Neuroscience and Biobehavioral Reviews, 36,* 271–284.

Aveyard, P., Massey, L., Parsons, A., Manasek, S., & Griffin, C. (2009). The effect of transtheoretical model based interventions on smoking cessation. *Social Science and Medicine, 68,* 397–403.

Baines, L. S., Joseph, J. T., & Jindal, R. M. (2004). Prospective randomized study of individual and group psychotherapy versus controls in recipients of renal transplants. *Kidney International, 65,* 1937–1942.

Baker, T. B., Mermelstein, R., Collins, L. M., Piper, M. E., Jorenby, D. E., Smith, S. S., . . . Fiore, M. C. (2011). New methods for tobacco dependence treatment research. *Annals of Behavioral Medicine, 41,* 192–207.

Baldwin, A. S., Kellerman, Q. D., & Christensen, A. J. (2010). Coping with chronic illness. In J. M. Suls, K. W. Davidson, & R. M. Kaplan (Eds.), *Handbook of health psychology and behavioral medicine* (pp. 494–507). New York, NY: Guilford Press.

Bandura, A. (1977). Self-efficacy: Toward a unifying theory of behavior change. *Psychological Review, 84,* 191–215.

Baroletti, S., & Dell'Orfano, H. (2010). Medication adherence in cardiovascular disease. *Circulation, 121,* 1455–1455.

Barrera Jr., M., Castro, F. G., Stryker, L. A., & Tolbert, D. J. (2012). Cultural adaptations of Behavioral health interventions: A progress report. *Journal of Consulting and Clinical Psychology.* doi: 10.1037/a0027085

Barsky, A. J., & Ahern, D. K. (2004). Cognitive behavior therapy for hypochondriasis: A randomized controlled trial. *Journal of the American Medical Association, 291,* 1464–1470.

Barth, J., Critchley, J., & Bengel, J. (2008). Psychosocial interventions for smoking cessation in patients with coronary heart disease. *Cochrane Database of Systematic Reviews* (1), CD006886.

Beck, A. T. (1976). *Cognitive therapy and the emotional disorders.* New York, NY: International Universities Press.

Beckner, V., Vella, L., Howard, I., & Mohr, D. C. (2007). Alliance in two telephone-administered treatments: Relationship with depression and health outcomes. *Journal of Consulting and Clinical Psychology, 75,* 508–512.

Belar, C. D., & Deardorff, W. W. (2009). *Clinical health psychology in medical settings: A practitioner's guidebook* (2nd ed). Washington, DC: American Psychological Association.

Belle, S. H., Burgio, L., Burns, R., Coon, D., Czaja, S. J., & Gallagher-Thompson, D. (2006). Enhancing the quality of life of dementia caregivers from different ethnic or racial groups: A randomized, controlled trial. *Annals of Internal Medicine, 145,* 727–738

Bennett, G. G., & Glasgow, R. E. (2009). The delivery of public health interventions via the Internet: Actualizing their potential. *Annual Review of Public Health, 30,* 273–292.

Bennett, G. G., Herring, S. J., Puleo, E., Stein, E. K., Emmons, K. M., & Gillman, M. W. (2010). Web-based weight loss in primary care: A randomized controlled trial. *Obesity, 18,* 308–313.

Berkman, L. F., Blumenthal, J., Burg, M., Carney, R. M., Catellier, D., Cowan, M. J., . . . Schneiderman, N. (2003). Effects of treating depression and low perceived social support on clinical events after myocardial infarction: The enhancing recovery in coronary heart disease patients (ENRICHD) randomized trial. *Journal of the American Medical Association, 289,* 3106–3116.

Bhattacharyya, M. R., & Steptoe, A. (2007). Emotional triggers of acute coronary syndromes: Strength of evidence, biological processes, and clinical implications. *Progress in Cardiovascular Disease, 49,* 353–365.

Blanchard, E. B. (1994). Behavioral medicine and health psychology. In A. E. Bergin & S. L. Garfield (Eds.), *Handbook of psychotherapy and behavior change* (4th ed., pp. 701–733). New York, NY: Wiley.

Blumenthal, J. A. (2011). New frontiers in cardiovascular behavioral medicine: Comparative effectiveness of exercise and medication in treating depression. *Cleveland Clinic Journal of Medicine, 78,* s35–s43.

Blumenthal, J. A., Babyak, M. A., Hinderliter, A., Watkins, L., Craighead, L., Caccia, C., …Sherwood, A. (2010). Effects of the DASH diet alone and in combination with exercise and weight loss on blood pressure and cardiovascular biomarkers in men and women with high blood pressure: The ENCORE study. *Archives of Internal Medicine, 170,* 126–135.

Blumenthal, J. A., Babyak, M., Keefe, F. J., Davis, R. D., Lacaille, R. A., Carney, R., …Palmer, S. M. (2006). Telephone-based coping skills training for patients awaiting lung transplantation. *Journal of Consulting and Clinical Psychology, 74,* 535–544.

Blumenthal, J. A., Babyak, M. A., Sherwood, A., Craighead, L., Lin, P. H., Johnson, J., …Hinderliter, A. (2010). Effects of the dietary approach to stop hypertension diet alone and in combination with exercise and caloric restriction on insulin sensitivity and lipids. *Hypertension, 55,* 1199–1205.

Blumenthal, J. A., Sherwood, A., Babyak, M., Watkins, L., Waugh, R., Georgiades, A., …Hinderliter, A. (2005). Effects of exercise and stress management training on markers of cardiovascular risk in patients with ischemic heart diseases: A randomized controlled trial. *JAMA, 293,* 1626–1634.

Bodenheimer, T., & Pham, H. H. (2010). Primary care: current problems and proposed solutions. *Health Affairs, 29,* 799–805.

Bogers R. P., Bemelmans, W. J., Hoogenveen, R. T., Boshuizen, H. C., Woodward, M., Knekt, P., …Shipley, M. J., for the BMI-CHD Collaboration Investigators. (2007). Association of overweight with increased risk of coronary heart disease partly independent of blood pressure and cholesterol levels: A meta-analysis of 21 cohort studies including more than 300,000 persons. *Archives of Internal Medicine, 167,* 1720–1728.

Bogner, H. R., Morales, K. H., de Vries, H. F., & Cappola, A. R. (2012). Integrated management of type 2 diabetes mellitus and depression treatment to improve medication adherence: A randomized controlled trial. *Annals of Family Medicine, 10,* 15–22.

Bolan, B., West, R., & Gunnell, D. (2011). Does smoking cessation cause depression and anxiety? Findings from the ATTEMPT cohort. *Nicotine and Tobacco Research, 13,* 209–214.

Bootzin, R. R., & Epstein, D. R. (2011). Understanding and treating insomnia. *Annual Review of Clinical Psychology, 7,* 435–458.

Bottonari, K. A., Safren, S. A., McQuaid, J. R., Hsiao, C. B., & Roberts, J. E. (2010). A longitudinal investigation of the impact of life stress on HIV treatment adherence. *Journal of Behavioral Medicine, 33,* 486–495.

Brandon, T. H., Vidrine, J. I., & Litvin, E. B. (2007). Relapse and relapse prevention. *Annual Review of Clinical Psychology, 3,* 257–284.

Bray, J. H. (2010). The future of psychology practice and science. *American Psychologist, 65,* 355–369.

Brennan, L., Castro, S., Brownson, R. C., Claus, J., & Orleans, C. T. (2011). Accelerating evidence reviews and broadening evidence standards to identify effective, promising, and emerging policy and environmental strategies for prevention of childhood obesity. *Annual Review of Public Health, 32,* 199–223.

Bricker, J. B. (2010). Theory-based behavioral interventions for smoking cessation: Efficacy, processes, and future directions. In J. M. Suls, K. W. Davidson, & R. M. Kaplan (Eds.), *Handbook of health psychology and behavioral medicine* (pp. 544–566). New York, NY: Guilford Press.

Brown, J. L., & Vanable, P. A. (2008). Cognitive–behavioral stress management interventions for persons living with HIV: A review and critique of the literature. *Annals of Behavioral Medicine, 35,* 26–40.

Brown, R. J. (2007). Introduction to the special issue on medically unexplained symptoms: Background and future directions. *Clinical Psychology Review, 27,* 769–780.

Brown, S. L., Smith, D. M., Schulz, R., Kabeto, M. U., Ubel, P. A., Poulin, M., …Langa, K. M. (2009). Caregiving behavior is associated with decreased mortality risk. *Psychological Science, 20,* 488–494.

Brownson, R. C., Boehmer, T. K., & Luke, D. A. (2005). Declining rates of physical activity in the United States: What are the contributors? *Annual Review of Public Health, 26,* 421–443.

Brownson, R. C., Haire-Joshu, D., & Luke, D. A. (2006). Shaping the context of health: A review of environmental and policy approaches in the prevention of chronic disease. *Annual Review of Public Health, 27,* 341–370.

Burgio, L. D., Collins, I. B., Schmid, B., Wharton, T., McCallum, D., & Decoster, J. (2009). Translating the REACH caregiver intervention for use by area agency on aging personnel: The REACH OUT program. *Gerontologist, 49,* 103–116.

Burns, J. W., Day, M. A., & Thorn, B. E. (2012). Is reduction of pain catastrophizing a therapeutic mechanism specific to cognitive-behavioral therapy for chronic pain? *Translational Behavioral Medicine.* doi: 10.1007/s13142–011–0086–3

Butryn, M. L., Webb, V., & Wadden, T. A. (2011). Behavioral treatment of obesity. *Psychiatric Clinics of North America, 34,* 841–859.

Byers, T. (2010). Two decades of declining cancer mortality: Progress with disparity. *Annual Review of Public Health, 31,* 121–132.

Campbell, M. K., Hudson, M. A., Resnicow, K., Blakeney, N., Paxton, A., & Baskin, M. (2007). Church-based health promotion interventions: Evidence and lessons learned. *Annual Review of Public Health, 28,* 213–234.

Caplan, B. (2010). Rehabilitation psychology and neuropsychology with stroke survivors. In R. G. Frank, M. Rosenthal., & B. Caplan (Eds.), *Handbook of rehabilitation psychology* (2nd ed., pp. 63–94). Washington, DC: American Psychological Association.

Carrel, A. L., Clark, R. R., Peterson, S. E., Nemeth, B. A., Sullivan, J., & Allen, D. B. (2005). Improvement of fitness, body composition, and insulin sensitivity in overweight children in a school-based exercise program: A randomized, controlled study. *Archives of Pediatric and Adolescent Medicine, 159,* 963–968.

Carrel, A. L., Clark, R. R., Peterson, S. E., Eichhoff, J., & Allen, D. B. (2007). School-based fitness changes are lost during summer vacation. *Archives of Pediatric and Adolescent Medicine, 161,* 561–564.

Casey, E., Hughes, J. W., Waechter, D., Josephson, R., & Rosneck, J. (2008). Depression predicts failure to complete phase-II cardiac rehabilitation. *Journal of Behavioral Medicine, 31,* 421–431.

Castell, B. D., Kazantzis, N., & Moss-Morris, R. E. (2011). Cognitive-behavioral therapy and graded exercise for chronic fatigue syndrome: A meta-analysis. *Clinical Psychology: Science and Practice, 18,* 311–324.

Charakida, M., Deanfield, J. E., & Halcox, P. J. (2009). Childhood origins of arterial disease. *Current Opinion in Pediatrics, 19,* 538–545.

Chida, Y., & Hamer, M. (2008). An association of adverse psychosocial factors with diabetes mellitus: A meta-analytic review of longitudinal cohort studies. *Diabetologia, 51,* 2168–2178.

Chida, Y., Hamer, M., Wardle, J., & Steptoe, A. (2008). Do stress-related psychosocial factors contribute to cancer incidence and survival? *Nature Clinical Practice: Oncology, 5,* 466–475.

Chida, Y., & Steptoe, A. (2009). The association of anger and hostility with future coronary heart disease: A meta-analytic review of prospective evidence. *Journal of the American College of Cardiology, 53,* 774–778.

Chida, Y., & Vedhara, K. (2009). Adverse psychosocial factors predict poorer prognosis in HIV disease: A meta-analytic review of prospective investigations. *Brain, Behavior, and Immunity, 23,* 434–445.

Chow, C. K., Jolly, S., Rao-Melacini, P., Fox, K. A., Anand, S. S., & Yusuf, S. (2010). Association of diet, exercise, and smoking modification with risk of early cardiovascular events after acute coronary syndromes. *Circulation, 121,* 750–758.

Cohen, F., & Lazarus, R. S. (1979). Coping with the stress of illness. In G. C. Stone, F. Cohen, & N. E. Adler (Eds.), *Health psychology* (pp. 217–254). San Francisco, CA: Jossey-Bass.

Cohen, S. Doyle, W. J., Alper, C. M., Janicki-Deverts, D., & Turner, R. B. (2009). Sleep habits and susceptibility to the common cold. *Archives of Internal Medicine, 169,* 62–67.

Cohen, S., Janicki-Deverts, Chen, E., & Matthews, K. A. (2010). Childhood socioeconomic status and adult health. *Annals of the New York Academy of Science, 1186,* 37–55.

Cole, S. W., (2008). Psychosocial influences on HIV-1 disease progression: Neural, endocrine, and virologic mechanisms. *Psychosomatic Medicine, Special Issue: Psychosocial Influences in HIV/AIDS, 70,* 562–568.

Conn, V. S. (2010). Depressive symptom outcomes of physical activity interventions: Meta-analytic findings. *Annals of Behavioral Medicine, 39,* 128–138.

Cosio, D., Jin, L., Siddique, J., & Mohr, D. C. (2011). The effect of telephone-dministered cognitive-behavioral therapy on quality of life among patients with multiple sclerosis. *Annals of Behavioral Medicine, 41,* 227–234.

Cowie, C. C., Rust, K. F., Byrd-Holt, D. D., Gregg, E. W., Ford, E. S., Geiss, L. S., . . . Fradkin, J. E. (2010). Prevalence of diabetes and high risk for diabetes using A1C criteria in the U.S. population in 1988–2006. *Diabetes Care, 33,* 562–568.

Coyne, J. C., Lepore, S. J., & Palmer, S. C. (2006). Efficay of psychosocial interventions in cancer care: Evidence is weaker that it first looks. *Annals of Behavioral Medicine, 32,* 104–110.

Coyne, J. C., Stefanek, M., & Palmer, S. C. (2007). Psychotherapy and survival in cancer: The conflict between hope and evidence. *Psychological Bulletin, 133,* 367–394.

Coyne, J. C., Thombs, B. D., & Hagedorrn, M. (2010). Ain't necessarily so: Review and critique of behavioral medicine interventions in health psychology. *Health Psychology, 29,* 107–116.

Cramer, J., Benedict, A., Muszbek, N., Keskinaslan, A., & Khan, Z. (2008). The significance of compliance and persistence in the treatment of diabetes, hypertension, and dyslipidaemia: A review. *International Journal of Clinical Practice, 63,* 76–87.

Cramp, F., & Daniel, J. (2008). Exercise for the management of cancer-related fatigue in adults. *Cochrane Database of Systematic Reviews* (2), CD006145.

Creer, T. L., Holroyd, K. A., Glasgow, R. E., & Smith, T. W. (2004). Health psychology. In M. J. Lambert (Ed.), *Bergin and Garfield's handbook of psychotherapy and behavior change* (5th ed., pp. 697–742). Hoboken, NJ: Wiley.

Crepaz, N., Marshall, K. J., Aupont, L. W., Jacobs, E. D., Mizuno, Y., Kay, L. S., . . . O'Leary, A. (2009). The efficacy of HIV/STI behavioral interventions for African American females in the

United States: A meta-analysis. *American Journal of Public Health, 99*, 2069–2078.

Cummings, K. M., Fong, G. T., & Borland, R. (2009). Environmental influences on tobacco use: Evidence from societal and community influences on tobacco use and dependence. *Annual Review of Clinical Psychology, 5*, 433–458.

Currier, J. M., Neimeyer, R. A., & Berman, J. S. (2008). The effectiveness of psychotherapeutic interventions for bereaved persons: A comprehensive quantitative review. *Psychological Bulletin, 134*, 648–661.

Curry, S. J., Keller, P. A., Orleans, C. T., & Fiore, M. C. (2008). The role of health care systems in increased tobacco cessation. *Annual Review of Public Health, 29*, 411–418.

Daley, M., Morin, C. M., LeBlanc, M., Gregoire, J. P., Savard, J., & Ballargeon, L. (2009). Insomnia and its relationship to health-care utilization, work, absenteeism, productivity and accidents. *Sleep Medicine, 10*, 427–438.

Davidson, K. W., Gidron, Y., Mostofsky, E., & Trudeau, K. J. (2007). Hospitalization cost offset of a hostility intervention for coronary heart disease patients. *Journal of Consulting and Clinical Psychology, 75*, 657–662.

Davidson, K. W., Goldstein, M., Kaplan, R. M., Kaufman, P. G., Knatterud, G. L., Orleans, C. T., ... Whitlock, E. P. (2003). Evidence-based behavioral medicine: What is it and how do we achieve it? *Annals of Behavioral Medicine, 26*, 161–171.

Davidson, K. W., Rieckman, N., Clemow, L., Schwartz, J. E., Shimbo, D., Medina, V., ... Burg, M. M. (2010). Enhanced depression care for patients with acute coronary syndrome and persistent depressive symptoms: Coronary psychosocial evaluation studies randomized controlled trial. *Archives of Internal Medicine, 170*, 600–608.

Davidson, K. W., Trudeau, K. J., Ockene, J. K., Orleans, C. T., & Kaplan, R. M. (2004). A Primer on current evidence-based review systems and their implications for behavioral medicine. *Annals of Behavioral Medicine, 28*, 226–238.

Deakin, T., McShane, C. E., Cade, J. E., & Williams, R. D. (2005). Group based training for self-management strategies in people with type 2 diabetes mellitus. *Cochrane Database of Systematic Reviews*, CD003417.

DeGeest, S., Schafer-Keller, P., Denhaerynck, K., Thannberger, N., Köfer, S., Bock, A., ... Steiger, J. (2006). Supporting medication adherence in renal transplantation (SMART): A pilot RCT to improve adherence to immunosuppressive regimens. *Clinical Transplantation, 20*, 359–368.

Devineni, T., & Blanchard, E. B. (2005). A randomized controlled trial of an internet-based treatment for chronic headache. *Behaviour Research & Therapy, 43*, 277–293.

De Vogli, R., Chandola, T., & Marmot, M. G. (2007). Negative aspects of close relationships and heart disease. *Archives of Internal Medicine, 167*, 1951–1957.

Dew, M. A., & DiMartini, A. F. (2011). Transplantation. In H. S. Friedman (Ed.), *The Oxford handbook of health psychology* (pp. 522–559). New York, NY: Oxford University Press.

Dew, M. A., Hoch, C. C., Buysse, D. J., Monk, T. H., Begley, A. E., Houck, P. R., ... Reynolds III, C. F. (2003). Healthy older adults' sleep predicts all-cause mortality at 4 to 19 years of follow-up. *Psychosomatic Medicine, 65*, 63–73.

Diabetes Prevention Program Research Group. (2002). Reduction of the incidence of type 2 diabetes with lifestyle intervention or metformin. *New England Journal of Medicine, 346*, 393–403.

Diez Roux, A. V., & Mair, C. (2010). Neighborhoods and health. *Annals of the New York Academy of Sciences, 1186*, 125–145.

Dickinson, H., Campbell, F., Beyer, F., Nicholson, D., Cook, J., Ford, G., & Mason, J. (2008). Relaxation therapies for the management of primary hypertension in adults: A Cochrane review. *Journal of Human Hypertension, 22*, 809–820.

Dixon, K. E., Keefe, F. J., Scipio, C. D., Perri, L. M., & Abernethy, A. P. (2007). Psychological interventions for arthritis pain management in adults: A meta-analysis. *Health Psychology, 26*, 241–250.

D'souza, P. J., Lumley, M. A., Kraft, C. A., & Dooley, J. A. (2008). Relaxation training and written emotional disclosure for tension or migraine headaches: A randomized, controlled trial. *Annals of Behavioral Medicine, 36*, 21–32.

Dunkel Schetter, C. (2011). Psychological science on pregnancy: Stress processes, biopsychosocial models, and emerging research issues. *Annual Review of Psychology, 62*, 531–558.

Eckel, R. H., Grundy, S. M., & Zimmet, P. Z. (2005). The metabolic syndrome. *Lancet, 365*, 1145–1128.

Edwards, A. G. K., Hulbert-Williams, N., & Neal, R. D. (2008). Psychological interventions for women with metastatic breast cancer. *Cochrane Database of Systematic Reviews (3)*, CD004253.

Eller, N. H., Netterstrom, B., Gyntelberg, F., Kristensen, T., Nielsen, F., Steptoe, A., & Theorell, T. (2009). Work-related psychosocial factors and the development of ischemic heart disease: A systematic review. *Cardiology Reviews, 17*, 83–97.

Elliott, A. F., Burgio, L. D., & DeCoster, J. (2010). Enhancing caregiver health: Findings from the resources for enhancing Alzheimer's caregiver health II intervention. *Journal of the American Geriatrics Society, 58*, 30–37.

Engel, G. L. (1977). The need for a new medical model: A challenge for biomedicine. *Science, 196*, 129–136.

Engel, G. L. (1980). The clinical application of the biopsychosocial model. *American Journal of Psychiatry, 137*, 535–544.

Epstein, L. H., Paluch, R. A., Roemmich, J. N., & Beecher, M. D. (2007). Family-based treatment, then and now: Twenty-five years of pediatric obesity treatment. *Health Psychology, 26*, 381–391.

Everson-Rose, S. A., & Clark, C. J. (2010). Assessment of psychosocial factors in population studies. In A. Steptoe (Ed.), *Handbook of behavioral medicine: Methods and applications* (pp. 291–306). New York, NY: Springer.

Fabricatore, A. N., & Wadden, T. A. (2006). Obesity. *Annual Review of Clinical Psychology, 2*, 357–377.

Fabricatore, A. N., Wadden, T. A., Moore, R. H., Butryn, M. L., Heymsfield, S. B., & Nguyen, A. M. (2009). Predictors of attrition and weight loss success: Results from a randomized controlled trial. *Behaviour Research and Therapy, 47*, 685–691.

Fawzy, F. I., Fawzy, N. W., Hyun, C. S., Elashoff, R., Guthrie, D., Fahey, J. L., & Morton, D. L. (1993). Malignant melanoma: Effects of an early structured psychiatric intervention, coping, and affective state on recurrence and survival 6 years later. *Archives of General Psychiatry, 50*, 681–689.

Fiore, M. C., & Baker, T. B. (2011). Treating smokers in health care settings. *New England Journal of Medicine, 365*, 1222–1231.

Fiore, M. C., Jaen, C. R., Baker, T. B., Bailey, W., Benowitz, N., Curry, S., ... Wewers, M. (2008). *Treating tobacco use and dependence: 2008 Update*. Rockville, MD: U.S. Department of Health and Human Services.

Fisher, E. B., Fitzgibbons, M. L., Glasgow, R. E., Haire-Joshu, D., Hayman, L. L., Kaplan, R. M., ... Okene, J. K. (2011). Behavior matters. *American Journal of Preventive Medicine, 40*(5), e15–e30.

Fisher, L., Mullan, J. T., Arean, P., Glasgow, R. E., Hessler, D., & Masharani, U. (2010). Diabetes distress but not clinical depression or depressive symptoms is associated with glycemic control in both cross-sectional and longitudinal analyses. *Diabetes Care, 33*, 23–28.

Flegal, K. M., Carroll, M. D., Kit, B. D., & Ogden, C. L. (2012). Prevalence of obesity and trends in the distribution of body mass index among US adults, 1999–2010. *JAMA, 307*, 491–497.

Flegal, K. M., Carroll, M. D., Ogden, C. L., & Curtin, L. R. (2010). Prevalence and trends in obesity among US adults, 1999–2008. *JAMA, 303*, 235–241.

Ford, E. S., & Capewell, S. (2011). Proportion of the decline in cardiovascular disease mortality due to prevention versus treatment: Public health versus clinical care. *Annual Review of Public Health, 32*, 5–22.

France, C. R., Masters, K. S., Belar, C. D., Kerns, R. D., Klonoff, E. A., Larkin, K. T., ... Thorn, B. E. (2008). Application of the competency model to clinical health psychology. *Professional Psychology: Research and Practice, 39*, 573–580.

Frank, R. G., McDaniel, S. H., Bray, J. H., & Heldring, M. (Eds.). (2004). *Primary care psychology*. Washington, DC: American Psychological Association.

Freedland, K. E., Mohr, D. C., Davidson, K. W., & Schwartz, J. E. (2011). Usual and unusual care: Existing practice control groups in randomized controlled trials of behavioral interventions. *Psychosomatic Medicine, 73*, 323–325.

Freedland, K. E., Skala, J. A., Carney, R. M., Rubin, E. H., Lustman, P. J., Davila-Roman, V. G., ... Hogue, C. W. (2009). Treatment of depression after coronary artery bypass surgery: A randomized controlled trial. *Archives of General Psychiatry, 66*, 387–396.

Friedman, M., Thoreson, C. E., Gill, J. J., Ulmer, D., Powell, L. H., Price, V., ... Dixon, T. (1986). Alteration of type A behavior and its effects on cardiac recurrences in post myocardial infarction patients: Summary of results of the recurrent coronary prevention project. *American Heart Journal, 112*, 653–665.

Fung, T. T., Chiuve, S. E., McCullough, M. L., Rexrode, K. M., Logroscino, G., & Hu, F. B. (2008). Adherence to a DASH-style diet and risk of coronary heart disease and stroke in women. *Archives of Internal Medicine, 168*, 713–720.

Gallicchio, L., & Kalesan, B. (2009). Sleep duration and mortality: A systematic review. *Journal of Sleep Research, 18*, 148–158.

Gariepy, G., Wang, J., Lesage, A. D., & Schmitz, N. (2010). The longitudinal association from obesity to depression: Results from the 12-year national population health survey. *Obesity, 18*, 1033–1038.

Garland, S. N., Carlson, L. E., Antle, M. C., Samuels, C., & Campbell, T. (2011). I-CAN SLEEP: Rationale and design of a non-inferiority RCT of mindfulness-based stress reduction and cognitive behavioral therapy for the treatment of insomnia in CANcer survivors. *Contemporary Clinical Trials, 32*, 747–754

Gaylord, S. A., Palsson, O. S., Garland, E. L., Faurot, K. R., Coble, R. S., Mann, J. D., ... Whitehead, W. E. (2011). Mindfulness training reduces the severity of irritable bowel syndrome in women: Results of a randomized controlled trial. *American Journal of Gastroenterology, 106*, 1678–1688.

Gehi, A. K., Ali, S., Na, B., & Whooley, M. A. (2007). Self-reported medication adherence and cardiovascular events in patients with stable coronary heart disease: The heart and soul study. *Archives of Internal Medicine, 167*, 1798–1803.

Gentry, W. D. (1984). Behavioral medicine: A new research paradigm. In W. D. Gentry (Ed.), *Handbook of behavioral medicine* (pp. 1–12). New York, NY: Guilford Press.

Glasgow, R. E. (2008). What types of evidence are most needed to advance behavioral medicine? *Annals of Behavioral Medicine, 35*, 19–25.

Glasgow, R. E., & Emmons, K. M. (2007). How can we increase translation of research into practice? Types of evidence needed. *Annual Review of Public Health, 28*, 413–433.

Glasgow, R. E., McKay, H. G., Piette, J. D., & Reynolds, K. D. (2001). The RE-AIM framework for evaluating interventions: What can it tell us about approaches to chronic illness management? *Patient Education and Counseling, 44*, 119–127.

Glasgow, R. E., Nutting, P. A., King, D. K., Nelson, C. C., Cutter, G., Gaglio, B.,...Whitesides, H. (2005). Randomized effectiveness trial of a computer-assisted intervention to improve diabetes care. *Diabetes Care, 28*, 33–39.

Glasgow, R. E., Vogt, T. M., & Boles, S. M. (1999). Evaluating the public health impact of health promotion interventions: The RE-AIM framework. *American Journal of Public Health, 89*, 1322–1327.

Glombiewski, J. A., Sawyer, A. T., Gutermann, J., Koenig, K., Rief, W., & Hofmann, S. G. (2010). Psychological treatments for fibromyalgia: A meta-analysis. *Pain, 151*, 280–295.

Goetzel, R. Z., & Ozminkowski, R. J. (2008). The health costs and benefits of work site health promotion programs. *Annual Review of Public Health, 29*, 303–323.

Goldbacher, E. M., & Matthews, K. A. (2007). Are psychological characteristics related to risk of the metabolic syndrome? A review of the literature. *Annals of Behavioral Medicine, 34*, 240–252.

Goldberg, J. H., & King, A. C. (2007). Physical activity and weight management across the lifespan. *Annual Review of Public Health, 27*, 145–170.

Golden, S. H., Lazo, M., Carnethon, M., Bertoni, A. G., Schreiner, P. J., Diez Roux, A. V.,...Lyketsos, C. (2008). Examining a bidirectional association between depressive symptoms and diabetes. *Journal of the American Medical Association, 299*, 2751–2759.

Gonzalez, J. S., Batchelder, A. W., Psaros, C., & Safren, S. A. (2011). Depression and HIV/AIDS treatment nonadherence: A review and meta-analysis. *Journal of Acquired Immune Deficiency Syndrome, 58*, 181–187.

Gonzalez, J. S., Peyrot, M., McCarl, L. A., Collins, E. M., Serpa, L., Mimiaga, M. J., & Safren, S. A. (2008). Depression and diabetes treatment nonadherence: A meta-analysis. *Diabetes Care, 31*, 2398–2403.

Goodheart, C. D. (2011). Psychology practice: Design for tomorrow. *American Psychologist, 66*, 339–347.

Gordon, L., Graves, N., Hawkes, A., & Eaken, E. (2007). A review of the cost-effectiveness of face-to-face behavioral interventions for smoking, physical activity, diet and alcohol. *Chronic Illness, 3*, 101–129.

Gould, K. L., Ornish, D., Scherwitz, L., Brown, S., Edens, R. P, Hess, M. J.,...Brand, R. (1995). Changes in myocardial perfusion abnormalities by positron emission tomography after long-term intense risk factor modification. *JAMA, 274*, 894–901.

Greeven, A., van Balom, A., Visser, S., Merkelbach, J., van Rood, Y., van Dyck, R.,...Spinhoven, P. (2007). Cognitive behavior therapy and paroxitine in the treatment of hypochondriasis: A randomized controlled trial. *American Journal of Psychiatry, 164*, 91–99.

Gross, C. R., Kreitzer, M. J., Thomas W., Reilly-Spong, M., Cramer-Bornemann, M., Nyman, J. A.,...Ibrahim, H. N. (2010). Mindfulness-based stress reduction for solid organ transplantation: A randomized controlled trial. *Alternative Therapies in Health & Medicine, 16*, 30–38.

Grundmann, O., & Yoon, S. L. (2010). Irritable bowel syndrome: epidemiology, diagnosis and treatment: An update for health-care practitioners. *Journal of Gastroenterology and Hepatology, 25*, 691–699.

Guh, D. P., Zhang, W., Bansback, N., Amarsi, Z., Birmingham, C. L., & Anis, A. H. (2009). The incidence of co-morbidities related to obesity and overweight: A systematic review and meta-analysis. *BMC Public Health, 9*, 88.

Gulliksson, M., Burrell, G., Vessby, B., Lundin, L., Toss, H., & Svardsudd, K. (2011). Randomized controlled trial of cognitive behavior therapy vs. Standard treatment to prevent recurrent cardiovascular events in patients with coronary heart disease: Secondary prevention in Uppsala primary care project (SUPRIM). *Archives of Internal Medicine, 171*, 134–140.

Haas, L. J. (Ed.). (2004). *Handbook of primary care psychology*. New York, NY: Oxford University Press.

Hackett, M. L., & Anderson, C. S., (2005). Predictors of depression after stroke: A systematic review of observational studies. *Stroke, 36*, 2296–2310.

Hackett, M. L., Anderson, C. S., House, A., & Halteh, C. (2008). Interventions for preventing depression after stroke. *Cochrane Database of Systematic Reviews (3)*, CD003689.

Hackett, M. L., Anderson, C. S., House, A., & Xia, J. (2008). Interventions for treating depression after stroke. *Cochrane Database of Systematic Reviews (4)*, CD0003437.

Hagedoorn, M., Sanderman, R., Bolks, H. N., Tuinstra, J., & Coyne, J. C. (2008). Distress in couples coping with cancer: A meta-analysis and critical review of role and gender effects. *Psychological Bulletin, 134*, 1–30.

Hall, K. L., & Rossi, J. S. (2008). Meta-analytic examination of the strong and weak principles across 48 health behaviors. *Preventive Medicine, 46*, 266–274.

Hall, M. H., Muldoon, M. F., Jennings, R., Buysee, D. J., Flory, J. D., & Manuck, S. B. (2008). Self-reported sleep duration is associated with the metabolic syndrome in midlife adults. *Sleep, 31*(5), 635–643.

Hall, S. M., & Prochaska, J. J. (2009). Treatment of smokers with co-occurring disorders: Emphasis on integration in mental health and addiction treatment settings. *Annual Review of Clinical Psychology,* 5, 409–431.

Hall, S. M., Tsoh, J. Y., Prochaska, J. J., Eisendrath, S., Rossi, J. S., Redding, C. A....Gorecki, J. A. (2006). Treatment for cigarette smoking among depressed mental health outpatients: A randomized clinical trial. *American Journal of Public Health,* 96, 1808–1814.

Harris, J., Lack, L., Kemp, K., Wright, H., & Bootzin, R. (2012). A randomized controlled trial of intensive sleep retraining (ISR): A brief conditioning treatment for chronic insomnia. *Sleep,* 35, 49–60.

Harvey, A. G. (2011). Sleep and circadian functioning: Critical mechanisms in the mood disorders? *Annual Review of Clinical Psychology,* 7, 297–319.

Hendershot, C. S., Witkiewitz, K., George, W. H., & Marlatt, G. A. (2011, July 19). Relapse prevention for addictive behaviors. *Prevention & Policy,* 6, Art ID 17.

Herring, M. P., Puetz, T. W., O'Connor, P. J., & Dishman, R. K. (2012), Effect of exercise training among patients with a chronic illness: A systematic review and meta-analysis of randomized controlled trials. *Archives of Internal Medicine,* 172, 101–111.

Hersey, J. C., Khavjou, O., Strange, L. B., Atkinson, R. L., Blair, S. N., Campbell, S.,...Britt, M. (2012). The efficacy and cost-effectiveness of a community weight management intervention: A randomized controlled trial of the health weight management demonstration. *Preventive Medicine,* 54, 42–49.

Herzog, T. A. (2008). Analyzing the transtheoretical model using the framework of Weinstein, Rothman, and Sutton (1998): The example of smoking cessation. *Health Psychology,* 27, 548–556.

Hettema, J., Steele, J., Miller, W. R. (2005). Motivational interviewing. *Annual Review of Clinical Psychology,* 1, 91–111.

Higgins, J. P. T., & Green, S. (Eds.). (2011). *Cochrane handbook for systematic reviews of interventions version 5.1.0* [updated March, 2011] The Cochrane collaboration. Available from www.cochranehandbook.org

Hoffman, B. M., Babyak, M. A., Craighead, W. E., Sherwood, A., Doraiswamy, P. M., Coons, M. J., & Blumenthal, J. A. (2011). Exercise and pharmacotherapy in patients with major depression: One year follow-up of the SMILE study. *Psychosomatic Medicine,* 73, 127–133.

Hoffman, B. M., Papas, R. K., Chatkoff, D. K., & Kerns, R. D. (2007). Meta-analysis of psychological interventions for chronic low back pain. *Health Psychology,* 26, 1–9.

Holroyd, K. A., Martin, P. R., & Nash, J. M. (2006). Psychological treatments for tension type headache. In J. Olesen, P. Tfelt-Hansen, & K. Welsh (Eds.), *The headaches* (pp. 711–719). Philadelphia, PA: Lippincott, Williams, & Wilkins.

Holtgrave, D. R., & Curran, J. W. (2006). What works, and what remains to be done, in HIV prevention in the United States. *Annual Review of Public Health,* 27, 261–275.

Holt-Lunstad, J., Smith, T. D., & Layton, J. B. (2010). Social relationships and mortality risk: A meta-analytic review. *PLoS Medicine*: e1000316.

Hopko, D. R., Bell, J. L., Armento, M., Robertson, S., Mullane, C., Wolf, N., & Lejuez, C. W. (2008). Cognitive-behavioral therapy for depressed cancer patients in a medical care setting. *Behavior Therapy,* 39, 126–136.

Howard, I., Turner, R., Okin, R., & Mohr, D. C. (2006). Therapeutic alliance mediates the relationship between interpersonal problems and depression outcome in a cohort of multiple sclerosis patients. *Journal of Clinical Psychology,* 62, 1197–1204.

Hunt, M. G., Moshier, S., & Milonova, M., (2009). Brief cognitive-behavioral internet therapy for irritable bowel syndrome. *Behaviour Research and Therapy,* 47, 797–802.

Ickovics, J. R., Kershaw, T. S., Westdahl, C., Magriples, U., Massey, Z., Reynolds, H., & Rising, S. S. (2007). Group prenatal care and perinatal outcomes: A randomized controlled trial. *Obstetrics and Gynecology,* 110, 330–339.

Ickovics, J. R, Reed, E., Magriples, U., Westdahl, C., Schindler Rising, S., & Kershaw, T. S. (2011). Effects of group prenatal care on psychosocial risk in pregnancy: Results from a randomized controlled trial. *Psychology and Health,* 26, 235–250.

Irwin, M. R., Wang, M., Ribeiro, D., Cho, H. J., Olmstead, R., Breen, E. C.,...Cole, S. (2008). Sleep loss activates cellular inflammatory signaling. *Biological Psychiatry,* 64, 538–540.

Jennings, J. R., Muldoon, M. F., Hall, M., Buysee, D. J., & Manuck, S. B. (2007). Self-reported sleep quality is associated with the metabolic syndrome. *Sleep,* 30, 219–223.

Jensen, M. P. (2011). Psychosocial approaches to pain management: An organizational framework. *Pain,* 152, 717–725.

Johnson, S. S., Paiva, A. L., Cummins, C. O., Johnson, J. L., Dymet, S. J., Wright, J. A.,...Sherman, K. (2008). Transtheoretical model-based multiple behavior intervention for weight management: Effectiveness on a population basis. *Preventive Medicine,* 46, 238–246.

Jungquist, C. R., O'Brien, C., Matteson-Rusby, S., Smith, M. T., Pigeon, W. R., Xia, Y.,...Perlis, M. L. (2010). The efficacy of cognitive-behavioral therapy for insomnia in patients with chronic pain. *Sleep Medicine,* 11, 302–309.

Kangas, M., Bovbjerg, D. H., & Montgomery, G. H. (2008). Cancer-related fatigue: A systematic and meta-analytic review of non-pharmacological therapies for cancer patients. *Psychological Bulletin, 134*, 700–741.

Kaplan, R. M. (2010). Behavioral epidemiology. In J. M. Suls, K. W. Davidson, & R. M. Kaplan (Eds.), *Handbook of health psychology and behavioral medicine* (pp. 203–216). New York, NY: Guilford Press.

Kaplan, R. M., & Groessl, E. J. (2002). Applications of cost-effectiveness methodologies in behavioral medicine. *Journal of Consulting and Clinical Psychology, 70*, 482–493.

Kapson, H. S., & Haaga, D. (2010). Depression vulnerability moderates the effects of cognitive behavior therapy in a randomized controlled trial for smoking cessation. *Behavior Therapy, 41*(4), 447–460.

Katz, D. L., (2009). School-based interventions for health promotion and weight control: Not just waiting for the world to change. *Annual Review of Public Health, 30*, 253–272.

Kazdin, A. E., & Blase, S. L. (2011). Rebooting psychotherapy research and practice to reduce the burden of mental illness. *Perspectives on Psychological Science, 6*, 21–37.

Keefe, F. J., Shelby, R. A., Somers, T. J., Varia, I., Blazing, M., Waters, S. J., . . . Bradley, L. (2011). Effects of coping skills training and sertraline in patients with non-cardiac chest pain: A randomized trial. *Pain, 152*, 730–741.

Keogh, K. M., Smith, S. M., White, P., McGilloway, S., Kelly, A., Gibney, J., & O'Dowd T. (2011). Psychological family intervention for poorly controlled type 2 diabetes. *American Journal of Managed Care, 17*, 105–113.

Kerner, J., Rimer, B., & Emmons, K. (2005). Introduction to the special section on dissemination: Dissemination research and research dissemination: How can we close the gap? *Health Psychology, 24*, 443–446.

King, C. R., Knutson, K. L., Rathouz, P. J., Sidney, S., Liu, K., & Lauderdale, D. S. (2008). Short sleep duration and incident coronary artery calcification. *Journal of the American Medical Association, 300*(24), 2859–2866.

Kiviniemi, M. T., & Rothman, A. J. (2010). Specifying the determinants of people's health beliefs and health behavior: How a social psychological perspective can inform initiatives to promote health. In J. M. Suls, K. W. Davidson, & R. M. Kaplan, *Handbook of health psychology and behavioral medicine* (pp. 64–83). New York, NY: Guilford Press.

Kline, C. E., Crowley, E. P., Ewing, G. B., Burch, J. B., Blair, S. N., Durstine, J. L., . . . Youngstedt, S. D. (2011). The effect of exercise training on obstructive sleep apnea and sleep quality: A randomized controlled trial. *Sleep, 34*, 1631–1640.

Knight, K. M., McGowan, L., Dickens, C., & Bundy, C. (2006). A systematic review of motivational interviewing in physical health care settings. *British Journal of Health Psychology, 11*, 319–332.

Knol, M. J., Twisk, J. W. R., Beekman, A. T. F., Heine, R. J., Snoek, F. J., & Fouwer, F. (2006). Depression as a risk factor for the onset of type 2 diabetes mellitus. *A meta-analysis. Diabetologia, 49*, 837–845.

Koenig, L. J., Pals, S. L., Bush, T., Pratt Palmore, M., Stratford, D. & Ellerbrock, T. V. (2008). Randomized controlled trial of an intervention to prevent adherence failure among HIV-infected patients initiating antiretroviral therapy. *Health Psychology, 27*, 159–169.

Kop, W. J., & Plumhoff, J. E. (2012). Depression and coronary heart disease: Diagnosis, predictive value, biobehavioral mechanisms, and intervention. In R. Allen & J. Fisher (Eds.), *Heart and mind: The practice of cardiac psychology* (pp. 143–168). Washington, DC: American Psychological Association.

Krebs, P., Prochaska, J. O., & Rossi, J. S. (2010). A meta-analysis of computer-tailored interventions for health behavior change. *Preventive Medicine, 51*, 214–221.

Kroenke, K. (2007). Efficacy of treatment for somatoform disorders: A review of randomized controlled trials. *Psychosomatic Medicine, 69*, 881–888.

Kwak, J., Montgomery, R. J. V., Kosloski, K., & Lang, J. (2011). The impact of TCARE® on service recommendation, use, and caregiver well-being. *Gerontologist, 51*, 704–713.

Lahmann, C., Röhricht, F., Sauer, N., Noll-Hussong, M., Ronel, J., Henrich, G., . . . Loew, T. (2010). Functional relaxation as complementary therapy in irritable bowel syndrome: A randomized, controlled clinical trial. *Journal of Alternative and Complementary Medicine, 16*, 47–52.

Lancaster, T., Hajek, P., Stead, L. F., West, R., & Jarvis, M. J. (2006). Prevention of relapse after quitting smoking: A systematic review of trials. *Archives of Internal Medicine, 166*, 828–835.

Lancaster, T., & Stead, L. F. (2005). Individual behavioral counseling for smoking cessation. *Cochrane Database of Systematic Reviews* (3), CDO 02852.

Landon, B. E., Gill, J. M., Antonelli, R. C., & Rich, E. C. (2010). Prospects for rebuilding primary care using the patient-centered medical home. *Health Affairs, 29*, 827–834.

Lange, T., Perras, B., Fehm, H. L., & Born, J. (2003). Sleep enhances the human antibody response to hepatitis A vaccination. *Psychosomatic Medicine, 65*, 831–835.

Lazarus, R. (1966). *Psychological stress and the coping process*. New York, NY: McGraw-Hill.

Lazarus, R. S., & Folkman, S. (1984). *Stress, appraisal, and coping*. New York, NY: Springer.

Lebow, J. L., Chambers, A. L., Christensen, A., & Johnson, S. M. (2012). Research on the treatment of couple distress. *Journal of Marital and Family Therapy, 38*, 145–168.

Ledesma, D., & Kumano, H. (2009). Mindfulness-based stress reduction and cancer: A meta-analysis. *Psycho-Oncology, 18*, 571–579.

Lee, C. D., Sui, X., Artero, E. G., Church, T. S., McAuley, P. A., Stanford, F. C., . . . Blais, S. N. C. (2011). Long-term effects of changes in cardiorespiratory fitness and body mass index on all-cause and cardiovascular disease mortality in men. *The aerobics center longitudinal study. Circulation, 124,* 2483–2450.

Lee, C. D., Sui, X., & Blair, S. N. (2009). Combined effects of cardiorespiratory fitness, not smoking, and normal waist girth on morbidity and mortality in men. *Archives of Internal Medicine, 169,* 2096–2101.

Lee, C. D., Sui, X., Hooker, S. P., Herbert, J. R., & Blair, S. N. (2011). Combined impact of lifestyle factors on cancer mortality in men. *Annals of Epidemiology, 21,* 749–754.

Lengacher, C. A., Johnson-Mallard, V., Post-White, J., Moscoso, M. S., Jacobsen, P. B., Klein, T. W., . . . Kip, K. E. (2009). Randomized controlled trial of mindfulness-based stress reduction (MBSR) for survivors of breast cancer. *Psycho-Oncology, 18,* 1261–1272.

Leonard, M. T., Cano, A., & Johansen, A. B. (2006). Chronic pain in a couples context: A review and interpretation of theoretical models and empirical evidence. *Journal of Pain, 7,* 377–390.

Lett, H. S., Blumenthal, J. A., Babyak, M., Strauman, T., Robbins, C., & Sherwood, A. (2005). Social support and coronary heart disease: Epidemiologic evidence and implications for treatment. *Psychosomatic Medicine, 67,* 869–878.

Leventhal, H., Breland, J. Y., Mora, P. A., & Leventhal, E. A. (2010). Lay representations of illness and treatment: A framework for action. In A. Steptoe (Ed.), *Handbook of behavioral medicine: Methods and applications* (pp. 137–154). New York, NY: Springer.

Lichtman, J. H., Bigger, J. T., Blumenthal, J. A., Frasure-Smith, N., Kaufman, P. G., Lesperance, F., Mark, D. B., . . . American Psychiatric Association. (2008). Depression and coronary heart disease: Recommendations for screening, referral, and treatment: a science advisory from the American Heart Association Prevention Committee of the Council on Cardiovascular Nursing, Council on Clinical Cardiology, Council on Epidemiology and Prevention, and Interdisciplinary Council on Quality of Care and Outcomes Research: Endorsed by the American Psychiatric Association. *Circulation, 118,* 1768–1775.

Linde, J. A., Simon, G. E., Ludman, E. J., Ichikawa, L. E., Operskalski, B. H., Arterburn, D., . . . Jeffery, R. W. (2011). A randomized controlled trial of behavioral weight loss treatment versus combined weight loss/depression treatment among women with comorbid obesity and depression. *Annals of Behavioral Medicine, 41,* 119–130.

Linden, W., & Girgis, A. (2011, September 1). Psychosocial treatment outcomes for cancer patients: What do meta-analyses tell us about distress reduction? *Psycho-Oncology.* doi: 10.1002/pon.2035

Linden, W., Phillips, M. J., & Leclerc, J. (2007). Psychological treatment of cardiac patients: A meta-analysis. *European Heart Journal, 28,* 24, 2964–2966.

Ljótsson, B., Falk, L., Vesterlund, A. W., Hedman, E., Lindfors, P., Rück, C., . . . Andersson, G. (2010). Internet-delivered exposure and mindfulness based therapy for irritable bowel syndrome—A randomized controlled trial. *Behaviour Research & Therapy, 48,* 531–539.

Lobel, M., Cannella, D. L., Graham, J. E., DeVincent, C., Schneider, J. & Meyer, B. A. (2008). Pregnancy-specific stress, prenatal health behaviors, and birth outcomes. *Health Psychology, 27,* 604–615.

Lopez, C., Antoni, M., Penedo, F., Weiss, D., Cruess, S., Segotas, M. C., . . . Fletcher, M. A. (2011). A pilot study of cognitive behavioral stress management effects on stress, quality of life, and symptoms in persons with chronic fatigue syndrome. *Journal of Psychosomatic Research, 70,* 328–334.

Lovallo, W. R. (2010). Emotions and stress. In J. M. Suls, K. W. Davidson, & R. M. Kaplan (Eds.), *Handbook of health psychology and behavioral medicine* (pp. 31–48). New York, NY: Guilford Press.

Lundahl, B., & Burke, B. L. (2009). The effectiveness and applicability of motivational interviewing: A practice-friendly review of four meta-analyses. *Journal of Clinical Psychology, 65,* 1232–1245.

Macea, D. D., Gajos, K., Calil, Y. A. D., & Fregni, F. (2010). The efficacy of web-based cognitive behavioral interventions for chronic pain: A systematic review and meta-analysis. *Journal of Pain, 11,* 917–929.

Magkos, F., Yannakoulia, M., Chan, J. L., & Mantzoros, C. S. (2009). Management of the metabolic syndrome and type 2 diabetes through lifestyle modification. *Annual Review of Nutrition, 29,* 223–256.

Mahoney, M. J. (1977). Reflections on the cognitive-learning trend in psychotherapy. *American Psychologist, 32,* 5–13.

Manne, S. L., Rubin, S., Edelson, M., Rosenblum, N., Bergman, C., Hernandez, E., . . . Winkel, G. (2007). Coping and communication-enhancing intervention versus supportive counseling for women diagnosed with gynecological cancers. *Journal of Consulting and Clinical Psychology, 75,* 615–628.

Markowitz, S., Friedman, M. A., & Arent, S. M. (2008). Understanding the relation between obesity and depression: Causal mechanisms and implications for treatment. *Clinical Psychology: Science and Practice, 15,* 1–20.

Martin, R. K., McNeil, D. W. (2009). Review of motivational interviewing in promoting health behaviors. *Clinical Psychology Review, 29,* 283–293.

Martire, L. M., Schulz, R., Helgeson, V. H., Small, B. J., & Saghafi, E. M. (2010). Review and meta-analysis of couple-oriented interventions for chronic illness. *Annals of Behavioral Medicine, 40*, 325–342.

Mathers, C. D., & Loncar, D. (2006). Projections of global mortality and burden of disease from 2002 to 2030. *PLoS Medicine, 3*, e442. doi:10.1371/journal.pmed.0030442

Matthews, K. A., & Gallo, L. C. (2010). Psychological perspectives on pathways linking socioeconomic status and physical health. *Annual Review of Psychology, 62*.

Matthews, K. A., & Gump, B. B. (2002). Chronic work stress and marital dissolution increase risk of post-trial mortality in men from the multiple risk factor intervention trial. *Achieves of Internal Medicine, 162*, 309–315.

McBeth, J., Prescott, G., Scotland, G., Lovell, K., Keeley, P., Hannaford, P., . . . MacFarland, G. J. (2012). Cognitive behavior therapy, exercise, or both for treating chronic widespread pain. *Archives of Internal Medicine, 172*, 48–57.

McCain, N. L., Gray, D. P., Elswick, R. K. Jr., Robins, J. W., Tuck, I., Walter, J. M., . . . Ketchum, J. M. (2008). A randomized clinical trial of alternative stress management interventions in persons with HIV infection. *Journal of Consulting and Clinical Psychology, 76*, 431–441.

McCaul, K., Hockemeyer, J. R., Johnson, R. J., Zetocha, K., Quinlan, K., & Glasgow, R. E. (2006). Motivation to quit using cigarettes: A review. *Addictive Behaviors, 31*, 42–56.

McDaniel, S. H., & Fogerty, C. T., (2009). What primary care psychology has to offer the patient-centered medical home. *Professional Psychology: Research and Practice, 40*, 483–492.

McGinnis, J. M., Williams-Russo, P., & Knickman, J. R. (2002). The case for more active policy attention to health promotion. *Health Affairs (Millwood), 21*, 78–93.

McHugh, R. K., & Barlow, D. H. (2011). The dissemination and implementation of evidence-based psychological treatments: A review of current efforts. *American Psychologist, 65*, 73–84.

Meichenbaum, D. H. (1977). *Cognitive behavior modification*. New York, NY: Plenum Press.

Meijer, A., Rosenman, M., Milette, K., Coyne, J. C., Stefanek, M., Ziegelstein, R., . . . Thombs, R. (2011). Depression screening and patient outcomes in cancer: A systematic review. *PLoS One, 6*(11), pe27181.

Miller, G. E., Chen, E., & Parker, K. J. (2011). Psychological stress in childhood and susceptability to the chronic diseases of aging: Moving toward a model of behavioral and biological mechanisms. *Psychological Bulletin, 137*, 959–997.

Miller, W. R., & Rose, G. S. (2009). Toward a theory of motivational interviewing. *American Psychologist, 64*, 527–537.

Mills, P. J., von Känel, R., Norman, D., Natarajan, L., Ziegler, M. G., & Dimsdale, J. E. (2007). Inflammation and sleep in healthy individuals. *Sleep, 30*, 729–735.

Mohr, D. C., Hart, S., Julian, L., Catledge, C., Honos-Webb, L., Vella, L. & Tasch, E. (2005). Telephone-administered psychotherapy for depression. *Archives of General Psychiatry, 62*, 1007–1014.

Mohr, D. C., Hart, S., & Vella, L. (2007). Reduction in disability in a randomized controlled trial of telephone-administered cognitive-behavioral therapy. *Health Psychology, 26*, 554–563.

Monin, J. K., & Schulz, R. (2009). Interpersonal effects of suffering in older adult caregiving relationships. *Psychology and Aging, 24*, 681–695.

Montgomery, G. H., Kargas, M., David, D., Hallquist, Green, S., Bovjberg, D. H., & Schnur, J. B. (2009). Fatigue during breast cancer radiotherapy: An initial randomized study of cognitive-behavioral therapy plus hypnosis. *Health Psychology, 28*, 317–322.

Morin, C. M., & Espie, C. A. (2003). *Insomnia. A clinical guide to assessment and treatment*. New York, NY: Plenum Press.

Morley, S., Williams, A., & Hussain, S. (2008). Estimating the clinical effectiveness of cognitive behavioural therapy in the clinic: Evaluation of a CBT informed pain management programme. *Pain, 137*, 670–680.

Moskowitz, J. T., Hult, J. R., Bussolari, C., & Acree, M. (2009). What works in coping with HIV? A meta-analysis with implications for coping with serious illness. *Psychological Bulletin, 135*, 121–141.

Moss-Morris, R., McAlpine, L., Didsbury, L., & Spence, M. J. (2009). A randomized controlled trial of a cognitive behavioural therapy-based self-management intervention for irritable bowel syndrome in primary care. *Psychological Medicine, 40*, 85–94.

Mustanski, B. S, Newcomb, M. E., Du Bois, S. N., Garcia, S. C., & Grov, C. (2011). HIV in young men who have sex with men: A review of epidemiology, risk and protective factors, and interventions. *Journal of Sex Research, 48*, 218–253.

Nation, D. A., Schneiderman, N., & McCabe, P. M. (2010). Animal models in health psychology research. In J. M. Suls, K. W. Davidson, & R. M. Kaplan (Eds.), *Handbook of health psychology and behavioral medicine* (pp. 163–181). New York, NY: Guilford Press.

Nestoric, Y., & Martin, A. (2007). Efficacy of biofeedback for migraine: A meta-analysis. *Pain, 128*, 111–127.

Nestoric, Y., Rief, W., & Martin, A. (2008). Meta-analysis of biofeedback for tension-type headache: Efficacy, specificity, and treatment moderation. *Journal of Consulting and Clinical Psychology, 76*, 379–396.

Nezu, A. M., Nezu, C. M., Felgoise, S. H., McClure, K. S., & Houts, P. S. (2003). Project Genesis:

Assessing the efficacy of problem-solving therapy for distressed adult cancer patients. *Journal of Consulting and Clinical Psychology, 71*, 1036–1048.

Nichols, L. O., Martindale-Adams, J., Burns, R., Graney, M., & Zuber, J. (2011). Translation of a dementia caregiver support program in a health care system—REACH VA. *Archives of Internal Medicine, 171*, 353–359.

Nicholson, A., Kuper, H., & Hemingway, H. (2006). Depression as an aetiologic and prognostic factor in coronary heart disease: A meta-analysis of 6362 events among 146,538 participants in 54 observational studies. *European Heart Journal, 27*, 2763–2774.

Nield, L., Moore, H. J., Hooper, L., Cruickshank, J. K., Vyas, A., Whittaker, V., & Summerbell, C. D. (2007). Dietary advice for treatment of type 2 diabetes mellitus in adults. *Cochrane Database of Systematic Reviews*, CD004097.

Noar, S. M., Benac, C. N., & Harris, M. S., (2007). Does tailoring matter? Meta-analytic review of tailored print health behavior change interventions. *Psychological Bulletin, 133*, 673–693.

Novak, D., Cameron, O., Epel, E., Ader, R., Waldstein, S. R., Levenstein, S., . . . Wainer, A. R. (2007). Psychosomatic medicine: The scientific foundation of the biopsychosocial model. *Academic Psychiatry, 31*, 388–401.

Ogden, C. L., Carroll, M. D., Kit, B. D., & Flegal, K. M. (2012). Prevalence of obesity and trends in body mass index among US children and adolescents, 1999–2010. *JAMA, 307*, 483–490.

Oken, B. S., Fonareva, I., Haas, M., Wahbeh, H., Lane, J. B., Zajdel, D., & Amen, A. (2010). Pilot controlled trial of mindfulness meditation and education for dementia caregivers. *Journal of Alternative & Complementary Medicine, 16*, 1031–1038.

Oldenburg, B., Absetz, P., & Chan, C. K. Y. (2010). Behavioral interventions for prevention and management of chronic disease. In A. Steptoe (Ed.), *Handbook of behavioral medicine: Methods and applications* (pp. 969–988). New York, NY: Springer.

Oldenburg, B., de Courten, M., & Frean, E. (2010). The contribution of health psychology to the advancement of global health. In J. M. Suls, K. W. Davidson, & R. M. Kaplan (Eds.), *Handbook of health psychology and behavioral medicine* (pp. 397–408). New York, NY: Guilford Press.

Ornish, D., Brown, S. E., Scherwitz, L. W., Billings, J. H., Armstrong, W. T., Ports, T. A., . . . Brand, R. (1990). Can lifestyle changes reverse coronary heart disease? The Lifestyle Heart Trial. *Lancet, 336*, 129–133.

Ornish, D., Scherwitz, L. W., Billings, J. H., Gould, K. L., Merritt, T. A., Sparler, S., . . . Brand, R. (1998). Intensive lifestyle changes for reversal of coronary heart disease. *JAMA, 280*, 2001–2007.

Orth-Gomér, K., Schneiderman, N., Wang, H. X., Walldin, C., Blom, M., & Jernberg, T. (2009). Stress reduction prolongs life in women with coronary disease: the Stockholm women's intervention trial for coronary heart disease (SWITCHD). *Circulation. Cardiovascular Quality and Outcomes, 2*, 25–32.

Orth-Gomér, K., Wamala, S. P., Horsten, M., Schenck-Gustafsson, K., Schneiderman, N., & Mittleman, M. A. (2000). Marital stress worsens prognosis in women with coronary heart disease: The Stockholm female coronary risk study. *JAMA, 284*, 3008–3014.

Pack, A. I., & Pien, G. W. (2011). Update on sleep and its disorders. *Annual Review of Medicine, 62*, 447–460.

Palmer, S. C., van Scheppinger, C., & Coyne, J. C. (2011). Clinical trial did not demonstrate benefits of screening patients with cancer for distress. *Journal of Clinical Oncology, 29*, e277–e288.

Patten, S. B., Williams, J., Lavorato, D., Khaled, S., & Bulloch, A. (2011). Weight gain in relation to major depression and medication use. *Journal of Affective Disorders, 134*, 288–293.

Pomerleau, O. F., & Brady, J. P. (1979). Introduction: The scope and promise of behavioral medicine. In O. F. Pomerleau & J. P. Brady (Eds.), *Behavioral medicine: Theory and practice*. Baltimore, MD: Williams & Wilkins.

Pomerleau, O. F., & Rodin, J. (1986). Behavioral medicine and health psychology. In A. E. Bergin & S. L. Garfield (Eds.), *Handbook of psychotherapy and behavior change* (3rd ed., pp. 483–522). New York, NY: Wiley.

Powell, K. E., Paluch, A. E., & Blair, S. N. (2011). Physical activity for health: What kind? How much? How intense? On top of what? *Annual Review of Public Health, 32*, 349–365.

Pradhan, E. K., Baumgarten, M., Langenberg, P, Handwerger, B., Gilpin, A. K., Magyari, T., . . . Berman, B. (2007). Effect of mindfulness-based stress reduction in rheumatoid arthritis patients. *Arthritis & Rheumatism, 57*, 1134–1142.

Prather, A. A., Blumenthal, J. A., Hinderliter, A., & Sherwood, A. (2011). Ethnic differences in the effects of the DASH diet on nocturnal blood pressure dipping in individuals with high blood pressure. *American Journal of Hypertension, 24*, 1338–1344.

Prejean, J., Song, R., Hernandez, A., Ziebell, R., Green T, Walker, F., . . . Hall, H. I., for the HIV Incidence Surveillance Groups. (2011). Estimated HIV incidence in the United States, 2006–2009. *PLoS ONE, 6*, e17502.

Prochaska, J. J., Hall, S. M., Humfleet, G., Munoz, R. F., Reus, V., Gorecki, J., & Hu, D. (2008). Physical activity as a strategy for maintaining tobacco abstinence: A randomized trial. *Preventive Medicine, 47*, 215–220.

Prochaska, J. J., Hall, S. M., Tsoh, J. Y., Eisendrath, S., Rossi, J. S., Redding, C. A., . . . Gorecki, J. A. (2008). Treating tobacco dependence in clinically depressed smokers: Effect of smoking cessation on mental health functioning. *American Journal of Public Health, 98*, 446–448.

Prochaska, J. J., Nigg, C. R., Spring, B., Velicer, W., & Prochaska, J. O. (2010). The benefits and challenges of multiple health behavior change in research and practice. *Preventive Medicine, 50*, 26–29.

Prochaska, J. J., & Prochaska, J. M. (2009). Multiple risk behavior change: What most individuals need. In S. A. Shumaker, J. K. Ockene, & K. A. Riekert (Eds.), *The handbook of health behavior change* (3rd ed., pp. 287–305). New York, NY: Springer.

Prochaska, J. J., Velicer, W. F., Prochaska, J. O., Delucchi, K., & Hall, S. M. (2006). Comparing intervention outcomes in smokers treated for single versus multiple behavioral risks. *Health Psychology, 25*, 380–388.

Prochaska, J. O., DiClemente, C. C., & Norcross, J. C. (1992). In search of how people change: Applications to addictive behaviors. *American Psychologist, 47*, 1102–1114.

Relman, A. S., & Angell, M. (2002). Resolved: Psychosocial interventions can improve clinical outcomes in organic disease (Con). *Psychosomatic Medicine, 64*, 558–563.

Renehan, A. G., Tyson, M., Egger, M., Heller, R. F., & Zwahlen, M. (2008). Body-mass index and incidence of cancer: A systematic review and meta-analysis of prospective observational studies. *Lancet, 371*, 569–578.

Rohrbaugh, M. J., Shoham, V., & Coyne, J. C. (2006). Effect of marital quality on eight-year survival of patients with heart failure. *American Journal of Cardiology, 98*, 1069–1072.

Rollman, B. L., Belnap, B. H., LeMenager, M. S., Mazumdar, S., Houck, P. R., Counihan, P., ... Reynolds, C. F. 3rd. (2009). *Telephone-delivered collaborative care for treating post-CABG depression: a randomized controlled trial Journal of the American Medical Association, 302*, 2095–2103.

Rotheram-Borus, M., Swendeman, D., & Chovnick, G. (2009). The past, present, and future of HIV prevention: Integrating behavioral, biomedical, and structural intervention strategies for the next generation of HIV prevention. *Annual Review of Clinical Psychology, 5*, 143–167.

Rutledge, T., Reis, V. A., Linke, S. E., Greenberg, B. H., & Mills, P. J. (2006). Depression in heart failure: A meta-analytic review of prevalence, intervention effects, and associations with clinical outcomes. *Journal of the American College of Cardiology, 48*, 1527–1537.

Saab, P. G., Bang, H., Williams, R. B., Powell, L. H., Schneiderman, N., Thoresen, C., ... Keefe, F. (2009). The impact of cognitive behavioral group training on event-free survival in patients with myocardial infarction: The ENRICHD experience. ENRICHD investigators. *Journal of Psychosomatic Research, 67*, 45–56.

Sackett, D., Rosenberg, W., Muir Gray, J., Haynes, R., & Richardson, W. (1996). Evidence based medicine: What it is and what it isn't. *British Medical Journal, 312*, 71–72.

Safren, S. A., O'Cleirigh, C., Tan, J. Y., Raminani, S. R., Reilly, L. C., Otto, M. W., & Mayer, K. H. (2009). A randomized controlled trial of cognitive behavioral therapy for adherence and depression (CBT-AD) in HIV-infected individuals. *Health Psychology, 28*, 1–10.

Satcher, D. (2006). The prevention challenge and opportunity. *Health Affairs (Millwood), 25*, 1009–1011.

Sallis, J. F., Cervero, R. B., Ascher, W., Henderson, K. A., Kraft, M. K., & Kerr, J. (2006). An ecological approach to creating active living communities. *Annual Review of Public Health, 27*, 297–322.

Schneiderman, N., Antoni, M. H., Penedo, F. J., & Ironson, G. H. (2010). Psychosocial-behavioral interventions and chronic disease. In A. Steptoe (Ed.), *Handbook of behavioral medicine: Methods and applications* (pp. 989–1008). New York, NY: Springer.

Schneiderman, N., Saab, P. G., Catellier, D. J., Powell, L. H., DeBusk, R. F., Williams, R. B., ... Kaufman, P. (2004). Psychosocial treatment within sex by ethnicity subgroups in the enhancing recovery in coronary heart disease clinical trial. *Psychosomatic Medicine, 66*, 475–483.

Schnur, J. B., David, D., Kangas, M., Green, S., Bovbjerg, D., & Montgomery, G. H. (2009). A randomized trial of a cognitive-behavioral therapy and hypnosis intervention on positive and negative affect during breast cancer radiotherapy. *Journal of Clinical Oncology, 65*, 443–455.

Schnur, J. B., & Montgomery, G. H. (2010). A systematic review of therapeutic alliance, group cohesion, empathy, and goal consensus/collaboration in psychotherapeutic interventions in cancer: Uncommon factors? *Clinical Psychology Review, 30*, 238–247.

Schulz, M. B., & Hu, F. B. (2005). Primary prevention of diabetes: What can be done and how much can be prevented? *Annual Review of Public Health, 26*, 445–467.

Schwarzer, R. (2011). Health behavior change. In H. S. Friedman (Ed.), *The Oxford handbook of health psychology* (pp. 591–611). New York, NY: Oxford University Press.

Scott-Sheldon, L. A., Fielder, R. L., & Carey, M. P. (2010). Sexual risk reduction interventions for patients attending sexually transmitted disease clinics in the United States: A meta-analytic review, 1986 to early 2009. *Annals of Behavioral Medicine, 40*, 191–204.

Scott-Sheldon, L. A. J., Kalichman, S. C., Carey, M. P., & Fielder, R. L. (2008). Stress management interventions for HIV+ adults: A meta-analysis of randomized controlled trials, 1989 to 2006. *Health Psychology, 27*, 129–139.

Seo, D. C., & Sa, J. (2008). A meta-analysis of psycho-behavioral obesity interventions among

US multiethnic and minority adults. *Preventive Medicine, 47,* 573–582.

Shields, C. G., Finley, M. A., Chawla, N., & Meadors, P. (2012). Couple and family interventions for health problems. *Journal of Marital and Family Therapy, 38,* 265–280.

Simon, G. E., Katon, W. J., Lin, E. H., Rutter, C., Manning, W. G., Von Korff, M., ... Young, B. A. (2007). Cost-effectiveness of systematic depression treatment among people with diabetes mellitus. *Archives of General Psychiatry, 64,* 65–72.

Smeets, R., Vtaeyen, J., Kester, A., & Knottnerus, J. (2006). Reduction of pain catastrophizing mediates the outcome of both physical and cognitive-behavioral treatment in chronic low back pain. *Journal of Pain, 7,* 261–271.

Smith, P. J., Blumenthal, J. A., Babyak, M. A., Georgiades, A., Hinderliter, A., & Sherwood, A. (2007). Effects of exercise and weight loss on depressive symptoms among men and women with hypertension. *Journal of Psychosomatic Research, 63,* 463–469.

Smith, P. J., Blumenthal, J. A., Hoffman, B. M., Cooper, H., Strauman, T., Welsh-Bohmer, K., ... Sherwood, A. (2010). Aerobic exercise and neurocognitive performance: A meta-analytic review of randomized controlled trials. *Psychosomatic Medicine, 72,* 239–252.

Smith, T. W. (2006a). Personality as risk and resilience in physical health. *Current Directions in Psychological Science, 15,* 227–231.

Smith, T. W. (2006b). Blood, sweat, and tears: Exercise in the management of mental and physical health problems. *Clinical Psychology: Science and Practice, 13,* 198–202.

Smith, T. W. (2010a). Conceptualization, measurement, and analysis of negative affective risk factors. In A. Steptoe (Ed.), *Handbook of behavioral medicine research: Methods and applications* (pp. 155–168). New York, NY: Springer.

Smith, T. W. (2010b). Depression and chronic medical illness: Implications for relapse prevention. In C. S. Richards & M. G. Perri (Eds.), *Relapse prevention for depression* (pp. 199–225). Washington, DC: American Psychological Association.

Smith, T. W. (2011). Measurement in health psychology research. In H. S. Friedman (Ed.), *Oxford handbook of health psychology* (pp. 42–72). New York: Oxford University Press.

Smith, T. W., Kendall, P. C., & Keefe, F. J. (2002). Behavioral medicine and clinical health psychology: A view from the decade of behavior. *Journal of Consulting and Clinical Psychology, 70,* 459–462.

Smith, T. W., Orleans, C. T., & Jenkins, C. D. (2004). Prevention and health promotion: Decades of progress, new challenges, and an emerging agenda. *Health Psychology, 23,* 126–131.

Smith, T. W., & Traupman, E. K. (2012). Anger, hostility, and aggressiveness in coronary heart disease: Clinical applications of an interpersonal perspective. In R. Allan & J. Fisher (Eds.), *Heart and mind II: Evolution of cardiac psychology* (pp. 197–217). Washington, DC: American Psychological Association.

Smith, T. W., Uchino, B. N., Berg, C. A., & Florsheim, P. (2012). Marital discord and coronary artery disease: A comparison of behaviorally-defined discrete groups. *Journal of Consulting and Clinical Psychology, 80,* 87–92.

Sparrenberger, F., Cichelero, F. T., Ascoli, A. M., Fonseca, F. P., Weiss. G., Berwanger, O., ... Fuchs, F. D. (2009). Does psychosocial stress cause hypertension? A systematic review of observational studies. *Journal of Human Hypertension, 23,* 12–19.

Sperl-Hillen, J., Beaton, S., Fernandes, O., Von Worley, A., Vazquez-Benitez, G., Parker, E., ... Spain C. V. (2011). Comparative effectiveness of patient education methods for type 2 diabetes: A randomized controlled trial. *Archives of Internal Medicine, 171,* 2001–2010.

Spiegel, D., Bloom, J. R., Kraemer, H. C., & Gottheil, E. (1989). Effect of psychosocial treatment on survival of patients with metastatic breast cancer. *Lancet, 334,* 888–891.

Spring, B. (2011). Translational behavioral medicine: a pathway to better health. *Translational Behavioral Medicine, 1,* 1–3.

Spring, B., Howe, D., Berendsen, M., McFadden, H. G., Hitchcock, K., Radenmaker, A. W., & Hitsman, B. (2009). Behavioral intervention to promote smoking cessation and prevent weight gain: a systematic review and meta-analysis. *Addiction, 104,* 1472–1486.

Spring, B., Pagato, S., Knatterud, G., Kozak, A., & Hedeker, A. (2007). Examination of the analytic quality of behavioral health randomized clinical trials. *Journal of Clinical Psychology, 63,* 53–71.

Spring, B., Pagoto, S., Kaufman, P. G., Whitlock, E. P., Glasgow, R. E., Smith, T. W., ... & Davidson, K. W. (2005). Invitation to a dialogue between researchers and clinicians about evidence-based behavioral medicine. *Annals of Behavioral Medicine, 30,* 125–127.

Stanton, A. L., Revenson, T. A., & Tennen, H. (2007) Health psychology: Psychological adjustment to chronic disease. *Annual Review of Psychology, 58,* 565–92.

Stead, L. F., Perera, R., Bullen, C., Mant, D., & Lancaster, T. (2008). Nicotine replacement therapy for smoking cessation. *Cochrane Database for Systematic Reviews (1),* CD 000146.

Stein, C. J., & Colditz, G. A. (2004). The epidemic of obesity. *Journal of Clinical Endocrinology and Metabolism, 89,* 2522–2535.

Stein, R. A. (2012). Exercise for the prevention and treatment of depression in patients with coronary heart disease. In R. Allen & J. Fisher (Eds.), *Heart and mind: The practice of cardiac psychology* (pp. 459–474). Washington DC: American Psychological Association.

Stefanek, M., Palmer, S. C., Thombs, B., & Coyne, J. C. (2009). Finding what is not there: Unwarranted claims of an effect of psychosocial intervention on recurrence and survival. *Cancer, 115,* 5612–5616.

Strange, K. C., Nutting, P. A., Miller, W. L., Jaen, C. R., Crabtree, B. F., Flocke, S. A., & Gill, J. M. (2010). Defining and measuring the patient-centered medical home. *Journal of General Internal Medicine, 25,* 601–612.

Strecher, V. (2007). Internet methods for delivering behavioral and health-related interventions (eHealth). *Annual Review of Clinical Psychology, 3,* 53–76.

Stroebe, M., Schut, H., & Stroebe, W. (2007). Health outcomes of the bereaved. *Lancet, 370,* 1960–1973.

Stroebe, W., Schut, H., & Stroebe, M. S. (2005). Grief work, disclosure and counseling: Do they help the bereaved? *Clinical Psychology Review, 25,* 395–414.

Stone, G. C., Cohen, F., & Adler, N. E. (1979). *Health psychology.* San Francisco, CA: Jossey-Bass.

Story, M., Kaphingst, K. M., Robinson-O'Brien, R., & Glanz, K. (2008). Creating healthy food and eating environments: Policy and environmental approaches. *Annual Review of Public Health, 29,* 253–272.

Stuart, S., Noyes, R. Jr., Starcevic, V., & Barski, A. (2008). An integrative approach to somatoform disorders combining interpersonal and cognitive-behavioral therapy and techniques. *Journal of Contemporary Psychotherapy, 38,* 45–53.

Stuart-Shor, J., Berra, K. A., Kamau, M. W., & Kumanyika, S. K. (2012). Behavioral strategies for cardiovascular risk reduction in diverse and underserved racial/ethnic groups. *Circulation, 125,* 171–184.

Suls, J., & Bunde, J. (2005). Anger, anxiety, and depression as risk factors for cardiovascular disease: The problems and implications of overlapping affective dispositions. *Psychological Bulletin, 131,* 260–300.

Suls, J. M., Luger, T., & Martin, R. (2010). The biopsychosocial model and the use of theory in health psychology. In J. M. Suls, K. W. Davidson, & R. M. Kaplan (Eds.), *Handbook of health psychology and behavioral medicine* (pp. 15–30). New York, NY: Guilford Press.

Sun-Edelstein, C., & Mauskop, A. (2011). Alternative headache treatments: Neutraceuticals, behavioral and physical treatments. *Headache, 51,* 469–483.

Surwit, R. S., van Tilburg, M. A. L., Zucker, N., McCaskill, C. C., Parekh, P., Feinglos, M. N., . . . Lane, J. D. (2002). Stress management improves long-term glycemic control in type 2 diabetes mellitus, *Diabetes Care, 25,* 30–34.

Surwit, R. S., Williams, R. B., & Shapiro, D. (1982). *Behavioral approaches to cardiovascular disease.* New York, NY: Academic Press.

Taylor, R. S., Brown, A., Ebrahim, S., Jolliffe, J., Noorani, H., Rees, K., . . . Oldridge, N. (2004). Exercise-based rehabilitation for patients with coronary heart disease: Systematic review and meta-analysis of randomized controlled trials. *American Journal of Medicine, 11,* 682–692.

Thieme, K., Turk, D. C., & Flor, H. (2007). Responder criteria for operant and cognitive-behavioral treatment of fibromyalgia syndrome. *Arthritis and Rheumatism, 57,* 830–836.

Thombs, B. D., de Jonge, P., Coyne, J. C., Whooley, M. A., Frasure-Smith, N., Mitchell, A., . . . Ziegelstein, R. C. (2008). Depression screening and patient outcomes in cardiovascular care: a systematic review. *Journal of the American Medical Association, 300,* 2161–2171.

Thorndike, A. N., Regan, S., McKool, K., Pasternak, R. C., Swartz, S., Torres-Finnerty, N., & Rigotti, N. A. (2008). Depressive symptoms and smoking cessation after hospitalization for cardiovascular disease. *Archives of Internal Medicine, 168,* 186–191.

Thorpe, A. A., Owen, N., Neuhaus, M., & Dunstan, D. W. (2011). Sedentary behaviors and subsequent health outcomes in adults a systematic review of longitudinal studies, 1996–2011. *American Journal of Preventive Medicine, 41,* 207–215.

Turk, D. C., Wilson, H. D., & Cahana, A. (2011). Treatment of chronic non-cancer pain. *Lancet, 377,* 2226–2235.

Uchino, B. N. (2006). Social support and health: A review of physiological processes potentially underlying links to disease outcomes. *Journal of Behavioral Medicine, 29,* 377–387.

Umpierre, D., Ribeiro, P. A., Kramer, C. K., Leitão, C. B., Zucatti, A. T., Azevedo, M. J., . . . Schaan, B. D. (2011). Physical activity advice only or structured exercise training and association with HbA1c levels in type 2 diabetes: A systematic review and meta-analysis. *JAMA, 305,* 1790–1799.

Van der Feltz-Cornelis, C. M., Nuygen, J., Stoop, C., Chan, J., Jacobson, A., Katon, W., . . . Sartorius, N. (2010). Effectiveness of interventions for major depressive disorder and significant depressive symptoms in patients with diabetes mellitus: A systematic review and meta-analysis. *General Hospital Psychiatry, 32,* 380–395.

Van der Feltz-Cornelis, C. M., Van Os, T. W., Van Marwijk, H. W., & Leentjens, A. F. (2010). Effect of psychiatric consultation models in primary care: A systematic review and meta-analysis. *Journal of Psychosomatic Research, 68,* 521–533.

van der Houwen, K., Schut, H., van den Bout, J., Stroebe, M., & Stroebe, W. (2010). The efficacy of a brief internet-based self-help intervention for the bereaved. *Behaviour Research and Therapy, 48,* 359–367.

van Kessel, K., Moss-Morris, R., Willoughby, E., Chalder, T., Johnson, M. H., & Robinson, E. (2008). A randomized controlled trial of cognitive behavior therapy for multiple sclerosis fatigue. *Psychosomatic Medicine, 70,* 205–213.

van Scheppingen, C., Schroevers, M., Smink, A., van der Linden, Y. M., Mul, V., Langendik, J. A., . . . Sanderman, C. (2011). Does screening for distress efficiently uncover unmet needs in cancer patients? *Psycho-Oncology, 20,* 655–663.

Veehof, M. M., Oskam, M., Schreurs, K. M. G., & Bohlmeijer, E. T. (2011). Acceptance-based interventions for the treatment of chronic pain: A systematic review and meta-analysis. *Pain, 152,* 533–542.

Vitiello, M. V., Rybarczyk, B., Von Korff, M., & Stepanski, E. J. (2009). Cognitive behavioral therapy for insomnia improves sleep and decreases pain in older adults with co-morbid insomnia and osteoarthritis. *Journal of Clinical Sleep Medicine, 5,* 355–362.

Vizza, J. (2012). Comprehensive lifestyle intervention and group support. In R. Allan & J. Fisher (Eds.), *Heart and mind: The practice of cardiac psychology* (2nd ed., pp. 401–416). Washington, DC: American Psychological Association.

Von Bertalanffy, L. (1968). *General systems theory.* New York, NY: Braziller.

Wadden, T. A., Foreyt, J. P., Foster, G. D., Hill, J. O., Klein, S., O'Neil, P. M.,...Dunayevich, E. (2011). Weight loss with naltrexone SR/bupropion SR combination therapy as an adjunct to behavior modification: the COR-BMOD trial. *Obesity, 19,* 110–120.

Wardle, J., Chida, Y., Gibson, E. L., Whitaker, K. L., & Steptoe, A. (2011). Stress and adiposity: A meta-analysis of longitudinal studies. *Obesity, 19,* 771–778.

Weidner, G., & Kendel, F. (2010). Prevention of coronary heart disease. In J. M. Suls, K. W. Davidson, & R. M. Kaplan, *Handbook of health psychology and behavioral medicine* (pp. 354–369). New York, NY: Guilford Press.

Weinstein, N. D., Rothman, A. J., & Sutton, S. R. (1998). Stage theories of health behavior: Conceptual and methodological issues. *Health Psychology, 17,* 290–299.

West, R. (2005). Time for a change: Putting the transtheoretical (stages of change) model to rest. *Addiction, 100,* 1036–1039.

Whalley, B., Rees, K., Davies, P., Bennett, P., Ebrim, S., Liu, Z.,...Taylor, R. S. (2011, August 10). Psychological interventions for coronary heart disease. *Cochrane Database of Systematic Reviews,* CD002902.

Whitebird, R. R., Kreitzer, M. J., Lewis, B. A., Hanson, L. R., Crain, A. L., Enstad, C. J., & Mehta, A. (2011). Recruiting and retaining family caregivers to a randomized controlled trial on mindfulness-based stress reduction. *Contemporary Clinical Trials, 32,* 654–661.

Whitlock, G., Lewington, S., Sherliker P., Clarke, R., Emberson, J., Halsey J.,...Prospective Studies Collaboration (2009). Body-mass index and cause-specific mortality in 900,000 adults: Collaborative analyses of 57 prospective studies. *Lancet, 373,* 1083–1096.

Wilamowska, Z. A., Thompson-Hollands, J., Fairholme, C. P., Ellard, K. K., Farchione, T. J., & Barlow, D. H. (2010). Conceptual background, development, and preliminary data from the unified protocol for transdiagnostic treatment of emotional disorders. *Depression and Anxiety, 27,* 882–890.

Williams, G. C., Lynch, M., & Glasgow, R. E. (2007). Computer-assisted intervention improves patient-centered diabetes care by increasing autonomy support. *Health Psychology, 26,* 728–734.

Williams, P. G., Smith, T. W., Gunn, H., & Uchino, B. N. (2011). Personality and stress: Individual differences in exposure, reactivity, recovery, and restoration. In R. J. Contrada & A. Baum (Eds.), *Handbook of stress science: Biology, psychology, and health* (pp. 231–246). New York, NY: Springer.

Williams, P. G., Smith, T. W., & Jordan, K. D. (2010). Health anxiety and hypochondriasis: Interpersonal extensions of the cognitive-behavioral perspective. In J. G. Beck (Ed.), *Interpersonal perspectives in the anxiety disorders* (pp. 261–284). Washington, DC: American Psychological Association.

Williams, R. B. (2008). Psychosocial and biobehavioral factors and their interplay in coronary heart disease. *Annual Review of Clinical Psychology, 4,* 349–365.

Wilson, D. K., St. George, S. M., & Zarrett, N. (2010). Developmental influences in Understanding child and adolescent health behaviors. In J. M. Suls, K. W. Davidson, & R. M. Kaplan (Eds). *Handbook of behavioral medicine* (pp. 133–146). New York, NY: Guilford Press.

Wilson, G. T. (1980). Cognitive factors in lifestyle changes: A social learning perspective. In P. O. Davidson & S. M. Davidson (Eds.), *Behavioral medicine: Changing health lifestyles* (pp. 3–37). New York, NY: Bruner/Mazel.

Witthoft, M., & Hiller, W. (2010). Psychological approaches to origins and treatment of somatoform disorders, *Annual Review of Clinical Psychology, 6,* 257–283.

Wright, A. A., Zhang, B., Ray, A., Mack, J., Trice, E., Balboni, T.,...Prigerson, H. G. (2008). Associations between end-of-life discussions, patient mental health, medical care near death, and caregiver bereavement adjustment. *JAMA, 300,* 1665–1673.

Zautra, A. J., Davis, M. C., Rich, J. W., Nicassio, P., Tennen, H., Finan, P.,...Irwin, M. (2008). Comparison of cognitive behavioral and mindfulness meditation interventions on adaptation to rheumatoid arthritis for patients with and without history of recurrent depression. *Journal of Consulting and Clinical Psychology, 76,* 408–421.

CHAPTER **18**

COMBINING MEDICATION AND PSYCHOTHERAPY IN THE TREATMENT OF MAJOR MENTAL DISORDERS

NICHOLAS R. FORAND, ROBERT J. DERUBEIS, AND JAY D. AMSTERDAM

INTRODUCTION

Mental disorders are increasingly understood to be chronic and recurrent conditions. Even when clinicians provide state-of-the-art psychotherapeutic or psychopharmacological treatment, a substantial proportion of patients do not respond, and many others are left with residual symptoms that cause significant distress and impairment (e.g., Judd, Schettler, et al., 2003; Kocsis, 2000; Yonkers, Bruce, Dyck, & Keller, 2003). In addition, relapse after successful treatment is all too common (Beshai, Dobson, Bockting & Quigley, 2011; Gitlin et al., 2001; Post et al., 2003; Yonkers, Bruce, Dyck, & Keller, 2003). Clinical researchers have investigated combining medication and psychotherapy as a means of improving response and preventing relapse. Combination treatments are thought to improve outcomes in two ways: by increasing the magnitude of response within individuals, or by increasing the odds that any given person will receive the "correct" treatment. In many cases, combined treatments have been found to provide incremental benefits in average response over medication or psychotherapy alone (e.g., Cuijpers, van Straten, Warmerdam, & Andersson, 2009; Furukawa, Watanabe & Churchill, 2006). On the basis of this evidence, combined treatments are recommended in the American Psychiatric Association (APA) Practice Guidelines, the National Institute of Health and Clinical Excellence (NICE) Clinical Guidelines, and other treatment guidelines, particularly for cases in which symptoms are either unresponsive or partially responsive to monotherapy.

Despite these recommendations and the widespread use of combination therapy (Olfson & Marcus, 2010), little is known about the longer-term risk/benefit and cost/benefit ratios of combination treatments relative to monotherapy. Findings supporting the efficacy of the combination treatment approach are often derived from short-term treatment studies, which provide little information about long-term risk and benefits. When longer-term analyses are conducted, the results are often more equivocal. For example, in the treatment of panic disorder and social anxiety disorder, investigators have found that combined medication and psychotherapy is less effective than psychotherapy alone in preventing relapse (Otto, Bruce, & Deckersbach, 2005; Otto, McHugh, & Kantak, 2010). Issues related to long-term response deserve careful consideration because the costs of combined treatment can be high. Compared to monotherapy, combined treatments are more complex and time-consuming, and they expose individuals to an increased chance of negative effects. Currently, there is little controlled clinic data to guide clinicians as to which monotherapy or combined therapy is most likely to produce a lasting benefit in any specific individual (i.e., there is limited research on prescriptive factors). In the absence of any prescriptive evidence, we argue that treatment selection should be guided by the expected benefit in symptoms or functioning in comparison to other available treatments *over the full course of the illness*. A review of the evidence suggests that simultaneous initiation of combination treatment is often not indicated when long-term outcomes are considered. Instead, we recommend a strategic approach to combining psychotherapy and medications with the goal of maximizing benefit-to-cost ratios.

In this chapter we examine the empirical evidence for combining therapies, and discuss whether the evidence justifies the additional costs. We confine our review to treatments for adult outpatients with anxiety, depressive, bipolar and schizophrenia spectrum disorders. When available, findings are highlighted pertaining to the long-term efficacy of combination treatments. We also present arguments and evidence for a strategic application of combined therapy, and areas for future research.

ANXIETY DISORDERS

Anxiety disorders present numerous treatment challenges, and therefore are a fitting place to begin. Both medications and psychotherapy (in particular, cognitive behavioral therapy, or CBT) are efficacious in the acute treatment of anxiety disorders (Kjernisted & Bleau, 2004; Norton & Price, 2007), but many individuals remain symptomatic (Pollack et al., 2008), and relapse is common (Thuile, Even, & Ruillon, 2009). Strikingly, at least three trials of medications combined with CBT have found that the combined approach is less effective than CBT alone over the longer term, leading authors to suggest that medication can interfere with exposure-based treatments (Foa, Franklin, & Moser, 2002; Otto et al., 2005). These findings call into question the widely held assumption that combined treatments are more effective than single treatments and that the only remaining questions concern the magnitude and mechanisms of the presumed advantage. On the other hand, studies have shown that nonanxiolytic medications such as D-cycloserine can augment exposure therapy by enhancing extinction learning (Hofmann, Smits, Asnaani, Gutner, & Otto, 2011), providing an example of a possible synergy between psychotherapy and medications. We begin by reviewing studies from each of the major anxiety disorders in which combination psychotherapy and medication have been initiated simultaneously. These include the studies showing evidence of treatment interference. This is followed by a discussion of possible drawbacks of this approach, and a description of alternatives such as nonsimultaneous combination strategies.

Panic Disorder

In panic disorder, both psychotherapeutic and pharmacological interventions have demonstrated short-term efficacy (Batelaan, van Balkom, & Stein, 2011; Hofmann & Smits, 2008). However, the literature provides only modest support for the value of combining them. A recent meta-analysis found that combined treatment for panic disorder was only 1.2 times more likely to produce a response than antidepressants alone (tricyclics or SSRIs) and only 1.2 times more likely to produce a response than psychotherapy alone (Furukawa et al., 2006). Longer-term outcomes were even less impressive; the effects of combined treatment were equal to those of psychotherapy alone after medications were discontinued. Similar short-term findings emerged from a meta-analysis of combined CBT and benzodiazepine treatments (Watanabe, Churchill, & Fukuwara, 2007). In this case, combined treatment was not superior to CBT on primary outcomes, although it showed additional benefit on some secondary measures. An analysis of follow-up data showed that CBT alone was superior both to medications and combination treatment over longer periods, providing some evidence that medications interfere with the enduring effects of CBT.

Evidence for treatment interference in panic disorder is derived from two separate trials. In the first of these, Marks et al. (1993) randomized 154 patients to 8 weeks of exposure (EXP) plus Alprazolam (ALP), EXP plus Placebo (PBO), Relaxation (RLX) plus ALP, and RLX plus PBO. At posttreatment, response rates were 71%, 71%, 51%, 25%, respectively. Groups receiving exposure demonstrated superior short-term response relative to those who received ALP or relaxation. However, at a 43-week medication-free follow-up, the sustained response rate in the combined treatment group fell to 36%, compared to 62% for the EX plus PBO, and 29% for the ALP alone group. EX plus PBO was superior to all other treatments, whereas combined treatment was no different from medication alone. In the second study, Barlow, Gorman, Shear, and Woods (2000) randomized 312 patients to CBT plus imipramine (IMP), CBT plus PBO, CBT, IMP, and PBO. After the 3-month acute phase and 6 months of continuation treatment, CBT plus IMP was superior to CBT and IMP alone (9-month response rates: CBT plus IMP: 57%, CBT plus PBO: 47%, CBT: 40%, IMP: 39%, PBO: 13%). However, at a 6-month medication-free follow-up, groups receiving CBT without IMP evidenced sustained response rates of 41% (CBT plus PBO) and 32% (CBT alone), each of which were numerically superior to the 25% rate in the combined treatment group. Among patients who entered the follow-up phase, both groups receiving CBT without imipramine had significantly better sustained response rates than the CBT plus IMP group, which experienced the highest relapse rate in the study. Thus, in panic disorder, combination treatments appear to be, at best, marginally superior to CBT alone in producing acute response (e.g., Van Apeldoorn et al., 2008), and at worst, associated with a higher probability of relapse in comparison to CBT monotherapy.

Social Anxiety Disorder

Clinical trials in social anxiety disorder offer a mixed picture for the efficacy of combined therapy. Some findings suggest that combined therapy is superior to monotherapy during short-term treatment. For example, in a study of 128 patients randomized to phenelzine (PHEN), cognitive-behavioral group therapy (CBGT), PHEN plus CBGT, and PBO, results showed that PHEN plus CBGT (response rate: 72%) and PHEN monotherapy (54%) were superior to placebo (33%), and CBGT (47%) after 12 weeks (Blanco et al., 2010). Results were similar after 24 weeks of treatment. Responders in the combined group evidenced larger average improvements than responders in each of the monotherapies, suggesting a within-individual additive effect of combined treatment (i.e., combined treatment responders received more benefit on average than monotherapy responders). As impressive as these findings are, a follow-up report is needed to determine the longer-term outcomes. This is particularly important because in a similar study an acute advantage for combined treatment relative to psychotherapy faded after treatment was discontinued. In that trial, Blomhoff et al. (2001) randomized 375 patients in primary care to 24 weeks of combined exposure (EX) plus sertraline (SERT) therapy, EX plus PBO, SERT monotherapy, or PBO. At end of the treatment period, response rates were 46%, 33%, 40%, and 24%, respectively. Active medication treatments were superior to placebo and EX plus PBO was not superior to PBO alone. However, at the end of a 28-weeks medication-free follow-up period, the EX plus PBO and PBO groups had continued to improve, whereas EX plus SERT and SERT monotherapy groups had experienced significant worsening on one symptom measure and indications of deterioration on others, suggesting that, similar to what is seen in panic disorder, medications might interfere with longer-term gains (Haug et al., 2003).

In contrast, three other clinical trials yielded no evidence of interference in social anxiety. However, these studies also failed to demonstrate short-term advantages of combined treatment relative to monotherapy. Davidson et al. (2004) found that fluoxetine (FLU) monotherapy, comprehensive CBT (CCBT), combined FLU plus CCBT, and CCBT plus PBO all yielded similar response rates after 14 weeks of treatment (51%, 52%, 54%, and 51%, respectively). Prasko et al. (2006) found CBT plus PBO and CBT plus moclobemide (MOC) to be superior to MOC alone after 6 months of treatment, and each of the CBT groups had lower rates of relapse after a 24-month treatment free follow-up (CBT + PBO: 48%, CBT + MOC: 64%, MOC: 79%). Finally, in one of only a few studies of combination treatment that did not use CBT, Knijnik et al. (2008) found that medication combined with psychodynamic group therapy did not result in greater symptom reduction than medication alone, but it did result in greater gains on a measure of clinical improvement. So, in social anxiety, there is mixed evidence for the efficacy of combined treatments versus monotherapy, and at least one example of treatment interference.

Obsessive Compulsive Disorder (OCD)

In the treatment of obsessive compulsive disorder, some studies suggest an advantage for combined treatments versus monotherapies, specifically in individuals with comorbid mood symptoms. In one of these, Cottraux et al. (1990) found no differences between fluvoxamine (FLV), exposure and response prevention (EXRP), and EXRP plus FLV after 24 weeks of treatment, and no differences in relapse-prevention during 48 weeks of follow-up. However, the combined treatment did produce a greater improvement in mood at 24 weeks. In another study, Hohagen et al. (1998) also found no differences in compulsions between those assigned to CBT plus FLV as compared to CBT plus PBO after 9 weeks of treatment, but combined therapy resulted in lower levels of obsessions and a higher response rate (88%) relative to monotherapy (60%). Combined treatment was also more efficacious for patients with substantial co-morbid depressive symptomatology.

In contrast, other studies have found no advantage of combined treatment (e.g., van Balkom et al., 1998). In one trial (Foa et al., 2005), patients were assigned to clomipramine (CMP), intensive EXRP, EXRP plus CMP, or placebo for 12 weeks ($N = 122$). At the end of acute treatment, EXRP plus CMP (response rate: 70%) and EXRP (62%) were each superior to CMP alone (42%) but not different from one another. After a 12-week treatment discontinuation phase, EXRP plus CLO and EXRP alone were each associated with fewer relapses than CLO alone (sustained response of 39%, 55%, and 17%, respectively), and no different from one another (Simpson et al., 2004). One important criticism of this study is that the period of intensive EXRP (15 2-hour sessions over 3 weeks) was completed before the effects of clomipramine could be realized, perhaps reducing the chance of finding a combined effect (Franklin & Simpson, 2005). Other evidence suggests that there is no difference between combined treatment and psychotherapy alone in preventing relapse and recurrence over a longer-term follow-up (Rufer et al., 2005). Therefore, in OCD, evidence for greater efficacy of combined treatments over the short term is mostly confined to individuals with comorbid depression symptoms. There is little if any evidence suggesting that there are long-term benefits of combined treatment, relative to CBT alone.

Posttraumatic Stress Disorder (PTSD)

Psychotherapy (i.e., CBT) and pharmacotherapy are each efficacious treatments for PTSD (APA, 2004a; NICE, 2005). However, there have been few controlled trials testing their simultaneous combination. In a recent randomized trial, paroxetine, in combination with prolonged exposure (a type of CBT), was more efficacious than prolonged exposure alone after 10 weeks of treatment (Schneier et al., 2012). Although this trial is suggestive of an acute advantage for combined treatment, there is as of yet no follow-up report on the long-term stability of these gains.

In contrast, findings from a study by van Minnen, Arntz, and Keijsers (2002) suggest that medications might interfere with the beneficial effect of psychotherapy. In this trial of 63 outpatients, self-reported use of concurrent benzodiazepines was associated with poorer outcomes in exposure therapy. Further evidence suggests that a course of CBT is more effective at preventing relapse than is a course of medications

of equal duration (Frommberger et al., 2004), and that medication maintenance is necessary for prevention of relapse and recurrence (Davidson et al., 2001). Without further comparisons between monotherapy and combined therapy, however, it remains unclear whether adding medications to CBT either enhances or inhibits the relapse prevention effect of CBT for PTSD.

Generalized Anxiety Disorder (GAD)

There is little evidence that combined therapy is more effective than monotherapy in the treatment of GAD. In the largest controlled study, Power et al. (1990) randomized 113 individuals to CBT plus diazepam (DZ), CBT plus PBO, CBT monotherapy, DZ, or PBO. After 9 weeks of therapy, combined treatment was superior to DZ alone but not to CBT plus PBO or CBT alone at reducing anxiety symptoms (response rates: 91% for CBT plus DZ, 83% for CBT plus PBO, 86% for CBT, 68% for DZ, and 37% for PBO). At a 6-month naturalistic follow-up, response rates in all conditions that contained CBT were better than those for DZ-alone conditions. There was no difference observed between the condition that combined CBT with DZ, relative to the CBT conditions that did not include medication, suggesting that DZ neither enhanced nor interfered with CBT's relapse prevention effect (Foa, Franklin & Moser, 2002). In another study, using a naturalistic design ($N = 87$), Ferrero et al. (2007) found no differences between brief dynamic therapy (BDT), BDT plus medication (i.e., antidepressants plus benzodiazepines), or medication alone after 3, 6, or 12 months of therapy. Overall, the lack of randomized comparisons between combined and monotherapies limits the conclusions that can be made about the relative effectiveness of these approaches in the treatment of GAD.

Summary of Simultaneously Combined Treatments in Anxiety Disorders

The findings summarized above suggest that the benefits obtained during combination treatment, which are of modest clinical significance in most trials, fade relative to psychotherapy after treatment is completed (Hofmann, Sawyer, Korte, & Smits, 2009). Even more concerning is the evidence that, in some cases, combined treatment is inferior to CBT alone at preventing relapse (Barlow et al., 2000; Haug et al., 2003; Marks et al., 1993). In these instances, medications appear to block some of the prophylactic benefits of exposure-based CBT.

Mechanisms of Treatment Interference in Anxiety

There are several plausible explanations of treatment interference effects in anxiety disorders, each focusing on how medications might disrupt the presumed therapeutic mechanisms of exposure therapy. One account, provided by Foa, Franklin, and Moser (2002), suggests that the anxiolytic effects of medication suppress the activation of fear-related cognitions during exposure, preventing the encoding of corrective information. Others have suggested that corrective information is encoded, but that this learning does not generalize across the contextual shift that accompanies medication discontinuation, leading to the return of anxiety after treatment (Otto et al., 2005). In a review of evidence from both animal and human neurobiological studies, Otto, McHugh, and Kantak (2010) propose that medications inhibit extinction learning by suppressing acute cortisol secretion. The secretion of cortisol, which normally facilitates the consolidation of memories (Lupien et al., 2005), is inhibited by benzodiazepines and antidepressants (e.g., Pomara, Willoughby, Sidtis, Cooper, & Greenblatt, 2005; Schüle, Sighart, Hennig, & Laakmann, 2006), thus potentially interfering with the consolidation of fear-incongruent learning during exposures.

In each of the proposed mechanisms, the presumed *therapeutic* effect of the medication disrupts the processes that mediate the effect of exposure. Thus it may be that the beneficial effects of one treatment undermine the beneficial effects of another superior treatment. Notably, interference findings have thus far been observed only when the two treatments are initiated simultaneously, and the interference effects are asymmetric in that there is no evidence that psychotherapy interferes with or inhibits the positive effects of medications.

Disadvantages of Simultaneous Combined Therapy in Treating Anxiety

A reexamination of the rationale for simultaneously combining medication and psychotherapy is required in light of repeated findings that these strategies are not superior to psychotherapy

in the treatment of anxiety disorders. Because combination treatments yield little advantage in sustained benefit relative to psychotherapy alone, it is likely that many individuals receive unnecessary treatment with medications. Duration of this unneeded treatment can be lengthy. Evidence suggests that medication use can continue for years after the intial response to combined therapy without providing a benefit in relapse prevention relative to CBT alone (Van Oppen, van Balkom, de Haan, & van Dyck, 2005). Other negative effects of combined treatment relative to psychotherapy have been noted, including increased cost, unwanted side effects, and an increased chance of dropout (Gould, Otto, & Pollack, 1995). Prolonged benzodiazepine use can also result in tolerance (Salzman, 1998; Woods, Katz, & Winger, 1992), and there is emerging evidence that prolonged antidepressant exposure might produce similar problems (Fava & Offidani, 2011; see the depression section). Moreover, individuals who relapse after discontinuation of medication therapy might need to restart and remain on medications indefinitely to prevent further relapses (Thuile et al., 2009).

In addition to the increased costs and risks, the opportunity to learn whether patients would have responded to a monotherapy is missed when both treatments are initiated simultaneously. In other words, when a patient is treated successfully with a combination therapy, it cannot be known if one of the monotherapies would have been sufficient, and if so, which one. On the other hand, if a monotherapy is effective, the patient and the provider acquire information about treatment response that can inform the longer-term management of the illness. Identifying effective and cost-effective treatment options is especially important for patients who seek additional therapy after an incomplete initial response, as well as for those whose symptoms return after treatment. Both scenarios are common in patients who are treated for anxiety disorders (Davidson et al., 2001; Durham et al., 2005; Keller, 2006; Rubio & López-Ibor, 2007; Rufer et al., 2005). Thus, the selection of a simultaneous combination treatment can be seen as disadvantageous when viewed within the context of longer-term care.

Other Combined Treatment Strategies.

An alternative to the simultaneous initiation of combination treatment is treatment sequencing.

In sequencing strategies, a monotherapy is the initial treatment, and additional or alternative therapies are introduced only if response is inadequate (Rodrigues et al., 2011). The sequencing strategies that have shown the most promise in the treatment of anxiety are those that involve the addition of psychotherapy or pharmacotherapy (i.e., augmentation) and those in which psychotherapy is used to assist in the tapering of medications.

Augmentation

Rodrigues et al. (2011) provide a systematic review of 17 studies in PTSD, panic disorder, or OCD that used CBT as an add-on treatment for pharmacotherapy non-remitters. In contrast to the common finding that combination treatments do not outperform monotherapies, positive findings have been obtained consistently from studies of CBT augmentation. For example, in a three-phase study of panic disorder, Simon et al. (2009) showed that nonresponders to back-to-back courses of sertraline treatment experienced a reduction in symptoms from either the addition of CBT or clonazepam, which did not differ from each other. In OCD, Simpson et al. (2008) found that partial responders to serotonin reuptake inhibitors showed greater rates of response when EXRP was added, relative to the addition of stress management. In PTSD, Hinton et al. (2005) showed that CBT improved outcomes after an inadequate response to SSRI plus supportive counseling. Benefits accruing from add-on CBT after an inadequate medication response have been observed in several other controlled trials (e.g., Kampman et al., 2002a; Tolin et al., 2007);[1] and in uncontrolled naturalistic studies (Heldt, Blaya, et al., 2006; Pollack et al., 1994; Tundo, Salvati, Busto, Di Spigno, & Falcini, 2007).

CBT augmentation might also have other advantages over simultaneous treatment combinations. Franklin (2005) proposed that, in the treatment of OCD, medications plus add-on EXRP might work synergistically, by allowing time for the medications to reach their full effective dose before EXRP is initiated. Once on their therapeutic dose, patients might more readily confront feared stimuli and refrain from engaging in safety behaviors. Add-on CBT might also be less susceptible to treatment interference. Some research indicates that cortisol response normalizes over the course of medication treatment, perhaps leading to a reduction in medication-induced inhibition of extinction learning (Otto, McHugh, & Kantak, 2010). Findings to date on the durability of add-on CBT have been positive (Heldt, Gus Manfro, et al., 2006; Hinton et al., 2005; and Pollack et al., 1994), but large-scale replication is lacking.

In contrast to add-on psychotherapy, surprisingly few controlled clinical trials provide data on the strategy of adding medications to psychotherapy (Albert & Brunatto, 2009). Findings from these studies paint a mixed picture of the benefits of this approach. In one study of panic disorder, paroxetine or pill placebo was added to CBT after a nonresponse ($N = 161$). At the end of treatment, 74% of patients in the CBT plus paroxetine group were panic free, compared to 47% in the CBT plus placebo group (Kampman et al., 2002b). Findings from two other panic disorder studies suggest that clear but modest gains accrue from the addition of clomipramine to exposure therapy (Hoffart et al., 1993), and from the addition of divalproex sodium (Depakote) to CBT plus standard medications (Baetz & Bowen, 1998). In contrast, Simon et al. (2008) found no benefit for the addition of paroxetine versus placebo to PE after an initial nonresponse to PE in PTSD. Indeed, although non-significant and small ($d = 0.35$), effect sizes favored the placebo group. A similar finding in panic disorder was reported by Fava, Savron, Grandi, and Rafanelli (1997). In this crossover design, patients were randomly assigned to three balanced treatment blocks involving exposure, exposure plus imipramine, and exposure plus cognitive therapy. Remission was observed most often after exposure alone regardless of treatment order. Moreover, a number of nonremitters to exposure assigned to exposure plus imipramine had difficulty tolerating the drug, and 43% had to be discontinued prematurely. The results of these two studies might suggest that (1) the duration of exposure treatment is inadequate in some psychotherapy nonresponders, and (2) the addition of other treatment "too early" could complicate the therapeutic process of exposure. Because the addition of medications to psychotherapy is popular in general practice (Albert & Brunatto,

---

[1] For an exception see Rothbaum et al., 2006, who found that adding PE to sertraline did not significantly improve response compared to continuing sertraline in PTSD. It should also be noted that, with the exception of Hinton et al. (2005) and Rothbaum et al. (2006) these studies lack comparison groups who continue their previous treatment, making it difficult to separate the effects of augmentation versus the passage of time.

2009), further studies are urgently needed, with specific attention paid to mediating and moderating variables that might identify those patients for whom the addition of medications is likely to enhance response, relative to a continuation of psychotherapy, or to a shift in the targets or methods of psychotherapy.

Psychotherapy for Medication Taper and Discontinuation

Other sequencing strategies address difficulties with discontinuing anxiolytic medications, a process that is associated with severe discontinuation syndromes, substantially increased anxiety, or relapse (Noyes, Garvey, Cook, & Suelzer, 1991). CBT has proven useful as a means of "bridging the gap," by preventing relapse during benzodiazepine taper in both panic and GAD (Gosselin, Ladouceur, Morin, Dugas, & Baillargeon, 2006; Otto et al., 1993; Otto, McHugh, Simon, et al., 2010). CBT might also reduce the negative effects of the discontinuation of antidepressant medications after successful treatment for panic disorder (e.g., Schmidt, Wolloway-Bickel, Trakowski, Santiago, & Vasey, 2002). These studies suggest that combination therapy in anxiety might help those who struggle to taper their medications after successful acute treatment.

Augmentation of Exposure Therapy With D-Cycloserine

Most augmentation strategies for anxiety add one anxiolytic therapy, whether psychotherapeutic or pharmaceutical, to another. In contrast, the glutamatergic N-Methyl-D-Aspartate (NMDA) partial agonist D-cycloserine (DCS) has no anxiolytic properties on its own, but has been shown to enhance response when combined with exposure therapy (Deveney et al., 2009). Specifically, DCS is thought to enhance extinction learning and thereby facilitate response to exposure therapy (Hofmann et al., 2011). Across several brief placebo controlled trials, DCS administered before exposures has been associated with greater symptom improvement in acrophobia (Ressler et al., 2004), social anxiety disorder (Guastella et al., 2008; Hofmann et al., 2006) and panic disorder (Otto, Tolin, et al., 2010). Although these results are promising, findings from some studies suggest that DCS becomes less effective with prolonged use, possibly due to drug tolerance (Kushner et al., 2007; Wilhelm et al., 2008). Further work is therefore needed to determine the

limitations and durability of the enhancing effects of DCS and other putative memory enhancers (e.g., yohimbine hydrochloride; see Hofmann et al., 2011).

Summary and Recommendations

Results for simultaneously combined treatments in anxiety vary by the specific anxiety disorder under study, but on the whole the evidence for improved efficacy over monotherapies is lacking. Thus, combination treatments are best reserved for cases that are refractory to monotherapy, and then used in such a way to maximize their benefit. Evidence suggests that adding psychotherapy for individuals who are non-responders to medication is efficacious acutely (Rodrigues et al., 2011), and that CBT is effective in helping individuals taper medications while maintaining treatment gains. Fewer studies assess adding medications to psychotherapy, and the benefits of this approach are not yet determined. In each case, more research is needed to identify prognostic and prescriptive factors for combination treatments (e.g., Maher et al., 2010) and to determine the durability of these approaches.

The prospect of increasing the potency of exposure therapy with pharmacological agents such as DCS is exciting and important. At this time, DCS is not widely available; however, as researchers refine the procedures and identify the populations for whom application of DCS is most effective, practitioners might be provided with a powerful tool. These approaches appear to retain the best features of CBT treatments (enduring effects, limited side effects), while at the same time increasing their efficacy.

DEPRESSION

Findings from research on combined therapies for depression share several features with those for anxiety disorders. Psychotherapy and antidepressant medication appear to have similar efficacy in short-term treatment trials (Cuijpers, van Straten, van Oppen, & Andersson, 2008; Spielmans, Berman, & Usitalo, 2011). Psychotherapeutic treatments, in particular CBT, might also confer an enduring benefit by preventing relapse and recurrence when compared to discontinuing medication (Dobson et al., 2008; Hollon, DeRubeis, et al., 2005; Imel, Malterer, McKay, & Wampold, 2008). However, as is true of antianxiety therapies, antidepressant therapies are only modestly effective during initial short-term treatment, with remission rates of less than 50% (Fava, Ruini & Belaise, 2007). Moreover, rates of recurrence after successful treatment for depression range from 40% to 85%, with an average time to recurrence of 3.2 years (Hughes & Cohen, 2009). Recent large-scale trials (e.g., Keller et al., 2000) and meta-analytic studies (Friedman, et al., 2004; Pampallona, Bollini, Tibaldi, Kupelnick, & Munizza, 2004) have revealed a small to moderate short-term advantage for combined therapy over various monotherapies of depression. As a result, treatment guidelines recommend the use of combined therapy as initial treatment for severe, chronic, and recurrent depression, as well as for individuals who have not responded to prior monotherapy (Davidson, 2010). We briefly review these positive findings, and then turn our attention to concerns with common combination approaches and discuss evidence for possible alternatives.

Short-Term Benefits of Combination Treatments

In head-to-head comparisons, estimates of the short-term advantage for combined treatment in depression are $d = 0.31$ versus medications (Cuijpers, Dekker, Hollon, & Andersson, 2009), and $d = 0.35$ versus psychotherapy (Cuijpers, van Straten, et al., 2009); although a large portion of the latter advantage could be accounted for by the placebo effect (Cuijpers, van Straten, Hollon, & Andersson, 2010). Further meta-analytic findings suggest that chronicity, rather than severity, might be the best predictor of an advantage of combined treatment (Cuijpers, Dekker, et al., 2009; Cuijpers, van Straten, Schuurmans, et al., 2010; see also Cuijpers, van Straten, Hollon, et al., 2010).

In addition to improving rates of response, combined treatment might increase the "breadth" of response relative to monotherapy by providing more rapid symptom reduction or improvements in a greater number of functional domains (Hollon, Jarrett, et al., 2005). In early studies of Interpersonal Therapy (IPT), a combination of IPT and medication was associated with greater gains in social functioning compared to medication alone (Weissman, Klerman, Paykel, Prusoff, & Hanson, 1974, Weissman, Klerman, Prusoff, Sholomskas, & Padian, 1981). Cognitive behavioral analysis system of psychotherapy (CBASP; a variant of CBT) combined with medication also appears to enhance the breadth of

response relative to monotherapy. In a trial of 656 patients with chronic depression, Keller et al. (2000) found the combination of CBASP and nefazodone to be more efficacious than either monotherapy (rates of remission for combined treatment: 48%, CBASP: 33%, and nefazadone: 29%). Secondary analyses from this trial revealed that combined treatment was associated with faster time to remission (Manber et al., 2008), and greater improvements in psychosocial functioning relative to either monotherapy (Hirschfeld et al., 2002).

Combination therapy with brief dynamic psychotherapy (BDT) might also be associated with added functional benefits. To date, two controlled clinical trials and one mega-analysis of combined therapy with BDT have shown short-term advantages of combined therapy over monotherapy (Burnand et al., 2002; de Jonghe, Kool, van Aalst, Dekker, & Peen, 2001; de Maat et al., 2008). Molenaar et al. (2007) also found that patients receiving BDT plus medications improved on more dimensions of social functioning than did those receiving medication monotherapy, although it is possible that these advantages were due to the superior effects of the combined treatment on symptoms of depression.

Thus, in addition to small advantages in symptoms, short term combined treatment has been shown to improve rate of response and some dimensions of social functioning relative to monotherapy.

Prevention of Relapse and Recurrence

As we have argued in our review of anxiety disorders, the long-term benefits of combination treatments must equal or exceed the benefits derived from monotherapies to justify their use as an initial treatment. Maintenance medications (Geddes et al., 2003), as well as initial and maintenance psychotherapy (Blackburn & Moore, 1997; Dobson et al., 2008; Hollon, DeRubeis, et al., 2005), have shown moderate efficacy in preventing relapse and recurrence of depression. The available evidence, although limited in scope, suggests that longer-term efficacy of combined treatments is on a par with but not superior to that of either monotherapy (e.g., Cuijpers, Dekker, et al., 2009; Vittengl, Clark, Dunn, & Jarrett, 2007). Comparisons between discontinued combination therapy with CBT versus discontinued CBT alone show no difference with respect to relapse prevention, with each condition being superior to discontinued medication (Blackburn, Eunson, & Bishop, 1986; Evans et al., 1992; Simons, Murphy, Levine, & Wetzel, 1986). Vittengl et al. (2007) estimated the risk of relapse or recurrence in individuals with prior CBT combined with medications to be 61% lower than in those with prior medication monotherapy. Again, prior combined therapy did not differ from prior CBT.

Data from a recently completed study also support the benefit of CBT combined with medications in producing a sustained response. The study comprised a large ($N = 452$) trial of CBT plus medications versus medication monotherapy for recurrent and/or chronic major depression. The aim of the trial was to treat patients to recovery, defined as a 26-week period without relapse, allowing for the detection of speed of recovery and therefore a comparison of combined treatment versus medications alone. Preliminary results show that rates of recovery were higher in combined therapy (73%) versus medication alone (62%) while rates of attrition were lower in combined therapy (18%) versus medication alone (27%; S. D. Hollon, R. J. DeRubeis, R. C. Shelton, J. Zajecka, & J. Fawcett, personal communication, May 7, 2011).

IPT or BDT in combination with medication might also provide some protection against relapse. Cuijpers et al. (2011) estimated that maintenance IPT in combination with medications is superior to medication maintenance alone, with an effect size of $d = 0.37$. Interestingly, the method that produced the acute response might be important for predicting recurrence. Frank et al. (2007) found that women on maintenance IPT who had remitted on IPT alone were less likely to have a recurrence than women who had remitted on IPT plus add-on medications. Other findings suggest that maintenance IPT plus medications is superior to IPT maintenance alone in preventing relapse (Reynolds et al., 1999). In regards to BDT, Maina, Rosso, and Bogetto (2009) found that the combination treatment resulted in a lower rate of relapse (28%) than the medication group (47%) over a 48-month naturalistic follow-up.

Disadvantages of Combined Therapy in Treating Depression

Taken together, the evidence for combined therapy of depression is largely positive. Unlike combined therapy for anxiety disorders, there is little evidence that treatments interfere with one another. However, the possibility of obtaining incremental gains from combined treatment must be balanced against other potential disadvantages.

One concern in combination therapy is the long-term care of depressive illness. Increasingly, depression is recognized as a chronic and recurrent disorder, suggesting that the longer-term management of the disorder should be considered during initial treatment selection (Fava & Ruini, 2006). As with anxiety disorders, having information about an effective treatment for any particular individual is potentially cost-reducing. If a patient evidences a good response to simultaneously initiated combination treatment, no information is obtained about how to prevent relapse or recurrence in *that individual*; that is, whether or not to continue to provide both, one, or neither of the therapies. An incorrect choice can have negative consequences: If medications produced the response, discontinuation could leave the individual vulnerable to relapse (Bockting et al., 2008). On the other hand, a decision to continue both treatments might leave an individual on two expensive and possibly unnecessary maintenance treatments. As previously noted, successful combination treatment also provides no information for selecting subsequent (and less costly) monotherapies if symptoms recur. Faced with these uncertainties, a common and recommended maintenance strategy in clinical practice is prolonged continuation of medication treatment (Petty, House, Knapp, Raynor, & Zermansky, 2006; Piek, van der Meer, & Nolen, 2010), which is expensive (Vos, Corry, Haby, Carter, & Andrews, 2005) and often ineffective (Bockting et al., 2008).

Moreover, the increased potential for negative or iatrogenic effects during combined treatment needs to be considered. Side effects during medication treatment (Warden et al., 2009) and the increased chance of relapse upon discontinuation of medications (Viguera, Baldessarini, & Friedberg, 1998), are well documented. There is also increasing evidence that prolonged antidepressant maintenance can worsen the course of depressive illness, at least in some cases (Fava & Offidani, 2011). Findings from long-term studies suggest that the efficacy of maintenance medication fades over time, with little additional benefit accruing after 3 to 6 months of maintenance (Kaymaz, van

Os, Loonen, & Nolen, 2008; Reimherr et al., 1998). Other studies have found evidence for tachyphylaxis, or progressive tolerance, defined as the recurrence of depressive symptoms during adequate maintenance treatment (Solomon et al., 2005). Tachyphalaxis might be functionally related to treatment resistance, in which individuals fail to respond to previously effective medications after a drug-free period (Amsterdam et al., 2009). Tolerance to antidepressant therapy may become more likely as the number of prior medication exposures increases (Amsterdam et al., 2009; Amsterdam & Shultz, 2005; Leykin et al., 2007). Discontinuation of medications can also result in "discontinuation syndromes," marked by worsening mood, agitation, and multiple somatic symptoms (Rosenbaum, Fava, Hoog, Ascroft, & Krebs, 1998). Fava and Offidani (2011) hypothesize that these effects are caused by compensatory changes in neurotransmitter systems, collectively known as "oppositional tolerance." Similar to iatrogenic effects in antipsychotic medications (e.g., tardive dyskinesia), oppositional tolerance is hypothesized to result from adaptations in synaptic structure and activity induced by the presence of antidepressant agents. Progressive change in these mechanisms might result in the return of depressive symptoms during treatment, or a rebound effect upon discontinuation.

There are also possible negative effects of psychotherapy. Research on harmful effects in psychotherapy has been hindered both by neglect (Lilienfeld, 2007) and by methodological difficulties (Dimidjian & Hollon, 2010), thus the identification of these effects in psychotherapy lags behind that of pharmacological interventions. However, a review of the literature indicates that 5% to 10% of adults deteriorate while in psychotherapy (Hansen, Lambert, & Forman, 2003), indicating that negative effects are possible. In established therapies for depression, findings regarding moderators of treatment outcome might suggest conditions under which treatment is toxic to some individuals, for example, in cases of comorbid personality disorder (Fournier et al., 2008) or low levels of therapist competence in CBT (Strunk, Brotman, DeRubeis, & Hollon, 2010).[2] Unethical or inappropriate actions by therapists, such as sexual relations with patients, are also an unfortunate and serious cause of potential harm (Berk & Parker, 2009). However, even presumably ethical and well-meaning therapists can produce negative outcomes. Okiishi et al. (2006) found that outcomes in outpatient treatment varied widely by therapist. Furthermore, Kraus, Castonguay, Boswell, Nordberg, and Hayes (2011) found that a surprising number of community therapists produced reliable deterioration in specific functional domains. For example, 10% of therapists reliably *increased* anxiety symptoms and 14% of therapists reliably *decreased* social functioning. This alarmingly high rate of deterioration (although largely domain specific, i.e., therapists might produce poor outcomes in one domain but not others) suggests that harmful effects of therapy might be more common than once thought. Even if it is innocuous, ineffective courses of psychotherapy are associated with more substantial "opportunity costs" relative to ineffective medications, because they require a greater investment in time and effort (Lilienfeld, 2007).

The findings that point to these problems in both medications and psychotherapy are not definitive; therefore, further investigation is required. However, the possibility of incurring one or more of these negative effects increases when two therapies are prescribed together. Treatment providers should consider this increased chance of harm when selecting initial treatment strategies.[3]

Other Combination Treatment Strategies

Similar to anxiety disorders, better cost/benefit and risk/benefit ratios might be achieved from sequenced treatment strategies, which might produce, on average, similar benefit with a lower chance for negative effects. Evidence exists regarding the effects of several sequencing strategies in depression, including (a) switching between therapies, (b) augmenting one therapy with another, and (c) clinical staging (Fava & Tomba, 2010). These strategies have been examined for their ability to improve both short-term and long-term responses.

---

[2] These findings do not provide evidence for harmful outcomes, per se. Rather, they identify conditions under which some individuals respond less well. It is possible that extreme values on these dimensions could make CBT toxic in some cases.

[3] It is not always the case that combination treatment increases the chance of harm. Some evidence suggests that combined treatments have lower dropout rates than medication monotherapy (Cuijpers, Dekker, Hollon, & Anderson, 2009).

Switching

Switch strategies involve a planned change from one treatment to another for patients who fail to respond adequately to the initial treatment. Evidence in favor of switching strategies has emerged from Keller et al. (2000) and the Sequenced Treatment Alternatives to Relieve Depression study (STAR*D). In Keller et al., individuals who did not respond to CBASP or nefazodone alone after 12 weeks were crossed over to the other treatment (Schatzberg et al., 2005). Individuals who were switched from nefazadone to CBASP experienced a significantly greater rate of response (57%) than individuals who were switched from CBASP to nefazadone (42%), a difference that the authors attributed to a lower rate of dropout in CBASP. In Stage 2 of STAR*D, nonresponders to citalopram could be assigned to switch to CBT or have citalopram augmented with CBT. Among those who were switched to CBT, 25% remitted, compared to 28% of those who were switched to another medication (Thase et al., 2007). Moreover, the switch-to-CBT group reported significantly fewer side effects than did the medication switch group. Thus, switching from medications to psychotherapy appears to be about as efficacious as the opposite strategy, but the longer-term efficacy of each strategy is unknown.

Augmentation

Add-on treatments have been studied for their ability to improve both short-term response and long-term efficacy. In STAR*D, add-on CBT at Stage 2 was equivalent to add-on medications in producing remission (rates of 23% versus 33%, respectively), although medication augmentation was associated with faster time to remission (Thase et al., 2007).[4] In one of the only studies to compare two different strategies for combining treatments, Frank et al. (2000) randomized women to IPT or combination IPT plus medications. In the IPT alone group, medications were added at 24 weeks if remission was not achieved. At the end of treatment, the augmentation treatment group showed a higher rate of remission (79%) than the combination treatment group (66%). Interestingly, in another study comparing IPT alone versus

---

[4]Unfortunately, due to the randomization strategy in STAR*D, too few patients were either augmented or switched to CT to permit a generalizable estimate of its efficacy as a second stage treatment.

IPT plus sequential medication augmentation, maintenance IPT was less efficacious at preventing recurrence in the augmentation group after the medication was discontinued (Frank et al., 2007). Other studies show less positive results for short-term augmentation. In the Research Evaluating the Value of Augmenting Medication with Psychotherapy (REVAMP) trial, nonresponders or partial responders to 12 weeks of sertraline treatment received equal—and surprisingly low levels of—benefit from each of the following treatments: 12 weeks of continued medication, add-on CBASP, and add-on supportive therapy (Kocsis et al., 2009). The authors conjectured that the lack of benefit from add-on CBASP could have occurred because individuals who preferred psychotherapy might have been discouraged from entering a trial that required an initial course of medication.

In trials testing relapse prevention strategies, the long-term efficacy of medication maintenance is consistently improved by add-on CBT. For example, mindfulness-based cognitive therapy (MBCT), a treatment designed to prevent depressive relapse by teaching patients to become mindful of and disengage from ruminative cognitive processes (Teasdale et al., 1995), appears to be particularly useful for preventing relapse in patients with recurrent depression. Two studies found that remitted depressed individuals with three or more previous episodes (but not those with two or fewer) receiving MBCT plus treatment as usual (TAU) were less likely to relapse over 60 weeks than those receiving TAU (Ma & Teasdale, 2004; Teasdale et al., 2000). Other studies suggest that the protective effect of add-on CBT for recurrent depression is durable. CBT added to maintenance medication was associated with decreased relapse rates versus medication monotherapy at 68 weeks (Paykel et al., 1999) and at 3.5 years (Paykel et al., 2005). CBT was also associated with cost-benefit advantages over medication monotherapy (Scott, Palmer, Paykel, Teasdale, & Hayhurst, 2003). Furthermore, Bockting et al. (2005) found that remitted depressed individuals with five or more depressive episodes had lower relapse rates in group CBT plus TAU than did those who received TAU alone (46% versus 72%, respectively). The enduring effects of CBT continued for individuals with four or more episodes at a 5.5-year follow-up (Bockting et al., 2009).

Similar to the Frank et al. (2007) finding reported above, evidence suggests that patients

who require augmentation to achieve acute remission are more likely to relapse than those who remit after unaugmented treatment. Rucci et al. (2011) reported that remitters to IPT or SSRI alone were one third as likely to relapse over 6 months of continued treatment as those who required add-on medications or IPT to achieve remission. These studies suggest that difficult-to-treat individuals might require more robust maintenance therapy in order to achieve recovery.

Clinical Staging

The augmentation literature, although promising, provides little guidance for making treatment decisions about when—or if—one should initiate psychotherapy or terminate medication treatment, and so on. A possible alternative to unguided augmentation is theory-guided staging of treatments. These approaches are derived from clinical staging models commonly used in medicine, and are receiving increasing attention in the psychiatric literature (McGorry et al., 2007; McGorry, Nelson, Goldstone, & Yung., 2010; Tomba, Fabbri, & Fava, 2009). Clinical staging defines the progression of the disorder and the individual's stage within this progression, allowing the selection of interventions best suited to these conditions (Fava & Tomba, 2010; McGorry et al., 2010). Proponents of staging models for depression hypothesize that the needs of patients change over the course of treatment. For example, patients might initially require acute relief of distress, but during the residual phase they would benefit from interventions to improve functioning and prevent relapse (Tomba et al., 2009). In Fava and Ruini's (2002) "sequential model," patients are treated to response with medications, and then switched to a variant of CBT, called well-being therapy (Fava, 1999), as medications are tapered. According to Fava and Ruini (2002), sequential treatment with CBT might (a) alleviate residual symptoms (known to be related to relapse), and (b) provide a prophylactic effect without the need for maintenance medications, eliminating the potential drawbacks of long-term medication use.

Some evidence is emerging to substantiate the clinical applicability of this and similar staging algorithms. Fava, Grandi, Zielezny, Canestrari, and Morphy (1994) found that, after successful antidepressant treatment, individuals randomly assigned to CBT during medication discontinuation had lower residual symptoms at the end of the discontinuation period than individuals assigned to clinical management. They also had lower rates of relapse at 4-year follow-up (35% versus 70%; Fava, Grandi, Zielezny, Rafanelli, & Canestrari, 1996), although these differences had faded after 6 years (50% versus 75%; Fava, Rafanelli, Grandi, Canestrari, & Morphy, 1998). In a similar study of individuals with recurrent depression, a group recieving CBT plus well-being therapy during antidepressant discontinuation evidenced lower relapse rates than a clinical management group at both the 2 year (25% versus 80%; Fava, Rafanelli, Grandi, Conti, & Belluardo, 1998) and 6 year (40% versus 90%; Fava et al., 2004) follow-ups. In another study of staged treatment using MBCT, remitted individuals were randomized to discontinued medications plus MBCT, maintenance medications, or placebo (Segal et al., 2010). The two active conditions were each superior to placebo and equal to one another in preventing relapse in "unstable" remitters (individuals who experienced brief symptom recurrence after remission) over 18 months, but they did not differ from placebo among "stable" remitters.

Staged approaches offer the possibility of a prescribed series of treatments that maximize the benefits of each (e.g., rapid symptom relief for medications, relapse prevention for CBT), while minimizing their potential weaknesses. Currently, though, the literature provides a somewhat limited investigation of possible staging strategies, as only medications have been tested as the first step in the sequence. Fava and Tomba (2010) suggest that state-dependent learning and cognitive deficits might inhibit depressed individuals from benefitting from acute CBT (e.g., Reus, Weingartner, & Post, 1979). Moreover, evidence that medications consistently outperform psychotherapy in producing an acute response, even severe depression, is equivocal (Cuijpers et al., 2008; DeRubeis et al., 2005; Elkin et al., 1989). Current staging models might therefore be based on an incorrect premise: That early stages of depression treatment require pharmacological intervention. One consequence of the limited scope of these investigations is that they provide little information about options for individuals refractory to medication treatment. Nevertheless, staging strategies are the first well-researched treatments for depression that integrate psychotherapy and medications into a coherent treatment model.

Summary and Recommendations

There is little doubt that combined treatments for major depression provide incremental improvements in response over monotherapies, particularly in subgroups such as those with chronic depression. At the same time, there is little reason to offer combined treatment for mild or moderate depression unless individuals do not respond to monotherapy. Concerns about the effectiveness and safety of medications over the long term and possible negative effects of psychotherapy suggest that the best strategy for implementing combined treatments is a non-simultaneous and time-limited approach (e.g., switching, augmentation, or staging). However, more research is needed to determine optimal treatment selection and timing of treatment changes. Particularly needed are studies that assess the efficacy of adding medications to psychotherapy when a course of psychotherapy does not lead to remission, given the somewhat surprising finding from one such study, in which the remission rate was higher for the augmentation strategy relative to a simultaneous combination (Frank et al., 2000). Despite the larger evidence base for medication-first strategies, there is no reason not to conduct research on psychotherapy-first strategies (e.g., Frank et al., 2011). In particular, acute remission on psychotherapy would offer the benefits associated with this treatment without requiring exposure to medication treatment and its associated risks. Finally, moderators of response for combination therapy versus monotherapy, that is, prognostic and prescriptive factors (e.g., Fournier et al., 2009; Frank et al., 2011), have also yet to be identified.

COMBINED TREATMENT OF PSYCHOTIC AND BIPOLAR DISORDERS

Combination treatment of bipolar and psychotic disorders presents a different set of issues. Unlike anxiety and depression, medications are known to be more efficacious than psychotherapy for reducing acute manic or psychotic symptoms. Medications are also the recommended treatment for prevention of relapse and recurrence of these disorders. However, medication monotherapy is often inadequate as an acute and preventive therapy for these disorders, and is often associated with poor compliance and side effects. These

problems have led researchers to explore an expanded role for psychotherapy. Because medications are considered the mainstay therapy, the majority of studies have examined psychotherapy as adjunctive treatment, and controlled trials of psychotherapy-first or staging strategies are therefore rare. The utility of add-on psychotherapy in these disorders depends upon whether the addition of second (or third, fourth, etc.) treatment is worth the additional cost and effort. Often, this appears to be the case, as adding psychotherapy to medication appears to improve acute outcome and provides some protection against relapse and recurrence relative to medications alone. In contrast, there is some emerging evidence that acute medication treatment might be contraindicated in some cases of psychosis, possibly indicating a larger role for psychotherapy as initial treatment. In the following sections we present the evidence regarding the acute and long-term efficacy of combined treatments in these disorders.

SCHIZOPHRENIA

Antipsychotics are recommended for the acute and maintenance treatment of schizophrenia and other psychotic disorders (APA, 2004; NICE, 2009). However, up to 30% of individuals show a poor initial response and an additional 30% of patients continue to experience symptoms (Lehman et al., 2004). In addition, medication side effects can be debilitating, resulting in poor adherence and reduced effectiveness (Lieberman et al., 2005). Schizophrenia spectrum disorders are also heterogeneous in their presentation and clinical course, suggesting that a "one-size-fits-all" treatment strategy is inappropriate (McGorry et al., 2010). A variety of adjunctive psychosocial treatments have been developed to enhance the effectiveness of medications at different phases of treatment, for example, to hasten recovery in acute psychosis, or to relieve chronic medication-resistant symptoms. Other treatments target comorbid problems such as substance use and weight gain. Some researchers have also examined the efficacy of delaying medication therapy, often in conjunction with psychosocial treatment, as an intervention for early episode psychosis.

Several well-established psychosocial treatments for schizophrenia are not readily classified as "psychotherapy" per se, but rather as rehabilitation or skills-training programs. Although a full description of these studies is outside the purview of this chapter, we briefly present some relevant evidence. Because combined treatments for schizophrenia are often delivered in inpatient settings, we broaden our review to incorporate studies that include inpatients.

Cognitive Behavioral Therapy

CBT for schizophrenia was developed to treat persistent, medication-resistant positive psychotic symptoms. Since its initial trials, it has also been examined for its efficacy in treating acute psychosis and in preventing relapse. In CBT models, cognitive and behavioral strategies are used to treat positive and negative symptoms directly. For example, individuals are taught to reappraise the power and source of halucinations (e.g., internal versus external), evaluate the veracity of delusions, or address motivational and other deficits (Gaudiano, 2006; Tarrier, 2010).

Findings from several trials suggest that CBT reduces symptoms of schizophrenia (e.g., Kuipers et al., 1997; Sensky et al. 2000; Tarrier et al., 1998). In one meta-analysis, effect sizes for CBT versus standard care[5] were estimated at $d = 0.40$ for targeted symptoms, $d = 0.37$ for positive symptoms, and $d = 0.38$ for general functioning, suggesting that CBT produces significant small to moderate effects (Wykes, Steel, Everitt, & Tarrier, 2008).[6] On the basis of these findings, CBT is classified as a recommended adjunctive treatment in NICE (2009) and by the Schizophrenia Patient Outcomes Research Team (PORT; Dixon et al., 2010).

The most compelling evidence for CBT effectiveness comes from treatment of chronic positive symptoms of schizophrenia. In a 3-arm, 87-subject trial comparing CBT plus standard care versus supportive therapy plus standard care versus standard care alone, Tarrier et al. (1998) found that CBT was superior to both groups in reducing the number and severity of positive symptoms after 3 months of treatment and at a 12-month follow-up (Tarrier et al., 1999). In

another study, Sensky et al. (2000) randomized 90 individuals with persistent symptoms to either CBT or a befriending intervention (described as empathic and nondirective). At the end of the 9-month treatment, there were no differences between groups, but at an 18-month follow-up, CBT was superior to befriending on schizophrenia symptoms. At a 5-year follow-up, the CBT group maintained superiority to befriending on overall symptoms (Turkington et al., 2008). Other evidence suggests that CBT can be helpful for more specific applications, such as increasing control over command hallucinations (Trower et al., 2004). Findings from a recent trial also suggest that CBT can reduce negative symptoms of schizophrenia in the most severely ill individuals. In a group of 60 low-functioning chronic schizophrenia patients, a type of patient that typically is excluded from CBT trials, Grant, Huh, Perivoliotis, Stolar, and Beck (2011) found that a modified form of CBT was superior to standard care at improving functional outcomes, as well as decreasing the severity of avolition, apathy, and positive symptoms.

Less evidence has accrued in support of CBT for speeding recovery from early (or first episode) psychosis. Lewis et al. (2002) randomized 315 individuals with early episode psychosis to standard care, CBT plus standard care or supportive counseling plus standard care. At Week 4, the CBT group showed a nonsignificant trend toward faster improvement than did the standard care group; however, these differences did not persist to the end of the 5-week treatment. At an 18-month follow-up, both CBT and supportive counseling were superior to standard care in relieving symptoms, but not different from each other (Tarrier et al. 2004). Notably, patients received only 9 hours of the CBT intervention on average, which, as the authors acknowledged, might have been insufficient to promote enduring change. Two studies by Jackson and colleagues conducted in the Early Psychosis Prevention and Intervention Centre (EPPIC) in Melbourne, Australia, also provide mixed evidence of CBT's efficacy. In the first, Cognitively Oriented Psychotherapy for Early Psychosis (COPE) was added to EPPIC's standard rehabilitation services ($N = 91$). This treatment did not improve symptoms or readmissions relative to EPPIC alone (Jackson et al., 2005). A second study examined a befriending intervention versus acute symptom intervention called *Active Cognitive Therapy for Early Psychosis* (ACE; $N =$

---

[5] Unless otherwise noted, all participants in the reviewed studies were treated with antipsychotic medications. Experimental treatments were generally added to "standard care," which at minimum consisted of medication management and regular treatment visits, and in some cases also included case management and other services.

[6] The estimates for the benefit of CBT are more modest when only higher-quality studies are considered (e.g., $d = 0.22$ for targeted symptoms; Wykes et al., 2008).

62). Participants receiving ACE showed a trend toward improvement in negative symptoms and overall functioning relative to befriending early in treatment, but there were no differences between groups at a 1-year follow-up (Jackson et al., 2008).

Two trials adapted CBT treatment for relapse prevention. Gumley et al. (2003) randomized 144 subjects at high risk for relapse to standard care plus 12 weeks of CBT (plus additional CBT if signs of relapse were detected) versus standard care alone. At 12 months, CBT was associated with significantly lower relapse rates (18% versus 35%), and more improvement in symptoms and functioning. In contrast, a more recent study of 128 recently relapsed individuals found similar and suprisingly low rates of remission (< 50%) after 9 months of standard care or standard care plus CBT (Garety et al., 2008). Relapse, defined as a reemergence or a significant worsening of positive symptoms, did not differ by treatment condition at either 12 or 24 months. In light of these conflicting results, further research is needed to determine the efficacy of CBT in reducing schizophrenic relapse.

Despite the broad application of CBT for schizophrenia, the evidence suggests that CBT is most effective for chronic medication resistant symptoms. Improvements in chronic symptoms following CBT also appear to be relatively enduring (Tarrier et al., 1999; Turkington et al., 2008). Currently, CBT does not appear to be more efficacious than supportive treatment for acute symptom relief, and evidence regarding relapse prevention is equivocal. Newer applications of CBT, such as CT for negative symptoms (Grant et al., 2011) and acceptance and commitment therapy in acute schizophrenia (Bach & Hayes, 2002; Gaudiano & Herbert, 2006) have shown promise, and are likely a fruitful area for continued inquiry.

Family Psychoeducation

Family psychoeducation treatments are intended to improve coping, reduce stress within the family, and encourage within-family behaviors that promote recovery (e.g., reduction in conflict and high expressed emotion). Interventions include psychoeducation, consultation, and elements from supportive and cognitive behavioral therapies (McFarlane, Dixon, Lukens, & Lucksted, 2003). More than 50 trials of family psychoeducation have been conducted, generally with relapse prevention as the primary outcome. Efficacy estimates are impressive, with early studies

achieving an estimated reduction in relapse risk of as high as 40% by the end of treatment, although the estimates are lower in comparisons of family treatments verus other adjunctive psychosocial treatments (Bustillo, Lauriello, Horan, & Keith, 2001; Pilling et al., 2002). In a recent Cochrane review, Pharoah, Mari, Rothbone, and Wong (2010) estimated that family interventions reduce the risk of relapse at 12 months (relative risk = 0.55), 18 months (relative risk = 0.64) and 24 months (relative risk = 0.64) relative to all comparison treatments.

Some research indicates that the prophylactic effects of family treatments can extend even longer. For example, one family treatment study found that patients in the treatment group whose families were judged to be high in expressed emotion had significantly lower relapse rates compared to subjects who received psychoeducation or standard care at 5 and 8 years (Tarrier, Barrowclough, Porceddu, & Fitzpatrick, 1994). In another study, Barrowclough et al. (1999) assigned patients and carers to a needs-based program with access to a family support worker, problem solving, behavioral family management, and/or CBT components. At 6 months, members of the control group, who also received a family support worker, were 2.6 times more likely to relapse than those in the treatment group (46% versus 24%). The advantage for the treatment group remained at 12 months (hazard ratio = 2.8; 72% versus 37%; Sellwood et al., 2001), and at 5 years (Sellwood, Wittkowski, Tarrier, & Barrowclough, 2007). Importantly, evidence suggested that the prophylactic benefits of the treatment were sustained across the full course of the 5-year follow-up.

Family interventions have also been found to improve outcomes for caregivers (Cuijpers, 1999; Hazel et al., 2004) and have been successfully implemented in a number of different ethnic groups and nationalities (Pharoah et al., 2010). Some preliminary work suggests that family treatments are also efficacious in preventing relapse in early psychosis (Bird et al., 2010).

However, family treatments do require the willing participation of a caregiver in close contact with the patient, making them inappropriate for some. At least one study has had difficulty recruiting enough families to adequately power a family treatment arm (Garety et al., 2008), and others have enrolled only a small percentage (22%) of potentially eligible families (Schooler et al., 1997). Thus, despite promising outcomes, family treatments have limited clinical utility for individuals whose family members are unable or unwilling to participate in treatment.

Other Psychotherapies

Studies of other adjunctive psychotherapies have produced mixed results. Recent meta-analyses of psychodynamic and supportive therapies for schizophrenia suggest that these treatments do not improve outcome relative to standard care (Buckley & Pettit, 2007; Malmberg, Fenton, & Rathbone, 2010; respectively). Furthermore, Hogarty's personal therapy (Hogarty et al., 1997a), which was designed specifically as an intervention for schizophrenia, produced some positive results with respect to relapse prevention (albeit only among those patients living with their families) and social adjustment (Hogarty et al., 1997b). However, despite these promising findings, no subsequent trials have been conducted to test this intervention.

Treatment for Comorbid Problems

Psychosocial treatments have also been tested for reducing medication side effects or treating comorbid conditions in schizophrenia. For example, psychosocial treatments have proven effective for addressing weight gain and metabolic dysfunction, which are common and potentially serious side effects of second-generation atypical antipsychotics (Falissard et al., 2011). Positive outcomes have been reported for both weight loss and weight gain prevention programs (for a review, see Alvarez-Jimenez, Hetrick, González-Blanch, Gleeson, & McGorry, 2008). In an example of the latter, Evans, Newton, and Higgins (2005) found individuals in a 3-month nutritional psychoeducation program had significantly less weight gain (4.4 pounds) than a TAU group (13.2 pounds). Lower weight relative to TAU was maintained at 6 months (4.4 versus 21.8 pounds).

Psychosocial treatments are also available for comorbid substance use disorders, which occur in 20% to 40% of individuals with schizophrenia (Mueser, Bellack, & Blanchard, 1992). In a small study ($N = 36$), Barrowclough et al. (2001) found that individuals with psychosis and substance use had better global functioning, a lower percentage of days using any substance, and somewhat better symptoms in a 9-month treatment that combined CBT, motivational interviewing, and family

intervention, compared to those in a standard care group. Relapse rates were also significantly lower in the treatment group at 12 months, but this difference was not maintained at 18 months (Haddock et al., 2003). Various other interventions for substance use in schizophrenia appear to produce some benefits in substance use and other relevant domains (for a review, see Dixon et al., 2010).

Psychiatric Rehabilitation and Skills-Training Interventions

In addition to traditional psychotherapies, there is a strong tradition of multidisciplinary rehabilitation programs in the psychiatric literature, many of which include psychosocial interventions. These programs are intended to promote rehabilitation or address various deficits common in psychotic disorders (e.g., work functioning, social skills). Although these efforts do not always include psychotherapy, per se, they are firmly rooted in the biopsychosocial model, and thus deserve consideration. Examples include intensive case management and community support. Reviews indicate that these services are effective for increasing contact with service providers and reducing rehospitalizations and homelessness (Coldwell & Bender, 2007; Nelson, Aubry, & Lafrance, 2007). Other efforts emphasize behavior management or teach skills needed for good functioning. Interventions such as token economies (Dickerson, Tenhula, & Green-Paden, 2005), supported employment (Bond, Drake, & Becker, 2008), social skills training (Kurtz & Mueser, 2008), social cognitive training (Kurtz & Richardson, 2011), cognitive remediation (Wykes, Huddy, Cellard, McGurk, & Czobor, 2011), metacognitive training (Moritz, Vitzthum, Randjbar, Veckenstedt, & Woodward, 2010), and social rehabilitation (Horan, Kern, Green, & Penn, 2008) have each shown beneficial effects in improving important skills or in reducing the targeted deficits.

In general, research suggests that skills based approaches are promising methods of improving deficits, but similar to other psychosocial interventions for schizophrenia, more research is needed to determine their durability and their generalization to wider domains of functioning. Those interested in learning more about the various other rehabilitation approaches are directed to reviews by Kurzban, Davis, and Brekke (2010) and Dieterich, Irving, Park, and Marshall (2010).

A Role for Psychosocial Treatment Alone?

As noted previously, there is a large body of evidence supporting the efficacy of antipsychotic medications in reducing acute positive symptoms of schizophrenia, especially in first-episode psychosis (Kahn et al., 2008). However, long-term maintenance of individuals on these medications can be problematic. Toxicities associated with first generation antipsychostics (tardive dyskinesia, akathesia, drowsiness; Bhattacharjee & El-Sayeh, 2008; Bola, Kao, & Soydan, 2012; Wirshing, 2001) and second generation atypical antipsychotics (diabetes, weight gain, metabolic syndrome; Asenjo Lobos et al., 2010; Gautam & Meena, 2011; Haddad, 2004) can be severe, and noncompliance with medications is common (Lieberman et al., 2005). Treatment with antipsychotics, especially clozapine, has been associated with rapid and severe relapse on medication discontinuation, suggesting that these medications have iatrogenic effects (for a review see Moncrieff, 2006). Although treatment guidelines recommend the immediate initiation of antipsychotic medication for nearly all individuals showing signs of psychosis (American Psychiatric Association, 2004b; NICE, 2010), there is evidence that a subgroup of individuals can recover without them. Indeed, the placebo response rate in controlled trials has been 25% or higher (Kemp et al., 2010; Kinon, Potts, & Watson, 2011). Evidence also suggests that some individuals can obtain stable functional recovery or prolonged periods of remission from schizophrenia without continued medication maintenance (Harrow & Jobe, 2007). These findings suggest that neuroleptics might not be the best intervention for all individuals in the early stages of psychotic illness (Francey et al., 2010).

Despite the prospect of medication free recovery, withholding medications is controversial in part because longer periods of untreated psychosis have been associated with a worse course of illness (Bottlender et al., 2003; Harrison et al., 2001). Nevertheless, a handful of studies have investigated the efficacy of intensive psychosocial interventions in combination with delayed medication. In these approaches, medications are postponed for a prescribed period and initiated only in the case of nonresponse or symptom worsening. Although these studies are of varying quality, their results are promising. A preliminary meta-analysis of studies with placebo or other medication free arms

found no evidence of long-term harm in comparison to groups receiving medications (Bola, 2006). In a review of medication delay studies, Bola, Lehtinen, Cullberg, and Ciompi (2009) described the outcomes of five experimental or quasi-experimental programs that provided active psychosocial treatment in combination with medication delay: the Agnews State Hospital Project (Rappaport, Hopkins, Hall, Belleza, & Silverman, 1978), the Soteria project in San Francisco (Mosher & Menn, 1978), the Soteria-Berne project (Ciompi et al., 1992), the Needs-Adapted Project in Finland (Lehtinen, Aaltonen, Koffert, Räkköläinen, & Syvälahti, 2000), and the Parachute Project in Sweden (Cullberg, Levander, Holmqvist, Mattsson, & Wieselgren, 2002). In the experimental conditions, 27% to 61% of treatment completers received no antipsychotic medications. The analysis revealed a small *advantage* for the experimental treatments in comparison to treatment as usual (composite advantage, weighted by sample size = 17%). At 2- to 3-year follow-up, 27% to 43% of individuals in the experimental groups were not receiving medications.

Other evidence supporting the effectiveness of psychotherapeutic treatment has emerged from a recent trial of cognitive therapy for individuals with schizophrenia who refused or discontinued medications. In a 9-month open trial ($N = 20$), Morrison et al. (2011) found CT to have significant medium to large uncontrolled effect sizes on all outcome measures, and response rates of 35% and 50% after acute treatment and 15 months of follow-up, respectively. A full-scale controlled trial is currently underway. In light of these preliminary findings, it seems likely that for some individuals with psychotic disorders, intensive psychosocial treatment alone is equally as effective as, or superior to, standard medication treatment.

Based in part on the evidence for medication delay approaches, some clinical researchers have called for the development of clinical staging approaches in psychotic disorders (McGorry et al., 2007; McGorry, et al., 2010). As in depression (Tomba et al., 2009), clinical staging approaches offer treatments tailored to the stage of the disorder as well as the individual's progression within the course of illness. In McGorry and colleagues' model, earlier, less severe stages are treated with simpler and more benign treatments, whereas later stages are treated more aggressively. Because the future course of psychosis cannot be known at onset (i.e., some patients will become chronically ill, others will recover), clinical staging treatments begin with milder psychosocial interventions, and step up the level of care in the case of worsening or nonresponse. In other words, clinical staging approaches reduce the chance of "overtreating" conditions that are benign but phenotypically similar to more severe pathologies. Some preliminary evidence on staging approaches suggests that programs using CBT alone (Morrison et al., 2004) or in conjunction with low dose antipsychotics (McGorry et al., 2002) can prevent so-called ultra-high risk individuals from transitioning to full-blown psychosis. Viewed in this way, a medication delay approach is a two-phase staging treatment.

At present, these approaches lack well-controlled clinical data to support them. However, a large controlled trial of a staging treatment with a medication-free arm is curently underway at the EPPIC program in Melbourne, Australia (Francey et al., 2010). It is hoped that this trial will provide much needed data on the efficacy of medication free treatment, including prognostic and prescriptive factors that might predict medication free response.

Summary and Recommendations

Overall, adjunctive psychosocial treatments appear to improve symptomatic and functional outcomes in individuals with schizophrenia spectrum disorders, and we recommend their use. Each of the available psychosocial treatments has specific strengths, however, and clinicians are advised to select treatments carefully based on these characteristics. CBT is best suited for treating chronic positive symptoms (and perhaps chronic negative symptoms, Grant et al., 2012), but its effect on relapse or recurrence is equivocal. Individuals judged to be at risk for relapses are likely to benefit from family psychoeducation, but only if they have close caregivers who are willing to participate in treatment. There are also several treatment options for individuals suffering from comorbid conditions.

Unfortunately, evidence for moderators of response to combined treatments is lacking. One exception is Hogarty et al. (1997a), who found that individuals in personal therapy living with their families had lower relapse rates compared to psychological treatment controls, whereas those living alone had higher relapse rates than controls. Because little is known

about who will benefit from which treatments in schizophrenia, including those who might benefit from less intensive treatments during the early course of the illness, future trials should include planned analyses of theory-specific mediators and moderators.

BIPOLAR DISORDER

The recommended treatments for bipolar depression and mania for initial and long-term therapy are mood stabilizers or anticonvulsants (APA, 2002; NICE, 2006). However, remission during medication monotherapy is not common, with only about one in four patients achieving symptomatic or functional recovery after 1 year of treatment (Keck et al., 1998). Medication responders often require complex medication regimens to achieve sustained response (Post et al., 2010). Relapse rates are also high, reaching and exceeding 70% after 4 to 5 years (Gitlin, Swendsen, Heller, & Hammen, 1995; Tohen, Waternaux, & Tsuang, 1990). In addition, adherence to medication treatment has often been poor, with up to 75% of individuals discontinuing or otherwise interrupting treatment (Keck et al., 1996; Unützer, Simon, Pabiniak, Bond, & Katon, 2000).

Psychotherapy has been studied as an adjunctive treatment for bipolar depression and mania (Frank et al., 2005; Miklowitz et al., 2007; Scott et al., 2006), and for preventing relapse (Colom et al., 2003; Lam et al., 2003; Miklowitz et al., 2000). The psychotherapy interventions with the most empirical support are CBT (e.g., Lam et al., 2003), Family Focused Therapy (FFT; Miklowitz & Goldstein, 1997), Interpersonal and Social Rhythm Therapy (IPSRT; Frank et al., 1994), and psychoeducation (e.g., Colom et al., 2003). Although each contains unique elements, several interventions are common across these treatments. All target known risk factors for relapse, such as poor medication adherence (Otto, Reilly-Harrington, & Sachs, 2003), and environmental triggers such as sleep-wake cycle disruptions and stressful life events (Johnson et al., 2000; Johnson & Roberts, 1995). They also promote self-monitoring as a means of normalizing routines and recognizing signs of relapse (Lam, Burbeck, Wright, & Pilling, 2009). Promising findings have been obtained in tests of these therapeutic models. In a large trial, CBT, IPSRT, and FFT combined with medications were associated with significantly higher rates of recovery over 1 year than medications combined with collaborative care (Miklowitz et al., 2007). With regard to relapse prevention, Scott, Colom, and Vieta (2007) estimated that adjunctive psychotherapy decreases relapse rates by 40% relative to pharmacotherapy alone.

Cognitive-Behavioral Therapy

Although CBT is the best-studied of these adjunctive therapies, trials of CBT as an initial treatment for bipolar disorder have produced mixed findings. A recent 5-month trial of CBT combined with medications in patients with treatment refractory bipolar disorder showed that CBT was of modest benefit, with a lower frequency of hospitalizations at a 12-month follow-up, as well as lower levels of depressive, manic, and anxiety symptomatology compared to medications alone at 6 and 12 months (Isasi, Echeburúa, Limiñana, & González-Pinto, 2010). In contrast, an earlier large-scale trial produced very different results. In that study, Scott et al. (2006) assigned 253 patients with severe and recurrent bipolar disorder (32% in active episode) to CBT plus TAU or TAU. Rates of relapse did not differ between the groups at any point during treatment or over follow-up (18 months). The authors did find an interaction between treatment and number of previous episodes, such that CBT was superior for individuals with 12 or fewer, perhaps suggesting that CBT is more efficacious for those with less chronic forms of bipolar disorder. Lam (2006) argued that, despite its large sample and good methodological controls, this trial is not indicative of CBT's efficacy in preventing relapse, because the inclusion of acutely ill patients might have interfered with treatment delivery.

Other trials have focused on CBT for relapse prevention in individuals whose symptoms have stabilized. Scott, Garland, and Moorehead (2001) found that CBT led to improved symptoms and functioning compared to a wait-list control, and resulted in a decrease in relapse rates of 60% relative to relapse rates prior to the trial. Lam et al. (2003) also found that a 6-month CBT treatment reduced relapse rates, and that this benefit extended to a 12-month follow-up (44% in CBT versus 75% in TAU). By the 30th month, the CBT group still showed significantly lower bipolar affective relapses (64% versus 84%), however, most of this benefit was seen during the first 12 months (Lam, Hayward, Watkins, Wright, & Sham, 2005). A similar finding emerged from Ball et al. (2006), who randomized 52 patients

to 6 months of CBT plus TAU versus TAU. At the end of treatment, patients in the CBT group had, on average, lower scores on measures of depression and dysfunctional attitudes, and a trend toward lower relapse rates (CBT: 20%, TAU: 33%) was also observed. However, this difference had faded by the 18-month follow-up. Findings from these trials suggest that the efficacy of CBT in preventing bipolar relapse might not be robust over longer periods (Szentagotai & David, 2010). Thus, further research is required to determine the conditions under which CBT interventions are most effective.

Family Therapy

Family treatments enlist patients' relatives in relapse prevention by targeting risk factors such as lack of social support or high levels of familial expressed emotion (Miklowitz & Goldstein, 1997). Like family treatments in schizophrenia, family therapies for bipolar disorder require the involvement of a close caregiver. In the treatment of acute bipolar symptoms, two studies provide evidence for the efficacy of family therapies. The first is the NIMH's Systematic Treatment Enhancement Program for Bipolar Disorder (STEP-BD) trial, in which Family Focused Therapy (FFT) was numerically (but not significantly) superior at one year to the other psychosocial treatments in individuals whose family members agreed to participate (recovery rates, FFT: 77%, IPSRT: 57%, CBT: 59% and collaborative care: 58%; Miklowitz et al., 2007). In the second study, Miller, Solomon, Ryan, and Keitner (2004) randomized 92 actively depressed or manic patients to TAU in combination with individual family therapy (one patient and family members), multifamily group psychotherapy (a group of patients and family members), or TAU. The authors found no differences between any of these groups on rates of recovery at 28 months. However, a follow-up analysis showed that only 5% of patients undergoing multifamily group therapy required hospitalization compared to 31% in individual family patient and 38% in TAU, suggesting that group family treatment might protect against hospitalization (Solomon, Keitner, Ryan, Kelley, & Miller, 2008).

Findings from other randomized studies suggest that FFT confers protection against bipolar relapse. In one study, Rea et al. (2003) randomized 53 patients to 9 months of FFT or individually focused patient treatment (described as supportive, problem-focused, and educational). Over the

2-year study period, there were no differences between groups on time to first relapse. However, a secondary analysis revealed that patients receiving FFT were less likely to relapse over the 1-year follow-up (28% versus 60%)—but not during the acute period—and that they had fewer relapses overall. In the other study, Miklowitz, George, Richards, and Simoneau (2003) randomized 101 patients to 9 months of either clinical management or clinical management plus FFT. They found that patients receiving FFT were less likely to relapse by the end of 24 months (35% versus 54%), and had longer mean relapse-free intervals (74 weeks versus 53 weeks). A difference in depressive symptoms favoring FFT was also found, but this difference emerged only after 6 months of treatment. The delay in relapse protection in Rea et al. (2003) and symptom improvement in Miklowitz et al. (2003) led Miklowitz and Otto (2007) to suggest that time is needed for patients and families to "absorb" the skills central to family treatments.

Interpersonal Social Rhythm Therapy

Interpersonal Social Rhythm Therapy (IPSRT) is based on Interpersonal Therapy (IPT) for depression (Klerman, Weissman, Rounsaville, & Chevron, 1984). In addition to IPT principles such as the identification of interpersonal problem areas, the treatment focuses on correcting disruptions in social and circadian rhythms that can lead to bipolar relapse (Frank et al., 1994).

IPSRT has been examined in two large-scale bipolar trials: the STEP-BD trial, the acute findings from which are reported above, and the University of Pittsburgh Maintenance Therapies in Bipolar Disorder trial. In the latter, Frank et al. (1999) randomized 82 patients in an acute affective episode to medication management plus IPSRT or intensive clinical management (CM). After an acute stabilization phase, patients were reassigned either to remain in the same psychosocial treatment or to switch to the other treatment over a 2-year relapse prevention phase. This created four treatment groups: CM/CM, CM/IPSRT, IPSRT/IPSRT, and IPSRT/CM. There were no differences over the first 52 weeks between the groups; however, relapse rates were significantly higher for those who switched treatments (41%) relative to those who remained in the same treatment (18%). The authors interpreted this result as evidence that stable treatment routines are important for preventing bipolar relapse. Notably, although no differences

emerged on rates of relapse, monthly symptom scores were worse in the group that had lost IPSRT, relative to the groups that gained IPSRT, stayed in IPSRT, or never had IPSRT at all. At 2 years, Frank et al. (2005) found that patients treated acutely with IPSRT had longer time to recurrence than those treated acutely with CM. Additional analyses indicated that acute IPSRT was associated with improved social rhythms, and that improved social rhythms were associated with a lower probability of recurrence across conditions, supporting the idea that IPSRT protects against recurrence by stabilizing interpersonal and circadian rhythms.

Psychoeducation

Psychoeducational treatments for bipolar disorder focus on improving medication adherence, stabilizing chaotic lifestyles, and promoting the early detection of prodromal symptoms (e.g., Colom et al., 2003; Perry, Tarrier, Morriss, McCarthy & Limb, 1999). In the first major randomized trial of psychoeducation for bipolar disorder, 7 to 12 sessions of psychoeducation plus TAU or TAU alone were provided to 69 individuals (Perry et al., 1999). Over an 18-month follow-up, the psychoeducation group had a longer time to manic relapse and a 30% lower rate of manic relapse than the TAU group. Other psychoeducational treatments have been provided in a group therapy format. Colom et al. (2003) randomized 120 euthymic bipolar individuals to medications plus a 20-week group psychoeducational treatment or an unstructured support group. Patients in the psychoeducation condition recurred at a lower rate during acute treatment (38% versus 60%) as well as during the 2-year follow-up (67% versus 92%). The treatment also extended time to recurrence for depressive, manic, and mixed episodes, and reduced the number and duration of hospitalizations, relative to the unstructured group. At a 5-year follow-up, the psychoeducation group continued to have fewer recurrences and a longer average time to recurrence for all episode types. Treatment had no effect on medication adherence. The durability of this treatment is particularly impressive considering that the prophylactic effects of other psychotherapies appear to fade over time (e.g., Lam et al., 2005; Ball et al., 2006). Indeed, Colom et al. (2003) found that the size of the prophylactic effect *increased* between 2 and 5 years. These results have yet to be replicated, but suggest that a group psychoeducational format might be a powerful intervention for prevention of relapse.

Other group psychoeducation treatments enlist patients' family members or close companions in relapse prevention. Reinares et al. (2008) compared a 12-session group intervention for caregivers of individuals with bipolar disorder to a group control treatment (N = 113). Patients did not attend the group meeting in either condition. The psychoeducation group was associated with a lower relapse rate (42% versus 66%), and a longer time to relapse over a 12-month follow-up, although this effect was primarily confined to manic episodes. Other group formats, including one in which a close companion of each patient is included in the group, have also shown positive effects for relapse prevention (D'souza, Piskulic, & Sundra, 2010).

Overall, group treatments have been shown to be effective in the prevention of relapse in bipolar disorder. Outside of Colom and colleagues' studies, the prevention effect has been evident primarily in regard to manic episodes. Because of the potential for these programs to improve outcomes to a larger number of individuals at a relatively low cost, group treatments are worthy of greater research attention.

A Role for Psychosocial Treatment Alone?

As is the case with schizophrenia, medication treatment outcomes for bipolar disorder remain relatively poor overall (Post et al., 2010). Even with high adherence to medication treatment regimes, individuals experience frequent depressive, manic, and mixed episodes, and residual symptoms between episodes are common (Judd, Akiskal, et al., 2003; Judd, Schettler, et al., 2003). It is also uncertain whether medication maintenance is superior to placebo in preventing relapse (Bowden et al., 2000). Considering that delayed or low dose medication in combination with appropriate psychosocial management can be successful in early psychosis (Bola, 2009), the potential role for reduced medication use in some cases of bipolar illness is worthy of study. The reviewed trials provide some suggestive results. One of the mechanisms through which psychosocial interventions are hypothesized to prevent relapse is by improving medication adherence. Surprisingly, several trials demonstrating positive prophylactic effects found no differences in adherence between treatment and control

conditions (Colom et al., 2009; Frank et al., 2005; Rea et al., 2003; Reinares et al., 2008). In another trial, differences in adherence were obtained, but they did not account for the benefits conferred by psychotherapy (Lam et al., 2005). Of all reviewed trials, only in Milkowitz et al. (2003) was a reduction in mania fully mediated by better medication adherence in the experimental condition.

Despite the widely held belief that mania is a "biological" mood state, placebo response rates in mania range from 11% to 43% (Charney et al., 2002) and psychosocial treatments also appear to prevent and shorten time in manic episodes (Colom et al., 2009; Perry et al., 1999; Reinares et al., 2008). These findings suggest that there might be a larger role for psychotherapeutic treatments in bipolar disorder, especially for individuals who cannot tolerate prolonged medication maintenance. Treatment might begin with stabilization on medication, followed by careful withdrawal of medications while the patient undergoes an intensive relapse prevention treatment, similar to clinical staging treatments in depression (Tomba et al., 2009). If manic relapse occurs, medications can be reintroduced as needed. Alternate possibilities include medication delay and intensive inpatient management for early episodes of mania, similar to the medication delay models for early psychosis (Bola et al., 2009; Francey et al., 2010). Such programs, if successful, could improve long-term outcomes for some individuals.

Summary and Recommendations

On the whole, empirically supported adjunctive psychotherapy is recommended in treatment of bipolar disorder. Current evidence suggests that CBT and IPSRT provide acute benefits, with some research suggesting longer-lasting effects. Perhaps the most promising treatments are family therapies and group psychoeducation, each of which has been shown to reduce acute symptoms and protect against relapse. Family interventions might be especially helpful for individuals who are unable to recognize the signs of an impending relapse. Indeed, it appears that patients do not have to participate in these treatments for them to be effective in preventing relapse (Reinares et al., 2008). Preliminary research on group psychoeducation has also yielded impressive long-term results (Colom et al., 2009). As with the other reviewed disorders, there is little research on predictors of treatment response in combination treatments of bipolar disorder. Some evidence suggests that patients who are acutely ill or those with more chronic illnesses might benefit less from adjunctive psychotherapy (Solomon et al., 2008; Scott et al., 2006), but these findings are not consistent (Frank et al., 2005; Lam et al., 2009). Further research is needed to identify the conditions under which combined treatments are most effective. Also, the overlap in the interventions between these treatments (Lam et al., 2009) makes it difficult to determine whether common or specific treatment elements are related to efficacy. Randomized head-to-head trials such as STEP-BD can be useful to determine moderators of treatment response, and we encourage researchers to look into these questions.

Finally, current models of treatment in bipolar are highly constrained, with only multiple combinations of medications and adjunctive psychotherapy available as alternatives in the case of nonresponse. This approach is inappropriate for a disorder that is increasingly recognized as heterogeneous (e.g., Angst, Gerber-Werder, Zuberbühler, & Gamma, 2004). We encourage the development and testing of alternative strategies that do not rely solely on indefinite medication use.

CONCLUSION

A central concept in any discussion of mental health treatment is the heterogeneity of psychiatric disorders. Recognition of heterogeneity, particularly in regard to therapeutic response, has contributed directly to the increase in research on combined treatments. These treatments are often considered a means to "correct" for diverse responses. As we have argued, however, a nonstrategic use of combined treatments often trades rather small average advantages in short-term response against effective longer-term management for specific individuals, while also increasing risks and costs. In light of these concerns, we have encouraged clinicians to think carefully about how to combine psychotherapy and medications to meet various patient needs. Recently, evidence has emerged to support a number of strategic approaches for combining therapies. Sequenced approaches, in which additional treatment is provided only when it is necessary or when it is known to improve longer-term outcomes (e.g., Rodrigues et al., 2011; Tomba et al., 2009), are likely associated with improved risk/benefit ratios over simultaneously combined therapies. Taken a

step further, theory-derived clinical staging protocols presume that treatment needs correspond to the clinical progression of the disorder, and thus promote the use of less intensive treatments at earlier or less severe stages (McGorry, 2010). A flexible, long-sighted approach to treatment using these or other treatment algorithms is better suited for treatment of heterogeneous disorders than are fixed, one-size-fits-all methods.

We acknowledge that some of our recommendations run counter to beliefs that are commonly held by clinicians and clinical scientists. For example, we argue that a potential delay in short-term response, as can occur in a sequenced or staged treatment, might be superior to an accelerated response produced by a simultaneous combination treatment (as in Manber et al., 2008). Although rapid relief of distress is appreciated by patients and clinicians, there is currently little evidence that rapid symptom relief is associated with improved longer-term outcomes. Indeed, emerging evidence indicates that, in some contexts, rapid early improvement in depression can be associated with increased risk of relapse (Forand & DeRubeis, under review). Thus, a prolonged period of recovery might be beneficial for longer-term stability in some individuals.

We also argue that possible complications arising from long-term medication management indicates that the use of these approaches might best be minimized. This argument is contrary to the recommendations of some practice guidelines and the clinical impressions of many. However, there is reason to believe that the design of clinical trials and typical clinical practices might lead to biased estimates of the safety and effectiveness of medications. For example, there is evidence that the probability of relapse is elevated over baseline rates when medications are discontinued (Baldessarini et al., 1999; Frank et al., 2011; Moncrieff, 2006). However, evidence supporting the use of long-term maintenance medication is based on comparisons between groups that continue medications versus groups that discontinue, sometimes abruptly, which invariably produce large effects in favor of the medications. The natural conclusion is that the likelihood of sustained recovery is maximized by aggressive, long-term medication use. This biased understanding of medication effects has likely fostered the prolonged use of maintenance medications in clinical practice (Petty et al., 2006; Piek et al., 2010) despite the questionable effectiveness of this practice (Bockting et al., 2008). We believe it is essential for clinicians to challenge their conceptions about treatment based on a careful (re)reading of the available evidence. Conceptualizing the goal of treatment as long-term recovery, as opposed to rapid symptom reduction and tenuous stability, might prove helpful in this endeavor.

New Trial Designs

Although sequenced and staging approaches represent advances over simple and inflexible treatment models, the literature supporting their use has limitations that must be addressed before definitive recommendations can be made. One concern is that sequencing trials often provide evidence for only one possible treatment algorithm even though other procedures might be equal or superior. In clinical staging, the research is limited by incomplete knowledge about disease progression, as well as by unreliable and insensitive diagnostic instruments. For example, although some have called for interventions at the prodromal stage of bipolar and depressive disorders (Berk et al., 2010; Fava & Tossani, 2007), efforts to identify sensitive and specific markers of progression from prodromes to full-blown disorders have produced equivocal results (e.g., Fava & Tossani, 2007; Howes et al., 2011). Thus, the development of valid sequencing or staging treatments presents a number of new challenges.

Recent advances in trial design and analysis might help address some of these problems (Collins, Murphy, & Strecher, 2007). One promising design is "sequential multiple assignment randomized trials" or SMART. SMART designs are used to develop "adaptive" sequenced treatments, in which treatment dose and type are adjusted repeatedly based on time-varying information such as treatment response (Collins, Murphy, & Bierman, 2004; Murphy, 2005). The goal of SMART is to develop a series of decision rules that optimizes overall outcome. These trials comprise multiple treatment phases, with randomization to various next-step treatments at each phase. Posttrial analyses determine the most efficacious treatment path as well as predictors of response to initial and subsequent treatment steps. Replication and refinement of decision rules occurs in subsequent trials (Murphy, 2005). SMART designs are well-suited to analyzing difficult-to-treat disorders because they can identify effective sequences of treatments

for individuals with particular prognostic or prescriptive features, including up-to-the-moment information about treatment adherence and response (e.g., Brooner et al., 2007; Marlowe, Festinger, Dugosh, Lee, & Benasutti, 2007).

Despite the promise of these designs, recent examples of SMART trials such as the STAR*D trial in depression (Rush et al., 2004), and the Clinical AntipsychoticTrials of Intervention Effectiveness (CATIE) for schizophrenia (Stroup et al., 2003) have produced somewhat disappointing results (Lieberman et al., 2005; Rush et al., 2006). Why promote these designs when two influential SMART trials have failed to improve overall outcomes? For one, more efficacious treatment algorithms might be identified if a greater variety of possible interventions are studied. These trials relied heavily (or in CATIE, completely) on sequences of pharmacological agents, all of which have similar mechanisms of action. In one sense, poor outcomes are not surprising, because non-responders to one drug are not likely to respond to another similar drug. Some evidence suggests that psychotherapy and medication work via different neurological pathways (Etkin, Pittenger, Polan, & Kandel, 2005; Linden, 2008; Roffman, Marci, Glick, Dougherty, & Rauch, 2005), perhaps indicating that response to one is poorly predicted by response to the other. Combining these approaches in a SMART design, in sequence or combination, allows a test of the relative strengths and weaknesses of medications and psychotherapy for different stages of treatment. Other treatment-enhancement methods, such as progress monitoring and practitioner feedback systems (e.g., Finch, Lambert, & Schaalje, 2001), have also been shown to improve outcomes in comparison to usual treatment (Shimokawa, Lambert, & Smart, 2010). Methods such as these could be integrated into combination treatment algorithms as a means of identifying those who might require a switch or adjunctive treatment, or redoubled efforts in their current treatment. Even though these approaches are time and resource intensive, they represent our best current option for optimizing and individualizing our treatments, and we encourage future investigators to consider them.

Maximizing the Potential of Psychotherapy

Throughout this chapter we have argued that the evidence supports a prominent role for evidence-based psychotherapy, either alone or in combination with medications. Although most studies of stepped treatments assume a medication-first approach (e.g., Fava & Ruini, 2006; Rodrigues et al., 2011), psychotherapy is an appropriate and advantageous first-phase treatment for many conditions. Nevertheless, the use of psychotherapy decreased in the United States from 16% in 1998 to 11% in 2007, while use of medications alone increased from 44% to 57%. Combined treatment with medications and psychotherapy has also decreased (Olfson & Marcus, 2010).

Several factors contribute to these trends. First, efforts of pharmaceutical companies to promote and market their products directly to the public have been extremely successful at increasing awareness and acceptance of medication treatments (An, Jin, & Brown, 2009; Bell, Taylor, & Kravitz, 2010; Wilkes, Bell, & Kravitz, 2000). Other factors include large differences in accessibility and availability between medication and psychotherapy (Hoge et al., 2007; Mark, Levitt, Buck, Coffey, & Vandivort-Warren, 2007), and limitations on coverage of psychotherapy by third-party payers (Teich & Buck, 2007). Still other factors, such as financial disincentives for psychiatrists to provide therapy (because medication management sessions are reimbursed at a higher pay per unit time), or cultural factors such as a wish for a "quick fix" might also contribute to this decline.

Clearly, improving access to psychotherapy in the United States would require extensive changes in culture, dissemination, and regulation. One model for such changes might be found in the United Kingdom's "improving access to psychological therapies" (IAPT) program, which is a national dissemination and training effort designed to increase access to government-mandated psychological services. As of 2011, IAPT has trained more than 3,600 CBT providers, and initial findings from evaluation studies of IAPT are encouraging (Clark, 2011). However, until such efforts achieve widespread support in the United States, the most feasible stepped treatments will be medication-first strategies, with psychotherapy used as an add-on, switch, or staged treatment when available. Insofar as short-term medication use is safe and efficacious for most individuals (Melnik, Soares, Puga, & Atallah, 2010; Papakostas, 2010; Vieta et al., 2010), these strategies are appropriate. However, we reiterate that long-term care must

be considered carefully. Clinicians should develop plans for both inadequate response and maintenance treatment, and these should include options for decreasing or discontinuing medications, especially if psychosocial treatment is also available. We recommend that medications be used in ways that emphasize their relative strengths (i.e., short term symptom relief), and minimize their relative weaknesses (the costs, financial and otherwise, of long-term maintenance).

Other Disorders

Our review has been limited to outpatient treatment of anxiety, mood, and psychotic disorders; however, there is little doubt that other psychiatric conditions would benefit from strategic thinking about combining medication and psychotherapy. Of particular importance are conditions that can be treated efficaciously with either medications or psychotherapy, such as substance use disorders (McHugh, Hearon, & Otto, 2010; Ross & Peselow, 2009). Childhood disorders also deserve careful attention. Recent high-profile research has highlighted the short-term efficacy of combined psychotherapy and medication for depression and anxiety in children (March et al., 2004; Walkup et al., 2008). However, because of the largely unknown effect of long-term treatment in children, concerns about increased risk of combination treatments are amplified, and more research in this area is urgently needed. As above, we encourage the development of strategic, adaptive treatment strategies for children designed to maximize long-term outcome while minimizing risk.

References

Albert, U., & Brunatto, C. (2009). Obsessive-compulsive disorder in adults: Efficacy of combined and sequential treatments. *Clinical Neuropsychiatry: Journal of Treatment Evaluation*, *6*(2), 6, 83–93.

Alvarez-Jiménez, M., Hetrick, S. E., González-Blanch, C., Gleeson, J. F., & McGorry, P. D. (2008). Non-pharmacological management of antipsychotic-induced weight gain: Systematic review and meta-analysis of randomised controlled trials. *British Journal of Psychiatry: Journal of Mental Science*, *193*(2), 101–107. doi: 10.1192/bjp.bp.107.042853

American Psychiatric Association. (2002). *Practice guidelines for the treatment of patients with bipolar disorder* (2nd ed.). Washington, DC: Author. Available at http://psychiatryonline.org/guidelines.aspx

American Psychiatric Association. (2004a). Practice guideline for the treatment of patients with acute stress disorder and posttraumatic stress disorder. Washington, DC: Author. Available at http://psychiatryonline.org/guidelines.aspx

American Psychiatric Association. (2004b). Practice guidelines for the treatment of patients with schizophrenia (2nd ed.). Washington, DC: Author. Available at http://psychiatryonline.org/guidelines.aspx

Amsterdam, J. D., & Shultz, J. (2005). MAOI efficacy and safety in advanced stage treatment-resistant depression—A retrospective study. *Journal of Affective Disorders, 89*(1–3), 183–188. doi: 10.1016/j.jad.2005.06.011

Amsterdam, J. D., Williams, D., Michelson, D., Adler, L. A., Dunner, D. L., Nierenberg, A. A., . . . Schatzberg, A. F. (2009). Tachyphylaxis after repeated antidepressant drug exposure in patients with recurrent major depressive disorder. *Neuropsychobiology, 59*(4), 227–233. doi: 10.1159/000226611

An, S., Jin, H. S., & Brown, J. D. (2009). Direct-to-consumer antidepressant ads and young adults' beliefs about depression. *Health Marketing Quarterly, 26*(4), 259–278. doi: 10.1080/07359680903303981

Angst, J., Gerber-Werder, R., Zuberbühler, H.-U., & Gamma, A. (2004). Is bipolar I disorder heterogeneous? *European Archives of Psychiatry and Clinical Neuroscience, 254*(2), 82–91. doi: 10.1007/s00406-004-0501-6

Asenjo Lobos, C., Komossa, K., Rummel-Kluge, C., Hunger, H., Schmid, F., Schwarz, S., & Leucht, S. (2010). Clozapine versus other atypical antipsychotics for schizophrenia. *Cochrane Database of Systematic Reviews (Online),* (11), CD006633. doi: 10.1002/14651858.CD006633.pub2

Bach, P., & Hayes, S. C. (2002). The use of acceptance and commitment therapy to prevent the rehospitalization of psychotic patients: A randomized controlled trial. *Journal of Consulting and Clinical Psychology, 70*(5), 1129–1139.

Baetz, M., & Bowen, R. C. (1998). Efficacy of divalproex sodium in patients with panic disorder and mood instability who have not responded to conventional therapy. *Canadian Journal of Psychiatry. Revue Canadienne De Psychiatrie, 43*(1), 73–77.

Baldessarini, R. J., Tondo, L., & Viguera, A. C. (1999). Discontinuing lithium maintenance treatment in bipolar disorders: Risks and implications. *Bipolar Disorders, 1*(1), 17–24.

Ball, J. R., Mitchell, P. B., Corry, J. C., Skillecorn, A., Smith, M., & Malhi, G. S. (2006). A randomized controlled trial of cognitive therapy for bipolar disorder: Focus on long-term change. *Journal of Clinical Psychiatry, 67*(2), 277–286.

Barlow, D. H. (2001). *Anxiety and its disorders* (2nd ed.). New York, NY: Guilford Press.

Barlow, D. H., Gorman, J. M., Shear, M. K., & Woods, S. W. (2000). Cognitive-behavioral therapy, imipramine, or their combination for panic disorder: A randomized controlled trial. *JAMA: The Journal of the American Medical Association, 283*(19), 2529–2536.

Barrowclough, C., Haddock, G., Tarrier, N., Lewis, S. W., Moring, J., O'Brien, R., . . . McGovern, J. (2001). Randomized controlled trial of motivational interviewing, cognitive behavior therapy, and family intervention for patients with comorbid schizophrenia and substance use disorders. *American Journal of Psychiatry, 158*(10), 1706–1713.

Barrowclough, C, Tarrier, N., Lewis, S., Sellwood, W., Mainwaring, J., Quinn, J., & Hamlin, C. (1999). Randomised controlled effectiveness trial of a needs-based psychosocial intervention service for carers of people with schizophrenia. *British Journal of Psychiatry: The Journal of Mental Science, 174,* 505–511.

Batelaan, N. M., Van Balkom, A. J. L. M., & Stein, D. J. (2011). Evidence-based pharmacotherapy of panic disorder: An update. *International Journal of Neuropsychopharmacology / Official Scientific Journal of the Collegium Internationale Neuropsychopharmacologicum (CINP),* 1–13. doi: 10.1017/S1461145711000800

Bell, R. A., Taylor, L. D., & Kravitz, R. L. (2010). Do antidepressant advertisements educate consumers and promote communication between patients with depression and their physicians? *Patient Education and Counseling, 81*(2), 245–250. doi: 10.1016/j.pec.2010.01.014

Berk, M., & Parker, G. (2009). The elephant on the couch: Side-effects of psychotherapy. *Australian and New Zealand Journal of Psychiatry, 43,* 787–794. doi: 10.1080/00048670903107559

Berk, M., Hallam, K., Malhi, G. S., Henry, L., Hasty, M., Macneil, C., . . . McGorry, P. D. (2010). Evidence and implications for early intervention in bipolar disorder. *Journal of Mental Health (Abingdon, England), 19*(2), 113–126. doi: 10.3109/09638230903469111

Beshai, S., Dobson, K. S., Bockting, C. L. H., & Quigley, L. (2011). Relapse and recurrence prevention in depression: Current research and future prospects. *Clinical Psychology Review, 31*(8), 1349–1360. doi: 10.1016/j.cpr.2011.09.003

Bhattacharjee, J., & El-Sayeh, H. G. G. (2008). Aripiprazole versus typical antipsychotic drugs for schizophrenia. *Cochrane Database of Systematic Reviews (Online)* (3), CD006617. doi: 10.1002/14651858.CD006617.pub3

Bird, V., Premkumar, P., Kendall, T., Whittington, C., Mitchell, J., & Kuipers, E. (2010). Early intervention services, cognitive-behavioural therapy and family intervention in early psychosis: Systematic review. *British Journal of Psychiatry: The Journal of Mental Science, 197*(5), 350–356. doi: 10.1192/bjp.bp.109.074526

Blackburn, I. M., & Moore, R. G. (1997). Controlled acute and follow-up trial of cognitive therapy and pharmacotherapy in out-patients with recurrent depression. *British Journal of Psychiatry: The Journal of Mental Science, 171,* 328–334.

Blackburn, I. M., Eunson, K. M., & Bishop, S. (1986). A two-year naturalistic follow-up of depressed patients treated with cognitive therapy, pharmacotherapy and a combination of both. *Journal of Affective Disorders, 10*(1), 67–75.

Blanco, C., Heimberg, R. G., Schneier, F. R., Fresco, D. M., Chen, H., Turk, . . . Liebowitz, M.R. (2010). A placebo-controlled trial of phenelzine, cognitive behavioral group therapy, and their combination for social anxiety disorder. *Archives of General Psychiatry, 67*(3), 286–295. doi: 10.1001/archgenpsychiatry.2010.11

Blomhoff, S, Haug, T. T., Hellström, K., Holme, I., Humble, M., Madsbu, H. P., & Wold, J. E. (2001). Randomised controlled general practice trial of sertraline, exposure therapy and combined treatment in generalised social phobia. *British Journal of Psychiatry: The Journal of Mental Science, 179,* 23–30.

Bockting, C. L. H., Schene, A. H., Spinhoven, P., Koeter, M. W. J., Wouters, L. F., . . . Kamphuis, J. H. (2005). Preventing relapse/recurrence in recurrent depression with cognitive therapy: A randomized controlled trial. *Journal of Consulting and Clinical Psychology, 73,* 647–657. doi: 10.1037/0022–006X.73.4.647

Bockting, C. L. H., Spinhoven, P., Wouters, L. F., Koeter, M. W. J., & Schene, A. H. (2009). Long-term effects of preventive cognitive therapy in recurrent depression: A 5.5-year follow-up study. *Journal of Clinical Psychiatry, 70*(12), 1621–1628. doi: 10.4088/JCP.08m04784blu

Bockting, C. L. H., ten Doesschate, M. C., Spijker, J., Spinhoven, P., Koeter, M. W. J., & Schene, A. H. (2008). Continuation and maintenance use of antidepressants in recurrent depression. *Psychotherapy and Psychosomatics, 77*(1), 17–26. doi: 10.1159/000110056

Bola, J. R. (2006). Medication-free research in early episode schizophrenia: Evidence of long-term harm? *Schizophrenia Bulletin, 32*(2), 288–296. doi: 10.1093/schbul/sbj019

Bola, J. R., Kao, D. T., & Soydan, H. (2012). Antipsychotic medication for early-episode schizophrenia. *Schizophrenia Bulletin, 38*(1), 23–25. doi: 10.1093/schbul/sbr167

Bola, J. R., Lehtinen, K., Aaltonen, J., Räkköläinen, V., Syvälahti, E., & Lehtinen, V. (2006). Predicting medication-free treatment response in acute psychosis: cross-validation from the Finnish need-adapted project. *Journal of Nervous and Mental Disease, 194*(10), 732–739. doi: 10.1097/01.nmd.0000243080.90255.88

Bola, J. R., Lehtinen, K., Cullberg, J., & Ciompi, L. (2009). Psychosocial treatment, antipsychotic postponement, and low-dose medication strategies in first-episode psychosis: A review of the literature. *Psychosis, 1*(1), 4–18. doi: 10.1080/17522430802610008

Bond, G. R., Drake, R. E., & Becker, D. R. (2008). An update on randomized controlled trials of evidence-based supported employment. *Psychiatric Rehabilitation Journal, 31*(4), 280–290. doi: 10.2975/31.4.2008.280.290

Bottlender, R., Sato, T., Jäger, M., Wegener, U., Wittmann, J., Strauß, A., & Möller, H.-J. (2003). The impact of the duration of untreated psychosis prior to first psychiatric admission on the 15-year outcome in schizophrenia. *Schizophrenia Research, 62*(1–2), 37–44. doi: 10.1016/S0920–9964(02)00348–1

Bowden, C. L., Calabrese, J. R., McElroy, S. L., Gyulai, L., Wassef, A., Petty, F., . . . Wozniak, P.J. (2000). A randomized, placebo-controlled 12-month trial of divalproex and lithium in treatment of outpatients with bipolar I disorder. Divalproex maintenance study group. *Archives of General Psychiatry, 57*(5), 481–489.

Brooner, R. K., Kidorf, M. S., King, V. L., Stoller, K. B., Neufeld, K. J., & Kolodner, K. (2007). Comparing adaptive stepped care and monetary-based voucher interventions for opioid dependence. *Drug and Alcohol Dependence, 88*(Suppl. 2), S14–23. doi: 10.1016/j.drugalcdep.2006.12.006

Buckley, L., & Pettit, T. (2007). Supportive therapy for schizophrenia. *Schizophrenia Bulletin, 33*(4), 859–860. doi:10.1093/schbul/sbm058

Burnand, Y., Andreoli, A., Kolatte, E., Venturini, A., & Rosset, N. (2002). Psychodynamic psychotherapy and clomipramine in the treatment of major depression. *Psychiatric Services* (Washington, DC), *53*(5), 585–590.

Bustillo, J., Lauriello, J., Horan, W., & Keith, S. (2001). The psychosocial treatment of schizophrenia: An update. *American Journal of Psychiatry, 158*(2), 163–175.

Charney, D. S., Nemeroff, C. B., Lewis, L., Laden, S. K., Gorman, J. M., Laska, E. M., . . . Solomon, S. (2002). National depressive and manic-depressive association consensus statement on the use of placebo in clinical trials of mood disorders. *Archives of General Psychiatry, 59*(3), 262–270.

Ciompi, L, Dauwalder, H. P., Maier, C., Aebi, E., Trütsch, K., Kupper, Z., & Rutishauser, C. (1992). The pilot project "Soteria Berne." Clinical experiences and results. *British Journal of Psychiatry, Supplement*(18), 145–153.

Clark, D. M. (2011). Implementing NICE guidelines for the psychological treatment of depression and anxiety disorders: The IAPT experience. *International Review of Psychiatry (Abingdon,*

England), *23*(4), 318–327. doi: 10.3109/09540261.2011.606803

Coldwell, C. M., & Bender, W. S. (2007). The effectiveness of assertive community treatment for homeless populations with severe mental illness: A meta-analysis. *American Journal of Psychiatry*, *164*(3), 393–399. doi: 10.1176/appi.ajp.164.3.393

Collins, L. M., Murphy, S. A., & Bierman, K. L. (2004). A conceptual framework for adaptive preventive interventions. *Prevention Science: The Official Journal of the Society for Prevention Research*, *5*(3), 185–196.

Collins, L. M., Murphy, S. A., & Strecher, V. (2007). The multiphase optimization strategy (MOST) and the sequential multiple assignment randomized trial (SMART): New methods for more potent eHealth interventions. *American Journal of Preventive Medicine*, *32*(5 Suppl.), S112–118. doi: 10.1016/j.amepre.2007.01.022

Colom, F., Vieta, E., Sánchez-Moreno, J., Palomino-Otiniano, R., Reinares, M., Goikolea, J. M.,...Martinez-Aran, A. (2009). Group psychoeducation for stabilised bipolar disorders: 5-year outcome of a randomised clinical trial. *British Journal of Psychiatry*, *194*(3), 260–265. doi: 10.1192/bjp.bp.107.040485

Colom, F., Vieta, E., Martinez-Aran, A., Reinares, M., Goikolea, J. M., Benabarre, A.,...Corominas, J. (2003). A randomized trial on the efficacy of group psychoeducation in the prophylaxis of recurrences in bipolar patients whose disease is in remission. *Archives of General Psychiatry*, *60*(4), 402–407. doi: 10.1001/archpsyc.60.4.402

Cottraux, J., Mollard, E., Bouvard, M., Marks, I., Sluys, M., Nury, A. M.,...Ciadella, P. (1990). A controlled study of fluvoxamine and exposure in obsessive-compulsive disorder. *International Clinical Psychopharmacology*, *5*(1), 17–30.

Cuijpers, P. (1999). The effects of family interventions on relatives' burden: A meta-analysis. *Journal of Mental Health*, *8*(3), 275–285. doi: 10.1080/09638239917436

Cuijpers, P., Dekker, J., Hollon, S. D., & Andersson, G. (2009). Adding psychotherapy to pharmacotherapy in the treatment of depressive disorders in adults: A meta-analysis. *Journal of Clinical Psychiatry*, *70*(9), 1219–1229. doi: 10.4088/JCP.09r05021

Cuijpers, P., Geraedts, A. S., van Oppen, P., Andersson, G., Markowitz, J. C., & van Straten, A. (2011). Interpersonal psychotherapy for depression: A meta-analysis. *American Journal of Psychiatry*, *168*(6), 581–592. doi: 10.1176/appi.ajp.2010.10101411

Cuijpers, P., van Straten, A., Hollon, S. D., & Andersson, G. (2010). The contribution of active medication to combined treatments of psychotherapy and pharmacotherapy for adult depression: A meta-analysis. *Acta Psychiatrica Scandinavica*, *121*(6), 415–423. doi: 10.1111/j.1600-0447.2009.01513.x

Cuijpers, P., van Straten, A., Schuurmans, J., van Oppen, P., Hollon, S. D., & Andersson, G. (2010). Psychotherapy for chronic major depression and dysthymia: A meta-analysis. *Clinical Psychology Review*, *30*(1), 51–62. doi: 10.1016/j.cpr.2009.09.003

Cuijpers, P., van Straten, A., van Oppen, P., & Andersson, G. (2008). Are psychological and pharmacologic interventions equally effective in the treatment of adult depressive disorders? A meta-analysis of comparative studies. *Journal of Clinical Psychiatry*, *69*(11), 1675–1685; quiz 1839–1841.

Cuijpers, P., van Straten, A., Warmerdam, L., & Andersson, G. (2009). Psychotherapy versus the combination of psychotherapy and pharmacotherapy in the treatment of depression: A meta-analysis. *Depression and Anxiety*, *26*(3), 279–288. doi: 10.1002/da.20519

Cullberg, J., Levander, S., Holmqvist, R., Mattsson, M., & Wieselgren, I.-M. (2002). One-year outcome in first episode psychosis patients in the Swedish Parachute project. *Acta Psychiatrica Scandinavica*, *106*(4), 276–285.

D'souza, R., Piskulic, D., & Sundram, S. (2010). A brief dyadic group based psychoeducation program improves relapse rates in recently remitted bipolar disorder: A pilot randomised controlled trial. *Journal of Affective Disorders*, *120*(1–3), 272–276. doi: 10.1016/j.jad.2009.03.018

Davidson, J. R. T. (2010). Major depressive disorder treatment guidelines in America and Europe. *Journal of Clinical Psychiatry*, *71*(Suppl. E1), e04. doi: 10.4088/JCP.9058se1c.04gry

Davidson, J. R. T., Foa, E. B., Huppert, J. D., Keefe, F. J., Franklin, M. E., Compton, J. S.,...Gadde, K.M. (2004). Fluoxetine, comprehensive cognitive behavioral therapy, and placebo in generalized social phobia. *Archives of General Psychiatry*, *61*(10), 1005–1013. doi: 10.1001/archpsyc.61.10.1005

Davidson, J., Pearlstein, T., Londborg, P., Brady, K. T., Rothbaum, B., Bell, J.,...Farfel, G. (2001). Efficacy of sertraline in preventing relapse of posttraumatic stress disorder: Results of a 28-week double-blind, placebo-controlled study. *American Journal of Psychiatry*, *158*(12), 1974–1981.

de Jonghe, F., Kool, S., van Aalst, G., Dekker, J., & Peen, J. (2001). Combining psychotherapy and antidepressants in the treatment of depression. *Journal of Affective Disorders*, *64*(2–3), 217–229.

de Maat, S., Dekker, J., Schoevers, R., van Aalst, G., Gijsbers-van Wijk, C., Hendriksen, M., ...deJonghe, F. (2008). Short psychodynamic supportive psychotherapy, antidepressants, and their combination in the treatment of major depression: A mega-analysis based on three randomized clinical trials. *Depression and Anxiety*, *25*(7), 565–574. doi: 10.1002/da.20305

DeRubeis, R. J., Hollon, S. D., Amsterdam, J. D., Shelton, R. C., Young, P. R., Salomon, R. M.,...Gallop. R. (2005). Cognitive therapy vs medications in the treatment of moderate to severe depression. *Archives of General Psychiatry, 62*(4), 409–416. doi: 10.1001/archpsyc.62 .4.409

Deveney, C. M., McHugh, R. K., Tolin, D. F., Pollack, M. H., & Otto, M. W. (2009). Combining D-cycloserine and exposure-based CBT for the anxiety disorders. *Clinical Neuropsychiatry: Journal of Treatment Evaluation, 6*(2), 75–82.

Dickerson, F. B., Tenhula, W. N., & Green-Paden, L. D. (2005). The token economy for schizophrenia: Review of the literature and recommendations for future research. *Schizophrenia Research, 75*(2–3), 405–416. doi: 10.1016/j.schres.2004.08.026

Dickinson, D., Tenhula, W., Morris, S., Brown, C., Peer, J., Spencer, K.,...Bellack, A.S. (2010). A randomized, controlled trial of computer-assisted cognitive remediation for schizophrenia. *American Journal of Psychiatry, 167*(2), 170–180. doi: 10.1176/appi.ajp.2009.09020264

Dimidjian, S., & Hollon, S. D. (2010). How would we know if psychotherapy were harmful? *American Psychologist, 65*(1), 65, 21–33. doi: 10.1037/a0017299

Dieterich, M., Irving, C. B., Park, B., & Marshall, M. (2010). Intensive case management for severe mental illness. *Cochrane Database of Systematic Reviews (Online)* (10), CD007906. doi: 10.1002/14651858.CD007906.pub2

Dixon, L.B., Dickerson, F., Bellack, A. S., Bennett, M., Dickinson, D., Goldberg, R. W.,...Kreyenbuhl, J. (2010). The 2009 schizophrenia PORT psychosocial treatment recommendations and summary statements. *Schizophrenia Bulletin, 36*(1), 48–70. doi: 10.1093/schbul/sbp115

Dobson, K. S., Hollon, S. D., Dimidjian, S., Schmaling, K. B., Kohlenberg, R. J., Gallop, R. J.,...Jacobson, N. S. (2008). Randomized trial of behavioral activation, cognitive therapy, and antidepressant medication in the prevention of relapse and recurrence in major depression. *Journal of Consulting and Clinical Psychology, 76*(3), 468–477. doi: 10.1037/0022–006X.76.3.468

Durham, R. C., Chambers, J. A., Power, K. G., Sharp, D. M., Macdonald, R. R., Major, K. A.,...Gumley, A. I.(2005). Long-term outcome of cognitive behaviour therapy clinical trials in central Scotland. *Health Technology Assessment (Winchester, England), 9*(42), 1–174.

Elkin, I., Shea, M. T., Watkins, J. T., Imber, S. D., Sotsky, S. M., Collins, J. F.,...Docherty, J. P.(1989). National institute of mental health treatment of depression collaborative research program. General effectiveness of treatments. *Archives of General Psychiatry, 46*(11), 971–982; discussion 983.

Etkin, A., Pittenger, C., Polan, H. J., & Kandel, E. R. (2005). Toward a neurobiology of psychotherapy: Basic science and clinical applications. *Journal of Neuropsychiatry and Clinical Neurosciences, 17*(2), 145–158. doi: 10.1176/appi.neuropsych.17.2.145

Evans, M. D., Hollon, S. D., DeRubeis, R. J., Piasecki, J. M., Grove, W. M., Garvey, M. J., & Tuason, V. B. (1992). Differential relapse following cognitive therapy and pharmacotherapy for depression. *Archives of General Psychiatry, 49*(10), 49, 802–808.

Evans, S., Newton, R., & Higgins, S. (2005). Nutritional intervention to prevent weight gain in patients commenced on olanzapine: A randomized controlled trial. *Australian and New Zealand Journal of Psychiatry, 39*(6), 479–486. doi: 10.1111/j.1440–1614.2005.01607.x

Falissard, B., Mauri, M., Shaw, K., Wetterling, T., Doble, A., Giudicelli, A., & De Hert, M. (2011). The METEOR study: Frequency of metabolic disorders in patients with schizophrenia. Focus on first and second generation and level of risk of antipsychotic drugs. *International Clinical Psychopharmacology, 26*(6), 291–302. doi: 10.1097/YIC.0b013e32834a5bf6

Fava, G. A. (1999). Well-being therapy: Conceptual and technical issues. *Psychotherapy and Psychosomatics, 68*(4), 171–179.

Fava, G. A., Grandi, S., Zielezny, M., Canestrari, R., & Morphy, M. A. (1994). Cognitive behavioral treatment of residual symptoms in primary major depressive disorder. *American Journal of Psychiatry, 151*(9), 1295–1299.

Fava, G. A., Grandi, S., Zielezny, M., Rafanelli, C., & Canestrari, R. (1996). Four-year outcome for cognitive behavioral treatment of residual symptoms in major depression. *American Journal of Psychiatry, 153*(7), 945–947.

Fava, G. A., & Offidani, E. (2011). The mechanisms of tolerance in antidepressant action. *Progress in Neuro-Psychopharmacology & Biological Psychiatry, 35*(7), 1593–1602. doi: 10.1016/j .pnpbp.2010.07.026

Fava, G. A., Rafanelli, C., Grandi, S., Canestrari, R., & Morphy, M. A. (1998). Six-year outcome for cognitive behavioral treatment of residual symptoms in major depression. *American Journal of Psychiatry, 155*(10), 1443–1445.

Fava, G. A., Rafanelli, C., Grandi, S., Conti, S., & Belluardo, P. (1998). Prevention of recurrent depression with cognitive behavioral therapy: Preliminary findings. *Archives of General Psychiatry, 55*(9), 816–820.

Fava, G. A., & Ruini, C. (2002). The sequential approach to relapse prevention in unipolar depression. *World Psychiatry: Official Journal of the World Psychiatric Association (WPA), 1*(1), 10–15.

Fava, G. A., Ruini, C., & Belaise, C. (2007). The concept of recovery in major depression.

Psychological Medicine, *37*(3), 307–317. doi: 10.1017/S0033291706008981

Fava, G. A., Ruini, C., Rafanelli, C., Finos, L., Conti, S., & Grandi, S. (2004). Six-year outcome of cognitive behavior therapy for prevention of recurrent depression. *American Journal of Psychiatry*, *161*(10), 1872–1876. doi: 10.1176/appi.ajp.161.10.1872

Fava, G. A., & Ruini, C. (2006). What is the optimal treatment of mood and anxiety disorders? *Clinical Psychology: Science and Practice*, *12*, 92–96. doi: 10.1093/clipsy.bpi011

Fava, G. A., Savron, G., Grandi, S., & Rafanelli, C. (1997). Cognitive-behavioral management of drug-resistant major depressive disorder. *Journal of Clinical Psychiatry*, *58*(6), 278–282; quiz 283–284.

Fava, G. A., & Tomba, E. (2010). New modalities of assessment and treatment planning in depression: The sequential approach. *CNS Drugs*, *24*(6), 453–465. doi: 10.2165/11531580–000000000–00000

Fava, G. A., & Tossani, E. (2007). Prodromal stage of major depression. *Early Intervention in Psychiatry*, *1*(1), 9–18. doi: 10.1111/j.1751–7893.2007.00005.x

Ferrero, A., Pierò, A., Fassina, S., Massola, T., Lanteri, A., Daga, G. A., & Fassino, S. (2007). A 12-month comparison of brief psychodynamic psychotherapy and pharmacotherapy treatment in subjects with generalised anxiety disorders in a community setting. *European Psychiatry: The Journal of the Association of European Psychiatrists*, *22*(8), 530–539. doi: 10.1016/j.eurpsy.2007.07.004

Finch, A. E., Lambert, M. J., & Schaalje, B. G. (2001). Psychotherapy quality control: The statistical generation of expected recovery curves for integration into an early warning system. *Clinical Psychology & Psychotherapy*, *8*(4), 8, 231–242. doi: 10.1002/cpp.286

Foa, E. B., Franklin, M. E., & Moser, J. (2002). Context in the clinic: How well do cognitive-behavioral therapies and medications work in combination? *Biological Psychiatry*, *52*(10), 987–997.

Foa, E. B., Liebowitz, M. R., Kozak, M. J., Davies, S., Campeas, R., Franklin, M. E., . . . Simpson, B. (2005). Randomized, placebo-controlled trial of exposure and ritual prevention, clomipramine, and their combination in the treatment of obsessive-compulsive disorder. *American Journal of Psychiatry*, *162*(1), 162(2005), 151–161. doi: 10.1176/appi.ajp.162.1.151

Forand, N. R., & DeRubeis, R. J. (under review). *Severity of anxiety and depression predict patterns of change in depression treatment*.

Fournier, J. C., DeRubeis, R. J., Shelton, R. C., Gallop, R., Amsterdam, J. D., & Hollon, S. D. (2008). Antidepressant medications v. cognitive therapy in people with depression with or without personality disorder. *British Journal of Psychiatry: The*

Journal of Mental Science, *192*(2), 124–129. doi: 10.1192/bjp.bp.107.037234

Fournier, J. C., DeRubeis, R. J., Shelton, R. C., Hollon, S. D., Amsterdam, J. D., & Gallop, R. (2009). Prediction of response to medication and cognitive therapy in the treatment of moderate to severe depression. *Journal of Consulting and Clinical Psychology*, *77*(4), 775–787. doi: 10.1037/a0015401

Francey, S. M., Nelson, B., Thompson, A., Parker, A. G., Kerr, M., Macneil, C., . . . McGorry, P. D. (2010). Who needs antipsychotic medication in the earliest stages of psychosis? A reconsideration of benefits, risks, neurobiology and ethics in the era of early intervention. *Schizophrenia Research*, *119*(1–3), 1–10. doi: 10.1016/j.schres.2010.02.1071

Frank, E, Grochocinski, V. J., Spanier, C. A., Buysse, D. J., Cherry, C. R., Houck, P. R., . . . Kupfer, D.J. (2000). Interpersonal psychotherapy and antidepressant medication: Evaluation of a sequential treatment strategy in women with recurrent major depression. *Journal of Clinical Psychiatry*, *61*(1), 51–57.

Frank, E., Cassano, G. B., Rucci, P., Thompson, W. K., Kraemer, H. C., Fagiolini, A., . . . Houck, P.R. (2011). Predictors and moderators of time to remission of major depression with interpersonal psychotherapy and SSRI pharmacotherapy. *Psychological Medicine: A Journal of Research in Psychiatry and the Allied Sciences*, *41*(1), 41(2011), 151–162. doi: 10.1017/S0033291710000553

Frank, E., Kupfer, D. J., Ehlers, C. L., Monk, T. H., Comes, C., Carter, C., & Frankel, D. (1994). Interpersonal and social rhythm therapy for bipolar disorder: Integrating interpersonal and behavioral approaches. *Behavior Therapist*, *17*, 143–149.

Frank, E., Kupfer, D. J., Buysse, D. J., Swartz, H. A., Pilkonis, P. A., Houck, P. R., . . . Stapf, D. M. (2007). Randomized trial of weekly, twice-monthly, and monthly interpersonal psychotherapy as maintenance treatment for women with recurrent depression. *American Journal of Psychiatry*, *164*(5), 761–767. doi: 10.1176/appi.ajp.164.5.761

Frank, E., Kupfer, D. J., Thase, M. E., Mallinger, A. G., Swartz, H. A., Fagiolini, A. M., . . . Monk, T. (2005). Two-year outcomes for interpersonal and social rhythm therapy in individuals with bipolar i disorder. *Archives of General Psychiatry*, *62*(9), 996–1004. doi: 10.1001/archpsyc.62.9.996

Frank, E., Swartz, H. A., Mallinger, A. G., Thase, M. E., Weaver, E. V., & Kupfer, D. J. (1999). Adjunctive psychotherapy for bipolar disorder: Effects of changing treatment modality. *Journal of Abnormal Psychology*, *108*(4), 579–587. doi: 10.1037/0021–843X.108.4.579

Franklin, M. E. (2005). Seeing the complexities: A comment on "combined psychotherapy and pharmacotherapy for mood and anxiety disorders in adults:

Review and analysis." *Clinical Psychology: Science and Practice*, *12*(1), 87–91. doi: 10.1093/clipsy.bpi010

Franklin, M. E., & Simpson, H. B. (2005). Combining pharmacotherapy and exposure plus ritual prevention for obsessive compulsive disorder: Research findings and clinical applications. *Journal of Cognitive Psychotherapy*, *19*(4), 19, 317–330. doi: 10.1891/jcop.2005.19.4.317

Friedman, M. A., Detweiler-Bedell, J. B., Leventhal, H. E., Horne, R., Keitner, G. I., & Miller, I. W. (2004). Combined psychotherapy and pharmacotherapy for the treatment of major depressive disorder. *Clinical Psychology: Science and Practice*, *11*(1), 47–68. doi: 10.1093/clipsy/bph052

Frommberger, U., Stieglitz, R.-D., Nyberg, E., Richter, H., Novelli-Fischer, U., ... Berger, M. (2004). Comparison between paroxetine and behaviour therapy in patients with posttraumatic stress disorder (PTSD): A pilot study. *International Journal of Psychiatry in Clinical Practice*, *8*(1), 19–23. doi: 10.1080/13651500310004803

Furukawa, T. A., Watanabe, N., & Churchill, R. (2006). Psychotherapy plus antidepressant for panic disorder with or without agoraphobia: Systematic review. *British Journal of Psychiatry: Journal of Mental Science*, *188*, 305–312. doi: 10.1192/bjp.188.4.305

Garety, P. A., Fowler, D. G., Freeman, D., Bebbington, P., Dunn, G., & Kuipers, E. (2008). Cognitive-behavioural therapy and family intervention for relapse prevention and symptom reduction in psychosis: Randomised controlled trial. *British Journal of Psychiatry: The Journal of Mental Science*, *192*(6), 412–423. doi: 10.1192/bjp.bp.107.043570

Gaudiano, B. A. (2006). Is symptomatic improvement in clinical trials of cognitive-behavioral therapy for psychosis clinically significant? *Journal of Psychiatric Practice*, *12*(1), 11–23.

Gaudiano, B. A., & Herbert, J. D. (2006). Acute treatment of inpatients with psychotic symptoms using acceptance and commitment therapy: Pilot results. *Behaviour Research and Therapy*, *44*(3), 415–437. doi: 10.1016/j.brat.2005.02.007

Gautam, S., & Meena, P. S. (2011). Drug-emergent metabolic syndrome in patients with schizophrenia receiving atypical (second-generation) antipsychotics. *Indian Journal of Psychiatry*, *53*(2), 128–133. doi: 10.4103/0019-5545.82537

Geddes, J. R., Carney, S. M., Davies, C., Furukawa, T. A., Kupfer, D. J., Frank, E., & Goodwin, G. M. (2003). Relapse prevention with antidepressant drug treatment in depressive disorders: A systematic review. *Lancet*, *361*(9358), 653–661. doi: 10.1016/S0140-6736(03)12599-8

Gitlin, M. J., Swendsen, J., Heller, T. L., & Hammen, C. (1995). Relapse and impairment in bipolar disorder. *American Journal of Psychiatry*, *152*(11), 1635–1640.

Gitlin, M., Nuechterlein, K., Subotnik, K. L., Ventura, J., Mintz, J., Fogelson, D. L., ... Aravagiri, M. (2001). Clinical outcome following neuroleptic discontinuation in patients with remitted recent-onset schizophrenia. *American Journal of Psychiatry*, *158*(11), 1835–1842.

Gosselin, P., Ladouceur, R., Morin, C. M., Dugas, M. J., & Baillargeon, L. (2006). Benzodiazepine discontinuation among adults with GAD: A randomized trial of cognitive-behavioral therapy. *Journal of Consulting and Clinical Psychology*, *74*(5), 908–919. doi: 10.1037/0022-006X.74.5.908

Gould, R. A., Otto, M. W., & Pollack, M. H. (1995). A meta-analysis of treatment outcome for panic disorder. *Clinical Psychology Review*, *15*(8), 819–844. doi: 10.1016/0272-7358(95)00048-8

Grant, P. M., Huh, G. A., Perivoliotis, D., Stolar, N. M., & Beck, A. T. (2012). Randomized trial to evaluate the efficacy of cognitive therapy for low-functioning patients with schizophrenia. *Archives of General Psychiatry*, *69*(2), 121–127. doi:10.1001/archgenpsychiatry.2011.129

Guastella, A. J., Richardson, R., Lovibond, P. F., Rapee, R. M., Gaston, J. E., Mitchell, P., & Dadds, M. R. (2008). A randomized controlled trial of D-cycloserine enhancement of exposure therapy for social anxiety disorder. *Biological Psychiatry*, *63*(6), 544–549. doi: 10.1016/j.biopsych.2007.11.011

Gumley, A., O'Grady, M., McNay, L., Reilly, J., Power, K., & Norrie, J. (2003). Early intervention for relapse in schizophrenia: Results of a 12-month randomized controlled trial of cognitive behavioural therapy. *Psychological Medicine*, *33*(3), 419–431.

Haddad, P. M. (2004). Antipsychotics and diabetes: Review of non-prospective data. *British Journal of Psychiatry*, *Supplement*, *47*, S80–86.

Haddock, G., Barrowclough, C., Tarrier, N., Moring, J., O'Brien, R., Schofield, N., ... Lewis, S. (2003). Cognitive-behavioural therapy and motivational intervention for schizophrenia and substance misuse. 18-month outcomes of a randomised controlled trial. *British Journal of Psychiatry: The Journal of Mental Science*, *183*, 418–426.

Hansen, N. B., Lambert, M. J., & Forman, E. M. (2002). The psychotherapy dose–response effect and its implications for treatment delivery services. *Clinical Psychology: Science and Practice*, *9*(3), 9, 329–343. doi: 10.1093/clipsy/9.3.329

Harrison, G., Hopper, K., Craig, T., Laska, E., Siegel, C., Wanderling, J., ... an der Heiden, W. (2001). Recovery from psychotic illness: A 15- and 25-year international follow-up study. *British Journal of Psychiatry: The Journal of Mental Science*, *178*, 506–517.

Harrow, M., & Jobe, T. H. (2007). Factors involved in outcome and recovery in schizophrenia patients not on antipsychotic medications: A 15-year multifollow-up study. *Journal of*

Nervous and Mental Disease, *195*(5), 406–414. doi: 10.1097/01.nmd.0000253783.32338.6e

Haug, T. T., Blomhoff, S., Hellstrøm, K., Holme, I., Humble, M., Madsbu, H. P., & Wold, J. E. (2003). Exposure therapy and sertraline in social phobia: 1-year follow-up of a randomised controlled trial. *British Journal of Psychiatry: The Journal of Mental Science*, *182*, 312–318.

Hazel, N. A., McDonell, M. G., Short, R. A., Berry, C. M., Voss, W. D., Rodgers, M. L., & Dyck, D. G. (2004). Impact of multiple-family groups for outpatients with schizophrenia on caregivers' distress and resources. *Psychiatric Services* (Washington, DC), *55*(1), 35–41.

Heldt, E., Blaya, C., Isolan, L., Kipper, L., Teruchkin, B., Otto, M. W., . . . Manfro, G. G. (2006). Quality of life and treatment outcome in panic disorder: Cognitive behavior group therapy effects in patients refractory to medication treatment. *Psychotherapy and Psychosomatics*, *75*(3), 183–186. doi: 10.1159/000091776

Heldt, E., Gus Manfro, G., Kipper, L., Blaya, C., Isolan, L., & Otto, M. W. (2006). One-year follow-up of pharmacotherapy-resistant patients with panic disorder treated with cognitive-behavior therapy: Outcome and predictors of remission. *Behaviour Research and Therapy*, *44*(5), 657–665. doi: 10.1016/j.brat.2005.05.003

Hinton, D. E., Chhean, D., Pich, V., Safren, S. A., Hofmann, S. G., & Pollack, M. H. (2005). A randomized controlled trial of cognitive-behavior therapy for cambodian refugees with treatment-resistant ptsd and panic attacks: A cross-over design. *Journal of Traumatic Stress*, *18*(6), 18, 617–629. doi: 10.1002/jts.20070

Hirschfeld, R. M. A., Dunner, D. L., Keitner, G., Klein, D. N., Koran, L. M., Kornstein, S. G., . . . Keller, M. B. (2002). Does psychosocial functioning improve independent of depressive symptoms? A comparison of nefazodone, psychotherapy, and their combination. *Biological Psychiatry*, *51*(2), 123–133.

Hoge, M. A., Morris, J. A., Daniels, A. S., Stuart, G. W., Huey, L. Y., & Adams, N. (2007). *An action plan for behavioral health workforce development*. Washington, DC: Department of Health and Human Services.

Hoffart, A., Due-Madsen, J., Lande, B., Gude, T., Bille, H., & Torgersen, S. (1993). Clomipramine in the treatment of agoraphobic inpatients resistant to behavioral therapy. *Journal of Clinical Psychiatry*, *54*(12), 481–487.

Hofmann, S. G., & Smits, J. A. J. (2008). Cognitive-behavioral therapy for adult anxiety disorders: A meta-analysis of randomized placebo-controlled trials. *Journal of Clinical Psychiatry*, *69*(4), 621–632.

Hofmann, S. G., Meuret, A. E., Smits, J. A. J., Simon, N. M., Pollack, M. H., Eisenmenger, K., . . . Otto,

M. W. (2006). Augmentation of exposure therapy with D-cycloserine for social anxiety disorder. *Archives of General Psychiatry*, *63*(3), 298–304. doi: 10.1001/archpsyc.63.3.298

Hofmann, S. G., Sawyer, A. T., Korte, K. J., & Smits, J. A. J. (2009). Is it beneficial to add pharmacotherapy to cognitive-behavioral therapy when treating anxiety disorders? A meta-analytic review. *International Journal of Cognitive Therapy*, *2*(2), 160–175.

Hofmann, S. G., Smits, J. A. J., Asnaani, A., Gutner, C. A., & Otto, M. W. (2011). Cognitive enhancers for anxiety disorders. *Pharmacology, Biochemistry, and Behavior*, *99*(2), 275–284. doi: 10.1016/j.pbb.2010.11.020

Hogarty, G. E., Greenwald, D., Ulrich, R. F., Kornblith, S. J., DiBarry, A. L., Cooley, S., . . . Flesher, S. (1997a). Three-year trials of personal therapy among schizophrenic patients living with or independent of family, II: Effects on adjustment of patients. *American Journal of Psychiatry*, *154*(11), 1514–1524.

Hogarty, G. E., Greenwald, D., Ulrich, R. F., Kornblith, S. J., DiBarry, A. L., Cooley, S., . . . Flesher, S. (1997b). Three-year trials of personal therapy among schizophrenic patients living with or independent of family, II: Effects on adjustment of patients. *American Journal of Psychiatry*, *154*(11), 1514–1524.

Hohagen, F., Winkelmann, G., Rasche-Rüchle, H., Hand, I., König, A., Münchau, N., . . . Berger, M. (1998). Combination of behaviour therapy with fluvoxamine in comparison with behaviour therapy and placebo. Results of a multicentre study. *British Journal of Psychiatry*. Supplement, (35), 71–78.

Hollon, S. D., DeRubeis, R. J., Shelton, R. C., Amsterdam, J. D., Salomon, R. M., O'Reardon, J., . . . Gallop, R. (2005). Prevention of relapse following cognitive therapy vs medications in moderate to severe depression. *Archives of General Psychiatry*, *62*(4), 417–422. doi: 10.1001/archpsyc.62.4.417

Hollon, S. D., Jarrett, R. B., Nierenberg, A. A., Thase, M. E., Trivedi, M., & Rush, A. J. (2005). Psychotherapy and medication in the treatment of adult and geriatric depression: Which monotherapy or combined treatment? *Journal of Clinical Psychiatry*, *66*(4), 455–468.

Horan, W. P., Kern, R. S., Green, M. F., & Penn, D. L. (2008). Social cognition training for individuals with schizophrenia: Emerging evidence. *American Journal of Psychiatric Rehabilitation*, *11*(3), 205–252.

Howes, O. D., Lim, S., Theologos, G., Yung, A. R., Goodwin, G. M., & McGuire, P. (2011). A comprehensive review and model of putative prodromal features of bipolar affective disorder. *Psychological Medicine*, *41*(8), 1567–1577. doi: 10.1017/S0033291710001790

Hughes, S., & Cohen, D. (2009). A systematic review of long-term studies of drug treated and non-drug treated depression. *Journal of Affective Disorders*, *118*, 9–18. doi: 10.1016/j.jad.2009.01.027

Imel, Z. E., Malterer, M. B., McKay, K. M., & Wampold, B. E. (2008). A meta-analysis of psychotherapy and medication in unipolar depression and dysthymia. *Journal of Affective Disorders*, *110*(3), 197–206. doi: 10.1016/j.jad.2008.03.018

Isasi, A. G., Echeburúa, E., Limiñana, J. M., & González-Pinto, A. (2010). How effective is a psychological intervention program for patients with refractory bipolar disorder? A randomized controlled trial. *Journal of Affective Disorders*, *126*(1–2), 80–87. doi: 10.1016/j.jad.2010.03.026

Jackson, H., McGorry, P., Edwards, J., Hulbert, C., Henry, L., Harrigan, S.,...Power, P. (2005). A controlled trial of cognitively oriented psychotherapy for early psychosis (COPE) with four-year follow-up readmission data. *Psychological Medicine*, *35*(9), 1295–1306. doi: 10.1017/S0033291705004927

Jackson, H. J., McGorry, P. D., Killackey, E., Bendall, S., Allott, K., Dudgeon, P.,...Harrigan, S. (2008). Acute-phase and 1-year follow-up results of a randomized controlled trial of CBT versus befriending for first-episode psychosis: The ACE project. *Psychological Medicine*, *38*(5), 725–735. doi: 10.1017/S0033291707002061

Johnson, S. L., & Roberts, J. E. (1995). Life events and bipolar disorder: Implications from biological theories. *Psychological Bulletin*, *117*(3), *117*, 434–449. doi: 10.1037/0033–2909.117.3.434

Johnson, S. L., Sandrow, D., Meyer, B., Winters, R., Miller, I., Solomon, D., & Keitner, G. (2000). Increases in manic symptoms after life events involving goal attainment. *Journal of Abnormal Psychology*, *109*(4), *109*, 721–727. doi: 10.1037/0021–843X.109.4.721

Judd, L. L., Akiskal, H. S., Schettler, P. J., Coryell, W., Endicott, J., Maser, J. D.,...Keller, M. B. (2003). A prospective investigation of the natural history of the long-term weekly symptomatic status of bipolar II disorder. *Archives of General Psychiatry*, *60*(3), 261–269.

Judd, L. L., Schettler, P. J., Akiskal, H. S., Maser, J., Coryell, W., Solomon, D.,...Keller, M. B. (2003). Long-term symptomatic status of bipolar I vs. bipolar II disorders. *International Journal of Neuropsychopharmacology/Official Scientific Journal of the Collegium Internationale Neuropsychopharmacologicum (CINP)*, *6*(2), 127–137. doi: 10.1017/S1461145703003341

Kahn, R. S., Fleischhacker, W. W., Boter, H., Davidson, M., Vergouwe, Y., Keet, I. P. M.,...Grobee, D.E. (2008). Effectiveness of antipsychotic drugs in first-episode schizophrenia and schizophreniform disorder: An open randomised clinical trial. *Lancet*, *371*(9618), 1085–1097. doi: 10.1016/S0140–6736(08)60486–9

Kampman, M., Keijsers, G. P. J., Hoogduin, C. A. L., & Hendriks, G.-J. (2002a). A randomized, double-blind, placebo-controlled study of the effects of adjunctive paroxetine in panic disorder patients unsuccessfully treated with cognitive-behavioral therapy alone. *Journal of Clinical Psychiatry*, *63*(9), 772–777.

Kampman, M., Keijsers, G. P. J., Hoogduin, C. A. L., & Hendriks, G.-J. (2002b). A randomized, double-blind, placebo-controlled study of the effects of adjunctive paroxetine in panic disorder patients unsuccessfully treated with cognitive-behavioral therapy alone. *Journal of Clinical Psychiatry*, *63*(9), 772–777.

Kaymaz, N., van Os, J., Loonen, A. J. M., & Nolen, W. A. (2008). Evidence that patients with single versus recurrent depressive episodes are differentially sensitive to treatment discontinuation: A meta-analysis of placebo-controlled randomized trials. *Journal of Clinical Psychiatry*, *69*(9), 1423–1436.

Keck, P. E. Jr., McElroy, S. L., Strakowski, S. M., Stanton, S. P., Kizer, D. L., Balistreri, T. M.,...West, S. A. (1996). Factors associated with pharmacologic noncompliance in patients with mania. *Journal of Clinical Psychiatry*, *57*(7), 292–297.

Keck, P. E. Jr., McElroy, S. L., Strakowski, S. M., West, S. A., Sax, K. W., Hawkins, J. M., Bourne, M. L., & Haggard, P. (1998). 12-month outcome of patients with bipolar disorder following hospitalization for a manic or mixed episode. *American Journal of Psychiatry*, *155*(5), 646–652.

Keller, M. B., McCullough, J. P., Klein, D. N., Arnow, B., Dunner, D. L., Gelenberg, A. J.,...Zajecka, J. (2000). A comparison of nefazodone, the cognitive behavioral-analysis system of psychotherapy, and their combination for the treatment of chronic depression. *New England Journal of Medicine*, *342*(20), 1462–1470. doi: 10.1056/NEJM200005183422001

Keller, M. B. (2006). Social anxiety disorder clinical course and outcome: Review of Harvard/Brown anxiety research project (HARP) findings. *Journal of Clinical Psychiatry*, *67*(Suppl. 12), 14–19.

Kemp, A. S., Schooler, N. R., Kalali, A. H., Alphs, L., Anand, R., Awad, G.,...Vermeulen, A. (2010). What is causing the reduced drug-placebo difference in recent schizophrenia clinical trials and what can be done about it? *Schizophrenia Bulletin*, *36*(3), 504–509. doi: 10.1093/schbul/sbn110

Kinon, B. J., Potts, A. J., & Watson, S. B. (2011). Placebo response in clinical trials with schizophrenia patients. *Current Opinion in Psychiatry*, *24*(2), 107–113. doi: 10.1097/YCO.0b013e32834381b0

Kjernisted, K. D., & Bleau, P. (2004). Long-term goals in the management of acute and chronic anxiety disorders. *Canadian Journal of Psychiatry. Revue Canadienne De Psychiatrie*, *49*(3 Suppl, 1), 51S–63S.

Klerman G. L., Weissman, M. M., Rounsaville, B. J., & Chevron, E. S. (1984). *Interpersonal Psychotherapy of Depression.* New York, NY: Basic Books.

Knijnik, D. Z., Blanco, C., Salum, G. A., Moraes, C. U., Mombach, C., Almeida, E., ... Eizirik, C. L. (2008). A pilot study of clonazepam versus psychodynamic group therapy plus clonazepam in the treatment of generalized social anxiety disorder. *European Psychiatry: The Journal of the Association of European Psychiatrists, 23*(8), 567–574. doi: 10.1016/j.eurpsy.2008.05.004

Kocsis, J. H. (2000). New strategies for treating chronic depression. *Journal of Clinical Psychiatry, 61*(Suppl. 11), 42–45.

Kocsis, J. H., Leon, A. C., Markowitz, J. C., Manber, R., Arnow, B., Klein, D. N., & Thase, M. E. (2009). Patient preference as a moderator of outcome for chronic forms of major depressive disorder treated with nefazodone, cognitive behavioral analysis system of psychotherapy, or their combination. *Journal of Clinical Psychiatry, 70*(3), 354–361.

Kraus, D. R., Castonguay, L., Boswell, J. F., Nordberg, S. S., & Hayes, J. A. (2011). Therapist effectiveness: Implications for accountability and patient care. *Psychotherapy Research, 21*, 267–276. doi: 10.1080/10503307.2011.563249

Kuipers, E., Garety, P., Fowler, D., Dunn, G., Bebbington, P., Freeman, D., & Hadley, C. (1997). London-East Anglia randomised controlled trial of cognitive-behavioural therapy for psychosis. I: Effects of the treatment phase. *British Journal of Psychiatry: The Journal of Mental Science, 171*, 319–327.

Kurtz, M. M., & Mueser, K. T. (2008). A meta-analysis of controlled research on social skills training for schizophrenia. *Journal of Consulting and Clinical Psychology, 76*(3), 491–504. doi: 10.1037/0022–006X.76.3.491

Kurtz, M. M., & Richardson, C. L. (2011). Social cognitive training for schizophrenia: A meta-analytic investigation of controlled research. *Schizophrenia Bulletin.* doi: 10.1093/schbul/sbr036

Kurzban, S., Davis, L., & Brekke, J. S. (2010). Vocational, social, and cognitive rehabilitation for individuals diagnosed with schizophrenia: A review of recent research and trends. *Current Psychiatry Reports, 12*(4), 345–355. doi: 10.1007/s11920–010–0129–3

Kushner, M. G., Kim, S. W., Donahue, C., Thuras, P., Adson, D., Kotlyar, M., ... Foa, E. B. (2007). D-cycloserine augmented exposure therapy for obsessive-compulsive disorder. *Biological Psychiatry, 62*(8), 835–838. doi: 10.1016/j.biopsych .2006.12.020

Lam, D. H. (2006). What can we conclude from studies on psychotherapy in bipolar disorder? *British Journal of Psychiatry, 188*(4), 321–322. doi: 10.1192/bjp.188.4.321

Lam, D. H., Burbeck, R., Wright, K., & Pilling, S. (2009). Psychological therapies in bipolar disorder: The effect of illness history on relapse prevention—A systematic review. *Bipolar Disorders, 11*(5), 11, 474–482. doi: 10.1111/j.1399–5618.2009.00724.x

Lam, D. H., Hayward, P., Watkins, E. R., Wright, K., & Sham, P. (2005). Relapse prevention in patients with bipolar disorder: Cognitive therapy outcome after 2 years. *American Journal of Psychiatry, 162*(2), 324–329. doi: 10.1176/appi.ajp.162.2.324

Lam, D. H., Watkins, E. R., Hayward, P., Bright, J., Wright, K., Kerr, N., ... Pak, S. (2003). A randomized controlled study of cognitive therapy for relapse prevention for bipolar affective disorder: Outcome of the first year. *Archives of General Psychiatry, 60*(2), 145–152. doi: 10.1001/archpsyc.60.2.145

Lehman, A. F., Lieberman, J. A., Dixon, L. B., McGlashan, T. H., Miller, A. L., Perkins, D. O., & Kreyenbuhl, J. (2004). Practice guideline for the treatment of patients with schizophrenia, second edition. *American Journal of Psychiatry, 161*(2 Suppl.), 1–56.

Lehtinen, V., Aaltonen, J., Koffert, T., Räkköläinen, V., & Syvälahti, E. (2000). Two-year outcome in first-episode psychosis treated according to an integrated model. Is immediate neuroleptisation always needed? *European Psychiatry: The Journal of the Association of European Psychiatrists, 15*(5), 312–320.

Lewis, S, Tarrier, N., Haddock, G., Bentall, R., Kinderman, P., Kingdon, D., ... Dunn, G. (2002). Randomised controlled trial of cognitive-behavioural therapy in early schizophrenia: Acute-phase outcomes. *British Journal of Psychiatry* (Suppl., 43), s91–97.

Leykin, Y., Amsterdam, J. D., DeRubeis, R. J., Gallop, R., Shelton, R. C., & Hollon, S. D. (2007). Progressive resistance to a selective serotonin reuptake inhibitor but not to cognitive therapy in the treatment of major depression. *Journal of Consulting and Clinical Psychology, 75*(2), 267–276. doi: 10.1037/0022–006X.75 .2.267

Lieberman, J. A., Stroup, T. S., McEvoy, J. P., Swartz, M. S., Rosenheck, R. A., Perkins, D. O., ... Hsiao, J. (2005). Effectiveness of antipsychotic drugs in patients with chronic schizophrenia. *New England Journal of Medicine, 353*(12), 1209–1223. doi: 10.1056/NEJMoa051688

Lilienfeld, S. O. (2007). Psychological treatments that cause harm. *Perspectives on Psychological Science, 2*(1), 2, 53–70. doi: 10.1111/j.1745–6916 .2007.00029.x

Linden, D. E. J. (2008). Brain imaging and psychotherapy: Methodological considerations and practical implications. *European Archives of Psychiatry and*

Clinical Neuroscience, 258(Suppl. 5), 71–75. doi: 10.1007/s00406–008–5023–1

Lupien, S. J., Fiocco, A., Wan, N., Maheu, F., Lord, C., Schramek, T., & Tu, M. T. (2005). Stress hormones and human memory function across the lifespan. *Psychoneuroendocrinology, 30*(3), 225–242. doi: 10.1016/j.psyneuen.2004.08.003

Ma, S. H., & Teasdale, J. D. (2004). Mindfulness-based cognitive therapy for depression: Replication and exploration of differential relapse prevention effects. *Journal of Consulting and Clinical Psychology, 72*(1), 31–40. doi: 10.1037/0022–006X.72.1.31

Maher, M. J., Huppert, J. D., Chen, H., Duan, N., Foa, E. B., Liebowitz, M. R., & Simpson, H. B. (2010). Moderators and predictors of response to cognitive-behavioral therapy augmentation of pharmacotherapy in obsessive-compulsive disorder. *Psychological Medicine, 40*(12), 2013–2023. doi: 10.1017/S0033291710000620

Maina, G., Rosso, G., & Bogetto, F. (2009). Brief dynamic therapy combined with pharmacotherapy in the treatment of major depressive disorder: Long-term results. *Journal of Affective Disorders, 114*(1–3), 200–207. doi: 10.1016/j.jad.2008.07.010

Malmberg, L., Fenton M, & Rathbone J. (2010). Individual psychodynamic psychotherapy and psychoanalysis for schizophrenia and severe mental illness. *Cochrane Database of Systematic Reviews, 3*, Art. No. CD001360. doi: 10.1002/14651858.CD001360

Manber, R., Kraemer, H. C., Arnow, B. A., Trivedi, M. H., Rush, A. J., Thase, M. E.,…Keller, M. B. (2008). Faster remission of chronic depression with combined psychotherapy and medication than with each therapy alone. *Journal of Consulting and Clinical Psychology, 76*(3), 459–467. doi: 10.1037/0022–006X.76.3.459

March, J., Silva, S., Petrycki, S., Curry, J., Wells, K., Fairbank, J.,…Severe, J. (2004). Fluoxetine, cognitive-behavioral therapy, and their combination for adolescents with depression: Treatment for adolescents with depression study (TADS) randomized controlled trial. *JAMA: The Journal of the American Medical Association, 292*(7), 807–820. doi: 10.1001/jama.292.7.807

Mark, T. L., Levit, K. R., Buck, J. A., Coffey, R. M., & Vandivort-Warren, R. (2007). Mental health treatment expenditure trends, 1986–2003. *Psychiatric Services* (Washington, DC), *58*(8), 1041–1048. doi: 10.1176/appi.ps.58.8.1041

Marks, I. M., Swinson, R. P., Baolu, M., Kuch, K., Noshirvani, H., O'sullivan, G.,…Sengun, S. (1993). Alprazolam and exposure alone and combined in panic disorder with agoraphobia. A controlled study in London and Toronto. *British Journal of Psychiatry: The Journal of Mental Science, 162*, 776–787.

Marlowe, D. B., Festinger, D. S., Dugosh, K. L., Lee, P. A., & Benasutti, K. M. (2007). Adapting judicial supervision to the risk level of drug offenders: Discharge and 6-month outcomes from a prospective matching study. *Drug and Alcohol Dependence, 88*(Suppl. 2), S4–13. doi: 10.1016/j.drugalcdep.2006.10.001

McFarlane, W. R., Dixon, L., Lukens, E., & Lucksted, A. (2003). Family psychoeducation and schizophrenia: A review of the literature. *Journal of Marital and Family Therapy, 29*(2), 223–245.

McGorry, P. D. (2010). Risk syndromes, clinical staging and DSM V: New diagnostic infrastructure for early intervention in psychiatry. *Schizophrenia Research, 120*(1–3), 49–53. doi: 10.1016/j.schres.2010.03.016

McGorry, P. D., Nelson, B., Goldstone, S., & Yung, A. R. (2010). Clinical staging: A heuristic and practical strategy for new research and better health and social outcomes for psychotic and related mood disorders. *Canadian Journal of Psychiatry. Revue Canadienne De Psychiatrie, 55*(8), 486–497.

McGorry, P. D., Purcell, R., Hickie, I. B., Yung, A. R., Pantelis, C., & Jackson, H. J. (2007). Clinical staging: A heuristic model for psychiatry and youth mental health. *Medical Journal of Australia, 187*(7 Suppl), S40–42.

McGorry, P. D., Yung, A. R., Phillips, L. J., Yuen, H. P., Francey, S., Cosgrave, E. M.,…Jackson, H. (2002). Randomized controlled trial of interventions designed to reduce the risk of progression to first-episode psychosis in a clinical sample with subthreshold symptoms. *Archives of General Psychiatry, 59*(10), 921–928.

McHugh, R. K., Hearon, B. A., & Otto, M. W. (2010). Cognitive behavioral therapy for substance use disorders. *Psychiatric Clinics of North America, 33*(3), 511–525. doi: 10.1016/j.psc.2010.04.012

Melnik, T., Soares, B. G., Puga, M. E. D. S., & Atallah, A. N. (2010). Efficacy and safety of atypical antipsychotic drugs (quetiapine, risperidone, aripiprazole and paliperidone) compared with placebo or typical antipsychotic drugs for treating refractory schizophrenia: Overview of systematic reviews. *São Paulo Medical Journal = Revista Paulista De Medicina, 128*(3), 141–166.

Miklowitz, D. J., George, E. L., Richards, J. A., Simoneau, T. L., & Suddath, R. L. (2003). A randomized study of family-focused psychoeducation and pharmacotherapy in the outpatient management of bipolar disorder. *Archives of General Psychiatry, 60*(9), 904–912. doi: 10.1001/archpsyc.60.9.904

Miklowitz, D. J., & Goldstein M. J. (1997). *Bipolar disorder: A family-focused treatment approach*. New York, NY: Guilford Press.

Miklowitz, D. J., & Otto, M. W. (2007). Psychosocial interventions for bipolar disorder: A review of literature and introduction of the systematic treatment enhancement program. *Psychopharmacology Bulletin, 40*(4), 116–131.

Miklowitz, D. J., Otto, M. W., Frank, E., Reilly-Harrington, N. A., Wisniewski, S. R., Kogan, J. N., . . . Sachs, G. S. (2007). Psychosocial treatments for bipolar depression: A 1-year randomized trial from the systematic treatment enhancement program. *Archives of General Psychiatry*, *64*(4), 419–426. doi: 10.1001/archpsyc.64.4.419

Miklowitz, D. J., Simoneau, T. L., George, E. L., Richards, J. A., Kalbag, A., Sachs-Ericsson, N., & Suddath, R. (2000). Family-focused treatment of bipolar disorder: 1-year effects of a psychoeducational program in conjunction with pharmacotherapy. *Biological Psychiatry*, *48*(6), 582–592. doi: 10.1016/S0006–3223(00)00931–8

Miller, I. W., Solomon, D. A., Ryan, C. E., & Keitner, G. I. (2004). Does adjunctive family therapy enhance recovery from bipolar I mood episodes? *Journal of Affective Disorders*, *82*(3), 431–436. doi: 10.1016/j.jad.2004.01.010

Molenaar, P. J., Dekker, J., Van, R., Hendriksen, M., Vink, A., & Schoevers, R. A. (2007). Does adding psychotherapy to pharmacotherapy improve social functioning in the treatment of outpatient depression? *Depression and Anxiety*, *24*(8), 553–562. doi: 10.1002/da.20254

Moncrieff, J. (2006). Does antipsychotic withdrawal provoke psychosis? Review of the literature on rapid onset psychosis (supersensitivity psychosis) and withdrawal-related relapse. *Acta Psychiatrica Scandinavica*, *114*(1), 3–13. doi: 10.1111/j.1600–0447.2006.00787.x

Moritz, S., Vitzthum, F., Randjbar, S., Veckenstedt, R., & Woodward, T. S. (2010). Detecting and defusing cognitive traps: Metacognitive intervention in schizophrenia. *Current Opinion in Psychiatry*, *23*(6), 561–569. doi: 10.1097/YCO.0b013e32833d16a8

Morrison, A.P., Hutton, P., Wardle, M., Spencer, H., Barratt, S., Brabban, A., . . . Turkington, D. (2011). Cognitive therapy for people with a schizophrenia spectrum diagnosis not taking antipsychotic medication: An exploratory trial. *Psychological Medicine*, *1–8*. doi: 10.1017/S0033291711001899

Morrison, A. P., French, P., Walford, L., Lewis, S. W., Kilcommons, A., Green, J., Parker, S., & Bentall, R. P. (2004). Cognitive therapy for the prevention of psychosis in people at ultra-high risk: randomised controlled trial. *British Journal of Psychiatry: The Journal of Mental Science*, *185*, 291–297. doi: 10.1192/bjp.185.4.291

Mosher, L. R., & Menn, A. Z. (1978). Community residential treatment for schizophrenia: Two-year follow-up. *Hospital & Community Psychiatry*, *29*(11), 715–723.

Mueser, K T, Bellack, A. S., & Blanchard, J. J. (1992). Comorbidity of schizophrenia and substance abuse: Implications for treatment. *Journal of Consulting and Clinical Psychology*, *60*(6), 845–856.

Murphy, S. A. (2005). An experimental design for the development of adaptive treatment strategies. *Statistics in Medicine*, *24*(10), 1455–1481. doi: 10.1002/sim.2022

Nelson, G., Aubry, T., & Lafrance, A. (2007). A review of the literature on the effectiveness of housing and support, assertive community treatment, and intensive case management interventions for persons with mental illness who have been homeless. *American Journal of Orthopsychiatry*, *77*(3), 350–361. doi: 10.1037/0002–9432.77.3.350

NICE. (2005). The management of PTSD in children and adolescents, in primary and secondary care. *Clinical Guideline 26*. London, United Kingdom: National Institute for Health and Clinical Excellence. Available at www.nice.org.uk

NICE. (2006). The management of bipolar disorder in adults, children and adolescents, in primary and secondary care. *Clinical Guideline 38*. London, United Kingdom: National Institute for Health and Clinical Excellence. Available at www.nice.org.uk

NICE. (2009). Core interventions in the treatment and management of schizophrenia in primary and secondary care (update). *Clinical Guideline 82*. London, United Kingdom: National Institute for Health and Clinical Excellence. Available at www.nice.org.uk

Norton, P. J., & Price, E. C. (2007). A meta-analytic review of adult cognitive-behavioral treatment outcome across the anxiety disorders. *Journal of Nervous and Mental Disease*, *195*(6), 521–531. doi: 10.1097/01.nmd.0000253843.70149.9a

Noyes, R. Jr., Garvey, M. J., Cook, B., & Suelzer, M. (1991). Controlled discontinuation of benzodiazepine treatment for patients with panic disorder. *American Journal of Psychiatry 148*(4), 517–523.

Okiishi, J. C., Lambert, M. J., Eggett, D., Nielsen, L., Dayton, D. D., & Vermeersch, D. A. (2006). An analysis of therapist treatment effects: toward providing feedback to individual therapists on their clients' psychotherapy outcome. *Journal of Clinical Psychology*, *62*(9), 1157–1172. doi: 10.1002/jclp.20272

Olfson, M., & Marcus, S. C. (2010). National trends in outpatient psychotherapy. *American Journal of Psychiatry*, *167*(12), 1456–1463. doi: 10.1176/appi.ajp.2010.10040570

Otto, M. W., Bruce, S. E., & Deckersbach, T. (2005). Benzodiazepine use, cognitive impairment, and cognitive-behavioral therapy for anxiety disorders: Issues in the treatment of a patient in need. *Journal of Clinical Psychiatry*, *66*(Suppl. 2), 34–38.

Otto, M. W., McHugh, R. K., & Kantak, K. M. (2010). Combined pharmacotherapy and cognitive-behavioral therapy for anxiety disorders: Medication effects, glucocorticoids, and attenuated treatment outcomes. *Clinical Psychology:*

Science and Practice. *17*(2), 91–103. doi: 10.1111/j.1468–2850.2010.01198.x

Otto, M. W., McHugh, R. K., Simon, N. M., Farach, F. J., Worthington, J. J., & Pollack, M. H. (2010). Efficacy of CBT for benzodiazepine discontinuation in patients with panic disorder: Further evaluation. *Behaviour Research and Therapy, 48*(8), 48, 720–727. doi: 10.1016/j.brat.2010.04.002

Otto, M. W., Pollack, M. H., Sachs, G. S., Reiter, S. R., Meltzer-Brody, S., & Rosenbaum, J. F. (1993). Discontinuation of benzodiazepine treatment: Efficacy of cognitive-behavioral therapy for patients with panic disorder. *American Journal of Psychiatry, 150*(10), 1485–1490.

Otto, M. W., Reilly-Harrington, N., & Sachs, G. S. (2003). Psychoeducational and cognitive-behavioral strategies in the management of bipolar disorder. *Journal of Affective Disorders. Special Issue: Validating the bipolar spectrum, 73*(1–2), 171–181. doi: 10.1016/S0165–0327(01)00460–8

Otto, M. W., Tolin, D. F., Simon, N. M., Pearlson, G. D., Basden, S., Meunier, S. A., . . . Pollack, M.H. (2010). Efficacy of D-cycloserine for enhancing response to cognitive-behavior therapy for panic disorder. *Biological Psychiatry, 67*(4), 365–370. doi: 10.1016/j.biopsych.2009.07.036

Pampallona, S., Bollini, P., Tibaldi, G., Kupelnick, B., & Munizza, C. (2004). Combined pharmacotherapy and psychological treatment for depression: A systematic review. *Archives of General Psychiatry, 61*(7), 714–719. doi: 10.1001/archpsyc.61.7.714

Papakostas, G. I. (2010). The efficacy, tolerability, and safety of contemporary antidepressants. *Journal of Clinical Psychiatry, 71*(Suppl. E1), e03. doi: 10.4088/JCP.9058se1c.03gry

Paykel, E. S., Scott, J., Cornwall, P. L., Abbott, R., Crane, C., Pope, M., & Johnson, A. L. (2005). Duration of relapse prevention after cognitive therapy in residual depression: Follow-up of controlled trial. *Psychological Medicine, 35*(1), 59–68.

Paykel, E. S., Scott, J., Teasdale, J. D., Johnson, A. L., Garland, A., Moore, R., . . . Pope, M. (1999). Prevention of relapse in residual depression by cognitive therapy: A controlled trial. *Archives of General Psychiatry, 56*(9), 829–835.

Perry, A., Tarrier, N., Morriss, R., McCarthy, E., & Limb, K. (1999). Randomised controlled trial of efficacy of teaching patients with bipolar disorder to identify early symptoms of relapse and obtain treatment. *BMJ (Clinical Research Ed.), 318*(7177), 149–153.

Petty, D. R., House, A., Knapp, P., Raynor, T., & Zermansky, A. (2006). Prevalence, duration and indications for prescribing of antidepressants in primary care. *Age and Ageing, 35*(5), 523–526. doi: 10.1093/ageing/afl023

Pharoah, F., Mari, J., Rathbone, J., & Wong, W. (2010). Family intervention for schizophrenia.

Cochrane Database of Systematic Reviews, (Online) (12), CD000088. doi: 10.1002/14651858.CD000088.pub2

Piek, E., van der Meer, K., & Nolen, W. A. (2010). Guideline recommendations for long-term treatment of depression with antidepressants in primary care—A critical review. *European Journal of General Practice, 16*(2), 106–112. doi: 10.3109/13814781003692463

Pilling, S., Bebbington, P., Kuipers, E., Garety, P., Geddes, J., Orbach, G., & Morgan, C. (2002). Psychological treatments in schizophrenia: I. Meta-analysis of family intervention and cognitive behaviour therapy. *Psychological Medicine, 32*(5), 763–782.

Pollack, M. H., Otto, M. W., Kaspi, S. P., Hammerness, P. G., & Rosenbaum, J. F. (1994). Cognitive behavior therapy for treatment-refractory panic disorder. *Journal of Clinical Psychiatry, 55*(5), 200–205.

Pollack, M. H, Otto, M. W., Roy-Byrne, P. P., Coplan, J. D., Rothbaum, B. O., Simon, N. M., & Gorman, J. M. (2008). Novel treatment approaches for refractory anxiety disorders. *Depression and Anxiety, 25*(6), 467–476. doi: 10.1002/da.20329

Pomara, N., Willoughby, L. M., Sidtis, J. J., Cooper, T. B., & Greenblatt, D. J. (2005). Cortisol response to diazepam: Its relationship to age, dose, duration of treatment, and presence of generalized anxiety disorder. *Psychopharmacology, 178*(1), 1–8. doi: 10.1007/s00213–004–1974–8

Post, R. M., Altshuler, L. L., Frye, M. A., Suppes, T., Keck, P. E Jr., McElroy, S. L., . . . Nolen, W.A. (2010). Complexity of pharmacologic treatment required for sustained improvement in outpatients with bipolar disorder. *Journal of Clinical Psychiatry, 71*(9), 1176–1186; quiz 1252–1253. doi: 10.4088/JCP.08m04811yel

Post, R. M., Denicoff, K. D., Leverich, G. S., Altshuler, L. L., Frye, M. A., Suppes, T. M., Rush, A. J., et al. (2003). Morbidity in 258 bipolar outpatients followed for 1 year with daily prospective ratings on the NIMH life chart method. *Journal of Clinical Psychiatry, 64*(6), 680–690; quiz 738–739.

Power, K. G., Simpson, R. J., Swanson, V., & Wallace, L. A. (1990). A controlled comparison of cognitive-behaviour therapy, diazepam, and placebo, alone and in combination, for the treatment of generalised anxiety disorder. *Journal of Anxiety Disorders, 4*(4), 4, 267–292. doi: 10.1016/0887–6185(90)90026–6

Prasko, J., Dockery, C., Horácek, J., Houbová, P., Kosová, J., Klaschka, J., . . . Höschl, C. (2006). Moclobemide and cognitive behavioral therapy in the treatment of social phobia. A six-month controlled study and 24 months follow up. *Neuro Endocrinology Letters, 27*(4), 473–481.

Rappaport, M., Hopkins, H. K., Hall, K., Belleza, T., & Silverman, J. (1978). Are there schizophrenics for whom drugs may be unnecessary or contraindicated? *International Pharmacopsychiatry, 13*(2), 100–111.

Rea, M. M., Tompson, M. C., Miklowitz, D. J., Goldstein, M. J., Hwang, S., & Mintz, J. (2003). Family-focused treatment versus individual treatment for bipolar disorder: Results of a randomized clinical trial. *Journal of Consulting and Clinical Psychology, 71*(3), 482–492. doi: 10.1037/0022–006X.71.3.482

Reimherr, F. W., Amsterdam, J. D., Quitkin, F. M., Rosenbaum, J. F., Fava, M., Zajecka, J., ... Sundell, K. (1998). Optimal length of continuation therapy in depression: A prospective assessment during long-term fluoxetine treatment. *American Journal of Psychiatry, 155*(9), 1247–1253.

Reinares, M., Colom, F., Sánchez-Moreno, J., Torrent, C., Martínez-Arán, A., Comes, M., ... Vieta, E. (2008). Impact of caregiver group psychoeducation on the course and outcome of bipolar patients in remission: A randomized controlled trial. *Bipolar Disorders, 10*(4), 511–519. doi: 10.1111/j.1399–5618.2008.00588.x

Ressler, K. J., Rothbaum, B. O., Tannenbaum, L., Anderson, P., Graap, K., Zimand, E., ... David, M. (2004). Cognitive enhancers as adjuncts to psychotherapy: Use of D-cycloserine in phobic individuals to facilitate extinction of fear. *Archives of General Psychiatry, 61*(11), 1136–1144. doi: 10.1001/archpsyc.61.11.1136

Reynolds, C. F. 3rd, Frank, E., Perel, J. M., Imber, S. D., Cornes, C., Miller, M. D., ... Kupfer, D.J. (1999). Nortriptyline and interpersonal psychotherapy as maintenance therapies for recurrent major depression: A randomized controlled trial in patients older than 59 years. *JAMA: The Journal of the American Medical Association, 281*(1), 39–45.

Reus, V. I., Weingartner, H., & Post, R. M. (1979). Clinical implications of state-dependent learning. *American Journal of Psychiatry, 136*(7), 927–931.

Rodrigues, H., Figueira, I., Gonçalves, R., Mendlowicz, M., Macedo, T., & Ventura, P. (2011). CBT for pharmacotherapy non-remitters—A systematic review of a next-step strategy. *Journal of Affective Disorders, 129*(1–3), 219–228. doi: 10.1016/j.jad.2010.08.025

Roffman, J. L., Marci, C. D., Glick, D. M., Dougherty, D. D., & Rauch, S. L. (2005). Neuroimaging and the functional neuroanatomy of psychotherapy. *Psychological Medicine, 35*(10), 1385–1398. doi: 10.1017/S0033291705005064

Rosenbaum, J. F., Fava, M., Hoog, S. L., Ascroft, R. C., & Krebs, W. B. (1998). Selective serotonin reuptake inhibitor discontinuation syndrome: A randomized clinical trial. *Biological Psychiatry, 44*(2), 77–87.

Ross, S., & Peselow, E. (2009). Pharmacotherapy of addictive disorders. *Clinical Neuropharmacology, 32*(5), 277–289.

Rothbaum, B. O., Cahill, S. P., Foa, E. B., Davidson, J. R. T., Compton, J., Connor, K. M., ... Hahn, C. (2006). Augmentation of sertraline with prolonged exposure in the treatment of posttraumatic stress disorder. *Journal of Traumatic Stress, 19*(5), 625–638. doi: 10.1002/jts.20170

Rubio, G., & López-Ibor, J. J. (2007). Generalized anxiety disorder: A 40-year follow-up study. *Acta Psychiatrica Scandinavica, 115*(5), 372–379. doi: 10.1111/j.1600–0447.2006.00896.x

Rucci, P., Frank, E., Calugi, S., Miniati, M., Benvenuti, A., Wallace, M., ... Cassano, G. B. (2011). Incidence and predictors of relapse during continuation treatment of major depression with SSRI, interpersonal psychotherapy, or their combination. *Depression and Anxiety, 28*(11), 955–962. doi: 10.1002/da.20894

Rufer, M., Hand, I., Alsleben, H., Braatz, A., Ortmann, J., Katenkamp, B., ... Helmut, P. (2005). Long-term course and outcome of obsessive-compulsive patients after cognitive-behavioral therapy in combination with either fluvoxamine or placebo: A 7-year follow-up of a randomized double-blind trial. *European Archives of Psychiatry and Clinical Neuroscience, 255*(2), 121–128. doi: 10.1007/s00406–004–0544–8

Rush, A. J., Fava, M., Wisniewski, S. R., Lavori, P. W., Trivedi, M. H., Sackeim, H. A., ... Niederehe, G. (2004). Sequenced treatment alternatives to relieve depression (STAR*D): Rationale and design. *Controlled Clinical Trials, 25*(1), 119–142.

Rush, A. J., Trivedi, M. H., Wisniewski, S. R., Nierenberg, A. A., Stewart, J. W., Warden, D., ... Fava, M. (2006). Acute and longer-term outcomes in depressed outpatients requiring one or several treatment steps: A STAR*D report. *American Journal of Psychiatry, 163*(11), 1905–1917. doi: 10.1176/appi.ajp.163.11.1905

Salzman, C. (1998). Addiction to benzodiazepines. *Psychiatric Quarterly, 69*(4), 251–261.

Schatzberg, A. F., Rush, A. J., Arnow, B. A., Banks, P. L. C., Blalock, J. A., Borian, F. E., ... Keller, M.B. (2005). Chronic depression: Medication (nefazodone) or psychotherapy (CBASP) is effective when the other is not. *Archives of General Psychiatry, 62*(5), 513–520. doi: 10.1001/archpsyc.62.5.513

Schmidt, N. B., Wollaway-Bickel, K., Trakowski, J. H., Santiago, H. T., & Vasey, M. (2002). Antidepressant discontinuation in the context of cognitive behavioral treatment for panic disorder. *Behaviour Research and Therapy, 40*(1), 67–73.

Schooler, N. R., Keith, S. J., Severe, J. B., Matthews, S. M., Bellack, A. S., Glick, I. D., ... Woerner, M.G. (1997). Relapse and rehospitalization during maintenance treatment of schizophrenia. The effects of dose reduction and family treatment. *Archives of General Psychiatry, 54*(5), 453–463.

Schneier, F. R., Neria, Y., Pavlicova, M., Hembree, E., Suh, E. J., Amsel, L., & Marshall, R. D. (2012). Combined prolonged exposure therapy and paroxetine for PTSD related to the World Trade Center attack: a randomized controlled trial. *American Journal of Psychiatry*, *169*(1), 80–88. doi:10.1176/appi.ajp.2011.11020321

Schüle, C., Sighart, C., Hennig, J., & Laakmann, G. (2006). Mirtazapine inhibits salivary cortisol concentrations in anorexia nervosa. *Progress in Neuro-Psychopharmacology & Biological Psychiatry*, *30*(6), 1015–1019. doi: 10.1016/j.pnpbp.2006.03.023

Scott, J., Garland, A., & Moorhead, S. (2001). A pilot study of cognitive therapy in bipolar disorders. *Psychological Medicine*, *31*(3), 459–467.

Scott, J., Colom, F., & Vieta, E. (2007). A meta-analysis of relapse rates with adjunctive psychological therapies compared to usual psychiatric treatment for bipolar disorders. *International Journal of Neuropsychopharmacology/Official Scientific Journal of the Collegium Internationale Neuropsychopharmacologicum (CINP)*, *10*(1), 123–129. doi: 10.1017/S1461145706006900

Scott, J., Paykel, E., Morriss, R., Bentall, R., Kinderman, P., Johnson, T., . . . Hayhurst, H. (2006). Cognitive-behavioural therapy for severe and recurrent bipolar disorders: Randomised controlled trial. *British Journal of Psychiatry: The Journal of Mental Science*, *188*, 313–320. doi: 10.1192/bjp.188.4.313

Scott, J., Palmer, S., Paykel, E., Teasdale, J., & Hayhurst, H. (2003). Use of cognitive therapy for relapse prevention in chronic depression: Cost-effectiveness study. *British Journal of Psychiatry*, *182*(3), 182, 221–227. doi: 10.1192/bjp.182.3.221

Segal, Z. V., Bieling, P., Young, T., MacQueen, G., Cooke, R., Martin, L., . . . Levitan, R.D. (2010). Antidepressant monotherapy vs sequential pharmacotherapy and mindfulness-based cognitive therapy, or placebo, for relapse prophylaxis in recurrent depression. *Archives of General Psychiatry*, *67*(12), 1256–1264. doi: 10.1001/archgenpsychiatry.2010.168

Sellwood, W., Barrowclough, C., Tarrier, N., Quinn, J., Mainwaring, J., & Lewis, S. (2001). Needs-based cognitive-behavioural family intervention for carers of patients suffering from schizophrenia: 12-month follow-up. *Acta Psychiatrica Scandinavica*, *104*(5), 346–355.

Sellwood, W., Wittkowski, A., Tarrier, N., & Barrowclough, C. (2007). Needs-based cognitive-behavioural family intervention for patients suffering from schizophrenia: 5-year follow-up of a randomized controlled effectiveness trial. *Acta Psychiatrica Scandinavica*, *116*(6), 447–452. doi: 10.1111/j.1600–0447.2007.01097.x

Sensky, T., Turkington, D., Kingdon, D., Scott, J. L., Scott, J., Siddle, R., . . . Barnes, T. R. (2000). A randomized controlled trial of cognitive-behavioral therapy for persistent symptoms in schizophrenia resistant to medication. *Archives of General Psychiatry*, *57*(2), 165–172.

Shimokawa, K., Lambert, M. J., & Smart, D. W. (2010). Enhancing treatment outcome of patients at risk of treatment failure: Meta-analytic and mega-analytic review of a psychotherapy quality assurance system. *Journal of Consulting and Clinical Psychology*, *78*(3), 78(2010), 298–311. doi: 10.1037/a0019247

Simon, N. M., Connor, K. M., Lang, A. J., Rauch, S., Krulewicz, S., LeBeau, R. T., . . . Pollack, M. H. (2008). Paroxetine CR augmentation for posttraumatic stress disorder refractory to prolonged exposure therapy. *Journal of Clinical Psychiatry*, *69*(3), 400–405.

Simon, N. M., Otto, M. W., Worthington, J. J., Hoge, E. A., Thompson, E. H., Lebeau, R. T., . . . Pollack, M. H. (2009). Next-step strategies for panic disorder refractory to initial pharmacotherapy: A 3-phase randomized clinical trial. *Journal of Clinical Psychiatry*, *70*(11), 1563–1570. doi: 10.4088/JCP.08m04485blu

Simons, A. D., Murphy, G. E., Levine, J. L., & Wetzel, R. D. (1986). Cognitive therapy and pharmacotherapy for depression. *Sustained improvement over one year. Archives of General Psychiatry*, *43*(1), 43–48.

Simpson, H. B., Liebowitz, M. R., Foa, E. B., Kozak, M. J., Schmidt, A. B., Rowan, V., . . . Campeas, R. (2004). Post-treatment effects of exposure therapy and clomipramine in obsessive-compulsive disorder. *Depression and Anxiety*, *19*(4), 225–233. doi: 10.1002/da.20003

Simpson, H. B., Foa, E. B., Liebowitz, M. R., Ledley, D. R., Huppert, J. D., Cahill, S., . . . Petkova, E. (2008). A randomized, controlled trial of cognitive-behavioral therapy for augmenting pharmacotherapy in obsessive-compulsive disorder. *American Journal of Psychiatry*, *165*(5), 621–630. doi: 10.1176/appi.ajp.2007.07091440

Solomon, D. A., Keitner, G. I., Ryan, C. E., Kelley, J., & Miller, I. W. (2008). Preventing recurrence of bipolar I mood episodes and hospitalizations: Family psychotherapy plus pharmacotherapy versus pharmacotherapy alone. *Bipolar Disorders*, *10*(7), 798–805. doi: 10.1111/j.1399–5618.2008.00624.x

Solomon, D. A., Leon, A. C., Mueller, T. I., Coryell, W., Teres, J. J., Posternak, M. A., . . . Keller, M.B. (2005). Tachyphylaxis in unipolar major depressive disorder. *Journal of Clinical Psychiatry*, *66*(3), 283–290.

Spielmans, G. I., Berman, M. I., & Usitalo, A. N. (2011). Psychotherapy versus second-generation antidepressants in the treatment of depression: A meta-analysis. *Journal of Nervous and Mental Disease*, *199*(3), 142–149. doi: 10.1097/NMD.0b013e31820caefb

Stroup, T. S., McEvoy, J. P., Swartz, M. S., Byerly, M. J., Glick, I. D., Canive, J. M., . . . Lieberman,

J.A. (2003). The national institute of mental health clinical antipsychotic trials of intervention effectiveness (CATIE) project: Schizophrenia trial design and protocol development. *Schizophrenia Bulletin*, *29*(1), 15–31.

Strunk, D. R., Brotman, M. A., DeRubeis, R. J., & Hollon, S. D. (2010). Therapist competence in cognitive therapy for depression: Predicting subsequent symptom change. *Journal of Consulting and Clinical Psychology*, *78*(3), 429–437. doi: 10.1037/a0019631

Szentagotai, A., & David, D. (2010). The efficacy of cognitive-behavioral therapy in bipolar disorder: A quantitative meta-analysis. *Journal of Clinical Psychiatry*, *71*(1), 66–72. doi: 10.4088/JCP.08r04559yel

Tarrier, N., Barrowclough, C., Porceddu, K., & Fitzpatrick, E. (1994). The Salford family intervention project: Relapse rates of schizophrenia at five and eight years. *British Journal of Psychiatry: The Journal of Mental Science*, *165*(6), 829–832.

Tarrier, N, Wittkowski, A., Kinney, C., McCarthy, E., Morris, J., & Humphreys, L. (1999). Durability of the effects of cognitive-behavioural therapy in the treatment of chronic schizophrenia: 12-month follow-up. *British Journal of Psychiatry: The Journal of Mental Science*, *174*, 500–504.

Tarrier, N, Yusupoff, L., Kinney, C., McCarthy, E., Gledhill, A., Haddock, G., & Morris, J. (1998). Randomised controlled trial of intensive cognitive behaviour therapy for patients with chronic schizophrenia. *BMJ (Clinical Research Ed.)*, *317*(7154), 303–307.

Tarrier, N. (2010). Cognitive behavior therapy for schizophrenia and psychosis: Current status and future directions. *Clinical Schizophrenia & Related Psychoses*, *4*(3), 176–184. doi: 10.3371/CSRP.4.3.4

Tarrier, N., Lewis, S., Haddock, G., Bentall, R., Drake, R., Kinderman, P., . . . Dunn, G. (2004). Cognitive-behavioural therapy in first-episode and early schizophrenia. 18-month follow-up of a randomised controlled trial. *British Journal of Psychiatry: The Journal of Mental Science*, *184*, 231–239.

Teasdale, J. D., Segal, Z. V., Williams, J. M. G., Ridgeway, V. A., Soulsby, J. M., & Lau, M. A. (2000). Prevention of relapse/recurrence in major depression by mindfulness-based cognitive therapy. *Journal of Consulting and Clinical Psychology*, *68*, 615–623. doi: 10.1037/0022–006X.68.4.615

Teasdale, J. D., Segal, Z., & Williams, J. M. G. (1995). How does cognitive therapy prevent depressive relapse and why should attentional control (mindfulness) training help? *Behaviour Research and Therapy*, *33*, 25–39. doi: 10.1016/0005–7967(94)E0011–7

Teich, J. L., & Buck, J. A. (2007). Mental health benefits in Employer-sponsored health plans, 1997–2003. *Journal of Behavioral Health Services &*

Research, *34*(3), 343–348. doi: 10.1007/s11414–006–9050–2

Thase, M. E., Friedman, E. S., Biggs, M. M., Wisniewski, S. R., Trivedi, M. H., . . . Rush, J. A. (2007). Cognitive therapy versus medication in augmentation and switch strategies as second-step treatments: A STAR*D report. *American Journal of Psychiatry*, *164*(5), 739–752. doi: 10.1176/appi.ajp.164.5.739

Thuile, J., Even, C., & Rouillon, F. (2009). Long-term outcome of anxiety disorders: A review of double-blind studies. *Current Opinion in Psychiatry*, *22*(1), 84–89. doi: 10.1097/YCO.0b013e32831a726d

Tohen, M., Waternaux, C. M., & Tsuang, M. T. (1990). Outcome in mania. A 4-year prospective follow-up of 75 patients utilizing survival analysis. *Archives of General Psychiatry*, *47*(12), 1106–1111.

Tolin, D. F., Hannan, S., Maltby, N., Diefenbach, G. J., Worhunsky, P., & Brady, R. E. (2007). A randomized controlled trial of self-directed versus therapist-directed cognitive-behavioral therapy for obsessive-compulsive disorder patients with prior medication trials. *Behavior Therapy*, *38*(2), 179–191. doi: 10.1016/j.beth.2006.07.001

Tomba, E., Fabbri, S., & Fava, G. A. (2009). The sequential model in the treatment of depression. *Clinical Neuropsychiatry: Journal of Treatment Evaluation*, *6*(2), 45–55.

Trower, P., Birchwood, M., Meaden, A., Byrne, S., Nelson, A., & Ross, K. (2004). Cognitive therapy for command hallucinations: Randomised controlled trial. *British Journal of Psychiatry: The Journal of Mental Science*, *184*, 312–320.

Tundo, A., Salvati, L., Busto, G., Di Spigno, D., & Falcini, R. (2007). Addition of cognitive-behavioral therapy for nonresponders to medication for obsessive-compulsive disorder: A naturalistic study. *Journal of Clinical Psychiatry*, *68*(10), 1552–1556.

Turkington, D., Sensky, T., Scott, J., Barnes, T. R. E., Nur, U., Siddle, R., . . . Kingdon, D. (2008). A randomized controlled trial of cognitive-behavior therapy for persistent symptoms in schizophrenia: A five-year follow-up. *Schizophrenia Research*, *98*(1–3), 1–7. doi: 10.1016/j.schres.2007.09.026

Unützer, J, Simon, G., Pabiniak, C., Bond, K., & Katon, W. (2000). The use of administrative data to assess quality of care for bipolar disorder in a large staff model HMO. *General Hospital Psychiatry*, *22*(1), 1–10.

van Apeldoorn, F. J., van Hout, W. J. P. J., Mersch, P. P. A., Huisman, M., Slaap, B. R., Hale, W. W., 3rd, . . . den Boer, J.A. (2008). Is a combined therapy more effective than either CBT or SSRI alone? Results of a multicenter trial on panic disorder with or without agoraphobia. *Acta Psychiatrica Scandinavica*, *117*(4), 260–270. doi: 10.1111/j.1600–0447.2008.01157.x van Balkom, A. J., de Haan, E., van Oppen, P., Spinhoven, P., Hoogduin, K. A., & van Dyck, R. (1998). Cognitive and behavioral therapies alone versus in combination with fluvoxamine in the treatment of obsessive compulsive disorder. *Journal of Nervous and Mental Disease, 186*(8), 492–499.

van Minnen, A., Arntz, A., & Keijsers, G. P. J. (2002). Prolonged exposure in patients with chronic PTSD: Predictors of treatment outcome and dropout. *Behaviour Research and Therapy, 40*(4), 439–457.

van Oppen, P., van Balkom, A. J. L. M., de Haan, E., & van Dyck, R. (2005). Cognitive therapy and exposure in vivo alone and in combination with fluvoxamine in obsessive-compulsive disorder: A 5-year follow-up. *Journal of Clinical Psychiatry, 66*(11), 1415–1422.

Vieta, E., Locklear, J., Günther, O., Ekman, M., Miltenburger, C., Chatterton, M. L., Aström, M., & Paulsson, B. (2010). Treatment options for bipolar depression: A systematic review of randomized, controlled trials. *Journal of Clinical Psychopharmacology, 30*(5), 579–590. doi: 10.1097/JCP.0b013e3181f15849

Viguera, A. C., Baldessarini, R. J., & Friedberg, J. (1998). Discontinuing antidepressant treatment in major depression. *Harvard Review of Psychiatry, 5*(6), 293–306.

Vittengl, J. R., Clark, L. A., Dunn, T. W., & Jarrett, R. B. (2007). Reducing relapse and recurrence in unipolar depression: A comparative meta-analysis of cognitive-behavioral therapy's effects. *Journal of Consulting and Clinical Psychology, 75*(3), 475–488. doi: 10.1037/0022–006X.75.3.475

Vos, T., Corry, J., Haby, M. M., Carter, R., & Andrews, G. (2005). Cost-effectiveness of cognitive-behavioural therapy and drug interventions for major depression. *Australian and New Zealand Journal of Psychiatry, 39*, 683–692. doi: 10.1111/j.1440–1614.2005.01652.x

Walkup, J. T., Albano, A. M., Piacentini, J., Birmaher, B., Compton, S. N., Sherrill, J. T., . . . Kendall, P.C. (2008). Cognitive behavioral therapy, sertraline, or a combination in childhood anxiety. *New England Journal of Medicine, 359*(26), 2753–2766. doi: 10.1056/NEJMoa0804633

Watanabe, N., Churchill, R., & Furukawa, T. A. (2007). Combination of psychotherapy and benzodiazepines versus either therapy alone for panic disorder: A systematic review. *BMC Psychiatry, 7*, 18. doi:10.1186/1471-244X-7-18

Warden, D., Rush, A. J., Wisniewski, S. R., Lesser, I. M., Kornstein, S. G., Balasubramani, G. K., . . . Trivedi, M.H. (2009). What predicts attrition in second step medication treatments for depression?: A STAR*D Report. *International Journal of Neuropsychopharmacology/Official Scientific Journal of the Collegium Internationale Neuropsychopharmacologicum (CINP), 12*(4), 459–473. doi: 10.1017/S1461145708009073

Weissman, M. M., Klerman, G. L., Paykel, E. S., Prusoff, B., & Hanson, B. (1974). Treatment effects on the social adjustment of depressed patients. *Archives of General Psychiatry, 30*(6), 771–778.

Weissman, M. M., Klerman, G. L., Prusoff, B. A., Sholomskas, D., & Padian, N. (1981). Depressed outpatients: Results one year after treatment with drugs and/or interpersonal psychotherapy. *Archives of General Psychiatry, 38*(1), 51–55. doi: 10.1001/archpsyc.1981.01780260053005

Wilhelm, S., Buhlmann, U., Tolin, D. F., Meunier, S. A., Pearlson, G. D., Reese, H. E., & Rauch, S.L. (2008). Augmentation of behavior therapy with d-cycloserine for obsessive-compulsive disorder. *American Journal of Psychiatry, 165*(3), 335–341; quiz 409. doi: 10.1176/appi.ajp.2007.07050776

Wilkes, M. S., Bell, R. A., & Kravitz, R. L. (2000). Direct-to-consumer prescription drug advertising: Trends, impact, and implications. *Health Affairs (Project Hope), 19*(2), 110–128.

Wirshing, W. C. (2001). Movement disorders associated with neuroleptic treatment. *Journal of Clinical Psychiatry, 62*(Suppl. 21), 15–18.

Woods, J. H., Katz, J. L., & Winger, G. (1992). Benzodiazepines: use, abuse, and consequences. *Pharmacological Reviews, 44*(2), 151–347.

Wykes, T., Huddy, V., Cellard, C., McGurk, S. R., & Czobor, P. (2011). A meta-analysis of cognitive remediation for schizophrenia: Methodology and effect sizes. *American Journal of Psychiatry, 168*(5), 472–485. doi: 10.1176/appi.ajp.2010.10060855

Wykes, T., Steel, C., Everitt, B., & Tarrier, N. (2008). Cognitive behavior therapy for schizophrenia: Effect sizes, clinical models, and methodological rigor. *Schizophrenia Bulletin, 34*(3), 523–537. doi: 10.1093/schbul/sbm114

Yonkers, K. A., Bruce, S. E., Dyck, I. R., & Keller, M. B. (2003). Chronicity, relapse, and illness—Course of panic disorder, social phobia, and generalized anxiety disorder: Findings in men and women from 8 years of follow-up. *Depression and Anxiety, 17*(3), 173–179. doi: 10.1002/da.10106

CHAPTER 19

TRAINING AND SUPERVISION IN PSYCHOTHERAPY

CLARA E. HILL AND SARAH KNOX

Extensive clinical training is required to become a credentialed mental health practitioner, and postdegree practitioners are also often mandated to participate in continuing education and supervision. Furthermore, credentialing agencies have recently proposed that the helping professions establish and adhere to specific benchmarks to verify that trainees are advancing in their development as professionals before they are allowed to continue in their training programs (e.g., Fouad et al., 2009). Most practitioners and trainers (including us) believe that such training, for the most part, is helpful. If we are to claim that training is necessary and effective, however, we need to provide evidence of this effectiveness.

In this chapter, we review existing evidence for the effectiveness of clinical training, following as much as possible the chronology of training itself. To that end, we first review the literature on training for novice therapists (undergraduates and graduate students). We then turn to research on individual supervision, most of which has been conducted with graduate students. Third, we review the research related to training for practicing professionals. Finally, we review studies that indirectly assess the effects of training.

To make the scope of this chapter manageable and its findings useful, we cover only empirical studies about training and supervision. We do not cover training and supervision for group and family therapy (with one exception), given the paucity of such research. In addition, although such research is fundamental to the provision of effective psychotherapy, we do not cover studies that focus on training for diversity, multiculturalism, social justice, assessment, diagnosis, or case conceptualization, nor do we cover

peer supervision. Similarly, we do not review the literature on trainees' own personal psychotherapy or their personal relationships, even though these experiences undoubtedly influence the well-being of trainees and thus their ability to function in a therapeutic setting. In addition, although instruction in basic psychology, research methods, and statistics is part of graduate education and thus probably affects graduate students' ability to conduct psychotherapy, we do not review the effects of such instruction because it is not directly linked to assessing the effects of training and supervision. Furthermore, due to our own limitations, we excluded studies that were not written in English. What we do focus on, then, is the training and supervision of English-speaking therapists at all levels (novice through experienced) who work with clients in individual therapy from any theoretical orientation. Narrowing our focus in this way allows us to closely examine a body of research that addresses the very heart of clinical education.

In locating the corpus of studies for the current chapter, we focused primarily on research conducted since the last chapter on training and supervision in this handbook (Matarazzo & Patterson, 1986), although we incorporated previous work as needed to tell a complete story in a particular area. To that end, we performed a manual search of the past 15 years in psychology journals most likely to publish articles on training and supervision (*Counseling Psychologist*, *Journal of Counseling Psychology*, *Journal of Consulting and Clinical Psychology*, *Professional Psychology*, *Psychotherapy*, *Psychotherapy Research*, and *Training and Education in Professional Psychology*), and then searched the reference lists of located articles to identify additional published articles. We also invited researchers in the training and supervision sections of the Society for Psychotherapy Research and the Society for Counseling Psychology to send us relevant studies.

When we speak about training in this chapter, we refer to structured education for groups of trainees; supervision refers to an individualized forum of a supervisor working with one trainee (supervisee) regarding specific clients. Thus, whereas training typically involves a standardized set of steps, supervision more often involves working individually with trainees to best meet their and their clients' needs. We note, however, that the distinction between training and supervision is often unclear, in that training programs often involve a supervision component, and supervision sometimes involves teaching using a structured approach. Nevertheless, we present these two literatures separately. Finally, we use "therapist" and "client," regardless of terms used in the literature reviewed.

TRAINING NOVICE THERAPISTS

We divide the studies in this section into two parts. First, we review studies related to helping skills training. Second, we review studies related to changes during the course of graduate training.

Helping Skills Training

The majority of training studies with novice therapists involved helping skills training, which refers to structured programs that teach facilitative conditions (e.g., empathy, warmth, genuineness) or specific verbal interventions (e.g., reflections of feeling, open questions, challenges) thought to facilitate empathy. Trainees in these helping skills programs are typically taught to implement the desired behaviors and to minimize the use of undesired behaviors (e.g., advice, interruptions) through instruction (reading and lecture/discussion), modeling, practice with classmates, and feedback. Students usually engage in helping skills training at the advanced undergraduate and beginning graduate level before seeing real clients under supervision in practicum settings so that they can focus on the development of their skills.

The origins of helping skills training trace back to Rogers (1942, 1957), who asserted that empathy, warmth, and genuineness were necessary and sufficient for therapeutic change. Rogers

(1942) initially posited that these facilitative conditions could be taught as skills (e.g., restatements, reflections of feelings), but later (Rogers, 1957) came to believe that the facilitative conditions were attitudes and could not be taught. Many of his followers (e.g., Truax & Carkhuff, 1967), however, continued to believe that empathy, warmth, and genuineness could be taught as specific skills.

A number of helping skills training programs were developed in response to Rogers' work. The three early programs that received the most extensive empirical attention were developed by Carkhuff (Human Relations Training, HRT; 1969), Ivey (Microcounseling, MC; 1971), and Kagan (Interpersonal Process Recall, IPR; 1984). HRT and MC focus on teaching specific verbal skills such as empathy or reflection of feeling, whereas IPR focuses on helping trainees articulate their thoughts and feelings about their interventions under the assumption that trainees are blocked from effectively using their native skills due to performance anxiety. We now review the empirical literature about these early training programs.

Evidence for the Effectiveness of Helping Skills Training Programs

Having been conducted primarily in the 1960s and 1970s, most of the research on helping skills training is relatively old. To provide an historical context, we briefly review this older literature, and then turn to more recent literature.

Narrative Reviews of Helping Skills Training

A number of narrative reviews have been written about the empirical research on helping skills training (Ford, 1979; Kasdorf & Gustafson, 1978; Lambert, DeJulio, & Stein, 1978; Matarazzo, 1971, 1978; Matarazzo & Patterson, 1986; Russell, Crimmings, & Lent, 1984). We focus here only on the reviews of training in the three early editions of the *Handbook of Psychotherapy and Behavior Change* by Matarazzo because these were the most comprehensive. Matarazzo concluded (contrary to Rogers' assertion) that warmth and empathy could be taught. More specifically, she asserted that there was sufficient evidence that Ivey's MC program could be taught in a relatively short period of time to appropriately selected students. In contrast, she dismissed the outcome studies of Carkhuff's HRT because of numerous methodological problems (e.g., skills not being operationally defined, crude and subjective assessment of skills, unspecified aspects of training, inadequate controls, identical rating scales used to assess training and outcome, use of analogue methods rather than actual interview behavior to assess outcome, inadequate training of judges for coding outcome measures, lack of attention to the optimal sequencing of training methods). No conclusions were drawn about Kagan's IPR.

In addition to the methodological problems in the helping literature previously discussed by Matarazzo (1971, 1978; Matarazzo & Patterson, 1986), Hill and Lent (2006) more recently noted several concerns that limit our confidence in the conclusions drawn from the early studies about the effects of helping skills training. The content of the training programs was seldom specified, most studies involved only one trainer (thus confounding the effects of training with the effects of the specific trainer), trainees were rarely randomly assigned to training vs. control conditions, training was far briefer than is currently considered adequate (about 20 hours versus the current one to two semesters), and outcome was typically assessed through written or taped responses to written or taped analogue stimuli, rather than through assessing therapist behavior or client outcomes in clinical settings.

A related area is the prediction of outcome based on trainee characteristics. In their review, Hill and Lent (2006) found five studies that predicted outcome from trainee characteristics. None of these studies used the same variables or measures, however, so it was not possible to draw any conclusions about whether some types of trainees profit more than others from helping skills training.

Meta-Analytic Reviews of Helping Skills Training

In addition to Matarazzo's narrative reviews, researchers have also completed meta-analyses of this helping skills literature. In their review of Ivey's MC, Baker and Daniels (1989) reported a larger effect size (1.18) for undergraduate trainees than for graduate trainees (.66). Goodyear and Guzzardo (2000) argued compellingly, however, that graduate trainees have had more clinical experience and thus there might be a ceiling effect on what they can learn from a helping skills training program. In a comparison of MC, HRT, and IPR, Baker, Daniels, and Greeley (1990)

reported a large effect (1.07) for Carkhuff's HRT, a medium effect (.63) for Ivey's MC, and a small (.20) effect for Kagan's IPR for graduate-level trainees. It should be noted, however, that this meta-analysis was based on a small number of studies (8 for HRT, 23 for MC, and 10 for IPR). There also may have been a confound between the type and amount of training, given that HRT averaged 37 hours whereas MC and IPR averaged 19 and 9.5 hours, respectively.

Maintenance of Skills Posttraining

If training is effective, the results should persist over time. We found only three studies that investigated whether those who had been trained actually maintained their skills over time. Across these studies, undergraduate trainees decreased in rated facilitativeness (Collingwood, 1971; Gormally, Hill, Gulanick, & McGovern, 1975), whereas beginning graduate trainees either maintained or increased in rated facilitativeness (Butler & Hansen, 1973; Gormally et al., 1975). Gormally et al. (1975) suggested that undergraduates were less likely to continue using the skills given that many did not go on to graduate school or work in mental health settings. Graduate students, in contrast, were more likely to continue using their skills in required practica, and so they were more able to maintain and enhance their skills.

Recent Research on Helping Skills Training or Empathy Training

Although research on helping skills training was broadly popular in the 1960s and 1970s, current research has focused mostly on Hill's (Hill, 2004, 2009; Hill & O'Brien, 1999) helping skills model, which integrates elements from HRT, MC, and IPR, as well as empirical findings from psychotherapy process research. The Hill model teaches skills in three stages. In the exploration stage, helpers use open questions, restatements, reflections of feelings, and disclosures of feelings to help clients explore their thoughts and feelings. In the insight stage, helpers promote insight through skills of open questions, challenge, interpretation, and immediacy. In the action stage, helpers use open questions, information, and direct guidance to help clients explore the idea of making changes in their behaviors. The training focuses on the specific skills by providing theory, empirical findings, and examples, followed by extensive practice in small groups and dyads. We note that the skills highlighted in this model are largely based on clinical wisdom rather than specific empirical evidence about the connection of the skills with client outcomes.

As opposed to previous studies that involved judges rating helpers' use of the skills in which they have been trained, Hill and Kellems (2002) developed the Helping Skills Measure, the Relationship Scale, and the Session Evaluation Scale. These are self-report instruments that allow clients to assess the frequency with which they perceive that the skills were used, the quality of the therapeutic relationship, and the quality of the just-completed session. Using these measures, Hill and Kellems found that undergraduate students were perceived as increasing across the course of a semester of training in the frequency of their use of exploration, insight, and action skills; in addition, they were better able to establish a therapeutic relationship and conduct brief sessions with volunteer clients. It is important to note that volunteer clients completed these measures after brief sessions with trainees, so this study provided more naturalistic data than were available in previous studies that used written/oral responses to written/oral stimuli.

A second study by Hill et al. (2008) investigated effects of helping skills training from multiple perspectives (helpers, clients, and judges). Hill et al. (2008) found that undergraduate students were more able (compared to their performance pretraining) to use exploration skills, were more empathic, talked less, and were evaluated as more effective in brief sessions with classmates after about 8 weeks (32 hours) of training in the exploration stage skills. In addition, at the end of a 15-week semester (60 hours), these trainees had higher self-efficacy for using helping skills than they had at the beginning of the semester. Interestingly, based on weekly ratings during the semester, confidence steadily grew during training in exploration skills, then declined during training in insight skills perhaps because insight skills are more difficult to learn, and again rose during the action stage perhaps because action skills are easier to master. The authors were not able to predict outcomes from initial grade-point average, trainee-rated empathy, or client-rated perfectionism, reflecting the lack of consistency in predicting who profits from training cited in the Hill and Lent (2006) review. Strengths of the Hill et al. (2008) study include the use of multiple perspectives of outcome, the use of actual brief sessions with volunteer clients, and the use of more than one trainer.

From a more qualitative perspective, Williams, Judge, Hill, and Hoffman (1997) found that beginning therapists had a great deal of anxiety and insecurity about being able to use skills in a clinical situation, a discomfort that was substantially reduced during training; trainees also perceived the training as positive overall. In a qualitative study of master's-level trainees (Hill, Sullivan, Knox, & Schlosser, 2007), trainees kept weekly journals about their experiences learning helping skills in the classroom and working with volunteer clients in weekly sessions. As the semester progressed, trainees reported being able to use exploration and insight skills more effectively (although they rarely mentioned action skills) and feeling better about themselves as therapists (less anxious, more self-efficacious, more comfortable in the role of therapist, less self-critical, and more able to connect with clients).

Nerdrum and Rønnestad (2002, 2004) conducted qualitative studies of the experience of empathy training. They found that trainees reported more empathic understanding in working with clients, more understanding of themselves as professionals, and positive effects on clients as a result of training focused on both cognitive and affective aspects of empathy.

Summary of the Effectiveness of Helping Skills/Empathy Training

Strong evidence has been found for the efficacy of various forms of helping skills training during the approximately 50 years that such training has been conducted. Effectiveness has been assessed in diverse ways, including changes in empathy, changes in skill usage, and client ratings of session effectiveness. As discussed previously, however, limitations in this research do exist especially in the early research, which may temper our confidence in these findings.

Despite a half-century of research in this area, questions remain regarding what is adequate training outcome. Some would argue that we should develop minimum thresholds (benchmarks) to determine whether a student has succeeded or failed in training. Such criteria could be used to assess the "quality" of training, just as some researchers assess the outcomes of psychotherapy by examining the number of clients who pass from the symptomatic to normal ranges of functioning. We would argue against such a trend, however, because the goal of helping skills training is to teach students to broadly think about the skills and practice them, to learn when and why to use skills, and to observe client reactions and adjust their approach based on clients' unique needs. Given that every client is different, and thus that therapists must respond to each client's needs, it is not only unfeasible, but perhaps even dangerous, to dictate what skills "should" be used in a given situation. Thus, the goals of training are to provide therapists with an armamentarium of skills upon which they can rely, and which they can astutely use, in the inevitably dynamic and varied clinical situations they will encounter. Furthermore, given the infinite variability in therapists, as well, we simply cannot determine what a "skilled" therapist will look like posttraining. In fact, there could well be a chilling effect on the training process were we to dictate exactly how trainees, or therapists, should behave with clients.

Although we have concerns about the use of benchmarks, as noted above, we remain in dogged pursuit of how best to conduct helping skills training, and thus how best to serve clients. One unresolved question, for instance, involves the sequencing of helping skills training. From our perspective (see also, Hill, Stahl, & Roffman, 2007), helping skills training is vital as a first exposure to the field because it allows trainees to examine their own behaviors before they are placed in settings where they must focus on client dynamics. Although it makes intuitive sense to provide helping skills training first, then introduce trainees to working with "easy" clients under in vivo supervision, and only later train students in specific treatment approaches (see later section), such sequencing of training experiences has not been investigated empirically.

Relatedly, it also makes sense, based on our experiences and based on the cognitive psychology literature about learning and expertise (e.g., Ericsson, Charness, Feltovich, & Hoffman, 2006; Georghiades, 2004; Hacker, 1998), that it would take 2 to 3 years for students to become relatively comfortable using the skills. Once they develop some proficiency in using the skills in an empathic, caring manner, they typically no longer focus on each individual skill (i.e., they do not think about doing a reflection of feeling), but rather begin to focus more on the client and the dynamics of the therapeutic relationship. Thus, the skills become automatic and recede into the background and other challenges (e.g., case conceptualization, session management) occupy the foreground of attention. Thus, we need to

assess the effects of helping skills training over extended periods of time. There is some hint that continued practice is necessary, so this would be particularly important to study.

Finally, we know very little about trainer and trainee effects. Undoubtedly, who the trainer is makes a difference in that some trainers inspire trainees, whereas others turn trainees off to pursuing a career as a therapist. Similarly, some trainees profit from training (perhaps those who are cognitively complex and naturally empathic), whereas others do not seem to "get" how to facilitate client change (perhaps those who have a hard time putting themselves in others' shoes). Such potential influences are also worthy of examination.

Effectiveness of Components of Helping Skills Training

In their examination of several narrative reviews of the effectiveness of specific methods used in training, Hill and Lent (2006) noted that modeling, rehearsal/practice, instruction, feedback/supervision, self-observation/confrontation, co-counseling, and deconditioning of anxiety have all been cited as effective in teaching helping skills. Most of this research was based on Bandura's (1969, 1997) social cognitive theory that postulated that instruction, modeling, practice, and feedback are essential components of the learning process. Thus, if we want someone to learn something, Bandura suggested that it is most effective to carefully define what is to be learned and give a theoretical framework for it, show how it can be used, provide opportunities for practice, and then provide corrective feedback.

As part of their review, Hill and Lent (2006) conducted a meta-analysis of the most often used methods: instruction (typically involved 5 to 10 minutes of written or taped didactic information about the definition and rationale for using a specific skill), modeling (usually involved watching short, less-than-30-minute videotapes of expert therapists demonstrating the target skill), practice, and feedback (typically involved immediate reinforcement visually via lights or verbally through earphones or speakers, or through a 20- to 30-minute feedback session). Across all studies, they found a large effect (.79) indicating that the aforementioned training methods (aggregated across all types) were better than no training. [Recall that an effect size of .79 suggests that only 31% of the untrained will be successful whereas

69% of the trained will be successful.] Further comparisons indicated medium to large effects for modeling (.90), feedback (.89), and instruction (.63), compared to no training. Medium effects across components were found for the two most frequently used outcome measures (.75 for judges' ratings of trainee empathy during short practice interviews, and .62 for judges' ratings of trainee empathy in written/taped responses to written/taped analogue stimuli). Relatively large effects across components were found for both graduate (.88) and undergraduate (.77) trainees.

The above meta-analysis was conducted on between-studies effects (e.g., participants were not randomly assigned to training versus control, but instead came from different studies). Another way of estimating training effects is through looking at studies that compare the target variables in the same study when researchers randomly assign participants to conditions versus control. Thus, Hill and Lent (2006) conducted a within-study meta-analysis, and reported a medium effect size (.67) favoring modeling over instruction and feedback. Furthermore, an additive effect (.51) was found, indicating that training using multiple methods yielded better results than training using any single method. These results suggest that the most influential training component is modeling, and that using several methods is better than relying on a single method of training.

Hill and Lent cautioned, however, against overreliance on any of the results of these studies about the components of training because of methodological problems. Most problematically, skills were typically taught in isolation rather than within the context of a training program. Because researchers did not want to confound training on a specific skill with training in general, they often used introductory psychology students and taught them the skill (e.g., reflection of feelings) within the space of 5 minutes to 1 hour, hardly giving participants the opportunity to learn the complexities of using this intervention. In addition, training for more advanced or difficult skills (e.g., interpretation, challenge, immediacy) that require a foundation of empathic ability was not studied at all. Furthermore, authors were often vague about how they defined and implemented training methods, and assessments of outcomes were restricted to simplistic written/oral responses to written/oral analogue vignettes. There was also considerable overlap between instruction and modeling (i.e., how do you model without defining what it is you are modeling?), and between

practice and feedback (i.e., how can you give feedback unless it is based on something a trainee has practiced?).

Investigators in three recent studies have attempted to correct some of these methodological concerns. Spangler et al. (2011), Chui et al. (2011), and Jackson et al. (2011) examined both quantitatively and qualitatively the effectiveness of using instruction (reading and lecture), modeling, practice, and feedback for teaching undergraduate students the skills of immediacy, challenge, and interpretation, respectively, within the context of semester-long training programs using the Hill (2009) model. These authors found considerable support for all four methods (instruction, modeling, practice, and feedback), although students consistently indicated that practice was by far the most helpful training method.

An alternative method for analyzing the effective components of training is through qualitative research. In a study of trainees learning empathic communication, for instance, Nerdrum and Rønnestad (2002) reported that trainees liked having training spread out over a long period of time and interspersing training and practice. Trainees reported that the most useful training methods were lectures about theory, role playing, and trainers demanding that trainees actively participate in the training. Trainees also valued trainers' responsiveness to their individual needs, supportiveness, and being credible models of empathic functioning. All trainees also, however, commented that being vulnerable about their abilities made them anxious. In reflecting about how they changed, trainees noted the influence of new knowledge and suggested that they learned by self-observation and by observing the effects of their interventions on clients. Finally, trainees noted that both time and effort were essential for internalizing learning.

In summary, considerable evidence has been found for the effectiveness of instruction, modeling, practice, and feedback in teaching empathy and reflection of feelings. We know less, however, about the best ways to learn insight and action skills. We also do not know much about other possible components of training, such as self-observation/confrontation, co-counseling, anxiety-reduction techniques, support, and transcribing and coding interventions used in sessions and receiving feedback from instructors about those interventions. In addition, paralleling the earlier question regarding the most effective sequence of training, a similar question arises here, for we do not yet know the best sequence for the components of training. Although it makes sense that trainees need to read first, then hear about a skill through lecture, then see models of the skill, then practice, and then receive feedback, other sequences might be as useful, and sequences might vary for different skills.

Summary and Recommendations for Research on Helping Skills Training for Novice Therapists

Across this body of research, we have evidence that helping skills training is effective; that skills have to be practiced for maintenance; and that instruction, modeling, practice, and feedback are helpful components of training. Methodological improvements in recent studies bolster our confidence in these findings. We have no evidence about trainer effects, however, and inconsistent evidence about trainee effects. Furthermore, we have only preliminary evidence for training of insight skills (e.g., challenge, interpretation, immediacy), and no evidence for training of action skills.

The bulk of the research for novice trainees has focused on helping skills training. We would suggest that this focus is prudent because trainees are learning to shift from communication that is appropriate in friendships to communication that is appropriate for therapy. Hence, they must learn to move from evenly shared conversations to listening more, giving less self-disclosure, and offering less opinion, while donning the mantle of professionalism and seeing themselves in the therapist role. It makes sense, then, to focus on these skills in very safe practice situations with volunteer clients so that trainees can begin to self-reflect and observe their behaviors in a supportive environment. Based on the extant research, we offer the following seven suggestions for future research:

1. Continued research is needed on training in basic helping skills. We need to know which helping skills programs are effective and what makes them effective.

2. In addition to learning the helping skills, trainers also hope that trainees become less anxious, have more self-efficacy, are better able to manage sessions, and become more self-aware. Thus, we also need to know what training approaches yield such effects for different types of trainees.

3. We need to know more about training for specific skills. As earlier noted, we have a lot of research on training for empathy/restatements/reflections of feelings, but need research on how to teach other skills such as interpretations, challenges, and immediacy. It would also be interesting to determine whether prior training in helping skills enables trainees to more effectively learn these advanced skills.

4. We also need to know more about trainer (e.g., dogmatism, charisma) and trainee (e.g., attitudes about psychotherapy, motivations for wanting to be a therapist, tolerance for ambiguity, self-awareness) characteristics that influence training outcomes.

5. We need to know more about the maintenance of helping skills after training. Thus, we urge others to follow-up on the idea that continued practice using the skills helps trainees maintain their skills.

6. We need to learn more about the interaction between attitudes and skills. In other words, we need to know more about how to train students not only to learn the skills, but how to use them in a caring, empathic manner.

7. More research is needed on methods of training novice therapists. For example, researchers need to investigate the effectiveness of having novice trainees begin by learning evidence-based treatment approaches rather than by learning basic helping skills.

STUDIES OF STRUCTURED TRAINING DURING GRADUATE SCHOOL

Several studies have examined other types of training during graduate education. These studies provide some evidence for the effectiveness of training, although the effects of training are typically confounded with other experiences (e.g., personal therapy, coursework, personal relationships). Although a few of these studies did include comparison conditions (i.e., different types of training), there was no random assignment to conditions, reducing our confidence in the results. The first set of studies assessed changes in therapist behaviors over time using brief, single sessions with volunteer clients. The second set of studies assessed changes in therapist behaviors across time with "real" clients. Trainees' self-reported changes over the course of training were examined in the final set of studies.

Assessing Changes in Graduate Trainees Using Analogue Sessions

Pope, Nudler, Norden, and McGee (1976) found that undergraduate mental health trainees decreased in the number of speech disturbances (reflecting anxiety) and increased in perceived warmth and genuineness over 3 years of training. These findings were based on judgments of trainee behavior in single, 15- to 45-minute sessions with volunteer clients.

Hill, Charles, and Reed (1981) assessed changes across graduate training for 12 counseling psychology doctoral students. Students completed two 10- to 15-minute sessions with volunteer clients during each of the first 3 years of graduate school. Results indicated increases in the use of minimal encouragers and decreases in questions. In contrast, no changes were found in activity level, anxiety, or judge-rated quality of sessions. In addition, no effects were found for experience level (half of the students had some clinical experience prior to the program, whereas half had none or minimal experience) prior to entering the program. In interviews, trainees reported making gains in ability to use advanced skills (interpretations, confrontation, silence); manage sessions (i.e., timing and appropriateness of interventions); conceptualize client dynamics; and feel more relaxed, natural, and spontaneous with clients.

In a follow-up study, Thompson (1986) compared the skills of 13 graduate students and 13 undergraduate psychology students in 20-minute interviews with volunteer clients at the beginning and end of an academic year. Graduate students were in a counseling psychology program that taught helping skills; undergraduates were in regular psychology classes with no exposure to counseling skills. Both graduate and undergraduate students used more information, closed questions, and restatements but fewer minimal encouragers over time. Graduate students also used more open questions and confrontations but fewer interpretations and "other" skills (e.g., small talk) over time. In contrast, undergraduates used more "other" skills over time. Interestingly, judge-rated quality of sessions increased for both groups over time. Finally, graduate students changed on scores on the Personal Orientation Inventory over time, evidencing more inner-directness and self-acceptance, whereas undergraduates decreased on these scales.

O'Donovan, Bain, and Dyck (2005) compared one group of students who participated in a traditional graduate program in clinical psychology with a second group who served an apprenticeship in which they obtained supervised workplace experience without organized training. Both groups had graduated with a 4-year undergraduate degree in psychology and had similar levels of clinical knowledge and practice ability at the beginning of training, although there was an unspecified age difference between the two groups. Students were not randomly assigned to condition, however, and nonrandom factors probably influenced which track students took. Although after 1 year of training, clinical psychology graduate trainees had gained more than apprentices in terms of clinical knowledge (didactic information about assessment, treatment, and evaluation), neither group changed in terms of practice ability (assessed by client and observer ratings of working alliance, empathy, and dropout probability based on trainees working with a standard client for 30 minutes). In additional analyses of the data, O'Donovan and Dyck (2005) found that if trainees had emotional problems (as defined by scores on the Eysenck Personality Questionnaire and the MCMI), they were more likely to be able to engage appropriately with clients after clinical psychology training than after an apprenticeship. Given the lack of details about the training experiences, it is difficult to interpret the results of both studies. It would seem, however, that the traditional program allowed students to learn more academic knowledge, but that students in both programs were equally proficient in the clinical skills.

Hess, Knox, and Hill (2006) focused on one of the most difficult situations faced by trainees and practicing clinicians—the management of anger. They compared three different approaches for helping trainees manage client anger. More specifically, they provided 62 graduate student trainees who had completed basic helping skills training with three types of more advanced but brief training for dealing with anger: supervisor-facilitated training (supervisors asked students to talk about their reactions and then worked with them during role plays to become more empathic and use more reflections of feelings and immediacy in response to client anger), self-training (students were asked to write about their reactions and then think of what they might do differently with the client), and bibliotraining (students read an article about a treatment model for anger disorders). Students received all three types of training in a random order. Training overall was rated as very helpful, and trainees rated themselves as having higher self-efficacy for working with client anger as a result of the training. Supervisor-facilitated training appeared to be the most beneficial training method, given that trainees rated it as most helpful and used more reflections of feelings after it. Although these results are intriguing, we do not know whether they would generalize to other challenging client behaviors, or to real clinical situations, especially after such brief training.

Crook-Lyon, Hill, Hess, Wimmer, and Goates-Jones (2009) examined the effects of didactic-experiential training, individual feedback, and practice for teaching novice therapists to do dream work as a therapeutic intervention. Therapist self-efficacy for working with dreams and attitudes towards dreams increased after didactic training. In addition, those who received individual feedback had higher process and outcome evaluations from clients in a dream session than did those who did not receive feedback. Furthermore, self-efficacy, attitudes toward dreams, and perceived self-competence in dream work steadily increased across the course of conducting five dream sessions. Although the sample size was small, these results support the effectiveness of didactic-experiential methods, feedback, and practice for training, which responds to the call we earlier made to examine various components of training in a more clinically realistic approach.

In sum, these studies show that graduate trainees do change over time. Summarizing across studies, however, is difficult because of the different research questions and the lack of replication of findings.

Assessing Changes in Graduate Trainees Using Real Clients

Multon, Kivlighan, and Gold (1996) examined changes in the use of psychodynamic techniques within a single, four-session case with a volunteer client for each of 36 masters-level students in a pr-practicum class on time-limited dynamic psychotherapy (TLDP). Across the four sessions, there was a linear increase in TLDP adherence and client-rated working alliance. Strengths include the relatively large number of trainees; limitations include the use of only one case

per therapist, so that we do not know whether learning would transfer to other cases.

In Hilsenroth, Ackerman, Clemence, Strassle, and Handler (2002), doctoral students who received structured clinical training in short-term psychodynamic psychotherapy produced higher client and therapist alliance ratings after Session 4 than did those who received no training. Hilsenroth, Defife, Blagys, and Ackerman (2006) then investigated changes in the ability to use psychodynamic techniques within and across the first two cases seen by each of 15 clinical psychology graduate students working in a psychology department clinic while learning to implement short-term psychodynamic psychotherapy. Hilsenroth et al. (2006) found increases in psychodynamic interventions between Sessions 3 and 9 in the first case (which could be due to experience with the client as much as training), but no comparable changes within the second case (which is puzzling). They also found that psychodynamic interventions were used more frequently in the second case as compared with the first case at Session 3 (which could indicate the effects of training), but no differences were found at Session 9 (which is again puzzling). Furthermore, no differences were found within or across cases for use of cognitive behavioral techniques, which makes sense given the lack of focus on these techniques in the psychodynamic training. Thus, evidence for the effects of training was somewhat mixed. Strengths of these studies include the use of data from real clients in a community-oriented clinic; limitations include the small sample of students all trained by one trainer/supervisor, the lack of attention to dropouts, and the use of only two cases per therapist.

Boswell, Castonguay, and Wasserman (2010) investigated the effects of training on 19 clinical psychology students (none of whom had any prior clinical experience) in their first practicum working with community clients. Students were trained using manuals in one of three different practica: psychodynamic, CBT, or humanistic-interpersonal (students were not randomly assigned to practica). The type of practicum had no effect on therapist postsession ratings of session process or on client-rated postsession outcome. Thus, per client report, students learned and implemented the three treatment manuals equally well (or equally poorly). Strengths of the study include the use of real clients; limitations include a lack of attention to dropouts, the use of a small sample all from one program, and the data collection period of only one semester.

Overall, the evidence for changes across time in graduate school using therapist behaviors with real clients is somewhat mixed. Evidence for therapists learning and applying psychodynamic techniques within one particular case was presented by Multon et al. (1996), Hilsenroth et al. (2002), and Hilsenroth et al. (2006), with some additional evidence across two cases by Hilsenroth et al. (2006). Boswell et al. (2010) found no differences among three approaches for training students. The lack of replication across studies and the lack of control conditions, however, make us cautious in interpreting these results of these studies. We also worry about the adequacy of assessing the effects of training with only one or two cases, given that clients can differ so dramatically, and thus results may reflect random variance rather than true change. Researchers may need to use several cases across the course of training to illuminate potential effects of training while controlling for differences across clients. We also note that it was unclear whether students in these studies had completed basic helping skills training; relatedly, we wonder whether having had helping skills training early in one's graduate career would help or hinder trainees in learning these other approaches.

Self-Reported Changes Across the Course of Graduate Training

Several studies examined self-reported changes across the course of graduate training. Although not as compelling in terms of providing evidence for the effects of training as observational measures of behavior, these studies assessed whether trainees experienced themselves as changing.

Freiheit and Overholser (1997) trained 40 clinical psychology students in CBT over the course of two semesters. Based on self-report, students learned CBT techniques and had more positive attitudes regarding CBT. Interestingly, however, a subsample of students who initially had negative evaluations of CBT did not change on attitudinal variables at the end of training. Limitations include the lack of a control group, the reliance on self-report measures, and the lack of observations of actual interventions with clients.

Pascual-Leone, Wolfe, and O'Connor (in press) conducted a qualitative study of trainees'

experience of learning experiential psychotherapy. They found consistent changes at both professional and personal levels.

In their review of the literature, Larson and Daniels (1998) concluded that therapist self-efficacy correlated positively with developmental level, such that more experienced therapists reported higher levels of self-efficacy than did those with less experience. Self-efficacy also correlated positively with satisfaction and negatively with anxiety about doing therapy, suggesting that indeed it is a relevant variable for assessing changes over training. In addition, Larson and Daniels (1998) reported that specific interventions in beginning practica (e.g., role-plays, modeling, and positive feedback) seem to promote increases in self-efficacy. In a more direct test of changes, Lent, Hill, and Hoffman (2003) and Lent et al. (2006) found changes in self-efficacy over the course of a semester of training. Given that self-efficacy is often used as a proxy for performance, the findings are encouraging.

These studies suggest that indeed graduate students perceive themselves as changing during training. Furthermore, the finding that a subsample of students with initial negative evaluations of CBT did not change on attitudinal variables at the end of training in the Freiheit and Overholser (1997) study is very interesting and begs replication because attitudes may determine whether trainees later incorporate training in their repertoires.

Summary and Recommendations for Research on Changes in Graduate Trainees Across Time

The evidence involving graduate students tentatively suggests that graduate training is effective. We cannot, however, rule out confounds with other experiences (personal therapy, work with clients). We may never be able to separate out the intertwining of these variables, and thus, discerning the effects of graduate training remains a challenging endeavor. We have four recommendations for further research:

1. We strongly recommend that researchers continue this avenue of research, despite its inherent challenges. It is especially important to assess for changes using longitudinal rather than cross-sectional designs if we are to attribute any findings to training.

2. Changes need to be studied across more than one or two cases to make sure that we discern

true changes rather than random variation among clients.

3. We need to learn more about what goes on during the time in which trainees receive training. To what extent are trainees in structured training, how much personal therapy are they receiving, and how many clients are they seeing (e.g., is there an optimal client load in ratio to the amount of supervision)?

4. Researchers can use data from both trained (standard or actor) and real clients for studying the effects of training. Trained clients are ideal because comparisons can more easily be made across time and trainees, but great care must be taken to standardize the presentation of the material so that it is highly consistent across trainees. Real clients are ideal because they present actual data and are more likely to respond naturally to trainees.

INDIVIDUAL SUPERVISION

As defined by Falender and Shafranske (2004), supervision involves a relationship between a supervisor and a supervisee that promotes the professional development of the supervisee through interpersonal processes, including mutual problem-solving, instruction, evaluation, mentoring, and role modeling of ethical practice. The goals of supervision include building on the supervisee's strengths, ameliorating weaknesses, and creating an environment that fosters clinical skill development, self-efficacy, and ethical decision making, while maintaining client welfare. Likewise, Bernard and Goodyear (2009) defined supervision as "an intervention provided by a more senior member of the profession to a more junior member...of that same profession. This relationship is evaluative and hierarchical, extends over time, and has the simultaneous purposes of enhancing the professional functioning of the more junior [person], monitoring the quality of professional services offered to the clients that she [or] he sees, and serving as a gatekeeper of those who are to enter the particular profession" (p. 7). Integrating these two definitions, we can define supervision as a relationship whose purpose and related activities support not only the professional development of the supervisee, but also the protection of her or his clients' welfare.

Our goal in this part of the chapter is to review studies of the effects (outcomes) of supervision in the mental health field. Most of the studies reviewed have involved graduate students.

We do not focus on studies that describe only the process of supervision: Although doing so may well shed light on what occurs within supervision, such a focus does not help us answer questions regarding supervision's effectiveness, the primary intent of the chapter. We focus only on individual supervision and do not include studies of group supervision. In organizing this content, we first seek to answer the question, "Is supervision effective?" We then turn to the question: "If so, what makes supervision effective?"

Within these two main sections, we separately consider quantitative and qualitative studies given the difference in the methods. Where possible we further organize our examination into subsections that reflect the foci of this literature: effects on the individual supervisee (e.g., satisfaction, competence, personal growth) and effects on the client (e.g., decreases in depression, improvements in quality of life). Holloway (1992) posited that "the ultimate goal of supervision is counselor competence" (p. 202), referring to the effects of supervision on supervisees. Others (e.g., Ellis & Ladany, 1997; Goodyear & Guzzardo, 2000), however, asserted that the most stringent and important criterion for supervision is client change.

Is Supervision Effective?

To adequately test the question about the effectiveness of supervision, researchers would have to conduct experimental manipulations in which they randomly assign trainees to supervision or no supervision (or a placebo condition) and then assess the effects on supervisee or client outcome. We found only one study of this sort (Bambling, King, Raue, Schweitzer, & Lambert, 2006), and thus we stipulate in advance that we do not have enough evidence to confidently assert the causal effects of supervision. Fortunately, there are a few other quantitative and a small handful of qualitative studies that address the topic of effectiveness, albeit not in ways that allow us to establish causality.

Quantitative Evidence

Bambling et al. (2006) evaluated the impact of supervision on clients, specifically on working alliance and symptom reduction in the brief treatment of depression. In this study, which notably was conducted in Australia with post-degree experienced therapists, 127 clients with major depression were randomly assigned either to supervised or unsupervised therapists to receive eight sessions of problem-solving therapy. Supervised therapists were randomly assigned either to eight sessions of alliance skill- or alliance process–focused supervision. Results indicated significant effects for all three conditions (i.e., supervised with alliance skill-focused supervision, supervised with alliance process-focused supervision, unsupervised) on working alliance (*ds* ranged from .57 to .74) and symptom reduction (*ds* ranged from .54 to 4.21), leading the researchers to conclude that the means by which supervision enhances alliance and treatment outcome is unclear. Clients treated by supervised therapists were, however, more satisfied than those treated by unsupervised therapists (as measured by clients' scores on a measure of treatment evaluation) and had a lower attrition rate (as measured by failure to complete eight sessions of therapy) than those with unsupervised therapists. Limitations include the inability to separate possible effects of supervision from those of a pretreatment orientation and training session, lack of a sufficient sample size to guard against Type II errors, and one researcher providing most of the supervision in both conditions.

Two other studies provided evidence of pre- to postchange as a result of supervision. Tryon (1996) examined the development of 25 advanced clinical and counseling psychology doctoral students completing a practicum at a university counseling center. Participants conducted 14 sessions per week of individual counseling with college students, for which they received 2 hours per week of individual supervision from experienced, psychodynamic supervisors. Across the semester, supervisees increased in self- and other-awareness ($d = 1.37$; large effect), autonomy ($d = 1.10$; large effect), and motivation ($d = .46$, small effect). All supervisees in this relatively small sample came from a single training program, and perhaps more importantly, there is no way to link the results to supervision itself (i.e., these findings may have arisen from trainees' clinical work rather than from supervision).

Also focusing on effects of supervision on supervisees, Ladany, Ellis, and Friedlander (1999) investigated changes in supervisory working alliance across time. In this study, 107 trainees who ranged from beginning practicum students to interns and postdocs received individual supervision for about 80 minutes per week. They completed measures of the supervision working alliance, supervisee self-efficacy, and supervisee personal reactions at the beginning and end of the semester. The results yielded minimal effects for supervision: Goals ($d = .02$; no effect), Tasks ($d = .04$; no effect), Bond ($d = .09$; no effect), self-efficacy ($d = .37$; small effect), and personal reactions ($d = .01$; no effect). Limitations of the study include its ex post facto design, the lack of random assignment, and the inability to make any causal links.

One other investigation provided possible evidence of supervision's effects. Cashwell and Dooley (2001) found that those who received supervision reported higher counseling self-efficacy at posttest than those who did not receive supervision (it was not possible to calculate an effect size given that the authors did not provide a standard deviation).

Collectively, what do these four quantitative studies tell us regarding the effects of supervision? With regard to effects on supervisees, supervision appeared to improve supervisee awareness of self and others, autonomy, motivation, and self-efficacy. Intriguingly, supervision appears to have had no effect on the supervisory working alliance, at least over the course of a semester. Now focusing on client effects, both skill- and process-focused supervision appeared to have had moderate effects on client-reported therapy alliance; however, unsupervised therapists yielded similar effects, so results were not likely due to supervision. Therapy outcome (i.e., reduction in depression symptoms) appeared to be strongly affected by therapists whose supervision attended to process issues; again, however, unsupervised therapists produced similar effects, raising caution about attributing the results to supervision. Thus, supervision may have some beneficial effects on supervisees, but its effects on clients are less clear. Our inability to assert strong and definitive findings here is surely influenced by the research itself: Few studies actually addressed the question of supervision's effectiveness, whether focusing on supervisees or clients. Those studies that did attend to this focus had several limitations, often related to the sample, but even more importantly, related to the inability to assert that any effects found were due to supervision.

Qualitative Evidence

We found a few qualitative studies on how supervision affects supervisees or their clients. Unfortunately, these researchers all explored different variables (e.g., counterproductive events in supervision, supervisor self-disclosure, corrective relational experiences in supervision, good supervision events), making it difficult to draw conclusions across studies.

In Hill, Sullivan, et al. (2007), supervisees suggested that supervision helped them cope with the anxieties inherent in learning to be therapists and in working with clients. In addition, Worthen and McNeill (1996) found that supervision seemed to build supervisees' self-confidence, fostered a deeper understanding of the therapy endeavor, enhanced supervisees' ability to conceptualize clients in a more sophisticated manner, and helped supervisees intervene with clients.

On the other hand, Gray, Ladany, Walker, and Ancis (2001) found some deleterious effects of supervision. Troubling events in supervision sometimes reduced supervisee self-efficacy, made supervisees more guarded and less likely to disclose to supervisors, increased supervisees' fear of a negative evaluation, weakened the supervision relationship, led to difficult interactions between supervisor and supervisee, and impaired supervisees' interactions with their clients. Such events sometimes also increased supervisee stress (health problems, obsessive analysis of their own behavior), self-doubt, feelings of powerlessness, and engendered questions regarding professional decisions and plans (Nelson & Friedlander, 2001).

In sum, supervision seemed to have both salutary and deleterious effects, whether on supervisees or their clients. As with the quantitative designs, this qualitative research also has its limitations, including participant self-selection and nondiverse samples, frequent reliance on a single event described from a single perspective (e.g., supervisor or supervisee), and the inability to assert that these effects were caused by supervision. The negative effects occasionally attributed to supervision also raise vital questions regarding how such difficulties may be resolved, if not avoided entirely, how long such effects last, and whether they occur more frequently with some supervisors than others.

What Makes Supervision Effective?

We have some tentative evidence from the above studies that supervision is effective. Hence, we now turn to an examination of the factors that might influence these effects.

Quantitative Evidence

Although a number of studies examined possible correlates of supervision outcome, no two studies included the same predictor or outcome variables.

Hence, it is not possible to draw conclusions about the predictors of supervision outcome. In the following section, then, we present a preliminary review of possible predictors.

Some of the basic mechanics of supervision may be related to its effectiveness. The (a) frequency with which supervisor and supervisee met and (b) the time spent in supervision each week were positively related to supervisee-rated satisfaction ($rs = .30$ and $.30$, respectively), supervisee ratings of supervisor helpfulness ($rs = .27$ and $.29$, respectively), the amount that supervisees thought they learned ($rs = .29$ and $.32$, respectively), and how well prepared for practice supervisees felt ($rs = .29$ and $.31$, respectively; Knight, 1996).

The supervision relationship may be positively related to supervision's rated effectiveness, as well, whether measured globally or in its traditional tripartite structure (goals, tasks, bond). For example, the relationship as reported by the supervisee has been linked to supervisee satisfaction ($r = .41$) and to self-efficacy ($r = .09$) (Ladany, Ellis, & Friedlander, 1999).

Inman (2006) found that elements related to diversity may also be related to supervision effectiveness. Supervisor multicultural competence was positively linked with supervisee satisfaction and supervisee-rated supervision alliance ($rs = .62$ and $.62$, respectively), but negatively linked with supervisee ability to differentiate and integrate cultural factors when conceptualizing the etiology of clients' presenting concerns or conceptualizing the treatment approach ($rs = -.14$ and $-.09$, respectively).

The effects of particular supervisory behaviors have also been examined, with mixed effects reported. Supervisor openness was related to supervision effectiveness. More specifically, supervisors explaining their own and supervisees' roles, sharing their thoughts, encouraging feedback from supervisees, and nurturing open discussions with supervisees were, paralleling the above findings, positively linked with supervisee satisfaction, helpfulness, the amount supervisees reported learning, and how well prepared they felt for practice (explaining roles: $rs = .60, .61, .52, .57$, respectively; sharing thoughts: $rs = .44, .43, .40, .41$, respectively; encouraging feedback: $rs = .60, .60, .51, .54$, respectively; nurturing open discussions: $rs = .75, = .71, .61, .65$, respectively; Knight, 1996). Similarly, Knight (1996) also found that supervisors' understanding supervisees' feelings and encouraging their autonomy were positively correlated with the same outcomes (understanding feelings: $r = .70$, .66, .58, .62, respectively; encouraging autonomy: $rs = .62, .58, .51, .57$, respectively).

Furthermore, Riggs and Bretz (2006) found that supervisor angry withdrawal, supervisor compulsive care-seeking (i.e., overactive seeking and dependence on attachment figures for care and help), compulsive self-reliance (i.e., extreme form of avoidant attachment characterized by excessive self-sufficiency and distancing, inhibition of attachment feelings and behaviors, and strong mistrust and fear of depending on others), or compulsive caregiving (i.e., solely taking on care-giving roles and prioritizing others' needs while also being unable or unwilling to receive care from others) were, somewhat surprisingly, not related to supervisee ratings of supervision goals, tasks, or bond. However, supervisor nonadherence to ethical guidelines (e.g., adequate performance evaluations, maintenance of confidentiality, ability to work with alternate perspectives) was correlated with reduced supervisee satisfaction ($r = -.72$) and supervisee perception of impaired supervision alliance ($r = -.68$ [Bond], $r = -.78$ [Tasks], $r = -.73$ [Goals]) (Ladany, Lehrman-Waterman, Molinaro, & Wolgast, 1999).

What do these studies tell us? Many factors are likely related to the effectiveness of supervision, some having helpful and others having harmful influences. Frequent and appropriately long supervision sessions may contribute to supervision's effectiveness, as may supervisors' openness, empathy, and nurturance of supervisee development. The supervisory alliance, used in this research as both predictor and outcome, may well have a central role in supervision's effectiveness, although the mechanisms through which the alliance works are not clear. In addition, behaviors most would anticipate being negatively linked with effectiveness (e.g., supervisor nonadherence to ethical guidelines, angry withdrawal from supervisees and supervision) were indeed often negatively linked (modestly so), but they also sometimes yielded positive (though modest) effects.

Limitations exist in this research. Most importantly, correlational findings cannot speak to causality. In addition, we do not know whether there are additional intervening variables that also influence supervision effectiveness.

Qualitative Evidence

We found only a few qualitative studies about factors associated with the effects of supervision.

With regard to what may contribute to positive effects, supervisors providing instruction, support, and feedback, as well as facilitating exploration and occasionally challenging supervisees (Hill, Sullivan, et al., 2007) have been linked with positive effects, as has supervisors' normalizing supervisees' difficult reactions to clients (Ladany et al., 1997). Per supervisors' report, their use of supervisor self-disclosure (e.g., reactions to their own or to supervisees' clients, information about their personal life or professional development; Knox, Burkard, Edwards, Smith, & Schlosser, 2008) also yielded beneficial effects (e.g., strengthening the supervisory alliance, eliciting more supervisee self-disclosure). Similarly, supervisors noted that their facilitation of corrective relational experiences in supervision via openness and process/immediacy discussions likewise had positive effects (e.g., strengthened the supervision relationship, increased supervisee self-efficacy and comfort with disclosure, improved work with clients; Knox, Edwards, Hess, & Hill, 2011). In contrast, supervisees felt that supervisors' being unempathic or seeming to dismiss supervisee thoughts and feelings rendered supervision less effective (Gray et al., 2001), as did their apparent lack of investment in supervision and their unwillingness to acknowledge their own role in supervisory conflict (Nelson & Friedlander, 2001).

Thus, here, too, a range of possible contributors to supervision's effects, whether positive or negative, emerges. Those studies that yielded positive effects seem to focus on supervisors' efforts to support and connect with supervisees, to nurture them in the inherently difficult process of learning to become therapists, and to provide a safe place for them to discuss their inevitable struggles. Those studies that led to less beneficial effects, on the other hand, evinced supervisor insensitivity and disengagement, elements surely not conducive to supervisee or client development. As noted above, this research is limited by homogeneous samples and dependence on single, discrete events from single perspectives.

Summary and Recommendations for Research on Individual Supervision

This body of research indicates that supervision is indeed linked with positive effects for supervisees (e.g., greater awareness and autonomy), but effects in terms of client outcome are less clear. Furthermore, many factors are likely related to supervision's impact (e.g., frequency/length of meetings, supervisors' provision [or lack thereof] of facilitating conditions for supervisee development), some showing positive, and others negative, influences. Limitations in this research (few investigations directly addressed the effects of supervision, samples were idiosyncratic and nondiverse, qualitative studies relied on single events from one perspective, inability to assume causality due to the use of correlational or qualitative methods), however, suggest caution in applying these findings broadly. We make the following seven recommendations for further research on individual supervision:

1. We need more coherent and consistent investigations that build on and extend existing studies in an effort to create a solid corpus of literature that will enable more confident conclusions. For example:

   a. The extant literature has largely ignored the impact of specific supervisor interventions on supervisees or clients. If practice via role playing is a pivotal component of the effectiveness of helping skills training, for example, might this activity also lead to such effects when used in supervision? Similarly, immediacy has been shown to have positive effects in therapy (see Hill & Knox, 2009); what might be its effects when used in supervision?

   b. Some researchers are beginning to examine corrective experiences in supervision (e.g., Ladany et al., 2012). Continued investigation into the effects of such experiences, on supervisees and on clients, is fertile territory.

2. We urge researchers to attend more diligently not only to how supervision affects supervisees, but also to how it affects their clients. Thus, researchers might collect data from clients regarding the effectiveness of their supervised therapist (e.g., strength of supervision working alliance; helpfulness of interventions; resolution of concerns that brought them to therapy; reaction, if any, to knowing that their therapist was being supervised).

3. Goodyear (2011) proposed a process model of supervision in which supervisor interventions directly affect the supervisee (in terms of personhood, case conceptualization skills, and clinical interventions), which influence supervisees' in-session behaviors with clients, which then affect client outcomes. This model

is conceptually intriguing and in need of empirical examination.

4. We need additional investigations regarding how feedback may be effective in supervision. What are the circumstances, for instance, in which immediate versus delayed feedback is most helpful (Hattie & Timperley, 2007)? And which type of feedback is most helpful for which supervisees learning which skills? Furthermore, supervisory use of immediacy and supervisor encouragement of therapist use of immediacy in the therapy session may yield rich and valuable feedback that can be directly used in the supervision and therapy. Also related to feedback, what if the feedback that a supervisee receives consists of strong encouragement to adopt the supervisor's orientation, style, or approach, and as a result the supervisee is not able to develop his or her own identity? Supervisees may well receive plentiful feedback, but what are the short- and long-term effects of supervisors urging supervisees to adopt the supervisor's style versus supervisors encouraging supervisees to develop their own natural style?

5. When supervision yields deleterious effects on supervisees, what contributes to such outcomes? What supervisor and supervisee factors, for instance, may lead to such consequences, and how, if at all, does such difficult supervision affect supervisees' work with their clients? Of at least equal importance, how can such negative effects be reduced, if not avoided entirely? One possible method would be to routinely monitor supervisees' anxiety or confidence, for instance, and provide that feedback to supervisors during the course of supervision, much as Lambert and colleagues (e.g., Whipple et al., 2003) provide feedback to therapists regarding client progress.

6. When engaging in required supervision, supervisees are typically assigned a supervisor rather than being able to choose with whom they would want to work. What impact, if any, does selecting versus being assigned to a supervisor have on the effectiveness of supervision?

7. Similarly, supervisees engaged in required supervision as part of their training often switch supervisors after one or two academic terms. How do such changes affect supervisees and the clients with whom they work? Are such changes disruptive to the supervision or therapy process, or do they instead provide

useful and multiple perspectives from which supervisees may learn and thereby work more effectively with clients? Does this effect vary across type of supervisee?

TRAINING PRACTICING THERAPISTS

We focus in this section on training for practicing or postdegree professionals. We first discuss studies evaluating the effectiveness of training programs designed to teach highly select samples of experienced professionals to implement manual-guided treatments for randomized clinical trials (RCTs). We then turn to research evaluating attempts to disseminate manuals to practicing professionals. Finally, we examine attempts to assess the effects of continuing education for practicing professionals. We note at the outset that it is probably more difficult to find effects in research with practicing professionals than with novice therapists because experienced therapists already have a base of clinical skills, and thus have comparatively less room for improvement. In addition, because experienced therapists may have more investment in believing that what they do is adequate and are no longer in graduate training programs, they may have less motivation to change.

Training Experienced Therapists to Implement Manualized Treatments for RCTs

Several training programs have been designed to teach therapists to implement manualized treatments. Such programs were developed so that researchers investigating RCTs could justifiably claim that their therapists had been suitably trained and were implementing the targeted treatment at high levels of adherence and competence, thereby allowing researchers to conclude that any results identified were likely due to the treatment rather than to extraneous variables. Sholomskas et al. (2005) noted that training for manual-guided therapies typically consists of three phases: (1) selecting experienced therapists who are highly committed to the type of treatment they will be implementing, (2) an intensive didactic seminar including a review of the treatment manual and extensive role playing/practice, and (3) successful completion of training based on assessments of adherence and competence in at least one closely supervised training case.

Vanderbilt Study on Psychodynamic Training

Binder and Henry (2010) recently provided a retrospective overview of how the Vanderbilt Psychotherapy Research Team, under the leadership of Hans Strupp, developed the first research program for teaching therapists to implement time-limited dynamic psychotherapy (TLDP; Strupp & Binder, 1984). Therapists, most of whom were psychodynamically oriented, were licensed clinical psychologists and psychiatrists with about five years of experience. They served as their own controls, such that they first conducted two cases following their usual treatment approach, then participated in a year-long training program (about 100 hours of seminars and supervision) during which they saw an additional two cases using TLDP, and finally treated two additional cases using TLDP to test for the effects of training.

In the cases treated after training, therapists increased in technical adherence to TLDP but not in general interviewing skills (Henry, Strupp, Butler, Schacht, & Binder, 1993). Most surprisingly, however, therapists were, on average, more hostile, less optimistic, less supportive, less focused on feelings, more authoritarian, and more defensive with their patients following training. Henry et al. (1993) concluded that training contributed to a temporary deterioration in the therapists' ability to form alliances. Binder and Henry (2010) speculated that the negative effects were due to too much emphasis in the training on providing transference interpretations, which may not have been appropriate for short-term treatment and may also not have been implemented competently. We would also suggest that when therapists adhere too closely to a manualized approach, rather than incorporating these strategies more naturally and organically into their own repertoires, they may become anxious and overly rigid in how they implement the techniques, especially when they are being closely evaluated.

Training Therapists for the National Institutes of Mental Health Treatment of Depression Collaborative Research Program (NIMH TDCRP)

The NIMH TDCRP involved three conditions for which therapists were trained: interpersonal therapy (IPT), cognitive-behavior therapy (CBT), and clinical management with and without medication (an active drug and a placebo condition). Published studies related to training were found only for IPT and CBT.

For IPT, Rounsaville, Chevron, Weissman, Prusoff, and Frank (1986) trained 11 postdoctoral therapists in the NIMH TDCRP. These therapists were chosen from 28 applicants who were already competent in psychodynamic/interpersonal therapy. Training involved reading the manual and then treating three to four cases under supervision. Rounsaville et al. (1986) found no changes in therapist skillfulness in using IPT strategies, which they explained as a "ceiling effect," given that the ratings for implementing the techniques were already excellent for the first case. They confirmed this explanation in comparing the training effects for the TDCRP therapists with the training of seven non-TDCRP therapists who were not as experienced and who did not receive as intensive a training program. The non-TDCRP therapists started lower and increased more in skill usage across two cases than did the TDCRP therapists. A limitation of this study is its lack of a pretraining assessment, making it difficult to know whether the training itself had any effect.

Shaw and Wilson-Smith (1988) examined training for the TDCRP CBT therapists (different therapists from those used by Rounsaville et al., 1986). Trainees improved on the judge-rated Cognitive Therapy Scale, based on a therapy session with a standard-client actor after a 2-week training workshop. Therapists were able to set an agenda, obtain feedback, interview in relevant areas, and assign homework. Appropriate conceptualizations and judgments about interventions, however, took longer to develop over time in supervision. Knowledge of CBT theory and techniques (as measured through a written exam) did not predict performance in the training phase, although performance with the standard client did predict training outcome. Limitations of this study include the small sample and lack of control conditions.

Training Therapists for the National Collaborative Cocaine Treatment Study (NCCTS)

Researchers investigated the effects of training therapists to use supportive-expressive therapy (SE), cognitive therapy (CT), or drug counseling (DC) to treat cocaine addicts in the NCCTS.

The therapists for SE and CT were postdoctoral clinicians; many of the drug counselors were ex-addicts. Therapists were selected from a large group of applicants, yielding a highly select group of experienced therapists. In the training phase, trainees read the manual, attended 8 days of workshops, and treated four cases under supervision.

Using these data, Crits-Christoph et al. (1998) found a large effect for CT in terms of changes across cases in therapist adherence/competence and client-rated alliance, whereas changes were found for SE and DC within but not across cases, providing clear support for training only for CT (changes within a single case are potentially confounded by experience with the case, whereas change across cases shows that the therapist can transfer learning to new cases). A strength of this study was the large sample size (about 20 in each condition); a limitation is that there may have been a ceiling effect in the ability of therapists to profit from training, given that therapists were carefully selected from a large group of applicants and thus were probably relatively competent prior to training. Also, the authors duly noted that because CT is more technique-based, it may be easier to teach than SE or DC.

In Siqueland et al.'s (2000) investigation of therapist characteristics that might predict benefit from training in the NCCTS, no effects were found for race, degree, age, or sex for any of the treatments. Higher competence ratings before training were associated with more change in competence during training for SE and higher competence after training for DC. For CT, years of experience was associated with increased competence, but more pretraining supervision hours were associated with less change. Hence, there was minimal evidence across the treatment modalities for the effects of demographic variables, and there were mixed effects for initial levels of competence and experience. With such highly selected samples and without replication, however, these findings should be interpreted with caution.

Najavits et al. (2004) interviewed therapists who were trained and certified as competent in the NCCTS about their experiences with the training. Replicating earlier findings (Godley, White, Diamond, Passetti, & Titus, 2001; Najavits, Weiss, Shaw, & Dierberger, 2000), supervision was judged by the therapists as the most important element of training. Other highly rated positive influences were the desire to learn something new, intrinsic interest in the treatment, being recorded, and the training. The least influential variables were the pay and the threat of losing one's job for not implementing the protocol competently. Furthermore, it took those learning the individual drug treatment, group drug treatment, cognitive therapy, and supportive-expressive therapy an average of 8, 13, 35, and 63 weeks, respectively, to feel competent in delivering their treatments.

Summary of Training for RCTs

Although the above studies had some flaws (none included control groups that did not receive training; all trained highly selected therapists, which left little room for growth in skills), we can tentatively conclude that experienced therapists can be trained to implement manuals for psychodynamic, supportive-expressive, interpersonal, cognitive therapy, and drug counseling. Importantly, Najavits et al. (2000) provided evidence that it takes longer for therapists to feel competent in learning to use psychodynamic than cognitive-behavioral therapy or drug counseling.

Based on their experiences training therapists in interpersonal therapy, Weissman, Rounsaville, and Chevron (1982) discussed several challenges. First, random assignment means that therapists work with patients they do not necessarily want to treat and who may not be appropriate for the treatment approach; likewise, patients who might profit from a given treatment might not be assigned to that condition. Second, treatment is not open-ended, even though some clients may need long-term services. Third, patients are shared between therapist and research staff, sometimes making responsibility for various tasks unclear. Fourth, therapists often do not like being evaluated, and as a result might not perform as well as they would when not being evaluated. Fifth, adherence to manuals limits therapist flexibility, which is especially problematic if the new approach does not fit with the therapist's natural approach.

Given these challenges, Weissman and colleagues (1982) recommended that researchers carefully select therapists for training. They suggested using experienced, competent therapists who are committed to the method and whose natural orientation is similar to the new approach, and thus whose skills just need to be modified slightly. They also suggested that researchers be explicit about the requirements of participation, recruit more therapists than necessary in case of dropouts, provide both didactic information and supervision, monitor the training process carefully, and always remember the ethical maxim that patient care comes first. These recommendations are very apt for yielding highly trained therapists for RCTs, but they are of limited value in terms of assessing the general effects of training, given (as noted above) that highly experienced therapists likely have little room to change.

TRAINING COMMUNITY THERAPISTS TO IMPLEMENT MANUALIZED TREATMENTS

Studies in this section focused on teaching practitioners to use manuals, with such training typically conducted through 1- or 2-day workshops. As compared with the earlier reviewed RCT studies that used experienced, highly selected therapists who had to adhere to the treatment protocol or be dropped from the research project, community therapists often did not have to implement what they learned from training and thus may have had less motivation to learn specific skills or to change behavior. Furthermore, many of these therapists were less highly educated (often high school graduates up to master's level) than were the RCT therapists.

Dissemination of Training in Motivational Interviewing (MI)

In studies of the effects of 2-day MI workshops, Miller and Mount (2001) and Rubel, Sobell, and Miller (2000) found changes in knowledge of MI and ability of therapists to respond to written vignettes, but no change in client behavior. Based on what they learned in these two investigations, Miller, Yahne, Moyers, Martinez, and Pirritano (2004) designed one of the best studies we found on training. Each of 140 licensed substance abuse counselors who actively sought MI training received the MI therapist manual and seven training videotapes. Counselors were then randomly assigned to one of five conditions: (1) 2-day workshop only, (2) 2-day workshop plus emailed feedback based on judges' ratings of four work samples submitted over the course of a year, (3) 2-day workshop plus up to six individual coaching sessions in which trainees were allowed to consult and engage in problem solving and role-plays via telephone, (4) 2-day workshop plus feedback and coaching, and (5) a wait-list control in which therapists had to learn the method on their own. Workshops involved didactic material and demonstration as well as practice, and all were conducted by the same four leaders. Outcomes of training were assessed based on judge-rated assessments of counselor behavior in (a) work samples selected by participants to represent their best work submitted at baseline and then 4, 8, and 12 months after training; (b) an interview with a standard-client actor immediately after the 2-day workshop; and (c) responses to written client stimuli after the workshop. At the 4-month follow-up, large gains in MI skills were found for participants in the three workshop-plus conditions (with no differences among the three conditions), but participants in the workshop-only condition had only marginal gains, and those in the control condition had no gains. Furthermore, personality characteristics (self-esteem, aggression, achievement, nurturance, personal history of drug problems) did not predict response to training. These three studies provide evidence that MI can be taught to community practitioners, but even more importantly, the studies provide evidence for the importance of practice and feedback in enabling trainees to incorporate skills into their work with clients.

Dissemination of Training in Cognitive-Behavior Therapy (CBT)

A number of studies suggest that community practitioners can be trained in brief workshops to use CBT (Lau, Dubord, & Parikh, 2004; Milne, Baker, Blackburn, James, & Reichelt, 1999; Morgenstern, Morgan, McCrady, Keller, & Carroll, 2001; Sholomskas et al., 2005; Simons et al., 2010; Williams, Moorey, & Cobb, 1991). These studies were fairly similar in design and outcome, and showed that CBT training enabled trainees to feel more confident about using CBT skills. In addition, trainees were judged as more adherent and competent in using these skills, and clients reported relevant changes.

Strosahl, Hayes, Bergan, and Romano (1998) taught managed care therapists to use acceptance and commitment therapy (ACT), a type of CBT. Ten people who had received training the previous year in solution-focused therapy were compared with eight people who received 1 year of training in ACT (didactic workshop, intensive clinical training, monthly supervision). Clients of therapists trained in ACT reported better coping,

had more self-acceptance, and were more likely to have completed treatment within 5 months than were clients of solution-focused therapists. The lack of random assignment and high dropout rate make conclusions tentative, but these results suggest that therapists can be trained in ACT.

Comparison of Training for Professional and Nonprofessional Practitioners

Thompson, Gallagher, Nies, and Epstein (1983) provided 8 weeks of training in a manualized behavioral group therapy for depression in the elderly to 16 mental health counselors (ranging in education from baccalaureate to doctoral degrees) and to 16 paraprofessionals (non–mental health workers). Both training groups increased in knowledge of behavior theory and therapy, although professionals had more knowledge both before and after training. The training groups did not differ in terms of knowledge of problem-solving skills; attitudes toward the elderly; or ratings of competence, effectiveness, and nonspecific factors. Furthermore, although clients' outcomes were not different across groups at posttherapy in terms of reductions in depression, negative thinking, and pleasant events, or at follow-up in terms of overall depression or overall life satisfaction, those who were treated by professionals had higher life satisfaction posttherapy, rated their overall improvement higher, and rated the helpfulness of the group higher than did clients of paraprofessionals.

In a similar study, Bright, Baker, and Neimeyer (1999) trained professional (had completed formal clinical training with at least a master's degree in clinical or counseling psychology) and paraprofessional (had completed no formal training but had participated in support groups in self-help organizations) therapists in a workshop for either CBT or mutual support groups; all received weekly supervision. After training, therapists led either CBT or support groups for depressed clients, consistent with the training they had received. Regardless of type of therapy or professional status of therapists, clients improved in depression, negative thinking, and overall psychological distress.

The results of these two studies thus support the effects of brief training for both professionals and paraprofessionals. Differences between paraprofessionals and professionals were not substantial, although it is important to note that some of the paraprofessionals had a considerable amount of practical experience even though they had no formal training.

Training for Improving Alliance

Crits-Christoph et al. (2006) trained five therapists (each with 1 to 3 years of postgraduate experience and from a variety of theoretical orientations) in methods for improving the therapeutic alliance. In the pretraining phase, therapists each treated three clients using their natural style; they then treated three clients in the training phase, during which they tried to implement what they were learning in the training (which involved readings and workshops about specific techniques for increasing alliance and addressing interpersonal patterns; trainees also received individual supervision). In the posttraining phase, therapists again treated three clients using their own form of treatment with no requirement to apply what they had learned in training. Moderate to large effect sizes were found from pre- to posttraining in the alliance, although results were not significant with such a small sample. The researchers, however, noted variability in the results, such that three therapists had better alliances and two had worse alliances following training. Therapists' adherence to alliance techniques was significantly associated with subsequent client-rated alliance, and small to moderate effect sizes were found from pre- to posttraining in improvement in clients' depression symptoms and quality of life. The authors noted that these therapists may have already been able to address alliance issues, creating a ceiling effect on the data, and also acknowledged the difficulty of manualizing recommendations for improving alliances, given that the alliance is influenced by both the therapist and client.

Smith-Hansen, Constantino, Piselli, and Remen (2011) studied the effects of providing a 3.5-hour alliance-building workshop, which used lecture, role-plays, video demonstrations, and discussion to teach community mental health therapists about adopting a relational stance to address relational problems. No significant differences were found between those who had the workshop versus those in a control condition for (a) therapists' use of alliance-fostering strategies in a first session with a new client, (b) therapists' ratings of the working alliance in the session, or (c) client engagement (i.e., number of sessions

attended in the first 4 weeks of treatment). The authors noted that the brevity of the treatment and the lack of follow-up supervision may have made it difficult for therapists to incorporate what they learned into their repertoires. In addition, since no pretests of therapist behavior were conducted, we do not know if there was a ceiling effect, such that therapists already had sound alliance skills and thus had little room for change, as was true in the earlier Crits-Christoph et al. (2006) study.

In sum, the findings from these two studies suggest that it is difficult to train experienced therapists to improve alliances. From the earlier helping skills literature, we know that novice therapists can be trained in the facilitative conditions (which are associated with alliance formation), but perhaps these skills are already established and thus more difficult to alter in experienced therapists. Alternatively, it could be that other training approaches such as countertransference management or intensive supervision would be more helpful than the above approaches for improving alliances. Furthermore, such training might be more effective for therapists who have difficulties in alliance formation (e.g., low alliance ratings).

Summary of Effectiveness Studies

From these studies, we can conclude that MI and CBT can be successfully disseminated to clinicians working in the community, although less promising results were found for alliance-building training. The findings, however, suggest strongly that merely attending a workshop is not enough. Rather, trainees have to actively work at incorporating new skills into their repertoires. As Miller et al. (2004) indicated, "There is little empirical reason to believe that a one-shot training workshop (albeit the usual method for continuing education) would be sufficient to change durable practice behavior" (p. 1052).

A few methodological concerns must be addressed. On the one hand, the dissemination studies with practicing professionals more often included control conditions and had a wider range of initial therapist competence than did the RCT studies. On the other hand, many of the dissemination studies had large dropout rates and low compliance with the research, which may indicate that results apply only to those who complete the training and comply with the research. Perhaps those who did not like the approach or who felt that the approach was not compatible with their theoretical orientation were less likely to adhere to the approach.

In addition, we found it interesting that no dissemination studies were conducted of psychodynamic, supportive-expressive, or interpersonal therapy, even though RCT studies had been conducted for these approaches. These treatment approaches may be more complex and difficult to disseminate in brief workshops for community therapists than are MI and CBT.

CONTINUING EDUCATION FOR PRACTICING PSYCHOLOGISTS

Neimeyer, Taylor, and Wear (2009) noted that most states and provinces in the United States and Canada mandate that licensed psychologists engage in continuing education. The assumption is that continuing education keeps psychologists current with recent developments in the profession and helps them practice more effectively. Unfortunately, although there is some evidence that psychologists are satisfied with the quality of their continuing education and think that it is helpful for their practices, there is almost no empirical evidence that psychologists learn anything from such experiences or that their participation translates into better outcomes with clients (Neimeyer, Taylor, & Philip, 2010). Relatedly, within the medical field, meta-analyses of several studies have shown that traditional didactic programs had no significant impact on physicians' behaviors or patient-related outcomes, but interactive programs (especially if they had a supervised skill rehearsal) did have a significant impact on physicians' behaviors and a lesser impact on patient outcomes (Bloom, 2005; Davis et al., 1999).

In an effort to address this lack of empirical support for the effectiveness of required continuing education, Neimeyer et al. (2009) noted that what counts as continuing education needs to be clarified. A wide array of activities (workshops, reviewing for journals, supervision) has been used for continuing education, and these probably have different effects. They also recommended that outcomes include not only satisfaction, but also assessment of knowledge, skills, clinical competencies, and client outcomes.

Summary and Recommendations for Research on Training for Practicing Professionals

From these results, we can conclude that carefully selected experienced therapists who already espouse the relevant theoretical orientation can be trained to use manuals in RCTs. Furthermore, it appears that community practitioners can be trained to use MI, CBT, and ACT, although how much they use their learning in their clinical work is unknown. Less convincing evidence has been reported for training experienced therapists to improve their alliance skills. We have four recommendations for future research:

1. The similarity of the trainees' orientation to the approach espoused in the manual needs to be investigated.
2. We need to know whether novice therapists would be more able to learn manual-guided approaches if they had first been exposed to helping skills training.
3. The maintenance of skills learned in continuing education needs more investigation. Researchers could investigate, for instance, to what extent trainees later incorporate what they have learned into their repertoire of skills, and what may be associated with such greater versus lesser incorporation.
4. We need to construct new measures that better assess the effects of training for experienced therapists. Given that experienced therapists are typically honing skills rather than learning completely new skills, measures of self-efficacy or changes in belief systems may be more appropriate assessments of learning than are client outcomes.

INDIRECT ASSESSMENTS OF EFFECTS OF TRAINING

In an ideal world, as Stein and Lambert (1995) noted, we would have well-designed studies of training so that we could clearly assess its effects and attribute change in trainees to the training itself. There would be clear treatment and control conditions, random assignment to conditions, clearly specified interventions used in training, and clearly defined outcomes. Unfortunately, because of the complexity of graduate and postgraduate training (i.e., lack of clear criteria for selecting students, multiple components that comprise training, the influence of personal life during training, the impossibility of providing true control conditions), we have minimal direct evidence of the effects of training even during graduate school, let alone during the professional career span. Hence, less direct assessments are often cited as supporting or refuting claims for the effectiveness of training. In this section, then, we focus on these more indirect assessments as providing some, albeit tentative (and sometimes misleading because of methodological problems), evidence of the effects of training.

Reports About the Helpfulness of Training and Supervision

Orlinsky et al. (1999) asked 3,900 psychotherapists at all career stages in a variety of mental health professions and from several Western countries to complete a questionnaire about their development. Using a 5-point scale (5 = high), therapists across all experience levels perceived themselves as being above average in terms of therapeutic mastery ($M = 3.41$, $SD = .83$) and indicated that they were currently experiencing growth ($M = 3.55$, $SD = .79$). Perceived therapeutic mastery was strongly correlated (.53) with years in practice (which included years of formal training), indicating that the therapists who perceived themselves as most competent were those who were most experienced. In contrast, therapist reports that they were currently experiencing growth were not correlated significantly with years in practice ($r = -.02$), indicating that both inexperienced and experienced therapists equally considered themselves to be currently growing and developing as therapists. Finally, perceived therapeutic mastery was moderately correlated with current growth (.27), indicating that those who perceived themselves as most competent also perceived themselves as continuing to grow. Although the data were cross-sectional rather than longitudinal, the sample was not randomly selected, and the assessments were self-report, these results indicate that therapists perceived themselves as growing and changing over time, both during and after formal training, providing indirect support for the effects of training (although clearly results could be due to other factors such as personal therapy and clinical experience).

In addition, surveys have been conducted with a wide range of therapists across countries, experience levels, and mental health professions (Carlsson & Schubert, 2009; Fortune,

McCarthy, & Abramson, 2001; Kohl et al., 2009; Morrow-Bradley & Elliott, 1986; Orlinsky, Botermans, Rønnestad, & the SPR Collaborative Research Network, 2001; Rachelson & Clance, 1980; Skovholt & Rønnestad, 1992, 1995; Sontag et al., 2009). Results indicated that hands-on experiences with clients, engaging in personal therapy, and receiving supervision were perceived as the most important sources of learning. Much lower in terms of perceived influence, although still helpful, were coursework, seminars, and theories. Again, these results suggest that training and especially supervision are perceived by trainees as helpful, although other experiences are also viewed as somewhat helpful.

Rønnestad and Skovholt (2003) conducted interviews with 100 individuals across the span of the career range, from inexperienced to very experienced therapists. Many of the results were cross-sectional, but they also conducted a number of interviews over time with the same therapists, so there were longitudinal data as well. Based on their data, they delineated six phases of development: lay helper, beginning student, advanced student, novice professional, experienced professional, and senior professional. A number of the themes that spanned the development phases involved shifts in attentional focus and emotional functioning, the importance of continued self-reflection, and a life-long integration of personal and professional issues. Participants consistently described the influence of both personal life (early family history and adult interactions) and professional life (client interaction, working with professional elders, and interactions with peers) as significant sources of learning.

In sum, trainees at all levels have reported growth over time. This growth could be attributed at least partially to training or supervision experiences, although other experiences (e.g., hands-on experience with clients, personal therapy) were also important influences.

INFLUENCE OF EXPERIENCE ON CLIENT OUTCOME

In this section, we first review cross-sectional studies of the effects of therapist experience level on client outcome and therapy process. Next, we turn to reviewing studies related to comparing therapists who have had different types of training and comparing therapists versus untrained people.

Cross-Sectional Studies of the Effects of Therapist Experience Level on Client Outcome

Researchers have often included therapist experience level in studies in the hope of explaining variance in client outcome. The results of such studies are relevant to our examination of the effects of training, because experience may serve as a proxy for training. If training makes a difference, experienced therapists should have better outcomes than therapists-in-training do with their clients. Many other variables (e.g., practice, maturation) are reflected in estimates of experience, but it can still be argued that experience may serve as an indirect marker of the effects of training.

Stein and Lambert (1995) conducted a *between studies* narrative (i.e., only one experience level was represented in each study) meta-analyses. They concluded that there was modest support for a relationship between therapist experience and client outcome, but they noted that the limited range of experience in many studies may have constrained the results.

Stein and Lambert (1995) noted, however, that the foregoing between-study meta-analyses were limited because different populations were often used across studies. They suggested that better evidence would emerge from within-study comparisons of therapist experience level. They thus conducted a *within studies* meta-analysis of 36 studies that included therapists of varying levels of experience within the same study. They found that setting made a difference in the effects of therapist experience on dropout rate. More specifically, minimal differences were found between student trainees (e.g., practicum and internship students) and full-time MA-level and PhD-level staff in university counseling center settings. In other treatment settings with a greater range of training levels (e.g., BA-level staff and paraprofessionals to PhD-level staff), however, professionals with more training had fewer dropouts than did less experienced therapists. In addition, setting also made a difference in the effects of therapist experience on client-rated satisfaction and outcome. Experienced therapists had higher client-rated outcomes than did inexperienced therapists in university counseling centers (.27), but this effect was not found in other treatment settings (−.04). Stein and Lambert (1995) concluded overall that there were modest but fairly consistent effects for therapist experience on various outcome measures.

Beutler et al. (2004), in their review of therapist experience, found four studies that they evaluated as effectively separating therapist experience level from various other aspects of professional training. They suggested that these four studies generally supported the role of therapist experience but the effects were small (*rs* from −.19 to .48). In their review of therapist age (which could also be viewed as a proxy for training given that older therapists typically have had more training), Beutler et al. (2004) concluded that age did not play a role in treatment outcome. In contrast, in their review, Anderson, Ogles, Patterson, Lambert, and Veermeesch's (2009) concluded that older therapists had better outcomes and noted that "age serves as an indicator of the accumulation of clinical experiences needed to master the interpersonal qualities inherent in facilitative interpersonal skills" (p. 10).

Two recent analyses of very large numbers of therapists perhaps provide the most definitive evidence about therapist experience. Wampold and Brown (2005) found no effects for therapist experience level (years of practice) when they analyzed the outcomes of 6,146 clients seen by 581 therapists in a managed care setting (all therapists were postdegree). Similarly, Okiishi et al. (2006) found no effects of therapist experience level (pre-internship, internship, postinternship) on the speed of client improvement in their study of more than 5,000 clients seen by 71 therapists at a university counseling center.

In summary, these studies provide mixed support for the effects of therapist experience, with more recent studies involving large numbers of therapists showing no effects. Given that these studies did not explore the longitudinal effects of training, and thus unexplored sources of variance could explain differences among the therapists at different experience levels, this evidence is tentative. In addition, it is important to note that the definition of experience differed across studies, and that there is no standard definition or assessment of experience.

Cross Sectional Studies of the Effects of Therapist Experience Level on Psychotherapy Process

In addition to the outcome research just described, many researchers have examined the psychotherapy process for therapists at different levels of experience, again an indirect indication of the effects of training. Given that most of these studies are very old, we report just a sampling of the research rather than comprehensively reviewing this literature.

The first set of such studies involves therapists of differing experience levels responding to taped stimuli of actors playing clients. Such analogue studies are problematic because therapist behavior in simulated situations often does not generalize to interactions with real clients. For example, Kushner, Bordin, and Ryan (1979) found that therapists responded differently to a filmed client versus a real client in an intake session, concluding that therapist behavior is influenced by situational factors. Nevertheless, Strupp (1955) found that experienced (> 5 years in practice) Rogerian therapists used more exploratory and fewer reflective responses than did inexperienced (< 5 years in practice) Rogerian therapists, although no such differences were found between experienced and inexperienced psychodynamic therapists. Howell and Highlen (1981) found that in comparison to beginning or advanced graduate student therapists or postdegree therapists, untrained introductory psychology students used more direct guidance, were judged as providing lower quality responses, had less liking for the client as a person, and judged the clients as being less motivated to change. Few differences were found between the other three groups, suggesting that the most growth may occur very early in training. Tracey, Hays, Malone, and Herman (1988) found that in comparison with beginning and advanced graduate students, postdegree therapists used more confrontation and were more flexible but were less dominant, verbose, and gratifying of client demands.

A second set of studies involves therapists of differing experience levels interacting with actual clients. For example, based on data for between 7 to 96 sessions at a university counseling center, Barrett-Lennard (1962) found that expert therapists (all of whom had at least 2 years of experience and were staff psychologists) had higher levels of client- and therapist-rated level of regard, empathic understanding, congruence, and unconditionality than did practicum-level trainees (ds range from .29 to .95), although no differences were found on willingness to be known. Similarly, in Mallinckrodt and Nelson's (1991) study, more experienced therapists (postdoctoral staff at agencies) provided more of the facilitative conditions and had higher client- and therapist-rated working alliances than did inexperienced (graduate student) therapists. Caracena (1965) found that

experienced therapists (4 to 10 years postdegree) approached dependency (i.e., encouraged the client to talk) more than did inexperienced therapists (interns and practicum students).

It is difficult to draw conclusions from the two sets of studies because researchers did not use the same process measures and defined experience in different ways. Very broadly, however, we can say that researchers have found a multitude of process differences among therapists at different levels of experience. Once again, we need longitudinal data to make sense of these findings.

COMPARISON OF PSYCHOTHERAPISTS WITH DIFFERENT TYPES OF TRAINING

Howard (1999) compared the outcomes of treatment for anxiety disorders in an HMO for therapists who had a cognitive behavioral orientation and specialty training in anxiety disorders versus therapists who were not cognitive behavioral and had no specialty training in anxiety disorders (although this latter group perceived themselves as competent to treat anxiety disorders). Clients of therapists in the first group completed treatment significantly faster and had significantly lower rates of relapse over 2 years following therapy than did clients of therapists in the second group. Again, although not directly testing the effects of training, these results suggest that training (or having a cognitive behavioral approach) made a difference in client outcome.

COMPARISON OF PSYCHOTHERAPISTS VERSUS UNTRAINED PEOPLE

Though not directly investigating the effects of training, a study by Strupp and Hadley (1979) yielded major implications for our thinking about such training. They compared the outcomes of brief therapy for experienced male psychotherapists and friendly male college professors, each paired with three male college students who were high in depression, anxiety, and social introversion. The psychotherapists were selected on the basis of their reputation within the professional and academic community (three were psychoanalytically oriented, two were experientially oriented). The college professors had a reputation for being warm, trustworthy, and interested in students (none had any formal training or experience in therapy). The therapists and professors were comparable in terms of age, professional status, and years of professional experience. Both the therapists and professors had outcomes that exceeded those of controls, but there were no differences between them on any of the outcome measures completed by patients, therapists, and clinical judges. If college professors can achieve the same outcomes as highly trained and experienced psychotherapists, the value of formal training is indeed brought into question. Similarly, Burlingame and Barlow (1996) found no differences in process or outcome for clients randomly assigned to professional group therapists selected by peer nomination or "natural helpers" nominated by students in 15-session psychotherapy groups.

Anderson, Crowley, and Hamburg (in preparation) conducted an interesting follow-up study. They selected graduate students to be therapists based on having high versus low facilitative interpersonal skills, as assessed both by self-report measures of empathic ability and judgments of behavior in videotaped interactions with a standard client. Half of the therapists of each facilitative level were clinical psychology doctoral students with at least 2 years of clinical training, and half were students in a nonhelping doctoral program (e.g., biology, history). Clients, who were selected to have diagnosable problems but were not in therapy, were seen for seven sessions. Those therapists with high facilitative interpersonal skills had higher client outcomes and higher client- and therapist-rated working alliance than did therapists with low facilitative interpersonal skills. But most important to this review, the high facilitative doctoral students from nonhelping disciplines were just as effective as were the high facilitative clinical psychology doctoral students.

The results of these studies certainly do not provide direct evidence for the effectiveness of training; in fact, they call into question the very necessity of this training. Such findings led us to wonder about the effects of experiential learning versus structured training. Clearly, people can learn facilitative skills throughout their life by observing and modeling others who have such skills and by receiving feedback from their interactions with others. Similarly, some people become good teachers without ever having had a course in teacher education or supervision of their teaching skills. Quite likely, these highly effective teachers assess what works for them in an educational situation and carefully attend to feedback from students. Similarly, until recently clinical supervisors were not trained how to be supervisors, and yet many were excellent in this role; likewise, managers in the corporate world often receive no training, yet many also perform superbly at managing others. Clearly, then, people can learn interpersonal skills through informal observation, practice, reflection, and feedback, the very components of therapy training. Perhaps the biggest difference between facilitative people who are therapists and those who are not lies in the formers' commitment to learn and engage in the work of therapy. In other words, many people may have the ability to be therapeutic but not all of these people choose to utilize these skills as professional psychotherapists.

SUMMARY AND RECOMMENDATIONS FOR RESEARCH ON INDIRECT EVIDENCE FOR THE EFFECTS OF TRAINING

The indirect evidence suggests positive effects of training on therapists in that: (a) experienced therapists perceived themselves as more effective than did inexperienced therapists, and (b) therapists perceived themselves as changing and growing across the span of their development. No differences were found, however, between trained experienced therapists and friendly college professors or lay helpers, nor between clinical psychology graduate students and graduate students in nonhelping professions who were equally matched in terms of facilitative levels. Mixed results were reported in studies of the effects of experience level. Mixed results were also found in surveys of experienced therapists, given that hands-on experience with clients, personal therapy, and supervision were all perceived to be more effective than formal coursework in helping them learn to become therapists. Thus, the results do not provide adequate evidence of the value of training. Importantly, these results must be interpreted with caution given that the research designs employed do not allow us to make causal attributions about the effects of training. We have three recommendations for future research:

1. More research using longitudinal designs assessing changes in trainees over the course of several years of training.

2. Inclusion of therapist experience as a variable in outcome studies is fine, but we need better definition and operationalization of the construct of therapist experience (we return to this issue in the conclusions).

3. Replication of the work comparing facilitative and nonfacilitative therapists and nontherapists is needed. How do facilitative people who have not been formally trained become effective helpers? More work on such natural helpers would be interesting (see Stahl & Hill, 2008), and may provide valuable insights that can inform training practices.

CONCLUSIONS AND FUTURE DIRECTIONS

In this section, we first address the evidence related to the question: "Are training and supervision effective?" We then turn to evidence for the second question guiding this chapter: "If so, what contributes to making training and supervision effective?" Given the relative lack of evidence about the effectiveness of training and supervision, we describe some of the conceptual and methodological problems that make research in this area so difficult. We conclude by offering ideas for future research in this area.

Are Training and Supervision Effective?

We first focus on evidence for the effectiveness of training. Next, we turn our attention to the maintenance of gains from training.

Evidence of Effectiveness

After reviewing the literature, our conclusion is a very hesitant yes, training and supervision are effective. We base this conclusion on the following evidence reviewed in this chapter: (a) novice trainees can be trained in helping skills; (b) trainees improve over the course of training; (c) supervision enhances supervisees' awareness of self and others and increases their autonomy; (d) experienced therapists can be trained to use manuals, and these training approaches can be extended to practicing therapists in the community, particularly if they continue to use the skills beyond the initial training period; and (e) trainees value training and supervision.

Contrary evidence also exists, however, to call this conclusion into question. For example, (a) nonsupervised therapists did not differ from supervised therapists in terms of therapy alliance and client outcome; (b) supervision sometimes had detrimental effects on supervisees; (c) recent studies involving very large numbers of therapists showed no effects for therapist experience level; and (d) highly facilitative people who had no psychotherapy training were found to be as effective in helping clients as were trained therapists.

Maintenance of Effects

Even if we could definitively assert that training and supervision are indeed effective, we must also raise the question about the maintenance of any such effects. In a few studies in helping skills training, graduate students (who may have kept practicing skills) maintained the effects, whereas undergraduates (who may not have kept practicing) did not maintain skills (Butler & Hansen, 1973; Collingwood, 1971; Gormally et al., 1975). Furthermore, Miller et al. (2004) found that an initial workshop produced longer-term effects only when trainees received further input (e.g., coaching) beyond the workshop. With so few studies, however, we cannot draw conclusions about the maintenance of effects.

What Contributes to Making Training and Supervision Effective?

We first focus on the considerable evidence for the effectiveness of hands-on practice. We then briefly describe other possible contributors to the effectiveness of training and supervision.

Hands-On Experience

One major conclusion that emerges is that hands-on experience is a key component of learning to becoming a good therapist. Therapists retrospectively stated that they learned the most from experience with clients, and trainees indicated that practice was the most helpful component of their skills training. This finding has clear implications for how we train therapists: We must provide trainees with ample opportunity to practice what they are learning.

Similarly, Binder and Henry (2010, p. 299) described "inert knowledge," or conceptual knowledge of therapy techniques and principles for using them, as divorced from actually applying the knowledge. Relatedly, they posited that trainees may have ample declarative knowledge (conceptual knowledge) but relatively little procedural knowledge (applying knowledge under real-life situations), potentially rendering their eventual entry into the clinical world quite abrupt, especially if their training relies largely on theoretical and conceptual understanding. Binder and Henry (2010) described "deliberate practice" as having three components: (1) perform well-defined tasks at an appropriate difficulty level, (2) receive immediate and informative feedback (i.e., supervision), and (3) have many opportunities to repeat and correct performance errors. We would suggest that such direct experience be instituted early in training in appropriate doses so that trainees begin to encounter in vivo what they read about in their texts.

Other Contributors

Considerable evidence in the helping skills literature indicates that instruction, modeling, and feedback (supervision) are effective, providing support for Bandura's (1969, 1997) social cognitive model. Furthermore, supervisees noted that supervisors' openness, empathy, and supportive nurturance of supervisee growth, in the context of a safe supervision alliance, aided their development and their clinical work. There well may also be other key components of training (e.g., expectations, coaching, self-reflection, transcribing and coding sessions) that need to be studied.

Why Do We Know So Little About the Effects of Training and Supervision?

In light of the large number of studies reviewed, we were struck by how little we actually know about the effects of training and supervision. Several explanations can be offered.

Complexity of Training and Supervision

Therapy is complex and relationships differ with every therapist-client dyad, so one can never be completely trained or prepared for such inevitably varied experiences. In addition, the desired outcomes differ for every case, so we will likely never have a single battery of measures that fully assesses each supervisee's and client's needs and desired outcomes. Thus, we may never be able to completely measure, much less know, the effects of training and supervision.

In addition, consider the added confound that inexperienced therapists often receive comparatively easy cases and close supervision, and have small caseloads. In contrast, experienced therapists see many cases per week, often work with more difficult cases and frequently do so

without supervision, making any observed differences in client outcome between those working with novice versus experienced therapists even more murky. Experienced therapists may also experience compassion fatigue and burnout because they see many challenging cases and have many responsibilities (e.g., supervision, consultation, administration), circumstances that could alter their effectiveness with clients.

Furthermore, training and supervision might influence trainees in different ways, rather than having uniform effects. Based on our own experiences, some students profit considerably from training and supervision: They move from being anxious and awkward and not having skills, to becoming excellent therapists. Other students, however, may be able to learn everything they need to know solely via hands-on practice with clients, without targeted training and supervision, and in fact, might get derailed by negative experiences in supervision. Finally, there may be some students for whom training does not work and they do not become better therapists. If trainees indeed respond in such idiosyncratic ways, finding clear effects of training and supervision is rendered even more difficult. In addition, the needs and developmental goals of trainees and supervisees change over time, and thus different outcomes of training likely emerge at different stages in the career span.

Given this myriad of complications, we should not be surprised by the tentativeness of our conclusions. We should instead acknowledge the immense difficulty inherent in any attempt to assess the effects of training and supervision and embrace the challenge to model this complexity in our research efforts.

Methodological Problems

Although, as we have noted, there have been a huge number of studies related to psychotherapy training and supervision, we were struck by the lack of focus in and the marginal quality of much of the literature. For instance, we found no extended research programs on training or supervision. Furthermore, only a few well-controlled studies (with random assignment to treatment and control conditions, many trainers, well-defined treatments) were found.

Furthermore, several common limitations emerged in the studies cited in this chapter. Lack of clarity in definitions of training and supervision was rampant, as was substantial overlap between the domains of training and supervision. Most studies involved small and nonrepresentative samples from single training sites (e.g., most used female, European American, master's-level trainees from single programs). There was generally a lack of random assignment to condition, a lack of control conditions, and a lack of attention to dropout. In addition, there was a lack of detail about what took place in training and supervision, as well as a large range of time involved in training and supervision (some training lasted 5 minutes, whereas others spanned 3 years). Furthermore, much of the research relied on only one judge for observational measures, collected data solely via self-report, suffered from ceiling effects (high initial levels of functioning) that limited possible gains from training and supervision, used analogue stimuli or volunteer clients in brief sessions to assess the effects of training and supervision, did not include pretraining assessment, and did not collect follow-up data. Finally, in terms of statistical procedures, large numbers of analyses were often conducted, which was especially problematic given the frequently small sample sizes. Clearly, researchers cannot control everything in any given study, but they do need to be aware of the inherent limitations in what they do. Research on training and supervision is quite difficult: In addition to the challenges already noted, training and supervision are largely educational endeavors, subject to local pressures to train in a certain way, rendering rigorous empirical examination daunting.

Difficulty of Defining Expertise

Another explanation for the lack of definitive findings is the difficulty in assessing expertise in psychotherapy. Shanteau (1992) noted that it is easy to assess expertise in some domains, such as chess playing and livestock judging. In contrast, it is difficult to assess expertise in other domains, such as practicing psychology and playing the stock market. The major difference between these areas is that the former benefit from predictable structures and well-defined outcomes, whereas the latter suffer from ill-defined structures and outcomes. Given the complexity and lack of predictability of the process and outcome of psychotherapy, it makes sense that it would be difficult to define expertise but we need to keep trying without being overly rigid and theory-specific.

Future Directions

Based on these conclusions, we offer the following 16 overall recommendations (recall that we provided specific recommendations at the end of each main section earlier):

1. *We need better definitions of expertise and competence.* Given the growing international demand for competency benchmarks, we need to know how to define and measure expertise and competence of therapists. We thus encourage researchers to clearly operationalize both constructs, and also to develop psychometrically sound means of assessing them.

2. *We need better definitions and measures of therapist experience level.* A major limitation in the extant research involves the definition of therapist experience. Some studies defined experience based on level of training (e.g., beginning master's-level trainees, advanced doctoral trainees, interns, beginning professionals, seasoned professionals). One problem with using level of training, however, is that many people enter training with different levels of experience. Consider, for example, a person who has always been the "go-to" person for her friends when they had problems, has done peer counseling in high school, and has worked for several years on crisis hotlines as compared with a much older person who wants retraining to become a counseling psychologist after having been an engineer with no helping experience. Although these two people would both be classified as novice or beginning therapists, they clearly have different backgrounds of clinical experience. Others use, as an indicator of experience, number of years of practice; again, this indicator is flawed because people might see very different numbers of clients when in practice. Still others rely on numbers of sessions with clients, an index vulnerable to memory distortions (who can remember exactly how many sessions they have had?) and by type of experiences (e.g., work in crisis counseling yields different experiences than conducting long-term therapy). We do not have a solution, but rather suggest that researchers begin to tackle this definitional problem and develop valid standardized measures of experience.

3. *Researchers need to think carefully about outcomes.* Based on suggestions by Holloway (1984) and Rønnestad and Ladany (2006), we propose three types of outcomes. First

are client outcomes (e.g., engagement in psychotherapy, changes in symptomatology, changes in insight, behavioral change). Second are therapist outcomes (e.g., theoretical understanding, conceptualization ability, diagnostic skills, understanding of parallel process, self-awareness, intrapersonal characteristics such as self-efficacy and anxiety, basic helping skills, more advanced interventions, personal growth, professional identity). Finally, there is the supervisory relationship (e.g., alliance). Clearly, not every study on training or supervision can, or should, include all of these outcome variables. Hence, researchers need to deeply consider what they wish to study, and how best to do so. Furthermore, researchers need to study not only outcomes during and at the immediate end of training, but also longer-term outcomes.

4. *Both quantitative and qualitative methods will advance the field*. Both quantitative and qualitative methods provide important information about training and supervision. We can only detect causal connections through experimental manipulations, but we can learn vital information about the lived experiences of participants through qualitative studies. Most importantly, we need an accumulation of studies using both methods so that we can begin to perform quantitative and qualitative meta-analyses.

5. *Multisite longitudinal studies are especially needed*. Multisite longitudinal studies need to be conducted, including careful recording of amounts, types, and quality of training and supervision. In such studies, the amount and quality of personal therapy, personal relationships, and major life events also need to be recorded, because such variables likely interact with the effects of training and supervision. By collecting data at multiple sites, researchers would have large samples, and so would have enough power to investigate the effects of sites, type of training, supervisor characteristics, trainee characteristics, and client characteristics. Given that multisite studies have now been conducted for psychotherapy (e.g., NIMH TDCRP, NCCTS), we have models for how to conduct such research for training and supervision.

6. *The influence of trainer and trainee effects needs to be examined*. In Henry, Schacht, Strupp,

Butler, and Binder's (1993) training study, very different effects were found for two different trainers in terms of therapists' posttraining interviewing style and psychotherapy adherence (one trainer's trainees yielded effects sizes of 1.20 and 3.18, whereas the other yielded effects sizes of .25 and .53). Thus, researchers need to examine trainer characteristics (e.g., charisma, therapeutic competence) to determine what leads to effective training. Likewise, although no consistent results have been found because studies have not used the same predictors (see reviews of the helping skills literature, Hill & Lent, 2006), it makes sense that trainee characteristics (e.g., cognitive complexity, emotional intelligence, receptivity to feedback, flexibility, ability to engage in introspection) also influence the outcome of training and supervision, and are thus crucial variables to be examined.

7. *We need to know more about the effective components of training and supervision*. Research in helping skills training has pointed to the effectiveness of instruction, modeling, feedback, and especially practice for learning helping skills. These efforts need to be expanded to other components (e.g., coaching, self-supervision, monitoring of client outcomes) and areas (e.g., supervision).

8. *We need to explore how training and supervision interact with other experiences*. More research is needed about the interaction between training/supervision and personal therapy, didactic education, family and friendship relationships, and external events. Similarly, more work is needed about how and how much trainees learn from their experiences with clients (see also Stahl et al., 2009).

9. *We need to attend to developmental levels in thinking about the effects of training and supervision*. Bernard and Goodyear (2009) reviewed about 20 studies that provided support for developmental models of supervision. These developmental models could thus provide a conceptual structure that would help us understand the most effective approaches for training and supervision at different developmental stages. Furthermore, Mallinckrodt and Nelson (1991) indicated that a "review of the counselor training and supervision literature suggests that the two greatest and most abrupt increments in trainees' ability occur after the first practicum (Baker, Daniels, &

Greeley, 1990) and after completion of the internship (Holloway & Roehlke, 1987)" (p. 134). Although we did not see convincing evidence for these proposed jumps in trainee changes or client outcomes, it is an intriguing idea in need of further research.

10. *We need to examine how skills are incorporated over time.* An additional question is how trainees change their styles to incorporate new training. It may be, for instance, that trainees try new methods for a short while and then revert to their previous style of interaction unless they continue to practice the new techniques. Or perhaps some trainees gradually and diligently add new skills to their repertoire by conscious incorporation of these new skills and positive feedback from clients. If so, what accounts for such differences in trainees, and how do such differences affect trainee effectiveness as therapists?

11. *We need to attend to therapeutic approach in assessing the effects of training and supervision.* Therapeutic approaches differ in their beliefs about the components of effective therapy and in their definitions of competence. Thus, researchers need to attend to the particular approach under examination and the inherent values and expectations of its practitioners.

12. *We need to attend to the process of training and supervision.* In this chapter, we focused on outcomes and did not include research about process (other than examining the components of helping skills training). To make sense of the process, however, it may be helpful to have a conceptual framework of how all the pieces fit together. Strauss's (in press) and Stabingis and Gelo's (2011) generic models of input variables, process variables, and outcome variables could provide a framework for future research.

13. *We need to pay more attention to selection.* Whom we select as trainees may strongly influence the effects of training and supervision. To the degree that trainee characteristics determine training outcomes, a vital step in improving client outcomes is selection of candidates for the professions. Admissions committees, for example, often seek to admit those who will be the "best" psychiatrist, psychologist, or social worker but have little empirical evidence upon which to base their decisions. Furthermore, students often have to be selected to be both practitioners and researchers, roles that clearly demand different talents. Research is thus needed to determine how selection affects the outcomes of training and supervision.

14. *We need to learn from research in basic areas of psychology.* We could learn a great deal from research in cognitive and social psychology. Research in cognitive psychology, for example, has found that experts can be distinguished from novices in that they are more likely to "chunk" their specialized knowledge into meaningful patterns, differentiate relevant from irrelevant information, spend considerable time planning and formulating mental representations, be efficient and automatic in task performance, and engage in metacognition (Davidson & Sternberg, 1998; Dominowski, 1998; Goodyear, 1997; Jennings, Hanson, Skovholt, & Grier, 2005; O'Byrne, Clark, & Malakuti, 1997; O'Byrne & Goodyear, 1997; Sitko, 1998). Metacognition, or thinking about one's thoughts, might be particularly important in promoting expertise because it involves reflecting about the learning process, self-appraisal of skills and abilities, and self-management (Georghiades, 2004; Hacker, 1998). Relatedly, Rønnestad and Skovholt (2003) noted that novices form inadequate conceptual maps, which makes them formulate problems too quickly and give too much advice. We wonder, then, whether expert therapists form different types of cognitive maps than do novice therapists, and how such potentially different maps might affect functioning.

15. *We need to learn from research in teacher education.* We can also learn from research in teacher education. In biology, for instance, there are active efforts to transform teaching (e.g., Luft, Kurdziel, Roehrig, & Turner, 2004). As an example, Schlussel et al. (2008) described a semester-long training program where students read and discussed different teaching practices. Students also observed a variety of classes and identified examples of educational practices, reflecting on practices they liked and disliked. In addition, they wrote their own teaching philosophy and designed a course syllabus. As a result of this experience, students began to question traditional teaching practices, formulated a

teaching philosophy, and used more reflection. Clearly, these researchers addressed challenges similar to those inherent in our efforts to train students to be psychotherapists (e.g., helping students understand theory, observing models of behavior and reflecting on what works and what does not work, developing their own identity as therapists, applying their knowledge).

16. *We need to learn from research in medical education*. Likewise, medical educators have been struggling with how best to select and train physicians. The *New York Times* recently published an article (Harris, July 10, 2011) indicating that medical schools are now selecting applicants by assessing how they respond to a number of structured role plays about potential difficult situations. These responses are rated by the trained actors in terms of how the applicant made the actor feel. Similarly, medical schools often now test students' ability not only to diagnose, but also to quickly establish a bedside manner with standard role-play actors (e.g., Mavis, Turner, Lovell, & Wagner, 2006; Zabar et al., 2010). Perhaps such selection and assessment techniques would be helpful in the mental health fields, as well.

FINAL THOUGHTS

With the creation of special sections on training and supervision in the Society for Psychotherapy Research and the Society of Counseling Psychology, it seems that researchers have begun to recognize the importance of systematic investigation into these areas. We urge investigators to build on the existing research, and of at least equal importance, to address the many limitations inherent in those studies. It is indeed exciting to see the groundswell of enthusiasm and energy for examining these important clinical endeavors. Hopefully, researchers will approach such topics with openness and eagerness to learn what works and what does not work, so that we can improve our training and supervision practices, and thereby enhance client outcomes.

REFERENCES

Anderson, T., Crowley, M. E., & Hamburg, J. (in preparation). *Specifying a common therapist effect: An experiment of therapist facilitative interpersonal skills on outcome*.

Anderson, T., Ogles, B. M., Patterson, C. L., Lambert, M. J., & Veermeesch, D. A. (2009). Therapist effects: Facilitating interpersonal skills as a predictor of therapist success. *Journal of Clinical Psychology*, *65*, 755–768. doi: 10.1002/jcip.20583.

Baker, S. B., & Daniels, T. G. (1989). Integrating research on the microcounseling program: A meta-analysis. *Journal of Counseling Psychology*, *36*, 213–222. doi: 10.1037/0022–0167.36.2.213.

Baker, S. B., Daniels, T. G., & Greeley, A. T. (1990). Systematic training of graduate-level therapists: Narrative and meta-analytic reviews of three major programs. *Counseling Psychologist*, *18*, 355–421. doi: 10.1177/0011000090183001.

Bambling, M., King, R., Raue, P., Schweitzer, R., & Lambert, W. (2006). Clinical supervision: Its influence on client-rated working alliance and client symptom reduction in the brief treatment of major depression. *Psychotherapy Research*, *16*, 317–331. doi: 10.1080/10503300500268524

Bandura, A. (1969). *Principles of behavior modification*. New York, NY: Holt, Rinehart, & Winston.

Bandura, A. (1997). *Self-efficacy: The exercise of control*. New York, NY: Freeman.

Barrett-Lennard, G. T. (1962). Dimensions of therapist response as causal factors in therapeutic change. *Psychological Monographs* (76, Whole No. 562).

Bernard, J. M., & Goodyear, R. K. (2009). *Fundamentals of clinical supervision* (4th ed.). New York, NY: Pearson Allyn & Bacon.

Beutler, L. E., Malik, M., Alimohamed, S., Harwood, T. M., Talebi, H., Noble, S., & Wang, E. (2004). Therapist variables. In M. J. Lambert (Ed.), *Handbook of psychotherapy and behavior change* (pp. 227–306). Hoboken, NJ: Wiley.

Binder, J. L., & Henry, W. P. (2010). Developing skills in managing negative process. In J. C. Muran & J. P. Barber (Eds.), *The therapeutic alliance: An evidence-based guide to practice* (pp. 285–303). New York, NY: Guilford Press.

Bloom, B. S. (2005). Effects of continuing medical education on improving physician clinical care and patient health: A review of systematic reviews. *International Journal of Technology Assessment in Health Care*, *21*, 380–385. doi:10.1017/S026646230505049X

Boswell, J. F., Castonguay, L. G., & Wasserman, R. H. (2010). Effects of psychotherapy training and intervention use on session outcome. *Journal of Consulting and Clinical Psychology*, *78*, 717–723. doi: 10.1037/a0020088

Bright, J. I., Baker, K. D., & Neimeyer, R. A. (1999). Professional and paraprofessional group treatments for depression: A comparison of cognitive-behavioral and mutual support interventions. *Journal of Consulting and Clinical Psychology*, *67*, 491–501. doi: 10.1037/0022–006X.67.4.491

Burlingame, G. M., & Barlow, S. H. (1996). Outcome and process differences between professional and nonprofessional therapists in time-limited group psychotherapy. *International Journal of Group Psychotherapy, 46*, 455–478.

Butler, E. R., & Hansen, J. C. (1973). Facilitative training: Acquisition, retention, and modes of assessment. *Journal of Counseling Psychology, 20*, 60–65. doi:10.1037/h0033989

Caracena, P. F. (1965). Elicitation of dependency expressions in the initial stage of psychotherapy. *Journal of Counseling Psychology, 12*, 268–274. doi: 10.1037/h0022586

Carkhuff, R. R. (1969). *Human and helping relations* (Vols. 1 & 2). New York, NY: Holt, Rinehart, & Winston.

Carlsson, J., & Schubert, J. (2009). Professional values and their development among trainees in psychoanalytic psychotherapy. *European Journal of Psychotherapy and Counselling, 11*, 267–286. doi: 10.1080/13642530903230319

Cashwell, T. H., & Dooley, K. (2001). The impact of supervision on counselor self-efficacy. *Clinical Supervisor, 20*, 39–47.

Chui, H., Hill, C. E., Hummel, A., Ericson, S., Ganginis, H., Ain, S., & Merson, E. (2011). *Teaching novice therapists to use challenges.* Paper presented at the 27th Society for the Exploration of Psychotherapy Integration meeting, Washington, DC.

Collingwood, T. R. (1971). Retention and retraining of interpersonal communication skills. *Journal of Clinical Psychology, 27*, 294–296.

Crits-Christoph, P., Connolly Gibbons, M. B., Crits-Christoph, K., Narducci, J., Schamberger, M., & Gallop, R. (2006). Can therapists be trained to improve their alliances? A preliminary study of alliance-fostering psychotherapy. *Psychotherapy Research, 16*, 268–281. doi: 10.1080/10503300500268557

Crits-Christoph, P., Siqueland, L., Chittams, J., Barber, J. P., Beck, A. T., Frank, A., . . . Woody, G. (1998). Training in cognitive, supportive-expressive, and drug counseling therapies for cocaine dependence. *Journal of Consulting and Clinical Psychology, 66*, 484–492. doi: 10.1037/0022–006X.66.3.484

Crook-Lyon, R. E., Hill, C. E., Hess, S., Wimmer, C., & Goates-Jones, M. K. (2009). Therapist training, feedback, and practice for dream work: A pilot study. *Psychological Reports, 105*, 87–98. doi: 10.2466/pr0.105.1.87–98

Davidson, J. E., & Sternberg, R. J. (1998). Smart problem solving: How metacognition helps. In D. J. Hacker, J. Dunlosky, & A. C. Graesser (Eds.), *Metacognition in educational theory and practice* (pp. 47–68). Mahwah, NJ: Erlbaum.

Davis, D., O'Brien, M. A. T., Freemantle, N., Wolf, F. M., Mazmanian, P., & Taylor-Vaisey, A. (1999). Impact of formal continuing medical education: Do conferences, workshops, rounds, and other traditional continuing education activities

change physician behavior or health care outcomes? *Journal of the American Medical Association, 282*, 867–874. doi: 10.1001/jama.282.9.867

Dominowski, R. L. (1998). Verbalization and problem solving. In D. J. Hacker, J. Dunlosky, & A. C. Graesser (Eds.), *Metacognition in educational theory and practice* (pp. 25–45). Mahwah, NJ: Erlbaum.

Ellis, M. V., & Ladany, N. (1997). Inferences concerning supervisees and clients in clinical supervision: An integrative review. In C. E. Watkins (Ed.), *Handbook of psychotherapy supervision* (pp. 447–507). New York, NY: Wiley.

Ericsson, K. A., Charness, N., Feltovich, P., & Hoffman, R. (2006). *Handbook of expertise and expert performance.* Cambridge, United Kingdom: Cambridge University Press.

Falender, C. A., & Shafranske, E. P. (2004). *Clinical supervision: A competency-based approach.* Washington, DC: American Psychological Association.

Ford, J. D. (1979). Research on training therapists and clinicians. *Review of Educational Research, 49*, 87–130.

Fortune, A. E., McCarthy, M., & Abramson, J. S. (2001). Student learning processes in field education: Relationship of learning activities to quality of field instruction, satisfaction, and performance among MSW students. *Journal of Social Work Education, 37*, 111–124.

Fouad, N. A., Hatcher, R. L., Hutchings, P. S., Collins, F. L., Grus, C. L., Kaslow, N. J., . . . Crossman, R. E. (2009). Competency benchmarks: A model for understanding and measuring competence in professional psychology across training levels. *Training and Education in Professional Psychology, 3*, S5–S26. doi: 10.1037/a0015832

Freiheit, S. R., & Overholser, J. C. (1997). Training issues in cognitive-behavioral psychotherapy. *Journal of Behavior Therapy and Experimental Psychiatry, 28*, 79–86. doi: 10.1016/S0005–7916(97)00001–3

Georghiades, P. (2004). From the general to the situated: Three decades of metacogntition. *International Journal of Science Education, 26*, 365–383. doi: 10.1080/0950069032000119401

Godley, S., White, W., Diamond, G., Passetti, L., & Titus, J. (2001). Therapist reactions to manual-guided therapies for the treatment of adolescent marijuana users. *Clinical Psychology: Science and Practice, 8*, 405–417. doi: 10.1093/clipsy.8.4.405

Goodyear, R. K. (1997). Psychological expertise and the role of individual differences: An exploration of issues. *Educational Psychology Review, 9*, 251–265. doi: 1023?A:1024787208551

Goodyear, R. K. (2011, August). Supervision conventions and structures that limit its effectiveness. Presented as part of the symposium, *Expertise in Psychotherapy—Following the Yellow Brick Road?* (B. Wampold, Chair). Annual meeting of the American Psychological Association, Washington, DC.

Goodyear, R. K., & Guzzardo, C. R. (2000). Psychotherapy supervision and training. In S. Brown & R. W. Lent (Eds.), *Handbook of counseling psychology* (3rd ed., pp. 83–108). New York, NY: Wiley.

Gormally, J., Hill, C. E., Gulanick, N., & McGovern, T. (1975). The persistence of communication skills for undergraduate trainees. *Journal of Clinical Psychology, 31,* 369–372.

Gray, L. A., Ladany, N., Walker, J. A., & Ancis, J. R. (2001). Psychotherapy trainees' experience of counterproductive events in supervision. *Journal of Counseling Psychology, 48,* 371–383. doi: 10.1037/0022–0167.48.4.371

Hacker, D. J. (1998). Definitions and empirical foundations. In D. J. Hacker, J. Dunlosky, & A. C. Graesser (Eds.), *Metacognition in educational theory and practice* (pp. 1–23). Mahwah, NJ: Erlbaum.

Harris, G. (2011, July 10). New for aspiring doctors, the people skills test. *New York Times.*

Hattie, J., & Timperley, H. (2007). The power of feedback. *Review of Educational Research, 77,* 81–112. doi: 10.3102/003465430298487

Henry, W. P., Schacht, T. E., Strupp, H. H., Butler, S. F., & Binder, J. L. (1993). Effects of training in time-limited dynamic psychotherapy: Mediators of therapists' responses to training. *Journal of Consulting and Clinical Psychology, 61,* 441–447. doi: 10.1037/0022–006X.61.3.441

Henry, W. P., Strupp, H. H., Butler, S. F., Schacht, T. E., & Binder, J. L. (1993). Effects of training in time-limited dynamic psychotherapy: Changes in therapist behavior. *Journal of Consulting and Clinical Psychology, 61,* 434–440. doi: 10.1037/0022–006X.61.3.434

Hess, S., Knox, S., & Hill, C. E. (2006). Teaching graduate student trainees how to manage client anger: A comparison of three types of training. *Psychotherapy Research, 16,* 282–292. doi: 10.1080/10503300500264838

Hill, C. E. (2004). *Helping skills: Facilitating exploration, insight, and action* (2nd ed). Washington DC: American Psychological Association.

Hill, C. E. (2009). *Helping skills: Facilitating exploration, insight, and action* (3rd ed). Washington DC: American Psychological Association.

Hill, C. E., Charles, D., & Reed, K. G. (1981). A longitudinal analysis of changes in counseling skills during doctoral training in counseling psychology. *Journal of Counseling Psychology, 28,* 428–436. doi: 10.1037/0022–0167.28.5.428

Hill, C. E., & Kellems, I. S. (2002). Development and use of the helping skills measure to assess client perceptions of the effects of training and of helping skills in sessions. *Journal of Counseling Psychology, 49,* 264–272. doi: 10.1037/0022–0167.49.2.264

Hill, C. E., & Knox, S. (2009). Processing the therapeutic relationship. *Psychotherapy Research, 19,* 13–29.

Hill, C. E., & Lent, R. W. (2006). A narrative and meta-analytic review of helping skills training: Time to revive a dormant area of inquiry. *Psychotherapy: Theory, Research, Practice, Training, 43,* 154–172. doi: 10.1037/0033–3204.43.2.154

Hill, C. E., & O'Brien, K. (1999). *Helping skills: Facilitating exploration, insight, and action.* Washington, DC: American Psychological Association.

Hill, C. E., Roffman, M., Stahl, J., Friedman, S., Hummel, A., & Wallace, C. (2008). Helping skills training for undergraduates: Outcomes and predictors of outcomes. *Journal of Counseling Psychology, 55,* 359–370. doi: 10.1037/0022–0167.55.3.359

Hill, C. E., Stahl, J., & Roffman, M. (2007). Training novice therapists: Helping skills and beyond. *Psychotherapy: Theory, Research, Practice, Training, 44,* 364–370. doi: 10.1037/0033–3204.44.4.364

Hill, C. E., Sullivan, C., Knox, S, & Schlosser, L. (2007). Becoming psychotherapists: The experiences of novice therapists in a beginning graduate class. *Psychotherapy: Theory, Research, Practice, Training, 44,* 434–449. doi: 10.1037/0033–3204.44.4.434

Hilsenroth, M., Ackerman, S., Clemence, A., Strassle, C. G., & Handler, L. (2002). Effects of structured clinical training on patient and therapist perspectives on alliance early in psychotherapy. *Psychotherapy: Theory, Research, Practice, Training, 39,* 309–323. doi: 10.1037/0033–3204.39.4.309

Hilsenroth, M. J., Defife, J. A., Blagys, M. D., & Ackerman, S. J. (2006). Effects of training in short-term psychodynamic psychotherapy: Changes in graduate clinician technique. *Psychotherapy Research, 16,* 293–305. doi: 10.1080/10503300500264887

Holloway, E. L. (1984). Outcome evaluation in supervision research. *Counseling Psychologist, 12,* 167–174. doi: 10.1177/0011000084124014

Holloway, E. L. (1992). Supervision: A way of teaching and learning. In S. D. Brown & R. W Lent (Eds.), *Handbook of counseling psychology* (2nd ed., pp. 177–214). New York, NY: Wiley.

Holloway, E. L., & Roehlke, H. J. (1987). Internship: The applied training of a counseling psychologist. *Counseling Psychologist, 15,* 205–260. doi:10.1177/0011000087152001

Howard, R. C. (1999). Treatment of anxiety disorders: Does specialty training help? *Professional Psychology: Research and Practice, 30,* 470–473. doi: 10.1037/0735–7028.30.5.470

Howell, J. M., & Highlen, P. S. (1981). Effects of client affective self-disclosure and counselor experience on counselor verbal behavior and perceptions. *Journal of Counseling Psychology, 28,* 386–398. doi: 10.1037/0022–0167.28.5.386

Inman, A. G. (2006). Supervisor multicultural competence and its relation to supervisory process and outcome. *Journal of Marital and Family Therapy, 32,* 73–85. doi: 10.1111/j.1752–0606 .2006.tb01589.x

Ivey, A. E. (1971). *Microcounseling: Innovations in interviewing training*. Springfield, IL: Thomas.

Jackson, J., Hill, C. E., Ericson, S., Liu, J., Wydra, M., & Merson, E. (2011). *Training novice trainees to use interpretations*. Paper presented at the 27th Society for the Exploration of Psychotherapy Integration meeting, Washington DC.

Jennings, L., Hanson, M., Skovholt, T. M., & Grier, T. (2005). Searching for mastery. *Journal of Mental Health Counseling*, *27*, 19–31.

Kagan, N. (1984). Interpersonal process recall: Basic methods and recent research. In D. Larson (Ed.), *Teaching psychological skills: Models for giving psychology away* (pp. 229–244). Monterey, CA: Brooks/Cole.

Kasdorf, J., & Gustafson, L. (1978). Research related to microtraining. In A. E. Ivey & J. Authier (Eds.), *Microcounseling: Innovations in interviewing, counseling, psychotherapy, and psychoeducation* (pp. 323–376). Springfield, IL: Thomas.

Knight, C. (1996). A study of MSW and BSW students' perceptions of their field instructors. *Journal of Social Work Education*, *32*, 399–414.

Knox, S., Burkard, A. W., Edwards, L. M., Smith, J. J., & Schlosser, L. Z. (2008). Supervisors' reports of the effects of supervisor self-disclosure on supervisees. *Psychotherapy Research*, *18*, 543–559. doi: 10.1080/10503300801982781

Knox, S., Edwards, L. M., Hess, S. A., & Hill, C. E. (2011). Supervisor self-disclosure: Supervisees' experiences and perspectives. *Psychotherapy*, *48*, 336–341.

Kohl, S., Barrow, S., Brahler, E., Fegert, J. M., Fliegel, S., Freyberger, H. J., ... Strauss et al. (2009). Psychotherapy training from the perspective of the trainers: Results of a survey made among lecturers, supervisors, and leaders of self-awareness groups within the framework of the research report. *Psychotherapeut*, *54*, 445–456.

Kushner, K., Bordin, E. S., & Ryan, E. (1979). Comparison of Strupp and Jenkins' audiovisual psychotherapy analogues and real psychotherapy interviews. *Journal of Consulting and Clinical Psychology*, *47*, 765–767. doi: 10.1037/0022–006X.47.4.7652

Ladany, N., Ellis, M. V., & Friedlander, M. L. (1999). The supervisory working alliance, trainee self-efficacy, and satisfaction. *Journal of Counseling and Development*, *77*, 447–455.

Ladany, N., Inman, A. G., Hill, C. E., Knox, S., Crook-Lyon, R., Thompson, B. J., ... Walker, J. A. (2012). Corrective relational experiences in supervision. In L. G. Castonguay, & C. E. Hill (Eds.) (2012), *Transformation in psychotherapy: Corrective experiences across cognitive behavioral, humanistic, and psychodynamic approaches* (pp. 335–352). Washington, DC: American Psychological Association.

Ladany, N., Lehrman-Waterman, D., Molinaro, M., & Wolgast, B. (1999). Psychotherapy supervisor ethical practices: Adherence to guidelines, the supervisory working alliance, and supervisee satisfaction. *Counseling Psychologist*, *27*, 443–475. doi: 10.1177/0011000099273008

Ladany, N., O'Brien, K. M., Hill, C. E., Melincoff, D. S., Knox, S., & Petersen, D. A. (1997). Sexual attraction toward clients, use of supervision, and prior training: A qualitative study of predoctoral psychology interns. *Journal of Counseling Psychology*, *44*, 413–424. doi: 10.1037/0022–0167.44.4.413

Lambert, M. J., DeJulio, S. S., & Stein, D. M. (1978). Therapist interpersonal skills: Process, outcome, methodological considerations, and recommendations for future research. *Psychological Bulletin*, *85*, 467–489.

Larson, L. M., & Daniels, J. A. (1998). Review of the counseling self-efficacy literature. *The Counseling Psychologist*, *26*, 179–218. doi: 10.1177/001100098262002

Lau, M., Dubord, G., & Parikh, S. (2004). Design and feasibility of a new cognitive-behavioural therapy course using a longitudinal interactive format. *Canadian Journal of Psychiatry*, *49*, 696–700.

Lent, R. W., Hill, C. E., & Hoffman, M. A. (2003). Development and validation of the Counselor Activity Self-Efficacy Scales. *Journal of Counseling Psychology*, *50*, 97–108. doi: 10.1037/0022

Lent, R. L., Hoffman, M. A., Hill, C. E., Treistman, D., Mount, M., & Singley, D. (2006). Client-specific counselor self-efficacy in novice counselors: Relation to perceptions of session quality. *Journal of Counseling Psychology*, *53*, 453–463. doi: 10.1037/0022–0167.50.1.97

Luft, J. A., Kurdziel, J. P., Roehrig, G. H., & Turner, J. (2004). Growing a garden without water: Graduate teaching assistants in introductory science laboratories at a doctoral/research university. *Journal of Research in Science Teaching*, *41*, 211–233. doi: 10.1002/tea.2004

Mallinckrodt, B., & Nelson, M. L. (1991). Counselor training level and the formation of the psychotherapeutic working alliance. *Journal of Counseling Psychology*, *38*, 133–138. doi: 10.1037/0022–0167.38.2.133

Matarazzo, R. G. (1971). The systematic study of learning psychotherapy skills. In A. E. Bergin & S. L. Garfield (Eds.), *Handbook of psychotherapy and behavior change* (pp. 895–924). New York, NY: Wiley.

Matarazzo, R. G. (1978). Research on the teaching and learning of psychotherapeutic skills. In S. L. Garfield & A. E. Bergin (Eds.), *Handbook of psychotherapy and behavior change* (2nd ed., pp. 941–966). New York, NY: Wiley.

Matarazzo, R. G., & Patterson, D. (1986). Research on the teaching and learning of therapeutic skills. In S. L. Garfield & A. E. Bergin (Eds.), *Handbook of psychotherapy and behavior change* (3rd ed., pp. 821–843). New York, NY: Wiley.

Mavis, B., Turner, J., Lovell, K., & Wagner, D. (2006). Faculty, students, and actors as standardized patients: Expanding opportunities for performance assessment. *Teaching and Learning in Medicine*, *18*, 130–136. doi: 10.1207/s15328015tlm1802_7

Miller, W. R., & Mount, K. A. (2001). A small study of training in motivational interviewing: Does one workshop change clinician and client behavior? *Behavioural and Cognitive Psychotherapy*, *29*, 457–471. doi: 10.1017/S1352465801004064

Miller, W. R., Yahne, C. E., Moyers, T. B., Martinez, J., & Pirritano, M. (2004). A randomized trial of methods to help clinicians learn motivational interviewing. *Journal of Consulting and Clinical Psychology*, *72*, 1050–1062. doi: 10.1037/0022–006X.72.6.1050

Milne, D. L., Baker, C., Blackburn, I, James, I., & Reichelt, K. (1999). Effectiveness of cognitive therapy training. *Journal of Behavior Therapy and Experimental Psychiatry*, *30*, 81–92. doi: 10.1016/S0005-7916(99)000–11-7

Morgenstern, J., Morgan, T. J., McCrady, B. S., Keller, D. S., & Carroll, K. M. (2001). Manual-guided cognitive-behavioral therapy training: A promising method for disseminating empirically-supported substance abuse treatments to the practice community. *Psychology of Addictive Behaviors*, *15*, 83–88. doi: 10.1037/0893–164X.15.2.83

Morrow-Bradley, C., & Elliott, R. (1986). Utilization of psychotherapy research by practicing psychotherapists. *American Psychologist*, *41*, 188–197. doi: 10.1037/0003–066X.41.2.188

Multon, K. D., Kivlighan, D. M., & Gold, P. B. (1996). Changes in counselor adherence over the course of training. *Journal of Counseling Psychology*, *43*, 356–363. doi: 10.1037/0022–0167.43.3.356

Najavits, L. M., Ghinassi, F., Van Horn, A., Weiss, R. D., Siqueland, L., Frank, A.,...Luborsky, L. (2004). Therapist satisfaction with four manual-based treatments on a national multisite trial: An exploratory study. *Psychotherapy: Theory, Research, Practice, Training*, *41*, 26–37. doi: 10.1037/0033–3204.41.1.26

Najavits, L. M., Weiss, R. D., Shaw, S. R., & Dierberger, A. E. (2000). Psychotherapists' view of treatment manuals. *Professional Psychology: Research and Practice*, *31*, 404–408. doi: 10.1037/0735–7028.31.4.404

Neimeyer, C. J., Taylor, J. M., & Wear, D. M. (2009). Continuing education in psychology: Outcomes, evaluations, and mandates. *Professional Psychology: Research and Practice*, *40*, 617–624. doi: 10.1037/a0016655

Neimeyer, C. J., Taylor, J. M., & Philip, D. (2010). Continuing education in psychology: Patterns of participation and perceived outcomes among mandated and nonmandated psychologists. *Professional Psychology: Research and Practice*, *41*, 435–441. doi: 10.1037/a0021120

Nelson, M. L., & Friedlander, M. L. (2001). A close look at conflictual supervisory relationships: The trainee's perspective. *Journal of Counseling Psychology*, *48*, 384–395. doi: 10.1037/0022–0167.48.4.384

Nerdrum, P., & Rønnestad, M. H. (2002). The trainees' perspective: A qualitative study of learning to empathic communication in Norway. *Counseling Psychologist*, *30*, 609–629. doi: 10.1177/00100002030004007

Nerdrum, P., & Rønnestad, M. H. (2004). Changes in therapists' conceptualization and practice of therapy following empathy training. *Clinical Supervisor*, *22*, 37–61. doi: 10.1300/J001v22n02_04

O'Byrne, K. R., Clark, R. E., & Malakuti, R. (1997). Expert and novice performance: Implications for clinical training. *Educational Psychology Review*, *9*, 321–332. doi: 10.1023/A:1024742505548

O'Byrne, K. R., & Goodyear, R. K. (1997). Client assessment by novice and expert psychologists: A comparison of strategies. *Educational Psychology Review*, *9*, 267–278. doi: 10.1023/A:1024739325390

O'Donovan, A., & Dyck, M. J. (2005). Does a clinical psychology education moderate relationships between personality or emotional adjustment and performance as a clinical psychologist? *Psychotherapy: Theory, Research, Practice, and Training*, *42*, 285–296. doi: 10.1037/0033–3204.42.3.285

O'Donovan, A., Bain, J. D., & Dyck, M. J. (2005). Does clinical psychology education enhance the clinical competence of practitioners? *Professional Psychology: Research and Practice*, *36*, 104–111. doi: 10.1037/0735–7028.36.1.104

Okiishi, J. C., Lambert, M. J., Eggett, D., Nielson, L., Dayton, D. D., & Vermeersch, D. A. (2006). An analysis of therapist treatment effects: Toward providing feedback to individual therapists on their clients' psychotherapy outcome. *Journal of Clinical Psychology*, *62*, 1157–1172. doi: 10.1002/jclp.20272

Orlinsky, D. E., Botermans, J. F., Rønnestad, M. H., & and the SPR Collaborative Research Network (2001). Towards an empirically grounded model of psychotherapy training: Four thousand therapists rate influences on their development. *Australian Psychologist*, *38*, 139–148. doi: 10.1080/00050060108259646

Orlinsky, D., Rønnestad, M. H., Ambuhl, H., Willutzki, U., Botermans, J., Cierpka, M.,...the SPR Collaborative Research Network (1999). Psychotherapists' assessments of their development at different career levels. *Psychotherapy*, *36*, 203–214. doi: 10.1037/h0087772

Pascual-Leone, A., Wolfe, B., & O'Connor, D. (in press). The reported impact of psychotherapy training: Undergraduate disclosures after a course in experiential psychotherapy. *Person-Centered and Experiential Psychotherapies*.

Pope, B., Nudler, S., Norden, J. S., & McGee, J. P. (1976). Changes in nonprofessional (novice) interviewers over a 3-year training period. *Journal of Consulting and Clinical Psychology, 44*, 819–825. doi: 10.1037/0022–006X.44.5.819

Rachelson, J., & Clance, P. R. (1980). Attitudes of psychotherapists toward the 1970 APA standards for psychotherapy training. *Professional Psychology, 11*, 261–267. doi: 10.1037/0735–7028.11.2.261

Riggs, S. A., & Bretz, K. M. (2006). Attachment processes in the supervisory relationship: An exploratory investigation. *Professional Psychology: Research and Practice, 37*, 558–566. doi: 10.1037/0735–7028.37.5.558

Rogers, C. R. (1942). *Counseling and psychotherapy.* Boston, MA: Houghton Mifflin.

Rogers, C. R. (1957). The necessary and sufficient conditions of therapeutic personality change. *Journal of Consulting Psychology, 21*, 95–103. doi: 10.1037/h0045357

Rønnestad, M. H., & Ladany, N. (2006). The impact of psychotherapy training: Introduction to the special section. *Psychotherapy Research, 16*, 261–267. doi: 10.1080/10503300600612241

Rønnestad, M. H., & Skovholt, T. M. (2003). The journey of the counselor and therapist: Research findings and perspectives on professional development. *Journal of Career Development, 30*, 5–44. doi: 10.1177/089484530303000102

Rounsaville, B. J., Chevron, E. S., Weissman, M. M., Prusoff, B. A., & Frank, E. (1986). Training therapists to perform interpersonal psychotherapy in clinical trials. *Comprehensive Psychiatry, 27*, 364–371. doi: 10.1016/0010–440X(86)90012-X

Rubel, E. C., Sobell, L. C., & Miller, W. R. (2000). Do continuing education workshops improve participants' skills? Effects of a motivational interviewing workshop on substance-abuse counselors' skills and knowledge. *Behavior Therapist, 23*, 73–77.

Russell, R. R., Crimmings, A. M., & Lent, R. W. (1984). Therapist training and supervision. In S. Brown & R. W. Lent (Eds.), *Handbook of counseling psychology* (pp. 625–681). New York, NY: Wiley.

Schlussler, E., Torres, L. E., Rybczynski, S., Gerald, G. W., Monroe, E., Sarkar, P., . . . Osman, M. A. (2008). Transforming the teaching of science graduate students through reflection. Journal of College Student Teaching, September/October, 32–36.

Shanteau, J. (1992). Competence in experts: The role of task characteristics. *Organizational Behavior and Human Decision Processes, 53*, 252–266. doi: 10.1016/0749–5978(92)90064-E

Shaw, B. F., & Wilson-Smith, D. (1988). Training therapists in cognitive-behavior therapy. In C. Perris, I. M. Blackburn, & H. Perris, *Cognitive psychotherapy: Theory and practice* (pp. 140–159). New York, NY: Springer-Verlag.

Sholomskas, D. E., Syracuse-Siewert, G., Rounsaville, B. J., Ball, S. A., Nuro, K. F., & Carroll, K. M. (2005). We don't train in vain: A dissemination trial of three strategies of training clinicians in cognitive-behavioral therapy. *Journal of Consulting and Clinical Psychology, 73*, 106–115. doi: 10.1037/0022–006X.73.1.106

Simons, A. D., Padesky, C. A., Montemarano, J., Lewis, C. C., Murakami, J., Lamb, K., . . . Beck, A. T. (2010). Training and dissemination of cognitive behavior therapy for depression in adults: A preliminary examination of therapist competence and client outcomes. *Journal of Consulting and Clinical Psychology, 78*, 751–756. doi: 10.1037/a0020569

Siqueland, L., Crits-Cristoph, P., Barber, J. P., Butler, S. F., Thase, M., Najavits, L., & Onken, L. S. (2000). The role of therapist characteristics in training effects in cognitive, supportive-expressive, and drug counseling therapies for cocaine dependence. *Journal of Psychotherapy Practice and Research, 9*, 123–130.

Sitko, B. M. (1998). Knowing how to write: Metacognition and writing instruction. In D. J. Hacker, J. Dunlosky, & A. C. Graesser (Eds.), *Metacognition in educational theory and practice* (pp. 93–115). Mahwah, NJ: Erlbaum.

Skovholt, T. M., & Rønnestad, M. H. (1992). Themes in therapist and counselor development. *Journal of Counseling and Development, 70*, 505–515.

Skovholt, T. M., & Rønnestad, M. H. (1995). *The evolving professional self: Stages and themes in therapist and counselor development.* Chichester, United Kingdom: Wiley.

Smith-Hansen, L., Constantino, M. J., Piselli, A., & Remen, A. L. (2011). Preliminary results of a video-assisted psychotherapist workshop in alliance strategies. *Psychotherapy, 48*, 148–162. doi: 10.1037/a0022184

Sontag, A., Glaesmer, H., Barrow, S., Brahler, E., Fegert, J. M., Fliegel, S., . . . Strauss, B. (2009). Psychotherapists' education from the perspective of trainees: Results of a survey in Germany. *Psychotherapeut, 54*, 427–436.

Spangler, P., Hill, C. E., Dunn, M. G., Hummel, A., Walden, T., Liu, J., . . . Salahuddin, N. (2011). *Teaching novice trainees to use immediacy.* Paper presented at the 27th Society for the Exploration of Psychotherapy Integration meeting, Washington DC.

Stabingis A. J., & Gelo, O. (2011) *Generic model for psychotherapy training.* Paper presented at SPR 42nd International Meeting, Bern, Switzerland.

Stahl, J., & Hill, C. E. (2008). A comparison of four methods for assessing natural helpers. *Journal of Community Psychology, 36*, 289–298. doi: 10.1002/jcop.20195

Stahl, J. V., Hill, C. E., Jacobs, T, Kleinman, S., Isenberg, D., & Stern, A. (2009). When the shoe is on the other foot: A qualitative study of intern-level trainees' perceived learning from clients. *Psychotherapy: Theory, Research, Practice, Training, 46*, 376–389. doi: 10.1037/a0017000

Stein, D. M., & Lambert, M. J. (1995). Graduate training in psychotherapy: Are therapy outcomes enhanced? *Journal of Consulting and Clinical Psychology, 63,* 182–196. doi: 10.1037/0022–006X.63.2.182

Strauss, B. (in press). Leaving splendid isolation: Why psychotherapy trainees and researchers should communicate with each other. In B. Strauss, J. Barber, & L. G. Castonguay (Eds.), *Visions in psychotherapy research: Reflections from the presidents of the society for psychotherapy research*. New York, NY: Routledge.

Strosahl, K. D., Hayes, S. C., Bergan, H., & Romano, P. (1998). Assessing the field effectiveness of acceptance and commitment therapy: An example of the manipulated training research method. *Behavior Therapy, 29,* 35–64. doi: 10.1016/S0005-7894(98)80017–8

Strupp, H. H. (1955). An objective comparison of Rogerian and psychoanalytic techniques. *Journal of Consulting Psychology, 19,* 1–7. doi: 10.1037/h0045910

Strupp, H. H., & Binder, J. L. (1984). *Psychotherapy in a new key: A guide to time-limited dynamic psychotherapy*. New York, NY: Basic Books.

Strupp, H. H., & Hadley, S. W. (1979). Specific vs. nonspecific factors in psychotherapy. *Archives of General Psychiatry, 36,* 1125–1136.

Thompson, A. P. (1986). Changes in counseling skills during graduate and undergraduate study. *Journal of Counseling Psychology, 33,* 65–72. doi: 10.1037/0022–0167.33.1.65

Thompson, L. H., Gallagher, D., Nies, G., & Epstein, D. (1983). Evaluation of the effectiveness of professionals and nonprofessionals as instructors of "Coping with Depression" classes for elders. *Gerontologist, 23,* 390–396. doi: 10.1093/geront/23.4.390

Tracey, T. J., Hays, K. A., Malone, J., & Herman, B. (1988). Changes in counselor response as a function of experience. *Journal of Counseling Psychology, 35,* 119–126. doi: 10.1037/0022–0167.35.2.119

Truax, C. B., & Carkhuff, R. R. (1967). *Toward effective counseling and psychotherapy*. Chicago, IL: Aldine.

Tryon, G. S. (1996). Supervisee development during the practicum year. *Counselor Education and Supervision, 35,* 287–294.

Wampold, B. E., & Brown, G. S. (2005). Estimating variability in outcomes attributable to therapists: A naturalistic student of outcomes in managed care. *Journal of Consulting and Clinical Psychology, 73,* 914–923. doi: 10.1037/0022–006X.73.5.914

Weissman, M. W., Rounsaville, B. J., & Chevron, E. (1982). Training psychotherapists to participate in psychotherapy outcome studies. *American Journal of Psychiatry, 139,* 1442–1446.

Whipple, J. L., Lambert, M. J., Vermeersch, D., Smart, D. W., Nielsen, S. L., & Hawkins, E. J. (2003). Improving the effects of psychotherapy: The use of early identification of treatment failure and problem solving strategies in routine practice. *Journal of Counseling Psychology, 50,* 59–68. doi: 10.1037/0022–0167.50.1.59

Williams, E., Judge, A., Hill, C. E., & Hoffman, M. A. (1997). Experiences of novice therapists in prepracticum: Trainees', clients', and supervisors' perceptions of personal reactions and management strategies. *Journal of Counseling Psychology, 44,* 390–399. doi: 10.1037/0022–0167.44.4.390

Williams, R. M., Moorey, S., & Cobb, J. (1991). Training in cognitive-behaviour therapy: Pilot evaluation of a training course using the cognitive therapy scale. *Behavioural Psychotherapy, 19,* 373–376. doi: 10.1017/S0141347300014075

Worthen, V., & McNeill, B. W. (1996). A phenomenological investigation of "good" supervision events. *Journal of Counseling Psychology, 43,* 25–34. doi: 10.1037/0022–0167.43.1.25

Zabar, S., Hanley, K., Stevens, D. L., Ciotoli, C., Hsieh, A., Griesser, C., . . . Kalet, A. (2010). Can interactive skills-based seminars with standardized patients enhance clinicians' prevention skills? Measuring the impact of a CME program. *Patient Education and Counseling, 80,* 248–252. doi: 10.1016/j.pec.2009.11.015

AUTHOR INDEX

813

SUBJECT INDEX